# The Enchantments of Mammon

# THE
# ENCHANTMENTS
## OF MAMMON

*How Capitalism Became
the Religion of Modernity*

Eugene McCarraher

THE BELKNAP PRESS OF
HARVARD UNIVERSITY PRESS

Cambridge, Massachusetts, and London, England · 2019

First printing

*Library of Congress Cataloging-in-Publication Data*

Names: McCarraher, Eugene, author.
Title: The enchantments of Mammon : how capitalism became the religion of modernity /
    Eugene McCarraher.
Description: Cambridge, Massachusetts : The Belknap Press of Harvard University Press,
    2019. | Includes bibliographical references and index.
Identifiers: LCCN 2019015075 | ISBN 9780674984615 (hardcover)
Subjects: LCSH: Capitalism—Religious aspects—History. | Economics—Religious
    aspects—History. | Romanticism.
Classification: LCC HB501 .M443 2019 | DDC 261.8/5—dc23
LC record available at https://lccn.loc.gov/2019015075

To Alecia, Alexandra, and Gabrielle,

and to the memory of my father, Eugene Thorne McCarraher

This Desert soil
Wants not her hidden lustre, Gems and Gold;
Nor want we skill or art, from whence to raise
Magnificence; and what can Heav'n show more?
Our torments also may in length of time
Become our Elements, those piercing Fires
As soft as now severe, our temper chang'd
Into their temper; which must needs remove
The sensible of pain.

—MAMMON, speaking to his fellow fallen angels, in Milton, *Paradise Lost,* Book II, 270–278


The world is charged with the grandeur of God.
It will flame out, like shining from shook foil;
It gathers to a greatness, like the ooze of oil
Crushed. Why do men then now not reck his rod?
Generations have trod, have trod, have trod;
And all is seared with trade; bleared, smeared with toil;
And wears man's smudge and share's man's smell; the soil
Is bare now, nor can foot feel, being shod.

And, for all this, nature is never spent;
There lives the dearest freshness deep down things;
And though the last lights off the black West went
Oh, morning, at the brown brink eastwards, springs—
Because the Holy Ghost over the bent
World broods with warm breast and with ah! bright wings.

—GERARD MANLEY HOPKINS, "God's Grandeur"

# Contents

# The Enchantments of Mammon

# Prologue

ONCE UPON A TIME, the world was enchanted. Rocks, trees, rivers, and rain pulsated with invisible forces, powers that enlivened and determined the affairs of tribes and empires as well. Though beholden to the caprice or providential design of a variety of spirits and deities, the world of enchantment could be commanded by magic or humbly beseeched through prayer. But with the Reformation, the Enlightenment, and industrial capitalism in Europe, the company of spirits was evicted from the cosmos. If the medieval Church had preserved the pagan phantoms in its sacraments and saintly relics, its sober and industrious Protestant antagonists began the demolition of enchantment. Gradually, the sciences dispelled the realm of mystery; the prose of reason hushed the poetry of superstition; greed and calculation fostered callous disregard for the earth and the bonds of community. Dispossessed from their ancestral homes, the remnants of enchantment fled into our private chambers of fantasy or faith. And as science, technology, and capitalism come to embrace the entire globe, the enchanted specters of other peoples will be duly banished or sequestered as well.

Entitled "the disenchantment of the world" by the German sociologist and historian Max Weber, this story is the predominant account of modernity in the West and increasingly beyond, and capitalism plays a pivotal role. In the course of releasing the making and exchange of goods from traditional restraints, capitalism evacuated sacredness from material objects and social relationships. Once capable of linking us to divinity or of binding us to one another, things lost their souls when they became commodities made and exchanged for profit. Avarice—once one of the seven deadly sins—morphed into the "self-interest" or "initiative" indispensable to wealth and innovation, while the inscrutable ways of Providence yielded to the laws of supply and demand. And if enchanted forces received our devotion, entreaty, and gratitude, disenchanted forces could be mastered with money and greater technological prowess. As the economist Robert Heilbroner once summarized the conventional wisdom, capitalism "is not sacred but secular" and "would be impossible in a sacralized world to which men would relate with awe and veneration."[1]

Indeed, nothing seems more thoroughly secular than the modern business corporation, the Leviathan of the twenty-first century and the preeminent institution of our gilded age. To its admirers, the corporation is the servant of a democratic market, an unfairly maligned and underappreciated creator of abundant commodified marvels. To its detractors, it is a remorseless gargantua despoiling the planet, an insatiable, globe-encircling syndicate reliant on mendacity and exploitation. Yet both admirers and detractors of the corporation agree on its thorough disenchantment. Corporations must mobilize profit and accumulate capital, organizing money, expertise, and technology with sober judgment and utmost efficiency. Whatever their owners, managers, or workers may believe in their homes or office cubicles, corporations cannot and dare not rely on magic, divination, or prayer. They must organize every "factor of production"—from fiber optic cables and "human resources" to the dreams of the ad department—and calibrate the marginal utility of every expenditure, exertion, and longing. No beatitudes here, no works of mercy, no yearning for paradise.

As we're reminded every time there's the slightest complaint about the lack of decency or justice, out of this disciplined hunger for money comes the splendor of capitalist civilization: its protean energy; its surfeit of pleasures; its exotic gallery of images; its ingenious, bustling, and exuberant indulgence of every paying desire. The roles of patron and moralist once assumed by religion are now leveraged by capital: the arts, athletics, and scholarship receive plentiful corporate largesse, while brands, slogans, and advertising supplant icons, chants, and commandments. For the four decades before the financial crisis unfolded in the fall of 2008, capitalism's lavish indifference to piety was a major selling point. In the fleshpots of American suburbia, where the armada of SUVs ferry the heavily indebted through the consumer republic, the spectacular reign of money seemed well nigh ubiquitous and irreversible. And to cultures still mired in the backwaters of enchantment, capitalist modernity was marketed as the greatest jubilee season in history. Breaking the shackles of immemorial customs, capitalism offered the sale of commodities, not the dutiful worship of relics; the fulfillment of the self, not subordination to the past; the romance of the present and the promise of the future, not a vale of tears and a hope beyond the grave. In the words of journalist Michael Lewis, capitalists are "practitioners of liberty" who "do not suffer constraints on their private ambition" and who "work hard, if unintentionally, to free others from constraint." Firmly committed to the real world of disenchanted, manipulable forces, they represent the "spiritual antithesis of religious fundamentalists" who thwart this labor of liberty "in the name of some putatively higher power." Karl Marx wrote much the same thing a century and a half earlier, with greater flourish and prophetic grandeur. "All that is solid melts into air; all that is holy is profaned." Capitalism's most unlikely celebrant, Marx observed how the market, far from being a bastion of conservatism, dissolves "all fixed, fast-frozen relations, with their train of ancient and venerable prejudices." History's assassin of enchantment, capitalism "drowns the most heavenly ecstasies of religious fervor . . . in the icy water of egotistical calculation."[2]

Yet despite the secular veneer of capitalist life, it's not at all clear that enchantment lies lifeless in the arctic mercenary deep. To journalist Naomi Klein, the neoliberal economics of the past forty years amounts to a veritable creed, "the contemporary religion of unfettered free markets." Indeed, "corporate business has always had a deep New Age streak," she observes, with branding as the most advanced form of "corporate transcendence." The Nike swoosh, the Starbucks siren, and other trademarks are neoliberal totems of enchantment. Journalist Barbara Ehrenreich discovers that, despite its reputation for a ruthless focus on the bottom line, corporate business is "shot through with magical thinking," inspired and mesmerized by a burgeoning portfolio of New Age quackery and bunkum. Evangelicals refer to Jesus Christ as their "CEO" or personal investment advisor, while management writers cull from Lao-tzu, Buddha, Confucius, and Carl Jung. Counting out "seven habits" or "four competencies" or "sixty-seven principles of success," business advice books can be as comically arcane as end-times prophecy, the oracles of Nostradamus, or another Dan Brown novel. Some writers see a sacramental significance in contemporary consumer culture. "Material things are shot through with enchantment," *New York Times* columnist David Brooks informs us. Suburban acquisitiveness stems from a "sacramental longing,"

Brooks believes, a desire to enter "a magical realm in which all is harmony, happiness, and contentment." Historian Steve Fraser believes that even in the stampede for consumer goods slumbers "a sacramental quest for transcendence, reveries of what might be."[3] In search of some material grace, more Americans than ever seem willing to be impaled on William Jennings Bryan's cross of gold.

Contemporary writers are not the first to note the persistence of enchantment in capitalist societies. Reflecting on the misery of industrial England in the 1840s, Thomas Carlyle detected the presence of "invisible Enchantments" that bewitched the "plethoric wealth" that had "yet made nobody rich." Owners and workers walked "spell-bound" in the clutches of a "horrid enchantment," beguiled by some power that lurked in the factories and inhabited the things they produced. Carlyle traced this sorcery to "the Gospel of Mammonism," the good news that money possessed and bestowed a trove of "miraculous facilities." While this could be dismissed as rhetorical flourish, even Marx and Weber used the language of enchantment to explain the power of capitalism. The capitalist, Marx and Engels wrote in *The Communist Manifesto,* "is like the sorcerer, who is no longer able to control the powers of the nether world he has called up by his spells." Later, in the first volume of *Capital,* Marx included a seminal passage on "the fetishism of commodities," the attribution of human or supernatural qualities to manufactured objects. Four decades later, after marking the epoch of disenchantment, Weber mused that "many old gods ascend from their graves," resurrected as the "laws" of the market—spirits of "the Gospel of Mammonism."[4]

Far from being an agent of "disenchantment," capitalism, I contend, has been a regime of enchantment, a repression, displacement, and renaming of our intrinsic and inveterate longing for divinity. There is more than mere metaphor in the way we refer to the "worship" or "idolatry" of money and possessions. Even if many (if not most) of us believe in a disenchanted, desacralized cosmos—a universe devoid of spirits and other immaterial but animate beings—capitalism has assumed, in its way, the status of an enchanted world. Like the blood-sacrificial rites of nationalism that sanctify the modern state, capitalism represents what the theologian William Cavanaugh has called a "migration of the holy," a forced march of sanctity and devotion toward new, putatively secular objects of reverence.[5]

To be sure, enchantment can take a variety of forms: magic; animism; the myriad shapes of the occult; or at its most elaborate, religion. Although Weber showed that capitalism, while an agent of disenchantment, had nonetheless received the sanction of Calvinist Protestantism, Walter Benjamin suggested almost a century ago that *capitalism* is a religion as well, a "cult" with its own ontology, morals, and ritual practices whose "spirit . . . speaks from the ornamentation of banknotes."[6] I take this as a point of departure and argue that capitalism is a form of enchantment—perhaps better, a *misenchantment*, a parody or perversion of our longing for a sacramental way of being in the world. Its animating spirit is money. Its theology, philosophy, and cosmology have been otherwise known as "economics." Its sacramentals consist of fetishized commodities and technologies—the material culture of production and consumption. Its moral and liturgical codes are contained in management theory and business journalism. Its clerisy is a corporate intelligentsia of economists, executives, managers, and business writers, a stratum akin to Aztec priests, medieval scholastics, and Chinese mandarins. Its iconography consists of advertising, public relations, marketing, and product design. Its beatific vision of eschatological destiny is the global imperium of capital, a heavenly city of business with incessantly expanding production, trade, and consumption. And its gospel has been that of "Mammonism," the attribution of ontological power to money and of existential sublimity to its possessors.

The Gospel of Mammonism sanctions the printing of counterfeit promissory notes, for the love of money misdirects our sacramental desire to know the presence of divinity in our midst. "The world is charged with the grandeur of God," as Gerard Manley Hopkins wrote. "There lives the dearest freshness deep down things"—a freshness spoiled, he ruefully added, "seared with trade, bleared, smeared with toil." *The Enchantments of Mammon* is an extended assay of the moral and metaphysical imagination: our ideals of self and the common good that emerge from the way we understand the nature of the cosmos—what philosophers and theologians would call our metaphysics, ontology, or cosmology.[7] What Carlyle dubbed "the Gospel of Mammonism" is the meretricious ontology of capital, in which everything receives its value—and even its very existence—through the empty animism of money. It proclaims that capital is the *mana* or *pneuma* or soul or *elan vital* of the world, replacing the older enlivening spirits with one that is more real, energetic, and productive.

Yet as Hopkins recognized, the dearest freshness "is never spent"; the sorcery of capital can ravage and deface but can never defeat the grandeur of God. The history of capitalism in America has been a tale of predation on that dearest freshness, an ambitious but inexorably grotesque and destructive endeavor in the manufacture of beatitude, and that story is arguably winding down to its conclusion. What better time to trace the outlines of that history and inquire into the possibilities that lie dormant in the present? I've written *The Enchantments of Mammon* out of the conviction that, rather than bewail or curse the twilight of American economic and geopolitical imperium, we should welcome the demise of our misenchanted way of life as an opportunity for repentance and renewal. But redemption can only come if we tell a different story about our country and its unexceptional sins.


How has the story of "disenchantment" been told, and why is now an opportune moment to revise it? The most cogent account is Weber's, contained in several scattered essays and in *The Protestant Ethic and the Spirit of Capitalism* (1905). According to Weber, the enchanted universe was inhabited by "mysterious incalculable forces" who animated or controlled the natural world. The enchanted world fused ontology and ethics—an account of what "is" was united with an imperative of what one "ought"—and so "the most ultimate and sublime values" formed part of the world's metaphysical composition. This infusion of the everyday world with sublimity undergirded enchanted communities; divinities of varying power and character provided the "*pneuma*" that "swept through the great communities like a firebrand." Embedded in the ontology of enchantment, the production and exchange of material goods were believed to partake of these forces. So they could never be left to the unregulated activity of "free" or "impersonal" markets; there was no "economy" unto itself, separate from other sacralized social relationships. As the historian Karl Polanyi explained in *The Great Transformation* (1944), "man's economy, as a rule" was considered by premodern peoples to be indivisible from "custom and law, magic and religion."[8]

Protestant theology and capitalism played crucial roles in Weber's tale of disenchantment. Rejecting the "foolish and doctrinaire" idea of a direct causal link between the two, Weber argued that the connection inhered both in the "elective affinities" of Protestant theology and capitalist enterprise and in the "psychological drives" for accumulation sanctioned by the new religious doctrines. The "elective affinities" of Protestantism and capitalism originated in the repudiation of Catholic sacramentalism—a Christianized form, he implied, of the earlier enchanted universe, a cultic ensemble of rituals and relics in which matter and human relationships were believed capable of mediating the supernatural. In Weber's view, the marrow of Protestant divinity was a mistrust of such "sensual and emotional elements" in religion—specifically, the sacraments, which Calvinists in particular rejected as magic. Lacking the assurance of salvation provided by Catholic sacramental rituals, the Calvinist allayed the inevitable anxiety through "tireless labor in a calling." So the "spirit of capitalism" was not, Weber argued, just another term for greed; it was the rationalized accumulation of wealth, undertaken, Calvinists convinced themselves, for the sake of God's glory and majesty. In the process, Calvinist capitalists achieved a "sanctification of worldly activity" and cultivated an "innerworldly asceticism," which, once loosened from its theological moorings, became the classic trinity of bourgeois virtues: diligence, thrift, and self-restraint. Thus, the nexus of Protestantism and capitalism lay in a "disenchantment of the world," which by denying matter any sacramental character, unleashed upon it—and upon human beings—both the capitalist's energies of mastery and acquisition and the scientist's desire for knowledge.[9]

While popular notions of disenchantment usually trace its origins to science, Weber insisted that capitalism was the primary culprit in the eclipse of the sacred. As "the most abstract and impersonal element that exists in human life," money displaced *mana* and dissolved the enchanted bond between ontology and "ultimate values." By demolishing this enchanted ontology, capitalist markets rendered the exchange of goods "ever less accessible . . . to any imaginable relationship with a religious ethic of brotherliness." Enchanted assumptions of abundance, fluidity, and generosity—articulated, in the Jewish and Christian traditions, by the opening verses of Genesis—gave way to the disenchanted verities of scarcity and competition, while shamans, magicians, and priests yielded to businessmen, bureaucrats, and technicians. Life in modernity's iron cage embodied Hobbes's infernal vision: "a perpetual and restless desire of power after power, that ceaseth only in death." As Weber wrote in his bleak conclusion to *The Protestant Ethic*, the disenchanted world labored under "specialists without spirit, sensualists without heart" who presumed to have "attained a level of civilization never before achieved."[10] For Weber, the triumph of capitalism dispelled enchantment, mandated impersonality, and nullified the prospect of commerce as a material expression of beloved community.

The consensus of disenchantment is so pervasive and stubborn that even religious thinkers take it for granted. Charles Taylor, for instance, one of the most renowned students of secularity and its discontents, restates the conventional narrative, with a twist, in *A Secular Age* (2007). In the premodern epoch of enchantment, Taylor explains, the boundary that separated our world from the sacred was porous and indistinct; traffic between the two spheres was frequent, if not always desired or friendly. Now, having left the enchanted universe behind, we disenchanted dwell within the moral and ontological parameters of an "immanent frame": the world as apprehended through reason and science, bereft of immaterial and unquantifiable forces, structured by the immutable laws of nature and the contingent traditions of human societies. What Taylor calls the "buffered self" is a kind of "immanent frame" that insulates the inner from the outer world, thus precluding any sense of the numinous or any notion that "nature has something to say to us." Although Taylor foresees that "the hegemony of the mainstream master narrative of secularization will be more and more challenged" and hopes that "its overcoming [will] open up new possibilities," the contour and substance of his account of disenchantment do not differ fundamentally from Weber's. Where he parts from Weber and the consensus is in the prospect he discerns along "the unquiet frontiers of modernity" for a "re-enchantment of the world"—not necessarily a return to religious orthodoxies, but a recovery of a sense of the numinous, adumbrated in Romantic poetry and philosophy and visible today in "New Age" spirituality untethered to traditional doctrines and institutions.[11]

Yet any "re-enchantment" that presumes the hegemonic tale of disenchantment would likely prove to be an abortive exercise in willful self-delusion. It would seem difficult if not impossible to re-enchant the world without a paralyzing degree of self-consciousness; like a deliberate effort at spontaneity, the re-enchantment of a disenchanted world would be a futile enterprise in psychological calculation. Such a re-enchantment would occur solely in our heads, where the irrefragable and irksome reminders of disenchantment would still lurk, repressed in the shadows. Whether as art, or poetry, or play, or spirituality, re-enchantment would amount to little more than a tenuous and self-defeating therapy of consolation. Thus Taylor's hope for a "re-enchantment of the world" depends on telling a different story about disenchantment, one that does not rest on the ontological and historical foundations of the reigning account. To be genuine and enduring, a "re-enchantment of the world" must begin in a dissent from the prevailing wisdom about disenchantment. Just as Bruno Latour has argued that "we have never been modern"—that we have never differentiated nature and society as cleanly and rigidly as we suppose—might it be better to claim that we have never been disenchanted?[12] Perhaps the story we've told about the evacuation of the sacred from everyday life has been a fable; perhaps the "immanent frame" has always been permeable, while the "buffered selves" that ward off transcendence have been more porous than we ever imagined.

Weber himself left clues for a rather different account of our condition. In this story, we abide between two eras; "we live as did the ancients when their world was not yet disenchanted of its gods and demons," as Weber speculated in "Science as a Vocation" (1915)—"only we," he wrote, "live in a different sense." Antiquity witnessed a long twilight of the gods, only to be followed by the dawn of a new one, whose own demise appeared to be the final senescence and annihilation of all enchantment from the world. Indeed, Weber observed, while "many old gods ascend from their graves" they are quickly "disenchanted," taking "the form of impersonal forces." But is that the only way to understand the "different sense" to which Weber alluded so nebulously—that modernity marks the crossing of the final Rubicon of disenchantment? Perhaps the sociologist who considered himself "religiously unmusical" heard faint notes of enchantment in modernity; perhaps, despite their wounds, the old divinities had not risen to give consent to their euthanization.[13] Were they really "disenchanted" when they assumed their "secular" form? Or do they still roam among us in the guise of "secularization"? Capitalism has long been presumed to be a powerful solvent of enchantment—all that is holy is profaned, ecstasy is murdered in the waters of calculation. But what if those waters of pecuniary reason constituted a baptismal font, a consecration of capitalism as a covert form of enchantment, all the more beguiling on account of its apparent profanity?

Simon Critchley and Terry Eagleton might lend support to this conception of secularization as a disguise for enchantment. In *The Faith of the Faithless* (2012), Critchley rejects the axial assumption of most modern political thought: that the modernity of modern politics resides in its utter secularity, its lack of foundation in the will of divinity. Political order depends, he maintains, on allegiance to a "fiction," "an act of creation that brings a subject into existence"—like something performed by a writer, or a deity. This fiction, or "original covenant," as Critchley puts it, is a sacred, unquestionable tale whereby a people is brought—or rather, brings itself—into existence. If premodern polities traced their origins to the creative act of some divinity, modern "secular" political forms are, in effect, no different in their fictional character; whether fascism, communism, or liberal democracy, they represent "a series of metamorphoses of sacralization."[14]

Likewise, Eagleton has argued, in *Culture and the Death of God* (2014), that the Supreme Being "has proved remarkably difficult to dispose of"; ever since the Enlightenment, "surrogate forms of transcendence" have scrambled for the crown of the King of Kings: reason, science, literature, art, nationalism, but especially "culture." Providing cold, imperious Reason with the wardrobe of mythology, poetry, literature, and art, Culture, its devotees fervently hoped, would successfully impersonate religion. Displacing the clergy, philosophers and poets aspired to establish a new, post-Christian clerisy who would educate the masses with new myths, icons, and epiphanies, "the sacred discourse of a post-religious age." But the modern project of surrogate transcendence failed; even Nietzsche's *Übermensch* represented, Eagleton writes, a "counterfeit theology." In our incorrigibly ironic era of postmodernism, the venerable questions of meaning and destiny are sloughed off as unreal and coercive "metanarrative"; even revolutionary hope—another grasp at transcendence—yields to the conquest of cool, the imperium of a hip plutocracy. "The only aura to linger on," Eagleton sadly concludes, "is that of the commodity or celebrity."[15]

Although Eagleton insists that capitalism is "fundamentally irreligious . . . and totally alien to the category of the sacred," his perception of an "aura" around the commodity suggests that capitalism is a "surrogate form of transcendence," another "metamorphosis of sacralization," a modern vessel of primordial enchantment decked out in the apparel of secularity. As Marx himself hinted, despite the ostensible profanity of its pecuniary ethos, capitalism is hardly post-metaphysical: its metaphysics is money, the criterion of reality, meaning, and identity in a competitive commodity culture. In *Grundrisse* (1857), Marx referred to "the divine power of money" and its status as "the god among commodities." As the realm of the commodity widens, money not only purchases everything; it also seems to bring things into being from nothing, performing all manner of astonishing feats of moral and metaphysical alchemy. Money *can* buy you love: as the young Marx mused in an early reflection on "the power of money in bourgeois society," money enables its possessor to say "I am ugly, but I can buy for myself the most beautiful of women. Therefore I am not ugly, for the effect of ugliness—its deterrent power—is nullified by money."[16] Under capitalism, money occupies the ontological throne from which God has been evicted.

I want to go one step further than Eagleton and Critchley: The world does not need to be re-enchanted, because *it was never disenchanted in the first place.* Attending primarily to the history of the United States, I hope to demonstrate that capitalism has been, as Benjamin perceived, a religion of modernity, one that addresses the same hopes and anxieties formerly entrusted to traditional religion. But this does not mean only that capitalism has been and continues to be "beguiling" or "fetishized," and that rigorous analysis will expose the phantoms as the projections they really are. These enchantments draw their power, not simply from our capacity for delusion, but from our deepest and truest desires—desires that are consonant and tragically out of touch with the dearest freshness of the universe. The world can *never* be disenchanted, not because our emotional or political or cultural needs compel us to find enchantments—though they do—but because the world itself, as Hopkins realized, is charged with the grandeur of God.

Hence the importance of theology for this book, as I root my affirmation of the persistence of enchantment in a theological claim about the world: that the earth is a sacramental place, mediating the presence and power of God, revelatory of the superabundant love of divinity. In Christian theology, another way to say that the world is "enchanted" is to say that it is *sacramental;* in Graham Ward's words, the material world "bears the watermark of its creator." Of course, Christians are not alone in perceiving a sacramental quality in ordinary things; as anthropologist Marcel Mauss documented in *The Gift* (1922), tribal and ancient societies believed in various forms of what the Maori of New Zealand dubbed *mana*, an unseen presence that resided in things and knit together those who exchanged them. To be sure, unlike notions of *mana,* Christian theology (like its Jewish and Islamic relatives) asserts that things in themselves have no power apart from God. Still, material life has sacral significance, and how we make and use material goods has a sacramental and a moral dimension; there are sacramental—as well as perversely sacramental—ways of being in the world. Moreover, Christian ontology entails the conviction that abundance and peace are the true nature of things, not the scarcity and violence that leaven the cosmology of capitalist economics. As Pope Francis reiterated the sacramental imagination in his 2015 encyclical *Laudato Si,* while the Judeo-Christian religious heritage certainly "demythologized nature"—stripped it of divinity in itself—it nonetheless insists that divine love is "the fundamental moving force in all created things," and that the world is "illuminated by the love which calls us together into universal communion."[17]

That longing for "universal communion" is corrupted by a lack of trust in God, and our love spoils into a lust for power that mars the development of civilization. Without faith in the sacramental nature of the world, we anchor ourselves in the illusory and inevitably malevolent apparatus of domination: patriarchal lineages, property lines, police departments, surveillance networks, military-industrial complexes. This is what Augustine called the "earthly city," our inexorably unstable and unsuccessful attempt to construct a "celestial city" on the fissured foundation of our aberrant loves. Whether true or errant, our loves make us what we are; so if we are what we desire, history is the convoluted record of our loves in all their magnificent and ignoble forms. As the theologian Eric Gregory asserts, "love is the key to understanding world history." (Norman O. Brown once expressed much the same insight in psychoanalytic terms: "the riddle of history is not in Reason, but in Desire; not in labor, but in love.")[18] Capitalism is one such desire for communion, a predatory and misshapen love of the world. (Capitalism *is* a love story.)

However significant theology is for this book, I have relied on a sizable body of historical literature on the symbolic universe of capitalism. Much of this work suggests that capitalist cultural authority cannot be fully understood without regard to the psychic, moral, and spiritual longings inscribed in the imagery of business culture. As Jackson Lears puts it, the corporation may well be "a triumph of bureaucratic rationality," but its advertising speaks lissomely to desires for release from Weber's iron cage of disenchantment. Attuned to popular anxieties about an increasingly rationalized and impersonal world dominated by large institutions, Lears demonstrates that advertisers used a variety of aesthetic strategies to generate a "reanimation of the world under the aegis of major corporations." Likewise, Roland Marchand observed how corporate image professionals attempted to "reanimate" the corporation itself. Since the late nineteenth century—when it was first defined as a legal person—the corporation has often figured in popular culture as a soulless leviathan, destructive of the creativity and moral virtue once located (so it was thought) among proprietors and local communities. Responding to this crisis of moral legitimacy, public relations departments conjured, Marchand argued, a "corporate soul," an image of the corporation as a friendly neighborhood behemoth solely interested in community service.[19] It would seem that the iron in the cage of secularity has been leavened with enchanted materials.

Because I emphasize this enchanting carceral quality, some readers may complain that I overlook the real advances in human flourishing made possible by capitalism. Although I consider this objection a red herring, I want to make clear that I am not one of those churlish reactionary radicals who see nothing in capitalist modernity but one long, unrelieved nightmare of greed, brutality, and desiccating rationalization. The technological achievements of capitalism have surely improved the social and material conditions of billions of people; as none other than Marx asked in the *Communist Manifesto,* what earlier time "had even a presentiment that such productive forces slumbered in the lap of social labor?" Still—and this needs to be reiterated at a time of wavering but nonetheless ascendant capitalist triumphalism—these improvements would also not have been possible without labor unions, radical movements, welfare states, and political parties that mobilized unremitting popular struggle *against* the imperatives and institutions of capital. Moreover, it is essential to remember that, as Benjamin observed, every document of civilization is also a document of barbarism; during the tragically dialectical epoch of class struggle, all human achievement is tainted by oppression. It's a ruefully ironic observation with which Augustine would, I suspect, have concurred. Marveling in the *City of God* at "all the arts discovered and developed by human genius," Augustine still insisted that the aims and means of these arts could nonetheless be "dangerous and harmful" on account of our corruption.[20]

Thus, in the spirit of Augustine and Benjamin, I don't deny the reality of "progress," but I contend that the problem of "progress" is not as Christopher Lasch posed it in *The True and Only Heaven* (1991)—"progress and its critics"—but rather the *meaning* of "progress."[21] Despite caricatures of Luddism or technophobia, almost none of my anticapitalist protagonists desired a reversion to premodern technology and social relations. It is more accurate to say that the moral and ontological primacy of money in capitalist civilization has valorized a particular conception of "progress" that was, in their view, humanly and ecologically destructive despite all the material benefits it has conferred. (Even Marx succumbed to it.) Yet they did not call for the restoration of earlier social orders, nor did they believe that hammers and hoes would exhaust the technical possibilities of a world after capitalism. Their example suggests not that we should resurrect the past, but that we need to revisit what we mean by "progress," and not change the subject by invoking cyberspace or holding up the newest version of the iPhone.

Digital commodities now comprise the most recent items in the perverse iconography of consumerism, but this book is not yet another lengthy screed about "mindless," "materialistic" consumers. Because they often reduce consumption to a moral issue, critics of consumerism engage in a tiresome and largely ineffectual moralism. But historians and theologians might remind us that consumption is far more than a moral affair. However deftly and beguilingly the culture industries prey on some of the worst features of human nature, consumerism is a structural imperative of the modern capitalist economy; preaching jeremiads (religious or secular) has been of little discernible avail against the necessities of accumulation. Talking about *consumerism* is a way of *not* talking about *capitalism*. And besides, matter is good; material life should be cherished and savored as the sensuous gift of creation. Indeed, a sacramental sensibility and imagination constitute, in my view, the most compelling alternative to a pecuniary, instrumentalist desecration of people and the rest of the world. Thus, rather than rail against consumerism, I affirm John Ruskin's magnificent adage that "there is no wealth but life," as well as his distinction between "wealth"—that which helps produce "full-breathed, bright-eyed, and happy-hearted human creatures"—and "illth"—that which causes "devastation and trouble in all directions."[22]

The arc of my narrative traces the enchantment of capitalism since the seventeenth century. Emerging from the fields and factories of industrializing England, capitalist enchantment migrated to the American continent and became the marrow of a proprietary dispensation, represented enthusiastically by Puritans, evangelicals, Mormons. In the late nineteenth century, the proprietary order gave way to the corporate dispensation with a soulful corporation at its center. Through much of the twentieth century, the corporation presided over the Fordist endeavor to build a heavenly city of business, a celestial metropolis of capital achieved through the mechanization of production and communion. By the early twenty-first century, capitalism has reached its highest meridian of enchantment in the neoliberal deification of "the Market." The enchantments of Mammon have had their critics, to be sure, but pride of place in this volume will go to intellectuals, poets, novelists, and artists with profoundly religious sensibilities. From Gerard Winstanley and Ruskin to Herman Melville, James Agee, and Kenneth Rexroth; from John Muir, William James, Vida Dutton Scudder, and Dorothy Day to Lewis Mumford, Mark Rothko, Theodore Roszak, and Thomas Merton—a pedigree of prophets saw capitalist enchantment as a desecration of some invisible grandeur. As Henry Miller realized, "the earth is a Paradise. We don't have to make it a Paradise—it *is* one. We have only to make ourselves fit to inhabit it."[23]

Words such as "paradise" or "love" or "communion" are certainly absent from our political vernacular, excluded on account of their "utopian" connotations or their lack of steely-eyed "realism." Although this is a book about the past, I have always kept before me its larger contemporary religious, philosophical, and political implications. The book should make these clear enough; I will only say here that one of my broader intentions is to challenge the canons of "realism," especially as defined in the "science" of economics. As the master science of desire in advanced capitalist nations, economics and its acolytes define the parameters of our moral and political imaginations, patrolling the boundaries of possibility and censoring any more generous conception of human affairs. Under the regime of neoliberalism, it has been the chief weapon in the arsenal of what David Graeber has characterized as "a war on the imagination," a relentless assault on our capacity to envision an end to the despotism of money.[24] Insistent, in Margaret Thatcher's ominous ukase, that "there is no alternative" to capitalism, our corporate plutocracy has been busy imposing its own beatific vision on the world: the empire of capital, with an imperial aristocracy enriched by the labor of a fearful, overburdened, and cheerfully servile population of human resources. Every avenue of escape from accumulation and wage servitude must be closed, or better yet, rendered inconceivable; any map of the world that includes utopia must be burned before it can be glanced at. Better to follow Miller's wisdom: we already inhabit paradise, and we can never make ourselves fit to live in it if we obey the avaricious and punitive sophistry professed in the dismal pseudoscience.

The grotesque ontology of scarcity and money, the tawdry humanism of acquisitiveness and conflict, the reduction of rationality to the mercenary principles of pecuniary reason—this ensemble of falsehoods that comprise the foundation of economics must be resisted and supplanted. Economics must be challenged, not only as a sanction for injustice but also as a specious portrayal of human beings and a fictional account of their history. As a legion of anthropologists and historians have repeatedly demonstrated, economics, in Graeber's forthright dismissal, has "little to do with anything we observe when we examine how economic life is actually conducted." From its historically illiterate "myth of barter" to its shabby and degrading claims about human nature, economics is not just a dismal but a fundamentally fraudulent science as well, akin, as Ruskin wrote in *Unto This Last,* to "alchemy, astrology, witchcraft, and other such popular creeds."[25]

Ruskin's courageous and bracing indictment of economics arose from his Romantic imagination, and this book partakes unashamedly of his sacramental Romanticism. "Imagination" was, to the Romantics, primarily a form of vision, a mode of *realism,* an insight into the nature of reality that was irreducible to, but not contradictory of, the knowledge provided by scientific investigation. Romantic social criticism did not claim the imprimatur of science as did Marxism and other modern social theories, yet the Romantic lineage of opposition to "disenchantment" and capitalism has proved to be more resilient and humane than Marxism, "progressivism," or social democracy. Indeed, it is more urgently relevant to a world hurtling ever faster to barbarism and ecological calamity. I wrote this book in part out of a belief that many on the "left" continue to share far too much with their antagonists: an ideology of "progress" defined as unlimited economic growth and technological development, as well as an acceptance of the myth of disenchantment that underwrites the pursuit of such expansion. The Romantic antipathy to capitalism, mechanization, and disenchantment stemmed not from a facile and nostalgic desire to return to the past, but from a view that much of what passed for "progress" was in fact inimical to human flourishing: a specious productivity that required the acceptance of venality, injustice, and despoliation; a technological and organizational efficiency that entailed the industrialization of human beings; and the primacy of the production of goods over the cultivation and nurturance of men and women. This train of iniquities followed inevitably from the chauvinism of what William Blake called "single vision," a blindness to the enormity of reality that led to a "Babylon builded in the waste."[26]

Romantics redefined rather than rejected "realism" and "progress," drawing on the premodern customs and traditions of peasants, artisans, and artists: craftsmanship, mutual aid, and a conception of property that harkened back to the medieval practices of "the commons." Whether they believed in some traditional form of religion or translated it into secular idioms of enchantment, such as "art" or "beauty" or "organism," Romantic anticapitalists tended to favor direct workers' control of production; the restoration of a human scale in technics and social relations; a sensitivity to the natural world that precluded its reduction to mere instrumental value; and an apotheosis of pleasure in making sometimes referred to as *poesis,* a union of reason, imagination, and creativity, an ideal of labor as a poetry of everyday life, and a form of human divinity. In work free of alienation and toil, we receive "the reward of creation," as William Morris described it through a character in *News from Nowhere* (1890), "the wages that God gets, as people might have said time agone."[27]

Rendered gaudy and impoverished by the tyranny of economics and the enchantment of neoliberal capitalism, our sensibilities need replenishment from the sacramental imagination. As Americans begin to experience the initial stages of imperial sclerosis and decline, and as the advanced capitalist world in general discovers the reality of ecological limits, we may find in what Marx called the "prehistory" of our species a perennial and redemptive

wisdom. We will not be saved by our money, our weapons, or our technological virtuosity; we might be rescued by the joyful and unprofitable pursuits of love, beauty, and contemplation. No doubt this will all seem foolish
to the shamans and magicians of pecuniary enchantment. But there are more
things in heaven and earth than are dreamt of on Wall Street or in Silicon
Valley.

# PART ONE

## The Dearest Freshness
## Deep Down Things:
## Capitalist Enchantment
## in Europe, 1600–1914

"THE WORLD IS CHARGED with the grandeur of God," Gerard Manley Hopkins marveled in the winter of 1877. For Hopkins, the earth was a place of grace, a vast and glorious sacrament; it was not inanimate, but rather "charged," enlivened, always quickened by the presence of divinity. Since God dwells among us, the universe is radiant, "like shining from shook foil." Yet, oblivious to God's enchantment of the earth, "generations have trod, have trod," and as a result of our industrious inattention, "all is seared with trade; bleared, smeared with toil." The labor enforced by the lust for profit disfigures the face of creation; the malevolence and tyranny of money effaces and blasphemes the majesty of God. But Hopkins refused to despair, for despite our sacrilege, "nature is never spent"; even when despoiled, it confounds our defilement and remains a vessel of grandeur. God resides at the exuberant heart of creation and will not be dispossessed: "There lives the dearest freshness deep down things." God protects and mends the despoiled world, watchful, forgiving, and resplendent. "The Holy Ghost over the bent / World broods with warm breast and ah! bright wings."[1]

Hopkins bore a hopeful witness against the desecration of the enchantment of the world. Indeed, he believed that the waning of traditional religious faith and the future of capitalism—the "death of God" and the "social question"—were inextricably bound together. In the summer of 1871, Hopkins had written to a friend about the bloody suppression of the Paris Commune. "In a manner I am a Communist," he confessed, for the ideal of communism is "nobler than that professed by any secular statesman I know of." "Besides," he added curtly, "it is just." "It is a dreadful thing," he continued, "for the greatest and most necessary part of a very rich nation to live a hard life without dignity, knowledge, comforts, delight, or hopes in the midst of plenty—which plenty they make."[2] Though Hopkins's "manner" of being a communist would surely have failed any test imposed by Marx and his comrades in the First International, Hopkins was certain that reverence for God's grandeur demanded the end of capitalist iniquity.

Yet even if "some great revolution is not far off," Hopkins worried that workers had been mortally infected with the spirit of the "iniquitous order." With its ruthless and irrepressible dynamism, capitalism had extinguished or broken all traces of "the old religion, learning, law, art, etc." In books, music, and stone, medieval Christianity had preserved the ideal of a fellowship leavened by love; but that invaluable edifice was now succumbing to the mercenary forces of "wrecking." It was only from the memory of the past, Hopkins implied, that workers could fashion a communist future worthy of their human dignity. But thanks to the demolition of history by their exploiters, the working classes know "next to nothing" of this inheritance; and since most of its custodians were indifferent or hostile to their demands, the workers "cannot be expected to care if they destroy it."[3]

Hopkins echoed a long tradition of prophecy. The age of capitalist enchantment began in England in the sixteenth and seventeenth centuries. Sweeping away the sacramental moral economy of the medieval commons, a capitalist vanguard of landowners and merchants constructed a regime of "improvement." Spearheaded by Puritan improvers, the historical point men of capital were not disenchanting, mechanical accumulators; their Protestant ethic was perfectly compatible with omens, portents, and marvels. Protestant capitalists reworked the sacramental imagination of medieval Catholicism, aligning its conviction of metaphysical enchantment with the imperatives of dispossession, enclosure, and profit. From Puritan divines such as Richard Baxter to John Locke and the godfathers of liberalism, English Protestants espoused a systematic theology of the divine right of capitalist property. But other Protestants dissented from the gospel of improvement sanctified by Puritan divinity. Epitomized by Gerard Winstanley and the Diggers, a sacramental, communist materialism prefigured the modern, secular left.

By the early nineteenth century, the Puritan era of capitalist enchantment had given way to an evangelical successor. Proclaiming themselves heralds of a science of wealth whose laws had been decreed by God, "Christian political economists" were more widely read and admired than Adam Smith or David Ricardo. For the clerics of evangelical enchantment, God had manufactured the capitalist cosmology of property, market, and enterprise, with scarcity and struggle as His paternal inducements to labor, innovation, and riches. Marveling at the dreadful beauty of a strife commanded by the Creator, English evangelicals preached and imposed the gospel of capitalist freedom.

As the industrial revolution triggered by "improvement" advanced through the nineteenth century, a motley array of opposition to the gospel of capitalist enchantment arose. Karl Marx, for instance, detected the persistence of the spirits in capitalist modernity. From the oldest fabrication of gods and spirits to the superstition of "commodity fetishism," human beings had projected their own inherent powers onto illusory but oppressive beings. Through the science and practice of revolutionary socialism, human beings would reclaim their alienated powers; God would finally be exposed as humanity, and humanity would come into its own as God. Less "scientific" than Marx, Romantic writers affirmed a "natural supernaturalism," the unorthodox heir to sacramental theology. The Romantic sacramental imagination became prophecy in the work of Thomas Carlyle, John Ruskin, and William Morris. Carlyle's invective against the "Gospel of Mammonism" stemmed from a Romantic theology of wonder; yet for all his rhetorical thunder, Carlyle ended his career as a champion of the work ethic and the "Captains of Industry." The most renowned and formidable art historian of the nineteenth century, Ruskin was also a heretical political economist. Though derided, then and now, as a cranky medievalist scourge of technological progress, Ruskin was rather a passionate exponent of an alternative, sacramental modernity, countering the dismal science with one that taught the laws of "the Economy of Heaven." Following Ruskin, Morris longed to re-enchant the world—but without Ruskin's Christian theology. Like utopian socialists, anarchists, and members of the Arts and Crafts movement, Morris tried to revive the tradition of the commons, hoping to suffuse the people's republic with a naturalist replica of enchantment.

# 1

# About His Business

The Medieval Sacramental Economy,
the Protestant Theology of "Improvement,"
and the Emergence of Capitalist Enchantment

THE "DISENCHANTMENT OF THE world" is a myth. To be sure, the enchanted universe of medieval Catholicism collapsed, succumbing to Protestant theology, the new science and its quest for technological mastery, and the pecuniary reason and promethean ethos that emboldened capitalist enterprise. But Protestantism was a reformation of enchantment, not a herald of disbelief in an animate world. The new science replaced the old animate cosmos with a new "mechanical philosophy" of enchantment, a cosmology of matter and spirit conducive to industrial exploitation. Arising within the new metaphysical imagination, capitalism emerged as the moral and political economy of modern enchantment.

The medieval moral economy was enveloped in a "sacramental worldview," in Brad Gregory's words, in which the material world and social life could reflect and convey divine grace and power. For serf, lord, merchant, and artisan as for pope, archbishop, and scholastic philosopher, all of life was sacramental, pervaded by the presence of the triune God. Epitomized in the sacrament of the Eucharist, medieval culture displayed a profound conviction of material beatitude and beloved community; as Eamon Duffy observes, the crown of the sacraments could be used to sanction the most oppressive power relations only because "the language of Eucharistic belief and devotion was saturated with communitarian imagery." The medieval landscape was a topography of enchantment: churches, chapels, shrines, grottos, all manner of sacred spaces. Merging orthodox religion and beliefs in magic, sorcery, and other brands of the occult, popular religion featured cults of veneration of saints and relics, as well as numerous feasts and holy days when the ordeal of labor was suspended. Even the culture of "Carnival" held enchanted, eschatological meaning. At its pinnacle in the Feast of Fools—when lords and serfs changed places for a day, while laity mocked priests and bishops—Carnival included the temporary, utopian erasure of social hierarchies. Carnival was a glimpse of "the beatific vision" in fleshly, joyful plenitude; for a day, the gates of heaven opened, the future paid a visit to the present, and carnal splendor could provide a robust foretaste of the impending kingdom of God.[1]

Preparation for that kingdom was the point of economic life in the Middle Ages. Superintended by God the Almighty Father, patriarchal family and kinship relations were the models for all social and political affairs; manors, fiefs, and kingdoms were considered patrimonies, not sources of revenue, polities governed by divinely sanctioned elders. Leavened and structured throughout by Christian metaphysics and morality, this "theological economy," as Diana Wood has characterized it, was bound up with the medieval conception of a *communitas commutitatum,* a "community of communities" that embraced families, manors, guilds, cities, courts, parishes, fraternal associations, universities, and monasteries.[2]

With both earthly and beatific destinies in mind, property was hedged with innumerable restrictions, enveloped in a latticework of moral rules, legal codes, guild charters, and spiritual meanings. To be sure, the distribution of goods, money, and property buttressed the rule of nobles over serfs, artisans over apprentices, clergy over laity, men over women—the channels of medieval patriarchal dominion, the (alleged) handiwork of God that contained the calamitous consequences of the Fall. But philosophers, canon lawyers, and municipal officials constructed elaborate systems of just prices, just wages, and financial regulation to hold pandemonium at bay as well. Though regularly flouted or circumvented, medieval prohibitions of usury, for instance, reflected a view of interest on loans as an offense against both humanity and God. According to the thirteenth-century prelate and homilist Jacques de Vitry, usurers eat not the Eucharist but rather "the bread of impiety"—usury was, in this view, a desecration of the sacrament. The arduous and ultimately futile effort to control pecuniary delirium—to keep money embedded in the "theological economy" of Christian charity and piety—vexed theologians, lawyers, merchants, and municipal leaders throughout the Middle Ages. "Every other sin has its periods of remission," warned Caesarius of Heisterbach, another thirteenth-century moralist, but "usury never rests from sin. Though its master be asleep, it never sleeps, but always grows and climbs."[3]

The sacramental imagination imbued the urban guilds that arose in the tenth and eleventh centuries, as well as the rural moral economy of the feudal countryside. Besides furthering the material interests of merchants and artisans through restrictions on entry, trade, and production, the "essential aim" of medieval guilds, Anthony Black writes, "was to sacralize the cohesion of their members." Before the eleventh century, most guilds had been religious in character, dedicated to a patron saint. Guild rules and charters codified this spirit of communion, enjoining mutual aid; support for orphans and the poor; endowment of churches, hospitals, and universities; and the use of money, not for unfettered accumulation, but for charity. Thomas Brinton, a fourteenth-century Benedictine monk and canon lawyer, asserted that "merchants and faithful mechanics" were the left hand of the Mystical Body of Christ. As late as the fifteenth century, Florentine leaders beckoned to guilds as models of beloved community. "We long to preserve such a divine being," one municipal official exulted in 1427, "and to direct towards it our energies, love, loyalty, concord, truth and our soul, as loving the universal good most of all."[4]

In the countryside, a similar moral and theological economy prevailed: "the commons," as it was called in England. "Commons" meant not only the common fields and forests of a manor but also the assignment to the whole community of power to determine property rights, the provision of subsistence, and the organization of labor. Before the Norman invasions of the eleventh century, village land in Saxon England belonged, not to individual people or families, but to all residents of the village; individuals enjoyed rights of use, not ownership. Even after the Norman conquest, when village lands belonged to a lord, common rights remained, conditional on fealty and tribute to the manorial noble. Thus the commons was no utopian ideal; it reflected the historical and everyday experience of cooperation and mutual aid. In England, the two documents that enshrined the commons in law and morality—the Magna Carta and the Charter of the Forest, both forced on King John in 1215—possessed, in Peter Linebaugh's words, "the aura of power, the glamour of color, and the solemnity of religion." Because the world was a sacramental place, a violation of the commons, like the extraction of usury, put one's soul in eternal peril. Though subordinate to the interests of the seigneurial class, it offered the subaltern both political leverage and a trove of moral imagination.[5]

The commons also pointed to a barely repressed desire for communism that lurked as the political unconscious of medieval Christendom. "The ideal—if only man's nature could rise to it—was communism," as R. H. Tawney long ago recognized. Private property was considered a rueful concession to the circumstances of a fallen world; property was either a necessary evil, a right of use, or a social trust. One's land, workshop, or manor was a means of subsistence and a contribution to the common good, not a means of increasing one's wealth or of fostering accumulation as an end in itself. Under the medieval cope of heaven, property had to be directed toward the common good, not employed or aggregated for private gain; distributed as widely as possible, not concentrated in ever fewer hands; and dispensed to the poor after the requirements of one's "station in life" had been met. Monastic orders quarantined communal ownership in the otherworldly asceticism of their members, while scholastics such as Thomas Aquinas sublimated the desire for communism into the "universal destination of goods." God's creation belongs to all, in Aquinas's formulation, but after the Fall, private property oriented toward the common good would ensure that wealth is produced and distributed fairly.[6]

Yet the desire for communism surfaced with unprecedented force in the twelfth and thirteenth centuries as commercial and monetary relations spread in both the cities and the countryside, leading to more pressure on serfs, more rural and urban destitution, and more righteous fury among the exploited. Often drawn from the ranks of heterodox mystics and dispossessed peasants and artisans, medieval communists blended a powerful sense of divine immanence with common ownership, voluntary poverty, egalitarianism, and millennial proclamations of impending deliverance. They included Joachim of Fiore and his heterodox eschatology of "The Three Ages," the last of which was dawning; the lay mendicant Beguines and Beghards, exemplified by the ill-fated Marguerite Porete; and the Brethren of the Free Spirit, perhaps the most notorious, whose antinomianism owed a great deal to both Joachim and Porete. Convinced that love and poverty were tokens of friendship with God, these groups espoused what Simon Critchley has dubbed a "faith-based communism" in which common possession of material goods was believed to reflect the life of the Trinity. Many who remained within the bounds of orthodoxy witnessed to the ideal of communism. The popularity of St. Francis of Assisi in the early thirteenth century is incomprehensible outside the idealization of poverty and dispossession. A century later, William Langland asserted in *Piers the Plowman,* his mid-fourteenth century moral allegory, that "Christians should hold their riches in common, and none covet anything for himself." Where devotion to Mammon wrought misery and death, "Love," Langland wrote, "is the physician of life . . . the direct way to Heaven."[7] Medieval millenarianism suggests that a beatific, communist promise resides at the heart of Christianity—a promise whose vindication was rooted in a metaphysics and theology of sacramental love.

To be sure, the medieval "theological economy" was no Golden Age of communion. "The world we have lost" was one that most premodern men and women would almost certainly not want to recover. "The failure of medieval Christendom," Gregory writes, stemmed from "the pervasive, longstanding, and undeniable failure of so many Christians . . . to live by the church's own prescriptions and exhortations." The Latin Church's own clergy were among the most notorious and most vilified malefactors; many in the episcopate, and especially the cardinals and popes in the Vatican, spurned Lady Poverty and befriended Mammon through simony and luxurious consumption. Barons and guildsmen were hardly ever paragons of chivalry; nobles lived off the sweat of peasants; merchants cheated their customers; artisans exploited their journeymen; bankers turned the screws on creditors; scholastics like Aquinas wrote *Summas* and ruminated on the nature of being because serfs were treated like beasts. As Raymond Williams reminds us with stark and compelling gravity:[8]

> [For] the uncountable thousands who grew crops and reared beasts only to be looted and burned and led away with tied wrists, this economy, even at peace, was an order of exploitation of a most thoroughgoing kind; a property in men as well as land; a reduction of most men to working animals, tied by forced tribute, forced labour, or "bought and sold like beasts"; "protected" by law and custom only as animals and streams are protected, to yield more labour, more food, more blood.

Yet the innumerable transgressions against the sacramental order underscores the significance of its exalted character, as offenses against charity and justice could be identified as evils rather than as prices to be paid for abundance. The volcanic peasant uprisings that erupted in the fourteenth century—the Jacquerie in France in 1358 and the Peasant's Revolt in England in 1381, led by Wat Tyler and John Ball—were triggered, not by aspirations for market freedom or liberal democracy, but by violations of the medieval moral economy. The typical peasant, Rodney Hilton observes, felt a "permanent rage against nobles whom he blamed, as a whole, for not having fulfilled their duty of protection which tradition and mutual obligation demanded of them." Utterly bereft of illusions about the perfectibility of the human condition, medieval people were thereby free from the delusion of a concord achieved through venality. So as Tawney shrewdly observed, if medieval moralists were "naive in expecting sound practice as the result of lofty principles alone," they were also innocent of the contemporary "form of credulity which expects it from their absence or their opposite."[9]

Indeed, medieval moralists had steadily more of that "absence or their opposite" to confront as the European commercial economy expanded from the eleventh to the sixteenth centuries. The old medieval moral economy endured, if in an increasingly fragile form, as business practices and relationships remained enmeshed in networks of family and marriage until well into the sixteenth century. While monetized transactions proliferated most obviously and ostentatiously in towns from Florence and Venice to Bruges, Antwerp, Paris, and London, money and profit-maximizing practices had encroached into more and more rural areas by the thirteenth century. By the fifteenth century, well-to-do urban Christians could worship in opulent cathedrals, adorn themselves in sumptuous clothing, and donate to the poor and to religious orders thanks to their sophisticated banking, credit, and accounting systems. As commercial activity burgeoned in northern Italy and Flanders and the lures of "filthy lucre" multiplied, merchants, lawyers, and theologians gradually relaxed or abolished many of the traditional restrictions on interest-bearing loans; guilds bestowed more benefactions on charities, priories, universities, and hospitals; and avarice stepped out of the shadows of hell and into the light of respectability, if not of heaven. The new glorification of riches and acquisitiveness was evident among Renaissance humanists such as Poggio Bracciolini, whose fifteenth-century treatise On Avarice marked a halfway covenant between medieval and modern attitudes. Though careful to condemn avarice as a sin, Bracciolini noted nonetheless that without it, "all the magnificence of cities would be removed, all culture and ornament would be destroyed, no temples would be built, no colonnades, no palaces, all arts would cease, and then confusion of our lives and of the republic would follow." The unabashed delight in wealth was a gorgeous effrontery to the old morality of Christendom. When in 1515 Erasmus told his portraitist to depict him as a merchant—complete with purse and broadcloth gown—it was clear that the medieval ideal had waned, and that some new, more brashly venal world was coming. Thus, from the standpoint of economic cosmology and ethics, whether or not England, the Dutch Republic, or the Italian Renaissance city-states represented the first "modern" or "capitalist" economy is less important than the beleaguered persistence of the sacramental worldview.[10]

It was in the midst of this waning sacramental economy that the Reformation demolished the theological and institutional coherence of Latin Christendom. Yet neither the "magisterial" reformers—Martin Luther, John Calvin, Ulrich Zwingli—nor their "radical" counterparts—Anabaptists such as Thomas Muntzer and Menno Simons, and, as I'll argue, Gerrard Winstanley and the Diggers—were avid enthusiasts of competitive, endlessly expanding enterprise. Scandalized by the extravagance of the Church and the clergy's connivance in the corruptions of the rich, the Reformers believed, as Gregory puts it, that "economic behavior . . . needed a massive overhaul through an infusion of biblical morality"; they wanted "not to liberate but to restrict the runaway greed and sinful selfishness" they saw among prelates and their wealthy benefactors. Some—Muntzer, John of Leyden, the Swiss Brethren, Mennonites, and Moravian Hutterites—invoked the medieval ideal of communism, establishing (usually short-lived) experiments in community of goods, while Calvin and his brethren in Geneva enforced a tightly regulated commercial economy even as they ended traditional restrictions on usury.[11]

But if Protestantism did not *cause* capitalism, the Reformation did clear moral and metaphysical ground for a new "theological economy," one that, as we have seen, had been gathering momentum for several centuries. By destroying the Catholic sacramental architecture that sacralized medieval society, Protestantism made possible the transvaluation of values that culminated in capitalist enchantment. With its rejection of what Weber called the "magical" power ascribed to the sacraments, the Protestant repudiation of Catholic ritual—especially in its most virulent form in Calvinist theology—led to what Weber called "the sanctification of worldly activity": the consecration of a "calling" in which ordinary people served God in their daily labors.[12] Ironically, the rejection of *works* as means of salvation entailed a gospel of *work;* however worldly or secular these callings appeared, work inherited the sacral efficacy formerly ascribed to Catholic ritual. At the same time, by commencing the desacralization of nature—the denial of any sacramental character in matter—Protestants set the stage for pecuniary enchantment, the unwitting metaphysics of capital.

Yet just as the Reformation did not immediately usher in capitalism, so it did not immediately disenchant the world; indeed, what one scholar describes as a "distinctively Protestant popular religious and magical culture" continued to flourish in the sixteenth century and beyond. Protestants throughout Europe beheld omens and portents, revered relics, visited holy places, and attended to "special providences" that warned of damnation or heralded salvation. Familiar with "the sacraments of the Devil," they dreaded sorcery and divination, consulted astrologers, and prayed against demonic possession. The Protestant cosmology of enchantment embraced agricultural life, particularly in England, where medieval and Renaissance conceptions of nature as a living, nurturing, provident being long outlasted the sixteenth-century Reformation in England. Pervading almanacs, manuals, and planting and harvesting rituals—Maypole dances and offerings to spirits—English agricultural enchantment reflected a view of nature as, in Carolyn Merchant's words, "an animate mother, subservient to God yet a powerful actress in the mundane world." Far from being an inert, soulless heap of resources, Nature was God's "vice-regent" in the universe.[13]

Even the "mechanical philosophy" that was emerging as the intellectual armature of modern science was not as mechanical as it seemed. In early modern Europe, and especially in England, educated Protestants became a new clerisy of enchantment. Like their rural compatriots, they inherited a view of nature as a vibrant, spirit-filled realm. Their openness to science demonstrated that belief in an enchanted world did not preclude the pursuit of rational investigation and technological control. Sir Francis Bacon blended the animistic universe and the new mechanical conception of nature. Steeped in alchemical and Rosicrucian lore, Bacon believed that nature was liberally suffused by "spirits or pneumaticals" that thrived in the pores of matter. In

Bacon's view, even inorganic matter held spirits; gems, diamonds, and emeralds possessed virtues that "comfort and exhilarate" those who wear them. A similar animate cosmology flourished among Cambridge Platonists, who depicted a universe vivified by a *spiritus mundi,* or world spirit, which took life force from the world soul, *or anima mundi,* and infused it into the world body, or *corporea mundi.* Many among the Protestant intelligentsia—whether the Puritan clergy or the Anglican members of the Royal Society—took an avid and erudite interest in supernatural phenomena, occult practices, and esoteric cosmologies. If Puritan theologians such as William Perkins condemned magic and astrology, pioneers of the "mechanical philosophy," such as Bacon and Robert Boyle, championed Hermetic philosophy and Paracelsian alchemy. As Isaac Newton's alchemical and Rosicrucian passions suggest, Protestant enchantment and scientific thought overlapped well into the era of modernity.[14]

Though often regarded as the pious and steely vanguard of desacralization, English Puritans epitomized this Protestant enchantment. Just as the Protestant ethic has been seen as the template of sober and methodical labor, the Puritan conception of Providence has been considered a precursor of scientific law. Yet the Puritan doctrine of Providence accommodated a colorful array of wonders, portents, and prodigies. As Keith Thomas observes, the Puritan inclination to see omens and marvels in nature "sprang from a coherent vision of the world as a moral order reflecting God's purposes and physically sensitive to the conduct of human beings." Comets or eclipses "did not cease to be seen as divine warnings when . . . it came to be appreciated that they had natural causes and could be predicted." Precisely because of their faith in a divinely appointed order, Puritans still lent credence to premonitory dreams, illustrious providences, and presages of death and disaster. Though they associated much of magic and the occult with the lingering pestilence of Catholicism, they believed nonetheless in the diabolical efficacy of witchcraft, divination, alchemy, fortune telling, and astrology. They feared the powers of cunning-men and wizards no less than they despised Catholic priests. Late Tudor and Stuart England witnessed the proliferation of a vast elite and popular literature of Puritan enchantment. Reminding Christians that the world was *The Theatre of Gods Judgements* (1597), Thomas Beard—clergyman, theologian, and teacher of Oliver Cromwell—reflected that in and behind every object and occurrence lay the invisible hand of God.

"Is there any substance in this world that hath no cause of his subsisting? Doth not every thunderclap constraine you to tremble at the blast of his voyce?"[15] Although they assisted in the inaugural stages of the scientific dis- enchantment of nature, Puritans saw no incongruity between a universe governed by natural law and a cosmos rife with monstrous births, punitive hailstorms, and portentous comets.

At the same time, with their self-proclaimed "delight in secular employ- ments," enchanted Puritans emerged as the avant-garde of capitalism, arch- angels of divinely commanded "improvement"—the use of land for the prof- itable production of commodities. Puritan ministers revered and publicized the work of pamphleteers, such as Edward Misselden, Thomas Mun, Nich- olas Barbon, and William Petty, advocates for greater freedom in monetary policy, international trade, and enclosure. Through enclosure—the termina- tion of rights to the commons, the transformation of customary land tenures into rents, the fencing of common land, and the dispossession of tenants— Puritan nobles and gentry hastened the capitalist transformation of English agriculture. Meanwhile, Puritan merchants—especially those involved in overseas ventures in Africa, East India, the West Indies, and the Atlantic sea- board of North America—spearheaded a similar metamorphosis of urban trade and manufacturing. Moving from commerce into production, the new merchants joined agrarian entrepreneurs in enforcing the regime of im- provement. Puritans were also the shock troops in what Peter Burke has called "the triumph of Lent": the reduction of holy days, the curtailment of feasts, the grim cancellation of Carnival.[16]

Since Protestant theology and enchantment was the reigning religious cul- ture of seventeenth-century England, "improvement" required the sanction and discipline of God. Echoing older Catholic warnings against avarice, Pu- ritan ministers admonished merchants, artisans, "improving" landowners and tenants, and others for whom thrift and diligence were cardinal virtues in the newly competitive society of Stuart England. Exhortations to pursue one's "calling"—one's "secular employment" ordained by God—were hedged with reminders of the hellfire that awaited the covetous. Puritans constantly reminded themselves that they could not serve two masters. "The mixture of God and mammon in men's love . . . debaseth and destroyeth religion," the minister and theologian Richard Baxter warned in *A Christian Directory* (1678). Over the past three decades, many historians of trans-Atlantic Puritanism have taken these invocations of "godly commonwealth" at face value. As Stephen Innes argues, the Puritans sincerely believed that they labored "in the service of God, not Mammon."[17]

Contemporaries were less impressed by Puritan professions of antipathy to Mammon. In Thomas Hobbes's view, Puritans condemned lust and gluttony but never inveighed "against the lucrative vices of men of trade or handicraft." What Christopher Hill rightly identified as the Puritans' "cultural revolution" was rooted in their indomitable and lucrative faith in the divine imperative of profit. "When duty was so profitable," as Tawney asked sardonically, "might not profit-making be a duty?"[18] This sense of a mercenary calling was rooted in the Puritans' cosmological architecture. The same God who ordained the world's wonders and marvels made the market for pecuniary glory. Contrary to the oft-reiterated claim that Puritans separated the religious and economic realms, the saints affirmed that profit-making followed the grain of the universe. Cosmological enchantment and pecuniary calculation were complementary, not antagonistic. As a result, the Puritan conscience displayed considerable elasticity where profits were concerned; the cosmology of the saints harmonized much of the traditional dissonance between God and Mammon.

Indeed, the Puritan God commanded His saints to befriend the unrighteous Mammon. The coins that poured into Puritan coffers were signs every bit as revelatory as comets, storms, and apparitions. The Puritan God was the Celestial Improver with unrelenting demands for *more*. As Baxter ominously declared in his *Christian Directory*, "if God shew you a way in which you may lawfully get more than in another way"—without, of course, "wrong to your soul or to any other"—then "if you refuse this, and choose the less gainful way, you cross one of the ends of your Calling, and you refuse to be God's Steward." Of course, Baxter cautioned, we may not pile up "riches for our fleshly ends"; but "in subordination to higher things," the pursuit of wealth was justified, even mandatory.[19] Seldom has so plentiful and inexpensive a line of moral credit ever been extended. Formed in the crucible of improvement, the Puritan doctrine of calling was the first covenant theology of capitalism. Wrought under the aegis of Protestant enchantment, the Puritan transvaluation of values eased the traditional tension between God and Mammon. The Puritans ensured that later generations would trod and trod and trod, seared with trade and bleared with toil.

But Puritan avarice also revealed the depth of a sacramental desire. Especially during the reign of Charles II, Puritan clergy produced their own version of the abundant literature on enclosure and agricultural improvement. Addressing upwardly mobile merchants, artisans, and farmers, the clerics discerned a sacramental dimension in the life of capitalist enterprise. The ritual of improvement was the subject of volumes such as William Spurstowe's *The Spiritual Chymist* (1666), Edward Bury's *The Husbandman's Companion* (1677), and William Bagshaw's *Trading Spiritualised* (1696). In *The Weavers' Pocket-Book* (1675), for instance, John Collinges, a Presbyterian minister in Norwich, sought to "spiritualise" the craft by raising "heavenly meditations from the several parts of their work." John Flavel, a Presbyterian clergyman in Dartmouth, was even more insistent on the capacity of improvement to bring the worker closer to God. Flavel's *Husbandry Spiritualised* (1669) and *Navigation Spiritualised* (1671) were among the most popular booklets in the religious literature of improvement. The material world delivered "spiritual sweetness," Flavel wrote; "do we not feed with angels?" As Flavel reminded his readers, nature, to the eye of the believing Christian, was transparent to the radiance of God. "The world below is a Glass to discover the world above," Flavel marveled; natural objects bear "the figures and similitudes of many sublime and heavenly mysteries." Indeed, our diligent laboring with the earth could have more sacramental efficacy than the Eucharist. Through "skilful and industrious improvement," we could experience "a fuller taste of Christ and heaven, in every bit of bread . . . in every draught of beer that we drink, than most men have in the use of the sacrament."[20]

Other Protestants could be equally adept in the sacralization of improvement. From his vicarage in the rural parish of Bemerton, in Wiltshire, George Herbert dispensed advice to young priests when not busy writing poetry. In *The Country Parson* (1652), Herbert composed a clerical manual of agrarian capitalist enchantment. His sacramental conception of land reflected the metaphysical concerns of his verse. "Our Saviour made plants and seeds to teach the people," Herbert mused, "for he was the true householder." Since rural folk lack the time and talent for intellectual appreciation, God instructs them "by familiar things" that "slip more easily into the hearts even of the meanest." In the grass, flowers, trees, and animals of the Wiltshire countryside, Herbert saw "monuments of his Doctrine, remembering in gardens, his mustard-seed, and lilyes, in the field, his seed-corn, and tares." Ploughs, hatchets, bushels, and other "things of ordinary use" could "serve for lights even of heavenly truths." Herbert nowhere voiced the slightest unease with the new regime of enclosure and improvement, pointing to the industrious and accumulating farmer as the moral ideal of the future. Set on "the improvement of his grounds, by drowning, or drawing, or stocking, or fencing," the rural proprietor made profitable use of God's sacramental monuments. Echoing Baxter and other Puritans, Herbert reasoned that since riches are "a blessing from God," then "all are to procure them, honestly and seasonably, when they are not better employed."[21]

Improvement literature gave birth to a new utopian genre: the utopia of incessant research, innovation, industrial development, and economic growth. The prototype of industrial utopias was, of course, Bacon's *The New Atlantis* (1627), in which a band of English sailors discovers the island of Bensalem, a sanctuary of abundance and beloved community directed by a scientific and technical elite. Sworn to "the enlarging of the bounds of human empire, to the effecting of all things possible," the wizards work in "Salomon's House," a research-and-development center whose devotion to innovation and efficiency prefigured the ethos of modern laboratories and corporate bureaucracies. Salomon's House is the hub of a network of research, production, and amusement: "engine-houses" for machinery, "mathematical-houses" for computation, numerous other sites for the fabrication of silks, jewels, perfumes, and a host of culinary delicacies. Bensalem also sports an entertainment industry, with devices for "feats of juggling, false apparitions, impostures, and illusions" as well as for imitation of motion, "by images," in what resembles film or holograms. The island's intelligentsia relies on "Merchants of Light," businessmen who, concealing their identities, procure knowledge and inventions from all over the globe.[22] *The New Atlantis* spawned five centuries of technological beatific visions.

Yet while Bacon's celebration of "human empire" affirmed the desacralized, instrumental view of nature indispensable to capitalist enterprise, the search for what one character called "natural divinations" also suggests the persistence of enchantment. Bacon's ambiguous allegiance to alchemical and Rosicrucian ideas—recall the "spirits or pneumaticals" in which he believed—was evident in the mystical atmosphere of Bensalem and its scientific magi. As the sailors approach "Bensalem," they see "a great pillar of light" rising from the sea up toward the heavens, at the top of which is "a cross of light . . . bright and resplendent." The mandarins explain that the pillar is "a true Miracle," a suspension of natural law for some "divine and excellent end." Far from secular, the technicians' and researchers' daily routine includes "hymns and services" as well as prayers "for the illumination of our labours, and the turning of them into good and holy uses." As the prayers suggest, Bacon clearly feared that the growing inventory of "natural divinations" could be turned to fraudulent purposes. The denizens of Salomon's House aver that they "have so many things truly natural that induce admiration" that they could easily "deceive the senses," disguising the products of human artifice "to make them seem more miraculous."[23] Despite his commitment to the extension of human mastery, Bacon worried that the new empire of science and technology could conjure a host of counterfeit enchantments, works of human participation in the power of divinity that wrought malevolence in the guise of good.

Similar utopian tracts appeared in the 1640s and 1650s, all positing an indelible link between the human and divine activities of mastery: Gabriel Plattes's *A Discovery of Infinite Treasure* (1639) and *The Famous Kingdome of Macaria* (1641), as well as Samuel Gott's *Nova Solyma: The Ideal City, or, Jerusalem Regained* (1648). Gott's theology of industrial utopianism was overtly sacramental. "The world," one of the new Jerusalem's inhabitants explains, "is the *idolum*, or *imago*, of the Deity," who is "a wise and active and indwelling spirit." "Motes in a sunbeam," human beings "resemble the phantasies and spectres of an active brain"; we are "the Poems of God." Plattes—an alchemist and agriculturalist who influenced John Winthrop, Jr., in his colonization of Connecticut—called on his compatriots to abandon doctrinal disputation and to concentrate on wealth, the real "pith and substance of Religion," in his view. If they identified "the Finger of God in their creation," the industrious, Platte maintained, could enjoy the intimate companionship of His presence, "without whose blessing all is vanitie and lost labour." Plattes outlined a capitalist kingdom of innovation and technological deliverance. Calling for the abolition of feudal land tenures and their replacement with contractual wage relations, Platte contended that new property relations would leave both landlord and tenant free to "trie experiments" and "improve to the utmost."[24]

Thus, well before the invention of classical political economy in the eighteenth century, capitalism had acquired not only moral approval but also religious significance. Enclosures certainly "prepared for the proletarianization of the common people," as Linebaugh observes; but they did *not*, as he claims further, "destroy the spiritual claim on the soil."[25] In shredding the charter of the medieval commons and writing their own covenant of work, English improvers recast but did not abrogate the "spiritual claim on the soil"—or on the workshop or the counting-house. Contrary to Weber, Protestant capitalists did not disenchant the world; rather, they re-negotiated the terms of enchantment. If they no longer held that Catholic sacramental ritual was efficacious for salvation, they believed that they encountered God in the midst of material creation—and wealth. If Protestants had rejected Catholicism as a "gospel of works"—a scheme of salvation through enchanting external rituals rather than inward faith—the Protestant ethic was a gospel of work, with riches as the new eucharistic tokens of communion with divinity. To Puritans and other "improving" Protestants, the golden rules of capitalism codified a post-medieval theological economy.

Even John Locke thought of God as the Almighty Sponsor of Improvement. Some scholars have attempted to rescue Locke from the ideological lineage of what C. B. Macpherson called "possessive individualism," stressing his objections to the unfettered accumulation of wealth, his admiration for small proprietors, and his Christian suspicion of the morally corrosive impact of prosperity. Yet Locke's own moral imagination is thoroughly leavened with a pecuniary sensibility. An adviser to the first Earl of Shaftesbury—an improving landlord and colonial investor—Locke was steeped in the agricultural literature of late Stuart England. Read against that background, his *Second Treatise of Government* (1690) is much more than a patristic text of liberalism; it is a theological manifesto of Christian capitalism, an early promulgation of commercial metaphysics.[26]

Although Locke has been credited with espousing a "labor theory of value" in the *Second Treatise*—"'tis *labour* that *puts the difference of value on every*-thing"—a closer examination reveals that money is the final standard of valuation. Locke observed that God has given the earth to men and women "to make use of it to the best advantage of life and convenience"; indeed, we are "sent into the world by His order and about His business." Left without attention to "His business," land that "hath no improvement . . . is called, as indeed it is, *waste*." Like Baxter, Locke measured "advantage," "convenience," and "improvement" in almost wholly pecuniary terms; "improvement" meant not just the art of cultivation, but the science of profitable enterprise. An acre of land in America may be as fertile as an acre in England, he observes, but it is not worth 1 / 1,000 of the English acre, for "all the Profit an *Indian* received from it were it valued and sold here."[27] The value of the acre to the Indian as subsistence means little or nothing to Locke; what matters is the creation of exchange value, assessed in monetary terms and underwritten by the covert metaphysics of capital.

Locke's remarks on money offer an early intimation of this new pecuniary metaphysics. Distinguishing between use value and monetary value, Locke interpreted the latter as a human creation with far-reaching, transubstantive consequences. By making it possible to acquire more things than one could use, money, he wrote, "altered the intrinsick value of things"—their utility. As a vehicle of desire created and maintained in motion "by the tacit Agreement of Men," money in effect transformed—or rather canceled—"intrinsick value" and wrought what amounted to a metaphysical metamorphosis. At the same time, as Locke's comparison of European and Amerindian acreage indicated, money displaced labor and utility as a stand of valuation. Land in England and land in America possessed "the same intrinsic value," he conceded, but they now differed in monetary value—hence his dismissal of "all the *Profit* an Indian received from it." Locke remained well aware of the purely conventional nature of monetary value; he expressed astonishment that "a little piece of yellow metal" could "be worth a great piece of flesh or a whole heap of corn." But in the end, money's moral and metaphysical authority—affirmed by the profitable improvement it made possible—sufficed to muffle any further objections. Thus in Locke's view, "improvement," not labor, confers a right to property—improvement understood as God's appointed "business" of increasing profitable production.[28] "His business" is capitalist business: the systematic entrepreneurial development of land through enclosure from the commons. For Locke, the whole point of the commons is to be steadily diminished by gainful improvement; the land and labor themselves are evaluated in the terms of pecuniary reason and ontology.

So despite—or rather, precisely because of—his concern for the small agricultural proprietor, Locke remains, along with Hobbes, one of the premiere ideological architects of possessive individualism. Far from offering an apologetic for labor, Locke vindicated the divine right of capital, supplementing Hobbes's fabrication of enchantment in *Leviathan* (1651)—where the "commonwealth" is "a "mortal God"—with a theology of improvement. At the same time, in sanctioning the dispossession of indigenous peoples for their lack of prowess in "His business," the *Second Treatise* contained a theological warrant for English colonization and genocide.[29] For Locke—as for Baxter, Herbert, and subsequent chaplains for the mercenary armies of improvement—capitalism bore the mandate of heaven, and its emissaries held a divine license to consign their opponents to eternal damnation.

If Protestant enchantment sacralized "His business," it also inspired prophecy against the brave new world of money and "improvement." The religious allure of the new capitalist order obsessed numerous Elizabethan and Jacobean writers, from poets and playwrights to political economists and commercial pamphleteers. Mammon, Philip Spenser wrote in *The Faerie Queene* (1590), is "God of the world and worldlings . . . greatest god below the skye." Ben Jonson satirized the commercial culture of Jacobean London in *Volpone* (1606), whose eponymous protagonist—a greedy and salacious Venetian nobleman—greets the dawn with a gilded prayer:

Good morning to the day; and next, my gold,
Open the shrine that I may see my saint:
Hail the world's soul, and mine . . .
. . . let me kiss
With adoration, thee, and every relic
Of sacred treasure, in this blessed room.

"Our *summum bonum* is commodity," Robert Burton lamented in *The Anatomy of Melancholy* (1621), "and the goddess we adore, *Dea moneta,* Queen Money, to whom we daily offer sacrifice." Queen Money poisoned souls; divided friends; parted lovers; and reduced patriarchs, lords, and emperors to abject servility. She made a mockery of piety and revealed the face of perverse, sublunary desire: "Take your heaven, let them have money."[30]

Denunciations of Mammon and his minions persisted throughout the seventeenth century, even among Puritans, especially after the abandonment of the republican cause of the 1640s and 1650s and the restoration of the Stuart monarchy. From the ranks of artisans, traders, and other less successful members of the elect came John Bunyan, "a tinker and a poor man," a Puritan tribune convinced that God's people "are most commonly of the poorer sort." His morality tale set against the gaudy fleshpots of Restoration England, *The Pilgrim's Progess* (1678) is also a melodramatic homily of Puritan populism. En route to "the Celestial City," two pilgrims, Christian and Faithful, come upon "Vanity Fair," whose urbane and callous inhabitants deal in houses, lands, "Bodies, Souls, Silver, Gold, Pearls, Precious Stones." Faithful is murdered, but Christian makes his way to "Beulah," an "Inchanted Ground" whose vapors overwhelm him. (Later, Christian's wife Christiana crosses over Beulah and encounters the infamous Madame Bubble, "Mistress of the World" who reveals herself as the enchantress: "It is by Virtue of her *Sorceries* that this Ground is *enchanted*.")[31]

Christian awakens and proceeds to the Celestial City, "builded of Pearls and Precious Stones" and whose streets are paved with gold—in other words, the elements traded in the sinful markets of Vanity Fair. The City is the reality of which Vanity Fair is the enchanting but insidious simulacrum. Yet despite Bunyan's insistence that, as Christian says, "the soul of religion is the practical part," he counseled resignation to the inevitable sway of sin and mercenary morality. Bunyan surely looked backward to "the old laws, which are the Magna Carta, the sole basis of the government of a kingdom"; but Christian never avers that Vanity Fair can be destroyed, reformed, or redeemed.[32] Like Christian, we must carry our crosses and expect no justice in this vain and fallen world.

Light-years different from Bunyan in theology and sensibility, John Milton's bold and truculent disparagement of Calvinist predestinarianism—"though I may be sent to hell for it, such a God will never command my respect"—encapsulated his religious and political radicalism. Milton's radicalism stemmed in part, scholars now agree, from his embrace of an "animist materialism": an ontology in which the distinction between spirit and matter has been abolished. As the angel Raphael explains to Adam in *Paradise Lost* (1667), "One first matter all / Indued with various forms, various degrees / Of substance, and in things that live, of life; / But more refined, more spirituous, and pure." (In *Paradise Lost*, angels eat, drink, and make love.) Milton's animist materialism—a heterodox brand of sacramentality—could inspire a communist vision and a critique of accumulation. Paradise, the angel Raphael explains to Adam, is an image and likeness of the celestial homeland: "God hath here / Varied his bounty as with new delights, / As may compare with Heaven." Eden is innocent of property, enclosure, and hierarchy. With love as their "sole propriety," Adam and Eve share "a happy rural seat of various view" without mine and thine, or master and servant. "Among unequals what society / Can sort, what harmony or true delight?" While work is to be done in Eden, it is pleasant and moderate, uncompelled by profit or productivity. Before the Fall, they performed "no more toil than sufficed / To recommend cool Zephr, and made ease / More easy."[33]

Once Satan slithers into the Garden, this earthly beatitude ends, and the sinful regime of toil and accumulation commences. Milton suggests that the ethic of improvement is the spawn of Mammon. Milton's Mammon is the perfect example of perversion: a being who reveres and desires creation even more than he loves its Creator:[34]

> ... the least erected Spirit that fell
> From Heaven, for even in Heaven his looks and thoughts
> Were always downward bent, admiring more
> The riches of Heaven's pavement—trodden gold—
> Than aught divine or holy else enjoyed
> In vision beatific.

Milton portrays Mammon as the demon of possessive individualism. While Moloch and Belial rally the fallen angels for a second offensive against God, Mammon advises, not merely resignation, but strenuous, defiant self-reliance. Rather than be vassals in heaven, we damned, Mammon thunders, can "seek / Our own good from ourselves, and from our own / Live to ourselves ... Free, and to none accountable." Preferring "hard liberty" to heaven's "easy yoke / Of servile pomp," Mammon robustly preaches the work ethic, admonishing his fellow condemned to "work ease out of pain / Through labour and endurance." Indeed, Mammon voices the hidden desire at work in capitalist enterprise—the construction of a parody of the heavenly city:

> ... this desert soil
> Wants not her hidden luster, gems and gold;
> Nor want we skill or art, from whence to raise
> Magnificence; and what can Heav'n shew more?

As the prototype of industrious improvement, Mammon leads the excavation crew for Pandemonium, the capital city of Hell, and they erect "a Temple . . . with Golden Architrave." As Milton makes clear, the construction of Pandemonium is the paradigm for later human despoliation of the earth. Just as Mammon fractures the soil and mountains of hell for building materials, so men, "by his suggestion taught," seek to plunder and desecrate creation: They have "ransacked the center, and with impious hands / Rifled the bowels of their mother Earth / For treasures better hid."[35]

*Paradise Lost* records the experience of defeat shared by partisans of "the Good Old Cause": the abolition of monarchy, the disestablishment of the Church of England, the creation of a republic, and—at its most radical— the eradication of class. Milton gave melancholy voice to a desire that had been thwarted by Cromwell and the Stuarts: a godly, sacramental communism. The cultural revolution launched by the Puritans was not the only one envisioned in England. In the 1640s and 1650s, dissenters from Anglican and Puritan orthodoxy—itinerant craftsmen and displaced cottagers, often in league with young, iconoclastic graduates of Oxford and Cambridge— attempted to stage an alternative cultural revolution, one that looked backward to the tradition of the commons but also pointed to an egalitarian future. In the maelstrom of religious and political turmoil that defined the English Revolution, these nomadic, masterless men and women formed an underground of plebian saints. From the dispossessed rabble, they believed, the Holy Spirit would ascend, and Christ would, in Gerrard Winstanley's phrase, "rise up in sons and daughters" to establish his earthly republic of love.[36]

Before Cromwell's Protectorate quashed the Good Old Cause in 1653, England abounded with groups determined to turn the world upside down: Levellers, Familists, Fifth Monarchy Men, Adamites, Ranters, and "True Levellers," or Diggers. Like less radical Protestants, they blended magic, astrology, and alchemy with the "mechanical philosophy." Rejecting rituals, doctrines, and often the Bible itself, religious radicals placed more credence in individual judgment and mystical consciousness, repudiating priestly mediation for a wider democracy of sacramental experience. With sin defeated and consigned to oblivion, many radicals sought to reenter the splendor of the Garden of Eden before the Fall. However temporarily, the party of Carnival held Lent at bay and rehearsed for the people's republic of heaven. "My most excellent majesty and eternal glory," proclaimed Abiezer Coppe, an Oxford-educated Ranter, resides "in me ... who am universal love, and whose service is perfect freedom and perfect libertinism." God is "that mighty Leveller," Coppe avowed, who would, upon the glorious return of His Son, "overturn, overturn, overturn."[37]

The most profound challenge to the new regime of enclosure and commerce came from the Diggers, whose spokesman Winstanley addressed the question of property with remarkable theological bravado. In April 1649, Winstanley and several others occupied a piece of common land on St. George's Hill, in Surrey, just outside London. After tearing down fences and other enclosures, they planted vegetables and invited "all to come in and help them." Reviving the ethos of the medieval countryside, they declared that England would never be free until all enjoyed a "free allowance to dig and labor the commons." Harassed in court and bullied by local landowners, the Diggers were forced to abandon St. George's in August. The summer of love ended, and the sinful reign of law and order was restored. Other Digger colonies cropped up throughout England, but they, too, were quickly and ferociously suppressed.[38]

Never trained in philosophy or divinity, Winstanley forged his Christianity out of his own experiences of misery, doubt, and epiphany. Born in 1609, he had been a cloth merchant in London, but when his business failed in 1643, he was forced to move to Cobham, where he labored as a cowherd. In the tracts and pamphlets that he began writing at this time, Winstanley denounced the dubious ethics of commerce, recalling unscrupulous traders—including, perhaps, himself—who demanded "sometimes too much" for their goods. Having fallen into rural wage labor, Winstanley now knew from bitter experience the hardships and indignities of poverty: "sickness, frowns of friends, hatred of men, losses of his estate by fire ... being cheated by false-spirited men." Official religion had offered no help; though he had been an eager "hearer of sermons" and "a blind professor and strict goer to church," no denomination offered the poor anything beyond chastisement or the afterlife.[39]

From this maelstrom of personal ruin and despair, Winstanley fashioned a daring and compelling theology of communism. In an extraordinary four-year burst of writing (1648 to 1652), Winstanley published pamphlets and treatises that fused theology, metaphysics, history, and politics. Convinced, as he proclaimed in *The True Levellers Standard Advanced* (1649), that "the great Creator Reason made the Earth to be a Common Treasury," Winstanley narrated a story of original fraternity, descent into private property, and redemption back into communism. A "great mystery" had been unfolding on St. George's Hill, he believed, a spiritual revolution seen by "the material eyes of the flesh." It was "the fullness of Time," he and the Diggers believed; "that Scripture which saith *The poor shall inherit the earth*, is really and materially to be fulfilled."[40] The end of the world appeared to be impending. Winstanley's invocation of "the Creator Reason" has led Hill, his most influential interpreter, to claim that Winstanley was, if not an outright rationalist, at the very least a religious precursor to modern, secular communism. "The poetic, mythopoeic style . . . came naturally to him," Hill contends; Winstanley "was struggling towards concepts which were more precisely if less poetically formulated by non-theological materialisms." He was certainly unorthodox, mystical, and anticlerical. The conventional notion of God "held [him] under darkness," he confessed; he recounted ecstatic, episodes of "Vision, Voyce, and Revelation," "Vision in Dreams, and out of Dreams," as well as "Prophecies, Visions, and Revelations of Scriptures, of Prophets, and Apostles"; he despised the Anglican clergy for their unctuous obeisance to crown and property; and he scoffed at the divine inspiration of the Bible, freely engaging in allegorical interpretations.[41]

Yet Hill's contention that Winstanley was poetically "struggling towards" ideas articulated "more precisely" by "non-theological materialisms" reflects all the unexamined assumptions that underlie the narrative of "secularization," especially that poetical or mythopoeic forms of understanding and explanation stand in absolute, intractable antagonism to scientific, historical, and technological terms. If Hobbes's political imagination was thoroughly mechanistic, Winstanley's recalled the enchanted medieval "sacramental worldview," in which the divinity of reason allowed it to speak in a variety of dialects: nature, prophecy, revelation, and the "rising up of Christ in sons and daughters." At the same time, the position that pre-modern revolutionary ideas must be somehow liberated from their confinement within religious language rests on the assumption that religion is incapable of generating a genuinely revolutionary imagination. But Winstanley did not need dialectics of class analysis to respond to injustice; he denounced private property and the theft of the commons because they violated God's original communist mandate for creation—and that was enough to impel him to action. A representative of plebian Protestantism, Winstanley was not a proto-deistic infidel but rather a political theologian of the radical wing of the English Reformation; he was not "struggling toward" anything other than a prophetic remonstrance against the Lucifer of enclosure. His materialism was sacramental, his politics were religious, and his communism was redemptive.

Though resolutely unorthodox, Winstanley's theology of communism was robustly sacramental. Permeating all things without being identifiable with matter, Winstanley's God was purely, radically immanent, pervading and enlivening the material world. He does not reside above the firmament, or constitute a state of eternity untouched by the vicissitudes of time and place. "The Father is not confined to any one particular place for he is in every place, and in every creature," he wrote in *Truth Lifting Up Its Head above Scandals* (1649). "The whole creation," he observed, is "the clothing of God." "The Body of Christ is where the Father is, in the earth, purifying he earth, and his spirit is entered into the whole creation which is the heavenly glory where the Father dwells." Later, in *The Fire in the Bush* (1650), Winstanley reiterated that God "fills all with himselfe, he is in all things, and by him all things consist."[42]

But creation had fallen from the heavenly glory, and the Diggers proposed to lead the way back to paradise before the Fall. With the earth as his clothing and with men and women as his undefiled image and likeness, God had ordained common ownership of the planet as the original state of nature. Winstanley repeated, in post-dogmatic terms, the medieval ontology of love and abundance. "The Living Earth is the very Garden of Eden, wherein that spirit of Love, did walke." Imbued with Love and Reason, "every single man, Male and Female, is a perfect Creature of himself," and "the same Spirit that made the Globe, dwels in man to govern the Globe." Though man was created "a perfect Creature," the Fall was an act of idolatry, committed when man began to "delight himself in the objects of the Creation, more than in the Spirit Reason and Righteousness." This perverse "delight," led inexorably to private property, class conflict, and tyrannical government—"Civil Propriety," as he called the system of dominion that held the vast majority in mesmerized servitude. "Civil Propriety" blighted all of creation; "the Ayre and Earth is all poysoned, and the curse dwels in both, through mans unrighteousness."[43]

The form of idolatry and bondage that Winstanley's rural contemporaries knew was the "disturbing devil" of capitalist property. The earth was "hedged in to In-closures," he observed in *A Declaration from the poor oppressed people of England* (1649), while men were subjected to the demon of money, "the great god that hedges in some, and hedges out others." Enclosure was the mark of perverted desire for the sacramental goods of the earth. A year later, delivering *A New-Yeers Gift for the Parliament and Armie* (1650), Winstanley extended his prophetic range to include the entire political system, sounding the inaugural notes in what would become the tradition of modern anarchism. There are two kinds of kingly power, he explained: one, that of "Almightie God, ruling the whole creation in peace . . . the power of universall love," and the other "the power of unrighteousness, which indeed is the Devil," the monarchy that superintends the satanic regime of enclosure and money.[44]

Winstanley believed that the end of this infernal tyranny was nigh, to be followed by the restoration of the original communist state of nature. "We see it to be the fullness of Time," he wrote; the "New Jerusalem" was imminent, and "the glory of the Lord shall be seen and known within the Creation." But "we shall not do this by force of Arms," he declared, but rather through the "streaming out of Love in our hearts towards all." Citing the book of Acts, he described the descent of the Spirit on the brethren: "the Rich men sold their Possessions, and gave part to the Poor; and no man said, That ought that he possessed was his own, for they had all things Common." In the communist democracy of a new English Eden, the "great cheat" of buying and selling would cease, as would class, clergy, monarchy, and enclosure. "Universall love" would overwhelm the insidious enclosures of the Devil, and men and women would reenter "the state of simple plainheartedness or innocency." "They that are resolved to work and eat together, making the earth a common treasury, doth join hands with Christ to lift up creation from bondage, and restore all things from the curse."[45] The world turned upside down—which is to say, the world turned right side up and inside out—was a people's republic of heaven. More a herald of "liberation theology" than a harbinger of modern secularity, Winstanley illustrated the radical potential of the sacramental imagination.

And yet the Garden remained padlocked and guarded. When Cromwell became Lord Protector in 1653, he imposed a military government; God did not overturn, overturn, overturn. And when Charles II reclaimed the throne in 1660, Providence seemed to put a royal seal on the plutocracy of enclosure and improvement. Auguring the defeat of the Good Old Cause, Winstanley had reflected melancholically on the failure of his attempt to reenter Eden. "Knowledge, why didst thou come, to wound, and not to cure?" Milton and other radicals retired from politics; Winstanley himself fled into respectability, becoming a prosperous corn merchant, a member of the Society of Friends, and a resident of the fashionable Bloomsbury district of London.[46] The beatific vision of St. George's Hill must have seemed like the folly of a dream.

# 2

# The God among Commodities

Christian Political Economy, Marx on Fetishism,
and the Power of Money in Bourgeois Society

BY THE END of the seventeenth century, the juggernaut of improvement
had accelerated the pace and scope of rural enclosure. By 1750, having seized
control over the labor of agricultural workers and struggling skilled workers,
urban merchants were taking the initial steps in the degradation of artisanal
labor—the unleashing of "the unbound Prometheus," the "industrial revolution" against the order of craft, "the making of the English working class."
Meanwhile, new, more permissive attitudes toward consumption developed
among the urban middle classes, eager to emulate the tastes of the aristocracy, who in turn escalated the standards of consumption to stay ahead of
upstart bourgeois.[1]

Whether or not Hanoverian England was "the first consumer society," it
witnessed a profound metamorphosis in attitudes toward pleasure and consumption. How did a frugal and striving class of "improvers" give way to
avid consumers of textiles, pottery, and luxury items? Certainly, the old Puritan strictures against luxury retained much of their force; fears of degenerate, emasculating ease persisted into the nineteenth century. But among
Enlightenment luminaries such as Bernard Mandeville, David Hume, and
Adam Smith, the ideals of simplicity and asceticism were being supplanted
by a "rehabilitation of desire," in Christopher Lasch's words, in which the
incessant, indefinite multiplication of material wants was lauded as the engine of progress. Mandeville's *Fable of the Bees* (1714) was notorious for its
exuberant cynicism about the benefits of "vice." Writing in "Of Refinement of
the Arts" (1752), Hume contended that by stimulating initiative, ingenuity,
and sociability, "the pleasures of luxury and the profit of commerce" promote
an "encrease of humanity"—an expansion of the sphere of moral concern and
capacity for generosity. "*Industry, knowledge,* and *humanity* are link'd by an

indissoluble chain, and are found . . . to be peculiar to the more polished and luxurious ages." In *The Theory of Moral Sentiments* (1759) Smith mused on the beneficent ruses of avarice. "Enchanted with the distant idea of felicity," a poor boy "charmed with the beauty" of the luxuries abounding in the blue-blood world of pleasure will work and cultivate his talents to fulfill his desire for riches—only to discover that "wealth and greatness are mere trinkets of frivolous utility." Yet "it is well that nature imposes upon us in this manner," Smith observed, for "it is this deception which rouses and keeps in continual motion the industry of mankind."[2]

Yet the "rehabilitation of desire" was not purely a secular project of liberation. As Colin Campbell has argued, a nascent culture of consumption gestated within Protestantism itself. Beginning in the mid-seventeenth century, a loose coalition of moral pioneers—Cambridge Platonist advocates of "spiritual sensation," Arminian rebels against the rigors of Calvinism, and Lockean advocates of sensationalist psychology—forged what Campbell dubs "the Other Protestant Ethic": an affirmation of emotional experience that eventually culminated in evangelical religion and Romanticism. Through this "Other Protestant Ethic," the enchantment formerly attributed to the external world was relocated in the individual self. In the three centuries after the Reformation, Campbell argues, "wonder," "marvel," and other qualities once considered features of the medieval sacramental cosmos gradually became aspects within, not outside the self, subjective reactions to an otherwise desacralized world now understood by the standards of science. If the *world* was disenchanted, the *self* was not.[3]

This enchantment of subjectivity sanctioned a "Christian sentimentalism" in which individual sensibility served as the register of moral and religious truth. Idealized in the "Man of Feeling" who was exquisitely attuned to the emotions of others, Christian sentimentalism celebrated the experience of delight in righteous conduct. While Christian sentimentalism leavened an ethic of benevolence and humanitarianism that issued in abolitionism, factory reform, and the extension of the suffrage, it also constituted a new form of enchantment that provided the English bourgeoisie with a moral license to participate in fashionable consumption. Thus, Campbell implies, modern capitalism rests on a metaphysical fault line: a profane, inanimate external world given over to calculation and control, and a hedonistic, "enchanted" internal realm of daydream, fantasy, and romance. In a world increasingly understood in terms of Newtonian physics and mechanism, what John Brewer has dubbed "the pleasures of the imagination" became new enchantments of capitalist modernity.[4]

Yet for quite some time, the advance of rationalism, empiricism, and other "secular" forms of consciousness was not incompatible with Protestant enchantment. Take, for instance, Joseph Addison and Richard Steele's *Spectator,* one of the first periodicals to represent the worldview of the Hanoverian bourgeoisie. Aiming "to enliven morality with wit, and to temper wit with morality," the *Spectator* would seem to epitomize what historians have depicted as the urbane and stylish secularism of the English Enlightenment. As Whigs, Addison and Steele were enthusiastic promoters of commercial expansion, industrial development, and the civilizing pleasures of consumption. Yet they also saw the Almighty everywhere—even in the delights of the senses. As Addison wrote in a July 1714 issue of the *Spectator,* "His Being passes through, actuates and supports the whole Frame of Nature. His Creation, and every Part of it, is full of him. . . . His Substance is within the Substance of every Being, whether material or immaterial." Whether or not this is pantheism matters less than its avowal of metaphysical enchantment—the truth of which, Addison added, "Reason as well as Revelation assures us." In another issue, Addison mused further that "we may taste and see how Gracious He is, by His Influence upon our Minds, by those Virtuous Thoughts . . . secret Comforts and Refreshments . . . ravishing Joys and inward Satisfactions." Almost a month later, Addison concluded his religious reveries with an eloquent testimonial to the pleasures of enchantment, discerning in the fulfillment of our physical senses the voluptuous presence of divinity. "Why," he asked rhetorically, "should we exclude the Satisfaction of these Faculties, which we find by Experience as Inlets of great Pleasure to the Soul?"[5]

Blending virtue, reason, and comfort, Addison's apologia for the pleasures of the imagination—ratified, in his genteel sensibility, by God's pervasive presence in creation—was a Whiggish precursor to the evangelical cosmology of industrial capitalism. In the "Christian political economy" that arose in the early nineteenth century, British evangelicals defended unfettered markets and the new regime of factories and labor discipline as features of "the harmony and beauty, the symmetry and order of that system, which God and nature have established in the world," as one early expositor explained.[6] Indebted to Smith, David Ricardo, John Stuart Mill, and other worldly philosophers, God's evangelical economists espoused a theological economy of the Protestant Enlightenment: the laws of the market, discernible by science, were the edicts of an active and ever-present Almighty. Thus, fusing the moral vernacular of sentimentalism with the idiom of modern science, Christian political economists recast the theology of capitalist misenchantment. And as representatives of a rising class of merchants, factory owners, managers, and technicians, they refashioned the work ethic in terms of industrial technology and managerial authority.

Like the Puritan universe of improvement and omens, evangelical cosmology blended capitalist modernity with belief in enchanted powers. As Alison Winter has demonstrated, many evangelicals were enthusiasts of mesmerism. Much like the many Victorian scientists who investigated mesmerism, hypnosis, trances, and other "paranormal" phenomena, evangelicals straddled the boundary between the vestiges of occult and the canons of natural science. Belief in "influences," "correspondences," and "animal magnetism" was rife among the Victorian middle and upper classes, and many evangelicals either feared or succumbed to what one acknowledged as the "mysterious and subtle agency" of mesmerists. Like Puritans assessing the value of magic, evangelicals disputed, not the efficacy of mesmerism, but its contribution to spiritual health. One of the leading evangelical economists, Richard Whately, Anglican archbishop of Dublin, was a mesmerist and mesmeric patient who founded the London Mesmeric Infirmary in the 1850s. Despite Whately's open and passionate practice of mesmerism, he was never reproached by his brethren.[7]

Whately considered mesmerism both a spiritual practice and a body of knowledge—akin to the political economy he taught at Oxford in the early 1830s. Like his fellow "Christian economists," Whately held that the laws of the universe had been decreed by a mysterious but resplendent God. In his *Introductory Lectures on Political Economy* (1831) Whately declared that political economy was "a branch of Natural Theology," providing evidence of "striking marks of divine Wisdom" similar to those in astronomy or physiology. A Scottish Presbyterian clergyman as well as a lecturer on divinity, mathematics, and political economy at St. Andrew's and Edinburgh, Thomas Chalmers maintained that economic laws were beautiful as well as utilitarian. Celebrating the "thriving interchange of commodities" in *The Application of Christianity to the Commercial and Ordinary Affairs of Life* (1820),

Chalmers marveled at the "beauteous order" of the market, wrought by the "presiding Divinity" who "compasses all his goings." God's grace could enrapture and fructify the apparently sordid dealings of business, "impregnating our minutest transactions with the spirit of the gospel." Chalmers envisioned the plenitude of grace available to all who asked, a "great stream of supply, which comes direct from Heaven to earth." This grace-filled abundance ensured success in the market, the sign and seal of "a beauteous character."[8]

But as Thomas Malthus and other Christian economists proved, such beauty truly was in the eye of the beholder. Scarcity, evil, and suffering played positive roles in the evangelical theodicy of capitalism. To many of the evangelical economists, our expulsion from the Garden of Eden was not a punishment, but an opportunity. In the evangelical gospel of scarcity, privation was excellent news: the lashes of adversity and competition would compel us into moral and material improvement. Malthus and Nassau Senior led the way among evangelical economists in redefining evil as a necessary good. In his infamous *Essay on the Principle of Population* (1798) Malthus—an instructor at Haileybury College, the training school for administrators of the East India Company, as well as an Anglican pastor—asserted that want, conflict, and other agonies were parts of a godly metaphysical and moral architecture. Human life, he asserted, is "a state of trial and school of virtue preparatory to a superior state of happiness." Departing from the mainstream of Christian theology since Augustine, Malthus argued that moral evils and natural calamities were "absolutely necessary to the production of moral excellence . . . instruments employed by the Deity" to spur industriousness and ingenuity. Malthus's insistence on the goodness of disaster rested on a toilsome, penurious sacramentality, an ontology of dearth and meanness designed by an omnipotent but skinflint deity. Life is "the mighty process of God," he insisted, "a process necessary to awaken inert, chaotic matter into spirit." "The finger of God is, indeed, visible in every blade of grass that we see," and among the "animating touches of the Divinity" is the salutary character of evil. "Evil exists in the world not to create despair but activity." (If it failed to spur industry, then, Malthus wrote in the 1826 edition, "we should facilitate, instead of foolishly and vainly endeavoring to impede, the operations of nature in producing this mortality"—i.e., the death of the poor.) Senior—first professor of political economy at Oxford, and a protégé of

Whately's—told students in 1830 that God and nature "decreed that the road to good shall be through evil—that no improvement shall take place in which the general advantage shall not be accompanied by partial suffering." So rather than look to reform or revolution to end their miserable condition, evangelicals such as Cobden advised workers that they should abide by "the principle of competition which God has set up in this wicked world as the silent arbiter of our fate."[9] The God of Love consigned the poor and dispossessed to a lifelong Calvary road.

By the 1840s, many workers had been acquainted with that "principle of competition" through subjection to the industrial division of labor. Misenchanted and driven by the same imperatives that propelled earlier agrarian "improvers," Victorian manufacturers and merchants patented industrial forms of enclosure. The industrial revolution was a social and political process in which artisans and craftspeople were dispossessed, stripped of traditional skills which were then rationalized and embodied in new technologies, and subjected both to an increasing subdivision of labor and to the control of overseers and managers. The transformation of skilled workers into factory hands—the "proletarianization" of craft, a process every bit as coercive as the eviction of peasants from the commons—was essential to the introduction of industrial technology. As Andrew Ure acknowledged in *The Philosophy of Manufactures* (1835), "skilled labour gets progressively superseded, and will eventually, be replaced by mere onlookers of machines." Ure was well aware that capital's most formidable enemy was the skilled worker, so "self-willed and intractable" that the worker's stubborn insistence on independence would inevitably "do great damage to the whole"—of capital's plans, that is.[10] To design the technical and moral artillery for its warfare against the workers, capital enlisted the skills of a new and specialized breed of improvers: managers, scientists, engineers, and consultants, the vanguard of industrial progress. As the first general staff of industrial capitalism, individuals such as Ure and Charles Babbage devised the first strategies of modern class warfare.

But Babbage and Ure were also evangelists of management and chaplains of industrialism. Both were deeply religious men who thought of their work as a form of moral and natural theology. A mathematician who believed that the promotion of scientific education was also "the promotion of true religion," Babbage was also an amateur theologian of science who claimed that his "calculating engine" could establish the invariability of the laws of divine creation. While this was the language of natural theology, Babbage also employed an earlier rhetoric of magical enchantment. In *On the Economy of Machinery and Manufactures* (1832), his manual on the arts of industrial technics and managerial domination, Babbage had rhapsodized about the "living miracles" that proliferated throughout the natural world. This was a Christian language of sacramentality; and when he speculated about the technological future, Babbage hinted that modern inventors were the heirs of the discredited enchanters of old. The forces dimly perceived by priests, shamans, and wizards—"the unreal creations of fancy or of fraud"—would obey "a holier spell" when "called at the command of science, from their shadowy existence."[11] With their enchantments purified by Christian faith, managers and inventors were the magicians of industry, the shamans of automation.

Ure was an even more versatile and popular enchanter of mechanization. Educated in Glasgow, Ure was an evangelical polymath: in addition to his highly remunerative work as an industrial consultant to English, French, and Belgian manufacturers, he was also an astronomer, chemist, and "scriptural geologist," one of a dwindling number who aimed to reconcile the growing geological evidence with a literal interpretation of Genesis. But Ure's geological work was not merely another case study in fundamentalist folly. The same evangelical faith that inspired his geology also galvanized his managerial thought, for Ure considered his "philosophy of manufactures" a vindication of God's mechanical ways to human beings. An apparently mechanistic ontology underlay both Ure's promotion of industrial technology and his case for managerial prerogative. God's universe was a vast machine composed of moral and material parts. Thus, in *The Philosophy of Manufactures,* Ure could admonish the wise manufacturer to "organize his moral machinery on equally sound principles with his mechanical."[12]

Yet Ure's philosophy of managerial dominion was also leavened by a capitalist misenchantment. An enchanted sensibility lay underneath the moralistic and mechanical veneer; the dour consultant doubled as a priest in the cult of technological fetishism. Despite his relentless concentration on the productive benefits of automation, Ure revealed, on occasion, a profound allurement by the power and complexity of machinery. Ure was unmistakably enthralled by "the idea of a vast automatum, composed of various mechanical and intellectual organs, acting in uninterrupted concert for the production of a common object, all of them being subordinated to a self-regulated moving force." Elsewhere, drawing on classical mythology, Ure likened the automated factory to a giant industrial gendarme. With the Luddite uprisings of the 1810s still terrifyingly fresh in his memory, and with Chartist agitation for the suffrage gathering strength among the working class, Ure looked to industrial and technical means to quell proletarian disruption. At the bidding of Minerva—the Roman goddess of crafts and commerce—an "Iron Man, as the operatives fitly call it, sprung out of the hands of our modern Prometheus." By subjecting workers to the political fatigue induced by factory regimentation, this mechanical golem would "restore order among the industrious classes" and "strangle the Hydra of misrule." Whether in the workplace or on the gallows, workers were so many sacrificial animals offered up to the spirit of Minerva. Yet Ure also stepped forth as a herald of a beloved community of production. If allowed by virtuous owners and pliant workers to grace the factory, divine love could suffuse the division of labor, enabling "a new life to circulate through every vein of industry."[13] Ure believed devoutly that the kingdom of heaven could enliven the automated factory.

Ure's technological beatitude represented the heaven of evangelical misenchantment; evangelical policy in Ireland during the Great Famine of the 1840s embodied its infernal counterpart. To evangelical economists, the Almighty's didactic malevolence was evident. The starvation that racked the Irish people was "the judgment of God" on "the selfish, perverse, and turbulent character" of the Irish people, in the words of Sir Charles Trevelyan, prominent evangelical and chief administrator of famine relief; it was "the direct stroke of an all-wise and all-merciful Providence." (Though some economists grumbled that Providence had botched the job: Senior complained that a million deaths "would scarcely be enough to do much good.")[14] God's painful but ultimately beauteous providence had a benevolent purpose: shoving the indigent Irish along the Calvary road of industrial modernization. Followed with Malthusian piety, evangelical economics played a central role in prolonging and deepening the catastrophe in Ireland. To Christian political economists, the Great Famine was a beautiful, marvelous omen in the arduous comedy of God's judgment.

Historians seeking to burnish the penny-pinching image of "Christian political economy" have pointed out that evangelical economists supported voluntary humanitarian schemes in poor relief, religious instruction, and education. Other scholars have traced the origins of British consumer culture to evangelical moralism, contending that middle-class Christians reconciled their newfound wealth with their stated devotion to parsimony by attributing moral qualities to commodities. Yet such balancing acts were responses—usually inadequate—to the misery caused by the very policies blessed by evangelical economists. The brutal, impoverishing, and often lethal ordeal of proletarianization was, from their standpoint, an inextricable part of God's "beauteous order." Evangelical capitalists and their fawning clerisy induced the disease to which they offered a paltry, sanctimonious remedy. John Ruskin—who "unconverted" from his parents' evangelical faith—would later excoriate this heartless sentimentality. "You knock a man into a ditch, and then you tell him to remain content in 'the position in which Providence has placed him,'" he sneered in *The Crown of Wild Olive* (1866). "That's modern Christianity."[15]

Many of Ruskin's contemporaries were also dismissing "modern Christianity" and placing their faith in the emerging social sciences. Throughout the nineteenth century, what Weber would term the "disenchantment of the world" was the major catalyst for the science of sociology. Sociology originated in the 1820s as a search for a secular religion, with French sociologists as the premiere catechists of a new divinity for industrial society. Henri de Saint-Simon, for instance, contrived a "new Christianity," stripped of its cultic and doctrinal elements, to infuse his idealized industrial technocracy. (His missionary journal was entitled *Le Catechisme des Industriels—The Catechism of the Industrialists.*) In the late 1840s, Saint-Simon's student and secretary Auguste Comte constructed an elaborate "religion of humanity," complete with its own catechism, liturgy, sacraments, and theology. Society, for Comte, was "le vrai Grand-Etre," the True Great Being who compels our worship. Less exotic than Comte, Emile Durkheim remained confident that religion could be recovered and recast in secular modernity. As he argued in The *Elementary Forms of Religious Life* (1912), although "there are no immortal gospels, there is no reason to believe that humanity is henceforth incapable of conceiving new ones." If modernity had killed the traditional deities, its own gods were still being born. But if the inhabitants of industrial society sought modern equivalents of totemism—the emblems and objects believed by earlier peoples to possess extraordinary powers—they would have to look to industrial life for the sources of modern enchantment. Under the circumstances, this meant that any modern totems would have to emerge from industrial capitalism. Modern people lived in a state of suspension: "the ancient gods grow old or die, and others are not yet born."[16]

Weber foresaw a more melancholy future for secularizing capitalist societies. In *The Protestant Ethic,* he predicted the reign of professional and managerial experts, "specialists without spirit, hedonists without heart." The permanently disenchanted world would be a wasteland of mass-produced tedium and vanity, a "monstrous development" of "ossification, dressed up with a kind of desperate self-importance." Convinced that disenchantment was an irreversible condition, Weber dismissed the quest for new gods as futile and demeaning, and admonished the disenchanted to ignore the treacherous siren songs of religion. The godless must "set to work, and meet 'the demands of the day,'" he snarled like a burgher in "Science as a Vocation." Still, fearful of a future designed by soulless industrialists and technocrats, even Weber seemed at times to long for some renewal of the ancient verities of enchantment. Maybe, he mused in *The Protestant Ethic,* "new prophets" will arise and "powerful old ideas and ideals will be reborn."[17]

Marx and Engels acknowledged the endurance of a longing for the world of the old gods as well. Indeed, Marx focused his critique of capitalism on its fundamentally "religious" qualities. Despite its historical role as a force for secularization—as the *Communist Manifesto* put it, the pecuniary habit of mind encouraged by the rage to accumulate "drowns the most heavenly ecstasies in the icy waters of egotistical calculation"—capitalism generated its own peculiar forms of religious deception: the "alienation" of workers from their own labor and production, the "fetishism of commodities" that emerges from market exchange, and the brands of technological idolatry that arise with "machinery and modern industry."[18] For Marx, if "disenchantment" is one of the progressive features of capitalist science and technology, it can only be fully achieved through the thorough disenchantment of capitalism itself, the exposure of its own alienations and fetishes as duplicitous and oppressive phantoms.

Bound up with a radical critique of religion, Marx's account of "alienation"—our loss of control over our own powers and achievements—was part of a lineage of disenchantment. Like the "left Hegelians" he eventually repudiated, Marx secularized the work of G. F. W. Hegel, according to whom history unfolded as a series of dialectical conflicts within an "Absolute Spirit." Left Hegelians such as Bruno Bauer and Ludwig Feuerbach recast Hegel's "Spirit" as humanity, and contended that history was actually the story of human alienation and its eventual transcendence through scientific knowledge and philosophical materialism. In *The Essence of Christianity* (1841)—one of the most provocative and influential books of the nineteenth century—Feuerbach argued that "God" represented the hopes and capacities of humanity, projected onto a heavenly screen and then worshipped and feared as a being outside us. Once we realized that human beings are thoroughly and irreducibly matter, we could reclaim those powers and aspirations, ameliorate our condition, and finally flourish in plenty, justice, and love. We would, in other words, realize the essence of Christianity—that is, the essence of humanity.[19]

Working as a journalist and revolutionary agitator in the 1840s, Marx embarked on a kindred project of disenchantment. In his view, the problem with Feuerbach and other left Hegelians—indeed, a problem endemic to the Enlightenment—was that by stressing the need to change consciousness, they downplayed the primacy of material conditions and political struggle in shaping that consciousness. Marx's famous conclusion in his "Theses on Feuerbach" (1845) that "philosophers have only interpreted the world, in various ways; the point, however, is to change it" stemmed from a *historical* materialist position that consciousness—and specifically religion—arose from the evolving everyday realities of social and economic life. The origins of religion were indeed earthly, Marx agreed; but after locating those origins, Feuerbach and his followers proceeded to leave them untouched and even unexamined. To abolish the alienation that culminated in religion, the wretched earthly situation that produced it had to be transformed through politics. The antidote to religion was not atheism, but revolution. "After the earthly family is discovered to be the secret of the holy family, the former must then itself be destroyed in theory and in practice."[20]

In line with this historical materialism, Marx reworked "alienation" into a critique of capitalism. Like Feuerbach, Marx considered religion the most glorious and revealing mode of "alienation." Limited by their material and social conditions, men and women could not realize their capacities for free, versatile creativity in harmony with one another and nature. Compelled to fulfillment in some form, however spurious, humanity invented supernatural beings in whom it then invested its wholly natural but historically elusive longings. "The more man puts into God, the less he retains in himself," Marx asserted in the then-unpublished but now renowned "economic and philosophic manuscripts" of 1844. Yet if religion was the "opium of the people," as he had written in an essay published earlier that year, it was also "the soul of soulless conditions," an "illusory happiness," the "halo" for a "vale of tears." Marx admonished the enlightened radicals of his day that it was not enough simply to hector the oppressed about the opiate illusions of religion; they must mobilize the wretched to reclaim the means of humanity and thus eradicate their alienation. "To call on them to give up their illusions about their condition is to call on them to *give up a condition that requires illusions.*"[21] Again, religion would be overcome through political struggle and material development, not the secularist homilies of the intelligentsia.

At the same time, Marx was reading voraciously in ethnographical literature on "fetishism," the attribution of magical or supernatural powers to objects by archaic and ancient peoples. Fetishism is "a religion of sensuous desire," he wrote in 1842, in which the worshipper fantasizes that an "inanimate object will give up its natural character in order to comply with his desires." Marx plainly recognized the uncanny affinity of alienation and fetishism, and the two ideas wound up performing very similar labor in his writing. Marx first aligned them in the 1844 manuscripts—well before his discussion of "commodity fetishism" in the first volume of *Capital*. Tracing religious projection to the class relations of capitalism, Marx extended the concept of alienation to cover the process of capitalist production. With wage-laborers divorced both from the means of production and from their own products, capitalist alienation took a fetishistic turn, an ascription of life to objects produced by none other than the workers themselves. "The life which [the worker] has given to the object sets itself against him as an alien and hostile force," he mused. "If the product of labor does not belong to the worker, but confronts him as an alien power, this can only be because it belongs to a *man other than the worker.*"[22] The specter of this modern animism served to conceal the class rule of capital.

By retaining control over the production process, capital also established a metaphysics of money that resembled and supplanted traditional forms of enchantment. For Marx, "the power of money in bourgeois society" animated a pecuniary way of being in the world. Money is yet another mark of estrangement; like divinity, it represents "the alienated ability of mankind." But after drowning traditional religious faith in the vat of pecuniary reason, money became "the almighty being," the "truly creative power," the *de facto* ontological basis of reality in capitalist civilization. As the realm of the commodity widens, money not only purchases everything; like the God of Genesis, it also brings things into being from nothing and consigns all indigent things to oblivion. "If I have the *vocation* for study but no money for it, I have *no* vocation for study—that is, no *effective*, no *true* vocation. On the other hand, if I have really *no* vocation for study but have the will and the *money* for it, I have an *effective* vocation for it." As the metaphysical common sense of market society, it defines and even bestows all manner of qualities. "I am *stupid*, but money is the *real mind* of all things and how then should its possessor be stupid?" Money can even buy you love: "I am ugly, but I can buy for myself the most *beautiful* of women. Therefore I am not *ugly*, for the effect of *ugliness*—its deterrent power—is nullified by money."[23] Money confers powers once believed to belong to shamans, priests, and gods.

In the 1840s, Marx and Engels were confident that the secularizing momentum of capitalism would eventually dispel all modes of alienation and fetishism. As science and technology increased our power over nature, the need for supernatural narcotics would diminish; illusions would disappear, halos would fade, and the tearful vale would flower with the mortal splendor of material abundance. With the disenchantment wrought by technological progress and revolutionary politics, alienation and fetishism would wane— hence the watery death of heavenly ecstasy proclaimed in the *Communist Manifesto*. But as Marx was gradually realizing even as he wrote the *Manifesto*, the icy waters of capitalism do *not* drown the heavenly ecstasies; rather, they pool to form a new baptismal font for alienation and religious projection. In the *Grundrisse*—unpublished notebooks from the 1850s—as well as in the first volume of *Capital*, the new prominence of "fetishism" indicated Marx's more vivid awareness that religion had assumed a new guise in the allegedly secular world of capitalism. His ruminations on "the fetishism of commodities, and the secret thereof," as well as on the enchantments of industrial technology and factory organization, demonstrate that the philosophical and religious concerns of his youth persisted into the more "economic" period. Yet they also suggest that Marx's talent as a diagnostician outstripped his perspicacity as a prophet of disenchantment.

For Marx, the secret of the fetishism of commodities lay in their twofold character as "use-value" and as "exchange-value." The use-value of objects, he explained in volume one of *Capital,* resides in their particular, qualitatively different, incommensurable uses—shoes for feet, food for eating, shirts for adornment, etc. Their exchange-value resides in their status *as commodities,* as objects produced for sale in the market for the purpose of capital accumulation. For these commodities to be exchanged for money, their incommensurable use values must be obscured or erased; they must somehow be rendered qualitatively identical to other commodities. This abstract equivalence of otherwise different objects is rendered in terms of the equally abstract equivalence of money—"the god among commodities," as Marx dubbed it in the *Grundrisse.* Objects thus become "worth" so much in money; their value is defined in terms of money, not in terms of their utility for human purposes. In the market, this pecuniary alchemy induces the spell of "fetishism," by which people attribute a kind of agency and independence to commodities, the products of their own labor. (Later Marxists examined the culture industries of advertising, public relations, etc., which capture and cultivate the imaginative terrain opened up in the space between use-value and exchange-value.) Pervaded and commanded by the "god among commodities," objects are enchanted, enlivened, by money—the metaphysical substratum of capitalist society. Thus commodity fetishism is a specifically capitalist form of alienation, a modern recipe for the opium of the people. From the sardonic opening of the passage—the commodity, we learn, is "a queer thing, abounding in metaphysical subtleties and theological niceties"— through the exposure of "all the magic and necromancy that surrounds the products of labor as long as they take the form of commodities," Marx maintained that commodity fetishism amounts to the sacramental system of capitalism. (At one point, Marx compared the commodity fetish to the Eucharist.)[24] However secular their origins in property relations, commodity fetishism and the larger idolatry of the market are capitalist surrogates for enchantment.

Fetishism also envelops "modern industry," for which "the secret thereof" is also the enthralling alienation of human power. Machinery under capitalism has a twofold use-value: the production of ever-cheaper commodities for sale, but also—and in the end more important—the ever-greater subordination of the worker to the will of the capitalist. As Marx noted in *Capital*, technological innovation is propelled by capital's desire "to reduce to a minimum the resistance offered by that repellant yet elastic natural barrier, man." Made possible by the separation of producers from the means of production, the development of machinery, he observed in the *Grundrisse*, embodies "the historical reshaping of the traditional, inherited means of labor into a form adequate to capital." In both the *Grundrisse* and *Capital*, Marx described the indelible inscription of capitalist authority into modern technology. First, "capital destroys craft and artisan labor" in which the worker exercised both mental and manual acumen in production. After separating workers from direct access to productive property and mobilizing the latest science and technical prowess, capital dispossesses workers yet again—this time of their creative and intellectual skills, the very core of their human identity. "The separation of the intellectual powers of production from the manual labor" is followed by "the conversion of those powers into the might of capital over labor." Together, science and industrial technology "constitute the power of the 'master' . . . in whose brain the machinery and his monopoly of it are inseparably united."[25]

This annexation of creative prowess by capital is the precondition for technological fetishism. Once skill has been materially relocated in industrial technology, "it is the machine which possesses skill and strength in place of the worker," Marx wrote in the *Grundrisse;* the machine "is itself the virtuoso, with a soul of its own in the mechanical laws acting through it"; it towers over workers as "a mighty organism." Later, in *Capital,* Marx portrayed the industrial apparatus as "a mechanical monster whose body fills whole factories, and whose demon power, at first veiled under the slow and measured motion of his giant limbs, at length breaks out into the fast and furious whirl of his countless working organs." This was not mere melodramatic rhetoric, for it conveyed Marx's central contention about the nature of modern machinery and industry: that its "demon power" was, in the end, the stolen and disfigured productive potency of the workers themselves. Later Marxists would complement the master's insights into technology with attention to those who directly wield the "demon power"—the "professional-managerial class" spawned in the division of mental from manual labor. Enveloped in the aura of science and expertise, managers and technicians conjured what Alfred Sohn-Rethel has called "managerial fetishism," the belief that specialists possess recondite, almost esoteric knowledge, obtainable only through years of formal education.[26] But as with the phantasmagorical figures of religion and commodity fetishism, the source both of technological enchantment and of managerial fetishism lay in the expropriation from workers of their own inherent powers. For Marx, the industrial bourgeoisie is the class of magicians who oversee a mechanical sorcery.

"It is an enchanted, perverted, topsy-turvy world . . . this religion of everyday life," as Marx observed in the third volume of *Capital*.[27] Yet despite the allures of pecuniary enchantment, Marx and Engels believed that revolutionary theory and practice would disperse the charms of fetishism. With the sacramental glamor of capitalism exposed as the luster of their own alienated powers, workers would retrieve their own humanity—the natural source of what they now slavishly worshipped as divinity. Having recaptured mastery over the means of humanity, the communist society of the future would have no need for magical compensations. Yet Marx and Engels themselves provided ample reason to doubt that what they called the "pre-history" of the species would end in a *Götterdämmerung* of disenchantment. It was never clear that the reduction of the workers to industrial servitude would result in revolution, as money, that "god among commodities," exercised a potent and increasingly untrammeled authority in capitalist society. If all traditional sources of moral and ontological truth were pulverized in the course of capitalist development—if indeed, as they proclaimed in the *Manifesto*, "all that is solid melts into air, all that is holy is profaned"—nothing, it would seem, could generate the spirit of resistance to the rage to accumulate. And as the metaphysical regime of capitalism, monetary and commodity fetishism was at least as beguiling as any previous order of enchantment, especially as all its rivals were evaporating rapidly into quiescence or oblivion. If the moral imagination of the proletariat was so thoroughly permeated by pecuniary enchantment, and if the "real subsumption" of labor by capital was progressive and inexorable, why would the oppressed ever desire the transcendence of alienation and servility? With sufficient technical and political ingenuity—mass production, consumer culture, the welfare and regulatory policies of modern liberalism and social democracy—the sacramental sorcery of the system's fetishism could retard, assimilate, or even extinguish the growth of revolutionary consciousness.

The fetishism of technology could prove equally impervious to disenchantment. There was (and remains) a real and intractable tension between
the revolutionary objective of workers' control and the technocratic features
of modern production—a dissonance reflected in the contrast between the
Romantic humanism of Marx's early writing and his later celebration of
"machinery and modern industry." Marx's youthful portrayal of the human
essence as free, protean creativity echoed Friedrich Schiller's *Letters on the
Aesthetic Education of Man* (1799), where Schiller had elevated *play* as the
mark of genuinely human activity. Vestiges of this vision persisted into the
later, more "economic" work of both Marx and Engels. In *Capital,* Marx
maintained that despite the industrial degradation of traditional skills, that
process was nonetheless "revolutionary." It both increased the amount of
"disposable time"—which became "the measure of wealth"—and augmented
the dexterity of the worker, giving birth to "the fully developed individual, fit
for a variety of labors," able and happy to give "free scope to his own natural
and acquired powers." Of course, these possibilities could only be realized
in the world after capitalism—that is, in the world no longer bewitched by
the fetishism of machinery. As Engels asserted in 1878, "the old mode of
production"—the capitalist division of labor—"must be revolutionized from
top to bottom."[28]

Yet according to Marxist theory, socialism and communism had to emerge
from the crucible of capitalist enterprise; but if so, the industrial edifice of
production might well turn out to be resistant to "revolutionizing"—and
hence to disenchantment. Abandoning his earlier hope that the realms of
work and play could intermingle, Marx held in the *Grundrisse* that "labor
cannot become play"; work and free time were now conceived as strictly demarcated spheres of human life. The atrophy of this ideal stemmed, in part,
from Marx's contention that machinery's use-value for producing goods
would remain after the revolutionary supersession of capital—a use-value
that he himself demonstrated lay in the systematic subordination of workers.
Here Marx regressed into liberal, technocratic bromides about the "neu-
trality" of technology; but if indeed, as Marx himself had asserted, capitalists reshaped labor and machinery "in a form adequate to capital," then socialists would inherit a technological and organizational apparatus designed
expressly for the purposes of exploitation and techno-managerial command.
Pecuniary reason and enchantment had bred a gargantuan machinery of

subservience, and neither Marx nor Engels explained how a technics so thoroughly imbued with the sensibility of domination could be made democratic. While industrial despotism was precisely what was supposed to be "revolutionized from top to bottom," Engels employed the language of despotism itself to describe the process of revolution. As he insisted quite sternly in his 1872 essay "On Authority"—a volley in his ongoing battle with anarchists—machinery "is much more despotic than the small capitalists who employ workers have ever been." Because of the intricacy and precision of its mechanical elements and the vast interdependence it created, modern machinery, Engels admonished the anarchists, both exercised a "veritable despotism independent of all social organization" and underscored "the necessity of authority, and of imperious authority at that" even after the revolution.[29] Engels' authoritarian rhetoric was *prima facie* evidence that the "revolution" envisioned was not nearly profound enough, as the "despotism" entailed by modern industry signaled the persistence of alienation—the precondition for fetishism.

As Simone Weil later observed, if Marx fetishizes anything, it is surely matter—more precisely, "history," the realm of labor and productivity, "the open book of man's essential powers," as he wrote in 1844. Despite Marx's assertion that in the future wealth would be measured in terms of leisure, his portrayal of communism more often suggests a paradise of overachievers. His avowed mythological hero was, after all, Prometheus, and the ideal of perpetual achievement and innovation pervades his collected works. The work ethic of communism, as Marx described it, could seem more exacting than anything envisioned in the antiquated morality of Puritanism. As he declared in the "Critique of the Gotha Program" (1875), in communist society labor will become "not only a means of life but life's prime want." Although later, sympathetic expositors such as Herbert Marcuse and Marshall Berman would contend that Marx's Prometheanism was balanced by an Orphic appreciation of ease and sensuality, the balance was never even or permanent. As Berman himself concedes, in the dynamic, expansive, everrevolutionary conditions of modernity that Marx affirmed, such a friendship between Prometheus and Orpheus would require "an immense amount of Promethean activity and striving."[30]

Marx's commitment to endless economic growth and technological expansion is nowhere more evident than in the third volume of *Capital*, where he offered a sketch of "the realm of freedom" in the stateless communist future. As work and play remain separated, the realm of freedom begins, Marx asserted, where that labor ceases "which is determined by necessity and mundane considerations." Yet "the realm of necessity" seems never to recede, as the desires of post-capitalist humanity seem never to abate. With their rich and proliferating wants, communist men and women thereby enlarge the realm of necessity; with the colossal development of technology, "the forces of production which satisfy these wants also increase." Thus, the exponential generation and satisfaction of wants not only fosters but also enforces the need to incessantly strive, perform, and accomplish. Communism would seem to erase the distinction between freedom and necessity, but in a manner that alarmingly mimics the capitalist rage to accumulate. Theodor Adorno and Max Horkheimer were right when they later surmised that Marx wanted to turn the world into a factory, and that his vision of communism resembled "a gigantic joint-stock company for the exploitation of nature."[31]

Aside from the extensive ecological damage inflicted by this promethean tempest, the fetish of productivity would appear to intensify the exploitation of workers—indeed, by none other than themselves. Under Marx's auspices, Prometheus morphed into a technically proficient and always preoccupied Sisyphus, ever in search of new mountains and boulders to exhibit his accumulating powers. This is the real danger of Marx's communism: not authoritarianism or lazy, flaccid repose, but the freely chosen and restless enslavement to work, productivity, and achievement. Storming the gates of heaven to prove their own divinity, the modern devotees of Prometheus would work themselves and the earth to death.

# 3

# The Poetry of the Past

## Romantic Anticapitalism and the Sacramental Imagination

MARX AND ENGELS SUBJECTED other socialists to contemptuous dissection in the *Manifesto*, reserving the keenest vituperation for their "feudal," "Christian," and "petty-bourgeois" rivals. Engaging in "half lamentation, half lampoon, half echo of the past, half menace of the future," these socialists, they insisted, were hopelessly reactionary, clueless or befuddled about the nature of industrial society. To be sure, reactionary socialists shed light on the hypocrisies of classical economists, called attention to the ruinous effects of the industrial division of labor, and excoriated the concentration of wealth and the wanton destruction of nature. But because they valorized peasants and artisans, and harkened back to priestly and aristocratic oppression, these "socialists" stood in the way of a real resolution of the social question. In "a miserable fit of the blues," they sang haunting requiems for an epoch that would never return. Christian socialists were especially hapless lackeys, carrying "the Holy Water with which the priest consecrates the heart-burnings of the aristocrat." Four years later, in *The Eighteenth Brumaire of Louis Napoleon* (1852), Marx underlined once again the delusion and futility of nostalgia. In times of revolutionary crisis, people may "anxiously conjure up into their service the spirits of the past," borrowing costumes and language from history as they enacted something new. But in the end, modern revolution "could not draw its poetry from the past; it can only draw it from the future." Whatever virtues and beauties the past may have possessed, they must not impede the forward march of progress. Revolutionaries must "let the dead bury their dead."[1]

The poetry of the past composed a radical alternative to Marx and Engels, especially in the form of Romanticism. Usually considered a literary and artistic movement, Romanticism also produced a potent brand of opposition to the mercenary and instrumentalist values of industrial capitalism. But where Marx resolutely affirmed the spirit of capitalist modernity—iconoclasm, disenchantment, technological mastery—Romantics turned to precapitalist values and cultures for inspiration. Looking to the past for their sources of moral and political imagination—classical antiquity, the Middle Ages, the Renaissance, peasant and artisanal communities—Romantic anticapitalists sought, if not to literally resurrect and reinstate the past, then to revive in some modern form the values they cherished from premodern societies. From Blake's declamation against "dark, Satanic mills" to contemporary ecological activism, Romanticism has been an enduring current of witness against capitalist modernity. Pervading an extraordinarily wide range of aesthetic, political, and religious movements, Romanticism, in the words of Robert Sayre and Michael Lowy, "far from being a purely nineteenth-century phenomenon . . . is an essential component of modern culture."[2]

The invocation of premodern and precapitalist values has raised the recurrent—and not unjustified—fear that Romantic anticapitalism leads inexorably to irrationalism, reaction, and even fascism. Yet many Romantic anticapitalists affirmed both the Enlightenment and the French Revolution. Whether sympathetic to Jacobinism (Blake, Percy Shelley, Heinrich Heine), utopian and libertarian radicalism (Charles Fourier, Moses Hess, Pierre-Joseph Proudhon, Peter Kropotkin), or socialism (William Morris, Ernst Bloch, Herbert Marcuse), the Romantic left has embraced the scientific, cosmopolitan, and democratic legacy of the Enlightenment while also criticizing its limitations. They experienced a sense of exile and homelessness from some "true" home in the precapitalist past, identified that moment when humane values flourished as a template for utopia, and worked to reconstruct that lost paradise in some new form in the future. But where the Romantic right rejected the heritage of scientific reason and political democracy, the Romantic left considered what they called "imagination" as an extension and enrichment of the Enlightenment, sensing no fundamental contradictions among reason, democracy, and a re-enchantment of the world. The most incisive Romantic anticapitalists did not seek to resurrect or retreat into the past; rather, they looked to the past for a critical perspective on the present that was more penetrating and promising than the future held out by the disenchanted heirs of the Enlightenment.

Yet if Romantics were champions of spirit, nature, and memory, some scholars have suggested that, like their Enlightenment counterparts, they cleared a path to secular modernity, hastening, in M. H. Abrams' view, "the secularization of inherited theological ideas and ways of thinking." While drawing on myth and legend, Romantics offered a historical hospice for dying religious beliefs, preparing them for a secular afterlife. The process of secularization, Abrams explains, "has not been the deletion and replacement of religious ideas but rather the assimilation and reinterpretation of religious ideas." As Abrams demonstrates, Romantics recast the Christian mythos of creation, fall, history, and redemption. Born into a primal unity of self and world, humanity, Romantics believed, was now riven by self-consciousness and alienation. By unlocking its powers of imagination, humanity could overcome the baneful effects of that fall, and restore the old unity on a higher plane. In Abrams's words, Romantic eschatology envisioned "a rebirth in which a renewed mankind will inhabit a renovated earth where he will find himself thoroughly at home."[3]

Yet what Abrams dubs their "natural supernaturalism" was something more than the last refuge of enchantment. If, as Bernard Reardon has argued, Romanticism named "the inexpungable feeling that the finite is not self-explanatory and self-justifying"—that "there is always an infinite 'beyond'"—then natural supernaturalism was the heir to the Christian sacramental imagination. The visionary or rhapsodic quality of Romanticism was a sacramental consciousness, a capacity to see or sense divinity in the minutiae of finitude. In a poetic rather than a theological idiom, Romantic metaphysics often envisioned some reality that both transcended and pervaded the sensible world, some abiding mystery that left its alluring traces in the world of appearance. Some of the signature passages of Romantic poetry are modern sacramental epiphanies. In his "Auguries of Innocence," William Blake beckoned us

To see a world in a grain of sand,
And a Heaven in a Wild Flower,
Hold Infinity in the palm of your hand,
And Eternity in an hour.

Later, in "Tintern Abbey," William Wordsworth recorded

A presence that disturbs me with the joy
Of elevated thoughts; a sense sublime
Of something far more deeply interfused,
Whose dwelling is the light of setting suns,
And the round ocean and the living air,
And the blue sky, and in the mind of man:
A motion and a spirit that impels
All thinking things, all objects of all thought,
And rolls through all things.[4]

The sacramental rapture of those passages might serve to reinforce the caricature of Romantic hostility to reason. Yet Romantic writers of all kinds made clear that their nemesis was not reason but rather reason torn from the fabric of nature and humanity—a rupture that made a demon and idol of reason, a despoiled wreck of nature, and a beguiled slave of humanity. The "single vision" that terrified Blake was more than the abstract formulas of physics and mathematics. "Single vision" meant the occlusion or deception of sacramental sight, the optics of mastery and exploitation, the inability to see the world as anything more than material resources for misenchanted exploitation. Though divorced from orthodox theology, Romantic humanism echoed the traditional harmony of reason, love, and reality. When Romantics praised "enthusiasm," "reverence," and "imagination," they restated the venerable Christian wisdom that reason is rooted in love, that full and genuine understanding precludes a desire to possess and control. Against the imperious claims of "Urizen"—Blake's fallen "Prince of Light," *your reason* degenerates into measurement and calculation—Blake countered that "Enthusiastic Admiration is the First Principle of Knowledge & its last." "To know a thing, what we can call knowing," Thomas Carlyle surmised in *Heroes and Hero-Worship* (1841), we "must first *love* the thing, sympathise with it." Arising from a sacramental sense of the world as a "region of the Wonderful," Carlyle's incessant admonitions to "reverence" and "wonder" were, at bottom, exhortations to love.[5]

"Imagination" was the name Romantics gave to this erotic and sacramental consciousness. Yet imagination was not only a subjective enchantment, a lineal descendent of the "Other Protestant Ethic." In the Romantic sensibility, imagination was not a talent for inspiring fantasy, but the most perspicuous form of *vision*—the ability to see what is really there, behind the illusion or obscurity produced by our will to dissect and dominate. For Blake, imagination provided access to "the real and eternal world, of which this vegetable universe is but a faint shadow." If, to Samuel Taylor Coleridge, reason is "the Power of Universal and Necessary convictions, the Source and Substance of Truths above sense," imagination was its vibrant sacramental partner, "the living Power and prime Agent of all human perception . . . a repetition in the finite mind of the eternal act of creation in the infinite I AM." For Romantics, imagination did not annul but rather completed rationality. During the French Revolution, Wordsworth observed, reason seemed "most intent on making of herself / A prime Enchantress." Though warning of the brutality of instrumental reason—"our meddling intellect / Mis-shapes the beauteous forms of things; / We murder to dissect"—Wordsworth described imagination as "Reason in her most exalted mood."[6] Imagination is the ecstasy of reason.

In forging a sacramental imagination for modernity, Romantics posed a religious opposition to pecuniary, capitalist reason. The spirit of Langland, Joachim, Milton, and Winstanley resurfaced in Romantic anticapitalism. Aiming to root out "the spirit of evil in things heavenly," Blake traced the origins of desecration to the human capacity for idolatry. "Man must & will have Some Religion," Blake warned. "If he has not the Religion of Jesus"— meaning not the official Christianity of the churches but the undogmatic "Everlasting Gospel" of love and creative exuberance—"he will have the Religion of Satan." In one of his earliest poems, "Mammon," Blake recounted how one morning, while praying for riches, he realized that he had prostrated himself before the demon deity of money: "I took it to be the throne of God." Blake identified Mammon as the sponsor and architect of industrial capitalism, the proprietor of those "dark Satanic mills" that augured death and eternal damnation. (Urizen is his factory manager, "the great Work master.") Bankrolled and designed by the zealots of Mammon, the expanding apparatus of industrial might was a "Babylon builded in the Waste, founded in Human desolation."[7] Here was Ure's "vast automatum" and Marx's "mechanical monster," unveiled as a temple of Mammon.

Other English Romantics agreed that pecuniary enchantment sent humanity to its knees. Robert Southey bewailed the "undisputed and acknowledged supremacy" of the spirit of Mammon in England. "Commercial nations, if they acknowledged the deity whom they serve, might call him All-Gold," Southey wrote, warning that Mammon is "a more merciless fiend than Moloch." Wordsworth recoiled from the commercial frenzy of London, lamenting that "rapine, avarice, expense / These are idolatry; and these we adore." "Money, money is here the god of universal worship," he complained to his sister Dorothy. To the middle classes, "rapacity and extortion," he continued, were "glory and exultation." Coleridge rued that Britain had become a "monstrous, mammon-bloated Dives, a wooden idol of stuffed pursemen." Dismissing the maxims of evangelical economists as "solemn humbug," Coleridge surmised that what was true "of the little that is true in their dogmatic books" was the moral and religious wisdom "of any good man."[8]

Sadly, without a "Chariot of Fire," the visionary intensities of a Blake were unavailing against the sanctimonious humbug of capital. Though evocative of a deeper and more extravagant order of generosity and beatitude, Romantic verse could never counter the misenchantment of classical economics. Indeed, many Romantics ended their days on the political right, having made their peace, not only with throne and altar, but with "rapine, avarice, and expense." Though he fondly recalled his blissful youth as a supporter of the French Revolution, Wordsworth died a genial conservative. Coleridge epitomized the Tory paternalist, pontificating on the reciprocal duties of the classes and on deference to the Anglican clerisy. The answer to the social question was benevolence, not revolution. For many of those Romantics whom Raymond Williams inducted into the "culture and society" tradition— social critics who pitted the ideals of "culture" against the depredations of industrial "society"—art and literature eventually offered "not only a promise but a refuge."[9]

Even "Tory radicals" such as Carlyle and John Ruskin have been indicted as reactionaries. For all their eloquent invective against industrial capitalism, they nonetheless championed monarchy and feudalism in the age of rising liberal democracies, and they supported paternalist measures to dampen the militancy of the urban proletariat. They opposed Chartism, derided popular politics, and regarded servitude and British imperialism as necessary forms of moral instruction. (Carlyle's characterization of economics as "the dismal science" came in the midst of a *defense* of Jamaican slavery.) As Terry Eagleton has contended—echoing many other left and liberal writers—Carlyle and Ruskin provided Victorian capitalism with an "ideological stimulus and moral edification" its factories could never manufacture.[10]

How, then, do we explain their indelible impact on an array of writers, many of whose credentials on the democratic left are otherwise impeccable? The roster is long and illustrious: William Morris, Oscar Wilde, Leo Tolstoy, R. H. Tawney, G. D. H. Cole, Lewis Mumford, Raymond Williams, Norman O. Brown, Martin Luther King, Jr., Mahatma Gandhi, E. F. Schumacher, and Christopher Lasch, to name a few. (Carlyle was even cited favorably by Marx and Engels.) What appears to have elicited respect and even reverence for these reactionaries from partisans of the left was their "sense of the moral unity of the world," as Tawney wrote of Ruskin, their conviction that without some common end toward which art, politics, and economics tended, all human activities become "meaningless and in time degenerate."[11]

This "moral unity" was endangered by the "Victorian crisis of faith" that afflicted Carlyle, Ruskin, and their contemporaries. The onslaught of discoveries in biology, geology, history, and biblical scholarship appeared to inflict irreparable damage on Christianity. As many educated Victorians heard, along with Matthew Arnold, the "melancholy, long, withdrawing roar" of Christian faith, they realized that some other foundation for traditional morality would be necessary—or that traditional morality itself would need to be modified or supplanted. Out of this maelstrom emerged a secular if not always secularized intelligentsia alongside the Christian clergy: "public moralists," to use Stefan Collini's term, commentators on cultural and political issues who derived their moral authority, not from an ecclesial position, but from their own learning, talent, and persuasive force. Many among this new class of public intellectuals—Charles Bradlaugh, Herbert Spencer, Thomas Huxley—abandoned religion in favor of hardboiled, scientific secularism, while others—Arnold, George Eliot, Samuel Butler—affirmed some tragic form of humanism.[12]

Keenly aware that the intellectual stock of Christianity was crashing, other Victorians sought either to revitalize traditional faith or to create a new cultural form for religion. Defectors from evangelicalism such as John Henry Newman and the "Oxford Movement" of the 1830s and 1840s embraced Roman Catholicism; in the 1850s, F. D. Maurice and other Anglicans traveled in a decidedly more liberal Protestant direction. Carlyle and Ruskin embodied another alternative: a public moralism that doubled as religious prophecy, enchantment expressed in a modern idiom. Both men were "unconverted," as Ruskin put it, from the precepts of evangelicalism; yet both men desired to see divinity triumph against the world of industry and the cash nexus. Like Professor Teufelsdrockh, the philosopher-prophet of Carlyle's *Sartor Resartus* (1836), they longed to "embody the Spirit" of the gospel "in a new Mythus, in a new vehicle and vesture, that our Souls . . . may live."[13] The "sense of moral unity" in Romantic social criticism arose from a sacramental imagination.

Carlyle considered his work a form of modern prophecy. "For us in these days Prophecy (well understood) not Poetry is the thing wanted," he told his brother. "How can we *sing* and *paint* when we do not yet *believe* and *see?*" In his "heterodox heart," Carlyle conceded the increasing implausibility of traditional Christianity. "The Mythus of the Christian Religion," he wrote in *Sartor Resartus* ("the tailor retailored") did not inspire conviction in the nineteenth century "as it did in the eighth." If the tailor being re-tailored was Christianity, Carlyle's volumes were modern prophecies of an everlasting gospel. Almost alone among students of Carlyle, Lasch placed his curmudgeonly oeuvre in the lineage of Christian prophecy. Yet even Lasch overlooked the sacramental idiom of Carlyle's finest social criticism. Emphasizing Carlyle's affirmation of "wonder" for its "acknowledgement of our dependence on higher powers," Lasch missed its sacramental imagination, the perception of everyday, material grace. Prophecy, for Carlyle, was more than a reminder of humanity's reliance on God; it announced the company of divinity in the mundane and the particular. Fusing holiness and utility, the earth, for Teufelsdrockh, is both a tabernacle and a workplace. The truly blessed human being is one "to whom the Universe is an Oracle and a Temple, as well as a Kitchen and Cattle-stall." "Thy daily life is girt with Wonder, and based on Wonder, and thy very blankets and breeches are Miracles."[14] "Wonder" was Carlyle's new Christian mythology, a modern sacramental theology.

Carlyle condemned capitalism as a violation of "Wonder." Easily taken for evocative metaphors or "mere" theological relics, his numerous references to "Mammon" should be taken with full religious seriousness. "Testifying against the Mammon-god" in *Sartor Resartus,* Teufelsdrockh objected to the quality of tailoring in the deity's commercial culture, "Vanity's Workhouse and Ragfair." In *The French Revolution* (1837) Carlyle dubbed Mammon "the basest of known Gods, even of known Devils." But the most powerful indictment of Mammon came in *Past and Present,* Carlyle's angriest polemic on the condition of England. Converted to "the Gospel of Mammonism," England, Carlyle charged, had exchanged the beneficence of medieval Christianity for a "Mammon-Feudalism," a "brutish empire of Mammon." Both downtrodden workers and their heartless masters were "spell-bound" by a "horrid enchantment." "Enchantment," in Carlyle, is the counterfeit of "wonder," and the Gospel of Mammonism is a fraudulent religion, a decoy for the true mythology. The people of England worshiped "the frightfulest enchantment; too truly a work of the Evil One." The most numerous and devout of Mammon's disciples resided among the Victorian bourgeoisie. Disdainful of the bromides dispensed as gospel in Victorian Christianity, Carlyle surmised in "Signs of the Times" that middle-class religion was little more than "a wise prudential feeling grounded in mere calculation." More staid and mendacious than earlier forms of enchantment, Mammonism linked the fury of greed to the algebra of pecuniary reason. Believing that "some smaller quantum of earthly enjoyment may be exchanged for a far larger quantum of celestial enjoyment," the good Victorian tended his soul like a commodity future. "Religion too is Profit, a working for wages."[15] The "cash nexus" Carlyle excoriated now set its standard in the very heart of the wonderful.

If "enchantment," to Carlyle, was a perversion of wonder, only a rebirth of genuine wonder could pose a real threat to Mammonism. Carlyle's more unsettling and dangerous ideas make sense only in the context of his search for wonder, his quest to recover sacramental vision in the midst of a pecuniary age. His oft-maligned insistence on the need for *Heroes and Hero-Worship* was inseparable from "wonder." For Carlyle, the true hero is defined less by an achievement than by a kind of receptivity, a fortuitous, "blessed, heaven-sent" vocation to "discern the inner heart of things." Like that of the prophet—or of the saint, to whom the hero bears a striking affinity—the hero's calling is first to see, and only then to act accordingly. A Romantic seer on the stage of history, the hero is a prodigy of Imagination. Understood as a capacity for sacramental sight, heroism figures throughout Carlyle's work. Aghast at mechanical and commercial society, Teufelsdröckh experiences an epiphany that reveals a world pervaded by divinity. "The Universe is not dead and demoniacal, a charnel-house with spectres, but godlike," he realizes. Rejecting the utilitarian reason that compels predation on other men and women, the Professor perceives and embraces humanity as his alienated brethren. "With other eyes, too, could I now look upon my fellow-man; with an Infinite Love . . . I now first named him Brother." Rooted in his avowal of faith in the presence and unbounded love of God, Teufelsdrockh's heroic "Everlasting Yea" is a testimony against "the Mammon-god."[16]

Later, in *Past and Present*, Carlyle posed against the Gospel of Mammonism what amounts to a Gospel of Heroism, a joyous affirmation of sacramental presence. Despite its claims about the scarcity of nature and the rapaciousness of human beings, Mammon's gospel violates the laws of creation; endless accumulation cannot persist, for "the Universe is not made so." Those who enter into battle with Mammon must be heroes, possessed by wonder and love, abounding in "the faith in an Invisible, Unnameable, Godlike, present everywhere in all that we see and work and suffer." As a vehicle of that godlike presence, the hero of *Past and Present* is Abbot Samson, who rescued the monastery of St. Edmund's from moral and physical decay. Ruling the abbey with a firm but compassionate hand, the Abbot exemplifies the vocational paradox of heroism: the true leader must think and act as a servant, subordinating any will to power to the good of the community. "He that cannot be servant of many, will never be master, true guide and deliverer of many;—that is the meaning of true mastership."[17]

Still, "heroism" accounts for why Carlyle should not be enlisted in a populist tradition of anticapitalism. While he successfully defends Carlyle against charges of protofascism, Lasch ignores the authoritarian conclusion that Carlyle himself drew from his theology of wonder: that capacity for wonder confers political supremacy as well as lucid spiritual insight. "The Great Man was always a lightning out of Heaven; the rest of men waited for him like fuel, and then they too would flame." Abbot Samson is a stern paternalist; and in *Heroes and Hero-Worship* Carlyle idealized decisive and autocratic leaders, epitomized by Samson, Cromwell, and Napoleon. After the Chartist movement that he opposed subsided, Carlyle grew increasingly hostile to popular politics, ridiculing democracy in the name of heroism. By the time he published "Shooting Niagara," Carlyle had become a surly, elitist windbag, maligning "mobocracy" and harrumphing at the rabble's "amenability to beer and balderdash."[18] Carlyle could never fathom the possibility that all the Lord's people could be prophets and heroes.

Convinced that the talent for wonder was scarce as well as gratuitous, Carlyle succumbed to the more insidious implications contained in hero-worship. His even more unsavory positions are united by the conviction that the masses, incapable of wonder, required harsh and repressive education. His infamous defense of slavery in his "Occasional Discourse on the Negro Question" (1849) turned on the moral pedagogy of servitude—a notion that bore a grim resemblance to the theodicy of evangelical economists. Now vilified for his ugly and unashamed racism, Carlyle believed that white Englishmen, too, could use instruction in the arts of reverence. Indeed, Carlyle was closer to the evangelical worldview than his champions and detractors have imagined, for the moral economy of his "Everlasting Yea" turned out to be the Protestant ethic. "Love not pleasure, love God," Teufelsdrockh admonishes in *Sartor Resartus;* "Produce! Produce! Were it but the pitifullest infinitesimal fraction of a Product, produce it, in God's name!"[19]

This was homiletic bluster worthy of the Puritans and evangelicals; and the assertion that "the fraction of a Product" was worth producing suggested that Carlyle objected less to the industrial division of labor than to the reckless pursuit of profit. Yet the subdivision of labor was inseparable from the employment of industrial technology—the alarm at which Carlyle had been among the first to sound. The same man who coined the term "industrialism," who railed against the philosophy of "mechanism," and who had dubbed his era "the Age of Machinery" could also preach to the working class that alienated labor was a form of heroism.[20] The social and technological features of industrialism grew out of the very "Mammonism" that Carlyle reviled; the era was an Age of Machinery *because* it was an Age of Capital. Unlike Marx—or, later, Ruskin—Carlyle failed to link the hegemony of mechanism to the imperatives of capital accumulation. By the same token, it was never clear whether Carlyle saw "mechanism" or "Mammonism" as the primary demon of the time—in other words, whether the spirit of the age was disenchantment or the "frightfulest enchantment" of avarice.

By re-tailoring the Protestant ethic as a Gospel of Work for all classes, Carlyle defaulted on a politics of wonder. Instead, he became an unlikely ideological tailor for the Victorian bourgeoisie, fashioning the ideal of wonder to suit a nobility of industrial management. Though contemptuous of the greedy and philistine "Millocracy" in *Past and Present,* Carlyle rejected class politics, believing that exhortations to morality and wonder could convert the hearts of industrialists. Though as yet "only half-alive, spell-bound amid money-bags and ledgers," the enchanted industrial elite could evolve, Carlyle hoped, into an "Industrial Aristocracy." Imagining valorous "Captains of Industry" moved by "a Godlike stirring," Carlyle wagered that wonder could awaken a new kind of chivalry among the bourgeoisie. Carlyle's praise for his imaginary heroes of industry was effusive to the point of hyperbole. The Captains of Industry were "the true Fighters . . . Fighters against Chaos, Necessity, and the Devils . . . [they] lead on Mankind in that great, and alone true, and universal warfare . . . all Heaven and all Earth saying audibly, Well-done!" Far from demanding the overthrow of the enchanted empire of Mammon, Carlyle aimed at the moral transfiguration of its ruling class. Calling for a paternalist capitalism overseen by a directorate of chivalrous heroes, Carlyle sought to humanize, not to abolish, the diabolical cash nexus of Mammonism. "We must have industrial *barons,* of a quite new suitable sort," he once wrote to a Liberal member of Parliament, bluebloods of capital ruling kindly over "workers *loyally* related to their taskmasters—related in God . . . not related in Mammon alone!"[21] Beholden to the Gospel of Work, Carlyle's "Captains of Industry" would constitute an executive committee of wonder.

Ruskin would seem no more promising a critic, as his record of reaction, like Carlyle's, is indisputable. He extolled the virtues of monarchy; trumpeted the white-skinned splendor and benevolence of British imperialism; deplored the efficiency and productive power of industrial technology; and proposed paternalist compassion as an antidote to working-class political struggle. (As if all that weren't enough, even Ruskin's revered writing on art has been cited as evidence of his ideological complicity in colonialism.)[22] Once a hero to many on the British and American left, Ruskin now appears much less valiant, a relic as beautiful and reminiscent of oppression as the Gothic architecture he loved.

Ruskin's sins are well known, but there is exculpatory and mitigating evidence that argues for clemency and even redemption. He revered the Middle Ages and Gothic architecture—"The Nature of Gothic" in *The Stones of Venice* (1853) is a model of panegyric—yet he also maintained that no return to the medieval was either possible or desirable. "I am not one who in the least doubts or disputes the progress of this century in many things useful to mankind," he asserted in *The Two Paths* (1859). "We don't want either the life or the decorations of the thirteenth century back again." He insisted on the necessity and inevitability of hierarchies, and apologized for the rankest forms of servility. "No position is so *good* for men and women, none so likely to bring out their best human character," he told British workers and laborers in 1873, "as that of a dependent or menial." Yet he despised the English nobility and gentry as "the scurviest louts that ever fouled God's earth with their carcasses" and lavished his most venomous contempt on the godly affectations of the evangelical bourgeoisie. "You sit smiling at your serene hearths," as he portrayed them in "The Work of Iron" (1859), "listing comfortable prayers evening and morning, and counting your pretty Protestant beads, which are flat, and of gold, instead of round, and of ebony, as the monks' ones were."[23]

There was also more to Ruskin's relationship to the working class than condescension and paternalism. Long before radical historians called for a "history from the bottom up," he asserted that "the lives we need to have written for us are of the people whom the world has not thought of, far less heard of, who are yet doing most of the work." He offered courses on art and art history in the London Working Men's College, established by Tories in 1854 to provide a liberal education to "shop decorators—and upholsterers—and masons—and brickmasters, and glassblowers and pottery people." Although he considered the prospect of socialism to be "simply chaos," he could sound like a revolutionary orator summoning the subaltern to the barricades. "Whose is the Wealth of the World but yours? Where is the Virtue?" he asked in *Fors Clavigera,* a series of open letters to workers published in the 1870s. Though he referred to himself in his autobiography as a "violent Tory of the old school," in *Fors Clavigera* he had called himself a "Communist of the old school"—indeed a "dark-red Communist, reddest of the red." Tories like himself had to champion the cause of the working class, he explained, because the clergy were lackeys of the wealthy. "Have they so betrayed their Master's charge and mind in their preaching to the rich," he asked in another letter, "so smoothed their words, and so sold their authority, that . . . there is no man in England . . . who will have mercy on the poor?"[24]

Ruskin's fidelity to the "Master's charge and mind" is the key to his social criticism. The recent revival of interest in Ruskin as a scourge of capitalism tends to neglect or pass over his religious beliefs, yet anyone eager to enlist Ruskin in contemporary cultural and political struggles must inevitably come to terms with the religious roots of his moral imagination. Even Tawney's praise for the "moral unity" of Ruskin's artistic and social criticism missed this essential element. Of all his sympathetic expositors, only Williams—hardly a believer in the supernatural—clearly recognized that the deeper unity of Ruskin's vision was religious, not moral. "Both sides of Ruskin's work are comprised in an allegiance to the same single term, Beauty; and the idea of Beauty . . . rests fundamentally on a belief in a universal, divinely appointed order."[25]

After "un-converting" from evangelicalism, Ruskin retained a Romantic religious faith that harbored a sacramental imagination. From his earliest art criticism in the 1840s to his later speculations on climate, he wrote of natural beauty as an enchanted emblem of divinity. At their best, he argued in the first volume of *Modern Painters* (1843), artists such as J. M. W. Turner conveyed "that faultless, ceaseless, inconceivable, inexhaustible loveliness, which God has stamped upon all things." They "received the word of God from clouds, and leaves, and waves." Beauty, he wrote in the second volume (1846), is "that external quality of bodies . . . which, whether occur in a stone, flower, beast, or in man . . . may be shown to be in some sort typical of the Divine attributes." In animals, the appearance of these godlike qualities indicated "the felicitous fulfillment of function in living things"; in the human animal especially, beauty consisted of "the joyful and right exertion of perfect life in man." "In the midst of the material nearness of these heavens," Ruskin asserted in the fourth volume (1856), God desires that we "acknowledge His own immediate presence as visiting, judging, and blessing us."[26]

To Ruskin, nature was not inanimate, but rather soulful, even ethical, a vessel and barometer of moral and ontological vitality. In "The Work of Iron," he invited his audience to read the "curious lesson" in any pebble at their feet. "You look upon it . . . as if it were earth only." But the pebble possessed "a kind of soul," and if it could speak, it would inform us that "'I am not earth—I am earth and air in one; part of that blue heaven which you love, and long for, is already in me.'" Over the next three decades, as the factories spread and polluted the air and streams with industrial waste, Ruskin deciphered the signs of sacrilege. In *The Storm-Cloud of the Nineteenth Century* (1884)—his strange and ominous forecast of impending moral and ecological doom—Ruskin traced the violation of "the visible Heaven" of clouds, air, rain, and ice, reasoning that our sins infected the natural world, composed as it was of matter and spirit. "Blanched sun,—blighted grass,—blinded man"—the desecration extended everywhere. "Blasphemy," Ruskin pronounced it, that ruined "all the good works and purposes of Nature." The clouds were full of "bitterness and malice"; the "poisonous smoke" bellowing from factories consisted, in part, of "dead men's souls"; the climate bore traces of "iniquity." The restoration of nature's health depended, not on the application of remedial technologies, but on the cultivation of "Hope . . . Reverence . . . [and] Love." This sacramental ontology was the foundation of Ruskin's equally sacramental humanism. As he wrote in Volume 2 of *Modern Painters,* the "function" of a human being is "the full comprehension and contemplation of the beautiful as a gift of God." The "use and function" of a person is to be "the witness of the glory of God, and to advance that glory by . . . reasonable obedience and resultant happiness." "The direct manifestation of Deity to man is in His own image, that is, in man," he avowed in Volume 5 (1860). "The soul of man is a mirror of the mind of God"—"a mirror dark, distorted, and broken," he lamented, but reflective nonetheless of divinity.[27]

The broken grandeur of humanity was Ruskin's touchstone of judgment in a remarkable passage from "The Nature of Gothic," in the second volume of *The Stones of Venice* (1853). There, his long and impassioned philippic against the industrial division of labor turned on a sacramental portrayal of artisanal excellence. The artisan becomes Ruskin's icon of human divinity—a paradoxical paragon in that imperfection is his outstanding feature. Affirming human mediocrity, Ruskin warned that the ideal of perfection—taken to its fullest, fiendish zenith in the social and technical machinery of the factory—would disfigure the image and likeness of God. If we insist too severely on perfection, he reasoned, "all the brute animals would be preferable to man, because more perfect in their functions." Just as sin always bears an ironic testimony to the stature of human divinity—no other creature can possibly defy its Creator—so any shortcomings in labor suggest the magnificence of the worker, "for the finer the nature, the more flaws it will show through the clearness of it." Let even an inferior mind think and imagine, and "out come all his roughness, all his dullness, all his incapability; shame upon shame, failure upon failure, pause after pause; but out comes the whole majesty of him also, and we know the height of it only when we see the clouds setting upon him." "The principal admirableness of the Gothic schools of architecture," Ruskin surmised, is that they welcome "the labour of inferior minds." Out of such "fragments full of imperfection," the Gothic cathedral arose to the skies as "a stately and unaccusable whole."[28] Even weakness and deficiency could beckon to God.

But the industrial division of labor—dictated by the rage to accumulate—imposed an absolute precision of motion that led inexorably to deskilling and mechanization, "the degradation of the operative into a machine." "You must either make a tool of the creature, or a man of him," Ruskin insisted. "You cannot make both. Men were not intended to work with the accuracy of tools, to be precise and perfect in all their actions." The result was something worse than material deprivation: the loss of joyful, self-directed creation. The most pernicious offense of industrial capitalism against humanity "is not that men are ill fed, but that they have no pleasure in the work by which they make their bread." As anyone could see who cared to look at the uncalculated prodigality of nature, God was not interested in precision and efficiency. Thus those who adhered to Ure's "philosophy of manufacture" were, on Ruskin's account, stripping workers of their likeness to divinity. If precision, productivity, and profit rather than "majesty" are the goals of labor, workers *must* be made into machines; "you must unhumanize them." You must, in other words, desecrate them; and there would quite literally be hell to pay for this sacrilege. "This, nature bade not,—this, God blesses not,—this humanity for no long time is able to endure." None of Ruskin's subsequent declamation against "mammon-service" can be understood apart from this sacramental humanism. Men and women were only a little lower than the angels, and to cheapen and oppress them was, in Ruskin's eyes, a defilement as well as an injustice:[29]

Now it is a good and desirable thing, truly, to make many pins in a day; but if we could only see with what crystal sand their points are polished,—sand of human soul, much to be magnified before it can be discerned for what it is. And the great cry that rises from all our manufacturing cities, louder than their furnace blast, is all in very deed for this,—that we manufacture everything there except men; we blanch cotton, and strengthen steel, and refine sugar, and shape pottery; but to brighten, to strengthen, to refine, or to form a single living spirit, never enters into our estimate of advantages.

If, for Marx and Weber, capitalism was the dynamo of secular modernity, for Ruskin, it embodied a metamorphosis of the sacred, a perverse enchantment of the world. Ruskin clearly feared that "secularization" was really a capitalist form of idolatry—a rechristening of heavenly ecstasy in a cold baptismal font of money, a re-enchantment conducted under the gilded, unholy auspices of capital. In *The Political Economy of Art* (1857) Ruskin described the day of a typical businessperson as a regimen of spiritual discipline. "The worship of Mammon," he began, proceeds "with a tender reverence and an exact propriety" reminiscent of Jonson's Volpone. The merchant "rises to his Mammon matins with the self-denial of an anchorite" and asks forgiveness for the distractions that may keep him from his "Mammon vespers." Later, in *Munera Pulveris* (1871), Ruskin maintained that, far from a "secular" denial of the supernatural, capitalism had its own ensemble of gods, sacraments, and spiritual devotions. "We have, indeed, a nominal religion, to which we pay tithes of property and sevenths of time," he conceded. "But we have also a practical and earnest religion, to which we devote nine-tenths of our property, and six-sevenths of our time." The deity of this true Victorian faith was "the Goddess of Getting-on"—in male form, Mammon, "the great evil Spirit of false and fond desire, or 'Covetousness, which is Idolatry.'"[30]

Read in this light, *Unto This Last* (1862), Ruskin's best-known statement of his economic views, was both a manifesto of sacramental humanism and a theological critique of "the dismal science." Indeed, Ruskin went Carlyle one better and denied that economics is a science at all, comparing it to "alchemy, astrology, witchcraft, and other such popular creeds." Economics is worse than dismal, he contended; it is simply untrue, because its account of human nature is fallacious. A human being, he admonished his readers, is "an engine whose motive power is a Soul"—not autonomous and calculating self-interest—and "the force of this very peculiar agent . . . enters into all the political economist's equations . . . and falsifies every one of their results." Thus Ruskin dismissed the scientific pretensions of economics with indifference and disdain. "I neither impugn nor doubt the conclusions of the science if its assumptions are accepted," he sneered. "I am simply uninterested in them, as I should be in those of a science of gymnastics which assumed that men had no skeletons." To Ruskin, the mendacity of economics lay in its erasure of God's image from its account of human nature. When he declared that he knew "no previous instance in history of a nation's establishing a systematic disobedience to the first principles of its professed religion," those "first principles" were theological. The "mammon-service" that characterized laissez-faire capitalism exhibited "an idolatry abhorred of the Deity"—the *moral* evil of avarice arose from perverse *religious* veneration.[31]

The sacramental leavens all of Ruskin's account of what he calls "the real science of political economy." *Unto This Last* has been praised, even by its detractors, for its many elegant and moving passages, but the loveliness of the prose is not aesthetic finesse; the style of the argument is inseparable from the substance. At one point, Ruskin digressed—or appeared to digress—into a lyrical bucolic rhapsody. "No air is sweet that is silent," he mused;[32]

> As the art of life is learned, it will be found at last that all lovely things are also necessary—the wild flower by the wayside, as well as the tended corn; and the wild birds and creatures of the forest, as well as the tended cattle; because man doth not live by bread only, but also by the desert manna; by every wondrous word and unknowable work of God. Happy, in that he knew them not, nor did his fathers know; and that round about him reaches yet into the infinite, the amazement of his existence.

The pastoral imagery is so obvious—and so liable to dismissal as "reactionary"—that its sacramental import can be overlooked or evaded. Such passages convey Ruskin's fundamental assumptions throughout *Unto This Last*: that everything "reaches yet into the infinite," that the earth is resplendent with "amazement," that we live by and in the measureless, unfathomable wonder of a loving divinity. Unlike the world sketched out by Malthus and still preserved in the pages of economics texts, the world is not a hardscrabble land of unlikeness, parched and stricken by scarcity; it is charged with the grandeur of God.

This sacramental principle of "amazement" entailed the genuine enchantment of the dismal science. Convinced that material life is sacramental and that abundance is the basic ontological feature of creation, Ruskin labored to show how "real science" could permit a glimpse of what he called "the

Economy of Heaven": the economy we would build if we realized that the world "reaches yet into the infinite." If "the Soul" named the longing of incarnate beings to reach yet into the infinite, then political economy was first and foremost an education in desire: "the desire of the heart is also the light of the eyes." The true science of production instructs us first, not how to maximize profits, but how to "desire and labor for the things that lead to life, and . . . to scorn and destroy the things that lead to destruction." "Life" meant not merely biological survival, but the exuberant flourishing of all our powers of "love, of joy, and of admiration." Ruskin's famous declaration that "there is no wealth but life" stemmed from something more than a vitalist moralism; it was the motto of a sacramental economics in which life is the efflorescence of divinity.[33]

If "life" is the only true wealth, then to eyes illuminated by heavenly desire, a distinction appeared between "wealth" and what Ruskin cursed as "illth." Unlike the conventional, quantitative measurement of wealth—the total volume of "goods and services" irrespective of their impact on body or soul—Ruskin's calculus of wealth was exclusively qualitative: "the possession of the valuable by the valiant." Wealth depended on a relationship between the character of a thing and the character of its possessor; a valuable object in the hands of an unworthy person was a sadness, even a desecration, certainly not a "good." By the same token, the value of consumption resided in its contribution to the vibrancy of "life." "The final outcome and consummation of all wealth," he wrote, was not enlargement of production but rather the abundance of "full-breathed, bright-eyed, and happy-hearted human creatures." Hence Ruskin's assertion—sure to grate on the ears of contemporary scolds of "consumerism"—that consumption is indeed "the final object of political economy." Ruskin dimly realized that what we call "the culture of consumption" is really a covert culture of *production*, since profit, not pleasure, is its ultimate goal. The unending stimulation of desire and discontent is a means to magnify capital accumulation, not to increase or deepen our fulfillment; what goes by the name of "consumerism" represents the corruption of consumption by the work ethic. Thus the real alternative to the competitive hedonism of capitalist societies was not austerity but rather wisdom in consumption. Those who look to Ruskin's humanism as a philosophy for "the simple life" will be disappointed, as his economy of heaven is an invitation to delight, not to asceticism—"to use everything, and to use it nobly." The wealth that is life mandated "good method of consumption, and great quantity of consumption."[34] To Ruskin, self-denial is no part of the good life.

Against wealth, Ruskin posed not poverty but "illth," that which wreaks "devastation and trouble in all directions." Evaluated by this standard, much of "modern wealth" was a plethora of illth that inflicted a "dim-eyed and narrow-chested state of being." What appeared to economists as growth and dynamism could in fact be a metastasizing cancer. Indeed, if Ruskin implied that conventional economics is a pseudo-science of illth, then capitalism is the political economy of death. Because the dismal science enjoined envy and competition, Ruskin condemned it, not only as a falsehood but also as a discipline and practice of oblivion. Illth was lethal as well as shabby, for capitalist expansion was impossible without the corruption and death of the soul. In the warfare of "modern business," Ruskin observed, "the seeking of death is a grand expression of the true course of men's toil." If heavenly economics decreed the "Laws of Life," capitalist economics compiled the "Laws of Death."[35]

What form would the "Economy of Heaven" take on earth? As his answer unfolded over the 1860s and 1870s, Ruskin attempted to reconcile "old-school" Toryism and "old-school" communism in a sacramental imagination. The incarnate "Economy of Heaven" would blend the paternalism of the Tory tradition with the fraternal republican ethos of communism. In the preface of *Unto This Last,* he outlined a program that later became a model for the British welfare state: training schools for youth, public works projects, state-owned factories and workshops to absorb the unemployed, and provision of housing and medical care for the old and the destitute. In flagrant defiance of the "law" of supply and demand, Ruskin suggested that all workers in the same trade should be paid at the same rate, arguing that only in this way would workers be chosen on account of their quality rather than their cheapness. But Ruskin appeared less concerned with policy prescriptions than with the character of the English people, who had to be "unconverted," so to speak, from the enchantment of Mammon-service. Calling on his brethren to abandon the battle for status and illth, he admonished them to be modest "Givers of Calm," "peace-Creators" who exemplified the biblical injunction that justice and peace should kiss. "Not greater wealth, but simpler pleasure; not higher fortune, but deeper felicity; making the first of possessions, self-possession; and honoring themselves in the harmless pride and calm pursuits of peace."[36]

Ruskin's subsequent avowals of "communism" make sense only against the background of the Toryism of *Unto This Last*. In some of his first open letters to the English working class that comprise *Fors Clavigera*—written just after the establishment of the Paris Commune in March 1871—Ruskin explained that the "Economy of Heaven" was a communist republic of small producers. Alarmed by (spurious) reports that the Paris Communards had destroyed many of the city's most beautiful monuments, Ruskin felt compelled to distinguish himself from the radicals across the Channel. What he dubbed the "Parisian school of Communism" taught that all property was common property. But "we Communists of the old school"—"dark-red Communists," he emphasized, "reddest of the red"—while they, too, believed that "everybody must work in common, and do common or simple work for his dinner," they nonetheless upheld a kind of private property that was communist in principle and practice. "Our property belongs to everybody, and everybody's property to us." Old-school communists dwell in charity; since they "exist only in giving," and "dread, above all things, getting miserly of virtue," they considered property to be a mode of graceful self-expenditure, not a vehicle for accumulation. Thus there would never be any fear of unemployment; but there would be "great fear . . . lest we should not do the work set us well."[37]

This "old-school" communism differed from that of Marx in several respects, and the differences are traceable to Ruskin's Romantic sacramental imagination. If Ruskin was no simple reactionary—recall his recognition of "the progress of this century"—then perhaps the fundamental conflict of visions in the nineteenth century was not, as Lasch understood it, between "progress and its critics," but rather between what we might call promethean and convivial conceptions of progress. Sponsored under capitalist and Marxist auspices, the promethean project of industrial modernity assumed (even in its evangelical Protestant form) an irreducibly combative ontology. Ruskin repudiated promethean notions of progress, innovation, and secularism—all of which appeared, in the light of "amazement," as specious and destructive illusions, fables of dominion that blinded their adherents to the friendliness of the universe. Since, to Ruskin, the line between heaven and earth was so thin as to be almost indiscernible, and all finite things "reach yet into the infinite," the world did not need "improvement" so much as loving nurturance of its possibilities. The sacramental ontology at the root of Ruskin's communism sanctioned not a regressive or stationary state but a project of human and technological progress determined by the principle of "life."

Ruskin also defined communist property in a way that Marx would have scornfully dismissed—but which also underlined the serious flaws in the Marxist account of historical progress. Indeed, the conflict over the meaning of "progress" was also a contest over the meaning of *communism*. Modern communism has always had a twofold character: as a form of property— common ownership—and as a principle of morality—"from each according to ability, to teach according to need."[38] As his emphasis on "giving" indicates, Ruskin, like Marx, affirmed the communist principle of *morality*; but they differed profoundly about the proper form of communist *property*, and they would have quarreled over the "abilities" and "needs" to be cultivated and fulfilled. For Marx, the future form of common ownership was inextricably bound up with the course of capitalist development, as corporate consolidation prepared industry for collective expropriation and ownership by the revolutionary proletariat. But this meant that the communist principle of morality—the "abilities" and "needs"—would bear the marks of its promethean ancestor: its technocratic politics, its equation of "abundance" with industrial production, its defiant insensitivity to natural limits. Because he rejected this promethean account of progress, Ruskin thereby rejected the promethean account of communism. For Ruskin, consolidation and mechanized production embodied the defilement of human divinity, while "mammon-service" ensured, not the conquest of scarcity, but the triumph of productivity over love. Resisting what he considered the fraudulently progressive march of promethean modernity, Ruskin countered that communism could thrive with private, nonaccumulative, convivial property. His political economy of heaven was a society of friends, a beloved community of small proprietors who revived the spirit of the medieval commons, animated and united by a communist principle of giving and consuming in love—from each according to ability, to each according to need.

Following Marx, the left has tended to vilify Ruskin's kind of anticapitalism as "petty-bourgeois" fantasy. There is more than a little truth to this charge. Ruskin was at his best when playing the roles of critic, provocateur, and visionary; he failed utterly when he tried to be the architect of a fundamentally new economics, and that blend of genius and ineptitude augured more moderation than radicalism. Even in *Unto This Last,* Ruskin conceded too much to the realities of mammon-service: his proposal of equal wages, for instance, still assumed both wage labor and a competitive labor market. His forays into technical economics—epitomized in the uncharacteristically leaden prose and banal analysis of *Munera Pulveris*—failed to undermine and supplant the terms of conventional economics. But precisely because of its sacramental theology, Ruskin's ideal of small-producer communism remains invaluable. After two centuries of promethean technics and its irreparable ecological impact, the "bitterness and malice" he detected in nature seems less like dyspeptic projection and more like the groaning of a world in peril. A more convivial technology, more attuned to the earth's "amazement," must now be adopted as a necessity. By the same token, unlike the "despotism" that Engels foresaw as the rule in the "realm of necessity," convivial communism offered a way to preserve the creative autonomy of the worker—the image and likeness of God—against the managerial and technocratic encroachments of modern industrial organization. Against Marx's celebration of large-scale, mechanized production as the basis of freedom, Ruskin would undoubtedly lament automation as an exile from the realm of divinity, where an absolute duality of work and play is simply unimaginable. Automation would also elicit Ruskin's invective because its vision of abundance is utterly quantitative: more and more things for less and less work, irrespective of the quality of things and especially the quality of the worker. Wealth as the "possession of the valuable by the valiant"— rooted, like Ruskin's concern for the worker, in a sacramental humanism— implied a standard of abundance more profoundly humane than that of a mechanical cornucopia.

Alas, Ruskin's convivial communism never attracted much support among intellectuals or workers. He incurred the vituperation of the British intelligentsia, most of whom dismissed him as a crank. *Unto This Last* was "reprobated in a violent manner," as Ruskin himself put it drily; one reviewer wrote that it was full of "windy hysterics" and "intolerable twaddle," delivered in the tones of "a mad governess." Ruskin's Guild of St. George, established in 1877 to sponsor experiments in handicraft and cooperative farming, was in financial arrears in less than a decade. Although many trade unionists and Labour Party rank and file venerated *Unto This Last,* the larger working class—"the only body," Ruskin declared in *Time and Tide* (1867), "to which we can look for resistance to the deadly influence of moneyed power"—was indifferent to or ignorant of his work. Moreover, as Craig Calhoun, Gareth Stedman Jones, and other labor historians have contended, working-class revolutionary fervor, in Britain and elsewhere, has tended to wane rather than intensify with the progress of industrialization.[39] Over the course of Ruskin's life, large-scale industry increasingly set the boundary of the proletarian political imagination; the workers to whom Ruskin addressed his communism grew more interested in acquiring an ever-larger share of the fruits of mechanized production.

Ruskin often expressed his disappointment at the meagerness of workers' demands—a poverty of imagination he thought ultimately traceable to the mechanization of labor. Considering only "their immediate interest," unions, he lamented in *The Crown of Wild Olive,* never considered "the far more terrific power of [capital's] appointment of the kind and the object of labor." If they insisted only on higher wages—a demand that implicitly ratified both the wage system and the industrial division of labor—workers would become complicit in the system that corrupted their desires and degraded their skills. "It matters fearfully what the thing is, which [workers are] compelled to make."[40] Ruskin implied that, if they desired an authentic alternative to capitalism, workers would have to provoke a struggle over the *ends* as well as over the means of production. Unless workers reclaimed the birthright of human divinity stolen by industrial capitalists, Ruskin feared that any victory they won would prove pyrrhic, insipid, and short-lived. Thus Ruskin anticipated the concerns of Theodor Adorno, Max Horkheimer, and other "Western Marxists" vexed by the decidedly unrevolutionary consciousness of the working class. If the effects of industrial production and culture are so profoundly demoralizing, how can workers generate the political will to protest and transform their condition? Might they even consent to their own mechanization if the rewards are seductive enough? Ruskin foresaw that the denouement of industrialization might be acquiescence, not revolutionary upheaval.

A writer even more lucid and elegant than Ruskin, William Morris was another Romantic enchanter whose work deserves our attention. For a long time, scholars saw Morris through the prism constructed by E. P. Thompson, who claimed that Morris traveled "from romantic to revolutionary"—that is, from the medievalist and reactionary moralism of Ruskin to the scientific socialism of Marx and Engels. To Thompson, the trajectory of Morris's political evolution seemed clear. Enchanted as a student at Oxford by "the desire to produce beautiful things" and by "a hatred of modern civilization," Morris devoted himself to verse, fable, and handicraft, writing (in Thompson's words) "evasive" and "despairing" poetry such as *The Defence of Guenevere* (1858) and *The Earthly Paradise* (1868–1870) and designing splendid tapestries for the tasteful bourgeoisie. Along with Edward Burne-Jones, Dante Gabriel Rossetti, and other pre-Raphaelite artists and artisans, Morris hoped to overcome the ugliness and brutality of industrial capitalism through the revival of craftsmanship. Trained as an architect after leaving Oxford, Morris transformed himself into an artisanal prodigy, mastering ceramics, carpentry, weaving, printing, dyeing, and embroidery. Founder of a highly lucrative design firm, Morris also set up the Kelmscott Press, using the printing technology and typography of the fifteenth century. Morris might have been remembered as a versatile craftsperson and progressive capitalist; but in the early 1880s, he joined H. M. Hyndman, E. Belfort Bax, Eleanor Marx, and Edward Aveling in the Social Democratic Federation (SDF), Britain's first major socialist party. Having converted to Marxism, Morris embarked on his most productive phase: what Thompson dubbed the "Scientific Utopia" of *News from Nowhere* (1890) and a handful of magnificent essays that remain classics in the socialist canon. Thus, Morris's poetry and fiction, his advocacy for architectural restoration, and his work as a designer and craftsperson all became, in Thompson's narrative, a wayward albeit illustrious pilgrimage toward political enlightenment.[41]

Yet Thompson's claim that Morris "thought through" a fusion of the Romantic and Marxist traditions is refuted by many of Morris's own explicit statements. His own account of his political journey in "How I Became a Socialist" (1894) was a tale of an intellectual vagabond. Morris sketched his definition of socialism, not in the terminology of "scientific" socialism, but in the venerable lexicon of the commons: a "COMMONWEALTH" in which "there should be neither rich nor poor, neither master nor master's man . . . neither brain-sick brain workers, nor heart-sick hand workers." "This view," he continued, "which I hold to-day, and hope to die holding, is what I began with"—began, that is to say, in his days as a crafter of poems, romances, and tapestries. Indeed, Morris asserted that he "had no transitional period"; the SDF gave Morris "a hope of the realization of my ideal." But when asked "how much of a hope," he could only reply "I do not know."[42] These are hardly the words of a formidable theoretician, and Morris openly avowed—with a candor that must have unsettled his comrades and admirers—that he had little interest in the intricacies of socialist theory. "Blankly ignorant of economics" before he joined the SDF, he "put some conscience into trying to learn the economical side of Socialism," and he "even tackled Marx," specifically "that great work" *Capital.* Though he plumbed "the historical parts," Morris confessed to "agonies of confusion of the brain over reading the pure economics." Having recounted his meager theoretical prowess, Morris returned with relish (and not a little relief) to the source of his radical hope: the medievalist revival associated with "Carlyle and Ruskin." Morris seldom mentioned Carlyle, but Ruskin, he wrote plainly, was "my master." "How deadly dull the world would have been twenty years ago but for Ruskin!" Through Ruskin—not Marx—Morris "learned to give form to [his] discontent"—a discontent, he reiterated, that "was not by any means vague."[43]

Morris made no secret of his debt to Ruskin. After reading *Modern Painters* while at Oxford, he anointed Ruskin "a Luther of the arts." Despite Ruskin's Toryism, Morris felt no embarrassment or ambivalence in lavishing praise on his hero. In his foreword to the Kelmscott Press's 1892 reprint of "The Nature of Gothic"—published, like his account of his political journey, well into his allegedly Marxist period—Morris praised, not Ruskin the historian and critic, but "Ruskin, the teacher of morals and politics." Even though Ruskin's hostility to socialism was well known, Morris asserted that he had "done serious and solid work toward that new-birth of Society, without which genuine art, the expression of man's pleasure in his handiwork, must inevitably cease altogether, and with it the hopes of the happiness of mankind." As Morris summarized Ruskin's lessons, "art is the expression of man's pleasure in labour ... unless man's work once again becomes a pleasure to him, the token of which change will be that beauty is once again a natural and necessary accompaniment of productive labour, all but the worthless must toil in pain, and therefore live in pain." Writing while still a member of the SDF, Morris saluted Ruskin, not for any call for the equitable distribution of industrial production, but for his craft and aesthetic ideal of "the hallowing of labour by art."[44]

Bearing the gothic trademark of Ruskin, "the hallowing of labour by art" was the goal of Morris's Romantic socialism. The consecrating craftsperson, not the desecrated proletarian, was Morris's enduring icon. From his earliest lectures, Morris upheld aesthetic and sensual delight as the highest criterion of labor. Objecting to the invidious distinction between the "lesser" and the "higher" arts in "The Lesser Arts" (1877)—a talk delivered to an educational guild of artisans—Morris celebrated such allegedly lowly skills as carpentry, pottery, and weaving for their fusion of beauty and utility. The "lesser" arts "beautify the familiar matters of everyday life," while the "higher" arts minister to the vanity of the rich. Morris predicted that, if they remained separated, both arts would grow impoverished and joyless; the lesser ones would be mechanized and trivial, while the higher would produce "ingenious toys . . . dull adjuncts to unmeaning pomp." Later, in "Useful Work versus Useless Toil" (1885), one of the finest essays on labor ever written, Morris saluted the medieval artisan who "stamped all labour with the impress of pleasure." Degraded industrial workers should demand, not higher wages or shoddy abundance enjoyed in their hours of leisure, but "hope of rest, hope of product, hope of pleasure in the work itself." Workers should learn at least three crafts, Morris believed, and blend sedentary with outdoor labor.[45] Rather than simply release humanity from the realm of necessity—the Marxist hope for industrialization—Morris's Romantic socialism promised to leaven the realm of necessity with the joy of the realm of freedom.

This can hardly be squared with Marx's enthusiasm for industrialization. Still, Morris did make some attempt to align the historical dialectics of Marx with the romantic craftsmanship of Ruskin. His account of revolutionary unrest and upheaval in *News from Nowhere*—how the workers fight their way "from commercial slavery to freedom"—is a masterpiece in the fictional portrayal of proletarian struggle, a panoramic and violent eschatology of misery, mobilization, insurrection, and triumph. Yet neither *News from Nowhere* nor the socialist essays justify Thompson's contention that Morris achieved a harmonious blend of Ruskin and Marx. Morris's Marxism often seems dutiful; his keener perceptions are frequently at odds with historical materialist optimism. This ambivalence surfaced in the muddled conclusion of "How I Became a Socialist." Though claiming to sense a "consciousness of revolution stirring amidst our hateful modern society," Morris often seemed more convinced that the working class had renounced or evaded its historical mission. Sounding more like Ruskin than Marx, Morris worried that the average worker "scarcely knows how to frame a desire for any life much better than that which he now endures perforce." As Ruskin had feared—and as Morris now lamented—industrial technology and culture had crippled the moral imagination of the working class. In private, Morris was even gloomier about the workers' revolutionary potential. "It is obvious," he once wrote to a friend, that "the support to be looked for for constructive Socialism from the working classes at present is naught." Full of "vague discontent and a spirit of revenge," the typical worker with any gift for leadership "finds himself tending to rise out of his class" rather than remaining in a spirit of solidarity.[46]

Morris's doleful assessment of the working class was not unfounded. The recession of radicalism among workers that was evident to Ruskin had become even more pronounced by the 1890s. As Gareth Stedman Jones writes, "capitalism had become an immovable horizon" for the late-Victorian proletariat. The energies that formerly might have been devoted to revolutionary agitation were now absorbed by what Jones dubs "a culture of consolation" that provided workers with a packet of compensations for social and political impotence: trade unionism, which accepted industrial workplace discipline, and the new urban mass culture of commodified entertainment and distraction. Working-class politics shifted "from power to welfare," while socialism increasingly meant, not workers' control of production, but state provision of welfare, the redistribution of wealth, and the eradication of poverty.[47] The contraction of socialist ambition often attributed to Sidney and Beatrice Webb and the Fabian Society—as well as to Eduard Bernstein and the German Social Democrats—had already commenced among the urban working class. Gradualism and reformism were reflections, not diversions, of working-class political consciousness.

The narrowing horizon of working-class hope was evident to Morris, and he clearly realized that the dynamics of capitalist production and culture posed serious obstacles to the development of revolutionary consciousness. What if the everyday life of capitalism bred, not discontent and revolution, but rather discontent and acquiescence—or even contentedness and affirmation? What if the destruction of pre-industrial ideals celebrated by Marx left us, not with the freedom to write the poetry of the future, but with a protracted imaginative paralysis? Morris's desire for "hallowed labour" could have propelled him to challenge one of the central tenets of Marxist theory: that capitalism would create the material and cultural preconditions for revolution. Why did workers find it difficult or impossible to "frame a desire for any life much better" than one defined by competitive mobility and consumer goods? Ruskin would have answered, in part, the corruption of morality and sensibility—an answer that many Marxists and other socialists have dismissed as reactionary and elitist. But as Morris's remark suggested, without the sort of distinction between "wealth" and "illth" that Ruskin had drawn, the volume of material abundance could obscure any vision of a life beyond accumulation. Marx would have insisted that we must conquer the realm of necessity before we can enter the realm of freedom; but Morris realized that it was precisely the chasm imposed between those realms that needed to be eradicated. Necessity and freedom, labor and beauty, should be bound up together—and the craftsperson embodied this union. Gothic architecture proved that a materially less abundant civilization could create beautiful and ennobling objects. Why, then, suppose that beauty and goodness had to wait on the achievements of industrial plenitude—a bounty that was, in any case, so shabby and soul-destroying? As the historical treasury of craftsmanship proved, loveliness and virtue had already hallowed the realm of necessity. So for art—"the expression of man's pleasure in labour"— to be a form of moral imagination, workers had to learn the poetry of the past if they were to write any poetry of the future. "It is the province of art," Morris asserted, to envision and proclaim "the true ideal of a full and reasonable life."[48]

As Ruskin would probably have sealed the argument, humanity does not live by bread alone; seek first the kingdom of heaven, and all else shall be added unto you. Morris, however, deferred to his comrades: bread and then roses. Despite his conviction that roses were as essential as bread to human flourishing, Morris chided those who believed that "the question of art and cultivation must go before that of the knife and fork." Such well-intentioned dilettantes did not "understand what art means, or how its roots must have a soil of a thriving and unanxious life."[49] But as Morris's own life and work had testified so handsomely, this way of posing the issue was false. Too eager to see the final realization of his romantic artisanal ideal, Morris submitted to the apparently scientific certainty of the SDF—a triumph of impatience over wisdom.

Why did Morris betray the ideal of romantic craftsmanship? A large part of the answer lies in the allure of Victorian radical chic: to many on the British left, Marxism seemed to offer a more serious political and intellectual alternative to capitalist society than Fabianism, Christian socialism, or anarchism. But we must also consider Morris's abandonment of the sacramental imagination that was central to Ruskin's legacy. Like his master, Morris had been raised in an evangelical family; what he later excoriated as "rich establishmentarianism puritanism" was "a religion which even as a boy I never took to." Yet shortly before entering Oxford, Morris felt powerfully attracted to the religious culture of Anglo-Catholicism: he visited the cathedrals of northern France, moved in the high-church circles of the Oxford Movement, and even considered founding a monastery. Animated by his zeal for medieval history, Morris's Anglican enchantment persisted through most of his student years. But gradually, Morris drifted away, emerging from his Anglo-Catholic phase more or less hostile to institutional religion. He neither proselytized for atheism like Charles Bradlaugh, nor abided in Christian unorthodoxy like his master, Ruskin. With his usual effortless honesty, Morris declared himself, near the end of his life, "careless of metaphysics and religion . . . but with a deep love of the earth and the life on it."[50]

Still, despite his professed aloofness from religious and theological matters, Morris inflected his socialist writing with a compelling sacramental hope. In his essays, Morris combines the evangelical preacher and the medieval knight-errant, sworn to rescue a holy land from the infidels of capital. He clearly considered socialism a modern form of religion. As he told Georgie Burne-Jones, his close friend's wife, shortly after he joined the SDF, "the aim of Socialists should be the founding of a religion," an intense devotion to moral and aesthetic ideals. Socialism, he wrote in "The Hopes of Civilization" (1885), would provide more than an equitable distribution of wealth. It "bears with it its own ethics and religion and aesthetics"; it is "the hope and promise of a new and higher life in all ways." As he hinted in *News from Nowhere,* that new and higher life would be akin to divinity. When Morris asks his hosts from the future what they expect to be paid for their work, they gently chide him for his crass and grubby impertinence. They work for free—that is, they take pleasure in their labor. Our reward, one informs him, is "the reward of creation. The wages which God gets, as people might have said time agone."[51] In other words, God does not need or accept payment; His only remuneration is delight.

This was more than justice and beauty; it was redemption and exaltation, something larger and deeper than political revolution or romantic craftsmanship. In a remarkable passage in *News from Nowhere,* Hammond, the wise old teacher who guides Morris through the new society, reflects on the world after the revolution with an erotic, almost sacramental joy. "The spirit of the new days, of our days," he muses, is "delight in the life of the world; intense and overweening love of the very skin and surface of the earth on which man dwells, such as a lover has in the fair flesh of the woman he loves." Such a doting sensuality was difficult and fleeting in the world of commercialism, restricted as it was to the boundaries imposed by adherence to pecuniary reason. "More akin to our way of life," Hammond explains, is "the spirit of the Middle Ages." To the people of that era, "heaven and the life of the next world was such a reality, that it became to them a part of the life upon the earth; which accordingly they loved and adorned, in spite of the ascetic doctrines of their formal creed, which bade them contemn it." To be sure, the enlightened citizens of the new society could no longer share the medieval era's "assured belief in heaven and hell." But, Hammond assures Morris, nature assumes a luminous grandeur with the disappearance of the supernatural; the world and its inhabitants were now a beloved community of earthly beatitude. The "religion of humanity" was now easy to believe, Hammond told his visitor from the past. "The men and women who go to make up humanity are free, happy, and energetic at least, and most commonly beautiful of body also, and surrounded by beautiful things of their own fashioning, and a nature bettered and not worsened by contact with mankind."[52]

This was Blake's New Jerusalem, the return of the green and pleasant land, remade once the mills of Satan had been razed and their rubble carted away. It was also Carlyle's world of wonder and the Everlasting Yea—without the infernal Gospel of Work and the barons of industrial heroism. It was Ruskin's economy of heaven—in the absence of Ruskin's God. But it was also the hope of St. George's Hill dug up by Winstanley and his comrades; it was the heritage of the commons, the lineage of the guilds, the victory of Carnival, the abolition of Lent. Morris was well aware that medieval craft had been charged with religious hope, and that socialism represented a modern attempt to construct an alternative faith. "A revival of religion was one of the moving causes of energy in the early Middle Ages," he observed in his essay on Gothic architecture, and one of the salutary features of this faith had been its "enthusiasm for visible tokens of the objects of worship."[53] The beautiful people and things of Nowhere would be emblems of human divinity. Like his beloved medieval craftspeople, Morris desired that life on earth be leavened with the presence of heaven; what he sought in the people's republic of beauty was a re-enchantment of the world.

Morris's career marks the secular denouement of the Romantic sacramental imagination—"secular" in its longing for an utterly mortal and finite beatitude. But by that very token, it also marks the futility of secular attempts to re-enchant the world. Like other prodigal children in flight from Victorian evangelicalism, Morris believed he could dispense with Christian theology and still hold on to Christian wonder and ethics. As Nietzsche had noted of George Eliot and other adherents of the religion of humanity, "they are rid of the Christian God, and now believe all the more firmly that they must cling to Christian morality." But as Nietzsche realized with his pitiless clarity, the morality was embedded in the divinity; Christian ethics depended on a world understood as the creation of God. Eliot and those like her had postponed confronting the full implications of their apostasy; "for the English," Nietzsche wrote with mordant understatement, "morality is not yet a problem."[54] The same could be said of Morris's religion of socialism and beauty—his gorgeous substitute for sacrament. How could heaven inspire our love and adornment once we know it doesn't exist? Could paradise survive the inexorable course of material senescence and death? No beatitude has ever been so frail and melancholy.

John Ball knew better that justice and beauty needed firmer ontological foundations. Written two years before *News from Nowhere*, *A Dream of John Ball* (1888) is a similar tale of time travel, but to the past rather than the future. Recalling the ill-fated Peasants' Revolt of 1381, Morris became a socialist Malory, transforming the farmers and artisans of Kent into knights-errant of communism. In his speech to the insurgents at the foot of the village cross, Ball summoned their revolutionary spirit by invoking the marriage of heaven and earth. "Forsooth brothers, fellowship is heaven, and lack of fellowship is hell . . . I bid you not dwell in hell but in heaven, or while ye must, upon earth, which is a part of heaven, and forsooth no foul part." If their rebellion against the kingdom of hell was victorious, "the saints in heaven shall be glad, because men no more fear each other." Ball tells his men that even defeat will bear a sacramental witness: if they perish and decompose, they will be "part and parcel of the living wisdom of all things, very stones of the pillars that uphold the joyful earth."[55]

Yet the rebels fall victim not only to the nobles but also to the condescension of Marxist posterity. During Ball's oration at the foot of the village cross, Morris reflected on the detours that history would throw in the path of socialism. "Men fight and lose the battle, and the thing that they fought for comes about in spite of their defeat, and when it comes turns out not to be what they meant, and other men have to fight for what they meant under another name."[56] To Morris, socialism was the modern name of Ball's medieval dream—but Ball might well have protested that it wasn't exactly what he meant. While both Ball and Morris belonged to the lineage of "the commons," Ball's commons—envisioned at the foot of a cross—was a part of heaven on earth, in fellowship with the saints, an antechamber to the kingdom of God. For Ball and the peasants, divinity pervaded and sanctioned the commons; the injustice and tyranny of priests and nobles desecrated God's holy manor. Aiming to expropriate the clergy and the aristocracy, Ball's peasant crusaders had much larger hopes than the modern working class. Resigned to the permanence of capitalist society, the working classes—in England and elsewhere—made a tenuous peace with the barons of finance and industry. However resilient and even heroic in their efforts to effect reform, the culture of consolation was a pale reflection of the fellowship of heaven.

Morris's longing for a heavenly fellowship was shared by many in the Arts and Crafts movement. From Ireland to Finland, but especially in England, Arts and Crafts attracted numerous artists, architects, designers, and other disgruntled urban professionals. Often educated at Oxbridge, many English artisanal ideologues—Morris, Walter Crane, T. J. Cobden-Richardson, C. R. Ashbee, and Edward Carpenter—were self-taught craftspersons inspired by Ruskin and Morris. Appalled by the shoddiness of mass-produced goods and the blandness of industrial architecture, they traced the deformation of craft and architectural design to the capitalist imperative for low costs and maximum profit. Craftspersons were endangered, Crane contended, by "a misapplication of machinery, driven by keen competition of trade." But English artisanal ideologues aspired to more than aesthetically pleasing products. They aimed to efface the modern industrial distinction between art and life. Communities such as the Art Workers' Guild, the Guild of Handicraft, and the Bromsgrove Guild combined craftwork and agriculture in the hope that art and manual labor would gradually permeate society, supplanting the mercenary and mechanical civilization with a loving and organic community. Attempting to overcome power with beauty, artisanal advocates produced a cornucopia of books, essays, and catalogs; promoted exhibits and salesrooms; and set up numerous craft schools, workshops, and guilds.[57]

These small experiments in craft and husbandry could be dismissed as enclaves of apolitical withdrawal, romantic pining in industrializing England for what was left of Blake's "green and pleasant land." But we should recall how the participants saw them: as outposts of what many writers dubbed the "New Age," "the New Life," or "the Simple Life," living now with the exuberance and fullness one desired, not postponing paradise into the future. Artisanal advocates sought to revitalize—or even better, to create—a moral imagination for modernity. As many craft ideologues admitted, the figure of the artisan was a human ideal before it was a criterion for craftsmanship. "The real thing is the life," as Ashbee emphasized at his Guild of Handicraft in the Cotswolds. If workers or professionals found "freedom and personality" in the exercise of skill and autonomy, "it doesn't matter so very much if their metalwork is second rate."[58] Arts and Crafts aspired to make beautiful souls as well as handsomely usable objects.

But without social roots in the working class and metaphysical roots in theology, those beautiful souls stood defenseless against co-optation. Uncoupled from their hatred of industrial capitalism, their praise of the Gothic was easily enlisted in the service of the bourgeoisie. Though swearing fidelity to the spirit of Morris and Ruskin, the Arts and Crafts movement in both Britain and the United States became a form of aesthetic therapy for disgruntled bourgeois. Composed mainly of aesthetically earnest bourgeois, the British Arts and Crafts movement downplayed Morris's socialist politics and highlighted his designs for tapestry and furniture. Though deriding their "various elegant little schemes" for the revival of handicraft, Morris became an unlikely contributor to the aesthetic revitalization of the British ruling class.[59] Once an eloquent lion of socialism, Morris was housebroken

by tasteful consumers of domestic decoration. Through the alchemy of forgetting, Romantic opposition to capitalist squalor was transmuted into bourgeois bohemianism.

Morris's desire to mark labor with "the impress of pleasure" was shared
by the anarchist movement. Morris himself adamantly rejected anarchism;
anarchists themselves, he once told a friend, had convinced him "quite
against their intention, that Anarchism was impossible." Eager to maintain
his credibility with Marxists, Morris adopted their patronizing attitude,
chiding anarchists in "Socialism and Anarchism" (1889) for being "authoritative about authority, and not a little vague also." But Morris was an occasional contributor to *Liberty,* a short-lived English anarchist journal, and
he shared their distaste for electoral politics and their opposition to state
socialism. Moreover, Morris's celebration of artisanal autonomy both en-
deared him to craft ideologues and converged with the anarchist hatred of
the hierarchy that Marxists considered indispensable to modern industry.[60]
Both anarchists and Arts and Crafts writers expressed an antipathy to the
managerial and technocratic elitism against which Morris and Ruskin had
warned.

Anarchists (as well as artisanal idealists) have been routinely dismissed as
"romantic" and "backward-looking," unable or unwilling to board the train
of historical and technological progress. For instance, historians interpreted
anarchism as a dying, atavistic bray of the pre-industrial order, an ideological requiem of the petty bourgeoisie: artisans, peasants, shopkeepers, small
proprietors marked for extinction by agricultural and industrial modernization. Forged by members of declining classes—autodidact artisans like
Pierre-Joseph Proudhon, renegade aristocrats like Mikhail Bakunin, Leo
Tolstoy, and Peter Kropotkin—anarchist theory was the cry of freedom from
men being cast into the dustbin of history. But recent scholarship portrays
anarchism before World War I as a much more broadly based movement of
beleaguered small producers, insurgent industrial workers, and avant-garde
artists and writers. Like Marxists, anarchists identified the industrial
working class as the chief agent of revolutionary change. Yet they appealed
to all the displaced and disaffected, inviting all the wretched and alienated
of the earth, from patrician to *lumpenproletariat*.[61]

The discovery that anarchism was more than a form of petty-bourgeois
radicalism should not, however, obscure the salience of the artisanal ideal in

its moral imagination. Despite the obliteration of artisanal skills by the advance of mechanization, craftsmanship remained the moral and political unconscious of anarchism. Anarchists assured workers that they would not have to wait to obtain direct control of the means of production—a promise that Marxists could not make, and that Engels emphatically rejected. Marxists insisted that the proletariat would have to undergo an indefinite period of industrial tutelage from technical and managerial experts. Set against what Engels himself termed this "despotism," anarchist and syndicalist notions of "direct action" and the "general strike" make sense, not as infantile ideological disorders but as signs of faith in the capacity of workers to arrange and control their own affairs without permission or guidance from any vanguard. This confidence stemmed from the memory of artisanal and peasant customs of mutual aid. Anarchists were not simply or merely "backward-looking"; rather, they regarded the new industrial civilization through the lens of an artisanal sensibility. The often internecine struggle between Marxists and anarchists was a fight over the meaning and content of progress, not a duel between progress and its opponents.

If anarchism was "forward-looking" as well as artisanal, it was therefore a left-libertarian form of Romantic anticapitalism. Like other left Romantics, anarchists sought to reconcile pre-industrial values with Enlightenment principles of scientific reason, technological improvement, and individual freedom. The first two generations of anarchist thinkers lauded the ingenuity and resilience of craft and peasant communities. Peter Kropotkin, for instance, looked back to the guilds and cities of the Middle Ages as models for a libertarian communist modernity. Surveying the evolutionary history of cooperation in *Mutual Aid* (1902), Kropotkin echoed Ruskin and Morris. "Many aspirations of our modern radicals were already realized in the Middle Ages," he mused, and "much of what is described as Utopian was accepted then as a matter of fact": pleasurable work, reasonable hours, frequent holidays, festivals, and pageants. Peasant communes and urban guilds served Kropotkin, as they had Morris, as forerunners of fraternal, post-capitalist creativity. Unlike modern industrialists, guilds valued "the inventive skill of the worker" more than "rapidity of fabrication"; unlike the modern corporation, the guild (itself a corporate body) was a "brotherhood of men who knew each other [and] knew the technics of the craft."[62]

Anarchist forms of mysticism and spirituality also owed a great deal to Romanticism. Although anarchists denounced institutional religion as the incense surrounding the state—Bakunin declared that if God did exist, it would necessary to abolish Him—anticlericalism did not preclude a disposition to natural supernaturalism. In his nineteen-volume *The Earth and Its Inhabitants* (1886–1894), Elisée Reclus—like Kropotkin, a geographer— leavened his meticulous observation of nature with a poetic, ecologically enlightened sensibility imbued with traces of enchantment. Expressed in sensuous, lyrical prose, Reclus's love of the earth bordered on pantheism. "I have become part of the surrounding milieu; I feel as if I am one with the floating aquatic plants, one with the sand swept along the bottom, one with the current that sways my body." For Reclus, anarchism represented the fullest fruition of the oldest religious traditions, which had been, he believed, forms of natural enchantment before ossifying into priestcraft and moralism. "Our religion" of modernity, he asserted—which included "everything good that was contained in the ancient religions"—is "far from new and has always been practiced by the best people."[63]

The Romantic character of anarchism also explains its attraction for many fin-de-siècle artists and writers—the shock troops of European bohemia, the site of cultural modernity's earliest experiments in consciousness, manners, and mores. Like embattled craftspeople and peasants, the avant-garde had direct experience of unalienated production: the synthesis of conception and performance in writing, composing, painting, or sculpture remained indispensable to one's identity as an artist. But as freelance creators no longer tethered to the aristocratic and ecclesiastical systems of patronage, painters, sculptors, musicians, poets, novelists, and journalists jostled in a cultural bazaar dominated by bourgeois taste and moralism—the world of banal, sanctimonious avarice from which so many of them had sought escape. Along with their artisanal neighbors, the avant-garde bitterly resented bourgeois encroachment on their creative autonomy. Because of this craftlike conception of art, anarchism appealed to many avant-garde artists and writers who considered socialists too obsessed with centralization and uniformity, indifferent if not hostile to their desire for aesthetic independence and innovation. Galvanized by the prospect of liberation from the clutches of philistines, plutocrats, and administrators, the aesthetic vanguard—from Alfred

Jarry and Guillaume Apollinaire to Pablo Picasso and Wassily Kandinsky—
rallied beneath the black flag of anarchism.[64]

This desire for aesthetic freedom could also double as a modernist search
for enchantment. The anarcho-modernist quest for enchantment is best
illustrated by Kandinsky, who considered his theories about art and spirituality inseparable from anarchist political convictions. Moving among a
Munich avant-garde that took an avid interest in anarchism, medieval mysticism, occultism, theosophy, and pacifism, Kandinsky saw no dissonance between his interest in unorthodox spirituality and the anarchist repudiation
of religion. In his two most significant writings on art—"On the Question
of Form," his essay in the *Blaue Reiter* almanac (1911) that launched German
expressionism, and *Concerning the Spiritual in Art* (1912), a text widely read
and debated among artists and intellectuals—Kandinsky fused a mystical,
sacramental modernism with rebellion against capital and the state. Condemning bourgeois society for its "recognizing only what can be weighed and
measured," Kandinsky countered that the world is animated by the incalculable. "The world sounds. It is a cosmos of spiritually affective beings. Dead
matter is living spirit." Spirit is "concealed in matter" and "seeks its material-
ization." As a material vessel of spirit, contemporary art is "anarchistic"—it
"embodies as a materializing force that spiritual element now ready to reveal
itself." For Kandinsky, art was the outward and visible sign of an inner spiritual good, and anarchy was the free, spontaneous life of the same internal
grace. (His colleague and comrade Franz Marc predicted that modern art
would "belong on the altars of the coming spiritual religion.")[65] Often thought
to be a festive and insolent extravaganza of sensual excess, Bohemia could
host aesthetic experiments in the re-enchantment of the world.

Kandinsky's anarcho-enchantment had a political complement in the
work of the German libertarian socialist Gustav Landauer. A hero to many
German Jewish radicals (including the young philosopher and theologian
Martin Buber), Landauer broke with the Marxist orthodoxy of the Social
Democratic Party as propounded by Karl Kautsky and August Bebel. In *For
Socialism* (1911), his lyrically acerbic critique of Second International
Marxism—"the curse of the socialist movement," in his words—Landauer
excoriated what he viewed as its scientific pretensions and its imaginative
capitulation to bourgeois modernity. Against the Marxist claim to have over-
come "utopian" speculation and founded a science of revolution, Landauer

contended that "there is no science of the future"; human life is too various and volatile to be reduced to immutable laws. At the same time, Marxists' celebration of capitalist industrial development marked them not only as "worshippers of success" but as inadvertent acolytes of the very pecuniary enchantment they claimed to dispel. "Money, this God, is nothing else but spirit that has exited from man and become a living thing, an un-thing, the meaning of life changed to madness." Speaking for others on the non-Marxist left, Landauer proclaimed that "we are poets," not pedants armed with a fraudulent science, and that socialism is "a struggle for beauty, greatness, [and] abundance."[66]

In England, the artisanal romanticism of anarchism and Arts and Crafts found an eloquent oracle in Edward Carpenter, whose courageous defiance of Victorian morality grew out of a post-Christian spirituality. A friend and comrade of Morris and one of England's most popular writers and speakers from the 1880s until World War I, Carpenter embodied the unorthodox sanctity that permeated the late Victorian counterculture. Carpenter's open practice and advocacy of same-sex love and his support for sexual freedom reflected his scorn for "civilization," his term for the repressive property and erotic relations of industrial capitalism. Driven by insecurity and loneliness, Christian "civilization," in Carpenter's view, was harried, malicious, and violent; its hunger for property was insatiable, and its fear of the body's desires was boundless. Heaven-bent on riches and domination, its denizens renounced the only true joy: the resplendence of bodily health, which for Carpenter constituted the incarnation of "the divine *imago* within them." As the "cure" for "civilization," Carpenter prescribed "the old Nature-religion" of physical vitality and spiritual exaltation. With divine literati Emerson and Whitman as spiritual and poetic preceptors, Carpenter espoused an amorphous and expansive gospel of natural enchantment, a "sacredness of Life and Nature" in which "the distinction between spiritual and material disappears." In the ever-ancient and ever-new religion of nature, the "redeemed and delivered Man" was the one who experienced "divine life and love through all the channels of body and mind."[67]

In Carpenter's naturalist divinity, the artisan and the artist were saints of exuberance, icons of earthly enchantment. Although he considered himself a socialist, Carpenter's idealization of craftsmanship and rural life put him closer to Arts and Crafts and anarchism. (Adherents of both movements invoked his writing.) Never comfortable with Fabian statism, Carpenter evolved into an anarcho-communist by the end of World War I. Defining "industrial freedom" as workers' control of the means of production, Carpenter contended that smaller, decentralized communities would reskill and reinvigorate their inhabitants; the things they made would "radiate the spirit" of material divinity. Inspired by "a new gospel of Wealth," liberated craftspeople would abolish the monotonous servitude of the division of labor. More important, they would reclaim their rightful status as artists, "the only natural and healthy people," practitioners of "the arts of Life": the ordinary chores and routines that sustain and beautify everyday life, uncorrupted by the mercenary obligations of profit and productivity. Touched by the genius of the artist, ordinary objects were vessels of "Beauty," sacramental mementos that conveyed through matter "the sense of divinity in Nature and Life." For Carpenter—as for many radicals touched by the genius of Ruskin and Morris—beauty became the aesthetic and moral substitute for traditional Christian enchantment.[68]

Even where they relinquished the medieval spirit while seeking to recast medieval moral economy, anarchism and Arts and Crafts tried to thwart what Hopkins had called "the wreckage of the past"—a project of historical demolition that had proceeded much more rapidly across the Atlantic, in the United States. In *News from Nowhere,* Morris alluded to the ugliness of the American industrial landscape. Speaking after the revolution, Hammond tells Morris that the United States had been so disfigured by industrial capitalism that for a century now "the people of the northern parts of America have been engaged in gradually making a dwelling-place out of a stinking dust-heap." "There is still a great deal to do," he adds, "especially as the country is so big."[69] The most advanced capitalist society in the world, the United States had been engaged for almost three centuries in the business of improvement and progress. Pervaded by a more pristine economy and culture of capitalist enchantment, America already had—and would continue to compile—a long record of mammon-service.

# PART TWO

---

## A Hundred Dollars, a Hundred Devils: Mammon in America, 1492–1870

MORE SENSITIVE THAN MOST Americans to the brutal delusions of his country's messianism, Herman Melville discerned the sublimity and sham bound together in the national eschatology. In *White-Jacket* (1850), for instance, the eponymous narrator delivers an exhilarating oration on the destiny of America, expressing the vainglorious bravado of the Puritan errand and Manifest Destiny. "We Americans are the peculiar, chosen people—the Israel of our time," he declares, "predestinated" for greatness. Unlike the Persians, Romans, or other imperial peoples who conquered only to subdue and exploit, "with ourselves," he proclaims, "almost for the first time in history, national selfishness is unbounded philanthropy." When the new Israel steals land or takes commercial advantage, "we give alms to the world." Elsewhere, Melville captured the beatific vision at the core of business eschatology. Describing the Liverpool docks in *Redburn* (1849), Melville portrayed them as "an epitome of the world," a global communion created through trade. In "a grand parliament of masts," things and people commingle in fraternity:[1]

> Canada and New Zealand send their pines; America her live oak; India her teak; Norway her spruce; and the Right Honorable Mahogany, member for Honduras and Campeachy, is seen at his post by the wheel. Here, under the beneficent sway of the Genius of Commerce, all climes

and countries embrace; and yard-arm touches yard-arm in brotherly
love.

Yet Melville also discerned more insidious possibilities. The typical American, he observed in *Israel Potter* (1855), was "intrepid, unprincipled, reckless, predatory, with boundless ambition, civilized in externals but a savage at heart." Explaining "the metaphysics of Indian-hating" in *The Confidence Man* (1857), Melville maintained that the dreams of expansion were fantasies of powerlust. However crude and violent, the backwoodsman of the episode is a "captain in the vanguard of conquering civilization," a figure akin to "Moses in the Exodus, or the Emperor Julian in Gaul."[2] The same will to power remained in force in the more polite market society that followed in his wake. Well versed in self-delusion, the Confidence Man would have known what to make of White Jacket—or of the long, misenchanted lineage of believers in American anointment and exceptionalism.

The barely repressed madness that Melville detected in America's soul was also the spirit of malevolence at work in the expanding capitalist market. In "The Paradise of Bachelors and the Tartarus of Maids" (1855), young girls work in a paper mill at the bottom of a hollow named Devil's Dungeon. (In Greek mythology, Tartarus was the lowest region of the underworld.) Imprisoned in the industrial division of labor, the maids are servants of capitalist technology, sacrifices to the cults of pecuniary enchantment and technological fetishism. "Machinery—that vaunted slave of humanity—stood menially served by human beings, who served mutely and cringingly as the slave serves the Sultan." With "their agony dimly outlined on the imperfect paper, like the print of the tormented face on the handkerchief of Saint Veronica," the women stamp on their products the sacramental mark of their outraged human divinity. Later, in *The Confidence Man,* the shape-shifting "cosmopolitan" relies on misplaced confidence—that is, on manipulated faith. (The riverboat on which the narrative unfolds is called the *Fidele.*) The currency at the core of "confidence" becomes a sacramental token of evil. As a crotchety miser mutters at one point—and who better to know the enchantments of money—"A hundred dollars? A hundred devils!"[3]

Melville's sketch of a diabolical factory marked a denouement of the attempt to build a beloved community on the foundation of capitalism, and in his ambivalence about the promise of America, he captured the treachery of capitalist enchantment. A little over two centuries earlier, the Puritans had embarked on an "errand into the wilderness" that became an errand into the marketplace. Bearing the gospel of improvement from England, the saints of New England believed that love could be anchored in acquisitive property relations. Resting on the corpses of massacred natives and funded with credit from heaven, their "city on a hill" was the pious citadel of a covenant theology of capitalism. Yet as the wages of piety mounted throughout the seventeenth century, the community wandered far from the errand and softly descended from the heights of the city. Although ministers censured this declension in the "jeremiad"—a recollection of the errand, an acknowledgment of failure, and a call to rededication—they eloquently concealed the contradiction and futility inherent in the Puritan way.

The tensions in the Puritan errand remained repressed and unresolved in subsequent forms of capitalist enchantment in America. Between the Revolution and the Civil War, evangelicals and Mormons rewrote the terms of the covenant theology of business. Seeking to create a democracy of brethren while competing in the marketplace, they pioneered some of the fundamental features of modern American economic mythology: the alignment of pecuniary reason with the amazing grace of Christian divinity and the self-made entrepreneur in cahoots with the mercenary arc of the universe. With Americans in league with the unrighteous Mammon, the Puritan gospel of improvement morphed into the sublimity of technological progress, and the Puritan errand became the manifest destiny of pious white proprietors.

Like its counterpart in Europe, American Romanticism developed, in part, as a reaction to capitalist modernity, but its most penetrating sacramental witnesses were neither poets nor intellectuals. While members of Brook Farm and other utopian communities sought to savor "some aromatic root of wisdom," Walt Whitman and Ralph Waldo Emerson affirmed the justice, fraternity, and ontological veracity of proprietary capitalism. Whitman's democratic vistas embraced the popular stampede for riches, while Emerson's "soul's economy" was measured in "money as beautiful as roses." Compounded of Christianity and African enchantment, the religion of the slaves contained a more ominous version of Romantic prophecy. Epitomized in the confessions of Nat Turner, the slaves' faith in a sacramental universe afforded the clearest and most damning vision of American friendship with unrighteous Mammon.

# 4

# Errand into the Marketplace

## The Puritan Covenant Theology of Capitalism

BEFORE THE PURITANS SET out on their errand, other English explorers believed they had encountered an enchanted replica of Eden. Arthur Barlowe, captain of a ship dispatched to America by Sir Walter Raleigh in 1584, reported that he had hugged the shore of paradise. Virginian soil was "most plentifull, sweete, fruitfull, and wholesome," and the natives were "most gentle, loving, and faithfull . . . and such as live after the manner of the golden age." The enchantments of America provided abundant fare for poets and playwrights. In "To the Virginian Voyage" (1606), a celebration of English colonial destiny, Michael Drayton dubbed Virginia "Earth's onely paradise." Five years later, William Shakespeare modeled Prospero's island in *The Tempest* on voyagers' accounts of Virginia. As Leo Marx explains, Prospero represents a nascent commitment to incessant technological innovation. "With his magical incantations," Marx observes, Prospero is "a prophet of the emergent faith in progress." Free of the misery and oppression that plague the fearful old world of Europe, Prospero's enchanted isle—America embellished with utopian longing—is a "brave new world" of beatific abundance; "how beauteous mankind is!"[1]

Yet while marveling at the second Eden, the English also brought God and Mammon into closer proximity. Richard Hakluyt, a director of the Virginia Company and one of the premiere promoters of colonization in America, trusted that spreading the Gospel would bring extraordinary riches in its train. In his *Divers Voyages Touching the Discovery of America* (1582)—a quarto promoting Sir Humphrey Gilbert's voyage to plant a colony in America—Hakluyt regaled potential investors and colonists that God rewarded the industrious with material as well as spiritual wealth. Although "wee forget that Godlinesse is great riches," Hakluyt mused happily that "if

we first seeke the kingdome of God, al other things will be given unto us."
There were ample earthly returns on investment in the extension of God's
dominion. "Lasting riches do waite upon them that are zealous for the advancement of the kingdome of Christ." Recounting his own maritime career,
Hakluyt held up his success as a parable of special providence. Struggling
near the coast of Scotland, God gave Hakluyt and his crew, "through his
grace and accustomed goodnesse, a meetely favorable winde"; elsewhere,
God deigned to "send us very faire weather." Hakluyt's God also regulated
the commodity markets, enabling the discovery of a northwest passage to
China "for the bringing of the spiceries from India into Europe."[2]

Less pious promoters such as George Alsop and Thomas Morton appealed
to desires for enchantment before the Fall. After spending four years as an
indentured servant in Maryland, Alsop lavished gorgeous praise on the
colony in *A Character of the Province of Maryland* (1666). Alsop wrote with
some literary flair of the "superabounding plenty" of Maryland, fusing commercial appeal with Edenic longing. The colony was a perfect "situation for
the Soul of profitable Ingenuity," he wrote—"trafique" being "the very soul
of a Kingdom"—but it was also "a Landskip of Creation." Sacraments of original bliss, "the Trees, Plants, Fruits, Flowers, and Roots" were "Emblems or
Hieroglyphicks of our Adamitical or Primitive situation." Speaking in their
"dumb vegetable Oratory," the natural wonders of Maryland beckoned English colonists back to Eden, "Effigies of Innocency according to their original Grafts."[3] Alsop's Maryland was Bunyan's Beulah, an antechamber to the
kingdom of heaven.

A thorn in the side of the Puritan elite, Thomas Morton linked the animate
cosmology of early modern England with the emerging universe of improvement and commodities. Morton nursed a virulent and lifelong contempt
for Puritanism, having spent his short-lived legal career defending rural
farmers dispossessed by improving landlords, many of them Puritans. Tired
of fighting the good but hopeless fight, Morton ended up as a fur trader in
New Plymouth. Exchanging liquor and muskets for furs from the Narra-
gansett, Morton incurred the antipathy of the Puritan leadership. After
falling out with his partner, Morton turned their trading post into an
agrarian colony, "Merry Mount," complete with maypole, songs, and
drunken dancing. Openly scornful of Puritan probity, the Merry Mounters
swiftly attracted the opprobrium of elders such as William Bradford, who

vilified Morton in his doughty history *Of Plymouth Plantation* (1651). Horrified by the "mad Bacchinalians" and their shameless debauchery, Bradford took up the Puritan crusade against precapitalist enchantment and moral economy. Rebuking Morton and his band for their "base covetousnes," Bradford denounced the "idol May-polle" and other pagan sacramentals (other leaders called it a "Calfe of Horeb"), and dubbed Morton himself a "lord of misrule."[4]

Imprisoned by Puritan magistrates and packed off to England, Morton recounted his adventures in *New English Canaan* (1637), one of the earliest and most portentous documents of Anglo-American enchantment. Combining promotion, amateur anthropology, and colonialist exoticism, Morton sold New England to his compatriots as "Nature's Masterpeece." Addressing himself to "all such as are desirous of being made partakers of the blessings of God in that fertile Soyle," Morton warned that New England lay "fast bound in darck obscurity," a mystery revealed and channeled through the "pretty conjuring tricks" employed by the Indians. Morton was clearly of two minds about these "tricks"; though he considered the sachems but "weake witches," he reported that one Englishmen's injured hand had been cured through their congress with the Devil. Morton was just as divided about the natives' indifference to hard work and accumulation. They "passe away the time merrily," he noted enviously, living "the more happy and freer life, being voyde of care"—in stark contrast, he continued, to the solemnity and possessiveness "which torments the minds of so many Christians." Taking "no delight in baubles, but in usefull things," the natives shrugged at all the "superfluous commodities" that the English tried to sell them. And what "usefull things" they had, they shared without inhibition or complaint: "all things . . . are used in common amongst them. A bisket cake is given to one; that one breaks it equally into so many parts, as there be persons in his company and distributes it."[5]

Morton's favorable portrayal of the Indians obscured his commercial and aggressive intentions. Though he waxed Edenic on the nakedness of the Indians—"cloaths are a badge of sin"—he also saw a market for textiles, even as he conceded that "more variety of fashions" entailed "greater abuse of the Creatures." After doting on the region's forests, Morton soon recovered his pecuniary reason, giving the trees "a prime place in the Catalogue of commodities." Immediately after reporting on the natives' carefree open-handedness, Morton remembered that they were "ruled by the Devil"—the same spirit who vexed the acquisitive and restless Christians—and reverted to hackneyed but fateful caricatures of indigenous degeneracy. Morton's apparently tolerant attitude toward the Indians is belied by the very title of his book: the old Indian homeland was the new English Canaan, "a plaine parallel to Canaan of Israel," whose heathen inhabitants had been violently cleansed to make way for a chosen people. Like the Puritan elect he despised, Morton attributed the destruction of the natives to the Providence of the Almighty. Thanks to the "wondrous wisdom and love of God," the English would "sweepe away by heapes the Salvages," burying the natives underneath the foundations of their godly City on a Hill.[6]

The Puritans had arrived in America bearing belief in a world of wonders. As David D. Hall notes matter-of-factly, "the people of seventeenth-century New England inhabited an enchanted universe." If the American "wilderness" was a dangerous place to which the Puritans came with an "errand" of salvation, it was also a landscape of supernatural marvels. Like their brethren in England, the colony of the saints produced numerous books, almanacs, broadsides, and pamphlets abounding with reports of wonders. Theologians, physicians, printers, and teachers published works on alchemy, astrology, witchcraft, and other strange events and practices. John Winthrop filled pages of his journal with accounts of marvels, prodigies, and other signs of divinity. These "especial providences of God," he believed, "show the presence and power of God in his ordinances, and his blessing upon his people." Winthrop's son John—who later became the governor of Connecticut as well as the first colonial fellow of the Royal Society—was an alchemical magus steeped in the writings of Paracelsus, Rosicrucian masters, and Gabriel Plattes was one of the leading industrial utopians. Convinced that alchemy was at once religious quest, scientific project, and business enterprise, Winthrop the younger pointed to his salt-making venture as an example of how God "through the example of stones and fire enjoins constancy upon his worshippers." Increase Mather was awed by the "marvelous sympathies and antipathies in the natures of things," and worried that fortune-telling had "let loose evil Angels upon New England" before the 1692 Salem witchcraft trials. Later, his son Cotton studded his history of the errand, *Magnalia Christi Americana* (1702), with numerous episodes of "Illustrious, Wonderful Providences." Like the younger Winthrop's alchemical geology, the younger Mather's account of New England's history displayed a sacramental view of nature in which the world's outward, material objects signified invisible, spiritual realities. One of the key assumptions of *The Christian Philosopher* (1721), Mather wrote, was that the *"Footsteps* of a *Deity"* could be traced "in all the Works of Nature."[7]

The moral imagination of American capitalism was born in this Puritan cosmos of enchantment, for the God who dictated his covenant theology was the Author of the world of wonders. The saints accepted a charge to build a godly commonwealth—"a city on a hill," in Winthrop's words—and if they remained faithful to the covenant, the Lord would prosper their doings. But if they strayed from the path of righteousness—especially by succumbing to the blandishments of Mammon—the Almighty would punish His chosen and force them back onto the straight and narrow road to heaven. Puritan clergy often reiterated this covenant in the "jeremiad": a statement of the radiant ideal, a summons to recognize unrighteousness or "declension," remembrance of the meaning and destiny of the city, and rededication to the founding vision. The covenant was apparent in the colony's founding charter, approved by Charles I in 1629. The Massachusetts Bay Company—a profit-making venture established to generate handsome returns for investors and the Crown—declared that "the chief end of this plantation" was "the knowledge and obedience of the only true God and Saviour of mankind and the Christian Faith."[8] In the world of divine signs and wonders, the greatest marvel would be the Puritan community.

What Chris Lehmann has called "the Puritan social gospel" was embedded in the covenant theology. The Puritan social gospel sanctioned a communalist capitalism, a hierarchical but benevolent order that abounded in the works of charity and justice, not the baubles earned by greed and parsimony. "Among members of the same body," Winthrop declared in "A Modell of Christian Charity" (1630), a quintessential statement of early Puritan moralism, "love and affection are reciprocall in a most equall and sweete kind of Commerce." Since God instituted social inequality to promote mutual love and service, Winthrop exhorted wealthy Puritans to practice "liberality" toward their inferiors and insisted that "the care of the public" must oversway all private respects." To preserve the bonds of love and affection, Puritan clergy, theologians, and magistrates enforced strict sumptuary laws, price controls, and prohibitions of usury on merchants, artisans, and farmers. They inveighed mightily against avarice, formulating what Andrew Delbanco has described as "a powerful critique from within the early capitalist mind" of the anomie and callousness that beckoned with the erosion of medieval restrictions on market activity. John Cotton, one of the most revered of the first generation of New England clerics, observed in the 1620s that while a Christian might live "a most busie life in this world," he must be careful that "he lives not a worldly life." Cotton warned that avarice was a form of idolatry; "the love of Money" entailed a desire for "communion with the Creature," a perversion of the love owed only to the Creator.[9]

With that errant desire in mind, other Puritan clergy exhorted their congregations to abhor the "chattering and chaunging" merchant who cheated his customers—and thereby violated the bonds of "reciprocall" love and affection—with his "counterfeit balances, and untrue waightes." One infamous transgressor of the moral economy was the merchant Robert Keayne, often cited by historians as both a renegade and a harbinger of the future. Brought to court in 1639, Keayne was sharply chastised by Cotton, Winthrop, and others for his "false principles" of commerce, the most odious of which was "that a man might sell as dear as he can, and buy as cheap as he can." Braced by their aversion to modern market morality, Puritan leaders managed for at least a generation or two to hinder extensive participation in the trans-Atlantic and increasingly global economic networks of English Puritan merchants and financiers. As Delbanco remarks, the Puritans who disciplined Keayne and bridled the commercial energy of their congregants were "trying to keep the modern world at bay."[10]

Yet the New England Puritans were also at work assiduously bringing that world into being. The "powerful critique" to which Delbanco justly calls attention came, as he notes, from within a capitalist moral imagination. If, as the English Puritan moralist Richard Baxter would remind the saints in the 1670s, God *commanded* entrepreneurs to seek the most profitable avenues of investment, the line between greed and righteous enterprise would be harder and harder to discern. To the extent that unease with the embarrassment of riches was a part of "the Puritan ordeal," the saints of New England had only themselves to blame for their spiritual distress. With his "corrupt and covetous heart," Keayne was not only a portent of New England's commercial success; he was an avatar of the Puritans' conflicted present, their dream of a Christian commonwealth whose prosperity depended on pecuniary reason.

Fifteen years after his humiliating censure by the Puritan power elite, Keayne rebutted his accusers in a posthumously published apologia. Recounting his many civic accomplishments—honorable selectman, surveyor of highways, all-around public benefactor—Keayne insisted that his life had borne "good fruites and evidences of justification," pointing not only to "testemonyes in my spirit" but also to "my very outward estate." He had "not lived an idle, lazie or dronish life," nor had he lounged to "refresh myself with recreations."[11] Despite the almost comic fury of his self-righteousness, Keayne was merely echoing the gospel of improvement preached by English Puritans: God had rewarded his virtue with wealth.

The gradual demise of the Puritan social gospel was witness to the fundamental dilemma of the elect: their quest for a beloved community built on the foundations of capitalist enterprise. They resolved the dilemma with a covenant theology of capitalism, a creed whose doctrinal elements included the affirmation of wealth as a divine anointment; territorial conquest to enlarge the parameters of God's rich and faithful metropolis; a conception of the natural world as a providential storehouse of vendable wonders; and a jeremiad tradition to chastise moral failing and obscure the intractable persistence of the dilemma. Under the aegis of their halfway covenant with capitalism, the Puritan errand into the wilderness became an errand into the marketplace, and American life became an experiment in Christian friendship with unrighteous Mammon.

In the Puritan gospel of capitalist enchantment, wealth was God's benediction on the righteous, a reward from the Almighty to the archangels of improvement. Among the many ways God enabled his saints to "plainly see his providence," Cotton pointed to the profit acquired from business pursued "for merchandize and gaine-sake." "How shall I know that I have that life, in having of which, I may know I have Christ?" Cotton asked in *The Way of Life* (1641), the quintessential statement of Puritan moral economy. "Art thou diligent in thy calling, it is well." New England was never inhospitable to the entrepreneurial spirit; both rural and urban family producers engaged in surplus production for the market from the earliest days of colonization. As John Smith wryly observed in 1631 of the enterprising migrants to New England, "I am not so simple, to thinke, that ever any other motive than wealth, will ever erect there a Commonweale." Smith may have been cynical, but the Puritan clerisy saw no fundamental conflict between diligence and grace, savvy investment and reliance on faith, possessive individualism and predestined redemption. The City on a Hill was a palace of wealth *and* an abode for the elect, a place where Christian proprietors could procure what John Higginson pronounced "the Blessings of Time and Eternity." "The gospel hath brought in its right hand Eternal Salvation," another pastor observed, "and in its left hand, Riches and Protection from Enemies." When pastor Edward Winslow delivered the *Good Newes from New-England* (1624) that "religion and profit jump together," his fellow clerics agreed they skipped happily along in the towns and villages of the saints. For all their horror of Catholic works and "magick," the Puritan ethic became a form of divination to acquire the grace of the Almighty. "Let your business engross the most of your time," Mather counseled *A Christian at His Calling* (1701), but do not "expect that our business will succeed without God's blessing." Pray, honor the Sabbath, shun dishonesty, and give to the poor, and certainly, Mather assured his readers, "you will obtain the blessing of God upon your business." As Sacvan Bercovitch has noted archly of this economic revelation, "the wheel of fortune and the wheel of grace revolved in harmony."[12]

But first, the promised land of grace and riches had to be cleared of its sinful occupants. When they encountered the native Americans—cast in the role of Canaanites in a grisly reenactment of biblical drama—the Puritans recoiled from the idolaters whose degenerate customs deserved the wrath of God. The Indians' failure to "improve" the land offended the saints as unnatural, wasteful, and abhorrent. Confronted with such prodigal iniquity, God's chosen had a right, and in fact a duty, to evict the slothful inhabitants and put the land to profitable use. Frock-coated commissars of improvement, the Puritans embarked on a privatization drive to dispossess the native inhabitants. Well before Locke's justification of improving imperialism, Winthrop had sketched a theology of ethnic cleansing. Writing to his father after his first trip to America in 1628, Winthrop scoffed at "the Natives of New England" who "inclose noe Land, nor have they any settled habytation, nor any tame Cattle to improve the Land by." The saints, he resolved, must not "suffer a whole Continent as fruitfull and convenient for the use of man to lie waste without any improvement." Winthrop's God superintended their ventures with a volley of special providences, "sweeping away great multitudes of the natives" with a series of epidemics. "God hath hereby cleared our title to this place," wrote the modeler of Christian charity. After the Puritan victory over the Pequots in the 1630s, one devout commander—who had just presided over the immolation of four hundred men, women, and children—exulted that the Almighty had been so gracious as to "give us their Land for an Inheritance."[13]

The Puritans considered their "Inheritance" a paradise lost, reclaimed, and cleansed, an Eden whose lucrative marvels awaited the labor of godly men. Many New England farmers adhered to an enchanted and increasingly mercantile cosmology. Authors of almanacs and volumes on agriculture and husbandry regularly invoked astrology and the *anima mundi*. As late as 1713, Nathaniel Whittmore was telling readers of his *Almanack* that the best time to cut timber was in the winter months, "especially when the moon is in Pisces." As they became ever more enmeshed in the Atlantic commercial nexus, the colony's yeomen blended agricultural enchantment with an ever more scientific and entrepreneurial ethos. Under capitalist imperatives of "improvement," the *anima mundi* was subjected to the standards of pecuniary calculation. Among the political and clerical elite, men such as Edward Johnson and John Winthrop, Jr., exemplified the spirit of enchanted entrepreneurship. In his *Wonder-Working Providence of Sions Saviour, in New England* (1654), Johnson, a deputy to the Massachusetts General Court, waxed ecstatic at the prospect of a mercantile millennium. Once the natives were converted or exterminated, "the Lord will create a New Heaven," Johnson believed, "a new Earth, new Churches, and a new Common-wealth together." Thanks to the Lord of Hosts, the land was a cornucopia of exchange value: "every thing in the country proved a staple-commodity."[14]

"This Wilderness should turn a mart for Merchants," Johnson concluded smugly—and a bonanza for alchemists, as Winthrop the Puritan magus hoped. Well connected to an international network of Christian alchemists, Winthrop assumed the governorship of Connecticut in 1635 with plans to employ his science of enchantment for the economic development of the colony. Winthrop hoped to set up a "New London," an alchemical research and improvement plantation modeled after Bacon's Salomon's House, whose members would pursue work in metallurgy, mining, agriculture, medicine, and other industries. Devoted to the commercial expansion and technological progress of New England, Winthrop and his supporters saw no tension between the religious and metaphysical aspirations of alchemy and its potential as a profitable investment. Like his fellow Christian magi, Winthrop believed that the natural world was both a storehouse of raw materials and a book of divine allegories; salt-making, for instance, was, in William Woodward's words, "simultaneously a commercial venture, a metaphysical exploration, and a source of scriptural exegesis." Thus, in what Woodward terms Winthrop's "alchemical moral economy," the practice of alchemy fostered "God's work in the world," which "in no way ruled out making money." Winthrop's ambitious scheme never came to pass; the antinomian controversy that engulfed Anne Hutchinson and her sympathizers—stemming from the accusation that they believed that Christians were not subject to the moral law—cast a pall over anything that smacked of heresy, and so potential investors either withdrew or insisted that Winthrop scale back the project. Winthrop's vision of a Christian utopia succumbed to the imperatives of Puritan orthodoxy. Still, his kind of alchemical and hermetic philosophy retained a hold on the Puritan imagination; as late as 1721, the Connecticut minister John Wise was arguing that by employing the "*Lapis Aurificus* or *Philosopher's Stone* in our heads," we could "turn matter into Silver and Gold by the power of thought as soon as any other People."[15] The alchemical dreams of the Puritans foreshadowed later American hopes for a business millennium made possible by advanced technology.

By the early eighteenth century, as New England seaports became vital nodes of the British commercial empire, merchants had acquired an indefatigable faith in their appointment to saintly plutocracy. Vindicating the ways of Robert Keayne to humankind, urban elites demanded the renegotiation of the covenant theology of capitalism. As Mark Valeri and others have demonstrated, post-Puritan religious culture cleared away the last remaining obstacles to a recognizably modern capitalism. In the decades following the Glorious Revolution of 1688, New England divines, magistrates, and business leaders embraced a new trans-Atlantic culture of politeness, civility, and "reasonable" Christianity—"Christian sentimentalism," that intensification of emotional enchantment that prefigured the first consumer ethos. More at ease in the Zion of commercial refinement, the clergy embraced a dynamic, laissez-faire capitalism in which the "heavenly merchandize" of the gospel was the highest good of a larger commodity civilization. Equating Providence, science, and pecuniary reason, New England's post-Puritan intelligentsia read in the new economics, in Valeri's words, "a dialect of divine truth." From Samuel Sewall and Benjamin Colman to Jonathan Mayhew, New England's elite sanctioned practices previously vilified or closely regulated: usury, trade in securities, and pricing in accordance with market forces.[16] On credit extended by the clergy, Mammon had purchased a seat in the congregation from the heirs to the Puritan social gospel. Under the aegis of the covenant, the Puritans had marched from Egypt to Canaan, lingered briefly in Jerusalem, and settled in Babylon.

In Jonathan Edwards, the errand into the marketplace acquired the dimensions of a global vocation. Pastor of Northampton, Massachusetts, and the premiere theologian of the First Great Awakening, Edwards possessed a lyrically sacramental sensibility. Writing of his conversion in his personal narrative, Edwards related how, while he walked in his father's pasture after his acceptance of Christ, "the appearance of everything was altered; there seemed to be, as it were, a calm, sweet cast, or appearance of divine glory, in almost every thing . . . his wisdom, his purity, and love, seemed to appear in every thing; in the sun, moon, and stars; in the clouds, and blue sky; in the grass, flowers, trees, in the water, and all nature." Later, Edwards transformed this sacramental vision into theological speculation. "The beauty of the world" displayed, he believed, "the images or shadows of divine things." "Spiritual beauties are infinitely the greatest," Edwards explained, "and bodies being but the shadows of being, they must be so much the more charming as they shadow forth spiritual beauties." "The works of nature are intended and contrived of God to signify . . . spiritual things."[17]

Northampton in the 1730s and 1740s was an agrarian town with a vigorous and expanding commercial sector, and for a while Edwards feared that the new market forces were desecrating those "spiritual things." Yet despite his economic traditionalism in the pulpit—he denounced sloth, luxury, and "trickishness" in trade, and reminded the prosperous of their duties to the brethren—in his notebooks and essays, Edwards became a visionary of capitalist enchantment. If the works of nature bore the imprint of divinity, so, too, did what Edwards called the "art of man." Along with the marvels of nature, commerce and technology were signs and vehicles of God's redemptive purposes. Reflecting on the meaning of the revivals that swept through Northampton and the rest of New England in the early 1740s, Edwards envisioned a world redeemed through trade and technological progress. Christ's second coming would take place, Edwards believed, after a thousand years of Christian triumph and prosperity; his post-millennialism doubled as a capitalist eschatology. "'Tis probable," he believed, "that the world shall be more like Heaven" very soon, before the impending return of Christ, as business enterprise and technological advances would smooth a path for the Lord. "There will be so many contrivances and inventions," Edwards marveled; humanity will have "better contrivances for assisting one another through the whole earth by more expedite, easy, and safe communication between distant regions than now." To that end, he mused, the mariner's compass "is a thing discovered by God." Unified by commerce and innovation, "the whole earth," he wrote with beatific flourish, "may be as one community, one body in Christ."[18]

The prelude to the millennium would unfold in the New World; indeed, the Scriptures seemed "plainly to point out America, as the first fruits of that glorious day." The growth of material wealth in the colonies prefigured "what is approaching in spiritual things, when the world shall be supplied with spiritual treasures from America." From its trove of hallowed riches, America would effect, Edwards prophesied, "the most glorious renovation of the world." Comparing America to Joseph in his luxurious apparel, Edwards foresaw that his compatriots, "blessed with all manner of blessings and precious things, of heaven and earth" would "by the horns of a unicorn, push the people together, to the ends of the earth, i.e., conquer the world."[19] With his imperialist vision of a business millennium, Edwards commenced the long prophetic lineage of American capitalist globalism: missionaries for "manifest destiny," heralds of "the American Century," seers of the "global village," evangelists for "globalization."

If the Puritan errand evolved into consecration of capitalist expansion, one could argue that the jeremiad registered their arduous declension from the ideals of the covenant. As Delbanco puts it so powerfully, the Puritans, at their Augustinian best, dwelled in a conviction "that a transcendent realm of plenitude exists by which human beings can, if they are open to its influence, transcend their moral limitations, or even their mortality."[20] Yet the inexorable tragedy of the Puritan ordeal resulted from fidelity to the covenant, and that is why its mercenary character needs to be once again and vigorously emphasized. Puritan capitalism was a form of enchantment, for God so loved the world that He designed the market to enrich the elect. Among His magnificent providences, financial success was manna from heaven; riches were promissory notes of grace; profits were bills of credit from the transcendent realm of plenitude. From Cotton to Mather to Edwards, the benediction of wealth as a sign of God's favor resounds through Puritan theology and preaching. By widening the eye of the needle, the Puritans enabled the camel to pass and eased the passage of the rich into paradise.

The Puritan friendship with Mammon portended the course of American history. The tenacity of the jeremiad derived not only from the magnitude of the failure it admonished, but also from the scale of the contradiction it concealed. The jeremiad explained declension as a fall from piety, usually occasioned by prosperity; the love and authority of God, in this view, had been usurped by the unrighteous Mammon. If the people turn from greed and the love of luxury, they will regain the righteous city. Thus, the jeremiad demanded a renewal of devotion to the terms of the Puritan covenant. But if we recognize that the saints had already signed a tenuous contract with Mammon—if the belief that "religion and profit jump together" was the marrow of Puritan capitalist enchantment—then declension and jeremiad take on a different and much more unsettling significance. With whatever degree of ambivalence or hypocrisy, the Puritans attempted to build a beloved community on capitalist property; thus, the errand was doomed to fail from the very beginning of the Great Migration. If friendship with the unrighteous Mammon was really an unwitting fealty all along, then the holiness of the errand would be thrown into doubt; better to chastise themselves as unworthy than to cancel the errand and reconsider the covenant. The futility of the errand was an augury of all subsequent American dreams of a righteous commonwealth imbued with the spirit of mercenary enchantment. Alexis de Tocqueville was more prescient than he knew when he mused that "the entire destiny of America [was] embodied in the first Puritan to land on its shores."[21]

Although they wrought the most profitable fusion of pecuniary rationality and premodern superstition, the Puritans alone were not responsible for the American Pentecost of capitalist enchantment. As Lehmann reminds us, "popular religion in the colonial era"—from New England to the mid-Atlantic and the South—"was steeped in magic and folk belief," with many regional variations on what Catherine Albanese has called a "rural metaphysical culture" bound up with money and the quest for riches. Although Pennsylvania Germans, for instance, believed it an unfavorable bad omen to find money, they also thought that children could be cured of sickness by handling coins. Money would arrive and stay if one dreamed of clean water, or found a spider on one's clothes, or shook one's purse upon hearing the first springtime song of a cuckoo or a whippoorwill. Virginia gentry such as William Byrd II—point men in the creation of Southern slavery—consulted cunning folk about weather, planting, and trade as well as romance, travel, and health; they also credited dice, horses, and cards with magical abilities to determine fortunes. Morever, alchemy, hermeticism, and folk healing survived in many parts of New England and Pennsylvania well into the eighteenth century, and their many practitioners attributed supernatural powers to money and precious metals. By the early nineteenth century, both Christian and occult forms of capitalist enchantment were rife in the new republic.[22]

# 5

# The Righteous Friends of Mammon

Evangelicals, Mormons, Slaveholders,
and the Proprietary Dispensation

COMPOSED OF A WANING Puritanism and a prodigiously exotic meta-physical lore, this popular culture of pecuniary ontology percolated under the skeptical eyes of the nation's liberal republican elite. In the early years of the new republic, Thomas Jefferson, John Adams, and other founding mandarins idealized a yeoman republic of virtue, a paradise of small, patriarchal producers devoted to family labor and subsistence agriculture. Averse to the fleshpots of luxury, the independent proprietor of the liberal republican imagination was a Protestant Cincinnatus, devoted not to the pursuit of riches but to a comfortable competence for himself and his family. But if the Revolution had freed Americans from British imperial rule, they remained inextricably ensnared in the volatile entanglements of the transatlantic market. Indeed, by the end of the eighteenth century—with a rising overseas demand for American foodstuffs and a growing domestic market for household manufactures—the republican ideal was fading quickly, as more and more farmers produced for the market. By the 1820s, the national expansion of markets and the introduction of industrial technology in agriculture and manufacturing led to a boom in business incorporation, as firms needed larger and more dependable forms of capitalization than could be provided by families or partnerships. Thus in the two generations after the ratification of the Constitution, the United States became, as Gordon S. Wood put it, "a scrambling business society dominated by the pecuniary interests of ordinary working people."[1] In a nation without a nobility or an established church, the capitalist marketplace was becoming the new *religio,* the bond of what passed for fraternity among competitive Protestant Americans.

This business society was also a bedlam of enchantments—an "antebellum spiritual hothouse," in Jon Butler's words, teeming with magic, animism, astrology, and divination, as well as evangelical Protestantism. The culture of the occult that combined magical belief and Christian theology persisted in the early republican Northeast well into the nineteenth century. Farmers and artisans continued to employ witchcraft, consult astrological charts for propitious planting and harvesting, and protect their homes and crops with the judicious application of witch hazel to their doors. The mid-Atlantic region was the epicenter of the occult in eighteenth- and early nineteenth-century America, swarming with diviners; money-diggers; and cunning folk in search of gold, silver, jewels, and other buried riches. Diviners coaxed hidden treasures to "bloom" to the surface with incantations; one upstate New York money-digger advised that the best time to find troves of gold was in the summer, "when the heat of the sun caused the chests of money to rise to the top of the ground." The occult also survived along the New England coastline, where numerous villages lay outside the surveillance of the weakening regime of orthodoxy. Hundreds joined "money-digging companies" in search of treasures supposedly buried by pirates or Spanish adventurers. Hermetic mysticism and alchemy blended with shards of Christian doctrine to produce a bizarre bricolage of enchantment. The "New Israelites," for instance, who resided in Vermont in the 1790s, were treasure-diviners who mixed magic and biblical literalism as they searched for gold "to pave the streets of the New Jerusalem." With farmers' almanacs and dream books, seer stones and divining rods, Americans conducted what Alan Taylor has called a "supernatural economy," an extensive and vigorous trade in the paraphernalia of enchantment.[2]

By the 1820s and 1830s, the supernatural economy had converged with what Jackson Lears has dubbed the "carnivalesque" spirit of a burgeoning market culture. Fueled by evangelical emotionalism, the commercial culture of early national America featured new forms of enchantment and sacramentality, from worries about the "influence" of peddlers to widespread belief in the healing or transformative powers of elixirs, patent medicines, and jewelry. Plenty of middle-class landowners employed any fool or con man with a divining rod to locate water, metals, or treasure. Other rodsmen assured farmers that their instruments could protect their houses and fields from natural calamities. (The villain of Herman Melville's 1854 short story

"The Lightning-Rod Man" gulls his credulous customers with claims to magical power: "Say but the word, and of this cottage I can make a Gibraltar by a few waves of this wand.") Gamblers and speculators—then, as now, not easily distinguishable—consulted dream books for guidance on bets and investments. The dream of metamorphosis through purchase sustained the thriving markets in vendable enchantment.[3]

Still, the Protestant sacred canopy persisted, as evangelical Protestantism remade the nation's spiritual landscape between 1790 and 1860. As Protestants who rejected classical predestination, American evangelicals enlarged the sense of freedom and agency of the individual believer. Like their British counterparts, American evangelicals combined intense and often flamboyant emotionalism, an individualist and democratic ethos, and an instrumentalist conception of reason. With their zealous pursuit of souls through missionary activity, revivalism, and cross-denominational societies, evangelicals widened the scope of Protestant authority. Evangelicals achieved a cultural hegemony that could be every bit as coercive and exclusionary as the Puritan city on a hill, a moral establishment that Tocqueville registered when he observed that Christianity possessed "more actual power over souls in America than anywhere else."[4]

Tocqueville traveled through America in the midst of what historians have dubbed "the Market Revolution" of the 1820s and 1830s, the seismic upheaval in pre–Civil War society that laid many of the foundations of modern American capitalism: the breakdown of the household economy; the rapid spread of commercial farming; the emergence of the factory system; the development of a continental market for agricultural and manufactured goods; and the proliferation of canals, roads, and railways. The Market Revolution was the second great awakening of American capitalism, and evangelicals rewrote the terms of the Puritan economic covenant. Tocqueville and other foreign observers captured the nascent reformation of the covenant theology. "The passions that move Americans most deeply are commercial rather than political," he observed, adding that those commercial passions were encouraged, not bridled, by evangelical clergy and moralists. Both bemused and appalled by the unseemly practicality of many Protestant ministers, Tocqueville marveled at how "American preachers refer to this world constantly and, indeed, can avert their eyes from it only with the greatest difficulty"; listening to them, he could not determine "whether the chief object of religion is to procure eternal happiness in the other world or well-being in this one." Tocqueville was echoed by Thomas Hamilton, a Scottish academic who was also traveling through America in the early 1830s. Though charmed by popular candor, Hamilton recoiled from what he considered the ubiquitous obsession with money, something that religion did nothing to curb and everything to intensify. Americans were so "wholly devoted to money-making" that they referred to their "pecuniary resources" in even the most trivial conversations. Although he never set foot in the United States, Karl Marx captured the covetous, competitive nature of evangelical religious culture. In the "bourgeois society of North America," he wrote in 1843, brotherly love was now defined as fellowship in market antagonism. "Religion has become the spirit of civil society, the sphere of egoism, the *bellum omnium contra omnes*."[5]

Marx's sardonic comments shed light on the evangelical brio of American capitalism. Under the cope of the evangelical heaven, pecuniary reason and amazing grace were wedded in holy matrimony, spawning the entrepreneurial spirit of an evangelical-proprietary dispensation. American evangelicals attempted to reconcile Christianity both with the Enlightenment ideal of secular reason and with the liberal ideal of autonomy. Thus, many scholars have implied that evangelicalism in America reflected and even hastened the "disenchantment of the world." Certainly, by the 1850s, middle-class American Protestants had largely abandoned the world of wonders that enthralled the Mathers and Jonathan Edwards. Thanks to theologians, clergy, scientists, and other acolytes of evangelical rationality, belief in miracles, special providences, and other marvels had abated by the time Darwinian biology reached America. Yet even when stripped of portents and other marvels, evangelical cosmology retained enormous spiritual import. Even if special providence gave way to general Providence—the invariant will of God manifested in natural law—that Providence was intimate and personal, a divinity amenable to human entreaty and effort.[6] More at ease with calculation and hustling than their piously venal Puritan precursors, evangelical entrepreneurs still believed that the world was charged with the grandeur of God.

American evangelicalism was the perfect Christian vehicle of enchantment for a newly unfettered capitalist economy. Baptizing the ambitions of masterless strivers in the maelstrom of laissez-faire—merchants, small factory owners, enterprising planters, aspiring mechanics, prairie farmers eager for cash and credit—evangelicalism was the perfect Protestant enchantment for people on the make. With its volatile mixture of passion and rationality, evangelicalism embraced and composed the tensions between the carnivalesque and the rational, between the romantic and the empirical, between the molten self displayed in revival meetings and conversion experiences and the steely self-mastery increasingly demanded for middle-class sexual probity and economic success. Its spiritual individualism and emotional fervor dovetailed nicely with the fluid, unpredictable conditions of a turbulent national market. Its Baconian conception of reason and science as the accumulation of facts blended well with the quantitative, pecuniary rationality central to the capitalist ethos. "Business is the very soul of an American," the immigrant journalist Francis Grund reflected in 1837, and the ardor for profit was as great "as any crusader ever evinced for the conquest of the Holy Land, or the followers of Mohammed for the spreading of the Koran."[7] Far from inhabiting a disenchanted world, antebellum evangelicals banked on a righteously lucrative agreement with God and Mammon.

The preachers whose worldly homilies puzzled Tocqueville were expounding a new covenant theology of economics. They believed as strongly as Mather and Edwards that capitalism had been inscribed into the world by God, and they turned the moral maxims of the Puritans into a science of market society. The nation's "clerical economists," as Stewart Davenport has dubbed them, placed Adam Smith's economics on a par with Newton's physics and William Paley's natural theology.[8] Representing the entrepreneurial classes of the Northeast and the expanding West, these prophets of prosperity aspired to transform economics into a cheerful science. In the new evangelical economic cosmology, natural law and invisible forces lay down together in harmony; pecuniary reason discerned and enforced the economy decreed by God. Fusing the science of economics and the science of divinity, America's first economists comprised a clerisy of evangelical enchantment.

To the clerical economists, "Political Economy is an offspring of the Christian religion," as one Methodist journal declared in 1863. Horace Bushnell and others explained the metaphysics of Christian capitalism. As the Congregationalist pastor to the merchants and bankers of Hartford, Connecticut, Bushnell offered Christian nurture to the creditworthy souls of the Protestant patricianate, informing his congregants that their wealth was "a reward and honor which God delights to bestow upon an upright people." "If the outer world is the vast dictionary and grammar of thought we speak of," he continued, then it is also itself an organ throughout of Intelligence"—the "Intelligence" of "the universal Author." Francis Wayland asserted in *The Elements of Political Economy* (1837) that his discipline described the "the systematic arrangement of the laws which God has established." Surveying the "machinery of commerce and finance," Henry A. Boardman—a Presbyterian pastor in Philadelphia and author of *The Bible in the Counting-House* (1856), an oft-cited collection of sermons—reminded readers that "the power that moves it is out of sight." Likewise, Orville Dewey, Unitarian pastor in Gloucester and New Bedford and a popular lecturer, preached that commerce was "the germ, the original spring, that has put all other springs in action." As the "possessor and dispenser of all the riches of the universe," God was present "in every counting-room and warehouse of yonder mart"; indeed, His presence made them "holy ground." Dewey prevailed on bankers and other lawful conjurers of early finance capital to refurbish "the temple of mammon" into "the temple of God."[9] Yet Dewey and other homilists could never clearly distinguish between the fearsome magic of the devil and the wholesome sacraments of the marketplace.

The greatest circuit rider for Christian capitalism was Charles Grandison Finney, the star revivalist of the Second Great Awakening. Once an up-and-coming attorney, Finney turned to the Presbyterian ministry after a powerful conversion experience. Savvy, charismatic, and blessed with the vernacular charm of the hustling preacher, he soon became pastor of New York's Broadway Tabernacle, a church founded, attended, and bankrolled by Lewis Tappan, scion of one of Gotham's leading mercantile families. The capitalist market was, in Finney's view, the earthly bourse of God's cosmic estate. As the "proprietor of the universe," God entrusted His property to the faithful businessperson, who as "God's steward" was obliged to "take advantage of the market . . . to improve every opportunity to promote [God's] interest." "You have God's money in your hands," he reminded his well-remunerated Christian stewards; on Judgment Day, an accounting would be required of every penny in the Almighty's portfolio. Finney warned that the enlargement of material wealth would be a high but not exclusive priority in that posthumous audit. Besides a report on their accumulative prowess, God's chosen moneymen would be judged by their support of churches, schools, ministries, and philanthropies.[10]

Yet Finney was also ambivalent about the fusion of faith and pecuniary reason that he fostered. While he warned that Christians "are by no means to conform to the business maxims of the world," he increasingly feared that those very maxims were now the marrow of Christian stewardship. After he left the Tabernacle and moved to northern Ohio (where he soon became president of Oberlin College, another Tappan venture), Finney lamented his own complicity in erasing the line between stewardship and avarice. Schooled in what he called "the arithmetic of faith," too many revivalists, he asserted, were denaturing genuine preaching into mere "practical skill in the art of bringing about an excitement." Relying on "so much policy and machinery, so much dependence upon means and measures, so much of man and so little of God," the saving of souls was looking more and more like the accumulation of capital. Still, fretful that he had "erred in manner and spirit," Finney could offer nothing beyond pious boilerplate to clarify the difference between faith and self-delusion, between "God's money" and Satan's coin, or between "stewardship" and exploitation. Exhorting their listeners to be "friends of the unrighteous Mammon," evangelical preachers, Finney rued, had inadvertently indentured them to two masters.[11]

As masters of all they surveyed, Southern planters understood their own servility to Mammon as the practice of "order and regulated freedom," in the words of John Henley Thornwell, one of the more erudite theological champions of chattel slavery and the expansive "empire of Cotton." Until fairly recently, racial slavery in the antebellum South had been seen as "in but not of" North Atlantic capitalism—precapitalist, inefficient and unprofitable, and paternalist or "seigneurialist" in its ethos. Historians now consider Southern slavery a crucial feature of mid-nineteenth-century capitalism; its planters were not atavistic feudal barons but profit-maximizing entrepreneurs. Trailblazers in finance, accounting, and management, their money headed north for investment by assiduous evangelical bankers and industrialists. Enlisting in capitalist modernity as eagerly as their northern evangelical brethren, southern divines and regular clergy defended slavery as "proceeding from the Lord." They justified the repression and violence of King Cotton as "interwoven with the progress of Christianity," as one minister in Virginia asserted in 1861; and some even contended that slavery itself was a school of instruction in free labor, since "freedom" meant the development of the bourgeois virtues of self-restraint and methodical enterprise. However the evangelical case for black servitude was made, "the stronghold of slavery is in the pulpit," Frederick Douglass told a New York audience in 1847; southern evangelicals, clerical and lay, pronounced the most ardent benedictions on the bustling traffic in African-American flesh. "Revivals of religion and revivals in the slave-trade go hand-in-hand together," he wrote in his autobiography. "The dealer gives his blood-stained gold to support the pulpit, and the pulpit, in turn, covers his infernal business with the garb of Christianity."[12]

Like the northern "machinery of commerce and finance" supervised by Finney's "proprietor of the universe," the evangelical apparatus of white supremacy in the South envisioned God as the Cosmic Overseer, the Master whose dominion extended from natural phenomena to the vicissitudes of history. Just as "a sparrow cannot fall to the ground without a special Providence," as one pastor mused in 1861, so history, one of his earlier brethren had declared, had "permitted the black man to be brought here and subjected to the disciplines of slavery." "However dark, mysterious, and unpleasant these dispensations may appear to you," a Mississippi Baptist convention told slaves, rest assured that "we have no doubt they are founded in wisdom and goodness." Provided through preaching and whipping, the Master's tutelage in the Gospel aligned lissomely with the lucrative tyranny endemic to Southern slavery. Despite the fact that you possess immortal souls, one Kentucky captor told his human commodities, "the great God above has made you for the benefit of the Whiteman." Once enslaved—or rather, liberated from the bondage of paganism for the profit of evangelical entrepreneurs—the Master's oversight was inescapable. "Let Servants serve their masters as faithfully behind their backs as before their faces," the Georgia clergyman and planter Charles C. Jones catechized in 1837. "God is present to see, if their masters are not." When the masters were present to see, the more religious among them were remembered by slaves to be especially greedy and punitive. One ex-slave recalled that his master, "a religious man . . . couldn't see anything but cotton bales," while a freedwoman recalled in 1863 that "the Christians oppress you more." "Religious slaveholders are the worst . . . meanest and basest," Douglass reflected, recounting the tale of one master, a devout evangelical and a robust practitioner of the "pushing system," who preemptively brutalized slaves for sins or crimes before they committed them. Aiming at evangelicalism in general, Douglass denied that this pious and self-serving brutality was peculiar to slaveholder Christianity. Enjoining patient submission to injustice was "strictly true of the overwhelming mass of professed Christians in America."[13] As essential to the evangelical-proprietary dispensation as Indian dispossession and genocide, antebellum slavery was a form of white Christian bondage to the enchantments of Mammon.

Trading in yet another parody of freedom, self-improvement writers joined evangelical businesspeople and planters in befriending the unrighteous Mammon. "Apostles of the self-made man," these tutors in upward mobility were folk theologians and moral philosophers. The maxims and business advice contained in self-improvement literature are drearily familiar. Methodical at work, unremitting in frugality, leery of liquor and "dangerous" women, observant of the Sabbath, and literate in the Bible— these traits defined the quintessence of evangelical capitalist humanism. Yet some writers realized that a profound contradiction lay at the heart of the gospel of self-creation: how could people "make themselves" and still remain utterly dependent on the will of the Creator? The more ingenious purveyors of self-improvement resolved the problem by turning self-creation into a partnership with divine power. Though self-improvement tracts and manuals focused on the cultivation of good and remunerative habits, an ontology of divine participation lurked in the interstices of bourgeois moralism. As John Frost, author of several popular volumes on self-improvement, informed *The Young Merchant* (1841), God, as "the supreme disposer of all things . . . giveth thee power to get wealth."[14]

The most metaphysically adept of the self-improvement apostolate was Timothy Shay Arthur, a regular contributor to *Godey's Lady's Book* and the author of *Ten Nights in a Bar-room and What I Saw There* (1854), a classic of temperance fiction. Arthur opened his *Advice for Young Men on Their Duties and Conduct in Life* (1847) with what might seem to be an odd disquisition on the subtleties of theology and philosophy. "The natural body is the material form with which the spiritual body clothes itself." However amateurish Arthur's metaphysical speculations may appear, they point to the persistence of enchantment in the culture of self-creation. In *The Ways of Providence* (1852), a popular collection of short stories and vignettes on success, Arthur frequently invoked divine agency rather than individual effort as the crucial factor in business. One story, "Don't Be Discouraged," features Henry Grant, a pious and hard-working young man who has nevertheless failed in all his business ventures. In despair, Henry seeks counsel from an older entrepreneur, Mr. Linton. "The fates, I believe, are against me," he broods. Rather than offer moral advice to the young failure, Linton corrects Henry's theological errors. "What do you mean by the fates? . . . You can only mean, of course, that Divine Being, who is the author of our existence and the controller of our destinies." Henry walks away unconvinced, but after yet more failure, debt, and despondency, he experiences an epiphany, realizing that "happiness must flow from an internal state"—fellowship with the Controller of Our Destinies. Epiphany also plays a role in "The Merchant's Dream," in which Algeron, a wealthy clothier, feels that his life is worthless. One night, a beautiful woman visits Algeron in a dream: a Beatrice of moral economy, she leads the merchant past a cottage, a shop, and a farm, reminding him that his calling clothes and employs their inhabitants. "I have been taught," he reflects the next morning, "not by a mere phantom of the imagination, but by Truth herself—beautiful truth."[15]

At the top of the self-improvement clerisy sat Freeman Hunt, whose career suggests that American business journalism arose, in part, as a religious enterprise. An editor and publisher with magazines in Boston and New York, Hunt was first and foremost a proselytizer for American business who worried that "not a single magazine, of high or low pretensions" existed to "represent or to advocate the claims of commerce." Eager to promote the gospel, he founded, in 1839, *Hunt's Merchants' Magazine,* the first monthly business periodical in America. Providing statistical reports and analyses of every sector of the national economy—from agriculture, trade, and manufacturing to banking, navigation, and business law—*Hunt's* was the nation's leading business publication before the Civil War. But *Hunt's* also blended business reportage with moral instruction and religious pedagogy, providing an unsystematic theology for the nation's entrepreneurial vanguard. In addition to the encyclopedic business data, *Hunt's* often featured profiles of successful merchants, bankers, and manufacturers, all of whom exemplified the classic traits of the self-driven Protestant workhorse. Near the end of his life, Hunt edited two volumes dedicated to the *Lives of American Merchants* (1858). The Plutarch of merchant capital, Hunt resolved to place businesspeople on the level of monarchs, philosophers, artists, and saints. Paragons of moral and intestinal fortitude, Hunt's merchants were "men of enterprise, men of intellect, men of religion."[16]

Hunt's portrayal of the American capitalist reflected a pecuniary form of enchantment. As his hefty volume of lessons on *Worth and Wealth* (1856) attests, Hunt was a theologian of business culture, portraying commercial life as a liturgical practice, a mercenary way of being in the world. Far from being a secret outpost of Mammon, the Christian merchant's counting-house or shop was instead "a sanctuary," a tabernacle of the Lord. Indeed, Hunt depicted the little chapel of accumulation as the gilded antechamber to paradise. For the upright proprietor, "his profession of religion is all practice . . . a good man is just as near Heaven in his shop, as in his church; at work, as at prayer." Intimate with divinity in his daily affairs, the businessperson was a chaplain of capital, celebrating the eucharistic consecration of the market. "He makes all work sacramental; he communes with God and Man in buying and selling—communion in both kinds." At his best, the capitalist entered the communion of saints. Peter, Paul, Benedict, Francis, Catherine of Siena— "No Saint stands higher than this Saint of Trade," Hunt declared; "the Saint of the nineteenth century is the Good Merchant." Beatified on account of his pecuniary prowess, the holy man of business should command our reverence in every venue of religious practice. "Build him a shrine in Bank and Church, in the Market and the Exchange."[17]

Hunt might have added the inventor and the pioneer to his list of modern saints, as the evangelical partnership with Mammon inspired two brands of American eschatology: what Perry Miller and David Nye have dubbed "the technological sublime"—the mesmerizing veneration of technology and its creators—and the conviction that the nation had a "manifest destiny" both to possess the continent and to superintend the redemption of the world.[18] Among evangelicals, the Protestant errand into the marketplace authorized both a promethean mission of technological mastery and a ruthless adventure in imperial expansion.

Preceded by John Winthrop Jr.'s alchemical passions and Jonathan Edwards's enthusiasm for "contrivances," the evangelical technological sublime dovetailed with the popular culture of early American science, which often blended the fading world of marvels with the emerging universe of scientific modernity. Like the line that separated the genuine from the fraudulent in

the bustling market economy, the distinction between inventor and moun-
tebank was often difficult to draw. Students of electricity, for instance, recalled the alchemical magi in their enthusiasm. If more pious Protestants
suspected scientists of playing with "God's fire," many others greeted developments in electrical science with amazement and anticipation. Often itinerant salespeople, many of the earliest electrical scientists skirted the boundaries between science, technology, and entertainment. While the proliferation
of lightning rods testified to the more practical hopes for electricity, electrical scientists also provided spectacles of convulsion in parlors, churches,
barns, and theaters. Yet electrical science also ministered to more ineffable
spiritual desires. In the 1780s and 1790s, advocates of what James Delbourgo
has called "electrical humanitarianism" marketed "electrotherapies" that
enlisted what one physician, T. Gale of upstate of New York, dubbed "the soul
of the universe" in the cure of mental and physical diseases. For Gale, his
fellow electrotherapists, and their numerous patients, electricity was a material current of divine love; matter and spirit, nature and grace, were different aspects of a single reality. God, for Gale, was the "spiritual sun" whose
love was "spiritual nutrition"; electricity was that spiritual substance in material form, "participation of the same element as the natural sun diffused
through all the natural world." There was, in Gale's view, "no animation in
the natural world" except by the heat of the "ethereal fire." Echoing Edwards,
Gale believed that the discovery of electricity and its divine healing properties augured a worldwide Christian millennium.[19]

As the vanguard of the millennium, evangelicals claimed technology for
Christ in the years preceding the Civil War, recasting the Enlightenment
commitment to invention as a project in Christian dominion. Although as
late as 1856, one evangelical writer was warning that technological euphoria
proved that "Mammon has the heart of the age," most of his brethren greeted
technology with millennial expectation. The expanding infrastructure of canals, railroads, and turnpikes was "a moral machine," one writer argued in
1836, an enormous device to "perfect the civilization, and elevate the moral
character of the people." Celebrating the opening of the Cleveland and Columbus Railroad in 1851, one minister greeted the "great thoroughfare" as a
sign of "the evolution of divine purposes, infinite, eternal," evidence of "the
progress of Christianity and the coming reign of Christ." The editors of
*Scientific American* agreed, welcoming improvements in hay-making

technology in 1860 with eschatological fanfare. "Are not our inventors absolutely ushering in the very dawn of the millennium?" Amid the innovations in transport, communication, and production technology—the latter exemplified in the "American System" of manufacture of interchangeable parts—Edwards's prophecy of "contrivances" appeared to have been vindicated.[20]

The postmillennial eschatology of technological progress received support from writers such as Jacob Bigelow. Appointed Harvard's first Rumford Professor of "the Physical and Mathematical Sciences as Applied to the Useful Arts" in 1819, Bigelow later served as president of the American Academy of Arts and Sciences. Expressly targeting his popular survey of the *Elements of Technology* (1831) "for the use of seminarians and students," Bigelow provided state-of -the-art reports, accessible to laypeople, on developments in everything from printing and lithography to machinery and metallurgy. "We accomplish what the ancients only dreamt of in their fables," he wrote buoyantly, and Bigelow left no doubt that Americans would witness an even greater magnitude of progress. As a chronicle of efforts "to convert natural agents into ministers of our pleasure and power," Bigelow's history of technology blended seamlessly with postmillennial faith in the impending arrival of God's Kingdom on earth.[21]

Yet despite Bigelow's popularity with seminarians and the general reading public, his avoidance of Christian vocabulary points to alternative forms of the technological sublime. Among the New England intelligentsia, Unitarians took the lead in uncoupling commitment to technological development from evangelical Christianity. The abolitionist, Unitarian minister, and Transcendentalist Theodore Parker mused in 1841 that Adam's curse would soon be annulled by the use of labor-saving devices. "Labour will be a pleasant practice," he predicted. "The Fable of Orpheus is a true story in our time." Defending technical advances against the skepticism of Carlyle, Timothy Walker, a rising star in American jurisprudence, issued a "Defence of Mechanical Philosophy" in the *North American Review* in 1831. Walker's brief for technological progress assumed a sacramental understanding of nature and humanity. "The stupendous machinery of the universe" conveyed "an idea of the infinite attributes of the Supreme Being." Exerting the power of mind over nature, technology enabled humanity to attain its godlike status. Like "the Omnipotent Mind, of which it is the image," the human mind becomes the "powerful lord of matter." With the multiplication of inventions, the image and likeness of God would live a life of repose, devoted to contemplation and self-perfection. "Machines are to perform all the drudgery of man, while he is to look on in self-complacent ease." Walker beckoned toward a future of mechanical rapture. "Atlantis, Utopia, and the Isles of the Blest are nearer than those who first descried them."[22]

Walker's confidence in technology paled before that of the American technological utopians who emerged in the decades before the Civil War. Heirs to Bacon, Plattes, and Winthrop, Jr., antebellum techno-utopians augured a post-Christian brand of technological enchantment, setting the stage for later mavens of technology, such as Edward Bellamy, Harold Loeb, and Ray Kurzweil. In his boisterous tract, *The World as a Workshop* (1855), Thomas Ewbank—an engineer and inventor who served as commissioner of patents under President Zachary Taylor—tied his call for unlimited technological advance to a sacramental view of matter. "There is a Divinity in every particle of matter," he mused; "the material everywhere refers to the immaterial." Because matter is "the agent on which God has printed his thoughts," science and technology were no less than "the study and application of [divine] principles impressed upon matter." As "the enlightened elaborator of matter," humanity's closest imitation of God was the endless invention of new technologies—a stern necessity imposed by the Almighty. Redolent of Carlyle's "Gospel of Work," Ewbank's techno-utopia was implacably promethean. In "the divine economy of the world," Ewbank wrote, "man [is] to have nothing—absolutely nothing—done for him that he could possibly do for himself." "God employs no idlers—creates none."[23]

John Adolphus Etzler was the most prescient of all the antebellum enchanters of technology. Born in Prussia, Etzler emigrated to America twice: once in the early 1820s and then again in 1831, this time along with John A. Roebling, later the architect of the Brooklyn Bridge. Settling in Pittsburgh, Etzler worked on his first and greatest utopian tome, *The Paradise within the Reach of All Men* (1833), copies of which he sent to President Andrew Jackson and members of the Senate. For the next ten years, he produced other utopian tracts, as well as ideas for inventions and engineering projects. After failing to gather sufficient financial backing in America for his utopian schemes and technical designs, Etzler wandered to Haiti, England, and finally to Venezuela, where he disappears from history.[24]

As Steven Stoll has shown, Etzler's faith in technology exemplifies the "great delusion" of capitalist modernity: the belief that economic growth can go on forever, regardless of ecological limits. Etzler urged inventors, companies, and the federal government to embark on a gargantuan project of research and development. Returning to Eden with the assistance of machinery, men and women would be "free of all labors, full of endless delights and pleasures." With sophisticated technology harnessed to the goal of exponentially increasing consumption, the common materials of the earth, he predicted in *Paradise,* could provide "so enchanting and unheard of abodes, sceneries, ornaments, dress, comforts, luxuries, delights." But Etzler's beatific vision of automated, mass-produced bounty was also a metamorphosis of enchantment. Like other prophets of abundance, Etzler hinted at the sacramental desire that enlivened the fetishism of production. Despite his hostility to organized religion, Etzler believed that material plenty would offer "a fore-taste of heaven" and make us "so much the better prepared for another paradise hereafter." At the same time, Etzler also revealed the aspirations to divinity at the heart of technological utopianism. In the techno-paradise of the future, "man is powerful like a god—lord of the gigantic powers of nature."[25] On this point, Etzler joined hands with postmillennial Protestants seeking to reestablish Adam's dominion over nature. Yet by auguring the technological fabrication of enchantment, he also portended the cybernetic millennium of fully automated production.

Etzler hoped to attract his American hosts by appealing to imperial vanity. "Americans," he declared, "it is now in your power to become within ten years a nation to rule the world." He was invoking the American belief in a special mission and destiny—residue of the older Puritan errand, recycled through liberal republicanism and postmillennial eschatology. Over the eighteenth and nineteenth centuries, the city on a hill became the homestead on a plain, while the company of saints morphed into a master order of white proprietors. In his Federalist Paper #10, James Madison insisted that Americans needed to "extend the sphere" of their republic, seizing the land that was necessary to avert class conflict, provide the material basis for white patriarchal democracy, and enlarge the scope of commercial activity. Jefferson agreed, contending that westward settlement would magnify the "empire of liberty," an imperium of yeoman farmers and artisans. Hoping to acquire not only the land west of the Mississippi but also Cuba, Mexico, and Canada, Jefferson envisioned a republican empire that "has never [been] surveyed since the creation." As a member of the first committee to choose a Great Seal for the new republic, Jefferson favored a depiction of the Hebrews following the light of Yahweh.[26]

The Founders' hopes for proprietary dominion were echoed by Protestant leaders. Perhaps the most extravagant imperial manifesto came from Ezra Stiles, president of Yale College and the country's leading Congregationalist minister. In his oft-reprinted 1783 homily to the new General Assembly of Connecticut, "The United States Elevated to Glory and Honor," Stiles channeled the spirit of Edwards and heralded a millennial trove of riches. The Puritan theology of racial cleansing remained: the erasure of Indians and their replacement by whites followed happily from "God's good providence." With the red menace swept aside, "the political welfare of God's American Israel" was assured, and its victory was "allusively prophetic of the future prosperity and splendor of the United States." By expelling the Indians and throwing off the yoke of English monarchy, Americans had overcome the last remaining obstacles that "obstruct the progress of society towards perfection." Portraying the young republic as a heavenly landscape of proprietors, Stiles waxed rapturous on the passions of acquisition and the pleasures of mastery. "The rewards of [liberty], with property, have filled the English settlers in America with a most amazing spirit. Never before has the experiment been so effectually tried, of every man's reaping the fruits of his labor and feeling his share in the aggregate system of power." If their westward expansion were left unimpeded, American institutions of property and government promised the "inevitable perfectibility of man."[27] Summoning Americans to begin the construction of a proprietary paradise, Stiles's oration was a premonitory epistle of evangelical capitalist eschatology.

By the middle of the 1840s, the predestination of the elect had evolved into the manifest destiny of all; the Puritan errand and the liberal empire became the quest for evangelical dominion. Alongside clerical economists, such as Francis Wayland and Henry Carey, ministers such as Lyman Beecher preached an evangelical gospel of empire. In his *Plea for the West* (1835), Beecher implored Americans to mobilize their "pecuniary and moral power to evangelize the world." Referring explicitly to Edwards, Beecher held that "all providential developments since, and all the exiting signs of the times, lend corroboration" to Edwards's eschatological vision. Admonishing his eastern readers that the west prefigured the fulfillment of America's mission—"her destiny is our destiny"—Beecher also portended the redemption of the globe—"the joy of the whole earth," Beecher exulted. A decade later, the Democratic journalist John O'Sullivan echoed Beecher's augury, coining a memorable and contagious phrase in the vernacular of empire. Writing in the *Democratic Review* at the crest of the national debate over the annexation of Texas, O'Sullivan argued that the absorption of the Republic of Texas would fulfill a divine commission to subdue and replenish North America. It was, he proposed, "the manifest destiny of the United States to overspread the continent allotted by Providence for the free development of our yearly multiplying millions."[28]

Yet lebensraum for the white republic was not the only concern of Providence. As O'Sullivan had contended in an earlier essay for the *Democratic Review,* this "manifest destiny" embraced not only the continent, but the rest of the world as well. In "The Great Nation of Futurity," O'Sullivan echoed Edwards and Stiles in staking out the terms of an American millennium. With its democratic institutions and material prosperity, the United States demonstrated "the excellence of divine principles"; and as other nations hurried to emulate our example, "the boundless future will be the era of American greatness." O'Sullivan's eschatology was echoed and amplified by William Gilpin, explorer, soldier, editor, and first governor of the Colorado Territory. In the midst of a tireless career of imperial service in the western provinces, Gilpin found time to discern the "deep designs of Providence" in the high Sierras. His widely read account of *The Central Gold Region* (1860) doubled as travelogue and religious tract. Evoking the "fantastic, sublime, [and] *bizarre*" topography of the mountains and mesas, Gilpin also saw portents of American dominion. "The pioneer people . . . clear open the track of empire," he proclaimed, "pushed onward by the hand of God." Advancing with "all the solemnity of a Providential ordinance," settlers were God's emissaries; indeed, the remaining indigenous peoples, he thought, still "receive the white man as a new divinity." Bearing the ark of the republican covenant, the archangels of white democracy aimed at "the *industrial* conquest of the world." After the Civil War, Gilpin wrote of the Anglo-Saxon vocation with even more outlandish religiosity. Reissuing his book in 1873 as *Mission of the North American People,* Gilpin explicitly deified the economic and

technological advance of industrial capitalism. Beholding the white imperium, Gilpin wrote, "the American realizes that 'Progress is God.'"[29]

Gilpin's eschatology of progress was shared by many evangelicals, who
read harbingers of Christian dominion in the sublunary pages of nature and
history. To the Baptist audience of the *Christian Review,* for instance, the
stones themselves proclaimed the American capitalist coming of the Lord.
One remarkable article published in the magazine's January 1856 issue—
"The History and Destiny of Coal"—implied that minerals were sacramental
signs of America's beatific future. The continent's abundance of coal, iron,
and other natural resources had been felicitously "thrown by the Creator into
the hands of the Anglo-Saxon race." God bestowed his geological gifts for
the hallowed and vigorous extraction of profit, and He had cleft the rock of
ages to stoke the engines of American economic and political supremacy.
"What prophecies of the future God Himself has written on the solid rocks,"
the *Review* rejoiced, "mute prophecies graven thereon in ages long past."
What Baptists saw in rocks, the Reformed theologian and historian Philip
Schaff discerned in science and technology. In a rhapsodic sketch of America, Schaff envisioned a day—not far off—when the world would be united
in beloved community by the scientific and industrial triumphs of capitalism. "The extreme ends of the civilized world will be brought together by
the power of steam and electricity, the wonderful achievements of modern
science, the leveling influences of the press and public opinion"—all enlivened, Schaff believed, by "the more silent, but deeper and stronger workings
of the everlasting Gospel." Anointed and driven by the Spirit, "the distinctive mission of the *American* nation," he declared, is to lead humanity into
"the millennium of righteousness." However violent, avaricious, and wayward, the evangelical empire of capitalist enchantment could count on the
Almighty's favor. "God delivered us from greater dangers," Schaff concluded,
"and will not forsake us."[30]

The evangelical-proprietary dispensation extended to the most unlikely
quarters—for instance, to the Mormons, among whom the aurora of the dispensation shone with a special intensity. Despite the obloquy of evangelicals, the pioneers and settlers of the "Great Basin Kingdom" were legitimate
heirs of John Winthrop and the Puritans. From its birth in western New York
in the 1830s to the death of Brigham Young in Utah in 1877, Mormonism
insisted on the blessed symbiosis of material and spiritual riches. Relocating

the city on a hill to a kingdom of latter-day saints in a valley, Mormonism was a bizarre but authentic revision of the covenant theology of business, conveying with mythological bravado the pecuniary essence of capitalist enchantment.[31]

While New York's "burned-over" district was set ablaze by waves of fiery revivalists, it had also been enflamed by the passions of diviners, magicians, and other mavens of the occult, who lived and thrived among the region's beleaguered independent farmers and artisans. By the late 1820s, these self-sufficient, patriarchal households were besieged by small factories owned by urban merchants and manufacturers from eastern New York and New England. The losers soon became human debris in the Market Revolution; some became Shakers, some took up spiritualism, some joined utopian communes organized on Christian or Fourierist principles. Methodist and Baptist churches gathered in many more of the dispossessed, providing consolation and guidance in the arts of market competition. To many embattled skilled workers and landowners, the vagaries of the market looked very much like the inscrutable ways of the Almighty; success went to those who surrendered themselves (and others) to His remunerative providence. In manufacturing towns such as Utica and Rochester, evangelical economics enjoined master craftspeople to compete with godly savvy—and relinquish responsibility for their journeymen. Hammering out souls in a new diviner's fire of competitive family enterprise, evangelical Protestantism afforded enchantment for fledgling entrepreneurs.[32]

At the same time, the "supernatural economy" thrived, as economic desperation fueled a burgeoning of magic, divination, and treasure hunting. Occult tracts, almanacs, pamphlets, and booklets inundated western New York, detailing the powers of stars, rods, stones, and talismans. While the vanguard of improvement in eastern New York scoffed at rural superstitions, the impoverished hedged on the power of Christ by consulting astrological tables. Willard Chase, for instance, a busy treasure-seeker in Ontario County, was also a Methodist minister; another evangelical, Josiah Stowell, was a Presbyterian in Palmyra who enlisted the services of one Joseph Smith, Sr., to divine the location of some buried Spanish bullion. Smith had moved to Palmyra from Vermont in 1816 after his export business had failed. Hard pressed to pay the mortgage on their farm, Smith and his wife Lucy supplemented their meager income with divining and money-digging. They never, she later insisted, "stopt [their] labor and went at trying to win the faculty of Abrac drawing Magic circles or sooth saying to the neglect of all kinds of business."[33]

The Mormon gospel of wealth emerged from this cauldron of mercenary preternaturalism. As a young boy, Joseph Smith, Jr., learned the arts of divination from his father. But as numerous tongues of evangelical fire engulfed the region in the early 1820s, he endured a spiritual crisis, reading and praying for a sign to tell him which denomination preached the true gospel. His search for truth took a fateful turn in the fall of 1823, when an angel, "Moroni," revealed the existence of golden plates that recounted America's early history. For four years, Moroni denied Smith access to the plates, but he relented in 1827, charging Smith to translate the narrative and preach the gospel contained therein. Smith's divinatory skills came in handy: to decipher the plates, he used the "Urim and Thummim," sacred stones used by ancient Hebrew high priests to communicate with the divine. Smith's spiritual metamorphosis did not prevent him from engaging in divination: two years after his first encounter with Moroni, Smith, bearing his trusty seer stones, accompanied treasure-hunting expeditions in New York and Pennsylvania. In 1830, Smith completed his translation of the plates—which Moroni promptly retrieved—published the *Book of Mormon*, and set up the Church of Latter-Day Saints in Palmyra and several other towns. Local residents recalled his ne'er-do-well days as a shady money-digger, so Smith, his young wife, and their followers embarked on a pilgrimage to Missouri.[34]

Though vilified by evangelicals as the sacrilegious scheme of a confidence man, Mormonism wedded evangelical and magical prescriptions for earthly prosperity. To the growing bevy of followers who joined Smith through the 1830s and 1840s—from New York to Missouri to Ohio to Illinois—his alloy of Protestantism and the occult was good news in the maelstrom of the market. Endowed with a febrile imagination and an extraordinary talent for religious syncretism, Smith transformed his obsession with gold into a quintessentially American religion, a grand narrative that aligned God and Mammon even more perfectly than evangelicalism did. In a brilliant, outlandish mélange of Protestantism and divination, Christ and Moroni promised the advent of a cosmic patriarchal millennium. And as Mormon patriarchs proved at least as avid and shrewd as any born-again businessperson, Mormon theology sanctioned America's first unadulterated prosperity gospel. However many ways it directly contravened the tenets of orthodox Christianity, Mormonism was, to its adherents, the apotheosis of proprietary enchantment. Like its Puritan predecessor and its evangelical antagonist, the Mormon catechism of wealth was a triune covenant theology of capital: an ontology of divine immanence; a moral economy of "stewardship" in which riches are manna from heaven; and a tale of declension, renewal, and destiny that defined a chosen people's exceptional character. To the horror of orthodox Christians, Mormon ontology was bluntly and exuberantly materialist. "We differ from the Christian world in our religious faith and belief," Young reminded worshippers in the Tabernacle in Salt Lake City in 1871, "and we do so very materially." Unbelievers feared that such a high estimation of matter would subvert conventional morality, but Mormon materialism was religious, even sacramental, before it was economic. Mormon metaphysicians barely distinguished between matter and divinity; denying the creation of matter by God, Mormons insisted on its eternity and indestructibility. "The elements are eternal," Smith asserted in 1837. In place of creation out of nothing, Mormons substituted creation out of matter—even the creation of God. As Smith once explained, God himself "was once a man like one of us . . . [who] once dwelled on earth." "God never made something out of nothing," Young asserted to his Tabernacle audience. The Holy Spirit, one Mormon writer asserted in 1855, was a "spiritual fluid" that pervaded and united all material substance in the cosmos. "Spirit and element, inseparably connected, receive a fullness of joy," Smith had declared; "the elements are the tabernacle of God."[35] Where God, in Christianity, is immaterial and perfect, the Mormon God—like a hard-working merchant or self-improving mechanic—achieved His limitless glory and dominion, becoming the prototype of the self-made man.

The centrality of matter in Mormon theology lent enormous significance to accumulation. Since divinity was immanent to matter, the earth contained inner drives to "improvement"; and as God was (quite literally) an enterprising man, His servants must be enterprising saints as well. Thus property, money, commodities, and trade took up much of Mormon religious culture; as Leonard J. Arrington points out, of Smith's 112 "revelations," eighty-seven concerned economic affairs. Non-Mormons were put off by what they considered the Mormons' ignoble and shameless rapacity. After visiting a Mormon community in Ohio in the late 1830s, a Unitarian editor complained that his hosts displayed "too great a desire for the perishable riches of this world—holding out the idea that the kingdom of Christ is to be composed of 'real estate, herds, flocks, silver, gold,' etc. as well as of human beings." Yet Mormons themselves proudly maintained, as one writer avowed in the *Deseret News* in 1878, that their faith was preoccupied with "dollars and cents, with trade and barter, with the body and the ordinary things of life."[36]

Born amidst the decay of the pre-industrial world, Mormon economics displayed all the ambivalence of the evangelical moral imagination, where visions of patriarchal mutuality jostled with entrepreneurial hustle. Much of the appeal—and the dread—of early Mormonism stemmed from its theocratic collectivism. Emulating the early Christians, Mormons officially held their property in common; families were required to "consecrate" their possessions to the church, whose elders redistributed them according to need. The *Book of Mormon* traces the origins and laments the evils of inequality: the fall of the Nephites—the ancient Hebrews who journeyed to America and comprised the continent's aboriginal residents—commenced when they "began to be divided into classes."[37] Later critics of Mormonism (as well as later Mormons) often downplay or overlook this communalist ideal of the Latter-Day Saints. Though hardly egalitarian and certainly short-lived, Mormon communalism reflected a desire to eradicate the capitalist market, forsaking the lucrative agony of competition for love and mutual aid.

Yet the luster of lucre tinged even the most generous expressions of Mormon fraternity. "Be familiar with all and free with your substance," the *Book of Mormon* enjoined—"that they may be rich like unto you." In these and other passages—as well as in the prophetic canon of Smith, Young, and other Mormon elders—virtue looks like an investment strategy for patriarchs thinking about the morrow. The early Mormons equated material wealth with the favor of the Almighty—Himself a former man who had risen in the world to achieve His exaltation and divinity. In Mormon cosmology and history, the earth is a quarry of metallic luxuriance awaiting the sedulous pioneer. Although believers were warned about the subtle corruptions of avarice and prosperity, their scriptures and prophecies were leavened with a gold-tinged vision of terrestrial plenitude, an earth and a cosmos rendered beatific by the labor of accumulation. Throughout the *Book of Mormon*, for instance, America appears as a treasure trove awaiting the exploitation of the pious. America, Moroni told Smith, "doth abound most plentifully" in "gold, silver, and all manner of precious ores," a clear exhortation to fashion its abundance into a gilded patriarchal Zion.[38]

In the pursuit of this-worldly fortune, Mormons readily adopted the personal and political economy of evangelical capitalism. Evangelicals were so scandalized by Mormon theology and polygamy that they never recognized their affinity with the heretics: affirmation of the gospel of work and proprietorship, the gospel of the evangelical dispensation. The character armor forged in the evangelical fire—thrift, sobriety, and perseverance—was worn to embolden and protect an army of abstemious, well-scrubbed accumulators, "men of truth and soberness . . . neat and comely" crusaders for material sainthood. Though it appeared to outsiders like a collectivist theocracy, the Mormons' tight-knit ecclesia was a vanguard of proprietors on another errand into the marketplace. Wherever they settled, Smith and his followers fused mundane business with seraphic aspiration. When Smith and other elders founded the Kirtland Safety Society Bank Company in Kirtland, Ohio, in 1837, they wrote the bank's charter in such a way that it blended finance and eschatology. Stipulating that its funds would be used "for the promotion of our temporal interests, and for the better management of our different occupations, which consist in agriculture, mechanical arts, and merchandising," they also made no secret of their desire for a global pecuniary imperium. "Like Aaron's rod," Smith declared, Kirtland would "swallow up all other Banks . . . and grow and flourish and spread from the rivers to the ends of the earth." Later, in Utah in 1868, Young established Zion's Cooperative Mercantile Institution, which both patrolled the boundaries of the Mormon economy—even to the point of employing spies to report on wayward church members—and sponsored numerous small retail, manufacturing, and agricultural businesses. Members of the Institution posted signs above their storefronts that displayed an all-seeing eye accompanied by the phrase "Holiness to the Lord."[39]

Even consecration was always less than it appeared to be. Consecration was never a very popular doctrine; although it remained a nominal requirement of church membership, it languished as the Saints grew in numbers and wealth, and Young's attempt to revive the practice in the mid-1870s was a crashing and definitive failure. (Young himself refused to consecrate his own substantial property, which by then included a textile factory and more than ten thousand acres of farmland.) Thereafter, tithing replaced consecration as the economic tender of communal solidarity; at 10 percent charity for the church, brotherly love was now safely vouchsafed at a lower and always dependable rate. Besides, the Mormons' polygamous patriarchy introduced a tension between the common good and family interests. The elders reconciled the tension through "stewardship": though all possessions and estates were consecrated, elders displayed considerable latitude in setting the parameters of need, and lesser patriarchal stewards were, in turn, allowed considerable freedom of enterprise with their money and property.[40] As a surrogate for collectivism or mutual aid, stewardship and tithing comprised a consecration of the property interests of the saints. After the 1870s, the Mormon patriarchal millennium was more unambiguously identified with capital accumulation.

Yet Mormon patriarchs longed for something grander than a heavenly city of the propertied. In the doctrine of "eternal progression," they imagined their own "exaltation," their transfiguration into gods. Of course, the eventual divinization of humanity—*theosis*—had long been a teaching of orthodox Christianity. But where *theosis* is granted to humanity on account of God's gracious, unmerited love, Mormon "progression" and "exaltation" are robustly human labors and achievements. "You have got to learn how to make yourselves Gods," Smith admonished his followers early on; as one of his chief disciples, Lorenzo Snow, put it pithily, "as man now is, God once was; as God is now, man may be." A man makes himself a God, Smith taught, "by going from a small capacity to a great capacity, from a small degree to another, from grace to grace . . . from exaltation to exaltation." Eternal progression was upward mobility transformed into a cosmic process; hustling ascended from the market into the heights of ontological sublimity. In the heavens as it is on earth, class distinctions—now "levels of glory"—would remain among the patriarchy: the "celestials" raptured in the highest estate, while "terrestrials" and "telestials" basked in lower, less respectable echelons of beatitude. But for those at all levels of exaltation, the reward for their moral enterprise on earth was sovereignty over the elements. In a sermon delivered in 1853, Young foretold the omnipotence that awaited celestials in the sanctum of their upper-class heaven. The "Celestial Kingdom" would arrive, he declared, "when we can call gold and silver together from the eternity of matter in the immensity of space, and all the other precious metals, and command them to remain or move at our pleasure; when we can say to the native element, 'Be thou combined, and produce those commodities necessary for the use and sustenance of man.'"[41]

The celestials' arrival in their kingdom would mark the culmination of a history in which America played a starring and exceptional role. The *Book of Mormon* is a story about America, retold in Hebraic typology and recast as a Mormon jeremiad, an unfinished story of commitment, declension, and summons to renewed fidelity. Out of an unschooled but combustible ingenuity forced to grapple with tumultuous change, Smith produced the grandest statement of American exceptionalism since Cotton Mather's *Magnalia Christi Americana*. In the sixth century BC, a band of Israelites flees Jerusalem just before the Babylonian captivity. After wandering through Arabia and Africa, they make their way to America, a "land of promise" that is "choice above all other lands." They swiftly divide into two warring peoples: the white and upright Nephites and the licentious Lamanites, whose infidelity God punishes by darkening their skin. Like white Christians whose conquest of the continent would soon be anointed "manifest destiny," the Nephites are described as pious proprietors who are "industrious, and labor with their hands." Like the indigenous peoples whose subjugation and slaughter must clear the way for evangelical imperium, the Lamanites are portrayed as "lazy and idolatrous . . . wild, ferocious, and blood-thirsty," incapable of the diligence and self-restraint required to maintain a civilization. For six centuries these peoples live in a state of homicidal animosity; but when Jesus Christ visits America after his ascension, the Nephites and some of the Lamanites acknowledge his lordship, and harmony is restored. (The Lamanites retain their dark skin, however.) But the peace is tense and short-lived: the Lamanites fall away again, and the Nephites, enervated physically and morally by their wealth, are overcome and destroyed by their enemies.[42] When Smith accepted and translated the golden plates from Moroni, he (and his followers) accepted a charge to take up the Nephites' mission. The Mormons considered themselves heirs to a covenant, saintly envoys of an errand into the market, prophets recalling a delinquent people to an arduous but lucrative commission.

Burning with entrepreneurial zealotry, Mormons and evangelicals had continued and extended the Puritan errand into the marketplace. And like their predecessors, they confronted a fundamental contradiction: the simultaneous allegiance to God and Mammon, the effort to forge a mercenary fraternity. Under the auspices of both Whigs and Jacksonian Democrats, the evangelical friendship with unrighteous Mammon blessed the "democracy of cupidity," the fellowship in venality that Richard Hofstadter considered the marrow of the American political tradition. To borrow Ralph Waldo Emerson's pithy phrase, the evangelical-proprietary dispensation was "the soul's economy" of antebellum America.[43]

Under the signs of "producerism" or "labor republicanism," historians have made much of farmers, craftspeople, and journeymen who dissented from the evangelical dispensation as large-scale manufacturing expanded throughout the Northeast from the 1810s to the 1830s. But most workers who railed against the nascent "dominion of satan and antichrist," as one New York artisan put it, advanced alternatives that bore a telling resemblance to small-scale capitalism. "Let no one accuse us of enmity to capitalists," as a writer for the *Voice of Industry,* the leading antebellum labor weekly, cautioned in 1847. To Stephen Simpson, author of *The Working Man's Manual* (1831), "equality of wealth or a community of property" was nothing less than "a perversion." Producerism both reflected and was eventually destroyed by the very order it called into question. In the tenacious proprietary fantasy of producerism, competitive market relations had no long-term casualties; the dependency that characterized wage labor was temporary and always escapable. As the Benevolent Master of the Market, God could not consign any hard-working steward to a lifetime of industrial servility. "Can it be," the economist Henry Carey asked rhetorically, "that a beneficent Providence has so adapted the laws under which we live that laborers *must* be at the mercy of those who hoard food and clothing with which to purchase labor?"[44] The answer turned out to be yes: the rage to accumulate unleashed by evangelical fervor undermined the evangelical economy. As more and more artisans succumbed to the pressures of competition from factory production, proprietorship became more unreal as a possibility and more urgent as a compensatory ideal.

Enlisted by Christopher Lasch in the "populist campaign against 'improvement,'" Orestes Brownson offers a colorful case study in the ironies of the evangelical-proprietary dispensation. One of the most prolific and controversial journalists in antebellum America and now known primarily as one of American Catholicism's most formidable apologists, Brownson undertook a protracted and quixotic pilgrimage before joining the Church of Rome. Born a Congregationalist, he sampled the Presbyterian, Unitarian, and Transcendentalist faiths. In the 1820s, after ordination as a Unitarian minister, Brownson took a lively interest in labor politics, championing the Working Men's Party. Moving to Boston to minister to the city's poor, he befriended George Ripley and other Transcendentalists and founded the *Boston Quarterly Review,* a forum for his fellow spiritual adventurers. He achieved literary and political notoriety in 1840 with "The Laboring Classes," a blazing philippic against the new market society. A mercurial blend of the curmudgeon, the pedant, and the prophet, he embraced, in the span of a decade, Jacksonian Democracy, John C. Calhoun and the plantation grandees, Abraham Lincoln and the Republican Party, and finally a pugnacious Catholicism. Brownson's changes of opinion were so rapid and dizzying that James Russell Lowell dubbed him a "weathercock." "He shifts quite about, then proceeds to expound / That 'tis merely the earth, not himself, that turns round."[45]

Turn round he did, in just a few years, from an ardent voice for the new working class to a cranky spokesperson for the industrial elite. From the start of his literary career—in *New Views of Christianity, Society, and the Church* (1836) as well as in the pages of the *Boston Quarterly Review*—Brownson wrote of political economy as a matter of religious, sacramental importance. "If you will serve the devil," he warned in "The Laboring Classes," "you must look to the devil for your wages." Affirming Carlyle's evidence of "horrid enchantment," he railed that "Mammonism has become the religion of Saxondom." Since "the universe is the revelation of the Deity," he mused in 1840, then "whoso wrongs a man defaces the image of God, desecrates a temple of the living God."[46]

Yet however gifted his polemics, Brownson never expounded a "Christian radicalism," as Lasch once summarized his views. Indeed, the roots of his later conservatism, often attributed to his Catholic conversion, are clearly visible in his earlier work. A prototype of the fire-breathing moderate, Brownson was a proprietary believer in merit. After writing the incendiary essays of his Jacksonian period, he grew quickly despondent about democracy, recoiling from the "hard-cider" and "log cabin" antics of the 1840 presidential campaign. As the decade progressed, Brownson made his peace with the devil. Writing in the *Boston Quarterly Review* in 1841—not even a year after "The Laboring Classes"—Brownson launched into a sturdy defense of wage labor. "Let each man be an independent proprietor," he gushed with republican brio—unless he fails, in which case he must accept the judgment of the market, which was governed by "a stern and unyielding necessity." Moreover, since, Brownson reasoned, proprietors endure "all the vexation and labor of superintending," they deserve the greater share of benefits; "let the workingmen limit their desires to what is their due"—the wages, now no longer paid by Satan. Part of what was due to the propertyless was the rule of a wise and benevolent hierarchy. "There must be in all branches of human activity, mental, social, industrial, chiefs and leaders." Reform, he wrote in the *Democratic Review* in 1843, should be left to "the natural chiefs of industry": "bank presidents . . . directors of insurance offices, of railroads and other corporations; heavy manufacturers and leading merchants." Brownson's remarks demonstrate clearly that what Lasch hailed as "the political economy of republicanism" was not the antidote, but rather the prelude, to industrial plutocracy.[47] As so often happens with populist firebrands, the erstwhile tribune of the laboring classes became a champion of the professional and managerial elite. The sworn enemy of Mammonism morphed into a celebrant of the upper echelons of capitalist enchantment. Brownson was the American Carlyle, a herald of wonder at the captains of industry.

# 6

# Glows and Glories and Final Illustriousness

Transcendentalism, the Religion of the Slaves, and the Romantic Imagination in Antebellum America

BROWNSON SANG HIS HOSANNA to the industrial elite just a year before he converted to Catholicism, repudiating the Transcendentalist cause that was then at the crest of its vigor. During its heyday in the 1840s, Transcendentalism was the most vibrant intellectual movement in the country, claiming the adherence or sympathy of many of the nation's leading thinkers: Ralph Waldo Emerson, Henry David Thoreau, Margaret Fuller, Theodore Parker, Bronson Alcott, George Ripley, and others in what William Henry Channing anointed the "brotherhood of the 'Like-Minded.'" Transcendentalists embraced some of the radical causes of the day: women's suffrage, the abolition of slavery, prison and educational reform, workers' rights, utopian communities. The Transcendentalist moment gradually ended in the 1850s as the argument over slavery embittered American cultural and political life. Still, several of its luminaries became American icons—Emerson and Thoreau in particular—while its intellectual influence extended into the pragmatism of William James and the "New Thought" of spiritual seekers in the 1890s.[1]

Because the "Like-Minded" rejected the very idea of a common creed or philosophy, defining Transcendentalism has been difficult if not impossible. Scholars have traced its roots to Unitarianism and to the German idealism of Hegel, Johann Gottlieb Fichte, Friedrich Schelling, and Friedrich Schliermacher, who wedded idealist philosophy to liberal Protestant theology. To liberal Unitarians and idealists, the human spirit flourished when unencumbered by the dogmatic and liturgical trappings of religion. As Charles Mayo Ellis, a Boston lawyer and a popularizer of the movement's ideas, explained in 1842, Transcendentalists affirmed God's "immanent presence in the world" and the "substantive, independent existence of the soul of man." This soul or "religious sense," this "love for beauty and holiness," was unfettered by dogmas and inexpressible through rituals. The soul's transactions with God were "not dependent on education, custom, command, or anything beyond man himself." In his characteristically buoyant fashion, Emerson conveyed the movement's sense of joy and possibility. The Transcendentalist, Emerson wrote in 1842, exuded a "Saturnalia or excess of Faith"; he "believes in miracle, in the perpetual openness of the human mind to the new influx of light and power."[2]

As F. O. Matthiessen recognized, Emerson expounded a "romanticism of the future" that contrasted with the medievalist nostalgia common among many Romantics in Europe. If Transcendentalism was an American branch of Romanticism, then it was also a search for a natural supernaturalism, a sacramental imagination for a post-Protestant America. Transcendentalist Romantics exhibited an enchanted sensibility emancipated from the strictures of orthodox Christianity. Yet if they did not long for the past, the past abided in them; Transcendentalism, Matthiessen wrote, was "romanticism in a Puritan setting." "The aroused intellect," Emerson asserted, studies "facts, dull, strange, despised things," but it soon discovers "gold and gems in one of those scorned facts"; indeed, it beholds that "a fact is the Epiphany of God." "The wise man wonders at the usual," he reflected elsewhere, and finds "the miraculous in the common." Cotton Mather and Jonathan Edwards would have agreed—as would evangelical preachers and theologians, with whose cultivation of inner experience Transcendentalists bore an unlikely affinity. Puritan divines might even have appreciated Thoreau's epiphany in a snow-covered forest in the winter of 1855. "Thrilled and enchanted," Thoreau recorded in his journal that he "had seen into paradisiac regions, with their air and sky, and I was no longer wholly or merely a denizen of this vulgar earth." Once nature appears to the enchanted eye in this edenic "beauty and significance," he concluded, "the age of miracles is each moment thus returned."[3]

Like European Romanticism, the sacramental imagination of American Transcendentalists could have had radical implications. As the first generation of American intellectuals to rely on a national marketplace for the dissemination of their views, most Transcendentalists were, like Fuller, "disgusted with the vulgarity of a commercial aristocracy" who reduced everything to "vulgar earth" and pecuniary calculation. Transcendentalists founded or joined many of the numerous utopian communities that cropped up between 1800 and the Civil War, most appearing during the prolonged depression of the 1840s. The names of these communities form a melancholy roster of utopian hope and disappointment: among them, Alcott's Fruitlands; Adin Ballou's Hopedale; John Humphrey Noyes's Oneida; Robert Owen's New Harmony (modeled after his New Lanarck community in Britain); the Northampton Association (dubbed "Eden Jr." by a starry-eyed visitor); and Ripley's Brook Farm, the most renowned. Bringing together some of "the oddest of the odd," as one Brook Farm inhabitant put it, antebellum utopian communities aimed to dispel the ideal of perpetual striving, abolish the industrial division of labor, and end the primacy of pecuniary reason. Cajoling Emerson to support the venture, Ripley—a minister who left his Boston pulpit—claimed that Brook Farm would "insure a more natural union between intellectual and manual labor" and blend harmoniously "the agricultural and mechanic arts." One Brook Farmer later recalled that he and his fellow communards had attempted to build "a panorama of industrial beauty and universal happiness."[4]

Founded as enclaves from the Market Revolution, communal societies were also outposts of anticapitalist enchantment. If "the great truth," as Elizabeth Peabody asserted, is that "all labor is sacred, when done for a common interest," then utopia would resacralize human life as well as abolish capitalism. The Romantic desire to restore a sacramental way of life inspired Sylvester Judd, one of the few Transcendentalist novelists. Highly praised by Emerson and Fuller, his heavily didactic novels *Margaret* (1845, 1851) and *Richard Edney and the Governor's Family* (1850) doubled as Transcendentalist social criticism. The eponymous heroine of the popular *Margaret* is "a transparent, articulate revelation of God," who, when admiring the natural world, sees "an unknown realm of purity and peace . . . the faintly-revealed inferior heavens." Likewise, Richard Edney—a poor farm boy from Maine who leaves home to seek his fortune—affirms "the love and gladness at the core of all things" and trusts that nature harbors at its metaphysical center "a luminousness of Good Intent." Both characters discover that avarice has corrupted the luminous gladness. Richard travels to Woodylin, a rising manufacturing town (modeled after Lowell), and at first reacts joyously at the sight of the industrial scenery. "The Factories appeared like an abode of enchantment . . . hundreds of bright windows, illuminated every night in honor of Toil . . . the Factories, and factory life, how it glowed at that moment to his eye!" Alas, Richard discovers that the factories are dens of misery and exploitation. Facing a similar disenchantment, Margaret and her husband set up "Mons Christi," a liberal Christian utopia of lush natural beauty, effortless tolerance, and unaffected *agape*.[5]

As Nathaniel Hawthorne wrote of Brook Farm in *The Blithedale Romance* (1852), the "modern arcadians" embarked on an "exploded scheme for beginning the life of Paradise anew." Based loosely on Hawthorne's eight-month residence at Brook Farm in 1841, *The Blithedale Romance* is the first modern novel of utopian disappointment, foreshadowing the darker dystopian lineage of Zamyatin, Huxley, and Orwell. Blithedale's modern arcadians recoil from the disturbance of market upheaval. "Everything in nature and human existence was fluid, or fast becoming so," laments the narrator, Miles Coverdale. "It was a day of crisis, and we ourselves were in the critical vortex." Repulsed by the greed and callousness dictated by competitive market relations, the pilgrims to Blithedale aspire to create a beloved community of labor. With their sweat as a kind of baptism, work, they hope, will be a liturgical performance, creating a sacramental connection to the world. In the first days of their idyllic experiment, they enjoy, Coverdale reports, "delectable visions of the spiritualization of labor. It was to be our form of prayer, and ceremonial of worship." Patient field labor will uncover some "some aromatic root of wisdom," while rest will afford "glimpses into the far-off soul of truth."[6] The stench of manure, they hope, will become the felicitous fragrance of Eden. Blithedale promises a new soul's economy in the reunion of labor and love.

But paradise remains elusive. Pioneers of agrarian chic, visitors to Blithedale praise the arcadians for "imbuing the ordinary rustic occupations with a kind of religious poetry"—verse *they* would never labor to compose. Yet as the arduous days wear on, the poetry curdles into the uninspired prose of drudgery, futility, and resentment. For all their hoeing, milking, and shoveling, the pastoral bohemians fail to usher in the re-enchantment of the world. Despite the professed desire to "wear out our old clothes," the wardrobe of habit proves difficult to shed: jealousy, avarice, laziness, and other vices bedevil the arcadians. They also quickly discover that the liturgy of labor is a sweaty and grueling ritual. "The clods of earth, which we so constantly belabored and turned over and over, were never etherealized into thought. Our thoughts, on the contrary, were fast becoming cloddish." Yet if mental and manual labor cannot be reconciled, the erasure of class divisions is impossible. "Intellectual activity is incompatible with any large amount of bodily exercise," Coverdale concludes. "The yeoman and the scholar . . . are two distinct individuals, and can never be melted or welded into one substance." Once again, paradise must be postponed. Blithedale—like Brook Farm—is a failed romance, a fruitless search for a modern sacramental way of being in the world. Hawthorne's disenchantment reflected that of many other Brook Farmers. Alluding to Hawthorne, Ripley, Margaret Fuller, and other utopians, John Thomas Codman recalled that their ideas of labor "extended only to planting flowers or washing with care a few muslins to adorn their beautiful selves." The modern arcadians were unprepared to lead the world into a reconstructed Garden.[7]

Thoreau had visited Brook Farm in the winter of 1841. He was underwhelmed: "I think I had rather keep a bachelor's room in Hell than go to board in Heaven." A few years after declining his invitation to utopia, Thoreau set out on his own to elude the new religion of the market. Disgusted by the greed of his neighbors in Concord, Massachusetts, he escaped to a small cottage in the woods near Walden Pond, just south of town, in the summer of 1845. As he wrote in *Walden,* for two years Thoreau sought refuge from "the whole curse of trade," an activity that "curses everything it handles." Now "an authority as impersonal as the Fates," the market was not, to Thoreau, a forum of freedom but a glittering servitude. "We worship not the Graces . . . but Fashion." Aghast at the mercenary civility of traders and enterprising farmers in Concord, Thoreau condemned their "mean and sneaking lives." Especially appalled by one prosperous farmer who had named a pond after himself, Thoreau exploded in a volley of dudgeon. Though ostensibly devout, the megalomaniacal rube would "carry his God to market if he could get anything for him." Indeed, the farmer "goes to the market *for* his god as it is." Thus, though amoral and rapacious, the mercenary farmer, Thoreau perceived, was not quite disenchanted: like the rest of Concord's yeomen, he "sacrificed . . . to the infernal Plutus."[8]

In addition to its moral depravity, Christian capitalism wrought metaphysical havoc—a desolation that Thoreau's protest, however sacramental, could do little to reverse or repair. The farmer who roused Thoreau's bile, for instance, transmuted nature with every sale, since "fruits are not ripe for him till they are turned into dollars." Indeed, the "ambrosial and essential part" of his wares "rubbed off" in the cart on their way to Boston's markets. Recoiling from a Christian hypocrisy that commodified everything, Thoreau beckoned to a premodern animate cosmology and adapted it to his Trancendentalist Romanticism. In *Walden,* for instance, his curse upon trade follows a description of an Indian "feast of first fruits." Applauding their festivals of dancing and singing to welcome and bless the harvest, Thoreau remarked that he had "scarcely heard of a truer sacrament, that is, as the dictionary defines it, 'outward and visible sign of an inward and spiritual grace.'" Yet if Thoreau echoed the Puritans and evangelicals when he dubbed nature "the art of God," his God was not the Patriarch of proprietary Christians, Who had fashioned the earth into a marketplace. "The earth I tread on," he mused in his journals, "is a body, has a spirit, is organic and fluid to the influence of its spirit." The planet was "not a fossil earth, but a living earth; compared with whose great central life all animal and vegetable life is merely parasitic." "A mortal feels in himself Nature . . . his Mother stirs within in him, and he becomes immortal with her immortality." "He must be conscious of a friendliness in her." Yet Thoreau's personal dissent was memorable but unavailing, as individual nonconformity could achieve little when disconnected from any broader collective purpose. Indeed, in Thoreau's case, austerity provided a rich stock of capital for spiritual exhibitionism; as Alcott remarked sardonically, the sage of Walden Pond wore poverty "as an ornament about himself."[9]

The "friendliness" that Thoreau found in nature was discovered by Walt Whitman in the world of commodities. Whitman has, for good reason, been celebrated as the poet laureate of American democratic promise, but he should also be read, to use his own terms, as a divine literatus of proprietary capitalism. Democracy rests on "an aggregate of middling property owners," he asserted in *Democratic Vistas* (1871), who possessed "houses and acres, and . . . cash in the bank." Whitman marveled at the acquisitive spirit of the republic, affirming the "practical, stirring, worldly, money-making, even materialistic character" of its people. "Our farms, stores, offices, dry-goods, coal and groceries, enginery, cash-accounts, trades, earnings, markets, etc., . . . the extreme business energy, and this almost maniacal appetite for wealth . . . are parts of amelioration and progress." Whitman saw no ultimate tension between democracy and capitalism; his democratic vistas included "riches, and the getting of riches, and the amplest products, power, activity, inventions, movements, etc." "In the labor of engines and trades and the labor of fields / I find the developments," he observed in "A Song for Occupations," "and find the eternal meanings." "A new worship I sing," he chanted in "A Passage to India":[10]

> You captains, voyagers, explorers, yours,
> You engineers, you architects, explorers, yours,
> You, not for trade or transportation only,
> But in God's name, and for thy sake O soul.

Whitman's acclamation of capitalist dynamism is more than a hymnody of boosterism. Like Hopkins, Whitman intuited a dearest freshness that inhered deep down in things. Near the end of his life he professed a belief in the "ultimate vivification" of worldly things, "the glows and glories and final illustriousness" without which they were "incomplete." "Invisible spiritual results, just as real and definite as the visible, eventuate all concrete life and materialism." Yet Whitman identified the grandeur of God with the blear of trade and toil. His cosmology of capitalist enchantment is most vivid in his "Song of Occupations," where he describes a world of enlivened objects as an affable and generous place, an animate world, a beloved, democratic community of people and things:

> When the psalm sings instead of the singer,
> When the script preaches instead of the preacher,
> When the pulpit descends and goes instead of the carver that
>     carved the
> supporting desk,
> When the sacred vessels or the bits of the eucharist, or the lath and
> plast, procreate as effectually as the young silversmiths or bakers, or
> the masons in their overalls . . .
> When the minted gold in the vault smiles like the nightwatchman's
> daughter,
> When warrantee deeds loafe in chairs opposite and are my friendly
>     companions . . .

> I intend to reach them my hand and make as much of them as I
>    do of
> men and women.

Whitman feels thoroughly at home, for he remains fully conscious that this spirited world is made by the carver, the baker, and the mason. "You and your soul enclose all things, / regardless of estimation." Though Whitman knows that his animated objects draw life from human beings, he is not "disenchanted," for he sees divinity in the human power and presence that reside in objects. All products of thought and labor bear sacramental witness to their human makers:[11]

> Will we rate our cash and business high? I have no objection . . .
> We consider bibles and religions divine—I do not say they are
> not divine,
> I say they have all grown out of you, and may grow out of you
> still,
> It is not they who give the life, it is you who give the life . . .

Although it is "you who give the life," Whitman's natural supernaturalism was not a human usurpation of divinity. One of the divine literati of capitalist enchantment, Whitman considered all those houses and cash in the bank as tokens of a profoundly auspicious power. As he argued in *Democratic Vistas*, "at the core of democracy, finally, is the religious element," he asserted, "a deep, integral, human and divine principle." The venality that galvanized the republic partook of a benevolent cosmic enchantment; "within the purposes of the Kosmos"—pervading the marketplace as well as the rocks, the animal world, and the heavens—"there is a moral purpose," Whitman asserted, "a visible or invisible intention, certainly underlying all." This moral purpose required "intuition, faith, idiosyncrasy, to its realization," and the supernal vitality that coursed through the market would lift Americans into "the pure ether of veneration."[12] The American scramble for money and possessions was a vanity fair of beatitude.

If Whitman's Romanticism was buoyantly populist about the possibilities residing in the market, Emerson's contained more ominously sanguine portents about the capitalist future. The most renowned and beloved American intellectual of the nineteenth century, Emerson continues to elicit the reverence of even the most critical intellectuals. Even though he considers Emerson a "petty bourgeois libertarian" and a mandarin for the enlightened business elites of his time, Cornel West still hails him as a Transcendentalist precursor of the pragmatist tradition. Emphasizing Emerson's Puritan inheritance, Lasch portrays him as the exponent of a "theology of producerism," contending that he carried "the political economy of populism . . . into the higher register of moral and ontological speculation." Far from being a philosopher-booster for commerce and industrial expansion, Lasch's Emerson is a homilist of proprietary rectitude, inveighing against decadence and rapacity. Yet is this the Emerson who mused that money "is, in its effects and laws, as beautiful as roses"? Or who thought that the nostrums repeated by Carey and Hunt were "laws of the Universe"? If, as Lasch realized, *theology* is indeed the appropriate idiom, Harold Bloom was closer to the mark when he dubbed Emerson the inventor of "the American religion" of self-divinity and personal power.[13] A heretic from the covenant theology, Emerson heralded the eventual supersession of the Protestant economic dispensation, becoming an American Romantic seer of post-Christian capitalist enchantment.

After studying divinity at Harvard and pastoring the Unitarian Second Church in Boston, Emerson began to doubt his faith after the death of his first wife, Ellen. "The profession is antiquated," he confided to his journal in June 1832. "In an altered age, we worship in the dead forms of our fathers." Emerson soon resigned from his pulpit—but he never lost the desire to preach. Settling in Concord, Emerson quickly detected the potential in the growing Lyceum movement that enabled thousands of middle- and working-class people to attend lectures and debates on contemporary issues. Opening up intellectual life to more Americans than ever before, the lyceums and the new cultural market hastened the emergence of a new American clerisy, a secular but not yet secularized intelligentsia alongside the Protestant clergy. As a popular lecturer and essayist, Emerson became a celebrity fixture in the antebellum culture industry. He soon acquired the stature of high priest among American intellectuals, dispensing inspiration and counsel for a people increasingly unfettered from old Protestant and republican constraints. Anointing himself an enlightened heir to the Protestant cultural estate, Emerson naturally assumed the roles of prophet and theologian.[14]

Emerson's first post-Christian homily was "Nature," which made him a supernova in the firmament of New England intellectual life. Speaking to the Transcendental Club in Boston in the summer of 1836 near the end of the young republic's most extended period of economic growth, Emerson had good news for his friends, dwelling on the message he'd divined in nature. "All things with which we deal, preach to us," the former Unitarian minister declared. "What is every farm but a mute gospel," he asked, "a sacred emblem" from planting in spring to the snowy somnolence of winter? The farmer was not alone in receiving good news from the silent pulpit of nature: "the sailor, the shepherd, the miner, the merchant . . . have each an experience precisely parallel." What did things reveal when they preached? A universal moral law that lies in "the pith and marrow of every substance, every relation, every process" and "radiates to the circumference." Things possessed this homiletic property because they were more than mere evanescent matter. "In all their boundless changes," Emerson mused, things make "an unceasing reference to spiritual nature." Yet if Mather, Edwards, or other Puritan divines might have agreed about the sacramental character of nature, none of Emerson's predecessors would have dared to assert "I am part or parcel of God."[15] While "Nature" bore witness to the persistence of enchantment, evoking a faith that the earth could still harbor the presence of the holy, the erasure of the line between humanity and divinity would underlie his consecration of capitalism.

Over the next two decades, while building a career as an itinerant specialist in prophetic oratory, Emerson deciphered the economics contained in the silent gospel of nature. With the onset of the panic of 1837 and the ensuing hard times of the 1840s, Emerson denounced the dominion of money that accompanied the expansion of the marketplace. Emerson's essays and journal entries of the time abound with foreboding at the spread of capitalist enterprise. "The trail of the serpent reaches into all the lucrative professions and practices of man," he complained to an audience of mechanics' apprentices in 1841; it introduced a "system of selfishness . . . of distrust, of concealment, of superior keenness, not of giving but of taking advantage." "We eat and drink and wear perjury and fraud in a hundred commodities," he warned in "Man the Reformer." Because they "have not Faith and Hope," he lamented, Americans "rely on the power of a dollar." When Emerson looked beyond America, he saw a similar autocracy of Mammon. Recounting his second trip to England in 1847 in *English Traits* (1856), Emerson marveled at the progress of science and technology but rued "the tyranny of trade" and the inability of the people to "resist and rule the dragon Money."[16]

To slay the dragons of commerce and "Money," Emerson turned to the spiritual power inherent to a true and loving economics. Calling on readers to "learn the meaning of economy," he expounded an enchanted metaphysics of labor, goods, and property. He opened his lesson by asserting that "every man should be open to ecstasy." If "ecstasy" might seem a rather exalted concern for reformers, Emerson countered that the whole purpose of improving conditions and institutions was to make humanity fit for "intercourse with the spiritual world." "Economy is a high, humane office, a sacrament, when its aim is grand." When practiced for the sake of accumulating riches, thrift, Emerson scowled, was nothing but "a baseness"; but when practiced for the sake of "ecstasy," it was "frugality for gods and heroes." The man of ecstasy looked not to the enlargement of his estate but rather to "the prosecution of his love; to the helping of his friend, to the worship of his God." Such a man was a sacramental emissary, "a mediator between the spiritual and the actual world."[17]

Emerson's sacramental economy was also an economy of love. Besides re-vivifying "this great, overgrown, dead Christendom of ours," love "would put a new face on this weary old world in which we dwell as pagans and enemies." Emerson gestured toward an economics of love in "Gifts" (1844), a testament to the splendor of gratuity that offered a glimpse of a world innocent both of avarice and of property, an economy of charity like those being built in the utopian communities of the day. Leavened by "the majesty of love, which is the genius and god of gifts," the universe conducted the most intimate en-counters through a commerce averse to profit. Matter could handle the traffic in love, Emerson thought, as gifts were tokens of a transubstantiation more real than that imagined in theology. "A man's biography is conveyed in his gift," and its acceptance was a "flowing of the giver unto me, correspondent to my flowing into him." "The only gift is a portion of thyself," Emerson in-sisted; "thou must bleed for me." Into what did a giver's blood congeal? "The poet brings his poem; the shepherd, his lamb; the farmer, corn; the miner, a gem; the sailor, coral and shells; the painter, his picture; the girl, a handker-chief of her own sewing." Heedless of the property lines drawn on the earth or around the fearful self, the spirit of gift was at once erotic, artisanal, and transcendent. The economy of gift was a civilization of love, a beatific communism. "All his are mine, all mine his." Unlike gifts, commodities were anonymous substitutes for genuine communion, and their transaction could never be anything but "a cold, lifeless business." Written around the time that he was considering joining the communards at Brook Farm, "Gifts" was Emerson's votive offering to the utopian imagination, an epistle for those who believed it possible to live "the life of Paradise anew."[18]

Yet over the next two decades, Emerson warmed to the "cold, lifeless business" of commodity production and sale. The thaw is perceptible in "Compensation" (1841)—an essay pivotal to Lasch's explication of Emerson's producerist theology, "still another expression," in his words, "of the folk wisdom that condemns every attempt to get something for nothing." Aside from the implicit dismissal from such "folk wisdom" of any hope of grace or mercy—both of which involve getting something for nothing—Emerson's conception of compensation is embedded in a thoroughly capitalist cosmology. In "Compensation," all the world is a market, and everything and everyone merely buyers and sellers in it. "In Nature, nothing can be given, all things are sold." "The doctrine that everything has its price" was, to Emerson, "not less sublime in the columns of a ledger than . . . in all the action and reaction of nature." Praising all the maxims about frugality, diligence, and equivalence that are "hourly preached in all markets and workshops"—"tit for tat; an eye for an eye; a tooth for a tooth; blood for blood; measure for measure; love for love"—Emerson expounded an exemplary morality of exchange value. Over and throughout the universal market reigns a Supreme Accountant, "a third silent party" who superintends "all our bargains" and "makes square the eternal account."[19] Gone is the God who makes His sun to rise on *both* the evil *and* the good.

We could speculate that Emerson's growing fame and income wrought a kinder disposition toward the market, but the reasons for his change of heart toward "cold, lifeless business" are less important than the post-Protestant enchantment toward which he beckoned. Emerson's imprimatur on industrial capitalism stemmed from the cosmology he developed in the decade after leaving the Protestant ministry. He had already declared that the practice of "Economy" was "a high humane office, a sacrament, when its aim is grand." To Emerson, the invisible force that the world revealed was unbounded, divinized power. Beginning in the 1840s, Emerson ascribed sacramental force to this ruthless "power of Commerce," a supernatural current conveying America toward its destiny as "the country of the Future."[20]

Emerson's religion of power arose from the ashes of Protestant Christianity. Since "God builds his temple in the heart on the ruins of churches and religions," he explained in "Worship" (1860), then the decline of Protestantism "need give us no uneasiness." After leaving his pulpit and forsaking Christianity, Emerson embarked on a long spiritual quest, reading voraciously in neo-Platonism, the Hindu scriptures (especially the *Bhagavad-Gita*), English and German philosophical idealism (as interpreted by his friend Carlyle), and the tradition of Christian mysticism from Jakob Boehme to Emmanuel Swedenborg. Eclectic to the point, rather often, of incoherence, Emerson's "transcendentalism" is a masterpiece of syncretism, a mélange of astral pieties squarely in the American pedigree of spiritual bricolage: "New Thought," "mind cure," and "New Age." The universe is a part of "the eternal ONE," as he called it in "The Over-Soul," "an emanation of God," as he asserted in "The Method of Nature." "Everything is an emanation, and from every emanation is a new emanation, and that from which it emanates is an emanation also." This endless procession of emanations shows that change and becoming are the essential principles of being. "There are no fixities in nature," he proclaimed in "Circles." "The universe is fluid and volatile . . . in nature every moment is new."[21]

While Emerson's appeal, then and now, owes much to these wistful platitudes, they obscure the centrality of power and conflict to his view of human life. "Life is a search after power," he stated flatly in "Power" (1860)—a joyless, Hobbesian maxim, it would seem, until we see the metaphysical background. For Emerson, humanity and divinity were aspects of a single reality he dubbed "the ONE." "I am nothing; I see all: the currents of the Universal Being circulate through me; I am part or particle of God." As "emanation" and "transparency" suggest, Emerson's humanism rested on a fundamental denial of our creaturely nature. "Everything divine shares the self-existence of Deity," as he wrote in "The Transcendentalist." "The height, the deity of man is, to be self-sustained, to need no gift, no foreign force." This is certainly "self-reliance," but it is no "theology of producerism"—no acceptance of human finitude, no posture of humility. To be self-sustained is to be self-created—in other words, to be divine. Thus the proprietary "self-reliance" that Emerson championed was rooted in self-divinization, the anointment of the self by the self as its own metaphysical and moral foundation. Yet as Emerson himself asserted, if one's own self is divine, so are all the others—each is "his own world." So when Emerson enjoined his audiences to "live after the infinite Law that is in you," he sanctioned the endless combat of wills that defines the capitalist order. Unlike many of his current progressive admirers, Emerson never hesitated to draw the economic conclusions from his humanism of divinized power. As he pointed out in "The Transcendentalist," the distribution of property illustrated the "laws of being" with "wonderful fidelity of details."[22] If the "laws of being" were those of self-creation, this was, to say the least, a more extravagant claim about capitalist property than any made by the Puritan or evangelical clerisy. More so than Protestant economics, Emerson's theology of power captured the nihilistic energy of capitalism.

This enchantment with power leavened Emerson's exuberant affirmation of the marketplace. With his religion of divinized power in mind, we can see that for Emerson, the tempest of the market reflected deeper, intractable, and beneficent realities. As the economy recovered in the mid-1840s, he hailed the vigorous renewal of trade and manufacturing. In "Wealth"—his most popular and oft-reprinted lecture, first delivered in the early 1850s—he applauded the mercenary spirit of capitalist production and commerce. Now, far from being "a cold, lifeless business" that drowned love in the icy waters of egotistical calculation, commodity exchange was a vital feature of the world's metaphysical architecture. "The laws of nature play through trade, as a toy-battery exhibits the effects of electricity." The philosopher of gifts now looked to money as a touchstone of the human condition. "The coin," Emerson noted, "is a delicate barometer of civil, social, and moral changes," with an especially pronounced "susceptibility to metaphysical changes." It was "the finest barometer of social storms, and announces revolutions." Hallowing pecuniary reason, Emerson revered the patristic texts of capitalist economics, echoing the evangelical economists who believed that the dismal science was a canon of revelation. "Political Economy," he declared in "Wealth," "is as good a book wherein to read the life of man . . . as any Bible which has come down to us." Rather than inveigh against the wreckage wrought in the maelstrom of the marketplace, Emerson thought laissez-faire was inscribed in the ontological composition of the cosmos. Recycling his views in "Compensation," Emerson assured his readers that "the counting-house maxims liberally expounded are laws of the Universe. The merchant's economy is a coarse symbol of the soul's economy."[23]

In Emerson's new "soul's economy," both the Good Book and Political Economy denied any spiritual grandeur to poverty; "men of sense esteem wealth," Emerson preached, for "power is what they want." Though "the pulpit and the press have many commonplaces denouncing the thirst for wealth," if we took these moralists seriously and lived lives of penurious holiness, they would soon "rush to rekindle at all hazards this love of power in people, lest civilization be undone." Besides, it was an irrevocable law of the soul's economy that "each man feed himself," inflicting "pain and insult" on himself and others "until he has fought his way to his own loaf." Condemning the "low political economy" of tariffs and embargoes in "Worship" (1860), he rehearsed the competitive humanism of classical economics: "the way to conquer a foreign artisan, is, not to kill him, but to beat his work." Once fallen competitors were beaten, their care and sustenance were none of our concern. "Are they *my* poor?" Emerson asked with a tart annoyance in "Self-Reliance."[24]

The Sage of Concord also echoed the sado-moralism of British evangelical economists. "Debt, grinding debt, whose iron face the widow, the orphan, and the sons of genius fear and hate . . . is a preceptor whose lessons cannot be foregone, and is needed most by those who suffer from it most." Dickens's Gradgrind could not have said it so deftly. Like evangelicals, Emerson believed that the logic of business could be tempered, but not altered, by love. "Do you complain of the laws of Property?" he asked the casualties of the market. "Let into it the new and renewing principle of love, and property will be universality." This infusion of capitalist property by "love" made socialism as unnecessary as it was pernicious. Reflecting on the revolutions in France in 1848, Emerson harrumphed like a stodgy bourgeois that the cessation of profit, rent, and interest would "make all men idle and immoral." Most of the poor, he added for good measure, "have made themselves so," and under socialism would "only prove a burden on the state."[25]

Unlocked by adherence to the competitive "laws of Property," magical possibilities for power resided in commercial and manufacturing energies—embodied, for Emerson, in the prolific productive capacities of industrial technology. "Machinery and Transcendentalism agree well," he had mused in his journal in 1843. "Stage-Coach and Railroad are bursting the old legislation like green withes." Notarizing this agreement in "The Young American" (1844), Emerson admonished his compatriots to "conspire with the new works of new days." This venal and destructive conspiracy with the new looked forward to an age of filial abundance and love. Admiring "the rage for road-building," Emerson fastened on "railroad iron" as an enchanting "magician's rod," conjuring communities at the junctions of trade more quickly than farmers grew crops. The Sage of Concord sensed that even greater progress would depend on corporate enterprise. Noting the incipient efforts "to plant corn, and to bake bread by companies," Emerson hailed "the movement which made the joint-stock companies for manufacture, mining, insurance, [and] banking." "Founded in labor and in love," the nascent corporations emerged from the same desire for communion that animated Brook Farm and other utopian ventures.[26] For Emerson—as for the evangelical economists and for the rising clerisy of capital—commercial expansion and industrial might were constructing a beloved community.

With its plentiful resources and promethean will, America was the vanguard of humanity. "Here, here in America, is the home of man." Enchanted and directed by "a sublime and friendly Destiny," Americans marched "under Divine leading, going forth to receive and inhabit their patrimony." Like Henry Luce a little less than a century later, Emerson chastised leaders who slept or straggled in the service of Destiny. Lamenting the absence of "a high national feeling" among ministers, journalists, and politicians, Emerson looked to a new intelligentsia for a culture of manifest destiny. "Who should lead the leaders, but the Young American." Emerson called upon a rising clerisy—prototypes of Whitman's divine literati—to affirm the promise of the market. "Trade planted America," he stipulated, and the cultivation of mercantile and industrial progress would usher in "a new and more excellent social state than history has ever recorded." Speaking at the Smithsonian in January 1862 before President Abraham Lincoln and other Washington notables, Emerson bestowed the mandate of heaven on American civilization. Echoing the Puritans and their evangelical heirs, Emerson declared to the Union elite that "our whole history appears to be a last effort of Divine Providence in behalf of the human race."[27]

If "The Young American" is a brash epistle of capitalist millennialism, it also exhibits the ontology of violence and competitive humanism. An essential text in the canon of American imperial ambition, Emerson's tale of

America is also a grim Malthusian comedy. "Only what is inevitable interests us," he pontificated, "and it turns out that love and good are inevitable, and in the course of things." Yet the course of love and goodness is strewn with mangled souls and bodies; struggle, failure, and death are the sacred emblems of Nature, now "infused" with the Genius or Destiny of American enterprise. Steeling his audience against the cries of the weak or unfortunate, Emerson observed that "this Genius, or Destiny, is of the sternest administration." With "a grinding economy," it "crushed and straitened" we "poor particulars," subjecting all to the harsh and unforgiving millage of remorseless, divinized power. Surveying the Malthusian sublime, Emerson approved its "cruel kindness, serving the whole even to the ruin of the member." Emerson warned that no rain of mercy should be allowed to fall on this carnage; however brutal and tragic, the Genius of capitalist liturgy required its quotient of human sacrifice. Subverting our relief laws, Malthus's "principle of population is always reducing wages to the lowest pittance on which human life can be sustained." Charity only worked to preserve the lives of the undeserving losers. "The law of self-preservation is surer than any legislation can be." Draped in roseate beauty, the pith and marrow of the soul's economy turned out to be the spirit of Hobbes. "Our condition is like that of the poor wolves," wrote the theologian of "compensation." "If one of the flock wound himself, or so much as limp, the rest eat him up incontinently."[28]

Emerson provides a genteel instruction in the enchanting mendacity of power. It's not surprising that Nietzsche—another theologian of power—was one of Emerson's fondest admirers. Indeed, Emerson is the American Nietzsche, conferring divinity on remorseless power and on the self that finds freedom in its service. If Emerson summoned Americans to "build altars to the Beautiful Necessity," the pitiless and austere freedom of the market held his compatriot's love of fate.[29] His divinization of capitalist power would resound through the next two American centuries: in the nostrums of philosopher-businesspeople, in the casuistry of management writers, in the pieties of cheerfully merciless executives, journalists, and libertarians. Though appealing to the deepest human desire for communion with divinity, Emerson's promise of freedom in the "soul's economy" was a ruse of servitude to Mammon.

Prisoners of King Cotton—Mammon's overseer in the antebellum South— slaves bore the hardest and most horrific burden of Emerson's "grinding economy." Yet they also bore the most arduous and compelling witness against the mercenary beast, especially in a lineage of rebellion that called on the spirits of their sacred cosmos. More populous, lively, and intrepid than Transcendentalism or the evangelical market cosmology, the universe of slave religion was a motley enclave of sacramental imagination and its abiding revolutionary potential. A plebeian form of Romanticism, the enchanted world of the slaves both enabled them to fathom the depth of atrocity in slavery and to envision the possibility of deliverance from a world enchained to the spirit of Mammon.

Despite what Jon Butler has called the "African spiritual holocaust"—the fragmentation of tribal beliefs and practices in the African diaspora to the South—by the eve of the Civil War, slave religion had coalesced into a compound of vestigial West African enchantment and Baptist or Methodist Christianity. Conjuring, divination, spirit possession, and folk medicine blended with faith in Christ's amazing grace; charms, beads, bones, and talismans complemented hymns, crosses, and sermons in African-American communion with divinity. Barred from or surveilled in the churches controlled by their anxiously reverent owners, slaves had their own sacred spaces—cabin rooms, "prayin' grounds," and "hush harbors"—while the preacher who enjoined submission shared authority with witches, sorcerers, and conjurers. White evangelicals often complained of the slaves' effervescent and unbecoming enthusiasm, and rued the spiritual miscegenation of African sacramentality and Protestant orthodoxy. After seeing "actual negro dancing" at a service—the slaves cavorted, he carped, in the "merry chorus-manner of . . . the husking-frolic method"—one scandalized Methodist condemned such "gross perversions of true religion." Author of one of the South's most popular evangelical catechisms, Charles C. Jones complained often of the slaves' stubbornly creative syncretism. Although the Gospel had made inroads in the quarters, "paganism" persisted among slaves in Georgia, Jones lamented, in "second-sight, in apparitions, charms, witchcraft, and in a kind of irresistible Satanic influence." In part, this admixture stemmed from the long reluctance of the masters to inculcate Christianity in their slaves; although the Gospel was usually recommended as an effective bromide for insurrectionary impulses, masters knew that it could also act as an unpredictable catalyst for "sauciness" or sedition. But the slaves' religious bricolage also reflected a desire for autonomy and a resistance to the discipline and degradation imposed by planters as a condition of their own servility to the market.[30]

Slaves could be acutely aware of evangelical hypocrisy and enthrallment to pecuniary value. In an 1821 letter to one white parson, a Georgia slave asserted that the reverend faced the whites and not the blacks when preaching "because they give you money," and reminded him that "we are the very persons that labor for this money." Indeed, he continued, "money appears to be the object weare carid to market and sold a heathen or christian." "If the question was put, did you not sel a christian what would be the answer," he inquired. "I cant tell you what he was gave me my price that's all was interested in." Harriet Jacobs recalled that one North Carolina clergyman, "a sort of god among the slaveholders," left his congregation to go "where money was more abundant." One of her earliest religious instructors, a Methodist town constable, also beat his black brothers and sisters at the public whipping post; he was "ready to perform that Christian office for fifty cents." Jacobs also remembered that as one particularly avaricious slaveholder died, he cried that he was "going to hell; bury my money with me." Solomon Northup wrote that his owner Edwin Epps—a man who remarked about the "virtue and power in money"—could have watched his slaves "burned to ashes over a slow fire, or gnawed to death by dogs, if it only brought him profit." Although Frederick Douglass eventually espoused a liberal, rationalist Protestantism, his denunciations of the "hypocritical Christianity of this land" were rooted in the slaves' perception of white evangelical enchantment by Mammon. "Corrupt, slave-holding, women-whipping, [and] cradle-plundering," southern white Christianity perpetuated these evils enveloped in a mercenary sublime. In his autobiography, Douglass described slave merchants as "devils dressed in angels robes" and the auctions themselves as "hell presenting the semblance of paradise."[31]

Unbelievers in the cult of capital accumulation that poisoned the souls of the masters, the slaves rejected and fought the new industrial rituals imposed by their overseers. They imagined a world liberated from servitude to the imperatives of the cotton empire. Subjected to the time-and-work rhythms decreed in the regime of planation management, the slaves did all they could to retard or circumvent the Protestant work ethic, because God and the spirits did not follow any schedules; as one ex-slave recounted God's message to him, "'I am a time-God. Behold I work after the counsel of my own will and in due time I will visit whomsoever I will.'" Slaves believed they could follow the counsel of their wills in "heaven," "Canaan," or "the Promised Land," the kingdom of freedom so often rhapsodized in their spirituals. But as Eugene Genovese, Lawrence Levine, and Albert Raboteau have contended, the slaves' invocation of heaven was not escapist or compensatory. Like the medieval sacramental imagination, the slaves' cosmology denied any imper-meable, depoliticizing boundary between earth and heaven, and so their hope for paradise was political precisely because it was religious. White clergy suspected as much. Preaching about the Exodus to a group of slaves in 1862, one Methodist preacher in Charleston was mortified by the chasm between his own interpretation of the story and that of his captive audience. To the preacher, Exodus was a "spiritual" tale about "relief from the servi-tude of sin"; but his congregation took it "literally in the good time coming, which of course could not but make their ebony complexion attractive, very." Perhaps emboldened by the commencement of the Civil War a year before the preacher's sermon, the slaves' herald of a "good time coming" was terrestrial as well as spiritual. So if, as W. E. B. Du Bois wrote, the spirituals expressed "a faith in the ultimate justice of things," they did so because the slaves knew that justice was built into the very nature of the cosmos, and that slavery embodied a perversion of that order.[32] (Martin Luther King, Jr., re-hearsed the wisdom of the slaves when he asserted that the moral arc of the universe bent toward justice.)

As the most renowned slave rebellions demonstrated, the enchanted world of antebellum African-Americans could reveal moral and metaphysical evil with incisive and terrifying vividness. Two of the insurgencies—Gabriel's Rebellion and the Vesey Conspiracy—testified to the political potential residing in the slaves' religious syncretism. Gabriel Prosser's foiled revolt in Richmond, Virginia, in 1800 originated in slave "preachings" or religious meetings where Gabriel and his brother Martin, himself a preacher, recruited for and planned the insurrection. Declaring that "their cause was similar to the Israelites," Martin and Gabriel would engage their coconspirators in long discussions over biblical exegesis. Though they relied primarily on the Lord, the Prossers did not turn away the African spirits; one conspirator suggested contacting slaves who knew how to "deal with Witches and Wizards." Den-

mark Vesey's thwarted rebellion in Charleston in 1822 was similarly ecumenical in inspiration. "All his religious remarks were mingled with
slavery," one witness at his trial testified; two conspirators were religious instructors in Charleston's African Methodist Episcopal Church. One of
Vesey's associates, "Gullah Jack" Pritchard, was a member of the church and
a respected conjurer who allegedly told the rebels that they would be impervious to bullets if they put a crab-claw in their mouths after eating parched
corn and groundnuts.[33]

But the most visionary and unsettling document of rebellious slaves was
Nat Turner's confession, given after the failure of the bloody uprising in
Southampton, Virginia, in 1831. Although doubts persist about the reliability
of Thomas R. Gray, the attorney who was Turner's interrogator, the spiritual
odyssey he recounts seems too bizarre for him to have fabricated. Although
he professed at one point that he could not decide whether Turner was insane or playing the lunatic, Gray belittled his ill-fated interlocutor, dismissing
him as a "gloomy fanatic . . . revolving in the recesses of his own dark, bewildered, and overwrought mind . . . endeavoring to grapple with things beyond its reach."[34] Precisely because Gray found it unlikely that a slave could
"grapple with things beyond [his] reach," his appalled condescension to
Turner's testimony suggests that his report is dependable. And besides, in all
their marvelous and terrible grandeur, Turner's confessions reflect the sacramental and eschatological fervor of slave cosmology.

Like those of Augustine, Turner's confessions recount a life story: his preternatural boyhood, "revelations" in the 1820s, and a call to visit divine retribution on slaveholders and their families. At the age of three or four, he told
Gray, he described an incident that had occurred long before with such ex-
actitude that his parents considered him "a prophet, as the Lord had shewn
me things that happened before my birth." Blessed with a quick and prodigious intelligence, Turner not only learned to read but also to develop a kind
of prescience; whenever he looked into a book, he would see "many things
that the fertility of my own imagination had depicted to me before." As
he grew up, his "superior judgment . . . perfected by Divine Inspiration"
confirmed him in a sense of some exalted destiny, and so he began to avoid
others, "wrapped myself in mystery," and devoted himself to fasting and
prayer. In or around 1821, a spirit told him to "seek ye the kingdom of

Heaven"—"the Spirit," he clarified to Gray, "that spoke to the prophets in former days"—and four years later, Turner received "revelations" that unveiled, not only the architecture of the cosmos, but the true magnitude of slavery's horror. The Spirit opened the doors of Turner's perception, revealing "the knowledge of the elements, the revolution of the planets, the operation of tides, and changes of the seasons." He saw "white spirits and black spirits engaged in battle, and the sun was darkened—the thunder rolled in the Heavens, and blood flowed in streams." Laboring one day in a field, he found "drops of blood on the corn as though it were dew from heaven"; shortly thereafter, he discovered "hieroglyphic characters, and numbers" on the leaves of trees in a nearby forest. On May 12, 1828, the Spirit warned Turner that "the Serpent was loosened" and enjoined him to take on the yoke of Christ, for "the time was fast approaching when the first should be last and the last should be first." On a sign from heaven, he began to plot the insurgency, and on August 22, 1831, he and his fellow rebels launched their grisly and disastrous insurrection.[35]

"Do you not find yourself mistaken now?" Gray asked with the icy derision of a Pilate; "Was not Christ crucified?" Turner replied to his undoubtedly nonplussed interrogator.[36] Gray thought the prisoner deluded, but Turner's confession was more penetrating and veracious than all the grandiloquence of an Emerson. Supercharged with wonders, signs, and premonitions, Turner's narrative conveyed an account of a world of absolute ontological transparency, in which the material world possessed an emblematic, sacramental corporeality. Seeing no barrier between the world of divinity and that of human affairs, Turner was anything but "bewildered and overwrought"; he discerned the malevolence of slavery with perfectly lucid precision and judgment. The turbulence of race and class struggle on earth reverberating throughout the heavens; corn bearing the marks of violence that shed the blood of slaves and therefore of Christ; a beatific overturning of the powers and principalities that perverted the order of creation—Turner's revelations raised the iniquity of slavery to the level of cosmic outrage. They recalled the epiphanies of medieval millenarians, Gerard Winstanley, and the Romantic adversaries of Mammon.

Turner's affidavit of transcendent barbarism and redemption was perhaps the most powerful and disturbing testimony of slave Romanticism. Delivered by the poorest of Emerson's "poor particulars" crushed by the "grinding economy," it captured the truth about the evil of slavery—as well as the industrial capitalism whose growth depended on its bloodstained products—and did so without any erudition in political economy. The sacramental theology of the slaves—inhabitants of an enchanted world bereft of any secular, immanent frame—bore the keenest critique of the enchantments of Mammon before the Civil War.

# PART THREE

## The Mystical Body of Business: The Corporate Reconstruction of Capitalist Enchantment, 1870–1920

LOOKING BACK ON the disastrous year of 1893, Henry Adams recalled that "something new and curious was about to happen to the world." Triggered by the collapse of railroad companies made vulnerable by overspeculation, the ensuing financial panic eventually led to a four-year depression—the second major slump since the Civil War, and the worst in the nation's history. Thousands of businesses failed; thousands of farms were foreclosed; hundreds of thousands of workers lost their jobs, and many lost their homes. Faithful to the evangelical dispensation, ministers, editors, and public officials counseled endurance and prayer. But as savings ran out, bread lines lengthened, and mites of charity dwindled, ever fewer Americans saw the hand of God in squalor and starvation. Populist agitation had already been rising; anarchism and socialism gained strength in the cities; the bloody Homestead strike of 1892 now seemed a dress rehearsal for Armageddon. By the spring of 1894, "Coxey's Army" of unemployed, desperate men was marching on Washington, demanding jobs and public works; soon after, the Pullmann strike paralyzed railways in the West and the industrial North. The senescence of the old dispensation was apparent, even to many business leaders.[1]

Adams had excellent personal reasons for thinking the old order decrepit: his distinguished family almost lost its fortune in the panic and was saved from ruin only by the monetary wizardry of the bankers he loathed. After the storm had passed, Adams traveled to the World's Fair in Chicago. Featuring an array of bazaars, temples, amusements, and machines, the World's Columbian Exposition was a Vanity Fair of white modernity, the latest Victorian display of industrial power and imperial hegemony. In the enormous Machinery Hall, Adams "lingered long among the dynamos, for they were new, and they gave to history a new phase." In the presence of the Westinghouse generators, he admitted to himself that his cranky dislike for "bankers and capitalistic society" now felt "antiquated"; he had "known for years that he must accept the regime." Desperate to preserve what was left of their fortunes, the old guard had coalesced behind the corporate order—"capitalistic, centralizing, and mechanical"—and "had joined the banks to force submission." If Adams was wrong to fear for his fellow patricians—their concordat with finance and industrial capital ensured the persistence of the old regime—he had no doubt that corporate business was the indomitable vanguard of modern America. "The whole mechanical consolidation of force," he concluded, had spawned firms "capable of controlling the new energies that America adored."[2]

Americans "adored" corporate capitalism because, as Adams realized, the new economy was a new regime of enchantment. Seven years after the Chicago World's Fair, Adams experienced another epiphany at the Exposition Universelle in Paris, another *tableau vivant* of progress. Wandering again among the dynamos, he mused, with a blend of marvel and horror, that "man had translated himself into a new universe which had no common scale of measurement with the old." Adams now saw the dynamo not only as a vehicle of corporate power but as a "symbol of infinity." "Power seemed to have outgrown its servitude"; the sorcery had overwhelmed the sorcerer. Now "an occult mechanism," industrial technology was the modern liturgical system of corporate society; and like worshippers of any divinity, "one began to pray to it; inherited instinct taught the natural expression of man before silent and infinite force." Though it represented power rather than love, abundance rather than sacrifice, the dynamo exerted "a moral force much as the early Christians felt the Cross." Adams came to think that the new X-rays were even more beguiling and portentous. Bearing "a revelation of mysterious energy," they manifested what medieval theologians would have called "immediate modes of the divine substance."[3]

Adams stood at a dawn of the idols; the trusts and corporations had vanquished Christianity and established their own devotions. Beckoning to a beatific vision of plenty, corporate science and technology had supplanted theology and philosophy with "prosperity never before imagined, power never yet wielded by man, speed never reached by anything but a meteor." Adams likened the demise of the old enchantment to the twilight of classical antiquity. Adept in the increasingly irrelevant disciplines of orthodox Christianity, the educated man of 1900 stood "as bewildered and helpless, as in the fourth century, a priest of Isis before the Cross of Christ."[4] Christ would follow the pagan gods into the warehouse of divinities, and the Dynamo would take his place. If Adams was right, then the dynamo really was an occult mechanism, a graven image of capitalist modernity. And as the sponsors of industrial fetishism, the corporations and trusts were the new ecclesia, successors to the Protestant regime.

Yet others were buoyant at the prospect of a new dispensation of capitalist enchantment. In *Crowds: A Moving-Picture of Democracy* (1913), Gerald Stanley Lee—a popular journalist and lecturer who was also an ordained Congregationalist minister—provided a "spiritual census of modern civilization." Surveying the customers in Marshall Fields, Wanamaker's, and Woolworth's, Lee proclaimed the great department stores "the new steeples of the business world." "Measuring out their souls before God in dress goods, shoes, hats, boas, silk, and bread and butter," the customers were worshippers in "the religion of business." (Recalling his visit to the United States, the British historian G. Lowes Dickinson also remarked on "the religion of business.") But the reverend refrained from delivering a homily about greed and materialism; the "religion of business," he immediately added, was that of "the real and daily things."[5]

Lee lavished praise on the temples of production as well as the chapels of commerce. "There is no reason why a factory, if enough soul is poured in with the money at the top, should not be as spiritual as a church," he wrote in *Inspired Millionaires* (1908). Earlier, listening to *The Voice of the Machines* (1906), Lee, like Adams, had determined that "machinery . . . is an expression of the soul"; technology embodied a spiritual essence, "the god in the body of the man." "Every new invention is a spiritual masterpiece." Corporations, Lee insisted, had souls, and "the soul must be as supreme in business as it is in everything else." The state of the corporate soul depended on its management, the episcopal elite of the new capitalism. "The controlling factor, the strategic position in industry . . . belongs to the superintendent, the man who has the ideas, the great faith of the business—who is the soul of the business." Erasing the distinction between market valuation and spiritual discernment, Lee heralded the day when an executive's compensation should "approximate the actual market value a soul has, in this modern business world."[6]

Others expressed the same pecuniary enchantment in the post-Christian tones of Emerson. Take, for example, Orison Swett Marden, one of the most prominent exponents of "New Thought," descendant of Transcendentalism and precursor of New Age spirituality. A self-made hotel magnate, Marden was almost ruined by the depression of 1893. Managing to hold on to a hotel in Chicago, he devoted the rest of his life to writing advice for success in business. In more than a dozen books and in his magazine *Success,* Marden expounded a blend of metaphysical sublimity, personal gratification, and old-fashioned bourgeois moralism. While New Thought has been identified as a form of "positive thinking," the popularity of Marden and other writers also suggests the persistence of enchantment in the megalithic structures of corporate capitalism. When Marden urged his readers to visualize "the stream of plenty, of unlimited opulence," he evoked a beatific vision in the enchanting cadence of consumer extravagance. To Marden, the acquisition of goods and money is clearly a form of sacramental desire. "Every cell is in the closest touch with the Divine force"; once we know our proximity to this force, we achieve "conscious union with the Divine," a oneness with the "great creative, sustaining principle of the universe." The drive for success was a "divine injunction to be perfect, even as He is perfect"; success was the fruition of our "God-self." This was the gospel according to Emerson. And Marden (who claimed the Sage of Concord as a personal hero) updated Transcendentalist metaphysics and ethics in the new rhetoric of corporate business. The "God-self" was also a "happiness-machine," a dynamo of divinity every bit as powerful as Adams's Westinghouse generator. Still, despite the plenitude provided by the Divine, nature remained a capitalist, "a great one-price storekeeper who hands out what we ask for if we pay the price": struggle and proficiency in "scientific methods, the practical common-sense methods . . . businesslike efficiency methods."[7] The only possible evidence of oneness with divinity was success in the market, measured in terms of monetary metaphysics and scientific management.

Adams, Lee, and Marden wrote while Max Weber was declaring "the dis-enchantment of the world"; but the blueblood, the minister, and the herald of New Divinity were arguably more discerning, for all three realized that the new corporate order was an unprecedented form of enchantment. A compelling totem of industrial might, the Dynamo appeared in the midst of the corporate reconstruction of American capitalism. Hallowed by the evan-gelical dispensation and demolished by the market it sanctioned, the en-semble of proprietary dogmas collapsed before the onslaught of corporate industry. Like the deities vanquished by Catholic conquistadores, Calvinist saints, and evangelical pioneers, the God of the Protestant proprietors no longer seemed capable of protecting his people; the corporate metamor-phosis of American business provoked a crisis of capitalist enchantment. If, as Jackson Lears has contended, Americans living in the shadow of the Civil War were searching for "regeneration"—a "rebirth that was variously spiritual, moral, and physical"—many were longing to amend or annul the covenant theology of capitalism. Divinity did not disappear among the skyscrapers, dynamos, and stopwatches. Rather, its ways were reinterpreted by a corporate intelligentsia of economists, journalists, architects, management writers, and advertisers—the point men in the corporate reconstruction of capitalist enchantment.[8]

Though demonized by its opponents as a godless monstrosity, the "soulful corporation" replaced the proprietor as the center of the soul's economy. The philosophy of corporate enchantment appeared most clearly in manage-ment theory, usually considered the colorless quintessence of bureaucratic rationality. Epitomized in Frederick W. Taylor and the acolytes of "scientific management," early management theory was a mechanization of commu-nion, a professional reconstruction of charisma. Meanwhile, architects, ad-vertisers, and other professional artists recast the visual enchantments of capitalism. Fighting to establish themselves as fine artists, they attempted not only to embellish the commodity but also to kindle and impress what Maxfield Parrish called "the spirit of the thing" on the popular imagination. At the same time, "corporate liberalism" replaced the free-market supersti-tions of evangelical enchantment with a new conception of political economy: "modern communion," in Walter Lippmann's words, a religious surrogate for secular Progressives.

# 7

# God Gave Me My Money

## The Incorporation of America and the Persistence of Evangelical Enchantment

IN THE YEARS BETWEEN Reconstruction and the end of World War I, the modern corporation supplanted the small proprietorship as the center of the nation's political economy. Especially from 1890 to 1916, and reaching a crescendo in the years between 1897 and 1903, leading bankers, investors, and industrialists orchestrated the consolidation of enterprises across the entire range of US capitalism, from sugar, tobacco, paper, and petroleum to metals, coal, machinery, and railways. The pace of combination was swift, and its magnitude was gargantuan. By 1899, corporations comprised one-eighth of all manufacturing firms but employed almost two-thirds of all workers in the manufacturing sector; just six years later, they made up almost a quarter of all manufacturing establishments and employed nearly three-quarters of all wage earners in the sector. Corporate consolidation was enabled by favorable changes in jurisprudence and statutory law. In its 1886 *Santa Clara* decision, the Supreme Court bestowed on corporations the rights and privileges of natural persons under the Fifth and Fourteenth Amendments. Later, corporate personhood was ratified in the provisions of the Sherman Antitrust Act of 1890. In the Standard Oil case of 1911, the Court's "rule of reason" interpretation of the Sherman Act put a judicial imprimatur on corporate concentration. With the establishment of the Federal Reserve System in 1913, and with the passage in 1914 of the Federal Trade Commission Act and the Clayton Antitrust Act, the main legal, regulatory, and financial architecture of corporate consolidation was complete. The Invisible Hand of the evangelical dispensation was replaced by the visible hands of managers, administrators, technicians, and other experts, united in an anticompetitive consensus. In those sectors still embroiled in the old-fashioned competitive ethos, smaller firms scrambled, or serviced the titans. David now worked for Goliath.[1]

The modern corporation marked a Copernican revolution in the cosmology of American capitalism, triggering a protracted conflict over the nature and destiny of American democracy. By separating ownership and effective control of the enterprise, the corporate form broke the traditional link between property and productive labor. By appropriating the craft knowledge and organizational prowess once possessed by artisan-proprietors, corporate managers and technical professionals—the "professional-managerial class"—decreed the divorce of mental and manual labor. Since the evangelical ancien regime tied citizenship to mastery of property, the prospect of a large and permanent proletariat seemed to augur the dissolution of the covenant and the end of the evangelical "soul's economy." At the same time, what Alan Trachtenberg dubbed "the incorporation of America" set off a contest over the meaning of modernity. Much of the cultural turbulence of the era stemmed from the demise of evangelical dispensation. The transformation of the independent male proprietor into a waged or salaried worker, together with the exodus of women from the household into the wage labor force, precipitated the sexual revolution that unsettled evangelical conventions of gender, sexual conduct, and reproduction. Feminism emerged from the collapse of the evangelical patriarch's estate. Evangelical religious culture reeled under the demographic assault of Jewish and Catholic immigrants, imported as low-cost labor to feed the mills of the Protestant covenant. And as evangelical theology waned, liberal Protestant leaders blessed the scientific knowledge and professional expertise essential to corporate business. In the wake of evangelical hegemony came a new consumer culture, disseminating visions of being in the world at odds with the ole-time gospel: advertising; marketing; museums; motion pictures; the popular, resplendent venues of metropolitan commerce and entertainment.[2] Corporate capitalism seemed to be enabling Americans to forsake the Puritan-evangelical covenant.

Historians have quarreled over the meaning of the incorporation of America. Did the demise of proprietary capitalism eviscerate liberal democracy, leaving us with only its hollow forms—or did it portend a consummation of democracy, embracing the Whitmanesque multitudes? Did consumer culture offer Americans the promise of liberation from skinflint Protestant strictures—or is it a gilded distraction from our corporate indenture, a new, more pleasant, "therapeutic" servility to advertising, marketing, and professional authority? Did corporate enterprise enable the first arduous steps toward freedom from possessive individualism—or did it merely fashion a new social form for accumulation and its discontents? Was it, as James Livingston describes the alternatives, "the last act of a bitter tragedy" or "the first act in an unfinished comedy?"[3]

We should reject this Manichean framework; the incorporation of America was a tragicomic blend of civilization and barbarism. We should also dispute the notion that the corporation has been a major sponsor of "disenchantment." With the coming of corporate society (so the story goes), the sacred Protestant canopy of capitalism collapsed, to be replaced by a secular firmament of cultural and political authority—managerial, professional, technical, and scientific. As William Leach contends, the new corporate commercial culture "dropped the older religious dimension." In a similarly stark fashion, Lears maintains that the postbellum era witnessed a "transition to secular and corporate modes of modern culture"; the nascent America of incorporation bore "a secularizing culture, where larger frameworks of meaning were fading." As the moral and metaphysical vernacular of Protestant producerism became unintelligible, the idiom of managerial and professional expertise helped "redefine the old republican vision of the public good in corporate and technocratic terms." Meanwhile, appeals to secular expertise merged with calls for virility and imperial adventure to galvanize the "regeneration" of the white Protestant establishment. Thus, corporate domination fostered and ratified the disenchantment of American culture.[4]

To be sure, the inherited frameworks of meaning were fading. Traditional Protestantism plays little, if any, role in the popular tales of pluck and success by Horatio Alger, Jr., the postbellum laureate of self-improvement. Unlike Timothy Shay Arthur, Alger never assigned God a prominent role in his tales. When Walter Conrad, hero of *Strive and Succeed* (1872), thanks God "for having so ordered events as to lead to [his] good fortune," his gratitude to Providence is rare for a character among Alger's dramatis personae of winners. More sensitive literary observers such as William Dean Howells feared that God was a victim of industrial progress. Like Basil March, the protagonist of *A Hazard of New Fortunes* (1890), Howells glimpsed a "lawless, godless world" in the maelstrom of urban industrialization. Yet Howells could also hint at the spiritual residue of the old regime. In *The Rise of Silas Lapham* (1885), Howells's comedy of manners and social mobility, the eponymous protagonist, a paint manufacturer, assesses the mysterious value of his product. "I believe in my paint," Lapham says. "I believe it's a blessing to the world. I mix it with *Faith,* and after that I grind it up with the best quality of boiled linseed oil that money will buy."[5] Lapham's paint is a proprietary enchantment, a material substance leavened with the spirit of the entrepreneurial believer.

With varying degrees of discretion, some business titans violated the canons of Protestant orthodoxy. Encouraged by his friend Victoria Woodhull, the flamboyant advocate of free love and spiritualism, railroad magnate Cornelius Vanderbilt attended séances where the dear departed offered stock tips. J. P. Morgan—an Episcopal vestryman—toyed with the occult and astrological charts. Andrew Carnegie considered clergy of all persuasions a league of mountebanks; organized religion, he once said, was "clap-trap." After reading the evolutionary philosophy of Herbert Spencer, Carnegie "got rid of theology and the supernatural," he recalled in his autobiography, and "found the truth of evolution." Yet Carnegie clung to his own superstitions. Perhaps most telling was his memory of an episode from his early days in business, recounted in the spring of 1896 for *Youth's Companion,* a popular weekly aimed at children and young adults that featured sentimental fiction, inspirational tales, and evangelical piety. After receiving his first dividend check—for five dollars, from a railroad company—Carnegie brandished it in front of his friends. "None of us had ever received anything but from toil," he recalled; "a return from capital was something strange and new." Carnegie and his companions marveled at "how money could make money, how, without any attention from me, this mysterious golden visitor should come."[6] Capital was a kind of magic, conjuring riches without labor, perseverance, or even concentration. Contemptuous of traditional religion, Carnegie believed—or at least traded on belief—in the mercenary sorcery of capital.

Still, even as corporations undermined and remade the foundations of American capitalism, the symbolic universe of the evangelical dispensation did not simply disappear. Rather than forsake the mythology of evangelical economics, many Americans adapted it to the new conditions of capital accumulation. The nascent corporate order was dressed in the costume of the proprietor, and Americans gave the starring roles in the drama to a cast of promethean heroes and villains, putting faces on the impersonal furies of consolidation: Carnegie, Rockefeller, Morgan, "robber barons," "titans," or "captains of industry." Faced with the inexorable crumbling of the evangelical capitalist cosmos, many in the business intelligentsia redoubled their devotion to orthodoxy.

The virtues of the godly entrepreneur were extolled by the business clerisy, who continued to teach the metaphysical principles of the laissez-faire cosmology. In textbooks, journals, and middle-class periodicals, prewar economics put the mandate of heaven on the fortunes amassed in the new capitalism. Epitomized by Arthur T. Hadley of Yale and Amasa Walker of Amherst, the professors of economics affirmed the capitalist ways of God to humanity. "Science accepts our Lord's method," as W. D. Wilson of Cornell pontificated; the discipline of economics traces the "footsteps of providential intelligence," as Arthur Latham Perry intoned. Confronted by restive industrial workers, postbellum economists displayed less cheer than their clerical predecessors; they drew more heavily on the Protestant-Malthusian lineage of sanctimonious cruelty. With his signature relish for severity, William Graham Sumner of Yale observed that "before the tribunal of nature"—convened from before time by the Almighty—"a man has no more right to life than a rattlesnake." "The Lord maketh the selfishness of man to work for the material welfare of his kind," proclaimed Edward Atkinson, cotton manufacturer and popular economist.[7]

The theology of evangelical laissez-faire remained vibrant among businesspeople and their apologists. God still strode through the boss's office as gracefully as He'd walked through Eden—"a partner in every business transaction," as one fortunate businessman asserted. Stephen Merritt, a flourishing New York undertaker, bragged of his "co-partnership" with Yahweh, a venture that produced "a history of wonders in my business affairs." Henry J. Latham, a prosperous manufacturer, observed that after his conversion, "mistakes and accidents which at first seemed disastrous resulted to [his] advantage." "Some One," Latham concluded, was "silently guiding and guarding" these apparently fortuitous events. Alexander S. Bacon, a prominent attorney, claimed that "God furnishes the capital and directs the counsels" of every successful enterprise. The Almighty's omnipotence and versatility extended into every branch of commercial activity. As a Brooklyn merchant averred, "the Lord is my Banker, my Insurer, my Deliverer, my Patron, and my Blessed Guardian of temporal things."[8]

Evangelical enchantment pervaded the literature of business success well into the early twentieth century. If God was absent from Alger's pages, He appeared frequently in those of William Taylor Adams and William Makepeace Thayer. Writing under the pseudonym Oliver Optic, Adams, a Massachusetts teacher and politician, proffered religious instruction and success advice for thousands of young boys, both in his novels and in *Oliver Optic's Magazine,* published in the 1860s and 1870s. In *Work and Win; or, Noddy Newman on a Cruise* (1865), Optic regaled readers on God's material rewards for holiness, perseverance, and "patient, plodding labor." Echoing the academic economists, Thayer assured his readers that "God uses the transactions of this world to give all who do His will the highest success here, and the greatest glory hereafter." Heir to the legacy of Finney, Thayer justified Christianity by pointing to its investment portfolio. "Christianity has proved itself worthy of general confidence by practical operations," he wrote in *Ethics for Success* (1893), a reader aimed at high school students. The Bible, he added, is "a business manual of exceptional quality." Beseeching young men to acquire the market virtues of *Tact, Push, and Principle* (1882), Thayer professed the "divine rules" of business, stressing to his pious go-getters that "religion demands success." In *Onward to Fame and Fortune* (1897), he provided a gilded lesson in the theology of monetary fetishism. "Money is bread; money is raiment; money is shelter; money is education, refinement . . . is science, invention, discovery, [and] enterprise."[9]

Other heralds of business success shared Thayer's evangelical enchantment. Popular volumes such as *God in Business* (1885) and *The Wonders of Prayer* (1885) brimmed with stories and vignettes of divine intercession in the capitalist universe. The marketplace remained a theater of God's judgments, produced and directed by Providence. If God's general providence still superintended the accumulation of capital, He retained the option of a special providence in commercial and pecuniary matters; as one minister opined, the laws that governed the economy remained in force, but the covenant still recognized "an exigency that may make necessary their suspension" to remind us of God's presence and solicitude. Readers pored over anecdotes of God's marvelous gifts to the striving, faithful, and disciplined: consecrated currency ("a ten-dollar bill with remarkable associations"); recoveries of stolen money and bonds; and deliverances from debt, insolvency, and ruin ("That Wonderful $25—Another Evidence of the Ever-Present Spirit of God"). While settling debts and circulating bank notes, God also furnished capital, softened the hearts of creditors, arranged for carriages, and paid hotel bills on business trips.[10]

Business journalists and other apologists for pecuniary metaphysics often used a sacramental, fetishistic vernacular. Announcing that "it is the duty of some men to make a great deal of money," Josiah Strong told *Our Country* (1885) that money "confers on the wise man a kind of omnipresence." Money is "the modern miracle worker; it has a wonderful multiplying and transferring power." Expounding his "philosophy of successful human activity" in *The Science of Business* (1905), Arthur Frederick Sheldon, a well-known business teacher and eminence of Chicago's Rotary Club, told listeners and readers that the honest character, infused by God, was "the inward and spiritual grace of which temperament is the outward and visible sign." Outlining "The Ten Laws of Success" in the summer of 1910 for the National Association of Accountants and Bookkeepers, John R. Meader asserted that financial moguls possessed "a sort of halo." Far from being mementos of plunder, their fortunes were "the outward and visible sign" of blessing on their ingenuity. William Peter Hamilton, editor of the *Wall Street Journal,* mused that while Cecil Rhodes had needed money for his Cape-to-Cairo Railway, the line was an "outward and visible sign" of his "spiritual significance." (Hamilton failed to mention that the railway was never completed.) Arthur Nash, a successful men's clothing manufacturer, contended that his profits were "material results of his faith," an "outward and visible sign" of his adherence to "the golden rule in business." The sacramental theology of business received its pithiest statement from Rev. M. D. Babcock, who asserted in his widely read *Thoughts for Every-Day Living* (1901) that "business is religion and religion is business." Like Freeman Hunt and earlier theologians of business, Babcock claimed that since "the world is God's workshop," entrepreneurs were unwavering stewards of the Almighty's otherwise unregulated factories. God's remunerative design of the cosmos "makes life sacramental, turning water into wine."[11]

Like Babcock, Russell Conwell proselytized the gospel of wealth in the evangelical timbre Pastor of Grace Baptist Church in Philadelphia—the largest and most affluent Baptist congregation in the country—and first president of Temple University at its founding in 1888, Conwell became famous as a preacher, traveling to churches, colleges, and conventions to deliver his sermon "Acres of Diamonds." (He preached the homily more than six thousand times.) First published as a booklet in 1890, "Acres of Diamonds" is a masterpiece in the annals of capitalist evangelism. The title itself recalled the city depicted at the end of the book of Revelation, where sapphires, rubies, and other jewels adorn the streets of heaven. Conwell pithily restated the evangelo-capitalist faith: "To make money honestly is to preach the gospel." His crassness could be disarming; seldom in the literature of evangelical economics has monetary fetishism been so brazen: "money printed your Bible, money builds your churches, money sends your missionaries . . . money is power, money is force, money will do good." Like earlier sages of mercenary divination, Conwell insisted that spiritual discipline paid handsome material dividends. As he observed in another popular sermon—aptly titled "Praying for Money"—prosperity provided evidence for "the power of consistent prayer in producing objective results."[12]

These "objective results" could be traced to the monetary leaven of divine creation. Conwell's world is charged with the drudgery of God; the lilies of the field were beauteous, hard-working tokens of the Protestant ethic. "If a lily could speak," he reflected in another of his homilies, you would hear "the songs of the angels." Yet forgetting that Jesus had recommended the lilies for their *lack* of toil and spinning, Conwell heard those seraphic voices sing of careful, assiduous labor. Consider the lilies, he suggested; they display an "industrious foresight" in spreading their roots to acquire water.[13] For Conwell as for other devotees of the evangelo-capitalist covenant, nature was an Eden of capital goods, and profit was the grain of the universe. In Conwell's proprietary metaphysics, the earth was a garden of financial delights, studded with acres of diamonds. To his audiences—dreaming of independence in a corporate age—this message endowed their fruitless perseverance with the glamor of divinity.

One of Conwell's friends and admirers was John Wanamaker, the merchant and merchandising virtuoso. Owner of stores in Philadelphia and New York and one of America's richest men, Wanamaker believed that God was the chief executive officer of his stores. "One Hand alone has made it possible for us to have this day of felicity," he told employees at a ceremony in June 1910. "Plainly written over all these years, guiding and guarding, is the one signature of the good God." Reflecting the old evangelical synthesis of divinity and pecuniary reason, Wanamaker believed that God was always a factor in business decisions. "It is a poor oversight to leave God out of our calculations"—calculations based on a mercenary ontology. "The earth is a vast magazine of materials," Wanamaker maintained, and "man is the artisan placed in the world to collect, subdue, and form them for their proper use"—the production and sale of vendible commodities.[14]

Although Wanamaker once called money "the most helpless god," he himself cast a powerful spell over the subjects of his mercantile dominion. Comparing Wanamaker to Lincoln, Jefferson, and Washington, Joseph H. Appel, one of the company's chief executives, gushed that his boss had been "called by God . . . to lead the way" in the evolution of merchandising. One liturgical consummation of the Wanamaker cult was "Jubilee Night," the fiftieth anniversary of the Philadelphia store on October 28, 1911. The ceremony was the high point of a yearlong series of events, including a homage from President William Howard Taft, who invoked "the blessing of God" on Wanamaker's "power of concentration and cooperation." Celebrated in the store's Grand Court—"a veritable cathedral," as Wanamaker once marveled, with stained-glass windows and seraphic statuary—"Jubilee Night" featured encomia from business and labor leaders, clergy, and politicians. After the hymns of praise, employees festooned the chief and his son Rodman with florid charms of *mana*, presenting Wanamaker with a bouquet of fifty yellow chrysanthemums—"emblems of human perfection and enduring worth," the accompanying card read, as well as symbols of "your Achievement, and our reverence." Rodman received a bouquet of fifty white chrysanthemums as "Emblems of the Rising Sun / Symbolic of the strength and power / Required and possessed by you."[15] The Jubilee was a gorgeous ritual of servility to a misenchanted plutocracy.

A generous benefactor of charities, Wanamaker was one of the more benign devotees of the declining evangelical gospel, as some of the defenders of the old-time capitalism had a sharper, more ferocious edge. When William Graham Sumner, professor of sociology at Yale, explained *What Social Classes Owe Each Other* (1884)—in a word, nothing—he reiterated the evangelical economic cosmology in Darwinist terms. "God and Nature have ordained the chances and conditions of life on earth for all." The market was the sacred crucible of agony where character and progress developed. Along with war, market competition comprised "that great discipline of adversity and prosperity by which God makes men and nations strong." Sumner was always keenly aware of the religious nature of economic life. In *Folkways* (1906), Sumner traced the origins of property and money to the tribal universe of enchantment, "amulets, trophies, and ornaments" believed to be "abodes of powerful spirits."[16]

The surliest ombudsman of the evangelical covenant was George F. Baer, one of Morgan's more adroit and indefatigable lawyers, who was also president of the Philadelphia and Reading Coal and Iron Company. When the United Mine Workers struck eastern Pennsylvania's anthracite coalfields in May 1902, the mine owners asked Baer to direct their legal counteroffensive. When union president John Mitchell recommended mediation of the strike by a committee of prominent businesspeople and clergy, Baer rejected any outside arbitration, declaring that "anthracite mining is a business, and not a religious, sentimental, or academic proposition." Yet in private, Baer asserted that coal mining was indeed a religious proposition. In a letter to a minister that was leaked to the press in the midst of the showdown, Baer justified his intransigence in terms of evangelical enchantment. Workers should entrust their welfare, he asserted, not to "labor agitators" but to "Christian men to whom God in His Infinite wisdom has given the control of the property interests of the country." Baer's maxim of plutocratic sanctimony bore witness to the skinflint vigor of the Puritan-evangelical covenant. In the theology of American capitalism, Baer remained a fundamentalist, an "old covenanter," as one magazine profile described him. Baer never renounced his conviction of capital's divine and benevolent despotism, attributing strikes and class conflict to blasphemous envy and pride. "Strikes began with Genesis . . . Cain was the first striker," he mused to a gathering in Colorado Springs shortly after the anthracite strike. "He killed Abel because Abel was the more prosperous fellow."[17]

John D. Rockefeller, Sr., was more laconic than Baer about the source of his enormous fortune: "God gave me my money," he once famously claimed without a trace of irony or facetiousness. Pilloried as a ruthless criminal by the muckraker Ida Tarbell, the founder of Standard Oil was a devout and austere Baptist who affirmed the evangelical covenant. Rockefeller's parents had embodied the symbiosis of market carnival and Protestant enchantment. His father, William "Doc" Rockefeller, was a traveling salesman who peddled trinkets, potions, elixirs, and patent medicines. Advertising himself as an "herbal doctor" and "botanic physician," Doc—also known to his neighbors in Richford, New York, as "Devil Bill"—was the consummate charlatan, a vagabond master of bunkum who preyed on the credulity of his rural customers. Often disappearing from Richford for months as he sold his wares on the road, Doc would return with a fat wad of cash, a livery of horses, and a fashionable wardrobe. For his debt-ridden family, every return of the patriarch was an extravaganza; as Rockefeller's biographer puts it, money, for John, was "God's bounty, the blessed stuff that relieved all of life's cares." Doc's long-suffering wife Eliza took refuge in the Baptist church. From Eliza and her Baptist brethren, John and his siblings first learned the virtues of hard work, frugality, and charity. "Willful waste makes wasteful want," she preached to her thrifty brood. Where Doc indulged his children with money, Eliza taught them the Protestant ethic with a Bible and a well-worn birch. Unsparing with the rod while Doc spoiled the child, Eliza gave moral and metaphysical sanction to John's lifelong passion for lucre.[18]

Rockefeller's cold and insatiable venality stemmed from his evangelo-carnival upbringing. "I never had a craving for anything in my life," the richest man in the world once claimed. From his earliest days in business to his imperium in the oil industry, Rockefeller accumulated riches with a phlegmatic, amoral sanctimony. (H. G. Wells once remarked on Rockefeller's "mild, pleasant, thin-lipped face," which in his view belied all "melodramatic nonsense" about the personal villainy of capitalists.) In the mid-1850s, at age sixteen, Rockefeller found work as a bookkeeper for a produce firm in Cleveland. One day, the owner stashed a four-thousand-dollar bank note in the company safe. Rockefeller recalled much later that, several times during the day, he would open the safe and "gaze longingly" at the note.[19] Like Jonson's Volpone, Rockefeller longed to open the shrine so that he could behold his saint: the holy relic, the tabernacle bread, the *mana* in the shell, the blessed boodle that Doc would bring home.

Despite his stolid veneer, Rockefeller effervesced about the numinous properties of the world whose money God gave him. "The whole process seems a miracle!" he once said of the petroleum industry. "What a blessing the oil has been to mankind!" Pecuniary prowess was also a bequest from God, a talent intended, not for one's own enrichment, but for the sake of the larger, less talented multitude. "The power to make money is a gift from God," Rockefeller explained to the *New York American* in 1906. "Having been endowed with the gift I possess, I believe it is my duty to make money and still more money." But Rockefeller considered his fortune a trust, with himself as the wise and responsible steward. The money God gave him was "for the good of my fellow man according to the dictates of my conscience." Rockefeller's philanthropy was not some lavish penance for his business practices; rather, as Ron Chernow recognized, it was a form of "spiritual double-entry bookkeeping." Mammon piled up the money; God spent it, according to Rockefeller's lights. Thus Rockefeller saw no corruption or scandal in his mercenary homilies to Sunday-school students. It was, he preached to the unsuspecting children, "a religious duty to get all the money you can, fairly and honestly." Echoing Richard Baxter's warning that a man would be punished for every mite of profit he forgoes, Rockefeller maintained as "religion," one business partner recalled, that "no man has done his business properly who has missed a single dollar he could have secured in the doing of it."[20] Be ye perfect in accumulation.

Rockefeller also pointed to the incorporation of capitalist enchantment. "Faith and work were the rocks upon which Standard Oil was built." Rockefeller never doubted that Standard Oil was a vehicle of godly purpose. The Standard's annihilation of competitors was "Godlike," Rockefeller once mused, for it had pulled "this broken-down industry out of the Slough of Despond." Thus, the company was not the malevolent behemoth denounced by Tarbell and other critics. It was rather "an angel of mercy," as he told the *New York World* in 1917; Standard Oil had descended from heaven to battle the demons of ineptitude. Rockefeller and his fellow captains of enchantment were "missionaries of light," steering "the car of salvation" to its divinely appointed destination. Rockefeller conceded that the modern corporation relied on expertise as well as on the ways of Providence; the angel enlisted the earthly labors of the professional-managerial class. Success in business depended, not only on prayer and the will of God, but on "rational, sane, modern, progressive administration." Uneasy with the Darwinism promulgated by titans such as Carnegie, Rockefeller maintained that the angel of mercy represented a higher phase of business evolution. If earlier, more primitive periods of capitalism had enjoined the law of competition, Standard Oil and other corporations "preached the doctrine of cooperation."[21] Under the aegis of the corporate form, Standard Oil represented yet another synthesis of Protestant enchantment and pecuniary reason.

# 8

# The Soulful Corporation

## Corporate Fetishism and the Incorporation of Enchantment

ROCKEFELLER'S DIVINIZATION OF STANDARD Oil displayed the spell of corporate fetishism. As the godly male proprietor yielded to the legal fiction of the corporation, the corporate reconstruction of capitalist enchantment entailed an all-encompassing metamorphosis in the tenets of the covenant theology. The corporate soul's economy mandated a new jurisprudence of corporate personhood; an ideal of a "corporation with a soul"; management theory and its mechanization of communion; a pecuniary metaphysics of advertising; an idyll of "modern communion" idealized in the ideology of corporate liberalism; and a progressive imperialist eschatology. By the end of World War I, a new beatific vision lay at the heart of the moral imagination of American capitalism: the mass production of a beloved community founded on corporate property relations.

Charles Francis Adams, Jr.—Henry's older brother, and like him, a historian—had a premonition of corporate enchantment shortly after the Civil War. An astute investor, a member of the Massachusetts Railroad Commission, and a president of Union Pacific Railroad, Adams was no enemy of business. Still, he recoiled from the scale of corruption he witnessed in American business, and his tirade *A Chapter of Erie* (1869)—an account of the "Erie War" between financial moguls for control of the Erie Railway—was one of the earliest and most eloquent alarms at the magnitude of corporate malevolence. Fought by a colorful cast of warriors—the wily Cornelius Vanderbilt, the treacherous Jay Gould and Jim Fisk, as well as Tammany Hall—the Erie War was a spectacle of venality, complete with secret meetings at plush hotels and banquets at Delmonico's. Wall Street "revealed itself as a haunt of gamblers and a den of thieves," Adams wrote; "the offices of our great corporations appeared as the secret chambers in which trustees plotted the spoliation of their wards."[1]

Those secret chambers worried Adams more than the chicanery of Tammany Hall; he rued the enchantment of corporations more than he loathed municipal corruption. After reporting on the Erie War, Adams dwelled on the meaning of the carnage, sounding all the portentous notes of republican umbrage and rectitude. Although they were creatures of state legislatures, corporations were already "establishing despotisms which no spasmodic popular effort will be able to shake off." "Corporations have no souls," Adams asserted, reiterating "the old maxim of the common law." Yet Adams foresaw a time when corporations—given souls and then mastery of the common life—would infiltrate and destroy representative democracy. If Vanderbilt represented "the autocratic power of Caesarism introduced into corporate life," then the executive branch of republican government would itself be compelled to "put Caesarism at once in control of the corporation and the proletariat, to bring our vaunted institutions within the rule of all historic precedent."[2] Adams strongly implied that corporate ensoulment led inexorably to authoritarian government. Whitman's democratic vistas would be permanently gilded by corporate fetishism.

At the time of the Erie War, corporations occupied an ambiguous place in the evangelical capitalist cosmos—their existence was undeniable and even efficacious, but their metaphysical and moral legitimacy was questionable. In the 1819 Dartmouth College case, for instance, Chief Justice John Marshall had conferred rights, privileges, and immortality on entities whose artificiality he openly acknowledged. But while the Supreme Court's finding in *Santa Clara* that corporations were persons under the Fifth and Fourteenth Amendments was certainly not unprecedented, the decision was remarkable for its cavalier brevity. Bereft of any argument whatsoever, *Santa Clara* was more an arbitrary edict than a carefully considered opinion; neither Chief Justice Morrison Remick Waite nor Justice John Harlan (who delivered the decision) presented any defense of their position. Indeed, they could not, as their equation of corporations with natural persons went beyond anything in previous jurisprudence.[3]

The first jurist to recognize the significance of the case was Delphin M. Delmas, the attorney for the county of Santa Clara, whose eloquent failure was a harbinger of metaphysical and political battles to come. Besides arguing his case on constitutional grounds, Delmas engaged in a futile polemic against the metaphysics of corporate personhood. Dissenting from what he considered an odious perversion of the Fourteenth Amendment—corporations possessed rights and privileges "which are not enjoyed by any man in his individual capacity," he conceded, but the principle of equal protection under the law did not "require that corporations should be governed by the same laws as natural persons"—Delmas hinted that the nondecision bore even larger moral and metaphysical implications. The intent of the amendment, he reminded the Court, had been "to raise the humble, the downtrodden, and the oppressed," not "to make the creature of the State—the bodiless, soulless, and mystic creature called a corporation—the equal of the creature of God."[4] Delmas clearly implied that the stakes in the case were religious as well as political: if the Court ruled in favor of the railroad company, corporations would acquire the image and likeness of God that belonged only to natural persons.

American jurists addressed the issue of corporate ontology only after the *Santa Clara* decision, exhibiting an impatience with metaphysical speculation and a keen awareness of the dangers of fetishism. As University of Chicago law professor Ernst Freund wrote in *The Legal Nature of Corporations* (1897)—one of the seminal texts in the post–*Santa Clara* discussion of corporate personality—it was pointless to hope for an "unattainable metaphysical unity" in our thinking about personhood. More than a decade later, Maurice Wormser, professor of law at the University of Illinois, eschewed any hope of identifying "the true anatomy of the corporate concept." In a landmark 1911 essay on "Corporate Personality" in the *Harvard Law Review,* Arthur Machen confessed the confusion of American jurisprudence. "A corporation cannot possibly be both an artificial person and an imaginary or fictitious person," he declared. "An artificial lake is not an imaginary one, nor is an artificial waterfall a fictitious waterfall." ("In such metaphysical mazes," Machen observed, "it is easy to lose one's self.") The solution, they all agreed, was pragmatic and pecuniary: corporations needed and even deserved the status of personhood in order to facilitate business. The attribution of personhood to a business corporation is "a matter of discretion," Freund asserted, determined by "practical requirements" and "practical purposes"—"practical" defined as capitalist. Likewise, Wormser opined that the irreducibly social and material nature of corporations was "the essential root and gist of things." Although Machen was more inclined to write of corporate personality as "real"—the corporation is an "objectively real entity," he believed—it still derived, in his view, from a "group of men . . . whose membership is changing."[5]

Jurists acknowledged that a strong and irresistible propensity to fetishism existed in the human imagination. Echoing Durkheim, Sir James Frazer, and other contemporary students of archaic enchantment, legal students of corporate personality ventured into religious territory. Wormser feared that corporate personality could be easily "exalted into a fetish." If corporate personhood was a convenient fiction for economic and legal purposes, the corporation itself must not be "converted into a fetish," he warned a convention of lawyers and legal scholars in 1923. "It must not be worshipped in the way savages worship a red cow or an ornamental totem pole as a supposed incarnation of a sacred spirit." Machen cautioned readers of the *Harvard Law Review* that the corporation should not be "exalted into a divinity," a deity before which "we must stand in reverent awe, believing where we cannot prove." "There is no command to fall down and worship the imaginary corporate personality, like the golden image which Nebuchadnezzar set up."[6] In the presence of Standard Oil, U.S. Steel, and other corporations, jurists experienced intimations of idolatry, an ominous sunrise of the mercenary gods.

Like the jurists, other Americans struggled to make sense of the emerging dispensation. The American people were "writing the epilogue of one drama," the economist Simon N. Patten mused in *The New Basis of Civilization* (1907), while "the curtain was rising upon the prologue of another presenting a new cast of characters." "The economic revolution is here, but the intellectual revolution that will rouse men to its stupendous meaning has not done its work." That "intellectual revolution" of language and imagery occupied a wide range of writers. Journalists, economists, and reformers referred politely to "consolidation" and "combination," while Populists fulminated against "plutocracy," "the money power," or industrial and financial "Bourbons." Carnegie hailed *The Empire of Business* (1913), while W. J. Ghent marveled at *Our Benevolent Feudalism* (1902), "graced by a sense of ethics and somewhat restrained by a fear of democracy."[7]

The incorporation of enchantment depended on popular acceptance of corporate "personhood"—and the spell of this fetish was by no means guaranteed. In the evangelical soul's economy, personhood and moral responsibility inhered in flesh-and-blood proprietors: local farmers, artisans, shopkeepers, and bankers were readily known and accountable. The incompetent or dishonest businessman could be rebuked in his shop, rumored about in the street, or shamed in church on Sunday. In the new economy of the latter nineteenth century, the national scale of corporations introduced an unprecedented anonymity to American economic life. As ownership, production, and distribution grew more collective and subdivided, praise and blame became difficult if not impossible to assign. Owners and employees, executives and workers, producers and customers no longer necessarily knew one another. As the writer Seymour Eaton (creator of the Roosevelt or "Teddy" Bear) observed in his *Sermons on Advertising* (1907), people "prefer to know individuals. They like to feel that they are being served by men." If they want to kick someone in frustration, it is "unsatisfactory" to "kick an Express Company or a Railroad or Brown, Smith, and Company."[8] Increasingly deprived of the human scale of proprietary personality, Americans suspected something insidious in the impersonality of corporations. In the 1890s, the popular imagery of corporate industry assumed its modern form: gargantuan factories, shrouded in smoke, enslaving workers reduced to cogs by an inscrutable and ravenous corporation.

Popular opposition to corporations stemmed as much from a sense of their existential illegitimacy as from a fear of their unbridled power. In the 1890s and 1900s, corporate "soullessness" opened a new chapter in the history of popular metaphysics: the corporation's eerie mixture of personhood and impersonality. How could a corporation be both personal and impersonal at once? A company with a name, yet anonymous, unaccountable, even immaterial? As Populist firebrand James H. "Cyclone" Davis explained in 1894, the corporation was "a mere ideal being, an artificial creation of imaginary workmanship, set up as a person . . . to move among natural persons." This illegitimate person was "without one human sympathy," and one of its most pernicious effects was to drain "natural persons" of their own humanity, as the owners and employees of the corporation "feel no personal concern for the moral quality of the acts that produce money."[9]

Forged in the fire of populist polemic, "soulless corporation" and kindred terms became weapons in the rhetorical arsenal employed by critics of corporate business, especially after the great merger wave that ended in 1903.

(William Futhey Gibbons, a popular scribe for the social gospel, was especially fond of the phrase. In 1902, Gibbons published both a nonfiction philippic against *The Soulless Corporation* and a novel about striking coal miners, *Those Black Diamond Men,* whose first chapter was entitled "The Soulless Corporation.") Critics railed against the corporation's diabolical blend of metaphysical and moral evil. In Frank Norris's *The Octopus* (1901)—a story of conflict between ranchers and a railroad company in the San Joaquin Valley—Presley, the poet-protagonist, describes the corporation as "the soulless Force, the iron-hearted Power, the monster, the Colossus, the Octopus." Later, in *The Titan* (1914), Theodore Dreiser rued "the day of the trust" as a moment when Americans beheld "a set of giants—Titans—who, without heart or soul . . . were setting forth to enchain and enslave them." Writing in *Everybody's Magazine* in early 1912, radical journalist C. P. Connolly inveighed that the blood of a man crippled by a railroad freight car had "stained the right of way of a soulless corporation." Even businesspeople occasionally joined the critics of corporate soullessness. The editors of *Commerce and Finance* felt compelled to lament in 1917 when a Missouri state court "upheld the soulless corporation" in a price-fixing case. As late as 1920, A. P. Richardson, a prominent accountant and editor of the profession's most respected journal, wondered what it would take to convince businesspeople that "a corporation has no soul," and that "without a soul the relations of man to man degenerate."[10]

This swelling chorus of popular opprobrium forced beleaguered corporate executives to defend the soulfulness of their firms. John H. Patterson, president of the National Cash Register Company, insisted in 1899 that "it is the duty of the company to show . . . that it is not a corporation without a soul." Insurance company executive George W. Perkins—also a representative of Morgan on the board of U.S. Steel and later a Progressive politician— observed in 1903 that business needed to "disarm the prejudice against the trusts." Acutely aware that they and their employers inhabited a moral and existential limbo, the business intelligentsia moved to endow the modern corporation with a soul. The strategies of soulfulness varied greatly in manner and effectiveness. "Welfare capitalism"—the provision by companies of numerous programs, benefits, and amenities to their employees— began in part as a response to the problem of soullessness. At its most inept, this approach was dismissed as a cynical ploy to avert class conflict and government regulation; at its most skillful, it produced Gertrude Beeks, director of International Harvester's welfare programs, who found herself anointed an "angel of peace" in the business and popular press.[11]

The invention of a soul for the corporation led to the professionalization of image production. As Roland Marchand and other historians have shown, the profession of public relations arose, in part, as the conjurers of a "corporate soul," a vision that transformed a satanic leviathan into the friendly neighborhood behemoth. Public relations experts and advertisers labored mightily to convince a skeptical public that when a company communicates, "a man is talking," as adman Claude C. Hopkins put it, "a man who takes pride in his accomplishments—not a soulless corporation." One common and effective strategy depicted the corporation as a humble servant, an indefatigable minister to the wishes of the sovereign consumer. In a typical paean to corporate service and soulfulness, the *American Underwriter* observed in 1917 that "'soulful corporation' seems an apt title for the greatest of all life insurance companies, the Metropolitan Life Insurance Company of New York." In a 1922 issue of *Printer's Ink,* the leading advertising journal, Hugh E. Agnew described how Pacific Gas and Electric "makes itself a personality" through carefully crafted imagery. Its image professionals succeeded in portraying the corporation as "a strong tireless servant . . . a servant so domesticated that it warms, lights, and makes comfortable the homes of the land." Although many Americans continued to withhold their affection from soulful corporations, these strategies of ensoulment could be remarkably effective in winning hearts and minds. In 1915, after the Santa Fe Railroad agreed to pay damages for lives and property lost when one of its cars exploded in Ardmore, Oklahoma, the town's citizens erected a billboard to the company: "Great is the Santa Fe: One Corporation with a Soul."[12]

To be sure, the ensoulment of corporations by image professionals was a way to assuage popular unease and disarm criticism. But something more exalted and disturbing was at work in the movement for corporate soulfulness. As early as 1879, economist John Bates Clark had forecast that "when the corporation shall fairly pass the point in its development when it acquires a fully grown corporate soul, it will become a cooperative society." By the eve of World War I, management professor Patten could assert that the corporation was now "the social basis of religion." The campaign for corporate ensoulment suggested that the corporation was being recast as the object of longings for beloved community. It was not only that, as one spokesperson for the National Association of Manufacturers wrote in the association's journal in 1918, corporations demonstrated that "God's work is done through man's hands." The corporation was a vessel of other, more sublime intentions of divinity. Carroll D. Wright, Massachusetts commissioner of labor and later chief of the US Bureau of Labor, asserted in 1882 that the corporation was "an instrument of God for the upbuilding of the race." Two decades later, Wright reiterated his faith in the mission of the soulful corporation. Representing "the coordinate works of the Creator and His grandest creation—man," the technological and organizational prowess of the corporation "allies man to his Creator." At the same time, with its careful division of labor and its peaceful resolution of workplace conflict, the corporation "follows the Pauline plan of adjusting a difficulty arising between two members of a church."[13]

These views of the soulful corporation as a form of beloved community were widespread among business writers and executives. In the summer of 1908, for example, John Kimberly Mumford—a prolific journalist and a tireless booster for corporate enterprise—searched "the heart of a 'soulless corporation'" in a series of articles in *Harper's Weekly*. Twenty years earlier, Mumford recalled, the size of corporations had suggested to Americans "an impertinence greater than Lucifer's." Now, more and more Americans realized that "the boundless needs which the corporation and its vast expansion have created" were the modern "furnace in which God for His own purposes tries out the race of man." Focusing especially on International Harvester's welfare programs, Mumford contended that the cafeterias and company picnics bore "the visible signs of a new order, a change of the world's heart." (Marie Goss, Beeks's successor as welfare manager, had "the face of an Apostle.") The impending transformation of capitalist society would be so complete that Mumford fell back on the oldest terms of enchantment to explain the change. "It is the age, a magician releasing new spirits on earth, that has wrought the change, and from this time forth the *djinn* will never return to the bottle."[14]

Other business journalists hailed executives as the vanguard of a corporate millennium. Having made her reputation as a crusader with her history of Rockefeller's Standard Oil, Tarbell became an acolyte of soulful corporations with her paean to *New Ideals in Business* (1916). Profiling Henry Ford and his Motor Company in the *American Magazine* in 1914, Tarbell praised the firm's "Sociological Department"—charged to "put Jesus Christ in my factory" and headed by an Episcopal minister—as the harbinger of "the Golden Rule in Business." In a trilogy of books on the steel industry, Arundel Cotter, an editor and correspondent for the *Wall Street Journal,* marveled at the "absolute harmony" achieved by executives such as Elbert H. Gary of U.S. Steel and Charles M. Schwab of Bethlehem Steel. In *United States Steel: The Corporation with a Soul* (1921), Cotter not only described the company as "a true democracy" and "the highest form of socialism," but portrayed the firm as a model of efficient, productive, soulful community. "The man who gives gets," as one manager parroted, and Cotter wrote of the charitable spirit that animated the "vast human machinery" of U.S. Steel. Corporate executives seconded these lavish affirmations of corporate community. In the March 1912 issue of *World's Work,* for example, William G. McAdoo, president of the Hudson and Manhattan Railroad Company and later treasury secretary under President Woodrow Wilson, let readers inside "The Soul of a Corporation." The Hudson and Manhattan was more than a railway line, McAdoo explained; it was a beloved community of transport. The corporation possessed an "esprit de corps" of service to each other as well as to the public. "We are all working together for the good of each other," McAdoo asserted; executives, managers, and railroad workers shared "a spirit of common devotedness, of common sympathy."[15]

Soulful firms needed temples in which to house their beloved communities, and architects supplied the blueprints. Epitomized in the skyscraper, the rapid evolution of American corporate architecture provided ready material for sensitive observers. George Santayana used architecture as a metaphor for the divisions in American culture. "The American Will inhabits the skyscraper," he wrote in 1911, a monument to "aggressive enterprise." One obstacle to the creation of a corporate architecture lay in the fine arts tradition to which most American architects and critics were beholden. To traditionalists such as Russell Sturgis, a prominent critic and enthusiast of Ruskin, commercial and industrial needs were irrelevant and even inimical to the pursuit of beauty in architecture. "Fine art and active mercantile pursuits are mutually exclusive," Sturgis asserted in a 1908 issue of the *Architectural Record.* "Business requirements are ... the very defeat, the very ruin, of architectural effect." Still, architects needed to make a living in a raucous business civilization, and as a result, they differed sharply over the aesthetics of business architecture. Yet even as Sturgis was writing, his high-brow orthodoxy was waning. Beginning in the 1880s, a cohort of architects and critics—including John Wellborn Root, Peter Brooks, H. H. Richardson, Daniel H. Burnham, Louis Sullivan, and Montgomery Schuyler—had advanced the view that commerce and industry did not preclude aesthetic merit. Sometimes, their reasoning was bluntly pecuniary: as Burnham told the Merchants' Club of Chicago in 1897, "beauty has always paid better than any other commodity, and always will." But others discerned a genuine splendor in the might of the corporate metropolis. Oscar Lovell Triggs, a professor of English at the University of Chicago and a frequent commentator on architecture, marveled at the skyline traced by the city's escalating business buildings. Radiating "daring, strength, Titantic energy, intelligence, and majesty . . . the commercial temple is the exact equivalent of the modern business ideal," Triggs wrote in 1898.[16]

Comparisons of department stores (and, later, shopping malls) to temples, churches, or cathedrals have by now become tedious and even misleading clichés. Yet it remains true that many architects, businesspeople, and critics saw enchanting implications in the new corporate architecture. If corporations could have souls, then their headquarters were shrines, as devoted as any ancient temple complex to trafficking in the wares of enchantment. While traveling through America in 1908, G. Lowes Dickinson discerned a religious longing in corporate architecture. Gazing across the East River from his hotel room in Brooklyn, he admired the "blazing basilicas" of Manhattan, "outshining the firmament of stars" with their powerful, towering electrical lights. While he knew they were citadels of business, Dickinson sensed that the skyline was still "divine somehow in its potentialities." Even Ezra Pound—soon to be a far-right critic of usury and finance capital—couldn't help but be enchanted by the nocturnal skyline when he visited Manhattan during a brief trip home from London in 1910. On a brilliant night, "the great buildings lose reality and take on their magical powers." "Here is our poetry," Pound wrote, "for we have pulled down the stars to our will."[17]

The Metropolitan and Woolworth buildings in New York exemplified the architecture of corporate enchantment. In 1905, John R. Hegeman, president of Metropolitan Life, commissioned Napoleon Le Brun to design a new headquarters at 24th and Madison. He instructed Le Brun to use as his model the campanile of St. Mark's in Venice, one of Hegeman's favorite civic and religious monuments. Completed in 1909, the Metropolitan was the tallest structure in the city. Six years later, speaking at the annual Metropolitan Life convention, art historian William Henry Atherton complimented Hegeman and his board of directors for their choice of model, "for a tower, with its light and its belfry, has always been a source of inspiration." By the time Atherton spoke, the Woolworth Building had surpassed the Metropolitan as the highest building in Gotham. Designed by Cass Gilbert in 1913 as the corporate headquarters for Frank W. Woolworth, it was the epitome of Business Gothic: glazed terra cotta panels, a tower of sheeted copper, a grand arcade with glass mosaics and marble imported from Greece. A sensation in the architectural and popular presses, its grandeur was magnified four years later by its manager, Edwin A. Cochran, who dubbed it *The Cathedral of Commerce* (1917). A veritable devotional manual, Cochran's booklet featured a foreword by Rev. S. Parkes Cadman, a prominent Congregationalist pastor from Brooklyn. Like the temples and cathedrals of antiquity and the Middle Ages, the commercial edifices of the modern age reflected "the spiritual aspirations they embodied and expressed." Not that Cadman bemoaned these spiritual aspirations. Far from being a temple to Mammon, the Woolworth Building pierced into space "like a battlement of the paradise of God which St. John beheld." A vessel of the image of God, the Woolworth was a "chosen habitation of that spirit of man which . . . binds alien people into unity and peace." Woolworth himself received the unctuous flattery desired by any potentate. "The name Frank W. Woolworth has been indelibly inscribed throughout the length and breadth of our land and abroad." (His opulent office was named the Empire Room.)[18]

Corporate architecture had its most eloquent advocate in Louis Sullivan, whose writing blended professional acumen with grandiose metaphysical speculation. After a brief and unhappy stint at MIT learning "a misch-masch of architectural theology," Sullivan moved to Philadelphia and then to Chicago, where he worked briefly for Burnham before joining Dankmar Adler in 1878. Over the next twenty years, Sullivan recast the Chicago cityscape with the Auditorium Building (1889); the Chicago Stock Exchange Building (1894); and the Carson, Pirie, Scott, and Company Building (1896). Together with the Wainwright Building in St. Louis (1891) and the Guaranty Building in Buffalo (1896), Sullivan's business edifices announced the commencement of architectural modernism. They also reflected Sullivan's conviction that architecture was essentially religious. "With me, architecture is not an art, but a religion."[19]

From early in his career, Sullivan articulated an unsystematic theology of architecture. While at MIT, he later recalled, he had resolved to effect through his work "a complete reversal and inversion of the commonly accepted intellectual and theological concept of the nature of man." Rejecting original sin, Sullivan began to "worship man as a being, a presence containing wondrous powers, mysterious hidden powers." Rather than trust in the Christian God, Sullivan put "faith in the Earth, faith in Life, faith in Man." Obscuring any distinction between the human and the divine—"the spiritual," he mused in his autobiography, is "a term interchangeable with the physical"—Sullivan expounded a secular parody of a sacramental view of the world—and of architecture. "The essence of things," he thought, is always "taking shape in the matter of things." Thus Sullivan's maxim that "form ever follows function" did not indicate a crass practicality; the "function" of a building was always expressive of spiritual as well as pecuniary meaning. If matter was "interchangeable" with spirit, Sullivan could see architecture as the outward and visible sign of something inward and invisible. "As you are, so are your buildings; and, as are your buildings, so are you."[20]

Like Emerson, Sullivan affirmed the divinization of power. Hailing "the Doer—ever growing in power," Sullivan avowed that power and its infinite expansion was the core of human divinity. The architect was a model of the divinized power that suffused the universe. At its best, architectural design reflected a "Great Spirit" which resides both in the architect's "silent subjectivity" and in "the unfailing bounty of nature." Determined to overcome the stifling legacy of Christian humility, Sullivan lauded "the Ego—the 'I am'—the unique" as "the most precious of man's powers." (If Ayn Rand's egotistical architect Howard Roark in *The Fountainhead* has a precursor, it is Sullivan, not Frank Lloyd Wright.) Yet this egoism was not malevolent. The Great Spirit that embraced the architect's ego enabled him to enter into that "extraordinary communion that the sacred writers called to 'walk with God'." Since human divinity was untrammeled power, Sullivan hallowed the forces of the market. Outlining his eschatology of capitalism at the annual convention of the American Institute of Architects in October 1894, he expressed his apprehension at the "murky materialism" of corporations—"so prodigious, so grotesque, so monstrous"—yet asserted nonetheless that this very monstrosity "contains the elements of change." "From its own intensity, its own excess, its own complex striving," the rage to accumulate "predetermines the golden age of the world." Through the scientific and technological development sponsored by corporate enterprise, humanity had arrived at "a materialism so profound, so exalted as to prove the fittest basis for a coming era of spiritual

splendor."[21]

The draftsman of "spiritual splendor" was an avid celebrant of corporate power, saluting the talent and ambition of urban financiers, managers, and professionals. Chicago, he wrote in 1891, owed its greatness to its "brainy men," whose avarice and savvy were qualities "as noble, daring, and inspired as ever quickened knights of old to deeds of chivalry." In "The Tall Office Building Artistically Considered" (1896), one of the finest paeans to corporate architecture ever written, Sullivan asserted that in the skyscraper "a new grouping of social conditions has found a habitation and a name." Acknowledging that it was the "joint product of the speculator, the engineer, [and] the builder"—and not, apparently, the workers who actually built it—Sullivan boasted that the architect imparted to this edifice of strife and greed "the higher forms of sensibility and culture." The "lofty" form of the skyscraper followed the loftiness of the social function that Sullivan attributed to corporate business. "The force and power of altitude" stemmed from "the glory and pride of exaltation"; the skyscraper was "the new, the unexpected, the eloquent peroration of most bold, most sinister, most forbidding conditions." "From bottom to top," the skyscraper was "a unit without a single dissenting line."[22] In Sullivan's architectural theology, the skyscraper was a seamlessly integrated tabernacle of the soulful corporation.

Sullivan's corporate sublime was a beatific vision rendered in concrete and steel, and it reminds us that "the soulful corporation" had very visible, tactile features. Emerging from the moral imagination of the professional-managerial class, the soulful corporation was their answer to popular moral and metaphysical suspicions. In the course of bestowing a soul or personality on an impersonal legal fiction, business ideologues converted the corporation into an enchanted colossus of capital. The mystical body of the corporation was also a counterfeit beloved community, a holy family whose products and services bore the soulful personality of the company. The image and likeness of the enchanted corporation would appear in public relations and advertising; its canon law and technology of community would take form as management theory. Under the sign of the corporate soul, the corporation inherited the title to the venerable American errand: the establishment of a heavenly city on the property relations of capitalism.

# 9

# Blazers of the One True Way

## Corporate Humanism, Management Theory, and the Mechanization of Communion

However "soulful" the corporation, class conflict remained an indelible feature of industrial capitalism. In the three decades after the Civil War, the American economy was shaken by two shock waves of labor unrest: the Great Railroad Strike of 1877—the climactic episode of the panic that began in 1873—and the Homestead and Pullman strikes of 1892 and 1894. Eager to end class warfare and avert the radicalization of workers, business reformers of the 1880s and 1890s urged capitalists to abandon the old ways of accumulation. As the minister and journalist Nicholas Paine Gilman wrote in 1899, the source of industrial unrest lay in the "personal alienation of the employer from his fellow-men who work for him." To overcome this estrangement, restore tranquility, and ensure profitability in the future, businesspeople needed to seek "the sagacious application of ideal justice and righteousness to the employer's function." In the spirit of Andrew Ure and the British evangelical clerics of capital, Gilman imagined the industrial workplace as a beatific site of production, a factory pervaded by "humaneness, kindness, and fraternity."[1]

Gilman's hopes were taken up by corporate management, while management theory offered a new covenant of "humaneness, kindness, and fraternity" from within the culture of corporate professionalism. The emergence of a professional stratum of managers to oversee and coordinate the activities of the modern corporation was one of the defining developments of modern America. Heir to the proprietor's organizational labor, the manager increasingly seemed to be the only figure capable of understanding, leading, and humanizing the promethean forces unleashed by corporate business. In this view, managers, like other professionals, possessed sophisticated, even recondite skills whose deployment enables them to master the complexities of markets, administration, and technology. Thus the "visible hand" of management displaced the invisible hand of the market as the orchestrating force of capitalism. Meanwhile, the convergence of corporate management with the rising cadre of engineers, scientists, and technicians gave birth to the "professional-managerial class," whose varieties of skilled expertise comprised the fund of knowledge on which the corporation and corporate society relied.[2]

Historians have tended to treat management literature as a scientific body of knowledge about the efficient organization of large-scale business enterprise. Writing of Du Pont, U.S. Steel, and General Electric, Olivier Zunz asserts that the earliest managerial theory represented "a concerted effort on the part of men in charge to think about managerial structure, investment strategies, expert knowledge, and employee relations." In this view, management theory is the anatomical science of corporate capitalism. Yet other historians have depicted the growth of management and management theory not as responses to the emergence of corporate enterprise but as instruments in its very creation. Consummating the "philosophy of manufactures" first sketched by Babbage and Ure, management theory was, in their view, part of a larger strategy by corporate capital to expropriate the technical and organizational skills of workers and give them to "experts" more amenable to capitalist imperatives. If, as Big Bill Haywood of the Industrial Workers of the World (IWW) put it, "the manager's brains" lay "under the workman's cap," then corporate capital needed to dispossess the worker of his intelligence as well as his access to production. The crusade of enclosure that began in England now engulfed American industry, and like their evangelical predecessors in improvement, American corporate leaders had to "strangle the Hydra of misrule." Much of the professional-managerial class arose from this war of annexation; "management" is, in this view, simply class war by other means. Enveloped in the aura of "expertise," management theory has been what David F. Noble dubs a "technology of social production," a toolkit of industrial exploitation.[3]

Beginning with the "scientific management" movement of the 1910s associated with Frederick W. Taylor and the Taylor Society, management theory has evolved as a method of dispossession, surveillance, and control. No managerial ideologue has ever been clearer than Taylor himself about the basis for management's claims to power and authority. Taylor never attributed the need for a managerial class to technological or organizational complexity. With an almost disarming candor, he acknowledged that management originated in the owners' desire to assert complete control over workers and the labor process through an industrial form of enclosure. "Workmen," Taylor wrote in *The Principles of Scientific Management* (1913), "possess the mass of traditional knowledge a large part of which is not in the possession of management." Because managers either lacked workers' knowledge or possessed it only deficiently, "the shop was really run by the workmen and not by the bosses." Taylor realized with chagrin that "the combined knowledge and skill of the workmen who were under him was certainly ten times as great as his own."[4] The issue was power, not "complexity," the mesmerizing talisman of the managerial mandarins.

Yet management theory has always been more than a weapon in the arsenal of corporate hegemony. To understand why, we need to fully think through the implications of what Alfred Sohn-Rethel has dubbed "managerial fetishism."[5] Like the "soulful corporation," corporate management thinking emerged from the turbulent transformation of the evangelical moral and political economy. From its inception in the late nineteenth century, management theory has marked an attempt to forge a beloved community on the foundations of corporate capitalism. In the wake of a waning evangelical hegemony, the corporate intelligentsia offered managerial "expertise" as the surrogate for Protestant theology and moralism. Management theory contains a corporate conception of selfhood, a corporate humanism, in which the business corporation—legally a person—becomes a site of personal fulfillment and devotion. At the same time, if management literature has provided a "technology of social production," it has also recorded the American quest for community in cupidity. Despite its professional veneer, management theory represents a refashioning of enchantment under corporate auspices, the animation of rational authority with the galvanizing charge of charisma. Like the "soulful corporation" for which it provides a canon law and moral theology, management theory is another form of fetishism: it beguiles, captures, and codifies the deepest human aspirations. At its most ardent and insidious, management theory has sought to realize the mechanization of communion.

Although the genesis of management theory can be traced to corporate "welfare departments"—especially to the celebrated Sociological Department of Henry Ford's automobile plant in Detroit—its enchanting character can be seen in the professional culture of engineering. As the ranks of civil, mechanical, and electrical engineers swelled between the Civil War and the Armistice, the engineer became one of the principal icons of industrial modernity, appearing in exhibitions and advertisements as well as popular and highbrow fiction. Fusing the romantic, the practical, and the mercenary, the figure of the engineer embodied utopian longing, technological mastery, and scorn for waste and inefficiency. Often, this ideal expressed a desire for magus-like power and imagination. Jack Hale, the hero of John Fox, Jr.'s *The Trail of the Lonesome Pine* (1908), has "the vision of a seer" when he surveys Cumberland Gap, believing it "the heaven-born site for the unborn city of his dreams." In Harold Bell Wright's *The Winning of Barbara Worth* (1911), the protagonist—eager to reclaim a desert area, "The Palm of the Hand of God"—dubs the coming days of engineering splendor "the age of the Seer and his companions." Zane Grey wrote of engineering with eschatological grandeur In *The U. P. Trail* (1918). Engineers, Grey marveled, were infused by "the spirit of some great thing to be . . . that strange call of life which foreordained a heritage for the future." For many Americans, engineers were heroic magi, not soulless technocrats; unlike Weber's disenchanted technicians, they were specialists with spirit. Conquering nature and extending the bounds of beneficent technical empire, they planned the extension of the American errand to improve and redeem the planet. In the popular imagination, engineers, in Cecilia Tichi's words, "renewed the spiritual mission embedded for over two and a half centuries in the national experience."[6] Heirs to Bacon, Winthrop, and the antebellum technologists, engineers were the new magi of the covenant.

The magical powers of engineering had been captured by Mark Twain in *A Connecticut Yankee in King Arthur's Court* (1889). Like William Morris in *A Dream of John Ball,* Twain sent his protagonist *back* in time: knocked unconscious during a fight, Hank Morgan, "head superintendent" of a gun factory, awakens in sixth-century England. After narrowly escaping execution (remembering the date of a solar eclipse, he predicts and thus "causes" the incident), Morgan swiftly debunks and usurps the official regime of Arthurian enchantment, especially Merlin the magician, who becomes his most intrepid antagonist. Anointed "the Boss," he embarks on an arrogant and energetic project of modernization, directing the construction of an enormous apparatus of industry, transport, and communication. All over the realm, he plants "the nuclei of future vast factories, the iron and steel missionaries of my future civilization." Spells, incantations, and prayers give way to scientific enlightenment and technological mastery. Everywhere, commerce and wage labor undermine the foundations of feudal subordination and chivalry: serfs learn to read, nobles become railway conductors, knights exchange errantry for careers as salespeople of mouthwash, toothpaste, and polish.[7]

Yet if Twain's fable affirmed the victory of industrial modernity over superstition, it also hinted that technical and managerial experts were the new regime of enchantment. Morgan is often referred to as a "magician," a "wizard," or an "enchanter," and he himself describes his rivalry with Merlin as "a duel between two mighty magicians; a duel not of muscle but of mind, not of human skill but of superhuman art and craft; a final struggle for supremacy between the two master enchanters of the age." Reading from the unfinished manuscript to an audience in Baltimore in January 1888, Twain paused and asked his listeners to "consider the trivial miracles and wonders wrought by the humbug magicians and enchanters of that old day, and contrast them with the mighty miracles wrought by science in our day of steam and electricity."[8]

Morgan's attempt to impose modernity was a form of social engineering, and it suggested that the quest of engineers to master nature would embrace human nature as well. Before World War I, most management theorizing took place in the professional periodicals of engineers; by the 1910s, engineers were the vanguard of managerial science, extending its sway from machine shops into electrical and chemical manufacturing firms. Centered in the American Society of Mechanical Engineers (ASME), the drive to create a coherent body of managerial literature first appeared in the 1880s. In an 1886 paper to the ASME, Henry Towne, an engineer and manufacturer from Stamford, Connecticut, issued a clarion call to his colleagues. While the science of engineering had a large and systematic literature, "the management of work is unorganized, is almost without literature, [and] has no organization or medium for the interchange of experience." Towne urged the ASME to establish a clearinghouse for managerial experience and reflection. At the same time, Towne underscored the conflation of technical efficiency, pecuniary reason, and beloved community that marked all subsequent management theory. Noting that the ASME's monogram—the symbol of the dollar—was "frequently conjoined to the figures of an engineer's calculations," Towne reiterated that "the final issue" of an engineer's work was "a question of dollars and cents." The returns to capital remained the standard by which the new social engineers would "subordinate each to the harmonious development of the whole." Over the next decade, other engineers echoed and amplified Towne's hopes for a science of management. In his presidential address to the American Society of Civil Engineers in 1895, George S. Morison, the nation's premiere bridge engineer, informed his colleagues that "we are the priests of material development . . . we are the priests of the new epoch, without superstitions." (Morison's 1903 tract, *The New Epoch,* was a banal but popular artifact of mechanical utopianism.)[9] The exalted engineers of popular fiction were replicated in the minds of the engineering elite.

The new business schools joined the engineering profession in forging a corporate clerisy. Upholding the priesthood of all proprietors, the evangelical dispensation had largely refrained from formal business education. Until well after the Civil War, most training in business was informal and unsystematic; "commercial colleges" offered brief courses of study in literacy, numeracy, and bookkeeping. In the 1880s, in tandem with the corporate construction of the professional and managerial apparatus, business education assumed the disciplinary and pedagogical trappings it wears today. Over the next two decades, a consensus emerged among executives, economists, and journalists that the longevity of corporate capitalism depended more on the creation of a business intelligentsia than on the accumulation of capital. As one writer opined in *World's Work* in 1904, "the success of the great corporation today depends primarily upon the possibility of securing not capital but brains."[10] What Ruskin had vilified as alchemy and witchcraft now donned the robes of the academy.

Business schools of all kinds proliferated, offering instruction in everything from finance and marketing to advertising, fashion, and industrial design: the Wharton School at the University of Pennsylvania (1881), the College of Commerce and Politics at the University of Chicago (1898), the College of Commerce at the University of California at Berkeley (1898), Harvard Business School (1908), the New York School of Fine and Applied Art (1909, later the Parsons School), the School of Retailing at New York

University (1919). Meanwhile, artistic and scientific institutions such as the Brooklyn Museum, the Newark Museum, and the American Museum of Natural History sponsored expositions of industrial products and embarked on extensive collaborations with urban merchants, manufacturers, and designers. Many advocates of formalized business education saw the new schools as outposts of a civilizing mission. President of Bethlehem Iron (later Steel) Corporation and a cofounder of Swarthmore College, Joseph Wharton envisioned his "School of Finance and Economy" as an academy for philosopher-executives. In his founding charter for the school, Wharton asserted his hope that professional managers would emerge as "a class of men likely to become pillars of the State." In addition to running successful businesses, the new class of mandarins would also contribute to "the solution of the social problems incident to our civilization." John Cotton Dana, curator of the Newark Museum and a leading proponent of partnership between business and the arts, rejected religion and turned instead for moral improvement to the pecuniary and technological rationality of corporate capitalism. "Business runs the world," Dana pontificated in 1909. "The world gets civilized just as fast as men learn to run things on plain business principles."[11]

By the eve of World War I, the growth of corporate management in numbers and prestige had culminated in the founding of the National Association of Corporation Schools (NACS), the first professional society of managers. The very name underlined the symbiotic relationship of managerial expertise and corporate hegemony. (The NACS changed its name to the American Management Association in 1923.) The NACS could exude an eerily religious fervor to "vocational guidance" and other branches of professional management. At the NACS's annual convention in Buffalo in 1917, one speaker enthused, without a trace of irony, that vocational education and other kinds of corporation training portended "the surrender of the soul to the machine-made God of the Twentieth-Century Utility." In his apparently undisputed opinion, the gospel of efficiency was a modern brand of Christianity. "I see in efficiency," he continued, the individual "as Christ saw him, in his soul." Calling on his brethren to teach "the holiness of labor," he proclaimed his confidence that, properly managed, the average worker could experience "joy, progress, and reward in the things he does."[12]

"Joy" was the goal of the most infamous species of management thought: "Taylorism" or "scientific management." Scientific management is easily—and rightly—vilified as a form of social engineering, a program for dehumanization, a beatific vision for control freaks. Historians have long recognized that Taylor's time-and-motion studies marked a pinnacle—or perhaps a nadir—in the development of the modern superego, the bourgeois quest to bring desire and impulse under systematic, rational control. Just as other Victorian prodigies of self-mastery sought to bring sexual life and erotic fantasy under the authority of reason (witness John Harvey Kellogg and his regimen of diet, enemas, and girdles), Taylor extended the empire of reason into the smallest details of the workplace.[13] Thus, in this view, Taylorism and scientific management represent archetypes of disenchantment: if, as Weber contended, the modern project of rationalization began in Protestant theology and moralism, Taylor and his colleagues brought the process under the aegis of science and technology.

But rationalization and enchantment have never been mutually exclusive; from early Puritan modernity in England to the evangelical dispensation in America, pecuniary reason and instrumental rationality have overlapped with intimations of divinity in the world. Undertaken during the decline of evangelical hegemony, the corporate reconstruction of American capitalism was no less a crusade for beloved community: witness the ideal of the "soulful corporation." Like other prophets of management, Taylor thought of his industrial research as more than a science of workplace authority. As one of his first biographers revealed, Taylor thought of himself as one of *The Dreamers* (1910) praised by Herbert Kaufman, a newspaperman and popular specialist in inspirational twaddle. "Their vision lies within their souls . . . through all the ages they have heard the voice of Destiny call to them from the unknown vasts . . . they are the chosen few—the Blazers of the Way."[14] That might seem exalted for time-and-motion studies, but Taylor believed that his science of work was a blueprint for brotherly love.

Like many a prophet, theologian, or philosopher, Taylor transformed his inner demons into a powerful moral imagination. Raised among the Quaker bluebloods of Philadelphia, Taylor lived the explosive contradictions of a privileged but repressive upbringing. His father was a gentle and somewhat lackadaisical lawyer; his mother, Emily, was an erudite and spartan pillar of

Victorian propriety. Emily's parental style was Dickensian, by way of Thomas Gradgrind: she subjected young Fred and his siblings not only to a regimen of "work, drill, and discipline," but also to a fierce competition in which "child [was] remorselessly pitted against child." Later, while a student at Philips Exeter, Taylor sought to acquire complete control of his mind and body. Rather than wander pleasurably in the woods, he measured the length of his walking stride so as to cover the greatest distance with the least expenditure of energy. Afraid of nightmares caused, so he thought, by lying on his back, he slept in a harness rigged with sticks to prick him when he reclined. Before he arrived at dances, he would carefully categorize all the girls in terms of their relative attractiveness. An indefatigable killjoy, he insisted fanatically on strict adherence to the rules of any game he was playing. This behavior would seem to suggest the most leaden and thoroughgoing disenchantment; but as Sudhir Kakar observes, these ritualistic habits were "akin to magical thinking"—the repetition of thoughts or actions in order to subdue the unpredictable.[15] Fearful and trembling in the valley of the wonderful—forests, slumber, women—young man Taylor relied on reason, stripped of imagination and reduced to technology. Though longing for ecstasy, Taylor rued the uncontrollable; so the repressed returned with a prosaic vengeance, overwhelming him with a fanatical devotion to order. Rooted in a similar effort to master the intractable material of humanity, scientific management arose, in part, from the psychic regions of enchantment.

The story of Taylorism has been told many times: Taylor's own two-decade apprenticeship in shop floor technology and politics; his (considerably oversold) accomplishments at the Midvale Steel Works, embodied in "Schmidt," the Ajax of scientific management; his stormy tenure as president of the ASME (1906–1907); the publicity afforded by the Eastern Rates case of 1910, in which Louis Brandeis drew on Taylor's principles of efficiency to argue for wage hikes without railroad rate increases; the 1911 strike at the federal arsenal in Watertown, Massachusetts, which both occasioned a much-publicized Congressional investigation of the movement and prompted Taylor to write *The Principles of Scientific Management,* an exposition and defense of his work. In the same year, Taylor's followers in the ASME—or, as they dubbed themselves, his "disciples"—broke with the organization to form the Society to Promote the Science of Management, or the "Taylor Society." Through its bulletin as well as other evangelizing projects—

conventions, lectures, and numerous books and essays—the Taylor Society disseminated the master's teachings: the wresting of all technical knowledge from workers and its reconstruction as "science" in the possession of management; the scientific study and selection of workers; the reunion of science and the worker under the direction of managers; the breakdown of tasks to determine the most efficient method of their performance—the "one best way."[16] Fulfilling the dreams of Ure and Babbage, scientific management was the most comprehensive ideology of capitalist authority yet devised.

Critics of Taylorism abounded. The most formidable enemy was Robert F. Hoxie, a University of Chicago labor economist and a special investigator for the US Commission on Industrial Relations. After berating Taylor and his disciples for overstating their science's contribution to productivity, Hoxie added insult to injury by noting that the movement was "cursed with fakirs" and "industrial patent medicine men," charlatans with clipboards and stop watches. Helen Marot, executive secretary to the Women's Trade Union League, observed in 1914 that "the difference between scientific management and organized labor is that the aim of the latter is to make men, the aim of the former is to make goods."[17]

Yet the aim of scientific management *was* to "make men" and rebuild their characters; indeed, as Taylor and his disciples often pointed out, the reconstruction and even redemption of men was its primary goal. Repelled by the apparent soullessness of engineering specs and blueprints, critics of technocracy and other scientific utopias often forget the desires for communion that impel the embrace of mechanized mutuality. It's banal to reiterate that scientific management was a form of human engineering; what's more intriguing, as well as more disturbing, is its larger and deeper aspirations. Taylor's ominous pronouncement in *The Principles of Scientific Management*—"in the past the man was first. In the future the system will be first"—was, to his mind, an augury of beatitude, a declaration of industrial interdependence in which all would find fulfillment. Taylor always presented scientific management not merely as a technique of productive efficiency but also as a program for a corporate humanism. Taylor insisted on the profoundly humane implications of industrial discipline. Musing that "a life which is one continuous struggle with other men is hardly worth living," Taylor saw the end of this Hobbesian war in the embrace of his managerial wisdom. With the adoption of scientific management, class war in the workplace would give way to "close, intimate, personal cooperation between the management and the men." In a visionary gesture to the end of alienation, Taylor imagined a corporate self, a moral personality constructed on the basis of labor and scientific knowledge. In a properly managed workplace, "each man possesses his own individuality and loses none of his originality and proper personal initiative," while at the same time agreeing to be "controlled by and . . . work harmoniously with many other men."[18]

Taylor repeated these utopian claims even in the face of withering skepticism. Testifying before the special Congressional committee charged to investigate the Watertown strike, Taylor expounded with prophetic ardor on the prospects for industrial amity. Yes, he crowed, productivity would increase with frictionless class relations: "the size of the surplus created by their joint efforts is truly astounding." But then Taylor dwelled on the broader moral and spiritual renovation made possible by scientific management. The embrace of industrial cooperation under the auspices of trained managerial professionals constituted a "great mental revolution," he declared—not so much for efficiency, but for "the substitution of peace for war . . . of hearty brotherly cooperation for contention and strife; of replacing suspicious watchfulness with mutual confidence; of becoming friends instead of enemies."[19] Taylor restated the American dream first imagined by Puritans and evangelicals: the consummation of history in the felicitous, lucrative rapport of labor and capital.

Though the master himself was indifferent to conventional religion, his "disciples," as the inner circle in the Taylor Society dubbed themselves, bore the ark of the covenant with the zeal of converts and the haughty self-assurance of clerics. Lawyer and jurist Felix Frankfurter was not engaging in hyperbole when he berated the Taylor Society for its imperious and "dogmatic faith" in scientific management. Writing of a prominent scientific manager he had befriended, Randolph Bourne remarked that his self-assured proficiency suggested "a walking evangel, an insistent, reiterate note of a new thing that is to dominate mankind." This "new thing" combined religious devotion, philosophical subtlety, and the precision of productive efficiency. One of a "mystic number" of seven men chosen by "the great Founder" Taylor, the managerial evangelist preached a "new gospel" of scientific knowledge and industrial peace. Though resisted, like any missionary, by benighted heathens—manufacturers and labor leaders locked in unregenerate class struggle—the new manager trusted that the truth of the gospel would overcome those who seemed to him, as Bourne put it, "as foolish as the obscurantists who opposed Galileo." Bourne feared that apostles of the new religion—"the one best way"—would seek the extension of Taylorist principles to areas of life outside the purview of managerial scrutiny. His friend maintained that the new management theory was "a course in character-building," a regimen of virtue akin to the wisdom of antiquity. Surveying the empire of business with "Stoic calm," the scientific manager was "an industrial Marcus Aurelius."[20]

The religious character of scientific management was evident not only to contemporary observers but also to members of the movement as well. As the members of the Efficiency Society avowed their enchantment in the inaugural issue of their journal in 1913, they were "apostles of a single faith, a faith so large, so universal, that it benefits all fields, and in varying guises inhabits all nature, animate and inanimate." Testifying before the Interstate Commerce Commission in the fall of 1910, Frank Gilbreth nodded in agreement when one commissioner observed that scientific management had "become a sort of substitute for religion with you." Gilbreth's fellow disciples were at least as evangelical. Taylor, H. L. Persons declared, was a "Seeker of Truth." Morris Cooke asserted that Taylor had taken the Sermon on the Mount and turned it into "a practical, profitable, working formula." The promise of Christianity awaited the day when "the principles of scientific management have permeated every nook and cranny of the working world." (Cooke fondly quoted a French priest who had sermonized that "the love of God is the Taylor system of the inner life.") H. L. Gantt concluded *Organizing for Work* (1919) by tracing a direct historical line from Christ to Taylor. Christ, Gantt explained, was the real founder of scientific management, "the first great Economist." Indeed, scientific management was merely "applied Christianity." Although "the great leaders of the Church of the middle ages" had recognized Christ's status, their scholastic "intellectualism" had obscured His managerial wisdom—which implied that Taylor and his disciples were the heirs of medieval clerical authority. But if medieval clerics and Protestant proprietors had awaited the fullness of redemption at the end of time, scientific managers bore witness to a consummation on this side of paradise. Harrington Emerson, for instance, opened his textbook *Efficiency as a Basis for Operation and Wages* (1919) by assuring readers of the capacity of scientific management to confer on modern civilization attributes formerly attributed to divinity: "infinite goodness, infinite wisdom, infinite power."[21]

To be sure, many writers and enthusiasts were coldly pragmatic about Taylorism. Even as they shared the movement's religious spirit, they stated clearly and unapologetically that managers aimed at class subordination and the enlargement of surplus value. Gilbreth asserted forthrightly in his *Primer of Scientific Management* (1912) that one of the chief purposes of the new science was to mystify and mechanize workers. "The laborer does not understand it, nor is he expected to understand it." Originally one of Taylor's most trusted disciples, Gilbreth became one of the master's most hated competitors, recoiling from the humanistic cant so common among managerial missionaries. "It is the aim of Scientific Management to induce men to act as nearly like machines as possible," he admitted proudly. Hugo Munsterberg—one of the founders of industrial psychology and a prominent public face of scientific management—conceded that the principal objective of what he dubbed "economic psychotechnics" was to "produce most completely the influence on human minds which are desired in the interests of business."[22]

Despite these avowedly mercenary pronouncements, Progressives lauded scientific management as the social technology of communion. Brandeis praised Taylor's "infinite patience and genius," hailing him as a "revelator of industrial truth." After visiting Ford's Sociological Department, Ida Tarbell became a promoter of enlightened corporate leadership. In a series of articles for *American Magazine* in 1914, Tarbell waxed ecstatic as she described "the Golden Rule in Business." Trained in scientific management, the corporate manager was an "entirely new type of employer," an "educator" and "friend of men" whose factory was a school of character. Even the staff of the *New Republic* succumbed to the mystique of scientific management. "Mr. Taylor and his followers have made a major contribution to civilization," as one editorial concluded near Christmas 1916. Walter Lippmann enthused that the managerial class would administer the "modern communion" portended by corporate organization. If patriarchal avarice had driven "the old chop-whiskered merchants," he wrote in *Drift and Mastery* (1914), the "civilizing passions" of science and public service inspired managers, who tempered "the primal desire to have and to hold and to conquer." Herbert Croly anointed Taylor's handiwork "the great critical and regenerative influence in business organization," a utopian discourse that revealed "the relation between scientific business and economic democracy."[23]

The many faces of management theory—one "mechanical" and "scientific," the other "brotherly" and even religious—fused more completely and lissomely after World War I. Prompted by the labor militancy of the war years, the emergence of what came to be called "industrial" or "human relations" marked an evolution, not a repudiation, of Taylorism and scientific management. Eager to wash his hands of the blood spilled in the Ludlow massacre of April 1914, John D. Rockefeller, Jr. ("Junior") espoused a "new industrial creed" when speaking to the Chamber of Commerce in Atlantic City in December 1918. W. L. Mackenzie King, a Canadian politician who also worked as an industrial relations consultant for General Electric, Bethlehem Steel, and the Rockefellers, exhorted businesspeople in *Industry and Humanity* (1918) to bring "the economy of God" to earth.[24]

King's advocacy of enlightened management inspired those who hoped for a "soulful" corporation. Two of the more portentous documents of industrial relations were *Industrial Goodwill* (1919) and *Industrial Government* (1921), a two-volume collection of reports by industrial researchers working under the direction of John R. Commons. Originally a missionary for the social gospel, Commons had been dismissed from Syracuse University for his advocacy of workers' rights and the living wage. Hired by the University of Wisconsin, Commons embarked on a career as a labor historian and industrial relations specialist, serving on the US Commission on Industrial Relations and establishing the first program in the field at Wisconsin. Although Commons had dismissed Ford's Sociological Department and other managerial schemes as mere schemes of industrial autocracy, he warmed to scientific management when he accompanied Taylor on factory tours during the 1910s. Impressed by Junior Rockefeller's penitent professions of benevolence and reform, Commons put aside the childish things of youth and assumed the maturity of corporate management. Commons and his colleagues presented a semi-ecclesial account of the corporation and its human members. "A corporation is said to have no soul," but Commons replied that its soul resided in its "goodwill." Goodwill—which Commons used interchangeably with "soul" and "personality"—signified the sum total of human relationships in the corporate workplace. A "multiple of all the different personalities that keep the business going," goodwill was "a spirit of brotherhood" that united workers and employers in the consciousness of a common cause. From this mystical body, corporate selfhood projected "personality" into its products, advertising, customer service, even its stocks and bonds. Indeed, Commons wrote, "the modern corporation specializes in personality."[25]

Corporate personhood consisted, the Commons team maintained, in "zeal for progress and pride in a great enterprise," an excitement that lit up "the most menial and stupefying task with the rays of a great industrial vision." If this seemed quite a bit to expect from pushing a broom, feeding a machine, or typing yet another letter, Commons and his researchers insisted that, through the imaginative vistas opened up by corporate production, the modern firm afforded "more chances for personality than ever were known before in industry." Led by the new professional-managerial workers—who annulled the old covenant of authoritarian proprietorship and replaced it with the new law of "personality"—corporations would move from "business to humanity." As one of Commons's researchers put it without a trace of irony, management was moving "from figures to feelings as instruments of control." Thus, "the new humanism" in management was the magnanimous orchestration of emotional and spiritual life.[26]

The managerial shift from "business to humanity" was a glimpse of the corporate future. Searching, like the evangelical economists, for amity in the midst of competition, managerial clerics developed a science and technology of brotherhood. Finney's "arithmetic of faith"—the evangelical fusion of religious emotion and pecuniary reason—assumed a new form in the time-and-motion studies of Taylor, Gilbreth, and other scientific managers. The fabrication of sentiment, implicit in Taylor's work and clearly recommended by the Commons team, would inspire the "human relations" lineage of Mary Parker Follett, Elton Mayo, Peter Drucker, and later philosophers of management. In its subtle move "from figures to feelings," management theory extended the American technological sublime into the realm of human personality. At the same time, the cultivation of good feelings, once originally directed toward the paternal proprietor, could now be lavished on the corporate person. The attribution of "soul" and "personality" to the capitalist firm epitomized the corporate reconstruction of charisma.

# 10

# The Spirit of the Thing

## Advertising and the Incorporation of the Beatific Vision

WHILE MANAGERS PURSUED the mechanization of charisma and communion at the point of production, other corporate professionals took the point of consumption as a gateway to enchantment. The rise of modern consumer culture in the half-century after the Civil War has sparked a sizable literature, and at this point, we should need no further persuasion that commodities bear enormous psychic and existential freight. Yet this trove of knowledge about consumer culture is also an embarrassment of riches, for historians remain deeply divided about its ultimate historical significance. For a long time, the dominant view of consumer culture was negative and censorious. In this view, the atrophy of producerist values left Americans suspended in a metaphysical and moral vacuum, prey to the wiles of commodity fetishism. Dispossessed from property and production, unbound from the work ethic, and indentured to corporate hierarchies, they increasingly embraced what Lears has called "a gospel of therapeutic release." With the erosion of Protestantism, traditional aspirations to transcendence gave way to "self-fulfillment and immediate gratification"—goals that, given economic growth, no longer seemed sinful or unattainable. But while it freed Americans from the more onerous strictures of evangelical morality, consumer culture also imprisoned the self in a culture of advertising, marketing, and professional advice. With enviable aesthetic and moral virtuosity, corporate-image professionals redefined freedom and happiness as access to consumer pleasures. Unlike heaven, "the dream life of capitalism," as Leach dubs it, is an endless pageant of goods and services. Democracy became, in Marchand's words, a "Republic of Goods," while the image of the human person became, as Leach describes it, "an insatiable, desiring machine . . . an animal governed by an infinity of desires." The horrible irony of American consumer culture is that, despite its claims to foster liberation, the "land of desire" or "culture of narcissism" is more thoroughly controlled through pleasure and anxiety than through threats of physical coercion.[1]

Yet in another, more optimistic view, consumer culture is a great emancipator, emptying the Protestant dungeons of patriarchy, privation, and parochialism. The apocalypse of the producers' republic becomes the advent of a moral revolution. By sweeping away the family farm and workshop, corporate capitalism dethroned the patriarch, emasculated evangelical moralism, and cleared space for new political movements—feminism, racial equality, sexual liberation. Thanks to the corporate form of ownership, proprietorship and labor began to recede as the primary sources of personal identity; thanks to industrial productivity, thrift and self-denial began to give way to self-fulfillment as the axis of moral order. In dance halls, department stores, and amusement parks, and in the images of plenty disseminated by advertising, consumers entertained the prospect of living beyond the strictures of scarcity. Enlarging the material and conceptual boundaries of human possibility, consumer culture enabled Americans to envision the transcendence of pecuniary reason. "In the midst of plenty, the imagination becomes ambitious," as Walter Lippmann observed in *Drift and Mastery*. "Rebellion against misery is at last justified, and dreams have a basis in fact."[2] Champions of consumer culture see, not decadence, but a new order of justice and generosity. Far from raising a pandemonium of nihilists, consumer culture is a new school of character, a soul's economy rooted in abundance.

Whether they see consumer culture as a form of bondage or as a prophecy of impending jubilee, historians agree that it draws its power from the deepest recesses of desire. Indeed, as James Livingston has written of advertising, it represents "the last utopian idiom of our time." For their own avowedly pecuniary purposes, the inventors of modern consumer culture recruited these ineffable aspirations. They knew that consumers desired more than a mere accumulation of objects; they studied and captured the immortal longing for an enchanted, beloved community. Just as Walt Whitman wanted things and people to become his "friendly companions," advertisers and other late–nineteenth-century enchanters attempted, in Lears's words, to effect "the reanimation of the inanimate world under the aegis of major corporations."[3]

I would venture further than Lears or Livingston. Consumer culture is a counterfeit beatific vision, a realm of coruscating misenchantment, a corporate atlas for a parodic sacramental way of being in the world. Conjured up to intensify, not to mellow, the rage to produce and accumulate, consumer culture served the managerial quest for communion through mechanization. Advertisers *were* appealing to human desires for self-transfiguration; they *were* employing the language of religion for avowedly commercial purposes. But they also believed that the goods they marketed possessed spiritual and moral treasures. Like soulful executives and scientific managers, admen believed that the culture of consumption held a promise of beloved community.

Although the history of advertising is well-trodden ground, it remains an essential point of departure in any tale of consumer culture. In the decades after Reconstruction, the modern advertising industry emerged from the bedlam of patent medicine peddlers, sideshow barkers, circus impresarios, and other itinerant performers. Indelibly marked by bunkum, fraud, and exotic sensuality, the antebellum carnival culture bore no shred of respectability. Outside the world of carnival, advertising was an almost entirely local affair, controlled by small-town merchants and newspaper editors. With the rise of corporations and a national marketplace, ambitious and far-seeing editors and salespeople saw the opportunity to create a new market for commercial imagery. Beginning in the 1870s, a new breed of advertisers— George P. Rowell, Francis Wayland Ayer, Albert Lasker, J. Walter Thompson, and Charles Austin Bates—sought both to establish durable connections to national corporations and to purge commercial imagery and its creators of any hint of dishonesty. One of the primary objectives of advertising agencies was the achievement of professional recognition and legitimacy. Ayer, who had founded N. W. Ayer and Sons in 1869, pioneered the use of marketing surveys and other statistically-based methods that lent to advertising an aura of scientific veracity. Trade journals such as *Fame, Publicity,* and *Printers' Ink* proliferated; the latter, founded by Rowell in 1888, was the fledgling profession's premiere periodical until well into the next century.[4]

Over the next twenty years, Claude C. Hopkins, Earnest Elmo Calkins, Ralph Holden, and other admen completed the metamorphosis of advertising from a species of carnival into a respected profession. As Calkins and

Holden proudly asserted in *Modern Advertising* (1905), where the older advertising had been "an untrustworthy instrument of quacks and charlatans," the new advertiser sought to transform it "from an art to a science—or, at least, to a profession worthy of the ambition and energy of trained minds." Employing "plain speech" rather than carnivalesque playfulness, advertisers increasingly invoked the epistemological conventions of modern science, whose cultural authority was rising among the middle and working classes. Calkins, Hopkins, and other admen drew on the work of applied psychologists, such as Walter Dill Scott, director of Northwestern's psychological laboratory and an instructor in the university's business school. Like their counterparts in scientific management, Scott and other advocates of "scientific advertising" believed that business now required an empirical, experimental basis. "The day of reckless, sporadic, haphazard advertising is rapidly coming to an end," Scott crowed triumphantly in *Atlantic Monthly* in January 1904. Business could now "establish advertising on a theoretical basis deduced from psychology." By the end of World War I, advertisers had overcome associations with the carnivalesque successfully enough to join managers as members of the professional-managerial class. Speaking with numerous businesspeople while visiting the United States, G. Lowes Dickinson observed that they considered advertising "a serious, important, and elevating department of business," a discipline rooted in "a profound study of human nature." Former President William Howard Taft could declare, at a testimonial dinner for Ayer in 1919, that advertising had been cleansed "of many of its evil tendencies," and that it was now "a form of publicity so useful and elevating, which might have been vicious and deplorable."[5]

Just as advertisers sought professional repute, the actual makers of commercial imagery—illustrators, photographers, graphic artists—aspired to aesthetic respectability. The market for commercial art expanded along several lines. Illustrators found opportunities with book publishers and with general interest magazines, such as *Collier's, Ladies Home Journal,* the *Saturday Evening Post,* and *Everybody's.* The growth of advertising agencies and corporate advertising departments, together with technological developments in lithography and photography, offered unprecedented opportunities for artists to design posters, billboards, calendars, and print advertisements. Artists with a decidedly pecuniary or administrative bent gravitated toward art direction; the Art Directors Club was founded in 1920 with considerable encouragement from Calkins. While the new political economy of commercial art afforded steady and occasionally quite lucrative employment, it also raised issues about the aesthetic character of images produced for mercenary purposes. Indeed, the increasing ubiquity of mass-produced commercial images between 1890 and 1920 triggered a heated and sometimes acrimonious debate about the meaning and boundaries of art. This art war of the early twentieth century pitted stalwart defenders of the fine art tradition—often housed in museums and academies—against the practitioners and partisans of commercial art in agencies and corporations. To a remarkable degree, this conflict forged the terms of artistic debate with which we are all too familiar: the creative independence of the artist against subservience to the imperatives of business; the affirmation of purely aesthetic considerations against the need to cater to popular sensibilities; art as beauty, transcendence, and truth against art as marketable commodity. This antagonism saw its most renowned literary portrayal in Dreiser's *The "Genius"* (1915), in which the painter Eugene Witla is corrupted and destroyed by "the presence and dangled lure of money."[6]

Yet if Dreiser affirmed the ideals of self-expression and aesthetic integrity, the new generation of commercial artists—from Charles Dana Gibson and Howard Pyle to Maxfield Parrish—contended that they could arrange a rapprochement between art and corporate business. Insistent that their work was as aesthetically accomplished as that of their highbrow peers, commercial practitioners demanded to be taken seriously as artists as well as productive workers. Even scientific advertisers such as Scott and Calkins promoted these aesthetic ambitions. "The designer of advertisements must be something more than a skilled artisan," Scott wrote in *The Theory of Advertising* (1903). "He must be an artist and must be able to put soul into his work . . . the art demands the work of an artist." Although his status as a cultural warrior for business rose mainly after World War I, Calkins was, almost from the beginning of his career, a tireless advocate for the inclusion of commercial illustration in the realm of the fine arts. Calkins organized the first advertising art exhibits in 1908, and his push to establish the Art Directors Club stemmed from his conviction that commercial art was a worthy aesthetic pursuit. Indeed, as Michelle Bogart and others have demonstrated, the boundaries between highbrow and popular art in America were much more permeable at the turn of the century than they later became. In 1907, when the Museum of Modern Art considered establishing a collection of black-and-white advertising illustrations, it received the support not only of illustrators but also of leading painters, such as John Singer Sargent. Such a collection was necessary, one curator argued, to distinguish illustrations of genuine aesthetic merit from the "mass of commercial trash that under the name of art is daily being dished up to an unsuspecting public."[7]

To be sure, many agency executives and art directors dismissed the aesthetic aspirations of their artists. In the churlish refrain of bourgeois culture, they were in business to make money; "art" was a pastime of fashionable women, effeminate men, and bohemian longhairs. Too much aesthetic virtuosity—"oversmartness," as one executive called it—risked confusing or offending clients and customers. Yet while plain speech persisted in much of advertising copy and imagery, more and more agencies and art departments came to recognize the aesthetic and commercial value of visual "oversmartness." In an increasingly crowded marketplace of commodities and images, manufacturers and advertisers needed to distinguish their products from those of their competitors, and visual appeal was an obvious and powerful weapon in the battle for sales. Industry leaders began to assert that advertisements had to do more than convey information about a product; they had to generate an aura that invested the object with immaterial properties. As the ad executive James H. Collins observed in *Printers' Ink* in 1901, the successful advertiser now embedded his product in an "economy of symbols," a constellation of words and images that evoked emotional associations over and above straightforward use values. The most effective ads not only hawked goods; they elicited hopes, told edifying stories, built camaraderie with the merchandise. Smiling faces and personable products began to abound in American advertising in the first decade of the twentieth century; well before Roland Barthes revealed the "mythologies" encoded in advertisements, industry professionals and journalists were spreading the new folklore of commodities. In the first of a series of *Collier's* articles on "The New American Trade" in 1909, Samuel Hopkins Adams called attention to the "decent and companionable myths" that enveloped Cream-of-Wheat, Campbell's Soups, and Quaker Oats. The myths were evidently so decent and companionable that they rather charmed Adams—one of the more indefatigable and prolific muckrakers—who wrote pleasantly of the "hale old friends" and "round-eyed chubs" who crowded the new visual universe.[8] Whitman's "friendly companions" were everywhere.

Adams's appreciation of "myths" undoubtedly impressed W. R. Emery, an advertising manager for *Everybody's* and a salient cleric in the new capitalist "economy of symbols." Writing on "the personality of a product" in a 1910 issue of *Printers' Ink,* Emery produced a theoretical essay on the corporate ensoulment of commodities. "Every machine, every enterprise, every product has its personality which may contribute to the advancement of the salesman, the distributor, and the manufacturer himself." The attribution of life to a standardized object was not visual flourish or humbug; as Emery explained, it was a product's personality "that vitalizes an inanimate object, that makes it mean more than a mere expression of power, that kindles enthusiasm, that brings about the intimacy of acquaintanceship."[9] As Marcel Mauss might have put it, advertisers endowed commodities with the mana of a corporation. Of course, Emery underlined the pecuniary rationale for the corporate enchantment of products. Like the "soul" of a corporation, the personality of a commodity was a "tangible asset when capitalized"—it achieved a fuller, or its fullest, reality when converted into capital. Thus Emery's insistence that products had souls was more than mercenary sophistry. The animation of commodities followed naturally from the pecuniary metaphysics of corporate enchantment.

Emery's promotion of enchantment had already been lampooned by H. G. Wells in *Tono-Bungay* (1908), an indictment of the new advertising culture that was far more elegant and perspicacious than Dreiser's. Though set in Britain, Wells's send-up of market amorality was readily appreciated by American readers: "Tono-Bungay," the eponymous tonic, was modeled after Carter's Little Liver Pills, a patent medicine concocted by Samuel J. Carter in 1864 and still popular forty years later. "Tono-Bungay" is invented by Edward Ponderevo, a failed pharmacist and genial quack determined to get rich and hobnob with the aristocracy. To promote the product, he enlists his nephew George, a scientist who's painfully ambivalent about the duplicity. Ashamed to be peddling "rubbish for the consumption of foolish, credulous, and depressed people" (the claims he and his uncle make for the tonic's restorative powers are a "Ton O' Bunk, eh?"), George carries his bad conscience all the way to the bank. Yet he comes to realize he's also trafficking in powerful human desires. His epiphany arrives when he chats with Ewart, an artist employed to embellish the elixir who descants on "the poetry of commerce." Far from being a crassly manipulative affair, the relationship of adman to customer is, to Ewart, one of vatic sublimity, "poet answering to poet—soul to soul." Trapped in the humdrum tyranny of the workplace, people are frustrated artists, Ewart tells George: "Think of the little overworked clerks and jaded women and overworked people . . . nobody wants to keep sticking labels on silly bottles at so many farthings a gross."[10] In addition to curing physical ills, Tono-Bungay salves the wounds inflicted by mechanization and managerial control.

Yet Ewart muses that the potion also allays other, more ontological maladies as well. In a brilliant meditation on the fraudulent paradise depicted in advertising, Wells limns the disfigured sacramental desire that enlivens commodity fetishism. "My special and distinctive duty," Ewart declares, is "to give Tono-Bungay substance and an outward and visible bottle." Offering a beatific vision, advertising enchants both lifeless things and enervated, impoverished souls. As Ewart explains to George, the advertiser is a magician of meaning, bestowing value on mass-produced objects. He "takes something that isn't worth anything—or something that isn't particularly worth anything—and he makes it worth something." Transfiguring the world of goods through the consecrating alchemy of commercial art, advertising is "mercy—it's salvation. It's rescue work! It takes all sorts of fallen commodities by the hand and raises them." With their longings for rapturous fulfillment, ordinary people are like fallen commodities, exiles from the garden of enchantment. They are "overstrained with wanting to be," Ewart asserts; they have a "hunger to be—for once, really alive—to the finger tips!" "That's what this—in the highest sense—muck stands for," he insists: the achievement of existential exuberance, the transubstantiation of humanity. "Health, Strength, and Beauty—in a bottle—the magic philtre! Like a fairy tale." An epitome of commodity fetishism, Tono-Bungay is a false promise of eternal happiness, a simulacrum of sacramental presence. As Uncle Edward reminds his vexed protégé, "we mint Faith, George"—a misguided and exploitable longing for bodily and spiritual exhilaration.[11]

As a good Fabian socialist, Wells considered most advertising a thoroughly cynical business. His comparison to religion was invidious as well as incisive: like priests and magicians, advertisers were the latest investors in the exploitation of credulity. American advertisers could have supplied Wells with even more ample and shameless evidence that advertising played on religious faith. Take, for instance, *Sermons on Advertising* (1907) by Seymour Eaton, a Philadelphia journalist, promoter, and creator of the "Teddy Bear." Published the same year as *Tono-Bungay* by the J. Walter Thompson Agency, it consisted of short "sermons"—each prefaced by a biblical passage— contained in a book that was framed as a church to be attended by an elect. With a faint gesture to Calvinist theology, the cover emphasized that the volume was a "Limited Edition" and that it had been "Published Exclusively for Original Pew Holders." The next page was an "Entrance Door Mat" which instructed the readers / congregants to "Please leave Umbrellas and Wraps in the Vestibule." Once the faithful were assembled, Eaton delivered his hom- ily—for the most part, a collection of advertising nostrums decked out in biblical allusions. Advertising must appeal to "the substance of things hoped for, and the evidence of things not seen." Commodities resembled the lus- cious vintage of Eden—sensuous, forbidden, the property of divinity. Goods were like "the apple on the tree of life," an "exclusive fruit reserved specially for the gods. That is why we want it." "We are all Adams and Eves," Eaton observed. Having preached the Word, he concluded the book by announcing that "the Congregation is now dismissed." Yet Eaton laced his sermons with a biting and discordant cynicism that suggested a tongue lodged firmly in cheek. "All conventional life is more or less sham," he snarled at one point, "as spotted with hypocrisy as a child with measles." Elsewhere, Eaton advised that "a strong personality can add a heavenly halo to a very ordinary hobo lie."[12] This unabashed mendacity suggested that the line between truth and falsehood was not so much clear as irrelevant to Eaton—as well as to J. Walter Thompson and other advertising professionals.

Others in the industry lacked Eaton's blend of solemnity and prevarica- tion. Even as they acknowledged the fabricated quality of product "person- ality" and symbolism, neither Emery nor Collins exhibited anything but sin- cerity. For them, no moral or metaphysical crisis attended the attribution of personality to a mass-produced commodity. Like others among the ideolog- ical vanguard of corporate America, the first generation of advertisers were true believers in the promise of commodity civilization. When, in 1899, L. Frank Baum—author of *The Wonderful Wizard of Oz* (1900) and editor of *The Show Window,* a leading decorative periodical—wrote that successful window displays evoke the "possibilities lying dormant in the beautiful goods," he articulated the existential aspirations of commodity fetishism.[13]

Often the sons of ministers, some of the leading advertising agents and theorists openly expressed their hostility to Protestant strictures against display and self-gratification. Drawing moral lessons from the carnival tent, admen often defended their profession as an enterprise in moral and spiritual education—or, rather, re-education, as evangelical Protestantism was a common background and enemy. Hopkins exemplified the pattern of strict upbringing and measured rebellion. Raised by harsh, poor fundamentalist parents in rural Michigan, he learned that pleasure was a snare and a delusion; "every joy in life was a sin," as he remembered bitterly. In a dramatic episode at the age of 18, Hopkins—then a student for the ministry—preached a sermon in his local church that ended with a stem-winding tirade against asceticism, countenancing "the harmless joys of life which had been barred to me." He left the church, and never looked back. Over a long and lucrative career, during which he worked for Lord and Thomas (Palmolive, Quaker Oats, and Pepsodent were a few of his clients), Hopkins pursued advertising as a surrogate for the ministry, referring to his work as his "vocation." Though he never shed the Protestant work ethic—he worked, he wrote, "for the love of working"—he asserted that advertising earned him "many rewards beyond money." As his autobiography clearly suggests, those "rewards" included the slow attrition of evangelical disapproval of indulgence in sensual delight. When Hopkins attributed his vocational success to his "love of simple things, of common people" and to his "love and knowledge of the masses," he linked his sense of fellowship to the rejection of skinflint morality.[14] Though he eschewed evangelical moralism, Hopkins remained a moralist, a cleric in the advertising ministry.

As the author of the textbook *Scientific Advertising* (1923), Hopkins reflected the striving of professionals and managers for personal perfection through science and technology. Promulgated by advertising, what Lears has called the "perfectionist project" recast old Protestant yearnings for regeneration in the idiom of scientific mastery. The fluid, expansive conception of the self at the heart of revivalism and carnival merged with ideals of managerial "efficiency." Thus, however different and even antagonistic they may appear to writers such as Daniel Bell—who saw in the opposition of work and consumption a "cultural contradiction of capitalism"—management and advertising bore greater affinities than we often realize. Hopkins's conception of his work as a "vocation" was indeed akin to the "calling" of professional management—the search for a technology of communion. As committed to scientific psychology as Hopkins was, Calkins anointed the advertising profession the avant-garde of the modern moral imagination, an heir to the tradition of religious prophecy. Advertising, he explained in 1905, "modifies the course of a people's daily thoughts, gives them new words and phrases, new ideas, new fashions, new prejudices and new customs." People "buy, believe, and think the things that the advertiser wants them to buy, believe, and think." Commencing a theme on which he would expand in the 1920s—when he would call on business to occupy the place once held but now lost by religion—Calkins compared the modern ad man to "Peter the Hermit, or a Savonarola, fiercely and earnestly impressing a crowd with his convictions."[15]

These were far from isolated sentiments among advertisers and their ideologues, many of whom piously expounded on the religious, enchanting nature of advertising. Speaking to the Sphinx Club at the Waldorf-Astoria in 1897, Artemus Ward—renowned as a pitchman for Sopolio soap—declared that advertising rested on a "foundation of faith." It was evil to "pervert the God-given opportunities which advertising offers in dealing with our fellow men." Calling on his profession to remain "inviolate" and "untarnished," Ward launched into a peroration on the sacred office of advertising. "It stands to me as an aspiration, a religion." Ward had been equally grandiloquent five years earlier, marveling in *Fame* on the capacity of goods to offer intimations of the supernatural. The enjoyment of commodities hinted that "beyond our touch, beyond our waking, beyond our working, and almost in the land of dreams, lie things beyond our present thought, greater, wider, stronger, than those we lay hold on now." "To each a world opens," he beckoned; "to everyone possibilities are present." "Our greatest and most successful advertisers are mystics," one contributor to *Printers' Ink* mused in 1904 in an essay on "the occult-mystical side of advertising." Capable of inducing "soulful vibrations" in consumers, these mystics possess "a keener insight into the nature of things." Over a decade later, the leading advertising journal was still sounding this soulful note. The advertising department of a corporation was "the invisible department," wrote another professional; it was "the soul department." Most of the incompetence and vice of advertising agents could be traced to their harboring a "wobbly soul." In 1920, Thomas Masson, managing editor of *Life,* opined in *Printers' Ink* that "advertising is the master spirit of the age." Arguing that the advertiser must be "converted to the value of his product" and "experience it in just the way one experiences religion," Masson concluded with sacramental flourish that an ad must be "the outward and visible sign of an inward and spiritual conviction."[16]

Few epitomized the advertising culture of enchantment better than Elbert Hubbard, one of the country's most popular promoters and lecturers before World War I. Hubbard was a virtuoso of artifice. Though best known today as the founder of the Roycroft Arts and Crafts colony in East Aurora, New York, Hubbard was no implacable foe of industrial degradation. After a spell as a salesman for Larkin Soap, Hubbard found his true calling as a writer of "publicity preachments," jingles for "everything from toothpicks to motor trucks" that he sold to local businesses and corporations. Though a self-proclaimed socialist and admirer of William Morris, he socialized with class enemies like Elbert H. Gary and John D. Rockefeller. Although Roycroft's shares were owned by workers—furniture, bookbinding, and metalwork were the most profitable endeavors—Hubbard was a benevolent managerial despot. Eventually, he repudiated his socialist convictions and devoted his life to spirited defenses of free enterprise. In *A Message to Garcia* (1899)—a best-selling (and still popular) encomium to business success—Hubbard maintained against reformers and radicals that "all employers are not rapacious and high-handed."[17]

Fusing the artist and the businessman, Hubbard was a pioneer of bourgeois bohemianism. "Business should be beautiful," he wrote in 1915, "and it is fast becoming so." In his handsomely illustrated monthly publications, *The Philistine* ("A Periodical of Protest") and *The Fra Magazine* ("Exponent of the American Philosophy"), Hubbard blended satire with advertising and exhortations to self-improvement. All of life was a market, and "all men are advertisers . . . the only man who should not advertise is the man who has nothing to offer the world." A precursor of the corporate conquest of cool, the self-styled "Fra Elbertus" was among the first to see eccentricity as a valuable marketing tool; his "protest" was usually mere quirkiness, and his heterodoxy stopped with "the American Philosophy" of unregulated competition. With his long hair, Quaker hat, and calculated nonconformity, Hubbard was a prototype of the hipster-entrepreneur. The put-on was fairly obvious even then: in a 1911 profile of Hubbard for *Cosmopolitan,* one writer quipped that the advertiser-bard had "struck pay-dirt on Parnassus." Hubbard was no gypsy spirit; he was in fact "as sane as a cash register." "In the Roycroft religion, the collection is the supreme sacrament!" Hubbard was "a Moses turned real-estate promoter, and booming lots in the promised land."[18]

Yet when the *Cosmopolitan*'s profiler noted that money was the "supreme sacrament" of the "Roycroft religion," he touched, however sardonically, on a real truth about Hubbard. Precisely in his savvy with surfaces, Hubbard evinced his unwavering faith in "the American Philosophy." As one of his friends recalled after Hubbard and his wife went down with the Lusitania, Fra Elbertus "deified commerce" and "religionized his business." Dismissive of theology and organized religion as old-fashioned scams, Hubbard reserved his piety for capitalism. "We believe in Big Business and the Religion of Business," he proclaimed in *Fra.* "There is room in business for all your religion, all your poetry, all your love." Rather than wait for a Protestant heaven of flinty self-denial, advertisers and promoters like himself were "intent upon bringing about paradise, here and now." Advertising was the homiletic and visual evangelism of the Religion of Business. "When I want to hear really good sermons nowadays, we attend a weekly lunch of the ad club." (Hubbard's regular column in *Philistine* consisted of random musings, "Heart-to-Heart Talks with Philistines by the Pastor of his Flock." As always with Hubbard, the line between authenticity and bunkum was almost invisible.) Hubbard's Religion of Business merged the divine and the profane under the sign of the dollar. "There is no gulf between the secular and the sacred," he once pontificated. "The useful is the divine, and the helpful is the sacred." Profitable investment and labor was a priestly office of capitalist enchantment, as entrepreneurial adventure channeled the power of divinity. "I make my appeal to the Divinity in men," Hubbard once asserted. "Man's business is to be a good conductor of the divine current."[19]

Maxfield Parrish conducted the current of divinity in his popular images, which brought to an exquisite level of visibility the enchantment of commercial art. Best known for his lush and dreamlike prints, Parrish achieved the consummate point of corporate image production: the transition from enchantment *of* commodities to enchantment *as* a commodity. Known as "the Peter Pan of illustrators," Parrish was the most successful and beloved commercial artist of the twentieth century. Versatile and prolific, he produced an extensive portfolio of advertisements, prints, posters, murals, calendars, and book and magazine illustrations. (Known especially for "Parrish blues," his work was so ubiquitous that F. Scott Fitzgerald could refer in one of his earliest stories to "the color of Maxfield Parrish moonlight.") Though born and raised (like Frederick Taylor) among Philadelphia Quaker patricians, Parrish catered to middle-class tastes; his prints (especially *Daybreak*) graced the walls of millions of homes. Although he longed for acceptance by modernist painters who dismissed him as a hack and a sellout, Parrish came to take a kind of relish in his status as a vendor of exoticism. "I've always considered myself a popular artist," he said late in his life, and throughout his career he took unashamed and lucrative advantage of the corporate economy of art. Money assuaged any pain he felt at rejection by the avant-garde; "art is long, but business is business," as he once wrote to one of his clients.[20] Yet the quality of his work cannot be reduced to purely mercenary factors. While Parrish was one of the most gifted masters in the history of commodity fetishism, he aspired not only to animate and embellish but also to market beatitude itself. Parrish's work is a gallery of beatific visions, the mass production of visual enchantment.

Born in 1870 into a wealthy Quaker family (his father was a painter and self-styled bohemian), Parrish intended to become an architect when he enrolled in Haverford College. The future businessman-artist was the very embodiment of starry-eyed romanticism: his roommate recalled that Parrish possessed "a liberal allowance of Make-Believe" and inhabited "a cosmos entirely of his own concoction." (Their room became famous for its wall decorations, painted almost entirely by Parrish.) While a student at the Pennsylvania Academy of Fine Arts, Parrish traveled to the Chicago World's Fair, where the Fine Arts Building confirmed his convictions about the truth of the imagination. "One has only to come here," he wrote to his mother, "to find that what is known as caricature is after all a literal rendering of truth." When Howard Pyle, one of the country's leading commercial illustrators, praised a portfolio that Parrish had sent him, the young artist embarked on his career. Handsome and affable as well as talented, he made numerous contacts in the world of commercial art, and by the mid-1890s, he was the most up-and-coming book illustrator in the country. Over a dozen years, Parrish won praise for *Mother Goose in Prose* (1897), *Knickerbocker's History of New York* (1897), Edith Wharton's *Italian Villas and Their Gardens* (1904), and

*The Arabian Nights* (1909). At the same time, he took commissions for covers and illustrations from *Collier's, Scribner's, Hearst's, Harper's, Good House-keeping,* and *Everybody's.* He illustrated catalogues for Wanamaker's; painted murals such as *Florentine Fete* for the Curtis publishing headquarters in Philadelphia; decorated Christmas gift boxes for Crane's Chocolates (featuring the *Rubaiyat, Cleopatra,* and the *Garden of Allah*); glamorized Edison-Mazda bulbs for General Electric; and designed posters for Royal Baking Powder, Colgate, and Santa Claus Soap.[21]

Working to erase the line that divided fine art from commercial illustration, Parrish pushed the imaginative possibilities of advertising to what were then its farthest limits. As he wrote to a lithographer of an advertisement for Jell-O—"The King and Queen Might Eat Thereof and Noblemen Besides" (1921)—he wanted his images to offer "a contrast to the usual run of realism and prettiness." Parrish's distinctive economy of symbols—medieval, Renaissance, or "Oriental" settings full of knaves, jesters, maidens, knights, princes, monarchs, and mythological and fairy tale characters—often overwhelmed the merchandise. His pictures could be so captivating that, as one industry critic complained, the public "stared and delighted but forgot to notice what the pictures advertised." (Though in his most gorgeous advertisements for General Electric—"Spirit of the Night" and "Prometheus"—the bulb is clearly visible.) The Crane's chocolate boxes were typical. The *Rubaiyat* depicts a young couple reading together, foregrounded against luminous mountains; *Cleopatra* portrays a garlanded monarch, reclining in a boat, surrounded by slaves and attendants; the *Garden of Allah* shows three young women lounging alongside a pool. While working for Crane's, Parrish created similar scenes for Djer-Kiss Cosmetics, with girls sitting on swings or frolicking with elves.[22] Rendered with the vivid, almost photographic verisimilitude that characterized all of Parrish's work, the settings evoke perennial longings for *luxe, calme, et volupte.* The only things missing are the chocolates and cosmetics.

The premiere commercial artist of his time admitted openly that the actual commodity held little interest for him. Rather than merely festoon a product with pretty pictures, Parrish sought to exhibit "*the spirit of the thing* . . . in which we take the most joy and happiness in life." Indeed, Parrish's images are perhaps better described as commercial evocations rather than illustrations. The product per se was not the point; the issue, for Parrish, was the elusive, the transcendent, the *mana* of the thing. In Parrish's world of commodities, Crane's chocolates were tokens of paradise; General Electric's bulbs and lamps were gifts from Prometheus or the torches of Mazda, the Persian god of light; Fisk Tires were vehicles of Mother Goose, with red cape unfurling gloriously in the wind. What Parrish said about his landscape paintings to an interviewer in 1952 could have been said as aptly of his commercial work: "Realism should never be the end in view."[23]

Yet "realism" and "the spirit of the thing" were never antithetical in Parrish's mind. Ridiculing him for catering to middlebrow sensibilities, his detractors overlooked the obvious: Parrish appealed to popular romanticism. While in no way overtly religious (the Friends terminated his membership on account of his "want of interest"), Parrish exhibited what one of his enthusiasts described as a "strong sense of romance"; and if romanticism is a modern form of desire for a sacramental way of being, then his imagery was a magnificent refraction of sacramental rapture into commercial art. When he told a friend that he wanted viewers of his work to "take delight in the trivial qualities of the material world," he invoked, in however inadvertent a fashion, the Romantic search for ecstasy. Parrish was never as reconciled to the values of business civilization as he sometimes professed to be; the Peter Pan of illustration was a simple, unabashed believer in Beauty who once confided to a client that he would rather "do things like ideal gardens, spring, autumn, youth, the spirit of the sea, the joy of living." While engaged in his commissioned work, Parrish continued to paint, mainly landscapes whose style and composition are often indistinguishable from his commercial work.[24] On canvases such as *Dream Castle in the Sky* (1908) and *Young Girl in a Landscape* (1918), as well as on the *Dream Garden* mosaic for the lobby of the Curtis building in Philadelphia, Parrish painted an alternative world—majestic, vivacious, yet also serene, bereft of fetishized commodities and the need to advertise and accumulate. Depicting a glory that he believed resided at the ineffable heart of the world, Parrish's dreamland of goods arose from his misdirected faith in a world of wonder—a world whose revelation could only be shared, he thought, through commodified images. Having mastered the art of fetishizing commodities, Parrish quickly and avidly mastered the art of commercializing enchantment.

Very similar in style to his landscapes, the best examples of Parrish's commodification of enchantment are the prints he began to produce and market in the late 1910s. Charles Crane—president of Crane Chocolates, as well as father of the author Hart Crane—had already commissioned the Chicago Art Publishers to make color prints of the candy box decorations, and by 1919 they were turning a considerable profit. Seeing an opportunity to escape from advertising, Parrish contracted with the House of Art, a New York fine arts publishing firm, to make paintings that would be sold as color reproductions. These prints—especially *Daybreak* (1922), *Interlude* (1922), *Stars* (1926), and *Dreaming* (1928)—depict scenes of arcadian repose and reverie: young women in various degrees of undress, set amidst floral canopies, columns, starry nights, and rocky shores. Whether lounging on porticos or sitting on rocks, their nudity or diaphanous raiment suggest a state of erotic innocence, a felicitous world where sensuous beauty is at peace with contemplative leisure. The scenes lack any hint of narrative; they evoke a timeless, placeless world of unending youth and guiltless pleasure. "I couldn't tell a single thing about *Daybreak*," he replied to the House of Art when it asked him to write a brief "story" about the print. "There isn't a single thing to tell: the picture is all there is, there is nothing more." The prints were a sensational success, adorning dormitory walls, living room mantels, shop windows, department stores, and hotel lobbies. Together with his calendars and advertising work, they became both Parrish's main source of income and his claim to popular esteem. At the crest of Parrish's popularity in the early 1930s, J. L. Conger, art director for General Electric, asserted that his imagery "appeals to vast numbers of people who are left emotionally unmoved by the work of others."[25]

Parrish's popularity suggests that Walter Benjamin may have been wrong, or at least premature, to assert that technological reproduction would deprive art of its status as "an instrument of magic."[26] He produced his prints for the explicit purpose of mass reproduction, yet he just as explicitly intended them to act as vessels of some kind of enchantment, intimations of an unseen world, evocations of the spirit of things. The prints are portraits of sensuous grace, windows onto eternity, an iconography of enchantment in which flesh and spirit embrace in immaculate tranquility. In a world where evangelical certitudes were crumbling, Parrish helped millions maintain a faith in the dearest freshness of things. Yet the prints were, at the same time, commodities; the glimpse of beatitude came at a price, not only in dollars, but in the hope of a broader communion. *Stars,* for instance, depicts a single young woman, admiring the heavens as she sits on a rock near the ocean; *Interlude* shows us three young friends enjoying a round of lute-playing. For all their intimations of transcendence, the Parrish prints are portrayals of solitude. For the owners as well as for the figures in Parrish's world of commodified enchantment, communion with the world of grace is a limited, even wholly private affair.

# 11

# Modern Communion

## Corporate Liberalism and Imperialist Eschatology

THE CORPORATE RECONSTRUCTION of enchantment set the stage for the "corporate liberalism" that united many businesspeople, professionals, labor leaders, and Progressive politicians and intellectuals. Convinced that the laissez-faire principles of classical liberalism no longer obtained in an age of corporate enterprise, corporate liberals sought to harmonize relations among corporate capital, labor, and the state. From the 1890s to the present day, corporate liberalism has encompassed attempts to rationalize and regulate the accumulation of capital through the corporate administration of markets; to make more or less grudging concessions, on the part of corporations and the government, to workers, farmers, and other subaltern groups; and to create more or less stringent government regulation of business activity. Eager to avoid more radical reconstructions of the American moral and political economy, corporate liberals endorsed a range of social and political reforms: worker's compensation, public utility regulation, minimum wages, restrictions on child and women's labor, and a powerful bureaucratic apparatus of financial and commercial regulation. Corporate liberalism brought together business executives and professionals in the National Civic Federation; union officials such as Samuel Gompers of the American Federation of Labor; politicians such as Theodore Roosevelt, Woodrow Wilson, and Robert La Follette; and Progressive intellectuals such as Patten, Walter Weyl, Walter Lippmann, Herbert Croly, and Jane Addams. Progressive in their concern to regulate capital in the interests of the commonweal, corporate liberals were conservative in their fundamental commitment to the preservation of capitalist property. In the words of journalist Will Irwin, the National Civic Federation and other reformist groups sought to "subordinate certain private interests to the interests of the whole body commercial." As businessman and politico Mark Hanna told the Executive Committee of the National Civic Federation in 1903, enlightened corporate leaders promoted "the elevation of the working class to a higher plane."[1]

Relying on the social sciences and the varieties of business and professional expertise, corporate liberalism would appear to be a thoroughly secular mode of thinking. Nothing would seem less enchanted than a corporate liberal political economy. Yet since they arose from a still profoundly Protestant religious culture, corporate liberals inherited the hopes of the Puritan errand. They received the halo of the saints on the city on the hill and the evangelical *herren;* they accepted the manifest destiny of beloved communion in accumulation. As Robert Crunden once wrote of Progressives, corporate liberals harbored an "innovative nostalgia": longing for the sense of neighborly community once defined in evangelical, paternalist terms, they enlisted the science and technique of modernity to achieve their desire in a world now grown to ever-expanding proportions.[2] In the new economy of the post-Civil War era, corporate liberals looked to the soulful corporation as the vessel of American communion.

John Bates Clark's prediction of a "cooperative society" suffused by the "corporate soul" was an early premonition of corporate liberal communion, as was Patten's evocation of the "socialized capitalism" enlivened by "social religion." Their eschatological dreams anticipated those of Progressive intellectuals and politicians. Though usually considered antagonists of business, Progressives were among its most enlightened acolytes, convinced that a reformed capitalism constituted the "cooperative commonwealth" desired by populists. As we will see, populist critics of the corporate order were themselves hardly antimodern; but Progressives embraced the corporate moment as the denouement of the American errand. To Josiah Royce—one of the triumvirate of philosophy at Harvard, along with William James and George Santayana—corporate enterprise modeled the "Beloved Community" he imagined in *The Problem of Christianity* (1913). Eager to find a surrogate for the weakening bonds of organized religion, Royce longed to discover or create a community united by love in "one individual soul." In *War and Insurance* (1914), one of the oddest volumes of moral speculation in the history of American philosophy, Royce found a paradigm for beloved community in, of all places, the insurance industry, a growing and oft-maligned subdivision of finance capital. Royce regarded insurance as a momentous moral achievement, encouraging "a large regard for the general welfare, thrift, and charity." Along with banking and other businesses, insurance, Royce wrote, brought an individual "into a true and active union of interest with his possible beneficiary." This harmony was enabled by the corporate form. "Artificially created but marvelously fruitful" and possessing an "essentially intangible soul," the business corporation was a paragon of "human relations which call out our most active loyalty, our most constructive devotion, our highest energy." The corporation was a force "for the unity of mankind . . . a life of peaceful construction . . . a life of a true love of mankind." Three years later, this religious conception of insurance would receive the imprimatur of the industry itself. Addressing the annual convention of the Illinois Life Insurance Company in Chicago in January 1917, corporate vice-president R. W. Stevens proselytized for "the religion of life insurance." Stevens preached to the assembled salespeople that devotion to the financial well-being of clients that "an agent should feel in the deepest recesses of his heart."[3]

Lippmann and Croly, cofounders of the *New Republic,* echoed Royce's affirmation of corporate society in their philosophical charters for corporate liberalism: Lippmann's *Drift and Mastery,* and Croly's *The Promise of American Life* (1909) and *Progressive Democracy* (1914). Both men portrayed the corporation as the economic vessel of a beloved modernity. Musing that champions of proprietary capitalism were "pilgrims to an empty shrine," Lippmann noted and applauded the demise of the old "magic of property." The modern corporation had dispelled the "old sanctities of private property," loosened the shackles of possessive individualism, promoted technological and organizational innovation, and forged a cosmopolitan sensibility. While doing so, it released millions from the strictures of property, custom, and myth; as "immigrants in the industrial world," they were also "immigrants spiritually." Like all immigrants, moderns longed for the safety of ancestral ways to which they knew they could never return; indeed, many realized that the old sanctities were best left in empty shrines. Creatively destructive in spiritual as well as industrial and political matters, corporate capitalism was clearing a path for modern forms of enchantment. It fostered what Lippmann called "modern communion"—the recovery of that "old sense of cosmic wonder" to which "the old religions could point as their finest flower."[4]

Raised by his parents in Auguste Comte's "religion of humanity," Croly welcomed the new corporate era as an arduous but liberating "pilgrimage" toward a "holy city" or "consummate community." Like Royce, Croly beheld in the corporation a new ark of religious identity, a bearer, along with the nation-state, of the "progressive democratic faith" that was needed in the wake of the older orthodoxies. Against the competitive individualism worshipped at Lippmann's "empty shrine," Croly posed, as *The Promise of American Life*, a "constructive individualism" that would reach its apotheosis in the holy city of consolidation. As the more enlightened among the pilgrims through modernity, contemporary adherents of "progressive democratic faith" dwelled in a love that—"like that of St. Paul"—was, to Croly, "an expression of the mystical unity of the human race." United by this "common faith that sanctifies those who share it," the people of the corporate era could draw upon a "spiritual heritage," a "fund of virtue" conserved and enlarged by a modern clerisy—"learned or holy men" exemplified by the "democratic administrator" and the "scientific manager."[5] In the Holy City of Progressives, the expertise of corporate professionals simulated the aura of Protestant divinity.

Like the Protestant archangels of virtue, corporate liberals claimed the inalienable right to admonish and smite the heathen—here and abroad. Progressives did not deny the coercive and imperialist thrust of "modern communion"; the journey to the beloved community would require legions as well as missionaries. In *Progressive Democracy,* Croly explained the eschatological rationale for domestic "pressure" and foreign interventionism. Like righteous proselytizers for any faith, Progressive liberals were obliged to bring "pressure to bear" on their "less emancipated or more stubborn fellow pilgrims." While Croly hoped that they could exert this pressure "not necessarily by force," he admitted tersely that violence was "probably necessary." In *The Promise of American Life*—a book favored by Theodore Roosevelt and a source of New Nationalist inspiration—Croly pointed to unrest and insurrection in Latin America to argue that "no American international system will ever be established without the forcible pacification of one or more such centers of disorder." Lippmann's panegyric to the modern corporation lay behind his defense of imperialism. "The new imperialism is no simple affair," he observed in *Drift and Mastery;* though thuggish and avaricious, it also underscored the fact that "the real interests of the world have overflowed frontiers." Sounding a note that would define his career as the Plato of corporate liberalism, Lippmann insisted that only America could sponsor modern communion. If, as Lippmann wrote in 1915, American business activity promoted the "interrelation of peoples," then "any real friend of mankind" must be "passionately devoted to the regeneration of those territories which constitute the stakes of diplomacy": China, Africa, the Balkans, and other "backward" areas of the globe in need of capital investment.[6] Freedom was mandatory; corporate eschatology admitted of no liberty to refuse the offer of "modern communion." Like the earlier Puritans and Indian-haters, the new vanguard of the errand had to remember that violence is a start-up cost for redemption. Aligned with Jonathan Edwards and Emerson, Lippmann restated the global pretensions of American capitalist enchantment.

As clerics and missionaries of the American errand, Progressives and other corporate liberals joined an imperialist crusade that was already well under way. Between the Mexican War and the Spanish-American War of 1898, the United States embarked on a quest for foreign markets and material resources. As the continental frontier for territorial expansion receded, the architects of postbellum economic and foreign policy looked beyond North America, especially to Latin America and Asia. The hunger for markets derived not only from the need for raw materials and investment opportunities but also from the desire to avert the acerbic class war that was raging at home. Especially after the frontier was declared officially closed in 1890—thus depriving the nation of an enormous palliative for social discontent—prominent Americans came to believe that the only solution to underconsumption and social conflict lay in overseas economic expansion. Shortly after the Pullman and Homestead strikes of the early 1890s, Henry Cabot Lodge warned that unless the nation discovered new markets, it would be "visited by declines in wages and by great industrial disturbances."[7]

As the United States became Great Britain's leading imperial rival, the old expansionist eschatology lingered, even as it added Darwinist terms to its rhetorical repertoire. Some of the most prominent imperial ideologues, such as Brooks Adams (yet another of Henry's siblings), typified the Darwinian turn in expansionist eschatology. Writing in *America's Economic Supremacy* (1900) that the nation was "fitted to survive in the contest of the twentieth century," Adams assigned to natural selection the role once given to divine Providence. America's path to imperial supremacy was "determined by forces which override the volition of man." Adams's Darwinian eschatology was less popular than the more Christianized Darwinism of Josiah Strong and Albert J. Beveridge. In his best-selling *Our Country* (1885), Strong—a Congregationalist minister and secretary of the American Evangelical Alliance—predicted that the world was entering a new and final phase of history: *"the final competition of the races for which the Anglo-Saxon is being schooled."* Having filled North America, Protestant whites would descend upon Latin America, swarm over Africa, and move on to Asia, displacing or "civilizing" the native inhabitants. In his saner and more benign moments, Strong conceded that lesser breeds could be Anglo-Saxonized through elevation of their consumer tastes. "What is the process of civilizing but the *creating of more and higher wants?"*—the wants, that is, "of a Christian civilization."[8] For Strong, religion and profit could still jump together as they had for his Puritan forebears.

Similarly, Beveridge—Republican senator from Indiana, stalwart ally of President Theodore Roosevelt, and Progressive reform politician—urged his compatriots to undertake the tasks imposed by a wise and Anglo-Saxon Providence. In speeches that were often reprinted, Beveridge expounded a more benign but nonetheless coercive eschatology of Anglo-Saxon predominance. Telling a packed Senate chamber in 1900 that God had "marked us as His chosen people, henceforth to lead the regeneration of the world," Beveridge denied that the quest for empire had anything to do with avarice. Indeed, he prayed that "Mammon and the love of ease" would not "debase our blood" and weaken our resolve to exercise worldwide dominion. Still, like the Puritans, Beveridge saw lucre as a fitting remuneration for performing the mandate of heaven. "The divine mission of America," he assured his fellow senators, held "all the profit, all the glory, all the happiness possible to man." Providence and capital went hand in hand in Beveridge's millennial vista. As he had told an audience while campaigning for his seat just after the end of the Spanish-American War, America's "march toward the commercial supremacy of the world" was inseparable from its accomplishment of "Heaven-directed purposes."[9]

European visitors such as H. G. Wells, G. K. Chesterton, and W. T. Stead were equally convinced that American corporate hegemony was unstoppable. Discovering *The Future in America* (1906), Wells recoiled from the capitalist ethos while admiring the industrial efficiency it spawned. He endured "much talk about the romance of business"—"quite horrible stuff morally," as readers of *Tono-Bungay* would soon discover—but believed that American industrial methods would overtake and enrich the planet. Visiting America shortly after World War I, Chesterton, a Catholic conservative, deplored the very mechanization that Wells applauded. Though charmed by American vitality, Chesterton resented Americans' penchant for "Americanising everything," and feared "what amounts to religious persecution" in their zeal for industrial progress. (He noted the "religious fire" of a salesman who accosted him on the art of salesmanship.) Chesterton worried that Americans appeared to think that the world should be "one vast model factory."[10]

Already well known to American readers as the author of *If Christ Came to Chicago* (1894), Stead—editor of the *Pall Mall Gazette*—predicted *The Americanization of the World* (1902). Surpassing the British Empire in population, resources, and vitality, the United States, Stead contended, now led "the providential mission which has been entrusted to the English-speaking Race." Indeed, Stead leavened his book with providentialist, millennial fervor. American primacy exemplified "the great law which presides over the evolution of human society," and Stead urged his compatriots to "cheerfully acquiesce in the decree of Destiny." What Stead dubbed "the principles of Americanism" were, he wrote, illustrative of a divine order, "part and parcel of the sacred deposit of truth." Throughout, Stead marveled that peoples around the planet were embracing American commodities and techniques. From typewriters, cigarettes, and sewing machines to blast furnaces, photographic equipment, and management methods, the industrial cornucopia of American capitalism enriched a thankful world. Formerly a friend of Cecil Rhodes until he broke with him over the Boer War, Stead considered American global dominance to be a peaceful brand of imperialism, in which production and trade, not bullets and warships, would resolve hostilities among nations. Still, even as he thought the Americanization of the world an irresistible and happy achievement—an "end of history," as it were—Stead conceded that the road to Destiny could be a harsh and ugly path. The relentless commotion of American life was "an unlovely spectacle," he mused, and he concluded his book of revelation with the biblical question: "What shall it profit a man to gain the whole world, and lose his soul?"[11]

Woodrow Wilson might have countered that a man could gain his soul *and* gain the whole world, while making a handsome profit as well. Historians have long appreciated the impact of Wilson's Presbyterian background on his political career. From the New Freedom to the League of Nations to his interventions in Central America and the Caribbean, Wilson's domestic and foreign policies exuded a haughty moralism that could put off friends as well as opponents. "Wilsonian internationalism" in particular is often interpreted as a secular version of the Puritan errand: in this view, the quest to build a city on a hill became, with Wilson, the imposition of liberal values on the world.[12] But Wilson wrought no "secularization" of the American theology of expansion. For him, business activity was inextricably bound up with idealism, not antithetical to it; American corporate modernity was, to his mind, a model of virtue and a providential assignment. Business was not a hindrance to the crusade for freedom; business *was* a crusade for freedom. Echoing Puritan covenant theology and Manifest Destiny, Wilson's providentialist conception of America suggests that, contrary to the parsing of US foreign policy as a conflict between "idealism" and "realism," Wilsonians have considered the pursuit of economic and geopolitical advantage to be a moral goal in itself. Fusing prophecy and profits, Wilsonian internationalism was a potent rendition of corporate eschatology.

The specter of predestination loomed whenever Wilson dwelled on America's history and future. "I believe very profoundly in an over-ruling Providence," he once confided to a friend. As Providence directed the course of history, Wilson echoed the Puritan sense of an unsought but sacred and ennobling mission. "We did not of deliberate choice undertake these tasks" of "promoting freedom and prosperity throughout the world," he asserted in 1901. "The great pressure of a people moving always to new frontiers, in search of new lands, new power, the full freedom of a virgin world, has ruled our course and formed our policies like a Fate," he wrote in the *Atlantic Monthly* a year later. "Fate," to Wilson, was another word for God. From his days as a professor of political economy at Princeton, Wilson held that God worked through our mercenary ways to perform His redemptive wonders. He was not being a vulgar materialist when he told students in 1898 that "in the main, the conduct of men is determined by economic motives." As products of those motives—fashioned, he thought, "by operation of irresistible forces"—corporations represented "another chapter in the natural history of power and of governing classes." The laws of that "natural history" had been decreed by a wise and munificent Providence. Three years later, writing again in the *Atlantic Monthly,* Wilson reflected that, in the face of the global power exerted by corporations, "every man knows that the world is to be changed—changed according to an ordering of Providence."[13]

Painting in broad eschatological strokes, Wilson portrayed the arrival of a commercial millennium constructed in accordance with "a great preconceived plan," as he wrote in 1901. The fate of all the world's peoples was to be included as "part of the universal world of commerce." That republic of trade was cast in the image and likeness of Euro-American capital, and the rest of the world had no choice but to submit to the regime of economic freedom. Alluding to the Open Door controversy, Wilson echoed Lippmann and Croly when he declared that "the East is to be opened and transformed," and that "the standards of the West are to be imposed upon it." Like other corporate liberals, Wilson resolved this paradox of compulsory freedom by resorting to eschatological comedy. All manner of things shall be well, he assured himself, because American business was providing, "in the spirit of service, a government and rule which shall moralize them by being moral." If the Puritans had moralized the Pequots with muskets, modern liberals would moralize the world with goods and services. This faith in the civilizing promise of capitalism lay behind Wilson's most tragic political failure. When, as President, Wilson presented the Versailles Treaty to the Senate in July 1919, he professed the same eschatological conviction. "The stage is set, the destiny closed . . . the hand of God [has] led us into this way. . . . We can only go forth, with lifted eyes and freshened spirit, to follow the vision . . . America shall in truth show the way."[14]

Wilson expressed the same faith when he spoke directly to business audiences. Although he professed to loathe the "dollar diplomacy" of his predecessor William Howard Taft, his homily to the World's Salesmanship Congress in Detroit in July 1916 shows how central corporate business was to the eschatology of Wilsonian internationalism. Wilson told the salespeople that they were vending, not just commodities, but the "democracy of business." With high-minded Presbyterian bravado, Wilson exhorted his audience to embark on a "peaceful conquest of the world," since "permanent peace can grow in only one soil": the "actual good will" generated through commercial camaraderie. Wilson exhorted the salespeople to "go out and sell goods that will make the world more comfortable and more happy, and convert them to the principles of America." Salespeople were missionaries preaching the gospel of corporate liberal internationalism. "Lift your eyes to the horizons of business," Wilson swelled; salespeople were "meant to carry liberty and justice and the principles of humanity wherever you go."[15]

One salesman who had lifted his eyes to the horizons of business was King Camp Gillette, inventor of the safety razor—and author of corporate utopian tracts. Gillette's fame as an inventor and businessman have overshadowed his utopian speculation, especially *The Human Drift* (1894), *World Corporation* (1910), and *The People's Corporation* (1924), the latter a collaboration with Upton Sinclair. Gillette had acquired a disdain for business while working as a salesman; during his years on the road selling bottle caps for the Crown Cork and Seal Company, he witnessed (and no doubt committed) innumerable acts of fraud and duplicity. Perhaps as penance for his itinerant sins, Gillette wrote down his utopian dreams while still peddling caps and corks. Like Edward Bellamy—whose best-selling utopian novel, *Looking Backward* (1887), was a prototype for other technological edens—Gillette maintained that corporate consolidation would lead to global abundance and peace. Competition among corporations was reducing their number and enlarging their scope; huge national and international firms, while ruthless and frightening, were also becoming more familiar. After a "bloodless revolution," all men and women would be stockholders in a "United Company" or "World Corporation" that subsumed all necessary production and distribution. The "New Civilization" would be lovely and plentiful, an "endless vista of beauty." People and production would be concentrated in "Metropolis," a super-industrial megamachine in the vicinity of Niagara Falls, which—connected to an enormous infrastructure of dynamos—Gillette believed could power the city. (He envisioned several such megalopolises on every continent.) Metropolis featured massive, glass-domed apartment complexes with courtyards and dining halls; spacious boulevards, lawns, and plazas; labyrinthine highways and tunnels; and subterranean walkways for strolling during inclement weather.[16]

While scholars have pointed to Gillette as a technological utopian, his true faith lay in the prowess of the managers and professionals he employed as an executive. Gillette may have recoiled from the everyday moral compromises of commercial life, but he always espoused "free enterprise" and never apologized for being a salesman; "I am a business man . . . a commercial traveler," he proudly declared in *The Human Drift*. For a utopian, Gillette remained profoundly faithful to the canons of pecuniary reason. "I look upon the consolidation of business and its centralization from a purely business standpoint," he asserted. Admiring the accomplishments of corporate enterprise, Gillette entrusted the leadership of the United Company to "successful business and professional men," "our wealthy and progressive men." If the people's corporation was a cooperative commonwealth, it was hardly democratic; as Gillette observed, consolidation and its bloodless denouement "does not need the support of a majority of the people." "Promoters" were the true socialists, he claimed in *World Corporation,* achieving in "a practical business way" what reformers and radicals vainly sought through class war or legislation.[17]

Gillette also reflected a post-Protestant turn in capitalist enchantment. Bound up with his praise for corporate expertise, the language of magic, sorcery, and divinity suffused his utopian reveries. Expressions such as "like magic" and "as if by magic" recurred throughout, and at one point, Gillette described the corporation as an instrument of economic sorcery: "We have found Aladdin's lamp. Let us profit by its possession." At his most extravagant and revealing, Gillette echoed the transcendentalist proclamations of Emerson. In *World Corporation,* Gillette wedded Emerson's theology of power to notions of corporate personality. Like Rockefeller's "angel of mercy," the unstoppable advance of consolidation was an eschatological force. "Heaven will be on earth," Gillette predicted, and God will work "through the great Corporate Soul." Through this "Corporate Soul," humanity had evolved into a stockholding (if nonvoting) partner in divinity. In the remarkable caption to a silly illustration—a muscular male, dressed in a kind of girdle, holding and contemplating a globe—Gillette portrayed "Man Corporate." "He absorbs, enfolds, encompasses, and makes the world his own. He will do work; he will penetrate the confines of space, and make it deliver up its secrets and power, for Mind, the Child of the Great Over-Soul of Creation, is Infinite and Eternal."[18] Uniting the human race in a joint-stock venture directed by managers and technocrats, the World Corporation would be a beloved community, a holy city of productivity.

Gillette's World Corporation was a post-Christian restatement of the capitalist covenant theology; the Puritan-evangelical errand had become corporate liberal internationalism. But Gillette's was not the only beatific vision to appear at the dawn of the corporate dispensation. If business apologists contended that the soulful corporation could be a commonwealth of love, other Americans believed that it stunted and perverted human flourishing. While Randolph Bourne agreed that the corporation had acquired "a sense of the miraculous," he wondered whether it also was not "inhibiting broader and more crucial visions."[19] Writing on the eve of American entry into World War I, Bourne alluded to a rich and contentious generation of alternative Americas, visions of "the cooperative commonwealth." To believers in *that* democratic promise, the corporation, if soulful, was nonetheless irredeemable; redemption lay only in other forms of community, other ways of being in the world.

# PART FOUR

*The Beloved Commonwealth:*
*Visions of Cooperative Enchantment,*
*1870–1920*

THOUGH HE FEARED the rule of the dynamo and its cult of "infinite force," Henry Adams had no regrets about the collapse of the Protestant dispensation; he never delivered a jeremiad, never admonished a wayward people to renew their devotion to the covenant. Too mindful of the past to take refuge in it, Adams put aside any hope for a proprietary Protestant restoration. "The current of his time was to be his current, lead where it might." So when Adams asserted that "the new man" of the future "could be only a child born of contact between the new and the old energies," he rejected whatever "old energies" remained from the Puritan-evangelical past. Indeed, by the time he wrote his "Prayer to the Virgin of Chartres" (1901), Adams was depicting the Puritan migrants as sanctimonious marauders. "Crossing the hostile sea, our greedy band / Saw rising hills and forest in the blue; / Our father's kingdom in the promised land!" Conquering a new world, they lost their souls—they "seized it, and dethroned the Father too." With the Westinghouse dynamo never far from his mind, Adams hinted that the Puritan quest had now reached the nadir of idolatry: "Ourselves we worship, and have no Son." The dynamo marked the culmination and transcendence of the Puritan-evangelical covenant.[1]

The "old energies" on which Adams now hoped to draw belonged to medieval Catholicism. Like many other Protestant bourgeois who suffered from nagging religious doubts, Adams turned to Catholic art and ritual. Adams grew steadily more absorbed in the religious culture of the Middle Ages, traveling to French monasteries, studying Gothic architecture, contemplating the cults of the Virgin Mary and the populous communion of saints. Enchanted by devotion to Mary and the saints, Adams enshrined the Madonna in the heart of his own idiosyncratic faith. As he wrote in *Mont Saint Michel and Chartres* (1913), the Virgin was, after her Son, "the greatest philosopher and musician and theologian that ever lived on earth." If medieval sinners cowered in terror at Christ's majesty and justice, "not even the weaker human frailty could fear to approach his Mother." In the ardor and radiance of the Virgin's love, all distinctions of class and merit dissolved: lord and serf, monarch and subject, rich and poor, deserving and undeserving. Mistress of the liberal arts, the Virgin also possessed, in Adams's estimation, "perfect mastery of economics"—"most of her great churches were built in economic centres," reminding the guilds of a standard for trade and production that was higher than profit.[2]

As with the Virgin, so with Francis of Assisi, Adams's favorite among the saints. To Francis, "humility, simplicity, and poverty were alone true science. They alone led to Heaven." The Franciscan science of wealth was rooted in a lavish sacramental imagination: "all nature was God's creature. The sun and fire, air and water, were neither more nor less brothers and sisters than sparrows, wolves, and bandits."[3] The Virginal and saintly opposition to corporate enchantment could not have been clearer. Emanating from an infinite source, their power could not be purchased with money or harnessed by industrial machinery. Divine love could elude and confound the calculations of pecuniary reason; divine power could overcome and annul the forces of economic and technological compulsion. To a degree unusual in a professional scholar, Adams acknowledged, almost despite himself, the power of love in history.

Facing the Virgin of Chartres, Adams finally grasped the meaning of history: "the struggle of [man's] littleness to grasp the infinite." The swinish avarice of railroad speculators; the plaints of the unemployed and the homeless; the hubris of the new corporate professionals, on display in their science and technology—all exhibited a longing for the illimitable power that moves the sun and other stars. "All that the centuries can do is express the idea differently—a miracle or a dynamo; a dome or a coal-pit; a cathedral or a world's fair." The world's fairs were sacred spaces, the modern equivalents of temples and churches that housed the infinite power. But where the masonry and glasswork of Chartres had revealed this infinite power as love, the fairs and factories were sanctuaries of infinite power as corporate mastery. Enthralled yet terrified by the dynamo, Adams longed to escape its enchantment and devote himself to the service of the Virgin. "I feel the energy of faith / Not in the future science, but in you!" Yet Adams remained too much of a skeptic to kneel before the Lady of Chartres; the forces that lay behind the dynamo appeared more real, proximate, and ominous. If, as Jackson Lears has claimed, Adams was "an antimodern modernist," he was a believing unbeliever, yearning for the power of infinite love yet uncertain of its ontological reality.[4]

Adams doubted that the popular movements of his time could bridge the chasm between power and love. In Adams's view, the "new men" would not arise from farmers' alliances, labor unions, or radical parties. "So complex and so concentrated a machine" as a modern economy, he wrote, could not be understood or governed by "Southern and Western farmers in grotesque alliance with city day-laborers."[5] Love and power could not be fully reconciled in a "grotesque alliance" of the people.

Historians have celebrated that "grotesque alliance" in spite of its ultimate failure to achieve the "cooperative commonwealth" or the "workingmen's democracy" or the "house of labor" or the "populist moment." In this view, the champions of the cooperative commonwealth demonstrated that Fordism and consumer culture were not the only, inexorable future. Beholden to the proprietary republic, an alternative America *was* possible, more humane, generous, and neighborly in spirit than the venal technocracy that prevailed. And if we remember this aborted future with sufficient vividness and fidelity, we might spark contemporary efforts to build our own cooperative commonwealth.[6] This story is a jeremiad: a glorious ideal, an account of declension, a call to rededicate ourselves to the vision. The movements were, and their historians are, the heirs of the Puritans and evangelicals; and like previous jeremiads, the legend of the cooperative commonwealth continues to obscure some intractable difficulties. What exactly was this "cooperative commonwealth"? Populism, for example, has been seen as a heroic defense of "producerism." In this view, populists stood athwart "improvement" or "progress"; they sought to prevent the world of bureaucratic administration, professional and managerial hegemony, technological fetishism, and consumer culture.

And yet, appealing to the same producerist ethos, socialists such as Eugene V. Debs embraced corporate modernization. How could the producerist imagination sanction both resistance and assimilation to corporate modernity? Was popular resistance to corporate power as fundamental and adamantine as it has been portrayed? Was the "cooperative commonwealth" yet another beatific vision of capitalist enchantment?

Although Populists considered financiers and industrialists to be traitors to the covenant—the forces of Mammon against the God of the producers—they were not opposed on principle to the incorporation of America. Indeed, many populists considered "combination" a marvelous principle of divine cosmology. Reaffirming the presence of divinity in the midst of the people's labors, they continued the errand into the marketplace, recasting the proprietary order in the form of the "cooperative commonwealth." Like the "modern communion" and the "soulful corporation" celebrated by corporate liberals, the cooperative commonwealth was a beatific vision, an ideal of enchanted modernity. The cooperative commonwealth was a reformation of the covenant theology of capitalism; the populist jeremiad continued to postpone a reckoning with the errand's futility.

More ostensibly radical movements also recast the jeremiad. When they welcomed corporate consolidation, Debs and other socialists were not simply affirming Marxist accounts of historical development; they were reconciling socialism with the American producerist tradition. Even where they rejected the conventional Protestant form of the jeremiad, they created heterodox forms of the covenant theology. But in paying this high and fateful tribute to the proprietary dispensation, American socialists reinforced the possessive individualism of their supporters. Under the aegis of socialism, Protestant enchantment morphed into a cooperative commonwealth of proletarian consumers. As a result, American socialism—like its counterpart in Europe—accepted wage labor, large-scale production, and hierarchical forms of management.

Anarchism and the Arts and Crafts movement carried on a Romantic critique of incorporation. Proclaiming art and beauty as the paradigm of work and espousing an artisanal ideal, both movements posed incisive and fundamental challenges to the ideal of industrial concentration. The artisanal ideal called into question not only the necessity but also the desirability of mechanized production, promethean technics, centralized power, and managerial supervision. To the extent that even champions of art remained teth-ered to the old dispensation, the artisanal ideal became an upscale therapy, a bohemian enclave of corporate capitalism. But at their most visionary and uncompromising, American arts-and-crafters continued the Romantic op-position to capitalism; they upheld the practice of craft as an enchanted way of life, a sacramental way of being in the world.

Recast as the search for a "passionate vision," the Romantic quest for en-chanted experience animated three other American critics: John Muir, Wil-liam James, and Vida Dutton Scudder. Searching for God in the California redwoods, Muir was more than a patron saint of environmentalism; he was a Romantic naturalist, a theologian of natural supernaturalism. Longing to "become worthless as a practical being" in order to divine the "limitless sig-nificance in natural things," James articulated a form of pragmatism that was, at its best, an American Romantic anarchism. Scudder turned to Anglo-Catholicism for fulfilling metaphysical experience. Although she embraced the centralization to which other socialists attached their hopes, Scudder harbored another ideal: the Franciscan way of poverty, a path of disposses-sion rooted in a confident, premodern ontology of love.

# 12

# The Producers' Jeremiad

## The Populist Reformation of the Covenant Theology

EMERGING FROM POSTBELLUM LABOR unions and the numerous farmers alliances, "populism" stemmed from the incorporation of America, which brought together city and country in a new and volatile interdependence. After the Civil War, the spread of mechanization in the factories of the industrial North threatened skilled workers with unemployment, falling wages, degradation of craft, and dislocation from the small towns and villages that, in the 1870s, were still home to the bulk of American manufacturing. As the widespread support for the massive strikes that engulfed the nation in the last quarter of the nineteenth century demonstrated—the Great Railroad Strike of 1877, the Great Upheaval of 1886, the Homestead Strike of 1894—industrialization unsettled not only artisans, unskilled workers, and local farmers, but also the small-town merchants and professionals who comprised the petty-bourgeois business elites. At the same time, the Midwest experienced rapid economic development and population growth. Farmers relied on urban hubs such as Chicago for transport, marketing, tools, and finance, while cities depended on the countryside for foodstuffs and raw materials. The settlement of the prairie states triggered a frenzy of railroad construction, avid and unregulated land speculation, and a sharp rise in the indebtedness of farming families for freight charges, machinery, and mortgages. Rural resentment at urban bankers, distributors, and railroad executives ran deep, while metropolitan contempt for the countryside grew equally intense. Meanwhile, the post-Reconstruction South witnessed the rise of crop-lien and sharecropping economies that sparked a rise in farm tenancy. Many Southern cotton farmers, white and black, descended into debt peonage, sweating to repay loans from bankers and merchants for seeds and tools. In the West and the South, all these stresses were exacerbated in the mid-1880s by poor harvests and a precipitous worldwide drop in agricultural prices. The global agricultural cataclysm aggravated the already exorbitant shipping charges; increased the already usurious interest rates; accelerated foreclosures on farm mortgages; and underscored, with brutal clarity, the dependence of farmers on a structure of finance and distribution controlled by distant monopolies and trusts.[1]

Beginning in the 1870s, some organizations arose for mutual aid and eventually for political action: the Knights of Labor, the Grange, the National Farmers' Alliance, the Northern and Southern Farmers' Alliances (the latter also known as the National Farmers' Alliance and Industrial Union). The "populist movement" was a motley social and political coalition of labor, agrarian, and other reform organizations that traversed the line between city and countryside. By the early 1890s, these groups had begun to coalesce at "industrial conferences"; "populism" became a broad-gauged reform movement that ventured well beyond agrarian relief. Spearheaded by the People's Party formed in 1892—a "Confederation of Industrial Organizations"— populists called for women's suffrage, workers' right to organize and bargain collectively, a graduated income tax, federal insurance for bank deposits, and greater regulation (if not nationalization) of railroads and telegraph lines. They envisioned a system of producers' cooperatives, community-owned-and-operated banks, an enlargement of the paper money supply through free coinage of silver, and the abolition of the gold standard. At their most ambitious, they advocated the "sub-treasury" plan sketched out by C. W. Macune: the federal treasury would provide low-interest credit to farmers through certificates for which, in return, they would store crops in government warehouses—"sub-treasuries." As the lords of finance capital realized with horror, the sub-treasury plan would place the nation's monetary policy under the control of the Treasury—hence under greater democratic supervision—and break the hold of big-city merchants and commercial banks on American farmers.[2]

Based on a common antipathy toward "the town clique," hundreds of thousands of Southern and Midwestern farmers and laborers launched a blazing and fearsome insurgency. Almost all historians of populism capture the blend of indignation and critical intelligence that suffused the populist press; the exhilaration of the rallies, encampments, and lectures that mobilized ordinary people; and the rhetorical power and flamboyance of populist orators and writers such as Ignatius Donnelly, Mary Elizabeth Lease, and Leonidas K. Polk. Yet the desire for quick success overwhelmed the need for vision and patience. A chasm opened between free-silver advocates and supporters of the more comprehensive reform agenda. In 1896, free-silverites convinced their fellow party members to fuse with the Democrats; the eloquence of William Jennings Bryan—a former lawyer and debt collector—supplanted that of Donnelly, Polk, and Lease. The Democrats' defeat by William McKinley and the Republicans both sealed the fate of the People's Party and demoralized the populist movement. The Knights of Labor dwindled and waned; Samuel Gompers and the American Federation of Labor acceded to industrial discipline and "business unionism." As agricultural prices rebounded and farm debt diminished, the passion of agrarian rebellion waned. Over the first two decades of the twentieth century, farmers gradually resigned themselves to the incorporation of agriculture. The ideal of the family farm gave way to "every farm a factory."[3]

Populism offers a Rorschach test of scholarly and political thinking. Were the insurgent farmers and workers a new model army of the producers' republic? Or were they luckless and resentful petty capitalists, protecting themselves from the judgments of a market whose decrees they had previously affirmed? Were they clear-sighted critics of capitalist plutocracy? Or were they backward-looking votaries of a pastoral mythology, eloquent hayseeds blind to the virtue and necessity of industrial modernity? In *The Age of Reform* (1955) and in several subsequent essays, Richard Hofstadter painted an indelibly abrasive and unflattering portrait of populists, depicting them as the precursors of Cold War reaction and *ressentiment,* "the paranoid style in American politics." Populism, Hofstadter contended, was the latest version of an "agrarian myth" in which the yeoman farmer was the omni-competent icon of labor and virtue, the favored son of God, the origin of all wealth, the Cincinnatus of the American republic. Spellbound by this agrarian myth, populists cast the farmers' plight as a moral and political melodrama in which they played the roles of "innocent pastoral victims of a conspiracy hatched in the distance." In reality, Hofstadter argued, the same forces that propelled Jacksonian democracy also unleashed "an entrepreneurial zeal probably without precedent in history, a rage for business, for profits, for opportunity, for advancement." The farmers who supported the Alliances and the Populist Party were not hard-working naifs; they were "an organic part of the whole order of business enterprise that flourished in the city."[4] Hofstadter's populists were sore and befuddled losers, protesting the outcome of a game they had previously played with acquisitive relish.

Challenging Hofstadter, historians galvanized by the social movements of the 1960s claimed populism for a lineage of dissent from capitalism. To Lawrence Goodwyn and Christopher Lasch, for instance, populism represented, in Lasch's words, "the producers' last stand" against the forces of "progress": wage labor, large-scale, mechanized production, and the redefinition of democracy in terms of access to consumer goods. In this view, the Alliances and the People's Party contained, not bewildered losers, but prophets. As Goodwyn writes tersely, "they saw the coming society, and they did not like it." Far from sharing the accumulative ethos of urban capitalist elites, populists, in this view, upheld the traditional moral economy of work, small property, and evangelical religion. In this celebratory account of populism, the chief significance of the movement lay in its prescient critique of modernization. As Goodwyn argues, populists rejected "the shared presumptions of 'progress' that unite capitalists and socialists in a religious brotherhood." Populism, in Alan Trachtenberg's words, "established itself as an opposing culture, an alternative view not only of 'politics' and 'economics' but of the world as such." In the election of 1896, the archangels of the cooperative commonwealth suffered, Lasch writes, "a crushing and conclusive defeat from which they never recovered"—and in which subsequent generations have languished, absorbed into corporate modernity.[5]

One of the main virtues of recent scholarship on populism is its demolition of this dichotomy. As Charles Postel muses, Lasch and Goodwyn "projected [their] ambivalence on the unwitting farmers, laborers, and other common folk of the nineteenth century." Without returning to Hofstadter and the "agrarian myth," Postel contends that populists were much more favorable to profit-seeking, "opportunity," and corporate modernization than his predecessors had acknowledged. In the emerging account of populism, populists become, not opponents of "progress," but contestants over its meaning and content; determined on what Norman Pollack calls "modernization from below," they were less defenders of a yeoman past than prophets of an agrarian modernity. Likewise, small producers were not necessarily hostile to large-scale organization and bureaucracy, even by the corporation and the state. As envisioned by the populists, the network of producers' cooperatives and sub-treasuries was, after all, a large-scale political economy—a "hybrid," as Postel characterizes it, between "the chaos of competitive capitalism and the organization of state monopoly." Populists discerned democratic promise in, not against, the fruition of modernity; they saw the coming society, and they liked it, as long as it could work for ordinary people. Thus the significance of populism lies, for Postel, in its role as an incubator for "alternative models of capitalism."[6]

But if populism was an alternative model *of* capitalism, it was never an alternative *to* capitalism. Hofstadter's contempt for rural folk does not discredit the stubborn truth he captured about American populism: it has never imagined a fundamental revision of property relations in America. "History from the bottom up" was supposed to uncover a people of prophets speaking truth to power; but what if the truth the prophets uttered was the truth of power, expressed in a populist style and vernacular? Perhaps it is better to understand populism as a jeremiad, a call to renew the Protestant covenant theology. The populist "cooperative commonwealth" was a reconstruction of the ideal of fellowship in accumulation. Populism was a beatific vision, a producerist myth of capitalist enchantment.

The populist moment of enchantment was evident in the Knights of Labor, founded in 1869 by Uriah P. Stephens, a Philadelphia tailor, and taken over in 1878 by Terence V. Powderly, a Philadelphia machinist. Calling for the eradication of wage labor and its replacement by a "cooperative industrial system," they created a movement culture of libraries and reading rooms, parades and pageants, picnics and concerts, sports teams, dances, and Labor and Independence Day festivities. Calling themselves a "Noble and Holy Order," the Knights cobbled together an assortment of rituals, symbols, and convictions—documented and illustrated in their manual, the *Adelphon Kruptos* (Greek for "secret brotherhood")—which drew from Catholicism, Freemasonry, and the still-vigorous evangelical ethos. Their assembly halls were "temples" or "tabernacles"—"the dwelling-place of God among men," as Stephens had admonished them—and their lodges were "sanctuaries," "holiest of holies," each with a "vestibule." The ritual of induction included a "Master Workman" and a "Venerable Sage," who welcomed the inductee "to this Sanctuary, dedicated to the service of God by serving humanity." Surrounded by hooded figures, the new member swore an "oath" to never reveal any of the "signs, mysteries, arts, privileges, or benefits" of the Order "except in a legal, authorized manner." The Knights also developed a meta-physics and theology that undergirded their sense of beloved community. As "the Philosopher's Stone," labor, they believed, possessed the real Midas touch: "everything it touches turns to wealth." The "Great Seal of Knight-hood" was an equilateral triangle signifying "elements which are essential to man's existence and happiness, land, labor, and love." The Great Seal also displayed the Knights' famous and stirring avowal of fraternity: "An injury to one is the concern of all," a declaration redolent of the Pauline doctrine that Christians are members of one another.[7]

However bizarre and eclectic—Engels once scoffed at their rites and be-liefs as "little absurdities"—the Knights' culture of beloved community tes-tifies to the persistence of enchantment. Its religious character was certainly evident to Catholic bishops, who saw in the Knights both a revolutionary cabal and a competitor for spiritual allegiance, sensing a rival sacramental system in the Order's moral, metaphysical, and ritual ensemble. As Catholic membership swelled to that of half the Order by the early 1880s, Powderly was compelled to make some grudging concessions to Catholic prelates: some of the secrecy was lifted, some rituals were altered, the "oath" of initia-tion became a "vow." These changes elicited a firestorm of protest from Prot-estant (and many Catholic) Knights who considered the local temples to be "workingmen's churches." To these stalwarts of the Order, Powderly's con-cessions constituted heresy and appeasement. They certainly failed to as-suage the bishops, who condemned the Knights in 1884. Although the American Church softened its position toward the Order in 1891 with the publication of Pope Leo XIII's *Rerum novarum,* the Knights' indictment of pro-business clergy continued to exhibit all the passion of religious zeal. One of the Knights' more stem-winding spokesmen, Alexander Wright, admon-ished his brethren in an 1891 issue of the Order's newspaper to ignore "the smooth-tongued orations of sleek-fed priests."[8]

Wright was preaching to a dwindling congregation, since by the early 1890s, the Knights were hemorrhaging members, many of whom had bolted to the American Federation of Labor or the various socialist parties. Weak-ened by internal strife and opposition from employers, the Knights progres-sively withered. While historians often point to factional disputes and ex-ternal pressures to explain the Order's demise, we must also wonder whether it was blinded and crippled by its fidelity to the capitalist covenant theology.

As inductees were told during the initiation rite, the Knights had "no conflict with legitimate enterprise, no antagonism to necessary capital"; they sought not to abolish distinctions of class but to "harmonize the interests of labor and capital."[9] Crooned in the dulcet tones of bourgeois Christianity, "harmony" was the siren song of evangelical producerism. The Knights' populist jeremiad was unavailing precisely to the extent that it repeated the ideal of the covenant: the convergence of desire for communion with the imperatives of mercenary property relations.

Despite a similar invocation of yeoman virtue and enchantment, the agrarian producers' jeremiad envisioned a corporate, industrial future. Populists often invoked the Founders as the sages of the producers' republic. They followed "the line laid out by the revolutionary fathers," as James H. "Cyclone" Davis put it; they adhered to "the Jefferson theory of Democracy." Thanks to the rhetorical gifts of Davis and numerous other writers and orators, the modern, forward-looking character of agrarian populism remains difficult to appreciate. The agrarian demonology of Wall Street, for instance, is a case study in bucolic melodrama. Sweaty, overworked farmers groaned in debt-laden servitude, while the satraps and pharaohs of Wall Street lit cigars with the money they extorted. "When the pious Mr. Rockefeller makes his offerings to the Lord," one firebrand asked in 1895, "does he ever think of the drops of blood from broken hearts, the groans from squalid misery, the tears from human agony, which have been coined into each shining dollar?" As epitomized in the works of Ignatius Donnelly—especially *Caesar's Column* (1890)—the apocalyptic imagination of agrarian populism seems anything but progressive.[10]

Yet when Donnelly and other agrarian populists described the future *after* the plutocracy, it often looked like a business paradise. Writing in 1896, Donnelly condemned "every interference with the freedom of trade and market, and the right of a human being to sell where he can for most and buy where he can for least." Donnelly echoed Nelson Dunning, chief publicist for the Farmers' Alliance, who had urged farmers in 1891 to adopt the "business standpoint." Farmers should mobilize, he wrote, to secure "individual benefits through combined effort." The Alliance, he added, offered the individual farmer a way to advance "your business" in "a selfish world." Like Whitman's, Dunning's populist vista was a democracy of petty capitalists: "moderate fortunes, moderate sized farms, and moderate business enterprises."

Other Alliance figures were equally adamant about the "business stand-point" of the movement. A lifelong enthusiast of Adam Smith, Macune, to-gether with Polk, insisted that the Alliance was above all "a business organ-ization for business purposes." Government, Macune argued, "should be reduced to business terms, placed upon a business basis and attended to by business agents." Thorstein Veblen—who, as the son of a prosperous Min-nesota farmer, knew a lot about "the business standpoint"—was right on target when he later wrote that American yeomen were "cultivators of the main chance as well as of the fertile soil."[11]

The "business standpoint" of agrarian populism explains the movement's ambivalence about corporations. The Farmers' Alliance often railed against trusts and monopolies as threats to liberty and virtue. Corporations, one of its newsletters lamented in 1890, had "absorbed the liberties of the commu-nity and usurped the power of the agency that created it." In *Caesar's Column,* Donnelly's protagonist and narrator, the wool merchant Gabriel Weltstein, rues how corporations have "reduced the people to slavery" as "the robber barons of old did the original owners of the soil of Europe." "I should abolish all corporations," Weltstein tells his brother. The most ominous and bellig-erent populist philippic against corporations came from "Cyclone" Davis, an itinerant Texas firebrand renowned for his oratorical and polemical skills. In *A Political Revelation* (1894), Davis portrayed the corporation as a venal, soulless golem, a "money-machine" bent on reducing the republic to regi-mented anonymity.[12]

Yet most populists objected, not to corporations per se but to their power to administer markets and fix the conditions of capital accumulation—in short, to "take advantage of the people," as one Alliance spokesperson put it. The agrarian intelligentsia often exhibited considerable admiration for the modern corporation. The California Grange urged its members in 1889 to "study well the lesson which these great corporations that dominate the country are teaching": that "in intelligent cooperation, there is strength, there is power." "We must do as the corporations are doing," it concluded, "meet combinations of capital and brains with like combinations." Alliance leader and historian W. S. Morgan wrote in 1891 of corporate executives as "men of ability, and integrity, too." Morgan condemned not all corporations, but those that entered into "a conspiracy against legitimate trade." Dunning stated the populist case for combination with the greatest concision and clarity. "To all progressive minds," he counseled, "organization" was "absolutely necessary for success in modern business." "Nothing could withstand their power," Dunning insisted, "if the farmers of America would organize as intelligently and solidly as the Standard Oil Company has." Populists reasserted the traditional legal concept of the corporation as an artificial and therefore dependent creature, subject to the will and sufferance of the people. As Tom Watson observed, "we have created the corporations. They are our legal offspring"—and children should obey their parents.[13]

Despite the persistence of the folksy, homespun, straight-talkin' rural icon, populism represented the ideals of an agrarian avant-garde. Most farmers simply wanted an end to their plight: reasonable freight rates, lower interest on loans, more paper money, and protection from foreclosure. Their spokesmen, however, looked further into the future. Far from being retrograde hayseeds, Macune, Dunning, Polk, and others in the agrarian intelligentsia both displayed and exhorted farmers to adopt an omnivorous interest in science, technology, marketing, manufacturing, and agricultural innovation. Agrarian populists desired a middling modernity: a society of small-scale proprietors, all enmeshed and flourishing in the large-scale labyrinth of corporate technology and organization. The agrarian vanguard believed in progress; they reconciled the agrarian myth with the nascent fable of modernization. In the new mythology of agrarian modernity, the family farm thrived in yeoman splendor alongside the corporate homestead. In their view, far from being a tragedy, the incorporation of American agriculture was a providential blessing. In the words of John Tetts, a member of the board of directors of the Louisiana farmers' union, "monopoly is the outgrowth of a beautiful principle of combination."[14]

Most agrarian activists and reformers saw the cleansing of capitalism as a prelude to the Second Coming. "The populists of today," Lease explained in 1892, "represent a demand for the enactment into law of the truths taught by Jesus; the truths which must prevail before Christ's kingdom can be established." The movement itself, Thomas Nugent assured a crowd in 1894, was evidence of "the sure unfoldings of God's providence." Recounting "the purposes of the Farmers' Alliance" in 1891, Macune—who after leaving the organization became an itinerant Methodist preacher in Texas—declared that "business contests or political fights" were "incidental" to the movement's more exalted aspirations. The Alliance was not just an interest group;

it was "a living, active, practical, and present embodiment of the cause of Jesus Christ." Following in the footsteps of "the Divine Master," it was an *imitatio Christi,* resembling the Galilean who "gave up his life as an example of the devotion due to principle." In agrarian populist eschatology, the Farmers' Alliance prefigured the communion of humanity at the end of time. Committed to the mission of the covenant, the agrarian vanguard renewed the Puritan errand and the evangelical quest for the millennium. As Lorenzo Lewelling roared to an outdoor rally in 1893, the "enduring faith" of the agrarian insurgency was that "the great march of destiny is forward."[15]

Henry George, crusading journalist and mayoral candidate in New York in 1886, was the economist laureate of agrarian enchantment. In his widely read and cherished *Progress and Poverty* (1879)—as well as in the lesser-known *The Science of Political Economy* (1897)—George echoed the optimism of the clerical economists. Although "Political Economy has been called the dismal science," it could still, George believed, be "radiant with hope." Certainly populists gave a hearty amen to George's charge that only "blasphemy" could attribute "to the inscrutable decrees of Providence the suffering and brutishness that come of poverty." Yet George also attributed whatever justice, fraternity, and abundance humankind had achieved to a "Law of Human Progress" that was preached "by One who eighteen hundred years ago was crucified."[16]

The very title of George's revered volume indicates that the meaning of progress, not its defeat, was at stake in the populist moment, as the "Law of Human Progress" was part of a broader metaphysics and eschatology. Nature—and especially land—was a bounty of "gifts of the Creator," suffused with divine and infinite powers "streaming through the material universe." Human labor enabled humanity to work in tandem with God, employing the energy "with which the universe sprang into being." George marveled at "the godlike quality of modifying and controlling conditions," and held up not only the farmer but also any producer as the bearer of sacred power. Thus progress, to George, was the march of humanity toward ever fuller participation in divinity; and in the opening section of *Progress and Poverty,* George celebrated technological and scientific modernity with an exuberance like that of Marx and Engels in the *Communist Manifesto.* Awestruck by "the new powers born of progress," George chided reformers who opposed "combination" as agents of historical and moral regression. If tempered by justice and fraternity, the new forces of progress would build the metropolis foreseen in the Book of Revelation. In the final pages of George's magnum opus, he concluded that St. John the Evangelist had beheld the producerist consummation of America. Announcing "the Golden Age of which poets have sung," John had witnessed in his trance at Patmos "the culmination of Christianity— the City of God on earth, with its walls of jasper and its gates of pearl!" Constructed with "the new powers born of progress," the City would be ready for the only monarchy recognized by republican producers: "the reign of the Prince of Peace!"[17] Thus, George's Single Tax movement was a religious crusade to recapture the sacral powers indispensable for building a beloved community—one whose outlines were little different from the evangelical-proprietary dispensation.

Despite the populist debt to evangelicalism, the movement was also awash in a sea of modern heterodoxy. Many in the agrarian intelligentsia dabbled in or embraced spiritualism, theosophy, Swedenborgianism, "mental science," "New Thought," and other forms of spiritual modernism. Pioneers of the soul as well as the soil, agrarian reformers forged a modernist spiritual idiom that affirmed scientific and technological progress. When a Farmers' Alliance editorial of 1891 contended that reform would "kindle the divine spark which is torpid in the soul," the divinity was not necessarily Christian. Henry Demarest Lloyd—author of *Wealth Against Commonwealth* (1894), one of the first muckraking polemics of the era—told a People's Party rally in 1894 that they were "incarnating in the lives of the common people the fullness of the divinity of humanity," but he made no reference to Christianity. In *Civilization's Inferno* (1893), Benjamin Orange Flower—admirer of Emerson; populist advocate; champion of faith healing and spiritualism; and editor of the *Arena,* one of the most audacious and effervescent reviews at the turn of the century—warned that "the divine in man cannot blossom or life yield its richest treasures while gold is society's god."[18]

Revered by hundreds of thousands, if not millions, of readers, Donnelly was the ideal populist prophet. Born in Philadelphia in 1831, he lost his father as a boy, but his mother scraped together enough money to send him to the city's best high school. Though he studied law and won a prestigious clerkship, his practice was only moderately successful. Eager to make his mark, he became a leading booster in Nininger, Minnesota, one of many settlements that sprang up in the state in the 1850s. After his boomtown went bust during the panic of 1857, Donnelly embarked on a political career. As a Republican, he served Minnesota as lieutenant governor, state senator, and Congressman. Dissatisfied with politics, he returned to practicing law, but in his spare time he indulged an array of intellectual obsessions: the lost city of Atlantis, catastrophist accounts of the earth's prehistory, the "real" authorship of Shakespeare's plays. Enthused with magpie interests and a febrile imagination, he penned a trilogy of amateur scholarship in the 1880s: *Atlantis: The Antediluvian World* (1882), *Ragnarok: The Age of Fire and Gravel* (1883), and *The Great Cryptogram: Francis Bacon's Cipher in the So-Called Shakespeare Plays* (1888). While cranking out his books, Donnelly returned to politics, running for Congress as a Democrat in 1884 and then helping to found the Minnesota Farmers' Alliance. Joining the People's Party, he wrote the preamble to its 1892 platform and became a virtuoso orator and polemicist.[19]

Donnelly's autodidact erudition flew in the face of the academic specialization that was beginning to engulf intellectual life—an enclosure movement of knowledge, much like the expropriation of craft under way among corporate professionals and managers. But if Donnelly's effrontery toward the university elite was rooted in producerism, he was also groping toward a new religious basis for producerism itself. If there's a thread running through Donnelly's erratic life, it is the search for a substitute for the Christianity he rejected as a young man. Donnelly had been baptized and raised a Roman Catholic. His father renounced the faith when Donnelly was a boy, and his mother apparently provided no formal religious instruction. Donnelly left the Church in the mid-1850s, and he remained hostile to orthodox Christianity for the rest of his life—a collection of "incredible yarns," as he confided to his diary. His aversion to traditional Christianity occasionally surfaced in his trilogy. Noting approvingly in *Atlantis* that "among the Gauls men would lend money to be repaid in the next world," he added sardonically that "no Christian people has yet reached that sublime height of faith." Still, although an avatar of populist modernism, Donnelly employed the rhetorical arsenal of evangelicalism all his life, and he believed Christianity might still contain something of "the spirit and purpose of God."[20]

This search for "the spirit and purpose of God" animated Donnelly's amateur scholarship, which is replete with biblical exegesis and religious speculation. The stories he narrated—the reality of the ancient but technologically advanced civilization of Atlantis, the destruction of the city and other early civilizations by comets and other natural calamities—rested on a wild interdisciplinary froth. In addition to perusing comparative religion and mythology, Donnelly collected an enormous range of material from geology, astronomy, archeology, and paleontology, drawing startling and often bizarre conclusions from the flimsiest of evidence. Yet the ineptitude and sensationalism of Donnelly's scholarship is less important than the enchantedly progressive lesson it conveyed. "Modern civilization is Atlantean," he mused in *Atlantis*. "The inventive faculty of the present age is taking up the great delegated work of creation where Atlantis left it thousands of years ago." Progress unfolded through creation, disaster, and further creation; as he concluded in the last few pages of *Ragnarok*—Norse for "destiny of the gods"— "after every cataclysm the world has risen to higher levels of creative development." This law of progress-through-destruction is the decree of the Supreme Being: "not a particle of dust is whirled in the funnel of the cyclone but God identifies it, and has marked its path."[21]

Donnelly's providential catastrophism was bound up with a producerist cosmology. Since "in truth, the universe is industry," he wrote in *The Great Cryptogram,* "no man should shrink from labor. Energy is God's glorious stamp set on his creature." Humanity was the image and likeness of a deity who was an independent, tireless proprietor. God was the "the Great Worker—a worker without a task-master—who never pauses, never wearies, and never sleeps." The beatitude of work and the abomination of sloth are the moral principles of Donnelly's metaphysics. Once the inhabitants of Atlantis are overcome by luxury and greed, they are destroyed by a divine cataclysm. Similarly, Donnelly argued his tirelessly contemptuous case against Shakespeare in the moral lexicon of producerism. Hailing Bacon as "a man of extraordinary and phenomenal industry," he maligned the Bard in terms usually reserved for the Wall Street financial oligarchy. Like bankers and speculators, Shakespeare was an unproductive, decadent wastrel who profited from another man's ingenuity and labor. After calling him a "poacher, fugitive, [and] vagabond," Donnelly added that he was also a "money-lender [and] land-grabber." Like the exploiters of Minnesota's yeomen, Shakespeare was a "thrifty, money-making, uncharitable, cold-hearted man" who lent money "at usurious rates of interest."[22]

But in Donnelly's producerist cosmology, the law of progress would put all things right. At the end of *Ragnarok,* Donnelly launched into a populist homily that makes sense only as a prophecy of impending destruction and renewed "creative development." He imagined a modern-day Dives (the rich man in the parable of the rich man and Lazarus) and his "unexpressed belief that heaven is only a larger Wall Street." Put no faith in your riches, the prophet warned, for if the law of terrestrial cataclysm is any guide, another comet might "overwhelm you and your possessions, and your corporations, and all the ant-like devices of men in one common ruin." He urged the new Dives to repent—"put out your tentacles toward the great spiritual world around you," Donnelly implored, and "the angels will exult over it in heaven."[23]

Clearly, Donnelly trembled at the thought that the angels were unhappy in the late 1880s, and the work he published over the next dozen years grew at once more politically and religiously charged. Donnelly's angels must have exulted as the coalescence of the myriad farmers' alliances, the meteoric rise of the People's Party, and the economic convulsions of the 1890s created a superheated political climate that forced him to clarify his populist vision. Into yet another trilogy—*Caesar's Column, The Golden Bottle* (1892), and *The American People's Money* (1896)—Donnelly poured a populist social criticism that doubled as religious prophecy. Rehearsing the jeremiad, the volumes describe corporate plutocracy as a malevolent form of enchantment; outline an eschatology of judgment, deliverance, and producerist redemption; and imagine a beloved commonwealth of proprietors, based on a sacramental view of the world.

Donnelly understood the tyranny of money as a fundamentally religious plight. "The gospel of grab," as he dubbed it in *The American People's Money,* appealed to the "hog in human nature." The hog in human nature was aroused and bewitched by the worship of precious metals. For Donnelly—as for the bearers of the gold standard—the money issue was not simply an economic or political matter. If, for the goldbugs, the gold standard represented and ensured the stability of civilization, the obsession with precious metals pointed, in Donnelly's view, to our inclination to misenchantment and idolatry. Gold and silver "were not made money by law"; they were "first the sacred metals of our ancestors," adorning the temples of early civilizations, "and then became the precious metals." Their use is "a survival of primeval superstition." In *The Golden Bottle,* Ephraim Benezet—a People's Party candidate who becomes president—regales Congress on the history of monetary fetishism. "It was religion that rendered gold and silver valuable by making them sacred, dedicating them to the worship of the sun and moon." Precious metals were "the religious, metallic, prehistoric emblems for those things that man has to eat or wear, or use, and which are therefore real wealth." Just as "in old times men carved, out of wood and stone, figures of men, and called them gods," so the acolytes of gold and silver held up their metals and "prostrated themselves before them." (As Weltstein says in *Caesar's Column,* "the adoration of gold and silver is a superstition of which the bankers are the high priests.") Calling for demonetization of precious metals, Benezet urges Congress to "relegate the worship of gold and silver to the region of witchcraft and spooks."[24]

To Donnelly, the American ruling class itself resided in that region of iniquity, and he excoriated their gilded wickedness to greatest effect in *Caesar's Column.* Set in New York in 1988 (close to the 1987 portended by Edward Bellamy in *Looking Backward*), *Caesar's Column* describes a United States ruled by "the Plutocracy," a callous and decadent business elite. Though the country is blessed with technological wonders, the benefits accrue only to the wealthy; republican institutions are theatrical sets concealing a tyranny of money. Christianity has been replaced as the nation's religion by a vicious but well-mannered nihilism. In one sermon, Dr. Odyard, a learned and thoroughly abominable character, expounds the essentials of Plutocratic theology. Preaching in what Gabriel describes as "a club-house of the rich," Odyard proclaims a barbarous gospel to his well-heeled congregation. The blind and remorseless decrees of Nature cannot be questioned or abrogated; she "is omnipotent . . . with stony eyes the thousand-headed goddess sits, serene and merciless."[25]

In Odyard's Plutocratic cosmology, it is pointless and even irreverent to lament the affliction and misery of the weak. Mocking "the impotent charity of Christendom," he absolves his gorgeous listeners of any moral responsibility for the poor. "We did not make them; we did not ask Nature to make them . . . it is nature's business to feed them, not yours or mine." Echoing Emerson's paean to nature's "grinding economy" of "cruel kindness," Odyard sees a ghastly but beneficent providence in the distribution of ordeal and felicity. "It was said in ancient times, 'Many are called, but few are chosen.' Our ancestors placed a mystical interpretation on this text; but we know what it means—many are called to the sorrows of life, but few are chosen to inherit the delights of wealth and happiness." Having explained the ways of God to the winners, Odyard envisions a saturnalia for patricians, an endless festival of exquisite consumption, leavened by melancholy and sadism. "On with the dance! Though we dance above graves"—eventually, he concedes, their own. Rather than close their eyes to suffering, the charmed should behold the lowly, for the sight of their anguish will sharpen pleasure and "add a flavor to our viands."[26] Donnelly's point is all too clear: the Plutocracy is an infernal Atlantis, a hideous antechamber of hell in which the reign of money betokens a horrific misenchantment.

In *Caesar's Column* and *The Golden Bottle* (in the latter, a similarly fiendish plutocracy exploits and demeans the people), Donnelly offers two different visions of judgment and redemption. In *Caesar's Column,* the Plutocracy is eventually overthrown by "the Brotherhood," a clandestine international conspiracy. Just as the enervated citizens of Atlantis suffered divine retribution, the lords of the heartless megalopolis perish in a righteous revolutionary paroxysm. Led by "Caesar," the rebels and the masses exact a deliriously sanguinary vengeance; as the violence escalates, the corpses pile up and have to be stacked and hidden in concrete—"Caesar's Column." As angry farmers descend on New York to join in the final conflagration of the city, Gabriel watches with sorrow, not schadenfreude, for the spiritual cancer that originated with the rulers has metastasized among the people. "They were no longer the honest yeomanry" of the antebellum republic; now they are "brutalized . . . fierce serfs—cruel and bloodthirsty peasants."[27]

Donnelly wrote *Caesar's Column* at a time of gathering political turmoil; he published *The Golden Bottle* during the campaign of 1892, intending, as he wrote in an apologetic preface, "to explain and defend . . . some of the ideas put forth by the People's Party." Ephraim Benezet, a poor Kansas farmboy, is visited by a spirit—"the Pity of God"—who hands him a golden bottle whose liquid can turn anything into gold. Empowered and emboldened by this enchanted gift, Ephraim—now a Midas without the curse—resolves to end the world's economic plight by increasing the supply of gold. He swiftly galvanizes a massive popular insurgency, buying up mortgages and settling debts with his limitless supply of gold. Forming a "Brotherhood of Justice," he runs successfully as the People's Party candidate for president;

passes, in tandem with Congress, a roster of populist reforms; and then invades Canada and Europe, setting up a "Universal Republic" with its capital in the Azores—on the site of the sunken Atlantis. But then Ephraim awakens, and discovers that his brilliant career has been nothing but a dream! Distraught and almost suicidal, he sees another apparition: an elderly gentleman from the seventeenth century who explains the meaning of his fantasy. One lesson is in monetary policy: the Golden Bottle represents "the power of government to create its own money," money so plentiful that "the credit system will cease, debts will disappear."[28]

But the deeper lesson is in metaphysics and theology: everything is charged with the grandeur of divinity. Channeling Blake and the early Emerson through Henry George and the Farmers' Alliance, Donnelly's metaphysics and theology represented a populist romanticism. "The world is full of spirits, cycles upon cycles of creators, universe unfolding universe of activities and labors, endless arrays of angels and archangels, cherubim and seraphim." The earth is enchanted and sacramental. "This is not a barren universe," the spirit continues. "It does not consist of the Un-named at one extremity, and man at the other, with only vacuum between . . . every inch of matter is packed with life; for life is only spirit with its clothes on." Ephraim's visitor echoes Gabriel in *Caesar's Column,* who assures one of the Brotherhood that "the humblest blade of grass preaches an incontrovertible sermon . . . every blade of grass points with its tiny finger straight upward to heaven." In *The Golden Bottle,* the grass and everything else is an illimitably enchanted field of labor. Harkening back to *The Great Cryptogram*—where he had written that "the universe is industry" and that God labored as "the Great Worker"—Donnelly argued that while the universe is a home to the angels, it is also "nothing but *work,*" as the spirit tells Ephraim, "and we all of us . . . have no place in it but as *workers.*"[29]

Suffused by this laboring enchantment, Donnelly's populist utopia recalled the community of the Protestant covenant. After settling in Uganda, Gabriel and his cohorts set up a republic to recapture this ideal, making "dependence on Almighty God" the first article of the constitution. Rooted in producerist divinity, Gabriel's utopia is the consummate cooperative commonwealth of populism: universal suffrage, education, and health care; abolition of interest on loans; ceilings on wealth and land ownership, achieved through progressive taxation. "A sentiment of brotherly love dwells in all hearts" of Gabriel's republic, "a garden of peace and beauty, musical with laughter . . . God smiles down upon them from this throne beyond the stars." Gabriel's utopia is the beloved community of *The American People's Money*: a middling populace, educated and industrious, a scene "over which the angels hang with delight, and which lights up the face of Divinity with smiles."[30] Yet this "God" or "Divinity" is only sketchily Protestant, or even Christian; Donnelly could not openly avow his spiritual modernism. Still, the Protestant harangue persisted in both *Caesar's Column* and *The Golden Bottle*: community, declension, confession of waywardness, and renewal of community.

Although it departed from the hallowed script, Donnelly's modernist enchantment restated the American capitalist jeremiad, reflecting a deeper, more fateful incoherence at the heart of the populist vision: the futility, pursued with zeal since the Puritans, of reconciling the imperatives of capitalist power with those of evangelical fraternity. Like others before and since, the populist jeremiad foundered on the fissures in the covenant itself. Although, for instance, he castigated corporations and "labor-saving devices" as sources of moral and spiritual degeneration, Donnelly could never grasp that both emerged from the "freedom of trade and the market" he endorsed. Even celebrants of corporate modernization such as Macune and Polk never quite grasped that the logic of "combination" would ravage the evangelical republic of small property. From the "business point of view," the centralization and mechanization of American farming that accelerated after World War I was not only a great success; as Postel himself observes, its foundations had also been laid by many of the agricultural cooperatives championed by the agrarian vanguard. Even those farmers' monopolies composed of small and middle-sized proprietors tended, over time, to succumb to the necessities of profit and industrialization. "Call us a trust, if you will, but we're a benevolent one," as the head of the California raisin association said in 1920.[31]

The populist reformation of American capitalism found a fitting champion in none other than William Jennings Bryan, whose career underscores the affinity of producerist theology and corporate modernity. Then and now, many partisans of populism cast Bryan in the role of an imposter, an eloquent caricature of genuine populism, the author of the "fusionist" strategy that led genuine populists into a fatal alliance with the Democrats.[32] Yet the fusionists won over a majority of the delegates at the People's Party's 1896 convention, and their victory—preceded by many fusions with one of the two major parties in previous state and local elections—suggests at the very least that populists had enough in common with the Establishment they vilified to broker electoral alliances. Indeed, since agrarian populists sought to reform, not to abrogate, the capitalist covenant, then the fusionist strategy marked less a betrayal than a culmination of their modernizing program; Bryan was an acolyte of the populist vision, not a false prophet come from the plutocracy.

Like many in the agrarian intelligentsia, Bryan had no problem with corporate enterprise. (He certainly had no problem with business—as a young lawyer in Lincoln, Nebraska, he had spent much of his time collecting debts that local farmers owed to corn suppliers.) "We are not hostile to corporations," the Great Commoner assured the Senate in 1894 while arguing for a graduated income tax. "We simply believe that these creatures of the law, these fictitious persons, have no higher or dearer rights than the persons of flesh and blood whom God created."[33] Bryan did not say that these "persons" had no rights at all, even as he openly recognized their fictive metaphysical status. Unlike "Cyclone" Davis and other populist skeptics of corporate personality—whom we must now recognize as a minority of the movement—Bryan never bemoaned the *Santa Clara* decision, nor did he ever challenge the moral or ontological standing of business corporations. Like other populist writers and politicians, Bryan adopted "the business standpoint."

The essential harmony of Bryanism, agrarian populism, and the evangelical dispensation was evident in Bryan's renowned acceptance speech at the Democratic Convention in 1896. The "Cross of Gold" has become so famous for its defiant concluding line—"you shall not crucify mankind on a cross of gold"—that its fundamental endorsement of "the business standpoint" has been overlooked or minimized. Declaring that the Democrats had behind them "the producing masses of this nation and the world, supported by the commercial interests, the laboring interests, and the toilers everywhere," Bryan introduced this sea of humanity as a "broader class of business men." "The definition of a business man," he complained, "is much too limited in its application." "The man who is employed for wages is as much a business man as his employer," Bryan said. In a passage from which Donnelly, Macune, Polk, George, or even Powderly would not have dissented, Bryan went on to enlarge the definition of businessman: "the attorney in a country town," the "merchant at the cross-roads store," the "farmer who goes forth in the morning and toils all day . . . and who by the application of brain and muscle to the natural resources of the country creates wealth, is as much a business man as the man who goes upon the board of trade and bets upon the price of grain."[34] From industrial worker to Wall Street speculator, every man was a businessman in Bryan's universe—a cosmos which, in its beautiful fruition, would bustle with virtuous, middling strivers, over whom Donnelly's angels would fly in acquisitive jubilation.

Populism has long been America's favorite fable of popular righteousness: the "working people," "the grass roots," or "the 99%" against "business," "the elites," or "the 1%." The fable has been moving, and often effective. Even in co-opted form, the Populist movement was, as Postel wryly notes, "far more successful dead than alive," as many populist reforms were eventually adopted in the first two decades of the twentieth century. Yet the mythology remains so strong that even Postel, going against the grain of his own evidence, can write that the Populist vision of the late nineteenth century was "increasingly eclipsed by a corporate vision."[35] But populism *was* a corporate vision—"an alternative model of capitalism," to recall Postel's own description—and the populist jeremiad underwrote a reformation of the capitalist economic theology. Like their Puritan and evangelical communion of saints, Populists kept one eye on God and one eye on the main chance. They did not dissent in any fundamental way from the tenets of the capitalist covenant.

# 13

# The Cross Is Bending

## The Socialist Jeremiad and the Covenant Theology

SOCIALISM WOULD SEEM TO have promised a more thorough repudiation of the covenant than populism. The call for a revolutionary overthrow of capitalist society, coupled with the secular effort to dispel the effects of the "opium of the people," struck at the heart of the Protestant moral and political imagination. The identity of capitalism and Christianity in the Protestant mind was nowhere more evident than in religious polemic against socialism. "Socialism places the will of the collectivity above the will of the individual," one clergyman inveighed in 1909, while "Christianity maintains the absolute freedom of individual choice." A year later, another minister noted that because he wanted to use the Apostles' money for the poor, "Judas was the only Socialist among professed Christians." (Not to be outdone in vituperative ingenuity by Protestants, one Jesuit maligned socialists as "Hell's lowest vomit.")[1]

To be sure, many American socialists shared Marx's hostility to religion or enchantment in any form. Yet they often downplayed their secularism or tolerated comrades who saw no conflict between religious faith and socialist commitment. Indeed, many socialists wrote of the cause as a religious crusade. Describing a meeting of radical workers, Hutchins Hapgood—Greenwich Village bohemian and self-described "pagan"—reported admiringly that the spirit of labor resembled "an emotional relationship to religion." Writing in *The Larger Aspects of Socialism* (1913), journalist and labor reformer William English Walling reflected that, because it promised relief from injustice and poverty in this life rather than the next, socialism, "provides a substitute for religion." John Spargo—one of the movement's most prolific writers and popular public speakers—believed that class conflict was "essentially a spiritual struggle." To Spargo, the spiritual significance of modern socialism lay in the realization that social and economic equality was "the only basis on which the divine fabric of human brotherhood can be raised." Jack London captured the religious passion of the socialist crusade in *The Iron Heel* (1907), his ominous tale of reactionary tyranny. As the protagonist Avis Everhard writes of the revolutionary devotion she shares with her ill-fated comrades, "the Revolution took on largely the character of religion . . . it was the divine flashing through us."[2]

This religious élan goes a long way toward explaining why, before World War I, socialism was the broadest and strongest radical movement in the United States. American socialism was both remarkably ecumenical—embracing Marxist militants such as Daniel de Leon, Protestant ministers of the "Social Gospel," and self-styled progressives—and sociologically diverse—Boston students, Manhattan bohemians, Chicago meatpackers, and Oklahoma farmers. While journals such as the *Masses* extolled the delights of "paganism"—free love, modern art, iconoclasm, indolence—periodicals such as the *Appeal to Reason,* published by Julius Wayland out of Girard, Kansas, made the case for socialism in more respectable, even impeccably bourgeois terms. Where metropolitan "pagans" such as John Reed or Max Eastman brashly denounced patriotism and religious orthodoxy, Wayland would invoke "the revolutionary red, white, and blue of our forefathers."[3] Affirming the spirit if not the letter of the Protestant republican tradition, American socialism reimagined the covenant and revised the jeremiad.

If American socialists relied on the powerful residue of Protestantism, most Protestant critics of capitalism never carried the revolutionary banner. The Social Gospel was rarely a *socialist* gospel, and most of the "Christian socialism" that appeared was, as in Europe, tepid and ameliorative. Led by theologians, clergy, and seminarians, the Social Gospel exuded the musty air of the small-town pastor's parlor; when its acolytes sought to "Christianize the social order," they signaled their acceptance of capitalist property and industrial regimentation. Long on prophetic exhortation but lamentably short on analytical acuity, most preachers of the Social Gospel settled for the bromides of "industrial partnership."[4]

Lyman Abbott and Washington Gladden typified the modesty that characterized much of the Social Gospel. Successor to Henry Ward Beecher in the pulpit of Brooklyn's Plymouth Church, Abbott was a prophet of industrial reform sure to comfort his affluent congregation. "The remedy for industrial ills is less a new organization than a new spirit," Abbott proclaimed in *Christianity and Social Problems* (1896)—the good news of a revitalized capitalism. Abbott's ardor for spiritual rather than political transformation was shared by Gladden, a Congregationalist minister in Columbus, Ohio, and a frequent champion of workers. Explaining the differences between Christianity and socialism, Gladden concluded that "the deepest need is not a change of forms, but a change of aims and purposes and tempers." Echoing the evangelical call to individual purity of character, Gladden opined that "the genuine Socialism is that of the heart, in the spirit, not the letter."[5]

Another Congregationalist pastor and writer who made justice a tally of individual changes was Charles Sheldon. Best known for his novel *In His Steps* (1897)—from which countless Protestants have taken "What would Jesus do?" as the gold standard of reform and morality—the Topeka minister was a champion of workers' rights, racial equality, women's suffrage, and temperance. Although *In His Steps* became his signature work, it cannot be read apart from essays and other novels—*The Heart of the World* (1903) and *Jesus Is Here!* (1914), the sequel to *In His Steps*—in which Sheldon imagined a capitalist order invested with loving kindness. The traditional Protestant cosmology persisted in Sheldon's moral universe. When Stanton—a conservative preacher turned righteous radical and the hero of *Heart of the World*—brings a greedy mill owner to spiritual regeneration, "the very air seemed pulsing with the divine presence; the Holy Spirit pervaded the room." Later, when Jesus returns to earth in *Jesus Is Here*—"like an average man, only different"—the divine strides through the world with palpable force but without leaving any physical traces. (An omnipresent but shadowy Savior, Jesus eludes capture by modern photography.) Yet to judge by the changes that Sheldon envisioned, what Jesus would do was certainly benign and emollient but hardly radical. The "Programme of Socialism" in *Heart of the World* combines common ownership of certain necessities and utilities with "fair wages" in an otherwise capitalist system, plus a heavy dose of evangelical moralism: temperance, sabbatarianism, and a rejuvenated family life. In *In His Steps*, Milton Wright, a newly converted merchant, "revolutionize[s] his business" with "personal love." Wright's firm becomes a "system of cooperation," a "real sharing in the whole business" that is not, as Sheldon goes out of his way to insist, "a patronizing recognition of inferiors." The Jesus of *Jesus*

*Is Here* inveighs against alcohol (it's all water and no wine for this divine prohibitionist), and harangues businesspeople who show "no feeling of sympathy or affection" for their employees.[6] For Sheldon as for most Social Gospel reformers, the cooperative commonwealth was capitalist property through which Jesus had gently stepped.

The Social Gospel spoke to popular demands for justice and desires for metaphysical renewal. Eager to address these longings, the most popular socialist writers and orators—Laurence Gronlund, Edward Bellamy, Julius Wayland, Henry Demarest Lloyd, and Eugene V. Debs—portrayed the arrival of the cooperative commonwealth as a religious consummation, an achievement of sacramental communion with the forces that enlivened the universe. In his trilogy of socialist theory—*The Cooperative Commonwealth* (1884), *Our Destiny* (1891), and *The New Economy* (1898)—Gronlund, a former member of the executive committee of the Socialist Labor Party who rejected violent revolution, argued that socialism reflected "the Will of the Universe" and its "Providence for Humanity." Socialism, he believed, "vouchsafes us a complete, true revelation of the Supreme Will." "Animated throughout by God's spirit," the commonwealth would represent "the Kingdom of God on earth" where "God's presence will be a demonstrated fact." Before writing his best-selling utopian novel *Looking Backward* (1887), Bellamy filled unpublished notebooks with musings on a "Religion of Solidarity" in which socialism would afford the individual soul "a more perfect realization of its solidarity with the universe." After gaining fame as the author of the muckraking classic *Wealth against Commonwealth* (1894) Lloyd likewise filled journals with "notes on a new religion" in which socialism figured as "the Eden of the past and Heaven of the future." In his posthumously published *Man, The Social Creator* (1906), Lloyd envisioned socialism as a realm of enchantment in which humanity would realize its divinity. "All life is incarnation," he wrote, "and there is no dead matter . . . we are coming to see God in everything that lives." Love was "foreordained" to "crown and consummate"—"like magic"—the long historical struggles of men to be godlike in power and goodness.[7]

Yet the instrumental and pecuniary rationality that formed part of the evangelical ethos vitiated even these rapturous visions of socialist communion. The regimented, technocratic character of Bellamy's utopia in *Looking*

*Backward* (1888) is one of its most conspicuous features; as William Morris put it in his perceptive review of the novel, Bellamy exhibited a "curiously limited" imagination, and his "Boston beautified" was an antiseptic bourgeois fantasy "organized with a vengeance." (Morris was so appalled by *Looking Backward* that he countered with *News from Nowhere*.) Lloyd asserted that the love animating the world was eminently "usable"; we should "get this God at work" performing "the chore of to-day." "Love," Lloyd insisted unromantically, "needs now to be discussed in matter-of-fact language, as though it were mechanics, or arithmetic, or housekeeping." Echoing the Knights, Lloyd the self-proclaimed socialist told readers of a liberal Protestant magazine that "all men will become capitalists and all capitalists co-operative."[8]

The Protestant proprietary legacy was most pronounced in Wayland, whose *Coming Nation* and *Appeal to Reason* were the most popular radical newspapers in the country before World War I. In the *Coming Nation*, Wayland argued that socialism was the contemporary form of Christianity, and for most of his career, he evangelized for socialism in this Protestant vein. Socialists preached "the gospel of Christ—a Higher civilization," he wrote in 1893. Yet Wayland's socialism was eclectic to the point of incoherence. Like other radical magazines, *Appeal to Reason* published exposes, fiery editorials, and lacerating cartoons, but it also accepted advertising from capitalists, featured promotional fanfare indistinguishable from that of the bourgeois press, and avidly competed with other socialist magazines. More a collection of yarns and homilies than a rigorous theoretical system, the "One-Hoss Philosophy" Wayland preached was a small-town socialist boosterism in which the Chamber of Commerce joined comradely hands with the Second International. Businesspeople who prayed for the millennium on Sundays were "not intentionally bad or hypocritical," Wayland wrote in one typical editorial. "They are simply ignorant of what it takes to have the prayer realized." Reading through Wayland's "One-Hoss" sermons, one often gets the impression that socialism is just a sharper brand of business sense. "Capitalism is not wholly bad," he wrote near the end of his life. While it exploited workers and crushed small businesspeople, it also demonstrated that "goods can be made and distributed under the system of largest production with the least amount of labor." Most of Wayland's most devoted readers were impeccably Protestant in habits and outlook; their letters exhibit an abiding fealty to thrift, hard work, temperance, monogamy, and faith in a loving Providence.[9]

Anointed by millions with what a biographer called "a status near to divinity," Debs was the first and final saint of American socialism, infusing industrial modernity with the small-town evangelical sublime. Debs was an unlikely and reluctant evangelist. He openly detested clergymen as pious minions of the ruling class who "prostitute the name and teachings and example" of Jesus "to the power of Mammon." Skeptical of saviors, Debs sought to dissociate himself from his own messianic image. "If you are looking for a Moses to lead you out of this capitalist wilderness, you will stay right where you are," he told a typically large and spellbound crowd in Detroit in 1906. Yet his halo was well deserved, for Debs was a pious if unorthodox devotee of the Protestant covenant. Growing up in Terre Haute, Indiana, during and after the Civil War, Debs heavily imbibed the producerist ethos of industry, perseverance, and republican civility. As a member of the Brotherhood of Locomotive Firemen, and later as head of the American Railway Union, Debs sang hosannas to the "progressive, enterprising working class," and insisted that hard work and social mobility were "standards by which Christ measured men." As leader of the American Railway Union during the Great Northern Railway strike of 1894, Debs explained to jubilant workers after the union's victory that the battle had been about ending class conflict as much as winning material demands. Convinced that "an era of close relationship between capital and labor is dawning," Debs imagined a time near at hand of "mutual justice" when "employer and employee can respect each other."[10] In Debs's and the other strikers' eyes, the Great Northern had violated the spirit and letter of the Protestant ethic.

This commitment to the Protestant covenant shaped Debs's conception of socialism. Debs joined the movement while serving a six-month prison term for his participation in the Pullman Strike; while in prison, he read Marx, Karl Kautsky, Gronlund, Bellamy, and other socialist writers. The subsequent timbre of Debs's oratory and writing suggest that his conversion owed much to Gronlund's evocations and Bellamy's ideal of mass-produced abundance. Indeed, for Debs, as for countless followers and admirers, the socialist movement was a modern jeremiad: a proclamation of ideals, a confession of declension, and a reclamation of corrupted but redeemable promise. Debs envisioned the socialist future as an eschatological consummation. As he wrote in the *Arena* in November 1908, socialism partook of "the nature of a religious movement and awakens something of a religious enthusiasm among its adherents." On occasion, traces of providential animation surfaced in Debs's homilies to radical workers. Speaking to the founding convention of the Industrial Workers of the World in Chicago in June 1905, Debs asserted that "the working class is permeated with the conquering spirit of the class struggle, and as if by magic the entire movement is vitalized . . . we move forward to certain and complete victory." Debs took so seriously the glorious preamble to the Wobblies' constitution—declaring that the union was "forming the structure of the new society within the shell of the old"—that he could write in 1908 that a man could be "so completely consecrated" to the socialist cause that "he lives within the realization of it even now."[11]

Debs's own prophetic magnetism drew on what remained of the current of Protestant divinity. "Like a John of Patmos," as one speaker described him to the Social Democratic convention in March 1900, Debs had revealed "a vision of things that were to be, of the new kingdom, of the new era." "It was like a sacrament to meet him," Max Eastman, editor of *The Masses*, recalled; Debs was a vessel of "the old real love, the miracle love that utterly identifies itself with the needs and wishes of others." Though uncomfortable in his role as a saintly tribune, Debs could not have been unaware of the parallels made between his own travails and those of an earlier messiah. Marveling in 1914 at "Jesus, the Supreme Leader," Debs venerated the "master proletarian revolutionist" and the "completeness of his transcendental consecration." Preaching "pure communism" and vilifying private property as "a sacrilege," Jesus was martyred by the Rockefellers of his day; but his generosity and courage in the face of martyrdom "gave to the ages his divine inspiration." Debs's own divine inspiration reached an eloquent pinnacle at his trial for sedition in September 1918. Debs had openly opposed American entry into World War I, and when he called for resistance to the draft in June 1918, he was arrested and indicted. At his sentencing hearing four months later, Debs addressed the court with all the lyrical, quotidian majesty of radical hope. Speaking for everyone "seized in the remorseless grip of Mammon," Debs reflected that

When the mariner, sailing over topic seas, looks for relief from his weary watch, he turns his eyes toward the Southern Cross, burning luridly above the tempest-vexed ocean. As the midnight approaches, the Southern Cross begins to bend, and the whirling worlds change their places, and with starry finger-points the Almighty marks the passage of time upon the dial of the universe. . . . Let the people take heart and hope everywhere, for the cross is bending, midnight is passing, and joy cometh with the morning.[12]

Debs's oration was the finest rhetorical moment in the history of American socialism, aligning the history of proletarian struggle with the designs of a loving Providence. But because that Providence was a metaphysical relic of Protestant producerism, it wasn't clear that the mariner's weariness would end, or that the morning would arrive with joy. Socialists shared with their antagonists a belief in the historical necessity of competition; the merciless contest of the marketplace would, in their view, produce a corporate leviathan that could be civilized into a democratic cooperative commonwealth. At the same time, sharing the old proprietary devotion to unending economic growth, socialists were committed to retaining—while somehow transfiguring—the capitalist apparatus of industrial technology and professional-managerial supervision. Debs often asserted that socialism meant direct control of industry by workers themselves, the end of alienation from production and product, and the commencement of a new community of neighborly, felicitous, artisanal labor. "The whole people will take the title-deed of Rockefeller's trusts and operate the machinery of production and distribution." In the cooperative commonwealth, he wrote in 1905, each worker will "express himself in his work and work with joy." Here Debs sounded like John Ruskin and Morris; but his favorable view of corporate consolidation was fundamentally at odds both with workers' control and with pleasurable endeavor. Convinced that large-scale, routinized production was beneficial and inevitable, Debs—like most other socialists—defined the cooperative commonwealth as an oligarchy of benevolent experts, presiding with managerial chivalry over a mass of fraternal proprietors. "The whole industry will represent a giant corporation in which all citizens are stockholders," he asserted in 1908, and the state will be "a board of directors acting for the whole people." "Details of organization and performance may well be left to the experts."[13]

True to Marx's and Engels's endorsement of industrial despotism, this acquiescence in the Fordist technics of corporate domination was common among socialists; as anarchists and other communists recognized at the time, they supported what amounted to "state capitalism"—the retention (under capitalist or socialist auspices) of the hierarchical relations and methods of capitalist property and production. Indeed, Debs's failure to recognize any conflict between democracy and corporate consolidation was shared by Lenin, who famously embraced "the Taylor system"—thereby confirming that the authoritarian features of Soviet industry were modeled directly after the most imperious brand of American corporate discipline. Convinced that material abundance was the essential precondition of justice and emancipation, both Lenin and Debs ratified managerial and technocratic authority in the workplace; equated democracy with distributive equity, not active participation in production and planning; and affirmed the mega-technics of control over nature and humanity in the name of freedom. Thus, precisely to the extent that it recast the producerist ethos of hard work and practicality in Fordist terms, Debsian socialism lent an unwitting sanction to the authority of industrial management. The producerist tradition to which Debs is regarded as the socialist heir did not and could not serve as a reliable, let alone effective, source of opposition to corporate power.[14] Like scientific managers and corporate liberals, American socialists accepted and even celebrated the corporate mechanization of communion.

The socialist assent to corporate modernity was challenged by Christian socialists unsatisfied by the sheepish reformism of the Social Gospel as represented by Abbott, Gladden, and Sheldon. Convinced that socialism and Christianity were not irreconcilable enemies, they were confident that, as the theologian Walter Rauschenbusch wrote, the future belonged to "those who can effect the completest amalgamation of the two." Parting company with other knights of the Golden Rule, Christian socialists joined in a broader Anglo-American effort to reconstruct socialist thought. Worried that Fabian socialists such as Sidney Webb and Beatrice Webb were succumbing to the undemocratic features of capitalist production, some writers attacked the socialist consensus on industrialization. For instance, "distributists" such as Hilaire Belloc, G. K. Chesterton, and A. J. Penty called for a disassembly of the industrial apparatus and a restoration of small farms and workshops.

Renegade Fabians such as G. D. H. Cole advocated "guild socialism": the abolition of wage labor; the elimination of a distinct managerial stratum; and the control of industry by "guilds," trade unions reclaiming full technical prowess and political power in the workplace. Uniting the workers' cause with the Romantic quest for beauty in the manner of Ruskin and Morris, guild socialism offered left-wing Anglicans a chance to reconcile socialism and Christianity. Anglican socialists such as Stewart Headlam, J. N. Figgis, and Maurice Reckitt preached a "sacramental socialism"—in their view, a fuller and richer materialism than the secular Marxist variety.[15]

Like their British counterparts, Christian socialists in America were maverick pastors and intellectuals determined to win the workers for the Gospel—not through calls to individual regeneration but through "social salvation" and sacramental radicalism. "Christianizing the social order" meant eradicating production for profit and replacing it with production for love. As the members of the Christian Commonwealth Colony outside of Columbus, Georgia, proclaimed in 1898, they were a "love-ruled fraternal, non-profit-seeking body." Christian socialists drew water from many of the same wells that nourished their Anglican comrades: references to Ruskin, Morris, and Tolstoy abounded in Christian socialist literature. Writers such as Rauschenbusch, W. D. P. Bliss, George D. Herron, Bouck White, and Vida Dutton Scudder refused to follow in the timorous steps of Sheldon's rabble-soothing Jesus. Instead, they beckoned Americans to bring heaven down to earth, end the reign of Mammon, and live in beloved, sacramental community. Denying the covenantal bond between Christianity and capitalist property, they came closer than anyone before them to repudiating the terms of the jeremiad tradition. Calling for "a universal communism of spiritual and material goods," Herron called in *The Christian State* (1895), for "common possession of the machinery, forces, and production of great industrial monopolies."[16]

For the knights of the socialist vision, the cooperative commonwealth was the earthly prelude to the fullness of the kingdom of God. In an 1890 issue of the *Dawn*, Bliss—pastor of Boston's Church of the Carpenter, an archetypal labor church—asserted plainly that "on earth we are to realize heaven." Harkening back to some of the earliest, forgotten hopes of Christianity, Bliss wrote that in the coming socialist millennium, "even God is not to rule over man; man is to be one with God, and God is to be realized in men." Bliss criticized less radical acolytes of the Social Gospel for equating socialism with reform; socialism was "no system of profit-sharing, no individualistic scheme, no associated charities and model houses and aristocratic patronage."[17] Following Jesus in his steps should lead to the abolition of the capitalist property system.

The socialist Jesus walked in workman's shoes. Jesus the Proletarian abounded in the radical literature of the early twentieth century: from cartoons in the *Masses* and the *Call* to John Richard Brown's *Jesus the Joyous Comrade* (1911), the Savior appeared in overalls preaching a muscular socialist Christianity. In her academic but accessible study of *Social Ideals in English Letters* (1898), Scudder upheld William Langland's *Piers Ploughman* as a model of a "workman-Christ." One of the more lyrical and cantankerous exponents of Christian socialism, White depicted Jesus as a working-class rebel and seer in several popular volumes. In *The Call of the Carpenter* (1911) and *The Carpenter and the Rich Man* (1914), White argued that Jesus—with a hale, brawny, "red-blooded masculine make-up"—augured, not a heaven beyond the stars, but "a paradise in the Here and Now, an industrial commonwealth." He anointed the labor movement "earth's holiest holy" and proclaimed that the cause of the workers bent not with the cross but with the arc of the cosmos. (Debs was so moved by *The Call of the Carpenter* that he praised it as the "truest interpretation of Jesus.") Claiming in *Letters from Prison* (1915) that socialism was the "lineal offspring of Christianity," White reasoned that the moral imagination of the left must therefore be "as big as the universe." As grandiose as this advice may sound, it stemmed from a materialist ontology, as White contended that the doctrine of the Incarnation put a blessing on material life. Embracing rather than rejecting materialism, White admonished his brethren that it "neither bereaves the race of its halo, nor degrades the story of the past into chronicles of a pigsty and the kennel."[18]

Echoing the medieval and Romantic lineage, socialist theologians espoused a sacramental materialism, an account of the world as a vessel of supernatural grace, power, and love. Just as Ruskin had drawn a line between illth and wealth, these theologians distinguished between the lethal rites of capital and the eucharist of the socialist future. Writing in *Dawn* in 1894, Bliss described George Pullman's industrial village as "a devil's sacrament," revealing the inner secret of "the system in the midst of which we live and move and have our being." By contrast, the beloved communitarians of the

Commonwealth Colony portrayed their work in 1898 as "a continuous sacrament which conveys the Divine life and love to each and all." Preachers, farmers, and mechanics dwelled in "a most delightful common fellowship . . . a 'communion of the saints.'" In *Christianizing the Social Order* (1912), Rauschenbusch attributed sacramental significance to socialist reconstruction. When invested with "great religious hope," the socialist movement was akin to "the cup of water [that] becomes a sacrament when it is hallowed by the thought of Christ."[19]

As the most flamboyant of the Protestant avant-garde, Herron was obligingly baroque in his account of socialism as an enchanted world. Material goods are "sacraments of grace," he wrote in *The New Redemption* (1893), through which "God creates and unfolds the powers of men." Even after he had repudiated organized Christianity, Herron remained a sacramental materialist. "All material things are the common coin of the spiritual realm," he told the Social Democratic Party in Chicago in 1900. (His speech was so well received that the radical publisher Charles H. Kerr included it in the Pocket Library of Socialism, a popular collection of radical tracts.) The graceful transparency of matter made property a religious as well as moral affair. Property forms must promote "communion with God and brotherhood with men," Herron taught in *The New Redemption; "*property is a sacrament of the unity of life," he asserted in *The Christian State* (1895), "and through its use men enter into fellowship with each other and communion with God." Thus Herron vilified capitalist business as "mammon worship" through which profiteers "crucify the Son of man afresh." To Herron, socialism was the inexorable consequence of Christian metaphysics. As the sign of beloved community, "mutualism of property . . . is the logic of any Christian doctrine of property," he concluded in 1894, "the political economy of the Lord's Prayer."[20]

Yet many Christian socialists succumbed to the allure of industrial centralization. Bliss, for instance, deemed the *Fabian Essays* "the best all around statement of modern practical scientific Socialism." Rauschenbusch vacillated between hopes for a restoration of the early Christians' "primitive communism" and technocratic concessions to the corporate present. Like Debs, Bliss, and the Fabians, Rauschenbusch discerned in corporate society "the evolution of a cooperative economic organization" and put considerable faith in the idealism of experts, trusting in their presumed capacity for disinterested mediation between classes—their talent, in his words, for "interpreting each to the other." Even Herron beheld a providential necessity in the unfolding of capitalist industrialization. Progress, he wrote in *The Christian State*, is "a divine journey, a sacred pilgrimage." "As progress ascends" in "the movement of history toward unity," God employed even the avarice of capital to serve His ultimate purposes. Alluding to the corporate concentration of industry, Herron declared that God was directing "the selfishness of mammon to teach the lessons of brotherhood," and investing "the gold of mammon to pave the streets of the New Jerusalem."[21]

Almost alone among Christian socialists, White remained unenchanted by the mythology of industrial progress. Educated at Harvard and Union Theological Seminary, he welcomed socialists, anarchists, Wobblies, and bohemians to his "Church of the Social Revolution" in lower Manhattan. He denounced American entry into World War I, urged young men to resist conscription, and burned the flag as a symbol of nationalist idolatry. A masterpiece of prophetic theater, White's inflammatory witness for peace overshadowed the social criticism in his earlier work. Articulated in *The Call of the Carpenter* and *The Carpenter and the Rich Man*, White's "philosophy of the universe" portrayed the world as charged with the grandeur of God, unstinting to those who treat it with love and refrain from predation and avarice. "Stinginess is not Earth's natural disposition," he wrote in *The Carpenter and the Rich Man*. To those enamored with money and production, scarcity is the fundamental fact of the world; exhibiting "an infidel distrust in the competency of Mother Earth to nourish all of us," they create the combative privation they fear. But those in league with the Galilean share his faith in a universe "alive and restless." Jesus could herald a "paradise in the Here and Now," because he trusted in "the native kindliness of the earth." Bearing the mark and bounty of divinity, "broad-bosomed Earth has store of nutriment for all her numerous progeny." Diametrically opposed to the barbarous fantasy at the heart of capitalist economics, this "romance of the favorable earth" told the truest story about the world.[22]

Because White cherished the "broad-bosomed Earth," he remained ambivalent about industrialization and its degradation of artisanal skill. Asserting that "every work bench [is] an altar," White decried the profanation and debasement of the worker's tabernacle by pecuniary enchantment. Invoking Ruskin and Morris, he wrote that Mammon, "besides being immoral and untrue," is "ugly of feature, a hideousness to behold . . . wreaking upon the workshop an imperious cupidity, to the vitiating of craftsmanship." Socialism, for White, meant the restoration of artistry and craftsmanship in labor's sanctuary. Once they recaptured the means of production from the clutches of the infidel, workers would be "permitted to be artists, finding in one and the same task self-support and self-expression." Like Morris's revolutionary medievalism, White's ideal of the liberated artisan blended the best of Marx and Ruskin. Indeed, Jesus the carpenter was "the patron of industrial art." "To the extent that a workman is wholly free, he goes a craftsman; incarnates himself in his product . . . enshrining mystic values."[23]

This "philosophy of the universe"—a "romance of the favorable earth"—also contained a critique of the modern dread and horror of poverty. While White never denied the brutality and meanness enforced by scarcity, he also observed that "some of the greatest achievements of the human spirit have been amidst a material environment which today would be called beggarly." People were capable of such moral and artistic sublimity only if they trusted in the reality of abundance—an abundance that could not be equated with possessions. "Humanity can get along without wealth, and has," he reminded his socialist readers. White dissented from the prevailing wisdom on the left, because he feared that the workers' movement could be corrupted by the very mistrust of the world that propelled the fury of capitalism. If the "native kindliness of the earth" was real, then the frenzy of accumulation was delusional as well as iniquitous; the gargantuan technics of industrialization were unnecessary as well as destructive; and the joy of creative expenditure in beautiful production was not an illusion. When White insisted that workers needed a new "philosophy"—with Jesus as its "patron of industrial art"—he was beckoning toward a romantic socialism of artisan-communards. "Once let the labor movement be touched with the spaciousness and grandeur of spiritual things, it will open to all mankind the closed doors of paradise."[24]

Alas, the doors of paradise remained bolted, as the great majority of American socialists, Christian or otherwise, found White's sort of philosophy unconvincing or irrelevant. As labor's war for industrial democracy came to naught, Christian socialists receded even further to the margins of mainline Protestantism. Convinced that the future lay with the extension of mechanized, hierarchical production, Protestant leaders made their peace with the incorporation of America, following Sheldon's Jesus down the path of clerical stewardship to corporate capital. When the Federal Council of Churches issued its statement *The Church and Industrial Reconstruction* (1919), it confronted the corporate order with insipid admonitions to employers to provide the "fullest consideration of human values."[25]

# 14

# The Priesthood of Art

## Anarchism, Arts and Crafts, and the Re-enchantment of the World

BOUCK WHITE'S ROMANTICISM POINTED to two other sources of opposition to corporate enchantment: the anarchist and Arts and Crafts movements. "Enshrining mystic values," in White's words, the artisanal ideal cast a powerful spell over many middle-class professionals who feared industrial displacement and objected to industrial aesthetics. At the same time, familiar with anarchists through his work at the Church of the Social Revolution, White praised them as valiant and invaluable allies in the march to the doors of paradise. Though dreaded by all respectable folk as the theory and practice of hell, anarchism, White mused in one of the Church's pamphlets, was rather "the most spiritual idea ever born among men."[1]

Upholding an artisanal ideal, anarchists and Arts and Crafts enthusiasts posed the most fundamental challenges to the incorporation of America. Unlike populists and socialists—who accepted the trajectory of the corporate juggernaut and sought to master rather than reverse it—anarchists and artisanal crusaders aimed to arrest, not hasten, the process of consolidation. Profoundly influenced by the Romantic lineage of opposition to industrial capitalism, they insisted that wisdom about the *ends* of production must inform any struggle over the *means* of production. Embracing the ideal of the artist, they spoke beauty as well as truth to power; defied the industrial division of labor as a desecration of the human person; insisted on pleasurable work that united loveliness and practicality; and resisted the mechanization of communion promoted by mass production. Yet in the end, they proved unable to mount a convincing and effective offensive against incorporation, and much in their beautiful crusades was eventually absorbed into bourgeois culture.

The American anarchist and Arts and Crafts movements have met with considerable ambivalence from historians. Anarchists are praised as crusaders for feminism, sexual freedom, and civil liberties; they are remembered as courageous opponents of American participation in World War I. When aligned with the bohemians of Greenwich Village, they are applauded as partisans in the revolt against prudery, superstition, and banality, the toppling of the Victorian regime of reticence, repression, and propriety. Espousing both personal liberation and self-expression while calling for the overthrow of capitalism, they arranged what they thought would be the indissoluble marriage of cultural and political radicalism, idealizing, in Christine Stansell's words, a self full of "rich possibilities fated to be joined felicitously with others." Yet they also never received support from more than an infinitesimal fraction of the working class; and even worse, as Christopher Lasch contended, the alliance of radicalism and bohemia had devastating consequences for the American left. Typified by the Armory Show and the Paterson Strike Pageant of 1913, the coalescence of culture and politics under the auspices of bohemia exposed the left, in Lasch's view, to an "insidious kind of exploitation": the transformation of "radical politics into entertainment." Easily uncoupled from the broader project of economic and political change, "paganism" and "self-expression" replaced class politics and popular mobilization; personal happiness supplanted or was even equated with revolutionary transformation. Indeed, in this view, bohemian radicalism augured colorful new styles in corporate cultural authority, staging a rehearsal for the "conquest of cool."[2] The "the lyrical left," in this view, was an exotic, iridescent laboratory for commodity fetishism, a vibrantly unprofessional research-and-development division of the culture industry.

Similarly, historians have lauded Arts and Crafts as an attractive and incisive protest against the banality of mass production, the alienation of industrial labor, and the triumph of managerial hierarchy. Encompassing a broad and often disparate range of reformers and activities, the movement attempted to restore moral, aesthetic, and spiritual meaning to increasingly monotonous work. But even sympathetic scholars maintain that it failed to become anything more than a balm for affluent bohemians, yet another incorporation of dissent. Reduced to hobbies and weekends in the country for artistically inclined bourgeois, Arts and Crafts became a therapeutic project of personal rejuvenation and fulfillment.[3]

Yet even if these forms of resistance to industrial capitalism degenerated into the lifestyle politics of "bourgeois bohemians," it remains essential and rewarding to revisit the promise these movements once held—and might still possess, if we knew how to educe it. The much-maligned "therapeutic ethos" preys on real needs for healing and reparation, and it resonates with our most enduring desires for integrity and beatitude. What sounds today like the lissome, manipulative cant of therapy and management—"self-expression," "potential," "liberation," "creativity"—gives voice to unsatisfied longings for joy and communion. Therein lies the secret of the therapeutic ethic: the dream of beloved community achieved through gratifying expenditure of self. Conceived as a cure of souls whose health resides partly in useful work, the politics of production contains a radical therapy of desire. By insisting on the erasure of the lines between delight and utility, the anarchist and Arts and Crafts movements beckoned to a world populated by Whitman's "friendly companions"—a paradise of people and things, a realm of earthly enchantment. Thus, in a manner unlike that of bourgeois sociology, they identified, in the language of artistry and beauty, the deepest source of modern discontent. They realized that "at bottom," as Lears observed, "discontent was religious," and that happiness depended, not on the timetable of progress, but on living joyfully in the here and now.[4] Arts and Crafts and anarchism were siblings under the skin, as artisanal idealists and anarchists sought sacramental ways of being in the world.

Both the anarchist and artisanal movements drew on European as well as indigenous sources: Ruskin, Morris, Kropotkin, Tolstoy, Carpenter. The Americans aimed squarely at the Protestant-proprietary heritage, broaching an incipient repudiation of the covenant theology and its perennial jeremiad. The attack was led by "Young Americans" such as Van Wyck Brooks, Waldo Frank, and Randolph Bourne; anarchists such as Emma Goldman, Alexander Berkman, and their allies in American bohemia; and Arts and Crafts writers such as Horace Traubel and Ralph Adams Cram. Recalling the antebellum American Renaissance, they enlisted art, beauty, and craftsmanship in a heretical phalanx against capitalist enchantment.

An early example of the artisanal-aesthetic critique was William Dean Howells's Altrurian novels, A Traveler from Altruria (1894) and Through the Eye of the Needle (1907). Set in the midst of the Gilded Age, the Altrurian volumes portray the American journey of Aristides Homos, an erudite and gracious emissary from the classless society of Altruria. Shocked by the squalor of the new industrial cities, Homos recounts to his incredulous hosts the rise and fall of "the Accumulation"—like Ignatious Donnelly's "Plutocracy," a venal and decadent oligarchy—and its replacement by an egalitarian community, "the kingdom of heaven on the earth." In Altruria, the worker is not jostled in a labor market or overseen by managerial stewards; rather, he "follows his fancy as to what he shall do, and when he shall do it, or whether he shall do anything at all." Altrurian workplaces are tabernacles of labor; they "look like temples, and they are temples, dedicated to that sympathy between the divine and human which expresses itself in honest and exquisite craftsmanship." Unlike Americans who worship businessmen—a veritable "priesthood," as one banker tells Homos—Altrurians idealize artisans and artists. As "the human type which is likest the divine," the artist works "from the love of his work" and is, in Altruria, "the normal man."[5]

Edgier and more iconoclastic than Howells and other genteel Protestant reformers, intellectuals associated with *Seven Arts* magazine—self-proclaimed avatars of a "Young America" still in the early years of "a renascent period"—repudiated the entire Puritan-evangelical inheritance of pecuniary culture, embracing beauty, grace, friendship, and love as their touchstones of social and cultural criticism—in Bourne's words, "the good life of personality lived in the environment of the Beloved Community." The *Seven Arts* group hated business as much for its banality as for its avarice; as Frank later recalled of the *Seven Arts* circle—himself, Bourne, Brooks, James Oppenheim, Paul Rosenfeld, and others—they loathed American business, "not because we knew it would not work, but because we judged it, even in success, to be lethal to the human spirit." From this standpoint, there was no point in a jeremiad that would only reaffirm the very worst in the American past. With "no tradition to continue," as the editors put it in 1917, the Young Americans, Frank declared in *Our America* (1919), were "the first generation . . . consciously engaged in spiritual pioneering."[6]

To the *Seven Arts* radicals, the most nefarious enemy of the human spirit in America was Puritanism. "The Puritan Theocracy is the all-influential fact in the history of the American mind," Brooks wrote in *America's Coming-of-Age* (1915), as its theology bestowed a benediction on the country's "catchpenny opportunism." The devout accumulators of New England "unleashed the acquisitive instincts" and repressed the aesthetic impulses. Puritanism continued to wreak havoc in the form of industrial civilization—"the clamped dominion of Puritan and Machine," in Frank's words, sustained by what Bourne termed the "Puritan will-to-power." Obliged by their God to acquire omnipotence over nature and their own desires, the American descendents of the Puritan idealized a ferocious and aesthetically analgesic productivity. Insensitive to beauty, reproachful of idleness, and obsessed with sin and decline, Puritans imparted to subsequent generations an abhorrence of sheer delight. "A race that has never cultivated life for its own sake," Americans lacked any criterion of value beyond business or technical utility. Even the revered Emerson came under fire as a divine literatus for business: Emerson, Frank asserted, "supplied the needed philosophic decoration for the seats of learning where men were prepared for the Business of life." Burdened with this "spiritual history," young American intellectuals felt "the chill of the grave," Brooks reflected with anger and melancholy in 1917.[7]

Brooks and Frank surveyed pre-industrial ages and peoples for a cure to the malady of Puritanism. Brooks surmised that, suffering from an "immemorial inhibition of our humane impulses," Americans should forsake the Puritan past and look to Europe for a cultural renaissance. "In Europe," he argued in 1917, "the great traditional culture, the culture that has ever held up the flame of the human spirit, has never been gutted out." More attuned than Puritanism to the "poetry" and "charms of life," this pre-industrial culture had enabled "human nature to get its back up" as soon as the dark satanic mills first appeared. Constructing a romantic modernist lineage of opposition to industrial capitalism, Brooks praised Carlyle, Ruskin, and Morris for "rediscovering the beautiful and happy art of the Middle Ages." Brooks touted Morris in particular in *America's Coming of Age* (1915). With his creatively unrepressed and "contagious personality," Morris had "opposed the ideal of craftsmanship to the ideal of cheapest work and largest money" and "substituted for the inhumane stimulus of competition the humane stimulus of fellowship."[8]

Frank was less optimistic about the appeal of craft traditions, doubting that the artisanal ideal would have any purchase on the American imagination. Because the average American "has no peasant or guild background," Frank believed that the memory and "articulations of craft" would "mean little to him." Still, he explored and celebrated the animistic varieties of Native American spirituality, Pueblo culture and mythology in particular.

Astonished by the Pueblo's unaffected and unassuming sense of natural enchantment, Frank noted how "the Great Spirit" touched upon "his dwellings, upon his pottery, upon his jewelry and ceremonials and dress." Like many middle-class intellectuals infatuated with the "primitive," Frank hoped to borrow an ancient sense of the sacred to enliven a flagging spiritual vigor. But like the peasants and guildsmen of yesteryear, the Great Spirit and its charms were marked for extinction by the westward march of industrial disenchantment. Frank regretted that the Pueblo way of life, like those of other indigenous peoples, would soon be swept into oblivion by progress. "The Indian is dying and is doomed."[9]

If Brooks hoped that the revival of craft would breed a moral and spiritual rebirth, Frank's path of "spiritual discovery" took a more overtly religious direction. Musing in *Our America* (1919) that "there can be no such thing as an irreligious people," he set out in the 1910s to imagine "a new religion" for modern America. In *The Unwelcome Man* (1917), an autobiographical novel, Quincy Burt, alienated from the business world in which his wealthy father flourishes, seeks escape from the prison of mercenary masculinity. "To be a man" in industrial America, Burt reflects, "was to be moved by ugly things—like business and money and machinery." In his love for his mother and in subsequent relationships with women, Burt seeks the virtues of a feminine ideal—receptiveness to nature, openness to feeling, and renunciation of striving and possessiveness. As he gradually rejects the life of "business and money and machinery," the patriarchal deity of enterprise yields to a mystical, womanly enchantment. When praying as a child, Burt's hands clutched in prayer touch "not God at all, but a still older, more eternal Mother." Throughout his life, some semblance of this nurturing divinity pervades the natural world, and Burt experiences occasional epiphanies in which he recaptures the childlike sense of union. In these mystical episodes, Burt slips "the bonds of body," and exults "in communion" with nature "in tremulous unison with the earth and the other stars."[10]

In *Our America*, a modernist sequel to Walt Whitman's *Democratic Vistas*, Frank transformed this mystical consciousness into a religion for American modernity, forsaking, like Brooks, any futile appeal to the Protestant jeremiad. With little in the American past to summon for a new religion, Frank turned increasingly to modernist art as the vessel of modern enchantment. He had long thought that the goal of poetry and fiction was to provide compelling "proofs of God"; the writer's highest objective was the re-enchantment of the world, to "make stones sing—without their ceasing to be stones." In *The Unwelcome Man,* nature was a hymnbook of feminine divinity; in *Our America,* art became the basis of religion and politics, the materialized "passion of beauty" that conveyed the ever-ardent "immanence of God." Frank importuned contemporary artists to seize the sacerdotal status of the clergy. As the acolyte of a new divinity—"love of life, love of *being*"—the artist is "the servant of the soul, worshipper of the revelations of life." Art was "the directest route to human consciousness"; the more fervently a man pursues art, "the more surely he finds God." In an effusive encomium to Alfred Stieglitz and his Manhattan gallery "291," Frank sketched a modern life of the saints and their preternatural powers of aesthetic witness. One who "has seen God and has dared to speak," Stieglitz was "the prophet... the true Apostle of self-liberation" who "takes up the ancient destiny." His gallery was "a religious fact; like all such, a miracle." With a priesthood that included Marsden Hartley, Georgia O'Keefe, and other artists, it was a "church consecrate" for those who "had left old gods, and whose need was sore for new ones." 291 was a tabernacle, a liturgical site where Stieglitz's photographs were miniature modernist sacraments, revealing "the being of depth beyond the surfaces of space and time."[11]

This religion of art attracted converts outside the *Seven Arts* circle. Greenwich Village bohemians wedded modernist art and revolutionary politics, pronouncing the vows in the oracular, magniloquent tones of aesthetic ontology. "The priesthood of art," *Masses* editor Max Eastman explained in 1913, was "not to bestow upon the universe a new aspect, but upon the beholder a new enthusiasm." Through poetry, painting, and the other arts, we are "re-born alive into the world," receiving a "spirituous refreshment" as our souls are "made naked to the touch of beauty." The divinity of art was consecrated and proclaimed most energetically by the Village's anarchists. Reflecting in 1910 on the "tendencies of modern literature," one writer for Goldman's *Mother Earth* asserted that "modern art is religious, and God-seeking in its tendency." Like religion—"true religion," he emphasized, "not the religion of the church"—art brings humanity "near to God, to goodness, and to beauty." Goldman was an especially enthusiastic acolyte of the anarchist religion of art. "Art," she rhapsodized, was always "reaching towards the heavens, itself a star on the firmament of life." For Margaret Anderson, founder of the *Little Review,* art and anarchism were complementary forms of a single spiritual devotion. "A temple was what I wanted," she recalled of her days among the bohemian intelligentsia. "A temple of the great, the permanent, versus the transient, exquisite." The sanctuary of art belonged to the "anarchist religion" of love and freedom from possessions. If modern art was a herald of the triumph of beauty, anarchism was an omen of historical consummation. "Anarchism, like all great things, is an announcement."[12]

American anarchists appealed to art as a surrogate for traditional enchantment, acclaiming beauty as a legitimate, even primary standard for social and economic progress. The *élan vital* of bohemian anarchists was a post-Romantic naturalism, an affirmation of the goodness of nature without recourse to orthodox religious metaphysics. Not that the attempt was altogether successful in eradicating the traces of religion. As Stansell observes, the anarchist celebration of modern, secularized notions of self-expression echoed "an older, Protestant evangelical tradition" that pushed against barriers "between the self and cosmic creation." Anarchists such as Goldman, she writes, sought to "fire the soul for a secular age." Contemporaries also remarked on the religious vehemence of anarchist conviction. "Although a large part of their activity is employed in scoffing at and reviling religion," Hutchins Hapgood wrote in *An Anarchist Woman* (1909), "all the anarchists I have known have, more or less, the religious temperament"—a sense of a "beyond-world" that Hapgood identified with Wordsworth's "something far more deeply interfused." (Hapgood himself was obsessed with God. "God pursued him and he pursued God," bohemian patron Mabel Dodge later recalled, "looking into every dustbin for him.")[13]

Thus, there was more than ostentatious rhetoric in Goldman's homage to "the truth and beauty of Anarchism." For Goldman as for many intellectuals, the sensuous delights of art and nature replaced organized religion as the vessel of moral and ontological wisdom. "I have never known a people more rabid about art than the anarchists," Anderson later recalled. "Anything and everything is art for them." As an instructor at the Ferrer School in New York averred, anarchism allowed him to enter a more capacious and resplendent world: "art, music, craftsmanship, creative imagination of literature." Under the sign of beauty, anarchists and their bohemian fellow-travelers embarked on the highest vocation of modernism: the reunion of art and life, the transformation of daily existence into a commonplace world of wonder. Scorning the fraudulent, platonic aesthetics of ruling-class theology—the conventional Christian postponement of paradise into a distant, ethereal afterlife—anarchists announced the arrival of an everlasting but earthly dispensation of love. Once released from its bondage to religious metaphysics, "Beauty," Goldman wrote in 1916, would no longer be considered "a gift from heaven"; men and women would realize that it constitutes the very "essence and impetus of life" on earth. Anarchism was, in Goldman's rapturous, eschatologically redolent peroration, "the great, surging, living truth that is reconstructing the world, and that will usher in the Dawn."[14]

If anarchism announced the impending radiance of freedom from capitalism, the present darkness bore the ugly, censorious scowl of "Puritanism." Contending for the human soul, Puritanism and anarchism were, to Leonard Abbott, "the two most vital spiritual tendencies of the age." Here, Goldman's anarchism merged with the paganism espoused and pursued by metropolitan bohemians—the uninhibited, guiltless enjoyment of the senses, unrestricted and uncontaminated by Victorian morality and sensibility. But before it was a noxious sexual code that poisoned and enervated pleasure, Puritanism was a rage to accumulate sanctioned by a callous, patriarchal deity. Representing more than the sanctimonious prurience of Mrs. Grundy, Puritanism connoted the feral and boorish compulsions of the Protestant ethic. A volley in the attack on Victorian morality, Goldman's diatribe against "the hypocrisy of Puritanism" was also a declaration of independence from the Protestant covenant theology. To Goldman, prudery and sexual repression were the grim monastic disciplines of possessive individualism. "Full of the horrors that have turned life into gloom, joy into despair, naturalness into disease," Puritanism wrought these afflictions for the sake of its "profit-taking, soul-destroying purpose."[15]

The bohemian advent of sexual modernity exemplified this apostasy from *herrenvolk* enchantment. From Goldman and Hapgood to Bourne, Floyd Dell, and other proponents of sexual liberation, the bohemian pioneers of a new morality were often at pains to distinguish free love from libertinism. As the Victorian regime of sex and love grew more untenable and etiolated among the college-educated bourgeoisie, bohemians responded with a new ethic of polyamorous but morally earnest intimacy. Yet while they rejected the sacramental vernacular of Christian patriarchal marriage, bohemians and anarchists relied on a kindred language of metaphysical romanticism. Although never an anarchist, Bourne celebrated the experimental life in love as well as in politics. Sexual love partakes of "a cosmic quality of a divine personality," Bourne wrote in *Youth and Life* (1913). "Diffusing our life with a new beauty," it embodied a "subtle corroboration that we feel from some unseen presence wider than ourselves." Since sex was one of the strongest and most fundamental forces in nature, there is "no tragic antithesis" between eros and devotion to the collective good, Bourne assured. Indeed, they are "beautifully compatible. They tend to fuse, and they stimulate and ennoble each other."[16]

Though more venomously antireligious than Bourne, Goldman wrote of erotic life in similar terms of existential sublimity. Goldman promoted free love as impassioned earthly communion, a voluptuous transcendence of the alienation enforced by Protestant mercenary culture. Open relationships and frank conversation about sex fostered "true companionship and oneness," she asserted. Sex was a rapturous physical premonition of beloved community; erotic freedom "invigorates the body and deepens our vision of human fellowship." (Stansell notes that Goldman's letters to her lover Ben Reitman oscillate between graphic sexual details and ruminations on "the omniscience of the great, good, and beautiful.")[17] For the bohemian pioneers of sexual modernity, erotic freedom was not ultimately about liberation from codes, emotional restrictions, or reproductive necessity. For Goldman and other sexual revolutionaries, eros would generate the ecstatic solidarity once produced by common faith in divinity.

Having forsaken the patriarchal, pecuniary metaphysics of Protestant enchantment, anarchists adopted a Romantic, naturalist idiom of ontological wonder. The extravagant veneration of nature and beauty that characterized so much anarchist literature suggests a desperate effort to re-enchant the cosmos by sheer sublimity of aspiration. *Mother Earth* was an evocative emblem of naturalist reverence: maternal warmth, affectionate abundance, and the loving kindness of a verdant and animate world. The cover of the early issues featured an unmistakable reference to Eden: free from chains lying broken in the foreground, Adam and Eve, unashamedly unclothed, beckon hopefully to a rising sun. Anarchy was paradise re-entered upon the fall of religion, property, and the state. A frequent contributor to *Mother*

*Earth* and an icon in bohemian circles, poet and critic Sadakichi Hartmann urged readers of *My Rubaiyat* (1916) to "commune with trees and
birds / With the soil and the mossgreen roads, / And pray at the shrine of
the gods."[18]

In his *Prison Memoirs of an Anarchist* (1912), Alexander Berkman
recounted two epiphanies that sustained his revolutionary zeal. During his
trip to Pittsburgh in 1892 to assassinate the steel mogul Henry Clay Frick,
Berkman's train stopped briefly in Washington, DC. While waiting to reboard,
Berkman gazed at the early morning sun; "golden and generous," the sun's
amber rays enveloped the building with "soft caresses" as if to "dally" with
the branches and leaves. The Capitol, the trees, and the avenue "quiver with
new-born ecstasy, all nature heaves the contented sigh of bliss, and nestles
closer to the golden giver of life." At that moment, Berkman felt "the great
joy, the surpassing gladness, of being." Fourteen years in prison did not
weaken his piety; awaiting his impending release, Berkman vowed to renew
his joy and gladness of being. "Close to the breath of Nature I will press my
parched lips, on her bosom I will pass my days, drinking sustenance and
strength from the universal mother." He would "kneel on the warm sod, and
kiss the soil and embrace the trees, and with a song of joy give thanks to Nature of the blessings of sunshine and air."[19] Within the would-be assassin lay
a devotee of nature, a Franciscan girded with a pistol.

Berkman's "song of joy" and his willingness to murder suggested a conflict between beauty and power that beset the anarchist imagination. An idealized world of beauty and craft pervaded anarchist visions of the future.
Explaining in 1910 what anarchism "really stands for," Goldman echoed the
Ruskin of *Unto This Last,* asserting that "real wealth consists in things of
utility and beauty, in things that help to create strong, beautiful bodies and
surroundings to live in." This genuine wealth was generated wherever "man
is free to choose the mode of work, the conditions of work, and the freedom
to work" once liberated from the grubby obligations of capitalist property.
The true maker was an artisan stepping from the pages of Morris or Carpenter, "one to whom the making of a table, the building of a house, or the
tilling of the soil is what the painting is to the artist and the discovery to the
scientist." Goldman's summoning of anarchism's artisanal archetype was
echoed in Berkman's own periodical, *The Blast,* where one writer lamented
in 1916 that "the machine drove out the artisan (and art)."[20]

For Goldman, the reclamation of Eden entailed the communist decentralization of industry. She chided her socialist comrades and others "who extol the deadening method of centralized production as the proudest achievement of our age." Centralized industry was "the death-knell of liberty, but also of health and beauty, of art and science." (Later, almost twenty years after the Bolshevik Revolution from which she fled in terror and disappointment, Goldman would condemn the Stalinist economy as "a sovietized Taylor system . . . the crassest form of state capitalism.") The true "revolutionary philosophy of labor" was syndicalism, whose vision of social reconstruction along "autonomous industrial lines" was "the economic expression of anarchism." With a repressive state rendered unnecessary, workers would create voluntary associations of production and exchange, "gradually developing into free communism."[21]

As Goldman's artisanal communism demonstrated, anarchists believed that a world of beauty could be built by ordinary people; yet she, like many other radicals, affirmed the aristocratic hauteur of Nietzsche. Reading Nietzsche, she swooned, transported her to "undreamed-of-heights" of "magic" and "rapture." Nietzsche's frisson for cultural radicals was obvious: his brash and unbridled contempt for the decrepit morality of Victorian Christianity augured a twilight of those idols still remaining in the tabernacle of proprietary Protestantism. The American bohemian Nietzsche was a heroic crusader against "Puritanism." Among Nietzsche's American epigones, the *Übermensch* morphed into the Emersonian ideal of creative genius, self-legislating sage, vessel of innocent, unencumbered power. Often linking him to Emerson and Whitman, cultural radicals sketched Nietzsche into their democratic vistas of beloved metropolitan community. But as Jennifer Ratner-Rosenhagen points out, they also "bleached" many of Nietzsche's more unsettling and reactionary ideas, overlooking or creatively misinterpreting the more unsavory features of his work.[22] No friend of the New Woman could have tolerated Nietzsche's brazen and virulent misogyny; the philosopher with a hammer was never a friend of democracy, socialism, or anarchism, all of which represented, in his eyes, modern mutations of Christian herd morality.

Goldman may have soared to rapturous, undreamt-of heights when she first read Nietzsche, but ordinary people seemed small and bovine from so lofty an altitude. For a tribune of the lowly, Goldman could exhibit an extravagantly vituperative spleen toward those she championed. Convinced that "the masses" were too fearful and superstitious to be capable of self-emancipation, Goldman shared—and cited—Emerson's Brahmin lament: "the masses are crude, lame, pernicious in their demands and influence, and need not to be flattered, but to be schooled." In true Emersonian fashion, Goldman rehearsed the Nietzschean melodrama of *Ubermensch* and doltish herd. With barely concealed self-pity, Goldman often implied that she felt like Zarathustra, proclaiming the death of the gods to a stupid, indolent, and ungrateful rabble. "Always, at every period, the few were the banner bearers of a great idea," she wrote in "Minorities versus Majorities"; "not so the mass, the leaden weight of which does not let it move." The people "crave display . . . a dog show, a prize fight, or a lynching." Industrial workers were "brainless, incompetent automatons"; most people desire "to be dominated, to be led, to be coerced." Dismissing the suffrage as a bromide, Goldman complained that the typical woman was "a fetish worshipper" who wore her patriarchal chains like jewelry.[23]

Indebted to Emerson and Nietzsche and their mythos of the unfettered spirit, Goldman and other cultural radicals draped a bourgeois ontology of power in the exotic raiment of bohemia. Thus, although she condemned "rugged individualism" as a counterfeit of genuine freedom, her own version was at least as atomistic as the competitive anthropology of laissez-faire. Society was a "collection of individuals"—the social contract fiction of liberal politics from Thomas Hobbes to Margaret Thatcher—and the individual, she declared, was "the fountainhead of all values," a "cosmos in himself"—a grandiosity worthy of Emerson, and soon to be elaborated into a middlebrow theology of money by Ayn Rand.[24]

As it turned out, bohemia was great for business; the divine literatus came into his (or her) own as a cultural impresario. In bohemian Americanism, the artisanal unconscious of anarchism merged with the capitalist romantic ideal. Bohemia comprised the founding fathers and mothers of the modern countercultural republic, ancestors to subsequent "creative" classes and their lucrative insurrections in style. America's first modernist intelligentsia consisted not only of writers, artists, and political dissidents, but also of designers, booksellers, restaurant owners, and other "converts from the ranks of the enemy," as Malcolm Cowley observed. Yet as Cowley quickly surmised, the path of conversion had two lanes, not one; the traffic between Greenwich

Village and Main Street was always busy and unrestricted. By the time
Cowley and the second wave of immigrants from middle-class Protestantism
had arrived after World War I, "many of the Villagers had already entered
business for themselves, and many more were about to enter it." The erstwhile scourges of the petty bourgeoisie had opened "tea shops, antique
shops, book shops, bridge parlors, dance halls, night clubs and real-estate
offices." Exploiting labor and extracting surplus value with keener aesthetic
panache, they accumulated capital in "a delightfully free and intimate atmosphere . . . on the best principles of business accounting." Upwardly mobile
promoters of fiction, poetry, art, and ideas, their counterparts were the
graphic artists, marketing specialists, and art directors of corporate advertising agencies. As Cowley was among the first to observe, bohemia heralded
the eclipse of the "production ethic" by a new "consumption ethic."[25] Containing multitudes of nonconformity, the incorporation of America could
proceed under the maverick auspices of professional bohemians. Dionysus
descended from Olympus and settled into an office at an advertising firm.

All this is not to simply rehash the familiar tale of cooptation. To be sure,
"paganism" was the bohemian prototype of what would later be called "consumerism," the sublimation of potentially revolutionary desire into mass-
marketed joie de vivre. But ironic accounts of cooptation can obscure the
persistence of longings for enchantment. Fashion—where so much of the
modern temper for self-expression was ensnared in consumer culture—
suggests the profoundest tragedy in the industrialization of bohemian allure. Like many other trenchant accounts of the annexation of bohemia by
the culture industry, Cowley's portrayal of sold-out, gentrified radicalism
captured the irony but not the aspiration of Bohemia's apostles of beautiful
living. Fashion has always offered moralists a perfect (albeit ever-moving)
target. Every fad and every model gives occasion for reminders of our vanity,
avarice, and injustice; in the dudgeon of anticonsumerism, fashion drapes
our enslavement to appearance, as well as our callous indifference to the ugly
machinery of accumulation. But if fashion conceals finitude and blemish in
a camouflage of mass-produced glory, it also expresses the eternal desire for
material beatitude: the body rescued and transfigured, not only from decay
but also from the everyday doom of banality. It preserves, in the lexicon of
style and couture, the ancient religious conviction that beauty is a sign of
metaphysical enchantment, a countenance of the transcendent.

This more overtly religious understanding of beauty resonated in the Arts and Crafts movement in America. Like its English parent and counterpart, American Arts and Crafts arose from a traditional professional class and members of a new intelligentsia: architects, academics, clergy, writers, and artists, all fearful of displacement, subordination, or irrelevance in the new industrial epoch. Alarmed by the acceleration of the division of labor and the entrenchment of managerial oligarchy, Arts and Crafts attempted both to bridle and circumvent the forces of incorporation. The movement aimed to promote the revival of handicraft, restore an ethos of craft that extolled joy in work and producers' control of technology, and—to a degree that was especially American—reconcile the regeneration of artisanal culture with the advantages of mechanization and mass production. Arts and Crafts spawned a variety of styles in domestic architecture, interior design, ceramics, jewelry, furniture, and glassware. It gave rise to a number of craft societies, experimental communities, and artisanal enterprises: the Boston Society of Arts and Crafts (BSAC) and the Chicago Arts and Crafts Society; the National League of Handicraft and the Industrial Art League; William Lightfoot Price's Rose Valley outside Philadelphia; Edward Pearson Pressey's New Clairvaux in Montague, Massachusetts; Ralph Radcliffe Hamilton's Byrdcliffe in Woodstock, New York; Elbert Hubbard's Roycroft in Aurora, New York; and Gustav Stickley's United Crafts furniture firm. The movement's philosophy appeared in a handful of handsomely crafted periodicals: *The Craftsman, The Artsman, Handicraft,* and *Country Time and Tide.*[26]

Arts and Crafters failed to obstruct industrialization and incorporation. They produced precious objects and homes for the wealthy, but even the rich eventually tired of and rejected the simplicity of many Arts and Crafts designs. Their attempt to reconcile handicraft and Fordism proved abortive; many of them ended up applauding "efficiency" and scientific management. Yet we may not have exhausted the meanings of its brief but vigorously lovely efflorescence. If the Romantic drive to restore a sense of enchantment animated much of their work, then Arts and Crafts may have represented one of its most robust and concentrated expressions. In its many, often wildly divergent forms, Arts and Crafts ideology conceived a beloved synthesis of work, beauty, and fellowship. But at its most expansive and profound, it envisioned a sacramental way of being in the modern industrial world.

Arts and Crafts writers rooted their ideal in a romantic, artisanal humanism. Recounting the story of New Clairvaux in 1910, Pressey recalled that it had envisioned a unity of "brain power, character, [and] culture" based on a conviction that "the brain, the hand, and the moral nature" were inextricable. The archetypal artisan was a saint of making and a master craftsman of beloved community. Writing in the BSAC's *Handicraft* in 1903, Mary Ware Dennett—bookbinder, suffragist, and future crusader for birth control—asserted that handicraft combined "a love of justice" and "a love of beauty," and insisted that its flourishing would revivify the "most vital and essential relations between art and democracy." As "the expression of true life"—"art for life's sake"—handicraft was a moral and aesthetic pursuit that demanded not only talent but also faith and sacrificial devotion. Addressing his fellow craft reformers in Boston in 1901, Arthur A. Carey had mused that every craftsman should ask, before embarking on his career, "Do I care so much for the pleasure of making useful, beautiful things, that I am content never to be rich in money?" Although such dedication was praised, craft ideologues longed for the day when such a dire choice would be unnecessary. Especially when linked to socialism, the Arts and Crafts movement beckoned toward a broader political economy of friends. In a 1904 issue of Rose Valley's *Artsman*, Morrisite socialist Peter Burrowes declared that with the arrival of socialism and the restoration of craftsmanship, "the earth shall become [an] atelier, not for bread alone, but for beauty and fellowship."[27]

Because the artisanal ideal was so exalted, craft writers condemned mechanization not only for the degradation of workers' skills and the deluge of shoddy items, but also for the desecration of human nature. Will Price, Philadelphia architect and a founder of Rose Valley, averred in the *Artsman* in 1903 that "the real motive" of craftsmanship was to "make us worth while, to make us fit to love and be loved"; by stripping men and women of manual and artistic prowess, mechanization made us unloving and unlovable. Stickley complained in the *Craftsman* in 1906 that mass production "has so intoxicated us that we have gone on producing in a sort of insane prolificness, and our imaginary needs have grown with it." Modern industry, he rued, has "befuddled our standards of living." Explaining the introduction of arts and crafts education into the curriculum of Hull House, Jane Addams asserted that she and Ellen Gates Starr saw "the children of Art devoured" by "the uncouth stranger, Modern Industry." (The Chicago Arts and Crafts Society opened a shop at Hull House in the mid-1890s, and Starr founded a bindery.) "Why do we permit the waste of this most precious human faculty, this consummate possession of civilization?" A Harvard-educated printer with a shop in Pressey's New Clairvaux, Carl Purington Rollins contended in *Handicraft* in 1911 that "the revolt of the proletariat" would erupt when industrial workers realized that they were "denied something of our inspiration and hope." Thus Pressey was not engaging in hyperbole when he characterized Arts and Crafts in 1903 as "a soul-reaction from under the feet of corporations and the wheels of machines."[28]

The craft intelligentsia used religious terms to describe both the blight of mechanization and the mission of artisanal revival. They depicted industrial work and technology as an evil liturgy, and they feared that the extension of human power over nature led to anomie, animosity, and violence. In one ruefully representative essay, a rabbi reflected in a 1902 issue of the *Craftsman* that "we have worshipped machines so long that we are tired of the iron gods." A contributor to *Country Time and Tide* traced mechanization, alienation, and ugliness to the modern obsession with terrestrial comfort and happiness. Pouring all their spiritual energy into "the best methods of producing and distributing material commodities," moderns suffered the ironic fate of fatigue and lassitude—"neurasthenia," in the parlance of the time. Against this pervasive idolatry, craft crusaders recognized that their mission was religious as well as industrial. Chiding other BSAC members who put faith in schools of handicraft or industrial education, Dennett emphasized that "the Arts and Crafts Problem is at bottom, not an educational, so much as an economic, moral, and religious problem."[29]

The most fervent advocates for handicraft considered the movement an urgent religious crusade against the "disenchantment of the world." In his *Chapters in the History of the Arts and Crafts Movement* (1902)—a compilation and chronicle of craft ideals in England and America—Oscar Lovell Triggs, architectural critic and an officer of Chicago's Industrial Arts League, asserted that the movement was part of "the growing religious perception of our time." Often blending a medievalist sensibility with modern, heterodox religious views, Arts and Crafts ideologues insisted that religion lay at the heart of their struggle to reinvigorate the artisanal ideal. Dennett's view of handicraft as a "religious problem" stemmed from her belief that the fusion of beauty, pleasure, and character had been ordained by "a most kind Providence." Noting in the *Craftsman* in 1902 that St. Francis's life and teachings were "quite subversive of all orthodox principles of political economy," Ernest H. Crosby, a journalist and poet, hoped to supplant the dismal science so as to "fructify the coming ages with the truest wealth." Echoing Ruskin, Crosby argued that a Franciscan science of wealth would enrich us through "communion with the Eternal." Crosby's invocation of Francis underscored the medievalist character of craft ideology. American acolytes inherited from Ruskin, Morris, and English craft writers the modal figures of anti-industrial dissent: the competent and contented artisan, the closely-knit village, the fraternal guild, and the handcrafted object, all enveloped in a religious penumbra. Artisanal ideologues repeatedly quoted Ruskin and Morris in books, articles, and catalogues, while invocations of medieval guilds and craftspeople abounded in Arts and Crafts publications.[30]

Some writers pointed to non-Western pre-industrial cultures as models of sacramental design and handicraft. One art historian explained in *Handicraft* in 1903 that since they believe that "everything—animate or inanimate—has a spirit," Native Americans thought of craft as manual dexterity with the divine, "an act of religion." In a 1904 issue of the *Craftsman*, another writer maintained that Oriental rugs bore sacerdotal meaning and power. "We tread on thoughts of eternity and themes of deity and the soul," she admonished readers. Though used as interior decoration by Westerners, the rugs were "sacred among the people who wrought them . . . they spoke great religious truths." Weavers were contemplatives who "translated the beatitudes of their religion into beauty itself." Many craft intellectuals were especially fond of the work of Lafcadio Hearn, whose popular books about Japanese life portrayed what appeared to be a more spiritually tranquil, craft-based alternative to the brutalities of Western industrialism. In volumes such as *Kokoro* (1896), Hearn—journalist and quintessential purveyor of Orientalist exotica to the middle classes—contrasted the graceful, penurious freedom of Japanese artisans with the burdensome riches of Americans. "With us," Hearn wrote, "the common worker is incomparably less free than the common worker in Japan," who "produces his miracles" in a small, simple workshop "without the help of machinery and large capital." Hearn attributed the beauty of Japanese handicraft to the Buddhist "doctrine of impermanency," the belief that transience and imperfection had their own real if evanescent splendors. If this was not quite Western sacramentalism, it aligned material life with a religious metaphysics and humanism, and recalled Ruskin's appreciation of human limitation and inexactitude. In Hearn's view, the Western obsession with eternity compelled reliance on the "Babels of machinery" to ensure a false, anxiety-ridden security.[31]

The sacramentalist nature of Arts and Crafts surfaced vividly in two craft communities: New Clairvaux and Rose Valley. Founded in 1901 by Pressey, a Harvard-educated Unitarian minister, New Clairvaux was an experiment, as one inhabitant wrote in *Country Time and Tide* in 1904, in making "the mechanic and the liberal arts subserve theology." Naming the colony after the Cistercian monastic community established by Bernard of Clairvaux in the twelfth century, Pressey declared that a revitalization of the arts and crafts would "show forth the redemption of this present world." Pressey and his fellow redeemers drew on a motley variety of inspirations: New England transcendentalism, British Arts and Crafts, Kropotkin's vision of decentralized fields and factories, and John Dewey's educational ideas, all enveloped in liberal Protestant medievalism. Combining handicraft and agriculture, New Clairvaux's residents (never numbering more than two dozen) produced textiles, furniture, baskets, dyes, and prints. Relying on subsistence farming and the sale of craft products in the "Village Shop," New Clairvaux always struggled to survive, and it eventually folded in 1909.[32] The re-enchantment and redemption of the world through handicraft was postponed indefinitely.

Shortly after the community dispersed, Pressey idealized the experiment in *The Vision of New Clairvaux* (1909), a brief but exemplary testimony to the hopes that inspired his comrades in redemption. To be sure, Pressey could not hide the colony's failure; he cautioned readers that the volume was a "sheer Utopian *tour de force*" and that several episodes were "purely imaginative." Still, Pressey's portrait of artisanal beatitude displayed their ardent desire for enchantment. Though its witness was unsuccessful, New Clairvaux represented, Pressey believed, "the awakening of a new generation fresh from their young dreams in God." Eager to "build the city of God," the communards had devoted themselves to "the law of God, the law of love [and] the light thereof." Blending craft, farming, and religion, New Clairvaux was a site of realized eschatology, "the Socialism that is already beginning to be." The future-in-the-present was "a special resort for skilled mechanics, artists and authors . . . it was life and industry itself . . . it was a church, a discipline, a new ideal of society." Each workshop had been "a temple . . . a living temple and not a dead sanctuary"; the Village Shop had pioneered in "elevating the idea of work and for bringing practical religion down from the skies."[33]

Like New Clairvaux, Rose Valley was established in 1901. Its founders, Will Price and Hawley McLanahan, were Philadelphia architects with progressive social and political views: in the same year, Price helped to set up a single-tax community in nearby Arden, Delaware, and both men were enthusiasts of Ruskin, Morris, and Ashbee. With money provided by McLanahan, wealthy local investors, and Swarthmore College, Price purchased eighty acres studded with old and abandoned barns, farmhouses, cottages, and mills. Over the next nine years, Rose Valley attracted craftsmen in ceramics, furniture, and book-binding; the products were sold out of Price's home in Philadelphia. The colony sported a library and a theater; the print shop published the *Artsman,* one of the most prominent and attractively illustrated periodicals of the Arts and Crafts movement. The residents enacted a morality play of medievalist modernity: calling themselves the Rose Valley Folk, they met in a "Guild Hall," dubbed their community government the "Folk Mote," and extended the suffrage to all inhabitants, male and female, over the age of five. In the exhilarating days of the experiment's commencement, Rose Valley thought of itself as a bold, irrepressible anti-industrial vanguard. In the inaugural issue of the *Artsman* in 1903, McLanahan proclaimed that the community, in "trying some experiments in economic gravitation," was leading "a general protest against the often vulgar product of the modern machine and against the consequent degradation and ruin of the craftsman."[34]

In the eyes of Rose Valley's proponents and residents, the artisanal haven was also a liturgical and sacramental space. Price once referred to the *Artsman* as "a kind of parish record," and the journal included a regular section titled "Rose Valley Scriptures" that featured snippets from Emerson, Thoreau, Whitman, Ruskin, Morris, Carpenter, Tolstoy, Kropotkin, and other sources of craft ideology. In the years of the *Artsman*'s publication (1903–1907), contributors often dwelled on the enchanting character of craft, remarking in sacramental terms about Rose Valley's attempt, as McLanahan put it, to "revise industry in the interests of the soul." In a 1903 issue, Triggs opined that "art at its best" consists of "materials transfused, sublimated, idealized." In 1904, Burrowes—a New York socialist and editor of the *Comrade*—dilated on the "sacrament of common things." The restoration of beauty and dignity to everyday useful objects was a religious vocation, a "recognition of sacraments." Investors who supported ventures like Rose Valley "use their money sacramentally." A year later, Percival Wiksell, a Boston dentist and president of the city's Whitman Fellowship, observed that, drawing on "the joy-forces of the universe," the craftsman "put something out of the fullness of himself freely and plentifully into the work." Calling for the beautiful omnipresence of "art in daily life," Ernest Newlandsmith—a British musicologist devoted to the reconciliation of art and religion—wrote in 1906 that art "manifests the divine spirit," and that people and their objects were sacramental tokens, vessels of loving enchantment. "Everyone is himself a work of art, in the sense that he is an outward material manifestation of an inward spiritual essence or content." Together with the "Rose Valley Scriptures," the *Artsman* left no doubt that Rose Valley was a venture in enchantment as well as a commune of craft. As Horace Traubel summarized what amounted to Rose Valley's sacramental theology of handicraft, "In Rose Valley, labor is creed and ritual. the Rose Valley shops are temples. Here men pray in their work . . . practice fellowship in their work . . . I can see God woven in tapestries and beaten in brasses and bound in the covers of books."[35]

Traubel was editor of the *Artsman,* and his career illustrates the merger of religion and radicalism that animated much of Arts and Crafts. Born to German immigrants in 1858, Traubel was raised in Philadelphia, where his father worked as a lithographer. Young Traubel read voraciously as a child, acquiring a wide erudition on which he drew later as a journalist and critic. Leaving school at the age of twelve, Traubel worked as a newsboy, printer's assistant, bank clerk, and reporter. After marrying, he settled across the Delaware River in Camden, where he befriended the aging Walt Whitman, to whom he became an apostle and amanuensis. With his growing fame as Whitman's Boswell, Traubel swiftly moved to the center of the Philadelphia bohemian scene that emerged in the 1890s. He founded the *Conservator* in 1891, a journal highly regarded by the literary intelligentsia; his volumes of free verse—especially *Chants Communal* (1904) and *Optimos* (1910)—garnered praise among radicals in America and Europe. Traubel corresponded with Goldman, Jack London, Upton Sinclair, and many other reformers, artists, and writers. He met Price through mutual progressive friends in

Philadelphia, and during his editorial tenure the *Artsman* was the most radical handicraft journal in America.[36]

Even before his death in 1919 Traubel had elicited a lavish and gushing hagiography: one of his admirers anointed him a "great prophet" and a "great mystic," a bard who expressed "the great and central idea of modern art—the divinity of all life." With his "faith in the immanence of God," Traubel, this writer insisted, articulated "a vision of the unity of all life and of the divine reality of our relationship with one another." Traubel's eminence as an oracle is well deserved, as his verse clearly echoed Whitman and Carpenter as the record of a modern search for enchantment. Whitman, he had written in 1893, forecast "new religious and political revelations," and Traubel devoted his life to sketching the lineaments of a sacramental vista. As he wrote in *Chants Communal*, the goal of socialism was not simply justice and plenty but "ecstasy," Traubel asserted; "we should go about our business each day chanting hymns." Socialism is "the new earth. Yes, the new heaven too." As his portrayal of Rose Valley's workshops indicates, Traubel hoped that the socialist nexus of heaven and earth would be a realm of *poesis*, an artisan's grove of useful and beautiful production. In 1908—a year after the *Artsman* folded, and two years before the Rose Valley experiment ended—Traubel lauded Howells's Altrurian trilogy in the *Conservator* as "a sacred invocation to which my heart jubilantly responds."[37]

The theology of Traubel's ecstatic vista could be found in his poetry. Like Whitman, Traubel longed to be a divine literatus, arriving with a post-Christian, materialist divinity to replace the enervated dogmas of the churches. As an enlightened merchant descants in a poem in *Optimos*, "the savor of my soap counter is as sweet to God as your incense, O priest!" For Traubel as for many other left intellectuals, art, poetry, and labor supplanted theology as the vernacular of modern enchantment. "I am not inanimate dust. I am animate song," as he declared in *Chants Communal*. Socialist artisans could chant hymns while working because God no longer resided outside the boundaries of time and space. Traubel's God was in some ways eminently traditional: in *Optimos*, God sustains "the last atom of substance and the last pulse of life"; God "pushes the tides along and holds the stars to their courses and says nothing, / God sticks very closely to business day and night with- / out a word." Yet this God was also utterly humble and familiar, "common to the commonest earth," performing quotidian wonders in "this sacred enclosure, this holy open." Traubel's ontology was utterly hopeful and harmonious: despite real and manifest evils, "nothing is finally wrong with the world," he concluded in *Chants Communal*. A vague eschatological certitude energizes Traubel's socialist verse; this commonest God appears to be leading or driving humanity to a glorious destiny. "Something is moving us on," as he closes the final poem of *Optimos;* "something that takes no / account of castes—that only takes account of love."[38]

Traubel's democratic, socialist vista was not the only political prospect that emerged from the Arts and Crafts movement. As the life and work of Ralph Adams Cram makes clear, a sacramental and anticapitalist imagination did not ensure a democratic vision of the future. Born in New Hampshire in 1863 to a Unitarian minister and his wife, Cram always considered himself one of the "last of the squires," caught in the decline of New England's rural elite. Moving to Boston to study architecture in the 1880s, Cram became a luminary in the city's small but effervescent bohemian community, who shared an intense conviction that "the last desiccated remnants of the Victorian age had to be destroyed." "The aim of destruction was sure," he recalled, "but the substitute revelation was murky in the extreme." To Cram, the "substitute revelation" became clear during a trip to Rome in 1887, when he underwent a powerful conversion, and for the rest of his life, he remained a High-Church, Anglo-Catholic Episcopalian. After returning to the United States, he set up an architectural firm in Boston, commencing what became an illustrious career in Gothic Revival architecture.[39]

Although never officially associated with the Arts and Crafts movement, Cram was an enthusiastic fellow-traveler; his religious opposition to industrial civilization echoed that of many craft ideologues. Despite his high Anglicanism, Cram retained the bohemian malcontentedness of his youth, transmuting his hunger for "spiritual realities" into a theology of architecture and material life. Indeed, as his professional success accelerated in the 1910s—capped by commissions for the Cathedral of St. John the Divine in New York and Princeton University Chapel—his polemical drive and pugnacity increased. Written in between designing and supervising, Cram's books and lectures of this period—especially *The Ministry of Art* (1914), *Six Lectures on Architecture* (1917), and *Walled Towns* (1919)—comprise a trove of right-wing craft ideology, a theology of reactionary sacramentalism.

The sacramentality of matter was the leitmotif of Cram's ruminations on art, architecture, and society. Sacramentalism, to Cram, was "the very underlying law of life itself, extending into the farthest reaches of being." Art is both a realm of "simple, sensuous joy and refreshment" and the vessel of "a secret spiritual grace through an outward and visible form." Through art and architecture, men and women receive "some faint adumbration of the Beatific Vision." Cram waxed incessantly on the sacramental character of art, beauty, and the cosmos. Art is "itself a sacrament"; beauty is "one of the sacraments in a universe wholly and absolutely sacramental in its nature." Thus, "the unbeautiful or the ugly thing is the thing of the wrong or evil shape, whether in art or religion, philosophy, government, or the social fabric." The talent for shaping sacramental beauty belonged, not merely to an aesthetically privileged caste of genius, taste, or wealth, but to all working people; beauty as a sacramental presence could be wrought "through power of craftsmanship." As the craftsman possessed a sacred skill, he bore an exalted responsibility; he could be either "one of the greatest agencies of righteousness and light" or "the servant of domination." For Cram, the Middle Ages represented the apotheosis of sacramental art and society. "Medieval art was at bottom sacramental"; only medieval art would permanently endure, since it alone was "in eternal conformity with life, which also is essentially and unchangeably sacramental." Medieval architecture in particular was a monument to and vehicle of divinity. "All the joy of life, the vivid vitality, the human romance, and mysticism . . . find outlet through the wrought stone and wood, glass, and metal that assembled under eager hands and at the impulse of ardent brains." The enchantment of the triune God supplied, in Cram's view, "the *elan vital* of the Middle Ages," pervading social and commercial life with a "sense of divine immanence."[40]

In Cram's tale of declension, the medieval Eden was poisoned by capitalism and modernity—but an age of renewal might be at hand. Like other medievalist critics, such as Belloc and Chesterton, Cram traced the genesis of capitalism to greedy monarchs, avaricious lords, and heretical Protestants. Capitalists destroyed the guilds that once nurtured craftsmanship and freedom, and they supplanted beauty and sacramentality with an idolatry of money, quantity, and mechanical efficiency. Epitomized in scientific management, capitalist mechanism fostered "religious infidelity and state-worship";

blighted the landscape with "the pestilence of bill-boards, the gross humbug of the art fakir"; and infected democracy, socialism, and communism with its vapid soullessness. Cram believed for a time that capitalism was heading toward a final catastrophe, and that a new medievalism would arise from the ruins of godless, mechanical modernity. Speaking at the Art Institute of Chicago in 1915, he asserted that the war in Europe had exposed "the shallow and meaningless nature of our own civilization"; the modern West's self-congratulation on its scientific and material successes had ended in rapine and butchery. The "chariot wheels" of industrialism had ground to a bloody halt, and Cram waited for "signs and wonders" portending the arrival of a postcapitalist epoch. Near the end of the war, in an essay on *The Great Thousand Years* (1918) of medieval culture, Cram declared that, if secular modernity contained "no powers of regeneration," the wellsprings of renewal lay within a revival of Christianity. The times would produce, he hoped, "a new prophet, son of Saint Benedict," who would release the West from its secular captivity.[41]

Cram's new monasticism never appeared—but even if it had, it would hardly have appealed to many people. Calling for "joyful living through simplicity," Cram could not have been more out of step with an urban, industrial America more devoted than ever to the unsimple life. In *Walled Towns,* for instance—the very title redolent of fear—Cram envisioned the eradication of industrial capitalism, the abolition of usury, the restoration of the guild system and family proprietorship, the discouragement and regulation of advertising, and the imposition of sumptuary laws—all capped by the disappearance of Protestantism. In his survey of *The Nemesis of Mediocrity* (1918), Cram bellowed an even more shrill and ugly indictment of American life, advocating strict controls on immigration and taboos on racial intermingling. Insisting on "the just and normal barriers of race," he lamented "the substitution of the mongrel for the product of pure blood by reason of the free and reckless mixing of incompatible strains."[42]

Cram's right-wing romanticism may have assuaged the anxieties of conservative professionals; but to workers increasingly inured to factory labor and industrial technology, his medieval idyll would have seemed utterly bizarre and more than a little invidious. Cram once hoped that labor unions would see that guilds were "quite in harmony with the high ideals they openly avow"; but as the American Federation of Labor concentrated ever more resolutely on "more," the labor movement faded from Cram's political imagination. Dismissive of democracy and progressive reform, he eventually put faith in an alliance of enlightened businesspeople and professionals like himself. This medievalist bourgeoisie would, he hoped, transform itself into an anticapitalist vanguard through a second naivete—a re-enchantment of themselves, if not of their contemporaries. In his autobiography, Cram claimed that "the guiding idea" for the design of his estate—"Whitehall"—was "to think and work as would pious but quite ignorant peasants who knew nothing about architecture."[43] In Cram's view, the renaissance of sacramental handicraft depended on the hearts of chastened professionals, who, like Carlyle's "captains of industry," would constitute a modern guild of wonder.

Cram's medievalist retreat into enlightened professionalism partook of the broader vitiation of Arts and Crafts in the decade before World War I. Like many other former partisans of handicraft, Cram had effectively abandoned the movement by the mid-1910s. "A movement that once seemed to promise so much" had been corrupted by the very division of labor it had once denounced, Cram wrote in 1914; more and more craft idealists were reverting to industrial production, "one man making the design, the other carrying it out." Cram was registering the swift reconciliation of artisanal ideals with industrial realities, corporate imperatives, and managerial hegemony. Indeed, both observers of and participants in the movement had predicted or assisted in its demise from the beginning. As we've seen, even sympathetic acolytes of art, such as Waldo Frank, had doubts about the appeal of Arts and Crafts to an America lacking a peasant or guild tradition. Reviewing Triggs's history of Arts and Crafts in 1902, Thorstein Veblen, though sympathetic to the movement, worried that Arts and Crafts would become "an anemic fad upon the fringe of modern industry." Over a decade later, Veblen had grown less sympathetic and even sardonic toward Triggs and his allies. In *The Instinct of Workmanship* (1914), he maintained that the mental habits of handicraft attributed an "anthropomorphic coloring of personality" to machines, thus inhibiting the cultivation of the scientific consciousness that he deemed indispensable to modern, democratic production.[44]

Veblen's critique of Arts and Crafts pointed to a fundamental flaw in the movement's vision: its ambiguity about the future of mechanization. Few craft writers could ever elucidate, beyond vague generalities, the relationship between machinery and handicraft. Indeed, Arts and Crafts advocates could be as enchanted by industrial technology as any technocrat, executive, or progressive. In his history of the movement, Triggs proclaimed that "the machine is an object of wonder, one of the special triumphs of the age, and worthy of all homage." Echoing Veblen, Dennett predicted that, in a society of artisans, machinery would be "a true saver of labor," providing "the majority of people . . . the time for leisure, cultivation, [and] education." While aesthetically rejuvenated workers would perform all the beautiful, "inspiring work," machines would be "accomplishing all the degrading or stupefying work that needs to be done." Thus, Dennett argued, rather than diminish in importance, machinery would, in the new order of craft, "have a much wider scope than its present one."[45]

If the crucial issue was how to identify "degrading or stupefying work," many Arts and Crafts supporters increasingly resolved—or rather, evaded—the problem by relying on business imperatives. Despite their frequent avowals of reverence for beauty and skill over profit and money, craft partisans also insisted on their sturdy business sense. H. Langford Warren, an architect and member of the BSAC, spoke for many professionals and businesspeople when he asserted that Arts and Crafts shops and salesrooms should be run "on business principles." Seeking, in part, to dispel caricatures of Arts and Crafts as a quixotic, sentimental folly, the founders of both New Clairvaux and Rose Valley emphasized that their beloved communities of sacramental labor were also solid business enterprises. As Pressey reminded both customers and prospective investors in a 1902 issue of *Country Time and Tide,* "We carry on a *Productive* Business." Similarly, McLanahan emphasized in the very first issue of the *Artsman* that while Rose Valley was reforming industry "in the interests of the soul," it was "not an impractical or visionary undertaking but a concrete business proposition."[46]

Hubbard and Stickley were the most openly and successfully entrepreneurial participants in Arts and Crafts. Believing that "business should be beautiful," Hubbard veiled the increasingly conventional industrial practices of Roycroft with his carefully crafted mystique of nonconformity. "The Roycroft began as a joke," Hubbard told a friend in 1903, "but did not stay one; it soon resolved itself into a Commercial institution." Although Hubbard dutifully parroted artisanal rhetoric—"work is for the worker . . . it's not so much what a man gets in money wages, but it's what he gets in terms of life"—he ruled his English Gothic domain like a benevolent lord of business, disparaging unions, regulating employees' spending, and supplementing low wages with gifts. (The socialist *Call* smirked that Roycrofters were "paid in privileges and flowers.") The Henry Ford of Arts and Crafts, Hubbard recast handicraft as a form of industrial paternalism. Though far less flamboyant than Hubbard, Stickley—founder of Craftsman Furniture and editor of the *Craftsman* (1901–1916)—was more overtly managerialist. Stickley's *Craftsman* published a range of articles on craftsmanship, design and designers, Japanese and native American crafts, manual arts, gardening, furniture—and socialism, the conception of which, however, was so amorphous and elastic that references to Morris or Carpenter could sit alongside practical business advice. Indeed, as Stickley's furniture attracted more and more affluent customers, ruminations on the joy of work and craft yielded to pieces on technical skill, salesmanship, and advertising. By 1911, Stickley had turned from the celebration of art and craft to the malediction of waste and inefficiency, calling waste "our heaviest national liability" and admonishing unions to "combine for greater efficiency." He praised Frederick W. Taylor and extolled the aesthetic as well as the industrial merits of scientific management. Since "the very idea of waste is unlovely," Stickley mused, the efficiencies achieved through Taylorist methods would offer "a sense of beauty."[47]

Craft intellectuals were following Stickley's example, subordinating the religious and political goals of the movement to profit and industrial efficiency. Although handcrafted objects should be judged by their aesthetic merits, "everything must stand the test of the market," Denman Ross, a design professor at Harvard, told BSAC in 1903. Other members of BSAC came to share Ross's enthusiasm for craft and industrial competition. Arthur A. Carey, his Harvard colleague, while conceding that "there is a real antagonism between business for the sake of gain and art for the sake of use and beauty," asserted reassuringly that "the antagonism is between the motives, not between the business and the art." In Warren's view, "commercialism, the subdivision of labor, and the machine" had brought "larger opportunities to so much larger numbers than at any other time in the world." In Chicago, Triggs—who had declared the machine "worthy of all homage"—looked, like Cram, to an enlightened elite to sponsor the revival of handicraft, idealizing some "philanthropic proprietor" who would endow schools and libraries dedicated to craftsmanship and craft literature.[48]

The willingness of more and more partisans of craft to compromise with the devil induced despair among the movement's true believers. A. R. Orage complained in 1907 that, on both sides of the Atlantic, the craft crusade had lost its aesthetic and political vitality. In words almost identical to Veblen's, Orage charged that "the disappearance of sociological ideas" was rendering the movement "pale and anemic." Pointing to the failure of artisanal idealists to capture the imagination of the working class, Ashbee disparaged American Arts and Crafts as "a narrow and tiresome little aristocracy working with high skill for the very rich." Pressey echoed these cries of betrayal, asserting that handicraft was devolving into a pastime for the "intellectual dilettante class." As Pressey quickly discovered, even working for the wealthy was no guarantee of success: Rose Valley went under in 1908, New Clairvaux folded in 1909, and other craft communities and companies closed their doors during the war. By 1920, the dilettantish fate of the movement was sealed, as Arts and Crafts firms found themselves appealing to an ever more narrowing market: wealthy customers were rejecting simplicity, while poor and working-class consumers preferred ornate, elaborate styling for furniture and other domestic goods. As one historian of the movement puts it delicately, Arts and Crafts products increasingly reached Americans in a handicraft style "as distilled by manufacturers who were not always philosophers."[49]

It was a melancholy end for what little remained of the apostolate of Arts and Crafts, as the promise of sacramental production gave way to the embellishment of Fordism, the decoration of domesticity, and the amusement of middle-class bohemians. The therapeutic culmination of the craft revival—its artful composure of religious aspirations for labor with industrial capitalism—derived from the reluctance of many of its adherents to repudiate the spirit of the covenant theology. Their extraordinary evocation of the sacramental character of work, together with their devotion to heralding and crafting a new enchantment of the world, flourished alongside and eventually yielded to the accumulative canon of business. Once incorporated, Arts and Crafts became a studio for mechanical enchantment; during the 1920s and 1930s—the heyday of the Machine's ubiquitous presence as an icon of American modernity—a new breed of "industrial designers" would press the spirit of Ruskin and Morris into the service of a corporate technological vision.

The enlistment of the craft ideal in the service of mechanical enchantment was foreshadowed by Frank Lloyd Wright, whose legendary architectural career has obscured his prominence as a prophet of mechanization. Once head draftsman for Louis Sullivan, Wright fell out with his mentor in the early 1890s over business differences. Although the separation was bitter, Wright always considered Sullivan his "dear master," and he shared his former boss's vitalist theology. He also shared Sullivan's inclination to cryptic pronouncement and abstruse prose style, both of which leaven two of his key early speeches: "A Philosophy of Fine Art," delivered at the Art Institute of Chicago in 1900, and his homily on "The Art and Craft of the Machine," a talk he gave to the Chicago Arts and Crafts Society at Hull House in March 1901 at the invitation of Jane Addams.[50] However enigmatic and even incoherent Wright's thinking about art, craft, and machinery, he captured the allure of artisanal enchantment for disaffected but hopeful professionals, and he offered sublimation of their aesthetic and religious desires in the forms of machinery. While proclaiming his spiritual and aesthetic hostility to Mammon, Wright assisted in the corporate reconstruction of enchantment.

Although the Chicago or Prairie school of architecture with which Wright has been associated was friendly to Arts and Crafts, Wright came to think that the movement was doomed to anachronism and irrelevance. The Prairie school's "organic" philosophy of design lent itself readily to craft ideology, and Wright's speeches invoked the Romantic, artisanal heritage of Ruskin and Morris. At a time when the machine was "deluging the world with a murderous ubiquity" and wreaking "the damnation of art and craft," Ruskin and Morris "professed the artist" and affirmed the glory of art. For Wright the Romantic architect, art possessed a divine metaphysical status, pervading the moral, aesthetic, and material lineaments of civilization. "We say that God is Love—well, Art is the very Genius of Love!" he proclaimed at the Art Institute. If Art was divine, then ugliness represented "the incarnation of sin"; "there is not, nor ever was, room in right living for the ugly." At the core of all things, art was "the great conservator of the finer sensibilities of a people"; it was "their only prophecy" and "the only light" by which civilization made its institutions commensurate to its conditions. Art and civilization constituted "a magic process," Wright asserted.[51]

Yet in "The Art and Craft of the Machine," Wright proceeded to reconcile Art with mechanization. Although "the Machine has dealt Art in the grand old sense a death blow"—dealt a blow, in other words, to the old Genius of God—Wright believed nonetheless that "in the machine lies the only future of art and craft." After the death of the old god, we are now entering "the Machine Age," Wright declared, and he described the arduous transition in terms of a new religious dispensation, one that would preserve the divinity of old in mechanical, industrial forms. Thus, while the new epoch entailed what Wright gingerly called an "adjustment" on the part of our heretofore "cherished gods," and however "perplexing and painful in the extreme the fire of many long-honored ideals," they would "go down to ashes to reappear, phoenix-like, with new purposes." Transfigured and redeemed by machinery, Art would reciprocate by breathing "the thrill of ideality" into the Machine— "A SOUL!" Clearly enchanted by industrial technology and its potentially soulful incorporation, Wright attributed a supernal agency and power to mechanization, urging his Hull House audience to "make some good impression upon the Machine, the destroyer of [our] present ideals and tendencies, their salvation in disguise."[52]

Yet Wright feared the power of another deity: Mammon. While waxing romantic about the aesthetic and spiritual promise of the Machine, Wright remained conflicted about the business culture that promoted mechanization. In the early 1900s, Wright began to express his lifelong ambivalence toward capitalist architectural practice. At Hull House, he complained of architects and their business clients who erected "a pantheon to the god of money," their edifices comprising "a mammoth aggregation of Roman monuments, sarcophagi, and Greek temples." Even "the patient retinue of the machine"—architects more open to the art and craft of the machine— pursued the "unhallowed ambition" of personal enrichment, an "insult to ancient gods." And yet, aware of his own ineluctable blasphemy, Wright finally, albeit reluctantly, deigned to accommodate the pecuniary spirit. In the summer of 1901, shortly after his talk at Hull House, Wright published a short piece in *The Brickbuilder*, a prominent architectural monthly, in which he reconciled his devotion to Art and the Machine with the demands of Mammon. Sketching plans for a generic bank, Wright referred disdainfully to the structure as "the town strongbox . . . a temple to the God of Money," but he saw no alternative to arraying Mammon's tabernacle with a specifically modern beauty. If people wanted to embellish their temples, Wright was glad to oblige; indeed, he thought their impulse to gild their pecuniary shrines was worthy of all respect, "for back of it are probably the only instincts that make life bearable or desirable." Bending if not violating his own canon of Art, Wright suggested that these "modern mercantile machines" could be tolerated—not redeemed—by the cosmetic application of modern design. Infused with "the thrill of ideality," architecture under corporate capitalism must aspire to a syncretic enchantment, endowing the shrines of mechanization and venality with a varnish of romanticism.[53]

# 15

# Another Kingdom of Being

The Crisis of Metaphysical Experience
and the Search for Passionate Vision

WRIGHT'S HOPE THAT ARCHITECTS could imbue their structures
with "the thrill of ideality" hinted at the desire for some new experience of
enchantment in the corporate dispensation. Among Protestant bourgeois,
the stability and meaning of everyday life seemed ever more insubstantial
and unreal; many complained of "neurasthenia," a feeling of anomie, listlessness, and boredom in the midst of unprecedented comfort and abundance.
But with Protestantism increasingly unconvincing as metaphysics and morality among educated Americans, they turned to other ways of being in the
world that promised more of the "thrill of ideality" than the waning dispensation of experience. Drifting away from their Protestant moorings, they embarked on a variety of quests to revivify lives fatigued by unbelief, success,
and "over-civilization": idealizations of military adventure that eventually
helped sanction imperialism; cults of "the strenuous life"—exemplified by
the exploits of Theodore Roosevelt—that aimed to reinvigorate middle-class
masculinity; Orientalist attempts to appropriate the "primitive" and supposedly regenerative qualities of non-Western peoples; medievalist excursions
in Gothic romance or Catholic religious culture.[1]

The incorporation of America was the prime source of this crisis of metaphysical experience. In transforming the American moral imagination, incorporation entailed a new iconography for the "thrill of ideality," with advertising and management bestowing a new holiness on the increasingly
corporate profane: image professionals fashioned a mosaic gallery of earthly
delights, while managerial ideologues mapped out a mechanized path to
"modern communion." But there was resistance to professionalized enchantment, attempts to locate sources of meaning outside the corporate soul's
economy. Three alternative modes of metaphysical experience stood out:

naturalist writing, including John Muir, John Burroughs, Mary Austin, and novelists such as Frank Norris; the pragmatism of William James; and the Anglo-Catholic sacramentalism of Vida Dutton Scudder. All three were Romantic pursuits of what James called "passionate vision": insight into and contact with some ineffable, ecstatic realm, encounter with the dearest freshness and grandeur available through sensuous experience.

John Muir's adventure in sacramental experience began in defiance of the evangelical heritage. Born in Scotland in 1838, Muir arrived in Portage, Wisconsin, at the age of eleven when his father, Daniel, a grain merchant in Dunbar, sold his business and moved his family to America. Daniel insisted on a strict and even abusive religious training for his children, forcing them to memorize long Biblical passages; if they ever failed to recite any passage on demand, he would, his son recalled, "thrash us industriously for our good." Working on his 60-acre farm, the patriarch led a life that was "steadily toilsome and full of enthusiastic endeavor." By his workaholic standards, the local Winnebago Indians were "unproductive" savages, whose pagan, loutish possession of the soil "could never have been the intention of God."[2]

Young John found refuge in nature from his father's punitive holiness. Whether in Scotland or in Portage, "no punishment, however sure and severe, was of any avail against the attraction of the fields and woods." Forest, hills, creeks, bushes, bluebird nests—all of nature was "wooingly teaching her wonderful gleaming lessons, so unlike the dismal grammar ashes and cinders so long thrashed" into him. Gradually, he rejected his father's Christianity, especially its "mean, blinding, loveless doctrine" that animals have no minds or souls. Muir's daily experience on the farm taught him that the love of a cow for her calves "in no way differed from the divine mother-love of a woman in thoughtful, self-sacrificing care." Unlike the rough christening he received from his father, Muir's "baptism in Nature's warm breast" made him "utterly happy."[3]

In the fall of 1860, Muir left Portage for Madison to enroll in the state university, whose records mark him as "Irregular." Far from the reach of the patriarch, Muir went "flying to the woods and meadows in wild enthusiasm." He never finished a degree; in 1864, with the Civil War raging, he hastened to Canada to dodge the draft. He spent the next two years on the Ontario side of Lake Huron, collecting plants and working in a sawmill. Returning in 1866, Muir settled in Indianapolis, Indiana, where he found work making wheels in another sawmill. One March day in 1867, he lost his grip on the sharp end of a file that struck him in the cornea of his right eye. For the next six weeks, Muir lay half-blind and desperate in a darkened room—and then an epiphany arrived. "This affliction has driven me to the sweet fields," he told a friend. When he recovered fully, Muir determined to be "true to myself" and "walk with Nature." After a thousand-mile trek from Indiana to Florida, Muir abandoned his plan to go on to South America and instead made his way to Yosemite Valley, where he had a beatific vision among the Sierra Nevada Mountains. "No temple made with hands can compare with Yosemite," he recorded, "the grandest of all spiritual temples of Nature."[4] The prodigal son returned home to his mother.

For the rest of his life, Muir preached and practiced a gospel of nature, a modern evangel of enchantment that he shared with capitalists, politicians, and the broader reading public. Although he had abandoned evangelical theology, he never lost its zeal for conversion. Arguing with a "grave old Mormon," Muir plucked a handful of lilies and thrust them in the man's face. "Here are the true saints," he shouted, "ancient and Latter-day, enduring forever." The evangelical style of indictment persisted as well: Muir loathed the "abomination" of gold prospectors and the "barbarous wickedness" of hunters. To spread the gospel, Muir made himself all things to all people. He hobnobbed with Edward H. Harrimann, the railroad baron, and befriended President Theodore Roosevelt, with whom he camped in Yosemite in 1903. Writing of sequoias and alpine glaciers, he acquired a large and admiring readership who deluged him with letters and requests.[5]

The gospel Muir preached was a Romantic religion of natural supernaturalism akin to that of Wordsworth, Thoreau, and Emerson. Nature, to Muir, was sacramental, charged with the grandeur of God, enlivened by "sparks of the Divine Soul variously clothed upon with flesh, leaves . . . rock, water." This Divine Soul was also "an essential love, overlying, underlying, pervading all things." Imbued with a great love deep down things, Muir's universe was animate and friendly, "full of charming company, full of God's thoughts." It delivered "sermons in stones, storms, trees, flowers, and animals brimful of humanity." "The very stones seemed talkative, sympathetic, brotherly." The human body was one of many enchanted receptacles of divinity, "our flesh and bone tabernacle." Since every body was a sanctuary, Muir saw no need for the traditional rites of anthropomorphic religions, sending his readers to the hills and valleys and forests for salvation. "In God's wilderness lies the hope of the world—the great fresh, unblighted, unredeemed wilderness"—"unredeemed" because it needed no redemption.[6]

Muir's natural supernaturalism inspired his ecological politics. Writing to Roosevelt in 1908, Muir excoriated "capitalists" and their "miserable dollarish" plans to turn Yosemite National Park into a Vanity Fair for nature-lovers. He railed unceasingly about the "money madness" of America, "our dollar-seeking, dollar-sick nation." His cofounding of the Sierra Club in 1892; his collaboration (and rancorous break) with the conservationist Gifford Pinchot; his lobbying on behalf of natural preservation; and especially his seven-year, futile effort to prevent the damming of the Hetch Hetchy Valley in Yosemite, near San Francisco—all stemmed from Muir's commitment to revere and protect nature's material divinity. To Muir, the Hetch Hetchy affair was more than a disagreement over the disposition of natural resources. When the city government of San Francisco applied to the Department of the Interior in 1906 for rights to dam Hetch Hetchy for drinking water and hydroelectric power, it sparked what Muir considered a religious controversy. Those who wanted to dam the valley were, in his view, sacrilegious "temple-destroyers, devotees of ravaging commercialism," adherents of the "gobble-gobble school of economics." "Instead of lifting their eyes to the God of the mountains," he fumed, these blasphemers "lift them to the Almighty Dollar." "Dam Hetch Hetchy!" he roared in 1912, just before his final defeat. "As well dam for water-tanks the people's cathedrals and churches, for no holier temple has ever been consecrated by the heart of man."[7]

Muir was not alone among American naturalists in searching for a new divinity. John Burroughs, for instance, was at least as popular as Muir among American readers and was even more pronounced in his adoption of a post-Christian form of natural enchantment. From his small farm in West Park, New York, Burroughs produced a body of work that blended vivid and sensitive observation, paeans to rural life, and moral and theological reflection. He wrote of the "rural divinity" of cows in *Birds and Poets* (1877); of "divinity-school days in the mountains" in *Locusts and Wild Honey* (1879); of "sermons in stone" in *Signs and Seasons* (1886). "We must recognize only Nature, the All," he asserted in *Accepting the Universe* (1920), the summation of his naturalist divinity. Since Nature was God, every day was like a lovely summer Sunday. "Every walk in the woods is a religious rite, every bath in the stream is a saving ordinance. Communion service is at all hours, and the bread and the wine are from the heart and marrow of Mother Earth."[8]

Yet Burroughs's keen and graceful evocations of birds, orchards, and vineyards rested happily alongside mites of Social Darwinism. Echoing Emerson's "grinding economy," Burroughs mused sagely in *Accepting the Universe* that "in the strife and competition of nature, the separate units fall that the mass may prosper." If Burroughs's popularity rested on his psalms of natural and agrarian rectitude, careful readers learned that if "the whole order of the universe favors virtue and is against vice," then strife and competition were both ontological fixtures and signs of moral probity. Thus, while acquiring renown as a sage of simplicity, Burroughs befriended and vacationed with captains of industry, such as Carnegie, Rockefeller, Ford, Harvey Firestone, and E. H. Harriman.[9] The homilist of natural communion was a companion of the lords of capitalist misenchantment.

Still, even when couched in Darwinist terms, naturalist divinity did not always issue in deference to corporate titans and their decrees. The "naturalist" fiction of Frank Norris, for instance, is sometimes inflected with a potent sense of natural divinity. In the metaphysical and moral cosmology of *The Octopus* (1901), his epic story of struggle between wheat farmers and railroad barons in the San Joaquin Valley, Nature is both divine destroyer and divine nurturer, bestowing both irrevocable judgment on the evil and prolific blessing on the loving. When Presley, the wandering poet and protagonist, experiences the Darwinian epiphany that "FORCE only existed," the nature of that "FORCE" is both malevolent and kindly, ineluctable and awesomely benevolent:

> FORCE brought men into the world ... FORCE made the wheat grow.... It was the mystery of creation, the stupendous miracle of re-creation, the vast rhythm of the seasons ... the eternal symphony of reproduction swung in its tremendous cadences like the colossal pendulum of an almighty machine—primordial energy flung out from the hand of the Lord God himself.

Yet if "FORCE" is procreative, it also imposes capital punishment on the avaricious and unjust. At the end of the novel, Nature passes sentence on

Behrman, the banker who represents the Pacific and Southwestern Railroad—itself depicted as a malicious divinity, a "great monster, iron-hearted, relentless, infinitely powerful." Smothered in a grain elevator, Behrman dies at the hands of "FORCE," which executes judgment on individual and corporate venality with pitiless aplomb. As Behrman gasps for breath, "no human agency seemed to be back of the movement of the wheat . . . the grain seemed impelled with a force of its own." As Behrman lies dead, Norris emphasizes the natural divinity of the grains: "Upon the surface of the Wheat, under the chute, nothing moved but the Wheat itself."[10]

If Behrman is buried by the Wheat, Presley's friend Vanamee is liberated and revitalized. A drifter given to visions, Vanamee believes in "a sixth sense, or, rather, a whole system of those unnamed senses beyond the reach of our understanding." This sixth sense is possessed by people who "live much alone and close to nature"; "touch this sixth sense," he muses, "and it acts with absolute fidelity." Vanamee relies on this sense as he longs for a vision of Angele Varian, a girl he once loved who died in childbirth. Throughout the novel, Vanamee feels Angele's presence, and at one point, while sitting in a garden at night, Vanamee has "a Vision" of Angele's daughter, and the sixth sense unveils the natural world as a place of limitless rapture. As Vanamee contemplates the wheat fields, "a cathedral hush overlay all the land, and a sense of benediction brooded low—a divine kindliness manifesting itself in beauty, in peace, in absolute repose." Renewed by the sight of Angele's daughter, Vanamee exults in the splendor of "the eternal green life of the growing Wheat." The grains embody a natural divinity, an immense, imperishable cycle of growth, evanescence, decay, and fecundity. "The Wheat! The Wheat! . . . Life out of death, eternity rising from out of dissolution . . . The seed dying, rotting and corrupting in the earth; rising again in life unconquerable, and in immaculate purity."[11] For Norris, Darwinian naturalism did not preclude the reality of a munificent, redemptive enchantment.

Norris's natural divinity was populist in politics: speaking to a farmer's rally, Presley discovers his true poetic voice as a bard and prophet of the people. "The voice of God is the voice of the People," he tells the crowd; "Don't you hear God speaking in us?" For Norris's fellow Californian Mary Austin, the spirits of nature augured a return to a sacred gift economy. Growing up among the farmers of Carniville, Illinois, in the 1870s and 1880s, Austin (nee Mary Hunter) imbibed the hardscrabble Methodism of her parents and their neighbors—"a conventional, pew-fed religion" as she later described it. But proprietary-Protestant Biblicism proved no match for the charisma of nature. "God happened" to her one day at the age of seven as she stood under a walnut tree; after this arboreal epiphany, she realized that God was available everywhere, and that "luminous contacts" could be had "in the brook, in the bird, in the flower." For the next twenty years, she struggled to reconcile Methodist piety and natural mysticism, and her turmoil drove her to read widely and incessantly in religion, literature, and history. Bright and strong-willed, she insisted on a college education, and she graduated from local Blackburn College in 1888.[12]

After moving to California in the late 1880s, Mary taught school, endured a brief and unhappy marriage (to another teacher, Stafford Austin), and joined in the social and political turbulence that roiled the southern part of the state: labor struggles; battles for the rights of Mexican immigrants; fights to protect the land and customs of native Americans; the "Water Wars" that raged among ranchers, farmers, environmentalists, and Los Angeles businesspeople and city officials. Often stymied and melancholy, Austin found comfort and inspiration in the work of Jane Addams and Charlotte Perkins Gilman. Joining a salon in Carmel that included Jack London and Ambrose Bierce, she discovered kindred souls and found encouragement for her growing literary ambitions. She also resolved her spiritual disquiet, parting company with the Methodist God and His rigid, misogynist strictures. On the death of her mother in 1896, she saw "the dark cloud of the Hebrew Tribal God lift and dissolve," and His tenuous hold on Austin relented.[13]

Austin turned to the desert and its people for spiritual refuge and renewal. Residing in the Owens Valley between the Sierra Nevada and the Mojave Desert, Austin lived among Paiute, Mojave, and Shoshone Indians and wandered among the whitewashed adobe huts of Catholic Mexican miners. In an unlikely bestseller, *The Land of Little Rain* (1903), Austin conveyed a wisdom of the desert as sacramental as that of any ancient monastic. "Weather does not happen," she wrote of the arid and austerely beautiful climate. "It is the visible manifestation of the Spirit moving itself in the void." Unlike American Protestants who "go to church to be edified"—and who defile and mutilate nature with "an environment of asphalt pavements"—Indians and Mexicans encounter their gods in the "divinest, clearest air." Among the Mexican families of El Pueblo de Las Uvas, "the little town of

the grape vines," Austin discovered a moral economy of humility and effortless sharing. Far from miserable and degrading, the poverty of the people
encouraged peace, generosity, and plentiful leisure. Since "there is little
wealth and that to be had for the borrowing," there was no theft or murder
among the Mexicans, none of the status anxiety and emulative consumption
that obsessed and ravaged Protestants. Living without much thought for the
morrow, they produced and exchanged for survival as well as for frequent
communal festivities; richness and depth of experience made up for what
they lacked in material possessions. Austin realized that the wages of the
Protestant covenant were death, and she invited her readers to put aside the
acquisitive ethic and emulate the peoples of the desert. "Come away, you who
are obsessed with your own importance in the scheme of things, and have
got nothing you did not sweat for, come . . . to the kindliness, earthiness, and
ease of El Pueblo de Las Uvas."[14]

Later, in books and plays such as *The Basket Woman* (1904); *The Arrow-
Maker* (1911); *A Woman of Genius* (1912); and her autobiography, *Earth
Horizon* (1932), Austin embraced even more fully the enchanted Native
American cosmos, and she espoused a sacramental economy of gift and sacerdotal craft. In *The Basket Woman*, Austin embraced Amerindian cosmology, writing easily of talking streams, coyote-spirits, cheerful glaciers,
rabbit people, and "enchanted mesas." "Everything speaks of God in its own
way," she wrote, "and it is only a matter of understanding how." As she reflected on her time in the desert, she came to understand the God of the
walnut tree as "the Wakonda of the universe," the "Friend-of-the-Soul-
of-Man," fully present in "the running of the quail, the creaking of the
twenty-mule team, the sweep of motion in a life-history, in a dance, a chant."
It also inhabited Indian arts and crafts, which expressed "the spirit of existence" and pointed to "the fine moralities of nature." These "fine moralities"
were violated by the capitalist economy of commodities and accumulation,
and Austin urged a return to the spirit of what she considered some archaic
communism. In *The Arrow-Maker*, for instance, the medicine woman
Chisera realizes that her gift for healing belongs not to herself but to the
entire community, bestowed by "direct communion with the gods." The
protagonist of *A Woman of Genius* says God is "the Distributor of Gifts." By
the 1920s—after a period of dalliance with Greenwich Village radicals and
the dream of "the Social Revolution"—Austin was writing glowingly of the

gift-economies described by anthropologists such as Bronislaw Malinowski and Marcel Mauss, labyrinths of friendship imbued with the fecund, munificent spirit of *mana*. Archaic peoples did not live in fear, she asserted; they dwelled in the "easy conviction of an animal in all nature, similar to the *anima* of man . . . the Spirit resident in created things."[15]

Austin's evocation of indigenous enchantment had no political traction—an impotence shared by almost all other varieties of naturalist divinity. By the eve of World War I, Norris's populism was already a memory, and Burroughs's brand of social Darwinism was becoming unfashionable—or at least unmentionable—among political and corporate elites. Of all the forms of naturalist divinity, Muir's was the most popular—and, it turned out, the most amenable to incorporation. Despite his contempt for the "gobble-gobble" school of economics, Muir's theology of the redwoods did not rule out the possibility of capitalist progress. Muir was no enraptured anchorite; his house in Martinez, California, was equipped with electric lighting, a telephone, and a typewriter. He devoted most of his 2,600-acre ranch to the growing of grapes and pears for the market—ready access to which he gained thanks to a railroad trestle that cut across his property, built after negotiations with the Santa Fe Railroad Company.[16]

Muir's friendship with the railroad baron Harrimann is even more illustrative. Organizing an expedition to southern Alaska in 1899, Harrimann assembled botanists, geologists, ornithologists, artists—and Muir, whose reputation as a naturalist was by then impeccable. Although he found Harrimann personally distasteful—and even suspected that he was actually reconnoitering for further railroad expansion—Muir warily accepted the invitation. As the trip proceeded, Muir warmed to this particular devotee of the Dollar. When Harrimann died in 1909, Muir delivered the eulogy at his funeral, lauding his friend for "developing the country and laying broad and deep foundations of prosperity." Muir hailed Harriman as "a great maker and harvester of crops of wealth . . . fortunes grew along his railroads like natural fruit."[17]

Unlikely as praise from a romantic naturalist to a robber baron seems today, Muir's panegyric to Harrimann reflected Muir's commitment to a Progressive moral economy. Like those of Lippmann and Croly, Muir's political instincts were unerringly elitist: cruise with Harrimann along the coast of Alaska, chat with Roosevelt by the light of a Yosemite campfire. If

Muir indicted monopolists, the Almighty Dollar, and the "gobble-gobble" of laissez-faire, he never condemned capitalism as a system, prefiguring the accommodation of many later environmentalists with the necessities of capitalist expansion. Muir reconciled his naturalist theology with industrial growth by relying on an ecological clerisy. He always recoiled from class politics; his lack of interest in the social turmoil that rocked the country in the 1890s has been noted even by sympathetic interpreters. This indifference to the injustice of industrial life rendered Muir all the more susceptible to the unctuousness of a Harrimann, who once assured Muir that his appetite for accumulation had little to do with money: "What I most enjoy," he told the sage of Yosemite, "is the power of creation, getting into partnership with Nature in doing good."[18]

The "partnership" of corporations and the commonweal was a staple of the Progressive moral imagination, and the conservationist movement that Muir helped launch partook of its benevolent elitism. The Sierra Club drew most of its members from the professional middle class, who constituted Progressives' primary spiritual and political constituency. Many if not most of Muir's readers were college graduates, who—whether corporate employees, independent professionals, or citizens of the republic of arts and letters—had abandoned orthodox Christianity and desired alternative forms of enchantment. Since most would never reside in the charms of God's wilderness sanctuary, Muir provided vicarious beatitude for the urban bourgeoisie. Writing from Portland, Oregon, one of Muir's many fans captured the appeal of the long-bearded mystic of the mountains. "We, who are not able to keep in constant communion with the great outdoors, need some-one to bring that vast domain to our desk and our evening lamp."[19] The religion of nature, like the religion of art, was an enchantment compatible with incorporation. By inviting industrialism into the sanctum of Nature, Muir suggested that beloved communion could abide with capitalist property; naturalist enchantment could sanctify commitment to the once-Protestant covenant theology. Like Transcendentalism and later, similar brands of New Age spirituality, Muir's naturalist divinity belongs in the lineage of bourgeois enchantment and moralism.

William James was another wanderer in search of divinity. Along with his brother Henry, William lived under the mercurial rule of Henry James, Sr., a dabbler in spirituality: Platonism, Fourierist socialism, a pinch of

Transcendentalism, and Swedenborgianism. Buoyed by the patriarch's fortune, the James family moved at least half a dozen times, on two continents, depending on the elder's whim. William and Henry knew no stable residence or education, living in New York, London, Geneva, Paris, and Boston, and attending over a dozen different schools. William James's early adulthood appears erratic, even irresponsible; "just like a blob of mercury," as his sister Alice once described him—fondly. He vacillated over whether to enlist in the Union army; he went back and forth between science and painting as a career, chose science, then abandoned science for a degree in medicine—a profession he never practiced. Appointed to Harvard in 1872, he taught, in rapid succession, physiology; psychology; and finally, philosophy. Unburdened by a conventional academic training, James brought to philosophy the freshness and verve of the superintelligent amateur. Even to those critical of pragmatism, James is one of the most readable and likeable thinkers in the history of philosophy; his exuberant openness to the variety of the world remains compelling and infectious. "Philosophy is more a matter of passionate vision than of logic," as he wrote in *A Pluralistic Universe* (1909).[20]

Despite his (easily misinterpreted) interest in the "cash-value" of ideas, James's conception of philosophy as "passionate vision" marks him as a Romantic—a pilgrim, however beholden to science, in search of a modern sacramental imagination. "At a single stroke," he wrote in 1881, theism "changes the dead blank it of the world into a living thou, with whom the whole man may have dealings." Reflecting "On a Certain Blindness in Human Beings" (1899), James implied that the malady was an inability to appreciate some invisible but magnanimous order, some dimension of being that eludes without invalidating scientific or rational investigation. Alluding to Wordsworth, Shelley, and Whitman as seers of "a limitless significance in natural things," James called on his Harvard audience to discover the "mystic sense of hidden meaning" affirmed in what he would call "the varieties of religious experience." This receptivity to the most uncanny experiences was evident, not only in James's avid interest in spiritualism but also in his endorsement of "radical empiricism." Eager to "unstiffen all our theories," James wanted scientists in particular to loosen up their epistemological categories and embrace forms of evidence from which they habitually recoiled. Conceiving "a world of pure experience," James contended for the possibility of powers beyond the grasp of ordinary rational apprehension. Men, he wrote in the

*American Magazine* in 1907, "use only a small part of the power which they actually possess" because "we never push through the obstruction"—the obstruction, that is, of a rigid metaphysics that narrowed the range of possibility.[21]

James's Romantic imagination infused his civic republicanism, his opposition to American imperialism, and his search for an alternative to war. Speaking in Boston on Memorial Day, 1897, at the unveiling of the Robert Gould Shaw Memorial, James praised Gould's martyrdom for "our American religion": "the faith that a man requires no master to take care of him, and that common people can work out their salvation." Compelled and guided by the "inner mystery" of civic virtue, such people "have no need of war to save them," he asserted; "God's judgments do not have to overtake them fitfully in bloody spasms and convulsions of the race." Still, unlike many of his fellow members of the Anti-Imperialist League, James respected and even revered the martial impulses he hoped to sublimate. Speaking to an international assembly of pacifists in Boston in 1904, James attributed war, not only to economic and political interests but also to "a vague religious exaltation"; war was a "passionate vision," of sorts. "It is a sacrament," he asserted, "a mystical blood-tax" paid to the community to which the soldier belongs. Later, in "The Moral Equivalent of War"—published in *McClure's* in August 1910, the same month as his death—James wrote of war as a spiritual adventure. Recounting the history of reflection on war from Homer and Thucydides to the militarists of his day, James concluded that war was both the "romance of history" as well as "a sort of sacrament." Envisioning a vast program of public works, James contended that such national service would channel the energies now expended in butchery: self-sacrifice, heroism, and solidarity. After building dams, bridges, schools, roads, ports, and skyscrapers, young men would have "paid their blood-tax"—in other words, performed their sacramental duties.[22] For James, the search for a moral equivalent of war was a quest for new forms of romance and sacrament.

If James considered war a "sacrament," he thought obsession with wealth an equally formidable obstacle to passionate vision. In his *Principles of Psychology* (1890), James came close to defining avarice as a spiritual disease as well as a psychological trait. Looking closely at the miser, James observed that he "transfers the bodily pleasures associated with the spending of money"—the enjoyment of material things—to "the money itself." Gold especially becomes a material cipher for something else—a sacrament, as it were, of the miser's real life. Avarice turns out to be a form of impoverishment, not only moral but physical and spiritual as well. (The wealthy pay a soul-tax at confiscatory rates.) If, as the miser believes, it is "better to live poor now, with the *power* of being rich, than to live rich at the risk of losing the power," then it is the desire for power that prevents the miser from living richly—that is, fully and passionately.[23] The miser takes all thought for the morrow, and dies in the here and now.

If the nascent consumer culture of James's day was undermining miserliness, he still believed that the inordinate desire for possessions induced a form of metaphysical blindness. We fail to see the "limitless significance" of things, he mused in "A Certain Blindness," because our vision is occluded by "the clamor of our own practical interests," the unexamined and corrupting exigencies of making a living in capitalist society. Things could be "mortgages on the soul," he mused in The *Varieties of Religious Experience* (1902); the property owner is "buried and smothered in ignoble externalities and trammels." Money-making and spending induced an insipid and cowardly shabbiness in our lives for which no amount of riches could compensate. Echoing Nietzsche's contempt for "the Last Man"—the nadir of bourgeois banality, with "his little pleasures for the day, and his little pleasures for the night"—James warned that wealth was making Americans all too pampered, boring, and ignoble. In "What Makes a Life Significant?" (1899), James reported his disgust with "the middle-class paradise" he saw at a Chautauqua camp. After surveying "this dead level and quintessence of every mediocrity"—soda-fountains, bicycles, lectures, picnics, endless smiles and civilities—James retched at the "atrocious harmlessness." "Sweat and effort, human nature strained to its uttermost, yet getting through alive"—life's arduous romance had been obscured by a veil of bowdlerizing niceness. With the arrival of the material abundance that humanity had so painfully and hopefully acquired, "an irremediable flatness is coming over the world." In *Varieties,* James directed the ire he had hurled at Chautauqua at his fellow college-bred. Among "the so-called better classes," the "worship of material luxury and wealth" produced "a certain trashiness of fibre." For all their hirsute and bombastic imperialism, the elites of business, politics, and culture were "scared as men were never scared in history at material ugliness and hardship." Profoundly fearful of any discomfort or misfortune, "we put off marriage until our house can be artistic, and quake at the thought of having a child without a bank-account and doomed to manual labor." Born of a lack of faith, the futile desire for complete security would literally kill us off. "It is time for thinking men to protest against so unmanly and irreligious a state of opinion."[24]

Under what banner should the thoughtful march in pursuit of a passionate vision? James's answers—"poverty" and "saintliness"—were unsettling to say the least. If, James reasoned in *Varieties,* we consider the depth to which the lust for possessions has infected "the very bone and marrow of our genera-tion," then the reassertion of poverty as a "worthy religious vocation" might well be "the spiritual reform which our time stands most in need of." As James explained, the ideal of poverty, far from enjoining resignation to misery, challenged its adherents to a life of freedom, courage, and generosity. Reversing the conventional wisdom of modernity—capitalist or socialist—James declared that, when freely chosen, poverty was a liberation, a reser-voir of strength, even an unsuspected trove of riches. Immune to the lure of material inducements, the man of poverty was an "unbribed soul," willing to throw away even his life in the service of truth and other unpopular causes. Unlike the accumulator of money or commodities—who experiences a kind of death-in-life, hoarding, postponing, barricading with possessions—the man of poverty lives life to the fullest through reckless, even joyful, expen-diture. He knows he is truly blessed with riches: confident in some realm of abundance, he trusts he can afford to claim nothing as his own, and gives everything he does not have to others. In an eloquent and bracing passage, James imagined the fruits of the passionate vision recovered by dedication to poverty:[25]

> We need no longer hold our tongues or fear to vote the revolutionary or reformatory ticket. Our stocks might fall, our hopes of promotion vanish, our salaries drop, our club doors close in our faces; yet, while we lived, we would imperturbably bear witness to the spirit, and our example would help to set free our generation.

What manner of person could afford this poverty? In "A Certain Blind-ness," James had mused that, to plumb "limitless significance"—"to attain to any breadth of insight into the impersonal world of worths as such"—one must "become worthless as a practical being." Blinded by their possessions—profit, power, religious orthodoxy, scholarly convention—practical beings could not afford to dispense with their accumulated wealth of interests. True knowledge required divestiture of ties, burdens, places. "Only your mystic, your dreamer, or your insolvent tramp or loafer, can afford so sympathetic an occupation." In *Varieties,* the name James affixed to this sympathetic occupation was "saintliness": "a feeling of being in a wider life than that of this world's selfish little interests." (As John Ruskin had written, there is no wealth but life.) Broader, deeper, and more joyful than morality, saintliness is a way of being in the world, not a restrictive code of conduct. Having divested themselves of worldly cares, saints live outside of themselves and fully in the world—they live, in other words, in ecstasy. Saints are complete romantics, dwelling in "rapture" and "ontological wonder." To the world, of course, saints are fools; living without the usual defenses of money, power, and guile, they are perfectly, terrifyingly vulnerable. "You may be a prophet, at this rate," James exhorted and warned his readers, "but you cannot be a worldly success." Yet to saints, this failure was triumph, for in living without cover their love was unbounded; helping even the hateful and undeserving, they upend all standards of justice and prudence that the world erects to preserve its interests. Despite our professions of reverence for holiness, the very real threat that it poses to our safety explains, James noted, why the saint's existential extremity "makes us admire and shudder at the same time." Indeed, the path of love involves such a break with "the present world's arrangements" that the saint offered entry "into another kingdom of being."[26]

Whether that other "kingdom of being" was real seemed less important to James than its morally exhilarant enchantment. In "The Moral Philosopher and the Moral Life" (1891), one of his most passionately envisioned essays, James adamantly maintained that only religion could overcome the "trashiness of fibre" that lamed our efforts to build an "ethical republic." Morality was possible in a godless world, he argued, but "our moral energy falls short of its maximal stimulating power." To be sure, life without God is "a genuinely ethical symphony," but it is "played in the compass of a couple of poor octaves, and the infinite scale of values fails to open up." With God, however, "the scale of the symphony is incalculably prolonged." The divine music of the spheres awakens what James called "the strenuous mood"—the capacity to endure adversity in the present for the sake of a greater, perhaps distant good. "It saith among the trumpets, ha ha; it smelleth the battle afar off, the thunder of the captains and the shouting." For the unbribed souls with religious faith, "every sort of energy and endurance, of courage and capacity for handling life's evils is set free." "On the battlefield of human history," James concluded, those strengthened by a faith in divine presence will "always outwear the easy-going type and religion will drive irreligion to the wall."[27]

Yet James could also maintain that that "kingdom of being" was the ordinary, everyday world—revealed, however, in all its marvel and possibility. The kingdom is here, all around us, its fullness hidden and repressed from view by the scramble for pecuniary utility. In his essays, James beckoned toward that hidden kingdom. In "A Certain Blindness," James cited an Indian chief's mordant observation that white farmers, obsessed with their commercial imperatives, can never truly live. "When they have finished ploughing one field, they begin to plough another; and, if the day were not enough, I have seen them plough by moonlight!" Always thinking about the remunerative morrow, the farmers lose their lives in the effort to preserve them. Life, the chief sighs, "is nought to them"; but since his people "live in the present"—"the most enchanting of all things"—they know happiness.[28]

James saw the same compulsiveness in the blasé commotion of urban capitalism. Distracted by the struggle for riches, "your ordinary Brooklynite or New Yorker" sees the world through a "jaded and unquickened eye," through which all appears "dead and common." But to anyone blessed with the capacity for sight—to anyone enlivened and enriched by the virtues of poverty and saintliness—the "dead and common" world was animate, enchanted. "What is life on the large scale," James asked, but "the same recurrent inanities, the same dog barking, the same fly buzzing, forevermore?" The inanities were indeed inane—pointless, bereft of exchange value. But it was precisely in their uselessness that James discovered the most profound significance. "Of the kind of fibre of which such inanities consist is the material woven of all the excitements, joys, and meanings that ever were, or ever shall be, in this world." To the unholy and mercenary eye, these idle and profitless moments are "meaningless and vacant tracts of time." No, James countered; these "holidays of life are its most vitally significant portions," for they cast a "magically irresponsible spell." "Rapt with satisfied attention . . . to the mere spectacle of the world's presence."[29]

At times, James gestured toward the implications of "passionate vision" for political economy. Historians have seen James as a social democrat and as an unwitting Marxist, but his conceptions of saintliness and heroism inclined him toward anarchism. In *Varieties,* anarchists, along with radical workers, were among the latter-day saints who exhibited "antipathy for lives based on mere having." "I am more and more an individualist and anarchist and believer in small systems of things," he once told William Dean Howells. James was frightened by the scale of modern social and economic organization. He refused to worship the "bloated idol termed 'modern civilization,'" he wrote in 1899. Complaining to a Boston newspaper in the same year about the American occupation of the Philippines, James asserted that the Army's treatment of the Filipino rebels resembled "the infernal adroitness of the great department store, which has reached perfect expertness in the art of killing silently and with no public squealing or commotion as in the neighboring small concern." This was the populist dudgeon of the little man, but James told an anarchist poet in 1901 that he embraced "Tolstoianism"—adding, with exquisite self-consciousness, that he himself lay "in the bonds of mammon."[30]

James's valiant defense of the oppressed suggests that Lewis Mumford was at least a little unfair when he condemned "the pragmatic acquiescence" in power; but without firmer ontological foundations, pragmatism could easily become a philosophical camouflage for power. The most trenchant critique of pragmatism along these lines came from none other than Randolph Bourne—exemplary "Young American," herald of "Beloved Community," and a star student of Dewey's at Columbia. As an apostle of "the experimental life" among the Greenwich Village left, Bourne was an avid and eloquent proponent of Romantic pragmatism, observing in "The Experimental Life" (1913) that while the world "despises poets, fanatics, prophets, and lovers" it has nevertheless been "those who experimented with life, who formed their philosophy of life as a crystallization out of that experimenting, who were the light and life of the world." But the debate among progressives and radicals over American entry into World War I undermined Bourne's buoyant faith and alerted him to the lethal shortcomings of pragmatism. Over the spring and summer of 1917, Bourne watched in painful disbelief as his fellow progressives—even his beloved Dewey—enlisted in the intellectual brigades and baptized themselves in "the sewage of the war spirit." Bourne was especially enraged by Dewey's rationale for supporting the war: that it offered progressives the chance to experiment with the technical and organizational prowess they would need for postwar social reconstruction. In "Twilight of Idols" (1917) and "The State" (1918)—the latter a treatise left unfinished due to his death from influenza—Bourne both reconsidered "the pragmatic dispensation," the intellectual and moral climate of his generation "who had taken Dewey's philosophy almost as our American religion," and sought to explore and demystify the enchantment of the modern state.[31]

How could people so learned and humane become such credulous warriors? Dewey meant to "start with values," Bourne contended, but he left an "unhappy ambiguity" as to "just how values were created." Bourne argued that in the bellicose climate of 1917, the void created by this ambiguity was filled by nationalism, which in "The State" becomes "a mystical conception," a surrogate for traditional communities of salvation. The State was the "invisible grace" of which the government was the sacramental vessel, "the visible sign, the word made flesh." "The State is a jealous God, and will brook no rivals." A perverse and bloodthirsty deity, the State demanded the taking and sacrifice of life in war, offering the individual citizen a sense of existential beatitude through death on the battlefield: "his apotheosis," as Bourne put it. As the means of its necrophiliac vitality, "war," Bourne famously proclaimed, "is the health of the State"; as James had written, it is indeed a sacrament.[32]

Turning to James after repudiating Dewey, Bourne hoped to redeem "the pragmatic dispensation" by recovering a passionate vision that would be at once more critical and more peaceable—a Beloved Community that could offer a persuasive moral equivalent to war. But if, as he wrote to Van Wyck Brooks, the pragmatic disappointment indicated that America needed "a new gospel," the good news remained unclear. Affirming James's "poetic vision" in "Twilight of Idols," Bourne deemed it central to the "malcontentedness" indispensable to social and political criticism. Yet he still could not explain how epiphany or iconoclasm could generate values without ontological warrant. For all his ebullient intelligence, James was as nebulous and evasive as Dewey about the origin and creation of values. If what Bourne himself called that "unhappy ambiguity" could not be resolved, then any "passionate vision" could never claim to be more than a vigorous personal zeal. But if the void at the heart of the pragmatic dispensation remained ambiguous and unfilled, then pragmatism offered no assurance of protection from the idolatrous enchantment of the state or the corporation. As Louis Menand observes, pragmatism "takes interests for granted; it doesn't provide for a way of judging whether they are worth pursuing apart from the consequences of acting on them."[33]

The abyss at the core of the pragmatic dispensation was filled, for James's saint, by "ontological wonder," and one seeker of wonder who found power in the saints was Vida Dutton Scudder. Born in Madura, India, in 1861 to Congregationalist missionaries, she also belonged to a prosperous Boston family of literary accomplishment; her uncle Horace Scudder was an editor of the *Atlantic Monthly*. Vida received a first-rate education, graduating in 1880 with the first class of the Boston Girl's Latin School. Traveling extensively in Europe with her mother, she visited galleries, cathedrals, and libraries, especially in France and Italy. Her travels made an indelibly Catholic impression on "the young Protestant girl," she later recalled. Increasingly alienated from the cultural and religious relics of Puritan Boston, Vida fell in love with Gothic art and architecture. "Cathedrals, sacred art, liturgies . . . bore a witness I could not repudiate." Although she joined the Episcopal Church, the splendor of Catholic Europe "determined what sort of person I should be . . . devotion to beauty, and awed intuition of the human past."[34]

After graduating from Smith College in 1884—"a little intellectual snob," she wrote later—Scudder enrolled in Oxford as one of its first female students. She attended Ruskin's lectures on art, and "strange things began to happen": his ardor and eloquence "threw wide to [my] awakening soul the portals of the temple of beauty," and she learned how to "read the declaration of the glory of God in the heavens." Ruskin also taught her that art and social criticism were intimately related; "the Ruskin of *Modern Painters* . . . was one with the Ruskin of *Fors Clavigera*." Perusing *Unto This Last* "marked a turning point in my mental, and later in my outward life."[35]

Inspired by Ruskin's "economy of heaven," Scudder both joined the Salvation Army and volunteered at Toynbee Hall, a settlement house in London's East End that served as a kind of station of the Cross for Anglican reformers. Realizing her insulation from "real life," she regretted "the plethora of privilege in which my lot had been cast"; she had encountered "too much at second hand," and she felt false, empty, and cheated, cloistered inside an "imitative life" of genteel and anesthetic pedantry. Like many other young middle-class intellectuals near the close of the nineteenth century, Scudder longed to escape from what she experienced as the inauthenticity of bourgeois life, believing that immersion in the lives of the poor would relieve her sense of unreality. Having arrived in England a coddled highbrow, Scudder left in 1886 determined to plunge into "real" experience.[36]

Scudder struggled to reconcile her "plethora of privilege" with her longing for a "real" life. In the fall of 1887, she took a position teaching English literature at Wellesley College, earning tenure five years later. Secure in the ivory tower, Scudder became one of Wellesley's most popular and revered professors, often "walking on air" after a successful lecture or seminar discussion. Yet teaching, she confided to a colleague, prevented her from doing "any of God's work." Like Jane Addams, Scudder turned to settlement house work to allay vague religious and existential doubts with the "sentiment of universal brotherhood"; unlike Addams, she thought of her service to the poor as a religious vocation, an imitation of Christ that enabled reformers to partake of the life of divinity. In the fall of 1889—two weeks before Addams opened Hull House in Chicago—Scudder and other idealistic Wellesley faculty and students opened a settlement house in New York; over the next three years, they established others in Philadelphia and Boston. At the same time, they founded the College Settlements Association, dedicated, in Scudder's words, to "righteous living" in harmony with "a purely spiritual ideal." Settlement houses, Scudder asserted, should be "centers of revelation" through which residents could follow "the example of the Master."[37]

Settlement work could be easily dismissed as another opiate of the bourgeoisie. Yet while it certainly assuaged the guilt felt by many young middle-class Christians, settlement work could also breed a much more capacious moral imagination. Scudder herself used "every scrap of freedom" from teaching and writing to work at Boston's Denison House, where she believed she acquired "a vivid feeling of life in the social depths." Service to the poor freed Scudder and others, however briefly, from the bonds of privilege. Performing their modern corporal works of mercy, Scudder and her fellow settlement workers were "busy cutting the wires which held us to our own class." In the callous world of industrial incorporation, Scudder approached the ideal of saintliness that James had heralded for their generation, bearing a witness to the spirit, a passionate vision in a venal and ferocious age.[38]

Scudder's work at Denison House convinced her that even the most zealous philanthropic service was insufficient and even anodyne, so she finally turned to socialism as an even greater *imitatio Christi,* perceiving in its march for justice a political vehicle of supernatural grace. After reading in Marxist and Fabian literature, Scudder joined the socialist cause in the early 1890s, committed to ending the distrust and alienation between socialists and Christians. Precisely because it represented humanity's greatest hope for a beloved modernity, the religious transfiguration of socialism was imperative, Scudder believed, lest the movement inadvertently spell "the worst disaster of any experiment in collective living that the world has ever seen." Christianity would, in her view, enlarge and embolden the socialist imagination. In *The Life of the Spirit in the Modern English Poets* (1895), Scudder drew a religious and political distinction between Shelley the secular modern and Dante the medieval believer. As a bard of romantic but unbelieving radicalism, Shelley put his faith in a natural world whose life was "abounding but elusive"; but Dante, enchanted by a "Beatific Vision of the Most High," could impart an "audacity impossible to the poet of revolution."[39] For Scudder, the face of Beatrice bestowed more boldness and strength than the brawn of Prometheus unbound.

Laboring mightily to plight a fruitful troth for Beatrice and Prometheus, Scudder embarked on a career as a socialist missionary to the Christians as well as the pagans. A congregant in W. D. P. Bliss's Church of the Carpenter and a contributor to the *Dawn,* Scudder hoped that radicalized churches could be "shrines of social practice" uniting "thinkers and laborers." A founding member of the Society of Christian Socialists, Scudder also set up the American branches of the Christian Socialist League and the Church Social Union; sat on the Episcopal Church's Commission on Social Service; served as a board member, with Addams and Lillian Wald of the National Women's Trade Union League; and helped establish the Church League for Industrial Democracy. One of the Christian socialist movement's most learned and assiduous evangelists, she spoke in churches, lecture halls, union meetings, and settlement houses, and wrote tracts and pamphlets as well as essays for the *Atlantic Monthly* and other middle-class periodicals.[40]

One casualty of Scudder's socialist commitment was her devotion to Ruskin. Impressed by the empirical heft of Fabian sociological research, Scudder repudiated Ruskin's Gothic Romanticism after reading the *Fabian*

*Essays.* "Poets and dreamers fed my imagination," she wrote, but in Fabian socialism, she discovered "practical, constructive ideas." In *Socialism and Character* (1912), her most important book, Scudder praised Ruskin's "sensitive intelligence" but disowned his reliance on patrician benevolence and his glorification of craftsmanship. She urged religious socialists to close their volumes of Ruskin and Tolstoy and "open your Engels, your Bebel, your Jaures."[41] Scudder's beatific vision would appear to have been the city of industrial modernity, mechanized and consolidated by corporate capitalism, then seized by a consecrated working class.

Yet Scudder never fully harmonized Christianity and modern socialism: the troth of Beatrice and Prometheus remained unconsummated. In a series of essays and books—especially *The Witness of Denial* (1895), *Social Ideals in Modern English Literature* (1898), *Socialism and Character,* and *The Church and the Hour* (1917)—she produced the most sophisticated socialist theology in America, and even then she remained ambivalent. Scudder worked her sacramental imagination into a materialist theory of history that joined Anglo-Catholic sacramental theology to historical materialism. If the world is "the Sacrament of God's Presence," as she asserted in *The Church and the Hour,* then "the sacramental system will afford the very interpretation of life for which a perfected democracy must yearn." In *Socialism and Character,* Scudder advanced a sacramental materialism that would, she hoped, rival the secular materialism of Marx. "The material universe," she explained, "is a sacrament ordained to convey spiritual life to us." God is "so manifest in the life of nature and the social whole that it is easy to confuse Him with the very world which he inspires." Since material things have "sacramental sanctity," human flesh is a vessel of divine grace and power; there is a "sacramental unity between flesh and soul." Concerned with both flesh and soul, economic life is therefore "not a dead thing"; in fact, what Marxists understood as "'determined,' automatic forces, which mechanically generate our passions and power" were also "messengers, fulfilling a central Will."[42]

Because work and property are sacramental matters, they really are "as sacred as the most sententious conservative conceives." Seen in this light, class struggles became internecine clashes over the means of material beatitude, and only socialism—and eventually communism—would put an end to this fratricidal warfare. "The Church has always given birth to communists," she observed, even if it quickly disavowed them. Scudder saw class conflict through the lens of Trinitarian and Eucharistic theology—in her view, not relics of metaphysical humbug but the only warrants for socialist hope. The doctrine of the Trinity had direct social implications for a being created in the image of God. "The abiding reality" is "fellowship; not self-seeking, but in giving of self to the uttermost; not personality shut in upon itself, but in an equal interchange of love." As the crowning celebration of that love, "the Eucharistic Feast beautifully sanctifies the union of the life of Nature with human labor"; it is "the consummation of all toil, the beautiful, sacramental consecration" of our works and days.[43]

Scudder posed an ingenious alternative to the prevailing tale of disenchantment, but she sensed that socialism might become a more egalitarian form of "the plethora of privilege." Her ambivalence stemmed, in part, from her reluctance to challenge the hegemony of Marxism in radical circles. Like Morris, Scudder succumbed to late-Victorian radical chic: the belief that Marxism offered a more realistic theory of historical and political transformation than did other forms of socialism. From this perspective, Ruskin and others who lacked the theoretical lexicon of Marxism appeared as mere "moralists" and "idealists," too unscientific to understand the laws that governed social and economic change. Yet despite the marriage over which she presided in *Socialism and Character,* Scudder harbored doubts about the veracity and efficacy both of Fabian gradualism and revolutionary Marxism.

Scudder's commitment to revolutionary socialism was never quite as ardent as she imagined it to be. Try as she might to mute the Romantic moralism of Carlyle and Ruskin, the echoes of Ruskin's *Unto This Last* and *Fors Clavigera* resounded in her work. "Quite possibly men would be better off in the socialistic state," she speculated in 1896, "but it is much more important to know whether they would be any better." Sounding like an inveterate acolyte of Ruskin, Scudder mused that the tedium of socialist literature was a clue to its deficiency as an ideal. Most socialist utopias were, she lamented, "dreary, lacking in color, interest, life; painfully dull in their suggestions of enervating material prosperity." Even the Fabians were, she eventually concluded, "bureaucratic [and] limited." In *Socialism and Character,* Scudder wondered if, as socialists aimed to "supplant love by justice," some of the finest human qualities would atrophy. "Free giving and uncalculating sacrifice" would disappear in the arithmetic of planning; personal idiosyncrasy and intimate community would yield to mechanism and bureaucracy, "impersonal and inevitable as gravitation." Elsewhere, Scudder fretted that the friends of socialism could be its worst enemies. Though repelled by industrialists, Scudder deemed the psychology of most labor leaders "no less capitalistic than that of industry"; Samuel Gompers's demand for "more" was essentially the same as John Rockefeller's.[44]

Despite her enthusiasm for the Bolshevik Revolution of 1917, Scudder inclined, in her own words, "rather toward St. Francis than toward Marx." Scudder's fondness for Francis and other medieval saints beckoned toward another kind of anticapitalist radicalism, indebted to socialism yet critical of its faith in economic and technological panaceas. Unable to fully resist the intellectual glamor of Marxist dialectics, Scudder, at her most acute, still realized its incongruity with Christian eschatology. Like the scarcity of Protestant capitalism, the Marxist metaphysics of conflict was incompatible with an ontology of peace—the conviction voiced by Hilda Lathrop, the protagonist of *A Listener in Babel* (1903), that "at the heart of the universe may be Love."[45] Scudder's most passionate vision emerged from her quest for mystical intimacy with God—from her longing to enter "another kingdom of being," as James had written of sainthood.

Scudder's most enduring personal passion was sacramental mysticism, communion with divine life through prayer, ritual, and contemplation. Sacramental mysticism thrived among Anglican social gospelers: the two Anglican monastic orders in the United States, the Society of St. John the Evangelists (also known as the Cowley Fathers) and the Order of the Holy Cross, combined the contemplative life with missionary work and social reform. Founded in 1866, the Cowley Fathers performed educational and charitable work among the poor of Boston and Philadelphia, and supported labor unions and "industrial cooperation." The cofounder of the Order of the Holy Cross in 1884, Father James Huntington, was a follower of Henry George, a member of the Knights of Labor, and head of the Church Association for the Advancement of the Interests of Labor. Often stymied by Episcopal officials and failing to attract any more than a handful of brothers, Huntington and his fellow monks ended their activism in the 1890s, retreating to a monastery in rural New York to cultivate the spiritual life.[46]

The withdrawal of both groups from class struggle would appear to suggest that mysticism and contemplation are indeed incompatible with political commitment. Yet the saintly ideal was itself a form of social protest, a statement both about capitalist iniquity and about the possibility of a more cooperative order. Withdrawal is not necessarily an expression of indifference or hopelessness; it may mark a strategic refusal to deal with a society on its own corrupt terms. Seen in this light, Anglican monastics did not abandon social reform for religious protest; rather, religious protest *was* their social reform, their deliberate effort to change society by example rather than through "activism." As with the Arts and Crafts communities in England and America, monastic opposition to capitalist modernity took a path of indirect but nonetheless genuine defiance.

Scudder, of course, chose the more direct path of socialist agitation; still, driven by her quest for "real life," her restless soul found a measure of stillness in sacramental mysticism. Perpetually haunted by a sense of inauthenticity, Scudder often lived near the abyss of despair, dreading what she called, in *The Witness of Denial*, the "blank nescience which envelops our pitiful humanity"—a sense of the futility of all human endeavor, the sound and fury that signify nothing. It was no wonder that Scudder, wracked by interminable doubt about the reality of God and the promise of socialism, should turn to mysticism for comfort and strength in the face of recurrent failure. However revolutionary her politics, Scudder remained a traditionalist of the spirit, refusing many of the compromises with bourgeois modernity struck by more liberal believers. She faulted liberal Protestantism both for its dilution of orthodoxy and for its equation of faith with an insipid moralism. "We are suffering from a diffusion of Christianity at the cost of its intensity," she warned in 1912.[47] Yet this stern disavowal of liberal theology dovetailed, in Scudder, with unwavering opposition to the orthodoxies of capitalism. Indeed, at her most bracingly traditional, Scudder gestured toward a communion of the humble and imperfect more generous and free than the prudent new world of industrial abundance.

Scudder's mystical pilgrimage began in 1889 when she joined the Society of Companions of the Holy Cross, an Episcopal women's group affiliated with Huntington's order who devoted themselves to prayer, self-education, and social work. Meeting in homes and retreats, the Companions fostered, as their manual explained, "Intercession, Thanksgiving, and Simplicity of Life." They recited prayers to mark the hours, reflected on the lives of saints, and dwelled on the grace that flowed from the Eucharist and the other sacraments. "Strengthened with the grace of the saving Food," they offered prayers for immigrants, workers, and capitalists, as well as for students and artists. Though never explicitly political, they prayed both to "enlighten all employers of labor" and for "the sanctification of labor in every calling and handicraft." Through psalms, hymns, oblations, prayers of penance and Eucharistic devotions, Scudder and her Companions sought spiritual formation, a traditional therapy of desire. Prayer, to the Companions, was not only petition but the generation of saintliness, the subjective necessity to live as Christ did; as their manual put it, "to begin to lead his life here."[48]

Scudder's sacramental mysticism surfaced in her work of the 1890s. In *The Witness of Denial*—a meditation on the varieties of religious doubt and renewal in nineteenth-century thought—she wrote that "spiritual desire is the prevailing modern mood," evident in even the most brashly secular writers and movements. "Out of the very depth of denial speaks the witness of the shadows; a reflected light mingles with darkness"—an assertion that echoed her own tribulation. In *Social Ideals in English Letters,* she observed that the contemporary Christian socialist movement in England owed an enormous spiritual and theological debt to the Oxford Movement. While John Henry Newman and his cohorts had little interest in social and economic reform, their insistence on "the sacramental conception of life" provided a salutary and invaluable spiritual energy to Christian socialism. The Oxford Movement's sacramental sensibility reminded crusaders against capitalism that "the sanctification of the flesh"—not only redistribution of wealth—should be the ultimate goal of socialism. The lesson for Scudder was clear: the apparently apolitical mysticism of the Oxford Movement had prepared the way for the radicalism of the Church Socialist League. "The social impulse in the Church is always effect and not cause of her deepest life"—the life, that is, of sacramental mysticism.[49]

As her dark night of the soul continued and deepened, Scudder came to understand that this "deepest life" held political implications that she continued to hold at arm's length. While recuperating in Europe after a nervous breakdown in 1901, Scudder turned to the study of medieval saints. After wandering through the English countryside, she sailed to the Continent and ended up in Italy, where she traveled through Umbria and Tuscany—the old haunts of St. Francis of Assisi. She immersed herself in the life of St. Francis and also of St. Catherine of Siena, the fourteenth-century Dominican mystic and theologian who was bold enough to admonish not one but two popes.

In the years after returning to Wellesley in 1903, she published *A Listener in Babel* (a thinly veiled autobiographical novel); edited a volume of Catherine of Siena's letters; wrote a historical novel, *The Disciple of a Saint* (1907), about one of Catherine's followers; and completed *Socialism and Character*. These books contain the lineaments of a political imagination rooted in sacramental mysticism, one that blended socialist and artisanal elements in a metaphysics of "real life."[50]

Like James, Scudder underlined the fundamentally ontological confidence of medieval saints. Francis and Catherine, for instance, displayed an abundance of faith in the nature of reality; the earth, for medieval saints, was an "image or sacrament of the Unseen." For both the renegade from mercantile wealth and the coarse, barely literate young firebrand, trust in the love of God was more indicative of wisdom than pecuniary reason or academic erudition. Frail, troubled, and often disillusioned, Catherine never capitulated to fatigue or despair because of her "absolute perception of the Love of God as the supreme reality of the universe." Mysticism was not mystification; it was what James would have called a "passionate vision"; it was Carlyle's "wonder," a receptivity to the infinite of far greater grandeur than any moral regimen.[51]

Scudder insisted that saintliness was not archaic, naive, or sanctimonious. Precisely because they spoke from a plenitude of love, Catherine and Francis saw no need for the moral austerity imposed by any alleged political necessity. "The saintly voice . . . is more living than our own," Scudder surmised, because it can pierce, without calculation, to the heart of any matter. Saints were not icons of credulity; Scudder maintained that Catherine's letters—addressed to prisoners, nobles, merchants, lawyers, soldiers, monarchs, and prelates—revealed a very keen, even savvy wisdom about the ways of the fallen world. Saints knew that ordinary people—including themselves—were sinful, and they expected nothing more. Infirmity and blemish were our fallen condition; but rather than exhort their fellow creatures to impossible feats of moral achievement, saints knew that holiness lay more in desire than in some fraudulent possession of moral stature. "Holy Desire" was the "true key to her personality," Scudder wrote of Catherine. Echoing the Ruskin of *The Stones of Venice*, Scudder even quoted the saint on the divine disregard of imperfection: "Care not to present an unfinished work to God Who is

Infinite Love and demands from thee only infinite desire."[52] Longing, not achievement, was the essence of sanctity.

Only in the light of "holy desire" does Scudder's praise for *poverty* make any sense. To be sure, Toynbee Hall and Denison House had disabused her of any illusions about the ennobling effects of destitution. As a socialist, Scudder hoped for the abolition of poverty through expansion of production and redistribution of wealth; yet as a student of mysticism and saintliness, she felt obliged to affirm the ideal of poverty. Without calling on her comrades and the proletariat to embrace the Franciscan life of voluntary penury, Scudder went a remarkable distance in lauding the virtues of dispossession. "Poverty in itself is neither good nor bad," she wrote in *Socialism and Character*—an egregious heresy against the liberal and socialist versions of the progressive creed. The "bad" side of poverty was misery, fear, powerlessness, and indignity; the "good" side—if freely chosen and shared—was freedom, generosity, and joy.[53] As Scudder, like James, understood, poverty could only be *defended* in terms of its richness in spiritual benefits, its capacity to enlarge and liberate the soul into the image and likeness of God.

St. Francis was the icon of this blissful freedom from money and personal property, and in *Socialism and Character*, Scudder dwelled at some length on Francis, intimating a subtle and powerful challenge both to the Protestant capitalist ethic and to the socialist gospel of wealth. In her view, Francis's "cult of poverty sprang from no ascetic distrust of natural good, but from a passionate recognition that only the meek possess the earth"— "meekness" understood as "holy desire" and the humility and gentleness it engendered, and "possession of the earth" understood as the common inheritance from a heavenly father. When Scudder observed that "no condition could possibly be more inimical . . . to the ideal of the Beatitudes than that of the modern wage-earner," she did not mean that improvement of living conditions or control over the means of production would enhance the virtue or holiness of the workers. Jesus and Francis urged their listeners to consider the lilies and take no thought for the morrow; the poor are "harassed by ceaseless care," driven by competition and beguiled by the emulative futility idealized in advertising. Christian poverty enabled a giving of self, an expenditure of personal gifts; capitalist life compelled both capitalists and workers to cry forever "More!" Poverty for the sake of "holy desire" conferred peace, patience, vigor, even ecstasy; modern poverty induced bitterness, envy, fatigue, and endless, useless toil.[54]

As Scudder realized, Francis represented a challenge to the modern association of freedom with material wealth. To the liberal tradition from Hobbes and Locke, possessive individualism both generated prosperity and ensured political freedom; private property erected the boundary lines that constituted the architecture of bourgeois liberty. In the Marxist tradition, the realm of freedom rested on the collective conquest of the realm of necessity; the abolition of class would unleash the technological instruments of liberation. In the Franciscan imagination, possessions were obstructions of the beatific vision, baggage that weighed us down on the road to heaven. The way of St. Francis entailed the rejection of vexing, burdensome riches—and hence of the disciplined frenzy to produce them. Fewer personal possessions would mean, not worry and pain, but a richer, more relaxed, more pleasurable life. Thus, Franciscan poverty cheerfully confounded the utopian vision of the emerging culture of Fordism. Against the strenuous life of production and consumption, it posed the grace of idleness, the delight of being without justification through work and productivity.

Scudder's reclamation of the Franciscan ideal pointed toward a gift economy. If the triune God was the original giver, then creation itself was a gift; if poverty was a lack of private possessions and a state of uninhibited giving, it was quite compatible with joyful work and a plenitude of material goods. The affinities among the Franciscan way, anarchism, and the artisanal ideal were not lost on Scudder: she characterized Francis and his band of brothers as "heavenly anarchists," and mused that anarchists may "read to a greater depth . . . the ultimate hope in the Mind of Jesus." She conceded that Christ's injunction to perfection—followed with exemplary inattention to the laws of the State by saints like Francis—beckoned toward a world without the governmental machinery of repression and violence. At the same time, with its affirmation of "life" as unbounded charity, her account of Franciscan poverty made it seem like the practice of Ruskin's maxim that "there is no Wealth but Life." Try as she might, Scudder could never dispel the charms of the author of *Unto This Last*. Even long after her conversion to socialism, Scudder never repudiated what she had written of craft in the early 1890s: "really artistic or beautiful objects can only result from the personal impress of the worker on his work." Alluding to the Arts and Crafts movement,

Scudder lauded their "healthy return to sound principles of workmanship, and simple and graceful conditions of life."[55]

Well aware that her homage to poverty would sound appalling—coming as it did from an academic still snugly nestled in a "plethora of privilege"—Scudder held her own ideal at arm's length, mocking the hypocrisy of progressives like herself but also undermining her saintly paragon. In an uncharacteristically sardonic passage, Scudder derided the modern compromise with Lady Poverty. "We live in sensible times," she wrote archly in *Socialism and Character;* even the most fiery and incandescent ideals "must be softened to pleasant domestic warmth." Unlike Francis, we woo, not Lady Poverty, but her "tame little sister, The Simple Life." This nicely echoed James and his scorn for the "trashiness of fiber" among the middle classes; yet Scudder herself conceded, in the end, that "there is something to be said for the worldly point of view."[56] Mechanization and science made a world of plenty unimaginable in Francis's time, and bureaucratic administration was more timely and efficient than personal performance of charity. So, to Scudder and her comrades, the Franciscan way appeared not so much impossible as irrelevant in the modern world.

Scudder never quite repressed the alternative radicalism that lurked in her Franciscan reveries, and it surfaced in *A Listener in Babel.* Set near the end of the nineteenth century, the novel is a fictional portrayal of Scudder's life as a young academic and settlement worker. Hilda Lathrop, an idealistic young artist and college student, feels "enclosed . . . in clique and class prejudice," and seeks "vital intercourse with those most alien and remote." Yet while much of the narrative relates episodes from Wellesley and Denison House, Hilda is also a portrait of Scudder as she thought she might have been.[57] If Hilda is Scudder as Franciscan radical, then the unlived life is worth examining; *A Listener in Babel* is the story of a soul who longs for the riches of poverty.

Like her creator, Hilda yearns to escape from her bourgeois captivity. She joins Langley House, an urban settlement in "Brenton," where Hilda and other idealists believe in the promise of American life. But instead of experiencing "life," Hilda feels a growing disaffection; her service to the poor seems unavailing, and her friends grow increasingly exasperated with the resignation of the working class. The colloquies at Langley, once intense and absorbing, now strike her as sterile babble. Even her faith in American democracy wanes, as Hilda now sees venality and plutocracy draped in patriotic splendor. Democracy was her "religion"; "I trusted it was liberating love: it is liberating greed." Assumed as a way into the excitement of real life, "the philanthropic attitude became more and more abhorrent."[58]

Confused, despairing, but unwilling to return to the incarceration of bourgeois comfort, Hilda accompanies a friend to an Episcopal monastery outside the city—much like Huntington's Holy Cross Monastery, it appears to have "escaped our restive imprisonment in time." Wandering into a chapel, she meets Father Phillips—a fictional persona for Father Huntington, "a man much at odds with his generation, yet modern in his very fibre." Unable to resist the strange allure of piety, she calls on Father Phillips and lays bare her anguish. Warning Hilda that "my answers are all very old-fashioned," Phillips explains that the desire of the heart is the light of the eyes. "We live in the light of a great though tremulous expectation," he says; if "the Holy City ever dwells on earth, it will be a visualized prayer." Prayer offers more than consolation and petition; it unites us with the longings of the past and with the power that enlivens and envelops the cosmos. "The prayers of the ages, slowly gathering, liberate a mighty force," he tells her; "it moves secretly, it moves slowly, but it moves surely." There is no dialectical or unilinear path to the cooperative commonwealth; Phillips has no faith in "the sweep of history" or in that "pleasant, good-natured belief" called progress. When Hilda asks if he really believes that what he desires will ever appear, Phillips answers only, "I do not know." "You cannot know," he tells Hilda; "but you can direct your stumbling steps thither"—via "the path of love, of voluntary poverty." Even though we will never vanquish evil, Phillips admonishes Hilda to remain steadfast in the struggle, not out of desire for political supremacy but out of loyalty to the power at the core of creation: "at the heart of the universe may be Love."[59] Like Scudder the socialist, Phillips grounds political action in traditional theology; like Scudder the Franciscan, he renounces illusions about progress and affirms a faith in the way of dispossession.

Rejuvenated by Phillips's "old-fashioned" answers, Hilda decides to leave Langley House and join the workers' movement—though as a peculiarly artisanal variety of socialist, redolent of Ruskin, Morris, and the American Arts and Crafts communities. "I am an artist," she declares, and commits herself to study "the possible field for handicraft in modern industry." In embracing the life of the working class, Hilda embarks on the path of poverty;

but as she tells her skeptical friends, her dedication to reviving the arts and crafts arises from a newfound faith in the heart of the universe. "Pouring forth her words with joyous energy," Hilda espouses an eschatology of hope that echoes Phillips's reverie in the monastery. We may never live to see our hope accomplished, she muses, but

> All through this strange, sad civilization of ours I feel forces at play making for social salvation—organic filaments weaving the new society to be. Weaving goes on silently and slowly; often the threads bewilder us, crossing and tangling; all the weavers guess at the design, none sees it yet.

The novel ends (all too neatly) with Hilda and her friends anticipating the glorious commonwealth on the horizon. "A new century will soon dawn," as one of them exclaims with breathless millennial enthusiasm.[60]

We live in the wake of that century, and the beloved commonwealth that Scudder desired seems as distant and ethereal as ever. The prayers of the ages indeed gather slowly; the force they liberate is surely bewildering and, it seems, anything but mighty. If Scudder's mysticism and veneration of St. Francis hold any lessons for opponents of Mammon, they lie in how to endure and draw renewal, even joy, from the experience of defeat. Rooted in a metaphysics of love, the prayerful, saintly ideal engenders greatness of soul in times of calamity, assuring in the face of disappointment that our desires accord with the grain of the universe. Against the promethean delusion of total dominion over nature and history, it sets the diminutive realism of finitude, weakness, and humility. Against the liberal paranoia of freedom and security procurable by acquisition and property, it sets the realism of our radical insecurity and the folly of any effort to insulate ourselves from pain, sorrow, senescence, and death. It prefers wisdom to theory, mercy to retribution, and the fidelity of a losing witness to a specious triumph purchased with violence. When defeated, it rejoices in the knowledge of a truth that will eventually forgive and transcend all falsehood. The way, not of the Dynamo, but of St. Francis and the Virgin.

# PART FIVE

## *The Heavenly City of Fordism: Enchantment in the Machine Age, 1920–1945*

SPEAKING TO FELLOW AMHERST alumni in February 1916, Calvin Coolidge, then the lieutenant governor of Massachusetts, mused that "the man who builds a factory, builds a temple, and the man who works there, worships there." Nine years later, as president, Coolidge enlarged the scope of his benediction. "The chief business of the American people is business," he told the American Society of Newspaper Editors in January 1925. Coolidge's remarks were typical mites of proprietary-Protestant divinity, pithy declarations of American reverence for property and its possessors. But even as Coolidge was delivering his homilies, the moral economy he invoked was under assault from corporate capital. The emergence of the modern corporation—a person, but not a human being; a legal fiction, not a factory—had demolished the moral and metaphysical foundations of the Protestant capitalist covenant. Like the six-day creation in Genesis, the economy described in the ancestral theology looked more and more like a fable. Fusing the roles of owner, manager, and artisan, the character enshrined in the Protestant firmament was becoming as archaic as Adam. The disjunction between Coolidge's sermons and the world led Walter Lippmann to write that Coolidge represented a "Puritanism *de luxe*," praising the "classical virtues" of thrift and simplicity "while continuing to enjoy all the modern conveniences."[1]

Presiding over his own temples—especially the River Rouge plant in Dearborn, Michigan, a Luxor of industrial capitalism—Henry Ford employed thousands of wage-worshippers in his mechanized holy of holies. Already revered as a tinkering titan, Ford became an amateur theologian in the late 1920s. Unimpressed with the moral and spiritual performance of organized religion, Ford proposed a model change. In his sacred labyrinth of assembly lines, Ford saw the body of a savior more effective than the exhausted corpus of Christendom. Machinery is "the New Messiah," he wrote in 1928, "accomplishing in the world what man has failed to do by preaching, propaganda, or the written word."[2] If Henry Adams had stood in fear and trembling at the sight of the Westinghouse dynamo, Ford glimpsed a mass-produced redemption more certain than those promised in Christian eschatology. To Ford, the industrial world comprised a surrogate regime of the sacred, an enchanted realm in which human inventions were the angels, principalities, and powers.

Ford's hosanna to technology was echoed by others. In the fall of 1927, before he published his messianic insights, Ford had commissioned the painter and photographer Charles Sheeler to create a montage of the River Rouge temple complex. For six weeks, Sheeler wandered like a pilgrim through the furnaces, conveyors, and coal bunkers of the sanctuary, and he quickly produced a classic portfolio in the iconography of industrial power. Appearing in the February 1928 issue of *Vanity Fair*, Sheeler's photographic essay made a Virgin of Adams's Dynamo: bereft of almost any human beings, the temple machinery was innocent of toil, impregnable by injustice, unsullied by lust for power or profit. The caption to the most famous photo, "Criss-Crossed Conveyors," paraphrased Matthew 7:16—"By Their Works Ye Shall Know Them"—while the copy praised Ford himself as "an almost divine Master-Mind," and dubbed his mechanized tabernacle "America's Mecca." The River Rouge plant, *Vanity Fair* proclaimed, was an "American altar of the God-Objective of Mass Production, an architectural symbol that defines America just as the Pyramids defined Egyptian civilization." (A year later, Eugene O'Neill, in *Dynamo*, would call the dynamo "the Divine Image on Earth," "the Great Mother of Eternal Life, Electricity." "Her power houses," O'Neill added, "are the new churches.") Two years later, Sheeler reflected on the spiritual meaning of industrial architecture. With the River Rouge plant undoubtedly in mind, Sheeler made the case for the factory as temple. "In a period such as ours when only a comparatively few individuals seem to be given to religion . . . our factories are our substitutes for religious expression."[3]

Sheeler's friend, the photographer Paul Strand, was no less rapturous about mechanization. Photographing parts of his own Akeley motion picture camera in 1922, Strand turned the device into a miniature River Rouge, exploring the iconic potential of technology on a more diminutive scale. The photos, along with Strand's remarks, appeared in *Broom,* a small magazine published by Harold Loeb, later a leader of the "Technocracy" movement. Accompanied by portraits of drills, lathes, and other machines, the photos composed a sacramental collage affording access to a new divinity. Like Sheeler, Strand explained his photos in religious terms, but with more theological panache. "The deeper significance of a machine, the camera, has emerged here in America, the supreme altar of the new God." That new God, Strand continued, had been constructed by man, who in forging the means of production had "consummated a new creative act, a new Trinity: God the Machine, Materialistic Empiricism the Son, and Science the Holy Ghost." Yet Strand also hinted at the peril that lurked in these modern industrial deities. "Not only the new God but the whole Trinity must be humanized unless it in turn dehumanizes us."[4]

John Dewey shared Strand's hope for the spirit in the age of mechanization. The urgent assignment for Americans, he wrote shortly after the start of the Depression, was "turning a machine age into a significantly new habit of mind and sentiment." Echoing the Progressive religiosity of Herbert Croly, Lippmann, and Josiah Royce, Dewey perceived a nascent spiritual culture developing in the industrial era. The technical and organizational necessities of a machine age were promoting a "mental and moral corporateness," a vivid and expansive sense of interdependence in work, education, entertainment, and sport. Dewey candidly acknowledged that "corporate society was as yet an epoch . . . lacking in solid and assured objects of belief and approved ends of action." But to revitalize "the spiritual factor" of the nation's life, Americans needed "a new psychological and moral type" adequate to the demands of "corporateness." A moral imagination as well as a product of technological reason, "corporateness" entailed what Dewey would soon call "a common faith": "allegiance to inclusive ideal ends."[5] Dewey saw a new religion emerging in the midst of industrial modernity, a complex of rituals, temples, and codes in the millennium of mass production.

Thus, to contemporary observers, what historians have understood as the political and moral economy of "Fordism" was also a vast mechanical apparatus of enchantment. As a *political* economy, "Fordism" names both a mode of production and a state formation. The mode of production consisted of product standardization; mechanization, together with a high degree of division of labor that mandated the breaking up of workers' tasks into discrete and measurable routines; the spread of managerial expertise and supervision in the workplace and the market; the concentration of workforce and technology into a single, centralized plant; relatively high wages to ensure the consumption of mass-produced commodities. The state formation included "the New Deal order;" the political alignment of government agencies, organized labor, and sectors of corporate capital; and the "military-industrial complex:" the Cold War coalition of the Pentagon, military contractors, and Sunbelt politicians.[6] The Fordist or New Deal state attempted to temper class conflict, stabilize the business cycle, and promote economic growth, relying primarily on the stimulation of consumption through fiscal policy and military spending.

As a *moral* economy, Fordism complemented a new producer culture suited to mechanized production with a full-fledged "consumer culture." Buffeted by the Great Depression, this consumer culture solved what Warren Susman described as a crisis of "culture and commitment": a search for, in his words, "a special collective relationship in which all Americans might share, a new sense of common belief, ritual observance, and common emotional sharing." That collective relationship becomes, for Roland Marchand, a "Democracy of Goods," a redefinition of democracy as access to material abundance; for Jackson Lears, a "new gospel of therapeutic release," an evangel of self-fulfillment spread by advertisers, public relations specialists, and other experts in the culture industries; for Michael Denning, a "laboring of American culture," the unprecedented visibility of working-class Americans in the imagery of corporate media, through which workers could stake claims on the republic of goods and hear the good news of fulfillment.[7] In all of these guises, the culture of consumption rested on an institutional network of corporate advertising; public relations; consumer credit; and the maturing symbolic industries of film, broadcasting, popular music, and theater.

But if Fordism was a "common belief, ritual observance, and common emotional sharing," it was also a new phase in the corporate assertion of title to capitalist enchantment. Fordism was Dewey's "common faith" of "inclusive, ideal ends"; it was Strand and Sheeler's "supreme altar" for the "new God of Mass Production"; it was Ford's eponymous temple complex for the "New Messiah" of machinery. Despite its appearance of soulless mechanism, the "Machine Age" was the most beatific moment to date in the history of technological sublimity. Corporate leaders and intellectuals recognized that an emerging "business civilization" required a new cosmology and moral imagination that pivoted around the machine. They joined other corporate mandarins as those Thurman Arnold called the spiritual governors of America, exemplified by the publisher Henry Luce and the filmmaker Walt Disney. Management theorists transmuted Taylorism into a philosophy of human relations through which they hoped to master, in Elton Mayo's words, "the human problems of industrial civilization." Meanwhile, advertisers, art directors, and industrial designers imagined a future of streamlined, utopian commodities, whose visual appeal and sensuous texture would enchant the world of mass production. Rapt in the gears of a mechanical charisma, the corporate intelligentsia set out to construct a heavenly city of Fordism.

# 16

# Business Is the Soul of America

## The New Capitalism and the Business Millennium

EVEN AFTER THE TUMULTUOUS reconstruction of American capitalism before World War I, the Protestant-proprietary ethos persisted. Fearful of renewed labor unrest after an upsurge of strikes in 1919, many employers created company-sponsored unions, workers' councils, shop committees, and pension plans. But most workers remained untouched by these reforms, as the prevailing mood in business circles was aggressively anti-union. Akin to the Protestant fundamentalism that blazed across the country in the 1920s, proprietary fundamentalism witnessed a strong and bilious resurgence. The most militant sentiment crystallized in "the American Plan," a crusade to rid industrial workplaces of unions and union agitation by creating open shops. Meanwhile, among numerous Rotary Clubs, in the Chamber of Commerce and the National Association of Manufacturers, and in the pages of *Nation's Business* and other periodicals, the paragon of the assiduous proprietor elicited pugnacious devotion and eloquence. Especially in the wake of the Bolshevik Revolution, businesspeople felt the need to reassert the faith that stood threatened by enemies within and without. "Business," declared Merle Thorpe, editor of *Nation's Business,* "is the soul of America."[1]

Proprietary fundamentalism found voice in various stalwart redoubts: the National Association of Manufacturers; the Chamber of Commerce and its organ, *Nation's Business;* as well as *American Industries,* the *Rotarian, Kiwanis,* and other business and civic periodicals. Lecturing to the clerics in his 1925 presidential address to the National Association of Manufacturers, John E. Edgerton declared that "the Great Ruler of the universe" had decreed the bylaws of business and the hierarchy of classes. Business writers produced a bevy of Decalogues—"Ten Commandments" for numerous industries—to keep owners, workers, and the general public mindful of capital's moral and cosmological legitimacy. The most strident assertion of the old-time gospel was Charles N. Fay's *Business in Politics* (1926), a classic in the canon of business agitprop. A well-known Chicago utilities executive and vice president of the National Association of Manufacturers, Fay was the Billy Sunday of the Rotarian set, an evangelist for free trade, small government, weak unions, and untrammeled business authority. Like Sunday, Fay made up in passion and bluster what he lacked in sophistication. The Bolshevik Revolution, he opined, was "the biggest business failure in history." Bolsheviks, socialists, and liberals refused to abide by those laws of human nature written into their genes by "the Creator." The Creator "seems to have so ordained the world that every man must carry his own weight, and be selfish (or self-supporting) enough to do so." As the system decreed by Providence, "selfish capitalism," Fay humbly intoned, "is absolutely vital to human progress."[2]

Yet Fay's very shrillness suggested that the old proprietary gospel was losing its credibility. As the economic theology of those H. L. Mencken called "the booboisie," proprietary nostrums sounded ever more hollow and alarmist, at least to many of the nation's intellectuals. In his much-discussed reflection on *Our Business Civilization* (1929), James Truslow Adams posed the basic rhetorical question: "Can a great civilization be built up or maintained upon the philosophy of the counting-house?" The assumption that "spiritual and intellectual progress" attended unregulated accumulation had become, Adams lamented, "a sort of American religion with all the psychological implications of religious dogma." Likewise, in Harold Stearns's renowned symposium, *Civilization in the United States* (1922), many contributors dismissed proprietary wisdom as nostalgic and pernicious nonsense. Walton H. Hamilton, Amherst professor of economics and a former member of the War Labor Board, noted that most economists and business editorialists were just "a scant generation or two removed from the country or the small town." Despite the emergence of corporations, most businesspeople inhabited an "Eden of free enterprise" that existed only in their fantasies. Because of the widening chasm between doctrine and reality, the older proprietary creed required "a more rigid and absolute statement." Dimly aware that corporate organization had pushed them out of the Garden, many business leaders remained so adamant that they camouflaged new realities in "the symbolic language of ritual." Humorist and former advertising agent J. Thorne Smith maintained that looking through "the magic portals of the advertising world," Americans beheld a "World That Never Was," an Eden, not of free enterprise, but of "well-regulated bowels, cornless feet, unblemished complexions, and completely equipped kitchens." Atheism was "less of a crime against the tenets of modern American civilization," he wrote, than disbelief in the power of an institution which "can rise up in our midst gods, kings, and other potentates."[3]

Even more acerbic was Sinclair Lewis's *Babbitt* (1922), the period's most memorable and enduring broadside against the bunkum of the boobsoisie. Real-estate broker, Rotarian blowhard, and Presbyterian hypocrite, George F. Babbitt is one of the most blubbering fiends in American fiction, a glad-handing monster of pecuniary reason. Babbitt and his friends blend Christianity and Rotarian twaddle, extolling the evangelist Mike Monday (a painfully obvious reference to Billy Sunday) for "keeping the overhead of spiritual regeneration down to an unprecedented rock-bottom basis." One of the underappreciated features of *Babbitt* is the religious quality Lewis ascribes to business itself. Though Lewis opens the novel with a misty vision of "the towers of Zenith" that are "neither citadels nor churches," by the end of chapter one, Babbitt is staring out his window at the Second National Tower, "a temple spire of the religion of business, a faith passionate, exalted, surpassing common men." Averse to doctrinal disputation but insistent on the virtues of diligence and thrift, Babbitt prefers "a real virile hustling religion," full of "pep and piety." And as Lewis realizes in one of his keenest insights, the God of business is the businessman himself, a harrumphing study in self-deification. In a scene set in the washroom of the Zenith Athletic Club, Lewis describes "a line of men bent over the bowls inset along a prodigious slab of marble as in religious prostration before their own images in the massy mirror."[4]

The proprietary faithful reacted to *Babbitt* with swift and acrimonious pride. "Dare to be a Babbitt!" the editors of *Nation's Business* urged their readers in 1925, retorting that Babbitt was "a kindly soul with an eagerness to work and play with his fellow-men." In a later issue, the magazine featured "Babbitt Ballads" such as this lame rejoinder to Lewis:

Babbitts—though we jeer and flout them—
We could never do without them.

Artists all—we would be beggars
Were it not for Butter'n'Eggers.

Some of Lewis's fellow intellectuals saw the limitations of *Babbitt*. Charles Beard complained that Lewis and Mencken posed as "self-constituted guardians of the higher sophistication." Lippmann—whose admiration for the achievements of corporate enterprise grew steadily after World War I—thought Lewis had created a straw man in George Babbitt, exhibiting "an extraordinary talent for inventing stereotypes." Attacking Lewis's entire corpus of invective, Lippmann retorted that Babbitt was "a creature of the passing moment" whose "taproots have been cut." The Protestant culture to which Babbitt was indebted for his ridiculous economic homilies was dying, Lippmann argued. While *Babbitt* was a clever send-up of provincialism, it did not portray the most potent forces at work in American capitalism, those through which Babbitt and others were "groping to find new ways of life."[5]

One way of "groping to find new ways of life" was undertaken by the adman and journalist Bruce Barton. Son of a Congregationalist minister, Barton helped found, in 1919, Barton, Durstine, and Osborne, which quickly became one of Madison Avenue's most prestigious advertising agencies, attracting lucrative accounts with U.S. Steel, General Motors, General Mills, and General Electric. (When they merged with Samuel Batten's firm in 1928, they became the better-known BBDO.) Like Norman Vincent Peale and Dale Carnegie, Barton has become an emblematic emissary of the therapeutic ethos, reducing Christianity to "positive thinking," the repetition of bromides to guarantee vitality, personal magnetism, and business success. Yet by the same token, Barton was a Protestant pastoral counselor guiding Americans from the proprietary faith to the new corporate dispensation. The story of Jesus that Barton related in *The Man Nobody Knows* (1925) was a tale of passage from artisanal to professional-managerial labor. In the episode where Jesus famously admonishes his mother Mary, "Wist ye not that I must be about my Father's *business?*," Barton describes Joseph's business as a "prosperous carpenter shop." But in the preface, Barton portrays Jesus as a deft executive who "picked up twelve men from the bottom ranks of business and forged them into an organization that conquered the world." Despite Barton's echo of Ford that "all work is worship; all useful service prayer," it was clear that work and service were conceived in managerial and professional terms. Indeed, Barton believed that corporate business was God's indispensable partner in dominion over the planet. "Whoever works wholeheartedly at any worthy calling is a co-worker with the Almighty," Barton swelled, a laborer in "the great enterprise which He has initiated but *which He can never finish without the help of men.*" In short, God needs our help. (As James Rorty—a radical journalist who once worked in Barton's agency—later wrote, Barton had sketched in *The Man Nobody Knows* "the *reductio ad absurdum* of the Protestant Ethic.")[6]

While Barton provided a Protestant idiom for the sanctification of corporate life, others sought a less overtly Christian legitimation for the new world of Fordist capitalism. Not all American intellectuals were as hostile to business as Lewis and other satirists, and their own hopes for a redemptive denouement to corporate modernity surfaced in yet another anthology about the prospects for "civilization": Charles Beard's two-volume panorama, *Whither Mankind* (1928) and *Toward Civilization* (1930). Where Stearns and his colleagues had seen the graveyard of culture in the mass-production factory, Beard perceived "something of cosmic mystery about the creative urge at work in machine civilization." Proclaiming that the machine process was "a great demiurgic movement," Beard contended that the religious significance of machinery was an idea with ample precedent in Christian theology. "In the minds of the highest Christian thinkers," Beard argued, "there has always been a close affiliation, never an antithesis, between spirituality—divine inspiration—and labor with material things." Elsewhere, Beard was even more unrestrained in his confidence. At the conclusion of *The Rise of American Civilization* (1927), he and his wife Mary marveled at the power of industrial technology in "subduing physical things to the empire of the spirit." "It is the dawn, not the dusk, of the gods."[7]

This mechanical enchantment reappeared throughout the two volumes, and especially in *Toward Civilization*—published just a year after the stock market crash. Dewey, writing on "Philosophy" in *Whither Mankind,* rued that machinery had become "the devil of a wide-spread cult." Calling the machine "the authentically embodied *Logos* of modern life," Dewey drew an unmistakable parallel between the instrumental reason in modern technology and the Incarnation of Christ. Michael Pupin, a Columbia University physicist, asserted that, like every medieval cathedral designed and built by men, "every modern machine has a soul . . . the soul of its inventor and of the patient souls of the men who developed it." (In *Romance of The Machine*, published in the same year, Pupin wrote that the machine "is the visible evidence of the close union between man and the spirit of the eternal truth which guides the subtle hand of nature.") In perhaps the most portentous essay—"Power," whose first letter the author capitalized several times—C. F. Hirschfeld, a mechanical engineer and research director for the Detroit Edison Company, declared that machines were "prime movers," the modern equivalents of Aristotle's God. Harnessing and distributing Power, machines were enabling men and women to "practice greater charity." Machine production afforded, for the first time in human history, "a wide-spread, real, and practical recognition of the brotherhood of man . . . a leaven more fruitful of practical results than all the preachings of the ages."[8]

While these engineers and scientists were forging the lineaments of a new technological fetishism, philosopher-executives were creating a credo for the corporate dispensation. Heirs to the "soulful corporation," a vanguard of business leaders worked zealously to enshrine corporate liberalism as the orthodoxy of American capitalism. The new corporate moral economy arose from a new breed of "industrial statesmen," as the business press anointed them: among others, Owen D. Young (General Electric, RCA); Gerard Swope (GE); Walter Teagle (Standard Oil); Walter S. Gifford (AT&T); Myron Taylor (U.S. Steel); and Edward A. Filene, the renowned mass merchandiser. The industrial statesmen of the 1920s were the point men of the "New Capitalism": the reorientation of the capitalist economy toward consumption through higher wages, the introduction of corporate-sponsored benefit plans, and the cultivation of more harmonious relations between corporate capital and labor. A constellation of business practice, social thought, and exalted aspiration, the New Capitalism foreshadowed the managerial economy of the Cold War era.[9]

As the leading organ of corporate liberalism in the 1920s, *Forbes* led the business press in advertising the New Capitalism. Just after the Armistice in 1918, *Forbes* forecast that "business hereafter will be conducted on a higher plane." The postwar era promised a "reformation and rebirth in the business world," a new era in which capitalists "set a new value upon the things of the spirit." Ten years later, pointing to the adoption of new business practices in many industries—pension plans, disability insurance, and profit-sharing—*Forbes* celebrated the enlightened corporate titans who had performed their "solemn responsibility" to employees and the wider public. But *Forbes* was not alone in championing the New Capitalism. In the spring of 1924, the Chamber of Commerce issued a statement of its "Principles of Business Conduct," which, when promulgated later in *Nation's Business,* assumed Mosaic status as "The Fifteen Commandments of Business." Once a conclave of proprietary dogma, the Chamber was slowly opening its doors to the forces of heterodoxy. "We are acquiring a new industrial philosophy," one of its directors avowed proudly in 1929. By the late 1930s, with its conversion to a modified form of Keynesian economics, the Chamber had almost fully embraced corporate liberalism.[10]

At their most flamboyant, industrial statesmen and the business intelligentsia saw the New Capitalism as the consummation of history. Indeed, the extravagance of business rhetoric in the 1920s would be unmatched until the 1990s, when similar and even more fulsome palaver would inflate yet another "New Economy." Like its woolly-headed descendent, New Capitalist fustian identified the new business era with the triumph of economic democracy. As Secretary of Commerce Herbert Hoover wrote in *Nation's Business* in 1924, the epoch of corporate enlightenment heralded an "industrial democracy" in which workers became capitalists with their higher wages and shareholding plans. But clerics for the New Capitalism saw more transcendent achievements in the enlightenment of corporate business. Chamber of Commerce President Richard F. Grant reflected in *Nation's Business* in 1925 that "business does not exist for itself alone." Rather, promoting "spiritual development," corporate leaders should "inspire men to give the best that is in them for the common good." Haley Fiske, president of Metropolitan Life, told readers in 1927 that in "the new business era" the exemplary executive was "serving God to serve well his fellow men." For many, this brand of selfless capitalism augured the arrival of a classless society. Benjamin Javits and Charles Wood, authors of *Make Everybody Rich* (1929), maintained that the new business dispensation ensured that, soon, "the rule of class will for the first time in human history utterly disappear."[11]

Anointed as the vanguard of history, the new breed of executives was also recast as a modern School of Athens. Once derided as philistines, corporate leaders became, in the 1920s, Platonic sages and utopian visionaries. As syndicated columnist E. W. Howe wrote in *Nation's Business* in 1921, the wisdom of businessmen is "the truest, fairest, and most important." "Business men," he reassured his readers, exhibit "better ability and philosophy, and are more useful than writers, soap box orators, politicians and statesmen." "Commerce leads the way," one journalist declaimed in the *Forum* in 1922, "and all arts, all professions, all culture follow." In a 1924 issue of *World's Work*, Edward W. Bok, editor of *Ladies' Home Journal* and a prominent spokesperson for business reform, hailed "the American business man of discernment, of vision, and of ideals." One writer for *World's Work* praised Alfred P. Sloan, Jr., president of General Motors, for blending "the man of action and the philosopher." Indeed, "in real wisdom," the publisher and journalist William Feather wrote in 1927, "the intelligent business man has far outdistanced the theoretic philosopher." According to Charles Mitchell, president of the National City Bank of New York, the benevolent and profitable industrial practices of corporate statesmen were "bringing to a nearer realization the dreams of Utopians."[12]

One of the most illustrious summits of industrial statesmen was the symposium convened in the spring of 1929 by J. George Frederick, managing editor of *Printer's Ink*. Already renowned as the sage of "progressive obsolescence"—the ancestor of "planned obsolescence"—Frederick edited a two-volume collection of papers by businessmen, *A Philosophy of Production* (1929–1930), an epistolary of the New Capitalism. Frederick assembled a synod of corporate prelates: Taylor, Young, Earnest Elmo Calkins of the advertising firm Calkins and Holden, and Walter Gifford of AT&T, among others. Invoking a cavalcade of "great thinkers" from Aristotle to Filene, Frederick contended that, especially in the midst of the deepening Depression, modern capitalism prompted "new questions of destiny and meaning." Fearful of class conflict and state intervention, Frederick called for "a new humanism" in industry, a beloved community of workers, managers, professionals, and stockholders suffused by "the ideality of the human spirit" throughout "our vast mechanism of production." Capitalists needed to jettison the "economic wisdom of the centuries," Calkins wrote, and attend to people and their souls as well as to productivity and profits. Henry P. Kendall, president of the Kendall Corporation (a conglomerate of manufacturing and service companies), conveyed the temper of the gathering with a blend of sanctimony, boosterism, and technocratic scrupulosity. The true executive, Kendall mused, lived "in the realm of the spirit," a "humanistic spirit" leavened by a "passion for precision and excellence."[13]

At their best, contributors contended, the upper echelons of the corporate hierarchy aimed to supply more than cheaper goods and services. Dedicated to the spiritual as well as the material well-being of the American people, "our ultimate objectives," Kendall concluded, "are found in the intangible, rather than the tangible realm." Young was more sardonic but in his way no less resplendent in his estimation of corporate modernity. The intellectual and spiritual traditions of the past had been superseded, in his view, by the intelligence cultivated in the everyday lives of citizens in a mass-production age. Scholastic philosophy may have been "an interesting pastime" for monks, he snorted, but it couldn't compare to the thrill of "a cross-word puzzle today." In Young's view, the shelves of technical and scientific literature held the scriptures of redemption for the age of machinery. When the medieval priesthood asked how people would be saved without churches or sacramental rituals, "we can look back and see the answer."[14]

Filene and Calkins were the most visionary and grandiloquent of all the philosopher-businessmen. Both believed that mass production augured a glorious new stage in human history—a "business millennium" as Calkins put it with eschatological flair. Made possible by technology and a shorter workday, material abundance and ample free time gave Americans the opportunity, in Filene's words, to "partake of the life which the artists and poets and preachers are forever talking about." As pioneers and settlers in the paradise of mass production, corporate managers and professionals were the avant-garde of human possibility, pointing the way to the final demolition of all obstacles to fulfillment. Advertisers, Calkins asserted, possessed some of "the best brains in the world," eager and able to take on "not the mere problems of production and distribution, but the greater problem of humanity, of civilization."[15]

Grandiose as all this seemed, neither Filene nor Calkins was ever quite sure about the motives behind these millennial prospects. Filene could write, in *Successful Living in This Machine Age* (1931), that corporate business was developing "a more inclusive loyalty, a sense of the oneness of all humanity" while asserting that the new capitalism had simply discovered that "it pays to give service." Calkins was equally ambiguous, if also more florid. As the epigraph for *Business the Civilizer* (1928)—a mostly light-hearted potpourri of anecdotes, business advice, advertising tips, and prognostication—Calkins chose Emerson's wry dictum from *Works and Days:* "The greatest meliorator of the world is selfish, huckstering trade." In that spirit, Calkins wrote that beauty is a "new business tool," implying that visual or sensuous delight was yet another mercenary ruse, a cold calculation of the marginal utility to capital provided by radiance. Yet elsewhere, Calkins appeared to set aside the implacable ledgers of pecuniary reason, waxing romantically medieval about the spiritual adventure of modern capitalism. Through its sponsorship of science and technology, the corporation offered to its most skilled employees "the glory that in the past was given to the crusader, the soldier, the courtier, the explorer, and the martyr." Indeed, the finest executives and professionals toiled, not for the money, Calkins thought, but because "there are no longer any long, slimy, green dragons holding captive maidens in durance vile, no holy sepulchers to be reft from the infidel, no Pacifics to be viewed for the first time." Corporate enterprise was our epoch's "Field of Gold," Calkins rhapsodized, the modern venue for faith, conquest, and heroism.[16]

If corporate enterprise was the modern surrogate for knightly heroism and saintly devotion, corporate society was also the heir to the aspirations of religious tradition. Like Walter Lippmann, Filene and Calkins agreed that the "business millennium" marked an unprecedented form of religious life. "The right and power to buy must lead to a great new religious awakening," Filene proclaimed, "a religious experience such as humanity has never had an opportunity to know before." Mass production and consumption enabled what he called "humancraft," an "emancipation of the very soul of man" from the privations and terrors of scarcity. Sounding much like Dewey on "corporateness" and "common faith," Filene rejoiced that, free from dogmas and irrational restrictions, the religious culture of a mass-production society would be "a seven-day religion" of "constant, creative participation in human life." Calkins was even more audacious in his vision of corporate enchantment. Angered by charges that business was a sinful and unworthy pursuit, Calkins regaled Fredericks's symposium with tales of Italian and Dutch merchants who, ashamed of their wealth, commissioned religious art "to square things with Heaven." There was nothing to square, Calkins asserted; businesspeople were as capable of artistic patronage and moral discernment as the churchmen and traders of an earlier age. Like Ford, Calkins was impatient with the earthly corruption and ineptitude of traditional religion, and he ended *Business the Civilizer* with a daring assertion of corporate moral and sacral ambition. "That eternal job of administering this planet must be turned over to the business man. The work that religion and government have failed in must be done by business."[17] In Calkins's beatific vision, advertisers, managers, and other professionals were the clerics of the corporate millennium.

Frederick echoed Calkins's audacious claim on the moral imagination, concluding the *Philosophy of Production* symposium with a brash insouciance toward religious conceptions of the afterlife. In the past, he reflected, material privation and bodily suffering had been "alleviated only by a (now declining) trust in a heavenly Utopia." Burdened and stupefied by "too much theology," humanity had labored under the "philosophic snobbery" of clergy, academics, and other masters of asceticism. The new and growing desires for material goods will seem sinful to these elitists "without insight," he wrote, but others will see the "sprouting of a great harvest." Indeed, future historians would note that, in the twentieth century, "the common man was raised to the tenderly elect of the gods." Because of the productivity of our "vast mechanism of production," more Americans were "untroubledly sure ... that supernaturalism is unimportant, even if we willfully retain a vestige of mysticism." Fulfilled on earth by rewarding labor in the apparatus of soulful production, "homo Americanus" could "partake of an exhilarating feeling of co-creation with God." The new corporate humanism demolished class walls, leapt over ivory towers, and transcended all national and religious boundaries. Even if a ruling class remains, it is "a spiritual aristocracy," Frederick explained, a breed of virtuosi adept in the techniques of leadership toward "the good life."[18] For Frederick—as for other scholastics in the corporate clerisy—the commencement of the business millennium augured a heavenly city of Fordism.

One remarkable testimonial to Frederick's brand of assurance came from Edward Sandford Martin—a founder of *Harvard Lampoon* and the original *Life,* and a popular humorist known for his wry conservative moralism. In the February 1925 issue of *Harper's,* Martin asked "Shall Business Run the World?" and answered in an utterly ingenuous affirmative. "The world is becoming spiritualized," he marveled, and business was the spirit's leading sacramental vessel. Arks of the soul of America, these "ecclesiastical corporations" were "material combinations for spirit to work through," providing a "link between the visible and invisible worlds." Indeed, they had "touched the hem of Christ's garment and felt the virtue that comes out of him." Though employing a more Christian idiom, Martin echoed Calkins's annunciation of business' panoptic and irrefutable sovereignty. "If Business is to manage the world," Martin asserted, "it must be Big Business: very big, indeed—comprehending all things."[19] The expansive enchantment of corporations augured the grand finale of human history.

# 17

# The American Century
# and the Magic Kingdom

## Mythologies of the Machine Age

TO BE SURE, heralds of a "business millennium" served very immediate political purposes between the world wars, especially after the stock market crash of 1929 threatened to discredit the corporate dispensation. Bestowing the imprimatur of inevitability on the existing social order, they obscured or invalidated challengers: what remained of the movement for industrial democracy, Bolshevism, the Soviet experiment, and close collaborations between the state and corporate capital such as "corporatism" or "fascism." But the business millennium was politically useful only to the extent that it was effective as a *myth:* a tale that purported to explain and justify an entire social order. Interest in the political uses of myth was pervasive among American intellectuals in the 1930s: from literary theorist Kenneth Burke and theologian Reinhold Niebuhr to political scientist Harold Lasswell and anthropologist Ruth Benedict, the study and affirmation of myth pointed to a recognition of the need, to recall Warren Susman's phrase, for "common belief, ritual observance, and common emotional sharing."[1] As myths require mythmakers—fabulists adept in the arts of summoning belief, crafting rituals, and eliciting emotion—the fabrication of business hegemony called for a new breed of theologians, artists, and bards. Three figures offer case studies from the pinnacle of the Fordist corporate dispensation: Thurman Arnold, Henry Luce, and Walt Disney.

Often celebrated (or vilified) as one of the most urbane satirists in the history of American social criticism, Arnold was also one of the keenest students of American economic theology. A lawyer and professor at Yale Law School before he took over the Justice Department's antitrust division in 1938, Arnold penned two books—*The Symbols of Government* (1935) and *The Folklore of Capitalism* (1937)—that contained a sardonic analysis of the

American business creed. As resistance to the New Deal persisted and mounted in the mid- and late 1930s, "mythology" impressed Arnold as one of the ineradicable conditions of social life, and he traced the difficulties of his predecessors to their ineptitude, not as planners, but as mythmakers and theologians. Cheerfully cynical about the sorcery he studied, Arnold was an anthropologist of capitalist enchantment and a herald of a new iconography. "The true faith is Capitalism," he stated in *Folklore,* and "its priests are lawyers and economists."[2]

Arnold's praise for elite dissimulation arose in part from his impatience with the Supreme Court's hostility to the New Deal. (Before he entered the Justice Department, he had supported FDR's Court-packing scheme.) He was especially infuriated by the Court's demolition of the National Recovery Administration, as it represented a quintessential example of how, to use Arnold's terms, "theological" and "metaphysical" thinking had trumped science and empiricism. Belief in free markets and unfettered private property struck Arnold as "pure mystical idealism," given the realities of modern economic life and the urgency of ending the Depression. In particular, the "mythology of private property" inscribed in the Court's decisions obscured the fact that corporations were clearly not private enterprises in any meaningful sense. More brashly than Adolph Berle, Jr., and Gardiner Means—whose study *The Modern Corporation and Private Property* (1932) described for economists the separation of ownership and management—Arnold argued that proprietary mythology was as ridiculous and harmful as "medieval myths which impeded medical knowledge." Disillusioned as well as impoverished by the Depression, Americans needed a moral economy that offered "the mystery, the romance and magic" that once informed the proprietary culture. Corporate liberals required, not only expertise, competence, and programs, but also symbols, talismans, and fables of sin and redemption. Since "social institutions require faiths and dreams to give them morale," Arnold wrote in *The Symbols of Government,* would-be reformers must become adept in the arts once practiced by shamans, priests, and artists.[3]

According to Arnold's general theory of enchantment, all societies have two governments: a "spiritual government" presiding over symbols, ideals, "mythology," and "magic," and a "temporal government" supervising the daily business of production and politics. No society survives without spiritual governors: indeed, Arnold asserted, "there is no evidence that the human race is going to . . . get along without a priesthood, whether it be religious, civil, or economic." In times of stability, the spiritual and temporal governments align in tranquility: the "magic words" crafted in the spiritual order appear to describe the material and organizational realities mastered in the temporal realm. Crises occur when a conflict arises between the verbal and visual enchantment of the priesthood and the realities of the temporal world. At first, when the conflict between "magic words and reality" becomes so clear that the formulas begin to lose their effect, institutions rally to revitalize their charm. Until the Depression, for instance, the mere pronouncement of "'thrift' or 'the law of supply and demand'" seemed sufficient to "make the evil spirits disappear." Thus, when economists and the Supreme Court vilified the early New Deal reforms, the "priestly portals" were merely providing "order when the magic words were losing their magic." But with the events of the 1930s, the discrepancy between the economic theology and the economic reality had now grown so vast that the proprietary sorcery had finally lost its power. The myths of the spiritual governors had been belied by the temporal realm.[4]

Changes in the clerisy and its sacral language were often prolonged and arduous, but eventually they culminated in a new board of spiritual directors with a new religious vernacular. In American economic theology, the hallowed verities of the nineteenth century—the Protestant ethic, small-scale property, thrift, and self-restraint—were now quaint and harmful illusions that obstructed a view of the real world: technological innovation, large-scale enterprise, and the need for ever-expanding consumption. Any emerging spiritual government had two historical assignments: de-mythologize the obsolescent order and equip the new one with an efficacious enchantment. In addition to requiring new temporal arrangements, corporate capitalism also needed a new mythology and spiritual government.

Arnold urged New Deal liberals and regulatory bureaucrats to gracefully euthanize the old spiritual government. Since proprietary mythology and magic retained so tenacious a hold on the American imagination, Arnold advised the rising "spiritual government"—the "new class"—against openly renouncing accepted doctrine, a course so abrupt it might disenchant the flock and trigger revolutionary upheaval. Instead, they should subtly add new features, however contradictory, and mystify away the anomalies. When administrators staffed or regulated corporations, for instance, *they* had to know that corporate personhood was an enchanting fiction. When they addressed the less theologically learned, they had to employ proprietary language. Sharing with Lippmann and H. L. Mencken a wan contempt for democracy, Arnold underscored his lack of faith in popular rationality by suggesting that "from a humanitarian point of view," the best form of government was "that which we find in an insane asylum." Doctors do not instruct or argue with the inmates about their delusions; rather they make them "as comfortable as possible, regardless of their respective moral deserts."[5] The lesson for the "new class" was clear: since the masses can't handle too much reality, keep them spellbound with empty incantations.

Critics of Arnold such as Christopher Lasch have been so put off by this cynicism that they find it hard to give the devil his due. To Lasch, Arnold exemplified the condescending expert, disdainful of popular wisdom and subtly dangerous to democracy. With his bemused contempt for common people, Arnold represents, in this view, a new, more technocratic form of liberalism that relied less on republican virtue and more on professional virtuosity.[6] But those who share Lasch's populist umbrage must explain the persistence of popular enchantment in the face of a system so exploitative. By remaining sardonically detached from the customs of the natives and the idols of the tribe, Arnold was able to account for the tenacity of business power in a way that cut deeper than populist grumbling about the malevolence of corporate elites.

Educated at Hotchkiss and Yale, Henry Luce was one of those mandarins straight out of populist melodrama. With his trio of magazines—*Time* (1923), *Fortune* (1930), and *Life* (1936)—Luce held a near-monopoly in the field of high-middlebrow journalism. Derided as a realm of "sophisticated kitsch" by Dwight Macdonald (who wrote for *Fortune* during the 1930s), the Luce empire was a River Rouge complex of the American culture industry, providing general information about political, economic, and cultural affairs for busy upper-middle class readers. Landmarks in the evolution of modern American journalism, the Luce publications were central to the sentimental education of the business elite—and thus indicative of Luce's status as a member of the corporate spiritual government.[7]

Aimed at the professional and managerial ranks, *Fortune* played the leading role in Luce's clerical enterprise. Launched in February 1930 just after the Depression began, *Fortune* quickly displaced *Forbes* as the ideological bellwether of corporate liberalism, a position it held from the 1930s to the 1960s. Fusing business journalism, social thought, and aesthetic modernism, *Fortune* was the most ambitious attempt yet to make the corporate intelligentsia into an American clerisy and avant-garde. *Fortune* stood out from other business periodicals for its motley and illustrious editorial board (Luce, Archibald MacLeish, Ralph Ingersoll, Eric Hodgins, Russell Davenport, and Peter Drucker, among others); its groundbreaking repudiation of boosterism and hagiography; and its reliance on modernist aesthetics in its illustrations, photo essays, and advertisements. *Fortune*'s contributors in reportage, commentary, illustration, and photography formed a gallery of American arts and letters, including Macdonald, James Agee, Walker Evans, Margaret Bourke-White, Diego Rivera, Lewis Mumford, and John Kenneth Galbraith. Although Luce himself was a Republican who backed Wendell Wilkie in 1940, *Fortune* provided a high-profile venue for corporate liberal intellectuals: "industrial statesmen" from the 1920s, such as Gerard Swope, Owen Young, and Walter Teagle, as well as the Business Advisory Council (1933) and the Committee for Economic Development (1944), two leading forums for the reception and dissemination of Keynesian economics.[8]

Luce envisioned *Fortune* as a monthly herald of the business millennium. In the summer of 1929, he circulated a prospectus to potential investors and contributors that sketched out an illustrious business epoch. *Fortune,* Luce promised, would not be just another pedestrian recitation of business news, nor would it churn out puffery about moguls and entrepreneurs. Instead, he assured his readers, *Fortune* would "portray Business in all its heroic present-day proportions" and convey "a sustained sense of the challenging personalities, significant trends, and high excitements of this vastly stirring Civilization of Business." Addressed to "the aristocracy of our human civilization," *Fortune* would reconcile art and commerce, broker a deal between the classes, and conclude an alliance between the warring fiefdoms of Wall Street and Greenwich Village. An ad for the advertising firm of Young & Rubicam captured the splendor of Luce's corporate mythology. "No longer is business a column of figures, or work a daily grind," the ad proclaimed. "Here is epic enterprise, a panorama of romance, adventure, conquest—with beauty in factories and derricks." *Fortune* would provide the icons and tales of corporate business mythology. During the 1930s and 1940s, *Fortune* regularly profiled business leaders who displayed a cosmopolitan sensibility, employed sophisticated management methods, and exuded enthusiasm for scientific and technological progress. Luce spoke for and to many in what Thomas Ferguson has called the new "hegemonic bloc" of the New Deal coalition: investment firms, capital-intensive industries, mass merchandisers, and internationally-oriented commercial banks.[9]

If Luce used *Fortune* as a venue of fables for the professional and managerial ranks, he preached to the humbler faithful in *Life*, whose large circulation gave him optimal range for his homiletic talents. His greatest didactic oration was "The American Century," published in *Life*'s February 1941 issue. Though rife with banquet doggerel and the strenuous bray of martial virility, "The American Century" is Luce's Epistle to the Americans, one of the boldest eschatological visions in American history, a scripture of revelation that announced the advent of a capitalist kingdom on earth. The essay is leavened from start to finish with biblical sensibility and allusion. Like an evangelical pastor preparing the flock for the troubles preceding the end-times, Luce rallied his readers for what he called "the great test" when destiny arrived at its American moment. With an array of vexations in mind—especially the Great Depression and the rise of fascism—Luce reassured his readers that "in all our trials and tribulations of spirit," they could discern a transformative episode, when "the meaning of our time" would be brilliantly revealed as the arrival of "an authentic 20th century—our Century." To Luce, the mission of the United States is to embark on a salvific enterprise, "lifting the life of mankind from the level of the beasts to what the Psalmist called a little lower than the angels."[10]

Evoking the Puritan errand and the expedition of Manifest Destiny, Luce justified US global supremacy in strikingly eschatological terms. Americans, Luce declared, were a chosen people, a historical vanguard, "the inheritors of all the great principles of Western civilization." At times, whetting his readers' millennial desires with a foretaste of the kingdom, Luce wrote as if the American Century was already breaking upon us; the emporium of goods uniting far-flung peoples was an intimation of beatitude. "There is already an immense American internationalism. American jazz, Hollywood movies, American slang, American machines and patented products, are in fact the only things that every community in the world, from Zanzibar to Hamburg, recognizes in common . . . America is already the intellectual, scientific, and artistic capital of the world." Here was Filene's "oneness of humanity," as well as Calkins's business executives repairing what priests had bungled. Here also was John Winthrop's "city on a hill," now extending its environs to the outermost limits; Jonathan Edwards's "most glorious renovation of the earth"; Ezra Stiles's American Israel "Elevated to Glory and Honor." Here was John O'Sullivan's "Great Nation of Futurity" and Emerson's "sublime and friendly Destiny"; Walter Lippmann's "modern communion" and Woodrow Wilson's "democracy of business."[11]

Like previous imperial projects, the American Century required artisans, proconsuls, priests, and legions, and Luce situated the political and moral economy just below the level of the seraphim. With the United States at its "dynamic center," a "vital international economy" would pave the way for "an international moral order"—a Civilization of Business like the one championed in the pages of *Fortune*. This corporate order would supply "the skillful servants of mankind," and these humble servants included "engineers, scientists, doctors, movie men, makers of entertainment, developers of airlines, builders of roads, teachers, [and] educators." Luce fully expected the world to greet these technical and cultural specialists as liberators, with the United States "eagerly welcomed" as a "good Samaritan" by the backward and wretched of the earth.[12]

Luce hinted that the Good Samaritan would on occasion have to act as the American Centurion. As the "powerhouse from which ideals spread around the world," we must be ready, he wrote ominously, to "exert upon the world the full impact of our influence, for such purposes as we see fit and by such means as we see fit." Launching into jeremiad mode, Luce lamented that, preoccupied with the Depression, apprehensive about events in Europe and Asia, and fearful of global responsibility, Americans had not "accommodated themselves spiritually and practically" to their power, stature, and destiny. Suffering from "the virus of isolationist sterility," the nation could not complete its redemptive mission unless there coursed "strongly through its veins . . . the blood of purpose and enterprise and high resolve."[13] Pulsating with imperial vivacity, the United States could either sell a *Pax Americana* or impose it like previous hegemons. Either way, neither America nor the rest of the world could resist the corporate trajectory of history. As the grandest undertaking in the history of capitalist enchantment, the American Century would be a long, victorious, and lucrative march toward the heavenly city of business.

Two cohorts of Luce's "skillful servants"—the radio industry and the Disney studios—were already well entrenched as spiritual governors by the eve of World War II. In *Our Master's Voice* (1934), his acerbic critique of advertising, the copywriter-turned-radical James Rorty flatly called the radio industry, together with the newspapers, "the machinery of the super-government." Rorty was far less sanguine than other left-wing writers about the prospects of revolutionizing that machinery, and his pessimism stemmed from a rueful appreciation of the culture industry's capacity for enchantment. Though radio was a fundamentally commercial affair, its unseen voices, speaking to millions simultaneously, inevitably suggested analogies with submission to invisible divine authority. As one 1943 NBC publication, *What Goes On behind Your Radio Dial?* suggested, corporate radio professionals fully appreciated the enchanting character of their medium. Deeming the radio "a modern cathedral of the air," NBC beckoned listeners to enter "a wonderland far surpassing anything dreamed up by the most imaginative storyteller."[14]

CBS was even more grandiose. In one 1939 broadcast, "Seems Radio Is Here To Stay," listeners were informed that radio originated, not in corporate laboratories and studios, but in the maelstrom of creation in the primeval past; the audience learned that "the mystic ethers" on which radio depended "were established well before the first word passed between men." These intimations of primordial divinity persisted throughout the broadcast. Later, the studio engineer and the chairman of the Federal Communications Commission were conflated into godly omnipotence. The "High Commissioner" deserves "homage," the announcer declared, as he "Who first assigned these frequencies to earth." "He is the same who fixed the stars in place," the voice continued, "Who set afire the sun . . . who puts some molecules together in a way to make a man." Possessing "the formula for genesis and death," the engineer's "hand rests on a dial bigger than infinity." After listening for hours to this rotomontade in his home on Riverside Drive, Theodor Adorno concluded that radio was a technology of modern enchantment. Noting that many a radio set even looked like "a tabernacle," Adorno detected a psychic affinity between the corporate "radio voice" and God that underscored the authoritarian nature and design of the corporate media.[15]

Walt Disney was an even more diligent and extravagant enchanter, feeling obliged, as Steven Watts has argued, to "re-enchant a modern world often devoid of play, fantasy, and magic." Yet the visual rapture of Disney films was not simply compensatory; the "Magic Kingdom" was not merely a fillip to atone for the tedium of everyday life. Even during the Depression, critics and other students of Disney's films realized that they provided much more than "tonic for disillusion," as one *New York Times* writer misunderstood. Some— like *Snow White* (1937) or *Dumbo* (1941)—contained, in Watts's words, "populist parables," tales of tribulation and triumph by the downtrodden. Others—especially *Fantasia* (1940)—exhibited what Watts calls a "sentimental modernism," a cinematic endorsement of Victorian virtues garnished by elements of avant-garde art.[16] Still, by defining "enchantment" in solely aesthetic or psychological terms, Watts and others miss the metaphysical longings depicted in Disney's phantasmagoria. Disney was much more than a mass entertainer; he was an astute mythologist and metaphysician of capitalist modernity. The Disney Company was a branch of the spiritual government, linking faith in technological mastery to desires for rapturous connection to the world. Reconciling corporate civilization with the most mysterious forces of the universe, the Magic Kingdom was a heavenly city of Fordist enchantment.

Disney himself was certainly no populist—he was, after all, the head of a corporate studio whose animators' union he broke in 1941—and as a rambling 1935 memo to animators indicated, Disney's modernism was more than "sentimental." Dwelling on his own "responsibility as a mass entertainer," Disney admonished his cartoonists to carefully study bodily motion, first to "richly possess sincerity and contact with the public" but then to venture into "the fantastic, the unreal, the imaginative." As Disney explained, animation lifted repressions and exposed to view a collective dreamworld. Indeed, the highest and most difficult calling of the animator, he continued, was to "picture on the screen things that have run through the imagination of the audience to bring to life dream fantasies and imaginative fancies that we have all thought of during our lives." But unlike Freud, Disney did not consider his archeology of fantasy a disenchanted analysis of desire. More like Carl Jung—with his theory of primordial images or "archetypes" in the "collective unconscious"—Disney unearthed and employed motifs as mythical therapy for the Machine Age.[17]

Some of Disney's contemporaries perceived the scope of his mythical, enchanting ambitions. A champion of Disney since his defense of mass culture in *The Seven Lively Arts* (1923), the critic Gilbert Seldes praised the all-encompassing nature of Disney's cultural magic. Writing in the late 1930s, Seldes observed that Disney achieved a "complete enchantment" of the culture industry, from studio inception to audience applause. Combining the artist, the moralist, and the scientific manager, Disney, Seldes grasped, offered not one but two case studies: the first in the rationalization of enchantment, and the second in the enchantment of rationalization. At the point of production, the Disney company was a paragon of Taylorization. In the same way that scientific management had rationalized industry by replacing humans with machines, Disney had demonstrated that he could "hire people to make animated drawings, always obedient, perfectly under control, and doing the work better than the living players." When the seven dwarves whistled happily on their way to the mine in *Snow White,* their refrain must have sounded siren-sweet to Disney and other corporate managers. At the same time, Disney's attempt to rationalize animation was also an effort to animate rationalization. Like Charlie Chaplin—whose *Modern Times* (1936) Disney imitated in *Modern Inventions* (1937)—Disney, Seldes thought, was a "great satirist of the machine age." In short films such as *Santa's Workshop* (1932) and *Mickey's Amateurs* (1937)—and arguably later in *Pinocchio*—Disney sought to reconcile audiences to the technology of mass production. Sensing the blend of fascination and distrust in popular attitudes toward industrial technology, Disney endowed machines with souls. In Disney animations, "the machine becomes human," Seldes surmised, "just when humanity is afraid mankind will be turned into a machine."[18]

Like Seldes, Walter Benjamin lauded Disney's talent as a mythmaker for modernity. In Benjamin's view, Disney, far from being a spokesman for Victorian propriety, was in fact one of the first artists in the culture industry to adopt "the cause of the absolutely new." Benjamin attributed to Disney films the same "double meaning" he saw in the cinema generally: the depiction of "figures in a collective dream," enacting both the nightmare of the present and the prospect of utopian transformation. One of these figures was Mickey Mouse, who appeared throughout Benjamin's essays and jottings of the 1930s. Benjamin observed that in the earliest cartoons, Mickey is insolent, amorous, and brutal. Living by his wits in a cruel and unpredictable world, the Mouse sustained a barrage of injuries and indignities, yet always managed to outwit and survive his tormentors. "The public recognizes its own life in them," Benjamin wrote of the cartoons—a life of everyday insult redeemed by small, evanescent triumphs. Mickey's mocking endurance demonstrated that "a creature can still survive even when it has thrown off all resemblance to a human being." Indeed, "in these films," Benjamin remarked, "mankind makes preparations to survive civilization," to persist beyond the horrors of mechanized oppression. At the same time, Benjamin contended, the technical prowess of the animations promised "a redemptive existence," a future of harmony between humanity and the machines it has made. But over time, Benjamin discerned a more repressive agenda, not only in the rodent's comic antics but also in all of Disney's work. Especially through the Mouse's misadventures, Disney both encouraged sadistic violence and immunized audiences against mass psychosis. Representing collective longings on screen in such a way as to vent and then neutralize them, Disney triggered "a therapeutic explosion of the unconscious" with no revolutionary consequences. To the same end, his portrayal of peace between people and technology fabricated an illusory rapport "between human beings and the apparatus."[19]

The most remarkable praise for Disney's enchantment came from the Soviet director Sergei Eisenstein. The maker of *Potemkin* and *October* would seem an unlikely admirer of Disney, but Eisenstein followed Uncle Walt's career from the very earliest animations. (Eisenstein met Disney in Hollywood in 1930, when he was being courted—unsuccessfully, in the end—by Paramount.) Like Benjamin, Eisenstein was first enthralled by Mickey Mouse, and his respect for Disney grew as *Snow White* (1937), *Pinocchio* (1940), and *Fantasia* appeared. Over the winter of 1940–1941, Eisenstein ventilated his thoughts about Disney in a theoretical essay on cinema. He conceded the obvious escapism in Disney films; if Disney sang "a marvelous lullaby," who among Americans, "whose lives are graphed by the cent and dollar," wouldn't want to forget being "shackled by hours of work . . . by a mathematical precision of time"? Precisely because it afforded release, escapism was a form, however temporary, of emancipation from Fordist drudgery. Liberating audiences for a few enchanting hours from "the time-clock mechanism of American life," Disney enabled his audience to stage a "revolt against partitioning and legislating."[20]

But in Eisenstein's view, the "revolt" imagined in Disney films was metaphysical as well as political. Like all lullabies, Disney's transported us to the world of dreams, and there, possessing "the magic of all technical means," he sifted through and refined "all the most secret strands of human thought, images, ideas, [and] feelings." To Eisenstein, Disney was a modern metaphysician, reversing disenchantment and leading his audience toward a "Paradise Regained." Endowing inanimate objects with "life and a soul," Disney augured what Eisenstein called a new "totemism" leavened by "pure ecstasy . . . the immersion of self in nature and animals." Drawing on "vague ideas and sensations of the interconnection of all elements and kingdoms of nature," Disney conjured "an unexpected rebirth of universal animism"—the primordial sense of *mana,* the all-pervading soul of the material world. But Disney's renaissance of enchantment was taking place in a world brought ever more thoroughly under technological subjugation. It was no accident, Eisenstein noted, that magic—the manipulation of cosmic forces for human purposes—was so prominent in Disney's films. In "a society that has so completely enslaved nature—namely, in America," magic was now embodied in industrial technology. Through his depictions of magic, Disney connected desires for metaphysical transfiguration with submission to Fordist technics. Enabling an untrammeled imaginative freedom, animation issued "a unique protest against the metaphysical immobility of the once-and-forever given." "You tell a mountain: move, and it moves. You tell an octopus: be an elephant, and the octopus becomes an elephant."[21] More than any of his contemporaries, Disney wedded the desire for enchanted communion to the drive for total dominion.

The immediate catalyst for Eisenstein's remarks was almost certainly *Fantasia,* then the most technically and aesthetically sophisticated of Disney's animations. *Fantasia* is a portmanteau of enchantment, a composite of technology, fantasy, and fable that ends with a vision of communion. For a "fantasia," the film contained some oddly "disenchanting" features. The "Rite of Spring" episode, for instance, was a condensed account of geological and biological evolution from volcanoes to the dinosaur extinctions. "Science, not art, wrote the scenario of this picture," as the music critic Deems Taylor asserted in his narration. The entire film featured Fantasound, a stereophonic system that required more than thirty large and very visible speakers mounted to theater ceilings. (Indeed, Fantasound was so cumbersome that *Fantasia* opened in only a dozen theaters.) And in the most self-consciously disenchanting fashion, Disney frequently called explicit attention to the artifice of the film itself. Taylor introduced each segment by explaining the musical score (which included pieces from Bach, Tchaikovsky, Stravinsky, Beethoven, Mussorgsky, and Schubert). *Fantasia* opens with curtains parting to reveal the Philadelphia Orchestra, conducted by Leopold Stokowski, entering and assuming their places on stage. At intermission, the orchestra leaves for a short break, and when they return, a clarinetist leads a jazz session, followed by "Meet the Soundtrack," in which the sounds of orchestral instruments are animated as waveforms.[22]

But the unconcealed artifice of *Fantasia* coincided with a deeper technological rapture. Animation and Fantasound liberated objects from the bonds of natural law, while the science affirmed in "The Rite of Spring" coexisted easily with magic, mythology, and religion. Three episodes—"The Sorcerer's Apprentice," "The Nutcracker Suite," and "Dance of the Hours"—exemplified the metaphysical liberation identified by Eisenstein. In the first of these segments (based on Goethe's poem), Mickey Mouse plays the ornery apprentice to a sorcerer, learning the arts of magic that preceded modern science and technology. When his master retires to bed one evening, Mickey—tired of performing household chores—opens his master's book of spells and gets a broom to do his drudgery. When Mickey loses control of the spell and almost floods the house, only the sorcerer's swift response prevents catastrophe. The obvious lesson—don't fool around with things you don't understand—had a political import: the marvels of modern technology should be left in the hands of professionals. The other two episodes displayed the wonders of enchantment under professional control. "The Nutcracker Suite" celebrates the seasons with a festival of dancing fairies, fishes, flowers, and mushrooms, while "Dance of the Hours" is a ballet performance by elephants, alligators, hippos, and ostriches.

The final episode, "Night on Bald Mountain," portrays the "triumph of hope and life over the powers of despair and death" by harmonizing technology, fantasy, and faith in a consummation of pious tranquility. On Walpurgisnacht—a pagan holiday adapted by Christians—the demon Chernabog summons up goblins, witches, ghosts, and other phantasms for a night of revelry and destruction. Recalling Mickey's loss of control over sorcery, Chernabog's orgy of malevolence ends when an Angelus bell strikes in the distance, signaling the arrival of the Christian faithful from a nearby village. Light from heaven illuminates a procession of believers, bearing candles and singing the *Ave Maria*. (Walpurgisnacht had been transformed by Christians into May Day, a celebration of the Blessed Virgin.) Adapted by the children's writer Rachel Field from Schubert's original composition, *Ave Maria* makes only the vaguest reference to Christian religiosity: "The Prince of Peace your arms embrace . . . Oh save us, mother full of grace, / In life and in our dying hour." Making their way through cathedral ruins, the reverent assemble under trees that bend to form a verdant Gothic canopy. *Fantasia* closes on a note of pastoral, maternal beatitude: a world of potentially violent enchantment pacified in the womb of nature—an arboreal paradise depicted through the science and technology of animation.

Disney's enchantment went deeper than pixie dust, demons, and dancing mushrooms. As Eisenstein saw, Disney merged the longing for enchantment with submission to the power of modern technology. The animated replication of enchantment would pacify, but not fulfill, that desire; it would even encourage a flight from reality into the worlds of computer generation, fostering an indifference to material reality that is now crucial to the maintenance of the corporate state. Not content to administer the production and distribution of goods, the civilization of business would manage our experience through the endless fabrication of what Chris Hedges has dubbed an "empire of illusion."[23] Conjuring an enchanted universe, the imagineers became the most spellbinding clerics in the corporate spiritual government.

# 18

# A New Order and Creed

## Human Relations as Fordist Moral Philosophy

CORPORATE MANAGERS COMPRISED the least exotic branch of the interwar "temporal government." After an upsurge of growth in the profession of personnel management during World War I (partly in response to struggles over Taylorism and "industrial democracy"), the number and power of personnel specialists increased more slowly during the 1920s. Thanks mainly to the success of the American Plan and to open-shop campaigns, most companies successfully avoided or suppressed labor strife until the middle of the Depression and the passage of the Wagner Act in 1935, which spurred the most combative and illustrious decade of unionization in American history. Hit hard by the Depression, the managerial class, both on the line and in the personnel office, rebounded in response to the CIO union drives of the mid-1930s. By the end of World War II, a new managerial hierarchy superintended corporate business, setting the stage for the managerial capitalism that flourished until the 1980s.[1]

This "managerial revolution," as James Burnham labeled it in 1941, coincided with an evolution in the ideology of scientific management. Stoked by the Bolshevik Revolution and by the brief but powerful wave of strikes in 1919, the persistent fear of labor unrest prompted the corporate intelligentsia to examine more studiously than ever what the Harvard Business School's Elton Mayo called "the human problems of industrial civilization." Though occasioned by the need to prevent class war and repel unionization, the emergence of what management writers and historians have dubbed "human relations" was more than a strategy of class domination.[2] As a theory of "spiritual government," human relations brought to fuller fruition a moral and spiritual aspiration nascent in scientific management: the mechanization of communion, a beloved family of production reconciled and sacralized by a corporate form of humanism. Leavening the techniques of Taylorism with psychology, philosophy, and religion, human relations became the scholasticism of corporate management.

After World War I, many of Frederick W. Taylor's disciples integrated the rhetoric of industrial democracy with the more humane idioms of scientific management—a Taylorism with a human face. Led by Morris Cooke, industrial relations specialists and personnel managers connected to the Taylor Society joined hands with labor leaders such as Sidney Hillman of the Amalgamated Clothing Workers of America. These managerial progressives and unionists—the nexus of the "new unionism" that would give birth to the CIO—converged with representatives of the corporate liberal intelligentsia (the Twentieth Century Fund and the Russell Sage Foundation), mass merchandising (Filene's and Macy's), finance capital (Goldman Sac's and Lehman Brothers), and a host of other industries with an interest in enlarging the mass consumer market. Many postwar Taylorists hoped to foster a more democratic Fordism, a republic of mechanization in which unionized workers would embrace the semi-skilling of labor in exchange for access to economic and cultural abundance. As Cooke put it, workers would receive both "the full garage" and "the world's highest culture" as compensation for the loss of control and craft pride.[3] But because this brand of Taylorism was too benign for most business leaders, other management writers invented "human relations" as a surrogate for industrial democracy. Arising from Taylorist scientific management, "human relations" was a Fordist variety of humanism, moral philosophy, and business enchantment.

The shift to "human relations" marked the work of Mary Parker Follett, a Boston activist and political theorist who was one of the foremost writers and speakers on management in the 1920s. Follett's prewar work in vocational guidance piqued an interest in industrial relations, and she quickly joined the ranks of Boston's business elite. Moving easily among Filene, the manufacturer Henry Dennison, and management specialists Meyer Bloomfield, Frank Parsons, and Henry C. Metcalf, Follett rose to the summit of American and British industrial relations circles. In numerous addresses to the Taylor Society, the Bureaus of Personnel Administration in Boston and New York, the Harvard Business School, and the London School of Economics, Follett articulated a corporate humanist conviction that, as she told a management conference in 1926, "industry is the most important field of human activity, and management is the fundamental element in industry."⁴

Recycling Taylorism through pragmatism, psychology, and a nebulously religious sensibility, Follett crafted a managerial imagination that enchanted the corporation, promised sacramental labor, and veiled subordination to the imperatives of business. To Follett, the workplace was a portal to aesthetic, metaphysical, moral, and spiritual truths. "Our daily living may itself become an art," she prophesied in *Creative Experience* (1924). "In commerce we may find culture, in industry idealism, in our business system beauty, in mechanics morals." Providing more than commodities, profits, and paychecks, the corporation offered "our greatest spiritual nourishment," she wrote, a "sacrament of life." Corporate managers and executives were the clerisy of this moral and sacramental economy. "The real service of business" to the community, she asserted in a typical 1925 talk, was "the better organization of human relationships." The manager was the moral paragon of the corporate sacramental order. "Long after the clerks have departed from the office of a big corporation you can see lights burning in the rooms of the executives." Their overtime reflected not an obsession with money or a crackpot devotion to work, but rather "the craftsman's love of doing a job well." Follett lauded the loyalty of the corporate leader to "the soul of his work," a dedication that was "the highest romance as it is the deepest religion." Indeed, the "high adventure of business," Follett waxed, was its release of "the deeper thing within every man, transcending every man, which you may call your ideal, or God, or what you will." "No occupation," she concluded, "can make a more worthy appeal to the imagination."⁵

In *Creative Experience*, Follett outlined an anthropology of management that mixed pragmatism, Gestalt psychology, and shards of theology. Selfhood, for Follett, emerged "in the relating, in the activity-between," a fluid and expansive conception of identity that she encapsulated in the "crescent self"—a "soul at home," who lived from that "sacrament of life" ritualized in corporate labor. The creation and flourishing of this "crescent self" was "the real service of business," whose innumerable productive activities constituted "those manifold, interweaving activities of men by which spiritual values are created." (As Coolidge had said, the factory was a temple.) This "crescent," corporate self required a new managerial philosophy: "dynamic administration" or "progressive integration," which Follett espoused in numerous talks to business leaders in the 1920s. If the proprietary autocrat had practiced "coercive power" or "power-over," the "progressive integrator," attuned to human relationships, would practice a "coactive power" that brought managers and workers together in a genuine industrial democracy. "Dynamic" or "integrated" solutions to problems arose from "constructive conflict" through which "both sides found a place, and neither side . . . had to sacrifice anything." Follett's oracular rhetoric often suggested that dynamic, coactive industry augured the erasure of class lines. "The distinction between those who manage and those who are managed is fading somewhat," she observed, dismissing the conventional dichotomy that set "that modern beneficent despot, the expert" against a "muddled, befogged 'people.'"[6] Follett's vision of corporate community seemed, at points, to resemble the producers' millennium imagined in anarchism, syndicalism, and the guild ideal.

Still, in the end, "dynamic administration" ratified the maintenance and extension of managerial hierarchy. Speaking in the spring of 1927 to a conference of personnel administrators—"pioneers," she flattered her audience, "working out something new in human relationships"—she observed that "business men are quietly . . . working out a system of organization which is not democratic in our old understanding of the word, but something better than that." This new corporate system was based "neither on equality nor on arbitrary authority, but on functional unity." The new manager was "the man who can energize his group, who knows how to encourage initiative, how to draw from all what each has to give." Even Follett's ostensibly mutualist conception of power could end up meaning, as she explained to a conference of managers in the winter of 1925, that nonmanagers manage when they "use their own judgment *in regard to the manner of executing orders.*"[7] Follett's recondite account of authority suggests that, while leavened with appeals to religious longing—"sacrament of life," "soul at home," "deepest religion"—the spiritualized parlance of pragmatism and psychology obscured the continuing power of management.

Other management theorists shared Follett's conviction that corporate managers were a moral and existential vanguard. Wallace B. Donham, dean of the Harvard Business School from 1919 to 1942, used his position as a pulpit to sermonize on the calling of corporate leadership. Backed enthusiastically by Harvard's president, A. Lawrence Lowell, Donham presided over a remarkable period of expansion in the Business School: a new campus, a Harvard Fatigue Laboratory, the founding of the *Harvard Business Review,* and the addition to the curriculum of courses in psychology, physiology, sociology, and anthropology. The laboratory and the curricular changes were motivated in large part by Donham's belief that, as he told Lowell in 1925, "the subject of human relations is one of the most important things in the whole field of business." Donham found support from none other than Harvard's premier philosopher, Alfred North Whitehead. In *The Aims of Education* (1929), Whitehead robustly defended postgraduate business schools. Since "business is now a highly intellectualized vocation," Whitehead reasoned, its inclusion in the university was a logical and appropriate addition to theology, medicine, and law. Whitehead pronounced that businessmen, along with theologians, scientists, and lawyers, were among the "intellectual pioneers of our civilization."[8]

But for Donham, "human relations" was part of a larger managerial form of social and cultural criticism. As he mused in the Business School's alumni bulletin in 1926, since much of the confusion in the modern world stemmed from the scientific and technical advances sponsored by capitalism, corporate executives needed more "depth and perspective on vital social problems." In part, Donham was trying to meet objections from the political left; when he wrote in the *Harvard Business Review* in 1927 that American society required a "socialization of industry from within on a higher ethical plane," he was clearly hoping to avert a socialization of industry from *without.* Still, like Follett, Donham recoiled from the Babbittry of the Chamber of Commerce. He considered corporate management one of the last bastions of civilization against an onslaught of cultural barbarism. Donham lamented the "materialism" of his time, tracing it to "certain mechanistic working hypotheses" associated with Newtonian physics. As a result of this disenchanting rationalization, "a lot of the idealism has gone out of the more intelligent and better-educated group of the community." If this mechanical materialism was not confronted by the business intelligentsia, a new dark ages might ensue in the midst of "this amazing material development of the race."[9]

Donham's call for a "higher ethical plane" designed by corporate management was taken up by Elton Mayo and Fritz Roethlisberger, two of his colleagues at the Business School. Mayo and Roethlisberger are best known for their study of Chicago's Hawthorne Works of Western Electric. Hired by the company to study employees' attitudes in order to improve productivity, they ended up investigating workers' desire for fellowship and creativity. Mayo—a lifelong charlatan with a phony doctoral degree who spent a total of six days at the Hawthorne Works—clearly conceived of his industrial research as a contribution to a corporate humanism. Calling for a "wide research into the nature of man" in a series of *Harper's* essays over 1924 and 1925, Mayo derided the "uncivilized reason" of most business leaders and promoted scientific management to assuage worker discontent and cultivate "morale." Later, reflecting on the Hawthorne study in *The Human Problems of an Industrial Civilization* (1933), Mayo focused on the workers' "mental preoccupations," their ambivalent feelings toward Western Electric. The Hawthorne employees considered Western Electric "an almost mythical entity" whose perceived combination of power, solicitude, and indifference produced "a sense of human defeat." Mayo realized that even as Fordist rationalization mechanized and degraded workers' labor, "the desire for continuous and intimate association in work with others remains a strong, possibly the strongest, human capacity." Indeed, despite their technocratic demeanor, Mayo and Roethlisberger perceived the religious longings in the Fordist workplace. Mayo's perception of the corporation as a "mythical," quasidivine entity dovetailed with Roethlisberger's insight in *Management and Morale* (1941) that the "system of sentiments" among factory workers bore a telling resemblance to tribal moral economies. Drawing on the work of the anthropologist Bronislaw Malinowski, Roethlisberger argued that "the forces which make collaboration possible [in tribes] are only in part economic," and that tribal productive life was "essentially social and religious," governed by numerous "ceremonials and rituals." Thus, the chief task of managers and executives was the generation of "morale" through liturgies of mass production. It was no mere figure of speech when, shortly after World War II, Mayo told a Harvard Business School audience that management theory could effect in workers "the strong and simple religious feeling of medieval times."[10] Though a sleek and proficient professional, the new administrator was also a cleric of that "mythical entity," the corporation, just as corporate capitalism had inherited the religious aura of a believing age.

The most prescient managerial philosopher was Peter Drucker, who produced a voluminous body of work that three generations of managers have revered. Drucker's frequent description as a management "guru" only hints at his moral and spiritual concerns, and it helps explain his renown outside corporate business circles. (By the 1940s, even W. H. Auden—a socialist a decade before—was recommending Drucker's work to friends.) A consummate corporate humanist, Drucker glided easily through the corridors connecting finance, journalism, academia, and industry. Born and raised among the liberal burghers of pre–World War I Vienna, Drucker had been a rising star in Catholic political thought; a financial reporter in Europe in the early 1930s; a political commentator for *Harper's,* the *New Republic,* and the *Saturday Evening Post;* an editor at the Luce manors of *Time* and *Fortune;* a professor of economics and humanities at Bennington College; and a much sought-after consultant for General Motors and other corporations.[11]

From the beginning of his career in the turbulent Austrian Republic of the late 1920s, Drucker sought to reconcile corporate enterprise with Christian standards of economic and personal conduct. Drucker perused both papal encyclicals—*Rerum novarum* (1891) and *Quadragesimo anno* (1931)—and the work of Austrian Catholic corporatists who influenced the Christian Social Party of Engelbert Dollfuss, chancellor and then dictator of Austria in the early 1930s. Though put off by the protofascist elements of Catholic corporatism, Drucker affirmed its undemocratic conception of authority, its paternalist insistence on the duties of property owners, and its promotion of "organic" economic institutions that would link personal responsibility with the common good. Although Catholic corporatists recoiled from the cosmopolitanism they associated with large capitalist enterprises and their leaders, Drucker contended that corporatists should embrace large-scale capitalism and concentrate their efforts not on reviving small proprietorship, but on both promoting innovation and Christianizing corporate firms, especially their managers and executives.[12]

When Drucker arrived in the United States in 1937, he joined in a search for new forms of business authority in the wake of the Great Depression, the reforms of the New Deal, and the militancy of the CIO. One strategy, exemplified in the work of Adolf Berle, Gardiner Means, and James Burnham, was to identify a "managerial revolution" that legitimated the hegemony of technocrats. In *The Modern Corporation and Private Property,* Berle and Means argued that because major corporations had separated ownership and management, the ascendant class of managers and professionals should perform what Keynes had dubbed "the euthanasia of the *rentier*"—the disenfranchisement of the functionless stockholder—and put decision-making power into the hands of a "purely neutral technocracy." Almost a decade later, the ex-Trotskyite Burnham offered similar claims and solutions in *The Managerial Revolution* (1941) and *The Machiavellians* (1943), contending that a government of experts should be supplemented by at least a facade of democracy.[13] Sparked by the Wagner Act and the formation of the CIO, union militancy in the late 1930s suggested to many corporate leaders that this openly technocratic approach was too brashly elitist to be acceptable to Americans. Hoping to inhibit union organization and to limit union power where it was already entrenched, executives and business intellectuals advocated a more populist brand of hegemony. Centered in the Business Advisory Council and the Advertising Council, borrowing from Popular Front culture, and honed in public relations and advertising departments, this method stressed the "participation and belonging" afforded by consumer culture, translating the corporate symbolic government into "the American Way of Life." In industry, companies expanded personnel programs, many of which incorporated elements of "human relations" theory.[14]

In portentously titled books, such as *The End of Economic Man* (1939) and *The Future of Industrial Man* (1942), Drucker entered this debate by challenging corporate managers to save Western civilization from what the Spanish philosopher Ortega y Gasset had dubbed the "revolt of the masses." Western society, Drucker maintained, was no longer a "community of individuals bound together by a common purpose" but rather a "chaotic hubbub of purposeless isolated monads" driven by "demonic forces." Fascism, Bolshevism, and consumer culture were all bogus "creeds," in his view, upholding "false gods" for worship. This was standard Euro-conservative cultural pessimism, but Drucker departed from others on the classical right by pinning his hopes for cultural renewal on corporate capitalism itself. "There has never been a more efficient, a more honest, a more capable and conscientious group of rulers than the professional management of the great American corporations today." These corporate overlords were the main repositories of the "Christian concept of man's nature: imperfect, weak, a sinner, and dust destined unto dust; yet made in God's image and responsible for his actions." Far from being the greedy and soulless swine of left-wing caricature, these men, Drucker believed, upheld a corporate moral economy permeated by a refurbished Christian ethic, "a new order and creed."[15]

For the next four decades, Drucker never strayed from this mandarin conception of corporate management, celebrating the business corporation's unprecedented prominence in the nation's moral imagination. Hoping for a postwar rehabilitation of business in American culture, Drucker called on executives and managers in *Concept of the Corporation* (1946)—a book-length reflection on his consulting work with General Motors during the war—to hold out "the promise of adequately fulfilling the aspirations and beliefs of the American people." Drucker charged the managerial elite with this mission, because the corporation was now "our representative social institution." Having supplanted the church, the family, and the state as the pivot of American society, the corporation provided the "symbol" and "standard for the way of life and the mode of living." Drucker's analysis aligned well with the corporate populism of the Advertising Council and public relations departments. While they reintroduced the corporation to America as a kindly behemoth, a "good neighbor," Drucker and others in the corporate intelligentsia could represent it to themselves as the vessel of that "new order and creed" for which the declining West had been longing.[16] Drucker's managerial philosophy marked the convergence of Catholic conservatism and corporate liberalism, an odd but fruitful marriage of neofeudalism and human relations theory. In Drucker, the soulful corporation had found its first and most erudite postwar chaplain.

# 19

# Beauty as the New Business Tool

Advertising, Industrial Design,
and the Enchantment of Corporate Modernism

AS THE CLERICS of Fordism, management writers and economists defined the boundaries of corporate orthodoxy; but just as previous spiritual orders had relied on the image as well as the word, the corporate spiritual government needed a sacred symbolic firmament: advertising, commercial art, public relations, and industrial design. Oddly, neither Peter Drucker nor Thurman Arnold had much to say about the apparatus of corporate iconography. Yet the interwar period witnessed an extraordinary growth not only in the number of corporate image professionals but also in their self-assurance, aesthetic sophistication, and claim to spiritual authority. Especially during the 1920s, "beauty" became the comely shibboleth of visual and design expertise as advertisers and designers incorporated modernist aesthetics into their work. But there was more than artistic aspiration at work in the desire, as *Fortune* put it, to instill the "beauty in factories and derricks." If cultural professionals regarded themselves as heralds of modernity, they were also oracles of the "business millennium" proclaimed by Earnest Elmo Calkins. Indeed, advertisers and designers provided the most visible, palpable evidence for Calkins's assertion that business had inherited the sacral supremacy formerly claimed by religion. When James Rorty wrote of his years as a copywriter for BBDO that he and his fellow scribes had been acolytes of "the religion of Beauty-in-Advertising," he recalled a genuine devotion.[1] For Rorty and others in the symbolic elite, beauty was the aesthetic refuge for enchantment in the corporate business millennium—or, as Romantic critics would have it, a capitalist parody of the sacramental imagination. The quest for beauty was a project of metaphysical transformation, an attempt to endow corporate commodities with the numinous aura of sacred objects.

With the resurgence of American industry after World War I, the 1920s saw a rise in the demand for commercial art and commercial artists. But the exuberance that characterized the advertising profession stemmed from more than economic prosperity. Engineered by George Creel and the Committee on Public Information—who enlisted graphic artists and illustrators such as Charles Dana Gibson and N. C. Wyeth—the success of wartime propaganda bestowed an impressive imprimatur on the power of mass-produced imagery. At the same time, art directors and advertising executives increasingly believed that their industry rested on sound empirical foundations. Relying on numerous studies conducted by psychologists, sociologists, statisticians, and market researchers, they contended that advertising had outgrown its carnivalesque origins and was now a genuine profession. To be sure, the veneer of professionalism concealed a theoretical maelstrom: advertising manuals and textbooks reflected a magpie assimilation of the new psychological sciences, whether Gestalt, psychoanalysis, or behaviorism. Still, when in 1920, John B. Watson, the founder of behaviorism, quit his academic post at Johns Hopkins and joined the J. Walter Thompson Agency, the scientific and professional status of advertising appeared, at long last, impeccable. (Though it was also far from credible. Agencies paid little serious attention in practice to psychology until the 1940s, and Watson himself came to think that its promise had been "greatly oversold.")[2]

Emboldened by their new respectability, advertising industry leaders and artists swelled to an exalted sense of their importance to the nation's moral imagination. "Your run of the mill ad-man," Rorty observed, "is positively messianic about his profession." "We advertising writers are privileged to compose a new chapter of civilization," the esteemed copywriter James Wallen wrote in 1925. "We are second only to statesmen and editors in power for good." Such bravado resounded through the business press. Merle Thorpe, editor of *Nation's Business,* told advertisers and art directors in 1931 that they had been charged with a duty to "direct public taste toward a higher beauty in the material expressions of our civilization." Their highest responsibility was not to please clients or increase profits but to foster among the American people "a common understanding, common feelings, common reactions"— something akin to the "modern communion" envisioned by Walter Lippmann and earlier progressives. The epochal import of advertising was recognized outside the business intelligentsia, even among its enemies. Speaking to the Advertising Club in New York in 1927, William Allen White remarked that "the real revolutionist" is not the Bolshevik but "the advertising man. Could I control the advertising publications of this country I would control the entire land." In 1931, New York governor Franklin D. Roosevelt told *Printer's Ink* that if he could start life over again, he would "go into the advertising business." "It is essentially a form of education," he flattered his readers, "and the progress of civilization depends on education." In the same year, Edmund Wilson paid a kind of homage to advertising when he denounced it in the *New Republic* for corrupting American idealism. "Our buoyance, our hope, our faith, has all been put toward stupendous campaigns of advertising, behind cyclones of salesmanship."[3]

Wilson was echoed by Clement Greenberg, who excoriated commercial art in 1939 as "the debased simulacra of genuine culture." Greenberg's hostility to advertising was inseparable from his promotion of modernism; creative autonomy and devotion to medium characterized the "avant-garde," while the prosaic, mechanical sentimentality of "kitsch" was represented not only by Soviet socialist realism but also by "popular, commercial art and literature with their chromeotype, magazine covers, illustrations, [and] ads." Many writers, artists, and intellectuals who had worked in the industry shared Greenberg's loathing for commercial culture. Former adman Sherwood Anderson rued that "thought and poetry died or passed as a heritage to feeble fawning men who also became servants of the new order." After a decade working for N. W. Ayer, Rockwell Kent told Margaret Bourke-White in 1936 that he felt soiled and unfaithful. Although art, he told her, was "the enshrinement of the best in heart and soul that men have in them," he confessed to having whored with commerce, "the great prostituting patron of the arts." Toiling in what he considered Bruce Barton's brothel, Rorty thought himself one of "the male hetaerae" of consumer culture. The dependence of serious art and artists on the pecuniary imperatives of business was conceded by none other Greenberg, who acknowledged that, like earlier forms of genuine, highbrow art, modernism was connected by "an umbilical cord of gold" to the interests of the dominant class.[4]

Still, as keen a critic of modernism as he was, Greenberg clearly failed to peruse advertisements with the perspicuity he directed at the avant-garde. Throughout the 1920s and well into the 1930s, modernist techniques were salient elements in the aesthetic repertoire of advertising. Although interest in modernism had been piqued by the Armory Show of 1913, art directors and artists were reluctant to challenge the sensibilities of their clients, who resisted "over-smartness" or "high hat" styles. After the war, industry leaders, centered in the Art Directors Club, took advantage of the profession's growing numbers and stature to mount an offensive against conventional taste. When the Art Directors Club sponsored its first exhibit of advertising art at the National Arts Club in New York in March 1921, its catalog stated that its primary purpose was to show that advertisers were "using as high a standard of art" as that used in "the average exhibition of studio painting." As evidence, the exhibit highlighted the work of Maxfield Parrish, Jules Guerin, and other well-known illustrators. The campaign received an even greater boost in 1925, when the International Exposition of Modern Industrial and Decorative Arts in Paris generated new and sustained interest in the design and promotional potential of modern art. Although the Exposition focused on the luxury market, it introduced a generation of American advertising professionals to Cubism, Bauhaus, Futurism, and Art Deco.[5]

Over the next ten years, both agencies (N. W. Ayer, Calkins and Holden, and J. Walter Thompson) and clients (Macy's, Eveready, and Delco) grew increasingly comfortable with impressionist, cubist, and surrealist techniques. Although modernism itself had arisen in part as a protest against the banality of mass production, its formal palette was easily used to embellish the fruits of industrial technology. Eager to appropriate the formal vernacular of modernism, illustrators and photographers employed diagonal lines, off-center layouts, montage, and exaggeration in the advertisement of everything from perfumes and batteries to automobiles and pistons. While industry artists honed their commercial modernism, corporate and agency art directors—epitomized by Charles Coiner of N. W. Ayer—directly commissioned modernist artists for advertising campaigns. For clients ranging from the Container Corporation of America and Dole Pineapple to French Line and DeBeers, Coiner enlisted an illustrious roster of painters, photographers, and graphic artists: Pablo Picasso, Lázló Moholy-Nagy, Fernand Leger, Georgia O'Keefe, Georges Rouault, Salvador Dali, Man Ray, Edward Steichen, Raoul Dufy, A. M. Cassandre, and Gyorgy Kepes. With so many artists crossing the allegedly inviolable boundary between avant-garde and kitsch, the advertising intelligentsia proudly announced the rapprochement of money and modernism. "Beauty," Calkins proclaimed in the *Atlantic*

*Monthly* in 1927, was "the new business tool." Both modernist art and contemporary industry "break with tradition" and "strike out in new and unknown worlds of imagination."[6]

The new advertising style developed in tandem with the corporate patronage of modernist art. Resenting the indictments of philistinism often directed at the bourgeoisie, business ideologues retorted that modern corporate leaders were more erudite and cosmopolitan than their boorish, chopwhiskered ancestors. As Calkins asserted in 1930, "business can be and may be as stimulating a patron of the arts as the cardinals, prelates, and popes who represented the church in the fifteenth century." Assuming the mantle of patron once worn by a Pope or a J. P. Morgan, corporations—led by Container Corporation of America and its president, Walter Paepcke—assembled collections of modern art. By hiring artists, sponsoring exhibits, and launching cultural campaigns (such as its famous "Great Ideas" series after World War II), Container Corporation of America stood in the vanguard of corporate modernism. Paepcke shrewdly cultivated an image of Container Corporation of America as a "new and progressive, modern corporation." By the mid-1940s, observers in both art and business circles agreed that corporate America had gone a long way toward "assuming the role of patron held by the Church and aristocracy in past ages," as a writer for *Art Digest* put it in 1943.[7]

Of course, many businesspeople rejected modernism as the bunkum of bohemia. A contributor to *Printer's Ink* expressed dismay in 1926 at the spread of "nightmare art" in advertising. Even Christine Frederick complained in 1929 that "no crime that could possibly be committed in the name of *art moderne* has been left uncommitted." Yet while they probably spoke for many in the business world, these dissident voices were unavailing. Recognizing the affinity between the urge to make it new and the oldfashioned rage to accumulate, modern art and modern industry had united to forge a new and popular symbolic universe. The wall separating the modernist vanguard from the kitschy vendor had been breached—from both sides. By consummating what Jackson Lears has called "the courtship of avant-garde and kitsch," advertisers achieved what amounted to a corporate reconstruction of modernism.[8]

The success of corporate modernism convinced industry leaders that they had practically defeated the forces of fine arts snobbery. "An artist who makes advertisements is an artist pure and simple," Calkins asserted in 1930, "exactly as is an artist who makes murals and paintings." Drawing on the aesthetic strategies of modernist painting and sculpture, a constellation of executives, artists, copywriters, and designers believed that they had reconciled the ideals of Art and the imperatives of Business. This new sense of status as artists pervaded the advertising world, from its most prominent representatives to the lowliest illustrators and writers. Thanks to the aesthetic expertise and accomplishment of modern advertising artists, businesspeople who had previously kept them on a short leash now exhibited "an increasing willingness to let them work in their own way and according to their own genius," Calkins observed. There was "less disposition to curb them with meaningless and silly limitations."[9]

Everyday commercial artists shared Calkins's lofty conception of their work. "Try as they might to sell out," Michele Bogart writes, many admen "were so indoctrinated with romantic ideals that they had difficulty embracing commercial practices wholeheartedly." Even if they worked in the industry to pay the rent while they worked on "serious" art, many advertising professionals thought of themselves as "an amiable band of poets," as Matthew Josephson claimed. When written with "the poet's cast of mind," advertising copy, Richard Surrey argued in *Printer's Ink* in 1925, could reach the level of belles lettres. While working under Barton, Rorty and his peers "developed an esthetic of advertising art and copy, a philosophy, a variety of equally fantastic creeds." Indeed, Rorty asserted that many admen were "more interested in beauty than in selling." "Not money alone could buy the devotion of these weary-eyed night workers," he remembered with a blend of fondness and horror. There was "something strange, incredible, miraculous" about their dedication to advertising, Rorty noted—a hope and faith that resembled religion. In their prose, illustrations, and photography, commercial artists and copywriters laid "pious oblations at the shrine of Beauty," votive offerings in the liturgical rites of the "religion of Beauty-in-Advertising."[10]

Rorty's remarks were (partly) sardonic, but they captured a real aspiration that was shared by many advertising professionals. Despite the obvious pecuniary motives of business, modernism supplied corporations and their cultural elites with more than aesthetic resources and prestige. By eschewing the prosaic and strictly representational, modernism provided a visual inventory of enchantment, a way to suggest that the visible, material world of commodities opened onto something transcendent. Historians of advertising have recognized this, however dimly. Marchand, for instance, wrote of advertising as a "secular iconography," while Lears discerned a desire to "reanimate the world."[11] But if secularity is a metamorphosis of the sacred, and if "re-animation" is another word for re-enchantment, then we need to confront the full religious significance of corporate imagery. Corporate modernism was a capitalist simulacrum of the sacramental imagination, an enchantment of the world sponsored and regulated under the auspices of corporations.

Artists and their employers acknowledged the metaphysical dimensions of advertising imagery, even as they yoked them to the crassest of motives. James Wallen, for example, straightforwardly blended the enchanting, the mercenary, and the ideological. "You do not sell a man tea," he explained in *Printer's Ink* in 1925, "but the magical spell which is brewed nowhere else but in a tea-pot." While the teleology of commerce remained in force—sell the product—copywriters and artists, Wallen advised, should endow products and their process of manufacturing with an aura appropriate to the Machine Age. If you depict a foundry, he wrote, put "the wonderful miracle of industry" into the picture—not "the hardships of labor." For Wallen, forsaking pictorial realism was a way not only to obscure the reality of alienation but also to enchant the industrial world. Other image professionals were more ingenuous and earnest about their mediation of invisible grace. "There are great spiritual values in material things," Glen Buck, a Chicago advertising executive, asserted in *This American Ascendency* (1927), his paean to the glories of commercial civilization. "Materials are the substances of which spirituality is the shadow." Rene Clarke, president of Calkins and Holden, took to the pages of *Advertising and Selling* in 1932 to lecture his fellow advertisers on the sacramental artifice of their craft. "I'm tired of looking at things as they are," he declared. "You are entrusted with the responsibility of showing others what they cannot see for themselves. If your eyes see only what is seen by others, from where will the vision come?"[12]

The "vision" enjoined upon advertising artists took a variety of forms: "atmosphere," "romance," "magic," "halo." Walt Whitman's hope of making objects friendly was most apparent in commercial photography, whose blending of realism and technical experimentation lent even greater power to modernist technique. As Lejaren Hiller, one of the era's premiere advertising photographers, told the Photographers' Association of America in 1927, "we photograph in order to get into these things a little more of what is known as atmosphere." A writer for *Commercial Photographer* praised W. M. Westervelt's shots of hats for Dobbs and Company for giving each hat "a personality, an atmosphere." Illustrators did not lag behind photographers as sorcerers of commodity fetishism. In two 1925 articles for *Printer's Ink* on the "tricky" and "magical effects" obtained by illustrators, the art director W. Livingston Larned marveled at the enchanting powers of industry professionals. One ad for New Jersey Zinc enveloped "a commonplace industry" in "romance," while another ad for Squibb Pharmaceuticals demonstrated that bottles of liver oil and boxes of soda could be transfigured as if with "a magic wand." Two years later, Larned lavished accolades on another ad for surrounding electric lamps with a "powdered brilliance" reminiscent of Parrish prints. The illustration showed, he wrote, that talented artists could enhance "industrial subjects with a shimmering halo."[13]

Indeed, halos and other emanations of light abounded in corporate modernism. In innumerable advertisements, a mock-heavenly radiance bathed the most lowly and quotidian of commodities. Shafts of light streamed on garbage cans and automobiles; beams that had once favored saints now illuminated Coldspot refrigerators and Hoover vacuum cleaners. One ad for Duco synthetic lacquer, published in the August 1928 issue of *Good Housekeeping*, blurred the distinction between an automobile showroom and a cathedral. Although a car dominated the foreground, a large stained glass window was visible in the back, complete with mosaic fluorescence. Yet it wasn't quite true that, as Marchand put it, supernal light "had become a secularized image without entirely losing its spiritual overtones."[14] If the image was "secularized," its "spiritual overtones" had not been lost or eroded; they had been appropriated and transformed by the clerisy of corporate business. The beatific vision of corporate modernism was a world redeemed by commodities.

The moral and religious dimensions of advertising were apparent to many in the business intelligentsia. Paul Nystrom, for instance, was a senior member of the corporate clerisy who tied the vicissitudes of consumption to the search for alternatives to religion. President of the New York Sales Manufacturers Club and a director of the Retail Research Corporation and the

Associated Merchandising Corporation, Nystrom also taught marketing at Columbia University's School of Business, where he offered the first college course on fashion. Cited by later historians for his "philosophy of futility"—the cultivation of evanescence essential to a dynamic consumer culture—Nystrom hinted that fashion traded on desires for personal metamorphosis and eternal transcendence. In *Economics of Fashion* (1928), one of the most engaging and mordant business textbooks ever written, Nystrom echoed Simon Patten by linking interest in fashion to escape from monotonous labor. For Nystrom, the corporate modernist pictorials in *Vogue, Vanity Fair,* and *Harper's Bazaar* displayed a world beyond toil and alienation. The average (usually female) consumer who flipped through the ads experienced a transformative moment, a state of "being a different person" after "a hard day of disappointment and defeat."[15]

Before modernity, Nystrom contended, religion had addressed this sense of futility with promises of a better life to come—after death. But as more and more people depart from "old-time standards of religion" and fail to develop "forceful views to take their places," they adopt by default a "philosophy of futility" that embraces and hallows impermanence. Hence the hostility of traditional religious authorities, whose aversion to fashion strongly suggested that its roots were partly religious. Becoming a kind of Augustine for advertisers, Nystrom reasoned that chic was anathema to clergy, not simply because of its "tending to evil" but also because of its counterfeit of good, its gorgeous impersonation of absolute beauty. The futilitarian view of life—"or lack of a view of life," as Nystrom put it shrewdly—was indispensable to advertisers, as business wooed, betrayed, and wooed yet again the restless heart of the consumer.[16] With its endless pageant of beautiful people and perfectly contoured raiment, fashion provided a beatific vision for a culture of futility.

Despite his position in the clerisy, Nystrom always nurtured a healthy sense that fashion was a storyline in a larger human comedy. As the pitchman for "business the civilizer," Calkins was a more zealous and outspoken ideologue for the enchantments of corporate modernism. Writing for the business press and for periodicals such as the *Atlantic Monthly,* Calkins both lauded the corporate benefaction of culture and emphasized its religious import. It is simply "an error," he claimed, to think that traditional religious paintings were more beautiful or inspiring than advertisements; indeed,

Calkins thought the number of religious works in European and American galleries "appalling." All those angels, Madonnas, and crucified Christs—full of "monotony," in his judgment, boring portraits of woe and misery enjoining us to huddle in our vale of tears. Besides, Calkins noted, the typical patron of medieval and Renaissance religious art had been an ecclesiastical big shot, or some "Florentine butter-and-egg man" who, guilt-ridden on account of his riches, commissioned some artist to "square things with Heaven." Corporate business, Calkins brashly asserted, could be a more discriminating patron of the arts than the imperious clergy or the anxious bourgeoisie. Indeed, the bishops, princes, and burghers of yesteryear were being displaced by a new aesthetic clerisy of art directors, public relations specialists, and corporate officials, an executive committee of beauty intent on revolutionizing popular taste. Calkins made no secret of the fact that corporate modernism was a form of aesthetic oligarchy. Just as technical professionals and managers controlled the means of material production, so artistic experts now possessed the means of loveliness and spiritual enrichment. "Beauty . . . must be imposed at the top by fiat," Calkins bluntly declared. "It cannot be imparted by the workman who has become a machine-tender."[17]

Besides reflecting the aesthetic supremacy of the professional-managerial class, corporate modernism was also, for Calkins, an outward sign of pecuniary grace. During the 1920s, at the crest of his stature in the advertising industry, Calkins philosophized everywhere about the fine art of the business millennium, lauding its marvelous capacities for metaphysical and moral transfiguration. "Beauty," for Calkins, was an ontological elixir, transforming goods into commodities and curing the existential maladies of modern souls. Hawking the "new business tool" in the *Atlantic Monthly* in 1927, he explained that beauty is "introduced into material objects to enhance them in the eyes of the purchaser"—an aesthetic corollary of monetary metaphysics. Three years later, in his contribution to Fredericks's "Philosophy of Production" symposium, Calkins defended the mercantile enlistment of modernism by asserting that it mitigated and even abolished "the ugliness and spiritual poverty" wrought by mechanization. Long after he retired from Calkins and Holden in 1931, he extolled the power of commercial art to convey intimations of transcendence. Modernism, he recalled in 1946, had availed advertisers of "the opportunity of expressing the inexpressible."

Yet despite all his paeans to art, Calkins—like the rest of the advertising apparatus—made "beauty" an instrument of pecuniary reason.[18] Originating as a form of artistic expertise and lending an exotic and graceful facade to the process of accumulation, corporate modernism reigned as the consummate aesthetic of professional-managerial hegemony.

Calkins left the industry in the midst of the Great Depression—a "*Gotterdammerung*," in Rorty's words, that ravaged firms, agencies, artists, and copywriters. The crisis was aggravated by an already powerful wave of public scorn for advertising, which was now associated, not with prosperity and modernity, but with waste, fraud, and decadence. Since the early 1920s, critics such as the journalist Stuart Chase had vilified advertising as "the life blood of quackery." In *Your Money's Worth* (1927), Chase had aimed squarely at the enchanting strategies of corporate modernism, castigating its "fanfare and trumpets" and its "Wonderland of fancy packages [and] soaring words." The Depression only amplified Chase's brand of moralism, and, chastened by the backlash, many admen beat their breasts in repentance. In the months before the crash, Theodore MacManus had scolded his fellow professionals in the *Atlantic Monthly* and in *Printer's Ink* for taking America to "the nadir of nothingness." Advertisers, he thundered with alliterative umbrage, had "mistaken the surface silliness for the same solid substance of an averagely decent human nature." After the crash, buffeted by unemployment and criticism, more admen donned sackcloth and ashes; as one penitent adman acknowledged in the *Atlantic Monthly* in 1932, his profession had become "a stench in the nostrils of the civilized world."[19]

Spearheaded by journalists such as Chase, a revitalized consumer movement, in tandem with New Deal reformers, set out to clean up and regulate the industry. Yet despite aggressive consumer activism, advertisers united with other sectors of corporate capital to limit and denature any regulatory legislation. While it amended the Federal Trade Commission Act to prohibit "unfair or deceptive acts or practices in commerce," the Wheeler-Lea Act of 1938 was far less restrictive than Chase and other activists had hoped. The formation of the Advertising Council in 1941 to support the new war effort and burnish the profession's image signaled a revival of confidence, at least among advertisers. But public criticism had made the industry more aesthetically conservative, and agencies and art departments gradually abandoned the corporate modernist inventory over the 1930s. As Marchand reports, disgruntlement with modernist aesthetics combined with furious competition for consumer dollars to make advertising imagery more "loud, cluttered, undignified, and direct."[20]

The desires contained in corporate modernism also pervaded industrial design. From the late 1920s until the mid-1940s, industrial designers were the main acolytes of the machine aesthetic in everyday life. Like advertisers— from whose ranks many of them came—industrial designers achieved professional stature after World War I. Until well after the war, corporate industry paid little sustained attention to the aesthetics of product design. But the economic upturn of the 1920s triggered a revolution among the draftsmen of mechanized material culture. Once again, Calkins was an indefatigable spokesman. In the same 1927 *Atlantic Monthly* essay devoted to beauty in business, Calkins predicted the appearance of "art directors whose work will be to style products . . . in the aesthetic spirit of the age." Designed in accordance with the zeitgeist of the business millennium, the new commodities would express and disseminate "the beauty that already exists in the industrial world around us." Calkins was among the first members of the culture industry to see aesthetic potential in machinery. "If we are to have beauty, it must grow out of our modern industrial civilization." "We are just on the threshold of creating a new world on top of our modern industrial efficiency," Calkins proclaimed. Through "the much criticized machines," designers, engineers, and architects could "replace the beauty that the machines originally displaced"—much as they had dispossessed the artisans of old. As beauty had assumed the ontological status of divinity for Calkins, so the material abundance of industrial life became the consecrated fetishes of modernity. Beauty emanated from "our visual world, our landscapes, our architecture and the tools and furniture with which we perform the operation of living." "A really beautiful factory building," Calkins mused elsewhere, "is worth more . . . than a museum full of the choicest art of antiquity."[21]

Other members or fellow-travelers of the advertising guild echoed Calkins's dithyramb to corporate modernist design. As Thomas L. Masson, editor of the *Saturday Evening Post,* had written in 1931, advertisers might well "create a fairyland," but they stood on the "legitimate ground" of science and machinery—ground occupied by industrial designers. Writing in 1932, in the depth of the Depression—a time, one would think, when the beauty of commodities was the last thing on anyone's mind—design virtuoso

Norman Bel Geddes saw a promising future for his profession. Despite (or perhaps precisely because of) the poverty and shabbiness of the present, "the mass of people," Geddes intuited, "have a deep-rooted craving for satisfaction from the appearance of the things around them."[22]

Industrial design had emerged from a loose coalition of museum curators, industrial educators, architects, decorators, advertisers, and art critics. Among curators and educators, the most vociferous partisans were John Cotton Dana, director of the Newark Art Museum, and Richard F. Bach, head of the Metropolitan Museum of Art's industrial arts program. Dana (who earlier in the century had envisioned a future in which "business runs the world") sponsored the first exhibition of commercial products in a fine arts museum, and he established a "Business Branch" of the Newark library. Like his good friend Calkins, Dana helped fashion and promote the ideal of the businessman as industrial virtuoso. In a 1927 booklet, *The Industrialist as Artist,* Dana reasoned that the businessman's "artistry" in enterprise allowed him to "see and understand and enjoy the artistry which goes into any one of a thousand forms of art"—a sensibility that, if applied to mass production, would augment sales and profits. Though he remained more of a highbrow aesthete than others in the movement, Bach preached the gospel of industrial design and its democratic promise. Despite his fear that "design for industry" was degenerating into "industrialized design," Bach continued to showcase the talents of established and rising designers, sponsoring over a dozen industrial arts expositions at the Met during the 1920s and 1930s. He continued to believe, as he wrote in the *American Magazine of Art* in 1931, that "the machine as an economic factor" made design "a spiritual necessity." The mission of contemporary business, Bach declared, was to make the spiritualized fruits of design for industry "available in quantity to the mass."[23]

Other advocates of industrial design had professional roots in architecture and advertising. One of the most prominent and wealthy Art Deco furniture designers, Paul T. Frankl, began his career as an architect. Frankl's *New Dimensions* (1928) and *Form and Re-form* (1930) became popular handbooks among product and interior designers, illustrating how the "spirit of speed, compression, [and] directness" could be expressed in "skyscrapers, motorcars, airplanes . . . in department stores and great industrial plants." As the avant-garde of corporate modernism, advertisers were especially keen on industrial design. As *Printer's Ink* editorialized in the mid-1920s, "machine-made products . . . must be assimilated to the destiny of things not machine-like." Mass production, the journal continued, "must be translated into human terms." Robert R. Updegraff, author of *The New American Tempo* (1929), one of the earliest celebrations of industrial design, was an advertising executive who included his volume in a "Little Library of Self-Starters"—a series redolent of small-proprietary uplift. Determined to bring the aesthetic flair of corporate modernism from the advertising suite to the production line, Updegraff admonished "a new crop of business geniuses" to capitalize on the accelerating speed and variety of modern life. To profit from the modern tempo, manufacturers, he argued, had to become as savvy and "modern" about the styling of their products as they were about their advertising. Having already provided an ample supply of "business genius," advertising spawned many of the major industrial designers—Walter Dorwin Teague and Raymond Loewy, for example, had been fashion illustrators, while Geddes and Herbert Dreyfuss had been stage designers with adeptly cultivated business contacts in the profession.[24]

The apostolic mission of Updegraff, Frankl, and other professionals associated with the American Union of Decorative Artists and Craftsmen received support from commercial expositions, business journalism, and popular mercantile literature. Like their counterparts and friends in advertising, many future industrial designers traveled to Paris in 1925 to attend the International Exposition of Modern Industrial and Decorative Arts. Although the Paris Exposition actually contained "little that was new," Jeffrey Meikle has observed, it "affected American visitors more through its brashness than its novelty." When the Exposition toured New York, Boston, Chicago, and six other cities in 1926, even more American designers were galvanized by the possibilities it suggested. The Paris Exposition presaged a decade and a half of industrial design publicity. In the spring of 1927, Macy's sponsored its Exposition of Art in Trade, which featured modern designs in furniture, fabrics, pottery, and silverware. Over the next two years, Wanamaker's, Lord & Taylor, Abraham & Straus, and other department stores followed Macy's lead. In the business press, *Women's Wear Daily* inaugurated a column in 1928 entitled "Home Furnishings=Modern Art"; *Business Week* and *Printer's Ink* began promoting industrial design before the Depression, while *Fortune* took up the banner in the 1930s. *Popular Mechanics* and

*Popular Science Monthly* ran numerous articles by and about the most prominent designers.[25]

Consumers learned about industrial design through magazines, store catalogues, product manuals, and brochures; the spread of trade exhibitions (especially those sponsored by the automobile industry); and the appearance of industrial styling in the most common and useful objects. Streamlining, Art Deco, and other forms of corporate modernism appeared in Sears Coldspot refrigerators (designed by Loewy), Eastman Kodak's Beau Brownie cameras (Teague), and Hoover's Model 150 vacuum cleaners (Dreyfuss) The most lavish popular theaters for industrial design were the world's fairs: the "Century of Progress" (Chicago, 1933–1934), the California-Pacific Exposition (San Diego, 1935), the Golden Gate International Exposition (San Francisco, 1939), and the "World of Tomorrow" (New York, 1939–1940). As the "Century of Progress" and the "World of Tomorrow" suggested, these expositions amplified the corporate eschatology envisioned in Chicago's White City of 1893: a world made radiant, harmonious, and bountiful by the genius of corporate capitalism.[26]

Art critics joined the chorus of praise for the promise of industrial design, especially Sheldon and Mary Cheney, its most articulate and prolific advocates in artistic and literary circles. In *The New World Architecture* (1930) and *Art and the Machine* (1936), the Cheneys affirmed the human potential residing in the union of machine aesthetics and product design. Far from reducing humanity to the proverbial cog in the machine, the application of science and technology to architecture and mass production presaged, in their view, "the liberation of man's individuality, of his creativeness." Indeed, the Cheneys believed that the machine could be so efficient that "we rise beyond it to enjoy those serenities, those spiritual contacts" that only an elite could relish before the industrial revolution. Others shared the Cheneys' faith in the impending beatitude of mechanized everyday life. In *Men and Machines* (1929), Chase observed that although "the machine has ruthlessly destroyed a whole age of art," it was also "busy creating a new one" from the patterns of gears, turbines, belts, and dynamos. Around the same time, Margaret Bourke-White told the *New York Times* that dynamos "could be more beautiful than pearls." Soon to join Sheeler as an iconographer of industry with her photography for *Fortune* and *Life,* Bourke-White thought machinery and its products the only possible catalysts for a vital contemporary art. "Any important art coming out of the industrial age will draw inspiration from industry, because industry is alive and well." Industrial life exhibited a passion for veracity and precision that tolerated no deceptive embellishment. "The beauty of industry lies within its truth and simplicity: every line is essential and therefore beautiful." In *Technics and Civilization* (1934), Lewis Mumford—later a scourge of "the myth of the machine"—linked "the esthetic excellence of machine forms" to moral and intellectual progress: simplicity and economy of line, he argued, fostered sober and disinterested inquiry. Thus, as Alfred H. Barr, Jr., director of the Museum of Modern Art, concluded in 1934, the beauty of the machine, while yet to be fully realized, was an imperative for American civilization. In his introduction to the catalogue for "Machine Art," MOMA's celebrated exhibit, Barr issued a challenge not only to artists but also to leaders in science and industry. "Not only must we bind Frankenstein, but we must make him beautiful."[27]

These exalted hopes for industrial design had been anticipated by European architects such as Le Corbusier. Le Corbusier's *Toward a New Architecture* (1923) cast a powerful and enduring spell on a generation of American architects, urban planners, and product designers. Often praised or maligned as one of the last architectural utopians—beautiful buildings, he believed, could "produce happy peoples"—Le Corbusier was indeed a zealot, and a religious fervor was central to his appeal. The West faced a "moral crisis," he warned. "We perish in untruth," he lamented, "demoralized" by a stupid and tasteless bourgeoisie: the coarse plutocracy of "big business men, bankers, and merchants" who inflicted their philistinism on the urban scene. With its clean, simple lines, modern architecture could overcome the bourgeoisie and its gilded cityscapes. So if Le Corbusier was a "functionalist"—a house, he infamously declared, was "a machine for living in"—the "function" he envisioned was not practical in any narrow sense. Likewise, when he called on his fellow architects to "create the mass-production spirit," he meant more than mere consumerism. Like Louis Sullivan, Le Corbusier hoped that architecture would mold the *mores* and spirits of modern men and women. Mathematical forms of design enable us, he wrote, to "see beyond mere sensations" and to perceive "certain relationships" which "lift us into a state of delight." In this elevated consciousness, we flourish "in harmony with the universal laws that govern us and all our actions," employing "our full powers of recollection, reason, and creation."[28] The "mass-production spirit" promised peace and euphoric transparency. Because he was an evangelist of mechanical beatitude, Le Corbusier was a prophet of the celestial city of Fordism.

With his dazzling blend of audacity and mysticism, Le Corbusier provided an imprimatur for the ambitions of American design professionals. Like advertisers who thought of themselves as modern artists, industrial designers and their celebrants fused a sense of professional elitism; a commitment to the artisanal ideal; and a grand, even grandiose conception of their calling. In *Horizons* (1932), an illustrated survey of industrial design, Geddes called on his fellow practitioners to embrace and promote their work as a vocation. Like many in the advertising industry, artists employed in the industrial arts had done so, he conceded, "with condescension, regarding it as a surrender to Mammon." Yet Geddes predicted that over time—and with corporate support—his colleagues would achieve what at present seemed oxymoronic: "an adequate industrial craftsmanship." Moreover, Geddes prophesied that in the very near future, municipal governments would overcome the graft, politics, and poor taste that hampered urban planning and turn to aesthetic engineers trained in the arts of design and business. "The most capable people in the municipality," he wrote, "will run it in the same way that the best brains in a business manage it." "Embodying the brains of the community," benevolent technocrats would plan their cities in accordance with the expertise and sensibility of professional designers and architects.[29]

Teague was just as emphatic that "only the ablest minds" could grapple with the complexities of a mass-production society. "More important than either capital or labor," the professional guilds of "chemists, physicists, metallurgists and engineer inventors" were, in Teague's opinion, "the most powerful forces in modern industry." Yet when Teague insisted that the aim of industrial design was the introduction of beauty into "the common rounds of daily life," he echoed Ruskin, Morris, and the rest of the Anglo-American Arts and Crafts movement—as did the Cheneys, who claimed that industrial designers were the descendants of Cretan potters, Scythian liverymen, and medieval stone masons. Industrial design, in their view, augured the restoration of "a long-lost unity of art and practical life." The aesthetically enlightened industries of the day were seeking "an artist of acute sensibility" who expressed his talent in "concrete, machine-age creations." At the same time, trained to "coordinate their aesthetics with engineering and mechanics and merchandising," the new profession exemplified the felicitous interdependence of professional life.[30] Instead of beefy and brutal robber barons, trim, cosmopolitan industrial designers were the artisans of the business millennium.

Industrial designers envisioned a world enchanted and transfigured by beautiful commodities. Where Ruskin and Morris had argued that the restoration of beauty to everyday objects entailed the rejection or severe curtailment of industrial production, professional designers and their advocates contended that modern machinery had reached an auspicious level of technical and aesthetic sophistication. Encouraged by writers such as the British art critic Herbert Read—who thoughtfully explored the possibilities of industrial design in *Art and Industry* (1934)—they rejected the charge that mass production was inimical to visual splendor and spiritual vitality. Like their counterparts in advertising, the design community draped its purposes and hopes in the rhetoric of magic, occult, and religion. Frankl argued in *Form and Re-form* that the loveliness of mechanized life owed much to the "alchemy" of industrial chemistry and metallurgy, through which "base materials" were "transmuted into marvels of beauty, expressive of our own age."[31]

Ever the evangelists for the machine aesthetic, the Cheneys countered that mechanical production contained a trove of treasure for the soul. A mechanized world, they wrote in *Art and the Machine,* was "rich in spiritual resources" harnessed and sculpted by the industrial designer, who pursued a priestly, vaguely sacramental vocation. The "community of tomorrow," only imagined by the nineteenth-century captains of industry, would be "transubstantiated by the boldest of the pioneering abstract artists: the industrial designer." "In accord with the secret rhythm of his century," the designer thrived on "profound forces" akin to those that inspired "the masons of the last Romanesque churches." Like the naves of those sanctuaries, the factories, offices, and agoras of modern capitalism, once touched by the genius of designers and architects, would "leap, lighten, elongate, and hover like a wing over the generation that [is] arising." Because streamlining suggested fluid, unhindered movement, its smooth, curvilinear patterns were "a valid symbol for the contemporary life flow," a sign of "the intangible, pervasive twentieth-century atmosphere." Designers related products to the airplane, the Cheneys intuited, because it was "the most conspicuous symbol and inspiration of the age," just as "the reverent medieval mind related everything to the symbol of the cross." Elsewhere, the Cheneys used the language of fable and magic rather than of sublimity or religion. "The fairy tale" familiar to all cultures of "the laden table invoked by a magic phrase" would, they prophesied, find its fruition in the product design of "modern wizardries."[32]

As a kind of doyen among designers, Teague reflected the enchantment of his peers, if not always with streamlined simplicity. Son of a Methodist minister from Indiana, Teague started his business career in Calkins's advertising firm, where he aspired to be the next Maxfield Parrish. For twenty-five years, Teague worked as a commercial magazine illustrator, but after a 1926 trip to Europe during which he "burn[ed] his mental bridges," Teague left illustration for industrial design. For clients ranging from Ford, Texaco, and U.S. Steel to Du Pont and Eastman Kodak, Teague designed cameras, compressors, barometers, railroad coaches, heaters, and motors. His "Beau Brownie" for Kodak is one of the diminutive masterpieces of Art Deco, and its success catapulted Teague into the front ranks of design professionals. By 1939, when he directed the Ford and Consolidated Edison exhibits at the New York World's Fair, Teague was the most respected industrial designer in America, with a firm of twenty-five employees trained at MIT, Cornell, and New York University.[33]

Though impatient with "professional messiahs," Teague thought of himself and his fellow designers as an aristocracy of achievement, a nobility of "doers" who, unlike intellectuals, focus on "the immediate task" undistracted by "the foggy realm of words." Still, between supervising employees and procuring corporate clients, Teague managed to enter that realm with *Design This Day* (1940), a superbly illustrated if nebulous primer on the principles of industrial design. Placing himself in the lineage of Ruskin and Morris, Teague agreed with arts-and-crafts critics that mechanization had broken the old artisanal unity of hand and brain. At the same time, obsessed with sheer volume and profit, the pioneers of industrial production had forced a "retreat of beauty from the ordinary circumstances of daily life and work." But the "revolt against destiny" demanded by defenders of traditional craftsmanship was both futile and myopic, Teague thought, because they refused to see the new unity forged among corporate professionals. Like his colleagues, Teague considered the industrial designer to be the modern heir to the craftsman, reinventing the rapport of hand and brain in the styling of mass-produced objects. In airplanes, parkways, factories, and offices—as well as in kitchens, bathrooms, and cellars—industrial designers were gracefully tracing "the inevitable trend of our destiny." Undaunted by bread lines and industrial turmoil, Teague assured his readers that the Depression and the looming war in Europe marked the "final, violent crisis in the process of readjustment." With their blend of mathematical and aesthetic skills, designers, architects, and engineers were laying "the first stones of Utopia." Teague predicted that, when the final stones were set in place, the earth would be an Art Deco olympus to the demigods of industrial modernity, a "race of fair, god-like men who have been dreamed about and talked about for ages."[34]

Thus, the expertise of industrial design held yet another promise of the corporate millennium; and in prose that veered close to the comically pretentious, Teague produced a theological tract in the faith of commodity fetishism. Believing that industrial design was an irreplaceable part of "the technique of order in the Machine Age," Teague imparted a quasi-sacramental character to the fruits of mechanization. Like Calkins, his former employer, he anchored his philosophy of industrial beauty in a metaphysics of mass production. In accord with the "Laws of Relationships" that "derive their validity from the structure of the universe," the forms of human-made objects should be simple, clear, "harmonious and rhythmical"—"instinct with grace," Teague wrote. Beauty, he asserted, was "outward evidence of inward rightness"; well-made objects were tokens of moral and spiritual truth, affording "outward revelation of inward soundness and rightness." Echoing Henry Ford and the management clerisy, Teague added that factories, too, could be shrines of enchantment, and that the people who worked there could worship there. "A modern machine shop is often a sight beautiful to see"—an outward sign of inward rightness—"and the men who work in these settings respond to them with keen appreciation."[35]

Teague had already put his ontology to work at the most spectacular liturgy of industrial design: the New York World's Fair of 1939–1940, the last of the Depression-era expositions. Historians have seen the decade's Fairs as pageants of corporate science and technics. The official slogan of the Chicago Fair—"Science Finds—Industry Applies—Man Conforms"—was a blunt and ominous incantation of deference to corporate authority, and the New York Fair's call for acquiescence was less overt but equally uncompromising. But where the Chicago Fair had been historically minded and self-congratulatory—"a century of progress"—the tone of the New York Fair was forward-looking and even utopian: "the World of Tomorrow," or as Geddes's General Motors' exhibit "Futurama" specified, the world of 1960. The techno-futurist luster that pervaded the Fair brought together the mechanical and the oracular; as David Nye has noted all too briefly, the Fair was "a quasi-religious experience of escape into an ideal future."[36] A vast ceremonial of technological sublimity, the New York World's Fair was a River Rouge complex of capitalist eschatology, a collection of glamorous set designs for a corporate heavenly city.

Sponsored by an impressive consortium of investment banks, legal firms, and industrial corporations, the Fair was carefully and deliberately conceived as a utopian extravaganza. While many of the sponsors looked to the Fair to relieve the city's economic distress, its planners hoped to burnish the hegemony of business with displays of a mechanical heaven. Three years before it opened, Teague, one of the Fair's first and most sedulous planners, vowed that the world it would depict would be "free from the confusions, wastes, and frustrations that we see all around us today." In contrast to the all-too-obvious inefficiency and ineptitude of the present, the corporate exhibits should suggest that the world of tomorrow would embody "the perfect integration of parts we see today in some of our products that machine production makes possible." Other officials were equally lofty about the Fair's celestial, futuristic romanticism. Grover A. Whalen—public relations whiz, former police commissioner, and president of the Fair—declared that the exhibits displayed "enlightened and harmonious cooperation to preserve and save the best of our modern civilization." Whalen dubbed the Trylon—a three-sided white needle that soared 700 feet into the sky—a "pointer to Infinity," ascending to the heavens with all the longings of mortals. The Trylon and the Perisphere, the giant white dome adjacent to the needle, combined, Whalen continued, "the Greek idea of beauty of form and harmony with the Gothic conception of reaching ever upwards for a better world." Echoing Whalen, Frank Monaghan, a professor of history at Yale and research director of the Fair, proclaimed that the exposition expressed "the infinite aspirations of man." In this view, the Fair's corporate participants comprised the vanguard of an impending technological elysium. The aura of mechanized enchantment suffused the Fair's lavish official guidebook, which attributed millennial import to the dazzling and expensive artificial illumination. Enveloped in polychrome fluorescence, the Fair at night was "a city of magic," it said, "an enchanting vision hinting at the future."[37]

Several of the more popular exhibits displayed an unmistakable ambience of enchantment. General Electric's House of Magic, for instance, focused on special effects rather than science, presenting radio waves and magnetism as corporate conjuring tricks. (As Nye observes, "visitors left no wiser about electricity than when they had entered.") Outside the House of Magic, an enormous canvas painted by Rockwell Kent depicted a historical tale of progress from ignorance to enlightenment. Humanity, a brochure explained, traveled from "the superstition and misbeliefs of the Dark Ages" to "the more abundant life" enabled by science. Yet with its pervasive aura of magic, General Electric's pavilion suggested the replacement of one form of enchantment with another, the new one sanctioned by its commodified fruits conjured by a new class of shamans. A similar atmosphere enveloped Consolidated Edison's City of Light (designed by Teague and Frank J. Roads), a miniaturization of New York illuminated by 130,000 small bulbs. Taking up an entire block, the City of Light, the largest of the Fair's dioramas, sported model skyscrapers, a functioning subway, and a loudspeaker system that conveyed a "voice from the sky" presiding over a symphony of natural and urban sounds. According to Con Ed's brochure, London, Berlin, Paris, and other European cities were merely "strange earthbound cities of an older age" when compared to this incandescent metropolis—a city of tomorrow exalted by corporate technology above other terrestrial places.[38]

Teague's diorama for Ford, The Ford Cycle of Production, was a tabernacle of mechanization. Before viewing a rotating, animated "cyclorama" that explained the assembly of an automobile from resource extraction to finished product, visitors beheld a thirty-foot high "activated mural" equipped with moving puppets, gears, pistons, shafts, and rods. Mounted on a platform one hundred feet in diameter, a series of concentric steps rose toward the apex on which stood three Ford automobiles. Like visitors to the City of Light, pilgrims to the Cycle of Production witnessed a rite of consecration, performed on what one Fair committee member called "an altarpiece for science" that depicted "high ideals": the enlistment of science in industry, the bureaucratized mobilization of labor, and the standardized abundance of consumer culture. On the wall behind the mural, Teague interpreted the scene so as to leave no room for doubt: "From the earth come the materials to be transformed for human service by Ford men, management, and machines."[39] A ziggurat of industrial capitalism, the "mural" was one of the Fair's most revealing liturgical edifices.

Where the Cycle of Production was earnest and high-minded, Futurama was flashy and sleek, a glossy eschatological advertisement sponsored by General Motors. A motorized, automated vision of America in 1960, Futurama was the hit of the Fair, and it bore the unmistakable imprint of Geddes, who designed it for GM after first collaborating with Shell Oil. (GM lured away Geddes with a larger fee.) With its modish technological vision, Futurama was clearly a modernist pitch to prospective automobile customers. But when the *New York Sun* described the dark descent into the building as a journey of "pilgrims . . . bound for some magic shrine," its exaggeration captured the exhibit's quality as a catacomb of corporate eschatology. Once inside, visitors sat in moving chairs, each equipped with a speaker. The narrator informed them that they were about to embark on a "magic Aladdin-like flight through time and space." For the next sixteen minutes, they took a simulated flight into and over the United States. After gliding over countryside, they arrived at a technopolis: skyscrapers, wide spaces, and elevated skywalks for pedestrian traffic.[40]

It was surely a technocratic daydream, but as Nye points out, it was also a "realm of pure property": replete with cars, buildings, and machines, the City of Tomorrow—like Sheeler's photos of River Rouge—was bereft of identifiable human beings, who were reduced to stick figures navigating a world inhabited by corporate technology.[41] The absence of people from Futurama underscored two troubling and related features of the Fair's mechanical saturnalia: the replacement of politics by expertise, and the transfer of beatific longing to the science and technics of corporate industry. Like Teague's technocracy of "doers," Geddes's unseen, benign directors would obviate all nettlesome political conflicts. No vapors from the cars and smokestacks polluted the crisp and salubrious air; no pedestrians or workers exhibited a trace of boredom or discontent. The pilgrimage to 1960 called for no sacrifice, hardship, or dedication, just the will to believe in a magical journey to the corporate promised land. In its spacious, antiseptic, and automated grandeur, Futurama was the apotheosis of industrial design, a modular fantasia of American longing for a heavenly city of business.

Aiming to style common, mass-produced objects, industrial design augured the fullest incarnation of corporate modernist enchantment. In tandem with advertising, management theory, and the spiritual government of the culture industries, it marked another evolution of the covenant theology, translating its essence into the streamlined idiom and imagery of the corporate millennium. The errand into the marketplace had led to the city on a hill, then the homestead on a plain, and now the metropolis with gears and power grids. Once expressed in the language of Protestant Christianity, the American desire for a beloved capitalism now spoke in the vernacular of corporate humanism—like its Taylorist ancestor, a mechanization of communion. First envisioned by Puritan magi, the technological sublime was reconstructed according to the blueprints of the cult of the machine.

The "World of Tomorrow" was the pinnacle of corporate modernism, but the beautiful desires of commercial artists were no match for the pecuniary imperatives of business. By the end of World War II, Calkins's dream of a rapprochement between beauty and business had faded, and the chasm between fine and commercial art grew wider than ever. American modernism would become the preserve of the abstract expressionists, who shared Clement Greenberg's insistence on aesthetic autonomy, difficulty, and formal experimentation. Corporate businessmen would remain sponsors, even collectors and connoisseurs, but they would not enlist modernists as aesthetic engineers. Not until the advent of Pop Art and Andy Warhol would the problem of art and commercialism surface again. At the same time, industrial designers discovered that their beatific visions were just tony marketing techniques in the eyes of their clients.[42] Streamlining and Art Deco became frills, not elements of a coherent project to adorn and elevate the culture of Fordism. The cultural rehabilitation of free enterprise during the Cold War made the sort of planning suggested at the World's Fair seem authoritarian—even as corporations engaged in planning on a scale unimaginable before the Depression. Consigned to the illustrious debris of utopia, the celestial models of the Fair gave way to ranch houses, tailfins, and a plethora of chrome—as well as shopping mall complexes and the impenetrable austerity of the International Style.

The mechanized magic and religion of Fordism provoked a host of infidels. Although the Great Depression triggered indictments of capitalism for its instability and injustice, it also intensified a body of criticism that aimed at its toll in human desecration. In this prophetic modernism, unemployment, poverty, and alienation posed something far worse than a range of "social problems"; they were, as James Agee put it, "predicaments of human divinity," indisputable evidence of sacrilege against the image and likeness of God. To Agee and other defenders of "human divinity," Ford's "New Messiah" was a mechanized complex of idols to the enchantments of Mammon.

# PART SIX

## Predicaments of Human Divinity: Critics of Fordist Enchantment, 1920–1945

OFTEN VILIFIED BY the pious as an insidious prophet of secular humanism, John Dewey was one of the last of the great liberal Protestant theologians. Since its inception in the early nineteenth century, liberal Protestantism had represented a tenuous halfway covenant with modernity: an acceptance of scientific hegemony; a repudiation of myths and miracles; and a benediction of "progress" through the advance of commerce, technology, science, and democracy. In the United States, the liberal Protestant accommodation with the Enlightenment anticipated the Progressive religiosity of Josiah Royce, Herbert Croly, and Walter Lippmann: the buoyant faith that social and technological advances were ushering in a modern communion. Like the first generation of Progressive intellectuals, Dewey believed that industrial culture bore the possibility of a spiritual life more expansive and fulfilling than previous religions, and in the 1920s and during the Great Depression, he sketched the rudiments of an alternative divinity. Just as Earnest Elmo Calkins and other corporate modernists were heralding a business millennium, Dewey proclaimed the advent of a beloved republic embedded in modern industry. As he wrote in *The Public and Its Problems* (1927), a "Great Community" was gestating in the apparently dehumanizing processes of mechanical civilization, a fellowship in which technology would be subordinate to democracy—"a name," he wrote with religious flourish, for "free and enriching communion."[1]

In the wake of the Great Depression, Dewey elaborated on the prospects of this impending Great Community. In *Individualism Old and New* (1930), he viewed "corporate society"—the interdependent complex of manufacturing and cultural industries—as the matrix of "a mental and moral 'corporateness' for which history holds no parallel." This corporateness was building "a new type" of "mind and soul" and constructing what Dewey would soon call *A Common Faith* (1934). Blurring the traditional distinctions between sacred and secular, corporate society, Dewey thought, embodied "values that are religious in character"—cooperation, respect for individuality, and commitment to "inclusive, ideal ends"—that would only reach their fullest realization when liberated from the "money culture." Beyond the pecuniary metaphysic lay, he asserted in *Art as Experience* (1933), "a world beyond this world which is nevertheless the deeper reality of the world in which we live."[2] Dewey's common faith was a quasimystical augury of a corporate millennium.

The English journalist G. K. Chesterton had predicted a religious denouement for American industrialism. Reflecting on *What I Saw in America* (1922) during a lecture tour in the winter of 1921, Chesterton—like foreign visitors before him, from Tocqueville to H. G. Wells—was both charmed and appalled by the popular romance with money and business success. The American preoccupation with prosperity exemplified what Chesterton archly described as "a fine spirituality," a belief that money and possessions were not worthy in themselves but rather markers of virtue. The typical American thought of goods as tokens, outward signs of victory in competition; the Yankee was a strange kind of "mystic" who thought of life as "a perpetual game of poker." So while he admired the ubiquitous "hustle" and "uplift" that electrified American life, Chesterton noted that the romance with capitalism was "also a religion" with a "queer sort of morality attached to it": a man "making good" is "analogous to a man being good or a man doing good." If America was, as Chesterton put it, "the nation with the soul of a church," it remained ever faithful to the gospel of wealth and its promise of a gilded redemption.[3]

The American romance with Mammon was on resplendent display in Manhattan, where Chesterton meditated on the visual delights of the "fine spirituality" of Broadway. Strolling at night under "the artificial suns and stars of this tremendous thoroughfare," Chesterton avowed his enchantment by the incandescent majesty of the modern metropolis, declaring his "rather dark sympathy with those many-coloured solar systems turning so dizzily, far up in the divine vacuum of the night." Chesterton captured the sacramental energies that surged through New York's commercial culture. The republic of goods advertised in the signs was a "beautiful superstition in the skies," and the tableau of fashion competed with "the purple and peacock plumage of the seraphim." Chesterton attributed the power of these edenic surrogates to the talents of commercial magicians, conjurers busy designing the earliest enchantments of corporate modernism. As hypnotists holding the means of "pyrotechnic violence," the adman and the financier branded "their commands in heaven with a finger of fire." Yet that heaven would share the fate of all sinful pretension to fulfill the desire for beatitude. "Nothing remains at last of a flaming rocket, but a falling stick."[4] A sacramental desire fueled the hunger for riches; the hope for a heavenly city charged the mercentile jostle of capitalism.

Beguiled by the fraudulent salvation of commodities, Americans, Chesterton realized, were also entranced by the magic of machinery. Before and after his trip to America—in *Utopia of Usurers* (1917) and *The Outline of Sanity* (1927)—Chesterton contended that the culture of Fordism was a covert form of idolatry. Sardonically defending Henry Ford as "a good man, so far as it is consistent with being a good millionaire," Chesterton considered the American capitalist a magus in the spells of enchantment. Like earlier tyrants, "the great employer" rules not only by force but also "mostly by fairy tales." Though "the sight of a millionaire is seldom a enchanting sight," Chesterton observed, "nevertheless he is in his way an enchanter." The modern industrialist was "much more than a swindler," he mused; he was "a mesmerist and a mystagogue," a "sorcerer" like the one Marx and Engels had accused in *The Communist Manifesto*. If maladroit in the arts of enchantment, he hires a coven of magicians—otherwise known as advertisers—and pays extravagant fees for the fetishes they conjure. "Even if there is only the devil to pay," the industrialist-warlock foots the bill for the shamans of capitalist culture, whose charms of corporate sorcery studded the popular press. Coming upon a description of "the Happy Factory" in an American magazine, Chesterton noted how its vision of mechanization turned quickly and daftly seraphic. "From height to height of ideality" it soared "until it ended with a sort of hush, as of the ultimate opening of the heavens."[5]

Chesterton was part of a trenchant and sometimes hysterical wave of European cultural criticism that appeared after World War I. Although Fordism held vast popular appeal in Europe—from business leaders to industrial workers, and from liberals and social democrats to Bolsheviks—in the canon of books and articles about "Americanism" or "Fordism" that were published in Europe in the 1920s, the United States epitomized an iniquitous industrial modernity: unchecked mechanization, vapid consumerism, a "mass society" of hollow men and women. Jazz, the Ford car, Hollywood, retail stores, and phonograph records—the pure products of America were crazy portents of the end of civilization.[6]

The abomination of *Fordismus* could be traced, some European critics thought, to the perverse religion that animated the new American mercenary and mechanical world. From Oswald Spengler and Ortega y Gasset to T. S. Eliot, Aldous Huxley, and D. H. Lawrence, America was depicted as a land in thrall to what Kate Leslie, the protagonist of Lawrence's *The Plumed Serpent* (1926), called "the cult of the dollar." In his *Studies in Classic American Literature* (1923), Lawrence had identified Benjamin Franklin as the quintessential American devotee of Mammon. Franklin's God was "the supreme servant of men who want to get on, to produce. Providence. The provider." Held "aloft on a pillar of dollars" and indifferent to vice or virtue, Franklin's God was now "head of nothing except a vast heavenly store." Later, in Huxley's *Brave New World* (1932), Henry Ford's famous car provides a religious ornament in the era after "a thing called God": shorn of any broken or suffering Christs, "all crosses had their tops cut off and became Ts." The inhabitants of Huxley's techno-dystopia engage in a weekly "Solidarity Service" at which they consume "dedicated" soma tablets—consecrated eucharistic wafers of the body of "Our Ford," which leave them with "an expression of rapture . . . the calm ecstasy of achieved consummation."[7] Cheap, safe, and reliably blissful, Brave New World is a heaven of narcotic felicity.

Domestic critics of Fordism and "the money culture" agreed that the country was descending into a monotonous barbarism, but they disagreed among themselves about the way to restore a vibrant civilization. Like Dewey, most progressive or Marxist critics of Fordism maintained that if capitalism could be reformed or abolished, the technological genius and productivity of mass production could finally serve and not enslave humanity. The clouds of industrial smog obscured a golden age of plenty and freedom; the promised land once foretold in religion lay just beyond the technological horizon. But to other opponents, Fordism was not simply an unjust and oppressive system; it was the industrial apparatus of a new Dark Age, an unprecedented assault on the humanity of human beings. Rather than a great leap forward in ingenuity and productivity, mechanized production marked a quantum advance in the history of degradation. If a "common faith" was under construction in the corporate factories and offices, it was devotion to an idol who demanded the sacrifice of human nature and dignity. In the words of the radical journalist James Rorty, corporate industry was committing a "profound profanation of the human spirit."[8]

With our own "money culture" even more brazen and punitive than it was in Rorty's day, we might appreciate that Rorty's charge of profanation was not melodrama, but clear-eyed reportage. Opponents of the money culture saw the spell of mechanization; even secular critics such as Theodor Adorno detected the "distinctly magical and irrational authority" exercised by Fordist capitalism. In Adorno's words, only a vantage "from the standpoint of redemption" could perceive and begin to dispel the enchantment. When rooted in some religious humanism—in a faith akin to Dorothy Day's conviction that the person was "a temple of the Holy Ghost"—dissenters from the mechanical money culture were most profound and incisive. Like James Agee, they affirmed the reality of human divinity against the phantoms of capitalist enchantment.

# 20

# The Mysticism of Numbers

Postwar Enthusiasm for Technocracy

WHILE EUROPEAN AVERSION to Fordism was rooted in aristocratic, agrarian, or artisanal values, American criticism of mechanization and mass production had no such venerable foundations. Well before Henry Ford and Frederick Taylor, the technological sublime had been an indelible feature of the American moral imagination. John Winthrop Jr.'s Puritan alchemy; Jonathan Edwards's millennial contrivances; Johann Etzler's mechanical "paradise within the reach of all men"; Emerson's avowal of a fundamental rapport between "Machinery and Transcendentalism"; the metropolitan megamachine envisioned by engineers, scientific managers, and corporate utopians such as King Gillette—this was Ford's ideological ancestry, and it brooked no resistance. Even rural populists admired the ingenuity and productivity of modern agricultural technology. The indignation of a Luddite or a Ruskin was left to curmudgeons such as Henry Adams, or to obstinate romantics in the Arts and Crafts movement. By the 1920s, industrial labor and technology were seen by most Americans as not only unstoppable but also, with the proper adjustments, indisputably beneficent. Conflict over Fordism concerned the distribution of its fruits, not the methods of their production.

Some of the harshest critics of the corporate order between the world wars were technocratic enthusiasts of mechanization and scientific management, who considered the profit motive an obstacle to productivity and technological progress. Advocates of technocracy called for a coup against the *ancien regime* of businesspeople and politicians and the installation of a technical and managerial elite. Yet despite their aggressively empiricist veneer, technocrats imagined the ideal ruling class as a new kind of priestly estate. Masters of that "mysticism of numbers" identified by Weber as one of the modern forms of enchantment, they sought to compute a metric of joy. Indeed, technocrats harbored a desire for redemption through the rationalization of enchantment.

The first organized cadre of technocrats was the Technical Alliance, formed in New York in 1919. Assembled through the energy and guile of Howard Scott—an oddball who combined the militant and the hustler—the Alliance included (at least officially) Scott; Thorstein Veblen of the newly created New School for Social Research; the engineer Charles Steinmetz; the regionalist and urban planner Benton MacKaye, later an associate of Lewis Mumford; the liberal journalist Stuart Chase; and several other writers and disgruntled professionals. Appalled by the waste and inefficiency that they blamed on the ineptitude of business leadership, the Alliance conducted an "Energy Survey of America" over the 1920s, a vast tabulation of natural resources, industrial organization, and professional personnel that was finally published in 1934. The Alliance concluded that the American economy was beset by mismanagement, traceable to the narrow pecuniary interest of stockholders and executives. Unable to understand the technical and managerial realities of production, businesspeople, the Alliance maintained, posed the doughtiest obstacle to efficiency and abundance. Convinced that both politicians and labor leaders were even more unqualified than the business class, the Alliance recommended the placement of industry under the direction of a "technate" that would provide firm and proficient professional and managerial governance over the nation's economy.[1]

The Energy Survey was the last act of the Alliance—it gradually dissolved as Scott's "Technocracy" movement emerged in the early 1930s—but its ideology of competence struck a chord among many writers eager to discredit the authority of corporate business. Veblen, for instance, had already indicted businesspeople before the war for their corruption of the "instinct of workmanship." Encouraged by the success of the Bolshevik Revolution, Veblen hoped, for a time, that a moment had arrived when the business class was vulnerable. In his last two books, *The Engineers and the Price System* (1921) and *Absentee Ownership and Business Enterprise* (1923), he surveyed the demise of the proprietary credo—a miscellany of "sentimental, religious, or magical truths," in his view—and beckoned toward a technocratic replacement. Beholden to "the stricter observance" of the proprietary creed, business was still steeped in an illusory metaphysics; the doctrines of corporate personhood and limited liability in particular both "put a strain on the received canons of knowledge and belief" and ensured that the nation's economic resources remained in the hands of "absentee ownership"—"the substance of things hoped for and the reality of things not seen," as Veblen described it. Insistent that the welfare of the nation and the leadership of its industry could not be left to phantom proprietors and clueless plutocrats, Veblen called on engineers to seize control of major corporations and establish a "soviet of technicians," a technocratic intelligentsia to superintend the industrial apparatus without interference from superstitious businessmen.[2]

Veblen's soviet of technicians remained a utopian idyll. Absent a violent revolution, the technicians' only resort would have been to ally with the corporate elite, whose pecuniary standards were precisely the targets of Veblen's ire. Labor unions were unlikely to be friendly: the American Federation of Labor was itself one of "the Vested Interests," as Veblen pointed out, while the Industrial Workers of the World—by the 1920s an organization seriously weakened by police repression, political apathy, and the American Plan—was in his view a ragtag bunch of "irresponsible, wayfaring men." And besides, sober and rational by temperament and training, the experts themselves were "a harmless and docile lot." And Americans on the whole remained enchanted by businesspeople, regarding their every platitude as a mite of revelation. In contrast, technicians aroused popular suspicion as "a somewhat fantastic brotherhood of over-specialized cranks, not to be trusted out of sight except under the restraining hand of safe and sane business men."[3] Over the 1920s, Veblen drifted away from the Technical Alliance, grew ever more despairing and resentful, and died in August 1929, two months before the stock market crash.

If Veblen was too mordant and disdainful to be a prophet, the acolytes of Technocracy were the most colorful, if also the most stridently elitist, evangelists of managerial control. Led by Howard Scott and Harold Loeb, Technocracy had a small but vociferous and high-decibel following among engineers, management experts, and industrial journalists. In the latter half of 1932, Technocracy made a meteoric appearance on the national scene: its leaders were profiled in both mass-market and highbrow periodicals, and thousands packed lectures and seminars directed by spokesmen. "Technocracy is all the rage," the *Literary Digest* reported in December 1932. After a comically incompetent national radio address by Scott a month later, the movement quickly descended into factional dispute, and its members fell apart acrimoniously.[4]

Despite its can-do veneer of "competence," Technocracy was never a truly coherent or unified movement. Its two most prominent spokesmen, Scott and Loeb, never shared a common vision: although Scott later claimed that Technocrats "never advocated social change," Loeb's *Life in a Technocracy* (1933), the most concise and accessible statement of the movement's goals, is nothing if not a call for profound transformations in American society, economy, culture, and politics. Neither man met the technocratic specs: Scott had no certified training in engineering, while Loeb had pursued a vagabond career as an avant-garde writer and publisher. (Independently wealthy, he had bankrolled *Broom,* the expatriate arts journal in which Paul Strand had ruminated about the "New Trinity.") As personalities, the two men could not have been more mismatched. Scott was an indefatigable charlatan, a "sardonic bombaster," as *Time* called him. (When pressed too hard for specifics about his life or ideas, he would, *Time* noted, "silence questions with a pontifical belch.") After an unsuccessful stint as the owner of a paint-and-floor polish company in New York, Scott stumbled into debates raging among Greenwich Village progressives and decided that technocracy afforded smart but impecunious men like himself an opportunity to demonstrate their talents. Loeb, scion of a rich family and a cousin of Peggy Guggenheim, was something of a ne'er-do-well playboy. After graduating from Princeton, he led the bohemian life in Greenwich Village and Paris, where his blend of mediocrity and flattery so offended Ernest Hemingway that he made Loeb the model for Robert Cohn, a dabbler-on-the-make, in *The Sun Also Rises* (1926). Scott's anxiety about his humble background goes a long way toward explaining his fractious relationship with the more cosmopolitan Loeb. These differences of temperament, not to mention those of ideology, eventually incited a quarrel that split Technocracy in 1933. Scott founded Technocracy, Inc., which still exists in the obscure hinterlands of American fringe movements, while Loeb set up the Continental Committee on Technocracy, which disbanded in 1936.[5]

Members of both Technocracy, Inc. and the Continental Committee on Technocracy agreed that the absentee owners of American industry had to be evicted and replaced by technical and managerial experts. The Taylor Society had never envisioned anything so sweeping; indeed, they had clearly conceived of scientific management as an instrument in the toolbox of corporate capital. Given a kind of imaginative license by Veblen, Technocrats advocated what they considered the next logical step in mechanization: the displacement of profit by efficient, abundant production as the criterion of economic performance. Especially after 1929, the Technocratic message certainly seemed reasonable, if not quite plausible, to many in the uneasy middle class. The coincidence of Technocracy's moment in the limelight with the presidential election of 1932 was auspicious, as both Technocrats and FDR seemed to promise a break with an unpopular and apparently discredited business orthodoxy.[6]

Technocracy was always a madcap fusion of quackery, machismo, and utopianism. The hokum of charts, graphs, and jargon usually left audiences both wowed and confused. Sporting a fedora, leather jacket, high-laced boots, and red bandana, Scott presented a rough-and-ready demeanor—a clear contrast to the polished manners of financial barons and industrial magnates. This image of virile professionalism became indistinguishable from a proto-fascist personality cult. Scott's Technocrats formed motorcycle corps, kept a fleet of gray automobiles, and brandished armbands and lapel pins bearing an insignia, "the Monad." Scott's antics stole attention from Loeb, a more careful and engaging thinker who wanted to dispel the connotations of authoritarianism that clung to Technocracy. Loeb's initial attraction to the movement stemmed from an epiphany he experienced while living in France. Traveling through the countryside one day, he discovered an ugly, abandoned factory that gradually became more beautiful to him in a new, hitherto unappreciated way. Contrary to the Romantic aspersion cast on machinery by bohemians, modern industry could, Loeb came to believe, bring humanity to "look around and rejoice in what they saw."[7]

Read in this light, Loeb's *Life in a Technocracy* is less a blueprint for bureaucratic regimentation than a beatific vision of enchantment regained. The authoritarianism was certainly there: democracy would be eliminated and replaced by magnanimous elitism, and a voluntary eugenics program would produce "a race of men superior in quality to any now known on earth." Echoing Scott, Loeb also asserted that, unconstrained by capitalist priorities, technology would reach such a level of sophistication and productivity that a 16-hour work week would suffice for all. Yet Loeb was clearly less interested in engineering and administrative details than in the recovery of enchantment. Capitalism, he thought, was already a powerful but perverse form of the sacred. Throughout *Life in a Technocracy,* Loeb referred to capitalism as an established but discredited religion, "the Mysticism of Money," as he called it repeatedly. "In America, the fundamental faith is the Mysticism of Money." "Capitalism has assumed a religious sanctity," he wrote elsewhere, and "to attack its tenets has become a heresy." Defined as belief in "the validity of the money standard" and in the "intrinsic merit of money making," the Mysticism of Money had its pious disciples; its festive rituals of sports and movies; and its temple edifices, especially the skyscraper, "a direct expression of the religion." Not that the Mysticism of Money was wholly bankrupt. Loeb praised the technological achievements enabled by pecuniary mysticism; Technocracy, he assured readers, would "require the toys of capitalism as well as the instruments of capitalism." What Technocracy would discard was the Mysticism of Money, "that religion which makes avarice a virtue."[8]

Yet in Loeb's account, the eradication of the Mysticism of Money would not be simply another "disenchantment of the world." If Technocracy would end or mitigate hunger and disease—the two great occasions of traditional faith—the conventional clerics would still have the cultural work of "encouragement to joy" in the midst of plenty. Still, suspecting that the historical religions would indeed become irrelevant in a Technocratic society, Loeb turned to artists and scientists as the new clerisy of enchantment. Where technology might turn the world into a joyless warehouse of resources, art would restore "that sense of imminent wonder . . . which all live things are heir to." Dimly aware that even art might prove incapable of bearing that existential freight, Loeb enlisted magic and voodoo—sifted, of course, through scientific reason. Since, Loeb argued, men and women had always found the meaning of life in "moments of ecstatic tension" generated by spiritual practices, then scientific study of these experiences could allow citizens of a Technocracy to "attain them at will" through psychological or pharmaceutical techniques.[9] Rapture now followed, not prayer or contemplation, but advances in industrial chemistry. A Technocratic culture would ensure an unprecedented efficiency of beatitude; the will to believe would yield to the scientifically managed production of enchantment.

After the Continental Committee on Technocracy dissolved, Loeb drifted away from Technocracy and eventually supported the New Deal as the best hope for stabilizing American capitalism. By the beginning of World War II, Technocracy, Inc. had faded as well, joining other discarded contraptions in the glossy junkyard of techno-utopias. But similar enthusiasms for techno-cratic enchantment would emerge in the Cold War vogue for automation, as well as in countercultural exhilaration about the possibilities for a postin-dustrial cyberculture. The technocratic mysticism of numbers would remain a component of the pecuniary metaphysics of capitalism.

# 21

# Secular Prayers and Impieties

## The Cultural Front as Migration of the Holy

DESPITE THEIR ANTIPATHY TOWARD business leaders, Technocrats hyperbolized the corporate world's growing obeisance to professional expertise. Indeed, with its emphasis on productivity and efficiency sundered from the imperatives of capital, Technocracy represented a genetic mutation of pecuniary rationality. Yet not all corporate professionals were beguiled by the mechanical enchantments of Fordism. Not all industrial designers, for instance, shared the millennial visions of Cheney, Teague, and Geddes. A few, like Hugh Ferris and John Vassos, imagined bleak alternatives to the polished, technocratic urbanism of Futurama. A successful illustrator and architectural draftsman, Ferris acquired a reputation in the 1920s for his gloomy, foreboding sketches of buildings and skylines. Accompanied by his signature drawings, Ferris's *The Metropolis of Tomorrow* (1929) was a moody reverie on urban modernity. Looking out of his office window at the skyscrapers of lower Manhattan, Ferris shudders with portentous dread even as he marvels at the city's grandeur. The nasty realities of metropolitan capitalism are invisible from the heights of Gotham. Capped by their Parnassian suites of corporate power, the buildings stand in haughty, titanic splendor, slaking "the financial appetites of the property owners." With an enormity that seems to overwhelm all dissent, every tower bestows a kind of sanction on those appetites: with its wall of black glass, its brass-inlaid floor, and its cup-shaped, bottom-lit well, the lobby of the *Daily News* Building gives visitors and employees "the sense of large actualities, often lacking in the words of contemporary scientists and architects." But take the elevator to the ground floor, and the trip to the city street becomes "a little like Dante's descent into hell."[1]

Yet despite his fear of the "new order" embodied in the Byzantium of capitalist culture, Ferris remains true to a more humane urban vision. "The real mission of Architecture," he insists, is "the elevation and evolution of Man," not the escalation of property values. Suggesting "intimations of a life other, and greater, than his own," the genuine architect is an emissary of some vague celestial order. In a strange epilogue, Ferris recounts how he discovered a mutilated manuscript—possibly of "quite ancient origin"—that recalled a less gargantuan and avaricious polis, founded in reverence for the human person. The fading document features a diagram of the ideal city, divided into precincts for business, science, and the arts, each corresponding to the senses, thoughts, and feelings of a healthy personality. "THE CITY," the text declares, "could be made in the image of MAN," "WHO IS MADE IN THE IMAGE OF"—and here the manuscript is torn. It's unclear what Ferris intended to say with that absence. Is "GOD" the concluding word? Is "MAN" made in the image of nothing? Though Ferris simply asked, "Did it contain a clue?" his spooky conclusion hinted at the prospect of retrieving the ancient conviction of the image of God.[2]

Vassos's vision of the future was even more harrowing. After living in Greece, Turkey, and England, Vassos emigrated to Boston after World War I and enrolled in the Fenway Art School, where he studied under John Singer Sargent. While attending Fenway, he designed sets for the Boston Opera Company and promotional ads for Columbia Records. He set up his own studio in New York in 1924, offering services in advertising and illustration to Lord & Taylor, Bonwit Teller, and Saks Fifth Avenue. Attracting other clients, such as Macy's, Packard, and French Line, Vassos catered to the high-end quarters of consumer culture. Though less venal than Teague, Vassos rivaled the designer-philosopher in talent and longevity: his turnstiles remain in many metropolitan theaters; his lotion bottle for Armand, a classic of luxury product design, doubled as a hip flask in the last days of Prohibition; and his radio cabinets for RCA sold well into the 1960s. In the late 1920s, Vassos moved into book cover art and illustration: his graphics for an edition of Oscar Wilde's *Salome* (1929) are still renowned for their sinewy, Art Deco eroticism.[3]

Despite his illustrious resume, Vassos expressed, off the clock, an infernal vision of techno-capitalist control. Although later in life he reflected that industrial design "took the curse off mass production" and "graced its products with personality and desirability," he never believed the corporate credo of progress he was paid to espouse. When he told a conference of furniture designers in 1938 that "the world depends on obsolescence and new merchandise," he uttered what was, in his own mind, a rueful fact, not an ideal. Always the artist, Vassos loathed the shilling that was inextricable from his job. Openly cynical about his manipulation of RCA dealers, he always lectured the annual meeting—completely without conviction—about "how terrible our last year's line was . . . because I try and make the new line better than last year's." Vassos and his wife Ruth—herself a former fashion consultant for Saks—always harbored a virulent antipathy toward capitalism, and they supported a variety of liberal causes in the 1930s.[4]

The Vassoses' contempt for their corporate clients and the world they were creating took form in what was, in effect, a four-volume graphic oracle of catastrophe: *Contempo* (1929), *Ultimo* (1930), *Phobia* (1931), and *Humanities* (1935). Illustrated by John, most of the texts (except for *Phobia*) were written by himself and Ruth, and all four folios depict a planet ravaged by avarice and violence. In *Contempo*—a collection of illustrations accompanied by brief, often sardonic captions—the Vassoses proved prescient about the capitalist future. In "Suburbia," for instance, a gouache of grassy hills is dominated by a telephone pole, a billboard, a mock-classical colonnade, and tract houses, while underneath Ruth muses on "Bastard architecture. The large billboard of the development company." "Commercialism" noted two business imperatives: not only "harness men to desks" but also "chop down the forests," a premonition of ecological wreckage. But the Vassoses also captured something of the dark enchantment that lurked in American commercial culture. The frontispiece to *Contempo* presents several elongated, sinister figures who either guard or beckon us toward a vortex of elliptical and ever-darkening swirls—the mercenary world lambasted inside the folio. "Confusion and disintegration lie in the many false gods we worship," John warned in *Humanities,* deities who "lead us inevitably into dead ends and blind alleys." Indeed, *Humanities* features an array of duplicitous and savage gods with "the nimbus of divinity": nationalism, fascism, racism, imperialism—all tutelary deities of capital.[5]

A graphic fusion of *Metropolis* and *Brave New World, Ultimo* is the most haunting of the folios, relating a post-catastrophic tale of a subterranean metropolis. The overindustrialized society has wrought irreparable havoc on the biosphere, and the earth's inhabitants are forced to descend into a techno-paradise underground. With a "mild and pleasant temperature equable at all times," the city is bathed in artificial light, with a "soft and palely green" firmament. Adorned with "gem-like gardens of rare beauty and translucency," it also sports large, effervescent mineral springs in which the inhabitants bathe for health and sexual stimulation. The economy consists of centralized, Fordist industrial centers; a short working day; tube delivery of food and other goods, reminiscent of Edward Bellamy's *Looking Backward*. The citizens engage in a ceaseless and frantic life of production, for their lives depend on their marginal utility to the underground domestic product: "No one can exist who cannot do his allotted share."[6]

The quest for godlike mastery produces boredom, anomie, and madness; thoroughly rationalized, life underground is "soul-deadening and pernicious." Many steal away to illegal bloodsports for some experience of adventure or intensity: one favorite features animals, somehow captured above ground, forced into glass enclosures where they fight to the death. At the same time, the demand for safety and comfort has ironically induced a state of pervasive anxiety and panic. (In *Phobia*—created with the help of his friend, psychoanalyst Harry Stack Sullivan—Vassos traced an ever-escalating trajectory of psychic agony, culminating in "pantophobia," the fear of everything.) The inhabitants grow more and more restive in their mechanized, climate-controlled Atlantis, hungry for "something to strive for, something to explore, something to suffer!" As the discontent spreads, the city stirs with talk about a vehicle—"bullet-shaped" in good streamlined fashion, the "apotheosis of mechanical genius"—designed to ferry passengers to other worlds. The narrator decides to leave if possible, hopeful that on some other planet, humanity can prosper with "a far kinder guise, in far gentler habiliments" than the wretched perfection under the earth.[7]

John Vassos's support for progressive politics while pursuing his career in industrial design marks him as a member of what Michael Denning has called "the cultural front": a theater of battle in the cultural industries between owners and executives on one side and left-leaning cultural workers on the other for control of the mass-produced symbolic universe of words, images, and sounds. Until recently, the conventional historical account of the cultural front and of its broader progenitor, the Popular Front, had been constructed by liberals and social democrats. In prominent left-liberal periodicals (such as *Partisan Review*, and later, in the 1950s, in *Dissent*), Dwight Macdonald, Clement Greenberg, Irving Howe, and others maligned the

Popular Front as a lightweight but toxic cultural confection, a saccharine coating for the poison pill of Stalinism. In their view, however eloquent their solicitude for the Common Man or the rights of minorities, Woody Guthrie, Paul Robeson, and other "committed" artists were unwitting troubadors for totalitarianism. At the same time, so this tale continues, the Popular Front was the latest chapter in the rube-ridden history of populist politics. With its hokey iconography of "the people," the Popular Front served as a dress rehearsal for the postwar culture of consumerism and conformity. Under the aegis of "the American Way of Life"—a phrase minted on the 1930s left—popular desires for social justice were transfigured into domesticity, while radicalism morphed into the quixotic causes of "socially conscious" celebrities.

This account prevailed among scholars as well; as Warren Susman put it, the Popular Front displayed "a ludicrous attitude toward American culture." But in the 1990s, a more sympathetic portrait emerged that rejected the acerbic dismissal of the Popular Front as shallow and sentimental agitprop. Denning, for instance, depicted a movement with deep roots both in the multiethnic working class and in the ranks of the culture industries—the "cultural apparatus," as C. Wright Mill would later describe them. The Popular Front at its best was, in Denning's view, an American form of social democracy, a motley crusade to claim the fruits of Fordism for the generation of the CIO. When workers in the consciousness industries aligned with this struggle, they comprised Denning's "cultural front." Far from being a band of dupes manipulated by Stalin, this cultural front was an authentic orchestra of American democracy, playing a Whitmanesque symphony containing multitudes.[8] Thus the "cultural front" was attempting to shape what Susman has described as Americans' "special collective relationship"—their "sense of common belief, ritual observance, and common emotional sharing." In other words, it was trying to craft a new "spiritual government," a new kind of religious dispensation for a socialist consummation of Fordist modernity.

Compiling his reflections on American civilization in the 1940s as he worked with fellow Trotskyists in Detroit, C. L. R. James, for instance, saw the religious dimension of the popular arts of film, radio, and recordings. To be sure, Hollywood and other precincts of the symbolic apparatus filled the "psychological need of the vast masses" for romance, aggression, and consumption. But like Sergei Eisenstein meditating on Disney, James noted that the devotion of fans to their favorite stars resembled "the mass cults of more primitive peoples." The studios' star system, he observed, was akin to the hierarchy of saints adored by the early Christians. Thanks to their technical ingenuity and ubiquity, the mass media increasingly tended, James wrote, to promote "a comprehensive integration of modern life" that embraced "the spiritual, intellectual, [and] ideological life of modern peoples." James recalled a precedent for modern mass culture in ancient Greek drama—as he noted, an essential part of religious festivals. Greek dramatists had written for the entire Athenian polis, assembled for the worship of the gods. As the leading intellectual and spiritual force of their time, these dramatists addressed philosophical and religious ideas with the full participation of the audience. Ordinary Athenians could experience what Aristotle called catharsis, because "they believed in their society, felt so to speak that God was with them." Before the advent of mass communications, the closest parallel to Greek drama in American culture had been the revival meetings of emancipated slaves, with sermons on "the sufferings of Christ or the saints." Produced for a working class better educated than the Athenians, the popular arts, James believed, heralded yet another epoch of cultural and spiritual democracy. Though conveyed in a Marxist lexicon of secularity, James's analysis approached being a theory of the popular arts as a modern migration of the holy.[9]

As one of the era's most astute students of mythology, Kenneth Burke, the music critic for the *Nation* in the mid-1930s, was less reluctant than James to characterize the culture industries as modern enclaves for a sense of divinity. In his controversial address to the 1935 American Writers' Congress, "Revolutionary Symbolism in America," Burke expounded on the indispensability of mythology. Myths, Burke explained, are "psychological tools" for achieving solidarity, and when they work well they are "as real as food, tools, and shelter." Because myths become so firmly embedded in the psyche, the left had to respect and turn to advantage their tenacious hold on the imagination. A Thurman Arnold of the left, Burke advised his comrades to build on the existing American proprietary mythology. Opposing any premature use of symbols such as "proletariat" or "masses" to unite the American working class—these words, he implied, were perceived as too radical and European—Burke pointed to the populist vernacular of "the people" as a rhetorical clothing of "middle-class values" in which revolutionary thought could be draped. Burke explicitly likened this strategy to the religious strategy of the early Church, which had "invariably converted pagans by making the local deities into saints." In Burke's view, there was little psychological difference that distinguished the wiles of advertising, the exhortations of religion, and the appeals of revolutionary politics. Indeed, Burke underlined the similarities by suggesting that, if admen hawked cigarettes by depicting smokers in pleasurable situations, then radicals should portray the communist future as desirable as well as just, in the same way that "the best artists of the religious era recommended or glorified their Faith."[10]

In his subsequent work—*Permanence and Change* (1935), *Attitudes toward History* (1937), and *The Philosophy of Literary Form* (1941)—Burke elaborated on his remarks to the American Writers' Congress by constructing a theory of culture as "secular prayer." In this account, just as social history is a progression of class conflicts, cultural history is a succession of clashes over sacred symbols, a tale of sacral orders and "impieties," challenges to the dominant symbols of an era that became orthodoxies in their turn. At present, the "priests" or "spiritual bankers" of capitalism conducted their liturgical business in the culture industries, professional associations, and corporate bureaucracies. Though cynical and greedy, the capitalist clerisy was the most enlightened of all priesthoods, perceiving the fundamentally material nature of human desire and action. For Burke, "the capitalist vocabulary of behavior" offered up the most readily answerable of all secular prayers, an "ingenious and suggestive vocabulary" of supplication fulfilled by science and technology. As the most rational and secular institution created in the history of class conflict, the corporation was both a rapacious firm and the acme of social development, as well as the most powerful answer to our prayers. Drawing a straight line from *corpus Christi* to the corporation, Burke praised modern capitalism for stripping corporate identity of its "unwieldy mysticism" and for exposing the irreducibly material basis of human cooperation. "The member of the church, as the 'body of Christ,' became simply the holder of non-voting stock."[11]

John Dewey also believed that corporate society still dwelled in the aura of religion. Although he rejected dogmatic religion, Dewey remained too much the liberal Protestant to fully embrace the moral and metaphysical implications of secularism. Like other signatories of the "Humanist Manifesto" published by the American Humanist Association in 1933, Dewey concurred with the document's affirmation of *"religious* humanism" which erased "the distinction between the sacred and the secular." Properly reconstructed by philosophers along the lines of scientific and technological modernity, religion could become the most "synthesizing and dynamic force for today," the soul of the industrial world. By this time, Dewey had identified "corporate society" as the institutional vehicle for a religious humanism: the "free and enriching communion" he had heralded in *The Public and Its Problems,* the "inclusive ideal ends" of *A Common Faith.* This new religion would arise from what he augured in *Individualism* as the creation of new "cultural possibilities" by "sociologists, psychologists, dramatists, and poets." The common faith would be the labor of workers in the culture industries—the new "seat of intellectual authority," in Dewey's words.[12] The shamans and clergy of old would be supplanted by writers, artists, and social scientists; in the new industrial world of cultural production, Whitman's divine literati—aided by professional and technical experts—could finally exercise their Romantic vocation as the spiritual legislators of modernity. Charged with the grandeur, not of God but of a self liberated from the decaying orthodoxies of the past, corporate society would transcend the disenchantment of the world through art, technology, and science. Thus did Dewey become the heir to Emerson as a theologian of "the soul's economy."

Even if they dismiss Dewey's "common faith" as religious twaddle, intellectuals eager to reclaim him for a revitalized progressive politics have emphasized this positive conception of corporateness. Fastening onto his pronouncement in *Individualism* that "we are in for some kind of socialism," they overlook his proviso: "a socialism that is capitalistic." The "common faith" could turn out to be a pecuniary credo with accumulation as its "inclusive ideal end," and Dewey clearly considered this a real possibility. If, as he realized, labor remained under the direction of "the business mind," and if managers continued to possess "the more active and leading share in the intellectual direction of great industrial undertakings," then corporateness portended a humanism indentured to pecuniary reason. Business may not have occupied "the new seat of intellectual authority," but it certainly endowed the chair; and if capital owned and managed the means of production of the common faith, then all spiritual legislation would have to be approved by the executive committee of the bourgeoisie. Dewey himself conceded that this "capitalistic" conclusion to socialism was made even more likely by the erosion of any countervailing forces. As he observed in *The Public and Its Problems,* industrialization had seriously weakened those institutions—especially religion and family—which had at least attempted to tame acquisitiveness and to nurture civic spirit and generosity.[13] Without the ability to envision possibilities outside the parameters of the corporate imagination, the "new individual" might well be more rather than less susceptible to capitalist enchantment.

Dewey's bland concession that corporate society might have a mercenary denouement would have come as no surprise to James Rorty, who envisioned a dystopian denouement to the Machine Age. Rorty—father of philosopher Richard Rorty—is best known as a radical journalist who, along with Lewis Corey, Kenneth Burke, Malcolm Cowley, and Matthew Josephson, contributed to *Culture and the Crisis* (1932), an *ur*-manifesto of the cultural front calling on workers in the consciousness industries to support the Communist Party. For much of the next two decades, Rorty lived and wrote among the lively albeit insular culture of left Manhattan; "all decent people were, if not Trotskyites, at least socialists," as his son later recalled, and a two-volume set of Dewey's inquiry into the Moscow Trials sat prominently on his bookshelf. But before he became a full-time journalist, Rorty had spent almost two decades in and out of the advertising industry. Like many other admen, Rorty entered the business as a way to pay the bills while pursuing a literary career. After graduating from Tufts in 1913, he moved to New York to write poetry and novels. During the day, he worked as a copywriter for H. K. McCann, whose sole client was Standard Oil. Always a mercurial and pugnacious loner, Rorty left the agency after Standard Oil complained about his copy. Enlisting in the Army, he was shipped to France in December 1917. After service in the Argonne Forest (from which he acquired both a Distinguished Service Cross and a strong support for pacifism), he returned to New York and the advertising business. For the next ten years, Rorty labored in the New York and San Francisco offices of BBDO, spewing forth streams of "advertising vomit." In 1930, fed up with his increasingly outspoken involvement in radical politics—he edited *The New Masses* and wrote eloquently in support of Sacco and Vanzetti—BBDO fired him, releasing Rorty from the well-paid nausea of churning out copy for corporate capital.[14]

Rorty worked with BBDO in the heyday of corporate modernism, but he had no bittersweet memories of advertising's dalliance with modernist art. It was "a hack job," he later recalled, but one that came to be something of "a labor of love." Though often depicted as "knaves and rascals," Rorty and his fellow copywriters "knew what we were": corporate gigolos, "the male hetaerae of our American commercial culture." So why did Rorty remain a prostitute, persisting in a profession whose clients he detested and serviced with exquisite skill? Besides the money, it was "craft, what every genuine craftsman cares about." The artisanal ideal survived, even among the beauticians of commodified monotony in the advertising trade. While he cranked out copy for his philistine clients, Rorty's "real loyalty was to the Word, to the materials of my craft." Indeed, working at BBDO among some of the finest practitioners in the field, Rorty came to believe that the best admen, propelled by an "obsessed delight in the materials of our craft," unconsciously aspired to break the bounds of pecuniary reason and "sabotage advertising." To Rorty, "the religion of Beauty-in-Advertising"—Calkins's venture to make advertising "the artist's greatest medium"—was a heretical crusade against the Gospel of Mammonism, an inchoate desire to liberate beauty from the integument of the commodity form.[15]

Alas, as Rorty knew, beauty would always be disfigured by the imperatives of profit, and so advertising could never really be more than a "pseudoculture," a mortal "rival of the Christian culture" that addressed the deepest longings of the faithful. Throughout *Our Master's Voice* (1934), Rorty emphasized the religious nature of advertising, about whose value for civilization admen could be "messianic." As the artisans of commodity fetishism, they moved to monopolize the dreams and rituals that formed the human imagination. Advertisers enclosed the mind and soul in an "advanced system of dream-manufacture," a liturgical enterprise of "make-believe" invested with "the accumulated make-believe of past decades and past centuries." Trafficking dishonestly in faith and hope—certainly not in charity—advertisers practiced a "modern priestcraft" not unlike that of the Middle Ages. Defining "the material, oral, and spiritual content of the Good Life," their slogans, images, and trademarks comprised the iconography of capitalist faith.[16]

Ironically, Rorty's belief in the power of advertising enchantment eroded his political convictions. He coedited *The New Masses* with Mike Gold in the mid-1920s during one of his spats with BBDO and later joined several Popular Front groups. But the more he reflected on the impact of his former profession and the more he saw of what American life had become under Fordist auspices, the more certain he grew that revolution was a dream as fantastic and opiate as advertising. Rorty's account of his travels, *Where Life Is Better* (1936), was light-years in tone from any Work Projects Administration guide book. With outrage, contempt, and despair, Rorty concluded that the pseudocultural surrogate for Christianity had triumphed. Stupefied by the "obsolete stereotypes" served up by the print and broadcast media, many Americans languished in a "passive acceptance of their condition." Resigned to the fate decreed by the powerful yet beguiled by the charms of the ads, Americans kept hoping that life would get better through some miraculous feat of abundance. "Always the fetishism of commodities," Rorty sighed in lament at the success of his former trade; "everywhere the vulgarization of the concept of progress." The devastation of the spiritual landscape was matched by that of the despoiled ecosphere, raped and polluted by industrial pillage; both the people and the ground were accursed on account of capitalist accumulation. Echoing the tradition of ecological criticism stemming from John Muir, Rorty mourned that "some profound profanation of the human spirit had occurred, some fundamental dislocation of the natural ecology."[17]

This was hardly a reveille for "permanent revolution," and while Rorty remained a committed socialist well into the 1940s, his travelogue betrayed a pessimism quite out of keeping with Marxist dialectics. The enchantments of Mammon seemed to have duped the fearful proletariat, the beleaguered bourgeoisie, and the dwindling agricultural classes. In Detroit, Rorty saw the full magnitude of Fordist enchantment. Even the unemployed and destitute were entranced by the vision of technological deliverance. Mesmerized by the mass production of dreams, both middle- and working-class citizens believed that "human life could flourish as a kind of parasitic attachment to an inhuman, blind, valueless process, in which money begets machines, machines beget money, machines beget machines, money begets money." After walking through Ford's River Rouge complex, Rorty confirmed Charles Sheeler's portrayal of the plant as a religious edifice. "A mechanically gifted child's dream of heaven," River Rouge attracted children "of assorted ages, from seven to seventy," who "throng the gates of this heaven for to admire and to see." After leaving Detroit and driving through the Midwest, Rorty dismissed the populist sentimentality of his comrades in the Popular Front. Farmers, he observed, were "oppressed and dispossessed capitalists, still pretty much dominated by the individualist business man's psychology."[18]

Depressed by his journey, Rorty abandoned the class struggle for what his comrades would have called idealism. If there was to be a final conflict— "which I doubt," he added tartly—it would not take place between classes, but between "intelligence and stupidity, between sanity and fanaticism, between justice and injustice, between freedom and tyranny."[19] After the Nazi-Soviet Pact of 1939, Rorty slowly ambled rightward, and by the early 1950s he was a self-described Taft Republican, writing scripts for the Voice of America—in short, playing the gigolo once again.

Ratified by popular deference to the mechanized commands of the Master's voice, Rorty's pessimism about the cultural apparatus as an incubator of radical consciousness was shared by Theodor Adorno and Max Horkheimer. Living in New York in the late 1930s after fleeing Nazi Germany, both emigrés conducted meticulous studies of the culture industries in which Dewey placed his hopes for communion: Horkheimer as director of the Institute for Social Research (relocated from Frankfurt to Columbia University) and Adorno as a researcher for the Princeton Radio Project directed by Paul Lazarsfeld. Not surprisingly, the priority of profit—determined by a pliant and calculable public—suggested that pragmatism was just another form of pecuniary rationality. Echoing Lewis Mumford's excoriation of the "pragmatic acquiescence" in business civilization, Horkheimer dismissed pragmatism as the philosophical equivalent of "market research and Gallup polls." Draping "obdurate common sense" in the raiment of philosophy, Dewey's thought struck Adorno as an exemplary form of manipulative bourgeois reason, surveying life with "a worldly eye schooled by the market." Even when coupled with radical politics in the work of Sidney Hook— Dewey's Marxist protégé in the Popular Front—pragmatism displayed, Horkheimer wrote, "a businesslike attitude toward matters of the spirit." However benign and progressive, Dewey's utterly conventional faith in science and technology risked both an unwitting capitulation to the present and an atrophy of political imagination. Beholden to business and the state, scientific and technological rationality would always reinforce the corporate order; some other source of utopian reverie was needed to counter the corruption of reason.[20]

This search for a cure to the "derangement of reason" seemed increasingly arduous and futile, as Adorno and Horkheimer grew ever gloomier as their American hiatus lengthened. Moving to Los Angeles in the early 1940s, they joined an illustrious enclave of German expatriates: Arnold Schonberg, Thomas Mann, Bertold Brecht, Fritz Lang, and Otto Klemperer. Although most accounts of their years in Los Angeles stress their alienation from the swanky decadence of Tinseltown, Adorno and Horkheimer were hardly aliens from Hollywood's social and artistic scenes: they attended and sought invitations to parties, requested and received research money from studios, and even wrote and peddled a film script—*Below the Surface*—to several major producers.[21] Yet their proximity to the dream factory only deepened their despair, as the industrialized allure of Hollywood augured a glamorous servitude for reason. The melancholy Marxism that emerged from their years in America took shape amidst the palms and bungalows of Los Angeles—the headquarters of mass-produced enchantment, the capital city of what the Frankfurt highbrows must have thought was the gaudiest inferno in history.

That balmy and ostentatious setting was perfect for their diagnosis of secular reason, which commenced with *Dialectic of Enlightenment* (1947) and concluded in the early 1950s with Adorno's analysis of astrology and the occult. Marooned among the glitterati, Adorno and Horkheimer saw the cultural apparatus as a splashy and portentous finale of the Enlightenment, a culmination of the hubris of reason in the calculated tawdriness of entertainment. The road from Voltaire and Diderot to Warner Brothers and Walt Disney was long but straightforward. The eighteenth-century *philosophes* had believed that through "enlightenment"—the emancipation of reason from the fetters of magic, superstition, religion, and ignorance—secular moderns would dispel the terrors of the unknown, fathom and utilize the laws of nature to extend and enrich human life, and live well and justly without hope or fear of a realm beyond the grave. But as with magic and divination, the desire to dominate the world inevitably entailed the domination of human beings, and the quest for absolute mastery marred and perverted the promise of enlightenment. Unleashed from old religious restrictions and then harnessed to new technological forces, the longing for worldly fulfillment had evolved into an unbounded will to power, manic underneath the facade of reason. The more it became calculation and measurement, reason demolished, not only religion but also its own claim to illuminate the nature of reality. Having relinquished and even liquidated its capacity to understand the world rather than manipulate it, reason itself enabled power and profit to become the effective metaphysics of modernity. Reason hardened into technology, while enlightenment degenerated into "animistic magic" and reverted to "superstition and paranoia." Invested with the same enchantment it had originally sought to demystify, reason become "deeply engulfed in mythology," fables of progress at least as insidious as the tales of gods and demons. Under cover of bureaucratic and technological sobriety, reason and enlightenment morphed into the administered delirium of productivity. As Horkheimer wrote in *Eclipse of Reason* (1947), "the watchword of production" had become "a kind of religious creed."[22]

While German fascism embodied the "derangement of reason" at its most barbarous and homicidal, the American culture industries pointed to a future with its own brands of rationalized enchantment. The deformation of enlightenment into mechanized irrationality was especially egregious in radio, film, and advertising. Supervising the musical component of Lazarsfeld's radio research project in New York, Adorno—a classically trained pianist—perused industry literature, endured innumerable hours of radio broadcasts, and even examined the shapes of radio sets and cabinets— "hallowed and sacred shrines," he surmised, "each like a miniature tabernacle." The sacral radio reinforced the divinity of the broadcast voices, whose unseen yet definitive presences spoke quite literally to the deepest recesses of the mind. "The absence of visible persons," Adorno asserted, "makes the 'radio voice' appear more objective and infallible than a live voice." Like a hearth god of antiquity, "the mystery of a machine which can speak may be felt in atavistic layers of our psychical life."[23]

Later, in Hollywood, Adorno and Horkheimer saw an even more harrowing future prefigured in the film industry, "a model of the huge economic machinery which has always sustained the masses." Like other Fordist mass-production enterprises, the business of dreams was a lucrative investment of enlightened rationality. But besides indicting mass culture as a form of rationalized "mass deception," Adorno and Horkheimer implied that radio, film, and advertising were the heirs of religion and magic. The conservative lament that the decline of religion had led to cultural chaos was "disproved every day," they contended, by the sheer ubiquity of commodity fetishism, conveyed incessantly through Hollywood's "cult of celebrity" and the "psychotechnology" of corporate modernism in commercial illustration. A fetish complex in constant production, the culture industry "now impresses the same stamp on everything": exchange value, marketability, and the pecuniary soul of capitalism.[24] With all avenues of escape from commodity culture apparently closed, workers embraced the moral and political imagination of their managers and technocrats. The mechanization of communion that began with scientific management ended in the administration of dreams.

Yet Adorno and Horkheimer also discerned a return of the repressed, a regression into primordial superstition and credulity that ratified the corporate order. While comfortably subjugated by business and the state, and bewildered by the collapse of old moral and religious certainties, the populations of industrial societies regressed into "pre-historical" modes of thought and belief. Among intellectuals, Horkheimer observed a resurgence of "forced naivete," attempts to revive older forms of metaphysics and conviction discredited by enlightenment, especially Buddhism and neo-Thomism. (He was especially exercised by religious and secular thinkers such as Jacques Maritain, Robert Hutchins, and Mortimer Adler, whose resuscitation of scholasticism seemed, to Horkheimer, to unwittingly bestow an imprimatur on the bureaucratic rationality they professed to abhor.)[25]

The renaissance of shibboleths among dyspeptic intellectuals was matched by the more popular delusion of astrology, the latter epitomized in Carroll Righter's "astrological forecasts" in the *Los Angeles Times*. Adorno had planned to undertake a study of occultism and astrology, but the project languished after he returned to Germany in 1949. When he briefly returned to America in the fall of 1952, he embarked on a more detailed analysis, reading through every one of Righter's columns from November to February 1953. Adorno's reflections underlined the affinities of astrology, the occult, and Fordism. Adorno sought to understand what he considered, at first, the incongruity between Righter's "distinctly magical and irrational authority" and the banality of the advice he offered. The astrologer is a strangely insipid oracle, Adorno wondered, whose "sobriety, nay overrealism" seems out of synch with his invocation of fateful celestial motions. Adorno resolved the conundrum by contending that, far from being an escape into utter irrationality, astrology was an enchanting representation of real life, a mythology of corporate capitalism. "The stars seem to be in complete agreement with the established ways of life," he marveled; the "opaqueness and inscrutability" of the astrological forces, together with their depersonalized and "merciless" decrees, parodied the bureaucracies of corporate power. As ridiculous as it seems in a scientific age, the horoscope reads like a list of "official directives," while "number-mysticism" prepares readers for "administrative statistics and cartel prices."[26]

The popularity of astrology and the occult suggested to Adorno that Americans were replacing "the cult of God" with the much more legalistic and unappeasable "cult of facts." By "transforming the world of things into quasi-metaphysical powers," the cult of facts both lowered resistance to "mythological temptations" and sanctioned obedience to corporate expertise. Like other features of the culture industry, astrology represented the merger of empiricism and mystery that Adorno thought endemic both to enlightenment and to capitalist authority. The awe and deference once given to Providence was now invested in the mechanical movement of the stars. To Adorno, the astrological liturgy of the cult of facts had disturbing moral and political implications. If the deities of traditional religion, while exacting, were also intimate and merciful, the transcendent powers invoked in astrology are "abstract, unapproachable, and anonymous"—just like the bureaucratic monoliths in which many of Righter's fans were employed. Thus, if religion had at least preserved the possibility of resistance to injustice, astrology and the occult enjoined an exotic subordination. Thoroughly aligned with the instrumental reason of the state and corporate bureaucracy, the new spirituality assumed a role as "guardian angel of the established order."[27]

Surveying such an effulgent but politically barren landscape, the disconsolate duo of Western Marxism retreated into critique, an uncompromising negativity that was both a bastion of moral fortitude and a symptom of imaginative paralysis. Their adamant refusal of all fraudulent hopes served to sharpen their critical acumen, but it also imposed an exorbitant levy on their powers of utopian vision. Both men struggled to prevent their devotion to reason from collapsing into mandarin cynicism. With the promise of enlightenment betrayed or at least on long historical hold, any further progress toward emancipation entailed, in Horkheimer's view, opposition "to what is currently called reason." Yet they declined to join hands with other antagonists of instrumental reason—neo-Thomists, "neo-orthodox" Protestants (such as Paul Tillich and Reinhold Niebuhr), "New Humanists" (like Irving Babbitt and Paul Elmer More).[28] Neither traditional Christianity nor classical humanism offered an antidote to commercial and technical philistinism.

Yet almost despite themselves, Adorno and Horkheimer drew both on the legacy of Western philosophy and especially on the treasury of hope that still abided in Judaism and Christianity. While many scholars of the Frankfurt School stress their reliance on art as the vessel of a promise of happiness, both melancholy Marxists gestured to the future in the language of metaphysics, memory, and redemption. Enlightened enough to reject traditional metaphysics, Horkheimer, for one, came close to challenging the enlightened dismissal of metaphysics and ontology. Eager to recapture the ancient conception of reason as "substantive" rather than instrumental—attuned to the *logos* of ultimate reality rather than the *techne* of use—Horkheimer affirmed the classical principle, prevalent in the epoch before enlightenment, that "belief in the goodness or sacredness of a thing precedes . . . enjoyment of its beauty." Any future conviction of such goodness must preserve such a sense of "original absolute significance" while transcending its historical origins in injustice and superstition—and doing so without relying on considerations of social and political utility. Adorno's view of philosophy remained remarkably classical—"the teaching of the good life"—and his "reflections on damaged life" in *Minima Moralia* concluded on a religious, eschatological note. In a society saturated by images of happiness produced and administered by capital, the only radical way to speak of the self, he mused, is "theologically, as the image and likeness of God." Such a godly albeit godless humanism beckoned inevitably toward a beatific vision, if not quite beatitude. The only philosophy worth practicing, Adorno wrote in a luminous and enigmatic passage, was one that contemplated the world as it would look "from the standpoint of redemption." Rather than offer consolations dressed up in faddish progressive politics, such philosophers should reveal how "indigent and distorted" the world appears when illuminated by "the messianic light."[29] Philosophy done in this way was painful but fruitful, he reasoned, since unrelenting critique inevitably suggested a utopian image of its opposite.

If Adorno echoed Randolph Bourne, who had praised "malcontentedness" as "the beginning of promise," it was not a promising beginning. Secularized as "critique," the prophetic imperative to demolish idols could easily become an iconoclasm without end. The conviction that, as Horkheimer and Adorno wrote in *Dialectic of Enlightenment,* "the guarantee of salvation lies in the rejection of any belief that would replace it" was tantamount to the fetishization of criticism.[30] Without some account of that "standpoint of redemption," the ferocity of suspicion that leavened enlightenment threatened to devour the promise of beatitude. But with only reason to guide them—a reason damaged, perhaps irreparably, in the tortuous history of domination and enlightenment—Adorno and Horkheimer could neither spark nor illustrate the beatific imagination. If, as they argued, reason had embarked on the subjugation of nature and human beings from the very beginning, then "derangement" was an endemic feature of reason, not a tragic historical contingency. But if reason is inherently deranged, how could it heal itself? Any standpoint of redemption would be quickly immolated by the furies of enlightenment; human profanation—impiety toward what Adorno had recalled as the image and likeness of God—would continue, unabated and unstoppable.

As another denizen of Los Angeles, Nathanael West knew a bit about the furies unbound in the course of human profanation. While working in Los Angeles as a scriptwriter for Columbia and RKO Pictures, West composed three short novels—*Miss Lonelyhearts* (1933), *A Cool Million* (1934), and *The Day of the Locust* (1939)—that constitute a trilogy of degradation and resentment, depicting a people whose mass-produced fantasies can no longer ward off the demons. In *A Cool Million,* West imagined one kind of apocalyptic conclusion to the failures of corporate capitalism: Protestant fascism. The novel relates the sordid and often brutal misadventures of Lemuel Pitkin, a poor and credulous farm boy from Ottsville, Vermont. Early on, he falls under the spell of Shagpoke Whipple, a former US president who preaches the old proprietary gospel. "Scoffers," he warns Lem, will tell you that Rockefeller and Ford are thieves. "Do not believe them," he scowls. Veiling a small-town reality of corruption, rape, and molestation, Whipple's homilies conjure up a proprietary America in which hard work and honesty lead to success. "This is not a matter of opinion, it is one of faith," Whipple insists.[31]

Forced to leave for New York to earn money to save his family's house from foreclosure, Lem endures a surreal series of failures, indignities, and mutilations, all in the midst of a collapsing economy and a turbulent political climate. Lem joins Whipple's National Revolutionary Party, which espouses an all-American brand of fascism. (Whipple's office sports "a cracker barrel, two brass spittoons, a hot stove and a picture of Lincoln.") Anticipating Sinclair Lewis's *It Can't Happen Here* (1935)—where one character muses that if fascism ever comes to America, it will come draped in the flag and carrying a cross—West suggests that a homespun variety will appeal to the proprietary-Protestant myth. The economic planks of Whipple's program are a hodge-podge of proprietary dogma and corporatism. The party seeks to restore Americans' "inalienable birthright: the right to sell their labor and their children's labor without restrictions as to either price or hours." Innocent of class antagonism—"class war is civil war," Whipple explains to Lem—the new Lincoln republic of producers would be a classic fascist corporatism in which "Capital and Labor . . . work together for the general good of the country." Add on fear and loathing of the usual villains—Bolsheviks, intellectuals, labor unions, "nigger-lovers," Wall Street, and international bankers (i.e., Jews)—and the National Revolutionary agenda stands revealed as Protestant reactionary modernism. In the end, Lem becomes the party's leading spokesman, but he is assassinated—on Whipple's orders?—just as the revolution is about to succeed. With Lem elevated to the status of fallen hero, Whipple becomes the nation's Protestant fuehrer, delivering the country from "sophistication, Marxism, and International Capitalism."[32]

The only counter to Whipple comes from Israel Satinpenny, a Harvard-educated Indian chief who hopes to reclaim the continent from "that abomination of abominations, the paleface." Like Whipple, Satinpenny trades on belief in an idyllic past of unspoiled virtue. Once, he roars at an assembly of braves, this was "a fair, sweet land" of human communion with nature. But when the whites arrived with their commerce and technology, they "filled the sky with smoke and the rivers with refuse." Satinpenny condemns the depredations of Fordism and the glittering detritus of industrial design. Enlisting the earth's elements to turn "wheels within wheels within wheels within wheels," paleface capitalism churns out "clever cigarette lighters," "superb fountain pens," "paper bags, doorknobs, leatherette satchels," "painted boxes to keep pinks in, key rings, watch fobs." Conceding that "you can't put the clock back," he exhorts his followers to "stop that clock . . . smash that clock." If the past is unrecoverable, Satinpenny is silent about the future, so smashing the clock would leave only an eternal present. Satinpenny's fiery but vacuous rhetoric explains why, in the end, his uprising degenerates into an orgy of retribution. "The day of vengeance is here," he proclaims, and the warriors embark on a crusade of massacre, scalping and pillaging without any apparent political objective.[33]

If *A Cool Million* envisions a fascist restoration of the Protestant *herrenvolk* order, *Miss Lonelyhearts* and especially *The Day of the Locust* depict an inferno of beatific longings. Set in different precincts of the culture industry, both novels highlight the religious desires propelling the new forms of fetishism. An advice columnist for the *New York Post-Dispatch,* "Miss Lonelyhearts" (a man whose real name we never learn) is one of "the priests of twentieth-century America," as Shrike, his editor, describes him. "A comforter of the poor in spirit and a lover of God," Lonelyhearts receives thousands of letters every day containing "profoundly humble pleas for moral and spiritual advice . . . inarticulate expressions of genuine suffering." Though sharing mightily in Shrike's cynicism—"give us this day our daily stone"— Lonelyhearts fathoms the yearnings of his readers. "They wanted to talk about something besides clothing or business or the movies, because they wanted to talk about something poetic." Having plumbed through so many epistles of despair, he knows that the images of commercial enticement are more than mere frivolity and bunkum. In their poverty, infirmity, or domestic tribulation, his unhappy audience continues to hope for a future of fulfillment, abundance, and beauty. "He had learned not to laugh at the advertisements offering to teach writing, cartooning, engineering, to add inches to the biceps and to develop the bust," West writes. "Guitars, bright shawls, exotic foods, outlandish costumes—all these things were part of the business of dreams." As a kind of savior to his readers, Lonelyhearts himself is capable of "dreaming the Christ dream." In one episode, he ponders Father Zosima's wisdom from *The Brothers Karamazov:* "Love a man even in his sin, for that is the semblance of Divine Love and is the highest love on earth." When he needs to escape from New York, he travels with his girlfriend, Mary, to a village called Monkstown. Opposite the foot of his bed, Lonelyhearts has nailed an ivory figure of Christ, removed from the cross to which it had been attached.[34]

Like Lonelyhearts, Tod Hackett, a Hollywood set designer and the protagonist of *The Day of the Locust,* finds it difficult to disparage the beatific imagination in even its kitschiest forms. Though declaring that he's "an artist, not a prophet," Hackett senses—and fears—the utopian fury that keeps the culture industries in business. "It is hard to laugh at the need for beauty and romance, no matter how tasteless, even horrible, the results of that are," as West observes. And again like Lonelyhearts, Hackett feels but also distrusts the need for some ultimate deliverance from misery. Listening to a Bach chorale, "Come Redeemer, Our Savior," Hackett muses that "perhaps Christ heard. If He did, He gave no signs."[35]

Lacking evidence of Christ's presence, West's world of mad and lonely hearts casts wildly about for surrogates—"a continuous hunt for other models," as West puts it in *Day of the Locust.* Yet none of the substitutes fills the void, and most of them end up commodified in a roiling market of phony redemption. In *Miss Lonelyhearts,* Shrike identifies and dismisses many of the common replacements: art, sex, booze, drugs. Buoyantly blasphemous, he imagines "the First Church of Christ Dentist, Preventer of Decay" whose newfangled trinity is "Father, Son, and Wirehaired Fox Terrier." But in the end, Shrike echoes Henry Ford and Paul Strand in proclaiming technological efficiency as "the new thomistic synthesis," an assertion he illustrates with a newspaper clipping on an adding machine for prayers. In *The Day of the Locust,* Hackett wanders through a studio lot of discarded props and sets—"a dream dump," he muses, "a Sargasso of the imagination." Amidst the detritus lies a cardboard Greek temple to Eros, where "the god himself lay face downward in a pile of old newspapers and bottles." Later, Hackett undertakes a pilgrimage through Hollywood's exotic spiritual bazaar:

He visited the "church of Christ, Physical" where holiness was
   attained through

the constant use of chestweights and spring grips; the "Church Invisible" where fortunes were told and the dead made to find lost objects; the "Tabernacle of the Third Coming," where a woman in male clothing preached the "Crusade Against Salt"; and the "Temple Moderne" under whose glass and chromium roof "Brain-Breathing, the Secret of the Aztecs" was taught.

In the Tabernacle, a deranged man expounds a revelation of "dietary rules, economics, and Biblical threats." Having seen a "Tiger of Wrath" and a "Jackal of Lust," the manic rails like "an illiterate anchorite" hurling warnings at a "decadent Rome." Like the Hollywood spiritual hothouse, West's America abounds in "wild, disordered minds," hysterical with anger at their obsolescence in the land of Fordist efficiency.[36]

Full of "awful, anarchic power"—"they had it in them to destroy civilization," as Hackett notes of the congregants—the nameless extras in West's novels long for a bloody and cleansing apocalypse. "There would be civil war," Hackett predicts. "The Angelenos would be first, but their comrades all over the country would follow." Yet West offers no prospect of millennium beyond the horizon of apocalypse. For West, death and ruin are the toxic waste of America's business of dreams. "They realize that they've been tricked and burn with resentment," he concludes in *Day of the Locust.* "The cultists of all sorts, economic as well as religious, the wave, airplane, funeral and preview watchers—all those poor devils who can only be stirred by the promise of miracles and then only to violence." The horsemen of West's apocalypse are the exploited of Fordist America, longing for some spectacle to avenge the miscarriage of justice and edenic hope:[37]

> They were savage and bitter . . . and had been made so by boredom and Disappointment . . . all their lives they had slaved at some kind of dull, heavy labor, behind desks and counters, in the fields and at tedious machines of all sorts, saving their pennies and dreaming of the leisure that would be theirs when they had enough . . . if only a plane would crash once in a while so that they could watch the passengers being consumed in a "holocaust of flame," as the newspapers put it. But the planes never crash.

Unable to contain the forces they summon, and even half in love with them, the high priests of the culture industry succumb to the furies they cultivate. In the final section of *Miss Lonelyhearts*—"Miss Lonelyhearts Has a Religious Experience"—the columnist "welcome[s] the arrival of fever" because it promises "heat and mentally unmotivated violence." The heat and violence arrive in the form of a cripple who guns him down; but as West writes, Lonelyhearts runs toward his killer "with his arms spread for the miracle." Throughout *Day of the Locust,* Hackett has been working on a painting titled "The Burning of Los Angeles," and in the final episode of the novel, his vision comes alive when a crowd riots outside a theater. His imagination sharpened by the ferocity of the revelers, Hackett conceives an apocalypse wrought by the dispossessed and vindictive. Los Angeles becomes "the burning city, a great bonfire of architectural styles, from Egyptian to Cape Cod colonial," set ablaze by "a great united front of screwballs and screwboxes." "No longer bored, they sang and danced joyously in the red light of the flames." Like the Protestant fascists of *A Cool Million,* they seek to "purify the land"; but like Satinpenny's "day of vengeance," their apocalypse yields no final redemption.[38] Too angry and hysterical for any "enriching communion," the people in West's fiction ignite their homes, not a revolution.

Of course, there was nothing even close to a revolutionary denouement to the turbulence and misery of the Depression. (In Europe, the most successful mass movement was fascism, a populist brand of reactionary modernism.) As the political modesty of the CIO demonstrated, labor's imagination remained well within the bounds of the "business mind." Although many of the CIO's leaders and organizers were militant socialists with a class-based political vision, the rank-and-file seldom displayed any interest in "industrial democracy" or socialism. The labor movement remained fractured along lines of ethnicity and skill; racism persisted as a debilitating toxin in the body politic of the CIO; and the appeal of socialism was blunted by Catholic social teaching, whose exponents (such as Philip Murray) pursued an active antipathy toward the secular left. As a result, the CIO was always a "fragile juggernaut," in Zieger's words, and the New Deal coalition that emerged after World War II was an unstable and fractious (albeit long-lived) political constellation.[39]

The CIO's eventual deference to the prerogatives of corporate capital during and after World War II stemmed not only from the countervailing power of corporations and the New Deal state, but also from the nature of the Fordist workplace, the attendant impact of the culture industry, and the persistence of individualism in the American moral imagination. The attrition of craft and the mechanization of labor meant that CIO workers had, in Steve Fraser's words, a "functional and instrumental but not existential relationship to their work"—they neither derived nor expected any artisanal fulfillment in the temples of Fordist production. The CIO working class was "far more integrated as consumers into the mass market and more influenced by the media of mass culture." Ruskin and Morris were vindicated: the cumulative effect of industrial work and culture had been to limit, not enlarge, labor's moral imagination. Moreover, as Jefferson Cowie and Nick Salvatore have argued, the New Deal's turn away from antimonopoly and redistribution toward the promotion of a vibrant consumer culture served to abet the "deep and abiding individualism" at the core of the American ethos. Under the aegis of the New Deal, the meaning of individualism was migrating away from control over productive resources—now more than ever firmly in the hands of the managerial elite—to the enjoyment of commodified pleasures. Stabilized and expanded by New Deal fiscal policy, and given a political imprimatur from labor leaders such as Walter Reuther, a humane Fordism became the political horizon of the liberal and social-democratic left—"moral capitalism," as Lizabeth Cohen has dubbed it. Burke's spiritual bankers had invested wisely; eventually, the New Deal would prove to be, in Cowie and Salvatore's words, "a historical aberration," a genuine but short-lived anomaly in the longer *duree* of American capitalism.[40] Even as the covenant theology now accommodated labor unions and state intervention, capitalist enchantment remained the spiritual government of the managerial order.

# 22

# Small Is Beautiful

The Religion of Small Property and Lewis
Mumford's *Novum Organum*

To some, the self-immolation of Los Angeles would have been a just and inexorable judgment, a fitting and perhaps divine verdict on the city's frenetic and incorrigible perversity. American culture has always harbored a powerful strain of ambivalence shading into hostility toward cities—demonized as seductive hellholes of depravity; swarming with fearsome racial heterogeneity; glittering with sophisticates full of disdain for rural piety, wisdom, and tranquility. Despite the accelerating urbanization of America in the years between the world wars, these images persisted, not only in depressed farming towns and villages but also among metropolitan intellectuals. To intellectuals alienated from urban life—many of whom, like Malcolm Cowley, had fled their rural hometowns in search of an ineffable liberation—the city assumed a new malevolence as the vast, metastasizing homeland of the machine, while the country became the final redoubt of humanity against mechanized demoralization. Cowley spoke for many postwar writers who, attracted by the prospect of freedom and dynamism, had made the exodus from the heartland to the metropolis only to discover new forms of repression. After the initial exhilaration, the "crowds, whistles, skidding taxicabs, all the discomforts of the city were a personal affront." Cowley himself confessed to having "pleasant nightmares in which I feared that New York was being destroyed by an earthquake." Exhausted by the city's pace and calloused by its inhospitality, Cowley and many of his friends harbored "the desire to escape and the hope of living somewhere under more favorable conditions, perhaps in their own countryside, of which they still dreamed, perhaps on a Connecticut farm." Even at our most deracinated and cosmopolitan, "we carry," Cowley wrote of his "Lost Generation," "each of us an urn of native soil."[1]

In both America and Europe, this agonized quandary about the city and the country was a salient source of literary modernism. Uprooted from but still emotionally attached to the folkways of rural life, modernists inhabited the imaginative vortex of transition from a largely agrarian to an urban and industrial civilization. But a handful of writers and social critics longed to escape the crucible of industrial urbanism and recover the archaism of the countryside. In their view, the technological insolence of industrial society—consolidated in the modern metropolis—had warped our kinship with nature, disrupted our biological rhythms, and abetted and magnified our promethean ambition to subjugate the universe. Only by a return to manual labor could we reverse the depredations of the mechanical world, repair our relations with nature, bridle our cosmological hubris, and recover the sense of a divinity excluded from skyscrapers yet welcomed in forests and meadows. And if no retreat to the countryside was possible, some semblance of the virtues associated with rural life had to be created in the industrial metropolis.

Often expressed in overt opposition to Fordism, the renewal of interest in small-scale economy was also a neo-Romantic quest for a sacramental way of life. Echoing the "religion of small property" preached by G. K. Chesterton, Hilaire Belloc, and other British distributists, neo-Romantic ruralism in America took three exemplary forms: the *herrenvolk* ideal of Herbert Agar, Allen Tate, John Crowe Ransom, and other "Southern Agrarians"; the Catholic personalism of Dorothy Day, Peter Maurin, and the Catholic Worker movement; and the International Peace Mission of Father Divine, headquartered in Harlem. Southern Agrarians and Catholic Workers in particular sought a reduction in the scale of property and production, achieved through the attrition of industrial technology and a return to agriculture and handicraft. While not, in the end, fundamentally opposed to the prevailing economic order, Father Divine and the Peace Mission combined a sacramental religious sensibility with an attempt to forge a communalist capitalism.

Crusaders for small property were addressing harsh and intractable conditions in the American countryside. The Depression devastated farmers, especially in the South and Midwest, and so the revival of the nation's agricultural economy was a pressing concern for the Roosevelt Administration. The New Dealers created various programs—the Agricultural Adjustment

Administration, the Farm Security Administration, the Resettlement Administration—to provide relief to rural families, bolster prices for food-stuffs, and acquaint producers with new agricultural methods and technol-ogies. Yet if most farmers considered New Deal assistance an affirmation of family farming, many liberals favored scientific and technologically ad-vanced methods that promoted larger-scale agriculture. Stuart Chase, for instance, welcomed the demise of small production and its replacement by a scientific agriculture. Farming was once "a way of life," he wrote in 1934. "Now . . . it is just another business," and a doomed one at that. Like the small businessperson and the industrial worker, the small farmer was "just one more poor devil drowning in economic insecurity." But, Chase reasoned, since "mass production in agriculture follows close behind mass production in industry," local and inefficient proprietors would eventually give way to "a few skilled laborers and mechanics" supplied with the latest technical expertise.[2]

Over the 1930s, the cumulative impact of falling prices, bad weather, and foreclosure seemed to portend the end of family farming as a way of life, and the promises of modernization appeared increasingly futile, even false. In the Delta region, for instance, many farmers saw natural and economic tur-moil as the well-deserved reprimand of Providence. The Arkansas drought of 1930–1931 induced one farmer to call it "a national chastisement to make men think of Him." The Depression, another farmer asserted in 1932, was "one of the vials of wrath being poured upon the world as a just punishment for the sins of which we have been guilty." Suspicion of New Deal agricul-tural reforms among white farmers in the Delta stemmed, in large measure, from a premillennialist eschatology in which the portents of nature were em-issaries from a vindictive God.[3]

Yet it was precisely in rural America that some artists, writers, and intel-lectuals saw the possibility of moral and spiritual regeneration for industrial society. While few called for an outright abandonment of industrial civiliza-tion, they looked to pre-industrial locales as enclaves of joy, simplicity, friendship, mutuality, and spiritual contentment. In King Vidor's *Our Daily Bread* (1934), an unsuccessful urban couple renounces the cutthroat ways of business and starts what becomes a thriving agricultural cooperative. "Regionalist" painters such as Grant Wood, Thomas Hart Benton, and John Steuart Curry portrayed an agrarian America still replete with plebian tenacity and rectitude. As Benton remarked of his Works Projects Administration murals, he strove to capture "the peculiar nature of the American brand of spirituality." Although now so familiar as to be liable to parody, the couple depicted in Wood's *American Gothic* (1931) at the time formed an icon of the proprietary heritage—America's analogue to the "Gothic" past of Europe, the waning epoch of spiritual vitality.[4]

Other celebrants of pre-industrial values looked elsewhere for renewal. The Spanish and Mexican peasants romanticized by Waldo Frank eluded the clutches of what he called "mechanolatry," the adoration of industrial technology that Lewis Mumford dubbed "the religion of the machine." Recalling Mary Austin's sojourn among the Shoshone and Mexicans of California, Willa Cather, in *Death Comes for the Archbishop* (1927), idealized the reverence displayed toward nature by the Hopi and Navajo of New Mexico. Treading lightly in a land enchanted by spirits, they befriended the desert and the mountains and abjured any desire to wrestle and dominate the earth. "It was the Indian way to pass through a country without disturbing anything, to pass and leave no trace . . . to vanish into the landscape, not to stand out against it." While the white invaders marauded the country with their money and brutally extractive technology, the Indians "spent their ingenuity in another direction, in accommodating themselves to the scene in which they find themselves." Likewise, the Mexicans examined by Chase displayed a grandeur and grace inaccessible to acquisitive and industrious whites. In *Mexico: A Story of Two Americas* (1931), Chase juxtaposed two very different communities: Tepotzlan, the Mexican village studied by the anthropologist Robert Redfield, and "Middletown," the Midwestern city explored by Robert and Helen Lynd. Although Tepotzlan was not unaffected by modernity, Chase made clear that to the extent they retained their mixture of handicraft, farming, and pagan-Catholic festivity, the villagers were spared the anonymity of gargantuan cities, the visual and ecological blight of industry, the callous pursuit of accumulation, and the oblivion of the numinous by calculation and enterprise.[5]

Advocates of a proprietary restoration went one step further than Chase and other admirers of rural life: they called for the disassembly of corporate, industrial capitalism. Yet there was a division in the church of small property. Like other believers in the American errand before them, the Protestant Southern Agrarians delivered yet another jeremiad: America had fallen away from the ideal of family property and decayed into corporate power, mechanization, and godlessness. Only a return to small, patriarchal proprietorship could revive the Jeffersonian-Christian republic. To reverse the corporate declension from the original errand of Christian cupidity, Protestant restorationists rejected mass production in favor of independent farming and handicraft. While the Catholic Workers also favored the proprietary program of agriculture, handicraft, and decentralization, they refrained from joining in the jeremiad, coming closer to repudiating the covenant theology than any other previous critics of capitalist enchantment.

Besides portraying farmers, artisans, and shopkeepers as the yeoman avatars of virtue, the American religion of small property also rehearsed the populist argument against corporate metaphysics. If Burke and Dewey considered the corporation a progressive force in history, proprietary ideologues thought the corporate firm an example of metaphysical and moral perversity. As the agrarian economist Richard Ransom explained, the legal fiction of the modern corporation gave it a "permanent lease on life" that undermined any notion of moral responsibility. Ruralists such as Ransom held that corporations should be considered special and contingent legal entities whose existence was revocable at the will of the legislature. When they did not call for the abolition of corporations altogether, Ransom and his proprietary comrades advocated various reforms: abolition of corporate personhood, federal chartering of corporations, and heavy inheritance taxes on the transfer of corporate shares and assets. These measures, he believed, would not only curb corporate power but also achieve a moral counterrevolution against abstract, tyrannical impunity. The resubordination of corporations to the popular will would, Ransom hoped, inculcate "more direct personal responsibility" among all producers in the country and the city.[6]

Corporations were also the primary culprits in the crime of spiritual dispossession, the "profanation" decried by James Rorty. Blasphemously impersonating the "mysterious and powerful presence," they were now "the legal and economic gods of the century," as one contributor to Herbert Agar and Allen Tate's *Who Owns America?* (1936) saw them, usurpers expelling farmers and artisans from the eden of tactile friendship with God. Banished from what was left of the producers' paradise, workers suffered "spiritual sterilization," as one of the Southern Agrarians, Andrew Lytle, put it, an infertility caused by their separation from the means of material beatitude.

Meanwhile, exiled from the rhythms and textures of nature, industrial workers sought a spurious compensation in the consumption of mass-produced goods. Catholic Workers also objected to the specious materialism fostered by mechanization. By reducing the worker to a mindless, insensate appendage of industrial technology, Fordism both desecrated the sacramental nature of labor and dulled the sensuous capacities of the body. Day condemned capitalism for its fraudulent love of the world—"the worst materialism of all," she thought, one that enervated creative exuberance "when this dear flesh of ours is denied."[7]

Against the system of mechanized indignity, the proprietary front proposed a revival of farming and craft that would hallow, civilize, and beautify human life. Proprietary champions held that spiritual nourishment depended on genuine, virtuous property ownership, as the roots put down in the soil went through the earth all the way to divinity. When residing and working in what one of the Southerners, John Crowe Ransom, rhapsodized as "a certain terrain, a certain history, [and] a certain inherited way of living," men and women acquired knowledge of themselves, the natural world, and finally of divinity. "The genuine farmer never loses his belief in God," Lytle declared. Religion wanes, he argued, when men seek to conquer nature; leave the countryside for the mass-produced blandishments of the metropolis; and forget their never-ending, fundamental dependence on "a mysterious and powerful presence." Donald Davidson, another of the Southerners, contended that artisanal production would grace "the round of daily life" with the visual and sensual joy of well-wrought "pots and pans, chairs and rugs, clothing and houses." The Catholic Workers considered the restoration of a sacramental quality to work and technology to be a paramount religious mission. "A man who works with his hands as well as with his head is an integrated personality," Day asserted. Partaking of "God's creative activity," the artisan's agile and loving proximity to matter brought a deeper intimacy with God. "Using mind and brain to work on beautiful objects," the craftsperson or farmer was gifted with "a sense of the sacramentality of things, the holiness, the symbolism of things."[8]

Yet important and irreconcilable differences divided the acolytes of proprietary restoration. Both denominations assented to Tate's assertion in *I'll Take My Stand* (1930) that "economy is the secular image of religious conviction." But the Southerners harkened back to the Protestant dispensation.

John Crowe Ransom's *God without Thunder* (1930), a strange and sometimes bewildering volume, was a modernist restatement of Protestant proprietary theology, the theological prologue to *I'll Take My Stand*. "The religion of a people," Ransom wrote, "is that background of metaphysical doctrine which dictates its political economy." In Ransom's view, the metaphysics of industrial modernity blended liberal theology and the will to power. An "Amiable Rotarian" God sanctioned a covert religion of "service" in which "mankind proceeds to serve itself as hard as possible." Heedless of limits and bereft of reverence, industrial capitalism was a "wartime economy" that conscripted labor, nature, and technology in an unending campaign for power and riches. The "Amiable Rotarian" was a Babbitt in the heavens, and such a complaisant deity was no match for the will to power and riches. Ransom insisted that the only antidote to the enchantment of industrial progress lay in a renewal of faith in the "stern and immutable god" of Calvinism, the predestining deity who placed implacable restrictions on desire and accumulation.[9]

Ransom's Calvinist God smiled benignly, however, on slavery and segregation. In the Southerners' historical mythology—an extension of the "Lost Cause" that aimed to reconcile white Southerners to the defeat of the Confederacy—the antebellum and Jim Crow South became an idyll washed clean of slave auctions, overseers, and lynching parties. Few of the Southern partisans were as shameless as Davidson, who expressed his hope, soon after the publication of *I'll Take My Stand*, that "the Lost Cause might not be wholly lost after all"; the Christian chivalry of plantation society might still be redeemed from obloquy and oblivion. Tate contended that throughout history, slavery had made possible "high cultures" of leisure, learning, and magnanimity. The historian Frank Owsley was more disingenuous, arguing that slavery had played "no essential part of the agrarian civilization of the South." In his contribution to *I'll Take My Stand*—"The Briar Patch"—Warren was at least embarrassed enough to employ euphemism and circumlocution in his brief for racial segregation. Whitewashed of slavery and segregation, the "history" and "tradition" so reverently affirmed was the moonshine of erudite *herrenvolk*. This specious and poisonous *herrenvolk* romance was lambasted ferociously by Agee, who skewered the ruralist "solution / Neither Hearstian nor Roosian" for its racist, faux-classical nostalgia. In the New Dixie of Tate and Ransom, Agee saw "an indisputably Aryan / Jeffersonian Agrarian / settin' on the ole rail fence."[10]

After World War II and the rise of the civil rights movement, Warren and many of his proprietary comrades would mute or retract their support for segregation. But the "Southern tradition" of white democracy would continue in the work of Richard Weaver, M. E. Bradford, and other grandees of the postwar right who excoriated corporate capitalism. Even when they tried to slough off the racist legacy of the proprietary dispensation, the white disciples of small property could never quite dispel the charms of *herrenvolk* enchantment.

The racist romance of the *herrenvolk* order was in the process of being dispelled among white and black sharecroppers and activists in the Southern Tenant Farmers Union (STFU), the interracial vanguard of union organization and radicalism in the Depression South. Formed in 1934 to resist evictions that resulted from the crop reduction programs of the Agricultural Adjustment Administration, STFU was a fractious but vibrant coalition of tenant farmers, socialists, Communists, and Congress of Industrial Organizations organizers who operated in Arkansas, Oklahoma, Mississippi, Missouri, Tennessee, Alabama, and Texas. As many contemporary observers noted, the STFU resembled a religious revival; steeped in the Pentecostal and Baptist religious cultures shared by white and black laborers, many black locals would open meetings with a hymn, which would often be followed by what amounted to a sermon on the solidarity of the union. As Rev. Claude Williams, a white preacher and organizer educated in the social gospel at Vanderbilt, declared to members, the union sought to make "the revolutionary program of Jesus become effective in the life of the world." As founder of the People's Institute of Applied Religion, which distributed political and religious literature to tenant farmers, workers, and clergy, Williams described the sharecroppers' crusade in world-historical, even cosmic terms; there were "revolutionary fires already kindled," he proclaimed, "which are destined to bring a new renaissance, a new reformation, yea a new pentecost." Likening the spirit of the STFU to the charisma of the early Christians, Williams asserted that the same divine presence that inspired the church was galvanizing the union. "Now there is a new Pentecost," he told a black congregation in Missouri in 1936. The disciples received God's anointment and power "when they were organized . . . so Pentecost is unity."[11]

The religion of small property among struggling and dispossessed tenants indeed augured "a new Pentecost," as the STFU envisioned a redistribution of land from wealthy owners to the people who worked it. Although most members saw the union as a way to obtain better conditions of tenancy, the most radical STFU organizers called for common ownership of the land and its abundance—a political program blessed by God, as Howard Kester and Evelyn Smith's "Ceremony of the Land" announced. First performed at the STFU's national convention in Muskogee, Oklahoma, in January 1937, the ritual was a common prayer that affirmed a divine mandate for rural communism. "Thou didst establish the land and its fruit for all the people and Thou didst call us to be the Keepers of Thy good earth." Capitalism was a consequence of the Fall into private property and scarcity; "in man's greed for gold, he had destroyed the fruitfulness of the earth." Concluding that "the land is the common heritage of all," Kester invoked the spirit that had long ago animated the medieval commons. "Speed now the day when the plains and hills and all the wealth thereof shall be the people's own . . . we shall be Thy tenants alone." As Williams had explained, the STFU members were representatives of the people's republic of heaven, living by principles at odds with those of pecuniary reason and metaphysics. "The Kingdom is not of this world, but it is in this world."[12]

While secular radicals in the STFU were uncomfortable with the religious fervor of the membership, they drew on the hopeful tenacity of people who believed in visions, dreams, spirit-possession, and speaking in tongues. Some of the union's most courageous and popular heroes displayed a sacramental, incarnational conviction of the permeability of heaven and earth. Disdainful of both white and black clergy who acquiesced in the exploitation of tenant farmers and workers, Rev. Owen Whitfield, one of the union's most energetic black organizers and leaders, portrayed his conversion to plebian Christianity as a painful but liberating epiphany occasioned by an encounter with God. Resting in a field after a long day's work, he was stunned to be told by his young daughter that there was no food left for supper. Famished and desperate, he prayed. "You said the righteous and them that preached the Gospel would never go hungry," he recalled complaining to God. An answer came to him from within: "But you ain't been preachin' the Gospel," God admonished Whitfield. "I bless you with enough product to fill many barns. Somebody's gettin' it. If you ain't, that's your fault, not Mine." Set straight by the Lord, Whitfield stopped "whoopin' and hollerin' at God" and embarked on a career as a union militant. Don West—son of white Georgia sharecroppers, divinity student at Vanderbilt, Communist Party organizer, and then Congregationalist minister—had his own rendezvous with the Almighty that he traced in poetry he wrote while on the road. Distributed widely by the People's Institute of Applied Religion and later collected in *Clods of Southern Earth* (1946), West's verse suggested that radical politics was grounded in what Agee would call "human divinity." In "I've Seen God," for instance, West bore witness both to the grandeur and to the profanation of divine creation. "I've seen him smile / In the several hues of a rainbow / I've felt his warm breath / In the mists / The sun sets up / From the plowed dirt / After the summer rain"; but God also stared out from "the gaunt eyes / Of a factory worker," and West "heard him groan / From the hungry throats / Of miners' children."[13] This was not Ransom's "God of thunder" but rather the Saviour crucified by avarice.

Unlike Protestant Agrarianism and its storm-God, the Catholic denomination of small property rested on a triune theological matrix: Mystical Body theology, a liturgical movement, and the papal social encyclicals. Mystical Body theology was a prominent current in Euro-American Catholicism between the wars, re-emphasizing the communal nature of the Church against liberal individualism. Catholic Workers linked Mystical Body theology to the struggle against social injustice. As Day wrote, "the injustices borne by workers and dispossessed farmers" were part of the "mystery of the tremendous sacrifice of Christ." Where Ransom thought Americans should revive submission to a harsh and punitive God, Day offered the imitation of Christ: living in voluntary poverty, bearing the crosses of the poor and rejected, and regarding exploiters as prodigal brethren in need of forgiveness and love. Closely related to the Mystical Body was the liturgical movement, another Catholic import from Europe. Committed primarily to improving the aesthetic quality of church liturgy, art, and architecture, some liturgical reformers, such as the Benedictine Virgil Michel, considered the Eucharistic meal to be a template for social relations. Just as those who receive the Eucharist do not enjoy Christ as an exclusive possession, so natural goods should be shared. As Michel summarized the ideal, "what belongs to all belongs to each and what belongs to each belongs to all." Though insisting that this principle was not communist, Michel and the liturgical reformers contended that property should be embedded in a network of communal constraints and obligations.[14]

These theological currents galvanized many Depression-era Catholics, from supporters of the New Deal to the National Union for Social Justice founded by the "radio priest" Father Charles Coughlin. Calling for a living wage, workers' rights to unionization and collective bargaining, and tighter regulations of corporations, neither the National Union for Social Justice nor the New Deal wing of interwar Catholicism—Catholic union organizers, "labor priests," and activist-academics such as "Right Reverend New Dealer" Monsignor John Ryan—ever ventured beyond the political horizon of a moralized corporate capitalism. Both Ryan and Coughlin inveighed against socialism, and the industry council plan envisioned by Philip Murray assumed both the separation of ownership and control and the division of professional, managerial, and proletarian labor.[15]

Among Catholic Workers, however, Catholic theology underwrote a sacramental radicalism—"personalism," as they often called it—that sanctioned more radical changes in the American economy than either their fellow Catholics or the Protestant Southerners could endorse. Personalists condemned both absentee ownership and the separation of production and planning, and in their rural farming communities and urban "houses of hospitality," they attempted to erase the lines that divided property, management, and manual labor. Although they were abject (and sometimes comical) failures, the Catholic Worker farms on Staten Island and in upstate Pennsylvania were experiments in artisanal humanism in the lineage of Brook Farm, Rose Valley, and New Clairvaux. In their "houses of hospitality," where they ministered to the urban poor, Workers held weekly roundtable discussions of theology, philosophy, economics, and other subjects, open equally to intellectuals and workers—even to the drunks and prostitutes who came for hot soup and baloney sandwiches. Maurin—a cranky autodidact whose "easy essays" appeared regularly in the *Catholic Worker*—dismissed American higher education as a complex of "fact-factories" churning out technically proficient but morally paralyzed specialists. Looking to Kropotkin's "integral education," which combined humanist erudition and technical training, Maurin called for agronomic universities, modeled after the roundtable discussions, in which students would perform both intellectual and manual labor.[16]

Personalists departed dramatically from union leaders, progressives, and Marxists, who embraced the Fordist mechanization of industry for its provision of material abundance. Catholic Workers resisted the trend toward professional and managerial specialization on theological grounds. Because, Day explained, personalists rooted their opposition to industrial capitalism in Christian humanism—the person as a "Temple of the Holy Ghost"—they recoiled from the separation of mental and manual labor as a desecration as well as a source of class division. Thus Day upheld "de-proletarianizing the worker" as the objective of Catholic personalism; workers had to "recapture control of industry" down to the last detail of technics and organization. Day constantly admonished the Congress of Industrial Organizations to demand, not just higher wages and shorter hours, but also ownership and dignity. While conceding that Communists also desired these goals, Day retorted that their "idolatry of the machine" forced them to welcome the reduction of persons to proletarian "hands"—to be complicit in human profanation.[17]

Thus, among Catholic Workers, the sacramental humanism of personalist theology underwrote a program of workers' control: "utopian, Christian communism," as Maurin described it. Day summarized the Workers' vision as a mélange of anarchism, Arts and Crafts, and distributism: "ownership by the workers of the means of production, the abolition of the assembly line, decentralized factories, the restoration of crafts, and ownership of property." Eclectic and ecumenical, Day's thinking owed at least as much to Kropotkin as it did to Chesterton, Belloc, and Pius. Having worked as a journalist in Greenwich Village during World War I, Day had been a charter member of the bohemian left before converting to Catholicism, and she admired and befriended secular radicals long after she joined the Church that officially anathematized them.[18] Yet if her refusal to bow to the jealous divinity of the State put her in the unlikely company of Emma Goldman, Day's unwavering faith in the ontology of love aligned her more with Vida Dutton Scudder. Renewing Scudder's sacramental materialism, Day was closer in spirit to Ruskin and St. Francis than to Marx, Debs, and the Fabians.

Yet as Day and other believers in small property came to realize, fewer and fewer Americans seemed willing to pioneer on small farms or in village workshops. "Ours is indeed an unpopular front," she once sighed, and the Southern Agrarians would have had to agree. By the time the United States entered World War II, the crusade for proprietorship had dissipated, and its waning stemmed in part from the anomalies of the crusaders. Like the earlier inhabitants of Brook Farm, proprietary ideologues were often intellectuals disgruntled by metropolitan culture. A tale told by a wistful intelligentsia, the rural South of the Lost Cause became, in the writing of the Agrarians, a fabulous yeomanry of Horaces. With Ivy League and Oxbridge degrees, followed by jobs in academia or with periodicals based in Northern cities, most of the Southerners were indeed, as the Vanderbilt graduates called themselves, "Fugitives," intellectuals in secession from the South's embattled rural culture. Genteel refugees from Dixie, they imagined "agrarian society" as a kind of compensation for their own abandonment of the plow. Tate eulogized Stonewall Jackson and Jefferson Davis while living the bohemian life in Greenwich Village; Lytle, concluding that he could not be both a writer and a "proper farmer," chose, not the farm, but the editor's office at the distinguished *Sewanee Review*. Ransom pounded the pulpit about a deity without thunder without ever really believing in God, and by the end of World War II, he'd even repudiated agrarianism.[19]

The Catholic Workers were similar specimens of urban disaffection. Day's literary talent and highbrow reading tastes marked her as a middle-class intellectual. (A typical Day article in the *Catholic Worker* might refer to Kropotkin, Marx, Dostoevsky, or Tolstoy.) Like Hawthorne's Coverdale or Tolstoy's Levin, Catholic Workers attempted to wed the intellectual and the peasant: milk cows in the morning, plow in the afternoon, study and discuss Aquinas in the evening. They were often too tired to pore over the *Summa*, and as one of the leading historians of the movement concedes, the Worker's farm communes were "unmitigated disasters." At the same time, despite their support for the Congress of Industrial Organizations' organizing efforts, their ideal of voluntary poverty held no appeal for urban industrial workers, while Day and Maurin felt nothing but antipathy for the fleshpots of consumer culture.[20]

The incongruity of urban intellectuals extolling the bucolic virtues was not the only reason for the failure of the religion of small property. Despite the Southern Agrarians' high dudgeon against corporations, it was never at all clear that what they were advancing was an alternative to capitalism. In the eschatology of agrarianism, the heavenly village looked much like the *herrenvolk* utopia—the beloved community of white male accumulators at the heart of the old covenant theology. Like the Puritans and the evangelicals, the Agrarians assumed a felicitous rapport between Christian love and capitalist property. Yet, intoning the liturgical chant of petty-bourgeois moralism—God, hard work, and family—the "small business" invoked by proprietary writers could be as ruthless and rapacious as any corporate monstrosity. Inattentive to the competitive logic of small business, the contributors to *Who Owns America?* drew the wrong conclusion from their avowal that "small business is the capitalist system": "Big Business" was no disease or perversion of capitalism, but the inexorable denouement of competition.[21]

Descendants of slaves liberated from the Agrarians' idealized dispensation, Father Divine and the Peace Mission exemplified the dissonance within the religion of small property. Possibly born George Baker to emancipated slaves in Rockville, Maryland, near the end of Reconstruction, Father Divine proclaimed himself "the Eternal Father" in 1912 and began a long, itinerant career as a preacher, and by the time he settled in Harlem in the early 1930s, he had attracted thousands of followers to his International Peace Mission. Whether in urban apartments or in rural cooperatives like the 34-acre estate in Ulster County, New York, members practiced communal living to reduce the costs of food and housing. Peace Mission "angels" opened a variety of small businesses, from restaurants and garages to hotels and dress shops; the cooperatives were jointly owned and parceled into small tracts, where members grew fruit, vegetables, and poultry, and raised dairy animals. All net profits were returned to the Peace Mission and were redistributed by Father Divine. (The Peace Mission was the largest realty holder in Harlem by the mid-1930s, and his opulent lifestyle fueled speculation that the movement was a confidence scam.) His followers, he declared, "live consecrated to and for the good of all, even though they own all things individually, severally and collectively." Although they rejected what Father Divine called "'rugged individualism' of the super greed type" and refused insurance and borrowing from banks, they opposed socialism, the labor movement, and the New Deal, and blamed individual sloth for the persistence of the Depression. Despite Harlem's high unemployment, squalid living conditions, and violent racial subordination, Father Divine's "platitudes" about peace and brotherhood, one journalist observed, "betray him as blissfully unimpressed by anything passing as a well-formulated radicalism."[22]

This "communalist capitalism," as one historian has characterized it, was anchored in a materialist theology that resembled the Catholic Workers' sacramentality. (It seems that Baker's mother had been a Methodist with a strong attraction to Roman Catholicism.) In *New Day*, the Peace Mission's periodical, Father Divine espoused a doctrine of "tangibilization," in which spirit took material form. "The Material Food We Eat . . . Is the Actual Tangibilization of the Personification of God's Word, God's Love and God's Presence." God's presence was most tangible in the Holy Communion or "Agape" feasts that the Peace Mission sponsored every Sunday, lavish banquets accompanied by ecstatic performances of music, chanting, shrieking, and witnessing. Although one purpose was to feed Harlem's hungry, the Holy Communion service was an eschatological meal, a corporeal foretaste of the afterlife.[23] Like the Mass explicated in Catholic Mystical Body theology, the Sunday services pointed to a sacramental communism, but they never entailed a full repudiation of the capitalist ethos, as the "angels" remained embedded in the competitive arena of petty-bourgeois enterprise.

While they may have shared something of a sacramentalist worldview with Father Divine and the Agrarians, Day and other Catholic personalists upheld the most serious sign of contradiction yet offered to the covenant theology of capitalist enchantment in America. Their willingness to espouse a "utopian, Christian communism" was a valiant and unequivocal defiance of the American moral imagination. Their sacramental ontology contravened the metaphysics of monetary and commodity fetishism; their indictment of capitalism was more intense and thoroughgoing than that of the Southern Agrarians; and their pacifism—which cost them dearly in financial and moral support when they condemned American participation in World War II—traversed and highlighted the imperialist hubris of Henry Luce's American Century. Not until the 1960s—with the appearance of a new left indebted, in part, to Day's courageous moral tutelage—would Americans witness any comparable effrontery to the avarice and violence of their idols.[24]

Yet the Catholic Workers could never explain how, in American conditions, *their* religion of small property could avoid the fate of competitive enterprise. Even as they offered their spectacle unto the world, Catholicism in America was being rapidly assimilated into the mainstream of Fordist society, where ownership of productive property, where it was not yet corporate, meant ownership of capitalist property. "Small property" inevitably meant "small business" and its everyday liturgies of struggle. Precisely for those reasons, Catholic personalism—isolated from most American Catholics as well as from Protestants—was unable to acquire any purchase on the

American moral imagination. If they missed the desire for beatitude that animated consumer culture, they remembered that human happiness required a robust materiality, a sensuous grace for which commodity hedonism offered only an anemic and fretful surrogate. If they displayed an incorrigible animus toward technology, they also posed invaluable challenges to the mystifications of the technological sublime.

Lewis Mumford might have been a perfect interlocutor for Day and the Catholic personalists. A quintessential man of letters, Mumford was indifferent to the professional protocols and disciplinary boundaries of the modern university; "his affinities," as Leo Marx observed, "were with Bohemia, not Academia." (His early friends included Van Wyck Brooks and Waldo Frank of the *Seven Arts* circle.) Mumford ranged widely and audaciously, covering art, literature, technology, architecture, and urban history. In the catholicity of his interests, Mumford was a classic philosopher, if philosophy is defined as the love of wisdom rather than as a bashful minion of science—the role accepted and even celebrated by positivists and pragmatists such as Mumford's nemesis, John Dewey. In style and substance, Mumford posed a vigorous and elegant alternative to Dewey's progressive acquiescence in cultural and industrial centralization. Where Dewey hoped to generate a common faith from within the apparatus of Fordism, Mumford looked beyond the industrial era to a more organic civilization: a "neotechnic" or "biotechnic" order, as he called it, a reunion of the city and the country in which the technics and culture of mechanization would serve rather than disfigure human nature. Fearful of industrial technology's authoritarian discipline and creative sterility, Mumford is the American Ruskin, a romantic critic of capitalism who, though more affirming of modern technics, denounced the religion of productivity and professed that there is no wealth but life. Indeed, "life"—richness of experience, variety of action, fertility of body and imagination—lay at the heart of Mumford's Romantic humanism, a way of being in the world as, in his words, "holiness, beatitude, and beauty."[25]

A lifelong lover of New York since his birth there in 1895—just as a whale ship was Melville's Harvard and Yale, "Mannahatta," he once wrote, "was my university, my true alma mater"—Mumford deplored the city's accelerating growth, a reckless industrial metastasis marred by pollution, congestion, and social turmoil. Searching for ways to rescue Gotham and other cities from the consequences of their own economic success, he embraced the ideas of the British urbanists Ebenezer Howard and Patrick Geddes, founders of the "garden city" and "regionalist" movements in city planning and architecture. A polymath like Mumford, Geddes was an especially profound and indelible influence on his admirer's life and work. (Mumford befriended and corresponded with Geddes, whom he referred to as his "master.") Geddes's strapping and capacious principle of "life insurgent" made the deepest impression on Mumford. Antedating Henri Bergson's *elan vital*, "life insurgent" played the role in Geddes's work of a pervasive and synthetic metaphysical principle not only of evolutionary biology but also of sociology, aesthetics, and religion. Since "life insurgent" compelled evolution toward ever greater organic complexity, interdependence, and unity, Geddes saw human civilization as a conscious, consummate product of nature, not a mechanical contraption that could be engineered in defiance of biological processes. Such impertinence toward nature was, Geddes thought, a besetting sin of capitalism, and his interest in ecology was provoked, in part, by his outrage at the effects of unchecked industrialization on rivers, fields, farms, and cities. In books ranging from *The Evolution of Sex* (1889) to *Cities in Evolution* (1915), Geddes both narrated a history of technology (divided into "eotechnic," "paleotechnic," and "neotechnic" periods, a scheme later employed by Mumford) and adumbrated an ecological philosophy that made organic development the criterion of social and technological progress.[26]

Spanning the 1920s to the 1960s—from *The Story of Utopias* (1922) through *Technics and Civilization* to the two-volume critique of *The Myth of the Machine* (1967, 1970)—Mumford's career was a prolific vocation for the cause of "life insurgent." "Life," "organic," and kindred terms abounded lushly in Mumford's prose, conveying both his delight in the sumptuous, regenerative abundance of nature and his affirmation of exuberant vitality as a moral and metaphysical criterion. "Life," he exulted in his study of *Herman Melville* (1929), "Life purposive, Life formative, Life expressive, is more than living, as living itself is more than the finding of a livelihood." Life, to Mumford, was more than mere biological existence; it included music, literature, art, play, and other activities often dismissed as "luxuries" by philistines and technocrats. The "genuine power" of any technical device, he asserted in *Technics and Civilization,* lay in its "power to sustain or enrich life." "Our goal," he insisted, should not be the multiplication of machines and commodities but rather "organic fulfillment," the satisfaction of desires for creation and connection that could be achieved—and, he came to believe, could *only* be achieved—through a diminution of the industrial apparatus.[27]

Mumford's celebration of "the primacy of life" recalled William James's "passionate vision," his marvelously impractical "ontological wonder" at "the mere spectacle of the world's presence." At the same time—paralleling Alfred North Whitehead's "philosophy of organism" and anticipating Hans Jonas's "phenomenology of life"—Mumford gestured to a romantic *novum organum,* a reconception of nature and humanity on the order of Francis Bacon and the mechanical philosophy that inaugurated the scientific and technological revolutions of modernity. His prototype for "an organic ideology" in *Technics and Civilization* assumed, he wrote, that "we now have an insight into a larger world and a more comprehensive intellectual synthesis than that which was originally outlined in our mechanical ideology." Rejecting the distinction between facts and values inherent to the modern scientific paradigm, Mumford's prolegomena to a *novum organum* revived and renovated Aristotelian and medieval Christian ontological principles. "Even the most rigorous scientific description of the physical basis of life indicates it to be internally teleological," he asserted. "Values," he declared in *Faith for Living* (1940), are not "cemented on to the ugly structure of physical existence as in a bad piece of architecture." Rather they are "present from the very beginning." Indeed, he continued, these values are "religious in essence," hinting that the religious is somehow intrinsic, not external, to the natural world.[28] Encompassing and even uniting the material world and the realm of the sacred, "life" served for Mumford as a surrogate for the enchantment once defined in Christian terms of sacramentality.

"Life" also posed an organic, artisanal standard of technical, economic, and political arrangements. In Mumford's view, humanity was not first *homo faber,* but *homo symbolicus,* the creator and inhabitant of the imaginative realm of language, thought, dream, and desire, where the aspirations of the artist and the saint precede the ingenuity of the maker and inventor. What distinguishes humanity from other species, he argued in *Faith for Living,* is "the presence and persistence of the ideal." But as the "ideal" or the "religious" was inseparable from the biological, *homo symbolicus* was best as an artisan, an incarnation of *poesis* for whom beauty and labor formed a rhyming, organic couplet. "The craftsman," he observed in *Sticks and Stones,* his book on American architecture, "literally possesses his work, in the sense that the Bible says a body is possessed by a familiar spirit." Inspired by a sense of "vital superfluity"—an ontology of life's abundance—the artisan assumes a plenitude of material to be shaped in accordance with his vision, not just an order to be filled for money. Though chiefly designed for everyday use, much of handicraft needs no other justification than that it "bears the mark of a joyous spirit." Taking "the worker's delight in production" as the criterion of work and technology, Mumford echoed Ruskin, Morris, and the Arts and Crafts movement by redefining true wealth as "creation": personal, durable, and attractive making for the sake of one's community. A community low in production yet high in creation is richer, Mumford contended, than a more "productive" society whose quantitatively greater volume of objects and services is corrupting and deliberately obsolescent. "The only civilized criterion of a community's economic life is not the amount of things produced, but the ratio of production to creation." Mumford's work for the Regional Planning Association of America, a league of reform-minded economists, architects, and developers, reflected this organic, artisanal humanism. This Association's advocacy of regional scale, resources, and community stemmed, he explained in 1925, from more than economic or ecological concerns with sensible production and conservation. "A certain unity of climate, soil, vegetation, industry, and culture" was necessary, Mumford maintained, for the promotion of a "vivid, creative life."[29] A place of material and spiritual grace, the well-cultivated region was the geographical matrix of romantic humanism and organic enchantment.

Mumford's organic ideology permeated both his account of the history of technics and his vision of a postmechanical, postcapitalist era. Especially in *Technics and Civilization,* Mumford contended that mechanization had taken command of the human imagination before it seized the means of production. For Mumford, human beings, not machines, occupied the center of the story of technological development. The progression of technics—the "eotechnic" epoch (1300–1700) of water and wood power, artisanal workplaces, and small-scale but not "backward" technics; the "paleotechnic" period (1700–1900) of coal and steam power, large factories, and mechanized, capital-intensive production; and the "neotechnic" era (1900–1934) of hydroelectricity, smaller factories, and more highly trained workers—is at the same time a series of cultural transformations, a succession of humanisms. Technological stages commence, Mumford argued, with cultural metamorphoses that make them conceivable. The technics of the eotechnic phase, for instance, reflected both the marvel of premodern peoples at the sheer power and magnitude of nature and their desire to achieve an integration of beauty and practicality, art and utility. From magic to handicraft, eotechnics represented a search, "not [for] mere power alone, but a greater intensification of life: color, perfume, images, music, sexual ecstasy."[30]

Mumford discovered this eotechnic imagination not only among tribal and archaic peoples but also among the guilds of medieval cities. In *The Culture of Cities* (1938), but also in his studies of American literary and architectural history—*Sticks and Stones* (1924), *The Golden Day* (1926), and *The Brown Decades* (1930)—Mumford celebrated what he called "the dream of medieval theology": a harmony of human beings and the natural world enveloped in a spirit of love and reverence. Repelled by the venality of American industrialism, Mumford looked back to medieval churches, guilds, and universities as models of solidarity and purposeful, integrated life. By insisting on a human scale in all things, the medieval order maintained "an organic relationship" between economics and religion and between people and nature. With their sacramental sensibility, medieval guilds in particular kept people in touch with "the tangible realities of the world"—grain, livestock, houses, tools—and directed economic life, not toward accumulation and senseless growth but toward "the glorification of God." Mumford emphasized that medieval guilds, far from losing sight of practical affairs in their devotion to patron saints, upheld "high standards of design and workmanship."[31]

Why did the eotechnic era end? Why did the dream of medieval theology yield to the nightmare of paleotechnic mechanization? Mumford traced part of the reason to fissures in the eotechnic imagination itself. While magic partook of the eotechnic conception of nature as a dwelling place for divinity, it also harbored and stoked the promethean ambition for unfettered power and productivity. "Magic was the bridge that united fantasy with technology; the dream of power with the engines of fulfillment." By the same token, the highly centralized and tyrannical infrastructures of ancient kingdoms and empires testified to a human longing for unconstrained supremacy over the elements. Even medieval culture exhibited this yearning: with their clocks, their rule, and their enterprise, the Benedictines, Mumford mused, were pioneers of self-control and synchronization, becoming "the original founders

of modern capitalism." When he ascribed the origins of the modern industrial labyrinth to the measurement of time by medieval monks, the crucial
development was not the clock but the very notion of standardizing human
conduct. Thus what Mumford called "the machine"—not merely discrete
pieces of machinery but also "the entire technological complex" of modern
industrial civilization—had been gestating in the moral and political unconscious of humanity since the dawn of history. Mechanization had taken
command of the human imagination *before* it captured the means of production. In the bureaucratic edifices of Egypt, Mesopotamia, and Rome, and
even in the humble, prayerful exactitudes of Christian monasticism, Mumford identified the origins of a mechanical humanism that preceded mechanization. Seeking power and certainty in their relations with nature, "men
became mechanical before they perfected complicated machines."[32]

All this served as a prelude to the secularization narrative that has dominated Western intellectual life from Max Weber to Charles Taylor, and at
times Mumford repeated, with minor variations, the Weberian myth of disenchantment. Tracing the origins of "disenchantment" to the Renaissance,
not the Reformation, Mumford maintained that the Renaissance scholar and
merchant—motivated, respectively, by mastery and lucre—"reduced the rich
actuality of things to a bare description of matter and motion." Armed with
a new ideology of scientific knowledge rooted in mechanical humanism, the
gentleman-scholars of the Renaissance proceeded to dismantle the traditional artisanal fusion of mental and manual labor. As possessors of the new
science, they drew a rigid distinction between those who designed and those
who executed orders, a hierarchy that prefigured the industrial regime of
management and worker. Later, Protestants, hostile to the sacramental sensibility of medieval Christianity, hastened the evacuation of spirit from
matter. Meanwhile, the violent and fiscally demanding rise of bureaucratic
monarchies increased both the scale and cost of warfare. Eventually, the disciplined aggression necessary for military and mining operations became
the model for capitalist enterprise. Thus the wave of technical improvements
that began in the sixteenth century depended, Mumford wrote in *Technics
and Civilization,* on "the dissociation of the animate and the mechanical"; a
lifeless universe was the metaphysical prerequisite for the modern state and
capital accumulation. This grand offensive against the organic prompted
Mumford's emulation of Randolph Bourne: "war is the health of the machine,"

he intoned, the apotheosis of slaughter and the paradigm of moral and onto-logical annihilation.[33]

Yet Mumford also suggested the outlines of an alternative to the conventional tale of scientific and technological secularization. Where Weber had seen desacralization as a constituent and expansive feature of modern consciousness, Mumford suggested that enchantment had instead been redirected toward the paleotechnical apparatus of industrial capitalism. The "dead world of physics" and the "mechanical philosophy" expounded by Descartes and Bacon provided unwitting ideological camouflage for a new and equally passionate devotion: the cult of the machine, or as Mumford would later put it in the 1960s, "the myth of the machine." Commencing a line of critique that would climax with his philippic against "the megamachine," Mumford underlined the religious character of machinery and of the hopes invested in its dubious guarantees of limitless mastery and wealth. Mumford studded *Technics and Civilization* in particular with allusions to the counterfeit religious character of capitalist paleotechnics. "Mechanical invention," he argued, "was the answer to a dwindling faith," a "substitute religion" that supplanted a Christianity grown stale, implausible, and subservient. "Mechanics became the new religion, and it gave to the world a new Messiah: the machine." The alleged disenchantment of the world introduced, not a brave new world of secular reason and justice, but a "religion of power" embodied most frightfully and destructively in industrial capitalism. Indeed, Mumford discerned an eschatological aspiration in the worship of the machine. As a spirit and icon of the lust for domination that propelled the capitalist economy, the machine was a "new demiurge that was to create a new heaven and a new earth," a "new Moses that was to lead a barbarous humanity into the promised land."[34]

But the land of paleotechnic promise turned out to be a promethean maelstrom of barbarism. The paleotechnic quest for an industrial heaven precipitated a moral revolution: enabled by technical innovation and sanctioned by the new indulgence given to avarice, "the ideal of a powerful expensive life supplanted the ideal of a holy or humane one"; the lust for mammon obviated "any other mode of life or form of expression except that associated with the machine." If the devil once took the greedy to hell, now he took the hindmost in the capitalist race for riches and mechanical power. Enchanted by the prospect of absolute dominion mediated by money and machinery, the religion of power mandated the imposition of a sterile technological despotism over the natural and human worlds; imbued with a lifeless sensibility, the leviathan scale of modern society entailed an economy and culture of death. "Megalopolis," as Mumford dubbed modern urban life in *The Culture of Cities*, "subordinates life to organized destruction" in war and industrial enterprise. "By putting business before every other manifestation of life," Mumford charged in *Technics and Civilization*, "our mechanical and financial civilization has forgotten the chief business of life: namely, growth, reproduction, development," and so factories fouled and polluted the earth, constricting and poisoning its powers of renewal. Similarly, manufacturers degraded artisanal prowess, committing a "castration of skill"; by renouncing personal control over technology, "a man could achieve godhood," he mused, but the power acquired was "ripped loose from his flesh and isolated from his humanity." Meanwhile, ideologues elevated a "maniacal intensity of work" to the level of moral principle; both capitalist and proletarian were enslaved to the rhythms of mechanization. Even the ideal of democracy degenerated into a "psychological rationalization for machine industry," as workers exchanged control over the means of production for a plethora of commodities.[35] Life under the spell of paleotechnic enchantment was as brutish as it was productive.

Much of American history was, for Mumford, a long and unfinished chapter in this tale of enchantment by money and paleotechnics. When he observed in *Faith for Living* that capitalism has "tended to supplant Christianity as a practical working religion" among Americans—even as they paid their loud and hollow rhetorical obeisance to the gospel—the conclusion flowed from the inexorable trajectory of the nation's covenant theology. In *Sticks and Stones*, Mumford described the American obsession with riches and technology as religious enthusiasm. Despite what he called their "Yankee communism," the Puritans had forsaken their medieval inheritance by hallowing the ethic of success; Benjamin Franklin, heir to the Puritan ethos, had repudiated "gothick phantoms" while deferring to the "dominant myths of his own time: matter [and] money." The typical American was "enchanted," Mumford wrote, by "dreams of a great fortune in real estate, rubber, or oil." He saw ritual and stigmata in the despoliation of nature by industrial development: in the American cult of the religion of power, "the smoke of the factory [is] incense," he wrote, and "the scars on the landscape [are] the lacerations of a saint." Expressing a seraphic ambition to escape the bonds of nature through technology, the American skyscraper, Mumford wrote, is "an architecture, not for men, but for angels."[36]

Even the ostensible opponents of capitalism knelt down in idolatry of power. Mumford's antipathy toward pragmatism, for instance, stemmed from his belief that it ratified the worship of force. In *The Golden Day,* he pronounced James and Dewey, not the heralds of a secular, scientifically informed democracy, but the ideological sponsors of a "pragmatic acquiescence" in the cult of industrial power. Conceding that "an enormous distance" separated James from the business intelligentsia, Mumford insisted nonetheless that a clear and straightforward line connected them. Pragmatists' happy agnosticism about the ends of life left them defenseless against the blandishments of business and allowed an easy conscience to their students when they became "employees in advertising agencies, or bond salesmen, or publicity experts." "Without vision," Mumford declared with biblical flourish, "the pragmatists perish." By the eve of World War II, Mumford was lambasting liberals on similar grounds. Since, in his view, pragmatism had become the default philosophy of American liberals, Mumford contended that their limitations as reformers could be traced to their own acquiescence in corporate rule, a "covert worship [of] power."[37]

This religious servility to power beguiled the revolutionary antagonists of capitalism as well. Even the poor and the proletariat remained "hypnotized," he lamented in *Technics and Civilization,* by the promise of what Mumford called "the *goods* life." Because workers identified justice and dignity with greater access to commodities, the class struggles triggered by industrial exploitation led to higher wages and improved working conditions, but "the fundamental conditions remained unaltered." Despite his sympathy with the Marxist desire to overthrow the established order, and although he praised Marx as a brilliant student of economics and technology, Mumford perceived that Marxists shared with capitalists an enchantment with the paleotechnic drive for colossal productive power. In his view, Marx's willingness to favor the expansion of productive forces over the freedom and dignity of workers left a blemish on all forms of socialism. Because they considered capitalism a necessary (albeit excruciating) phase in the dialectical unfolding of history, the left, Mumford feared, endorsed a socialist acquiescence in the remorseless religion of power. The socialist celebration of capitalist ingenuity and dynamism sanctioned a ritual sacrifice of human beings on the altar of history, while the complaint that "capitalism does not go far enough" was belied by its amoral, predatory abandon. "It actually does go farther," Mumford noted dryly, and its protean energy would carry with it anyone—like socialists—deluded enough to think that it could be harnessed to do any other bidding than its own.[38]

Not that Marx was entirely mistaken, Mumford observed, to think that paleotechnic capitalism was forging the lineaments of a superior order. Mumford lauded the paleotechnic era for some genuine contributions to civilization: the machine fostered "cooperative thought," appreciation for the aesthetic excellence of straight lines and simple forms, experience with the "delicate logic of materials and forces," and cultivation of a "more objective personality" that was capable of understanding reality without distraction by prejudice, fantasy, fear, or desire. Indeed, only by assimilating the virtues of mechanism, abstraction, and impersonality could the coming neotechnic age advance toward a life "more richly organic, more profoundly human." Some of the cultural preconditions of the "neotechnic" or "biotechnic" civilization were gestating within capitalism, as the paleotechnical apparatus created interdependence among machines and among workers. But Mumford broke with Marx by insisting that any "communist" society must shed both the primacy of paleotechnic technology and the mechanical humanism from which it arose.[39] The iniquity of paleotechnics derived not only from specifically capitalist objectives but also from the religion of power to which the machine was both a liturgical edifice and a sacramental vehicle.

Since any new, more organic and humane civilization would have to be prepared in the paleotechnic present, Mumford needed to identify traces of a new moral and metaphysical imagination. He found harbingers of a new organicism among a motley and sometimes bohemian company: poets, artists, and novelists, as well as the new scientific and technical professionals spawned by corporate industry. What appeared to unite these prototypes of neotechnic civilization was an artisanal relationship to their work. Exerting personal control over their words and images, writers and painters defied the paleotechnic system simply by pursuing their passions, living as "useless creatives" in the midst of a civilization given over to utility and panoptical management. From Morris and the pre-Raphaelites to Thoreau, Gauguin, and Tolstoy, they sought "plain animal self-respect, color in the outer environment and emotional depth in the inner landscape, a life lived for its own values, instead of a life on the make." The Romantics received Mumford's most fervent accolades for their "an attempt to restore the essential activities of human life to a central place" in the industrial world—personal creativity, beloved community, and reverence toward the sources of being. Ruskin, Morris, and other Romantics had tried valiantly to salvage emotion, body, and religion from the wreckage wrought by paleotechnic capitalism, preserving "those vital and historic and organic attributes that had been deliberately eliminated from the concepts of science and from the methods of the earlier technics." Thus, Romanticism formed a vital link between the eotechnic and neotechnic periods, sustaining the human desire for a richly gratifying synthesis of sensual, emotional, and spiritual experience. Yet if, in its "animus," it was right, Romanticism as an alternative to the machine was "dead." Blind to the possibilities of the paleotechnic present, Romantics avoided or vilified the "energies" required for a more organic and beautiful existence: science, technics, and "the mass of the new machine-workers themselves."[40]

For most of the interwar period, Mumford was optimistic about the prospects for a neotechnic or biotechnic civilization. Pointing to experiments with power generation undertaken by the Tennessee Valley Authority, and heartened by the "greenbelt communities" constructed under the auspices of the Resettlement Administration, Mumford believed that the neotechnic era was drawing nigh. These embryonic sites also harbored the promise of an organic individuality, an eotechnic sensibility renewed and intensified through modern technological implements. If the traditional industrial proletarian was disappearing with the triumph of neotechnics, a "new worker" was taking his place: an "all-around mechanic" characterized by "alertness, responsibility, [and an] intelligent grasp of the operative parts." Mumford joined Kropotkin and other anarchists in heralding the abolition of industrial hierarchy, calling for "a deliberate effort to produce engineering and scientific and managerial talent" at all levels of production.[41] Mumford's modern artisan would flourish in an organically felicitous workplace, moving among different, freely chosen varieties of mental and manual labor.

Mumford's preface to a new philosophy was the most ambitious attempt since nineteenth-century Romanticism to reconcile the scientific and democratic lineages of modernity with the moral and religious ideals of premodern civilizations. Attentive to biology and technics, his "organic ideology" represented the most intellectually incisive attempt by any contemporary critic of industrial society to return the realities of the natural world to a central place in the moral imagination. If Marx and other champions of technological progress had maligned "the idiocy of rural life," Mumford embraced the lessons of the organic without ratifying the pieties of reaction. And yet, as keen and seminal a student of technics as he was, Mumford himself could succumb to the lures of expert authority and technological determinism. Invited by the liberal *Forum* to contribute to its "What I Believe" series in 1930, Mumford called on progressive economists, engineers, administrators, and other specialists to form a vanguard capable of shaping the "groping intelligence" and amorphous "underlying desires" of the majority. Later, in *Technics and Civilization,* he wrote approvingly of Frederick W. Taylor, Elton Mayo, and other theorists of scientific management for their development of managerial techniques that "fully respected" the worker. His misreading of the implications of scientific management was of a piece with his enthusiasm for automation, whose removal of human agency from production militated against his artisanal conception of work. "The machine is a communist," he wrote confidently—an enthusiasm he would retract in the late 1960s as he grew more despondent about the course of technological development impelled by "the myth of the machine."[42]

Mumford's hopes were already dwindling as the Depression wore on, and by the time the United States entered World War II, he had largely abandoned his earlier optimism. Despite the expectancy at the end of *Technics and Civilization*—"nothing is impossible"—Mumford rapidly grew despondent. Just two years after the publication of his greatest book, he left New York in 1936 to live in Amenia, a rural town eighty miles north, where he remained for the rest of his life. His departure from his lifelong home, he later told his friend and fellow generalist the architect Roderick Seidenberg, reflected his growing pessimism about American civilization. "This society is as fatally doomed as Roman society was in the third century." While its "case" is not "irremediable," it is "too sick to know that it needs a doctor." There had been hints of despair in *Technics and Civilization,* where Mumford noted that "paleotechnic ideals still largely dominate the industry and politics of the Western world." Neotechnics would never deliver its promise until the paleotechnic residue had been discarded and earlier forms of science and technics had been recovered and renovated. This required political as well as intellectual commitment, but Mumford never translated his organic ideology and romantic humanism into a politics of work and technics. In *Technics and Civilization,* he acknowledged that the birth of a biotechnic communism would require "an outright battle with the guardians of capitalism" over control of industry and agriculture. Although he seemed to be endorsing overt class conflict, Mumford never called explicitly for a workers' revolution, union militancy, or any organized effort to capture the state or the workplace. Later, in *Faith for Living,* Mumford complained that unions clung to a small and shabby vision, demanding "just a little more of the gravy"—an irrefutable but also unenlightening position.[43]

Reluctant to engage in political resistance, Mumford had no other option but to wait on events. He gave up on his compatriots, sniping in *Faith for Living* that Americans "bow in prayer with a soft cushion under their knees," and implore God not to force them "to renounce their dear possessions until the day of judgment." As American entry into the second global war looked ever more imminent, Mumford detected an opportunity to foster the spirit of sacrifice necessary to end "the crazy economy we once held so sacred."[44] In a sad but instructive irony, Mumford looked to the state and the corporate elite just as Dewey and the pragmatists had during World War I. Calling on the United States to enter the war, Mumford acquiesced pragmatically, admonishing political and corporate leaders to act as a vanguard of personal simplicity and public service. For a lifelong critic of capitalist predation, Mumford showed an inexplicable faith in the republican spirit of the business community.

Still, Mumford preserved a small measure of hope beside his feckless prescriptions to the paleotechnic elite. Increasingly convinced that mechanization was encroaching on imaginative life, he urged readers of *Faith for Living* to adopt some of the most ancient of meditative practices, if not the way of life they informed. Watching the atrophy of radical dreams and the impending confrontation with fascism, Mumford counseled his readers to retreat into themselves, not in resignation but in what amounted to a spirit of prayer—without the soft cushions. "Every human being is living through an apocalypse of violence," he observed; "not since the Black Plague had "terror and misery . . . stalked through the world on this scale." The only available antidote to such carnage, as well as the only source of fortitude to transcend the religion of power, lay in a "cultivation of the inner life by withdrawal, purposive contemplation, and self-communion." For now, he counseled, we have to "restore our own faith for living, and to lay the foundations of a world in which life . . . will once more be sacred."[45]

# 23

# Human Divinity

## F. Scott Fitzgerald, James Agee, and the Son of God

FOR MANY OF MUMFORD'S generation, the sacredness of life was a bitterly discredited illusion. After a century of shocks to Victorian culture, the savagery of World War I administered the coup de grâce both to Christianity and to the modern piety of endless progress. As Amory Blaine concludes in F. Scott Fitzgerald's *This Side of Paradise* (1920), many educated Americans had "grown up to find all Gods dead" and "all faiths in men shaken." Yet Fitzgerald hinted that not *all* gods were dead, and that not *all* faiths in men had been shaken: the new generation, Amory remarks, is "dedicated more than the last to the fear of poverty and the worship of success." Mammon was a fetching surrogate for moribund divinity and secular enlightenment; and yet something of the old ideals persisted and remained doggedly venerable. Declaring that there is "no God in his heart," Amory nonetheless acknowledges the existence of "a deposit on his soul": a "love of life" and "the faint stirring of old ambitions and unrealized dreams"—perhaps those "mistakes and half-forgotten dreams of dead statesmen and poets" on which the new generation is being "fed romantically." Despite his own disillusion and regret, Amory vows to struggle in the face of gilded meaninglessness. Opening his arms to "the crystalline radiant sky," he asserts that he knows himself, "but that is all."[1]

This blend of melancholy and defiance in the wake of modernity's broken promises became common and even fashionable in literary and intellectual circles before the Depression. It pervaded a volume such as Joseph Wood Krutch's *The Modern Temper* (1929), a minor masterpiece in the annals of despair. Veering between erudite commentary and flippant cynicism, Krutch's book elegantly captured a sense that the disenchantment of the world had produced its own brands of credulity and fraudulence. Confidently assuming that science had rendered religion obsolescent, Krutch proceeded to de-molish the secular substitutes for traditional belief. Technological progress, revolutionary politics, liberation from totems and taboos—the new shibbo-leths now lay in a rubble of anomie. Reduced in status from the image of God to a product of indifferent natural processes, humanity could no longer identify its ideals with the larger design of the cosmos. The once vigorous materialism that had vanquished theological phantoms now sanctioned a "vegetative existence" given over to pointless, enervating acquisition. "We have settled into a kind of bourgeois security, and bourgeois security has its own dull comforts," Krutch sneered, at himself as much as at other Ameri-cans. Though dismissive of those "weak and uninstructed intelligences" that still found succor in religion, Krutch conceded that, even with all its ad-vances, modern life is not "one tenth so luminous as it was to those who felt themselves playing an important part in a cosmic struggle." Still, Krutch urged his fellow moderns to continue the quest for the knowledge that enervates hope.[2]

This genteel, ostentatious gloom was no longer acceptable a decade later, as the Depression made ennui not only intellectually retrograde but politi-cally unfashionable. Krutch's aversion to idealism was anathema to writers facing bread lines, striking workers, dispossessed farmers, and a resurgent radical left. Anyone eager to mend what James Agee called the vast and "appallingly damaged group of human beings" could not afford to think that life is meaningless; if they did not believe that the struggle was "cosmic," its terrestrial import was vivid and significant enough to arouse their energies. Indeed, as Agee's *Let Us Now Praise Famous Men* (1941) demonstrated, what was up to that time the most serious crisis in the history of capitalism could occasion not only the renewal of political engagement but also a return to the metaphysical and religious questions Krutch had considered surpassed. More than an account of "social conditions" among Southern tenant farmers, his book, Agee wrote unabashedly, was "an independent inquiry into certain normal predicaments of human divinity."[3]

Set at the poles of American society, two books illuminate both the pas-sage from despair to commitment and the persistence of sacramental hope: Fitzgerald's *The Great Gatsby* (1925), his American Vanity Fair on Long Island, and Agee's *Let Us Now Praise Famous Men*, his metaphysical reverie on the lives of white sharecroppers in Alabama. Chronicling the extremes of wealth and poverty, Fitzgerald and Agee also traced the affinity of idolatry and desecration in capitalist culture. Both books are inquiries into the vicissitudes of men and women cast in terms of human divinity: Jay Gatsby's duplicitous and lethal self-fashioning into a phony "son of God," and modern bondservants revealed as the likenesses of God in conditions of appalling irreverence.

*The Great Gatsby* has been read by at least four generations of readers as a meditation on "the American Dream": the allure and ultimate emptiness of a life devoted to the pursuit of "success," the "green light" of ambition as intense as the one at the end of Daisy Buchanan's dock. Like many a poor and ingenious youth, Jimmy Gatz wants everything the world can offer. Transforming himself into Jay Gatsby through will, deceit, and what the narrator Nick Carraway calls "an extraordinary gift for hope," the most flamboyant hero in American literature acquires everything—but love. Rejected by Daisy, Gatsby and the green light fade—snuffed out, in the end, by another poor man whose life has been demolished in the traffic of avarice—and the "orgastic future" at which he and his compatriots grasp is violently canceled. Thus *Gatsby* is a story of modern enchantment, an account of metaphysical as well as moral failure, a tale of intense sacramental desire perverted toward accumulation. Fitzgerald gestured to this desperate longing in a letter to a friend that he wrote while finishing *Gatsby*. "That's the whole burden of this novel—the loss of those illusions that give such color to the world so that you don't care whether things are true or false as long as they partake of the magical glory."[4]

"Color" and "magical glory" were part of Fitzgerald's upbringing in St. Paul, Minnesota, where his strict Catholic parents introduced him to the liturgical splendor of the Church. Fitzgerald remained a practicing Catholic during most of his years at Princeton; in *This Side of Paradise,* Amory fondly recalls the "halls and cloisters," the "chastity of the spires," and the choral music that "drifted over the campus in melancholy beauty." Fitzgerald left the Church during his senior year, and his shadow never darkened a church door again; but Catholicism pervades all of Fitzgerald's novels and short stories, from the Gothic imagery of *This Side of Paradise* to the confessional tone of *The Crack-Up* (1945), his wry "check-up of my spiritual liabilities." Formed in an American Catholic culture still at odds with the Protestant mainstream yet envious of its economic and political power, Fitzgerald's metaphysical and moral imagination enabled him to be an incisive if apolitical critic of American capitalism. Born an outsider yet permitted to enter the inner sancta of American hegemony, Fitzgerald always felt like a parvenu; from Princeton to Hollywood, he remained, like Nick Carraway, "within and without, simultaneously enchanted and repelled" by the wealthy milieu he inhabited.[5]

Gatsby's search for "magical glory" began in a short story, "Absolution," that Fitzgerald originally intended as an explanatory prologue to the novel. Set in the Dakotas at the turn of the century, the tale opens in the rectory office of Father Adolph Schwartz, an aging priest whose repressions have become explosively untenable. The laughter of pretty Swedish girls outside his window both touches and frightens him, and the scent of soap from the local drugstore seems "desperately sweet upon the air"; the aroma "drifted, rather like incense, toward the summer moon." Into his office walks Rudolph Miller, a handsome young boy, confused and wavering in his faith, who's troubled by the sin of having lied in the confessional. Transfixed by Rudolph's "beautiful eyes" (a faint hint of sexual attraction?), the priest can no longer maintain his defenses against the delights of earthly life. "Do you hear the hammer and the clock ticking and the bees?"—the rule of the Protestant covenant ethic over the vast wheat fields outside. "Well that's no good. The thing is to have a lot of people in the centre of the world, wherever that happens to be." "Then," he marvels, "things go glimmering." "Did you ever see an amusement park?" he continues. The rides, the lights, the music, the smells— "everything will twinkle." Sparkling outside the realm of instrumental reason, "it won't remind you of anything. It will all just hang out there in the night like a colored balloon—like a big yellow lantern on a pole." Sitting in panic, Rudolph nonetheless feels confirmed in a suspicion: "There was something ineffably gorgeous somewhere that had nothing to do with God." Rudolph feels unburdened of God's constant surveillance, while Schwartz collapses on the floor, demented.[6] Both the boy and the priest have experienced absolution from adherence to oppressive restrictions.

For Rudolph—as for many Americans—a secular zone of the "ineffably gorgeous" was an exhilarating possibility, a chance to escape the dreary mores of an ebbing proprietary culture. But in *Gatsby,* Fitzgerald appears to conclude that such a place is a land of death and despair—a "valley of ashes" not unlike the stretch between West Egg and New York City. As all readers know, peering over that valley is a large billboard with the eyes and spectacles of Dr. T. J. Eckleberg, whose brooding but feckless gaze is taken to suggest God's death or indifference. But God is not dead in Fitzgerald's classic—he is played by Jay Gatsby, whose re-creation of himself is both quintessentially American and gorgeously Faustian. In *Gatsby*, Fitzgerald examines the metaphysical insolence that fuels the rage to accumulate. Assigning a role to Gatsby once reserved for God, Fitzgerald suggests that capitalist ambition is a quest for human divinity.

Fitzgerald himself tells us that Gatsby's self-invention is a grasp for divine creative power. The son of struggling farmers whom "he never really accepted as his parents at all" (in "Absolution," Rudolph nurses a similar denial), young Jimmy Gatz imagines that he is self-created, even eternal. True to the proprietary ethic, he fills his *Hopalong Cassidy* notebook with mites of self-exhortation worthy of Benjamin Franklin or Timothy Shea Arthur: "read one improving book or magazine per week." But Jimmy's enterprise in self-help goes much further than moral discipline. As Nick observes in the key metaphysical passage of the novel:

> The truth was that Jay Gatsby, of West Egg, Long Island, sprang from his Platonic conception of himself. He was a son of God—a phrase which, if it means anything, means just that—and he must be about His Father's Business, the service of a vast, vulgar and meretricious beauty . . . to this conception he was faithful to the end.

Jimmy spends two dismal weeks at a Lutheran college whose Christian ethos repels him with its "ferocious indifference to the drums of his destiny." Working as a clam digger by day, Gatz is a deity by night, spinning "a universe of ineffable gaudiness"—"something ineffably gorgeous somewhere." The everyday world is pale and flat in the eyes of this venal god, convinced of "the unreality of reality"—the worthlessness of a world not endowed with value by his ineffably gaudy desires. Extravagantly ambitious yet still unsuccessful, a despairing Gatz is saved by World War I. Although, as he tells Nick, he "tried very hard to die," his survival in the midst of slaughter convinced him that he "seemed to bear an enchanted life." After the war, endowing himself with a cache of phony medals and a bogus Oxford degree, he amasses a fortune from bootlegging. As a son of God about "His Father's Business," Jay Gatsby is his own meretricious idol.[7]

Gatsby's self-divinity is the grandest totem in a novel replete with fetishes—a "count of enchanted objects," as Nick describes the world in which he swans. The people and things in *Gatsby* comprise a universe of pecuniary phantoms: the "silver pepper of the stars" that dapple the firmament over Long Island, turkeys "bewitched to a dark gold," Daisy's voice that is "full of money," Nick's volumes on finance "promising to unfold the shining secrets that only Midas and Morgan and Maecenas knew." Inanimate objects come to life: slippers "shuffle the shining dust," the cocktails at Gatsby's parties "float . . . through the twilight." Holding the "wild promise of all the mystery and the beauty in the world," New York—glimmering in "the enchanted metropolitan twilight"—seems "built with a wish out of non-olfactory money." There are few if any references to the actual labor that makes this gilded cosmos possible: waiters, mechanics, and domestic servants, like the butler who presses the button on Gatsby's juice machine. (George Wilson, the gas station owner who kills Gatsby in the end, is the only character we actually see working. He's also the only one with any lingering belief in a just and omnipresent God: "God sees everything," he tells his wife Myrtle, mistress to Tom Buchanan, who is killed by Daisy with Gatsby's car.) All of the characters luxuriate in the radiance of Gatsby's commodity spectacle, but the protagonist himself remains a tawdry, duplicitous, and inscrutable deity. "I'll tell you God's truth," Gatsby swears to Nick as a prelude to a lie about his past—but truth and falsehood melt into each other in the glow of "the magical glory."[8]

As Gatsby spins his tale, Nick remarks that "his right hand suddenly ordered divine retribution to stand by." Nemesis does eventually crucify the gaudy son of God. Gatsby's romantic disappointment brought on by Daisy's rejection triggers a metaphysical crisis—the erosion of his divinity and the disenchantment of his world. As it dawns on Gatsby that Daisy has rejected him, his lustrous universe dissolves into nothingness, and the palpable world turns ugly and vacant. Lying in his pool as his killer approaches, Gatsby beholds "an unfamiliar sky through frightening leaves" and recoils from "what a grotesque thing a rose is." Deprived of Gatsby's once enlivening powers, "a new world, material without being real . . . drifted factitiously about."[9]

"Material without being real"—the world hangs suspended in a terrifying void once it is depleted of Gatsby's enchantment.

Yet Gatsby's death registers only a part of Fitzgerald's equivocal judgment on American enchantment. There are utopian, sacramental traces embroidered into *Gatsby*'s garish metaphysical tapestry. Festivals of profligacy, Gatsby's parties resemble potlatches, with their host, in the roles of chief and shaman, divesting himself of his "enchanted objects" in the hope of winning love. Contrary to the flinty moralism of the Protestant proprietary ethic, the dissipation at Gatsby's parties is not merely a symptom of depravity; the orgies of consumption and self-indulgence originate in a desperate desire for happiness. As Nick observes with generosity and tenderness, the revelers "came for the party with a simplicity of heart that was its own ticket of admission." In their amoral innocence, the partygoers resemble the Dutch sailors who constituted the first white presence on Long Island, and whose epiphanous rapture Fitzgerald recounts in the pensive conclusion of the novel, a reflection on America as the final, tragic refuge of precapitalist enchantment. Nick imagines their arrival three centuries ago to a verdant, seductive island, full of trees that "pandered in whispers to the last and greatest of all human dreams": that America was the setting for the beloved community that had eluded the inhabitants of Europe. For a "transitory enchanted moment," confronted by "something commensurate" to their ingenuous "capacity for wonder," the explorers encountered the mysterious, fructifying presence of material grace—"the fresh green breast of the new world," a force that compelled "an aesthetic contemplation" that was "neither understood nor desired." Gatsby, too, Nick perceived, had partaken of that wonder and magical glory; but the "dream" was "already behind him," buried "where the dark fields of the republic rolled on under the night." However awestruck by natural beatitude, the Dutch sailors—like the Puritans—had proceeded to establish a commercial imperium, the prelude to Gatsby's fortune. The green breast had been ravaged in the rage to accumulate; the whispering trees had been felled and silenced to make way for Gatsby's house, the tabernacle of objects acquired in his self-destructive quest for self-creation. To Fitzgerald, the American Dream—born in the transition from premodern divinity to the enchantments of capitalist modernity—was impossible from the beginning. Thus, *The Great Gatsby* is an exquisitely understated rejection of the American jeremiad tradition.[10]

If the "greatness" of Gatsby is a glimmering abyss, the "fame" of the people
in Agee's masterpiece manifests the presence of God. Scraping by as tenant
farmers in northern Alabama, Agee's people resided in a valley of ashes far
from the enchanted metropolis; but as he reminded readers on the very first
page, "they are our world, brothers and sisters."[11] Yet Agee refused to reduce
them to examples of wretchedness and oppression. In their poverty they testified to a glory without magic, and in Agee they had a champion sensitive to
the depth and variety of human sacrilege. Far more than a classic of documentary journalism, *Let Us Now Praise Famous Men* is a chorale of exaltation, a testament to the fleshly but ineffable reality of what Agee called
"human divinity."

Like Fitzgerald's modern-day satyricon, Agee's book of revelation has been
routinely deprived of its metaphysical and religious import. It is read either
in politically progressive terms as a cry against injustice or in politically innocuous postmodernist fashion as evidence for the impossibility of representation. Both readings call attention to real facets of the book, but they also
miss or misrepresent the point Agee set out to make. In the summer of 1936,
while a staff writer for *Fortune,* Agee, accompanied by Walker Evans, embarked on what was supposed to be an investigation of living conditions
among sharecroppers. After *Fortune*'s editors rejected Agee's original submission, he enlarged it into a book, turning it into the most magnificent reportage of the Depression era. Though *Famous Men* sold poorly at the time
of its initial publication, Lionel Trilling anointed Agee's and Evans's work
"the most important moral effort" of the period, and it later became an almost required text among students in the early New Left.[12] While the stature
of *Famous Men* as a piece of social criticism is assured, Agee's anguish over
its veracity—especially his anxiety about exploiting the farmers like a leftish,
self-righteous voyeur—raises perennial questions about the limits of any attempt to depict "reality."

But Agee's doubts about his venture were not, in the end, about the inherent
limitations of art, and his misgivings about the book extended to the genre of
social criticism itself. For Agee, the futility of representation stemmed from
the holiness of humanity, a mystery whose acknowledgement lay, he believed,
at the basis of any genuine and enduring revolution. "For one who sets himself
to look at all earnestly, at all in purpose toward truth, into the living eyes of a
human life," Agee asks at one point, "what is it he there beholds that so freezes

and abashes his ambitious heart?" "What is it," he answers, "but ... [what] one may faintly designate the human 'soul'." Evans later recalled that to Agee, "human beings were at least possibly immortal and literally sacred souls." As his friend the poet and critic Robert Fitzgerald later wrote, "the religious sense of life is at the heart of all of Agee's work." Read as a testament of religious humanism, *Let Us Now Praise Famous Men* becomes exactly what Agee described in the preamble: an effort to "recognize the stature of a portion of un-imagined existence ... an independent inquiry into certain normal predica-ments of human divinity." As poet, journalist, and flawed recording angel, Agee felt that he was *revealing,* not constructing or bestowing, the sanctity of "the common people." More than the inadequacies of language, the fact of human divinity foiled any attempt to "capture" reality; and it also tripped up any movement for justice that denied this ineffable sacredness. Agee acknowl-edged and even seemed to relish the discomfort he knew this assertion would cause his secular, progressive audience. Asserting that "murder is being done, against nearly every individual in the planet," he went on to suggest that "there are dimensions and correlations of cure which not only are not being used but appear to be scarcely considered or suspected." One such unsuspected "cure," Agee thought, was "the fear and joy of God."[13]

Agee's fear and joy of God began in Knoxville, Tennessee, where he was born in 1909. As a boy he was sent to St. Andrew's, a rural Episcopal school run by the Order of the Holy Cross, where he met Father James H. Flye, who became his lifelong friend, confessor, and correspondent. After admission to Philips Exeter Academy—where he befriended Dwight Macdonald—he spent vacations with the Cowley Fathers, the Anglican order that influenced Ralph Adams Cram and Vida Dutton Scudder. Although Agee later aban-doned orthodox Christianity while a student at Harvard, Anglo-Catholic lit-urgy left a permanent moral and aesthetic impression: he loved the "leaden melodies of the Lenten hymns," he recalled, while "destitute, despised, for-saken were words especially dear to him." He attended retreats with the Fathers while at Harvard—a "field between devil and God" for Agee, where the spirit warred unsuccessfully against the temptations of sex, cigarettes, and booze. (A typical Agee weekend included a gin-soaked bender on Sat-urday night followed by choir on Sunday morning.)[14]

After Agee graduated from Harvard in 1932, he moved to New York, where Macdonald got him a job on the Luce estate writing articles and book reviews for *Time* and *Fortune.* While working for Luce, Agee published *Permit Me Voyage* (1934), a short and precocious volume in the Yale Younger Poets Series. So when he headed south, Agee seemed headed for a brilliant career, festooned with literary accolades. But Agee was a turbulent and combustible soul, and the Christian faith that he never lost—however "unchurched" he remained—compelled him to be one of those, as he wrote in one of his poems, "enraged that have beheld / those practiced and gravely cumulated idiocies which, since this race / began, have been committed of man on men." While at *Fortune,* he witnessed quite a bit of the idiocy of bourgeois life. Writing on a wide and even laughably disparate array of topics—the TVA, modern furniture, carpet mills, cockfighting, cruise lines, and horse racing— Agee endured what he remembered as "three years of exposure to foulness" that nearly corrupted him into "cynicism."[15]

Yet Agee tempered his ferocity with hope for the salvation of the bourgeoisie. In "Dedication," a prose poem in *Permit Me Voyage,* Agee implored the rich to repent of their hideous and lucrative sins, hectoring "men who . . . make it their business to destroy concord and to incite war and to prolong it, for their profit in the commerce of armament." Summoning the spirit of Hieronymus Bosch, Agee imagined their righteous afflictions: "the loins thaw with a shrieking pain," "slow nails in the skulls of each," "the quintessence of pain very eternal." But the munitions makers could avoid their well-deserved fate if they "repent themselves straightaway and for good." Agee called on "merchants, dealers, and speculators in the wealth of the earth who own this world . . . its channels of advertisement and converse and opinion" to "repent their very existence as the men they are, and change or quit it." Short of changing their ways, they would inexorably and rightly "visit the just curse upon themselves." Agee's vision of the inferno matched the iniquity of the offenders' crimes, but his hope for their redemption raised his rant above malice and lent it the quality of mercy.[16]

This refusal to hate the class enemy has led scholars to characterize Agee as an apolitical writer who looked to spiritual remedies for injustice. As one historian expresses the conventional indictment, Agee "opposed reform and encouraged political withdrawal." There's certainly plenty of damning evidence. Agee recoiled from Popular Front culture, maligning Works Projects Administration artists in a 1944 *Partisan Review* essay as "mock-primitive [and] demagogic" and skewering Paul Robeson's "Ballad for Americans" as "esthetically execrable." Agee had no time for the Wisdom of the Common Man, so thoroughly had it been tainted by the culture industries. Thanks to these "machines for universal manure-spreading," the folk so beloved by the left had been "dangerously corrupted," being "quite as vulnerable" as the middle classes to the "bourgeois-folk art" of advertising. Add to that Agee's avowed aversion to "all factions and all joiners" and his skepticism about the motives of progressives, many of whom he considered naive and self-righteous. His basic instinct, inseparable from his Christian faith, was that the fallen human condition could not be "essentially changed." As he told Father Flye while working on *Famous Men,* "I certainly have lost a great deal in faith, hope, and optimism in a few years. I have little if any hope left that the cancer will ever be even slightly alleviated, far less cured."[17] Let us now condemn James Agee.

But the guilty verdict should be set aside—not only because the prosecution ignores some of his explicit political statements but also because it implies a view of religion that Agee himself was seeking to discredit. Agee supported the radical left quite openly, if not with a passion for all things proletarian. As he told the Guggenheim Foundation when he applied for a fellowship in 1937, he agreed with the "ideas and basic procedures of Communism." (His application was denied.) Later, in a short and acerbic section of *Famous Men,* he responded to questions from *Partisan Review* about "the role of the writer." He had once felt "forms of allegiance or part-allegiance" both to Catholicism and to the Communist Party, he replied, but he felt "less and less at ease with them" and was now "done with them." Still, he expressed a basic sympathy with the far left, though he couched it in an irony that no true believer would have shared. "I am certainly 'for' an 'intelligent' 'communism,'" he wrote in parody of progressive posturing. Agee backed away both from the populist boilerplate of the Popular Front and from the self-importance of *Partisan Review,* opining that the political tendency of American literature "smells no more nor less to heaven" than any other trend.[18]

Agee kept a principled distance from the American left, not because he opposed revolution, but because he thought the revolution they envisioned was not radical or transformative enough. As he explained to *Partisan Review,* the achievement of a communist society should be "only a part of much more, and a means to an end." Agee feared that by making communism into an ultimate good, the left was endangering a greater human blessing as well as the revolution. Even if they wanted only to avoid yet another form of barbarism, communists, he warned in *Famous Men,* would have to reckon with "mortal sin," especially pride, which could "wreck the human race as [much as] 'Greed' ever could." So when Agee declared in *Famous Men* that he was "a Communist by sympathy and conviction," his communism must be seen in the light of the two epigrams with which he opened his book. One is Marx's clarion call to the workers of the world to unite—a summons which, Agee asserted, is not "the property of any political party, faith, or faction." But the other is from *King Lear,* where the foolish monarch, dethroned, disgraced, and naked, now knows "to feel what wretches feel." Embracing the wisdom of dis-accumulation and redistribution to the poor—"shake the superflux to them"—Lear pronounces that charity will "show the heavens more just."[19] For Agee, the Revolution would have to vindicate, not the dialectic of history, but the glory, justice, and love of God.

The most radiant of those glories was the creation of humanity in the image and likeness of God, and the ineffable splendor of *Famous Men* derives from this assurance of "human divinity." Agee's sacramental vision illuminates the contents of the Gudgers' home: "this tabernacle," in his words, his portrait of which was so inadequate, he fretted, that it was a "desecration" on which he nonetheless proceeded "reverentially." (Agee chose as an epigram for the section on "Shelter" a line from Psalm 43: "I will go unto the altar of God.") Among the most precisely observed and graceful of the volume's passages, Agee's inventory of the Gudgers' belongings comprised a sacramental catalog, a doting roster of material graces that eluded the taxonomy of "living conditions." Refusing to reduce the Gudgers' misery to yet another advertisement for social reform, Agee's assertion that their space was sacred—"not to me but of itself"—implied that even the shabbiest objects were tokens of human divinity.[20]

But Agee's most powerfully sacramental prose appeared in his portrayal of the sharecroppers themselves. If the tenant farmers were undoubtedly "an undefended and appallingly damaged group of human beings," they remained the icons and children of God. Seeking to employ but also transcend the categories of social science, Agee conceded their necessity but refused to consider them sufficient. "'Tenant' 'farmers,' or 'representatives' of your 'class' . . . social integers in a criminal economy"—"it is in all these particularities," he granted, "that each of you is that which he is." Yet Agee knew that these designations obscured or concealed the real magnitude of human suffering. To reduce his subjects to "social integers" would "fail to yield their stature, meaning, power of hurt"; it would even be "impious." In the farmers' tribulations one found more than injustice; one discovered "the true proportions of the savageness of the world." Once the farmers stood truly revealed in all their defiled quotidian holiness, the evils inflicted on them stood out as outrages on the body of Christ, "generations upon generations unceasingly crucified." Propelled by his discernment of a transcendent presence in the dingy overalls and faces, the majesty of Agee's prose ascended when he turned to beleaguered divinity. Each embattled farmer became "a furious angel nailed to the ground by his wings"; in each desecrated man and woman he beheld "the most sanguine hope of godhead." Agee glorified and rued the birth of a child by noting that "his globe is rounded upon him and is his prison, which might have been his kingdom."[21]

Like a long line of poets—from Milton through Blake to Auden—Agee knew that the dimensions of politics were broader than most writers or politicians imagined. Because he rooted politics and economics in their proper metaphysical soil—the "predicaments of human divinity"—Agee's "apolitical" work posed the largest political challenges of the era or of any time. If, on this side of heaven, our fallen state could not be "essentially changed" nor the "cancer" of sin be removed, then communism could only promise, at best, a mild foretaste of the celestial city. For Agee, the modesty of that goal was no reason to abandon the struggle: it remained a sacrilege that a furious angel was crucified on the cross of property. But once that illustrious stature became clear, so would the impossible imperative of our efforts to repair its desecration. So if, like Agee, they grasped the true depth of their desire, communists would have to do more than contend for control of the means of production. In league with other terrestrial angels, they would have to transform their fury at injustice into the patient love of the unjust. To Agee, struggle is unavoidable; ultimate victory is not our doing; and any triumph in the war against human profanation must be worthy of human divinity.

Agee thought the prognosis for the "cancer" was gloomy. In "Christmas 1945," four months after the end of World War II, Agee celebrated the birth of Christ by mocking the Christian Nation's pretensions. The holy day would inspire the usual chorus of earnest and unfaithful pledges: "All each heart holds of love, resolves / Once more, today, in angry grief, / Enduring courage;

and dissolves/In unbelief." But in Agee's eyes, the "unbelief" of the heart
took shape as the common faith of Fordism. Consumer culture had turned
Yuletide into a season of spiritual graft—"The Magi's gifts are subtle
bribes"—and those standing watch outside the manger were devotees of industrial idolatry—"the shepherds worship clock and wage." In the burgeoning weapons of the victorious Allies, Agee detected the advent of a new
order of profanation. "In rattling arms, roared diatribes,/Wakes the new
Age."[22] Agee saw an American empire, and he trembled.

# PART SEVEN

## One Vast and Ecumenical Holding Company: The Prehistory of Neoliberal Enchantment, 1945–1975

"I SHOULD LIKE TO see a bottle of Coca-Cola on every table in England," Hector Dexter tells his luncheon companions in Nancy Mitford's novel *The Blessing* (1951). A long-winded American politician on a fact-finding tour through Western Europe, Dexter has been sharing his uninvited opinions on the state of postwar Britain. "This little island of yours is just like some little old grandfather clock that is running down." How could Britain and other nations shattered by World War II recapture their vigor, if not regain the imperial stature that now belonged to the United States? Import Coca-Cola— "the Pause that Refreshes."[1]

"But isn't it terribly nasty?" Dexter's host Grace Allingham interjects. Unfazed, he swells with a patriotic flourish:[2]

When I say a bottle of Coca-Cola . . . I mean an outward and visible sign of something inward and spiritual, I mean it as if each Coca-Cola bottle contained a djinn, and as if that djinn was our great American civilization ready to spring out of each bottle and cover the whole global universe with its great wide wings. That is what I mean.

The pause that refreshes is a mass-produced, sacramental phial of Americanism.

The corporate clerisy at *Fortune* would have applauded Dexter's commodity fetishism. In February of the same year, the magazine's editors published a special issue titled *U.S.A.: The Permanent Revolution*. In an appendix
to Luce's proclamation of "the American Century," they claimed that capitalism represented the longings of decolonizing peoples more authentically
than the revolutionary dreams of Marxist guerrillas. "The American Way
of Life embodies a mystery which is common to all men—the mystery of
the human spirit." As this awe-inspiring mystery partook of fundamental
"metaphysical" truths—Freedom, Prosperity, Progress—*Fortune*'s clerics
reasoned that imperialism was impossible, as all peoples aspire to capitalist
modernity: "the question of Americans thrusting themselves on anybody
can never really arise."[3] *Fortune* called on all men and women of good will to
join the permanent capitalist revolution—the latest and most cosmopolitan
form of the American errand into the marketplace.

Twenty-five years later, another fictional character divined the implications of *Fortune*'s revolutionary project. In *Network* (1976), Paddy Chayefsky
and Sidney Lumet's film satirizing the television industry, Arthur Jensen, the
chairman of a communications conglomerate, demonstrates that Dexter's
winged demon has already enveloped the globe. Alarmed by Howard
Beale—a newscaster whose populist harangues have made him "the mad
prophet of the airwaves"—Jensen invites him to a meeting in "Valhalla," the
dimly-lit corporate boardroom. Roaring to Beale that he has "meddled with
the primal forces of nature," Jensen proceeds to explain the universe:[4]

> There are no nations, there are no peoples . . . there is only one holistic
> system of Systems . . . one interwoven, interacting, multi-varied, multi-
> national dominion of Dollars. . . . It is the international system of cur-
> rency which determines the totality of life on this planet. That is the
> natural order of things today. That is the atomic and subatomic and
> galactic structure of things today.

The pecuniary cosmology of capital has never received a more audacious
exposition, and it allows Jensen to acknowledge some stark but intractable
truths about the state of the world: the delusion of democratic promise, the
open secret of corporate plutocracy, the supersession of all cultural and political limits on the power and authority of money. America itself is a front

for the consortium whose mercantile communion embraces the entire planet. A new Walt Whitman hailing plutocratic vistas, Jensen chants the new empire:

> There is no America. There is no democracy. There is only IBM and IT&T and AT&T, and Du Pont, Dow, Union Carbide, and Exxon. These are the nations of the world today.... We no longer live in a world of nations and ideologies.... The world is a college of corporations, inexorably determined by the immutable by-laws of business. The world is a business, Mr. Beale.... One vast and ecumenical holding company for whom all men will work to serve a common profit—in which all men will hold a share of stock. All necessities provided, all anxieties tranquilized, all boredom amused.

"And I have chosen you, Mr. Beale, to preach this evangel," Jensen says as he touches the mad prophet's arm and anoints him the bearer of the gospel. "I have seen the face of God," the demented herald murmurs. "You just might be right, Mr. Beale," Jensen replies. God and Mammon have finally merged into the largest monopoly ever contemplated.

Beale's ratings plummet when he delivers this "evangel," so the network's desperate executives have him assassinated on live television. Beale dies as a sacrificial victim to what Guy Debord called the "the spectacle": a society controlled by mass-produced images, a counterfeit democracy of consumption that, Debord contended, was entering into its fullest realization as he was writing in the early 1960s. In the society of the spectacle, production and consumption are subsumed under managerial and technocratic supervision more extensively than ever before; "the specialized science of domination" fragments into "psychotechnics, cybernetics, [and] semiology." While "spectacle" is a "material reconstruction of the religious illusion"—a technologically enhanced and more all-encompassing form of the fetishism of commodities—it marks an ironic advance on pre-industrial brands of superstition. "Spectacular technology"—the ever more sophisticated means of image production and distribution—has not, Debord explained, "dispelled the religious clouds"; it has only "tied them to an earthly base" more securely and explicitly than ever. The "fallacious paradise" of spectacular society is ruled by "a pseudo-sacred entity"—the spectacle, the profusion of images—

that "reveals itself for what it is": a thing made by human hands that nonetheless wields a power over its creators. The human origins of the spectacle remain thoroughly structured and leavened by the rage to accumulate: "the spectacle is capital . . . as an image."[5] In the symbolic universe of the spectacle, advertising, art, and business become indistinguishable; literally everything is enveloped in the metaphysics of money. Beale had indeed seen the face of God: the factitious god of capital, with Arthur Jensen as its emanation.

Yet Beale's demise leaves unexplored another path of opposition to the corporate spectacle. Before his encounter with Jensen, Beale describes to his friend Max Schumacher a rapturous vision of cosmic harmony. Denying Schumacher's contention that he needs psychiatric treatment, Beale tells him gently that this is rather "a cleansing moment of clarity . . . I'm imbued with some special spirit." He then witnesses to an epiphany reminiscent of Winstanley, Blake, Wordsworth, or Hopkins:[6]

> I feel vivid and flashing as if suddenly I'd been plugged into some great electro-magnetic field. I feel connected to all living things—to flowers, birds, all the animals of the world—and even to some great, unseen, living force, what I think the Hindus call *prana*. It is not a breakdown. I've never felt more orderly in my life. It is a shattering and beautiful sensation. It is the exalted flow of the space-time continuum, save that is spaceless and timeless—and of such loveliness. I feel on the verge of some great ultimate truth.

Beale collapses to the floor unconscious; his epiphany appears to be little more than a symptom of psychological exhaustion. Yet this "shattering and beautiful sensation" hints at an alternative to Jensen's corporate cosmology; both men envision the world as a web of vast metaphysical networks, one governed by the laws of accumulation and the other aligned by the charisma of "loveliness." Coming shortly after the upheavals in sensibility provoked in the 1960s—especially by the "counterculture"—Chayefsky's portrayal of an enchanted prophet may be more suggestive than he intended. Is Beale psychotic or imbued? Has he seen heaven in a wildflower, felt the dearest freshness deep down things? Does his fiery outrage at the state of the world stem from a dazzling augury of innocence? If the fruit of the permanent revolution is a gaudy, spectacular barbarism, would a counterrevolution of loveliness require its insurgents to speak beauty to power?

The years between Dexter and Jensen witnessed the rapid evolution of the American Century, its metamorphosis from an American errand into a corporate quest for "globalization"—the subsumption of all peoples into "one market, under God," as Thomas Frank remarked so ominously.[7] As Jensen foretold, at the end of history, the world is a business. Respecting no national boundaries, the djinn of pecuniary enchantment has burst the integument of American capitalism; the exceptional, providentially ordained people is now part of "a vast, ecumenical holding company." The permanent American revolution is an ever-bustling emporium beyond democracy, the consummate expression of the cosmos' fundamentally capitalist architecture of being.

Historians have portrayed most of this period as an era of relative stability and consensus. In this view, the United States was, in Robert J. Griffith's words, a "corporate commonwealth." This commonwealth encompassed the "military-industrial complex" of business, universities, and the Pentagon; "managerial capitalism," a structure of corporate governance in which managers and executives bridled the stockholders to maintain the tenuous social compact with labor; and the maturation of "Fordism," the mega-mechanical ensemble of industrial production and professional-managerial authority. Moderate expansion took precedence over entrepreneurial exuberance, and the managerial elite, restrained by organized labor, superintended the creative destruction always fundamental to capitalism. All parties agreed that steady economic growth, distributed with unprecedented equity, would mitigate class conflict; all disagreements would be conducted within the parameters of Keynesian economics, a welfare state, and anti-Communism. As in other North Atlantic democracies, American society and politics appeared to demonstrate what the liberal journalist and sociologist Daniel Bell dubbed "the end of ideology": the renunciation of utopia and the cessation of the war between capital and labor that had ravaged the social landscape for a century.[8]

Still, the djinn in Dexter's bottle was restless, unable to accept even the most pliant restraints. Behind and in spite of the "consensus," business leaders were embarking on the second corporate reconstruction of American capitalism. Behind the veneer of a "commonwealth," business exploited every opportunity to circumvent or abrogate the armistice with labor. By the early

1970s, a new wave of labor unrest, rising energy and transportation costs, and increased international competition obliged corporations to undermine and eventually renounce the grand postwar moratorium. Increasingly mocked by corporate ideologues themselves, the gray-flannelled managerial capitalist order was clearing the way for "investor capitalism" and its raucous reassertion of shareholder interests. The so-called "golden age of capitalism" turned out to be, in Paul Krugman's words, "an interregnum between Gilded Ages."[9] The origins of our "neoliberal" era lie in the muted but intractable tensions of that interlude.

It is becoming equally clear that the Cold War counterculture, so often considered a flamboyant adversary of "conformity" and virtuous consumerism, was in fact more amenable to pecuniary and technological rationality than it appeared to be. In the conventional wisdom, the counterculture erupted as a jacquerie against the pinstriped lords of the corporate commonwealth. The problem with this Manichean tale is that dissatisfaction with conformity and hierarchy emerged, not only from intellectuals, beatniks, and hippies, but also from within corporate culture itself. Well before any psychedelic antics began disturbing the peace of the bourgeois utopia, business was already forging a new moral and symbolic imagination, a universe where the conquest of cool converged with the triumph of pecuniary enchantment. Replacing "virtuous consumerism" as the quintessence of the American spectacle, the democratization of bohemia represented the final incorporation of Romanticism, the annexation of the modern sacramental consciousness into the empire of corporate iconography.[10]

The origins of neoliberal enchantment—the untrammeled sway of the spectacle and the saturation of the American moral imagination by the pecuniary metaphysic—must be sought in the corporate commonwealth. For an extended and illusory moment in the first two decades after World War II, the heavenly city of Fordism appeared to be a permanent corporate utopia, a coziness purchased in the existential currency of ennui and alienation. But insider critics of the corporation exposed a world of repression while also counseling a higher, ironic acquiescence. At their most penetrating, they revealed the religious longings that galvanized devotion to corporate life, yet they offered no alternative to the corporate system aside from an innocuous "nonconformity."

These private enclaves of impotent rebellion composed a dress rehearsal for the conquest of cool, as a more thorough reconstruction of business culture was commencing among a vanguard of engineers, managers, and advertisers—a corporate counterculture that antedated and absorbed its feckless bohemian antagonists. Unlikely brethren of the technological sublime, Norbert Wiener and other cybernetic pioneers joined Stewart Brand and other countercultural entrepreneurs in transforming the industrial sensibility of capitalism, enabling the mechanization of communion first heralded by Frederick Taylor and scientific managers. By the early 1970s, pecuniary metaphysics and promethean ambition were expressed in a creole of cybernation, systems analysis, mathematics, and Asian spirituality. Partners in the same industrialization of beatitude, an avant-garde of post-Fordist business theorists recast the disciplines of capital accumulation as "teamwork," "creativity" and "self-actualization." In this view, employees engaged in competitive enterprise were achieving not only higher productivity but also the exalted, godlike status of what Abraham Maslow called "the highest reaches of human nature." Meanwhile, prompted by structural upheavals in their own industry that peaked in the 1960s, admen and illustrators drew up new "strategies of desire" in the midst of a professional crisis in advertising. Recoiling from the pieties of suburban consumerism, they spawned new beatific visions of life in the beloved community of cybernetic abundance, conjuring a mellow psychedelic fusion of enchantment and commercialism. The corporate counterculture heralded the ecstatic finale of capitalist civilization, a planet blissfully supplied and superintended by the guardian angels of digital technology—"all watched over by machines of loving grace," in Richard Brautigan's cyber-pastoral rhapsody.

The corporate counterculture paralleled an insurgent libertarianism. Rejecting Keynesian economics, a loose coalition of free-market fundamentalists—recalcitrant business leaders, Austrian-school economists, classical liberal philosophers, and evangelical bearers of the proprietary flame—sparked an eventually victorious crusade to demolish the social truce and the corporate commonwealth. Right-wing Protestants envisioned an updated restoration of the *herrenvolk* republic, a revival of the evangelical dispensation in the gilded promised land of Sun Belt capitalism. At the same time, the ideological progenitors of neoliberalism—Friedrich Hayek,

Ludwig von Mises, Milton Friedman, and Gary Becker—argued for an unprecedented extension of the scope and magnitude of market relations, aiming to insulate the market from democracy and bring all of life into the volatile crucible of capital accumulation. The market, in their view, is the ontological architecture of the cosmos, an omniscient and inerrant being more righteous than mere quivering mortals. A way of being as well as a paradigm of what Sheldon Wolin has called "inverted totalitarianism"—the transformation of political democracy into a subsidiary of corporate capital— neoliberalism named the highest stage of pecuniary metaphysics, the meridian of capitalist enchantment.[11] The neoliberal imagination found its crudest and most popular expression in Ayn Rand, who brought the roseate capitalist romanticism of Emerson to a tawdry culmination.

If the new right contemplated a world transformed in the image and likeness of the market, liberals and the left envisioned some form of transcendence of capitalism. From John Kenneth Galbraith and David Riesman to Herbert Marcuse and Norman O. Brown, the spectrum of liberal-left intellectual life assumed the conquest of material scarcity and the advent of a "post-materialist society." Forecasting a postindustrial society in which automated production permitted greater leisure, the attrition of class conflict, and the extension of public welfare, liberals pointed to a world in which the market would recede as the principle of social order. But as the "consensus" was revealed to be a chimera by the mid-1970s, and as "postindustrial society" was appearing to be politically and ecologically unsustainable, liberals were forced to reconsider the prospects of liberal modernity itself. As Daniel Bell concluded, only some "return to the sacred"—a "re-enchantment of the world"—would resolve the contradictions of capitalism.

While the radical left shared liberals' optimism about the arrival of a postindustrial society, they called for a far more extensive renovation of the moral and ontological imagination. The newness of the "New Left" has been understood, in part, as its concentration on the world *after* capitalism, its adumbration of a postmaterialist culture in which the rage to accumulate had been rendered superfluous by the accomplishments of technological rationality. But some of the most incisive thinkers of the New Left—especially Marcuse and Brown—raised fundamental questions about the rationality of instrumental reason itself. Drawing on Marxism and psychoanalysis, they diagnosed the "secularity" of capitalist civilization as a form of ontological pathology, the latest and most deadly outbreak of the passion for domination that only Eros could cure. Determined to invalidate the mercenary and imperious metaphysics of capitalist modernity, they beckoned to a secular romanticism, the ambience of an animate ontology without the fetters and illusions of traditional religion.

If the party of Eros rejected religion, other critics of capitalism embraced it, if not always in its orthodox forms. Cold War heirs of the Romantic imagination, they included painters, poets, freelance intellectuals, monks, Christians, and Buddhists—more a loose federation of kindred souls than a movement. Harkening back to the anarchist and Arts and Crafts traditions, they called not only for the disassembly of the megamachine but also for the abolition of domination itself, a cure to the afflictions of fear and powerlust that composed the spiritual toxin of capitalism. The therapy of desire lay, in Theodore Roszak's words, in a "sacramental consciousness," a communion with the sources of being understood as superabundant love. Eluding the conquistadores of cool, Romantics were neither a subsidiary of corporate bohemia nor a hospice for bourgeois discontent. Here lay the foundation of a genuine counterculture that would dispel capitalist enchantment, refuse the burdens of the errand into the marketplace, and affirm a metaphysic of pleasurable labor against the techno-managerial sublime. In a period easily caricatured as a moment of delirium, they represented the fundamental sanity inherent in the longing for beatitude, the latest ecstatic eruption of wisdom against the folly of pecuniary reason.

# 24

## God's in His Heaven, All's Right with the World

The Political Economy of Containment
and the Economic Theology of the Cold War
Consensus

BY THE END of World War II, Americans had endured nearly two decades of uninterrupted emergency and turmoil. The cataclysm of the Great Depression, together with the prolonged and horrific war against the Axis Powers, had generated strong desires for security, peace, and economic prosperity. But with the worldwide resurgence of revolutionary Marxism—a threat compounded by the new possibility of nuclear annihilation—Americans quickly came to fear that the postwar world was spiraling yet again out of control. Yet while the global "containment" of these upheavals marked US foreign policy during the Cold War, the term also captures the tense confinement of domestic life in the two decades after 1945. As Elaine Tyler May has argued, "containment" served for Americans as "an overarching principle that would guide them in their personal and political lives." Focusing on the suburban hearth, domestic containment attempted to bridle an array of potentially disruptive demands: of women for greater autonomy, of workers for workplace power, and of nonwhites for legal and social equality.[1] The corporate commonwealth was a political economy of containment.

Under a bipartisan aegis, corporate business assumed the leading role in remaking American consumer culture into a gargantuan apparatus of containment, especially as New Deal liberals realized that high consumer demand could be an effective catalyst of economic growth, one that happily required a minimum of noisome interference with business prerogatives. As William J. Levitt, developer of Levittown, New Jersey, famously remarked in 1948, "no man who owns his own house and lot can be a Communist. He has too much to do." Bankrolled by steadily rising wages for organized labor and a plentiful reservoir of credit, the corporate economy of containment underlay what Lizabeth Cohen has dubbed "the Consumer Republic," an attempt to achieve "the socially progressive end of economic equality without requiring the politically progressive means of redistributing existing wealth." The consumer republic depended on recalibrating the balance between frugality and consumer pleasure—"virtuous consumerism," in May's words, the concentration of spending and debt on the family that "upheld traditional American concerns with pragmatism and morality, rather than opulence and luxury."[2]

However tentative the relaxation of strictures against consumption, the consumers' republic also depended on a political economy of production—a postwar producers' republic, as it were. While historians have concentrated on the New Deal social truce, the military-industrial complex, the Fordist apparatus of mass production, and the Bretton Woods financial architecture, another condition for this *pax economica* was the containment of corporate stockholders by managers and executives—the "managerial capitalism" that characterized the corporate sector of the US economy from 1945 to the mid-1970s. By the 1940s, the separation of ownership and control had given corporate leaders virtually unchecked mastery over the daily operations, investment strategies, and long-term objectives of the firms whose stockholders they ostensibly served. Corporate governance needed to keep a respectful but firm leash on the owners, as any unrestrained insistence by shareholders on the value of their equity could both disturb the fragile ceasefire between management and labor and foster unpredictable market conditions. For three decades, the effective disenfranchisement of the stockholders allowed management both to maintain the armistice with organized labor and to plan confidently for expansion and technological innovation. As John Kenneth Galbraith observed in *The Affluent Society* (1958), the corporate manager was more interested in stability than in entrepreneurial valor: "the development of the modern business enterprise," he reflected, was "a comprehensive effort to reduce risk," adding for good measure that the owners had neither the time nor the talent to run the firm.[3]

While free-market ideologues bewailed what Keynes had pronounced "the euthanasia of the rentier," most liberals considered a resurgence of the owners both unlikely and undesirable. They consigned the bravado of the old-fashioned proprietor to the realms of history and myth, and dismissed the contemporary stockholder as a passive and functionless figure, legally empowered but politically toothless. Echoing Thorstein Veblen, Adolph Berle, and Gardiner Means, Galbraith regarded stockholders as vestigial relics, a "purely pecuniary association" who exhibited no real daring, contributed nothing in the way of ingenuity and expertise, and deserved little or nothing in the way of approbation. Even Marxists noted the unprecedented power and autonomy of capital's appointed stewards. Paul Baran and Paul Sweezy, then America's most distinguished Marxist economists, observed in *Monopoly Capital* (1966) that "control rests in the hands of management" and that "'responsibility to the stockholders'"—the banquet doggerel served up by executives—was "a dead letter."[4]

Like Thurman Arnold before them, liberals such as Galbraith and Will Herberg perceived the ambivalence in the covenant theology of capitalism. "Man cannot live without an economic theology," as Galbraith noted in *American Capitalism* (1952). Despite their acceptance of administrative routines, middle-class Americans, Galbraith predicted, would continue to praise free enterprise and private property "long after its substance had deserted them." Where Galbraith was droll, Herberg was outraged at the inclusion of "free enterprise" as a shibboleth of the American civil religion. In *Protestant Catholic Jew* (1955), his study of the postwar "religious revival," Will Herberg denounced the revival's shallowness as a feature of "the American Way of Life." As "the operative faith" of the American people," the American Way of Life was a bona fide religion, Herberg argued, complete with "its rituals, its holidays and its liturgy, its saints and its *sancta*." Herberg listed the doctrinal elements of the American Way—capitalist economics, individual responsibility, a facile idealism—and noted its incarnation in a host of objects, from the flag to indoor plumbing to Coca-Cola bottles, the enchanted tokens of postwar capitalism.[5]

The American Way of Life found its proudest articulation in *Fortune's* 1951 *U.S.A.* issue—the announcement of "permanent revolution" that doubled as a statement of corporate ontology. To the editors' dismay, the nation's cultural and political leadership had sown "intellectual and spiritual confusion" at a time when clarity was necessary in the conflict with Marxism. *Fortune* resolved to dispel the confusion and clarify "the meaning of America," drawing from the canonical repertoire of business apologetics—technological advance, "human relations" management, abundance, the cosmopolitan effects of trade and travel. Declaring that "a vast dispersion of ownership and initiative" now characterized American society, the editors announced that "capital has become, not the master of society, but its servant," and that "U.S. capitalism is popular capitalism," since "the people as a whole participate in it and use it." *Fortune's* brief for "popular capitalism" swelled with confidence that the corporate commonwealth represented not only "a true industrial democracy" but also an exalted vehicle for that "mystery of the human spirit" that was the ontological essence of capitalism.[6]

*Fortune's* "permanent revolution" dovetailed with the happy perception among intellectuals that, as Lionel Trilling put it in 1952, business increasingly displayed "a tendency to submit itself to the rule of mind and imagination." Several venues for this "submission" appeared after the war. One especially prominent site was the Aspen Institute for Humanistic Studies in Aspen, Colorado, set up in 1947 by the Container Corporation's Walter Paepcke. Distressed by the lack of taste and sensitivity among American business leaders, Paepcke hoped to elevate "the great intellectually unwashed of Americans: *the businessman.*" Aspen was to be a Parnassus of corporate humanism, a summit where intellectuals, artists, and businesspeople would have "an opportunity to stimulate thinking and discussion about . . . 'the good life,'" a subject "infinitely more important . . . than the pursuit of material gain." With enough money, Paepcke was confident that he could lure "the scholar and the business man into the mountains and let them converse . . . on a high philosophical level." The Institute's numerous festivals, conferences, and summer symposia attracted a retinue of luminaries, from sages such as José Ortega y Gasset, Albert Schweitzer, and Reinhold Niebuhr to architects and designers such as Louis Kahn, Buckminster Fuller, and Eric Saarinen.[7]

A similarly tony and illustrative thinkfest assembled in Corning, New York, in May 1951: a conference on "Living in an Industrial Civilization." Reminiscent of the "Philosophy of Production" symposium of 1930, the gathering was sponsored by Corning Glass Works and the American Council of Learned Societies. It featured a cavalcade of notables from corporate business, academia, labor unions, and journalism. Taking "a candid look at our industrial civilization from the standpoint of *human values,*" intellectuals, executives, and labor leaders traded insights into the maladies of capitalist modernity. As what *Harper's* editor Eric Larrabee called "an act of faith in the virtue of roundtables," the Corning conference was an obvious success. Banalities made the spring air stale: knowing platitudes about the "constantly changing problems of our society," earnest and forgettable bromides about "mutual understanding" between management and labor. (Charles Fahs of the Rockefeller Foundation confessed to being "thoroughly confused" by the meandering conversations.) The lingua franca in which the conferees discussed "human values" was the corporate parlance of accountancy and industrial relations. When Stanford economist Eugene Staley described Corning's own shopfloor practices as "a little accounting in human values," he betrayed the enterprise as an episode in the higher containment.[8]

Not all of the corporate cognoscenti were as sumptuously vapid as the gatherings at Corning and Aspen. A virtuoso of corporate reportage, *Fortune* editor Russell Davenport was one of the last to practice business journalism as a form of humane letters. As a leading voice of the reformist, internationalist wing of the Republican party, Davenport had served as an advisor to Wendell Wilkie's unsuccessful presidential campaign in 1940. Urbane and irascible, Davenport was a magpie, dabbling in poetry, philosophy, history, and theology. He also had quirky spiritual interests: though a practicing Episcopalian, Davenport was also an amateur astrologer who drew up horoscopes for his friends and colleagues. Although he was the leading scribe for the renowned *U.S.A.* issue in 1951, Davenport appears to have undergone something of a dark night of the soul in the years before his death in 1954.[9] Where Carnegie, Calkins, or Filene had seen a virtually unlimited horizon of progress, Davenport parted from the tradition of corporate humanism by incorporating the tragic sense of life.

In *The Dignity of Man* (1955), his best-selling and posthumously published reflection on the human condition, Davenport expounded on what he perceived to be a growing spiritual crisis, not only in America but also throughout the Western world. Beguiled since the eighteenth century into believing that "man's lot is infinitely improvable," Americans were, Davenport feared, becoming shallow utilitarians for whom the only virtues were efficiency and accumulation. Echoing Lewis Mumford, Davenport considered the aesthetic shabbiness of American life a measure of the soul's disrepair. "We do not care how ugly our towns are, how cluttered our highways, how uninspiring our churches, how drab our houses, how dismal our furniture, how tasteless our food." Mesmerized by quantity, modern man had repressed his anomie and desperation under the fury of his productive talents, creating a vivid contrast between "the brilliance of his outer achievements [and] the darkness of his inner life." But now even these achievements threatened to destroy humanity in the fiery ingenuity of atomic holocaust. For the editor of *Fortune*'s most celebrated affirmation of capitalism, the discovery that "the tragedy of human life on earth . . . is catching up with America" was especially appalling. Abandoning *Fortune*'s upbeat clichés, Davenport warned that middle-class Americans were drifting into a playland of desperation that "identified the good life with the products of modern industry." More than any corporate humanist before him, Davenport suspected that the capitalist West was a glittering desert of nihilism. "It is Nothing that we must fear: the thought of Nothing, the sound of Nothing in our hearts. . . . The belief in Nothing."[10]

Davenport sought redemption in "mystery," a felicitous "relation of the inner and outer world" as well as the unacknowledged and irreducible basis of economic life. Since mystery did not "passively await the end of a given line of investigation," it often arrived unbidden and unannounced: it "comes to meet us, bearing with it the potentiality of revelation." As the radiant nexus of the person and the world, "mystery" resembled an older metaphysics of nature and grace in which matter was a sacramental vessel. The rediscovery of mystery was, to Davenport, the only way to avert the spiritual and physical annihilation of Western civilization, and its full revelation was being hastened, in his view, by the emergence of a new kind of capitalism— "the American Way of Life" of the "permanent revolution," the incarnation of the "mystery of the human spirit." Like earlier corporate humanists, Davenport ascribed an ecclesial significance to corporate capitalism, a redemptive mission whose fulfillment was portended in the managerial revolution. "The individual finds his real self-fulfillment, not just in himself, but in terms that are some sense social, and modern industrial society has greatly accentuated this truth." Davenport's idealized "*social* or *socialized* individual," recognizing "a spiritual brotherhood," recalled the hopes of Patten, Dewey, and other corporate progressives. Celebrating the dispossession of the capitalist from the center of capitalism, Davenport saw this bloodless revolution as the final stage in the fulfillment of "mystery." Thanks to technology, the growth of corporate enterprise, and a new balance of power enforced by unions and government, the capitalist had been "ousted from his classical position" of unchallenged authority, Davenport contended, and so his single-minded concern with profit was no longer the only imperative of the corporation. Led by the "new kind of social management" heralded in *U.S.A.*, managerial capitalism now harnessed "private initiative for social goals."[11] In their gray-flannel clerical garb, managers and professionals embodied "mystery" in the office suites of corporate modernity.

Like Davenport, a host of executives, human relations specialists, and management writers believed that the managerial revolution had empowered business leaders who aspired to more than further enriching the already affluent. As the stewards of "private initiative for social goals," many corporate leaders claimed a "social responsibility" for the material and moral welfare of America. On one level, the new keywords merely restated the aspirations of the New Capitalism asserted by corporate humanists and other business progressives since the early twentieth century. But the apparent achievement of managerial control over stockholders lent these declarations a new credibility. Crafted in part to counter popular portrayals of business-people as boorish and avaricious tyrants, corporate "creeds," "philosophies," and professions of "social responsibility" multiplied over the 1950s, becoming so numerous and earnest that one business journalist remarked in 1953 that they were "not only acceptable in leading business circles, but even fashionable."[12]

Even though skeptics of the trend abounded—*Fortune's* Peter Drucker wondered late in 1954 "when the managers of American business had any time for business" as they proclaimed their devotion to the common-weal—the corporate assumption of social responsibility seemed to entail, as Drucker himself had suggested, a more mandarin executive elite. If moral and spiritual problems were now a division of corporate operations, then businesspeople required all the erudition appropriate to a new breed of humanists. As Crawford Greenewalt of Du Pont wrote in the *Saturday Review* in 1957, just as "no sensible academician" would refuse corporate largesse, "no sensible businessman" could eschew "the critical and analytical activity of the academic man." Leading business periodicals featured articles on the cultivation of Renaissance executives who, in the manner of Walter Lippmann's Progressive industrialist, combined managerial acumen with liberal education. Seeking to counter or mitigate the effects of professionalization,

*Fortune* recommended the "wholeness" provided by liberal education as a way to "overcome the ill effects of training in our highly specialized society." This was no mere idyll to corporate journalists, as managerial capitalism was, in their view, setting the economic stage for a new era of executive mandarins. Since, according to *Fortune,* the "rough-and-tumble days of corporation growth are over," business had no further need for "robber barons or industrial daredevils." The domineering but unlettered captain of industry had to give way to the diplomatic and cultivated steward of human community. If "human relations . . . is now the key" to company peace and business success, then the new corporate leader needed what *Nation's Business* jokingly called "that stuff called culture."[13]

Not that the task would be easy. As *Fortune* ruefully acknowledged, even the upper strata of American business were a dismally parochial lot. Surveying the reading habits of executives in the spring of 1954, *Fortune* recoiled from the dreadful tastes of corporate management, most of whom were apparently supervising the "permanent revolution" with minds full of middlebrow history, inspirational tales, adventures, and detective stories. (Mickey Spillane was a favorite.) They "almost never read drama, great fiction, the philosophers, the poets," and those few who did were "looked upon by their colleagues with mingled awe and incredulity." In short, *Fortune* concluded, the all-too-typical executive simply didn't do "the reading he doesn't think is necessary to his success."[14] Admonishing corporate managers about their slovenly mental habits, *Fortune* also reminded them of the sublimity of their calling. Their minds littered with the offal of popular culture, executives had defaulted on what *Fortune* considered their two primary obligations outside of accumulation: "cultural leadership in the broadest sense" and the maintenance of "moral and philosophic standards." To recapture the commanding heights of culture, the corporate elite needed to substitute Dostoevsky for Spillane, Shakespeare for Hollywood, Cezanne for the appliance advertisements. Indeed, *Fortune's* idealized postwar managerial elite was a new Platonic ruling class, discussing the affairs of the free world in a creole of Christian morality, human relations, and liberal democratic humanism. The ideal corporate leader read the *Wall Street Journal* in the morning, perused divisional reports in the afternoon, opined on the Lake Poets over dinner, and studied the brushstrokes of Impressionists in the evening. By the end of the decade, even the most sardonic critics of corporate life were praising the slightest trace of humanist learning among the managerial elite. "A businessman who reads *Business Week* is lost to fame," Galbraith wrote, but "one who reads Proust is marked for greatness." Even the anarchist poet Kenneth Rexroth mused that "so many American businessmen are insecure that we forget that they aren't all Babbitts." Pointing to Wallace Stevens—the insurance company lawyer whose work, in his view, represented "Santayana civilized and interpreted by the Harvard Business School"—Rexroth reflected that "America would be a far less naughty land" if the habit of reading poetry "would spread in the upper echelons of the Power Elite."[15]

In line with this anxious attention to executive moral formation, *Fortune's* renowned profiles of corporate executives took a less edgy and ironic turn after the war. A typical portrait was that of Fowler McCormick, president of International Harvester. Though introduced as a "self-made man," McCormick bore little resemblance to the scruffy bootstrap-pulling heroes of yore. Thanks to his glamorous upbringing and his Princeton education, McCormick attended to matters more esoteric and ennobling than quarterly profits. His reading was an impressive bricolage: Elton Mayo, Carl Jung, and John Dewey jostled in the symposium of McCormick's mind. So despite McCormick's "hard, Rockefeller core," his stony business sense was "wound round with softer stuff." Like the stories of other savant-executives, McCormick's offered a case study in how "the caricatured capitalism of his forbears" could be transformed into "a harmonious and lasting way of life."[16]

Human relations specialists and executives appeared to vindicate this portrayal of the corporate clerisy. Business leaders represented human relations as the consummation of efforts to compose industrial conflict, humanize the corporate world, and sanctify our daily labors. Douglas McGregor, professor of management at MIT's Sloan School of Management, asserted in 1948 that, since the factory was a "microcosm" of the larger society, human relations specialists could "find answers to some of the fundamental problems of modern society." Around the same time, Clarence Francis, chairman of General Foods, discoursed that since "people are composed of body, mind, and spirit," all of these, "but particularly spirit," should be trained "to execute assigned tasks if maximum productivity is to be attained." Writing in the *Harvard Business Review* in 1951, Frank W. Abrams, chairman of Standard Oil, declared that managers could now discharge their "positive duty to work for peaceful relations and understanding among men—for a restoration of faith of men in each other." Management textbooks displayed a similar sacral ambition. In *Human Relations in Business* (1957), one of the most widely used and respected introductions to the field, Keith Davis rhapsodized about "the infinite potential of the human mind" which had "enabled mankind to advance from caveman to modern man." With its battery of audits, surveys, and interview techniques to appraise and elevate morale, human relations hastened the ascent of humanity from rocky hollow to climate-controlled office. But Davis cautioned managerial students that the beloved community of the corporate workplace could not interfere with production schedules and cost-benefit analysis. Distinguishing the "human values" of harmony and fulfillment from the "technical values" of efficiency and productivity, Davis employed the language of equilibrium to obscure the primacy of the latter. "The goal" of human relations, he clarified, is to "*balance* human and technical values, rather than to replace all technical values with human values."[17] The mechanization of communion remained, in the end, a project of pecuniary reason.

As the most respected of the postwar corporate humanists well into the 1960s, Drucker idealized the managerial moral character and the promise of corporate selfhood. In *The New Society* (1950)—a volume that amounted to a long managerial manifesto—Drucker recounted a revolution whose vanguard was "the new industrial middle class: technicians, engineers, supervisors, accountants, statisticians, and branch managers" who, having secured a "victory of the secretariat" over stockholders and corporate directorates, stood read to carry the West "beyond Capitalism and Socialism." With a "very high, almost unprecedentedly high, degree of imaginative and intellectual ability," the new managers deserved the respect once conferred on the nobilities and clerisies of old. Echoing Lippmann, Mayo, and Follett, Drucker asserted in *The Practice of Management* (1954) that, if "vision and moral responsibility define the manager," then perhaps management merited "the standing of a genuine 'aristocracy,' such as the Confucian scholar in China, the Senatorial Class in Republican Rome, or the 'gentleman' in eighteenth- and nineteenth-century England."[18]

In *The New Society*, Drucker asserted that "the proper study of mankind is organization," and the moral lexicon of the managerial society was "Human Relations," which provided an indispensable "diagnostic tool" in the workplace and a vernacular for "the whole area of the social life of the industrial society." Unlike his predecessors, Drucker rooted human relations in a vague Christian theology: "In hiring a worker," he wrote in *The Practice of Management,* "one always hires the whole man," an indivisible human personality whose "relationship with his Creator . . . underlies all of [his] life and achievements." But like any good evangelist, Drucker was unsatisfied with mere acquiescence to corporate imperatives, and he strove to impart the spirit as well as the letter of the law. Drucker argued that managers needed to inculcate a "managerial attitude" in the worker—not a directive capacity, to be sure, but rather an identification with the goals of managers. Such "management by objectives," he insisted, would enable managers to induce workers to "convert objective needs [of the firm] into personal goals" and foster an "aggressive *esprit de corps*"—a "common faith," as Dewey might have put it. Though disenfranchised by management and automation, all workers, "down to the last sweeper and wheelbarrow-pusher," could internalize a "'managerial attitude' toward their work and toward the enterprise" and embrace the corporation as a democracy of industrial citizenship.[19]

Clear and unapologetic about its moral and religious ambitions, Drucker's management writing crowned a generation of corporate humanist literature. Indeed, thanks to his conflation of managerial technique, moralism, and religiosity, Drucker's humanist penumbra extended far beyond the business elite. W. H. Auden recommended Drucker as an example of "Christian thought applied to management." In his brief for *The Sane Society* (1955), the psychoanalyst–social critic Erich Fromm appealed to Drucker's corporate studies both for evidence of worker alienation and for advice on its eradication. The political scientist Clinton Rossiter included Drucker among "the thankless persuasion" of American conservatism.[20] These encomiums suggest that Drucker's later reputation as a guru of management theory began, not with New Agey business writers, but among the most respected postwar intellectuals.

While Drucker represented the corporate magisterium at its apogee of magnanimity, other cultural professionals wrestled with doubts about the wisdom of prevailing orthodoxy. Insider critics of corporate business produced some of the richest social criticism of the 1950s, portraying the consensus as a decorous camouflage over alienation and resentment. Behind the facade of corporate amity lay a snake pit of "antagonistic cooperation," in David Riesman's words, a maelstrom of malice, envy, ambition, and cynical acquiescence.[21] Yet the Machiavellian jockeying of corporate politics wasn't everything; in their keener moments, insider critics offered a glimpse of the longing for beatitude in the offices and suites—the Crystal Palace of business, as Alan Harrington put it, the citadel of the Fordist necropolis.

Insider criticism seemed to rehearse some of the gloomy themes of the "mass society" literature that migrated from the preserve of alienated intellectuals into middlebrow culture in the 1950s, when books such as Riesman's *The Lonely Crowd* (1950), C. Wright Mills's *White Collar* (1951), Russell Lyne's *A Surfeit of Honey* (1956), and Erich Fromm's *Escape from Freedom* (1941) and *The Sane Society* were widely read or frequently cited in mass-circulation magazines of opinion. Readers learned that America either bore or was coming to bear the marks of a "mass society": the absorption of more and more activity by bureaucratic institutions; the depersonalization of relationships by bureaucracy and mass communications; the conformity required for the effective functioning of the entire bureaucratic apparatus. Yet where most intellectuals deplored these developments, insider critics accepted them as irreversible, or even applauded them as positive. If, as Daniel Bell observed, mass society theory lodged a "romantic protest against contemporary life," its corporate retailers registered an unromantic, ambivalent affirmation.[22] Though corrosive of individuality, mass society, they suggested, made up in security and plenty what it lacked in adventure, excitement, and daring. As they saw it, to a generation buffeted by the Great Depression and World War II, obedience to administrative norms—however subservient, plodding, and even perilous to the soul—paid its own kind of existential dividend in peace, stability, and pensioned longevity.

Thus, the most popular examples of insider criticism were also the most innocuous: Sloan Wilson's *The Man in the Gray Flannel Suit* (1955), Eric Hodgins's *Mr. Blandings Builds His Dream House* (1946) and *Blandings' Way* (1950), and William H. Whyte's *The Organization Man* (1956). Though critical of corporate conformity, all of them wound up as sympathetic, reassuring comedies of suburban manners—which goes a long way toward explaining their success. All were written by workers in the culture industry about the denizens of corporate business: Wilson was a reporter for *Time* who also drew on a friend's experiences in advertising; Hodgins was an editor at *Time* and *Fortune*; Whyte was a managing editor and roving reporter for *Fortune*.

Wilson's Tom Rath is a public relations writer for a corporate broadcasting firm; Hodgins's James H. Blandings is an advertising copywriter; Whyte's subjects were corporate professionals and managers living in Park Forest, Illinois. Rath comes across as an affable cynic afflicted with a case of the bourgeois blues. "The important thing is to make money," he laments as he commutes from Westport, Connecticut to work in New York one Monday morning. Money buys the bigger house, the bigger car, the private schools, the department store accounts for Betsy, his wife. Rath accepts the metaphysic of money without question but not without complaint:

> The important thing is to create an island of order in a sea of chaos, and an island of order obviously must be made of money, for one doesn't bring up children in an orderly way without money, and one doesn't even have one's meals in an orderly way, or dress in an orderly way, or think in an orderly way without money. Money is the root of all order, he told himself, and the only trouble with it is, it's so damn hard to get, especially when one has a job which consists of sitting behind a desk all day doing absolutely nothing.

Quietly acquisitive and tastefully conformist, Rath, his colleagues, and his neighbors run the rat race in pursuit of "a bigger house and a better brand of gin." Through much of the novel, he maintains this ironic distance, calculating the price of everything and the value of nothing. By the end—after rejecting a promotion and rekindling his love for his wife—Rath sees the way to his island of order on a path of resignation and rectitude. "I may not be able to do anything about the world," he sighs, "but I can set my life in order." Now that "God's in his heaven, all's right with the world," the Raths (and Wilson's readers) discover they can prosper with a usurious mortgage on their souls.[23]

Hodgins's James Blandings is an erstwhile novelist who now suffers the "painless torment" of churning out jingles for an advertising firm, laboring among "the hard-working, highly competent, and deeply miserable men" who "in another century might have written sonnets." Still, Blandings is determined to reap whatever advantages he can from his anguish, using the blood money paid for his talents to do something "in my personal life that's going to help me compensate for what I have to do in my professional life"—namely, invest in a country dream house that soon becomes a money pit. Blandings shows a bit more courage than Rath but succumbs as fully to the seductions of accommodation. Tired of living on "the depressive slope of his psychic curve" and writing copy for companies such as "International Screw," he becomes his town's resident liberal gadfly—a role he abandons after the town's conservatives successfully brand him a Communist. Returning to the agency with something less than enthusiasm, Blandings has a secular epiphany in a hamburger joint on Lexington Avenue. Life is "more easily endured," he tells himself, if "I narrow my focus to include only that for which I have a demonstrated capacity"—like singing the praises of International Screw. Victory over despair and injustice requires a revolution of lower expectations. He promises himself to "scale my peak, three words at a time, three words at a time, until at last I achieve my summit"—a place from which, as Hodgins writes chillingly, Blandings hopes "there is no longer anything visible at all."[24]

Whyte was more incisive than the novelists but in the end, he proved just as ironic and acquiescent. A graduate of Princeton, a former salesman for Vicks Vapo-Rub, and an intelligence officer for the Marine Corps during the war, Whyte was no radical railing against the system. While he criticized the mindlessness of bureaucratic routine in his first book, *Is Anybody Listening?*, he also lauded the "human relations capitalism of 1950" and complained that critics such as Riesman and Mills were "almost psychopathic" in their vituperation. Charged by *Fortune*'s managing editor Hedley Donovan to examine the lives of corporate managers, Whyte embarked in 1952 on a three-year sojourn through office suites and suburban developments, interviewing hundreds of managers, executives, professionals, technicians, and their wives. Publishing a few preliminary articles in *Fortune*, Whyte pulled together his material in *The Organization Man*, a sprawling, satirical, but charitable report on the lives of the corporate middle class. Far from an Isaiah railing against the abominations of conformity, Whyte chose the role of Erasmus, a sage in a gray-flannel suit, and produced a praise of corporate folly. As Thomas Frank has observed, while *The Organization Man* "may have been astute social criticism"—maybe even "one of the first sparks of the counterculture"—it was definitely "a management book, a sweeping study of American business and its problems."[25] How could one of the most popular documents of postwar social criticism also be a primer for corporate business? The answer lies in seeing Whyte as a cleric of the postwar consensus, a sophist reaffirming the covenant theology of corporate capitalism.

Whyte opened *The Organization Man* with an explicit and oft-overlooked disclaimer: "This book is not a plea for nonconformity." Scourges of middle-class life should take no aid or comfort from his work, he warned, for he delivered no "censure of the fact of organization society." He denounced the litany of "strictures against ranch [station]wagons, or television sets, or gray flannel suits"; exhibited no fondness for the bad old days of rugged individualism; and disavowed any "misplaced nostalgia" for unfettered markets and small proprietors. In his view, modern American history was not a woeful tale of declension that opens with a "paradise lost" in some "idyllic eighteenth century" and ends in the air-conditioned nightmare of a "dehumanized twentieth." The humanoid "mass man" loathed by European critics was "a person the author has never met." Rejecting the folklore of populism, Whyte found it "difficult to see the three-button suit as more of a strait jacket than overalls," and trusted that the Buick owner could resist the Organization as bravely and effectively as any bohemian or radical firebrand.[26]

As a member of the corporate clerisy, Whyte pronounced a benediction on the religious and moral aspirations of the organization men. On the very first page, he observed that the typical management student at a business school was "blood brother" to the seminarian, a devotee poised to take "the vows of organization life"; later, he compared the same fledgling manager to a bright young medieval man "off to join holy orders." After interviewing college seniors majoring in business administration, Whyte characterized their image of a personnel manager as a blend of "YMCA worker, office Solomon, and father confessor"—a nicely ecumenical and pluralist ideal straight from the work of Peter Drucker (a colleague at *Fortune*). For all his queasiness about the "spiritual fealty" sworn to the corporation, Whyte found—somewhat to his surprise—that corporate work and social life provided "a great deal of brotherhood" to the men in gray-flannel suits.[27]

Whyte's discernment of religiosity informed his appraisal of the "Social Ethic"—a "secular faith," as he described it, "almost a secular religion." In the Social Ethic, "the organization man seeks a redefinition of his place on earth," Whyte declared, something that "will do for him what the Protestant Ethic did once." Though fragments of that proprietary-Protestant symbolic universe still lingered in the organization man's vocabulary—"free enterprise," "private property," "individual," etc.—the realities of large-scale business bureaucracy rendered them ever more notional and nostalgic. In contrast, the Social Ethic was a vibrant "utopian faith" with shrines erected in business schools, corporate firms, and suburban neighborhoods. The corporate humanist tenets of the Social Ethic—the group as the source of creativity; "belongingness" or "togetherness" as the highest good; social science, and especially management theory, as the canons of earthly beatitude—all encapsulated the soul's economy of the corporate commonwealth.[28]

The religious quality of the Social Ethic was especially evident in "human relations" management literature; Whyte noted that Elton Mayo and his protégés were "evangelists as well as researchers," heralds of the good news of industrial harmony. Whyte was struck by the "quasi-religious overtones" with which organization men endowed human relations theory, and he described one convention of managers and industrial relations specialists as a "convocation of believers." Indeed, Whyte found that human relations ideology now impersonated theology and that a polite, unobtrusive pragmatism had obscured formerly sharp denominational differences. Residents of Park Forest wanted a "*useful* church," Whyte wrote, dwelling on "the more useful parts of doctrine,'" as one minister proudly told him.[29]

Despite these perceptively mordant comparisons of corporate ideology to religious conviction, Whyte's sympathy to managerial objectives undercut the indictment of conformity that made his reputation as a critic of business culture. To be sure, he feared that organization men were "imprisoned in brotherhood," and that while the old authoritarian proprietor wanted "primarily your sweat," the corporate manager "wants your soul." But to Whyte, these represented abuses, not fundamental problems, with the Social Ethic. Even the appendix—advice on how to cheat on personality tests—underlined Whyte's critical limitations: giving "the most conventional, run-of-the-mill, pedestrian answer possible" was nothing compared to challenging the Organization's right to administer the test in the first place.[30] More circumspect than spirited, Whyte's call for a bit more nonconformity amounted to a plea for the reinvigoration, not the destruction, of corporate humanism.

Some of Whyte's more perceptive critics were not fooled by his urbane and ironic prudence. Deriding Whyte's "Orgprose," Harold Rosenberg dismissed his book as a "dreary professional's ruse for holding on to the best of both worlds." Paul Goodman bluntly called Whyte a "cynic," but went further in probing the nihilism at the core of the "nonconformist" genre. Goodman saw the essential fraudulence and conservatism in Whyte's advocacy of private rebellion; under the circumstances, Whyte's "individuality" was, he wrote, a form of "one-upping," a specious brand of resistance that could easily be absorbed, redesigned, and marketed. The only hope, Goodman implied, lay with individuals who organized against the Organization, people who created collectively a political and religious alternative to the consensus. Part of that vision, Goodman argued, should partake of art and craftsmanship—that is, an individuality forged partly through truly creative and necessary work, an ideal hallowed in the sacramental consciousness of the Romantic and Arts and Crafts movements. Bureaucratic savvy would never compensate for the absence of "worth-while objects," Goodman wrote, invoking the standards of *poesis* to take the measure of Whyte's pseudo-dissent. As he noted, "the necessary, useful, and pleasant, and the good, true, and beautiful are not much mentioned in his book."[31] Bereft of these transcendental truths, Whyte could offer only a knowing pedagogy in the wisdom of the higher conformity.

A more trenchant if still ultimately futile criticism came from Alan Harrington. Harrington exemplified a generation of well educated, conscientious, and disillusioned corporate employees: Harvard class of 1939, Air Force pilot, wire-service correspondent, and a brief but sobering career in advertising and public relations with Standard Oil. His two books on corporate life—*The Revelations of Dr. Modesto* (1955), a novel, and *Life in the Crystal Palace* (1959), an autobiographical novel-cum-anthropological report—portray the business world as existential melodrama, a quest for religious meaning that reflected Harrington's personal history. When he was a boy, his mother, an eccentric Boston brahmin, had abandoned her marriage and family for several years in search of spiritual renewal. After traveling in Brazil and Haiti, she surfaced in Arizona, married to a Tohono O'odham shaman. A seeker himself, Harrington befriended some of the notables of the postwar counterculture: Jack Kerouac, Neal Cassady, Allen Ginsburg, and Timothy Leary. Enthralled by advances in cryogenics and biotechnology, he came to consider death "an imposition on the human race" and authored a treatise, *The Immortalist* (1969), in which he called on scientists to perfect "the engineering of man's divinity." (Harrington died in 1997.)[32]

Harrington's criticism of business was much more modest, but equally metaphysical. *Dr. Modesto* centers on the hapless Hal Hingham, a struggling life insurance salesman who hates his job and his dingy boarding house. (Kerouac turned Harrington into "Hal Hingham" in *On the Road*.) Despondent and close to suicide, Hingham finds hope in an ad for "Centralism," the philosophy of a Dr. Modesto from Broad View, Nebraska, who identifies happiness with complete, mind-numbing, self-obliterating communion with others. Explaining how to lose "the intolerable burden of self," Modesto's Centralist brochure outlines a contemplative mysticism of mediocrity that doubles as a philosophy of will to power:

STARE AT ONE OBJECT . . . stare at it until you lose yourself. Then begin the Centralist's Walk through the streets. . . . There will be a hush all around you. Hear the people. All the faces have bright eyes. Their voices come through the uproarious silence and whisper in your ear. You will obtain an instantaneous fix on many lonelinesses. Louts meditate for you. A cry of anxiety rings out of a horselaugh. After a while, all the ideas that inhabit the town inhabit you. When the sleepwalk is over, you wake up the Central Man in town. . . . And this gives you practically limitless power over others!

By practicing Centralism, Hingham turns his life around: he posts record sales for the company and rekindles his waning romance with his girlfriend Rose. But he founders when his boss sends him to the company's annual sales convention, and Rose begins to find him so eerily predictable that she ends their love affair. When Hingham travels to Broad View to meet Dr. Modesto, he discovers that his guru is an inmate in an insane asylum; the "revelations" that ignited Hingham's success have been the promulgations of a lunatic.[33]

*Dr. Modesto* gained enough critical attention that, with help from Carey McWilliams, editor of the *Nation,* and a grant from the Fund for the Republic, Harrington left business altogether to write *Life in the Crystal Palace,* a sardonic but not bitter account of his years in the consciousness industry. Taking his title from Dostoevsky's *Notes from the Underground*—whose protagonist lavishes contempt on a world of steady but soul-killing progress—Harrington recounted his days as a corporate apparatchik. Handsomely landscaped and expensively upholstered, the hilltop corporate headquarters provoked Harrington to ask himself the same question that haunted Dosto-evsky: "*Does not man, perhaps, love something besides well-being?*" Not that Harrington protested *too* much, thankful as he was for the "private socialist system" that his firm provided: decent hours, insurance, help with moving expenses, picking up half the lunch tab, and then a pension. Indeed, Har-rington conceded that he might simply be flippant in denouncing this "kindly capitalism," an "earthly paradise" whose comforts and protections were as widely coveted as they were easily derided.[34]

But the costs were real, and they mounted with every year Harrington re-mained safely ensconced in the Palace. Buoyed by disposable income and expense accounts, corporate men "contended with other poverties," deficits of desire and expression. Part of the price was aesthetic, as the corporation formed "a protective league for small talents" that sponsored a lifelong apprenticeship in mediocrity. But the heaviest toll was spiritual, as the gray-flanneled men were "alive but not kicking"; they harbored a secret but well-repressed longing for the disheveled and unpunctual life of bohemia. "We never heard guitars strumming on the dirty doorsteps," Harrington sighed. Moderate to the point of listlessness, they lacked the "divine impatience" that quickens the arts, confronts injustice, and enlivens religion.[35] Akin to Hodgins's James Blandings, the frustrated writer, a troupe of timid and with-ering spirits wandered through the Palace labyrinth.

Harrington nonetheless saw much that was "divinely" inclined among his fellow "incomplete rebels," and he underlined the continuities between reli-gious life and corporate culture. "Branches they bore of that enchanted stem," as he quoted Tennyson on Ulysses's crew. Tracing the ancestry of corporate munificence back to the medieval Church—"Church and Palace alike are sanctuaries in the jungle of unbridled competition"—the corporation, he wrote, was thus "the inheritor and vessel of a mighty tradition." The corpo-ration had its own metaphysics of finance, exemplified in "Jim Lent," an ac-countant who "judges things-as-they-are" in accordance with the rise and fall and shuffling of numbers. Harrington likewise pointed to the corporate world's scientific substitute for spiritual formation: the personality test, "a new kind of confessional." Instead of confiding to God through a priest "or to himself via a psychoanalyst," corporate man bared his soul to "the Form" in the hope of adjustment, not redemption. Confident in the benevolence that came with the package, Harrington could wax in a psalm of thanksgiving for the luxury of his discontent:[36]

> A mighty fortress is our Palace; I will not want for anything . . .
> I am led along the paths of righteousness for my own good.
> I am protected from tyrants.
> It guards me against tension and fragmentation of my self.
> It anoints me with benefits.
> Though we pass through hard times, I will be preserved.
> These strong walls will surely embrace all the days of my life.

But the most striking evidence of corporate enchantment was a cornerstone ceremony. "The rituals of enlightened capitalism are interestingly pagan," he remarked. Gathering to "dedicate a new shrine," a "Crystal Palace to the future," the employees formed a circle around the excavated site, eager to "insert [their] own sacred objects in the cornerstone." Into the mortar went "pieces of earth, rocks, and metals from the company's branch areas"— sacramental tokens from the grounds of numerous office plazas that symbolized "our present-day unity and drive toward a bountiful future." Harrington was admirably bereft of contempt for this frail eschatological hope, but he saw no exit from the Palace; uneasy but not divinely impatient, he made clear that he "wouldn't disrupt the system."[37] Long as he might for those dulcet guitars, Harrington concluded that it was wiser to accept the compensation package of resignation.

# 25

# Machines of Loving Grace

## Auguries of the Corporate Counterculture

HOWEVER ACQUIESCENT, HARRINGTON'S "incomplete rebels" still nurtured dreams of rebellion in their wood-paneled offices. Indeed, one lesson in Whyte's ironic pedagogy was that the Organization itself needed eccentrics and rebels in order to prosper. In an age of all-too-smoothly functioning bureaucracies, he wrote, "individualism is more necessary, not less, than it ever was." Convinced that a return to the Protestant ethic was both impossible and undesirable, Whyte called for a new kind of individualism that was compatible with the imperatives of the Organization, pointing to the research laboratories at Bell and General Electric as prototypes of corporate-sponsored unorthodoxy. "Tolerant of individual differences, patient with off-tangent ideas," scientists and engineers at these firms produced exceptional work with a minimum of supervision and fraudulent bonhomie, while their executives cared "not a whit if scientists' eyes fail to grow moist at company anthems." Still, "though the consequences of profit for The Organization are secondary to the scientist," Whyte reminded readers that "eventually there are these consequences."[1] Individualism was more necessary than ever for profits; the volume of surplus value still determined the parameters of nonconformity.

Whyte's kudos for "off-tangent ideas" adverted to a nascent corporate counterculture, self-styled rebels who hoped to harness the energies of "nonconformity" for American business. Well before the appearance of beatniks, hippies, and radicalized students, the corporate counterculture was generating what Luc Boltanski and Eve Chiapello have called the "new spirit of capitalism": an ideology of "autonomy," "liberation," "teamwork," and "vision" that enlisted aesthetic and spiritual desires in the service of new forms of labor discipline.[2] Theorized in the military science of cybernetics, automation embodied the beatific visions of its designers and corporate sponsors: the mechanization of production and communion envisioned by industrialists and scientific managers. New brands of managerial thinking—"Theory Y," as they were dubbed collectively—anticipated a post-Fordist workplace where employees were given greater autonomy in devising the means of their own exploitation. Meanwhile, the "creative revolution" in advertising both roused the industry from aesthetic fatigue and inaugurated a brave new era in the rituals of commodity fetishism. Automation, Theory Y, and the new advertising were auguries of a new business culture, a novel brand of capitalist enchantment that constituted the American society of the spectacle.

"Automation" entered the popular imagination in the early 1950s, as automated processes began to spread throughout American industry, from electronics, petroleum, and engine manufacture to telephones, banking, and baking. The proliferation of articles and books on the subject reached such a crescendo that it triggered an "automation hysteria," in the words of one skeptical economist. Like earlier American fascination with technology, the excitement surrounding automation fused anxiety and utopian hope. Acolytes of automation heralded the newest and most breathtaking chapter in the story of Progress, the ascent to an even higher, more ingenious and productive magnitude of technological sublimity. The fabled hard-boiled sobriety of the business intelligentsia gave way to romanticism. The editors of *Business Week* featured automation several times in the 1950s, hardly able to contain their wonder at the precision and dexterity of the new technologies: "automatic tools prove virtuosos," as they marveled in a typical 1959 article. *Fortune* eagerly predicted "The Automatic Factory" and a golden age of "Machines without Men" in November 1946; convened a celebratory roundtable of scientists, engineers, executives, and reporters for its October 1953 issue; rushed to muffle "technological alarms" in May 1955; and argued that automation portended "more jobs and a sounder dollar" in November 1958. One of *Fortune*'s eminent clerics, Peter Drucker, waxed on "the promise of automation" in *Harper's* in April 1953. Far from signaling "technocracy under another name," automation, he insisted, would upgrade the typical worker into "a highly skilled and knowledgeable technician." Countering *The Myths of Automation* (1966), *Fortune* writer and editor Charles Silberman maintained that its most significant and irreversible effect had been "to enlarge, not to restrict, the sphere of human action and choice." Silberman's affirmation echoed that of Gerard Piel, publisher of *Scientific American* and a tireless popularizer of science and technology. In essays for *Saturday Review,* the *Nation,* and the *Atlantic* as well as *Scientific American,* Piel proclaimed that automated abundance meant both that "human want is obsolete" and that the "end of toil" was nigh.[3]

If most assumed that automation would enlarge the domain of leisure, some observers argued that it would intensify work and extend the realm of necessity. Thomas Watson of IBM looked to "job enlargement" as an antidote to alienation. But "job enlargement" compensated for the erosion of skill by merely multiplying the number of things for workers to do—which may well have been part of the attraction of automation all along. Ralph J. Cordiner, president of General Electric, held that automation created employment, spawned new products and industries, and exerted "a stimulating and stabilizing effect on the economy." David O. Woodbury, a science journalist highly regarded in business and technology circles, contended that the most inspiring promise of automation was not to increase leisure but to prolong the life of the Protestant work ethic. Woodbury rejoiced that technological progress would enable us to work even harder, not less. It would be better, he argued, if workers "did not attempt to work less, but to become more ambitious instead." Rather than annul or mitigate the curse of incessant toil, automation would bestow an ecstatically promethean character to labor. Peering out to the horizon of technological possibilities, Woodbury declared that there was "practically no limit to the progress automation can make"—"progress" defined, that is, in terms of ever-escalating production.[4]

This hope that advanced technology would enforce a new regime of work appeared to belie the elysian reveries of the corporate business intelligentsia, and it suggests why not all observers were sanguine about the effects of automation. Recalling Lewis Mumford's invective against "the megamachine," European students of automation such as Georges Friedmann, Sigfried Giedion, and Jacques Ellul feared that the replacement of human beings in the industrial workplace would trigger a cultural and political crisis. In their view, the triumph of the machine might augment the surveillance and destructive power of the state; impose a regime of instrumental rationality that would subsume all standards of beauty and purpose; and erode the use of intelligence in work, one of the indispensable foundations of personal creativity and political freedom. Claims that automation would liberate humanity from toil and inaugurate an epoch of leisure were "technicians' abstractions," Friedmann wrote, which the evolution of the capitalist workplace had "cruelly contradicted." Though often maligned as technophobes or Luddites, European skeptics of automation were attempting to redefine rather than inhibit technological progress. "Never has mankind possessed so many instruments for abolishing slavery," as Giedion concluded in *Mechanization Takes Command* (1948). "But the promises of a better life have not been kept. All we have to show so far is a rather disquieting inability to organize the world, or even to organize ourselves."[5]

Automation and "automation hysteria" had their American naysayers. After conducting field research in factories and interviewing more than three hundred manufacturers and technicians, James R. Bright of the Harvard Business School concluded in *Automation and Management* (1958) that claims about the "upgrading" effect of automation on skill were unfounded. In the January 1965 issue of the *New York Review of Books*, Columbia sociologist Daniel Bell—former Marxist, former labor editor of *Fortune*, and future herald of "post-industrial society"—dismissed as "absurd" the claim that "technology is making manpower redundant." Economist Ben Seligman declared in 1966 that automation represented "technology's notorious victory," a triumph over toil that threatened nonetheless "to destroy the essential human qualities that have been thus far characteristic of man." Technological unemployment augured a desolate and antiseptic world of useless human beings. "With humans automated out of the factory and office, only the archon and his machine will be left to contemplate with equanimity the mountain of reports flowing out of the computer."[6]

Whatever foreboding appeared among the business and technical intelligentsia was allayed by acquiescence in the sheer inevitability of automation. John von Neumann of Princeton's Institute for Advanced Study, for instance, asked whether humanity could "survive technology" in a June 1955 *Fortune* essay that was uncharacteristically equivocal for the magazine. One of the intellectual architects of cybernetics—the preeminent science of automated processes—von Neumann feared that the scale and complexity of contemporary technology was outstripping humanity's political and imaginative capacities. Yet von Neumann—a starstruck admirer of businesspeople and a zealous, even rabid Cold Warrior—never questioned the desirability of automation, as technological modernization remained a necessary condition for productive efficiency and value. Conceding the "silent conquest" of "cybernation," Donald N. Michael, a consultant to the Brookings Institution and a research associate at the Center for the Study of Democratic Institutions, concluded in a 1962 report that despite the dilemmas produced by unemployment and material abundance, "we have no choice but to encourage the development of cybernation." Because technological innovation continued to be considered an unrelenting force of history, both elite and popular opinion about automation remained ambivalent and even muddleheaded. As philosopher and novelist Gerald Sykes observed in *The Cool Millennium* (1967), "man rushes first to be saved *by* technology, and then to be saved *from* it. We Americans are front runners in both races."[7]

Hysterical or not, the widespread concern about automation obscured more fundamental and intractable issues, as the fetish of technology diverted attention from its origins in capital's need to achieve complete mastery of the production process. Contrary to the portrayal of the postwar era as a period of relative peace between the classes, the decade after World War II witnessed numerous skirmishes between capital and labor: there were, between 1945 and 1955, more than 43,000 strikes involving 27 million workers, and more strikes during the Korean War than during the pugnacious years (1935–1939) of the birth pangs of the Congress of Industrial Organizations. Seen against this background, the introduction of automated machinery was, as David Noble has demonstrated, an essentially political and pecuniary maneuver. Capital's will to power was most bluntly exemplified in Lemuel Boulware, the pugnacious vice president of General Electric who rapidly became notorious as the pinstriped Ajax of corporate management. "The employees got the idea that they were in the driver's seat," he told a management convention in 1946, reflecting on the GE strike. "This is the attitude, gentlemen, that must be reversed. This is the fantasy that must be eradicated."[8]

The spurious peace between corporate capital and organized labor provoked top management to turn to automation as the ultimate weapon in class warfare. Well aware of technology's role as an agent of "disciplinary power," labor economist Neil W. Chamberlain observed that business leaders were "focusing attention on types of machinery and equipment." Labor officials realized that management's mystification of technology was a ruse in the battle over workplace hegemony. Recalling numerous battles over automation with General Electric, one district president of the United Electrical,

Radio, and Machine Workers asserted that "if they can make it a mystery, we are helpless in dealing with them in negotiation . . . we have to take away the mystery that the company likes to make of this stuff." Executives and engineers were candid about their intention to use automation to bring labor to heel. As the editors of *American Machinist*, the machinery industry's leading magazine, confirmed in 1952, automation "is a philosophy of control." Alfred Teplitz of U.S. Steel lauded MIT's servomechanical laboratory in 1952 for its invention of numerical control, which empowered "the control equipment itself rather than the operator." Nils Olesten, head of the numerical control department at Rohr Aircraft, hoped that automation would bring "the decision-making in many manufacturing operations closer to management," while Alan Smith, a prominent management consultant with Arthur D. Little, foresaw capital's complete "emancipation from human workers."[9] Like Andrew Ure a century before, American business leaders sought in automation an instrument with which to teach docility to the refractory hand of labor.

Yet if capital employed automation to forever dispel labor's "fantasy" of control, it thereby sought to consummate its own dream of absolute, opulent dominion. By promising to eliminate labor as both an existential necessity and as a factor of production, automation transcended even the mechanized ideal of the Fordist heavenly city. Releasing business from its nettlesome dependence on labor, corporate automation could realize the ambition embedded in pecuniary metaphysics: the complete transfiguration of all things into the venal image and likeness of capital. The GE engineer's reference to the "mystery" of automation hinted at this esoteric metamorphosis. This aspiration toward mercenary enchantment has not been lost on historians; as Noble perceived, "primitive enchantment and capitalist greed assumed the severely logical appearance of technical necessity."[10] Although Noble rightly traced this corporate enchantment to the ancient desires for divine control over nature and liberation from physical drudgery, he missed the deeper connection between "primitive enchantment" and "capitalist greed," as well as the link between postwar automation and the mechanization of beatitude. Automation was a beatific vision suffused by an ontology of corporate power explicated most mysteriously in cybernetics, the most powerful and sophisticated idiom of technological animism yet articulated. As with earlier forms of capitalist mastery, the inscription of managerial will into the new industrial technology was bound up with a perverted aspiration toward a sacramental way of being.

These entangled political and metaphysical longings surfaced in the more effusive industry celebrations of automation. A 1955 National Association of Manufacturers pamphlet anointed automation "a magical key to creation" that unlocked "the fairyland of the world to come"; "guided by electronics," it continued, "the magic carpet of our free economy heads for distant and undreamed of horizons." Even the urbane editors of *Fortune* proclaimed the metaphysical charms of automation in their issue on "the permanent revolution," explaining that the mission of scientists and engineers was not to "enchain the human soul" but rather to 'increase its power and scope." They allayed fears that "the individual human spirit" would become as standardized as "tools and machines" by recalling that Americans considered technological dynamism "a special cosmic arrangement"—an ontological proclamation as grandiose as that of any traditional theologian.[11]

*Fortune*'s perception of a "special cosmic arrangement" took its own reportage to a new level of grandiosity. In the November 1946 issue, *Fortune* had featured two articles on automation: "The Automatic Factory," an editorial that proclaimed that computerized production signaled the advent of yet "another industrial revolution," and "Machines without Men," a longer, more reflective piece coauthored by two Canadian technicians. The latter essay was a minor masterpiece of corporate humanist technophilia. The new machinery, the authors conceded, "may well loose waves of temporary unemployment" and "degrade the worker to an unskilled and tradeless nonentity"—prices for progress that *Fortune* considered well worth paying. Besides, the automated factory outstripped human beings in existential and well as productive superiority: machines could, in their words, "see better than eyes, calculate more reliably than brains, communicate faster and farther than the voice, record more accurately than memory."[12] Automation would thus embody, in capitalist conditions, the achievement of divinity through technology: corporate machinery as animate being, with prodigious powers of consciousness and control incarnate in computers, thermocouples, magnetized tapes, and photoelectric cells.

As one of the theoretical craftsmen of postwar automation, Norbert Wiener was a remarkably penetrating but ultimately equivocal critic of its enchantments. A professor of mathematics at MIT, Wiener had worked with the US Army during World War II to improve the accuracy of antiaircraft guns, and his ballistic research led him, by several winding turns, to information theory, neuropsychology, and biophysics. Along with von Neumann, Wiener developed cybernetics as a science that conceived both machines and human beings as flexible and ever-changing structures of information, incessantly incorporating and responding to feedback to achieve new levels of homeostasis. Yet he worried that cybernetics afforded an expansive and potentially insidious power to government and business. Appalled by the bombings of Hiroshima and Nagasaki, Wiener attributed the willingness of scientists and engineers to join the Manhattan Project both to racism and to the desire of these "popes and cardinals of applied science" to acquire "a new ace in the hole in the struggle for power." More skeptical than von Neumann of the military and corporate interest in cybernetics, Wiener refused to engage in military research (bravely explaining his reasons in the *Atlantic* in January 1947), kept a wary distance from industry, and even resigned from the National Academy of Sciences on account of what he considered its stifling impact on independent research.[13]

Wiener's earliest expositions of cybernetics—*Cybernetics* (1948) and *The Human Use of Human Beings* (1950), the latter a best-seller—were studded with passages of prophetic alarm. The pervasive tone reflected the cool positivism of the mathematician: impatient with "such words as life, purpose, and soul," Wiener dismissed these ancient phantoms as "question-begging epithets," hoary gibberish "grossly inadequate to precise scientific thinking." By transforming "life" or "soul" into the measurable data of "information," cybernetics dispelled such metaphysical palaver. As insipidly inanimate as this worldview appeared, its dispassion enabled Wiener to discern the inexorable effects of cybernetic technology on workers. Observing that "the machine plays no favorites between manual labor and white-collar labor," Wiener warned enthusiasts of automation that intellectual workers enjoyed no protection from its corrosive impact on skill. Precisely because they could be programmed with any conceivable form of information, cybernetic devices could arrogate and degrade professional and managerial skills. Indeed, as machinery decomposed and reabsorbed more ingenuity, the trajectory of capitalist automation accelerated toward a future of universal human stupefaction and subjugation. Because the automatic machine is "the precise equivalent of slave labor," anyone who competes with it "must accept the economic conditions of slave labor." Wiener's ominous forecast of technological servitude was even more prescient than his eschewal of military research and his diatribe against "megabuck science."[14]

Yet Wiener was at least as compelling when he reflected on the religious and metaphysical implications of cybernetic technology. In *Cybernetics*, he likened automatic machines to archaic "technologies of magic" and compared his fellow scientists and engineers to the legendary Rabbi of Prague, who awakened the Golem, a large statue of clay, through kabbalistic incantation. Years later, more disillusioned and apprehensive, Wiener parlayed this analogy in *God and Golem, Inc.* (1964), a long essay on the perils of industrial and military technology. Many of his friends and followers—the "gadget-worshippers" who staffed the research laboratories of corporate industry—were also "priests of power" who, contemptuous of fleshly limitations and evasive of personal responsibility, sought perfect subordinates who never disagreed, showed fatigue, or organized unions. These shamans and priests of modernity pursued their quest for absolute power with automated machinery, "the modern counterpart of the Golem." "Those who suffer from a power complex," he had written in 1950, "find the mechanization of man a simple way to realize their ambitions."[15]

In *God and Golem*, Wiener was a repentant cybernetic magus, subjecting the science he had pioneered to a premodern moral and metaphysical critique. The cybernetic postulate that biological reproduction and mechanical self-replication are "of the same order of phenomena" brought with it—somewhat rightly, he now seemed to think—"something of the reprobation that attached in earlier ages to the sin of sorcery." Turning to the language of "question-begging epithets" that he spurned as a scientist, Wiener rued the hubris and avarice that impelled the refinement of machinery, calling it "sin" to use "the magic of modern automatization to further personal profit." Thus Wiener insisted that cybernetic heresy also pointed to a truth about capitalist automation: if human beings and machines could make likenesses of themselves, then the rapacious purposes programmed into automated machinery revealed the iniquity of human beings, not of technology per se.[16] For Wiener, the malevolence of contemporary cybernetics resided in its deployment for labor discipline and capital accumulation. The corporate sorcery of automation was a form of pecuniary enchantment: the animation of technics with the spirit of capital. More feasibly than earlier ideologies of mechanization, cybernetics appeared to herald the most thorough pecuniary animation of technology ever achieved.

Invaluable both for its scientific literacy and its eschewal of any facile technophobia, Wiener's philippic against the inhuman uses of human beings still fell short of a truly radical critique. Although he realized that the "sorcery" and "magic" of automated technology were fundamentally pecuniary, Wiener never suggested even a moratorium on automation, and he never called on scientists and engineers to mount a concerted resistance to corporate control of technological design. To be sure, his one overture to organized labor had come to nothing. Writing to United Automobile Workers president Walter Reuther in the summer of 1949, Wiener had conveyed his alarm at "the very pressing menace of the large-scale replacement of labor by machine." "These ideas are very much in the air," he emphasized, adding that his own refusal to work with industry would not likely be emulated by other scientists. Reiterating his warning that workers competing with machinery would be reduced to what amounted to slavery, Wiener urged Reuther to "steal a march upon the existing industrial corporations" and develop an alternative technological policy that would secure the profits and benefits of automation for labor. Although the two men met in March 1950 and agreed to formulate a strategy for dealing with technological change, they never met or corresponded again.[17] Without support from organized labor, Wiener could do little more than make heartfelt appeals to the professional-managerial elite—hardly a propitious prospect, given his own acknowledgment that most scientists and engineers were eager to assist in the technological enslavement of workers.

Besides, Wiener's prophetic rage against servitude to the machine had no convincing purchase on the moral imagination. Near the end of his life, Wiener invoked the "common sense of humanity, as accumulated in legends [and] in myths" as an alternative to the mercenary alchemy of corporate managers and technocrats.[18] But that "common sense" arose from a worldview profoundly antithetical to Wiener's positivism—an ostensibly disenchanted account of reality, but one that cloaked the cupidity of monetary metaphysics in the dispassionate lexicon of scientific rationality. The positivism that underlay Wiener's rejection of "question-begging epithets" was a philosophy almost tailor-made to serve as a Trojan horse for capitalist enchantment. An heir to and critic of the promethean trajectory of science portended by Sir Francis Bacon, Wiener—unlike Lewis Mumford—could not affirm or envision an ontology that might shake the foundations of corporate neotechnics. He could only hope that the cybernetic machinery to which humanity's fate was being linked would be superintended by benevolent technicians and their overlords.

A similar ambivalence leavened *Player Piano* (1952), Kurt Vonnegut's futuristic novel about Dr. Paul Proteus, a brilliant but troubled engineer and manager. *Player Piano* grew out of Vonnegut's mounting unease while he worked as a technical writer at the GE headquarters in Schenectady, New York. He was one of the first to see a fully automated milling machine—"a secret then," he recalled later, for the obvious reason that it was a weapon in the hands of management. ("They wanted no publicity that time," he recalled.)[19] But while Proteus's growing misgivings about automation form *Player Piano*'s main storyline, Vonnegut traced the drive to dispossess and mechanize to a deeper, more pernicious aspiration to mastery.

That desire to control, Vonnegut suggests, is a bid for godhood on the part of Ilium General Forge and Foundry, "the great omnipotent and omniscient spook, the corporate personality," where Proteus is a rising star. Governed by a technocratic cabal, Ilium is divided into three sections: a pleasant enclave for scientists, engineers, and managers; a factory complex for the machines; and "Homestead"—an obvious reference to the 1892 strike—populated by what remains of the industrial working class and those displaced by automation. The experts exhibit a contempt for Homestead that reveals the underside of *Fortune*'s automated idyll: "the goddamned people," as a colleague complains to Proteus, "if it weren't for them, earth would be an engineer's paradise." Homestead's residents are indeed "goddamned," as the corporate system exhibits many of the attributes of divinity. Though Ilium's rulers speak in the secular idiom of "progress," their devotion is irreducibly religious. As one of the technocracy's surreptitious critics observes, the experts possess a "crusading spirit," and their extension of automated production is a "holy war" against scarcity and inefficiency. The managers and professionals do indeed think of themselves as a new kind of clerisy. Matheson, a manager in charge of "testing and placement," goes about his job with "the air of a high priest," while Kroner, a duplicitous executive, seeks to stiffen Proteus's ideological backbone by reminding him that "there is no higher calling" than professional labor. And like the religious orders of old, the ranks of trained specialists have a commitment to the corporation that fuses erotic passion and spiritual ardor. In their "lovers' devotion to the unseen," the organization men remind Proteus of "nuns' symbolic marriage to Christ."[20]

Likewise, corporate technology—exemplified in EPICAC XIV, the system's master computer network—embodies a panoptical parody of godlike vision and productive potency. (Vonnegut almost certainly modeled the network after ENIAC and UNIVAC, two of the first high-speed computers developed for military and commercial purposes.) EPICAC XIV is a veritable deity who rivals Calvin's God with its powers of predestination: "dead right about everything," it determines production quotas, job distributions, and aptitude levels. Though Proteus recognizes that EPICAC "devaluates human thinking," his colleagues are so enthralled by its powers that they praise its prowess endlessly. Only a visiting African dignitary discerns the evil incarnate in the computer's digital enchantment: after a tour of EPICAC's mainframe, he warns his hosts that their creation is "a false god" who will eventually betray and destroy them.[21]

Seeking to recapture the "pride in strength and important mystery" that he believes was once possessed by artisans, Proteus quits his job and joins the Ghost Shirt Society, a secret brotherhood dedicated to industrial sabotage. The Ghost Shirts take their name from the late-nineteenth-century Lakota adherents of the Ghost Dance religion who believed themselves impervious to bullets; as one of Proteus's new comrades explains, they long for the reappearance of a "magic" that will restore "the old values, the old reasons for being." Finally emboldened to launch a revolution, the Ghost Shirts fail, not only against the superior firepower of the corporate technocracy, but also against the stubborn enchantment of "the goddamned people" who cannot, in the end, seem to imagine a life without their televisions and soda machines. "Already eager to recreate the same old nightmare," Proteus sighs. With many of their brethren slaughtered (like the Ghost Dancers at Wounded Knee in 1890), Proteus and the remaining Ghost Shirts surrender to the forces of progress: "Hands up. Forward March."[22]

Although Vonnegut appears to suggest that resistance to automation is futile, the defeat of the Ghost Shirts is not what renders *Player Piano* an ambivalent critique of technological progress. As Vonnegut suggests, "the goddamned people," despite their poverty and demoralization, are as beguiled by machinery as the engineers; Proteus recoils at "what thorough believers in mechanization most Americans were, even when their lives had been badly damaged by mechanization." Enchanted by techno-fetishism, Americans cannot imagine a different kind of "magic" or "mystery" to set against the new order of mass consumption and technological disposses-sion. Vonnegut himself strikes a note of vacillation before the tale even be-gins, as his foreword reads like a prayer for a divinely enlightened technoc-racy. "Our lives and freedom depend largely upon the skill and imagination and courage of our managers and engineers," Vonnegut writes, "and I hope that God will help them to help us all stay alive and free."[23]

A different kind of ambivalence about automation marked the work of Marshall McLuhan, whose delphic pronouncements on the media would make him a celebrity in the 1960s. McLuhan was an unlikely clairvoyant of automation; as he mused in 1966, "I am resolutely opposed to all innovation." Educated in Canada and Britain in the 1930s, he was also a devout convert to Catholicism; a close friend of Wyndham Lewis, one of Britain's most vit-riolic reactionaries; and an admirer of G. K. Chesterton, Hilaire Belloc, and other theologians of distributism. As a young scholar and teacher at the Uni-versity of Toronto, he vilified "modern industrial humanism" for its mecha-nistic tyranny over nature and its "swift obliteration of the person." Add his later animosity toward the counterculture and feminism, and McLuhan's aversion to cultural modernity seems obvious—but also incongruent with his subsequent renown as a herald of "the global village," a planetary com-munity achieved through the enlargement of consciousness by media technology.[24]

McLuhan's own personal attitude toward contemporary technological developments is less important than the imprimatur he appeared to bestow on electronic media and production. His oracular and impressionistic writing style made his account of impending technological transformation seem much more celebratory than it was. Yet McLuhan was not always the im-probable Emerson of the cybernetic age. His first book, *The Mechanical Bride* (1951), was a bemused and sardonic foray into the soul of capitalist culture, combing for signs of spiritual longing in the iconography of the consciousness industries—"the folklore of industrial man," as he called it, expressing longings for divinity as urgently as the legends of archaic and medieval peoples. Noting "the religious intensity of modern technology and business," he argued that the monthly publication of *Fortune* was "a major religious liturgy celebrating the feats of technological man," a "Bayreuth festival in the most megalomaniac style." Advertising, he told a gathering of academics in 1954, was "pictorial and verbal magic" invoked by the modern descendants of "primitive witch-doctors." Like advertising, popular entertainment conveyed the market-researched charms of corporate enchantment. "Hollywood means 'sacred grove,'" he pointed out, "and from this modern grove has issued a new pantheon of gods and goddesses to fashion and trouble the dreams of modern man."[25]

Yet unlike many other reactionaries, McLuhan abstained from agrarian sentimentality and expressed an impatience with the technophobic moralism of his fellow humanists. As he later observed in *Understanding Media* (1966), the "moral point of view" so often adopted by critics of machinery "too often serves as a substitute for understanding in technological matters." McLuhan acquired his own education in technology in the 1950s, as, in the wake of praise for *The Mechanical Bride,* he embarked on a lucrative career as an academic and cultural entrepreneur. He chaired the Ford Foundation's Seminars on Culture and Communication, one of the highest-profile corporate venues for prominent intellectuals, politicians, and businesspeople; became director of Toronto's Centre for Culture and Technology, another ongoing synod of the high-profile intelligentsia; and transformed himself from a critic of industrial folklore into a well-paid corporate consultant, hobnobbing with executives and media strategists at General Electric, AT&T, and IBM.[26]

So McLuhan's augury of a new age in *The Gutenberg Galaxy* (1962) reflected a long and remunerative sojourn among the clerisy of corporate enchantment. Though still capable of remarking on the "incantatory spells" of advertising, McLuhan had grown more expansively visionary, as aspersions on "modern industrial humanism" yielded to omens of cybernetic communion. McLuhan declared that "the world has become a computer, an electronic brain," and that "electromagnetic discoveries," by fostering evergreater simultaneity in communication, had reshaped "the human family" in such a way that it was now "a 'global village.'" Given McLuhan's status as an academic impresario, it was inevitable that his central claim—that the "Gutenberg galaxy" of print and scientific rationality was yielding to some new, more "tribal" cosmology of electronically mediated relationships—would be read as an affirmation of corporate-sponsored technology. Indeed, pointing to the "miracles of mass production," he now praised industrial society for creating "the plateau from which all can now share the awareness of new scope and potential for everyday beauty." McLuhan seemed even more hopeful that cybernetics would undermine the hierarchies of Fordism, enabling new structures that would pivot around democratic "dialogue and participation." "In our electronic age," he marveled, "the specialist and pyramid forms of structure . . . are not any longer practical." Automation appeared to McLuhan to promise a communal paradise of leisure, "workless and propertyless communities" free from the selfish and venal gravitational principles of the Gutenberg galaxy.[27] However anxious about "the global village," McLuhan beckoned to a new communion achieved through the liturgies of cybernetic technics.

McLuhan's gloomy prognosis for "pyramid forms of structure" echoed contemporary managerial ideology. Unsettled by popular social criticism of "conformity," management mandarins had been drafting a new, post-Fordist corporate humanism that celebrated the social and technological novelties spawned by automated production. Automation appeared to call for a legion of highly trained technicians, maintenance workers, and operators—the "technostructure," as Galbraith dubbed them in *The New Industrial State* (1967)—whose intellectual and creative skills made them both indispensable to the corporate apparatus but also potentially more disruptive of corporate society. Because, it was thought, such workers would chafe at the restraints imposed by enormous, lethargic bureaucracies, management would have to charm as well as exploit their critical and iconoclastic capacities. Thus, the new aversion to large-scale structures among management writers stemmed, in part, from a sense of affinity with the frustrated poets languishing in the offices of the Crystal Palace. As Thomas Frank argues, many in the elite sectors of corporate America saw in Whyte, David Riesman, Vance Packard, and other critics "comrade[s] in their own struggles to revitalize American business and the consumer order generally."[28] Eager to revivify what they considered a stifling, sclerotic monolith, the postwar generation of managerial intellectuals assembled a new portfolio of authority. Seeking a soulful but agile corporation that fused the camaraderie of mechanized communion with the fury of creative destruction, they created a hip produation, a rejuvenated moral economy that contained a key element of contemporary business ideology: the entrepreneur as existential vanguard of the species, a being whose "creativity" channels the truth and goodness of the pecuniary metaphysic.

As the paramount corporate *philosophe,* Drucker took the lead in constructing a novel paradigm for management. Though wary of criticism of "the Organization Man," he conceded by the late 1950s that enlightened executives should heed Whyte's warnings about conformity and overcentralization. Thanks to automation and a perceptive avant-garde of business leaders and management consultants, Drucker saw new possibilities for a felicitous merger of high productivity, technical innovation, and participatory work relations. The future of capitalism lay, in Drucker's view, with "conservative innovators," savvy pioneers who harnessed the creative energies of the marketplace without direction from on high. Resembling economist Joseph Schumpeter's swashbuckling capitalist heroes who emerge triumphant from the maelstrom of "creative destruction," "conservative innovators" combined the rationality of the bureaucrat with the brashness and ingenuity of the entrepreneur. Conservative innovation would, Drucker predicted, inaugurate a new era of faster, smaller, more "flexible" structures that engaged in a "continuous process" of organizational evolution.[29] Like the dinosaurs, the bureaucracies of Fordism were lumbering toward extinction—guided to their graves by management.

"Conservative innovators" could rely on an expanding repertoire of psycho-managerial techniques: Kurt Lewin's "group dynamics," for instance, developed at MIT's Research Center for Group Dynamics, and Robert Tannenbaum's "sensitivity training," forged at UCLA's Graduate School of Business Administration. Both group dynamics and sensitivity training incubated a new managerial culture characterized by attention to the emotional texture and nuance of the workplace. Because both sensitivity training and group dynamics were seen as overtly technocratic by many in the corporate intelligentsia, the bromides of humanistic psychology appeared less overtly managerial and manipulative. Ranging from Gestalt theory to the revisionist psychoanalysis of Karen Horney and Erich Fromm, the humanistic psychology represented by Rollo May, Victor Frankl, Abraham Maslow, and Carl Rogers had arisen in the 1930s out of dissatisfaction with orthodox Freudianism. Downplaying sexual and aggressive impulses and renouncing Freud's intractable pessimism, humanistic psychologists focused on what

Maslow called the "potentialities, virtues, and achievable aspirations" latent in human nature. The ideal self, in this view, was almost infinitely protean, displaying, as Rogers explained in *On Becoming a Person* (1961), "an absence of rigidity, of tight organization . . . a maximum of adaptability, a discovery of structure in experience, a flowing, changing organization of self and personality."[30]

Maslow and Rogers—whose books, along with taped interviews and conferences, began to circulate widely in business circles in the early 1960s—proved especially adept at evangelizing the new psychology to middlebrow readers. "Discoverers of banality," as Russell Jacoby once described them, they peddled a farrago of uplift packaged as the latest psychological science. Maslow in particular was a virtuoso of platitude, a master in pawning off nuggets of cliché as extraordinary pearls of insight. Yet for all its empty profundity, humanistic psychology also represented a metamorphosis of the sacred, a translation of religious aspirations into the existentialist vernacular of "being" and "authenticity." At the top of his celebrated hierarchy of needs, Maslow placed self-actualization, the expression of human potential uninhibited by enervating inner conflicts or unnecessary external restraints. Self-actualizers, Maslow wrote in *Toward a Psychology of Being* (1962), comprised "a different breed of human beings," an existential elite of kinder, gentler *Ubermenschen* who had scaled "the highest reaches of human nature." Represented best by artists, writers, Olympic athletes, and other "achievers," they "perceived reality more efficiently, fully, and with less emotional contamination" than lesser breeds below them in the anthropological hierarchy. At the most celestial level of personal development, self-actualizers would have what Maslow anointed "peak experiences" that resembled encounters with divinity recounted by seers, mystics, and saints. In its preachy, etiolated fashion, humanistic psychology preserved what had previously been considered the experience of enchantment. Indeed, Maslow and others openly admitted that terms such as "peak experience" and "self-actualization" mimicked the traditional therapeutic vocabulary of religion. Humanistic psychology was a "larger, more inclusive science," Maslow argued, because it included what he called "the data of transcendence."[31]

While the reduction of transcendence to "data" exemplifies Maslow's philistinism, it would be unfair to dismiss humanistic psychology as merely an ideology of conformity—"social amnesia," as Jacoby dubbed it. The utopian longing for communion in labor had surfaced before in management theory as well as in anarchist and artisanal evocations of joy in self-directed creativity. Though it ultimately sanctioned therapeutic acquiescence in a new managerial culture, humanistic psychology addressed desires for liberation from the bureaucratic routines of Fordism. "Growth" and "self-realization" possessed a powerful critical import for Fromm, who devoted a good deal of *The Sane Society* (1955) and *The Art of Loving* (1956) to analyzing the destructive impact of corporate capitalism on the conditions for genuine self-realization. If, as Fromm believed, love sought the self-realization of others, and if work was an indispensable "mode of self-realization," then humanly authentic work was impossible or perverted in a capitalist society that was "incompatible with the principle of love." Although Herbert Marcuse excoriated him as a peddler of "conformism," Fromm pointed to the anarchists and syndicalists of Spain and France as models for a beloved community of labor. "Centered around the idea of workers' participation and co-management," their conception of work fostered personal development rather than sheer productivity.[32]

Yet humanistic psychology also proved useful to a new generation of management theorists and business chieftains. Maslow and Douglas McGregor oversaw the full inclusion of humanistic psychology in the corporate portfolio of hegemony. A professor of management at MIT's Alfred P. Sloan School of Management, McGregor conducted extensive field research among numerous firms in the late 1950s, summarizing his discoveries in *The Human Side of Enterprise* (1960), one of the most celebrated documents in the managerial canon. Clearly indebted to Maslovian psychology, McGregor complained that "we are a long way from realizing the potential represented by the human resources we now recruit into industry." The chief culprits in this waste of human talent were the Fordist and Taylorist principles of what McGregor disparaged as "Theory X": rigid hierarchy, centralization of command and authority, and meticulous specialization of tasks. Under the specter of Theory X, managers and executives led corporate structures full of repressed and alienated employees—the timorous inhabitants of the Crystal Palace. To unleash the potential blocked by Fordist monotony, managers needed to draw on the latest psychology and social science to fashion "an organizational climate conducive to human growth" which would, of course, raise profits as well. McGregor dubbed the new philosophy of wealth

"Theory Y," promising "developments with respect to the human side of enterprise comparable to those that have occurred in technology"—automated technology, to be precise, whose designers and operators were the brave new artisans of the cybernetic era.[33] Blessed with such intrepid and imaginative specialists, managers, he advised, should relax their grip, loosen and diversify their bureaucracies, and trust rather than command their employees.

Maslow provided a sanctimonious psychological complement to Theory Y. As the chief middlebrow preacher of "growth" and "self-actualization," Maslow was courted in business circles, and his reflections in *Eupsychian Management* (1965) grew out of his brief stint as a managerial consultant. In the summer of 1962, Maslow worked as a "sort of visiting fellow" with Non-Linear Systems (NLS), a southern California digital manufacturing firm. An avid reader of McGregor, Maslow, and Drucker, NLS's founder and president Andrew Kay grouped his workers into production teams of six or seven members who set their own pace, kept no records, and made their own internal rules, while an "executive council" set overall policy but refrained from supervision. As Kay explained to one of the many business reporters who trekked to his factory in search of the future, "we control the process, not the people"—having already controlled the people by rearranging the process. Kay was so proud of his industrial democracy that he invited Maslow to analyze the firm's management and human relations policies. Required to come only one afternoon a week, Maslow studied his own ideas in action and was, unsurprisingly, astonished by the refreshing and remunerative transparency of NLS's corporate ecology. Unlike conventional corporations with their stodgy autocracies, NLS was like "a well-integrated basketball team," with a "coach" confident enough to let his talented "players" exercise their skills with a minimum of oversight.[34]

Workplace harmony and efficiency weren't the only virtues that Maslow discerned in what he dubbed "eupsychian management." In his view, NLS heralded the advent of an eschatological epoch in which capitalism would finally resolve the contradictions of history. "What is good for General Motors is then good for the United States, what is good for the United States is then good for the world, what is good for me is then good for everyone else." By empowering workers, humane management—"synergy," in Maslow's words—was "a utopian or revolutionary technique," the final rapprochement of political democracy and capitalist economics. But it also represented a religious consummation, since—with all the vapid sincerity of humanistic psychology—it took religion "seriously, profoundly, deeply, and earnestly." Since "salvation is a by-product of self-actualizing work and self-actualizing duty," then the labor of the new economy could rightly be called "'mission,' 'calling,' 'vocation,' in the priest's sense." Uninhibited by fear and unhindered by hierarchy, the new corporate self was an utterly transparent "creative person," a glorious self-actualizer who could "unleash himself . . . show his talent or genius or skill without building up defenses or guards." Maslow augured an unending peak experience, a life in which a race of thriving *ubermenschen,* unshackled from the need to take thought for the morrow, would be "totally immersed in the here and now."[35]

Yet despite immersion in the "here and now," the new management theory remained, in the end, fixated on the bottom line. McGregor never pretended otherwise; the fundamental goal of any Theory Y manager was, he reiterated, "demonstrating to people how they can satisfy their own needs best by working toward organizational objectives"—namely, capital accumulation. While Maslow was more adept at expressing corporate objectives in psycho-existential twaddle, he was also chillingly honest about the Hobbesian underside of "eupsychian" economics. Despite Maslow's frequent allusions to postwar material abundance, an ontology of scarcity lurked behind the humanist bombast of self-actualization. You can trust people in an affluent society with "plenty of money, plenty of goods, [and] plenty of food," but all bets were off if things get tight. If, Maslow imagined, "there were one hundred people and there was food for ten, and ninety of these hundred would die," then, he announced with unsavory candor, "I would make mighty goddamned sure that I would not be one of those ninety." Standing atop a bloody heap in the hierarchy of need—there, surely, was a peak experience. Maslow advised the "creative person" to cultivate the art of the higher duplicity to avoid the fate of the uncreative ninety. Even in good times, he cautioned, the synergistic leader "ought *not* to be as expressive and open about himself as other people are permitted and encouraged to be."[36] This was the sordid, Machiavellian denouement of Maslovian managerial synergy.

Maslow underlined the persistence of conflict in the political economy of Eupsychia, cautioning that the humanistic principles he and McGregor outlined "held *primarily for good conditions, rather than for stormy weather.*" Alas, just as Maslow was finishing his book, stormy weather was hitting NLS.

In the summer and fall of 1964, orders began to decline as more convention-ally structured competitors made inroads into its aerospace market, and Kay had to lay off some of the people over whom he claimed to have no control. The executive council terminated the experiment in "synergy," and NLS reverted to a rigidly structured hierarchy, featuring greater managerial supervision. Apparently, Eupsychia would quickly retool as a dystopian oligarchy when profits were down, and the Theory Y manager would need to perceive and control reality more efficiently. (As Kay later confessed to *Business Week*, he had "lost sight of the purpose of business, which is not to develop new theories of management.")[37] For all the lissome palaver about openness, growth, and opportunity for self-actualization, the new managerial style continued to rely on deceit, repression, and ferocious competitive discipline.

A similar conservative revolution was under way in advertising, an industry in turmoil precisely at the zenith of American prosperity and confidence. With the waning of corporate modernism in the 1930s and 1940s, firms took fewer aesthetic risks; the hopes of a Calkins that advertising could usher in a "business millennium" gave way to more prosaic concerns. Advertising, so the new wisdom went, was a thoroughly mercantile enterprise, founded on the latest scientific expertise; artistic adventurism was for abstract expressionists. As journalist Martin Mayer wrote in 1958, the best admen relied not on "genius" but on "rigorous logical analysis" of surveys, polls, and questionnaires. The very title of Rosser Reeves's *Reality in Advertising* (1960) encapsulated the rejection of modernism's insistence on autonomy, eccentricity, and brilliance. Engaged in the "scientific" production of images, the institutional apparatus of advertising was aligned with the nostrums of "scientific" management; most agencies were Theory X bureaucracies, models of utilitarian and monetary rationality.[38]

As a result, advertising in the 1950s was a dry-bones desert of creative sterility. Having managed successful ad campaigns for Shell gasoline, Rolls-Royce cars, Schweppes tonic water, and Hathaway shirts, David Ogilvy—co-founder of Ogilvy and Mather and former researcher for George Gallup—felt justified in asserting in his *Confessions of an Advertising Man* (1963) that "most advertisements are infernally dull." An unmistakable consciousness of professional and aesthetic fraudulence came to pervade the field by the late 1950s; many admen could have seconded Vic Norman, the protagonist of Frederic Wiseman's *The Hucksters* (1946), who, fed up with compromising with clients and consumers, implores his colleagues, "Christ, we ought to face it. We're hustlers." So when Allen Ginsberg lamented that "the best minds of [his] generation" cranked out "blasts of leaden verse" in their offices on Madison Avenue, he both roared in prophetic dudgeon and recounted his experience in the consciousness industry: the author of "Howl" had endured a stint as an adman in New York and San Francisco in the early 1950s.[39]

Yet just as Ginsberg was howling, a new cohort of theorists and professionals was replacing the leaden verse of scientific advertising with a brash new poetry of consumer desire. What industry leaders and historians have called "the Creative Revolution" began in the mid-1950s as an institutional and aesthetic upheaval against the Fordist dream factories in advertising. Just as management writers denounced Theory X bureaucracies and leadership styles for their hindrance of entrepreneurial innovation, more and more advertising writers berated the leaden institutions that stifled their artistic freedom. The Creative Revolution featured a shift to "boutique" firms, outposts of Theory Y that lavishly advertised their independence from aesthetic conventions. Creative revolutionaries incorporated public distrust of advertising into a brash new universe of commercial imagery that relied on clever copy, ironic humor, and derision of propriety and stuffiness. In what Frank has dubbed "the conquest of cool," the Creative Revolution marked the bourgeois-bohemian convergence of Madison Avenue with the "counterculture."[40] While "creativity" appeared to supplant scientific research as the chief mode of legitimation, it obscured the persistence of the century-old ambition to merge instrumental reason with aesthetics, the freedom of the artist with the necessities of the vendor, the longing for a sacramental way in the world with the mandates of pecuniary metaphysics.

These structural and symbolic revolutions in advertising were accompanied by changes in what marketing researcher Ernest Dichter dubbed the "strategies of desire." The most prominent and controversial strategy of desire was "motivational research," pioneered by Dichter, George Katona, Burleigh Gardner, Louis Cheskin, and Pierre Martineau. Drawing on group dynamics, sociological surveys, and psychoanalytic theory, motivational researchers assembled a sophisticated repertoire of psychic inquisition: Rorschach inkblots, interviews, psychographs, thematic apperception tests, and demographic studies. Diagramming the vectors of longing, motivational researchers lambasted conventional advertising—a "dull, uninvolving chant of mechanica and ingredients," as Martineau complained—and admonished the industry to remember that humans do not live by information alone. "Men live by symbols," Martineau observed, and the job of the new inquisitors was to fathom the allegories of the restless heart.[41]

Business journalists recognized that motivational research was more intrusive than any previous advertising method. "Madison Avenue is preparing a concerted onslaught on the consumer to find out what makes him tick," *Business Week* alerted readers in 1953. A year later, the *Wall Street Journal* noted apprehensively that advertisers were venturing into the "strange wilderness" of the unconscious mind. Robert Graham worried in the *Reporter* that, in addition to prostituting their talents, social scientists would "feed dangerous material to an irresponsible adman." Yet despite the umbrage of critics such as Vance Packard—whose popular diatribe against *The Hidden Persuaders* (1957) portrayed Dichter and his colleagues as a shady Orwellian cabal of master manipulators—advertisers and their clients were eager to enter and profit from the libidinal labyrinth. "The creative process requires more than reason," as Ogilvy asserted. Most businesspeople and advertisers were unoriginal, he contended, because they paid too much fealty to "the tyranny of reason." Echoing humanistic psychologists, Ogilvy traced the banality of most advertising imagery to psychic repression: "their imaginations are blocked," he wrote of his cohorts, and motivational research allowed them to escape both their own and the public's neurotic confinement. By the mid-1950s, the new science of desire was all the rage in agencies and corporate advertising departments, with researchers plumbing and charting the volatile id of the marketplace. As Graham reported, motivational research had become "the Appian Way of the advertising world," with a reputation so impeccable that it constituted "the new liturgy" of the consciousness industry.[42] With advertisers leading a return of the repressed, virtuous consumerism was marked for extinction.

As the principal celebrants of this new liturgy, Martineau and Dichter expounded the metaphysics and humanism of motivational research. In articles published in the *Harvard Business Review,* as well as in his textbook, *Motivation in Advertising* (1957), Martineau—director of research and marketing at the *Chicago Tribune*—offered an elementary introduction to the science of libidinal inquiry and manipulation. His recognition that "men live by symbols" was bound up with a commodity humanism, an account of human identity as an evanescent and kaleidoscopic ensemble of consumer purchases. Pointing to research on "market segmentation"—the idea that there is not *the* market but rather markets, subdivided into "segments" or "niches"—he asserted that the individual consumer is an integer in a market niche, "profoundly different [from those in other segments] in his mode of thinking and his way of handling the world." "Where he buys and what he buys will differ not only by economics but in symbolic value." Hence, there was, for example, "an automobile for every personality." Thus the mission of the advertiser was not to provide information about the product but to conjure a "halo of psychological meanings," to fabricate an aura out of longings identified through the techniques of motivational research. Seeking to mystify—not explain—the commodity, the successful magician of consciousness constructed "a powerful symbol capable of lifting the brand completely out of the long, long parade of faceless products." Even something as apparently mundane and unromantic as gasoline, Martineau argued, could be bathed in the radiance of the psyche as refracted through the mercantile science of passion. Yet if "color schemes and designs have an intrinsic meaning" to consumers, he wrote, their meaning to sellers was wholly pecuniary.[43] Though aimed at the collective unconscious of consumers, motivational research was ultimately a form of training in sensitivity to capital.

If Martineau addressed his fellow image professionals, Dichter engaged the wider public, assuming Calkins's role as advertising's most passionate moralist and metaphysician. Dichter's rise in the marketing and advertising world was meteoric and immensely lucrative. Born in Vienna in 1907 and trained as a psychoanalyst by Alfred Adler, Dichter escaped Nazi Germany with his wife and arrived in New York in 1938, finding work with a market research firm in Manhattan. Riding the rising wave of American interest in psychoanalysis, Dichter wrote to several agencies, introducing himself as "a young psychologist from Vienna" who had "some interesting new ideas which can help you be more successful, effective, sell more and communicate better."[44]

One of the firms, the Compton Advertising Agency, hired Dichter to work on its Ivory Soap account. After conducting a hundred "non-directive interviews" in which he asked subjects to talk about their bathing habits and experiences, Dichter concluded that soap was not about hygiene but rather about erotic self-indulgence. "One of the few occasions when the puritanical American was allowed to caress himself or herself," lingering in the bathtub gratified the basic impulse of primary narcissism. Thus, Ivory needed to understand that it wasn't selling soap—it was selling sexual allure, voluptuous ecstasy, fleshly beatitude. Dichter advised Ivory to renounce the "somber, utilitarian, thoroughly cleansing character" it had attributed to its product and to give it a more sensuous, luxuriant "personality"—one more like that of a competitor, Cashmere Bouquet, which projected a more "glamorous" image. After Ivory took Dichter's advice—"Be smart and get a fresh start with Ivory Soap"—his profile became so prominent that other corporate clients enlisted his services: Chrysler, Proctor & Gamble, Exxon, General Mills, and Du Pont. Dichter's remuneration and professional renown grew rapidly, to the point where, in 1946, he established the Institute for Motivational Research in Montrose, New York, which soon had a dozen branches in North America and Europe.[45]

It would be easy to dismiss Dichter as a cynical peddler of statistically sanctioned hedonism. (One psychologist-turned-marketing director advised clients to "use this guy. Use his ideas. Milk him. But for Christ's sake don't tell me it's research.") Packard made this mistake in *The Hidden Persuaders*, where his Protestant proprietary indictment of Dichter and motivational research not only missed, but misunderstood, its target—so thoroughly, in fact, that he inadvertently made Dichter into a celebrity. (A year after Packard's book appeared, Dichter thanked its author for making "the whole world motivation research conscious.") Upholding self-restraint and frugality, Packard excoriated Dichter and his fellow strategists of desire for their encouragement of "materialism." Dichter's retorts to Packard and other scourges of consumerism were pointed and astute, certainly much more subtle and searching than Packard's tightwad moralism. In Dichter's view—laid out in *The Strategy of Desire* (1960)—while Packard garnered "easy applause" by thundering against "materialism," he and other self-appointed censors seldom "bothered to tell us what they really mean by material or spiritual values." If and when they did, he continued, it quickly became obvious that their idealism entailed some kind of material expression. "Justice," for instance, required redistribution of money and goods; "love," "family," or "religion" needed roses, home-cooked meals, or collection envelopes to be taken seriously. Dichter's conclusion was resolutely materialist—in theological terms, incarnational. "The division between materialistic goods and ideal-istic goals is an erroneous one," he wrote. "There is no sharp dividing line between materialistic and idealistic values."[46] If, as Martineau had realized, "men live by symbols," they lived by those symbols through material objects anointed by a halo of meanings.

As Dichter's riposte to Packard and other champions of prudence and sobriety indicated, Dichter was more than a huckstering psychoanalyst. Ensconced at the Institute for Motivational Research, he was also a formi-dable philosopher of futility, a worthy heir of Nystrom and Calkins. Offering a commercial cryptography of the id, motivational research, Dichter confi-dently asserted, constituted "a new and revolutionary way of discovering the soul of man." "Human desire is the raw material we're working with," he re-minded admen and marketers; business is selling not only products and ser-vices but also a "positive philosophy of life." In numerous articles and in a trilogy of books—*The Psychology of Everyday Living* (1947), *The Strategy of Desire,* and his *Handbook of Consumer Motivations* (1964)—Dichter mounted a defense of commodity fetishism, laying a libidinal groundwork for a new pecuniary metaphysics of morals.[47]

In Dichter's view, affluent societies like the United States were entering what he called a "psycho-economic age," in which high levels of employment and production required an exponential expansion of consumption. But to educate the public in the strange new moralism of consumer desire, image professionals had to counter the static and antiquated psychology of scarcity, the rationality of inhibition that sanctioned the now-obsolete virtues of thrift and self-denial. Basing their invective against advertising on this archaic model of psyche and economy, Packard and other scourges failed, Dichter argued, to recognize that needs are "plastic and expansive," and that im-provements in modern technology enabled and even mandated their satis-faction. At the same time, if change and variation are necessary for human flourishing, then perpetual dissatisfaction should be fostered, not lamented; an escalating cycle of disappointment and fulfillment was "a healthy goal of persuasion and education." What Nystrom had named "futility" Dichter re-packaged as "constructive discontent," the creative destruction of desire that fueled ever-greater investment and innovation.[48] In the age of "psycho-economics"—when advertising would come into its own as an industry devoted to the production of consciousness—the restless heart would stay forever restless, finding an evanescent repose in the eternal obsolescence of commodity culture.

Dichter's psycho-economic age entailed the creative destruction of personal identity through consumption, a search that ceaseth only in death— or lack of money, which amounted to the same. Defining the human in terms of consumer activity, Dichter reduced identity to an ensemble of commodities. In the tables of market research, a middle-class white male, he pointed out, was someone "who wears an Adam shirt, drives a Plymouth car, drinks PM whiskey, and wears Arrow ties and shirts." But to Dichter, commodities were more than markers of taste or signifiers of status; they awaken, liberate, and "permit us to discover more and more about ourselves." Things indeed preach to us, as Emerson had thought; the world was filled with friendly objects, as Whitman had hoped. Combining psychoanalysis, Gestalt psychology, and cultural anthropology, Dichter outlined what he called a "phenomenology" of goods—a capitalist theory of commodity fetishism—in which "objects have a soul," the soul of their prospective consumers. Enchanted by projection, objects are vessels of desire, tokens empowered by our futile search for fulfillment in the commerce of longing. (Dichter's meticulous attention to the psychic and sensuous texture of desire enlivened his tales of market research: the "emotional facets of glass," the "soul of metals," the "secret life of a fruit," the erotic messages of cigarette lighters.)[49]

The conclusion of Dichter's phenomenology was inexorable: a soul thus projected is redeemed through consumption, a consummation afforded only through the ritual of purchase and the sanctifying grace of money. Thus Dichter's philosophy of futility restated the foundation of pecuniary metaphysics: as the criterion of reality in capitalist life, money is the root and quintessence of all things. And as money must move for capital to accumulate, Dichter emphasized that the ceremonies of consumption must be constantly reenacted. Since people inevitably "project themselves into objects" and perpetually suffer from "constructive discontent," advertisers should promote and orchestrate this "dynamic relationship of constant interaction." Dichter realized that constructive discontent would be the axis of a new moral imagination, mandating a transvaluation of values as profound as any ever envisioned by Nietzsche. Echoing Calkins, Filene, and Frederick, he predicted that as motivational researchers opened up to view "the vast lands of the human soul and spirit," consumers could explore those regions once considered the domains of religion and philosophy. Indeed, those realms touched on metaphysical sublimity; the more adroitly corporations employed the strategies of desire to identify and satiate our longings, "the more we approach . . . a God within ourselves." But that pliable deity could achieve its omnipotence only by erasing the memory of transgression. To savor the unremittingly transient bliss of constructive discontent, "we have to learn to forget the guilt of original sin."[50] With this memory repressed, Augustine's restless heart could be an engine of progress in unceasing acquisitive motion.

With greater flair and audacity than his predecessors in the perennial philosophy of futility, Dichter had identified the sacramental desire that animates the fetishism of commodities: the passion for communion with divinity in the sumptuous plenitude of the material world. Equipped with a deliberately elusive cure of souls, advertisers and marketers were spiritual directors, with their charts and questionnaires comprising a corporate breviary of capitalist enchantment. The priest had departed; the divine advertiser had come.

Dichter's open and unambiguous challenge to conventional morality indicates that the more advanced sectors of the corporate world were poised to assimilate the "counterculture" that was coalescing in the early 1960s. In both popular consciousness and academic scholarship, this counterculture encompasses a kaleidoscopic realm of dissidence: Beat writers and artists and their descendants among "hippies"; rock music and the drug culture; experiments in communal living based on artisanal and small-scale agricultural labor; the sexual revolution that culminated in the revitalization of feminism and the emergence of gay liberation; the new interest in Zen Buddhism and other forms of spirituality outside the compass of Judeo-Christianity; and an unprecedented concern for the ecological health of the planet that revived the environmental movement. Both popular and academic narratives of the counterculture account for its appearance in much the same way: bourgeois boredom and disgruntlement; alienation from the bureaucratic conformity and technocratic rationalism of industrial society; and revulsion at the racism, violence, and sexual repression of American life—all condensed in the opposition to the war in Vietnam. Demanding release from the Apollonian prison of instrumental rationality, the counterculture beckoned to Orpheus and Dionysus unbound, a *gemeinschaft* of festivity, pleasure, and mysticism embodied in communes, rock concerts, "be-ins," handicrafts, and organic farming. Sponsoring a profusion of experiments in consciousness, it practiced "expressive individualism," in Robert Bellah's words, another Romantic celebration of unrestrained feeling and sensuality.[51]

Yet one of the more remarkable aspects of American culture in the 1960s was the *popularity* of countercultural apostasy—the affirmation and embrace of its mutiny and flamboyance not only by youth but also by many of their middle-class elders. The sheer ubiquity of sympathetic books and articles on the counterculture in the popular press—capped by Yale law professor Charles Reich's dulcet paean to *The Greening of America* (1970)—suggests that the "counterculture" may not have been as "counter" as both contemporaries and later observers thought. Reich's proclamation that a "revolution" was already "spreading with amazing rapidity" captured an inchoate but pervasive transformation of American culture as a whole.[52] To be sure, the counterculture remained unsettling enough to mute and bridle its immediate impact: the specter of antinomian revelry, or the dangers of pharmaceutical rapture, or the dread of post-Christian anomie, prevented most white middle-class Americans from fully enlisting in the cultural revolution. But if the hesitant changes in bourgeois mores were any indication, modernism had found its way into quiet suburban lanes as well as noisy metropolitan streets; bohemia, once an enclave for an elite of disaffection, was now becoming a democratic vista.

Thus, like the new prophets of corporate iconoclasm, the counterculture grew out of very real frustrations; it reflected a general crisis of capitalist enchantment. Yet it harbored two very different legacies. One continued the Romantic lineage of anticapitalism, repudiating the ideal of commodified abundance, rejecting the dogmas of pecuniary metaphysics, and calling for an enchanted, sacramental alternative to the counterfeit disenchantment of corporate modernity. The other—complicit with the conquest of cool—dovetailed perfectly with the stylistic, moral, and metaphysical lineaments of the nascent corporate counterculture. Often merging seamlessly and enthusiastically with automation, managerial "synergy," and the "creative revolution," the cybernetic counterculture was not so much coopted as it was recognized fraternally by the cultural and technological vanguard of corporate capitalism. It embodied a corporate assimilation of Romanticism, a foreclosure on bohemia, a copyright infringement of the sacramental imagination.

The counterculture merged with corporate bohemia most clearly in technology and advertising circles, as many of its adherents and fellow-travelers were utopian enthusiasts of science and technological progress. Often pointing to the electric guitars, recording equipment, and amplifying systems essential to rock music, even sympathetic accounts noted the countercultural affinity for the products of corporate industry. In *The Making of a Counterculture* (1969), his friendly but critical study, Theodore Roszak pointed out that when heroes of the drug culture such as Timothy Leary advocated "Better Living through Chemistry," they "mean it the way Du Pont means it." Convinced that "there exists a technological solution to every human problem," the blissed-out knights of what Roszak called "the great psychedelic crusade" shared the same faith in the technological sublime that animated *Fortune* and other mavens of automation. Although Reich rehearsed many of the standard complaints about technology, he believed nonetheless that "the machine itself" was the material basis of "Consciousness III," the emancipatory sensibility of sensuousness, self-discovery, and communal elation adumbrated in the counterculture. Reich's ecologically resonant encomium to the "greening" of America stemmed in part from his belief that cybernetics and automation were eradicating scarcity, abolishing the need for alienating labor, and permitting a more selective use of technology that would diminish despoliation of the environment. Originally designed to further an acquisitive and conformist way of life, "the machine itself has begun to do the work of revolution," he wrote exultantly.[53]

Richard Brautigan agreed. By the mid-1960s, Brautigan was one of the most prominent and revered poets of the counterculture, and his "All Watched Over by Machines of Loving Grace" (1967) swiftly became a classic of techno-romanticism, a felicitous, cyber-pastoral vision of harmony between nature and technology. Brautigan dreamed of "a cybernetic meadow / where mammals and computers / live together in mutually / programming harmony," as well as "a cybernetic forest / filled with pines and electronics / where deer stroll peacefully / past computers / as if they were flowers / with spinning blossoms." This "cybernetic ecology" was Marx's realm of freedom, unshackled from the realm of necessity but beautifully intertwined with its myriad creatures: we would be "free of our labors / and joined back to nature," relieved from toil by a naturalized technology and reunited with our "mammal/brothers and sisters." The entire planet would be guarded by an angelic presence, "all watched over/by machines of loving grace"—a state, not of insidious superintendence and control, but of blissful camaraderie and security. Brautigan peppered his eschatology of technological communion with hints of historical inevitability. "It has to be!" as he declares at one point, "the sooner the better!"[54] As Brautigan suggested, the countercultural Orpheus could be in league with the corporate Prometheus; the psychedelic longing for earthly rapture was not at all incompatible with the cybernetic quest for untrammeled mastery.

As Andrew Ross, Fred Turner, and others have demonstrated, high-tech hippies and countercultural ideologues who experimented with non-Western religious traditions were among the key progenitors of the "cyberculture" that shaped the discourse surrounding computers, digitalization, and eventually the Internet. In their view, the metaphysical tenets of Judeo-Christianity had been discredited by modern science, and its institutions had been compromised by their allegiances with the forces of avarice, imperialism, and conformity. Convinced that Asian and Native American religions provided the basis for a reconciliation between traditional enchantment and the world revealed by contemporary physics, writers such as Fritjof Capra, Gary Zukav, Robert Pirsig, and Stewart Brand contended that cybernetic technology portended a world in which personal autonomy and spiritual unity could be fostered through the unimpeded flow of information—the metaphysical substratum of the universe, even if apprehended differently by swamis, shamans, and scientists. So when Pirsig wrote in his best-selling *Zen and the Art of Motorcycle Maintenance* (1974)—one of the canonical texts of the countercultural imagination—that "the Buddha, the Godhead, resides just as comfortably in the circuits of a digital computer . . . as he does at the top of a mountain or in the petals of a flower," he hinted not only at the romance of cybernation but also at the ideological affiliation of countercultural mysticism and the emergent corporate world of research, networking, and techno-entrepreneurial zeal.[55]

One of the first and most tireless impresarios of the cyberculture, Brand was a prescient harbinger of the new technological sublime of capitalist enchantment. After graduating from Stanford and serving in the Army, Brand embarked on a spiritual odyssey in the early 1960s that led him to abandon

Christianity and embrace the metaphysical wisdom of the Blackfoot, Navajo, and Hopi tribes he visited in Arizona and New Mexico. Perusing McLuhan, Wiener, and rising stars of futurology such as Buckminster Fuller, Brand synthesized an eclectic blend of Native American spirituality and technological utopianism. As he wrote in 1964 in the personal journal he kept, the modern world was growing out of the desiccated "Protestant consciousness" of his youth and entering, with the help of electronics and automation, "an era of tribal endeavors and cosmic consciousness." Eager to experiment in post-Protestant sensibility, Brand dove into the nexus of the drug culture and the music industry, taking up with Ken Kesey and the Merry Pranksters to arrange the first "Trips Festival" in San Francisco in January 1966. Staged with the help of rock promoter Bill Graham—who together with Brand and Kesey cobbled together the LSD and the stroboscopic lights—the festival's psychedelic pageantry was a premonitory spectacle of hippie capitalism, replete with electronic media, sensory surrealism, and slick chromatic promotion.[56]

But Brand aspired to more than acid tests and rock concerts. Between 1966 and 1968, he led a campaign to force NASA to release what was then rumored to be a satellite photograph of the planet taken from space—the "whole earth" picture, as it was called. At the same time, Brand and his then-wife Lois ran a mobile Whole Earth Truck Store out of a 1963 Dodge truck. Traveling around the country, they enjoined hippies and other refugees from industrial perdition to start another "back-to-the-land" movement. Peddlers of countercultural yeomanry, they sold easy-to-use agricultural tools and domestic appliances to communes, and they allowed customers to order larger implements through an informal catalog they kept in the truck. Yet neither Brand's ruralism nor his promotion of what was then labeled "intermediate" or "alternative" technology that was friendlier both to the user and to nature signaled a repudiation of his earlier infatuation with cybernetics. Along with several prominent computer engineers and programmers associated with the Augmentation Research Center at Stanford, Brand participated in a December 1968 demonstration project—"The Mother of All Demos," as it was later remembered in the cyberculture—that showcased many of the features of contemporary personal computers: word processing, hypertext, and video conferencing.[57]

Brand's melange of aboriginal spirituality, ecological solicitude, and technological progressivism represented a vibrant amalgamation of the most popular and enduring currents of the counterculture, and like McLuhan, he became an entrepreneur of ideas. In the *Whole Earth Catalog* (1968) and the *Co-Evolution Quarterly* (1974), Brand and other techno-hippies both retailed alternative technologies and espoused a credo of cybernetic romanticism that echoed the transcendentalist enchantment of Emerson. "We *are* as gods and might as well get good at it," as Brand declared on the inside cover of every edition of the *Catalog*. Declaiming in the antihierarchical rhetoric of the New Left and the counterculture—rhetoric that morphed into "market populism" and the libertarian vernacular of Silicon Valley *ubermenschen*—Brand explained that he was "interested in the *Catalog* format being used for all manner of markets. . . . I'm for power to the people and responsibility to the people. Responsibility is individual stuff." Indeed, the *Catalog* read as a Sears and Roebuck for Emersonian divinity, hawking products that would enable the consumer to enter "a realm of intimate, personal power" in which he could "conduct his own education, find his own inspiration, [and] shape his own environment." Advertisements for gardening tools or calculators lay alongside visionary rhapsodies to information systems as beloved communities, replete with citations of Wiener, McLuhan, the *I Ching*, and Navajo folklore.[58]

Still, though presented as the savior from the Protestant malevolence of Fordist bureaucratic rationality, Brand's cyber-romanticism remained capitalist—albeit inflected with the flippancy of cool. "I've yet to figure out what capitalism is," he told an interviewer in 1970, "but if it's what we're doing, I dig it." Writing a new chapter in the technological sublime, Brand and his fellow cyber-mystics were indeed trying to "figure out what capitalism is"; conservative innovators of the technostructure, they forged the material and cultural milieu of post-Fordist accumulation. At its most grandiose, the cyberculture echoed McLuhan's pronouncement in a 1968 interview with *Playboy* that computers were creating "a Pentecostal condition" of unity in diversity; the computer, he rejoiced, promised "a state of absorption in the logos that could knit mankind into one family and create a perpetuity of collective harmony and peace." But cybercultural mysticism would find its ultimate incarnation in the predatory figure of Steve Jobs, whose status as a techno-visionary rested on the harshest conditions of industrial exploitation.[59] Although Brand clearly hoped that the supersession of Protestant industrialism and the spread of cybernation would inaugurate an age of digitalized communion, he assisted instead in creating a template for neoliberal technologies of the self and in wiring the ideological circuitry for the rise of a bohemian, technocratic plutocracy. The machines that would watch over all of us would not be imbued by any loving grace.

A similar preview of the new sensibility of capitalist enchantment was on display in advertising, the premiere iconographic factory of the spectacle. The "creative revolution" launched in the late 1950s accelerated over the ensuing decade, bringing the new strategies of desire into headlong embrace with countercultures outside the corporate world. For many younger image professionals, this meant substituting marijuana, LSD, or peyote for the standard elixirs of whiskey, gin, or martinis. Gesturing to the Day-Glo aesthetics associated with hippies, rock music, and hallucinogenic drugs, Dichter argued in a 1967 issue of *Advertising Age* that to "bring the product alive with new, more exciting meaning," admen need to practice "mind expansion" that would enable them to use "animation with psychedelic colors and motion." The elder statesman of market research wrote just as more and more artists, copywriters, and art directors were adopting the sartorial, recreational, and vernacular styles of the counterculture. Agencies and corporate art departments increasingly saw employees decked out in denims, flowered ties, Nehru jackets, and miniskirts, with men sporting longer hair, moustaches, and sideburns.[60]

The prevalence of drugs and therapy on Madison Avenue was less significant than the new sense of professionalism and aesthetic ambition that animated the creative revolutionaries. Especially in the "boutiques," creative antinomianism was the flip side of a revitalized conception of advertising as a profession. Advertisers in the 1960s were no less reliant than their predecessors on the scientific acumen of behavioral psychologists, market researchers, and other technicians of consciousness. This heightened awareness of professional stature dovetailed with a rehabilitation of aesthetic aspiration, the desire to wed commerce and fine art, to elevate the kitsch of mercantile imagery into the empyrean of the avant-garde. Creative revolutionaries admired the visual strategies of Roy Lichtenstein, Andy Warhol, and other pioneers of Pop Art, enlisting them both to associate their prod-

ucts with contemporary art and to validate their own sense of aesthetic sophistication. Like their corporate modernist forebears, "creative" advertisers
compared their work favorably to the museum art of the day. In a typical
proclamation in a 1965 issue of *Advertising Age,* one industry journalist
likened the portfolio of Doyle Dane Bernbach to the best not only of Pop
Artists (such as Warhol) but also of Paul Klee and earlier modernists.[61]

Yet admen eager to claim the mantle of fine art met Warhol and his con-
freres at precisely the moment when Pop artists were forsaking the modernist
vocation of "vanguard," erasing the boundaries between serious art and evanescent kitsch, and reveling in what critics had dismissed as the vulgarity
of mass-produced commodity culture. Relinquishing the ideal of aesthetic
autonomy that energized Jackson Pollack, Mark Rothko, and Barnett
Newman, they also eschewed their implicit disdain for the voluminous commodities of everyday life. Like the industrial designers of the interwar era,
Pop Artists ratified the aesthetic possibilities residing in mass production.
As Warhol later explained, they took as their subjects whatever "anybody
walking down Broadway could recognize ... comics, picnic tables, men's
trousers, celebrities, shower curtains, refrigerators, Coke bottles—all the
great modern things that the Abstract Expressionists tried so hard not to
notice at all." Pop Artists rejected the fervent and heroic spirituality of high-
modernist existentialism, emulating the works of mechanical reproduction
that threatened to put an end to the age of Art.[62]

But Pop Art's enthusiasm for commodity culture was not always what it
seemed. Especially when engaging Warhol's work, both detractors and celebrants of Pop Art have focused on its flatness or erasure of affect, its cheerfully empty replication of the glitzy aesthetics of celebrity culture. Warhol's
quip that "in the future, *everyone* will be famous for fifteen minutes" becomes either a herald of cultural democracy or a spectacular falsehood of
late capitalism, an oracle of—if there can be such a thing—the pathos of postmodernity. But one could also interpret Warhol's prophecy as a burlesque of
eschatological hope, a metamorphosis of exaltation into the luminosity of
marketing and promotion. As Robert Hughes once observed of Warhol's
silver-papered "Factory," where so many lost souls came seeking "approval
and forgiveness," it provided fame and absolution in "the only form American capitalism knows how to offer: publicity," whose gorgeous redemption
from banality is, Hughes noted, "a parody of Catholicism." Warhol's own

pictures of Elizabeth Taylor, Marilyn Monroe, and other stars represented, in Hughes words, "a sly and grotesque parody of the Madonna-fixations of Warhol's own Catholic childhood"—an upbringing he never altogether rejected.[63]

Warhol's fondness for "the great modern things" partook of a fervent, postmodern devotion. A consummate entrepreneur, Warhol was a celebrant in the liturgy of the spectacle, merging the machinery of mass-produced aura with the aesthetics of the sacramental imagination. He certainly made no secret of his mercenary estimation of art; as he put it flatly in *The Philosophy of Andy Warhol* (1975), "being good in business is the most fascinating kind of art . . . good business is the best art." Indeed, Warhol pronounced in art-historical fashion that "business art is the step that comes after Art." He underlined the point with a mite of wisdom deduced straight from the tenets of pecuniary metaphysics: if you want to buy a $200,000 painting, "you should take that money, tie it up, and hang it on the wall. Then when someone visited you the first thing they would see is the money on the wall."[64] According to the narrative of disenchantment, this would seem to mark the utter secularization of art, its complete absorption into commerce and the final annulment of its critical capacity. But if capitalism itself is a metamorphosis of the sacred, and if "the spectacle" represents a sacramental vision refracted through the lens of ironic detachment, then another account becomes possible: Warhol as iconographer of the spectacle, a virtuoso of prefabbed, disposable aura and its trashy pastiche of enchantment.

Warhol's commodity sacramentalism originated in the Byzantine Catholic religious culture of his youth. Born in 1928 in a working-class suburb of Pittsburgh, Andrew Warhola grew up in an impoverished Carpathian-Russian immigrant family. His mother, Julia, "liked going to church better than material things," filling the Warhola home with icons and attending a Byzantine Catholic church. Like the icons of other Orthodox traditions, those of Byzantine Catholicism were believed not only to represent the divine or its emissaries (saints, holy men and women, in addition to Christ and the Virgin Mary) but also to establish their real presence to the viewer, the kind of contact with the supernal afforded even more viscerally by the bread and wine of the Eucharist. The making of icons was never considered an aesthetic activity to be pursued for personal expression; icons were intended to be unoriginal copies of earlier images. Byzantine iconography had a variety of formats—circles, ovals, diptychs, and triptychs—and its premiere color was gold, the consecrated hue of holiness and eternity. After he graduated from the Carnegie Institute of Technology in 1949, Warhol left Pittsburgh for New York, dropped the "a" and became Andy Warhol, and worked throughout the 1950s doing commercial illustrations—for Bonwit Teller, Tiffany's, *McCall's, Harper's Bazaar,* and *Glamour*—populated by gold-embossed birds, cherubs, angels, magi, and Holy Families.[65]

Warhol incorporated the formal aspects of Byzantine iconography into Pop Art, evoking the sacramental power of icons for the American denomination of the spectacle. Rooted in the modernist shibboleth that art must stand athwart the world of mass production, the incomprehension and derision that Pop artists elicited indicated that their critics missed the point: as Warhol explained, "Pop Art is a way of liking things," a celebration of those "great modern things" that comprise the humble matter of everyday life—a realm where, in Orthodox tradition, the divine always manifests itself sacramentally. On the simplest level of imitation, his Campbell's Soup cans and Coca-Cola bottles—mass-produced objects with no personal signature—recalled the anonymity and deliberate repetitiveness of Byzantine iconographers. The reworking of Byzantine sacramental aesthetics is even more evident in Warhol's gilded, silk-screened portraiture of celebrities, the shooting stars in the firmament of the spectacle: the simulacra of Marilyn Monroe, Elizabeth Taylor, Jackie Kennedy, Elvis Presley, and other idols of the marketplace constituted a portfolio of postmodern enchantment.[66] Yet while Warhol transubstantiated the elite of mass culture into a communion of saints and madonnas, the silk-screening also highlighted the artifice of celebrity, underlining their status as creatures of mass production. The pecuniary imagery of the spectacle had never procured so sincere and grotesque a consecration.

Warhol's eucharistic parodies remained largely the chic of museums and galleries, but the work of his friend Peter Max reached a broader, less ferociously modish audience. Despite his adulation of celebrities and commodities, Warhol was never quite condemned as a "sellout": Pop Art's conflation of art and consumerism was still provocative enough to absorb the cachet that still clung to the notion of the avant-garde. Max never impressed the aesthetic aristocracy, but he did outrage countercultural ideologues. Even in the 1960s, critics vilified Max as a flamboyant traitor whose talent for psychedelic—and lucrative—illustration betrayed the aesthetic and spiritual ideals of the counterculture. Yet this verdict presumes that Max indeed violated some countercultural essence or ideal. As Max often asserted, even at the peak of his fame and imitability, he never perceived the slightest contradiction between spiritual self-discovery and pecuniary aggrandizement. Like Maxfield Parrish, Max was an audacious vendor of enchantment impervious to the sneers of the cultural elite.[67]

Born in Berlin in 1937, Max was brought by his Jewish parents to Shanghai in the following year to escape persecution by the Nazis. While growing up in Shanghai, Max lived near Buddhist and Hindu monasteries—an obvious source of the spiritual ambience of his later illustrations—and developed a lifelong fondness for Chinese and Japanese art. His father moved the family to Haifa when the state of Israel was formed in 1948, and then to Brooklyn five years later. Enrolling in the Art Students League in 1956, Max soon switched to the School of Visual Arts where, like many of his friends, he was torn between the aesthetic heroism of the modernist avant-garde and the siren appeals of the advertising business. Though professing to seek "a new form of expression that was not limited by the constraints of the market," Max followed other graduates into advertising. Once passionate to emulate Picasso or Pollack, "we discussed dynamic concepts," he later recalled, but now "for ads, book and magazine covers, record albums, and posters."[68]

Max never apologized for being an adept and well-remunerated professional producer of images. In the early 1960s, he ran a small advertising studio with a friend from the School of Visual Arts, making ads and illustrations for book publishers and record companies that garnered considerable attention in the industry. Yet while finding inspiration, like Lichtenstein and Warhol, in the pulpy ephemera of mass culture—comic books, movie posters, and billboards—Max found himself seeking out larger, more transcendent sources. Though not religious "in an orthodox sense," he felt stricken by some spiritual malaise in the midst of his success by the middle of the decade. In the summer of 1966, Max spent three straight sixteen-hour days working on a collage that he hoped, in representing "a cosmic truth," would afford him "a glimpse into the grand scheme of things and the meaning of life." Exhausted and frustrated by his inability to see into the "scheme," Max experienced an epiphany. As he remembered the episode some years later, a white-bearded man appeared out of a cloud and nodded, "as if to say, 'It's all right. I will come.'"[69]

The man in the cloud soon arrived, and Max finally understood "the grand scheme of things." A week after his vision, anticipating "something wonderful," his friend Conrad Rooks (heir to the Avon cosmetics fortune) introduced Max to Swami Satchidananda, an Indian yogi then living in Sri Lanka. (Though Max was reluctant to help Rooks make a movie with the Swami, Allen Ginsberg, and William S. Burroughs, he relented when his friend handed him "a very large check.") Under the Swami's guidance, Max took his first lessons in yoga and opened up a "vast creative reservoir," an "interior space" that seemed "just as vast as the enormity of outer space"; indeed, "they seemed to be one and the same." Although the Swami was supposed to return to Sri Lanka, Max insisted that he remain and share his spiritual enlightenment with other Americans. (Bringing the Swami to the United States was, Max later claimed, "the most spiritual and patriotic thing I have ever done.")[70]

Max's spiritual renewal—sanctified by very large checks—was a truly Aquarian moment. After meeting the Swami, "all the planets lined up for me"; the acres of diamonds once promised by the Protestant God were now sown by yogi. By the late 1960s, Max's ad illustrations and posters were netting him a multimillion dollar income. "Madison Avenue was a great education," he later mused. "I learned what the world was about." Hired by General Electric, Wrangler, Burlington Mills, Coca-Cola, and other corporations, he owned five advertising and design companies and licensed fifty others to use his work on dishes, napkins, belts, gloves, and shopping bags. He swanned through parties with Donovan, Andy Warhol, and the Beatles, and he mugged with Ed Sullivan and Johnny Carson. The peak experience of Max's celebrity came in September 1969, when *Life* profiled him in an admiring "Portrait of the Artist as a Very Rich Man." (On the day the issue appeared, Max was sitting in Time-Life's boardroom with the magazine's editors—and Warhol. "Oh, Peter, now you're a household name," the elfin Warhol sighed.)[71]

Thanks to his meteoric rise and enshrinement in the vault of popular culture, Max attracted widespread criticism and mockery as a countercultural fraud—the hippie with the Midas touch. One writer in *Esquire* tagged him in December 1970 as a "hip capitalist" whose fame and fortune demonstrated conclusively that the counterculture had been coopted by the corporate order. While this account assumed a pristine counterculture, it could have pointed to the secret of commodity fetishism, the desire for enchantment that was so obviously an element in Max's prolific imagery. As Max cheerfully told *Life*, "I try to give warmth to machine-made objects"—a description that makes sense not only of his work for corporations but also of his even more popular posters as well, all of which floated in serene continuity with the oldest aspirations of advertising. Composed in a Fauvist variation of Pop Art, Max's posters depicted a cosmopolitan, anarcho-psychedelic beloved community: gurus, gods, goddesses, flower children, cosmic butterflies, and levitating yogi, unfettered by the laws of gravity as they swirled over lakes, hills, meadows, and mountains. Like Maxfield Parrish's dreamy tableaux of fairy tale monarchs and idling lovers, Max's fluorescent community sought to capture or impute some "spirit of the thing," to convey some blissful freshness permeating the grand scheme or meaning of life. In the dorm rooms, art galleries, and recording studios where Max's republic of beauty resided, the Romantic sacramental imagination endured—on sufferance, for a price. *Life*'s cover illustration for its profile underscored perfectly the commodification of enchantment. Max's big, toothy smile was superimposed over a riot of stars, clouds, planets, and rainbows—a poster that, peeled back slightly, revealed underlying columns of green dollar signs.[72] As Max learned on Madison Avenue, the grand scheme of things and the meaning of life radiated with the monetary metaphysics of capital.

Max's world of supple and iridescent mobility—powered, as *Life* so crassly acknowledged, by the augmentation of surplus value—offered a spectacular premonition of the moral imagination of neoliberal capitalism. Draped in Brooks Brothers suits and accessorized with the latest electronic gadgetry, his figures could have stepped from the pages of Alvin Toffler's *Future Shock* (1970), a best-selling ware in the middle-class market in anxiety about the cultural and technological horizon. A former labor columnist for *Fortune* and a freelance consultant for IBM, Xerox, and AT&T, Toffler had spent a decade perusing the latest developments in cybernetic technology, management theory, psychology, and social forecasting. Written with the bracing and relentless momentum of historical inevitability, *Future Shock* was a glossy, breathless compendium of the corporate counterculture. Hailing the arrival of a "new Atlantis" in the midst of a "super-industrial society," and denouncing resistance to the cybernetic revolution as "Rousseauite romanticism," Toffler studded his book of revelations with marvels invented or imagined in the laboratories of the scientific and technological estate: cyborgs, space travel, underwater cities, and cloning and other forms of bioengineering, wonders formerly considered the fantasy world of comic strips and science fiction. But the greatest prodigies were new human beings, the cybernauts of digitalized destiny: freelance professionals, Theory Y managers, technical designers, and specialists—the "advance agents of man," the avant-garde of the twenty-first century. Like Max's limber and sprightly gurus, they comprised "a new race of nomads": "modular men," as Toffler dubbed them, pathfinders on the superindustrial frontier whose personal and professional lives were incessantly "changing, fluid, and varied."[73] These were the icons of flexibility outlined in countercultural management literature, the instigators of permanent creative revolutions in technology, culture, and business.

In Toffler's avid prognostication, the emerging political economy was a Theory Y paradise of decentralization, pivoting on a social and personal plasticity unprecedented in history. Rapid job turnover, Toffler wrote, would reflect both technological displacement and "the mergers and acquisitions" mandated as industries "frantically organize and reorganize themselves" in response to market conditions. Convinced that top-down bureaucracies faced imminent extinction, Toffler predicted that capitalist firms would evolve into "fast-moving, information-rich, kinetic organizations, filled with transient cells and extremely mobile individuals." This was the creative destruction of capitalism at its most militant and irrepressible, and it echoed other popular books such as Robert Townsend's *Up the Organization* (1970), in which the author—a former executive at Avis—admonished the managerial fraternity to pulverize the bureaucratic behemoths of corporate America. Praising Ho Chi Minh and the Viet Cong, Townsend called for a permanent revolution in business: managers and executives must cultivate "a passionate hatred for institutions and their practices."[74]

Reminiscent of Marx's and Engels's tempestuous account of capitalist dynamism—"uninterrupted disturbance of all social conditions, everlasting uncertainty and agitation"—Toffler's account of superindustrial society pivoted on a new kind of selfhood. Like the market whose accelerating velocity cast everything and everyone into constant oblivion, "modular man" had to cultivate a talent for perpetual, remorseless self-transformation. Thanks to the escalating rate of change triggered by "flexible" capitalism, the stable and dependable self of the classic bourgeois moral imagination had to yield to a protean model of evanescent, "serial selves," as Toffler put it. Needing to travel light in the world of hypermobility, modular men and women could not (and apparently would not want to) establish exclusive and enduring ties to companies, communities, or individuals, preferring relationships of "medium or short duration" and making "numerous and rapid on-off clicks in their interpersonal lives." Professionally, the modular person was "basically uncommitted to any organization"; personally, he sported a Whitmanesque multitude of identities, each expendable at the slightest dip in the market or fear of emotional entanglement.[75] Exhibiting optimal flexibility, capacity for teamwork, and eupsychian personal agility, these elastic corporations and the cadres who staffed them fulfilled every dream of cybernetic and management literature.

Thanks especially to cybertechnology, they would also raise the spectacle to a new level of hegemony, reproducing the religious illusion with even greater sophistication and potency in the means of enchantment. Having moved from material to symbolic commodities, modular capitalism, Toffler wrote, would accelerate "the psychologization of all production." On the level of mass culture, Toffler pictured "great globe-girdling syndicates"—"psych-corps"—specializing in the construction of "super-Disneys of a variety, scale, and emotional power that is hard for us to imagine." Crafting "fantastic simulations" and "complex live environments," the professionals employed by psychological corporations would peruse "the pages of Krafft-Ebing and the Marquis de Sade for ideas." The Marquis might have reminded Toffler that the scrutiny of the psyche by experts promised not only new market research in desire but also invaluable lessons in the science and technology of domination. Toffler himself extolled the merits of "exact scientific knowledge, expertly applied to the crucial, most sensitive points of social control," noting that psychologists were already devising "Time and Emotion Forecasts" to assess the energy "invested" in various activities. Conceding that these techniques were still "crude tools for personal planning," Toffler trusted that further research would yield "sharper instruments, more sensitive to differences in probability, more refined and insight-yielding."[76] However democratic its rhetoric, the regime of "flexibility" possessed its own uniquely capillary forms of unaccountable power, suffused by the gorgeously obsolescent imagery of a cyber-capitalist oligarchy. "Flexibility" depended on a fabulous, panoptical machinery of entertainment and surveillance—the highest stage of alienation and fetishism yet reached in the history of the spectacle. Presenting the future in the present tense, Toffler's portrait of "modular man" was a kind of realized eschatology: the elastic personality of spectacular capitalism was already here, dismantling the corporate commonwealth.

# 26

# The New Testament of Capitalism

The Resurgence of Evangelical Enchantment
and the Theology of Neoliberalism

TOFFLER'S "MODULAR MAN" WAS not the only existential prototype of the corporate counterculture. Shortly before he died in 1970, Maslow had composed an encomium to postmodern strivers in "Theory Z," a step beyond Douglas McGregor's Theory Y toward the final consummation of managerial philosophy. Theory Z idealized "transcendence," the achievement of "peak experiences" that constituted "the most precious aspect of life." As in Maslow's earlier work, transcendence and peak experience both restated traditional religious longings for sanctification and reduced them to vapid but uplifting clichés. "Transcenders," as Maslow dubbed them, were "highly creative or talented people": "poets, mystics, seers, profoundly religious men," but they could be found among "businessmen, industrialists, [and] managers" as well as among writers, artists, and musicians. Prone to being "innovators, discoverers of the new," transcenders inhabited a celestial realm well beyond the uncreative common clay; indeed, they are "more awe-inspiring, more 'unearthly,' more godlike" than their merely average fellow mortals. Gifted with a consecrating touch, "they can sacralize anything at will"; endowed with exceptional wisdom, they "could sit down and in five minutes write a recipe for peace, brotherhood, and happiness."[1]

Maslow's risible anointment of the capitalist class and its stewards reflected a revival of the entrepreneurial ideal that was already well under way. One of the common criticisms of the Organization Man was his aversion to risk and adventure, a preference for security that restrained the "creative destruction" endemic to capitalism. Among most corporate countercultural ideologues, this criticism never rose to the level of a challenge to the New Deal. But criticism of conformity was not restricted to countercultural business reformers and liberal social critics. In the immensely popular novels and philosophical broadsides of Ayn Rand, for instance, the figure of the entrepreneur—stifled at least as much by mediocrity as by any leviathan welfare state—connoted not only the creativity of capitalism but also its existential sublimity as well.

Rand's rehabilitation of the entrepreneur was bound up with a resurgence of belief in the moral and economic benefits of unregulated markets— "neoliberalism," as it is now called. The genealogy of neoliberalism stretches back at least to the 1940s, when an aspiring hegemonic bloc of intellectuals and business leaders hostile to the New Deal commenced an eventually successful crusade to recover the holy land of unfettered accumulation. Joined by conservative Protestant clergy and businesspeople baptized in the evangelical dispensation, neoliberals, in this account, both undermined the New Deal order and reinstituted a pristine culture of capitalism. The relative prosperity and tranquility of "the golden age of capitalism" hindered their quest for recognition and power; but the global economic crisis of the early 1970s created auspicious conditions for an assault on American liberalism and European social democracy and the restoration of the ancien régime. Stagnation and falling profits provoked capital throughout the North Atlantic to unilaterally break the social truce. Spearheaded by Margaret Thatcher and Ronald Reagan in the 1980s, and supplied with legitimacy by the new prominence and vigor of neoliberal academics and journalists, the ensuing forty-year assault on organized labor and the welfare state issued in a resounding victory for corporate business—brought to a head in the late 1990s by Bill Clinton and Tony Blair. In Thatcher's ominous declaration of triumph, "there is no alternative," either in reality or in the imagination. As David Harvey writes, neoliberalism has been both "a *utopian* project to realize a theoretical design for the reorganization of international capitalism" and "a *political* project to re-establish the conditions for capital accumulation and to restore the power of economic elites."[2]

Just how utopian neoliberalism is has not been appreciated until recently. While Harvey emphasizes political economy, Wendy Brown and Philip Mirowski have argued that neoliberals are much more totalizing in their ambitions. For neoliberals, Brown argues, the market becomes a Platonic epitome, "the true form of all activity"; they seek, Mirowski writes, to re-weave "the entire fabric of society" by "increasingly erasing any distinctions among the state, society, and the market." Much more than a paradigm of politics and markets, neoliberalism is an attempt to remake all of human life in the crucible of capital accumulation, right down to the recesses of personal identity. In the neoliberal imagination, a human being is, in Mirowski's words, an "entrepreneurial self," a package of vendible talents and qualities: "a product to be sold, a walking advertisement . . . a jumble of assets to be invested . . . an offsetting inventory of liabilities to be pruned, outsourced, shorted, hedged against, and minimized." Promulgating a "catechism of perpetual metamorphosis," neoliberalism denies the existence of a "true," invariant self and celebrates the "eminently flexible" personality always willing to submit to the unimpeachable verdicts of the all-sovereign market.[3] Encapsulated in Toffler's "modular man," neoliberal freedom is absolute subservience to the dictates of the market.

Mirowski's characterization of neoliberalism as a "catechism" suggests that it constitutes a moral and metaphysical imagination. Neoliberals, he writes, admonish the individual to relinquish her "selfish arrogance" and "humbly prostrate . . . before the Wisdom of the Universe"—a Wisdom contemplated with reverent awe by Friedrich Hayek and President Reagan. Justifying the ways of the market to mere mortals, Hayek insisted that the "spontaneous order" of competitive enterprise must not be disrupted by fallible human judgments. The Wisdom of the Market is inscrutable yet beneficent; as Reagan mused in 1982, "there really is something magic about the marketplace when it's free to operate." Indeed, "in an age when words took on magical properties," Daniel Rodgers maintains, "no word flew higher or assumed a greater aura of enchantment than 'market.'" This triumph of pecuniary enchantment in the form of neoliberalism marked the consummation of a quest that had animated the most visionary and energetic elements of Cold War conservatism. As DuPont executive Jasper Crane wrote to a friend near the end of World War II, Christianity "made little progress until . . . it had the writings of the New Testament; Communism got nowhere until Marx wrote *Das Kapital* . . . National Socialism needed *Mein Kampf* to be effective." What businessmen require, Crane concluded, was a "New Testament of capitalism," a "'bible' of free enterprise" that delineated the inerrant and inviolable edicts of the Market.[4]

The victory of neoliberalism in the United States stemmed, in part, from the endurance of Protestant evangelical enchantment. Although the Great Depression and the New Deal had seemed to discredit the evangelical dispensation, in the South—an enormous beneficiary of New Deal programs—evangelical religious culture fueled a dogged suspicion of activist government, part of a selective aversion to large-scale institutions that reflected the populist legacy. Southern evangelicals affirmed what Darren Dochuk has dubbed a "plain-folks" ideology, a modern evolutionary descendant of *herrenvolk* democracy: white supremacy, patriarchal dominance, small government, antipathy toward cultural and economic elites, and the Protestant work ethic. They "conflated the doctrines of Jefferson and Jesus" and longed for the restoration of the middling splendors of the Protestant producer's republic. At the same time, as long as labor unions and big government were not perceived as threats to the sacred groves of the proprietary order, they were welcomed as envoys from a helpful providence.[5]

This *herrenvolk* modernity enabled corporations in the South to prosper from what Bethany Morton has archly called "federally subsidized free enterprise." After World War II, Southern workers and farmers rapidly shed their antagonism to corporate capital and embraced a newfangled version of the old evangelical gospel of wealth. Whether displaced by agricultural modernization or attracted by the prospect of escape from poverty, millions of white evangelicals migrated from the South to the West, and especially to southern California, where federal military spending was bankrolling the erection of a corporate fantasia: aerospace, electronics, and information firms, alongside services, entertainment, and recreation—a live diorama of the post-Fordist future stretching from Bentonville to Disneyland. Thus when God's suburban warriors denounced what one preacher cursed as the New Deal's "pagan statism," they vilified the same infidel colossus whose regular subventions underwrote their prosperity.[6]

Sun Belt evangelicals were not the abstemious folk of antebellum or populist producerism; like suburban consumers elsewhere, they took their affluence to be manna from heaven, material grace of a providential market. When they railed against the welfare state and its socialist subsidies to heathen indolence and recalled the nation to the covenant theology of Christian capitalist enchantment, they recast the jeremiad as a redemptive account of virtuous, domestic consumerism. As Lisa McGirr observes, "they enjoyed the fruits of consumer culture, reveled in their worldly success . . . [and] found the suburban world of tract homes, private developments, and decentralized living space to their liking." In Orange County as in Puritan Salem, religion and profit could jump together; the neo-evangelical city in a valley was, in Dochuk's words, "a 'Christ enchanted' society," a promised land of high-tech abundance produced and ensured by the old-time religion.[7] Embracing economic and technological innovation while holding on to biblical inerrancy, Sun Belt evangelicals were reactionary modernist pioneers of the new cybernetic capitalism. Evangelicals became, by the mid-1970s, the amen chorus of corporate enchantment.

The most extensive and exuberant promulgation of evangelical capitalism came from a right-wing, lay intelligentsia, a cultural apparatus of colleges, universities, seminaries, para-church organizations, and publishing firms, flush with money from Howard J. Pew of Sun Oil and other Protestant business leaders. Proper religious indoctrination was central to the survival of capitalism, in Pew's view; if businesspeople "want to be free to continue in business, the leadership of the people of our country must believe in the fundamentals of Christianity." Convinced that higher education was occupied by Satan's minions—that is, New Deal liberals and socialists—evangelicals formed an archipelago of "Bible colleges" and other academic venues where Christians were instructed in a modern synthesis of biblical theology and neoclassical economics. George Pepperdine, for instance, had founded Pepperdine College in 1937 to protect students from the "cynical and materialistic professors" who corrupted young Christians at secular institutions. Pepperdine explicitly conceived of his college as a "school for workers"; under "conservative, fundamental Christian supervision," all Pepperdine's students received intensive instruction in "Business Administration and preparation for commercial life."[8]

The evangelical industrial-educational complex churned out graduates who often joined lay church groups committed to building God's city of business. For example, the Christian Business Men's Committee International included entrepreneurs, managers, and professionals who espoused an updated proprietary vision of "stewardship" and biblical paternalism. Protestant business crusaders could also join the American Council of Christian Laymen, the Committee for Constitutional Government, or Spiritual Mobilization, led by Rev. James Fifield—Los Angeles' "apostle to millionaires"—and funded by Pew, Crane, and Hutchinson. Committed to fighting the accursed New Deal, Spiritual Mobilization published a journal, *Faith and Freedom*, that featured a vitriolic stable of contributors, including Rev. Edmund A.

Opitz, who based his opposition to taxes and redistribution on the eighth commandment's injunction against theft; R. J. Rushdoony, the Calvin of "dominionist" or "Christian Reconstructionist" theology; and Murray Rothbard, a secular libertarian who wrote under a pseudonym until his atheism was discovered. Many of these writers also belonged to the Christian Freedom Foundation (backed by Pew and headed by Howard E. Kershner, who also edited *Christian Economics,* the Foundation's periodical) or to the Foundation for Economic Education. The Foundation for Economic Education was supported by Pierre Goodrich and led by Leonard Read, a member of Fifield's congregation, general manager of the Los Angeles branch of the Chamber of Commerce, and editor of the *Freeman,* an ecumenical venue for religious and secular libertarians.[9]

Kershner and Read were the best-known evangelists of the good news of laissez-faire. A conservative Quaker who grew increasingly alienated from "the Socialist Society of Friends," Kershner had been a friend and collaborator with another Quaker, Herbert Hoover. After a successful career in real estate and manufacturing, Kershner devoted himself to humanitarianism, working as director of European relief for the American Friends Service Committee in the early years of World War II. Kershner joined with Pew in soliciting money and support from Norman Vincent Peale and other right-wing pastors to found *Christian Economics* in 1950. A vehicle of "free enterprise—the economic system with the least amount of government and the greatest amount of Christianity," *Christian Economics* peaked at 200,000 biweekly readers in the early 1960s. Until the Pew family stopped covering the magazine's losses in 1972, Kershner occupied a national pulpit in the Church of Jesus Christ, Free Market Economist, proclaiming that "the laws of economics are part of the laws of God."[10]

Outlined lucidly in *God, Gold, and Government* (1957), Kershner's "Christian economics" placed a biblical imprimatur on competitive, hard-money capitalism, embedding the free market and the Protestant work ethic in a theo-metallic metaphysics and cosmology. Kershner's world was charged with the grandeur of divinity; hidden inside invisible atoms, he wrote, lies "the infinite power of God." The universe is "the handiwork of God," and since economics laws are divine legislation, conventional economic theory was not only science but theology as well. Thus, as God's primer on all of creation, "the Bible is the greatest book on business ever written"; those who lived in accordance with the business advice dispensed therein would be "free, self-governing, and prosperous." Insisting on the moral and religious imperative of hard-money financial policies, Kershner considered a gold-backed dollar the only reliable currency of divine omnipotence. In Kershner's goldbug theology, the defense of Christianity was inseparable from the restoration of the gold standard and the renewal of proprietary moralism. The "revival of real religion," he asserted, went hand in hand with the "reestablishment of honest money of intrinsic value" and a return to "the ancient virtues of hard work, thrift, and upright living."[11]

Kershner's theo-metallic metaphysics found popular expression in Read's strange essay "I, Pencil," first published in the *Freeman* in December 1958 and soon a classic of free-market philosophy. Born to an impoverished family in Michigan, Read was a hardscrabble businessman and autodidact resentful of the condescension he felt from liberal political and cultural elites. Alarmed by the popularity of the New Deal, Read joined Fifield, economist and *Business Week* editor Virgil Jordan, and other prominent southern California businessmen in calling for a concerted intellectual insurgency against reform and regulation, and "I, Pencil" was an accessible manifesto for the metaphysics of laissez-faire. Describing the production of a pencil as a global thaumaturgy of capitalism, "I, Pencil" fused theology and commercial cosmology into a narrative of market animism. Declaring itself "a complex combination of miracles," Read's Pencil avowed "the miraculousness which I symbolize," a wonder deriving not only from God but even more from human fabrication. "Since only God can make a tree," the Pencil insisted that "only God could make me"—"God" apparently meaning the entire process of production, something Read asserted was more marvelous than divine creation itself: "I am a mystery—more so than a tree or a sunset." The metaphysics of the market imparted this sublunary glamour to everyday objects as well as reconciled the autonomy of individuals with the irrevocable laws of economics. When we hold a pencil as the outcome of an unplanned but beneficent mechanism, "we find the Invisible Hand at work" orchestrating order from the apparent anarchy of self-interest.[12]

If plain-folks corporate modernity was the true and only heaven for millions of evangelicals, other right-wing intellectuals linked the proprietary legacy to what became known as neoliberal economics and political philosophy. The resurgent conservative movement that erupted in response to the

New Deal; the new generation of neoclassical economists associated with the University of Chicago, the Mount Pelerin Society, and other venues; and a cluster of writers, especially Ayn Rand, who popularized entrepreneurial values and libertarian political ideas—these overlapping circles formed the rising hegemonic vanguard of neoliberal capitalism. The new American right was far from monolithic: conservatives such as Russell Kirk and Richard Weaver looked askance on cosmopolitan corporations, and secularists such as Rand loathed Catholics such as William F. Buckley, Jr. But while they thought themselves besieged and persecuted by a (phantom) liberal consensus, their impact on the American moral and political imagination proved immense and indelible. Even—and perhaps especially—where neoliberalism was purportedly secular or disenchanted, it served to divinize market forces and exalt the entrepreneurial self, affirming the most complete apotheosis of pecuniary metaphysics in the history of capitalism.[13]

Although Lionel Trilling once memorably dismissed postwar conservatism as a set of "irritable mental gestures which seek to resemble ideas," its champions actually constituted a diverse and vigorous intellectual movement. Indeed, when Richard Hofstadter called in 1955 for "a formidable and reasoned body of conservative criticism," he demonstrated a broader liberal illiteracy about conservative intellectual life. There was already such a "reasoned body," one of whose major components was the agrarian localism of Richard Weaver and Russell Kirk. Weaver's *Ideas Have Consequences* (1948) and Kirk's *The Conservative Mind* (1953) were two of the canonical texts of postwar conservatism, both condensing dyspepsia at modern life and holding out the hope of reactionary restoration. Kirk and Weaver articulated a metaphysics of property, a materialism that rejected conventional economics and recast its successor as a handmaiden of theology. Believing that "a divine intent rules society as well as conscience"—a supernatural will anchored in a "natural aristocracy" of intelligence, morality, and vigor—Kirk concluded that "political problems, at bottom, are religious and moral problems." Since "property and freedom are inseparably connected," Kirk assumed that the bond was a godly decree, and that the status of property was emblematic of a society's spiritual condition.[14]

At this point, Weaver took up the banner of the Southern Agrarians, emerging as the exemplary metaphysician of conservative economics. Weaver asserted that humans fulfilled their nature, in part, through the use of matter, and so the acquisition and maintenance of property was a "meta-physical right." Just as a man bore a likeness to God, so property originated in a "mystery of imprint and assimilation" through which "man becomes identified with his things." Serving as a "sanctuary" for personality, property was a sacramental token, a medium through which "the person is at once conscious of his relationship to the transcendental and the living commu-nity." Weaver's conception of property underlay his aversion to the corpora-tion. "The abstract property of stocks and bonds, the legal ownership of en-terprises never seen" severed the connection between "man and his substance" and reduced "metaphysical right" to abstract, diabolical power. In his view, only the restoration of actual, working proprietorship over land and tools could heal the alienation between man and his sacramental nature.[15]

Weaver and Kirk might have been expected to call for the abolition of cor-porate capitalism and the revival of family proprietorship. Yet however nos-talgic they may have been for the dung-scented air of agrarian integrity, they, along with most other "conservatives," made a separate peace with corpo-rate business. On this score, they demonstrated the veracity of Corey Rob-in's analysis of "the reactionary mind": that conservatism has been, at bottom, less a concern for the preservation of tradition than "an animus against the agency of the subordinate classes," a determination that society remain "a federation of private dominions," especially in the workplace and the family. Kirk proved more ready than Weaver to reconcile "tradition" and modernity. To be sure, Kirk railed against "the age of the machine [and] the hellhole city," and issued summary indictments: "an indiscriminate destruc-tion of variety" by mass production, a disfigurement of "loveliness" by ad-vertising, and a desecration of "ancient rights" by commercial freedom and unlimited democracy. These depredations were the work of the new, non-propertied elites in the professional-managerial class, who were usually, he claimed, "recruited from the mob of the spiritually impoverished." Kirk con-cluded that a new conservative order could take root only among a faithful remnant of small merchants, bankers, and manufacturers, and so he called for the rehabilitation of the "old-style libertarian democracy"—the *herren-volk* order of yesteryear—against "the planners of the new order."[16]

This libertarian democracy would find its leaders, Kirk hoped, among small-town propertied notables, whom he now discovered to be "the great prop of American conservatism." As in the evangelical dispensation, male entrepreneurs played starring roles as executors of divine intent; businessmen composed a branch of the "natural aristocracy" who comprehended the transcendent will that structured and leavened any healthy social hierarchy. With property as the token of natural nobility, socialism or any other form of rule by the proletarian rabble was perverse as well as calamitous, for "domination by mediocrity is contrary to the will of nature." Of course, Kirk had to make concessions to the grubby realities of provincial business culture. Though often ignorant and "inordinately vain," these local grandees respected hard work, self-control, concern for the future, and the responsibilities of property ownership; even their prejudices were usually "generous and sound."[17] Diligent, faithful, and agreeably philistine, Kirk's petty-bourgeois archangel of providence was a stock figure straight from central casting, walking and grumbling amiably right out of the *Saturday Evening Post.* Kirk's elevation of small business owners into a "natural aristocracy" betrayed the perennial desire at the heart of the reactionary lineage: the protection of property and rank from democracy, not fidelity to "tradition." More committed to hierarchy than to Edmund Burke's "cake of custom," conservatives could make their peace with capitalism while weeping for a world lost to avarice.

Kirk and Weaver's *herrenvolk* enchantment was rejected by another, more acerbic and bellicose wing of the Cold War right: businesspeople, economists, political philosophers, journalists, and other writers who were the direct progenitors of "neoliberalism." Corporate executives bankrolled a labyrinth of institutes, foundations, and periodicals; economists extended the moral purview of neoclassical economics; philosophers turned the market from a site of commerce and production into a fundamental ontological reality; journalists and novelists spread the nascent evangel of laissez-faire to millions of middle-class readers. Yet while they eventually aligned with evangelical modernists and conservative libertarians—an alliance of convenience convened beneath the sign of the hallowed Entrepreneur—this movement constituted something far broader and more incisive than a revival of the old covenant theology. Neoliberalism marked a pure culture of capitalism, the most pristine regime of pecuniary enchantment, a covenant theology of pure market power first adumbrated in Emersonian transcendentalism.

Hosannas to laissez-faire from business executives comprised a sizeable portion of the market in middlebrow neoliberalism. Such volumes as Monsanto CEO Edgar M. Queeny's *The Spirit of Enterprise* (1943), industrial consultant Ernest L. Klein's *How to Stay Rich* (1950), and GM customer research director Henry Grady Weaver's *The Mainspring of Human Progress* (1953) added little but banal expressions of piety to the lineage of the philosopher-executive. A more sophisticated and deadly zeal for the market quickened the ranks of economists and philosophers devoted to vanquishing the welfare state and installing an untrammeled capitalist order. Associated chiefly with the "Chicago School" of neoclassical economics and the Mont Pelerin Society of intellectuals, businesspeople, politicians, and reformers pledged to the restoration of unregulated markets, what became known as "neoliberalism" appeared to originate in classical liberal anxiety at the growth of state power in the liberal and social democracies of the North Atlantic. Averse both to the term and to the ambience of "conservatism," many of the earliest neoliberals insisted that they were *liberals,* even radicals. Hayek referred to himself as an "Old Whig" who cherished liberty, reason, and progress, and he berated the conservative lineage so beloved by Kirk for its wariness of science and its disparagement of technology. Besides, he pointed out, conservatism's "modern votaries . . . invariably find themselves appealing to authors"—Tocqueville, Acton, or Macaulay—"who regarded themselves as liberals." In *Capitalism and Freedom* (1962), one of the charter documents of postwar libertarianism, Friedman capped his case against state certification of physicians by asserting that "liberal principles do not justify licensure." Lamenting that "liberalism" had been stolen and corrupted by Keynesian enthusiasts for activist government, Friedman continued to use the term because, in his view, "'conservatism'" was "not a satisfactory alternative." Indeed, the belligerent Friedman maintained, just as "the nineteenth-century liberal was a radical . . . so too must be his modern heir."[18]

As Friedman's polemical brio suggested, the new crusaders for capitalism were far more than combative custodians of the liberal tradition. Although neoliberalism is often considered synonymous with "deregulation of business," its acolytes have sought not so much to limit state power as to redirect it toward the promotion and extension of market activity. Hence the privatization of many state services; the reconstruction of those remaining public to resemble the institutions of corporate enterprise ("running government more like a business"); the diminution of the state's welfare provisions and the dramatic augmentation of its panoptical capacities for coercion, punishment, and surveillance; and the insulation of the market from the nettlesome scrutiny and interference by democratic governments. Faced with the modern realities of universal suffrage, labor unions, left-wing political parties, and decolonization, neoliberalism has been an attempt to reimagine governance in an age of mass democratic politics, an effort to, in Quinn Slobodian's words, "inoculate capitalism against the threat of democracy."[19] But these goals emanate from a project whose objective is far deeper than the revival of laissez-faire and the liberation of capital from burdensome restraints. Where traditional liberals thought of the market and the state as two separate and antagonistic spheres, neoliberals seek to remake the state—and everything else—into the image and likeness of the market. Aiming to refashion not only the state but also the moral and metaphysical imagination as well, neoliberals elevated the market to a position of absolute ontological sovereignty.

At the same time, if evangelicals called on the Christian God to sustain the ontological legitimacy of capitalism, American neoliberals represented an elusive repudiation of the jeremiad tradition. Neoliberals realized that a beloved community could not be built on capitalist property; but rather than reject the property relations, they renounced and maligned the hope of community. Even when they invoked tradition and religion, neoliberals echoed the roseate transcendentalism of money portended by Emerson. In the neoliberal theology of the market, the world is a business; money is the measure of all things; mercenary, professional, or technical talent is the existential equivalent of sanctity; and the successful entrepreneur is the autocratic icon of morality and beatitude.

The clerics and evangelists of neoliberalism reached a wide audience and enjoyed a lavish patronage. The Foundation for Economic Education, the Earhart Foundation, and the Volcker Fund sponsored a plethora of conferences, publications, and benefactions. The battle against the New Deal was waged from the pages of the *Freeman, Modern Age, Human Events, Newsweek,* the *Wall Street Journal,* and the *National Review,* the latter funded not only by William F. Buckley, Jr., but by other self-pitying patricians. Book publishers such as Leonard Read, Henry Regnery, and D. Van Nostrand complemented the periodicals; several neoliberal classics rolled off the press of the University of Chicago; and Rand's best-selling (and still beloved) novels bore the imprint of Random House. The most celebrated neoliberal *philosophes* occupied impressive perches in institutes, think tanks, university economics departments, and business schools. Mises taught in New York University's Graduate School of Business Administration; Friedman taught at the University of Chicago and eventually received a Nobel Prize; Hayek went from the London School of Economics to Chicago, where he rued the drift toward egalitarian serfdom as a member of the Committee on Social Thought. Chicago was, of course, home to the Chicago School of neoclassical economics: Friedman, Frank H. Knight, Theodore W. Schultz, Arnold Harberger, and Gary S. Becker, analyst of *Human Capital* (1964) and another Nobel laureate. The Vatican of free-market economics, Chicago was the seminary for at least two generations of academics, policy wonks, and functionaries, offering instruction to Donald Rumsfeld, George Schulz, and a roster of neoliberal technocrats who turned Augusto Pinochet's Chile and United States–occupied Iraq into workshops of unfettered capitalism. At the summit stood the Mont Pelerin Society, the Mount Horeb of neoliberalism—what Mirowski has called "a floating transnational agora" of intellectuals and politicians.[20]

The neoliberal cultural apparatus exhibited a religious zealotry. To be sure, Mises dismissed reliance on any "allegedly divine principle of justice," and remained, according to his student and "anarcho-capitalist" Murray Rothbard, "a caustic rationalist critic of Christianity and all religion." Hayek was an unwavering agnostic who saw little but impediments to market freedom in the metaphysics and ethical codes of traditional religions. The growth of capitalism had been stunted, he wrote in 1979, "by those very morals preached by prophets and philosophers." "We must admit," he continued, "that modern civilization has become largely possible by the disregard of these indignant moralists." Still, as defenders of "modern civilization" against both orthodox religion and socialism, neoliberals saw themselves as dogmatists and moralists, embattled catechists of capitalism. Although Friedman rejected his parents' Judaism, he once referred to himself as "an old-fashioned preacher delivering a Sunday sermon," while his colleague Harberger described himself as "a seriously dedicated missionary."[21]

The grand old man of the Chicago School (where he taught from 1927 until his retirement in 1955), Knight made religion a continuous theme of his work in economics and social philosophy. Born in 1885 and raised in a pious Illinois family, he had originally intended to enter the ministry. But after a brief and intense crisis of faith in college, he abandoned Christianity and decided to become an economist. In almost all of his books—especially in *The Economic Order and Religion* (1945)—Knight vilified Christianity as a morass of chicanery and delusion, sneering that its professed ideals of poverty and meekness amounted to "a hypocritical pose." "With negligible exceptions," he observed, "religious people clearly admire competence and the active courageous exercise of power and the quest for power." Still, Knight held unequivocally that enmity toward capitalist economics was "deeply embedded in our religion," and that the Beatitudes sanctioned "an antagonism to almost every feature of a free economic order."[22] Christian ontology both underwrote a profligate generosity and precluded the instrumentalist standards of pecuniary reason.

Still, Knight believed that if religion lacked economic realism, it abounded in ideological enchantment. Religious reformers advanced proposals informed by "romantic prejudice and screwy thinking"—which, it turned out, was precisely what capitalism required of religion. The "social function of religion," Knight asserted, was "to force men to accept the established order of things." If belief in providence inspired the acquisitive to labor for the glory of an illusory God, and if belief in heavenly rewards reconciled the losers to their subordination, then Christianity or any comparable brand of "screwy thinking" deserved respect and support from apostate economists. Economists, he insisted, must "inculcate" in their students the certitude that each element of laissez-faire theory is "a sacred feature of the system," an inviolable network of laws, the economist's metaphysical surrogate for divinity.[23]

As the wisest mandarin of neoliberalism, Hayek turned laissez-faire from an economic principle into an ontology, identifying capitalist enterprise as an exemplary emanation of cosmic design. Scoffing at what they consider the epistemological hubris of social democratic and socialist planners, neoliberals (and others) have praised Hayek for emphasizing the limits of human understanding. In this view, the humility enjoined by Hayek is the enabling virtue of capitalist markets, permitting the efflorescence of entrepreneurial ingenuity and the attainment of a "spontaneous order" without the arrogant and peremptory ministrations of government. "It is impossible," as he wrote in 1973, "to improve or correct this order by interfering in it by direct commands." Yet Hayek himself believed both that the "spontaneous order" of the market arose from human artifice and that this artifice must be concealed within a stupefying haze of metaphysical enchantment. Like his Chicago colleague Leo Strauss, Hayek advanced what Mirowski has dubbed a "double-truth doctrine": one truth for the neoliberal intelligentsia and their sponsors—the fabrication of markets and property relations by corporate capital and the state—and another for the credulous mob—the natural and therefore inviolable status of capitalist markets and property.[24] Hayek's cosmology of exploitation remains an archetype of capitalist ontology and moralism, a masterwork of pecuniary metaphysics.

Hayek embedded his neoliberal economics in a social and political ontology that distinguished between *cosmos*—the realm of impersonal, spontaneous order—and *taxis,* the realm of conscious, deliberate construction. To Hayek, the improvisation of *cosmos* constituted a "higher, supraindividual wisdom" greater than that of any single human being or collective; indeed, it is because "we normally do not know who knows best" that most decisions should be left to "a process we do not control." The metaphysical and vaguely theological character of *cosmos* could not be clearer, and Hayek capitalized on its import for political economy. He denounced as insane and murderous the conviction—essential, he claimed, to any form of economic planning— that "reason is capable of directly manipulating all the details of a complex society." Because of the inherent limits of the human mind, even the most perspicacious experts could not foresee all contingencies, discern all connections, or identify all possibilities. Appalled at the insolence of bureaucrats, Hayek marveled at the felicitous ignorance of market competitors, "how little the individual participants need to know in order to be able to take the right action." What he had called in *The Road to Serfdom* (1944) "the impersonal and seemingly irrational forces of the market" became, in his philosophical writing, a cosmic, dispassionate, but progressive providence. "It was men's submission to the impersonal forces of the market that in the past has made possible the growth of civilization." As the most dynamic of "the products of spontaneous social growth," the incalculable market of capitalism embodied the serendipitous quintessence of *cosmos.*[25]

If the market is a cosmic forum of spontaneity, then any attempt to accumulate knowledge or distribute it equally amounted, to Hayek, to an act of ontological impertinence. Refusal to yield to the wisdom of the market stems, Hayek argued in *The Road to Serfdom,* from "an incomplete and therefore erroneous rationalism." Thus the erudite liberal insisted on ignorance and submissiveness as cardinal virtues. "There is not much reason to believe," he asserted in *The Constitution of Liberty* (1960), "that, if at any one time the best knowledge which some possess were made available to all, the result would be a much better society." Although statements like these have induced his admirers to laud his insight into human limitations and their preclusion of economic planning, Hayek intended them to preempt any democratic restraint on the power of capital and its cadres of expertise. "The best knowledge which some possess" became a positive danger when exercised to regulate the economy in the interests of a democratic polity. "It is at least possible in principle," he mused in 1967, "that a democratic government may be authoritarian"—"authoritarianism" defined as any prideful attempt to obstruct or modify the impromptu order of the market. Hayek had no objections to democracy as long as it refrained from modulating the market or redistributing private property; otherwise, as he clarified in *The Road to Serfdom,* it should engage in "planning for competition," paving a road to liberty rather than a road to serfdom. The state, he asserted, should construct a legal and social infrastructure "in which competition will be as effective as possible."[26]

If ignorance and submissiveness were, for Hayek, virtues for the democratic (and presumably proletarian) rabble, they were inexcusable vices in capital and its syndicate of managers and technocrats. Skilled in the legerdemain of economics, the upper echelons of corporate business and the state had to know that conscious political choice lay behind the magic of spontaneous order. As Hayek wrote in *Law, Legislation, and Liberty* (1973), "an order which would have to be described as spontaneous" may in fact "rest on rules which are entirely the result of deliberate design." Brandishing this license for duplicity, Hayek openly professed that liberalism was the most advanced form of class domination in history, "a method of social control," he averred in *The Road to Serfdom,* that "should be deemed superior because of our ignorance of its precise results." Who had "deemed" the market order "superior"? Everyone, according to Hayek; "once we have agreed to play the game and profited from its results, it is a moral obligation on us to abide by the results even if they turn against us." Like earlier social-contract theorists,

Hayek never specified when this agreement had been concluded. Tracing the origins of liberal democratic capitalism to a contract enabled Hayek not only to endow it with an immaculate conception unblemished by dispossession and violence, but also to erase the distinction between liberty and compulsion in the mechanisms of the market. If we freely "submit to the adjustments which the market forces" on us, Hayek implicitly admitted that the market was a latticework of coercions from which the powerless were unable to dissent.[27] If Rousseau had asserted that the general will could force us to be free, Hayek demonstrated that the capitalist market freed us up to be forced. Rerouting the road to serfdom onto the freeway of wage servitude, capitalism constituted a capricious and unfathomable command economy of freedom.

But what if the market's losers refuse to accept its decrees and move to abrogate or modify the "contract"? What if they blasphemously reject the edicts of the Market and its erratic, unaccountable will? Hayek realized that capitalism needed to be protected from democracy not only by restructuring the state but also by enlisting the resources of culture and religion to prevent any popular enlightenment about the artifice of capitalist "spontaneity." To inoculate the masses against disenchantment, Hayek proposed that the authoritarian nature of free market economics could be shrouded most effectively in the incense of "tradition"—the spurious solemnities of Kirk and Weaver. If, elsewhere, Hayek had blamed "tradition" for raising impediments to accumulation—the "indignant moralists" of religion, for instance—he transformed it into a guarantor of capitalist liberty by conjoining it with market cosmology. "Submission to undesigned rules and conventions whose significance and importance we largely do not understand"—or at least submission to those "described as spontaneous"—"this reverence for tradition, is indispensable for the working of a free society." Hayek acknowledged that the rules of competitive enterprise endure, not because we honor a fictitious agreement to abide by a cosmological order, but because "the groups who observed them were more successful and displaced others." The winners drape their triumph in the mendacious robes of "tradition and custom," the raiment of reverence that repels the scrutiny of reason. And if tradition and custom fail, God can be recalled from His metaphysical oblivion. Dismissive of religion when it inhibited the progress of commerce and technology, Hayek conceded its utility in upholding the foundations of capitalist civilization. Religion itself depended on its instrumental value in preserving bourgeois morality. "The only religions that have survived," he reflected late in his life, "are those which support property and the family."[28]

Yet if Hayek's instrumental attitude toward religion might suggest that neoliberalism represents the most thoroughgoing disenchantment of the world, his own commitment to an ontology of "spontaneous order"—epitomized in the capitalist market and its providential tokens of money and property—indicates that he and his neoliberal comrades were devotees of the pecuniary metaphysic. Rightly sensing that unbounded exchange could never proceed within a hierarchy of goods, Hayek pointedly objected to "a complete ethical code" in which "all the different human values are allotted their due place." The spontaneous, competitive order of the market should determine the proper order of human values, not some "common good" defined by religious wisdom or democratic deliberation. Mises was even more blunt about the metaphysical and moral lineaments of neoliberal economics, vigorously reasserting the ontology of scarcity and the mercenary standard of value. As he pontificated with all the eloquence of the skinflint in his tirade against *The Anti-Capitalistic Mentality* (1956), "nature is not bountiful but stingy." At home in this grubby and graceless world, neoliberals upheld a muscular moralism of achievement, measured and recorded in an austere and implacable ledger of ethical accountancy. "The sway of the principle, *to each according to his accomplishments does not allow of any excuse for personal shortcomings.*"[29]

The accounting principles of that ledger were those of pecuniary reason. In his diatribe against socialism, "Economic Calculation in the Socialist Commonwealth"—first published in 1920 but revered among Cold War right-wing economists—Mises contended that the rejection of mercenary rationality was the fundamental problem with socialism. Asserting that "without economic calculation there can be no economy," Mises went on to argue that economic calculation could proceed only in monetary terms. In "a competitive society," he wrote, money's central role was in "determining the value of production goods." In the absence of a competitive market whose processes were quickened and ordered by money, "there would be no means of determining what was rational." Thus if, without money, it is "impossible to speak of rational production"—"rational" defined as profitable—then socialist production "could never be directed by economic considerations." What was true of commodities applied also to people; rationalized by money, pecuniary "man deals with other people's labor in the same way he deals with all scarce material factors of production": he treats it as a resource "bought and sold on the market." Because a socialist society would allocate goods and labor according to a different calculus of value, its economic rationality was not even genuine, in Mises's view, let alone productive, efficient, or just. The entire argument turned on a subtle and insidious conflation of reason with money; if, as Mises stated so unequivocally, money determined both the value and the rationality of human creativity, then both morality and reason were defined in its terms.[30]

The magnitude of this neoliberal transvaluation of values was evident to Mises, who realized how extensive the demolition of moral, aesthetic, and metaphysical conventions would have to be. As the accumulation of capital was a categorical imperative, all obstacles to efficiency and expansion had to be summarily obliterated. "No religious or ethical tenet," he declared in 1958, "can justify a policy that aims at the substitution of a social system under which output per unit of input is lower for a system in which it is higher." Mises's remarks on Adam Smith and John Ruskin underscored the breadth of the neoliberal metamorphosis. As imperishable as Smith's work would remain, even he, Mises lamented in 1957, could not "free himself from the standards and terminology of traditional ethics," which set limits on material accumulation. Mises was more withering, even intemperate, when he excoriated Ruskin in *The Anti-Capitalistic Mentality*. Ruskin, Mises fumed, was a "bigoted detractor" of markets, a know-nothing who "slandered" economics, and a "romantic eulogist of the guilds." Mises also belittled Ruskin's art criticism, declaring that "judgment about the merits of a work of art is entirely subjective . . . there is no yardstick to measure the aesthetic worth of a poem or of a building." No yardstick, that is, other than money, the most efficient measure of loveliness. "What counts in the frame of the market economy," Mises pronounced, are "the valuations actually manifested by people in buying or not buying."[31] Outside of money there is no reality, let alone salvation.

While Mises and Hayek aimed at intellectuals and policymakers, other writers—Rose Wilder Lane, Isabel Paterson, Cameron Hawley, and Ayn Rand—peddled middlebrow brands of libertarian philosophy and neoliberal capitalist romance. A prolific journalist and novelist, Lane was a strident merchant of *herrenvolk* nostalgia and market individualism. Daughter of

Laura Ingalls Wilder, author of the beloved *Little House* series, Lane wrote her own set of pioneer novels and contributed to *Harper's, Good House-keeping, Ladies' Home Journal,* and *Saturday Evening Post.* Her best-selling magnum opus, *The Discovery of Freedom* (1943), conveyed her visceral hostility to the New Deal. Although *Discovery of Freedom* celebrates capitalism's liberation of human potential—rooting it in fidelity to natural energies conjured into being by "the Creator"—she articulated her fundamental conviction more pithily in *Give Me Liberty,* redacted into a "Credo" for *Saturday Evening Post.* Praising America's "anarchy of individualism," Lane observed with approval that "each of us has been out to get all he could for himself and his family upon the simple rule and good old plan that he shall take who has the power, and he shall keep who can."[32]

A friend and libertarian comrade of Lane, Paterson preached the evangel of laissez-faire from a perch at the *New York Herald Tribune,* where her column in the book review section became a running fulmination against the New Deal. (She refused to enroll in the Social Security system, dismissing it as a "swindle.") To Paterson, the New Deal and Soviet communism exemplified the evils wrought by altruism; as she wrote in her popular historical treatise, *The God of the Machine* (1943), "most of the horror done in the world is done by good people . . . for what they consider a worthy object." Paterson's own "Christian philosophy" touted God as "the Source of energy" superintending an enormous and complex network for the creation of wealth and the flourishing of liberty. Fond of electro-mechanical metaphors, Paterson described society as a conduit of God's power, a "long circuit energy system" in which "private property is the inductor that initiates the flow. Real money is the transmission line." "Private property, money, freedom, engineering, and industry are all one system," she contended, an apparatus charged with the grandeur of God. Paterson's amalgamation of capitalism, religious faith, and technological progress was so impressive that it elicited praise even from the atheist Rand, who gushed that it "does what *Das Kapital* did for the Reds and what the Bible did for Christianity."[33]

Hawley and Rand went further than Wilder and Paterson, arguing for the moral rehabilitation of avarice and the utter repudiation of the Protestant covenant theology. Their leading characters are icons of promethean willpower who insist on individual freedom and submission to the moral metric of the dollar. Writing athwart the lineage of anticapitalist literature from

Balzac to Dreiser, they pioneered a capitalist romanticism: a genre that not only depicted business life in epic, heroic terms but also made money into a talisman of goodness, even a token of metaphysical ultimacy, enchanting the world through the lucrative self-divinization of the entrepreneur.

Business as a paradigm for life was the animating conceit of Hawley's novels. After twenty-four years as an advertising executive with the Armstrong Cork Company in Pittsburgh, Hawley turned his hand to fiction, where in each of his two boardroom melodramas—*Executive Suite* (1952) and *Cash McCall* (1955)—he imagined a knight of capitalist valor. Unlike the alienated organization men who stalked the pages of Hodgins and Harrington, both Avery Bullard of *Executive Suite* and Cash McCall exhibit "strength, dominance, [and] the ability to demand subjection." President of the Tredway Corporation, a successful furniture manufacturing company, Bullard is the archetype of the tough, straight-talking entrepreneur; one long-time friend harrumphs that Bullard "hadn't built the Tredway Corporation with his hands tied with red tape." Yet for all his pugnacity and resilience, Tredway's founder is a disciple of sorts. Professing to disdain a merely acquisitive interest in business—"A man can't work for money alone. Money is just a way of keeping score"—Bullard, one vice-president remarks, is "willing to give his whole life to a company—lay everything on the altar like a sacrifice to the god of business." Mammon exacts his final tribute in a particularly fitting way, as Bullard's sudden death from a cerebral hemorrhage fittingly ends his compulsive life: "a tiny artery finally yielded to the incessant pounding of his hard-driven bloodstream."[34]

Unlike Bullard, Cash McCall's very name announces his brazen and unapologetic venality. Where Bullard's Tredway Corporation makes furniture, McCall makes money: a financier who buys and sells troubled companies, he is the Platonic form of later corporate raiders such as Carl Icahn and T. Boone Pickens. "You're a *builder*," one man tells Gil Clark, a management consultant who regards McCall with an awed revulsion. "He's a *trader*." McCall is in business purely for the lucre; money is the whole game, not just the score. He shamelessly refers to himself as a "thoroughly vulgar character—I enjoy making money." Alluringly suave and amoral, McCall embodies all the meretricious properties of the postmodern monetary pirate; he is, as one envious competitor notes, "the cleverest of all the jackals and vultures who prey upon the laggard members of the business pack."[35]

McCall would appear to be the model of disenchantment, bereft of any faith even in the god of business to whom Bullard devoted his life. "It's a popular religion—this company worship," he observes to Lory, his girlfriend. "I couldn't accept the gospel." He recoils from Bullard's brand of zealotry, "the terrifying fanaticism that would make a man offer up himself as a human sacrifice." A skeptic among the corporate faithful, McCall knows that capitalism thrives by inflating the markets in longing and credulity; as he tells the righteously diligent Clark, riches accumulate, not through toil, frugality, and dedication, but by "buying a company in which someone had lost faith and selling it to someone else who could be made to have faith in it." You have to *own,* not work; *exploit* belief, not share it. And yet McCall is, in his way, a believer, telling Lory that he admires the Hindu deification of wealth and prosperity in the goddess Lakshmi. At least the Hindus are honest, he implies; unlike hypocrites such as Christians, they consecrate their desires for money and possessions. At one point, McCall vents to Clark his impatience with the antique Christian hostility to riches:

> We have a peculiar national attitude toward money-making. . . . We maintain that the very foundation of our way of life is what we call free enterprise—the profit system. We're so serious about it that we'll fight to preserve it—literally go to war—but when one of our citizens shows enough free enterprise to pile up a little of that profit, we do our best to make him feel that he ought to be ashamed of himself.[36]

Oddly enough, McCall echoes Ruskin: he knows no previous instance in history of a nation's establishing a systematic disobedience to the first principles of its professed religion. But where Ruskin indicted the disobedience, McCall (and presumably Hawley) repudiated the professed religion.

Rand rejected the religion with unequivocal scorn—and then sought to put a new one its place. Rand and her work have attracted three generations of devotees, spellbound by her tales and philosophical defenses of passionate and unbridled egoism. (Rand told an interviewer in 1957 that she was "the most creative thinker alive.") Like other postwar champions of "nonconformity," Rand tapped into a motherlode of disaffection from the blandness and compromise of the managerial order. As she wrote in 1961, she recoiled from the "grayness, the stale cynicism, the noncommittal cautiousness, [and] the guilty evasiveness" of public life—a sentiment shared by many a denizen of Haight-Ashbury, or many a member of Students for a Democratic Society. Her heroes are rebels against some establishment, "stalwart, lone individuals," in Rick Perlstein's words, "who chose authenticity and autonomy and risk over conformity and prosperity and ease." Rand's contempt for the decencies of the corporate commonwealth percolated through the American right, and especially in fictional form, her "objectivism" has made an indelible impact on the conservative moral imagination.[37] What set Rand apart from traditional conservatives was the brazen vitriol of her atheism—an unbelief that she had the temerity to assert was fundamental to capitalism itself. Fusing the virtuous with the mercenary, Rand's moral alchemy dissolved the hoary Christian theology of capitalist enchantment, exposing its fraudulence with all the acquisitive bravado of her fictional paragons.

But after smashing one idol, she crafted another: power, festooned in the moral and metaphysical investiture of money and commerce. In her way, Rand was a theologian, bringing to a graceless apogee the American divinization of power that began with Emerson. Like the sage of Concord, Rand realized that the rage to accumulate required some new justification in the wake of the Protestant regime. "A new faith is needed," as she confided in her journals, "a definite, positive set of new values and new interpretation of life." "We will give people a faith," she once wrote to a friend, "a positive, clear, and consistent system of belief." Objectivism was, as she put it, "a spiritual, ethical, philosophical groundwork for the belief in the system of free enterprise." One of many heralds of the death of God, Rand was indeed a pioneer in her nomination of the dollar as a worthy and durable surrogate. (At the tawdry conclusion of *Atlas Shrugged*, Galt traces the sign of the dollar, not the sign of the cross, in the empty heavens.)[38] A true believer in the magic of the market, Rand joined Hayek as a pioneer of neoliberal capitalist enchantment.

If Rand was, in Jennifer Burns's words, a "goddess of the market," her divinity emanated from a combustible compound of resentment and misanthropy. Her hardcore commitment to capitalism stemmed from her arduous and turbulent life: déclassé bourgeois in the early days of the Soviet Union; struggling screenwriter and playwright in Hollywood, hampered by poverty in her quest for recognition; right-wing artist embittered by the popular and critical success of her Popular Front peers. Loathing Marxism or any other form of egalitarian politics, she idealized the glamour she saw depicted in American cinema, seeing in its ostentation the apotheosis of capitalist democracy. The success of *The Fountainhead* (1943)—capped by that of the film version in 1949—brought Rand not only the riches and celebrity she craved but also an opportunity to strike back at her detractors, many of whom she denounced to the House Un-American Activities Committee in October 1947. Successful, despised, and still hungry for critical approval, Rand moved to New York, where she surrounded herself with obsequious acolytes—Nathaniel and Barbara Brandon, Leonard Peikoff, future Federal Reserve Board chairman Alan Greenspan—and worked on *Atlas Shrugged* (1957), the novel she conceived as the quintessential statement of the objectivist worldview.[39]

The cultural elite of Manhattan proved no more welcoming than Hollywood's, so Rand promoted the formation of an intellectual cadre dedicated to the unadulterated supremacy of capital. She looked on embattled capitalists as the genuinely wretched of the earth, laboring under the yoke of popular envy and government regulation. Businesspeople, she told a fawning executive shortly after the publication of *Atlas Shrugged*, were "the greatest victims for whom I am fighting," constituting, she lamented in 1961, a "persecuted minority" of "exploited scapegoats." Calling for what amounted to a right-wing strategy of cultural hegemony, Rand envisioned a "New Intellectual," a hybrid of egghead and industrialist who would embody "a reunion of the twins who should never have been separated: the intellectual and the businessman." Rand's organic intellectuals of the capitalist class would offer their patrons "the guidance of an intelligible theoretical framework." Unapologetically mercenary, the New Intellectuals must "fight for capitalism . . . as a *moral* issue." Theorizing this moral crusade for capital into what she labeled "Objectivism," Rand promulgated the doctrine in essay collections—*For the New Intellectual* (1961), *The Virtue of Selfishness* (1964), *Capitalism: The Unknown Ideal* (1966), and *The Romantic Manifesto* (1969)—while she and her associates disseminated the gospel in *The Objectivist Newsletter* (1962–1965), *The Objectivist* (1966–1971), and *The Ayn Rand Letter* (1971–1976). Models of haughty didacticism, Rand's most memorable fictional characters were New Intellectuals as well: in the long speeches that bestrew the narratives of *The Fountainhead* and *Atlas Shrugged*, both Roark and Galt descant on the philosophical principles of objectivism.[40]

On the surface, objectivism appeared to recapitulate the utopian vision of classical liberalism: individuals pursuing their own interests free of interference from one another or the state. "Civilization is the progress toward a society of privacy," as Roark tells Ellsworth Toohey, an architectural critic whose socialist politics legitimate his own inferiority and self-loathing. Rand's ideal is a society of cupidity, not of fellowship; no exemplary human being was ever "prompted by a desire to serve his brothers." Rand depicted such a promised land of privacy in *Atlas Shrugged,* where Galt and other renegades from altruism form an intentional community of self-seekers in the Rockies. Outraged when his employer, the Twentieth Century Motor Company, moves to freely share his invention of an electrostatic motor that would revolutionize the production of energy, the charismatic Galt quits the firm and rouses other individualists to create "Galt's Gulch," an "Atlantis" or "Utopia of Greed" for disaffected but radical entrepreneurs. A faithful remnant of private property and free enterprise, Galt's Gulch—located on land leased out by the aptly named Midas Mulligan, a banker and closet libertarian—is an enclave of proprietary capitalism, where men conduct their business unhampered by government supervision and onerous taxation. Galt's Gulch is an Eden of promethean striving, "a radiant state of existence," its eponymous guru waxes, "a paradise which is yours for the taking."[41]

Yet Rand ventured well beyond the boundaries of classical liberalism, which still relied on traditional moral sanctions to prevent market society from descending into an inferno of egotism and rapacity. The moral ecology of objectivism is thoroughly mercantile; commodity exchange is the exclusive and unforgiving paradigm of human life. As the copper tycoon Francisco d'Anconia echoes Emerson in *Atlas Shrugged,* "money is the barometer of virtue." Like Hayek and the principle of *cosmos,* Rand sublimated the trucking and bartering of the market into a universal catechism. Trade, she believed, is "the only rational ethical principle for all human relationships, personal and social, private and public, spiritual and material." The Randian individual "does not seek to be loved for his weaknesses or flaws, only for his virtues" (registered in dollars and cents); a meticulous accountant of morality, he "earns what he gets and does not give or take the undeserved." Unlike saints or other wastrels, Randian individuals seek the only real meaning of life: "We exist for the sake of earning rewards," as Galt explains to a puzzled audience. This is skinflint proprietary moralism draped in the venerable robes of philosophy, but it takes that dispensation to an extremity that Puritans and evangelicals would never have countenanced. As Rand's disquisition on love demonstrates, neoliberal morality is market activity without the market's Protestant God. For Rand, the most intimate affairs find their finest consummations in a monetary nexus. Love and friendship, she argued, constitute "spiritual *payment*" tendered for "the personal, selfish pleasure which one man derives from the virtues of another's character."[42] With a soul reduced to the utility preferences of asset and liability calculation, Rand's conditional lover is an austere precursor of the neoliberal entrepreneurial self.

Yet in pushing pecuniary reason and morality to their logical if grotesque culmination, Rand revealed—and even reveled in—the malevolence that always lurked in the capitalist moral imagination. Rand's dramatis personae often act in despicable, even hideous ways that she clearly commends or romanticizes. In *Atlas Shrugged,* she describes Ragnar Danneskjold, a pirate who commandeers relief ships, sells their cargoes, and gives the proceeds to the wealthy, as a "policeman" and an "avenging angel," reuniting the rich with the hard-earned money they lose to tyrannical humanitarians. More horrific still are the infamous rape scenes in both *The Fountainhead* and *Atlas Shrugged,* in which the protagonists violate or degrade women whom Rand depicts as desiring their own humiliation. Roark assaults Dominique Francon "like a master taking shameful, contemptuous possession"—"the kind of rapture," Rand writes, "she had wanted." (She eventually marries him.) In *Atlas Shrugged,* D'Anconia attacks Dagny Taggart in "a shocking intimacy that needed no consent from her, no permission"; later, Hank Reardon, a mill owner, informs Dagny the night after their first tryst that "I wanted you as one wants a whore"—to which she replies that her "proudest attainment" is to have slept with him, adding, with impeccably Randian moral propriety, "I had earned it."[43] Disdainful domination and gorgeous obedience—such is love among entrepreneurial selves, taking and being taken in accordance with the tempests of alluring and ferocious power.

This specter of universal exploitation suggests that Rand's atheism scandalized the postwar right because it threatened to rupture the alliance of American Christianity and capitalism. Rand denigrated Christianity— "the best kindergarten for communism possible"—for its exaltation of charity. In her journals, she railed against charity (as well as "altruism" and "philanthropy") as a dangerous and even sinister practice. In their "intellectual sloppiness," she fumed, Christians and other promiscuous lovers of humanity threatened to erase those distinctions of merit necessary for any social order. Charity, Rand asserted, should be bestowed like coins from a tightwad's purse; it should mark and augment both the power of the giver and the impotence of the recipient. "Charity to an inferior does not include the charity of not considering him an inferior," she explained; the lowly object of charity should "remember and acknowledge his position."[44] Charity, for Rand, is a strategy of domination, not an expression of love or a sacrament of conviviality.

And yet, to a degree unrecognized by William F. Buckley and other religious intellectuals of the right, Rand fathomed the magnitude of the moral revolution provoked by charity. "If charity (or mercy) is the conception of giving someone something he has not deserved"—if, as she added with palpable horror, charity grew "out of pure kindness or pity, and if this is considered good"—then the wisdom of the work ethic would be unveiled as foolishness; the moral edifice of merit would tremble and collapse on the heads of the diligent. To give anyone something for nothing was a kind of cruelty, Rand argued, an act of malice inflicted on the meritorious. "The ultimate viciousness of charity," she reflected, lay in its cavalier indifference to achievement as a criterion of human worth. "Ignoring his actual worth as a man"—a worth determined, as in Mises's moral economy, in the competitive marketplace—one hands to the weak "the moral and spiritual benefits, such as love, respect, consideration, which better men have to earn."[45] Rand was frightened more by the incalculable extravagance of charity than by anything else in Christianity, for it threatened not only to sanction a massive redistribution of wealth but also to demolish the moral infrastructure of capitalist property relations.

Charity contravened Rand's Manichaean axiology of "producers" or "creators"—businesspeople or professionals who survive and flourish in the strife of the marketplace—and the *lumpenhumanitas* of "moochers," "looters," "parasites," "second-hand souls," and "incompetents of the earth"—those defeated and captured in mercantile conflict, reduced to the deservedly servile status of wage labor or unrelieved poverty. Rand's "producers" such as Roark (an architect) and Galt (an engineer) exemplify a haughty and virile professionalism, a swaggering genius impatient with the acquiescent banality of organization men. The "moochers" or "second-hand souls" represent the nadir of mediocrity; whether fearful, decadent, or untalented, they hide their envy of success behind both their imprecation against money and their rhetoric of compassion. As D'Anconia warns, St. Paul's indictment of the love of money as the root of all evil is "the leper's bell of an approaching looter."[46] As her abhorrence of this morality for weaklings indicated, Rand echoed Nietzsche in maligning charity as the masquerade of resentment, and she appropriated for her fictional heroes the aristocratic hauteur and willpower of the *Übermensch.*

With their indomitable volition and cavalier disregard for the lives they unsettle in their quest for self-expression, Galt, Roark, and other Randian entrepreneurs are capitalist supermen, imperious and obdurate masters of their trades portrayed as existential prodigies engaged in a capitalist trans-valuation of values. Although Rand portrays them as romantic heroes of cre-ative self-actualization, they resemble Carlyle's archetypes of wonder much less than they mirror fascist avatars of steely, unyielding power. Indeed, as Corey Robin has observed, there is a chilling homology between Rand's glo-rification of the Entrepreneur and fascist panegyrics to the Leader; "she and the Nazis share a patrimony in the vulgar Nietzscheanism that has stalked the radical right, whether in its libertarian or fascist variants, since the early part of the twentieth century." "Vulgar" or not, her Nietzschean adoration of power and its vessels partook of an obsequious deference that can only be described as worship. For Rand's characters, power is an ontology as well as an aphrodisiac; as Whittaker Chambers observed while eviscerating *Atlas Shrugged* in the *National Review,* Rand "consistently mistakes raw force for strength, and the rawer the force, the more reverent the posture of the mind before it."[47]

Chambers's attribution of "reverence" suggested a religious quality to the novel—an enchantment toward which *Atlas Shrugged* only gestured, but which Rand's earlier work had made explicit. Chambers noted that like all prophets, Rand proclaimed what he sardonically called "The Message," and divided the world into the saved and the damned, "the Children of Light and the Children of Darkness." The Children of Light were, of course, the pro-ducers in Galt's Gulch, standing "at the center of a godless world"—and therefore acting in effect as the gods of a godless world. Moreover, Rand's concluding episode with the Sign of the Dollar—the emblem and touchstone of the new producerism—was for Chambers both a "sophomoric" blasphemy and a Great Commission to go forth and exploit all losers.[48]

If *Atlas Shrugged* depicted a beatific vision of capitalist *Übermenschen,* even more compelling evidence of a covert Randian theology lay in her earlier novels. In *The Fountainhead,* Roark—whom his victim-cum-spouse Dominique describes as having "the face of a god" concurs with one critic who observes that he is "a religious man . . . in your way. I can see that in your buildings." Roark's religion is his own creativity: creators, he declares, have never depended on anyone, as "the whole secret of their power" is that it is, like divinity, "self-sufficient, self-motivated, self-generated"; every creator is "a Prime Mover." But Rand's most explicit theological avowals appeared in *Anthem,* a seminal if little-discussed book written in 1937 but published in 1946 by Leonard Read—head of the Foundation for Economic Education, author of "I, Pencil," and acolyte of evangelical enchantment. Set in some unspecified place and future, *Anthem* narrates the journey of its first-person narrator, "Equality 7–2521," from selflessness to freedom. After "the Unmentionable Times"—a period apparently characterized by free-market capitalism, robust individuality, and stupendous technological innovation—the world has become a stifling hive of cooperation, conformity, and bureaucracy. Scraping by on the material remains of the Unmentionable Times, the postcapitalist order is ruled by "Councils," guild-like colloquies of elders who tightly regulate economics, science, and technology. Humanity languishes in this prison of benevolence, where individuality is warped and repressed in the name of the common good—that is, the welfare of the losers. Personal distinctiveness is so virulently feared that the very word "I" is forbidden; all citizens must use the plural pronoun "We" when speaking of themselves.[49]

Though inquisitive and technically proficient, Equality has been forbidden by the "Council of Vocations" from embarking on a scientific career. Undaunted, he discovers and explores an abandoned subway tunnel, where he begins to conduct forbidden scientific experiments in his free time; eventually, he rediscovers electricity and reinvents the light bulb. Meanwhile, Equality falls in love with Liberty 3000, a golden-haired peasant girl he sees working in the fields outside the city. Emboldened by his passion, Equality brings his scientific discoveries to the World Council of Scholars, who recoil in horror from the challenge his work poses to the stability of their mediocre world. When they attempt to destroy his invention and suppress his findings, Equality escapes into the mountains outside the city, where he rejoins Liberty and settles with her in an abandoned cottage whose walls are covered with books.[50]

In one of the books they read the forbidden word "I," and attribute to it a revolutionary significance: the identity of humanity and divinity. Equality renames himself "Prometheus"—thief of the arts of civilization from the stingy Olympians—while Liberty takes the name "Gaea," earth mother of the early Greeks. Like all subsequent Randian heroes, Prometheus recites a creed of undaunted individualism, tracing his moral and metaphysical roots to the mundane fact of his existence. Prometheus is one of Maslow's "transcenders," sacralizing everything he touches—first of all, himself. "My happiness needs no higher aim to vindicate it," he reasons, since "I need no warrant for being, and no word of sanction upon my being. I am the warrant and the sanction"—which thereby makes him his own object of worship. "This miracle of me is mine to own and keep, and mine to guard, and mine to use, and mine to kneel before!" Thus Rand bestows divinity on the individual ego: "This god, this one word: 'I.'" (Likewise, Gaea is to be "the mother of a new race of gods.") Where Christian charity emanated from thanksgiving for the gift of existence, Promethean liberty stems from a principled ingratitude. "I owe nothing to my brothers," he announces, and "I [do not] gather debts from them." Like Rand herself, Prometheus redefines brotherly love as a reward for achievement or services rendered; other people must "earn my love," he says with all the lyricism of a miser.[51]

This free market of love required the insulation of divinity from contaminating contact with other deities. "In the temple of his spirit, each man is alone," Prometheus says of his tabernacle to himself. "Let each man keep his temple untouched and undefiled." This insistence on purity helps explain not only why the sexual couplings in Rand's novels are so devoid of fleshly exuberance and delight but also why they never produce children.[52] Needy, helpless, and unproductive, children are the ultimate moochers. For all her bloviation about production and creativity, Rand's Promethean ideal is the most strenuous and barren beatitude ever imagined.

Chambers predicted that Rand's popularity would be a brief if nasty episode in cultural history; like many a "patent medicine," he mused, Rand's "brew is probably without lasting ill effects."[53] Alas, over half a century later,

Rand's tonic of avarice and powerlust continues to beguile the American imagination, blending with other brands of corporate moonshine to form a febrile elixir of enchantment. Though written at the meridian of the New Deal era, Rand's hateful and sanctimonious fables of selfishness supplied an intoxicating fillip for later captains of neoliberal depredation. Emboldening the piracies of finance capital, feeding the cyberculture's exhilarant ambitions of technological sublimity, and bracing a new plutocracy with a conviction of its own existential superiority, her kitschy and melodramatic tributes to greed augured an epoch of spectacular pillage.

# 27

# The Statues of Daedalus

## Postmaterialism and the Failure
## of the Liberal Imagination

AMERICAN LIBERALS CERTAINLY NEVER expected to see the restoration of a plutocratic vista, as most of the Cold War era was a time of relative optimism among corporate liberals and social democrats. The rising prosperity of capitalist democracies proved to be a propitious conjuncture for reformist intellectuals and politicians. Liberals could point to the success of the New Deal's mixed economy as evidence that the corporate commonwealth could both forestall more radical measures at home and offer an example to postcolonial nations attracted to revolutionary socialism. They may have winced when Vice President Richard M. Nixon invoked washing machines as tokens of capitalist success in his 1959 "kitchen debate" with Soviet Premier Nikita Khrushchev, but liberals shared his premise that consumer abundance would diminish the appeal of communism.[1]

Until recently, Cold War liberalism was seen primarily as a sobering moment in American intellectual life, as ex-radicals recovered from their youthful intoxication with Marxism during the Depression. Faced with the horrors of Stalinism and the waning of Popular Front enthusiasm, former socialists and Communists languished in what Daniel Bell called "the exhaustion of Utopia." Hence (so the story goes) the gray mood of liberals in the 1950s, exemplified in the rhetorical ensemble of "realism," "maturity," "responsibility," "complexity," and "irony"—virtues that countered the utopian vices of doctrinaire zeal and indifference to limits. Utopianism, so liberals contended, led inexorably to massacres and gulags; better to be skeptical, even cynical, about radical faith in historical destiny. Hence the affirmation—even by secular intellectuals—of theologians such as Reinhold Niebuhr, whose insistence on the reality and endurance of sin seemed to have been verified by the horrific events of the past two decades.[2]

Yet many liberals and social democrats also felt a new optimism about the prospects for American society. As Howard Brick and other historians have demonstrated, they foresaw the emergence of a "postindustrial" or "postmaterialist" society from the womb of corporate capitalism—a surrogate for the utopian hopes abjured in the wake of Stalinism. In this view, the material abundance generated by industrial and cybernetic technologies would permit an array of historical marvels. Automation, postmaterialist liberals believed, would entail both the gradual supersession of the work ethic and the guiltless enjoyment of leisure. Exponentially increasing prosperity would enable the composure and perhaps the erasure of class warfare and ideological conflict, thus releasing social energies to accomplish the unfinished tasks of racial and sexual equality. In conjunction with Keynesian economic policy, affluence would support the extension of the purview of public concern and planning, enabling the free provision of services of ever-greater quality and variety. Technological ingenuity and plenitude also heralded the liberation of personal authenticity, the relaxation of sexual mores, and the cultivation of aesthetic sensibilities and talents, all previously contained and distorted by the repressive conditions imposed by scarcity. At most, the achievement of sustained abundance augured the transcendence of capitalism itself—not through an abrupt and violent revolution, but through the progressive permeation of society by liberal values and institutions. Thus, what Daniel Bell identified in 1960 as the "end of ideology"—code for the ebbing of Marxism—presupposed an interlocking set of revolutions of unprecedented magnitude.[3]

The conviction that material abundance was ushering in a new age of justice and community heartened liberal and social-democratic intellectuals. "The solution of the technical problems of production is in sight," Riesman declared in *The Lonely Crowd*, later chastising Norbert Wiener and others who questioned or deprecated "our great human achievement of turning over productive routines to machinery." Galbraith rested his critique of "the affluent society" on the premise that "the problem of production" had been solved. In *The Accidental Century* (1965), Michael Harrington invoked Aristotle's "statues of Daedalus"—one of the earliest recorded references to self-acting machines—to argue that, once released from its capitalist integument, cybernetic technology permitted a socialist economy of plenty and leisure. Business continued to build "a collective society for private profit," he maintained, because "the political and social imaginations have not approached the revolutionary intelligence of its technology." In the 1962 "Port Huron Statement," the manifesto of Students for a Democratic Society and a "blueprint of civic paradise," Tom Hayden maintained that automation, now pursued within a system "of selfish production motives and elitist control," nonetheless afforded "the opportunity for men the world around to rise in dignity from their knees." As scarcity and acquisitiveness receded, "a love of man overcomes the idolatrous worship of things," and men and women could satisfy their "unfulfilled capacities for reason, freedom, and love."[4]

As Riesman told an MIT audience in 1953, "we have approached the accomplishment of one mission, and are searching for another"; we need, he insisted, to find an exhilarating "moral equivalent for capitalism." Postmaterialist intellectuals were confident that such a "moral equivalent for capitalism" could be found, as they ascribed a salvific significance to a new historical force for progress: the professional, managerial, and technical strata of advanced industrial societies. Convinced that cybernetic technology had spawned a "postindustrial society" in which the production of material goods was giving way to the production of services, symbols, and knowledge, postmaterialists contended that this sizable and growing army of workers— Galbraith's "technostructure," accompanied by the "educational and scientific estate"—was better equipped than Marx's industrial proletariat to construct the world after abundance. These "liberal middlebrows" were, in David Bazelon's estimation, "the vanguard of the managerial revolution." Like Veblen's "soviet of technicians," these benevolent experts remained committed to professional standards unsullied by pecuniary interest. "Not motivated primarily by money," as Galbraith described them, they "contributed their best regardless of compensation." These were clearly not the pedestrian organization men and women defended by William H. Whyte, nor the avaricious, condescending blowhards iconized in Ayn Rand's entrepreneurial allegories, nor the duplicitous philosopher-economists recommended in Friedrich Hayek's salutations to the market. In Bell's view—elaborated with vast erudition in *The Coming of Post-Industrial Society* (1973), the magnum opus of postindustrial prognosis—the hegemony of magnanimous specialists augured the replacement of "governance by political economy" with "governance by political philosophy."[5]

The governing philosophy of the postindustrial avant-garde would emanate, liberal writers hoped, from the new postwar university. Affirming the account of the "multiversity" provided by the new breed of university presidents such as Clark Kerr of Berkeley and James B. Conant of Harvard, liberals asserted that a coalition of scholarly and business intellectuals was fashioning a postmaterialist moral imagination from the humanist and scientific traditions now housed in academia. Bell argued that since both the producers of mass culture and the ranks of the corporations passed through "primarily a university culture," academics possessed an unprecedented power to shape future generations of the corporate cognitariat. Adolf Berle likened university professors to the medieval clerisy. Although he respected the "Lords Temporal"—the corporate executives lionized in *Fortune*—Berle contended that they needed to be checked and cultivated by the "Lords Spiritual": academics, journalists, and others among the humanist intelligentsia, secular successors to the priests and scholastics who civilized the feudal aristocracy. As our "spiritual elite," this liberal clerisy also played the roles of clergy and prophet, developing a "public consensus" based on empirical investigation and "demanding redress" for social injustice, much like "Elijah in the presence of Ahab." Berle exhibited an extraordinary, even grandiose faith that the university would tame the corporation. "Though all the armies of Madison Avenue were arrayed against Columbia or Princeton or Stanford," he proclaimed, "the future would be with the campus spires."[6]

Berle's comparison of the university intelligentsia to the medieval clerisy was even more apt than he realized. Heirs to Progressive spirituality, postmaterialist academics had taken over the quest for what Dewey had called "a common faith." In their capacity as what Bell termed "cultural arbiters," many postwar liberal academics turned to art, history, and literature for the moral and spiritual tutelage once assigned to religion. The "historical-literary mind," Lionel Trilling wrote in *The Liberal Imagination* (1950), is "the best kind of critical and constructive mind we have"—better, he emphasized, "than the theological." Yet Trilling's own academic career reflected both the domestication of modernism—now tame and canonical in seminar rooms and galleries—and the bureaucratization of the liberal imagination. In the disciplinary protocols of the postwar university, liberal humanists pursued their clerical roles with a keen sense of cultural professionalism—a sense of moral and aesthetic expertise much like that exhibited among scientists and technicians.[7]

Yet traces of the sacred—sleek mementoes of enchantment—surfaced among liberal social thinkers, especially in "futurology," one of the more flamboyantly optimistic discourses of postwar intellectual life. Although futurology originated in the military-industrial labyrinth of the RAND Corporation, the Hudson Institute, and the Institute for Defense Analysis, it swiftly became a significant feature of Cold War liberalism. Often funded by the Ford and Carnegie Foundations and formulated by distinguished intellectuals, liberal futurology included venues less compromised by direct links to corporate and military interests: the Center for the Study of Democratic Institutions, the Committee for the Future, the Commission on the Year 2000, among other forums. The major speculators in postindustrial futures included an array of dignitaries from academia and journalism: Bell, Riesman, Hedley Donovan, Wassily Leontieff, Zbigniew Brzezinski, Samuel Huntingdon, Daniel Moynihan, and other thinkers who swanned in the overlapping circles of higher education and public policy. Utilizing the latest information and research methodologies, liberal futurologists hoped to identify and direct current trends in technology, science, and social relations.[8]

With its reliance on the new intellectual technologies of cybernetics, game theory, operations research, and simulation modeling, futurology would appear to have been, as Bell described its technocratic mien, "quite opposed to the traditional and customary religious, aesthetic, and intuitive mode" of prophecy or Romanticism. Yet Bell himself discerned magical qualities not only in futurology but also in any other "venture in social forecasting"—the latter the subtitle of his own extended omen of postindustrial society. The goal of future-oriented studies was, he acknowledged, "to realize a social alchemist's dream: the dream of 'ordering' the mass society." With their computers and decision theories, futurologists longed to know and master human fate "just as Pascal sought to play dice with God."[9] Bell's comparison of social forecasting to alchemy underscored the affinity of secular futurology with earlier forms of science and prognostication. As Bell's own hopeful oracle of "postindustrial society" indicated, futurology represented the professionalization of eschatology, a secular science of divination that employed the modern sortilege of mathematical variables and algorithms.

A residue of enchantment appeared as well in liberal thralldom before cybernetics. Their munificent praise tended to ratify Wiener's likening of cybernetic technology to magic, while their reverence for technological progress corroborated his comparison of technicians to shamans. Almost alone among liberals and social democrats, Harrington worried that intellectuals, politicians, businesspeople, scientists, and technicians in advanced capitalist societies shared a "modern animism" that invests technology "with the spirits that once inhabited trees and stones." As Wiener and Vonnegut had dreaded, this animism—the cybernetic version of the technological sublime, conjured up by the magi of the corporate technostructure—pervaded all levels of American society, even where the disenchanted consciousness of modernity had allegedly vanquished superstition most thoroughly. Mesmerizing many postmaterialist writers as well, "modern animism" helped ensure that the liberal imagination would remain within the parameters of corporate capitalism. Far from envisioning some qualitatively different society, forecasts of "postindustrial society" allowed their diviners to "'explore' alternative futures," in Andrew Ross's words, "within the confines of the existing system."[10]

Hence the sense of sacrilege felt by many liberal academics when confronted by opposition from radical students and the counterculture. Bell perceived a coming crisis among the postindustrial clerisy as early as 1965. In his view, the recent upheaval at Berkeley in 1964 displayed the antinomianism, not only of beatniks, hippies, and other cultural outlaws, but also of respected scholars such as Norman O. Brown, whose *Life against Death* (1959) was a remonstrance against psychic repression and the secular rationality that enforced it. Looking nervously at the favorable reception accorded Brown among younger liberal and New Left intellectuals, Bell surmised that "the tension between the technocratic and the apocalyptic modes will be experienced most sharply in the university." Brown and more disheveled denizens of the counterculture were, Bell thought, descendants of the Brethren of the Free Spirit, the Ranters, and the bohemians of nineteenth-century Paris—a legacy of "libertinism" that also found expression in heterodox forms of body mysticism. Recognizing the force of countercultural claims about the sterility and violence of industrial society, Bell called on his fellow educators both to "humanize technocracy" and to "tame the apocalypse"—an eminently clerical proposal to renovate the existing structure while incorporating elements of the opposition.[11]

After the 1968 student uprising at Columbia, critiques of the university, the technostructure, and the professional estates multiplied rapidly, and the tension Bell sensed between "technocracy" and "apocalypse" reached a crescendo in the late 1960s. The teach-ins and work stoppages at MIT and thirty other universities in the spring of 1969 suggested to Paul Goodman, for instance, the outbreak of what he called a broader "religious crisis" among the younger intelligentsia. Meanwhile, popular books such as Ivan Illich's *Deschooling Society* (1970) and Theodore Roszak's *The Making of a Counterculture* and *Where the Wasteland Ends* (1972) voiced incisive and even eloquent rejoinders to the corporate liberal faith in the liberating promise of science and technology. Deriding "the myth of objective consciousness" as the surreptitious faith of what he labeled "the technocracy," Roszak called for the revival of archaic modes of moral and religious sensibility—that is, of enchantment. "Nothing less is required," he proclaimed, "than the subversion of the scientific world view" and its replacement with a culture—leavened by a "shamanistic vision" or "sacramental consciousness"—whose inhabitants "take fire from visionary splendor and the experience of human communion."[12]

Goodman shared Roszak's conviction that secular rationality had itself become a form of idolatry. As he observed in *New Reformation* (1970), science and technology, although cloaked as secular pursuits, were really the demiurges of a "system of mass faith," a "beneficent religion" with its own "ecclesiastical structure"—the professional and disciplinary associations to which postindustrial theorists looked with reverence, but which a growing number of younger intellectuals perceived as the brains trust of a soulless and even "diabolical" establishment. But what impressed Goodman most about the rebellious students and faculty was not their morality or political will but what he called their "metaphysical vitality," their exuberant if sometimes arrogant and foolhardy attempts to explore genuinely alternative futures. Unlike their liberal elders, they ventured into the restricted areas of ultimate meaning and ecstatic communion. "It is religion that constitutes the strength of the new generation," Goodman wrote proudly of the obstreperous but vibrant young.[13]

By the mid-1970s, these attacks on the status of scientific and technological reason converged with new, even more urgent concerns with energy depletion and ecological catastrophe to produce what amounted to a general crisis of the postmaterialist mentality. The rise of the environmental movement, together with the 1973 oil crisis, suggested that there might be insurmountable material obstacles to the achievement of a postmaterialist society. As a spate of books, articles, and think-tank reports indicated—capped by the Club of Rome's heretical proclamation of "The Limits to Growth" in 1972— the postmaterialist prospect was now threatened by a cluster of previously unforeseen problems: pollution, overpopulation, and petroleum shortages of increasing frequency and severity. Reviewing the grim auspices of scientists, engineers, politicians, and philosophers, economist Robert Heilbroner envisioned, in *An Inquiry into the Human Prospect* (1974), a bleak and violent future for industrial societies, whether capitalist or socialist. American capitalism in particular, he predicted, could expect declining rates of productivity growth, stagnation of real income, and social turmoil provoked by an increasingly inequitable distribution of wealth. The only hope for national and planetary survival lay, Heilbroner argued, in "the gradual abandonment of the lethal techniques, the uncongenial lifeways, and the dangerous mentality of industrial civilization itself"—hardly a popular set of prescriptions, and one that implicitly denied the progressive tendency of history essential to both the liberal and socialist imaginations. Bell made similarly dolorous prophecies in *The Cultural Contradictions of Capitalism* (1976). Departing from one of the most crucial tenets of the postmaterialist credo, Bell asserted that because the "revolution of rising entitlements" ensured an equally rising need to find resources to satisfy them, "we will never overcome scarcity."[14]

Both Heilbroner and Bell turned to the wisdom of the past to salvage what they could of the postmaterialist project—but in doing so, they revealed the limitations, and even the exhaustion, of the liberal and social democratic traditions. Heilbroner doubted that the impending turbulence could be averted or mitigated by reliance on better science and technology. Pointing to environmentalism as evidence of a nascent dissatisfaction with consumer culture, Heilbroner reasoned that because higher income, better diets, medical advances, and technological accomplishments do not necessarily "satisfy the human spirit," then "rationality has its limits with regard to the engineering of social change." What, if not reason, could improve the prospects for planetary survival in the wake of a stationary economy and irreversible ecological damage? Since "the driving energy of modern man has come from his Promethean spirit," he observed, "it is not only with dismay that Promethean man regards the future. It is also with a kind of anger." Incredulous of religious answers, Heilbroner turned to mythology, summoning against Prometheus the image of Atlas and his stoic perseverance in bearing the weight of the world. "To accept the limitation of our abilities" would be the most painful lesson capitalist society has to learn, Heilbroner conceded, but it will learn it, one way or the other.[15]

Bell echoed this insistence on limits but maintained that the "cultural contradictions of capitalism" ran deeper than Heilbroner imagined, and that their resolution required something more than highbrow stoicism. Along with other culturally conservative critics such as Philip Rieff and Christopher Lasch, Bell rued not only the counterculture but also its extensive penetration into the mores of even middle-class Americans. The transgression of bourgeois morality was now, Bell believed, the everyday life of affluent Americans, whose consumer culture sold them a daily bacchanalia of pleasure, indolence, and play. Capitalism had succeeded in promoting values and habits that directly contravened its traditional culture of production—hence the intensifying "cultural contradictions" of capitalism. Aside from eroding the perseverance indispensable to efficient and sustained production, the hedonist ethic undermined "the long-run ability of capitalist society to maintain its vitality as a moral and reward system."[16]

With an amoral postindustrial society looming, Bell looked to religion to provide the legitimacy depleted by consumer culture, since liberalism seemed "uneasy in trying to say why" impulses should be restrained. To confront the "spiritual crisis" engulfing American society, Bell called for "some conception of religion"—which he identified with a "tragic sense of life"— to subdue the roiling desires set loose by the cultural industries of capitalism. Bell's understanding of religion was thoroughly Western, abstract, and utilitarian: he recommended no specific tradition other than "the great historic religions of the West," concurred with their "tough-minded view of human nature," and employed keywords—"debt," "obligation," and "limit" abounded—that comprised a rhetoric of conservative moralism. Portraying a "world as it should be," religion decreed a realm of "'allotted portions,'" those concrete relationships in time and space that humbled pride and the longing for limitless experience. Against the counterculture and its "rites of release," Bell posed the "rites of restraint" he thought central to the tragic wisdom of religion.[17]

Bell's tragic conception of religion was bound up with his account of the "cultural contradictions of capitalism"—"contradictions" that were more apparent than real. Like other moralistic attacks on consumerism, Bell missed the persistence of the work ethic, the subordination of the "adversary culture," and the metamorphosis of pleasure itself into an endeavor. Consumer pleasure still carried a price tag: the commodification of saturnalia required most people to submit to the disciplinary strictures of wage labor and monthly budgets. At the same time, the alleged democratization of antinomianism marked a new zenith, not a repudiation, of the command economy of pleasure. From the new advertising agencies and public relations firms to the burgeoning ranks of service workers, capitalism remained very much a culture of production, leavened by a hip producerism wherein the entrepreneurial self was becoming the character ideal. In the coming neoliberal marketplace, the mandatory "flexibility" of entrepreneurial selfhood merged bourgeois sobriety with bohemian vagabondage. What Malcolm Cowley had described of his Greenwich Village cohorts was now true of more Americans than ever: the boundaries of administered consciousness had been enlarged, and its techniques now embraced bohemia. By depicting a "contradiction" between two rigidly demarcated realms—one of production, governed by the performance principle of pecuniary and technological rationality, and the other of consumption, governed by pleasure and distraction—Bell and other mandarin scolds overlooked the possibility that contemporary "hedonism" was the performance principle decked out in party clothes.[18] The invasion and degradation of pleasure by the standards of the work ethic would only intensify under neoliberal capitalism.

What Bell and other critics of contemporary mores were describing was less an epidemic of hedonism than the colonization of ecstasy by the spectacle, the incorporation of desires for enchantment and communion by the cultural apparatus of capitalism. Thus the problem was not, as Bell and other moralizers construed it, how to bridle human longing with religion—a reduction of religion to propriety and control. For all of "the great historic religions of the West," at least, morality has issued from a way of being in the world, an experience, as William James had described it, of "rapture" and "ontological wonder." But if ontological wonder, not "the tragic sense of life," was the essence of religion, and if yearnings for rapture and communion constituted the spiritual sustenance of the spectacle, then the problem of contemporary desire lay not so much in its restraint but in its therapy and transformation—a diagnosis with radical implications. Despite his pragmatic approach to religion as an enforcer of limits and conventions, Bell recognized that it also harbored the potential to be an "adversary culture" every bit as transgressive of bourgeois moralism as bohemia. "At crucial junctures in history," he conceded, religion has been "the most revolutionary of all forces."[19]

# 28

## To Live Instead of Making History

Herbert Marcuse, Norman O. Brown,
and the Romantic Eschatology of Immanence

AS BELL'S ACKNOWLEDGMENT SUGGESTED, the utopian impulse
had not completely atrophied. The very notion that material scarcity either
had been or would soon be overcome was itself redolent of ancient eschatological presentiments of recovered edens or heavenly cities. Bell himself had
admitted that "the end of ideology is not—should not be—the end of utopia
as well." Riesman had vaguely alluded to the persistence of utopia among *The
Lonely Crowd*. "The sources of utopian political thinking may be hidden and
constantly changing, constantly disguising themselves." Still, even when
liberals summoned enough imagination to visit utopia for a moment, their
insistence on pecuniary and technocratic rationality took the romance out
of the adventure. The ladder to the "City of Heaven," Bell warned, could not
be a "faith ladder but an empirical one," detailing both "the costs of the
enterprise" and "the determination of *who* is pay."[1] "Realism" remained the
Medusa's head raised to admonish all visionaries to stone.

In the face of liberal wise men, utopia had its champions in C. Wright
Mills, Norman O. Brown, and Herbert Marcuse, who dismissed liberal in-
junctions to "realism" and "maturity" as evidence of betrayal and resignation. Tutors of the American New Left, they called on radicals to challenge
the canons of rationality that both liberals and conservatives took for
granted. Mills indicted purveyors of what he called "crackpot realism," the
bogus "practicality" that underwrote the imperatives of capital and the state.
When used as a term of derision, "utopian," Mills wrote in his pugnacious
letter to "The New Left" (1960), connoted "any criticism or proposal that
transcends the up-close milieu" of academic, government, and business institutions. Cultivated in the corporate and educational estates of "postindustrial" society, the cosmopolitan affectations of liberals camouflaged a

"simple provincialism." Brown opened his brief for *Life against Death* by rejecting the sense of "sin, cynicism, and despair" that inhibited utopian thinking and paralyzed political action. "Utopian speculations," he urged, "must come back into fashion." By the end of the 1960s, galvanized by the call of French students in May 1968 to "be realistic—demand the impossible!," Marcuse was announcing that utopian speculation was not only urgent but also eminently practical. "What is denounced as 'utopian'," he wrote in *An Essay on Liberation* (1969), is not what is impossible but rather what is "blocked from coming about by the power of the established societies."[2]

Utopians shared with liberals the premise of an impending end to material scarcity and the predatory ethos it spawned. "The most realistic observers," Brown noted, are proclaiming "liberation from work—given by modern technology." As a result, Brown speculated, economics could now become "the science of enjoyment," the study of new forms of "erotic exuberance" heretofore repressed in the struggle for survival. Marcuse echoed Brown, writing in 1967 that the "end of utopia" was in sight. "Utopian possibilities are inherent in the technical and technological forces of advanced capitalism," he reiterated in 1969. "Science and technology are the great vehicles of liberation, and it is only their use and restriction in the repressive society which makes them into vehicles of domination."[3] This duality in science and technology led utopians to question the nature of reason itself. The utopian investigation of scientific rationality revealed a tyrannical agent of the rage to master nature and accumulate capital; its overtly lucid and astringent visage, thought since the Enlightenment to be the face of liberation, masked the machinations of repressed and malignant desires. In *Eros and Civilization* (1955), Marcuse contended that the struggle for existence had imposed a "repressive reason" reduced to the "performance principle," now a calculating tool for managers and technocrats intent on increasing productivity, not on nurturing and gratifying sensuous desires for truth, beauty, and goodness. For Brown, modern science represented the "dominion of death-in-life," the triumph of the ascetic quest to stifle and overcome the human senses. Against this lifeless and therefore deadly knowledge, Brown called for a science rooted in "an erotic sense of reality," one enlivened by "the more concrete deliverances of poetry."[4]

As Brown's hope for a poetical science indicated, utopians belonged to the Romantic pedigree of opposition to capitalism. Signifying the possibility of poetry in labor, their invocation of the artisanal ideal was the most apparent link to Romantic modernity. Against the drudgery that marks the reign of death within life, Brown appealed to John Ruskin and the delight of "enjoyable effort." Deliberately turning to the "utopian" Charles Fourier rather than the "scientific" Marx, Marcuse contended that technological advances were allowing "the possibility of freedom *within* the realm of necessity"—the union of play and work that was the quintessence of craftsmanship. Indeed, Marcuse speculated in 1972, "certain lost qualities of artisan work may well reappear on the new technological base." Rejecting what he dubbed the "labor metaphysic" of Marxism that identified the industrial proletariat as the historical agent of revolution, Mills departed from progressive orthodoxy by adopting what amounted to a craft metaphysic. In *White Collar,* he lauded Ruskin, William Morris, Tolstoy, and Carlyle for their "humanist view of work as craftsmanship." Craftsmanship, he told a meeting of industrial designers in Aspen in 1958, was both "the central experience of the unalienated human being" and "the highest human ideal." Through his union of beauty and utility, the artisan composed "a poem in action," a transubstantiation of labor into lyric. Craft even held a certain religious quality for Mills. If for more and more workers in industrial societies "work seems to serve neither God nor whatever they may experience as divine in themselves," the artisan "lives in and through his work, which confesses and reveals him to the world."[5]

Mills's allusion to "revelation" hinted at a broader Romantic hope: a demolition of the pecuniary and promethean imagination that subdued advanced industrial societies, and its replacement with an erotic sensibility of pleasure in the sensuous textures and possibilities of the world. Postwar utopians were continuing the Romantic pursuit of a modern form of enchantment—a "new sensorium" or "new sensibility," as Marcuse called it in his *Essay on Liberation,* the fullest consciousness of ontological reality beyond the boundaries of mercenary, scientific, and technological reason. On this score, Mills was the outlier among postwar utopians. Although his vision was as "passionate" as that of William James, his identification with the pragmatist tradition precluded any fundamental reliance on art, literature, mythology, or religion. Even where they respected the protocols of Enlightenment reason—logical thinking, coherent argument, and the use of properly attributed evidence—Brown and Marcuse enlisted them in an effort to transcend the limitations of modern rationality. Relying on psychoanalysis as the science of desire, and drawing on an array of poets, artists, philosophers, theologians, and mystics—Schiller, Blake, Novalis, Ruskin, Breton, Bohme, and St. John of the Apocalypse, to name a few—they fought to break through psychic and ideological barriers to a moral and ontological revolution more momentous than the overthrow of capitalism. In *Life against Death* (1959), Brown named this revolution "the resurrection of the body," the abolition of repression anticipated in Romantic poetry and Christian mysticism. Property and accumulation, Brown argued, were ruses of repression, obstructing and enervating a full consciousness of reality. Once the senses are "emancipated from the sense of possession," then "the humanity of the senses and the human enjoyment of the senses will be achieved for the first time." In *Eros and Civilization* Marcuse posed against "repressive reason" the "rationality of gratification" that reconciled reason and the pleasure principle, suffused work with joy and playfulness, and celebrated "receptivity, contemplation, and enjoyment." Pointing to Orpheus and Narcissus as paradigms of unrepressed humanity, Marcuse beheld "the image of joy and fulfillment; the voice which does not command but sings; the gesture which offers and receives; the deed which is peace and ends the labor of conquest; the liberation from time which unites man with god, man, and nature."[6]

Although he rejected religion in *One-Dimensional Man* (1964) as "no longer contradictory to the status quo," Marcuse had conceded in *Eros and Civilization* that, in their expression of indefatigable longings for earthly justice and gratification, religious "illusions still have a higher truth value" than the disenchanted data of science. As student upheavals in Europe and North American mounted in the late 1960s, Marcuse came into his own as a romantic visionary, and the almost unrelieved pessimism of *One-Dimensional Man* yielded to the prophetic vivacity of *An Essay on Liberation*. Just as advanced technology was permitting the realm of freedom an entrance into the realm of necessity, radicals needed to rehearse for the revolution, practicing a similar "ingression of the future into the present." The "existential quality" of socialist relations "must show forth, anticipated and demonstrated, in the fight for their realization." Marcuse's summons to embark on reconnaissance missions to the frontiers of utopia entailed a secularized version of realized eschatology, the realization of a beatific vision in the sinful conditions of a fallen world—a "liberation from time," however brief and embattled, that brought the future into the present tense.[7]

Marcuse's conception of nature was even more evocative of a new sensibility beyond the confines of instrumental reason. Stirred by the new interest in ecology, he proclaimed in *Counterrevolution and Revolt* (1972) that nature is being rediscovered as "an ally in the struggle against exploitative societies." Here, Marcuse once again sided with Fourier against Marx, praising the "outrageously unscientific, metaphysical" account of nature in Marx's youthful writings—one lost in the more "scientific" socialism that ratified the bourgeois reduction of the natural world to raw material for industrial exploitation. Repudiating the capitalist provenance of Marxist instrumentalism, Marcuse advanced a teleological, even animistic account of nature that recalled the ontology of nineteenth-century Romanticism. Far from being an inert mass of objects available for measurement and use, nature, he argued, is a "subject" or "*cosmos* in its own right, with its own potentialities, necessities, and chances." Although a return to premodern superstitions about nature was impossible with the advance of science, Marcuse maintained that a technological culture permeated by a new sensorium would enable nature to realize its dormant faculties. Once free of the compulsion to ravage the earth imposed by economic necessity, a liberated community could "redeem" the "blindness" of nature, to "open its eyes" and help it "become what perhaps it would like to be."[8]

Yet Marcuse harbored deep and abiding doubts about the likelihood of revolution. As he wrote in *Counterrevolution and Revolt,* "power to the people" could not mean power to the "majority of the population as it exists today"—people whose needs and desires have been produced by the system, and who actively resist their own liberation. Part of the left melancholia that pervaded *One-Dimensional Man* stemmed from Marcuse's identification of "false needs" and "repressive desublimation": the cultural industries fostered spurious needs to ensure the steady accumulation of capital, while the liberalization of sexual mores distracted from psychic and political repression. This pessimism persisted even after *One-Dimensional Man,* while Marcuse was becoming an avuncular mentor in revolutionary consciousness to the New Left. He continued to believe that "false needs" had proliferated to the point that the most urgent revolutionary task was "to transform the will itself, so that people no longer want what they now want." Shackled to the system by invisible chains of fraudulent wants and counterfeit freedom, the inhabitants of capitalist societies required a revolutionary transformation of desire. "A qualitative change must occur in the infrastructure of man."[9]

However, given Marcuse's unwavering commitment to the progressive pieties of Marxism, it was hard to see how such a change in "the infrastructure of man" could transpire. Where Ruskin, Morris, or Mumford had tied the atrophy of revolutionary desire to the mechanization and stupefaction of the labor process, Marcuse could see nothing but emancipatory potential in cybernetics and automation—unlike contemporaneous students of technology such as Harry Braverman, Stephen Marglin, and David F. Noble, whose histories of industrial technology and organization were calling into question the standard progressive orthodoxy about technological progress. The replacement of pointless "productivity" as an ideal with "the rationality of gratification," Marcuse wrote in *Eros and Civilization,* presupposed "a huge industrial apparatus, a highly specialized division of labor, the use of fantastically destructive energies, and the cooperation of vast masses." This ominous forecast did not prevent him from speculating in 1967 that "play with the potentialities of human and nonhuman nature" would soon be "the content of social labor." Fearful of "a romantic regression behind technology" and dazzled by the promise of industrial automation, Marcuse displayed both a serious misunderstanding of its technological scope and an indifference to its authoritarian possibilities. In "The End of Utopia," his identification of alienated labor with *physical* labor implied that *mental* labor could not be alienated—yet that very alienation was the essence of cybernetics. Indeed, the happy convergence of "technology and art . . . and work and play" was a perfection difficult to foresee on the basis of automation, which by its nature depended on the elimination of play from work and the subjection of production itself to systematized algorithmic programming. Marcuse foresaw that automation would concentrate this necessary labor among "technicians, scientists, engineers, etc.," but he overlooked the prospect of a postcapitalist technocracy. So when he predicted that advanced technology promised "the total control of human existence," Marcuse evaded the oligarchic implications of the cybernetic revolution.[10]

If Marcuse reverted to the Marxist faith in historical progress, Brown abjured the faith in progress itself. Recognizing how deeply Marxism was implicated in the malignancy of capitalist rationality, he determined that Marx's "Faustian and restless" humanism rendered him "unable to emancipate socialism or any other economy whatsoever from the motive of accumulation"; if ever achieved, socialism would be a "nightmare of infinitely expanding technological progress and human needs." Thus Brown opened his defense of *Life against Death* by assuming "the superannuation of the political categories" that had shaped modern revolutionary consciousness. In his view, the historical optimism common to both liberals and Marxists had been invalidated, not only by the horrific events of World War II but also by the pervasive sense of disappointment and betrayal that Brown perceived among the inhabitants of advanced industrial societies. Contrary to the promises of the Enlightenment, reason and material abundance had not made them happy; perhaps these attainments were not really what had been wanted all along. Demanding ever more economic and technological growth, humanity in the capitalist world was simply "making itself more unhappy and calling that unhappiness progress." "Unconscious of its real desires and therefore unable to obtain satisfaction," humanity was "hostile to life and therefore ready to destroy itself." Brown nonetheless declared his affinity with those terrified by "the inhuman character of modern civilization" yet "unwilling to abandon hope of better things." He enlisted Freud not only to diagnose capitalism but also "to reappraise the nature and destiny of man." Refusing to "recover optimism cheaply" like the Freudian revisionists that both he and Marcuse loathed, Brown became a far more original, unsettling, and radical critic than Marcuse, tracing the malady of capitalist civilization to the roots of the human condition itself. Thus Brown's urgently religious question: "What shall man do to be saved?"[11]

The religious temper of Brown's work—evident not only in *Life against Death* but also in *Love's Body* (1966) and *Closing Time* (1973)—is often overlooked both by sympathetic readers and by adversaries such as Philip Rieff and Daniel Bell, the latter ridiculing him as a "preceptor of Eros," an erudite but dangerous and irresponsible mentor in the art of abolishing the repressions necessary for culture and civilization. To be sure, Brown's affirmation of "polymorphous perversity"—the nonlocalized state of libidinal pleasure attributed to pre-Oedipal infants—portended a thoroughgoing assault on the psychic and moral ramparts of repression. As a "neurosis" produced in the course of repression, religion, Brown agreed with Freud, was also an attempt at cure "within the neurosis itself." But Brown was more generous than the master, recalling that all "substitute gratifications," whether religion, poetry, or dreams, "contain truth; they are expressions, distorted by repression, of the immortal desires of the human heart." Since religion—and especially the Christian hope for a "resurrection of the body"—originated in the unconscious demand for full and unending bodily delight, it preserved that insistent passion, even if in fantastical form. Yet because religion begins from our evanescent flesh, its redemptive failure lay, Brown wrote, in its "delusions of grandeur" about the body.[12] Better equipped, in Brown's view, to elucidate the "immortal desires" of the heart, psychoanalysis recognizes that religion resides at "the heart of the mystery" but carefully traces its enigma to the ungratified body. "Completing what religion tries to do"—and fails—psychoanalysis both "gathers to itself ageless religious aspirations" and becomes "the science of original sin." Psychoanalysis affords the possibility of redemption within the parameters of history, not outside them in an illusory heaven. The end of repression and the realization of desire would mean the transcendence of religion, a consummation foretold in the mysticism of Boehme and the clairvoyant cadences of Blake. Once cured of "the disease called man," a new humanity could begin "to live instead of making history, to enjoy instead of paying back old scores and debts, and to enter that state of Being which was the goal of Becoming."[13]

Humanity preferred "history" to "life," Brown believed, because it refused to accept the finality of death. Unlike Marcuse—who traced the origin of repression to the conflict between material scarcity and human wants—Brown followed the later Freud in seeing repression as the result of a struggle internal to the psyche: the desire for endless life and gratification against the fear of and rage at mortality. "The riddle of history," he discovered, "is not in Reason but in Desire; not in labor, but in love." Brown commenced his diagnosis of civilization from what Freud had labeled "the death instinct" or Thanatos, which arises from the desperate attempt to restore the original feeling of oneness with the mother that is ruined by the discovery of her separate existence. Thanatos spurs not only the Oedipal complex but also the project of history itself, as humanity creates endless surrogates for the ecstatic maternal world it has forever lost—in Freudian terms, history is sublimation, "projecting the repressed body into things." Determined to deny our inescapable annihilation and resentful of our fleshly limitations, we seek perpetuity through religious ceremonies, family lineages, technological control, and property accumulation, all of which entail some degree of domination over nature and other human beings. Yet these sublimations are ultimately and necessarily unsuccessful; especially under capitalism, "the more the life of the body passes into things, the less life there is in the body."[14] (Under conditions of repression, there is no life but wealth.) As the record of our brutal and futile attempts to achieve a vicarious immortality, "history," Brown maintained, has been Augustine's sinful desire to dominate, or Walter Benjamin's document of civilization that doubles as a document of barbarism.

To Brown, capitalism is another sublimation, a projection of life into things—and therefore a simulacrum of magic and religion. Though starting from the standard psychopathology of economics—money as symbolic excrement, economic conduct as the sublimation of unconscious "anal" concerns with aggression and mastery—Brown noted how this analysis remained "anchored in the secular." But after reviewing the vast historical and anthropological literature on money, Brown concluded that, to the contrary, money derived its power from "the magical, mystical, religious . . . the domain of the sacred." Besides, he asserted, the dichotomy between secular and sacred was unreal. "Secularization," he contended, "is only a metamorphosis of the sacred"—an observation he made, tellingly, in the course of criticizing "the illusion that modern money is secular." If the secular is a transfiguration of the sacred, then "the psychological realities of money" are, Brown declared, "best grasped in terms of theology." He speculated that the money complex is "the heir to and substitute for the religious complex, an attempt to find God in things."[15] Money is a sacrament of sublimation, a projection of life into inanimate objects.

In Brown's view, Protestant theology was a religious precursor to the psychoanalytical investigation of capitalism. Examining Luther's well-known scatological fixations, Brown echoed the Reformer's warning that, under capitalism, "power over this world has passed from God to God's ape, the Devil." The Devil as "personified evil" played a crucial role in Luther's theology, representing the stark and untrammeled reign of Thanatos and accounting for disobedience, death, and the growing hegemony of money. For Luther, Eros retreats into the sanctuary of the inner life, while Thanatos acquires the title deed to the world of society, economics, and politics. Since the goal of Satan is, in Brown's words, "the same as the fundamental aim of capitalism—to make himself *princeps mundi*," then the Reformation marks the victory of Thanatos and the exile of Eros to the realm of fantasy. "In the Protestant era," Brown declared starkly, "life becomes a pure culture of the death instinct."[16]

What is "the way out," as Brown put it—the path to salvation from capitalist enchantment? In *Life against Death,* Brown only beckoned lamely to an answer, struggling to envision a world whose features could be seen only through the mutilated imagination of repression. Once we had (somehow) accepted death, we could enjoy the "resurrection of the body": not a literal overcoming of physical cessation like that traditionally promised in Christian theology, but a recovery of sensual rapture, the polymorphous gratification that made the infant body so electric, charged with the grandeur of libido. Enfeebled now by our fear of extinction, the erotic impulse to full and joyful experience could flourish without anxiety or inhibition; the beatific vision of fleshly radiance and communion would have its thoroughly terrestrial fulfillment. In bodies "reconciled with death," we could regain paradise, however brief and vulnerable its enchantment. (Susan Sontag rightly characterized Brown's desideratum as "an eschatology of immanence.") The brave new world of Eros would still require production—or rather, *poesis*—as well as consumption—or rather, "enjoyment"—but Brown hinted that these would not constitute an "economy." Proceeding from Ruskin's maxim that "there is no Wealth but Life," resurrected human beings, making and enjoying without the specter of repression, would be "erotic rather than sadistic," seek "not mastery over but union with nature," and reward not "the inhuman principle of economizing" but rather "erotic exuberance."[17]

After *Life against Death* and its awed reception among intellectuals, Brown continued to only beckon toward the future, growing ever more portentous and oracular, beginning with his Phi Beta Kappa address at Columbia in May 1960, "Apocalypse: The Place of Mystery in the Life of the Mind." Proclaiming that we live in "age of miracles," Brown importuned the fledgling scholars to break free of "the bondage of books" and dwell instead in the state of "holy madness" that possessed "the maenad and the bacchant." In *Love's Body,* he abandoned even that level of logical coherence and linear argument, turning to a collage of aphorism, quotation, metaphor, and allusion, all drawn from his vast erudition. Renouncing psychoanalysis as his science of desire, Brown looked instead to animism, mysticism, and poetry for their intimations of enchantment and superiority to modern scientific objectivity. An aboriginal erotic science, primitive animism, he wrote, captured the "identification of subject and object" and embodied a "mystical participation" with the world. Infected by the death instinct, "civilized objectivity"—the reason and science of the Enlightenment—imposed "separation" and "dualism" and reflected the realities of "property and prison." Since politics and revolution were futile and murderous substitutes for real, "mystical" transformation, Brown urged "a return to the principle of ancient animistic science, mystical participation, but now for the first time freely; instead of religion, poetry."[18]

Yet Brown never let go of the language of religion, as was evident in his exchange with Marcuse about *Love's Body* in the pages of *Commentary* in the winter of 1967—a dispute which, while changing nothing in either man's position, still clarified the ontological and political stakes. Although Marcuse admired the intellectual daring of *Life against Death,* he berated Brown's attempt to play the oracle in *Love's Body.* One could revel in Brown's virtuosity with language, he conceded, but "then comes the hangover": the realization that wordplay was no substitute for revolution. Charging Brown with "regression" and "mystification"—two of the cardinal sins in the Marxist catechism—Marcuse condemned Brown for balking at "the grand leap into the realm of freedom and light" and taking instead "a leap backward, into darkness." Against Brown's holy fool, Marcuse played the sober, realistic revolutionary, inadvertently confirming Brown's portrayal of Marxism as yet another form of bourgeois epistemology. We must always keep in mind, he lectured Brown, "the decisive difference between real and artificial, natural and political, fulfilling and repressive boundaries and divisions."[19]

Marcuse could not have done a better job of making Brown's point by missing it so completely, as such "realism" was precisely what Brown wanted to revisit. Besides, Brown implied in his response, for all his dedication to "critique," Marcuse missed the point of iconoclasm: "not the abolition of the temple, but the discovery of the true temple." Iconoclasts were believers, Brown reminded Marcuse; they smashed idols in the service of divinity. The alternative to idolatry, Brown suggested, is not disenchantment but rather "mystery"—an acknowledgement of the unknown while refusing to reify it. Since, in Brown's view, religion no longer commanded assent among the educated except as a kind of poetry, poetry was now both the guardian of "mystery" and the archangel of the erotic imagination. Thus, Brown asserted, it was poetry and not politics that held "the real revolutionary power to change the world." With the student and countercultural movements undoubtedly in mind, he countered Marcuse by declaring that "the next generation needs to be told that the real fight is not the political fight, but to put an end to politics." We must pass, Brown concluded, "from politics to poetry."[20]

# 29

# Heaven Which Exists
## and Is Everywhere around Us

The Sacramental Vision of Postwar Utopians

IF BROWN ESCHEWED POLITICS in favor of poetry, others saw no chasm or incommensurability between the two realms. When *Life against Death* appeared, a rediscovery of Romanticism was already well under way in Britain, where E. P. Thompson and Raymond Williams—founders of the British New Left disillusioned by Nikita Khrushchev's denunciation of Stalinism in 1956—were revisiting the lineage of Ruskin, Morris, and other critics of industrial capitalism. "After William Blake," Thompson concluded in *The Making of the English Working Class* (1962), "no mind was at home" among both Romantics and radical artisans, "nor had the genius to interpret the two traditions to each other." In the failure of those traditions "to come to a point of juncture," Thompson regretted, "something was lost. How much we cannot be sure, for we are among the losers." Given Thompson's commitment to reversing the effects of "the enormous condescension of posterity," that judgment could be read as an invitation to take up the work left unfinished by Blake.[1]

In France, the Situationist International, led by Guy Debord, Raoul Vaneigem, and other anti-Stalinist leftists, concocted an unlikely but pyrotechnic compound of Marxism, anarchism, surrealism, and Dadaism, aiming to undermine the "society of the spectacle" through the deliberate creation of "situations": moments when unrepressed desires for pleasure and adventure could burgeon forth, awakened and liberated through poetry and art and unperverted by advertising. The "revolution of everyday life," as Vaneigem called it, would bring the spirit of the avant-garde into the streets to abolish the distinction between art and life imposed by industrialization. When it leaves the mausoleum of Art, Vaneigem wrote, poetry "belongs first and foremost in action, in a way of living and in the search for a way of living." Poetry "animates all great revolutionary carnivals, until the bureaucrats place it under house arrest in their hagiographical culture." Such a revolutionary moment came in May 1968, when radical students in Paris called for "all power to the imagination" and emblazoned Situationist slogans and ideas on posters, pamphlets, and buildings.[2] Young communards rejected a radicalism housebroken by the necessities of bureaucracy and compromise.

So if Brown's vatic renunciation of politics for "poetry" incensed Marcuse, the events of May 1968 in particular—as well as, by the time of *Love's Body*'s publication, the nascent convergence of the New Left and the counterculture—validated his perception of a crisis of political modernity. The aversion of radical students throughout the North Atlantic countries to both liberal democracy and "really existing socialism" convinced many observers that, as Barrington Moore, Jr., opined in 1967, "there is a sense in the air, especially among the young" not only that "Marxism and liberalism have in good measure ceased to provide explanations of the world" but also that they "have become part of what requires explanation." The sense that the two preeminent lineages of progress "required explanation"—that they were part of the problem, not part of the solution, as younger radicals put it—opened up a possibility for fresh and untested sources of revolutionary vision and vitality. Once the fiery antagonists of capitalism, the traditional left, Roszak sighed in 1969, was now "the lead-bottomed ballast of the status quo," the middle managers of a consumerist, technocratic civilization. Looking with both hope and desperation to the "garish motley" of the counterculture—"depth psychiatry, the mellowed remnants of left-wing ideology, the oriental religions, Romantic *Weltschmerz,* anarchist social theory, Dada and American Indian lore"—Roszak identified it as the last, best alternative to "an existence wholly estranged from everything that has ever made the life of man an interesting adventure."[3]

Roszak captured a vibrant religious sensibility that joined the countercultural longing for transcendent experience to the utopian desire for the abolition of capitalism and the downfall of the state. Abandoning the parties of "progress," a montage of poets, artists, writers, and religious figures comprised a new party of enchantment, denouncing the allegedly disenchanted orthodoxy that consecrated the techno-capitalist imperium. This postwar company of enchantment personified a new efflorescence of Romantic "imagination": the ecstatic fulfillment of reason, the capacity to see the reality of the world concealed beneath the avarice and powerlust that occluded and perverted a passionate vision. Although the vessels of "imagination" varied and intermingled—poetry, painting, sculpture, Catholic theology and mysticism, Hindu and Zen Buddhist spirituality, Amerindian animism—they converged on a moral and political economy of artisanal anarchism, a "visionary commonwealth," in Roszak's words, that abided in a "sacramental consciousness."[4]

The partisans of the "visionary commonwealth" overlapped with the ranks of postwar "personalism," a confluence of religious and secular philosophies: the Catholic personalism of Dorothy Day and the Catholic Workers; the Gandhian *satyagraha* disseminated by Richard B. Gregg and other pacifists; the existentialist theology associated with Martin Buber, Paul Tillich, and other modernist exponents of Judaism and Christianity; and the anarcho-pacifism of Dwight Macdonald, Paul Goodman, and other contributors to journals such as *politics* and *Liberation,* a forum for Christian, Jewish, Hindu, Buddhist, and secular pacifists. Alarmed by the gargantuan scale of modern social organization, the inability of science to provide a compelling morality in the wake of religion, and the tendency of modern technology to alienate workers and ravage the planet, personalists insisted on the reduction of social and political activity to "a modest, unpretentious, personal level," as Macdonald explained in "The Root Is Man," "one that is real in the sense that it satisfies, here and now, the psychological needs, and the ethical values of the particular persons taking part in it." Against the abstract, anonymous "individual" of liberal social and political thought, personalists upheld the dignity and happiness of "the person"—the embodied and limited human being, actively engaged with others in the creation of a democratic, egalitarian community.[5]

The personalist imagination represented a revival of the ideal of "beloved community." "Love" had appeared before as a virtue and objective in American radicalism: the arcadians of Brook Farm, the Social Gospellers, the "Young Americans," and Catholic Workers had all looked to what Randolph Bourne had called the "Beloved Community." Banished from Cold War liberal rhetoric in favor of "realism," "love" and the "Beloved Community" flourished among liberals and radicals on the margins. "Our ultimate end," declared Rev. Martin Luther King, Jr.—perhaps the greatest avatar of personalism—"must be the creation of the beloved community." Both the founding statement of the Student Non-Violent Coordinating Committee (SNCC) and the Port Huron Statement of Students for a Democratic Society declared love to be an ultimate goal of radical democratic politics. SNCC's vision, outlined in its founding charter in 1960, was "a social order of justice permeated by love," the "redemptive community." Two years later, Tom Hayden's manifesto for Students for a Democratic Society listed "reason, freedom, and love" as the primary aims of participatory democracy. By the early 1970s, as the personalist political sensibility of love brought the relationship of politics and personal life to an ever greater degree of visibility, the women's and gay liberation movements made examining the meaning of "love" central to their revisions of sexuality, marriage, and family.[6]

More attuned to the politics of personal life, and convinced that Marxism promised nothing more than a cosmetic change to what Simone Weil called "the Apparatus," personalists turned to the artisanal and anarchist traditions. Prefigured in Catholic Worker farm communes and houses of hospitality, communities founded on personalist principles proliferated after World War II—"experiments in creative living," as the editors of *Liberation* characterized them, that anticipated the wave of communes and cooperatives that arose in the 1960s. Religious personalists aspired to be the avantgarde of the *eschaton,* establishing outposts of heaven that joined personal fulfillment to beloved community. They determined that, as Buber asserted, "a real community . . . must consist of people who, precisely because they are comrades, have mutual access to one another and are ready for one another," a condition that required a "center" that is "transpicuous to the light of something divine." Founded on ecumenical religious principles, many cooperatives strove to be artisanal comrades in relation to a fulcrum of divinity. In Glen Gardner, New Jersey, for instance, the future antiwar activist David Dellinger and other Protestant pacifists set up a community devoted to farming and handicraft in which "everyone took his or her share of both intellectual and physical work," Dellinger and his fellow emissaries from beatitude abolished "artificial distinctions between owners, managers, skilled craftsmen, and laborers." As the Quaker and future New Left historian Staughton Lynd remembered of the Macedonia Cooperative Community in northeastern Georgia, the residents shared a "common religious experience" of *agape* while engaging in dairy farming and supplying playground equipment for elementary schools. Although many of these "intentional" communities—like Koinonia Farm, Clarence Jordan's "demonstration plot for the Kingdom of God" in Americus, Georgia—originated as attempts at racial reconciliation, almost all of them struggled to practice artisanal, communalist forms of production in the midst of corporate industrial society.[7]

Although they did not aim explicitly at the eradication of capitalism, many in the civil rights movement affirmed the personalist conviction of a pervasive divine presence in the world. While the religious nature of the movement's commitment to nonviolence has often been reiterated, the ontological roots of its pacifism—the foundation of its unarmed struggle in a theological account of the nature of the world—are easy to overlook or dismiss. If indeed, as David Chappell has argued, the movement should be understood as a religious revival—a great awakening replete with talk of miracles, conversions, and even sacraments—then its politics of direct nonviolent action drew on a faith in the architecture of creation. The "love" they invoked was a cosmic divine power, just as tangible—perhaps more so—than the conventional forces of politics. As one SNCC activist put it, the lunch counter sit-ins that dramatized Jim Crow and its evils constituted "a sacramental reenactment" of Jesus's encounters with the disinherited. Political action was a material sign of an invisible grace, "a chance for the word to become flesh." King had encountered "the word" during the Montgomery bus boycott in 1956. Emotionally exhausted by the stress he was enduring—even thinking, like Jesus in the garden of Gethsemane, of "a way to move out of the picture without appearing a coward"—King sat at his kitchen table and "decided to take my problem to God," confessing his weakness and despair. "At that moment," King recalled, "I experienced the presence of the Divine in a way I had never experienced Him before." Sensing the "quiet assurance of an inner voice" that promised divine assistance if he continued in the struggle, "I was ready to face anything." King abided in this hope, because he believed that love was not an emotion but rather the ontological leaven of the cosmos. His oft-cited claim that "the moral arc of the universe is long, but it bends toward justice" was more than an inspiring exhortation; it was a corollary to his theological conviction that "the universe is under the control of a loving purpose . . . in the struggle for righteousness man has cosmic companionship."[8] In line with Nat Turner's visions and Owen Whitfield's epiphany in the fields of Southern tenancy, many in the crusade for civil rights saw the movement as a sacramental sign of divine intervention in history.

Even personalists who considered themselves secular often turned to religious figures and vocabulary. Paul Goodman, for instance, sometimes wrote in an overtly religious dialect. In *Growing Up Absurd* (1960), Goodman characterized "absurdity"—the sense of meaninglessness felt not only by the young but also by many trapped in corporations—as "an actual religious plight." Induced by useless bureaucratic labor and unsuccessfully assuaged by consumer goods, absurdity, Goodman argued, could be eliminated only by the recovery of "vocation" or "calling" as the paradigm of labor. "What now passes for 'vocational guidance' or 'aptitude testing' is the exact contrary of vocation in the old sense, a man's natural or God-ordained work." Goodman tried to salvage whatever remained worthy in the Protestant ethic. "Vocation," Goodman explained, "is the way a man recognizes himself as belonging, or appoints himself, in the community life and work." Vocation required faith and was a channel of grace. For Goodman, faith was simply confidence that "the world will continue to support the next step" of one's evolving life, while grace arrived in a world abundant with "possible ways for activity and achievement." The person committed to a vocation enters a "state of grace" in which vexation about the meaning of one's life never arises.[9]

Goodman's fellow anarchist Macdonald displayed a fondness for religious radicals. Replying in "The Root Is Man" to the Marxist charge that the personalist viewpoint was "of necessity a religious one," Macdonald wrote that "if by 'religious' is simply meant non-materialistic or non-scientific, then this is true. But if God and some kind of otherworldly order of reality is meant, then I don't think it is true." While his own radical stance was "certainly compatible with religion," Macdonald added, "I personally see no necessary connection, nor am I conscious of any particular interest in religion myself." Yet he published a sympathetic profile of Dorothy Day in the *New Yorker* in 1952, and he remained a friend and admirer of a movement whose blend of conservative Catholicism and radical politics was "a chimera perhaps, in Marxist taxonomy—but also a phoenix," as he maintained in the *New York Review of Books* in 1971. The endurance, not only of the Catholic Workers but also of the appeal of the Christian love they exemplified, struck Macdonald as "one of those frequent, indeed chronic, irruptions of the unexpected that shows history is not a well-trained valet to any system of ideas . . . one of those surprises that make life life." A *kairos,* in another idiom, a divine moment of opportunity.[10]

A sacramental imagination also appeared among postwar modernist artists and writers. Foraging among and transfiguring the debris of capitalist civilization, Joseph Cornell, for instance, fashioned his "memory boxes" from faded ornaments, old photographs, and images of paintings he discovered in bookstores and thrift shops. Cornell's assemblages—"poetic theaters" as he called them—embodied more than an aesthetic of the discarded, as he intended his retrieval of found objects to bestow a second, more enchanting life on the detritus of commodity fetishism. A Christian Scientist, Cornell sought in the scraps he collected a spiritual therapy similar to that offered by his denomination's healing practices. Since, according to the metaphysics of Christian Science, the material world is a gateway for the mental, "real" world, Cornell thought of his work as a revelatory medium, not as art for museums and galleries. The typical Cornell collage is a makeshift sacrament of the mundane, a portal to divinity through bric-a-brac, "a world of complete happiness," as he wrote in his diary, "in which every triviality becomes imbued with a significance."[11]

Mark Rothko shared Cornell's aspiration to make art a form of material grace, some point of contact with transcendent reality, not, as middlebrow aesthetics would have it, a vehicle of self-expression. Despite the fame lavished on his color-field paintings, Rothko always angrily resisted categorization as an "abstract expressionist." As he told a gathering of art students at the Pratt Institute in 1958, he had "never thought that painting a picture has anything to do with self-expression." Self-expression, he warned, "often results in inhuman values." While any artist was inevitably expressing a self, that self should never be stripped of "will, intelligence, civilization." A painting was, to Rothko, not a revelation of one's innermost being but rather "a communication about the world to someone else." Thus, a painting had to be, above all else, truthful, and "truth must strip itself of self, which can be very deceptive." Thus Rothko eschewed the desire of Barnett Newman and other artists to make "cathedrals . . . of ourselves," as Newman had written in 1948. Yet Newman did hope to reunite the talent of the painter with the skill of the artisan and the vision of the seer, a performer of "mythical action," as he put it to an interviewer in 1959.[12]

Rothko had long felt obliged to articulate, if only to himself, a theoretical foundation for his work. The son of Russian Jews, Rothko always aspired to be a religious artist, and he descanted on art in almost rabbinical fashion.

Living and painting in Manhattan just before World War II, he began, together with his friends Newman and Adolf Gottlieb, to study Freud, Jung, and Nietzsche. Rothko's interest in archaic mythology and ritual prompted him to reflect on the mythic promise of American art. During the 1940s, in published essays as well as in private notebooks, Rothko pondered the myth-making responsibilities of modern artists. Calling himself a "mythmaker," Rothko theorized that modern artists had inherited the vocation once per-formed in antiquity by priests, prophets, and bards: the creation of my-thology, the construction of narratives in which human beings discovered their possibilities through contact with "intermediaries, monsters, hybrids, gods and demigods."[13] Fearful that a demonic business civilization had crafted its own fables of destiny, Rothko aspired to paint a mythology for a democratic, corporate age.

The portrait of the artist that emerges in these writings was both mytho-logical and sacramental. Art, Rothko confided to his notebook, provides a window onto eternity, and the artist gives tactile form to transcendence, con-necting timeless truths with tangible matter. "Informing human sensuality" by offering "direct contact with eternal verities," the artist seeks a "reduction of these verities to the realm of sensuality, which is the basic language for the human experience of all things." Artists are always mythmakers, and the creation of a myth always represents not only a "dissatisfaction with partial and specialized truths" but also a powerful longing for union with the fun-damental forces of the cosmos. The metaphysical and religious ambition of Rothko's aesthetics was urgent and unequivocal. The mythic aspiration of art manifested, in his words, "a desire to immerse ourselves within the felicity of an all-inclusive unity." "Men," Rothko asserted, "could not live long without gods."[14]

Rothko's quest for a modernist form of enchantment resembled that of Henry Miller, whose status as a pioneer of literary eroticism has obscured his lifelong spiritual pilgrimage. Though a self-proclaimed "pagan" who detested "Christian humbug," Miller's work chronicled his search for an enchantment beyond the grasp of Mammon, a moral and ontological break-through to achieve "the recovery of the dignity of man." Even the novels he wrote while an expatriate in Paris in the 1930s—banned in the United States until 1961—convey Miller's sense both of the diabolical nature of business and of the spiritual sources of resistance. In *Tropic of Capricorn*, for instance, the protagonist "Henry V. Miller" works in the personnel division of the Cos-modemonic Telegraph Company, a fictional version of the Western Union Company, for which Miller had worked while a young man in New York. Behind its affable corporate face, the Cosmodemonic is an all-pervasive and malicious tyranny, a "slaughterhouse" where the souls of desperate, servile workers are digested and excreted. "Lawless, violent, explosive, demonical," the Cosmodemonic only reflects the larger, inescapable universe of corpo-rate iniquity. The only relief from the Cosmodemonic comes in booze, sexual adventure, or the occasional epiphany. "Everything is sentient," Henry V. says. "Once this fact is grasped, there can be no despair."[15]

Miller's odyssey began in earnest when he visited Greece on the eve of the war. What began as "a long vacation" from the literary and erotic intrigues of Paris became a journey of personal metamorphosis. As he recalled in *The Colossus of Maroussi* (1941), the Greek landscape became a "Book of Revela-tion," triggering "a metaphysical bliss which makes everything clear." Standing in Agamemnon's tomb, Miller listened to "the heart of the world beat"; its steady, powerful rhythm encouraged him to "give up, to relinquish, to surrender, so that our little hearts may beat in unison with the great heart of the world." The sexual renegade of the Montparnasse began to sound like a desert father, rejoicing in renunciation: "free of possessions, free of all ties, free of fear and envy and malice," he found a peace he had never experienced in bohemia.[16]

Returning to America after the war, Miller embarked on a cross-country trip to reacquaint himself with his homeland. The two volumes this so-journ produced, *The Air-Conditioned Nightmare* (1945) and *Remember to Remember* (1947) are both classics of American self-flagellation and cata-logues of the "metaphysical bliss" that Miller professed to see in his native land. On one level, Miller wrote, America is "an Inferno which exceeds anything that Dante imagined": miles and miles of factories, dumps, sleazy hotels, bad food, and abject poverty—America never "seemed more hid-eous." Yet amid this American grotesquerie, Miller could affirm that "the earth is a Paradise, the only one we will ever know. We don't have to make it a Paradise—it *is* one." From the Amish to the Cherokee, Americans could be "poetic to the core and deeply religious"; scanning the hills around Al-buquerque in the advancing dusk, Miller pronounced it "a land of enchant-ment." In an African-American neighborhood in Chicago, Miller warmed to the message on the side of a run-down house: "GOOD NEWS! GOD IS LOVE!"[17]

Miller's most sacramental insight appeared in *Remember to Remember*, when, complaining about the disgrace of mass-produced bread, he traced its genesis to the breakdown of religious life. "Before Communism there was Communion," the practice of thanksgiving for the abundance of the world. But having lost its faith in divine beneficence, industrial societies tied their hopes to the scientific and profitable production of everything, including bread. Both capitalism and Marxism, those "bread-and-butter philosophies" Miller had come to distrust, applauded the manufacture of bogus and un-healthy substitutes for genuine nourishment. With a keener appreciation of the meaning of sacrament than many a devout believer, Miller praised a eu-charistic way of life. "Life begins with bread. And a prayer . . . a prayer of thanks. Bless God for his favors—air, water, sun, moon." "God wants you to enjoy the bread of life," he continued. "He never meant you to go out all day working at a job you loathe so that you can buy a loaf of store bread wrapped in cellophane." "God"—whatever Miller conceived the deity to be—had cre-ated the world out of a bounty whose expenditure required no compensation. "The world isn't kept running because it's a paying proposition," as Miller condensed the wisdom of the artist. "God doesn't make a cent on the deal."[18]

Despite the varieties of this "sacramental consciousness," a conviction that the everyday world harbored intimations of divinity united the partisans of the visionary commonwealth. In Allen Ginsberg, the Romantic provenance of the sacramental vision was unmistakable, as in "Howl" (1956), where he proclaimed the

Heaven which exists, and is everywhere around us!

In another early poem, Ginsberg declared that

This is the one and only
Firmament . . .
I am living in Eternity.
The ways of this world
are the ways of Heaven.

Ginsberg's friend and fellow Zen Buddhist Gary Snyder agreed. Invoking an array of what orthodox Christians would have considered pagans or heretics—Hopi, Gypsies, Quakers, Diggers, Albigensians, and the Brethren of the Free Spirit, comprising what he called "the Tribe"—Snyder claimed in 1962 that "the universe is not a dead thing but a continual creation . . . springing from the trance of Brahma." Snyder adduced as evidence his friend, a Wasco Indian logger who quit his job and sold his chainsaw because "he couldn't stand hearing the trees scream as he cut into them."[19]

Zen was not the only source of sacramental consciousness for romantic utopians. In *Where the Wasteland Ends,* one of the more sprawling and eloquent documents of the search for a new religious sensibility, Roszak—a lapsed Catholic—enlisted Romantic poets and Amerindian shamans and magicians as avatars of "visionary imagination." As the inherited Judeo-Christian catechism had become, like the technocratic vernacular it only lamely counterpointed, "a jackbooted parade of lifeless verbal formulas," the "resurrection" of sacramental or visionary consciousness was "an urgent project of the times." The pre-scientific world of what he called "the Old Gnosis" "delighted in finding the sacred in the profane"; it was "a visionary style of knowledge, not a theological one; its proper language is myth and ritual; its foundation is rapture, not faith and doctrine; and its experience of nature is one of living communion." One of the more popular religious writers of the Cold War era and eventually a prophet against the Vietnam War, the Catholic monk Thomas Merton conveyed a similarly sacramental sensibility without the jargon of theology. "Every blade of grass is an angel in a shower of glory," he exulted in *Raids on the Unspeakable* (1966); "every plant that stands in the light of the sun is a saint and an anthem."[20]

Poet, critic, anarchist, and by the mid-1950s, the gray eminence of American bohemia, Kenneth Rexroth epitomized an erudite synthesis of radical politics and sacramental imagination. An intellectual and spiritual polymath, Rexroth never believed that his art or his anarchist convictions precluded spiritual commitment. "Literature is work. Art is work. And work, said St. Benedict, is prayer," he reflected in 1958. The genuinely radical life had to be, in Rexroth's view, an *imitatio Christi.* "Anyone who tries to model his life on Christ and his apostles," he wrote in 1967, "is by definition alienated from a predatory society." As a young radical in the 1920s, Rexroth had been a postulant at the Holy Cross Monastery in West Park, New York—spiritual center of the Anglican social gospel espoused by Fr. James Huntington and Vida Dutton Scudder. Immersing himself in the daily monastic routines of prayer, reading, work, and liturgy, Rexroth grew convinced that Catholicism consummated "the most ancient responses to the turning of the year and the changing seasons, and the rhythms of animal and human life." Long after Rexroth left Holy Cross, he remained a frequent attendant at Anglican services, read Offices from a breviary, and chanted Compline before bed. Even when he later explored Buddhism and Taoism, Rexroth never repudiated the liturgical and sacramental imagination of Catholic religious culture.[21]

Presiding over San Francisco's anarcho-bohemian enclave, Rexroth never repudiated this Catholic sensibility, as it afforded, in his words, "the accessibility of bliss of vision, of total knowledge of significance." The sacramental vision both conferred and revealed the ennobling enchantment of daily life. "The fundamental activities and relationships of life—birth, death, sexual intercourse, eating, drinking, choosing a vocation, adolescence, mortal illness"—all enabled "the ceremonious introduction of transcendence." In verse, Rexroth conveyed a similar awareness of an abiding presence deep down things. A Gerard Manley Hopkins in the age of Einstein, he often rendered the grandeur of God in a scientific and ecological idiom more appealing to the modern mind. As he put it in a book aptly titled *The Signature of All Things* (1950), "The saint saw the world as streaming / In the electrolysis of love." The ontological source of that illustrious cascade was "God," whose "Indwelling encompasses / All reality."[22]

What Rexroth called the "electrolysis of love" was stymied, however, by the malevolent social and political forces of what Roszak called "the technocracy": the estate of corporate and government managers, scientists, and technical wizards—the purveyors of the "objective consciousness" that sanctioned the exploitation of workers, the despoliation of the natural world, and the repression of any trace of the sacramental vision from the consciousness of modern societies. For Ginsberg, it was "Moloch," the ancient Mesopotamian demon returning as the master deity of capitalist enchantment: "Moloch whose factories dream and croak in the fog!" Moloch is a behemoth of mercenary and technical nihilism, an abhorrent pollution deep down things:

Moloch whose mind is pure machinery!
Moloch whose blood is running money!
Moloch whose fingers are ten armies!

Moloch whose eyes are a thousand blind windows! . . .
Moloch whose love is endless oil and stone!
Moloch whose soul is electricity and banks!

For Rexroth, it was "the Social Lie," the organized system of deceptions through which a society and state enforce submission. As the poet laureate of American anarchism, Rexroth penned long disquisitions in verse on the spiritual rot of "the Enemy" or "the State," the leviathan into which the United States was turning on account of its swelling commodity fetishism:

America is today a
Nation profoundly deranged,
Demented, and sick, because
Americans with very few
Exceptions believe, or when
They doubt are terrified to
Be discovered doubting, that
Love is measured entirely
In an interchange of
Commodities.[23]

Like all loves, commodity fetishism had its "sacrament," and like that of all perverse loves it was a sacrament of death: the atomic bomb. To Rexroth, nuclear weapons represented

The Apotheosis of quantity.
The blazing mushroom cloud is
Just a mystical vision
As one would expect of the
Managers of the Du Pont
Industries.[24]

Merton was the Catholic eminence of sacramental radicalism. In *No Man Is an Island* (1955), Merton observed that people who light their cigars with money were displaying "a deep, pure sense of the ontological value of a dollar." Over the next decade, that remark grew into an exegesis of America's mercenary theology. In his "Letter to a White Liberal" (1964), Merton noted that the civil rights movement exposed the adherence of both segregationists and liberals to the ontological gold standard of white America: money. The effectiveness of bus boycotts and lunch counter sit-ins proved that "it was only when money became involved that the Negro demonstrations finally impressed themselves upon the American mind as being real." The cult of Mammon was the nation's real civil religion: "it is not the life of the spirit that is real to us, but the vitality of the *market*." Whatever Americans say about their devotion to "spiritual values," they don't believe in them unless they can be swiftly and profitably translated into "terms of buying and selling." But since money "has no ontological reality," then the capitalist market exchange it mediates is a network of "abstract operations"—codes, ceremonies, iconography devoted to the worship and service of nothingness. "The ritual that surrounds money transactions, the whole liturgy of marketing and of profit, is basically void of reality and of meaning."[25]

Merton reasoned that this monetary ontological sensibility shed light on American conceptions of freedom. "The most basic freedom of all is the freedom to make money." If American individualism meant, in the end, that "the freedom of the person is dependent on money," then "without money, freedom has no meaning." What was true for the person was true for the corporation—itself a "person" by the canons of pecuniary ontology. When most white Americans bloviate about "freedom," what they really mean, Merton charged, was "the unlimited freedom of the corporation." Thus, for Merton, the Cold War became the enforcement of capitalist metaphysics on the larger—and often unwilling—world. The American willingness to arm, bankroll, or overlook tyranny around the world indicated that the "free world" was "first of all the world in which *business* is free."[26]

Merton's prophecy no longer seems so overheated. In the neoliberal palaver of "globalization" and "privatization," the reign of money would soon be heralded as the end of history, the victory of reason, one market under God. The heavenly city of business for which Earnest Elmo Calkins had pined seemed to Merton not far from completion. In "Rain and the Rhinoceros," a haunting essay in *Raids on the Unspeakable*, Merton imagined the sad perversity of a world reduced to inventory. As he listened to showers in the forest near the Kentucky abbey where he lived, Merton hastened to convey the beauty of the rain before "it becomes a utility that they can plan and distribute for money." To Merton, this insatiable avarice indicated an evil much deeper than moral perversion; it emanated from a capitalist enchantment that only masqueraded as secularity. Business was launching a metaphysical revolution to enshrine the fundamental axiom that "what has no price has no value, that what cannot be sold is not real." In the cosmology of capital, "the only way to make something *actual* is to place it on the market." Graphing the rain on the commercial axis of effective demand and scarcity of supply, members of the cult of moneytheism would "not appreciate its gratuity." Yet for those who saw the world as the lavish largesse of a loving and prodigal God, "rain is a festival," a celebration of its own gifted and pointless existence that is open to everyone for free.[27]

It was in this spirit of the gift that Merton, like other sacramentalists, espoused what amounted to a communism reminiscent of Ruskin, Morris, and the lineage of anarchism and the Arts and Crafts movement. "A man cannot be a perfect Christian," Merton declared flatly in *Seeds of Contemplation* (1949), "unless he is also a communist." Against "the spurious communism of the Marxists," Merton posed God's own "communism of charity and grace." Since everything belongs to God, we must "either absolutely give up all right to possess anything at all, or else only use what he himself needs." In this communism of grace, the sacramental performance of labor, perverted by capital accumulation, would afford human beings the privilege of engaging in a "conversation with God," as he put it in *The New Man* (1961), the perfection of beatitude in labor expressed as artisanal *poesis*. The holy artisan of sacramental radicalism reappeared in *The Silent Life* (1957) among the monks who lavished care on their buildings, furniture, tools, and books like that given to "the sacred vessels of the altar." Work performed without this tender and meticulous attention was "a desperate anodyne," a truly laborious distraction from the emptiness of a life lived apart from the love of God. As Merton wrote in *New Seeds of Contemplation* (1962), "frantic, anxious work, work done under pressure of greed or fear or any other inordinate passion, cannot properly speaking be directed to God."[28]

Even those who rejected Merton's Christianity shared his sacramental conception of economics. Snyder—who asserted that Church, State, and "civilization" should be not only demolished but "exorcised" from the American soul and psyche—saw a time when we would "sacramentalize" new economic relationships, regarding them as "part of the divine ecology."

Looking to "Dharma revolutionaries" practicing the "joyous and voluntary poverty of Buddhism," Snyder advocated a "Buddhist anarchism" or "true Communionism," a mystico-anarchist version of the old Left's "free, international, classless world." The movement that Snyder envisioned combined the Wobblies and the Bodhisattva; "building a new world in the shell of the old" required learning the way of the Buddha, fusing the simplicity of the Eightfold Path with the solidarity of One Big Union:

Stay together
learn the flowers
go light.[29]

The Romantic imagination still animated Lewis Mumford. In an arc that went from *Art and Technics* (1952) and *The City in History* (1962) to the two-volume culmination of his career, *The Myth of the Machine,* Mumford continued his search for a *novum organum* that put "the primacy of life" ahead of productivity. As in *Technics and Civilization,* Mumford continued to perceive a macabre religious quality in the military-industrial technostructure. Especially in *The Pentagon of Power* (1970)—the second volume of *The Myth of the Machine*—he remarked that technological progress has now become "an Ersatz religion" in industrial societies. As the "masters of the secret knowledge of the Temple" and "willing servants of the Pharaoh," the scientific and technical elite constituted a "priesthood" every bit as enthralling as the clergy of old. Even worse, like Ginsberg's Moloch, "the religion of the megamachine demands wholesale human sacrifice"—not only in the liturgy of war but also in the funereal rite of unemployment, in which those deemed expendable are slain on the altar of the market for the gratification of Mammon.[30]

The latest deity in the pantheon of the megamachine was "the Computer," Mumford warned, with an omniscience and beguiling power comparable to that of the divinities forsaken by modernity. Automation, in his view, represented the epitome of technological enchantment, the culmination of those "magical aspirations" that had set the megamachine in motion at the beginning of civilization. Cybernetics and automation might elicit the "trancelike vaticinations" of a Marshall McLuhan, Mumford wrote, but the notion of a "global village" united by electronic communication remained, he thought, rapturous "humbug." Writing at the dawn of the widespread computerization of work and information processes, Mumford vigorously challenged the belief that automation was an instrument of human liberation. The extension of automated processes throughout society required the incorporation of more areas of life into the networks of mechanization, and our ever-greater dependence on mechanized systems forced us to submit to their requirements of technical efficiency and productivity. At the same time, when reason is so completely embodied in technology, human beings witness the atrophy of their creative capacities and regress into servitude to their basest and wildest impulses. If "daily work and religious ritual" no longer demand the personal exercise of rationality, we become hostage to "demonic" drives. "By funneling all order into the machine, man has cut himself off from those very repetitive acts and rituals" foster both self-discipline and creativity. Repenting of whatever technocratic illusions he had entertained during the Depression, he recognized that industrial automation fostered not a higher brand of intelligence but rather, as he wrote in *Art and Technics*, a "feeble-mindedness" indispensable to "docile productivity" as well as an "abdication of the human personality" in the anonymity and aesthetic indifference enforced by mass production.[31]

Mumford's conviction that the technological captivity of reason would both enervate and demonize human desire made him more skeptical of the counterculture than were Roszak or Rexroth. Ridiculing the "strictly money-making enterprise" of the Woodstock Festival in August 1969, Mumford pointed to its ruinous social and ecological effects—the "personality cult" of rock stars, traffic congestion, the piles of trash and garbage—and concluded that it "mirrored and even grossly magnified the worst features of the system." Because the counterculture was "attached by invisible electrodes to the same pecuniary pleasure center" that galvanized the entire corporate apparatus, the megamachine "has nothing to fear from this kind of reaction—equally regimented, equally depersonalized, equally under external control." Mumford contrasted the electro-delirium of the counterculture to the quieter but more compelling ceremonies of the antiwar movement. Participants in the Moratorium to End the War in Vietnam in October 1969 used "the lighted candle, an ancient religious symbol." Marching through Washington in inclement weather, these people, he contended, represented "a more vital counterculture."[32]

The marchers' reliance on an old and venerable form of technics underlined Mumford's continued affirmation of life and the artisanal ideal. Throughout the 1950s and 1960s, Mumford drew back somewhat from the neotechnic enthusiasm of *Technics and Civilization*. Still inspired by garden city urbanism, Mumford came to believe that humanity was not first *homo faber* but rather *homo symbolicus,* the "ritual enacting, god-seeking figure" in the animal world, as he wrote in *The Transformations of Man* (1956). Yet he remained true to the Romantic humanism of his prewar years. In *Art and Technics,* Mumford wrote of "the human person" in religious terms, demanding the restoration of its appropriate dignity as "a mirror of infinity and eternity." At the same time, he emphasized the bounty and extravagance of nature as the basis of human personhood. In *The Conduct of Life* (1951), for instance, Mumford grew incandescent when he marveled at the sheer superfluity of the natural world, whose standards of proliferation were less careful and exacting than the pecuniary and technical criteria of business. Unlike the regime of accountants and engineers, "nature," Mumford observed, "has patently not been so intent on the single goal of economy and efficiency." Like a joyful artist—or a loving god—nature was magnificently wasteful, uselessly prolific, beautifully spendthrift with its treasures. While nature certainly exhibited elements of precision worthy of any engineer, "the exuberance of life—exuberance and largesse—these make all our rational standards of economy seem mean and restrictive."[33]

"Exuberance and largesse" were the ontological bases for Mumford's affirmation of the artisan. The idealized artisan of *Art and Technics* was Mills's poet in action or Miller's spendthrift creator. "The craftsman, like the artist," Mumford rhapsodized, "lived *in* his work, *for* his work, *by* his work; the rewards of labor were intrinsic to the work itself, and the effect of art was merely to heighten and intensify natural organic processes." Wedding technical aptitude to expressive power, craft labor united "the artist and the technician" in one person, afforded the comradeship of equally talented workers, and allowed an exquisite "lingering with loving care" over processes and materials. The erotic resonance of Mumford's portrait of the artisan was more than literary ornament. Mumford strongly implied that handicraft was the model for a moral economy of life, and that the megamachine embodied an ontology of violence, despotism, and death. "The purpose of art," as he wrote in *The Pentagon of Power*, "has never been labor-saving but rather labor-loving."[34]

Still, Mumford remained profoundly ambivalent about the prospects for deliverance from the Machine. The hold it possessed on our material and imaginative lives was apparently unbreakable; even where we managed to shake free of our thralldom to its ideology of consumption and rationality, our complicity in its technological interdependence was so extensive that it was difficult to imagine living without it. Even the conventional methods of resistance were futile: with their need for precise coordination, Mumford thought that mass movements and political parties simply replicated the machine's hegemony. Real change would come, Mumford hoped, from individual resistance and small, collective undertakings "breaking routines and defying regulations." Such efforts seek to "slow down" the capitalist economy, "not to capture the citadel of power, but to withdraw from it and quietly paralyze it." Thus Mumford urged "quiet acts of mental or physical withdrawal . . . abstentions, restrictions, inhibitions" that would amount over time to "a steady withdrawal of interest, a slowing down of tempo, a stoppage of senseless routines and mindless acts."[35]

Mumford knew that such a revolution entailed an almost unimaginable metamorphosis in the common sense of capitalist societies, which were now so thoroughly misled by the sophistries of economic and technological reason. "For its effective salvation mankind will need to undergo something approaching a religious conversion," he mused near the end of *The Pentagon of Power*. In *The Conduct of Life*, Mumford had gestured to the early Christians as models of a slow but tenacious revolution, seeing in their perseverance a lesson and a source for contemporary regeneration. To be sure, the conversion of today would involve a very different language; it would have to replace the mechanical with an "organic" worldview that respected the realities of biology and ecology and restored to human beings the precedence now given to money and technology. But we would still have to call on the divine in ourselves, Mumford suggested cryptically. "The God who saves us will not descend from the machine," he concluded in *The Pentagon of Power*; "he will rise up again in the human soul."[36]

Roszak, too, looked to the early Christians as a saving remnant, albeit with a far more robust sensibility of enchantment than even Mumford's organicism could sustain. To Roszak, ancient Christianity was a cosmopolis of love in the midst of a moribund and collapsing civilization, "the protective shell," as he described it in *Where the Wasteland Ends,* "within which a purified, if much restricted sacramental consciousness could survive." Yet today's acolytes of sacrament could not descend into catacombs or retreat into the desert. "Once perhaps, the God-intoxicated few could abscond to the wild frontiers, the forests, the desert places to keep alive the perennial wisdom that they harbored." That time was over, Roszak declared. "They must now become a political force or their tradition perishes." Knowing more keenly than the technocracy that "politics is metaphysically and psychologically grounded," today's bearers of romantic imagination must rekindle the spirit to generate "the final radicalism of our society." There was, he insisted, no longer "any way to be significantly political" without relying on "magic and dreams," "science and alchemy," and "visionary poetry." The politics of sacramental consciousness drew, Roszak wrote potently, on "primordial energies greater than the power of our bombs."[37]

While these sibylline pronouncements earned Roszak a reputation as a credulous fellow-traveler of the counterculture, it is better to see him as, like Brown, one of its most gifted and versatile theorists. He accounted for the counterculture's appeal to a general audience (both *The Making of a Counterculture* and *Where the Wasteland Ends* were bestsellers) and discerned its inanities, while also harnessing its energy and genuine wisdom into a powerful statement of sacramental imagination. Trained as a historian, Roszak exhibited both a sharp critical eye and a generosity of spirit that enabled him to ferret out fraudulence while honoring the desires it enraptured and exploited. He vilified the drug culture as a "counterfeit infinity" ironically reflective of technological panaceas and "the worst sort of American commercialism," yet he also respected the longing for a richness of experience unattainable through scientific rationality. And although he aimed to discredit "the myth of objective consciousness" and the fealty to corporate expertise that it sanctioned, he never approved a facile or sweeping dismissal of modern science or technology. "It would be a ludicrous mistake," he cautioned overzealous readers of *The Making of a Counterculture,* "to contend that the things and forces with which science fills space and time"—cells, electrons, gravity, chromosomes—"are the cultural equivalents of centaurs and Valhallas and angelic beings." Like William James and "passionate vision," Roszak claimed that sacramental consciousness embraced and did not invalidate scientific knowledge, and that it offered no warrant for a general proscription of technological innovation. Agriculture, he reminded readers in *Where the Wasteland Ends,* "was invented by people living within a magical worldview," while "all the basic handicrafts were invented and expanded within the sacramental vision of nature."[38]

As he made so eloquently clear in his study of the counterculture, Roszak's goal was to "proclaim a new heaven and a new earth so vast, so marvelous that the inordinate claims of technical expertise must of necessity withdraw in the presence of such splendor to a subordinate and marginal status in the lives of men." To do that, he had to explain not only the sources of our submission to "the technocracy" but also the sources of our redemption from it. Like the earlier Mumford of *Technics and Civilization,* Roszak advanced two tales of disenchantment: one cogent and conventional, the other fragmentary but more explosive. The first story repeated the Weberian wisdom about disenchantment as "a relentless stripping down operation" that left nature "purged of its sacramental capacities": Protestantism, science, and capitalism evacuated matter of its inherent sacrality, leaving it inanimate, inert, and ready for technological control and industrial conquest. Embodied in technology, the power that derived from the disenchantment tale conferred extraordinary status on scientific and technical experts, whose knowledge, Roszak wrote, was akin to "the monopoly of the sacramental powers" held by the medieval clergy. Hence "science is our religion because we cannot, most of us, with any living conviction *see around* it." Yet as Roszak himself seemed half-aware, that very comparison suggested the outlines of a different narrative, in which modernity was characterized not by secularization, but by a covert sacramental sensibility that invested nature and science with the reverence once given to divinity. Nature "*has* become an idol," he observed, "the highest reality, the *only* reality"; but if, as Roszak remarked, idolatry is "a mistaken ontology . . . a flawed consciousness," then this idolatry was not a "disenchantment" so much as a "mistaken" or "flawed" enchantment.[39]

Although Roszak was unmistakably committed to the first story of disenchantment, the second account of a flawed enchantment better suited his hopes for a "visionary commonwealth." If the disenchantment narrative was correct, then the desacralization of nature could never really be reversed; a counterculture could confront the citadels of expertise with only beautiful but groundless fables—known to be such by intellectuals such as Roszak. But if, even in idolatrous form, modern science and technology are as "shot through with spiritual meaning" as the technics of ancient agriculture and handicraft, and if the cultural hegemony of "the technocracy" depended on adherence to a fallacious ontology, then the Romantic "battle cry of a new Reality Principle" could claim truth as well as poetic inspiration. Roszak himself wrote as if the second story were true. The magical consciousness, he argued, discerns but does not valorize the utilitarian features of the natural world; to call earth Mother Nature is "a brilliant and beneficial insight," not an anthropomorphic superstition. Similarly, Roszak contended that "in any healthy culture, invention would properly be indistinguishable from art and ritual; technological progress would be simultaneously a deepening of religious consciousness." He even longed for the day when "the sacramental vision of nature" would be "restored to science as a discipline of the sacred."[40]

Grounded in the myth of disenchantment, liberalism and Marxism—the primary vehicles of politics and progress—were useless and even inimical, Roszak thought, to the creation of the "visionary commonwealth." Anarchism, he maintained, is instead "the political style most hospitable to the visionary quest." Anticipated by the early Christians; Buddhists; and Taoists; the medieval mystical heretics and the radical Reformation sects; the loose tribal confederations of North America; and the Romantic, Transcendentalist, and utopian movements of the early nineteenth century, anarchism encapsulated the longing for self-fulfillment in a beloved community. "The stronger the mystical sensibility, the stronger the longing for anarchist brotherhood and sisterhood." Writing in the early 1970s as the New Left was fragmenting into a loose constellation of movements—feminism, gay liberation, environmentalism, the bevy of "lifestyle politics"—Roszak perceived the anarchist spirit in a jumbled assortment of experiments: organic homesteads, urban and rural communes, handicraft and farm cooperatives, and free schools and clinics, many inspired by Zen Buddhism and other forms of non-Western spirituality. To the standard "realist" complaint that this array was too disjointed to energize "mass movements and armed collectivities," Roszak retorted that that was precisely the point. People who have "tasted of the visionary splendors" have not the time or inclination for the callousness, duplicity, and pandering required for the game of power politics; "they want the peace and personal intimacy that alone allows for spiritual growth. And that means the life of small, congenial groups."[41]

Roszak upheld the British economist E. F. Schumacher as a philosopher of the "visionary commonwealth." With its advocacy of a "Buddhist economics" that repudiated "the soul and life-destroying metaphysics of the nineteenth century" epitomized in capitalism, Schumacher's unlikely bestseller, *Small Is Beautiful* (1973), became a canonical text of the counterculture. Rejecting the fundamental axioms of his discipline in a way not since John Ruskin's *Unto This Last,* Schumacher argued that our most intractable problems were religious, not economic or political. "We are suffering from a metaphysical disease," he wrote, and "the cure must therefore be metaphysical." "The task of our generation," he declared, "is one of metaphysical reconstruction." To Roszak, who wrote the introduction to the American edition of *Small Is Beautiful,* Schumacher was "the Keynes of postindustrial society," a society that has "left behind its lethal obsession with those very megasystems of production and distribution which Keynes tried so hard to make manageable." Dismissing the "phony plebiscite of the marketplace" and rejecting the dismal science and its "banal misanthropy," Roszak commended Schumacher's "nobler economics" and what he identified as its pedigree: Kropotkin, Landauer, Tolstoy, Morris, Gandhi, and Mumford, "the tradition we might call anarchism," whose spirit prospered amid "the fragile renaissance of organic husbandry, communal households, and do-it-yourself technics." The revolution would emerge from this peaceful, realized eschatology; the destruction of the capitalist technocracy would proceed through avoidance, subterfuge, and the quiet boldness of living now as one would live in the future. "There is never any telling," he wrote in *Where the Wasteland Ends,* "how far the power of imaginative example follows."[42]

Certainly there were problems with this amorphous road map to the "visionary commonwealth." Along with other opponents of "realism," Roszak failed to explain how these enclaves of beloved community could survive, let alone flourish, while surrounded by the ever-expanding apparatus of corporate capitalism; indeed, survival might entail the adoption of the very logic and practices that fostered the hegemony of the technocracy. The corporate counterculture was already embracing self-proclaimed mavericks such as Stewart Brand—included by Roszak among his roster of "visionary" pioneers.

Roszak himself had noted that the technocracy was "willing to flirt with social protest for the sake of containing it. It can let long hair grow in high places." It could also capitalize on wheat germ, pine nuts, granola, and artisanal bread. Moreover, the notion of "the technocracy" was itself misleading, as technical expertise remained subordinate to the requirements of capital accumulation. An even more fundamental quandary lay in the "garish motley" that characterized the varieties of sacramental sensibility itself. Not only did Amerindian animism, Buddhist karma, and Catholic sacrament differ enormously from one another, but it was also hard to tell how seriously Roszak himself took any single one of them, at least as anything other than a handy ideological counterpoint to "objective consciousness." What Jackson Lears has written of abstract expressionism might well have been true of postwar romantic radicalism as well. "Without some firmer ontological ground" than "sincerity" or "seriousness," Lears observed, the abstract expressionist "quest for authenticity could slide from sincerity to self-destruction."[43] As Roszak himself had remarked, political imagination is always inseparable from metaphysics. Thus, bereft of any firmer ontological ground than a vague sense of transcendence, the visionary commonwealth might flounder—even fail to ever appear—because its "sacramental vision" was neither clear nor common.

But as Roszak and other romantics might have retorted, that very ambiguity was part of the point, as well as the very essence of the adventure. In the wake of a Judeo-Christian lineage discredited both by science and by its subservience to earthly power, and in the face of a secular rationality that had proven at least as obsequious, an ecumenical, even crazily syncretic generosity was perhaps the only way to rescue and nurture the sacramental imagination. The record of conventional religion's complicity with capital was too voluminous for many rebellious spirits to take it seriously as an ally against pecuniary and technological reason. (As Schumacher—himself a convert to Catholicism—once quipped about "Buddhist economics," "if I had called it Christian economics, no one would have read it.")[44] As for the timidity of religion, so for "secularity," whose horizon of human possibility, whether in capitalist or socialist societies, seemed to extend no farther than the conquest of nature and the provision of consumer goods. If *manitou*, *prana*, shamanistic magic, Zen sutras, or Tantric yoga could reawaken wonder at a world beyond the clutches of human mastery—or rekindle a desire for communion irreducible to self-interested negotiation—then the exhausted or comatose traditions of the West would have to retreat and do penance, or expire. Perhaps the very hospitality of this sacramental vision would prove to be its cardinal virtue against capital's global democracy of cupidity.

Merton and Rexroth exemplified this ecumenical sacramental vision. By the mid-1960s, Merton—increasingly restless in his monastic vows and alienated from ecclesiastical authority—had become not only a respected social critic but also a Catholic emissary to Zen Buddhism. An early indication of his metamorphosis appeared in *The Wisdom of the Desert* (1960), his translation of sayings from the "desert fathers" of the fourth and fifth centuries. Clearly alluding to the liberal capitalist West, Merton observed that as the western Roman Empire collapsed, the first Christian hermits who fled to Egypt, Arabia, and Persia considered society "a shipwreck from which each single individual man had to swim for his life." But the ultimate purpose of expatriation was not simple "purity of soul"; they knew "they were helpless to do any good for others as long as they floundered about in the wreckage." Once they had "a foothold on solid ground," they had "not only the power but even the obligation to pull the whole world to safety after them." While "we cannot do exactly what they did," we—and Merton clearly engaged an audience of laity—had "a great and mysterious vocation" like that of the first monastics.[45]

Over the course of the next decade, Merton's stature as a prophet against the Vietnam War rose in tandem with his journey eastward to discover that "great and mysterious vocation." Joining the resurgent interest in Asian spirituality and religion that popularized expositors of Zen such as D. T. Suzuki, Thich Nhat Hanh, and Alan Watts, Merton honored Buddhism as a "sacramental, living, and objective view of the spiritual life," as he wrote in *Mystics and Zen Masters* (1967)—a sacramental life with political implications. Zen, he wrote in *Zen and the Birds of Appetite* (1968), both "implies a breakthrough, an explosive liberation from one-dimensional conformism"—an unmistakable reference to Marcuse—and points to "a dimension where the bottom drops out of the world of factuality and of the ordinary." In contrast, he continued, Western capitalism—even with its semi-official adherence to Christianity—has reached "the climax of an entire totalitarian rationality of organization" whose "rational machinery" foreclosed all rational protest.

Merton advised that Zen and Christian mysticism could enable us to "open our eyes and *see*" through the cataracts of one-dimensional consciousness.[46]

Near the end of his life, Merton had determined that the impairment of sacramental vision in the West was well-nigh irreversible. The conventional methods of political transformation in liberal democracies were not only worn out and ineffectual, he decided, but contributory to the triumph of technocratic capitalism. The only hope for salvation from the shipwreck of pecuniary civilization resided in the way of desert fathers and Zen masters— disengagement, contemplation, return, and renewal. In December 1968, at a conference of Christian and Buddhist monks in Bangkok, Merton delivered an address on "Marxism and Monastic Perspectives," in which he tied Marcuse's analysis of "one-dimensional society" to the contemplative tradition of monasticism, reinterpreted and extended into a great and mysterious vocation for all. Despite their adherence to the canons of empiricism, those caught up in the one-dimensional world of capitalist society do not, Merton told the gathering, "apprehend reality as it fully and really is"—unlike monks, whose devotion to the contemplative life provides them with the sacramental gift of a more capacious realism. But the monk, he argued, is not necessarily an individual who takes traditional monastic vows; he (or she) is someone who "knows the score," who believes that "the claims of the world are fraudulent" precisely because they rest on a perverted, desiccated unreality. Even the claims of liberal democracy were spurious, he continued, since both the United States and the Soviet Union were becoming "equally totalitarian in one way or another"—one through outright tyranny and the other through the occlusion of alternative ways of being. Thus Merton dismissed liberal political institutions as feckless anodynes. "You cannot rely on structures. The time for relying on structures has disappeared."[47]

Merton never had a chance to practice this new monasticism—he died a few hours after his speech. Meanwhile, Rexroth (a correspondent and admirer of Merton's) was coming to believe that the radical tempests of the time were winding down, and that the endurance and vitality of the sacramental imagination required a similar stratagem of forbearance. Although he could be blithely exuberant about the anarchist and mystical inclinations of the counterculture, Rexroth never set aside his critical faculties. Though often lauded (or reviled) as a godfather of the Beats, he soon soured on them as bohemian mediocrities, belittling Jack Kerouac in particular as a prolific generator of "gibberish." By the end of the 1950s, Rexroth was snarling that, while the Beats "may once have been human beings," they were now the "comical helots of the Enemy . . . bogies conjured up by the Luce publications." Later, in 1967, Rexroth complained that the sartorial flamboyance of hippies had sparked little more than a revolution in middle-class taste and fashion, "a craze for the conspicuous expenditure on senseless commodities—beads, couch cover serapes, and worn-out squirrel-skin chubbies." In 1969, he groaned that the Declaration of Independence and the Communist Manifesto had been supplanted rhetorically by "*Seventeen, Mademoiselle,* and *Playboy*"; a year later, he dismissed Abbie Hoffmann, Jerry Rubin, Stokely Carmichael, and Bobby Seale, "all readily recognizable by the *Time* researchers because they inhabit the same world"—the society of the spectacle, "the flickering simulacra of the television tube." Shortly after the first Earth Day in April 1970, he predicted that ecology would be "a fashionable evasion with the public and a profitable lie with Shell Chemical." Indeed, Rexroth was convinced that humanity as a whole was "facing extinction" and that those devoted to the preservation of what is left of the earth are "not likely to win."[48]

And yet despite his accumulating gloom, Rexroth tended an affirming flame. The remnant of sanity and sacramental consciousness might lose the battle for the earth, but they could die in the spirit of witness, creating—like Merton's enclaves of a new monasticism—a "subculture of secession," as Rexroth dubbed it in 1969, "a Kingdom in the face of Apocalypse, a garrisoned society of the morally responsible which will face extinction with clean consciences and lives as happily lived as possible." Secession did not necessarily mean geographical withdrawal, but rather a commitment shared by friends to live by ideals—or rather, by the light of a reality whose features were twisted or obscured by the Social Lie. Assuming that "it's always Armageddon," Rexroth reiterated that the weapons of nonviolent resistance to the Lie could be found in an assortment of spiritual and secular discourses: "the Buddha word, the myths of Northwest Indians, the I. W. W. [Industrial Workers of the World] preamble, and the technology of electronics." As compromised as the counterculture had been by the flatteries of advertising and marketing, "the best . . . and most effective demonstration" of its authentic realism "is simply to start living by the new values"—the "theological virtues," as Rexroth designated them, of "voluntary poverty, sexual honesty, and personal integrity." The cultivation of sacramental vision was taking place in communes, ashrams, and open universities whose inhabitants practiced "mutual affection, respect, interest, loyalty, and simple physical touch— *agape,* the love of comrades in a spiritual adventure."[49]

As Rexroth conceded, success was unlikely; and by the early 1970s, even he was slowly and melancholically reflecting on the fading promise of a dream. With the counterculture either descending into nihilism or rushing headlong toward corporate sponsorship, and with the New Left either fracturing or regressing into paleo-Marxist orthodoxies, the Social Lie stood victorious and vindictive, determined to prevent another outbreak of imagination from ever happening again. "What can we do about it? Probably very little," Rexroth sighed in 1969. The ennui showed in his prose: his survey of *Communalism* (1974) was informative but uninspired, ending grumpily with a description of a rural commune as an "eyesore" and a "disposal problem." Until his death in 1982, Rexroth concentrated on poetry, his own and his beautiful translations of verse from Japanese and Chinese literature. Full of graceful erotic and religious meditations, his work preserved the lineaments of a sacramental vision for a more propitious time. With the gathering forces of neoliberalism poised to reassert the sovereignty of Mammon, Rexroth, as he had written of Blake in 1968, "saw the oncoming Business Civilization and prepared a refuge, a symbolic fortress or haven."[50]

# Epilogue

THE VISIONARY COMMONWEALTH NEVER came to pass; the Business Civilization did, with a vengeance. Realizing Arthur Jensen's eschatology of corporate cosmopolitanism—"one vast and ecumenical holding company"—the United States and other advanced industrial societies extended the imperium of capital to every corner of the world over the next forty years. The American Century morphed into the neoliberal Market Everlasting: unfettered free trade and globalization, epitomized by the formation of the World Trade Organization in 1995; the privatization of public services and their lucrative relegation to the caprice of the marketplace; the "reinvention" of government agencies along the lines of corporate bureaucracies; and the maniacal deregulation of finance and industry under the rubric of "modernization," liberating corporations from "stifling" restrictions on their freedom to invest, pollute, and exploit. Under the aegis of the World Trade Organization, the World Bank, and the International Monetary Fund, globalization built a paradise of capital, with its incandescent minarets ascending on every continent, looming over multitudes pauperized into despair, impressed into the legions of wage servitude, or sedated by the opiates of the spectacle. With a faith in the omnipotence of the Market fortified with an arsenal of money and munitions, neoliberalism—"the Marxism of the ruling classes," as Steve Fraser has brilliantly characterized it—has come closer than any previous regime of capitalism to transforming the world into a business.[1]

The United States' own metamorphosis into a corporate plutocracy has progressed with remarkable alacrity. Always hated by business leaders, the New Deal and the corporate commonwealth were dismantled by a new breed of executives, investors, and politicians. Beginning in the 1970s, corporations began to abrogate the social truce with organized labor, deplete the already parsimonious welfare state, break unions and impose stringent wage and benefit restrictions that always seem to need further reductions. Computerized production and communications technologies empowered management to accelerate automation and introduce more intensive labor practices— both made possible by the new "flexibility" of labor—all ensuring submission to the will of capital, performed more readily thanks to decimated unions. The postwar managerial regime came under assault from mutual fund directors and other institutional investors eager to break all shackles on capital accumulation. The managerial order gave way to investor capitalism, marked by a virulent reassertion of stockholder interests and the primacy of financial institutions in the governance of other capitalist firms.[2]

This corporate perestroika has issued in a "political economy of auto-cannibalism," as Fraser characterizes it, in which the profitability of the most prominent sector of capital—finance—depends increasingly on buying up and liquidating productive assets in industry and manufacturing, using the proceeds for reckless (but government-guaranteed) speculation in what Marx dubbed "fictitious capital": stocks, bonds, derivatives, IPOs, currency markets, commodity trading, collateralized debt, all the recondite arts of monetary sorcery. This is the world of Cash McCall—"the cleverest of all the jackals and vultures"—ruled by a patricianate far removed from and even contemptuous of the misery and desperation far beneath them, sanctioned by a clerisy whose edicts are promulgated in the cuneiform of mathematical economics. The results are, by now, depressingly familiar: the greatest concentration of wealth among the top 1 percent since the early twentieth century; stagnant real wages for the past three decades, resulting in increased reliance on debt for health care, housing, and education; precarious employment, diminishing benefits, and shabbier working conditions; the potential elimination of whole classes of employment by automated production technology; and intensifying pressure for productivity on workers reminded every day of their utter dispensability.[3]

These assaults on the livelihood and dignity of workers have been justified as painful but necessary steps on the interminable road of Progress, guided by infallible market forces to which we owe homage and genuflection. Indeed, in the spirit of Arthur Jensen, the apostles of neoliberal theology attributed an eschatological imperative to the Market. President Bill Clinton informed a meeting of the World Trade Organization in Geneva in May 1998 that the worldwide spread of capitalism had ushered in "the fullness of time"; later, he told a San Francisco audience in February 1999 that "we must embrace the inexorable logic of globalization." In *A Future Perfect* (2000), John Micklethwait and Adrian Woolridge, Washington correspondents at the time for the *Economist,* wrote with no irony or embarrassment of the "broad church" of neoliberalism. Forecasting an "empire without end" directed by an elite of "cosmocrats," they aligned the sway of the United States with the neoliberal trajectory of history, citing Sir Robert Peel's Tory invocation of "the beneficent designs of an all-seeing Creator." The most grandiose and sweeping statement of neoliberal triumphalism came from Francis Fukuyama, a former State Department official in the Reagan administration. In 1989, just after the collapse of Soviet communism in Eastern Europe, Fukuyama proclaimed in *Foreign Affairs* that we had just witnessed "the end of history," the conclusion of "a single, coherent, evolutionary process." History had reached its *telos* in neoliberal capitalism, which had won the "ultimate victory as the world's only viable economic system." Fukuyama envisioned a "universal consumer culture," an imperial emporium signified by the video cassette recorder—the heir to Hector Dexter's Coca-Coca bottle and a talisman of neoliberal metaphysics. Though apprehensive at the prospect of a future infiltrated by the shabby amoralism of consumer culture, Fukuyama reflected that "we cannot picture to ourselves a world that is *essentially* different from the present one, and at the same time better."[4]

Conveyed in a flippant rhetoric of historical determinism—"inexorable," "irresistible," "irreversible"—these and other auguries of market predestination were volleys in what David Graeber has called a "war on the imagination": a blitzkrieg against utopian speculation, a mission to sabotage the capacity to even dream of a world beyond capitalism. Margaret Thatcher's infamous apothegm "there is no alternative" was only the pithiest piece of ordnance in this relentless barrage of hubris and intimidation. More swaggering (and verbose) than Thatcher was the New York Times columnist Thomas Friedman, who asserted in *The Lexus and the Olive Tree* (1999) that "the free market is the only ideological alternative left." Dismissing all dissent as the bray of the economically illiterate—he described demonstrators at the 1999 meeting of the World Trade Organization in Seattle as "a Noah's ark of flat-earth advocates"—Friedman attributed a rigorous historical necessity to the unobstructed sway of the Market. There is only "one road," he warned naysayers; "different speeds. But one road." To ensure that the peoples of the world never stray from the neoliberal straight-and-narrow, the United States, Friedman insisted, must become an omnipotent imperial constable, invested with transcendent authority and power and enforcing the sacrosanct rulings of the Market on wayward or refractory nations. Writing in the *New York Times Magazine* in March 1999, Friedman issued this peremptory fatwa:

> For globalization to work, America can't be afraid to act like the almighty superpower that it is. The hidden hand of the market will not work without a hidden fist. McDonald's cannot flourish without McDonnell-Douglas, the designer of the F-15, and the hidden fist that keeps the world safe for Silicon Valley's technology is called the United States, Army, Air Force, Navy, and Marine Corps.[5]

Friedman's weaponized theophany bears an eschatological import: a military-industrial business millennium signified by the Golden Arches gleaming proudly at the End of History.

Writing near the turn of the century, Friedman blustered from the ideological meridian of the belle epoque of neoliberalism, when laissez-faire enjoyed a spellbinding, full-spectrum dominance over the American moral imagination. For the past thirty years, corporations have exercised a monopoly on our symbolic universe, and the gospel and iconography of capital have achieved an unprecedented level of omnipresence. "The Market's Will Be Done" as management guru Tom Peters wrote in his treatise on *Liberation Management;* "One market under God" as Thomas Frank captured the rapturous ebullience of a second Gilded Age.[6] In advertising, marketing, and public relations; in management-speak and financial journalism; in the stream of stock prices that seemed to frame every image on cable news networks—Business inscribed its commands and desires in the firmament of popular culture. The Market ascended into the ontological sublime; the Entrepreneur and the Technological Innovator rose into the communion of saints and the pantheon of demigods; economists assumed holy orders as the number-crunching clerisy of a pecuniary civilization; the corporate plutocracy publicized itself as the hippest imperium in history. The Business Civilization consummated human striving in the permanent revolution of cool, while the Visionary Commonwealth languished in the memories of aging bohemians and radicals. What millennium had ever been so awesome? Bliss was it in that dawn to be a start-up, but to go public was very heaven!

Among evangelical Protestants, free-market capitalism has been "born again," Bethany Moreton writes, rechristened and politicized among the teeming congregations of "Wal-Mart country." The longstanding and passionate love affair of evangelicals and capitalism has spawned a large and beaming family of Protestant neoliberal apologias: "free-market theology," "Name It and Claim It," "health and wealth," "prosperity gospel," to name only some of the buoyant descendants of the antebellum proprietary dispensation. Accompanied by a chorus of hosannas to the Father who orchestrates the cosmology of affluence, evangelical neoliberalism continues the Cold War reactionary modernist quest to recapture the glory days of *herrenvolk* modernity, enabled by a piously quiescent proletariat and overseen by a paternalist management imbued with the bromides of "servant leadership." Even after the crash of 2008—surely evidence that the Patriarch of the Market was yet another fraudulent God that had failed—evangelical faith in the holiness of the capitalist order remains unshakable. As Chris Lehmann observes, "no rival movement has taken root within the nation's vast Protestant mainstream . . . to question the logic of sanctified capitalism."[7]

The votaries of New Age go one step further and divinize the market itself. New Age initiates turn to "spirituality"—the "nondogmatic dogma," as Kathryn Lofton explains, "that encourages an ambiguous theism alongside an exuberant consumerism," a harmonic convergence with the ontology and economics of the neoliberal enchantment of the Market. These New Age "religions without religion" are best understood, in Lofton's view, as "religions for an age in which markets make custom, consumption is the universal aspect, and celebrities are ostensible gods"—"replacement divinities," she calls them, the surrogate deities, demons, saints, and icons of the enraptured society of the spectacle. Although New Age is often seen as "some adolescent rebellion against the disciplined logic of secularization," it renders happily unto the logic of the Market.[8]

Paeans to a new age of technological sublimity were equally spectacular as well as popular, implying that humanity had reached an existential apotheosis through the magic of cybernetics. Techno-millennialism envisioned a planetary community of dot-com start-ups and entrepreneurs, whose microchips and fiber-optic cables joined the sacramental inventory of capitalist metaphysics. The era's techno-millennial ideologues anointed digital technology as a mechanism of exaltation, even as it was subjecting an ever larger number of workers to more intensive exploitation and surveillance. In *The Road Ahead* (1995) and *Business @ the Speed of Thought* (2000), Bill Gates, the ubergeek of the digital age, heralded a "friction-free capitalism" innocent of class warfare and international rivalries. Vast computer networks would provide a "digital nervous system" for the planet—a cybernetic apparatus of animism designed and controlled by corporations—while personalized technology would confer semi-divine powers, fulfilling the most ancient longings for omniscience and omnipotence, giving people "the power to do what they want, where and when they want, on any device."[9]

Other augurs of digital felicity composed prayers to technology that were even more euphoric. George Gilder—whose neoliberal treatise *Wealth and Poverty* (1981) became a handbook for the Reagan Administration—embarked on a career as a maven of technological transcendence in the mid-1980s. Besides contending that the market is a sacramental venue—"a vessel of the divine"—Gilder waxed ecstatic about "the magic of the solid-state world." The silicon chip, in his view, was a kind of Eucharistic host, a material conduit of divinity that enables an "ever-expanding circuitry of ideas" and harbors "a truth that sets us free." The digitalization of divinity would eventually empower a conventicle of technicians who—replacing Shelley's poets and Whitman's divine literati—would become "the true legislators for the silent and silenced majorities of the world." Meanwhile, Kevin Kelly's techno-enchantment flourished on another, more New Age plateau of ontological exhilaration and grandeur. A former associate of Stewart Brand at the *Whole Earth Catalog* and the *CoEvolution Quarterly*, Kelly was the founding editor of *Wired*, the premier venue of the heady business cyberculture of the 1990s. In *Out of Control* (1994), Kelly enumerated "The Nine Laws of God," most of which—"distribute being," "maximize the fringes," "cultivate increasing returns"—amounted to conventional commercial banalities draped in esoteric regalia. Yet in the "Nine Laws" and elsewhere in *Wired*, Kelly located the world of cyber-business in the midst of a biotechnological animism. Alluding to "the spooky nature of material things," Kelly maintained that capitalism flourishes in a seamless web of being wherein "the river of life . . .

flows through it all." The same forces that quicken the natural world pulsate through "computer chips, electronic communication networks, robot modules, pharmaceutical searches, software design, and corporate management." Technological breakthroughs occur "when the Technos is enlivened by Bios." In the December 2002 issue of *Wired,* Kelly described the mainframe of the Technos and the Bios: God, Who is "the Machine" or "the Ultimate Software and Source Code."[10]

The "Ultimate Software" malfunctioned twice in the 2000s—first in 2000 when the dot-com bubble burst and again in 2008 with the global financial collapse. Yet faith in the promise of the Business Civilization remains widespread and almost invincible, as the enchantment and eschatology of corporate capitalism remain embedded in the popular imagination. The aftermath of the crisis of 2008 is illustrative. Despite the most serious economic crisis since the 1930s, the plutocracy has suffered little or nothing in the way of incarceration, embarrassment, or ignominy. Indeed, many of those who designed and superintended the calamity remain in power, managing the lucrative reconstruction of the rubble with unrepentant, vainglorious aplomb. Protected and worshipped by legislators, pundits, and a craven business intelligentsia, our overlords have emerged even more acquisitive than during the mercenary delirium of the 1990s—and in President Donald J. Trump and his administration of tycoons, they have an executive committee of the bourgeoisie straight from the pages of Marx and Engels. So with capital more thoroughly entrenched than ever, the contemporary American scene appears to be bereft of anything but plutocratic vistas; even in the face of its manifest injustice, degradation, and ecological toxicity, capitalism remains for most Americans the horizon of moral and political possibility.

The depth and rapidity of our transformation into a plutocracy should astonish only those with little or no sense of the contours of American history. America has always been a Business Civilization, from the Puritan errand into the marketplace to the evangelical contract with the unrighteous Mammon, from the immaculate conception of the "soulful corporation" to the heavenly city of Fordism, from the mechanical futuramas of industrial designers to the cybernetic sublime of computer engineers and techno-entrepreneurs, from the first advertising animators of commodities to the shamans of the postmodern spectacle. Far from constituting a violation or disavowal of republican or populist principle, the triumph of neoliberalism is the highest stage of capitalist enchantment ever achieved in America, the culmination of a rage to accumulate that has never known any enduring inhibition.

Despite the populist umbrage that has surged through American political culture since the presidential campaign of 2016, most Americans remain far from serious about a new way of life not indentured to capital. Hillary Clinton won the Democratic nomination for president while espousing the techno-meritocratic creed that flatters the professional-managerial classes and the elites of finance and digital capital. Defining "merit" almost solely in terms of its utility to capital accumulation, Clinton and her minions in the cultural apparatus were blithely and disastrously indifferent to the human wreckage wrought by neoliberal capitalism. With a moral imagination so gilded and tutored by Wall Street and Silicon Valley, a Clinton presidency would have remained as beguiled as former president Barack Obama's by the enchantments of money and cybernetic technology. Her opponent Donald Trump's populist bluster turned out, of course, to provide a cynical and successful prologue to the most unabashedly plutocratic government since the 1920s. Yet despite Trump's execrable racism and misogyny, his appeal stemmed, in large measure, from the dogged persistence of the capitalist idyll. Trump's boorish defiance of political politesse might be seen as a form of the creative destruction embellished in our cult of the Entrepreneur. His actual incompetence as a businessman (demonstrated in a dreary record of failures, bankruptcies, and flimflammed partners) is of no account; having flourished so gaudily in the turbulence of the market, Trump clearly believes that his prowess in business is an infinitely convertible wisdom—a conceit sustained by the American inclination to attribute all manner of ingenuity and virtue to the scrappy victors of capitalist competition. For all its grandiose banality, Trump's campaign slogan—"Make America Great Again"—evoked the waning but still mesmeric hope for a revival of the promise of capitalism, as well as for a time when the purchasing power of the wages of whiteness and masculinity were high.[11] It would seem that most of "the 99 percent" want to "take back" the American Dream, not awaken from and definitively repudiate it; no depth or magnitude of failure seems capable of occasioning a fundamental reckoning with the futility of the original covenant.

Thus it would appear that the future of American capitalism will be irreversibly bleak and degenerative: "a consumerist Sparta," in Chalmers Johnson's words, a Huxwellian empire of consumption and militarism, or "rentism," as Peter Frase has dubbed it, a condition of plenty marred by wage stagnation, technological unemployment, and entrenched inequality. Perhaps the most dreary and terrifying scenario is that sketched by Wolfgang Streeck, who contends that capitalism has entered a protracted state of social and political senescence. Always "a fragile and improbable order," capitalism has always been in need of "ongoing repair work" to offset its tendency toward stasis and breakdown. But now—with economic inertia, ecological crises, and political impasse throughout the North Atlantic world—"too many frailties have become simultaneously acute while too many remedies have been exhausted or destroyed." And where reform or revolutionary movements once held out promises of a better future, capitalist society now disintegrates "but not under the impact of an organized opposition fighting it in the name of a better social order." Thus, Streeck envisions a revenant future, in which "before capitalism will go to hell" it will "hang in limbo, dead or about to die . . . nobody will have the power to move its decaying body out of the way." Capitalism, he concludes, "is facing its *Gotterdammerung*"— with no new divinities ascending in the dawn.[12]

Given the ghastly resilience of neoliberal capitalism, some of its most penetrating and articulate critics express a disheartenment that borders on despair. Surveying our "age of acquiescence," Fraser chronicles with a melancholy thoroughness the styles of resignation to the despotism of money: a "freedom" defined as reinvention of the self in accord with the vicissitudes of the Market, encouraging pathetic "delusions of self-reliance" and "hallucinations of self-empowerment"; a tranquilizing repertoire of digital devices and myriad forms of entertainment; and the analgesic pleasures of consumerism that allay a metastasizing boredom, solitude, and demoralization. But as long as Americans remain convinced that, in Fraser's words, "the evergreen hope that the road to self-enrichment remains open," their submissiveness will remain intractable; the reign of our "populist plutocracy" will remain thoroughly anchored in a plutocratic populism. If there really is no alternative, not even in the imagination, then conformity seems the sanest response to a world thoroughly structured by the metaphysics of capital. As

Fraser reports the melancholy wisdom spreading among the despondent and politically hopeless, if nothing better beckons over the horizon, "to acquiesce may be less dispiriting."[13]

What if we find acquiescence dispiriting? To mitigate, let alone prevent, our impending ecological and economic disasters, we desperately need, to borrow Naomi Klein's words, "a new civilizational paradigm." And yet, as Klein also realizes, "post-Enlightenment Western culture does not offer a road map for how to live that is not based on an extractivist, nonreciprocal relationship with nature."[14] Both the advanced and the advancing capitalist worlds must not only forsake the promethean passion for domination and the mammonesque lust to accumulate; they must develop those alternatives whose existence their leaders have spent the past two generations denying. On what imaginative resources can the overdeveloped nations in particular rely to conceive these alternatives? Can we envision a different civilization and challenge the criteria of realism and practicality canonized by capital and the state?

Over the past decade, a desire for some new civilizational paradigm has surfaced, in however inchoate a form. The support for Senator Bernie Sanders and his "political revolution" in the Democratic primary race of 2016 demonstrated a profound and widespread longing for a break with the existing order. To be sure, Sanders's "democratic socialism" was, on close inspection, a mélange of the best of New Deal liberalism and European social democracy. As Jedidiah Purdy observed, it represented an updated version of "Eisenhower and FDR's world if Reagan had never happened."[15] But it also named both a visceral and expansive disenchantment with the charms of neoliberalism and the persistence of a longing for solidarity and justice that was not shy about the language of "revolution."

Sanders's campaign was one efflorescence of the Occupy movement that had arisen in the fall of 2011. Not only in New York but also around the world, Occupy revived a languishing hope that capitalism was not the gilded End of History. The Occupiers rebuked the callous and insouciant rapacity that had marked the previous three decades, uttering heresies against the meretricious doxology of neoliberal economics. With their general assemblies, "peoples' mics," and free provision of food and medical care, Occupy appeared to represent an exotic uprising of apostates and infidels, as—however briefly—a gift economy supplanted the mercenary order of accumulation. It seemed like a joyous, pentecostal return of Mammon's forgotten but lingering victims, escaping the beast on a reconnaissance mission to the frontiers of paradise. Alas, it seemed that humankind cannot bear too much of heaven: Occupy and its tongues of fire were quickly extinguished or exhausted. The Occupiers dwindled as the weather grew cold and the times remained unmoved, and the police closed down and threw away what remained of the ragged outposts of utopia.

If it remains to be seen whether Occupy was, in Graeber's words, "the opening salvo in a wave of negotiations over the dissolution of the American Empire," its more immediate importance may lie in the realm of the spirit rather than the barricades. As Rebecca Solnit observed of Occupy San Francisco, "Occupy has some of the resonance of a spiritual, as well as a political, movement." Citing one declaration that "compassion is our new currency," Solnit marveled at the beloved community that transpired among the carnivalesque participants in utopia. However reformist their demands, the experiments in direct democracy were, in her words, "messy, exasperating, and miraculous"; leaderless meetings did not proceed or conclude in confusion, listlessness, or violence. The "people's mics" enabled and even required men and women to "become the keeper of [their] brother's or sister's voice." Talking with Occupiers after the closure of their experiment in stateless, moneyless ways of being, Solnit remarked on "the extraordinary richness of their experience," noting without any irony or condescension that the sojourners "call it love."[16]

The Occupiers exhibited the same existential joy that Solnit had chronicled among survivors of natural disasters in *A Paradise Built in Hell* (2009). Describing the aftermath of the San Francisco earthquake a little over a century before, Solnit marveled not only at the improvisational ingenuity of people whose city had been reduced to rubble but also at the spontaneous generosity they displayed in the midst of the most horrendous circumstances:

Imagine a society where money plays little or no role, where people rescue each other and then care for each other, where food is given away, where life is mostly out of doors in public, where the old divides between people seem to have fallen away, and the fate that faces them, no matter how grim, is far less so for being shared, where much once considered impossible, both good and bad, is now possible or present.

Disaster kicks open "a door back into paradise, the paradise at least in which we are who we hope to be, do the work we desire, and are each our sister's and brother's keeper."[17] This is hardly the sort of thing that can be readily translated into a technocratic or pecuniary idiom, the lingua franca of the digital and financial oligarchies who claim to monopolize the power to draw the boundaries of political possibility in our time.

The paradise that emerges from catastrophe embodies what William James called "another kingdom of being," that realm of "ontological wonder" that appears in the relinquishment of all desire for possession and supremacy. If nothing less than a new civilizational paradigm will enable us to weather and perhaps avert this century's maelstrom of impending disasters, it must be rooted in a deep and even rapturous ontological imagination of wonder. "We want larger selves and a larger world," Solnit writes, and people caught in disasters soon discover how multitudinous they and the world truly are. And yet, she muses, "we lack the language for that aspect of our existence . . . the language we need to describe what happens during disaster." What Solnit discerns in the history of calamities, Fraser sees in the broader story of modern America. Propelled by "ineffable yearnings to redefine what it meant to be human together," all the great crusades for justice began "in a realm before money" and looked to the fruition of "a realm beyond money." Even in the stampede for consumer goods slumbers "a sacramental quest for transcendence, reveries of what might be."[18] For both Fraser and Solnit, one enormous obstacle to a breakthrough into paradise is the moral and ontological edifice of capitalism.

We do have a language for the human magnificence we witness in the wake of devastation; we do have a language that expresses our longings both for a sense of the world's magnitude and for fleshly access to transcendence. Our best hope for an imaginative and political antithesis to capitalist enchantment resides in the lineage of Romantic, sacramental radicalism. It understands calamity, injustice, and degradation as predicaments of human divinity, hardships that can reveal our suppressed or perverted but nonetheless godlike nature. It views the material universe as a cosmic theater of divine vitality, charged with the grandeur of God. Beginning with the squatters on St. George's Hill, the pedigree of Romantic modernity maintained that we already live in paradise, and that our blindness to the heaven all around us is the source of our descent into the hell of property, rank, and dominion.

The capacity to apprehend paradise had several names—"imagination," "wonder," "passionate vision," "sacramental consciousness"—but it has always been a way of *seeing,* a perception of some truth and goodness and beauty intrinsic to the material world, a view that embraces without nullifying the knowledge obtainable through the sciences.

So if we ask, along with T. J. Clark, "how deep does [the] reconstruction of the project of Enlightenment have to go?," *all the way down* is the answer, right down to the ontological roots.[19] At its boldest, the sacramental vision has beheld a superabundant love as the ontological architecture of creation, harmoniously blending unfathomable power and gracious, immeasurable munificence. The sacramental way of seeing has behooved a sacramental way of being, one described by James as "saintliness": not a blissed-out, puritan-ical sanctimony, but rather a fearless, vibrant, and open-handed life, sus-tained by a confidence in the bounty of the world, available to every person on condition that she become "worthless as a practical being"—"worthless," that is, by the pecuniary criteria of capitalist metaphysics and rationality.

By repudiating the standards of worth and practicality that discipline the capitalist way of being, the Romantic sacramental imagination has always borne revolutionary implications. Romanticism has represented an alterna-tive modernity, a substantive critique of the Enlightenment's collusion with bourgeois sensibility and moralism that nonetheless never ended in utter re-pudiation. It has always rejected capitalism's ontology of pecuniary transub-stantiation, its epistemology of technological dominion, and its morality of profit and productivity. Because Romanticism's passionate vision sees the presence of divinity throughout the material universe—especially in human beings—Romanticism has entailed an understanding of nature, work, and technics very different from that of capitalist societies, whose misconception of the world is encapsulated in the secular superstition of "economics." In the combative technological world constructed by capitalism, "human beings and material objects no longer extend a friendly hand to one another," as Pope Francis has echoed Walt Whitman; "the relationship has become confrontational"—characterized by the violence of the extractive paradigm, poisoned by the "bitterness and malice" that John Ruskin descried in the English heavens.[20] Nature as revealed by the sacramental consciousness is both abundant and holy. Impressed with the trademark of its creator, it is not a stingy and punitive antagonist, but rather a fruitful, ever-evolving habitat, open to the rational and creative participation of humanity in its manifold generosity.

In this sacramental view, our laboring and technical collaboration with nature should take the form of self-development as well as production. Performed in conditions worthy of our human divinity, work would not constitute money-grubbing toil in pursuit of a rapacious enlargement of "productivity" but rather the care and cultivation of people—as Ruskin put it, "full-breathed, bright-eyed, and happy-hearted human creatures." Along with artists and poets, artisans have also been archetypes of convivial, unalienated labor: the union of reason, imagination, and creativity amounting to poetry in labor—an inspiring alternative to the slavery of wages and to the ennui that beckons with total automation. Fusing conceptual and physical labor, the Romantic ideal of the artisan contravened the industrial paradigm of efficiency and productivity defined in capitalist terms. The recent renewal of interest in craftsmanship testifies to the persistence of this Romantic paradigm. Contrary to claims by many on the left that "craftsmanship" is merely a fantasy of reactionary nostalgia, a recovery of artisanal values would entail neither a revival of the Protestant work ethic—the slave morality of capitalism—nor a rejection of the possibilities for greater free time afforded by technological advance. The Romantic figure of the artisan both beckons to the goal of workers' control of production and reminds us to ask more fundamental questions about the nature and purposes of work. If *homo faber* is also *imago Dei*—the quintessential sacramental image of divinity—then the first question about labor is not how much can be produced in the shortest period of time, but what kinds of labor and what kinds of goods best contribute to human flourishing. Against the neoliberal inferno of 24/7 labor and consumption, "better work and less of it" should be the rallying cry of a revitalized workers' movement.[21]

Romantic sacramentalism has evoked communist, anarchist, and artisanal visions, so pioneers of a postcapitalist future can draw on a rich imaginative trove of property forms and beloved communities. "Communism," of course, triggers nightmares of authoritarianism, misery, and incompetence; images of jackboots, prison camps, and queues would appear to dispel any resurrection of the hope for a communist paradise. Yet when even a Pope can write—and be tagged with the predictable epithet of "Marxist"—that "the earth is essentially a shared inheritance, whose fruits should benefit everyone," then "Communists of the old school," as Ruskin called himself—communists who appeal to the spirit of the medieval commons, not, like Marx, to the spirit of the industrial factory—have an opportunity to educate our contemporaries in the longer and broader tradition of *communitas*. Long after its dispossession from the fields and towns, the spirit of the commons persisted most heartily among the anarchist and Arts and Crafts movement, Romantics who envisioned some modern revival of the self-direction and solidarity practiced among artisanal guilds and peasant communities. Workers' control of technology and production, the eradication of class and the industrial division of labor, the removal of the commons from private ownership and its restoration to federated communities—consolidated in the word "socialism," these remain the compelling answers to the "social question" posed by capitalism.[22]

A Romantic left would also help their fellow citizens to awaken from the spell of the American Dream, the trance that animates the feverish somnambulism known as the American Way of Life. We may already be waking up—the acquiescence may be dissipating to reveal a miasma of betrayal, anger, and resentment, all of which will intensify as more Americans realize that their way of life is neither blessed nor imperishable. If the events of the past few years have demonstrated anything beyond dispute, it's that our ruling class is not only venal and corrupt but rotten and putrefying as well. Certainly, judged by Ruskin's criterion, the American Empire is neither happy nor noble: our country, so deluded as to think itself rich, may well be among the poorest in powers of love, of joy, and of admiration. Indeed, the decline of the American Empire will be one of the pivotal episodes of the twenty-first century. What will Americans make of their future—not to mention their past and present—when they begin to doubt their divine anointment and eschatological mission? What will they do when they conclude that they never enjoyed the mandate of heaven? They may redouble their efforts in denial, unwilling to relinquish or even temper their faith in the enchanting verities of the Market. If they harken to the delusions of nativist populism, they will intensify racial animosity while entrenching the power of their mercenary overlords. If they affirm a renovated neoliberalism, they may attempt to prolong their economic and geopolitical imperium. Yet even if they succeed, their victory will be brief and pyrrhic, for they will have purchased their temporary reprieve in the currency of fear, recrimination, and death. Other peoples—perhaps even many Americans themselves—will not tolerate the expenditure in money, blood, and repression required to sustain the American Way of Life.

Or Americans could welcome the demise of the Empire as a liberating moment of possibility. Those who sense the impending twilight of empire as a way of life could greet the erosion of our hegemony, not with lamentation about the best days behind us, but with gratitude and even jubilation at the prospect of a better and lovelier country. Once relieved of the burdens of empire, and dispelled of the illusion that the world cannot survive without the escutcheon of American superintendence, we would surely be weaker. But we would also be wiser, freer to assess and rearrange our affairs by truer, saner, and more generous standards than productivity and technological innovation. Such a deliberate renunciation of capitalist enchantment will be arduous and sharply vilified, condemned as lethal and improvident heresy by the patricians and curates of the plutocracy. But the only alternative to apostasy from Mammonism will be a perdition of corporate thralldom perpetuated with unending and unavailing war.

The disassembly of the American Empire will require the acolytes of sacramental consciousness to imbue our politics with a hopeful, even joyful spirit. The barbarism of our current political culture has led some to call for a kind of inner, Benedictine expatriation: "a new—doubtless very different—St. Benedict," in Alasdair MacIntyre's words, or a "Benedict option" of cloistered, like-minded exiles from the toxins and failures of modernity. I reject this Benedictine disengagement as both impossible and undesirable. Rather, as Michael Hardt and Antonio Negri have hinted, we need a new—doubtless very different—St. Francis as a model of revolutionary militancy. Amid the injustice and corruption of his own day, Francis discovered, they assert, "the ontological power of a new society"—"love, simplicity, and also innocence," an ontological wonder that entails anger at the profanation of human divinity. For those eager, in Charles Taylor's words, to "break beyond the limits of the regnant versions of immanent order"—for those "restless at the barriers of the human sphere"—any new radicalism must begin from a faith in this fundamental joy of being.[23] A realized eschatology: if you will, the future in the present tense. Living the new world in the wreckage of the old.

That new world has always been present; history has not deprived us of an abiding and infinitely generous divinity. We *can* reenter paradise—even if only incompletely—for paradise has always been around and in us, eagerly awaiting our coming to our senses, ready to embrace and nourish when we renounce our unbelief in the goodness of things. And we can do this in the midst of imperial decay and in the face of seemingly impossible odds. Knowing that the world has been and will always be charged with the grandeur of God, we can practice, in the twilight of a senescent empire, love's radiant, unarmed, and penniless dominion.

# Notes

## Prologue

1. Weber first used this phrase *(Entzauberung der Welt)* in "Science as a Vocation" (1915), in *From Max Weber: Essays in Sociology,* trans. and ed. H. H. Gerth and C. Wright Mills (New York, 2009 [1946]), 155; see also "The Social Psychology of the World Religions" (1915) and "Religious Rejections of the World and Their Directions" (1915), in Gerth and Mills, *From Max Weber,* 277–282, 331–359. Robert Heilbroner, *The Nature and Logic of Capitalism* (New York, 1985), 135.

2. Michael Lewis, "Why You?," *New York Times Magazine* (September 23, 2001), 17; Karl Marx and Friedrich Engels, "The Communist Manifesto" (1848), in *The Marx-Engels Reader,* ed. Robert C. Tucker (New York, 1978), 476, 475.

3. Naomi Klein, *The Shock Doctrine: The Rise of Disaster Capitalism* (New York, 2007), 126; Naomi Klein, *No Logo: Fighting the Brand Bullies* (New York, 2000), 22; Barbara Ehrenreich, *Bait and Switch: The (Futile) Pursuit of the American Dream* (New York, 2005), 226; David Brooks, *On Paradise Drive: How We Live Now (and Always Have) in the Future Tense* (New York, 2004), 227, 270, 281; Steve Fraser, *The Age of Acquiescence: The Life and Death of American Resistance to Organized Wealth and Power* (New York, 2015), 305.

4. Thomas Carlyle, *Past and Present* (London, 1899 [1843]), 2, 8, 139–144; Marx and Engels, "The Communist Manifesto," 478; Karl Marx, *Capital,* ed. David McLellan, trans. Samuel Moore and Edward Aveling (New York, 2008), 42–50; Weber, "Science as a Vocation," in Gerth and Mills, *From Max Weber,* 149.

5. William T. Cavanaugh, *Migrations of the Holy: God, State, and the Political Meaning of the Church* (Grand Rapids, MI, 2011). Although Cavanaugh focuses almost exclusively on the nation-state, I am extending his line of thought to capitalism.

6. Walter Benjamin, "Capitalism as a Religion" (1921), in *Walter Benjamin: Selected Writings,* vol. 1, *1913–1926,* ed. and trans. Marcus Bullock, Michael Jennings, and Howard Eiland (Cambridge, MA, 1996), 290.

7. Gerard Manley Hopkins, "God's Grandeur" (1877), in *The Major Works* (New York, 2002), 128.

8. Weber, "Science as a Vocation," in Gerth and Wright Mills, *From Max Weber,* 139, 155; Karl Polanyi, *The Great Transformation* (New York, 1944), 55–56.

9. Weber, *The Protestant Ethic and the Spirit of Capitalism,* trans. and ed. Peter Baehr and Gordon C. Wells (New York, 2002 [1905]), 36, 69, 74, 67–122.

10. Weber, "Religious Rejections of the World and Their Directions," in Gerth and Mills, *From Max Weber,* 331; Weber, *Protestant Ethic,* 124.

11. Charles Taylor, *A Secular Age* (Cambridge, MA, 2007), 539–593, 358, 534, 711–772.

12. Bruno Latour, *We Have Never Been Modern,* trans. Catherine Porter (Cambridge, MA, 1993 [1991]), esp. 32–35; the reappearance or persistence of "enchantment" has piqued the interest of a number of scholars over the past three decades. See, for example, Zygmunt Bauman, *Intimations of Postmodernity* (London, 1992), x–xi, who (rather abstrusely) characterizes postmodernity's affirmation of artifice as a "re-enchantment of the world"; Jane Bennett, *The Enchantment of Modern Life: Attachments, Crossings, and Ethics* (Princeton, NJ, 2001); Simon During, *Modern Enchantments: The Cultural and Secular Power of Magic* (Cambridge, MA, 2002); Joshua Landy and Michael Saler, eds., *The Re-Enchantment of the World: Secular Magic in a Rational Age* (Stanford, CA, 2009); Michael Saler, *As If: Modern Enchantment and the Literary Prehistory of Virtual Reality* (New York, 2012). The problem with all these accounts, in my view, is their conception of "enchantment" as a wholly subjective, interior phenomenon that is projected onto the world.

13. Weber, "Science as a Vocation," in Gerth and Mills, *From Max Weber,* 148–149. Turner cites Weber's remark about being "religiously unmusical" in his preface to the 2009 edition of *From Max Weber,* 25. As Chris Lehmann observes, "the disenchantment that supposedly crowned the historical evolution of the Protestant spirit of remorseless accumulation was far less secular—in all senses of the word—than [Weber] imagined": Lehmann, *The Money Cult: Capitalism, Christianity, and the Unmaking of the American Dream* (New York, 2016), 17–18.

14. Simon Critchley, *The Faith of the Faithless: Experiments in Political Theology* (New York, 2012), 40, 84, 38, 85–93.

15. Terry Eagleton, *Culture and the Death of God* (New Haven, CT, 2014), ix, 121, 161, 192.

16. Eagleton, *Culture and the Death of God,* 8; Karl Marx, *Grundrisse: Foundations of the Critique of Political Economy,* trans. Martin Nicolaus (New York, 1993 [1857]), 221, 225; Karl Marx, "Economic and Philosophic Manuscripts of 1844," in Tucker, *The Marx-Engels Reader,* 101–105, quote on 104.

17. Graham Ward, *Cities of God* (New York, 2000), 157; Marcel Mauss, *The Gift: The Form and Reason for Exchange in Archaic Societies* (New York, 2000 [1922]), 8–46; see also Marcel Mauss, *A General Theory of Magic* (New York, 2001 [1902]), 133–149; Pope Francis I, *Laudato Si: On Care for Our Common Home* (Huntingdon, IN, 2015), 38–39.

18. Augustine, *City of God,* trans. Henry Bettenson (New York, 1984), esp. 5–75; Eric Gregory, *Politics and the Order of Love: An Augustinian Ethic of Democratic Citizen-*

*ship* (Chicago, 2008), 260; Norman O. Brown, *Life against Death: The Psychoanalytical Meaning of History* (Wesleyan, CT, 1985 [1959]), 16.

19. Jackson Lears, *Fables of Abundance: A Cultural History of Advertising in America* (New York, 1994), 2; Roland Marchand, *Creating the Corporate Soul: The Rise of Public Relations and Corporate Imagery in American Big Business* (Berkeley, CA, 1998).

20. Marx and Engels, "The Communist Manifesto," in *Marx-Engels Reader*, 477; Walter Benjamin, "Theses on the Philosophy of History" (1940), in *Illuminations*, ed. Hannah Arendt (New York, 1969 [1968]), 256; Augustine, *City of God*, 1072.

21. Christopher Lasch, *The True and Only Heaven: Progress and Its Critics* (New York, 1991).

22. John Ruskin, *Unto This Last and Other Writings*, ed. Clive Wilmer (New York, 1997), 222, 211.

23. Henry Miller, *The Air-Conditioned Nightmare* (New York, 1945), 22–23.

24. David Graeber, *Revolutions in Reverse: Essays on Politics, Violence, Art, and Imagination* (New York, 2011), 6.

25. David Graeber, *Debt: The First 5000 Years* (New York, 2011), 21–42, quote on 22; Ruskin, *Unto This Last and Other Writings*, 119. Most attempts to put theology and economics into conversation end in moralistic platitude. An incisive exception has been that of my Villanova colleague Mary Hirschfeld, *Aquinas and the Market: Toward a Humane Economy* (Cambridge, MA, 2018). Hirschfeld is trained in both economics and theology.

26. William Blake, "Jerusalem" (1804), in *The Complete Poetry and Prose of William Blake*, ed. David V. Erdman (New York, 1988), 169.

27. William Morris, *News from Nowhere* (1890), in *News From Nowhere and Other Writings* (New York, 2004), 118.

## Part One: The Dearest Freshness Deep Down Things

1. Hopkins, "God's Grandeur," in *The Major Works*, 128.

2. Gerard Manley Hopkins, letter to Robert Bridges, August 2, 1871, in *Gerard Manley Hopkins: Poems and Prose*, ed. W. H. Gardner (New York, 1953), 172–173.

3. Hopkins, letter to Robert Bridges, August 2, 1871, 173. Hopkins was reacting, in part, to inaccurate reports that the Communards had destroyed many of Paris' churches, public buildings, and monuments. For a brilliant study of the legacy of the Commune, see Kristin Ross, *Communal Luxury: The Political Imaginary of the Paris Commune* (New York, 2015).

## 1. About His Business

1. Brad S. Gregory, *The Unintended Reformation: How a Religious Revolution Secularized Society* (Cambridge, MA, 2012), 32; Eamon Duffy, *The Stripping of the Altars: Traditional Religion in England, 1400–1580* (New Haven, CT, 1992), 91–92. My

characterization of medieval religious culture relies on Jacques Le Goff, *Medieval Civilization 400–1500,* trans. Julia Barrow (Oxford, 1990 [1964]), esp. 195–362; John Bossy, *Christianity in the West, 1400–1700* (Oxford, 1985); Miri Rubin, *Corpus Christi: The Eucharist in Late Medieval Culture* (Cambridge, 1991), esp. 213–287; Sara Beckwith, *Christ's Body: Culture, Identity, and Society in Late Medieval Writings* (London, 1996). On the centrality of the Eucharistic imagination in medieval culture, see also the very different assessments of Keith Thomas, *Religion and the Decline of Magic: Studies in Popular Beliefs in Sixteenth and Seventeenth Century England* (New York, 1971), 36–40, who sees the sacrament as an artifact of popular magical culture, reflective of a retrograde technology, and both John Bossy, "The Mass as a Social Institution," *Past and Present* 100 (August 1983), 29–61, and Duffy, *The Stripping of the Altars,* 266–298, both of whom attend to elite and popular religious beliefs on their own terms. On carnival, see Peter Burke, *Popular Culture in Early Modern Europe* (New York, 1994 [1978]), 201–286, and, of course, Mikhail Bakhtin, *Rabelais and His World,* trans. Helene Iswolsky (Bloomington, IN, 1984), esp. 145–277.

2. Diana Wood, *Medieval Economic Thought* (Cambridge and New York, 2002), 1. J. N. Figgis, *Churches in the Modern State* (London, 1914), 79–81, is a classic summary of the *communitas communitatum;* see also David Runciman, *Pluralism and the Personality of the State* (Cambridge and New York, 1997), 124–149; and Le Goff, *Medieval Civilization,* 255–324. See also Ernest Kantorowicz, *The King's Two Bodies: A Study in Medieval Political Theology* (Princeton, NJ, 1997 [1957]), 273–313, quote on 283, and F. W. Maitland, *State, Trust, and Corporation,* ed. David Runciman and Magnus Ryan (Cambridge and New York, 2003), 9–130; Antony Black, *Guild and State: European Political Thought from the Twelfth Century to the Present* (New Brunswick, NJ, 2009 [1984]), 32–95.

3. Jacques Le Goff, *Time, Work, and Culture in the Middle Ages,* trans. Arthur Goldhammer (Chicago, 1980), esp. 3–121, and *Your Money or Your Life: Economy and Religion in the Middle Ages,* trans. Patricia Ranum (New York, 2001 [1986]). On the "just price" in particular, see Raymond de Roover, "The Concept of the Just Price: Theory and Economic Policy," *Journal of Economic History* 18 (December 1958), 418–434, and Oscar Langholm, *The Merchant in the Confessional: Trade and Price in the Pre-Reformation Penitential Handbooks* (Leiden, 2003), esp. 244–256. Jacques de Vitry and Caesarius of Heisterbach are cited in Le Goff, *Your Money or Your Life,* 49, 30. On usury, see Benjamin Nelson, *The Idea of Usury: From Tribal Brotherhood to Universal Otherhood* (Chicago, 1948), and John T. Noonan, *The Scholastic Analysis of Usury* (Cambridge, MA, 1957). On medieval money in general, see Peter Spufford, *Money and Its Use in Medieval Europe* (Cambridge, 1988).

4. Black, *Guild and State,* 10. On medieval guilds, Stella Kramer, *The English Craft Guilds: Studies in Their Progress and Decline* (New York, 1927), is old but invaluable; see also Heather Swanson, *Medieval Artisans: An Urban Class in Late Medieval England* (Oxford, 1989), and Virginia Bainbridge, *Guilds in the Medieval Countryside: Social and Religious Change in Cambridgeshire, 1350–1558* (Rochester, NY, 1996). The significance

of guilds in medieval religious culture is explored in Sara Beckwith, *Signifying God: Social Relation and Symbolic Act in the York Corpus Christi Plays* (Chicago, 2001), esp. 42–55. Thomas Brinton is cited in Wood, *Medieval Economic Thought*, 120; the Florentine official is cited in Black, *Guild and State*, 72; see also Augustine Thompson, *Cities of God: The Religion of the Italian Communes, 1125–1325* (University Park, PA, 2005).

5. On "the commons," the authoritative text is arguably R. H. Tawney, *The Agrarian Problem in the Sixteenth Century* (New York, 1967 [1912]), esp. 237–253. See also Max Beer, *Social Struggles in the Middle Ages*, trans. H. J. Stenning (London, 1924); Joan Thirsk, *The Rural History of England* (London, 1984), 35–64; Peter Linebaugh, *The Magna Carta Manifesto: Liberties and Commons for All* (Berkeley, 2008), 1–68, quote on 271.

6. R. H. Tawney, *Religion and the Rise of Capitalism* (New Brunswick, NJ, 1998 [1926]), 32; on private property and the common good, see Wood, *Medieval Economic Thought*, 17–41; Hirschfeld, *Aquinas and the Market*, 161–190; and Christopher Franks, *He Became Poor: The Poverty of Christ and Aquinas' Economic Teachings* (Grand Rapids, MI, 2009), esp. 53–66.

7. On the Beguines and Beghards, see Walter Simons, *Cities of Ladies: Beguine Communities in the Low Countries, 1200–1565* (Philadelphia, 2001); on the Brethren of the Free Spirit, Robert Lerner, *The Heresy of the Free Spirit in the Later Middle Ages* (Berkeley, 1972), who does much to correct the misconceptions of Norman Cohn, *The Pursuit of the Millennium: Revolutionary Millenarians and Mystical Anarchists of the Middle Ages* (New York, 1957), esp. 148–186, 205–222, 234–280, 287–330. Critchley, *Faith of the Faithless*, 11 (see 117–136 on medieval millenarianism). The quotes are from William Langland, *Piers the Ploughman*, ed. J. F. Goodridge (New York and London, 1966), 172–173, 37.

8. Gregory, *The Unintended Reformation*, 366; see also 488, n. 67, on literature regarding church finances and popular criticism. Raymond Williams, *The Country and the City* (New York, 1973), 37–38. Norman F. Cantor's *Inventing the Middle Ages* (New York, 1991) is indispensable on the link between modern medievalism and reactionary politics, esp. 201–244 on J. R. R. Tolkien, C. S. Lewis, and other "Oxford fantasists."

9. On the peasant revolts of the fourteenth century, see the commentary and documents assembled in Samuel K. Cohn, ed., *Popular Protest in Late Medieval Europe: Italy, France, and Flanders* (Manchester, 2004), esp. 143–200 on the Jacquerie, and Rodney Hilton, *Bond Men Made Free: Medieval Peasant Movements and the English Rising of 1381* (London, 1973), quote on 131; Tawney, *Religion and the Rise of Capitalism*, 24.

10. On the expansion of the medieval commercial economy, see Robert S. Lopez, *The Commercial Revolution of the Middle Ages, 950–1350* (Cambridge, 1976 [1971]); Edwin S. Hunt and James M. Murray, *A History of Business in Medieval Europe, 1200–1520* (Cambridge, 1999). On the continuing matrix of commerce and social relations,

see Martha C. Howell, *Commerce before Capitalism in Europe, 1300–1600* (New York, 2010), 49–260. The Renaissance culture of avarice, luxury, and display is evoked with great enthusiasm and insight in Lisa Jardine, *Worldly Goods: A New History of the Renaissance* (New York, 1996), esp. 275–330, 377–424; Erasmus's directive to his portraitist is on 32–33. Bracciolini is cited in Wood, *Medieval Economic Thought*, 118. Jan de Vries and Ad van der Woude, *The First Modern Economy: Success, Failure, and Perseverance of the Dutch Economy, 1500–1815* (New York, 1997), argue that the Dutch Republic's was the first "modern" or "capitalist" economy.

11. Gregory, *Unintended Reformation*, 235–297 (quotes on 262, 263), provides a lucid overview of Reformation economic thought; see also Nelson, *Idea of Usury*, 29–82. On Calvin in particular, see Nelson, *Idea of Usury*, 77–82, and Andre Bieler, *The Social Humanism of John Calvin*, trans. Paul T. Fuhrmann (Richmond, VA, 1964). George Hunston Williams, *The Radical Reformation* (Kirksville, MO, 1995 [1962]), remains the most capacious survey of the more socially radical forms of Protestantism.

12. Weber, *The Protestant Ethic and the Spirit of Capitalism*, trans. and ed. Peter Baehr and Gordon C. Wells (New York, 2002 [1905]), 108–110.

13. R. W. Scribner, "The Reformation, Popular Magic, and the 'Disenchantment of the World,'" *Journal of Interdisciplinary History* 23 (Winter 1993), 475–494, is widely considered the breakthrough essay on this subject. See also Trevor Johnson, "The Reformation and Popular Culture," in *The Reformation World*, ed. Andrew Pettegee (London and New York, 2000), 545–560, from which the quote is taken on 557; Alexandra Walsham, *Providence in Early Modern England* (New York, 1999), and "The Reformation and 'the Disenchantment of the World' Reassessed," *Historical Journal* 51 (2008), 497–528. Most recently, Euan Cameron, *Enchanted Europe: Superstition, Reason, and Religion, 1250–1750* (New York, 2010), provides a lucid and colorful overview of the popular and clerical varieties of enchantment. See also Thomas, *Religion and the Decline of Magic*, and Carolyn Merchant, *The Death of Nature: Women, Ecology, and the Scientific Revolution* (New York, 1980). On the "animate cosmos" of Protestant farmers in England and early New England, see Carolyn Merchant, *Ecological Revolutions: Nature, Science, and Gender in New England* (Chapel Hill, 1989), 112–147, quote on 126.

14. On Bacon and "pneumaticals," see Graham Rees, "Francis Bacon's Semi-Paracelsian Cosmology and the Great Instauration," *Ambix* 22 (1975), 81–101. For a deft exposition of Cambridge Platonism and its cosmology, see Rupert Hall's study of one of its most renowned exponents, *Henry More* (Oxford, 199). William Perkins's indictment of the occult is cited in Thomas, *Religion and the Decline of Magic*, 300. Robert Boyle's alchemical interests and his debt to Hermetic philosophy are ably explored in Lawrence M. Principe, *The Aspiring Adept: Robert Boyle and His Alchemical Quest* (Princeton, NJ, 1998), esp. 138–213. Newton's immersion in Rosicrucian learning is examined in Frances A. Yates, *The Rosicrucian Enlightenment* (New York, 2002 [1972]), 247–261.

15. Thomas, *Religion and the Decline of Magic,* 105; Thomas Beard is cited in David Hall, *Worlds of Wonder, Days of Judgment: Popular Religious Belief in Early New England* (Cambridge, MA, 1989), 78.

16. On the early English political economists, see William Letwin, *The Origins of Scientific Economics: English Economic Thought, 1660–1776* (New York, 2003 [1963]), and Terence Hutchison, *Before Adam Smith: The Emergence of Political Economy, 1662–1776* (Oxford, 1988); but see also Andrea Finkelstein, *Harmony and the Balance: An Intellectual History of Seventeenth-Century English Economic Thought* (Ann Arbor, MI, 2000), who argues that these writers cannot be considered forerunners of modern economics. The Puritan merchants' incursion into the reorganization of production is examined especially in Robert Brenner, *Merchants and Revolution: Commercial Change, Political Conflict, and London's Overseas Traders, 1550–1653* (Princeton, NJ, 1993), 113–195; see also 274–281 on the new merchants and Puritanism. I have relied on Brenner's conceptualization of capitalism—as well as of the transition from feudalism to capitalism in England—because it emphasizes better than other approaches what is historically distinctive about capitalist enterprise. See also Ellen Meiksins Woods, *The Origin of Capitalism: A Longer View* (New York and London, 2002), 73–124. The "triumph of Lent" is chronicled in Burke, *Popular Culture in Early Modern Europe,* 289–334.

17. Richard Baxter, *A Christian Directory: Or, A Body of Practical Divinity, and Cases of Conscience* (London, 1825 [1678]), 4:515; Stephen Innes, *Creating the Commonwealth: The Economic Culture of Puritan New England* (New York, 1995), 43.

18. Thomas Hobbes, *Behemoth, Or the Long Parliament* (Chicago, 1990 [1668]), 25; Christopher Hill, *The World Turned Upside Down: Radical Ideas during the English Revolution* (New York, 1991 [1972]), 324; Tawney, *Religion and the Rise of Capitalism,* 246.

19. Baxter, *A Christian Directory,* 2:585–586.

20. On the agricultural improvement literature of seventeenth-century England, see Joyce Appleby, *Economic Thought and Ideology in Seventeenth-Century England* (Princeton, NJ, 1978), 24–72, and Neal Wood, *John Locke and Agrarian Capitalism* (Berkeley, 1984), 23–26. John Collinges, *The Weavers Pocket-Book, Or Weaving Spiritualised* (Edinburgh, 1723 [1675]), title page; Joseph Flavel, *Husbandry Spiritualised: Or, The Heavenly Use of Earthly Things* (London, 1794 [1669]), 60, 3.

21. George Herbert, *The Country Parson, The Temple,* ed. John N. Wall, Jr. (New York, 1981 [1652]), 88, 84, 101.

22. Francis Bacon, *The New Atlantis,* in *Three Modern Utopias: Utopia, New Atlantis, and Isle of Pines,* ed. Susan Bruce (New York, 1999), 177, 182–183. On the emergence of utopian literature at this time, see Amy Boesky, *Founding Fictions: Utopias in Early Modern England* (Athens, GA, 1996).

23. Bacon, *New Atlantis,* 184, 186, 158–159, 185, 183.

24. Gabriel Plattes, *A Discovery of Infinite Treasure, Hidden Since the World's Beginning* (London, 1639), 88, 3, 16; see also *A Description of the Famous Kingdome of Macaria, Shewing Its Excellent Government* (London, 1641). Samuel Gott, *Nova Solyma,*

*the Ideal City: Or, Jerusalem Regained,* ed. Walter Begley (London, 1902 [1648]), 1:188–190. Walter W. Woodward, *Prospero's America: John Winthrop, Jr., Alchemy, and the Creation of New England Culture, 1606–1676* (Chapel Hill, NC, 2011), 63–65, discusses Plattes's impact on Winthrop.

25. Linebaugh, *Magna Carta Manifesto,* 51.

26. C. B. Macpherson, *The Political Theory of Possessive Individualism: Hobbes to Locke* (Oxford, 1962); on Locke's interest in agricultural literature, see Wood, *John Locke and Agrarian Capitalism,* 15–48. For an example of Lockean revisionism, see Richard Ashcraft, *Revolutionary Politics and Locke's Two Treatises of Government* (Princeton, NJ, 1986); see also Christopher Lasch, *The True and Only Heaven: Progress and Its Critics* (New York, 1991), 198–201, for a summary of the revisionist position.

27. Locke, *Second Treatise of Government* (1690), in *Two Treatises of Government,* ed. Peter Laslett (New York, 2003), 298, 286, 271, 297. Roland Boer, *Idols of Nations: Biblical Myth at the Origins of Capitalism* (Minneapolis, MN, 2014), 47–86, is a perceptive analysis of Locke's account of the transition from original communism to private property.

28. Locke, *Second Treatise,* 293–294.

29. Hobbes, *Leviathan* (New York, 1985 [1651]), 227; on the colonialist warrant contained in Lockean liberalism, see Richard Tuck, *The Rights of War and Peace: Political Thought and the International Order from Grotius to Kant* (New York, 2001 [1999]), 166–196.

30. Edmund Spenser, *The Faerie Queene* (New York and London, 1987 [1590]), 207; Ben Jonson, *Volpone* (New York, 2004), 51; Robert Burton, *The Anatomy of Melancholy* (New York, 1863 [1621]), 33–34, 207. On the pervasive concern with money's spiritual qualities and effects at this time, see David Hawkes, *Idols of the Marketplace: Idolatry and Commodity Fetishism in English Literature, 1580–1680* (New York, 2001), and David Landreth, *The Face of Mammon: The Matter of Money in English Renaissance Literature* (New York, 2012).

31. Christopher Hill, *A Tinker and a Poor Man: John Bunyan and His Church, 1628–1688* (New York, 1989), is an insightful and sympathetic biography. Bunyan is quoted in Hill, *World Turned Upside Down,* 405; Bunyan, *The Pilgrim's Progress* (New York, 2003 [1678]), 91, 156, 159, 310.

32. Bunyan, *Pilgrim's Progress,* 157, 82; quote from Hill, *World Turned Upside Down,* 405.

33. Hill, *World Turned Upside Down,* 396–397; see also Christopher Hill, *Milton and the English Revolution* (New York, 1977). On Milton's "animist materialism," see Stephen M. Fallon, *Milton Among the Philosophers: Poetry and Materialism in Seventeenth-Century England* (Ithaca, NY, 2007), esp. 79–110. Milton on Calvinism is quoted in Weber, *Protestant Ethic,* 58; Milton, *Paradise Lost* (New York, 2008), 129, 128, 106, 91, 197, 301, 94.

34. Milton, *Paradise Lost,* 26.

35. Milton, *Paradise Lost,* 37–38, 27, 26.

36. Christopher Hill records the varieties of radical disillusionment in the 1650s in *The Experience of Defeat: Milton and Some Contemporaries* (New York, 1984). On the alternative "cultural revolution," see Hill, *World Turned Upside Down,* esp. 287–343.

37. Abiezer Coppe is quoted in Hill, *World Turned Upside Down,* 210.

38. The Diggers' occupation of St. George's Hill and subsequent events are related in Hill, *World Turned Upside Down,* 107–113, who quotes a contemporary observer on 110. Although Hill remains the preeminent historian of Winstanley and the Diggers, see also the essays in Andrew Bradstock, ed., *Winstanley and the Diggers, 1649–1999* (Oxford, 2000).

39. Gerrard Winstanley, "The Saints Paradice" (1648), in *The Complete Works of Gerrard Winstanley,* ed. Thomas Corns, Ann Hughes, and David Loewenstein (New York, 2009), 1:344, 345; Winstanley, "The New Law of Righteousness" (1648), in *Complete Works of Gerrard Winstanley,* 567.

40. Gerrard Winstanley, "The True Levellers Standard Advanced" (1649), in *Complete Works of Gerrard Winstanley,* 2:4; "New Law of Righteousness," in *Complete Works of Gerrard Winstanley,* 493; "A New-Yeers Gift for the Parliament and Armie" (1649), in *Complete Works of Gerrard Winstanley,* 2:144. On Winstanley's theology, see Christopher Hill, "The Religion of Gerrard Winstanley," in *Collected Essays of Christopher Hill,* vol. 2, *Religion and Politics in 17th-Century England* (Amherst, MA, 1986), 185–252.

41. Hill, "Religion of Gerrard Winstanley," in *Collected Essays of Christopher Hill,* 236; Winstanley, "Truth Lifting Up Its Head above Scandals" (1648), in *Complete Works of Gerrard Winstanley,* 1:414; "True Levellers Standard Advanced," in *Complete Works of Gerrard Winstanley,* 1:3, 13–14.

42. Winstanley, "Truth Lifting Up Its Head," and "A New-Yeers Gift," in *Complete Works of Gerrard Winstanley,* 1:421, 129; "Fire in the Bush" (1650), in *Complete Works of Gerrard Winstanley,* 2:176.

43. Winstanley, "Fire in the Bush," "True Levellers Standard Advanced," and "Truth Lifting Up Its Head," in *Complete Works of Gerrard Winstanley,* 2:176–177; 4, 6, 11; and 421.

44. Winstanley, "A Declaration from the Poor Oppressed People of England" (1649), "True Levellers Standard Advanced," and "A New Yeers-Gift," in *Complete Works of Gerrard Winstanley,* 2:32; 5; and 108–109.

45. Winstanley, "True Levellers Standard Advanced," in *Complete Works of Gerrard Winstanley,* 2:10, 14, 13; "The New Law of Righteousness" (1649), in *Complete Works of Gerrard Winstanley,* 1:485.

46. Winstanley, *The Law of Freedom and Other Writings,* ed. Christopher Hill (New York, 2006), 389.

## 2. The God among Commodities

1. Neil McKendrick, John Brewer, and J. H. Plumb, *The Birth of a Consumer Society: The Commercialization of Eighteenth-Century England* (New York, 1983 [1982]),

esp. 9–100; John Brewer, *The Pleasures of the Imagination: English Culture in the Eighteenth Century* (New York, 2013 [1997]), 15–108; David S. Landes, *The Unbound Prometheus: Technological Change and Industrial Development in Western Europe from 1750 to the Present* (New York, 1969), 41–123; E. P. Thompson, *The Making of the English Working Class* (New York, 1964 [1963]).

2. On the eighteenth-century "rehabilitation of desire," see Lasch, *True and Only Heaven,* 52–55; see also Albert O. Hirschman, *The Passions and the Interests: Political Arguments for Capitalism before Its Triumph* (Princeton, NJ, 2013 [1977]), 56–66, on the civilizing effects attributed to commerce and money-making. Bernard Mandeville, *The Fable of the Bees, Or, Private Vices, Publick Benefits* (London, 1714); David Hume, "Of Refinement in the Arts" (1752), in *Essays and Treatises on Several Subjects* (London, 1760), 2:28–30 passim; Adam Smith, *The Theory of Moral Sentiments* (London, 1761 [1759]), 263–278, quotes on 267, 271, 268, 272.

3. Colin Campbell, *The Romantic Ethic and the Spirit of Modern Consumerism* (Oxford, 1987), 99–137.

4. Campbell, *The Romantic Ethic,* 115–118, 138–160.

5. Joseph Addison, No. 565, July 9, 1714, in *The Spectator,* ed. G. Gregory Smith (London, 1913), 4:36–37; Joseph Addison, No. 571, July 23, 1714, in *The Spectator,* 4:54–55.

6. The best studies of evangelical economics are Boyd Hilton, *The Age of Atonement: The Influence of Evangelicalism on Social and Economic Thought, 1785–1865* (New York, 1991), esp. 36–202, and Anthony Michael C. Waterman, *Revolution, Economics, and Religion: Christian Political Economy, 1798–1833* (New York, 1991), esp. 58–112. Joseph Townsend, *A Dissertation on the Poor Laws: By a Well-Wisher to Mankind* (Berkeley, 1971 [1786]), 36. The "Christian political economists" arguably exercised a greater influence on British economic policy than Adam Smith; on Smith's delayed influence in British intellectual and political circles, see Michael Perelman, *The Invention of Capitalism: Classical Political Economy and the Secret History of Primitive Accumulation* (Durham, NC, 2000), 175–176.

7. Alison Winter, *Mesmerized: Powers of Mind in Victorian Britain* (Chicago, 2000), 249; see also 134, 156, and 272 on Richard Whately.

8. Richard Whately, *Introductory Lectures on Political Economy* (London, 1832 [1831]), 100, 101; Thomas Chalmers, *The Application of Christianity to the Commercial and Ordinary Affairs of Life, In a Series of Discourses* (Hartford, CT, 1821 [1820]), 61–62, 151, 18, 105, 197.

9. Thomas Malthus, *An Essay on the Principle of Population* (New York, 1982 [1798]), 200, 210, 202, 217; the 1826 edition of the *Essay* is quoted on 411 (my thanks to Iain Boal for bringing this passage to my attention); Nassau Senior, *Three Lectures on the Rate of Wages: Delivered before the University of Oxford, in Easter Term, 1830* (London, 1830), xv; Cobden quoted in Allen C. Guelzo, "Lincoln, Cobden, and Bright: The Braid of Liberalism in the Nineteenth Century's Transatlantic World," *American Political Thought* 4 (Summer 2015), 404.

10. Andrew Ure, *The Philosophy of Manufactures: Or, An Exposition of the Scientific, Moral, and Commercial Economy of the Factory System of Great Britain* (London, 1835), 20.

11. Charles Babbage, *Reflections on the Decline of Science in England: And on Some of Its Causes* (London, 1830), 137; Charles Babbage, *The Ninth Bridgewater Treatise: A Fragment* (London, 1838 [1837]), esp. 92–107 on "the Nature of Miracles"; Charles Babbage, *On the Economy of Machinery and Manufactures* (London, 1832), 318–319.

12. Ure's "scriptural geology" is exemplified in Andrew Ure, *A New System of Geology: In Which the Great Revolutions of the Earth and Animated Nature, Are Reconciled at Once to Modern Science and Sacred History* (London, 1829); Ure, *Philosophy of Manufactures,* 417.

13. Ure, *Philosophy of Manufactures,* 13, 367, 418. On the Luddites, see Kirkpatrick Sale, *Rebels against the Future: The Luddites and Their War on the Industrial Revolution* (Cambridge, MA, 1996 [1995]), and Kevin Binfield, ed., *Writings of the Luddites* (Baltimore, 2015), an invaluable anthology of letters, pamphlets, and speeches. David W. Noble, *Progress without People: New Technology, Unemployment, and the Message of Resistance* (Toronto, 1995 [1993]), is a passionate and erudite defense of the Luddite tradition.

14. Trevelyan is quoted in Kerby Miller, *Emigrants and Exiles: Ireland and the Irish Exodus to North America* (New York, 1988), 283; Charles Trevelyan, *The Irish Crisis* (London, 1848), 201; Senior is quoted in Terry Eagleton, *Heathcliff and the Great Hunger: Studies in Irish Culture* (London and New York, 1995), 16.

15. David Bebbington, *Evangelicalism in Modern Britain: A History from the 1730s to the 1980s* (London, 1989), 105–150, covers evangelical philanthropy; on the evangelical roots of modern British consumerism, see Deborah Cohen, *Household Gods: The British and Their Possessions* (New Haven, 2009); John Ruskin, *The Crown of Wild Olive* (1866), in *Works of John Ruskin,* ed. E. T. Cook and Alexander Wedderburn (London, 1905), 18:422.

16. On Saint-Simon, see Frank Manuel, *The New World of Henri de Saint-Simon* (Cambridge, MA, 1956); on Comte, see Andrew Wernick, *Auguste Comte and the Religion of Humanity: The Post-Theistic Program of French Social Theory* (Cambridge, 2001), esp. 81–115, 187–220; Emile Durkheim, *The Elementary Forms of Religious Life,* trans. Carol Cosman (New York, 2001 [1912]), 323, 314. Owen Chadwick, *The Secularization of the European Mind in the Nineteenth Century* (New York, 1975), remains the ur-text in the study of cultural and intellectual secularization.

17. Weber, *Protestant Ethic,* 121; "Science as a Vocation," in Gerth and Mills, *From Max Weber,* 155, 156.

18. Marx and Engels, "Communist Manifesto," in Tucker, *Marx-Engels Reader,* 475; on "alienation," see Marx, "Economic and Philosophic Manuscripts of 1844," in Tucker, *Marx-Engels Reader,* 70–81; on the "fetishism of commodities," see Marx, *Capital,* 42–50. Gareth Stedman Jones, *Karl Marx: Greatness and Illusion* (Cambridge, MA, 2016), nicely interweaves biography and theoretical exposition.

19. Warren Breckman, *Marx, the Young Hegelians, and the Origins of Radical Social Theory* (New York, 2001 [1999]), traces the connections between the religious and political concerns of Hegel's radical heirs. Ludwig Feuerbach, *The Essence of Christianity* (New York, 1957 [1843]), is the most lucid and eloquent statement of their post-theological humanism.

20. Marx, "Theses on Feuerbach" (1845), theses XI and IV, in Tucker, *Marx-Engels Reader,* 145, 144, respectively.

21. Marx, "Economic and Philosophic Manuscripts" (1844), in Tucker, *Marx-Engels Reader,* 72; "Critique of Hegel's *Philosophy of Right:* Introduction" (1844), in Tucker, *Marx-Engels Reader,* 54.

22. Marx, *The Ethnographic Notebooks of Karl Marx,* ed. Lawrence Krader (Assen, The Netherlands, 1974); Marx, "The Leading Article in No. 179 of the *Kolnische Zeitung,*" in Karl Marx and Friedrich Engels, *Collected Works,* vol. 1, *Karl Marx, 1835–1843* (London, 1975), 189; "Economic and Philosophic Manuscripts" (1844), in Tucker, *Marx-Engels Reader,* 72. For a helpful elucidation of Marx's early thinking on fetishism, see Roland Boer, *Criticism of Earth: On Marx, Engels, and Theology* (Leiden, 2012), 65–67.

23. Marx, "The Power of Money," in Tucker, *Marx-Engels Reader,* 102, 104.

24. Marx, *Grundrisse,* 221; Marx, *Capital,* 42–50, quotes on 42, 47.

25. Marx, *Capital,* 247, 261; Marx, *Grundrisse,* 694.

26. Marx, *Grundrisse,* 693; Marx, *Capital,* 235; on "managerial fetishism," see Alfred Sohn-Rethel, *Intellectual and Manual Labor: A Critique of Epistemology* (Atlantic Highlands, NJ, 1978), esp. 13–17, 148–159.

27. Marx, *Capital,* 479.

28. Marx, *Capital,* 292; Engels, "On the Division of Labor in Production," from *Anti-Duhring* (1878), in Tucker, *Marx-Engels Reader,* 720.

29. Marx, *Grundrisse,* 712; Engels, "On Authority" (1872), in Tucker, *Marx-Engels Reader,* 731; see also "Versus the Anarchists," excerpt from letter to Theodor Cuno, January 24, 1872, in Tucker, *Marx-Engels Reader,* 728–729. The most trenchant critique of Marx and Engels on this score is Murray Bookchin, *The Ecology of Freedom: The Emergence and Dissolution of Hierarchy* (Oakland, CA, 2005 [1982]), 307–314.

30. Simone Weil, "Is There a Marxist Doctrine?," in *Oppression and Liberty,* trans. Arthur Wills and John Petrie (Amherst, MA, 1973), 164; Marx, "Economic and Philosophic Manuscripts," in Tucker, *Marx-Engels Reader,* 89; Herbert Marcuse, *Eros and Civilization: A Philosophical Inquiry into Freud* (New York, 1962 [1955]), 144–156; Marshall Berman, *All That Is Solid Melts into Air: The Experience of Modernity* (New York, 1988 [1982]), 126–127, quote on 127.

31. Marx, "On the Realm of Necessity and the Realm of Freedom," from the third volume of *Capital,* in Tucker, *Marx-Engels Reader,* 439–441 (the title is Tucker's, not Marx's); Adorno's remark about Marx was made to Martin Jay, recounted in *The Dialectical Imagination: A History of the Frankfurt School and the Institute of Social Research, 1923–1950* (Boston, 1973), 57.

## 3. The Poetry of the Past

1. Marx and Engels, "The Communist Manifesto," in Tucker, *Marx-Engels Reader,* 491, 493; Marx, "The Eighteenth Brumaire of Louis Napoleon" (1852), in Tucker, *Marx-Engels Reader,* 597. As Stedman Jones reminds us, Marx and Engels had been embroiled in a dispute in the 1840s with Wilhelm Weitling, a Christian communist whom they eventually ousted from the League of the Just, a band of German émigrés living in London: Jones, *Karl Marx,* 213–216.

2. Michael Lowy and Robert Sayre, "Figures of Romantic Anti-Capitalism," *New German Critique* 32 (Spring-Summer 1984), 42–92, quote on 42. Lowy and Sayre later expanded this article into *Romanticism Against the Tide of Modernity,* trans. Catherine Porter (Durham, NC, 2001).

3. M. H. Abrams, *Natural Supernaturalism: Tradition and Revolution in Romantic Literature* (New York, 1973), 12, 13.

4. Bernard M. G. Reardon, *Religion in the Age of Romanticism: Studies in Early Nineteenth-Century Thought* (New York, 1985), 3; William Blake, "Auguries of Innocence," in *The Complete Poetry and Prose of William Blake,* ed. David V. Erdman (Berkeley, 2008), 493; William Wordsworth, "Lines Written Above Tintern Abbey," in *William Wordsworth: The Major Works,* ed. Stephen Gill (New York, 2008), 134.

5. Blake, letter to Thomas Butts, November 22, 1802; "The Book of Urizen;" and "Annotations to the Works of Sir Joshua Reynolds," in *Complete Poetry and Prose,* 722, 70–84, and 647, respectively; Thomas Carlyle, *On Heroes, Hero-Worship, and the Heroic in History* (Boston, 1901 [1841]), 122; Thomas Carlyle, *Sartor Resartus* (New York, 2008 [1836]), 201.

6. Blake, "Milton," in *Complete Poetry and Prose,* 127; Samuel Taylor Coleridge, *Biographia Literaria* (1815–1817) and "Aids to Reflection" (1825), in *Samuel Taylor Coleridge: The Major Works,* ed. H. J. Jackson (New York, 2008), 313 and 667, respectively; William Wordsworth, "The Prelude" and "The French Revolution as It Appeared to Enthusiasts at Its Commencement," in *Wordsworth's Poetry and Prose,* ed. Nicholas Halmi (New York, 2013), 337, 368; and 338, respectively.

7. Blake, "The Birds," "Jerusalem," "Mammon," and "The Four Zoas," in *Complete Poetry and Prose,* 479; 201; 169; 481; and 314, respectively. On Blake's fusion of religious and political radicalism, see E. P. Thompson, *Witness Against the Beast: William Blake and the Moral Law* (New York, 1993), and Christopher Rowland, *Blake and the Bible* (New Haven, CT, 2011).

8. Robert Southey, "The Manufacturing System," in *St. Thomas More: Or, Colloquies on the Progress and Prospects of Society* (London, 1831), 158, 169; Wordsworth, "Written in London" (1802), in *Wordsworth's Poetry and Prose,* 285; Wordsworth to Dorothy Wordsworth, cited in *Lyrical Ballads and Other Poetry, 1797–1800,* ed. James Butler (Ithaca, NY, 1993), 79; Samuel Taylor Coleridge, *Table-Talk of Samuel Taylor Coleridge* (London, 1884), 258, 186.

9. Raymond Williams, *Culture and Society, 1780–1950* (New York, 1973), 67.

10. On "Tory radicalism," see the succinct account in Mark Bevir, *The Making of British Socialism* (Princeton, NJ, 2011), 66–73. Carlyle and Ruskin were major figures in the "culture and society" tradition of anti-industrial criticism identified by Williams in *Culture and Society*, 71–88, 133–148. Carlyle dubbed economics "the dismal science" in "Occasional Discourse on the Negro Question," *Fraser's Magazine* 40 (December 1849), 671. Terry Eagleton, *The Ideology of the Aesthetic* (Oxford, 1990), 63.

11. On Carlyle's impact on Marx and Engels, see Sayre and Lowy, *Romanticism against the Tide of Modernity*, 90. R. H. Tawney, "John Ruskin" (1919), in *The Radical Tradition: Twelve Essays on Politics, Education, and Literature*, ed. Rita Hinden (London, 1964), 41.

12. On the Victorian crisis of faith, see A. N. Wilson, *God's Funeral: The Decline of Faith in Western Civilization* (New York, 1999), esp. 127–278; but see also Timothy Larsen, *Crisis of Doubt: Honest Faith in Nineteenth-Century England* (New York, 2006), for a more skeptical view. Matthew Arnold's line is from "Dover Beach" (1867), in *Dover Beach and Other Poems* (New York, 2012), 87; yet see Eagleton's astute examination of Arnold's agnosticism in *Culture and the Death of God*, 125–150. Stefan Collini, *Public Moralists: Political Thought and Intellectual Life in Britain, 1850–1930* (Oxford, 1991).

13. C. Brad Faught, *The Oxford Movement: A Thematic History of the Tractarians and Their Times* (University Park, PA, 2004), esp. 1–72, 101–126. Carlyle, *Sartor Resartus*, 147.

14. Carlyle, letter to his brother (October 1, 1833), in *Letters of Thomas Carlyle, 1826–1836*, vol. 2, *1832–1836*, ed. Charles Eliot Norton (London and New York, 1888), 123; Carlyle, *Sartor Resartus*, 147, 54, 205; Fred Kaplan, *Thomas Carlyle: A Biography* (New York, 1983), is the best narrative, but Lasch, *True and Only Heaven*, 239–243, quote on 239, recognizes Carlyle's prophetic identity.

15. Carlyle, *Sartor Resartus*, 160, 161; Thomas Carlyle, *The French Revolution: A History* (New York, 1897), 11:458; Carlyle, *Past and Present*, 169, 359, 315, 2, 316; Carlyle, "Signs of the Times" (1829), in *A Carlyle Reader*, ed. G. B. Tennyson (Cambridge, 1984), 49.

16. Thomas Carlyle, *On Heroes, Hero-Worship and the Heroic in History* (London, 1840), 130–131; Carlyle, *Sartor Resartus*, 140–149, quote on 143.

17. Carlyle, *Past and Present*, 171, 105.

18. Carlyle, *On Heroes*, 15; Thomas Carlyle, *Shooting Niagara—And After?* (London, 1867), 10, originally published in *Macmillan's Magazine* 16 (April 1867), 674–687.

19. Carlyle, *Sartor Resartus*, 149.

20. Carlyle, "Signs of the Times," in *A Carlyle Reader*, 34.

21. Carlyle, *Past and Present*, 200, 315, 314, 313; letter to James Garth Marshall (December 7, 1841), in *Collected Letters of Thomas and Jane Welsh Carlyle*, ed. Clyde de L. Ryals and Kenneth J. Fielding (Durham, NC, 1985), 13:317.

22. The most direct and acerbic attack on Ruskin's affirmation of British imperialism is in Edward W. Said, *Culture and Imperialism* (New York, 1993), 102–104. Tim Hilton, *John Ruskin* (New Haven, CT, 2002), 456–463, remains silent on the issue.

23. "The Work of Iron in Nature, Art, and Policy," in *The Two Paths* (1857), in *Unto This Last*, 129, 138; *Fors Clavigera*, letter 28 (April 1873), in *The Works of John Ruskin*, ed. E. T. Cook and Alexander Wedderbern (London, 1907–1910), 27:519; *The Bible of Amiens* (1885), in *Works of John Ruskin*, 33:48 n. 34.

24. Ruskin, preface to Francesca Alexander, *The Story of Ida: Epitaph on an Etrurian Tomb* (1883), in *Works of John Ruskin*, 32:6; letter to Pauline Trevelyan, cited in Hilton, *John Ruskin*, 202; *Unto This Last*, 223; *Fors Clavigera*, letter 89 (1880), in *Works of John Ruskin*, 29:408; *Praeterita* (1885), in *Works of John Ruskin*, 35:13; *Fors Clavigera*, letter 7 and letter 10 (1871), in *Works of John Ruskin*, 27:117, 122, 125 and 173, respectively.

25. Williams, *Culture and Society*, 135. The revival of interest in Ruskin as a social critic can be traced both to Williams and to P. D. Anthony, *John Ruskin's Labour: A Study of Ruskin's Social Theory* (Cambridge, 1983). Hilton, *John Ruskin*, 328–335, discusses what he calls Ruskin's "flexible beliefs" and emphasizes that he loathed what he once called the "dull-droning drowsing insanity" of Victorian Protestantism (331). I have relied heavily on Michael Wheeler, *Ruskin's God* (Cambridge, 1999), the most thorough examination of Ruskin's religious background and convictions.

26. John Ruskin, *Modern Painters*, vol. 1, in *Works of John Ruskin*, 3:48, 45; *Modern Painters*, vol. 2, in *Works of John Ruskin*, 4:64, 146; *Modern Painters*, vol. 4, in *of John Ruskin*, 6:113.

27. Ruskin, *The Two Paths*, in *Works of John Ruskin*, 16:378, 376; *The Storm Cloud of the Nineteenth Century* (1884), in *Works of John Ruskin*, 34:59, 34, 38, 80; *Modern Painters*, vol. 2, in *Works of John Ruskin*, 4:47; *Modern Painters*, vol. 5, in *Works of John Ruskin*, 7:462, 259–260.

28. Ruskin, *The Stones of Venice*, in *Works of John Ruskin*, 10:190, 192.

29. Ruskin, *The Stones of Venice*, in *Works of John Ruskin*, 10:194, 196, 192, 195.

30. Ruskin, *Two Lectures on the Political Economy of Art* (1857), in *Works of John Ruskin*, 16:138; *The Crown of Wild Olive* (1866), in *Works of John Ruskin*, 17:287; *Munera Pulveris* (1872), in *Works of John Ruskin*, 18:447–448.

31. Ruskin, *Unto This Last*, 167, 170, 168, 203.

32. Ruskin, *Unto This Last*, 209, 226.

33. Ruskin, *Unto This Last*, 226, 209, 222.

34. Ruskin, *Unto This Last*, 211, 220, 189.

35. Ruskin, *Unto This Last*, 211, 189, 190.

36. Ruskin, *Unto This Last*, 163–164, 173–174, 227.

37. Ruskin, *Fors Clavigera*, letter 7 (1871), in *Works of John Ruskin*, 27:115–117 passim, 119, 125.

38. Graeber, *Debt*, 94–102, is a lucid discussion of "communism" as both a principle of morality and a form of property.

39. Ruskin, *Unto This Last*, 161; the aspersions are cited by Clive Wilmer in his introduction to *Unto This Last*, 28. Cook and Wedderbern provide a lengthy and informative account of the Guild of St. George in the introduction to vol. 30 of *Works of*

*John Ruskin,* xxi–lxxvi; see also Hilton, *John Ruskin,* 588–591. Ruskin, *Time and Tide,*
in *Works of John Ruskin,* 17:442. On Ruskin's renown among British workers, see Jonathan Rose's magnificent study of *The Intellectual Life of the British Working Classes*
(New Haven, CT, 2003), esp. 393–438. Inexpensive editions of Ruskin's books enabled
him to have a national following among workers (193) and were more popular than
Dickens and the Bible among early Labour MPs (42). Workers who read him were more
likely to be socialists than those who read the racing papers—who tended to vote Conservative (50). On the reformist impact of industrialization on working-class politics,
see Craig Calhoun, *The Question of Class Struggle: Social Foundations of Popular Radicalism during the Industrial Revolution* (Chicago, 1982), and Gareth Stedman Jones,
*Languages of Class: Studies in English Working Class History 1832–1982* (Cambridge,
1983).

40. Ruskin, *Crown of Wild Olive,* in *Works of John Ruskin,* 18:391.

41. The two main biographies of Morris are E. P. Thompson, *William Morris: From
Romantic to Revolutionary* (New York, 2011 [1955]) (the quote is on 695), and Fiona Mc-
Carthy, *William Morris: A Life for Our Time* (London, 2010).

42. William Morris, "How I Became a Socialist" (1894), in *News from Nowhere and
Other Writings,* ed. Clive Wilmer (New York, 2004), 379.

43. Morris, "How I Became a Socialist," in *News from Nowhere,* 380, 381.

44. Morris's remark about Ruskin as "Luther of the arts" is cited in Hilton, *John
Ruskin,* 232; Morris, preface to the Kelmscott edition of *The Nature of Gothic* (1892), in
*News from Nowhere,* 369, 367.

45. Morris, "The Lesser Arts" (1877), in *News from Nowhere,* 234; "Useful Work
versus Useless Toil" (1884), in Morris, *News from Nowhere,* 301, 288, 300.

46. Morris, *News from Nowhere,* 132–156, quote on 133; "How I Became a Socialist,"
in *News from Nowhere,* 381, 382; letter to Georgiana Burne-Jones (August 26, 1883), in
*The Collected Letters of William Morris,* ed. Norman Kelvin (Princeton, NJ, 1987), 2:219.

47. Jones, *Languages of Class,* 237, 238.

48. Morris, "How I Became a Socialist," in *News from Nowhere,* 383.

49. Morris, "How I Became a Socialist," in *News from Nowhere,* 382–383.

50. Morris, quoted in Thompson, *William Morris,* 2; see 1–87 for Thompson's account of Morris's early life. Morris's remark on being "careless" is in "How I Became a
Socialist," in *News from Nowhere,* 382.

51. Morris, letter to Georgiana Burne-Jones, in *The Collected Letters of William
Morris,* 219; "The Hopes of Civilization" (1885), in *News from Nowhere,* 327; 122.

52. Morris, *News from Nowhere,* 158–159.

53. Morris, "Gothic Architecture," in *News from Nowhere,* 339.

54. Friedrich Nietzsche, *The Twilight of the Idols and The Anti-Christ,* ed. Martin
Tanner (New York, 1990 [1888]), 80–81.

55. William Morris, *A Dream of John Ball and A King's Lesson* (London, 1898 [1888]),
29, 41, 28.

56. Morris, *A Dream of John Ball,* 31, 121.

57. On the British Arts and Crafts movement, see Eileen Boris, *Art and Labor: Ruskin, Morris, and the Craftsman Ideal in America* (Philadelphia, 1988), 3–23; Wendy Kaplan, *Leading "the Simple Life": The Arts and Crafts Movement in Britain, 1880–1910* (Miami, 1999). See also Mary Greensted, ed., *An Anthology of The Arts and Crafts Movement* (London, 2005).

58. C. R. Ashbee, quoted in Boris, *Art and Labor,* 16.

59. William Morris, "The Revival of Handicraft," *The Fortnightly* 44 (November 1, 1888), 610.

60. Morris's remark about anarchism to a friend is cited in David Goodway, *Anarchist Seeds Beneath the Snow: Left-Libertarian Thought and British Writers from William Morris to Colin Ward* (New York, 2012), 22; see 22–24 on Morris's ambivalent relationship to anarchism; William Morris, "Socialism and Anarchism" (1889), in *Political Writings of William Morris,* ed. A. L. Morton (London, 1984), 210.

61. The dismissive characterization of anarchism as "petty-bourgeois" originated with Vladimir I. Lenin, *"Left-Wing" Communism: An Infantile Disorder* (Detroit, 1921), in which he excoriated anarchism and syndicalism as "a kind of punishment for the opportunist sins of the working-class movement" (27). There is a sizeable historical literature on anarchism; see, for instance, Goodway, *Anarchist Seeds;* and George Woodcock, *Anarchism: A History of Libertarian Ideas and Movements* (New York, 1962).

62. Peter Kropotkin, *Mutual Aid: A Factor of Evolution* (New York, 1902), 194–195, 209, 192.

63. On Reclus's anarchist geography, see John P. Clark and Camille Martin, eds., *Anarchy, Geography, Modernity: The Radical Social Thought of Elisée Reclus* (New York, 2004), quotes on 24, 50.

64. On artists and anarchism, see Roger Shattuck, *The Banquet Years: The Origins of the Avant-Garde in France, 1885 to World War I* (New York, 1968 [1955]), 20–24; Richard Sonn, *Anarchism and Cultural Politics in Fin-de-Siècle France* (Lincoln, NE, 1989); and Allan Antliff, *Anarchy and Art: From the Paris Commune to the Fall of the Berlin Wall* (New York, 2007), 17–48.

65. On Kandinsky's blend of spirituality and anarchism, see Rose-Carol Long, "Occultism, Anarchism, and Abstraction: Kandinsky's Art of the Future," *Art Journal* 46 (Spring 1987), 38–45; Wassily Kandinsky, "On the Spiritual in Art" (1912), in *Kandinsky: Complete Writings on Art,* ed. Kenneth C. Lindsay and Peter Vergo (New York, 1982), 140; "On the Question of Form" (1911), Lindsay and Vergo, *Kandinsky,* 250, 235, 242; Marc is quoted in Robert Goldwater, *Primitivism in Modern Art* (Cambridge, MA, 1986), 135.

66. Gustav Landauer, *For Socialism* (St. Louis, MO, 1978), 32, 50, 62, 136, 54. On Landauer's social thought, Martin Buber, *Paths in Utopia* (New York, 1949), 46–57, is a fine introduction; Eugene Lunn, *Prophet of Community: The Romantic Socialism of Gustav Landauer* (Berkeley, 1973), situates Landauer within the socialist tradition; but see also the essays in Paul Mendes-Flohr and Anya Mali, eds., *Gustav Landauer:*

*Anarchist and Jew* (Berlin, 2015), which make a stronger case that Landauer is best understood as a mystical anarchist.

67. Sheila Rowbotham, *Edward Carpenter: A Life of Liberty and Love* (London and New York, 2008), is a sensitive and incisive biography. Edward Carpenter, *Civilisation: Its Cause and Cure and Other Essays* (London, 1889), 36, 45, 47.

68. Edward Carpenter, *Towards Industrial Freedom* (London, 1918), 57, 75, 61; *The Healing of Nations: And the Sources of Their Strife* (London, 1915), 212; "The Art of Life," in *Angel's Wings: A Series of Essays on Art and Its Relation to Life* (London, 1908), 210–228.

69. Morris, *News from Nowhere*, 128.

## Part Two: A Hundred Dollars, a Hundred Devils

1. Herman Melville, *White-Jacket, Or the World in a Man-of-War* (New York, 2000 [1850]), 153; *Redburn, White-Jacket, Moby-Dick* (New York, 1983 [1849]), 181.

2. Herman Melville, *Israel Potter: His Fifty Years of Exile* (Evanston, 2000 [1855]), 120; *The Confidence-Man: His Masquerade* (New York, 1990 [1857]), 168.

3. Herman Melville, "The Paradise of Bachelors and the Tartarus of Maids" (1855), in *Billy Budd and Other Stories* (New York, 1986), 278, 285; Melville, *Confidence-Man*, 84.

## 4. Errand into the Marketplace

1. Barlowe and Drayton are quoted in Leo Marx, *The Machine in the Garden: Technology and the Pastoral Ideal in America* (New York, 1967), 37, 38; on *The Tempest*, see 34–72; Marx is quoted on 64.

2. Richard Hakluyt, *Divers Voyages Touching the Discovery of America and the Islands Adjacent* (London, 1801 [1582]), 13, 95, 87, 25. On the religious foundations of Hakluyt's mission, see David Armitage, *The Ideological Origins of the British Empire* (New York, 2000), 75–80, and Peter Mancall, *Hakluyt's Promise: An Elizabethan's Obsession for an English America* (New Haven, CT, 2010).

3. George Alsop, *A Character of the Province of Maryland* (Cleveland, OH, 1902 [1666]), 32–33, 65.

4. The most informative and sympathetic account of Morton's life is William Heath, "Thomas Morton: From Merry Old England to New England," *Journal of American Studies* 41 (Winter 2007), 135–168. William Bradford, *Of Plymouth Plantation, 1620–1647* (New York, 1981), 226–232, quotes on 227, 229.

5. Thomas Morton, *New English Canaan* (Boston, 1883 [1637]), 109, 114, 110, 150, 177–178.

6. Morton, *New English Canaan*, 177, 223, 171, 120.

7. Hall, *Worlds of Wonder*, 71; John Winthrop quoted on 91. Richard Godbeer, *The Devil's Dominion: Magic and Religion in Early New England* (New York, 1994), is another excellent introduction to the enchanted world of the Puritans. Peter Benes, "Fortune-Tellers, Wise Men, and Magical Healers in New England, 1644–1850," in

*Wonders of the Invisible World, 1600–1900,* ed. Peter Benes and Jane Montague Benes (Boston, 1995), 127–137, chronicles the presence of occult practices in the era of high Puritanism. On the Puritan "errand," the standard work is Perry Miller, *Errand into the Wilderness* (Cambridge, MA, 1956). Winthrop's son is quoted in Woodward, *Prospero's America,* 55. Increase Mather, *Remarkable Providences Illustrative of the Early Days of American Colonization* (London, 1856), 71; Mather quoted in Godbeer, *The Devil's Dominion,* 84; Cotton Mather, *Magnalia Christi Americana: Or, The Ecclesiastical History of New-England* (Boston, 1820), 2, 15; Cotton Mather, *The Christian Philosopher* (Boston, 1815), 311.

8. The greatest account of the Puritan covenant theology remains Perry Miller, *The New England Mind: The Seventeenth Century* (Cambridge, MA, 1982 [1939]), 398–492. On the jeremiad and "declension," see Miller, *The New England Mind: From Colony to Province* (Cambridge, MA, 1981 [1953]), 19–48, esp. 27–40; and Sacvan Bercovitch, *The American Jeremiad* (Madison, WI, 1978). "The Charter of the Colony of Massachusetts Bay" (1628), in *The Charters and General Laws of the Colony and Province of Massachusetts Bay* (Boston, 1814), 14; John Winthrop, "A Modell of Christian Charity" (1630), in *The English Literatures of America, 1500–1800,* ed. Myra Jehlen and Michael Warner (New York, 2013), 159.

9. Lehmann, *The Money Cult,* 3–20, quote on 25; Winthrop, "Modell of Christian Charity," in Jehlen and Warner, *The English Literatures,* 156; Andrew Delbanco, *The Puritan Ordeal* (Cambridge, MA, 1989), 60; John Cotton is quoted in Larzer Ziff, *The Career of John Cotton: Puritanism and the American Experience* (New York, 1962), 152, 157; Cotton, *A Practicall Commentary, Or, An Exposition with Observations, Reasons, and Verses upon the First Epistle of John* (London, 1656), 109. My description of the Puritans' communalist capitalism relies on Innes, *Creating the Commonwealth,* 64–106; Stephen Innes, *Labor in a New Land: Economy and Society in Seventeenth-Century Springfield* (Princeton, NJ, 1983); John Frederick Martin, *Profits in the Wilderness: Entrepreneurship and the Founding of New England Towns in the Seventeenth Century* (Chapel Hill, NC, 1991); Mark A. Petersen, *The Price of Redemption: The Spiritual Economy of Puritan New England* (Stanford, CA, 1997); and Mark Valeri, *Heavenly Merchandize: How Religion Shaped Commerce in Puritan America* (Princeton, NJ, 2010).

10. The quote about "chattering and changing" merchants is in Delbanco, *The Puritan Ordeal,* 69; quotes concerning Robert Keayne are from Valeri, *Heavenly Merchandize,* 37, and Innes, *Creating the Commonwealth,* 161; Delbanco, *Puritan Ordeal,* 223.

11. All quotations from Keayne's apologia are from Bernard Bailyn, "The Apologia of Robert Keayne," *William and Mary Quarterly* 7 (October 1950), 581, 582, 584, 587.

12. John Cotton, *God's Promise to His Plantation* (Boston, 1630), 5, 8; Cotton's *The Way of Life* is cited in James Henretta, "The Weber Thesis Revisited: The Protestant Ethic and the Reality of Capitalism in Early America," in *The Origins of American Capitalism: Collected Essays* (Boston, 1991), 37–38; John Smith is quoted in Stephen Innes, "Fulfilling John Smith's Vision: Work and Labor in Early America," in *Work and Labor in Early America,* ed. Stephen Innes (Chapel Hill, NC, 1988), 11; John Higginson, *The*

*Cause of God and His People in New-England* (Boston, 1663), 18; Edward Winslow, *Good Newes from New-England* (Bedford, MA, 1996 [1624]), 69–70; Cotton Mather, *A Christian at His Calling* (Boston, 1701), 48, 49; Bercovitch, *American Jeremiad,* 47.

13. John Winthrop, letter to his father, in *The Life and Letters of John Winthrop,* ed. Robert C. Winthrop (Boston, 1864), 310, 312; the Puritan commander is quoted in Richard Drinnon, *Facing West: The Metaphysics of Indian-Hating and Empire-Building* (Norman, OK, 1997 [1980]), 46.

14. Nathaniel Whittmore is cited in Merchant, *Ecological Revolutions,* 141; see 112–147. Edward Johnson, *Johnson's Wonder-Working Providences, 1628–1651,* ed. J. Franklin Jameson (New York, 1910 [1654]), 25, 246–247.

15. Johnson, *Johnson's Wonder-Working Providences,* 247; Woodward, *Prospero's America,* 43–159, 210–252, quotes on 55, 3, 12; Wise is quoted in John L. Brooke, *The Refiner's Fire: The Making of Mormon Cosmology, 1644–1844* (New York, 1996), 107.

16. Valeri, *Heavenly Merchandize,* 4; see especially 111–177 on Samuel Sewall. On the new political economy of British imperialism, see Armitage, *Ideological Origins of the British Empire,* 146–169; on the transformation of the Puritan moral economy, see Mark Valeri, "William Petty in Boston: Political Economy, Religion, and Money in Provincial New England," *Early American Studies* 8 (Fall 2010), 549–580, esp. 571–580, and James D. German, "The Social Utility of Wicked Self-Love: Calvinism, Capitalism, and Public Policy in Revolutionary New England," *Journal of American History* 82 (December 1995), 965–998.

17. Jonathan Edwards, "A Personal Narrative" (1740), in *A Jonathan Edwards Reader,* ed. John E. Smith and Harry S. Stout (New Haven, CT, 2003), 285; "The Images and Shadows of Divine Things" (1738) and "The Beauty of the World" (1725), both in Smith and Stout, *Jonathan Edwards Reader,* 19, 14, respectively; Jonathan Edwards, *The Images and Shadows of Divine Things,* ed. Perry Miller (New York, 1948), 66. On Edwards's view of nature, see George M. Marsden, *Jonathan Edwards: A Life* (New Haven, CT, 2004), 77–79.

18. Valeri, "The Economic Thought of Jonathan Edwards," *Church History* 60 (March 1991), 37–54, traces the evolution of Edwards's thinking on morality and the marketplace. Harvey G. Townsend, ed., *The Philosophy of Jonathan Edwards from His Private Notebooks* (Eugene, OR, 1955), 207–208. I am indebted to Avihu Zakai, *Jonathan Edwards' Philosophy of History: The Reenchantment of the World in the Age of Enlightenment* (Princeton, NJ, 2009), esp. 118–130.

19. Edwards, "Some Thoughts Concerning the Present Revival of Religion in New England" (1742), in *The Great Awakening,* ed. C. C. Goen (New Haven, CT, 1972), 353–358.

20. Delbanco, *Puritan Ordeal,* 26.

21. Alexis de Tocqueville, *Democracy in America,* trans. Arthur Goldhammer (New York, 2004 [1835]), 322.

22. Lehmann, *The Money Cult,* 22 (see 20–25 on folk religion and money); on the plethora of folk beliefs and "metaphysical culture," see Jon Butler, *Awash in a Sea of*

*Faith: Christianizing the American People* (Cambridge, MA, 1990), 67–97; Catherine Albanese, *A Republic of Mind and Spirit: A Cultural History of American Metaphysical Religion* (New Haven, CT, 2007), 73–79; John L. Brooke, *The Refiner's Fire: The Making of Mormon Cosmology, 1644–1844* (New York, 1996), 30–33.

## 5. The Righteous Friends of Mammon

1. On the liberal republican consensus among American intellectuals in the late colonial and early republican period, see Joyce Appleby, *Capitalism and a New Social Order: The Republican Vision of the 1790s* (New York, 1984), esp. 25–106; Joyce Appleby, *Liberalism and Republicanism in the Historical Imagination* (Cambridge, MA, 1992), 140–209; Gordon S. Wood, *The Radicalism of the American Revolution* (New York, 1992), 95–225, quote on 250. On the early national economy, see David R. Meyer, *The Roots of Industrialization in America* (Baltimore, 2003), 17–121, and John Lauritz Larson, *The Market Revolution in America: Liberty, Ambition, and the Eclipse of the Common Good* (New York, 2010), 12–97. Pauline Maier, "The Revolutionary Origins of the American Corporation," *William and Mary Quarterly* 50 (January 1993), 51–84, is a superb account of corporations in the early republic.

2. On the "antebellum spiritual hothouse," see Butler, *Awash in a Sea of Faith*, 225–256. Brooke, *The Refiner's Fire*, 91–148, covers the persistence of hermeticism in New England (quotations on 31, 103); Benes, "Fortune-Tellers," in Benes and Benes, *Wonders of the Invisible World*, 127–148; Alan Taylor, "The Early Republic's Supernatural Economy: Treasure Seeking in the American Northeast, 1780–1830," *American Quarterly* 38 (January 1986), 6–34.

3. Lears, *Fables of Abundance*, 49–74; Jackson Lears, *Something for Nothing: Luck in America* (New York, 2003), 97–146; Steve Fraser, *Wall Street: America's Dream Palace* (New Haven, CT, 2008), 55–96 passim; see also Ann Fabian, *Card Sharps, Dream Books, and Bucket Shops: Gambling in Nineteenth-Century America* (Ithaca, NY, 1990). Herman Melville, "The Lightning-Rod Man" (1854), in *Great Short Works of Herman Melville* (New York, 2004), 189.

4. On antebellum evangelicalism, see Mark Noll, *America's God: From Jonathan Edwards to Abraham Lincoln* (New York, 2002), 161–446, and Mark Noll, *A History of Christianity in the United States and Canada* (Grand Rapids, MI, 2000 [1993]), 165–190, 219–244; see also Daniel Walker Howe, *What Hath God Wrought: The Transformation of America, 1815–1848* (New York, 2007), 164–202. On the "moral establishment," see David Sehat, *The Myth of American Religious Freedom* (New York, 2011), 51–72. Tocqueville, *Democracy in America*, 336.

5. Charles Sellers, *The Market Revolution: Jacksonian America, 1815–1846* (New York, 1991), esp. 202–236 on evangelicals and the market; see also Stewart Davenport, *Friends of the Unrighteous Mammon: Northern Evangelicals and Market Capitalism, 1815–1860* (Chicago, 2008). Tocqueville, *Democracy in America*, 329, 623; Thomas Hamilton, *Men and Manners in America* (London, 1833), 115; Karl Marx, "On the

Jewish Question" (1843), in *Early Writings*, trans. Rodney Livingstone and Gregor Benton (New York, 1992), 221.

6. On "evangelical rationality," see Lears, *Something for Nothing*, 62, 76–92 passim. Noll, *America's God*, 93–157, details the prevalence of "common sense" Protestant theology and religious culture.

7. Francis Grund, *The Americans: In Their Moral, Social, and Political Relations* (Boston, 1837), 202.

8. Davenport, *Friends of the Unrighteous Mammon*, 19–84; see also Paul Conkin, *Prophets of Prosperity: America's First Political Economists* (Bloomington, IN, 1980). The battle lines over Protestantism and antebellum capitalism are drawn by Paul Johnson, *A Shopkeeper's Millennium: Society and Revivals in Rochester, New York, 1815–1837* (New York, 1978), and Sellers, *The Market Revolution*, esp. 202–236, who consider evangelicalism the self-disciplinary regimen of the business vanguard and the new opiate of the masses. Other historians depict the new economy as an engine of growth and prosperity while applauding evangelicalism as a vehicle of popular democracy, reform, and philanthropy: Howe, *What Hath God Wrought*, esp. 164–201 and 525–569; Davenport, *Friends of the Unrighteous Mammon*, esp. 213–219, which amounts to a carefully hedged defense of the evangelical economists; and Mark Noll, "Protestant Reasoning about Money and the Economy, 1790–1860: A Preliminary Probe," in *God and Mammon: Protestants, Money, and the Market, 1790–1860*, ed. Mark Noll (New York and London, 2001), 273, who claims that antebellum "market reasoning remained subordinate to intrinsically religious convictions." Yet up and down and across antebellum American life, "market reasoning" and "religious convictions" were merging to a greater extent than ever before, so much so, in fact, that evangelical enchantment became the religious leaven of proprietary capitalism. Even the oft-maligned Puritans had a much keener sense of the enmity between God and Mammon.

9. "Synopsis of the Quarterlies," *Methodist Review* 45 (January 1863), 162; Horace Bushnell, *God in Christ: Three Discourses, With a Preliminary Dissertation on Language* (London, 1850), 20–22; Horace Bushnell, "Prosperity Our Duty" (1847), in *Spirit in Man: Sermons and Selections*, ed. Henry Barrett Learned (New York, 1910), 137; Francis Wayland, *The Elements of Political Economy* (Boston, 1857 [1837]), 1; Henry A. Boardman, *The Bible in the Counting-House: A Course of Lectures to Merchants* (Philadelphia, 1856), 46, 82; Orville Dewey, *Moral Views of Commerce, Society, and Politics, In Twelve Discourses* (New York, 1838), 63, 65, 53–54, 59.

10. The best biography of Finney is Charles E. Hambrick-Stowe, *Charles G. Finney and the Spirit of American Evangelicalism* (Grand Rapids, MI, 1996). James H. Moorhead, "Charles Finney and the Modernization of America," *Journal of Presbyterian History* 62 (Spring 1984), 95–110, esp. 101–105, nicely summarizes Finney's role as a champion of the entrepreneurial ethic. Moorhead does note elsewhere that Finney was never "completely comfortable with the ethos of commercial or industrial capitalism": James H. Moorhead, "Social Reform and the Divided Conscience of Antebellum Protestantism," *Church History* 48 (December 1979), 428. Charles G. Finney, *Lectures on*

*Systematic Theology* (New York, 1847), 471; Charles G. Finney, "Stewardship," in *Sermons on Important Subjects* (New York, 1836), 209, 212.

11. Charles G. Finney, "Conformity to the World," in *Lectures to Professing Christians* (New York, 1837), 96; Finney, quoted in Sellers, *The Market Revolution,* 234; Finney, quoted in *The Religious Inquirer and Gospel Anchor* 14 (May 9, 1835), 47; Finney quoted in Hambrick-Stowe, *Charles G. Finney,* 217.

12. Thornwell is quoted in Elizabeth Fox-Genovese and Eugene Genovese, *The Mind of the Master Class: Faith and History in the Southern Slaveholders' Worldview* (New York, 2005), 397. Genovese was most responsible for the view of antebellum slavery as essentially precapitalist and paternalist; see Eugene Genovese, *The Political Economy of Slavery: Studies in the Economy and Society of the Slave South* (New York, 1965), and Eugene Genovese, *The World the Slaveholders Made: Two Essays in Interpretation* (New York, 1969). The view of Southern slavery as integral to capitalism has been advanced in Sven Beckert, *Empire of Cotton: A Global History* (New York, 2014), and Edward Baptist, *The Half Has Never Been Told: Slavery and the Making of American Capitalism* (New York, 2014). On proslavery religious thought, see Fox-Genovese and Genovese, *Mind of the Master Class,* 505–527, 613–635; Larry Tise, *Proslavery: A History of the Defense of Slavery in America, 1701–1840* (Athens, GA, 2004 [1987]), 238–285, 323–366; Mark Noll, *The Civil War as a Theological Crisis* (Chapel Hill, NC, 2006), 31–94 passim; and John Patrick Daly, *When Slavery Was Called Freedom: Evangelicalism, Proslavery, and the Causes of the Civil War* (Lexington, MA, 2015), who maintains that southern evangelicals considered slavery a form of free labor. Quotations are from Charles Irons, *The Origins of Proslavery Christianity: White and Black Evangelicals in Antebellum Virginia* (Chapel Hill, NC, 2009), 244; Frederick Douglass, "Love of God, Love of Man, Love of Country" (1847), in *The Narrative and Selected Writings,* ed. Michael Meyer (New York, 1983), 250; Frederick Douglass, *Narrative of the Life of Frederick Douglass, An American Slave,* ed. Houston Baker (New York, 1982 [1845]), 154.

13. Irons, *Origins of Proslavery Christianity,* 231, 217; Baptist, *Half Has Never Been Told,* 204; Charles C. Jones, *A Catechism, of Scripture Doctrine and Practice* (Savannah, 1837), 130; Albert Raboteau, *Slave Religion: The 'Invisible Institution' in the Antebellum South* (New York, 1978), 166; Douglass, *Narrative,* 117–119, 156.

14. John G. Cawelti, *Apostles of the Self-Made Man* (Chicago, 1965); John Frost, *The Young Merchant* (Boston, 1841), 203.

15. Timothy Shay Arthur, *Advice to Young Men on Their Duties and Conduct in Life* (Boston, 1847), 24; Timothy Shay Arthur, *The Ways of Providence* (Philadelphia, 1852), 198, 206, 215.

16. Freeman Hunt, quoted in David P. Forsyth, *The Business Press in America, 1750–1865* (New York, 1964), 82; Freeman Hunt, *Work and Wealth: A Collection of Maxims, Morals, and Miscellanies* (New York, 1856), 254. For an example of the clerical moralism expounded in *Hunt's,* see Henry Ward Beecher, "The Benefits and Evils of Commerce," *Hunt's Merchants' Magazine and Commercial Review* 24 (February 1851), 147–156.

17. Freeman Hunt, "The Good Merchant," *Hunt's Merchants' Magazine* 16 (May 1847), 510; see also Hunt, *Work and Wealth,* 29; Freeman Hunt, *Lives of American Merchants* (New York, 1858), 1:v.

18. David E. Nye, *American Technological Sublime* (Cambridge, MA, 1994), provides the most detailed and incisive account of this rapture with technology, but the idea can be traced back to Leo Marx, *Machine in the Garden,* 198, who writes of it as "an intoxicating feeling of unlimited possibility," and to Perry Miller, *The Life of the Mind in America: From the Revolution to the Civil War* (New York, 1965), 319–321. Howard P. Segal, *Technological Utopianism in American Culture* (Syracuse, NY, 2005 [1985]), 74–97, surveys American enthrallment with technology before the Civil War. John F. Kasson, *Civilizing the Machine: Technology and Republican Values in America, 1776–1900* (New York, 1976), examines the nineteenth-century debate over industrialization and republicanism. For an overview of technological development in this period, see David Hounshell, *From the American System to Mass Production, 1800–1932: The Development of Manufacturing Technology in the United States* (Baltimore, 1985 [1984]), 15–216, and Carroll Purcell, *The Machine in America: A Social History of Technology* (Baltimore, 2007 [1995]), 35–202. On "manifest destiny," see Anders Stephanson, *Manifest Destiny: American Expansion and the Empire of Right* (New York, 1996), 28–64, and Walter Hixson, *The Myth of American Diplomacy: National Identity and U.S. Foreign Policy* (New Haven, CT, 2008), 43–73.

19. James Delbourgo, *A Most Amazing Scene of Wonders: Electricity and Enlightenment in Early America* (Cambridge, MA, 2006), 200–238, quotes on 214, 217, 216, 204.

20. "Human Progress: Mr. Bancroft's Oration," *Church Review* 8 (1855–1856), 263; Nye, *American Technological Sublime,* 39, 58; "Improved Hay-Maker," *Scientific American* 2 (March 31, 1860), 216.

21. Jacob Bigelow, *Elements of Technology* (Boston, 1831), iii, 4. Nye, *American Technological Sublime,* 45, credits Bigelow with coining the word "technology."

22. Parker and Walker quoted in Leo Marx, *Machine in the Garden,* 201, 185–186.

23. Thomas Ewbank, *The World as a Workshop: Or, The Physical Relationship of Man to the Earth* (New York, 1855), 183, viii, 164, 29, 27. Kasson, *Civilizing the Machine,* 148–152, discusses both Ewbank and the enthusiastic response of Protestant leaders to his message.

24. Stephen Stoll, *The Great Delusion: A Mad Inventor, Death in the Tropics, and the Utopian Origins of Economic Growth* (New York, 2009), is an absorbing chronicle of Etzler's life.

25. Steven Stoll, *The Great Delusion: A Mad Inventor, Death in the Tropics, and the Utopian Origins of Economic Growth* (New York, 2008), esp. 45–94; John Adolphus Etzler, *The Paradise within the Reach of All Men, Without Labor, by Powers of Nature and Machinery: An Address to All Intelligent Men* (Pittsburgh, 1833), 47, 81, 49, 45.

26. Etzler, *Paradise within the Reach,* 43; James Madison, Federalist #10, in *The Federalist Papers,* ed. Richard Beeman (New York, 2012), 32; Jefferson, quoted in

Gordon S. Wood, *Empire of Liberty: A History of the Early Republic, 1789–1815* (Oxford, 2009), 376; on the Great Seal, see 554.

27. Ezra Stiles, *The United States Elevated to Glory and Honor* (New Haven, CT, 1783), 7, 10, 12, 35.

28. Lyman Beecher, *A Plea for the West* (New York, 1835), 10, 9, 27, 11; John O'-Sullivan, "Annexation," *United States Magazine and Democratic Review* 17 (July–August 1845), 5.

29. John O'Sullivan, "The Great Nation of Futurity," *United States Magazine and Democratic Review* 6 (November 1839), 427; William Gilpin, *The Mission of the North American People, Geographical, Social, and Political* (Philadelphia, 1874), 130, 142; William Gilpin, *The Central Gold Region: The Grain, Pastoral, and Gold Regions of North America* (Philadelphia, 1860), 84, v, 102, vi; William Gilpin, *Notes on Colorado* (London, 1870), 5.

30. "History and Destiny of Coal," *Christian Review* 21 (January 1856), 267–283, quotes on 281; Philip Schaff, *America: A Sketch of Its Political, Social, and Religious Character,* ed. Perry Miller (Cambridge, MA, 1961 [1855]), 4, 15–16, 18, 20, 24.

31. In much of what follows I have relied on Brooke, *The Refiner's Fire;* Leonard J. Arrington, *Great Basin Kingdom: An Economic History of the Latter-Day Saints, 1830–1900* (Chicago, 2005 [1958]); Harold Bloom, *The American Religion: The Emergence of the Post-Christian Nation* (New York, 1992), 67–130; and Lehmann's superb narrative in *The Money Cult,* 124–152.

32. The classic source here is Whitney R. Cross, *The Burned-Over District: The Social and Intellectual History of Enthusiastic Religion in Western New York, 1800–1850* (Ithaca, NY, 1950). On the prevalence of magic and the occult in the region, see Brooke, *The Refiner's Fire,* 209–234, but especially D. Michael Quinn, *Early Mormonism and the Magic World View* (New York, 1998 [1987]).

33. On Chase, see Quinn, *Early Mormonism,* 42; on Stowell, see Richard L. Bushman, *Joseph Smith: Rough Stone Rolling* (New York, 2007), 48–51; Lucy Smith, *Lucy's Book: A Critical Edition of Lucy Mack Smith's Family Memoir,* ed. Lavina Fielding Anderson (New York, 2001), 162.

34. Bushman, *Joseph Smith,* 8–176.

35. Brigham Young, *Doctrine of the Priesthood* (Salt Lake City, 1988), 139; on his disbelief in creation *ex nihilo,* see Leonard J. Arrington, *Brigham Young* (New York, 2012), 203; quotes from Smith and the Mormon preacher are in Brooke, *The Refiner's Fire,* 201, 207.

36. Arrington, *Great Basin Kingdom,* 5–6.

37. Arrington, *Great Basin Kingdom,* 22–33, 145–148; *The Book of Mormon* (Nauvoo, IL, 1840 [1830]), 501.

38. *Book of Mormon,* 124.

39. *Book of Mormon,* 366; Arrington, *Great Basin Kingdom,* 252; Brooke, *The Refiner's Fire,* 222; Arrington, *Brigham Young,* 350.

40. On the failure of consecration in the 1870s, see Arrington, *Great Basin Kingdom*, 323–352.

41. All quotes are from Brooke, *The Refiner's Fire*, 254, 274.

42. *Book of Mormon*, 60, 72, 171–172.

43. Richard Hofstadter, *The American Political Tradition: And the Men Who Made It* (New York, 1948), xxxxvi. Jeffrey Sklansky, *The Soul's Economy: Market Society and Selfhood in American Thought, 1820–1920* (Chapel Hill, NC, 2002), 13–31.

44. The most capacious and forceful statement of the labor republican argument is Alex Gourevitch, *From Slavery to the Cooperative Commonwealth: Labor and Republican Liberty in the Nineteenth Century* (New York, 2014). On resistance to capitalist industrialization by evangelical workers, see William R. Sutton, *Journeymen for Jesus: Evangelical Artisans Confront Capitalism in Jacksonian Baltimore* (University Park, PA, 2010); the New York artisan is quoted in Sean Wilentz, *Chants Democratic: New York City and the Rise of the American Working Class, 1788–1850* (New York, 1984), 161; "The System of Wages," *Voice of Industry* 3 (December 10, 1847), 2; Stephen Simpson, *The Working Man's Manual: A New Theory of Political Economy* (Philadelphia, 1831), 27; Henry Carey is quoted in Charles H. Levermore, "Henry Carey and His Social System," *Political Science Quarterly* 5 (December 1890), 570. Although Marx considered Carey "the only original economist among the North Americans," he also noted that where "economic relations confront him in their truth . . . his principled optimism turns into a denunciatory, irritated pessimism": Marx, *Grundrisse*, 884, 887. I am endorsing here what Hofstadter dubbed a "left consensus" view of American history; Hofstadter, *The Progressive Historians: Turner, Beard, Parrington* (New York, 1968), 451–452.

45. Lasch, *True and Only Heaven*, 184–194; the best biography is Patrick W. Carey, *Orestes A. Brownson: American Religious Weathervane* (Grand Rapids, MI, 2004), who quotes Lowell on xiii.

46. Orestes A. Brownson, "The Laboring Classes," *Boston Quarterly Review* 3 (July 1840), 376; "The Present State of Society," *United States Magazine and Democratic Review* 13 (July 1843), 24; Orestes A. Brownson, *Charles Ellwood: Or, The Infidel Converted* (Boston, 1840), 200, 202.

47. Lasch, *True and Only Heaven*, quotes on 194, 192; Orestes A. Brownson, "Conversation with a Radical," *Boston Quarterly Review* 4 (January 1841), 38, 39, 40; Brownson, "Present State of Society," 34, 37.

## 6. Glows and Glories and Final Illustriousness

1. Channing quoted in Philip Gura, *American Transcendentalism: A History* (New York, 2008), 5.

2. Ellis cited in Gura, *American Transcendentalism*, 10; Ralph Waldo Emerson, "The Transcendentalist" (1843), in *The Complete Essays and Other Writings of Ralph Waldo Emerson*, ed. Brooks Atkinson (New York, 1940), 92, 90.

3. F. O. Mathiessen, *American Renaissance: Art and Expression in the Age of Emerson and Whitman* (New York, 1968 [1941]), 547, 104; Emerson, journal entry (June 21, 1838), in *Emerson in His Journals,* ed. Joel Porte (Cambridge, MA, 1984), 190; Thoreau, journal entry (December 11, 1855), in *The Works of Henry David Thoreau,* ed. Bradford Torrey (Boston and New York, 1906), 14:44.

4. Fuller quoted in Gura, *American Transcendentalism,* 17; John Thomas Codman, *Brook Farm: Historic and Personal Memoirs* (Boston, 1894), 79, 101; George Ripley, letter to Emerson (1840), in *Selected Writings of the American Transcendentalists,* ed. George Hochfield (New Haven, CT, 2004 [1966]), 379. David Shi, *The Simple Life: Plain Living and High Thinking in American Culture* (New York, 1985), 132–139, is a judicious account of Brook Farm and its demise; Sterling Delano, *Brook Farm: The Dark Side of Utopia* (Cambridge, MA, 2004), provides a much more complicated narrative that aligns with Hawthorne's tale. From the copious literature on antebellum communes, see Carl J. Guarneri, *The Utopian Alternative: Fourierism in Nineteenth-Century America* (Ithaca, NY, 1991); Edward Spann, *Hopedale: From Commune to Company Town, 1840–1920* (Columbus, OH, 1992); Stephen J. Stein, *The Shaker Experience in America: A History of the United Society of Believers* (New Haven, CT, 1992); Spencer Klaw, *Without Sin: The Life and Death of the Oneida Community* (New York, 1993); Christopher Clark, *The Communitarian Moment: The Radical Challenge of the Northampton Association* (Amherst, MA, 2003).

5. Elizabeth Peabody, "Plan of the West Roxbury Community" (1841), in Hochfield, *Selected Writings of the American Transcendentalists,* 387; Sylvester Judd, *Margaret: A Tale of the Real and the Ideal, Blight and Bloom* (Boston, 1845), 1:67, 184; Sylvester Judd, *Margaret* (Boston, 1851), 2:227; Sylvester Judd, *Richard Edney and the Governor's Family* (Boston, 1850), 9–10.

6. Nathaniel Hawthorne, *The Blithedale Romance* (New York, 1983 [1852]), 38, 4, 89, 40.

7. Hawthorne, *The Blithedale Romance,* 51, 40; Codman, *Brook Farm,* 41.

8. Thoreau quoted in Shi, *The Simple Life,* 144; Henry David Thoreau, *Walden and Civil Disobedience* (New York, 2004), 96, 74, 26, 7, 212, 177. Robert D. Richardson, *Henry Thoreau: A Life of the Mind* (Berkeley, CA, 1986), is a fine overview of Thoreau's life and thought. John P. Diggins, "Thoreau, Marx, and the 'Riddle' of Alienation," *Social Research* 39 (Winter 1972), 571–598, is a nuanced analysis of two very different accounts of selfhood and the marketplace.

9. Thoreau, *Walden,* 212, 187, 72, 73, 330; *The Works of Henry David Thoreau, Journal 1851–1852,* ed. Bradford Torrey (Boston and New York, 1906), 165; *A Week on the Concord and Merrimack Rivers,* ed. Carl Hovde (Princeton, NJ, 1980), 378; *The Works of Henry David Thoreau, 1837–1846, 1850–1861,* ed. Bradford Torrey (Boston and New York, 1906), 252. Richardson, *Henry Thoreau,* 151–159, covers Thoreau's two years at Walden Pond; Alcott is quoted in Michael T. Gilmore, *American Romanticism and the Marketplace* (Chicago, 1985), 160 n. 20.

10. Walt Whitman, *Democratic Vistas and Other Writings* (London, 1888 [1871]), 29; "Song for Occupations," in *Walt Whitman: The Complete Poems,* ed. Francis Murphy (New York, 2004), 240; "Passage to India," in *The Complete Poems,* 429.

11. Whitman, "A Backward Glance O'er Travel'd Roads" (1888), in *The Complete Poems,* 572; "November Boughs" (1888), in *Walt Whitman: Selected Poems 1855–1892,* ed. Gary Schmidgall (New York, 1999), 384; "Song for Occupations," in *The Complete Poems,* 247, 243. The line referring to the "eucharist" appeared in the first 1855 edition of *Leaves of Grass* but does not appear elsewhere.

12. Whitman, *The Complete Poems,* 27, 75, 47. I find unsatisfying David S. Reynolds's argument that *Democratic Vistas* reflects Whitman's "conflicting tendencies toward conservatism and radicalism." Although Whitman had been "antipathetic to the business culture" of antebellum America, Reynolds maintains, after the Civil War he "became far more amenable to capitalistic enterprise": Reynolds, *Walt Whitman's America: A Cultural Biography* (New York, 1996), 484, 482. I see far more continuity in Whitman's views of the capitalist marketplace.

13. Cornel West, *The American Evasion of Philosophy: A Genealogy of Pragmatism* (Madison, WI, 1987), 9–41, quote on 40; Lasch, *True and Only Heaven,* 265–273, quote on 271; see also Jeffrey Stout, *Democracy and Tradition* (Princeton, NJ, 2004), 19–41, who discovers in Emerson the "natural piety" essential to a multi-religious democracy. Emerson, "Nominalist and Realist" (1844), in *Complete Essays,* 438; Emerson, "Wealth" (1860), in *Complete Essays,* 715. Bloom's assessment of Emerson is in Bloom, *The American Religion;* see also his "Emerson: The American Religion," in *Ralph Waldo Emerson,* ed. Harold Bloom (New York, 2007), 33–62. I have relied on Stephen Whicher, *Freedom and Fate: An Inner Life of Ralph Waldo Emerson* (Philadelphia, 1953); Robert D. Richardson, Jr., *Emerson: The Mind on Fire* (Berkeley, 1995), and Sklansky, *The Soul's Economy,* 38–52. Lehmann, *Money Cult,* 121–123, includes Emerson in the pantheon of American capitalist gnosticism.

14. Alfred Ferguson, ed., *Journals and Miscellaneous Notebooks of Ralph Waldo Emerson* (Cambridge, MA, 1964), vol. 4, *1832–1834,* 27; on the antebellum cultural marketplace, see Gilmore, *American Romanticism,* 52–70, and David S. Reynolds, *Beneath the American Renaissance: The Subversive Imagination in the Age of Emerson and Melville* (New York, 1988), 3–53, 92–112.

15. Emerson, "Nature," in *Complete Essays,* 23, 6. Bloom rejects the notion, advanced by literary and intellectual historians from Perry Miller to Sacvan Bercovitch, that Emerson is the heir of the Puritans: see "Emerson: The American Religion," in Bloom, *Ralph Waldo Emerson,* 48. While Emerson is certainly post-Protestant, I think that the continuities are too apparent to discount.

16. Emerson, "Man the Reformer" (1841), in *Collected Works of Ralph Waldo Emerson,* ed. Robert E. Spiller et al. (Cambridge, MA, 1971), 146, 147, 157; *English Traits* (1856), in *Complete Essays,* 548.

17. Emerson, "Man the Reformer," in *Collected Works,* 145, 154, 155.

18. Emerson, "Man the Reformer," 156, 159, 154. Emerson, "Gifts" (1844), in *Complete Essays*, 405, 404, 403.

19. Lasch, *True and Only Heaven*, 270; Emerson, "Compensation" (1841), in *Complete Essays*, 178, 182, 179, 184.

20. Emerson, "Self-Reliance" (1841), in *Complete Essays*, 152; Emerson, "The Young American" (1844), in *Essays and Lectures*, ed. Joel Porte (New York, 1983), 217.

21. Emerson, "Worship," in *Emerson's Collected Works: The Conduct of Life* (Boston, 1889), 196; "The Over-Soul" (1841), in *Complete Essays*, 262; "The Method of Nature," in *Emerson's Collected Works*, 124; "Circles" (1841), in *Complete Essays*, 279, 289.

22. Emerson, "Power," in *Emerson's Collected Works*, 55; "The Transcendentalist," in *Complete Essays*, 90; "Nature," in *Complete Essays*, 42; "An Address" (1838), in *Complete Essays*, 73; "The Transcendentalist," in *Complete Essays*, 89. My account of Emerson as a theologian of power echoes and amplifies Whicher's observation that Emerson's thought is "radically anarchic, overthrowing all the authority of the past, all compromise or cooperation with others, in the name of the Power present and agent in the soul": Whicher, *Freedom and Fate*, 56.

23. Emerson, "Wealth," in *Complete Essays*, 705, 702–703, 715.

24. Emerson, "Wealth," in *Complete Essays*, 698, 699, 695; "Worship," in *Emerson's Collected Works*, 214–215; "Self-Reliance," in *Complete Essays*, 149.

25. Emerson, "Nature," in *Complete Essays*, 21; "Self-Reliance," in *Complete Essays*, 160; *Journals and Miscellaneous Notebooks*, vol. 10, *1847–1848*, ed. Merton M. Sealts (Cambridge, MA, 1973), 312.

26. Joel Porte, ed., *Emerson in His Journal* (Cambridge, MA, 1984), 307; Emerson, "The Young American," in *Essays and Lectures*, 221, 213, 223.

27. Emerson, "The Young American," in *Essays and Lectures*, 228, 217, 226, 221, 230; "American Civilization" (1862), in *Collected Works of Ralph Waldo Emerson: Society and Solitude*, ed. Ronald Bosco and Douglas Emery Wilson (Cambridge, MA, 2007), 332.

28. Emerson, "The Young American," in *Essays and Lectures*, 217, 218, 219.

29. On Nietzsche's fondness for Emerson, see Jennifer Ratner-Rosenhagen, *American Nietzsche: A History of an Icon and His Ideas* (Chicago, 2012), 4–27; Emerson, "Fate," in *The Conduct of Life*, 51.

30. On the "African spiritual holocaust," see Butler, *Awash in a Sea of Faith*, 129–163. My account of slave religion relies on Raboteau, *Slave Religion;* Eugene Genovese, *Roll, Jordan, Roll: The World the Slaves Made* (New York, 1974), 161–284 (quote from Jones on 215–216); Lawrence Levine, *Black Culture, Black Consciousness: Afro-American Folk Thought from Slavery to Freedom* (New York, 1977), 3–80; Mechal Sobel, *Trabelin' On: The Slave Journey to an Afro-Baptist Faith* (Westport, CT, 1979), esp. 3–76, 137–218; Vincent Harding, *There Is a River: The Black Struggle for Freedom in America* (New York, 1981), 3–116; Sylvia Frey and Betty Wood, *Come Shouting to Zion: African-American Protestantism in the American South and British Caribbean to 1830* (Chapel Hill, NC, 1998); and Yvonne Chireau, *Black Magic: Religion and the African-American*

*Conjuring Tradition* (Berkeley, 2003), esp. 11–89. The outraged Methodist is quoted in Edward Baptist, *The Half Has Never Been Told: Slavery and the Making of American Capitalism* (New York, 2014), 202.

31. Slave cited in Frey and Wood, *Come Shouting to Zion,* 177–178; Harriet Jacobs, *Incidents in the Life of a Slave Girl* (New York, 2001 [1861]), 62, 41, 61; Solomon Northup, *Twelve Years a Slave* (New York, 2012 [1853]), 120; Douglass, *Narrative,* 153, 154.

32. On the slaves' rejection of the Protestant work ethic, see Genovese, *Roll, Jordan, Roll,* 285–324, quote on 288; on the impermeability of the earthly and the heavenly as expressed in the spirituals, see Levine, *Black Culture, Black Consciousness,* 17–55, and Raboteau, *Slave Religion,* 243–266; the Charleston preacher is quoted in Raboteau, *Slave Religion,* 208–209. W. E. B. Du Bois, *The Souls of Black Folk* (New York, 1996 [1903]), 213.

33. On Gabriel's Rebellion, see Raboteau, *Slave Religion,* 147, and James Sidbury, *Ploughshares into Swords: Race, Rebellion, and Identity in Gabriel's Virginia, 1730–1810* (New York, 1997), 74–79; on the Vesey Conspiracy, see Raboteau, *Slave Religion,* 163, though see also Douglas Egerton, *He Shall Go Out Free: The Lives of Denmark Vesey* (Lanham, MD, 2004), 113–115, who argues (unconvincingly, in my view) that Christianity had no influence on Vesey. I have also relied on James Sidbury, "Reading, Revelation, and Rebellion: The Textual Communities of Gabriel, Denmark Vesey, and Nat Turner," in *Nat Turner: A Slave Rebellion in History and Memory,* ed. Kenneth S. Greenberg (New York, 2003), 119–133.

34. Nat Turner, *The Confessions of Nat Turner, The Leader of the Late Insurrection in Southampton, VA, As Fully and Voluntarily Made to Thomas R. Gray* (Baltimore, 1831), 4. See David Allmendinger, *Nat Turner and the Rebellion in Southampton County* (Baltimore, 2014), 215–257, on the composition and authenticity of the *Confessions.* On Turner himself, see the compelling narrative in Harding, *There Is a River,* 77–81, 94–99. Turner's visions were very different from those of the free black Robert Alexander Young, whose mystically leavened *Ethiopian Manifesto* (1829)—provoked, its author claimed, by "the invigorating power of Deity"—prophesied the emergence of a black Messiah from "Grenada's Island" in the West Indies: see the full text in Sterling Stuckey, ed., *The Ideological Origins of Black Nationalism* (Boston, 1972), 32–38, quotes on 33, 37.

35. Turner, *Confessions,* 7–11.

36. Turner, *Confessions,* 11.

## Part Three: The Mystical Body of Business

1. Henry Adams, *The Education of Henry Adams* (Boston, 1918), 338; on the turmoil of the 1890s, see Nell Irvin Painter, *Standing at Armageddon: The United States, 1877–1919* (New York, 1987), 110–140, and Jackson Lears, *Rebirth of a Nation: The Making of Modern America, 1877–1920* (New York, 2009), 181–186.

2. Lears, *Rebirth of a Nation,* 342–345. On the Chicago World's Fair, see Alan Trachtenberg, *The Incorporation of America: Culture and Society in the Gilded Age* (New

York, 1982), 208–234. I have relied on the subtle and absorbing account of Adams's life in Jackson Lears, *No Place of Grace: Antimodernism and the Transformation of American Culture, 1880–1920* (New York, 1981), 261–297.

3. Adams, *Education*, 380–381, 383, 499.

4. Adams, *Education*, 500, 485, 499, 487.

5. Gerald Stanley Lee, *Crowds: A Moving-Picture of Democracy* (Garden City, NY, 1913), 138–141; G. Lowes Dickinson, *Appearances: Notes of Travel, East and West* (Garden City, NY, 1915), 173–179. Gregory Wallace Bush, *Lord of Attention: Gerald Stanley Lee and the Crowd Metaphor in Industrializing America* (Amherst, MA, 1991), is an informative account of Lee's career.

6. Gerald Stanley Lee, *The Voice of the Machines: An Introduction to the Twentieth Century* (Northampton, MA, 1906), 76, 189, 77; Gerald Stanley Lee, *Inspired Millionaires: An Interpretation of America* (Northampton, MA, 1908), 93, 184, 91–92, 75.

7. Orison Swett Marden, *The Miracle of Right Thought* (New York, 1910), 32, 320, 206, 199, 19, 10; Orison Swett Marden, *Choosing a Career* (New York, 1905), 74; Orison Swett Marden, *How to Get What You Want* (New York, 1917), 221. Wende Marden Sinnaeve, *Out of the Ashes: The Life Story of Orison Swett Marden* (Westerley, RI, 2004), is a brief and hagiographic biography. On "New Thought," the standard work is Donald Meyer, *The Positive Thinkers: Popular Religious Psychology from Mary Baker Eddy to Norman Vincent Peale and Ronald Reagan* (Middletown, CT, 1988 [1965]), but see also Catherine Tumber, *American Feminism and the Birth of New Age Spirituality: Searching for the Higher Self, 1875–1915* (Lanham, MD, 2002).

8. Martin J. Sklar, *The Corporate Reconstruction of American Capitalism, 1890–1916: The Market, the Law, and Politics* (New York, 1988), remains the most comprehensive account of the legal and institutional transformations of the time. Lears, *Rebirth of a Nation*, 1.

## 7. God Gave Me My Money

1. My account of the economic changes relies on James Livingston, *Pragmatism and the Political Economy of Cultural Revolution, 1850–1940* (Chapel Hill, NC, 1994), 49–67.

2. Barbara and John Ehrenreich, "The Professional-Managerial Class," in *Between Labor and Capital*, ed. Pat Walker (Boston, 1979), 5–45. I am summarizing a vast trove of historical literature here, exemplified but not exhausted by the following: Angel Kwollek-Folland, *Engendering Business: Men and Women in the Corporate Office, 1870–1930* (Baltimore, 1994); Olivier Zunz, *Making America Corporate, 1870–1920* (Chicago, 1990); Susan Porter Benson, *Counter Cultures: Saleswomen, Managers, and Customers in American Department Stores, 1890–1940* (Urbana, IL, 1986); Sharon Hartman Strom, *Beyond the Typewriter: Gender, Class, and the Origins of Modern Office Work, 1900–1930* (Urbana, IL, 1992); Clark Davis, *Company Men: White-Collar Life and Corporate Cultures in Los Angeles, 1892–1941* (Baltimore, 2000); Kathy Peiss, *Cheap Amusements:*

*Working Women and Leisure in Turn-of-the-Century New York* (Philadelphia, 1986); Christine Stansell, *American Moderns: Bohemian New York and the Creation of a New Century* (New York, 2000); John Bodnar, *The Transplanted: A History of Immigrants in Urban America* (Bloomington, IN, 1985), esp. 30–84; David Hollinger, "Justification by Verification: The Scientific Challenge to the Moral Authority of Christianity in Modern America," in *Religion and Twentieth-Century American Intellectual Life*, ed. Michael J. Lacey (New York, 1989), 116–135; Julie A. Reuben, *The Making of the Modern University: Intellectual Transformation and the Marginalization of Morality* (Chicago, 1996), 61–187.

3. Jackson Lears, "From Salvation to Self-Realization: Advertising and the Therapeutic Roots of the Consumer Culture, 1880–1930," in *The Culture of Consumption: Critical Essays in American History, 1880–1980,* ed. Jackson Lears and Richard W. Fox (New York, 1983), 1–38; Livingston, *Pragmatism and Political Economy,* xx.

4. William Leach, *Land of Desire: Merchants, Power, and the Rise of a New American Culture* (New York, 1993), 4; Lears, *No Place of Grace,* 58, 43; Lears, *Fables of Abundance,* 2; Lears, *Rebirth of a Nation,* 296.

5. Horatio Alger, Jr., *Strive and Succeed: Or, The Rise of Walter Conrad* (Boston, 1872), 352. On the relative absence of religion from Alger's fiction, see Carol Nackenhoff, *The Fictional Republic: Horatio Alger and American Political Discourse* (New York, 1994), 18–24. William Dean Howells, *A Hazard of New Fortunes* (New York, 1890), 244; *The Rise of Silas Lapham* (Boston and New York, 1922 [1885]), 22, 4.

6. Edward J. Renehan, Jr., *Commodore: The Life of Cornelius Vanderbilt* (New York, 2007), 266–269; Ron Chernow, *The House of Morgan: An American Banking Dynasty and the Rise of Modern Finance* (New York, 1990), 51; David Nasaw, *Andrew Carnegie* (New York, 2006), 352, 232, 731; Andrew Carnegie, *The Autobiography of Andrew Carnegie* (Boston and New York, 1920), 339; Andrew Carnegie, "How I Served My Apprenticeship," *Youth's Companion* 69 (April 23, 1896), 7.

7. W. D. Wilson, *First Principles of Political Economy* (Philadelphia, 1879), 349; Arthur Latham Perry, *Elements of Political Economy* (New York, 1875), 49; William Graham Sumner, "The Boon of Nature," in *Earth-Hunger and Other Essays* (New Haven, CT, 1913), 234. The best introduction to business thought at this time remains Edward C. Kirkland, *Dream and Thought in the Business Community, 1860–1900* (Ithaca, NY, 1956).

8. All quotations are from Henry J. Latham, *God in Business* (New York, 1885), 90, 61, 9, 34–35.

9. On Adams, see Daniel T. Rodgers, *The Work Ethic in Industrial America, 1850–1920* (Chicago, 1978), 136–140, quote on 137; William Makepeace Thayer, *Tact, Push, and Principle* (Boston, 1882), 344–345, 346, 354; William Makepeace Thayer, *Ethics for Success* (New York, 1893), 440, 438, 274; William Makepeace Thayer, *Onward to Fame and Fortune* (New York, 1897), 212–213, 240–241.

10. D. W. Whittle, *The Wonders of Prayer: A Record of Well Authenticated and Wonderful Answers to Prayer* (Chicago, 1885), 6, 336; for other examples, see Latham, *God in Business,* 59, 48, and Whittle, *Wonders of Prayer,* 211–212, 240, 282.

11. Josiah Strong, *Our Country* (New York, 1885), 198, 181; Arthur Frederick Sheldon, *The Science of Business* (Chicago, 1905), 20; John R. Meader, "Success," *American Stationer* 68 (July 23, 1910), 18; William Peter Hamilton, *The Stock Market Barometer* (New York, 1922), 18; Arthur Nash, *The Golden Rule in Business* (Chicago, 1923), 115; M. D. Babcock, *Thoughts for Every-Day Living* (New York, 1901), 71–72.

12. Russell Conwell, *Acres of Diamonds* (New York, 1915), 18, 20; Russell Conwell, "Praying for Money," in *Effective Prayer* (New York, 1921), 116. Albert Hatcher Smith, *Life of Russell H. Conwell: Preacher, Lecturer, Philanthropist* (Boston, 1899), is the only biography; see also Lehmann, *The Money Cult,* 186–193.

13. Russell Conwell, "Lilies of the Field," in *Fields of Glory* (Chicago, 1925), 13, 22.

14. John Wanamaker, "Completion Day Speech," June 11, 1910, in *Golden Book of the Wanamaker Stores: Jubilee Year, 1861–1911,* ed. Joseph Herbert Appel and Leigh Mitchell Hodges (Philadelphia, 1911), 126–127; John Wanamaker, *Maxims of Life and Business* (Philadelphia, 1916), 23, 38. On Wanamaker and his store, see Leach, *Land of Desire,* esp. 23–35, 73–75, 112–114.

15. Joseph H. Appel, "Private Tributes," in *Golden Book,* 110–111; Wanamaker to Booth quoted in Leach, *Land of Desire,* 35; Taft quoted in *Golden Book,* 340; "Jubilee Night," in *Golden Book,* 118–119.

16. William Graham Sumner, *What Social Classes Owe Each Other* (New York, 1884), 14; William Graham Sumner, "Memorial Day Address," in *The Challenge of Facts: And Other Essays* (New York, 1914), 360; William Graham Sumner, *Folkways* (Boston, 1906), 142.

17. Baer's infamous letter can be found in *Literary Digest* 25 (August 30, 1902), 258; "Baer, Grim Old Covenanter of the Coal Fields" (no author cited), *Current Literature* 52 (May 1912), 523; Baer's remark about Cain is quoted in Frederic William Unger, "George F. Baer: Master-Spirit of the Anthracite Industry," *American Monthly* 33 (May 1906), 547.

18. Ron Chernow, *Titan: The Life of John D. Rockefeller, Sr.* (New York, 1998), 54, 674, 3–14, 24, 10, 22.

19. Chernow, *Titan,* 48; H. G. Wells, *The Future in America: A Search After Realities* (London, 1906), 135.

20. Chernow, *Titan,* 153, 55, 191, 380.

21. Chernow, *Titan,* 153, 154. Originally serialized in *McClure's,* Ida Tarbell's expose of Rockefeller's business practices appeared in book form as *The History of the Standard Oil Company* (New York, 1904).

## 8. The Soulful Corporation

1. Charles Francis Adams, "A Chapter of Erie" (1869), in Charles Francis Adams, Jr. and Henry Adams, *Chapters of Erie and Other Essays* (Boston, 1871), 1, 5, 95. For an account of the Erie War, see Edward J. Renehan, *Dark Genius of Wall Street: The Misunderstood Life of Jay Gould, King of the Robber Barons* (New York, 2005), 115–137.

2. Adams, "A Chapter of Erie," 95–96, 97, 98.

3. Morton J. Horowitz, *The Transformation of American Law, 1870–1960: The Crisis of Legal Orthodoxy* (New York, 1992), 67–68. In Horowitz's view, *Santa Clara* did not represent "a significant departure from American constitutional jurisprudence," even though the "natural entity" theory on which it rested was "nowhere to be found in American legal thought when the case was decided."

4. Delphin M. Delmas, "Argument in the Railroad Tax Cases," in *Speeches and Addresses* (San Francisco, 1901), 204–206.

5. Ernest Freund, *The Legal Nature of Corporations* (Chicago, 1897), 77, 80, 82; I. Maurice Wormser, "Piercing the Veil of Corporate Entity" (1912), in *Disregard of the Corporate Fiction and Allied Corporation Problems* (New York, 1927), 43, 61; Arthur Machen, "Corporate Personality," *Harvard Law Review* 24 (February 1911), 257, 258, 259.

6. Wormser, "Piercing the Veil," in *Disregard of the Corporate Fiction*, 84; "Disregard of the Corporate Fiction—When and Why" (1923), in *Disregard of the Corporate Fiction*, 24; Machen, "Corporate Personality (Continued)," *Harvard Law Review* 24 (March 1911), 356.

7. Simon N. Patten, *The New Basis of Civilization* (New York, 1907), 13–14, 11; Carnegie, *The Empire of Business* (Garden City, NY, 1913); W. J. Ghent, *Our Benevolent Feudalism* (New York, 1902), 9.

8. Seymour Eaton, *Sermons on Advertising* (New York, 1907), n.p.

9. James H. Davis, *A Political Revelation* (Dallas, 1894), 240, 242, 245.

10. William Futhey Gibbons, *The Soulless Corporation* (New York and Chicago, 1902); William Futhey Gibbons, *Those Black Diamond Men: A Tale of the Anthrax Valley* (New York and Chicago, 1902), 15–26; Frank Norris, *The Octopus* (New York, 1901), 51; Theodore Dreiser, *The Titan* (New York, 1914), 399; C. P. Connolly, "Big Business and the Bench," *Everybody's Magazine* 26 (March 1912), 295; Richard Spillane, "Lights and Shadows on Current Events," *Commerce and Finance* 6 (May 2, 1917), 436; A. P. Richardson, "Cobbler and Last," *Journal of Accountancy* 30 (November 1920), 363.

11. Patterson, Perkins, and Beeks quoted in Marchand, *Creating the Corporate Soul*, 17, 22, 24; on "welfare capitalism," see Andrea Tone, *The Business of Benevolence: Industrial Paternalism in the Progressive Era* (Ithaca, NY, 1997), esp. 66–181, and Sanford Jacoby, *Modern Manors: Welfare Capitalism since the New Deal* (Princeton, NJ, 1997), 11–34.

12. Claude C. Hopkins, *Scientific Advertising* (New York, 1923), 54; "The Companies in 1916," *American Underwriter* 47 (February 1917), 55; Hugh E. Agnew, "Puts Flesh and Blood into 'Soulless Corporation': Pacific Gas and Electric Company Makes Itself a Personality by Advertising," *Printer's Ink* 119 (April 6, 1922), 121–122; "Ardmore Citizens Appreciative," *Railway Review* 57 (November 6, 1915), 575.

13. John Bates Clark, "The Nature and Progress of True Socialism," *New Englander* 38 (July 1879), 573; Simon N. Patten, *The Social Basis of Religion* (New York, 1911); William P. White, "The Inspiration of Memorial Day," *American Industries* 19 (Sep-

tember 1918), 13; Wright quoted in Trachtenberg, *The Incorporation of America,* 43; Carroll D. Wright, "The Value of Art and Skill in Industry," *Bulletin of the National Association of Wool Manufacturers* 34 (June 1904), 184.

14. John Kimberly Mumford, "This Land of Opportunity: The Attitude of Great Corporations toward Their Men," *Harper's Weekly* 52 (June 6, 1908), 22–25; "This Land of Opportunity: The Watchword of the Hour—Honest Business and Fair Play," *Harper's Weekly* 52 (June 13, 1908), 11, 20; "This Land of Opportunity: The Heart of a 'Soulless Corporation,'" *Harper's Weekly* 53 (July 11, 1908), 22–23; "This Land of Opportunity: The Heart of a 'Soulless Corporation,'" *Harper's Weekly* 53 (July 18, 1908), 21–22.

15. Ida M. Tarbell, *New Ideals in Business: An Account of Their Practice and Effect upon Men and Profits* (New York, 1916), intro. n. p.; Arundel Cotter, *United States Steel: A Corporation with a Soul* (New York, 1921), 132, 134, 141, 133; William G. McAdoo, "The Soul of a Corporation," *World's Work* 23 (March 1912), 585.

16. George Santayana, "The Genteel Tradition in American Philosophy" (1911), in *Selected Critical Writings of George Santayana,* ed. Norman Henfrey (New York and London, 1968), 2:86; Russell Sturgis, "The Larkin Building in Buffalo," *Architectural Record* 23 (April 1908), 315–316; Daniel Burnham, quoted in Kenneth Turney Gibbs, *Business Architectural Imagery in America, 1870–1930* (Ann Arbor, MI, 1984), 118; Oscar Lovell Triggs, "Democratic Art," *Forum* 26 (September 1898), 75.

17. On the cliché of mall as cathedral, see Julian Stallabrass, *Gargantua: Manufactured Mass Culture* (London and New York, 1996), 153. Dickinson, *Appearances,* 141–142; Ezra Pound, "Patria Mia" (1913), in *Ezra Pound: Selected Prose, 1909–1965,* ed. William Cookson (New York, 1975), 107.

18. William Henry Atherton quoted in Gibbs, *Business Architectural Imagery,* 136; see William Henry Atherton, *The Metropolitan Tower: A Symbol of Refuge, Warning, Love, Inspiration, Beauty, Strength* (New York, 1915), esp. 2–6; Rev. S. Parkes Cadman, foreword to Edwin A. Cochran, *The Cathedral of Commerce* (New York, 1921 [1917]), 1–2; Cochran, *Cathedral of Commerce,* 22, 18. Gail Fenske describes Cochran's promotional pamphlet as "a gilded, prayer-book-like booklet": *The Skyscraper and The City: The Woolworth Building and the Making of Modern New York* (Chicago, 2008), 265.

19. Louis Sullivan, *The Autobiography of An Idea* (New York, 1924), 188; letter to Claude Bragdon, cited in Claude Brangdon, *More Lives Than One* (New York, 1917), 159.

20. Sullivan, *Autobiography,* 248, 323, 178–179, 271; "The Tall Office Building Artistically Considered" (1896), in *Louis Sullivan: The Public Papers,* ed. Robert Twombly (Chicago, 1988), 111; "What Is Architecture? A Study in the American People of Today" (1906), in Sullivan, *Public Papers,* 186.

21. Sullivan, *Autobiography,* 264, 271; "Emotional Architecture as Compared with Intellectual: A Study in Subjectivity and Objectivity," address to the American Institute of Architects, October 1894, in Sullivan, *Public Papers,* 95–96; "The High-Building Question" (1891), in Sullivan, *Public Papers,* 93–94, 95–96.

22. Sullivan, "The High-Building Question," in Sullivan, *Public Papers,* 79; "The Tall Office Building," in Sullivan, *Public Papers,* 104, 105, 108.

## 9. Blazers of the One True Way

1. Nicholas Paine Gilman, *A Dividend to Labor: A Study of Employers' Welfare Institutions* (Boston and New York, 1899), 15, 14, 29.

2. Alfred D. Chandler, Jr., *Strategy and Structure: Chapters in the History of the Industrial Enterprise* (Cambridge, MA, 1962); *The Visible Hand: The Managerial Revolution in American Business* (Cambridge, MA, 1977); *Scale and Scope: The Dynamics of Industrial Capitalism* (Cambridge, MA, 1990), 47–234; Ehrenreich and Ehrenreich, "The Professional-Managerial Class," in *Between Labor and Capital,* 5–45.

3. Chandler, *Strategy and Structure,* 383; Olivier Zunz, *Making America Corporate, 1870–1920* (Chicago, 1992), 76–77; David F. Noble, *America by Design: Science, Technology, and the Rise of Corporate Capitalism* (New York, 1977), xxv. From a vast literature on the emergence of management out of struggles between capital and labor over control of the industrial workplace, see Harry Braverman, *Labor and Monopoly Capital: The Degradation of Work in the Twentieth Century* (New York, 1974); David Montgomery, *Workers' Control in America: Studies in the History of Work, Technology, and Labor Struggles* (New York, 1979); David Montgomery, *The Fall of the House of Labor: The Workplace, the State, and American Labor Activism, 1865–1925* (New York, 1987), Haywood quote on 45.

4. Frederick Winslow Taylor, *The Principles of Scientific Management* (New York, 1913), 32, 48–49, 53.

5. On managerial fetishism, see Sohn-Rethel, *Intellectual and Manual Labor.*

6. Steven Watts, *The People's Tycoon: Henry Ford and the American Century* (New York, 2005), 199–224, describes the "Sociological Department"; on the engineer as icon, see Cecelia Tichi, *Shifting Gears: Technology, Literature, Culture in Modernist America* (Chapel Hill, NC, 1987), 97–170, quote on 105; see also David E. Nye, *Image Worlds: Corporate Identities at General Electric, 1890–1930* (Cambridge, MA, 1985), 59–70, for an account of one corporation's efforts to encourage its engineers to see themselves as "members of a new industrial elite" (69); John Fox, Jr., *The Trail of the Lonesome Pine* (New York, 1912), 41, 44; Harold Bell Wright, *The Winning of Barbara Worth* (New York, 1911), 94, 86; Zane Grey, *The U. P. Trail* (New York, 1918), 16.

7. Mark Twain, *A Connecticut Yankee in King Arthur's Court* (New York, 1889), 6, 56, 71.

8. Twain, *A Connecticut Yankee,* 35, 217, 220, 222, 369. Twain's remarks are cited in Everett Carter, "The Meaning of *A Connecticut Yankee,*" in *On Mark Twain,* ed. Louis J. Budd (Durham, NC, 1987), 190.

9. On engineers and management at this time, see Noble, *America by Design,* 263–268; Henry Towne, "The Engineer as Economist," *Transactions of the American Society of Mechanical Engineers* 7 (June 1886), 428, 429, 430; George S. Morison, "The New

Epoch and the Civil Engineer," *Transactions of the American Society of Mechanical Engineers* 33 (June 1895), 484; George S. Morison, *The New Epoch as Developed by the Manufacture of Power* (Boston, 1903).

10. Leach, *Land of Desire*, 155, summarizes the state of business education before the late nineteenth century; Harlow Stafford Person, "Professional Training for Business," *World's Work* 8 (May 1904), 47–67. For other examples of the new importance attached to business education at the university level, see James B. Dill, "The College Man and the Corporate Proposition," *Munsey's Magazine* 24 (October 1900), 148–152; Edwin Grant Dexter, "A Study of Success," *Popular Science Monthly* 61 (July 1902), 241–251; Charles F. Thwing, "College Training and the Business Manager," *North American Review* 563 (October 1903), 587–600; William Rainey Harper, "A University Training for a Business Career," *Harper's Weekly* 48 (September 10, 1904), 1393–1394.

11. Wharton quoted in Steven A. Sass, *The Pragmatic Imagination: A History of the Wharton School, 1881–1981* (Philadelphia, 1982), 22–23; John Cotton Dana, "The Use of Print in the World of Affairs," *Library Journal* 35 (December 1910), 536. On the moral aspirations of management schools at this time, see Zunz, *Making America Corporate*, 67–101, and Nye, *Image Worlds*, 93–111.

12. E. St. Elmo Lewis, address to the Fifth Annual Convention of the National Association of Corporation Schools, in *Annual Proceedings* 5 (1917), 535, 541.

13. Lears, *No Place of Grace*, 13–14, locates Taylor within the modern search for rationalized methods of self-control.

14. On Taylor's fondness for Kaufman, see Frank B. Copley, *Frederick W. Taylor, Father of Scientific Management* (New York, 1923), 2:440. The quote is from Herbert Kaufman, *The Dreamers* (New York, 1915 [1910]), 6–7.

15. There is a plentiful literature on Taylor and Taylorism. Copley's two volumes, while hagiographic, are nonetheless informative. Sudhir Kakar, *Frederick Taylor: A Study in Personality and Innovation* (Cambridge, MA, 1970), is a psychobiography (indebted to Erik Erikson) that, for the most part, achieves the delicate feat of psychoanalyzing Taylor without reducing him to the sum of his neuroses. My account of Taylor's upbringing relies on Kakar, *Frederick Taylor*, 15–20. Robert Kanigel, *The One Best Way: Frederick W. Taylor and the Enigma of Efficiency* (New York, 1997), provides the most comprehensive account of the man and his movement. On Taylor's impact on workplace politics and class relations, see especially Samuel Haber, *Efficiency and Uplift: Scientific Management in the Progressive Era, 1890–1920* (Chicago, 1964); Daniel Nelson, *Managers and Workers: Origins of the New Factory System in the United States, 1880–1920* (Madison, WI, 1975), 55–78; Daniel Nelson, *Frederick W. Taylor and Scientific Management* (Madison, WI, 1980); Dan Clawson, *Bureaucracy and the Labor Process: The Transformation of U.S. Industry, 1860–1920* (New York, 1980), 202–253, esp. 246–250 (Clawson calls scientific management "the dictatorship of the bourgeoisie"); and Montgomery, *Fall of the House of Labor*, 216–256. Taylorism had a significant impact in Europe as well: see Charles S. Maier, "Between Taylorism and Technocracy: European Ideologies and the Vision of Industrial Productivity in the 1920s," *Journal*

*of Contemporary History* 5 (1970), 27–63, and Anson Rabinbach, *The Human Motor: Energy, Fatigue, and the Origins of Modernity* (New York, 1990), 238–270.

16. Kanigel, *The One Best Way,* 196–484; Braverman, *Labor and Monopoly,* 63–69, analyzes Taylor's work at Midvale; on the decisive experience at the Watertown arsenal, see Hugh G. J. Aitken, *Taylor at Watertown Arsenal: Scientific Management in Action, 1908–1915* (Cambridge, MA, 1960).

17. Robert Franklin Hoxie, *Scientific Management and Labor* (New York, 1915), esp. 101–117; Helen Marot, *American Labor Unions* (New York, 1914), 235, 242.

18. Taylor, *Principles of Scientific Management,* 7, 52, 26, 140–141.

19. Taylor quoted in Kanigel, *The One Best Way,* 472–473.

20. Felix Frankfurter, contribution to roundtable discussion on "The Manager, the Worker, and the Social Scientist," *Bulletin of the Taylor Society* 3 (December 1917), 6; Randolph Bourne, "The 'Scientific' Manager," *in The Radical Will: Selected Writings 1911–1918,* ed. Olaf Hansen (Berkeley, 1992), 290, 291, 292.

21. Charles Buxton Going, "The Efficiency Movement: An Outline," *Transactions of the Efficiency Society* 1 (1913), 11; the commissioner's remark to Gilbreth is cited in Kanigel, *The One Best Way,* 434; H. L. Person, "Frederick W. Taylor as a Seeker of Truth," *Journal of the Efficiency Society* 4 (April 1915), 8; Morris Cooke, "Forward," *Annals of the American Academy of Political and Social Science* 85 (1915), xi; H. L. Gantt, *Organizing for Work* (New York, 1919), 108–109; Harrington Emerson, *Efficiency as a Basis for Operation and Wages* (New York, 1919), 15. (Montgomery, *Fall of the House of Labor,* 254, dismisses Emerson as a "charlatan," a judgment shared by many of Emerson's contemporaries.) See also Ordway Tead, "The Field of Personnel Administration," *Bulletin of the Taylor Society* 8 (December 1923), 239, who described the personnel manager as a "missionary" for managerial practices that enhance "richness and fullness of life for the rank and file."

Historians have not been inattentive to the religious aura of scientific management. Haber opens his study by describing the "efficiency craze" as a "secular Great Awakening"; Haber, *Efficiency and Uplift,* ix. John Jordan briefly discusses the religiosity of Taylor's followers, going so far as to note the "sacerdotal overtones" of Taylorite publications as well as their rhetorical reliance on a "substantial sum of Christian moral capital"; John Jordan, *Machine-Age Ideology: Social Engineering and American Liberalism, 1911–1939* (Chapel Hill, NC, 1994), 53–55. Kanigel refers repeatedly to the "gospel" of scientific management and writes that religious words and phrases "dog any account" of the movement; Kanigel, *The One Best Way,* 412.

22. Frank Gilbreth, *Primer of Scientific Management* (New York, 1912), 48, 50; Hugo Munsterberg, *Psychology and Industrial Efficiency* (Boston and New York, 1913), 19, 144, 24.

23. Louis Brandeis, *Business—A Profession* (New York, 1914), 42, 52–53; Ida Tarbell, *New Ideals in Business* (New York, 1916), 26–27, 332; the Tarbell articles are "The Golden Rule in Business," *American Magazine* 87 (October 1914), 16–17, (November 1914), 11–17, and (December 1914), 24–29. Tarbell described her research in Detroit in Ida Tar-

bell, *All in the Day's Work: An Autobiography* (New York, 1939), 280–300. After World War I, Tarbell specialized in portraits of businesspeople, including Elbert H. Gary of U.S. Steel and Owen D. Young of General Electric and RCA. "Democratic Control of Scientific Management," editorial, *New Republic* 9 (December 23, 1916), 205; Walter Lippmann, *Drift and Mastery: An Attempt to Diagnose the Current Unrest* (New York, 1914), 277, 38, 49; Herbert Croly, *Progressive Democracy* (New York, 1914), 399, 406.

24. John D. Rockefeller, Jr., "A New Industrial Creed" (1918), in *Selected Articles on Problems of Labor,* ed. Daniel Bloomfield (New York, 1920), 368; W. L. Mackenzie King, *Industry and Humanity: A Study in the Principles Underlying Industrial Reconstruction* (Boston and New York, 1918), 363.

25. John R. Commons, *Industrial Goodwill* (New York, 1919), 19–20, 147, 151; Jennie McMullin Turner, "Thinking and Planning," in *Industrial Government*, ed. John R. Commons (New York, 1921), 7. On Commons, see Dorothy Ross, *The Origins of American Social Science* (Baltimore, 1991), 202–204.

26. Commons, *Industrial Goodwill*, 19, 61.

## 10. The Spirit of the Thing

1. Lears, "From Salvation to Self-Realization," in Lears and Richard W. Fox, *Culture of Consumption;* Leach, *Land of Desire,* 8, 385; Roland Marchand, *Advertising the American Dream: Making Way for Modernity, 1920–1940* (Berkeley, 1985), 218; Christopher Lasch, *The Culture of Narcissism: American Life in an Age of Diminishing Expectations* (New York, 1978). This perspective on consumer culture formed the backdrop for Thomas Frank, *The Conquest of Cool: Business Culture, Counterculture, and the Rise of Hip Consumerism* (Chicago, 1997).

2. Lippmann, *Drift and Mastery,* 253. The most vociferous proponent of the emancipatory view of consumer culture among historians has been Livingston: see *Pragmatism and Political Economy,* 158–294; James Livingston, *Pragmatism, Feminism, and Democracy: Rethinking the Politics of American History* (New York, 2001), 17–53; and James Livingston, *Against Thrift: Why Consumer Culture Is Good for the Economy, the Environment, and Your Soul* (New York, 2011), esp. 77–98, 115–161.

3. Livingston, *Against Thrift,* xi; Lears, *Fables of Abundance,* 292.

4. Lears, *Fables of Abundance,* 102–218.

5. Lears, *Fables of Abundance,* esp. 198–210; the Taft quote is on 94. Earnest Elmo Calkins and Ralph Holden, *Modern Advertising* (New York, 1905), 1, 5; Walter Dill Scott, "The Psychology of Advertising," *Atlantic Monthly* 93 (January 1904), 34; Dickinson, *Appearances,* 190.

6. Michelle Bogart, *Artists, Advertising, and the Borders of Art* (Chicago, 1995), 55–170; Theodore Dreiser, *The "Genius"* (New York, 1915), 437.

7. Bogart, *Artists, Advertising, and the Borders,* 127–170, 207–212, 234–242; quote from curator on 43; see also Lears, *Fables of Abundance,* 282–298. Walter Dill Scott, *The Theory of Advertising* (Boston, 1903), 31–32.

8. Joel Benton, "Oversmartness," *Fame* 2 (May 1894), 116; James H. Collins, "The Economy of Symbolism," *Printers' Ink* 34 (March 20, 1901), 2–4; Samuel Hopkins Adams, "The New World of Trade: I. The Art of Advertising," *Collier's* 43 (May 22, 1909), 14. On the "mythologies" of advertising, see Roland Barthes, *Mythologies,* trans. Annette Levers (New York, 1972 [1957]), esp. 36–38, 58–61. Raymond Williams made a similar point when comparing advertising to magic: advertising, he wrote, is a "cultural pattern" in which advertisers "associate consumption with human desires to which it has no real reference"; Raymond Williams, "Advertising: The Magic System" (1960), in *Problems in Materialism and Culture* (New York, 1980), 189.

9. W. R. Emery, "The Personality of a Product," *Printers' Ink* 72 (August 4, 1910), 42.

10. H. G. Wells, *Tono-Bungay* (New York, 1908), 158, 182, 181.

11. Wells, *Tono-Bungay,* 173, 182, 181, 258.

12. Seymour Eaton, *Sermons on Advertising* (New York, 1907), n.p. On one Sunday in June 1915, a battalion of Detroit admen—led by advertising managers from Ford, Dodge, and Burroughs—did, in fact, preach in forty Chicago churches: "Detroit Advertising Men to Preach in Chicago Pulpits," *Detroiter* 6 (June 14, 1915), 2. Williams insisted that "it must not be assumed that magicians—in this case, advertising agents—disbelieve in their own magic": Williams, "Advertising: The Magic System," in *Problems in Materialism and Culture,* 189.

13. L. Frank Baum is quoted in Leach, *Land of Desire,* 60.

14. Claude C. Hopkins, *My Life in Advertising* (New York, 1917), 9, 29, 206, 203.

15. Lears, *Fables of Abundance,* 162–195; Daniel Bell, *The Cultural Contradictions of Capitalism* (New York, 1976); Calkins and Holden, *Modern Advertising,* 7, 8, 3.

16. Artemus Ward, "Fraudulent Advertising," *Fame* 7 (January 1898), 6–7; Artemus Ward, "Stray Shots," *Fame* 1 (December 1892), 323; Frank Harrison, "The Occult-Psychic-Mystical Side of Advertising," *Printers' Ink* 46 (March 2, 1904), 47; John A. Hill, "John A. Hill on the Publisher's Relation to the Manufacturer," *Printers' Ink* 91 (April 29, 1915), 39; Thomas L. Masson, "What Is Advertising?," *Printers' Ink Monthly* 1 (January 1920), 15–16.

17. The sole biography of Hubbard is Freeman Champney, *Art and Glory: The Story of Elbert Hubbard* (New York, 1968); see also Leach, *Land of Desire,* 41–46. On Hubbard and Roycroft, see Eileen Boris, "'Dreams of Brotherhood and Beauty': The Social Ideas of the Arts and Crafts Movement," in *"The Art That Is Life": The Arts and Crafts Movement in America, 1870–1920,* ed. Wendy Kaplan (Boston, 1998 [1987]), 218–219, and Kaplan, "Spreading the Crafts: The Reform of the Schools," in *"Art That Is Life,"* 317, who notes that "Hubbard's forte lay in entrepreneurship, not in design"; Hubbard, *A Message to Garcia* (East Aurora, NY, 1899), 10.

18. Elbert Hubbard, "Big Business—and Little," *Fra* 14 (February 1915), 129; Harold Bolce, "Hubbard the Homo, Plus," *Cosmopolitan* 50 (March 1911), 514–516.

19. Hubbard, "Heart-to-Heart Talks," *Philistine* 38 (December 1913), 48; advertisement, *Fra* 14 (March 1915), xvi; "Heart-to-Heart Talks," *Philistine* 38 (May 1914), 192; "The Tools of Civilization," *Fra* 9 (May 1912), 63.

20. Parrish, letter to Charles Crane, July 11, 1918, cited in Alma Gilbert, *Maxfield Parrish: Master of Make-Believe* (London, 2005), 76; interview with *New York Times*, June 3, 1964, cited in Gilbert, *Maxfield Parrish*, 115; F. Scott Fitzgerald, "May Day" (1920), in *The Short Stories of F. Scott Fitzgerald*, ed. Matthew Joseph Bruccoli (New York, 1998), 154.

Coy Ludwig, *Maxfield Parrish* (New York, 1973), is a valuable introduction to Parrish's life and work. Sylvia Yount, "Dream Days: The Art of Maxfield Parrish," in *Maxfield Parrish 1870–1966*, ed. Sylvia Yount (New York, 1999), 14–121, and Gilbert, *Maxfield Parrish*, explore Parrish's impact on commercial art and consumer culture. Cultural historians have studied Parrish from a variety of angles. Leach (*Land of Desire*, 52–55) views Parrish as a master of the "magic of surfaces," a virtuoso of consumer desire. To Lears (*Fables of Abundance*, 296–298), Parrish exemplifies the romantic who grows weary and disgusted with the compromises demanded by the advertising business. Bogart (*Artists, Advertising, and the Borders*, 234–243) traces Parrish's attempt to draw and negotiate the boundaries between fine and commercial art.

21. Christian Brinton, "A Master of Make-Believe," *Century Illustrated Monthly Magazine* 84 (July 1912), 340, 342; on Parrish's early life and career, see Ludwig, *Maxfield Parrish*, 11–20 (letter cited on 13), and Yount, "Dream Days," 15–70.

22. Samuel Strauss and Kate Parsons, editorial, *The Villager* 3 (March 20, 1920), 183.

23. Quotes from Ludwig, *Maxfield Parrish*, 134, 185.

24. Quotes from Ludwig, *Maxfield Parrish*, 15, 23; J. H. Irwin, "Professor von Kerkomer on Maxfield Parrish's Book Illustrations," *International Studio* 29 (July 1906), 35.

25. Quotes from Ludwig, *Maxfield Parrish*, 135, and Yount, "Dream Days," 102; J. L. Conger, "Maxfield Parrish's Calendars Build Sales for Edison Mazda Lamps," *Artist and Advertiser* 2 (June 1931), 4. On the popular success of the prints, see Yount, "Dream Days," 100–108, and Bogart, *Artists, Advertising, and the Borders*, 235.

26. Walter Benjamin, "The Work of Art in the Age of Mechanical Reproduction," in *Illuminations*, ed. Hannah Arendt, trans. Harry Zohn (New York, 2007 [1968]), 217–252.

## 11. Modern Communion

1. Will Irwin, "The Awakening of the American Business Man," *The Century* 82 (May 1911), 121; Hanna quoted in James Weinstein, *The Corporate Ideal in the Liberal State, 1900–1918* (Boston, 1968), 118. From among numerous accounts of corporate liberalism, see Weinstein, *Corporate Ideal*; Ellis Hawley, "The Study and Discovery of a 'Corporate Liberalism,'" *Business History Review* 52 (Autumn 1978), 309–320; R. Jeffrey Lustig, *Corporate Liberalism: The Origins of Modern American Political Theory, 1890–1920* (Berkeley, 1982); and Sklar, *Corporate Reconstruction*, 34–40, 383–430. On the broader transatlantic intellectual and political contexts for corporate liberalism, see James T. Kloppenberg, *Uncertain Victory: Social Democracy and Progressivism in*

*European and American Thought, 1870–1920* (New York, 1986), and Daniel T. Rodgers, *Atlantic Crossings: Social Politics in a Progressive Age* (Cambridge, MA, 1998).

2. Robert M. Crunden, *Ministers of Reform: The Progressives' Achievement in American Civilization, 1889–1920* (New York, 1982), x, 90–162. Even though Crunden used the idea to examine literature, painting, music, and architecture, its relevance to social thought seems obvious.

3. On the "Beloved Community," see Josiah Royce, *The Problem of Christianity* (New York, 1913), 2:163–213; *War and Insurance* (New York, 1914), x, 63, 49, xxvii, 19, 60; Stevens quoted in "Selling Stuff and Sapient Suggestions from the Illinois Life Convention," *National Underwriter* 21 (January 11, 1917), 6.

4. Lippmann, *Drift and Mastery*, 50, 206, 211, 283. Lippmann's life is chronicled in Ronald Steel, *Walter Lippman and the American Century* (New York, 1980).

5. On Croly's youthful initiation into the "Religion of Humanity," see David W. Levy, *Herbert Croly of the New Republic: The Life and Thought of an American Progressive* (Princeton, NJ, 1985), 3–42; on his later spiritual interests, see also 65–67, 290–295. Croly, *Progressive Democracy*, 191–193, 353, 399–401, 409–410, 414–415; Herbert Croly, *The Promise of American Life* (New York, 1909), 411, 444–446. Kloppenberg, *Uncertain Victory*, 315, sees Croly's religious language as an attempt to reconcile "science and mysticism."

6. Croly, *Promise of American Life*, 300–307, quote on 302; *Progressive Democracy*, 192. Lippmann, *Drift and Mastery*, 163–164; Walter Lippmann, *The Stakes of Diplomacy* (New York, 1915), 90; Walter Lippmann, "What Position Shall the United States Stand for in International Relations?," *Annals of the American Society of Political and Social Science* 66 (July 1916), 61.

7. Walter LaFeber, *The American Search for Opportunity, 1865–1913* (New York, 1994); see also *The New Empire: An Interpretation of American Expansion, 1860–1898* (Ithaca, NY, 1998 [1963]). Lodge is quoted in Lears, *Rebirth of a Nation*, 201.

8. Brooks Adams, *America's Economic Supremacy* (New York, 1900), 81, 83; Strong, *Our Country*, 14–15.

9. Albert J. Beveridge, "Our Philippine Policy" (January 9, 1900), in *The Meaning of Our Time and Other Speeches* (Indianapolis, IN, 1908), 85, 87; "The March of the Flag" (September 16, 1898), in *The Meaning of Our Time*, 48.

10. Wells, *The Future in America*, 226, 221; G. K. Chesterton, *What I Saw in America* (New York, 1922), 241, 240, 104, 242.

11. W. T. Stead, *The Americanization of the World, or, The Trend of the Twentieth Century* (New York and London, 1902 [1901]), preface (not paginated), 163, 104, 9, 164, 443; see especially 132–146 on the American economy.

12. On Wilsonian "idealism," see David Steigerwald, *Wilsonian Idealism in America* (Ithaca, NY, 1994). On Wilson himself, see John Milton Cooper, *The Warrior and the Priest: Woodrow Wilson and Theodore Roosevelt* (Cambridge, MA, 1983), and *Woodrow Wilson: A Biography* (New York, 2000).

13. Wilson's remark on Providence is cited in August Heckscher, *Woodrow Wilson* (New York, 1991), 245; Wilson, "Democracy and Efficiency," *Atlantic Monthly* 87 (March 1901), 297; "The Ideals of America," *Atlantic Monthly* 90 (December 1902), 733; Wilson's remarks to students are cited in Sklar, *Corporate Reconstruction*, 415–417.

14. Wilson, "Democracy and Efficiency," 297, 298; remarks to the Senate are cited in Arthur S. Link, *The Higher Realism of Woodrow Wilson* (Nashville, 1972), 20.

15. Woodrow Wilson, "Wilson's Address at the Salesmanship Congress" (July 10, 1916), in *President Wilson's State Papers and Addresses*, ed. Albert Sloan (New York, 1918), 282–283.

16. King Camp Gillette, *The Human Drift* (Boston, 1894), 28, 21–29, 93, 84, 87–128; King Camp Gillette, *World Corporation* (Boston, 1910); King Camp Gillette, *The People's Corporation* (Boston, 1924). On Gillette's life and work, see Segal, *Technological Utopianism*, especially 19–44, who considers Gillette "the quintessential technocratic visionary" (42), and Tim Dowling, *Inventor of the Disposable Culture: King Camp Gillette, 1855–1932* (London, 2001), who notes the anomaly of a business executive excoriating capitalism but then fails to explore it.

17. Gillette, *Human Drift*, 5, 84, 23, 8, 46; *World Corporation*, 9.

18. Gillette, *Human Drift*, 75; *World Corporation*, 122, 240, 92–94 (see illustration); see also references to "magic" in *Human Drift*, 3, 28, 29, 34, 129, and *World Corporation*, 138.

19. Randolph Bourne, "New Ideals in Business," *Dial* 62 (February 22, 1917), 133.

## Part Four: The Beloved Commonwealth

1. Adams, *Education*, 460, 500, 416; Henry Adams, "Prayer to the Virgin of Chartres," in *Letters to a Niece and Prayer to the Virgin of Chartres* (Boston and New York, 1920), 126–127.

2. Henry Adams, *Mont Saint Michel and Chartres* (New York, 1986 [1904]), 88, 90, 91.

3. Adams, *Mont Saint Michel and Chartres*, 317, 324.

4. Adams, *Mont Saint Michel and Chartres*, 103; Adams, "Prayer to the Virgin," 131; Lears, *No Place of Grace*, 297.

5. Adams, *Education*, 344.

6. From among a copious literature on agrarian and working-class populism, see Leon Fink, *Workingmen's Democracy: The Knights of Labor and American Politics* (Urbana, IL, 1983); Montgomery, *Fall of the House of Labor*; Robert Weir, *Beyond Labor's Veil: The Culture of the Knights of Labor* (Philadelphia, 1996); Lawrence Goodwyn, *Democratic Promise: The Populist Moment in America* (New York, 1976); Nick Salvatore, *Eugene V. Debs: Citizen and Socialist* (Urbana, IL, 1982); John L. Thomas, *Alternative America: Henry George, Edward Bellamy, Henry Demarest Lloyd, and the Adversary Tradition* (Cambridge, MA, 1983); Charles Postel, *The Populist Vision* (New York, 2009); Gourevitch, *From Slavery to the Cooperative Commonwealth*; see also

Lasch, *True and Only Heaven,* 209–225; Michael Kazin, *The Populist Persuasion: An American History* (New York, 1995), 27–77; Steve Fraser, *Every Man a Speculator: A History of Wall Street in American Life* (New York, 2005), 193–246, and Fraser, *Age of Acquiescence,* 25–178.

## 12. The Producers' Jeremiad

1. Lears, *Rebirth of a Nation,* 133–221; see also the overview provided by Elizabeth Sanders, *Farmers, Workers, and the American State, 1877–1917* (Chicago, 1999), 13–29.

2. Sanders, *Farmers, Workers, and the American State,* 30–147.

3. Goodwyn, *Democratic Promise;* Charles Postel, *The Populist Vision* (New York, 2007), 25–68; Deborah Kay Fitzgerald, *Every Farm a Factory: The Industrial Ideal in American Agriculture* (New Haven, CT, 2003).

4. Richard Hofstadter, *The Age of Reform: From Bryan to F. D. R.* (New York, 1955), 23–130, quotes on 35, 39; Richard Hofstadter, "The Paranoid Style in American Politics" (1965), in *The Paranoid Style in American Politics and Other Essays* (New York, 2008 [1965]), 3–40; Richard Hofstadter, *Anti-Intellectualism in American Life* (New York, 1963), 154–155, where Hofstadter refers to a more generalized current of "populism." See also Daniel Bell, ed., *The New American Right* (New York, 1955).

5. Goodwyn, *Democratic Promise,* 553, 606; Lasch, *True and Only Heaven,* 217–221, quote on 218; Trachtenberg, *Incorporation of America,* 177. Earlier sympathetic views of populism included John D. Hicks, *The Populist Revolt: A History of the Farmers' Alliance and the People's Party* (Minneapolis, MN, 1955 [1931]); Walter T. K. Nugent, *The Tolerant Populists: Kansas Populism and Nativism* (Chicago, 1963); Norman Pollack, *The Populist Response to Industrial America: Midwestern Populist Thought* (Cambridge, MA, 1962); and Norman Pollack, *The Humane Economy: Populism, Capitalism, and Democracy* (New Brunswick, NJ, 1990).

6. Postel, *The Populist Vision,* 8, 133, 271; Pollack, *Humane Economy,* 66.

7. Weir, *Beyond Labor's Veil,* 22–38 and scattered throughout; Uriah Stephens refers to the "tabernacle" as "the dwelling-place of God" in "The Ideal Organization," *Journal of United Labor* 1 (July 15, 1880), 34. On the Protestant inflection of postbellum labor culture, see Herbert Gutman, "Protestantism and the American Labor Movement: The Christian Spirit in the Gilded Age," in *Work, Culture, and Society in Industrializing America* (New York, 1977), 79–117, and Robert H. Craig, *Religion and Radical Politics: An Alternative Christian Tradition in the United States* (Philadelphia, 1995), 6–45.

8. Engels and Wright are quoted in Weir, *Beyond Labor's Veil,* xv, 98.

9. Fink, *Workingmen's Democracy,* 7–12, and Lasch, *True and Only Heaven,* 223–225, emphasize external factors in the Knights' demise; quotes in Weir, *Beyond Labor's Veil,* 56.

10. Davis, *A Political Revelation,* 3, 133; Mildred Wriarson Howard, *The American Plutocracy* (New York, 1895), 46. On Donnelly, see below.

11. Ignatius Donnelly, *The Bryan Campaign for the American People's Money* (Chicago, 1896), 148; Dunning and Macune quoted in Postel, *The Populist Vision*, 33, 38; Nelson Dunning, ed., *The Farmers' Alliance History and Agricultural Digest* (Washington, DC, 1891), 5; Thorstein Veblen, *Absentee Ownership and Business Enterprise in Recent Times: The Case of America* (New York, 1923), 135.

12. Quoted in Hicks, *The Populist Revolt*, 79; Ignatius Donnelly, *Caesar's Column: A Story of the Twentieth Century* (Chicago, 1890), 115, 121; Davis, *A Political Revelation*, 245.

13. Dunning, *Farmers' Alliance History*, 81, 8, 182; California Grange quoted in Postel, *The Populist Vision*, 311; W. S. Morgan, *History of the Wheel and Alliance and the Impending Revolution* (Hardy, AK, 1889), 37–38, 16; Macune, quoted in Postel, *The Populist Vision*, 104; Tom Watson quoted in C. Vann Woodward, *Tom Watson, Agrarian Rebel* (New York, 1963 [1938]), 178.

14. Tetts quoted in Postel, *The Populist Vision*, 121.

15. Lease and Lewelling are quoted in Rhys Williams and Susan Alexander, "Religious Rhetoric in American Populism: Civil Religion as Movement Ideology," *Journal for the Scientific Study of Religion* 33 (March 1994), 8, 12, respectively; Nugent is quoted in Catherine Nugent, *Life Work of Thomas L. Nugent* (Stephenville, TX, 1896), 205; C. W. Macune, "The Purposes of the Farmers' Alliance," in Dunning, *Farmers' Alliance History*, 257, 259. For a view of the Farmers' Alliance as a middle-class evangelical insurgency, see Joe Creech, *Righteous Indignation: Religion and the Populist Revolution* (Urbana, IL, 2006), esp. 51–102.

16. Henry George, *Progress and Poverty* (New York, 1879), 557, 546; Henry George, *The Science of Political Economy* (New York, 1897), 202. On George's life and career, see Thomas, *Alternative America*, 102–202.

17. George, *Progress and Poverty*, 548, 547, 283, 325, 549.

18. On Populists' religious modernism, see Postel, *The Populist Vision*, 243–268; Farmers' Alliance editorial cited in Norman Pollack, *The Just Polity: Populism, Law, and Human Welfare* (Urbana-Champaign, IL, 1987), 131; Henry Demarest Lloyd, quoted in Thomas, *Alternative America*, 333; Benjamin Orange Flower, *Civilization's Inferno: Studies in the Social Cellar* (Boston, 1893), 198. On Flower's interest in faith healing and spiritualism, see Christopher Lasch, *The Agony of the American Left* (New York, 1969), 13.

19. Surprisingly little has been written about Donnelly. Martin Ridge, *Ignatius Donnelly: The Portrait of a Politician* (Chicago, 1962), focuses almost exclusively on his political career.

20. Lasch, *Agony*, 15, characterizes Donnelly's amateur scholarship as "an attack on the knowledge trust"; Ignatius Donnelly, *Atlantis: The Antediluvian World* (New York, 1882), 134. In addition to rejecting Christianity, Donnelly also exhibited contempt for organized religion in general that was laced with anti-Semitism. "I cannot believe that the maker of the universe with its hundred million visible stars . . . worked for twenty years at the carpenter's trade in Judea; and permitted a lot of lousy Jews to murder him":

cited in Ridge, *Ignatius Donnelly,* 266. Ridge's discussion of Donnelly's beliefs supports Postel's account of the populists' religious modernism.

21. Donnelly, *Atlantis,* 177; Ignatius Donnelly, *Ragnarok: The Age of Fire and Gravel* (New York, 1883), 439.

22. Ignatius Donnelly, *The Great Cryptogram: Francis Bacon's Cipher in the So-Called Shakespeare Plays* (New York, 1888), 467, 286, 65, 48.

23. Donnelly, *Ragnarok,* 440–441.

24. Donnelly, *American People's Money,* 22, 99–101, 103; Ignatius Donnelly, *The Golden Bottle: Or, The Story of Ephraim Benezet of Kansas* (New York, 1892), 129, 125, 130; Donnelly, *Caesar's Column,* 122.

25. Donnelly, *Caesar's Column,* 52, 207, 213, 214.

26. Donnelly, *Caesar's Column,* 214–216.

27. Donnelly, *Caesar's Column,* 327.

28. Donnelly, *The Golden Bottle,* 3, 15, 305, 308. Hofstadter once pointed out the "anthropomorphic treatment" of gold and silver in Populist discourse; "the metals," he noted, "were given human characters and fates": Hofstadter, "Free Silver and the Mind of 'Coin' Harvey," in *Paranoid Style,* 266.

29. Donnelly, *The Golden Bottle,* 305, 311–312; Donnelly, *Caesar's Column,* 205.

30. Donnelly, *Caesar's Column,* 52, 353, 361, 364, 367; *American People's Money,* 23.

31. California raisin association quoted in Postel, *The Populist Vision,* 277.

32. See, for instance, Goodwyn, *Democratic Promise,* 387–502.

33. William Jennings Bryan, "Income Tax" (January 30, 1894), in *The Life and Speeches of Hon. Wm. Jennings Bryan* (Baltimore, 1900), 234–235. On Bryan's career collecting debts for suppliers, see Michael Kazin, *A Godly Hero: The Life of William Jennings Bryan* (New York, 2006), 24.

34. William Jennings Bryan, "In the Chicago Convention" (1896), in *Speeches of William Jennings Bryan* (New York, 1909), 1:249, 240–241.

35. Postel, *The Populist Vision,* 22, 271.

## 13. The Cross Is Bending

1. Edward R. Hartmann, *Socialism Versus Christianity* (New York, 1909), 117; I. M. Haldeman, *The Signs of the Times* (Philadelphia, 1919), 287; the Jesuit is quoted in Ira Kipnis, *The American Socialist Movement, 1897–1912* (Chicago, 2004 [1952]), 268.

2. Hutchins Hapgood, *The Spirit of Labor* (New York, 1907), 109; William English Walling, *The Larger Aspects of Socialism* (New York, 1913), v; John Spargo, *The Spiritual Significance of Modern Socialism* (New York, 1912), 25, 30; Jack London, *The Iron Heel* (New York, 1907), 250.

3. Julius Wayland quoted in Salvatore, *Eugene V. Debs,* 191. There is a voluminous history on American socialism, but see especially Kipnis, *American Socialist Movement;* Lasch, *Agony,* 35–59; James Weinstein, *The Decline of Socialism in America, 1912–1925* (Boston, 1969); James Weinstein, *The Long Detour: The History and Future of the Amer-*

*ican Left* (New York, 2009 [2003]); James R. Green, *Grass-Roots Socialism: Radical Movements in the Southwest, 1895–1943* (Baton Rouge, LA, 1978); Elliott Green, *Talkin' Socialism: J. W. Wayland and the Role of the Press in American Radicalism, 1890–1912* (Topeka, KS, 1988); Salvatore, *Eugene V. Debs;* Stansell, *American Moderns;* Michael Kazin, *American Dreamers: How the Left Changed a Nation* (New York, 2012), 68–104. John Nichols, *The "S" Word: A Short History of an American Tradition . . . Socialism* (New York, 2011), is a brisk and informative survey.

4. As with socialism, the literature on the Social Gospel is immense. See, out of many examples, Henry May, *The Protestant Churches and Industrial America* (New York, 1949); Robert T. Handy, *The Social Gospel in America, 1870–1920* (New York, 1966); Susan Curtis, *A Consuming Faith: The Social Gospel and Modern American Culture* (Baltimore, 1991); Eugene McCarraher, *Christian Critics: Religion and the Impasse in Modern American Social Thought* (Ithaca, NY, 2000), 7–33.

5. Lyman Abbott, *Christianity and Social Problems* (Boston, 1896), 282; Washington Gladden, *Christianity and Socialism* (New York, 1905), 147, 148.

6. Charles Sheldon, *The Heart of the World* (New York, 1903), 206, 29, 126–143; Charles Sheldon, *Jesus Is Here!* (New York, 1913), 26, 216.

7. Little has been written about Gronlund's socialism; a valuable exception is Mark Pittenger, *American Socialists and Evolutionary Thought, 1870–1920* (Madison, WI, 1993), 43–63. Laurence Gronlund, *The Co-Operative Commonwealth: An Exposition of Modern Socialism* (Boston, 1884), 158, 254; Laurence Gronlund, *Our Destiny: The Influence of Socialism on Morals and Religion* (London, 1891), 130–131. On Bellamy's "Religion of Solidarity," see Thomas, *Alternative America,* 86–88; Henry Demarest Lloyd, *Man, The Social Creator* (New York, 1906), 34, 11.

8. William Morris, "Looking Backward" (1889), in *News from Nowhere,* 354, 352; Lloyd, *Man, The Social Creator,* 9, 11, 21; Henry Demarest Lloyd, contribution to symposium on "What May Be in the Twentieth Century," *The Congregationalist* 86 (January 5, 1901), 14.

9. Julius Wayland, editorial, *Coming Nation* 1 (October 21, 1893), 4; quoted in Elliott Shore, *Talkin' Socialism: J. A. Wayland the Role of the Press in American Radicalism, 1890–1912* (Lawrence, KS, 1988), 34; J. A. Wayland, *Leaves of Life: A Story of Twenty Years of Socialist Agitation* (Girard, KS, 1912), 188–189. On the "One-Hoss philosophy," see Shore, *Talkin' Socialism,* esp. 32–54, who interprets Wayland's (self-admittedly) contradictory views as intended to "bring about a growth of consciousness" (*Talkin' Socialism,* 33).

10. Ray Ginger, *The Bending Cross: A Biography of Eugene Victor Debs* (New York, 1949), 306; Eugene V. Debs, "Jesus—The Supreme Leader," *Coming Nation* 1 (new series) (March 1914), 2; quotes from Salvatore, *Eugene V. Debs,* 229, 62, 64, 124.

11. Salvatore, *Eugene V. Debs,* 150; "Speech of Eugene V. Debs," *Proceedings of the First Convention of the Industrial Workers of the World* (New York, 1905), 146–147; Eugene V. Debs, "Socialist Ideals," *Arena* 40 (November 1908), 432.

12. Salvatore, *Eugene V. Debs,* 175, 295; Max Eastman, *Heroes I Have Known: Twelve Who Lived Great Lives* (New York, 1942), 57; Debs, "Jesus."

13. Quoted in Salvatore, *Eugene V. Debs,* 192; Eugene V. Debs, "Industrial Unionism" (1905), *Eugene V. Debs Speaks,* ed. in Jean Tussey (New York, 1970), 134; Debs, "The Socialist Party's Appeal" (1908), in Tussy, *Eugene V. Debs Speaks,* 163.

14. V. I. Lenin quoted in Mark Beissinger, *Scientific Management, Socialist Discipline, and Soviet Power* (London, 1988), 23; The notion of "state capitalism" originated among anarchists, "left communists," and other revolutionary opponents of both Bolshevism and social democracy. For an example, see the work of the Dutch council communist Anton Pannekoek, especially *Workers' Councils* (Oakland, CA, 2002 [1946]), esp. 38–58, 111–120.

Well before he adopted a more "populist" stance in *The True and Only Heaven,* Lasch recognized that the sort of position adopted by Debs did not pose a fundamental challenge to the hegemony of managerial and technical elites. Although Lasch was writing about populists, we can say that socialists have not been, in his words, "reliably antitechnocratic": Christopher Lasch, "Populism, Socialism, and McGovernism," in *The World of Nations: Reflections on American History, Politics, and Culture* (New York, 1973), 165.

15. Walter Rauschenbusch, contribution to the *Christian Socialist* 11 (March 1914), 5. The distributist lineage is covered in Jay P. Corrin, *G. K. Chesterton and Hilaire Belloc: The Battle against Modernity* (Athens, OH, 1981). On Christian socialism in Britain, see Peter D'Arcy Jones, *The Christian Socialist Revival in Britain, 1877–1914: Religion, Class, and Social Conscience in Late-Victorian England* (Princeton, NJ, 1968), esp. 85–304.

16. "The Christian Commonwealth," *Social Gospel* 1 (October 1898), 25; George Herron, *The Christian State: A Political Vision of Christ* (New York, 1895), 103. On the Social Gospel and socialism in the United States, see Peter J. Frederick, *Knights of the Golden Rule: The Intellectual as Social Reformer in the 1890s* (Lexington, KY, 1976); Jacob Dorn, *Christianity and Socialism in Early 20th-Century America* (New York, 1998), and McCarraher, *Christian Critics,* 18–20, which focuses primarily on Rauschenbusch. David Burns, *The Life and Death of the Radical Historical Jesus* (New York, 2013) examines the depiction of Jesus among both religious and secular radicals.

17. W. D. P. Bliss, "What to Do Now," *Dawn* 1 (July–August 1890), 1–2.

18. Vida Dutton Scudder, *Social Ideals in Modern English Letters* (Boston, 1898), 41; Bouck White, *The Call of the Carpenter* (Garden City, NY, 1914 [1911]), 141, 351; Bouck White, *The Carpenter and the Rich Man* (Garden City, NY, 1914), 276; Bouck White, *Letters from Prison: Socialism a Spiritual Sunrise* (Boston, 1915), 62, 47; Bouck White, *Letters from Prison: Socialism Church of the Social Revolution,* 9; Eugene V. Debs, "Bouck White's Great Book," *Coming Nation* (May 10, 1913), 16.

19. W. D. P. Bliss, untitled editorial, *Dawn* 6 (October 1894), 145; W. D. P. Bliss, "A Brotherhood Organization," *Social Gospel* 1 (February 1898), 21, 22; Walter Rauschenbusch, *Christianizing the Social Order* (New York, 1912), 101.

20. George D. Herron, *The New Redemption* (New York, 1893), 46, 52, 55, 62; George D. Herron, *Why I Am a Socialist* (Chicago, 1900), 12; Herron, *The Christian State,* 100.

21. W. D. P. Bliss, "Our Library," *Dawn* 1 (May 15, 1889), 8; Walter Rauschenbusch, *Christianity and the Social Crisis* (New York, 1907), 394; Rauschenbusch, *Christianizing the Social Order,* 367, 460; Herron, *The Christian State,* 25, 48; Herren, *The New Redemption,* 67–68.

22. White, *Carpenter and the Rich Man,* 274, 281, 277; White, *Call of the Carpenter,* 348, 347, 341; see also Bouck White, "The Democracy of the Carpenter," *Craftsman* 25 (October 1913), 3–6.

23. White, *Call of the Carpenter,* 352, 347; White, *Carpenter and the Rich Man,* 262, 273, 267; White, *Letters from Prison,* 150.

24. White, *Call of the Carpenter,* 325; White, *Carpenter and the Rich Man,* 273.

25. Federal Council of Churches Committee on the War and the Religious Outlook, *The Church and Industrial Reconstruction* (New York, 1921 [1920]), 193, 95.

## 14. The Priesthood of Art

1. White, *Church of the Social Revolution,* 23.

2. Stansell, *American Moderns,* 177; Lasch, *True and Only Heaven,* 336–340, quotes on 338. See also Edward Abrahams, *The Lyrical Left: Randolph Bourne, Alfred Stieglitz, and the Origins of Cultural Radicalism in America* (Charlottesville, VA, 1986).

3. Lears, *No Place of Grace,* 59–96.

4. Lears, *No Place of Grace,* 96. Prominent critics of "the therapeutic ethos"—Lasch and Philip Rieff in particular—overlooked or dismissed these desires because they tended to see religion almost exclusively in terms of morality (or "interdiction," as Rieff liked to put it). See Lasch, *Culture of Narcissism,* and Philip Rieff, *The Triumph of the Therapeutic: Uses of Faith after Freud* (New York, 1966). I made a start at revising this account of "the therapeutic" in Eugene McCarraher, "Heal Me: 'Personality,' Religion, and the Therapeutic Ethic in Modern America," *Intellectual History Newsletter* 21 (1999), 31–40. See also Martha Nussbaum, *The Therapy of Desire: Theory and Practice in Hellenistic Ethics* (Princeton, NJ, 1994).

5. William Dean Howells, *A Traveller from Altruria* (New York, 1894), 304, 279, 278, 284, 293, 215.

6. James Oppenheim, editorial, *Seven Arts* 1 (November 1916), 52; Randolph Bourne, "Trans-National America" (1916), in Hansen, *The Radical Will,* 264; Waldo Frank, *Our America* (New York, 1919), 9. On the Young Americans, the invaluable point of departure is Casey Nelson Blake, *Beloved Community: The Cultural Criticism of Randolph Bourne, Van Wyck Brooks, Waldo Frank, and Lewis Mumford* (Chapel Hill, NC, 1990), who quotes Frank on 124.

7. Van Wyck Brooks, *America's Coming-of-Age* (New York, 1915), 8, 9; Van Wyck Brooks, "The Culture of Industrialism," *Seven Arts* 1 (April 1917), 655; Van

Wyck Brooks, "Enterprise," *Seven Arts* 1 (November 1916), 60; Randolph Bourne, "The Puritan's Will to Power," *Seven Arts* 1 (April 1917), 631–637; Frank, *Our America,* 73, 135.

8. Brooks, "Culture of Industrialism," 661, 662, 656, 663; Brooks, *America's Coming-of-Age,* 175.

9. Frank, *Our America,* 207, 114–115.

10. Frank, *Our America,* 222; Waldo Frank, *The Unwelcome Man* (Boston, 1917), 202, 37, 254–255. Blake offers a perceptive and nuanced reading of this novel in *Beloved Community,* 32–40.

11. Waldo Frank, *Memoirs of Waldo Frank,* ed. Alan Trachtenberg (Amherst, MA, 1973), 43, 64; diary entry from the early 1920s, quoted in Blake, *Beloved Community,* 127; Frank, *Our America,* 223, 230, 187, 186, 184.

12. Max Eastman, *Enjoyment of Poetry* (New York, 1913), 197, 198, 192; William Zuckerman, "Tendencies of Modern Literature," *Mother Earth* 5 (October 1910), 265–266; Emma Goldman, *Living My Life* (New York, 1970 [1931]), 1:174; Margaret Anderson, *My Thirty Years' War: An Autobiography* (New York, 1969 [1930]), 46, 55, 149. On anarchism in the United States, see Paul Avrich, *Anarchist Voices: An Oral History of Anarchism in America* (Oakland, CA, 2005 [1995]).

13. Stansell, *American Moderns,* 140; Hutchins Hapgood, *An Anarchist Woman* (New York, 1909), 203; Mabel Dodge Luhan, *Intimate Memories: The Autobiography of Mabel Dodge Luhan* (Santa Fe, NM, 2007 [1933]), 114.

14. Emma Goldman, preface to *Anarchism and Other Essays* (New York, 1910), v; Anderson, *My Thirty Years' War,* 133; Ferrer instructor quoted in Stansell, *American Moderns,* 141; Emma Goldman, "The Philosophy of Atheism," *Mother Earth* 10 (February 1916), 415.

15. Leonard Abbott, *Ernest Howard Crosby: A Valuation and a Tribute* (Westwood, MA, 1907), 12; Emma Goldman, "The Hypocrisy of Puritanism," in *Anarchism,* 173–183, quotes on 174, 181.

16. Stansell examines the sexual modernity of radical bohemia with great insight and subtlety in *American Moderns,* 225–308. Randolph Bourne, *Youth and Life* (Boston, 1913), 201, 172, 75.

17. Goldman, "Marriage and Love," in *Anarchism,* 245; Goldman, "Hypocrisy of Puritanism," 182; Stansell, *American Moderns,* 295.

18. Sadakichi Hartmann, *My Rubaiyat* (San Francisco, 1916), 21.

19. Alexander Berkman, *Prison Memoirs of an Anarchist* (New York, 1912), 10–11, 480, 485.

20. Goldman, "Anarchism," in *Anarchism,* 61; Charles Erskine Scott Wood, "What Is the Matter with Labor?," *The Blast* 1 (January 22, 1916), 3.

21. Goldman, "Anarchism," 61, 62; Emma Goldman, "There is No Communism in Russia," in *Red Emma Speaks: An Emma Goldman Reader,* ed. Alix Kates Shulman (Amherst, NY, 1996), 416; Emma Goldman, "Syndicalism: Its Theory and Practice," in *Red Emma Speaks,* 99.

22. Goldman, *Living My Life,* 172; Ratner-Rosenhagen, *American Nietzsche,* 109–192, quote on 153. In the preface to *Anarchism and Other Essays,* Goldman defended Nietzsche as a "giant mind" and argued that the *Ubermensch* augured a society that "will not give birth to a race of weaklings and slaves" (50).

23. Emma Goldman, "Minorities versus Majorities," in *Anarchism,* 81, 80, 75, 77; Emma Goldman, "Woman Suffrage," in *Anarchism,* 201–202.

24. Emma Goldman, "The Individual, Society, and the State," in *Red Emma Speaks,* 111.

25. Malcolm Cowley, *Exile's Return: A Literary Odyssey of the 1920s* (New York, 1994 [1934]), 58, 62.

26. Overviews of the Arts and Crafts movement include Robert Judson Clark, ed., *The Arts and Crafts Movement in America, 1876–1916* (Princeton, NJ, 1972); Eileen Boris, *Art and Labor: Ruskin, Morris, and the Craftsman Ideal in America* (Philadelphia, 1986), Wendy Kaplan, ed., *"The Art That Is Life": The Arts and Crafts Movement in America, 1875–1920* (Boston, 1998 [1987]). Works that feature discussions of the movement include Rodgers, *Work Ethic in Industrial America,* 78–82; Lears, *No Place of Grace,* 59–96; and Crunden, *Ministers of Reform,* 144–157. Lears provides the most succinct formulation of the movement's eventual cooptation: "In part a reaction against therapeutic self-absorption, the revival of handicraft ultimately became another form of therapy for an overcivilized bourgeoisie"; *No Place of Grace,* 65. Boris contends that by the 1920s, the promise of Arts and Crafts was "buried under handicraft stands in national parks and a proliferation of do-it-yourself kits"; Boris, *Art and Labor,* 189.

27. Edward Pearson Pressey, *History of Montague: A Typical Puritan Town* (Montague, MA, 1910), 214; Mary Ware Dennett, "The Arts and Crafts: An Outlook," *Handicraft* 2 (April 1903), 13, 27, 12, 19; Arthur A. Carey, "The Past Year and Its Lessons," address to the Boston Society of Arts and Crafts, November 22, 1901, reprinted in *Handicraft* 1 (April 1902), 11; Peter Burrowes, "Sacrament of Common Things," *Artsman* 1 (February 1904), 165.

28. Will Price, "What Is the Arts and Crafts Movement All About?," *Artsman* 1 (July 1904), 372, 364; Gustav Stickley, "The Use and Abuse of Machinery, and Its Relation to the Arts and Crafts," *Craftsman* 11 (November 1906), 204; Jane Addams, *Twenty Years at Hull House* (New York, 1981 [1910]), 265; Carl Purington Rollins, "A Principle of Handicraft," *Handicraft* 4 (June 1911), 94–95; Edward Pearson Pressey, "Editorial," *Country Time and Tide* 4 (September 1903), 168.

29. Rabbi Joseph Leiser, "Simplicity, A Law of Nature," *Craftsman* 2 (August 1902), 230; George N. Holcomb, "The Social Teaching of John Wycliffe," *Country Time and Tide* 7 (November 1904), 5; Dennett, "The Arts and Crafts," 27.

30. Oscar Lovell Triggs, *Chapters in the History of the Arts and Crafts Movement* (Chicago, 1902), 169; Mary Ware Dennett, "Aesthetics and Ethics," *Handicraft* 1 (May 1902), 33; Ernest Howard Crosby, "The Wealth of St. Francis: A Study in Transcendental Economics," *Craftsman* 2 (October 1903\), 33–48, quotes on 46, 48, 35.

Quotes from Ruskin and Morris abounded in the pages of the *Craftsman* and the *Artsman,* while Triggs spoke for many when he declared that Ruskin grasped and expressed "the fundamental principles of human intercourse and social economy": Triggs, *Chapters,* 21. For examples of Arts and Crafts medievalism, see especially Irene Sargent, "The Gilds of the Middle Ages," *Craftsman* 1 (December 1901), 1–33; Irene Sargent, "Brain and Hand," *Craftsman* 1 (January 1902), 41–44; Irene Sargent, "A Word Concerning Some Great Religious Orders," *Craftsman* 1 (February 1902), 38–42. Ralph Adams Cram, discussed below, was another champion of medievalism.

31. George Wharton James, "Indian Handicrafts," *Handicraft* 1 (March 1903), 272, 277; Jesse Kingsley Curtis, "Oriental Rugs: Their Design and Symbolism," *Craftsman* 6 (June 1904), 281; Lafcadio Hearn, *Kokoro: Hints and Echoes of Japanese Inner Life* (Boston, 1896), 27, 23, 34.

32. Holcomb, "Social Teaching of John Wycliffe," 6; Pressey, "Editorial," 32. On the life and death of New Clairvaux, see Boris, *Art and Labor,* 158–160.

33. Pressey, *The Vision of New Clairvaux* (Boston, 1909), 7, 90, 87, 29, 30, 28, 114–115.

34. On Rose Valley, see Boris, *Art and Labor,* 162–165; "A First Word from the Editors," *Artsman* 1 (October 1903), 2; Hawley McLanahan, "Rose Valley in Particular," *Artsman* 1 (October 1903), 13.

35. Price cited in David Karsner, *Horace Traubel: His Life and Work* (New York, 1919), 79; McLanahan, "Rose Valley in Particular," 18; Oscar Lovell Triggs, "The Idealism of the Day," *Artsman* 1 (December 1903), 80; Burrowes, "Sacrament of Common Things," 167, 166; Percival Wiksell, "The Love of Work," *Artsman* 2 (July 1905), 324; Ernest Newlandsmith, "Art in Daily Life," *Artsman* 3 (March 1906), 144, 145; Horace Traubel, "Rose Valley in General," *Artsman* 1 (October 1903), 24, 25.

36. Traubel has not attracted a biographer. Karsner's volume is informative but largely uncritical, as is Mildred Bain, *Horace Traubel* (New York, 1913).

37. Bain, 23, 14, 26, 61, 66–67, 135 (Traubel quote); Horace Traubel, "Walt Whitman: Poet and Philosopher and Man," in *In Re Walt Whitman,* ed. Horace Traubel (Philadelphia, 1893), 201; Horace Traubel, *Chants Communal* (Boston, 1904), 167; Horace Traubel, "Through the Eye of the Needle," *Conservator* 19 (August 1908), 93.

38. Horace Traubel, *Optimos* (New York, 1910), 308, 348, 121; Traubel, *Chants Communal,* 149, 68, 181.

39. Ralph Adams Cram, *My Life in Architecture* (Boston, 1936), 95; Ralph Adams Cram, "Will This Modernism Last?," *House Beautiful* 65 (January 19, 1929), 45. On Cram's life and work, see Douglass Shand-Tucci, *Boston Bohemia, 1881–1900: Ralph Adams Cram, Life and Literature* (Amherst, MA, 1995), and Douglass Shand-Tucci, *Ralph Adams Cram: An Architect's Four Quests, Medieval, Modern, American, Ecumenical* (Amherst, MA, 2005); see also Lears, *No Place of Grace,* 203–209.

40. Ralph Adams Cram, *The Ministry of Art* (New York, 1914), ix, x, 11, 94, 97, xi; Ralph Adams Cram, *The Gothic Quest* (New York, 1915 [1907]), 47; Ralph Adams Cram,

*The Substance of Gothic: Six Lectures on the Development of Architecture from Charlemagne to Henry VIII* (Boston, 1917), 9.

41. Cram, *Six Lectures,* 37; Cram, *Ministry of Art,* 133; Ralph Adams Cram, *The Great Thousand Years* (New York, 1918), 51, 35, 36.

42. Ralph Adams Cram, *Walled Towns* (Boston, 1919), 41–47, 52, 80–82; Ralph Adams Cram, *The Nemesis of Mediocrity* (Boston, 1918), 31, 35.

43. Cram, *Ministry of Art,* 164–165; Cram, *My Life in Architecture,* 233.

44. Cram, *Ministry of Art,* 160; Thorstein Veblen, "Arts and Crafts" (1902), in *Essays in Our Changing Order* (New York, 1934), 196, 198, 194, 197; Thorstein Veblen, *The Instinct of Workmanship: And the State of the Industrial Arts* (New York, 1914), 243, 241.

45. Triggs, *Chapters,* 187, 151; Dennett, "The Arts and Crafts: An Outlook," 14–15.

46. H. Langford Warren, "Our Work and Prospects," *Handicraft* 2 (December 1903), 193; advertisement, back cover, *Country Time and Tide* 1 (January 1902); McLanahan, "Rose Valley in Particular," 13.

47. Elbert Hubbard and the *Call* are quoted in Boris, *Art and Labor,* 143, 149; Elbert Hubbard, *Little Journeys* (New York, 1916), 24–25. For a sense of how Stickley's thinking evolved from William Morris to Frederick Taylor, see Gustav Stickley, "The Fire on the Hearth," *Craftsman* 25 (December 1913), 302; Gustav Stickley, "Als Ik Kan: Art True and False," *Craftsman* 9 (August 1908), 684; Gustav Stickley, "The Guild Stamp and Union Label," *Craftsman* 13 (January 1908), 377; Gustav Stickley, "Waste: Our Heaviest National Liability," *Craftsman* 20 (July 1911), 343–348; L. and J. G. Stickley, *The Work of L. and J. G. Stickley* (Fayetteville, NY, 1915), 3. On Stickley, see Miles Orvell, *The Real Thing: Imitation and Authenticity in American Culture, 1880–1940* (Chapel Hill, NC, 1989), 159–166, and Kevin W. Tucker, *Gustav Stickley and the American Arts and Crafts Movement* (New Haven, CT, 2010).

48. Denman Ross, quoted in Lears, *No Place of Grace,* 94; Carey, "The Past Year," 25; Warren, "Our Work and Prospects," 188; Oscar Lovell Triggs, "The Arts and Crafts," *Brush and Pencil* 1 (December 1897), 48; Triggs, *Chapters,* 191.

49. A. R. Orage, "Politics for Craftsmen," *Handicraft* 5 (September–October 1912), 99; C. R. Ashbee quoted in Wendy Kaplan, "The Lamp of British Precedent," in Kaplan, ed., *"The Art That Is Life,"* 58; Edward Pearson Pressey, "Wise and Witty Saws of Calvin Mack," *Country Time and Tide* 1 (October 1902), 20.

50. Ada Louise Huxtable, *Frank Lloyd Wright: A Life* (New York, 2008), 56.

51. Frank Lloyd Wright, "A Philosophy of Fine Art" (1900), in *Frank Lloyd Wright: Collected Writings,* vol. 1, *1894–1930,* ed. Bruce Brooks Pfeiffer (New York, 1992), 43.

52. Frank Lloyd Wright, "Art and Craft of the Machine," in Pfeiffer, ed., *Frank Lloyd Wright,* 59, 66.

53. Wright, "Art and Craft of the Machine," 66; Frank Lloyd Wright, "The 'Village Bank' Series, V," *Brickbuilder* 10 (August 1901), 160–161.

## 15. Another Kingdom of Being

1. Lears, *No Place of Grace*, 97–216.

2. John Muir, *The Story of My Boyhood and Youth* (Boston, 1913), 263, 34, 218; Donald Worster, *A Passion for Nature: The Life of John Muir* (New York, 2008), 19. See also Jedidiah Purdy's thoughtful account of Muir in *After Nature: A Politics of the Anthropocene* (Cambridge, MA, 2015), 116–147. On Daniel Muir, see Worster, *Passion for Nature*, 19–24.

3. Muir, *Boyhood and Youth*, 49, 63, 109, 94.

4. Muir, *Boyhood and Youth*, 282–283; Muir quoted in Steven Jon Holmes, *The Young John Muir: An Environmental Biography* (Madison, WI, 1999), 149; quoted in Worster, *Passion for Nature*, 115, who also chronicles Muir's days at the University of Wisconsin, 69–85; John Muir, *The Writings of John Muir*, vol. 5, *The Mountains of California* (Boston, 1917), 130.

5. Muir, *Writings*, vol. 8, *Steep Trails* (Boston, 1918), 134; Muir, *Boyhood and Youth*, 166; Muir, *Writings*, vol. 6, *Our National Parks* (Boston, 1916), 362; on Muir's friendships with Harriman and Roosevelt, see Worster, *Passion for Nature*, 359–363, 366–368, 408–410.

6. John Muir, *John of the Mountains: The Unpublished Journals of John Muir*, ed. Lianne Wolfe (Madison, 1979), 138; Muir, *Writings*, 6:86, 87; John Muir, *My First Summer in the Sierra* (Boston, 1911), 319, 20; John Muir, *Writings*, vol. 1, *The Story of My Boyhood and Youth and A Thousand-Mile Walk to the Gulf* (Boston, 1916), 355.

7. Muir quoted in Worster, *Passion for Nature*, 402, 414, 418; John Muir, *The Yosemite* (New York, 1920 [1912]), 261–262.

8. John Burroughs, *Birds and Poets: With Other Writings* (Boston, 1895), 115–138; John Burroughs, *Locusts and Wild Honey* (Boston, 1888), 33; John Burroughs, *Signs and Seasons* (Boston, 1902), 243; John Burroughs, "God and Nature," in *The Writings of John Burroughs* (Boston, 1905), 11:187; John Burroughs, *Accepting the Universe: Essays in Naturalism* (Boston, 1920), 116. Edward J. Renehan, *John Burroughs: An American Naturalist* (Hensonville, NY, 1998 [1992]), is an engaging account of its subject's life and work.

9. Burroughs, *Accepting the Universe*, 125; Burroughs, "Meditations and Criticisms," in *Writings*, 11:205; on Burroughs's friendships with industrialists, see Renehan, *John Burroughs*, 2, 182, 207–214, 229–231, 271–276.

10. Frank Norris, *The Octopus: A Story of California* (New York, 1971 [1901]), 426, 32–33, 430, 434.

11. Norris, *The Octopus*, 144, 260, 259, 262, 261.

12. Norris, *The Octopus*, 368; Mary Austin, *Earth Horizon* (Santa Fe, NM, 2007 [1932]), 51, 94.

13. Austin, *Earth Horizon*, 274, 52.

14. Mary Austin, *The Land of Little Rain* (Bedford, MA, 2000 [1903]), 99–100, 113, 12.

15. Mary Austin, *The Basket Woman: A Book of Fanciful Tales for Children* (Boston, 1904), 47, 104; Austin, *Earth Horizon*, 276, 289, 362; Mary Austin, *The Arrow Maker* (New York, 1911), xi; Mary Austin, *A Woman of Genius* (Garden City, NY, 1912), 355.

16. Worster, *Passion for Nature*, 387, 403.

17. John Muir, *Edward Henry Harriman* (Garden City, NY, 1912), 27, 4.

18. Muir, *Edward Henry Harriman*, 36.

19. Worster, *Passion for Nature*, 415.

20. James's remark about not having had any formal education is cited in Paul Jerome Croce, *Science and Religion in the Era of William James: Eclipse of Certainty, 1820–1880* (Chapel Hill, NC, 1995), 1:72; Alice James quoted in Louis Menand, *The Metaphysical Club: A Story of Ideas in America* (New York, 2002), 76; William James, *A Pluralistic Universe* (New York, 1909), 176.

On Henry James, Sr., and William's early life, see Croce, *Science and Religion*, 49–82, and Howard M. Feinstein, *Becoming William James* (Ithaca, NY, 1984), 39–315. James's thought has been examined by an array of intellectual historians: Kloppenberg, *Uncertain Victory*, esp. 173–175; George Cotkin, *William James, Public Philosopher* (Urbana, IL, 1994); John P. Diggins, *The Promise of Pragmatism: Modernism and the Crisis of Knowledge and Authority* (Chicago, 1995), 108–157; Livingston, *Pragmatism and Political Economy*, 158–180, 273–279; and Menand, *The Metaphysical Club*, esp. 351–360, 369–375.

21. William James, "Reflex Action and Theism" (1881), in *The Will to Believe: And Other Essays in Popular Philosophy* (New York, 1907 [1896]), 127; William James, "On a Certain Blindness in Human Beings," in *Talks to Teachers and Students* (New York, 1900), 244, 243; William James, *Pragmatism: A New Name for Some Old Ways of Thinking* (New York, 1907), 53; William James, "A World of Pure Experience," in *Essays in Radical Empiricism* (New York, 1912), 39–91; William James, "The Powers of Men," *American Magazine* 65 (November 1907), 57–65.

James's relationship to religion, and the connection of that relationship to pragmatism, together constitute one of the most vexing topics in US intellectual history. For an argument that religious belief grounded James's ethics, see Cotkin, *William James*, esp. 102–108, and Michael R. Slater, *William James on Ethics and Faith* (New York, 2009), 69–232. Throntveit, however, contends that James's defense of religion was "a strategy for refining . . . his philosophy of pragmatism"; Trygve Throntveit, *William James and the Quest for an Ethical Republic* (New York, 2014), 4; see esp. 39–81. Whether James was a "believer" of some sort is less important, in my view, than his conviction that an "enchanted" view of the world underwrote a powerful critique of avarice and instrumentalist reductionism.

22. William James, "Robert Gould Shaw: Oration by Professor William James" (1897), in *William James: Essays in Religion and Morality*, ed. Frederick Burckhardt (Cambridge, MA, 1982), 66, 73–74; William James, "Remarks at the Peace Banquet," *Atlantic Monthly* 94 (December 1904), 847; William James, "The Moral Equivalent of War" (1910), in Burckhardt, *William James: Essays*, 164, 165, 171, 172.

23. William James, *The Principles of Psychology* (New York, 1918 [1890]), 2:423–424; William James, *The Principles of Psychology* (New York, 1890), 1:599.

24. James, "On a Certain Blindness," 247; William James, *The Varieties of Religious Experience* (New York, 1902), 312, 357, 360; James, "What Makes a Life Significant," in *Talks*, 270, 271, 283, 273.

25. James, *Varieties*, 359, 360.

26. James, "On a Certain Blindness," 247; James, *Varieties*, 266, 274, 278–279.

27. William James, "The Moral Philosopher and the Moral Life," *International Journal of Ethics* 1 (April 1891), 341, 351–352, 353.

28. James, "On a Certain Blindness," 258.

29. James, "On a Certain Blindness," 252–254.

30. Kloppenberg (*Uncertain Victory*, 147, 73) argues that while James's own explicitly political views amounted to "desultory meditations," his thinking helped "illuminate the path leading to social democracy and progressivism." Pronouncing pragmatism what Kenneth Burke called a "frame of acceptance," Livingston describes it as "a narrative of the transition from proprietary to corporate capitalism . . . through which new shapes of solidarity and new species of the moral personality become recognizable"; Livingston, *Pragmatism and Political Economy*, xxvii, see also 273–279. Cotkin, *William James*, 173, suggests that James's political views "might be seen as developing in the direction of socialism" (see, for instance, his vague endorsement of socialism at the end of "Moral Equivalent of War"). Throntveit, *William James*, 109–138, portrays James as a kind of radical democrat. Most illuminating is Deborah J. Coon, "'One Moment in the World's Salvation': Anarchism and the Radicalization of William James," *Journal of American History* 83 (June 1996), 70–99, who takes seriously James's own self-description as an "anarchist." James, *Varieties*, 312; all other quotations are from Coon, "One Moment," 71, 78, 77, 83.

31. On "the pragmatic acquiescence," see Lewis Mumford, *The Golden Day: A Study in American Experience and Culture* (New York, 1926), 157–195, esp. 183–193 on James; Bourne, *Youth and Life*, 245; Randolph Bourne, "The War and the Intellectuals" (1917), in Hansen, *The Radical Will*, 307; Bourne, "Twilight of Idols" (1917), in Hansen, *The Radical Will*, 336–347; Bourne, "The State," posthumously published in Hanson, *The Radical Will*, 355–395.

32. Randolph Bourne, "Twilight of Idols" (1917), in Hansen, *The Radical Will*, 342; "The State," in Hansen, *The Radical Will*, 359, 358, 367, 361, 382.

33. Bourne to Brooks, cited in Blake, *Beloved Community*, 169; Bourne, "Twilight of Idols," 346; Menand, *The Metaphysical Club*, 375.

34. Vida Dutton Scudder, *On Journey* (New York, 1937), 43, 73. *On Journey* is an absorbing autobiography, but see also Theresa Corcoran, *Vida Dutton Scudder* (Boston, 1982); Frederick, *Knights of the Golden Rule*, 115–140; Lears, *No Place of Grace*, 209–215. Elizabeth L. Hanson-Hasty, *Beyond the Social Maze: Exploring Vida Dutton Scudder's Theological Ethics* (New York, 2006), examines Scudder's political theology.

35. Scudder, *On Journey*, 79, 83; Vida Dutton Scudder, "Recollections of Ruskin," *Atlantic Monthly* 85 (April 1900), 569, 570.

36. Scudder, *On Journey*, 84. In this respect, Scudder resembled Jane Addams, whose own hunger for "experience" and "real life" persisted in an even greater theological famine: see Lasch, *The New Radicalism in America, 1889–1963: The Intellectual as a Social Type* (New York, 1965), 3–37.

37. Scudder, *On Journey*, 96, 176, 181–190.

38. Scudder recounts her work in the settlement movement in *On Journey*, 135–140; see also Vida Dutton Scudder, "The Place of College Settlements," *Andover Review* 18 (October 1892), 347–349.

39. Scudder, *On Journey*, 149–163; Vida Dutton Scudder, *Socialism and Character* (New York, 1912), 187; Vida Dutton Scudder, *The Life of the Spirit in the Modern English Poets* (Boston, 1895), 134, 138.

40. Vida Dutton Scudder, "Democracy and the Church," *Atlantic Monthly* 90 (October 1902), 524. See also the Vida Dutton Scudder articles: "A Hidden Weakness in Our Democracy," *Atlantic Monthly* 89 (May 1902); "Democracy and Socialism," *Atlantic Monthly* 90 (September 1902); "The Socialism of Christ," *Dawn* 3 (December 18, 1890), 3–4. On Scudder's activism at this time, see Frederick, *Knights of the Golden Rule*, 126–129.

41. Scudder, *On Journey*, 161–163; Vida Dutton Scudder, "Socialism and Spiritual Progress—A Speculation," *Publications of the Church Social Union*, Series A, 10 (January 1, 1896), 8; Scudder, *Socialism and Character*, 130, 133.

42. Scudder, *On Journey*, 191; Vida Dutton Scudder, *The Church and the Hour: Reflections of a Socialist Christian* (New York, 1917), 33; Scudder, *Socialism and Character*, 147, 173, 108, 146.

43. Scudder, *Socialism and Character*, 290, 74, 352; Scudder, *Church and the Hour*, 256.

44. Scudder, *Socialism and Character*, 5, 105; Scudder, "Socialism and Spiritual Progress," 4, 6.

45. Scudder, *On Journey*, 149; Vida Dutton Scudder, *A Listener in Babel* (Boston, 1902), 263.

46. Lears, *No Place of Grace*, 200–201, briefly mentions both the Cowley Fathers and the Order. Little has been written about them by other historians of the social gospel. Scudder later wrote an admiring biography of Huntington: Vida Dutton Scudder, *Father Huntington, Founder of the Order of the Holy Cross* (New York, 1940).

47. Vida Dutton Scudder, *The Witness of Denial* (New York, 1895), 68; Scudder, *Socialism and Character*, 346.

48. *Manual of the Society of the Companions of the Holy Cross* (Boston, 1909), 7, 67, 88, 89, 11.

49. Scudder, *Witness of Denial*, 16, 142; Vida Dutton Scudder, *Social Ideals in English Letters* (Boston, 1898), 308, 309, 306.

50. Scudder, *On Journey,* 237–244; Vida Dutton Scudder, *Catherine of Siena as Seen in Her Letters* (New York, 1905); Vida Dutton Scudder, *The Disciple of a Saint: Being an Imaginary Biography of Raniero Di Landoccio Dei Paglieresi, Secretary to St. Catherine of Siena* (New York, 1907).

51. Scudder, *Catherine of Siena,* 2, 7.

52. Quoted in Scudder, *Catherine of Siena,* 58.

53. Scudder, *Socialism and Character,* 218.

54. Scudder, *Socialism and Character,* 101, 218.

55. Scudder, *Socialism and Character,* 105, 233, 400; Vida Dutton Scudder, *An Introduction to the Writings of John Ruskin* (Boston, 1890), 19, 21.

56. Scudder, *Socialism and Character,* 103, 231.

57. Scudder, *Listener in Babel,* 85; as Frederick remarks, "Hilda Lathrop makes all the decisions which Vida Scudder did not make" (Frederick, *Knights of the Golden Rule,* 128).

58. Scudder, *Listener in Babel,* 252, 184.

59. Scudder, *Listener in Babel,* 242, 243, 253, 255–256, 264, 263.

60. Scudder, *Listener in Babel,* 318, 317, 320, 321.

## Part Five: The Heavenly City of Fordism

1. Calvin Coolidge in 1916 quoted in Horace Green, *The Life of Calvin Coolidge* (New York, 1924), 101; Coolidge in 1925 is quoted in Robert Sobel, *Coolidge: An American Enigma* (Washington, DC, 1998), 313; Walter Lippmann, *Men of Destiny* (New York, 1927), 17.

2. Henry Ford, "Machinery—The New Messiah," *Forum* 79 (March 1928), 363–364.

3. "By Their Works Ye Shall Know Them," *Vanity Fair* 29 (February 1928), 62; Eugene O'Neill, *Dynamo* (1929), in *Complete Plays 1920–1931,* ed. Travis Bagard (New York, 1988), 874; Charles Sheeler quoted in Lowery Stokes Sims and Lisa Mintz Messinger, *The Landscape in Twentieth-Century American Art: Selections from the Metropolitan Museum of Art* (New York 1991), 97. Karen Lucic, *Charles Sheeler and the Cult of the Machine* (Cambridge, MA, 1991), esp. 75–117, examines Sheeler's enthrallment by industrial technology.

4. Paul Strand, "Photography and the New God," *Broom* 3 (November 3, 1922), 252–258, cited in Richard Guy Wilson, "America and the Machine Age," in *The Machine Age in America, 1918–1941,* ed. Wilson and Dianne Pilgrim (New York, 1986), 23. After the World War II, Strand prophesied against the new divinity, arguing that atomic weapons augured the possibility "of being quickly ground to pieces under the heel of the new God." One historian notes that Strand aspired to be "a theocide of sorts": David P. Peeler, *The Illuminating Mind in American Photography: Stieglitz, Strand, Weston, Adams* (Rochester, NY, 2001), 112–113.

5. John Dewey, *Individualism Old and New* (New York, 1930), 124, 134, 133, 41, 52, 83; John Dewey, *A Common Faith* (New Haven, CT, 1934), 33.

6. The urtext on Fordism is Antonio Gramsci, "Americanism and Fordism," in *The Antonio Gramsci Reader: Selected Writings, 1916–1935,* ed. Paul Forgacs (New York, 1988), 275–299; for a succinct and comprehensive exposition, see David Harvey, *The Condition of Postmodernity* (Oxford, 1990), 125–140. On the political anatomy of Fordism in the United States, see Ellis W. Hawley, *The New Deal and the Problem of Monopoly: A Study in Economic Ambivalence* (Princeton, NJ, 1966); Michael Denning, *The Cultural Front: The Laboring of American Culture in the Twentieth Century* (New York, 1997), 21–37; Robert H. Zieger, *The CIO, 1935–1955* (Chapel Hill, NC, 1995); Steve Fraser and Gary Gerstle, eds., *The Rise and Fall of the New Deal Order, 1930–1980* (Princeton, NJ, 1989).

7. Warren Susman, "Culture and Commitment," in *Culture as History: The Transformation of American Society in the Twentieth Century* (New York, 1984), 207; Marchand, *Advertising the American Dream,* 217–223; Lears, "From Salvation to Self-Realization"; Denning, *Cultural Front,* 151–159.

## 16. Business Is the Soul of America

1. On the Seattle general strike of 1919, see Dana Frank, *Purchasing Power: Consumer Organizing, Gender, and the Seattle Labor Movement, 1919–1929* (New York, 1994), 15–86; on welfare capitalism and the "American Plan" in the 1920s, see Allen M. Wakstein, "The Origins of the Open-Shop Movement," *Journal of American History* 51 (1964), 460–475, and Stuart Brandes, *American Welfare Capitalism, 1880–1940* (Chicago, 1976); for an excellent case study in one industrial city, see Lizabeth Cohen, *Making a New Deal: Industrial Workers in Chicago, 1919–1939* (New York, 1990), 159–211; Merle Thorpe, "Business, the Soul of America?," *Nation's Business* 15 (March 1927), 13; see also Merle Thorpe, "Business Is Business," *Rotarian* 25 (August 1924), 27, 54–57.

2. John E. Edgerton, "The President's Annual Address," *Proceedings of the National Association of Manufacturers* (1925), 11; business decalogues included Frank Crane, "Ten Commandments for Salesmen," *American Magazine* 89 (June 1920), 55, 152, 155–156, 159–160; L. V. Selleck, "Ten Commandments of Business," *Rotarian* 24 (May 1924), 28; "Ten Commandments of Kiwanis," *Kiwanis Magazine* 11 (March 1926), 169. "KIWANIS," the latter decalogue proclaimed, "hath brought thee out of the land of darkness." Charles N. Fay, *Business in Politics: Suggestions for Leaders in American Business* (Cambridge, MA, 1926), 92–93, 95, 111. Fay had been president of the Chicago Gas Trust Company and the Indiana Natural Gas and Oil Company, and vice president and general manager of the Chicago Telephone Company. James Warren Prothero, *The Dollar Decade: Business Ideas in the 1920s* (Baton Rouge, LA, 1954), remains an indispensable guide to business thought at this time.

3. James Truslow Adams, *Our Business Civilization: Some Aspects of Our Culture* (New York, 1929), 31, 36; Walton H. Hamilton, "Economic Opinion," in *Civilization in*

*the United States: An Inquiry by Thirty Americans,* ed. Harold Stearns (New York, 1922) 257, 260, 261, 262; J. Thorne Smith, "Advertising," in *Civilization in the United States: An Inquiry by Thirty Americans,* ed. Harold Stearns (New York, 1922), 383, 392, 381.

4. Sinclair Lewis, *Babbitt* (New York, 1996 [1922]), 87, 1, 11, 168, 51–52.

5. "Dare to Be a Babbitt!" *Nation's Business* 13 (June 1925), 46; Berton Braley, "Babbitt Ballads," *Nation's Business* 16 (January 1928), 29; for more in this vein, see Dr. Roy L. Smith, "Business Becomes More Christian," *Nation's Business* 15 (March 1927), 95–96 (by a Methodist minister who berates Lewis), and Caspar S. Yost, "Business Has a Spiritual Side," *Nation's Business* 17 (March 1929), 142–146; Charles Beard, "Is Babbitt's Case Hopeless?," *Menorah Journal* 14 (January 1928), 21–28; Lippmann, *Men of Destiny,* 73, 83.

6. On Barton, see Stephen Prothero, *American Jesus: How the Son of God Became a National Icon* (New York, 2003), 98–108, and Richard M. Fried, *The Man Everybody Knew: Bruce Barton and the Making of Modern America* (Chicago, 2005), esp. 84–113. Bruce Barton, *The Man Nobody Knows: A Discovery of the Real Jesus* (Indianapolis, IN, 1925), epigraph, 160–161, 19, 179–180; James Rorty, *Our Master's Voice: Advertising* (New York, 1976 [1934]), 318.

7. Charles Beard, "Introduction," in *Toward Civilization,* ed. Charles Beard (New York, 1930), 1, 19–20, 3; Charles Beard and Mary Beard, *The Rise of American Civilization* (New York, 1927), 1:800.

8. John Dewey, "Philosophy," in *Whither Mankind: A Panorama of Modern Civilization,* ed. Charles Beard (New York, 1928), 318, 317; Michael Pupin, "Machine Industry and Idealism," in Beard, *Toward Civilization,* 280; Michael Pupin, *Romance of the Machine* (New York, 1930), 29; C. F. Hirschfeld, "Power," in Beard, *Toward Civilization,* 89, 97.

9. On the New Capitalism, see David Brody, "The Rise and Decline of Welfare Capitalism," in *Change and Continuity in Twentieth Century America: The 1920s,* ed. David Brody, John Braemer, and Robert Bremner (Columbus, OH, 1968), 147–178; Kim McQuaid, "Young, Swope, and General Electric's 'New Capitalism': A Study in Corporate Liberalism, 1920–1933," *American Journal of Economics and Sociology* 36 (July 1977), 323–334; Kim McQuaid, "Corporate Liberalism in the American Business Community, 1920–1940," *Business History Review* 52 (Autumn 1978), 342–368; and Mark Hendrickson, *American Labor and Economic Citizenship: New Capitalism from World War I to the Great Depression* (New York, 2013), esp. 154–179.

10. Editorial, *Forbes* 3 (November 30, 1918), 588. On the significance of *Forbes,* see Morrell Heald, *The Social Responsibility of Business: Company and Community, 1900–1960* (Cleveland, OH, 1970), 48. Edwin B. Parker, "The Fifteen Commandments of Business," *Nation's Business* 12 (June 1924), 16–19; Wainwright Evans, "A Business Man of the New Day," *Nation's Business* 17 (April 1929), 89.

11. Herbert Hoover, "If Business Doesn't, Government Will," *Nation's Business* 12 (June 1924), 7–8; Richard F. Grant, "The Case for Business," *Nation's Business* 13 (June 1925), 19; Haley Fiske, "The New Responsibilities of Business," *Nation's Business*

15 (May 1927), 17; Benjamin Javits and Charles Wood, *Make Everybody Rich: Industry's New Goal* (New York, 1929), 280.

12. E. W. Howe, "The Submissive Business Man," *Nation's Business* 9 (February 1921), 12; John Candee Dean, "The Magic of Modern Industrialism," *Forum* 67 (June 1922), 507; Edward W. Bok, "When Money Is King and Business Our God," *World's Work* 48 (September 1924), 479; William Feather, "European Notes from a Yankee Cuff," *Nation's Business* 15 (August 1927), 20; Charles Mitchell quoted in Lewis Corey, *The Decline of American Capitalism* (New York, 1934), 6.

13. J. George Frederick, "Humanism as the Emerging American Philosophy," in *A Philosophy of Production*, ed. J. George Frederick (New York, 1930), 249, 258–259; Earnest Elmo Calkins, "The New Consumption Engineer and the Artist," in Frederick, *Philosophy of Production*, 117; Henry P. Kendall, "Change and the Common Sense of Industrial Management," in Frederick, *Philosophy of Production*, 182, 184.

14. Kendall, "Change and the Common Sense of Industrial Management," 182; Owen D. Young, "Humanizing Modern Production," in Frederick, *Philosophy of Production*, 4, 6.

15. Earnest Elmo Calkins, *Business the Civilizer* (Boston, 1928), 118; Edward A. Filene, *Successful Living in This Machine Age* (New York, 1931), 15.

16. Filene, *Successful Living*, 80, 79; Calkins, *Business the Civilizer*, 244, 232–233; see also Earnest Elmo Calkins, "Beauty the New Business Tool," *Atlantic Monthly* 140 (August 1927), 145–156.

17. Filene, *Successful Living*, 170, 195–196, 180; Calkins, "New Consumption Engineer," 127; Calkins, *Business the Civilizer*, 294–295.

18. Frederick, "Whither Production?," in Frederick, *Philosophy of Production*, 200, 202, 217, "Homo Americanus," in Frederick, *Philosophy of Production*, 242; "Humanism," in Frederick, *Philosophy of Production*, 249, 258–259.

19. Edward S. Martin, "Shall Business Run the World?," *Harper's* 150 (February 1925), 378–384.

## 17. The American Century and the Magic Kingdom

1. On corporatism between the wars, see Charles S. Maier, *Recasting Bourgeois Europe: Stabilization in France, Germany, and Italy in the Decade after World War I* (Princeton, NJ, 2016 [1975]), esp. 545–578; Philippe Schmitter and Gerhard Lehmbruch, eds., *Trends Toward Corporatist Intermediation* (Beverly Hills, CA, 1982); Wyn Grant, ed., *The Political Economy of Corporatism* (New York, 1983). On the interest in myth among intellectuals in the 1930s, see Susman, *Culture as History*; examples include Kenneth Burke, "Revolutionary Symbolism in America" (1935), in *The Strenuous Decade: A Social and Intellectual Record of the 1930s*, ed. Daniel Aaron and Robert Bendiner (Garden City, NY, 1970), 311–320; Reinhold Niebuhr, *Moral Man and Immoral Society* (New York, 1932); Harold Lasswell, *Psychopathology and Politics* (Chicago, 1930), 313–317; Ruth Benedict, *Patterns of Culture* (New York, 1934).

2. Thurman Arnold, *The Folklore of Capitalism* (New Haven, CT, 1937), 5.

3. Arnold, *The Folklore of Capitalism,* 3, 232, 50, 121, 47; Thurman Arnold, *The Symbols of Government* (New York, 1962 [1935]), 131, 229.

4. Arnold, *Symbols of Government,* 105–127.

5. Arnold, *Symbols of Government,* 232–233.

6. Lasch, *True and Only Heaven,* 429–439, while duly noting Arnold's merits, also overlooks his discussion of symbols and mythology. A generation earlier, Hofstadter had dismissed Arnold in similar terms. Disparaging Arnold's "need to pose as hard-boiled," Hofstadter contended that he "did not . . . successfully pose, much less answer, the very real and important questions that were suggested by his books concerning the relations between morals and politics, or between reason and politics": Hofstadter, *Age of Reform,* 324 n. 7.

7. On Luce, Alan Brinkley, *The Publisher: Henry Luce and His American Century* (New York, 2010), esp. 108–281, is indispensable. The closest examination of *Fortune* and the rest of Henry Luce's publishing empire is Michael Augspurger, *An Economy of Abundant Beauty: Fortune Magazine and Depression America* (Ithaca, NY, 2004), where Dwight Macdonald is cited on 76. See also Kevin Reilly, "Dilettantes at the Gate: *Fortune* Magazine and the Cultural Politics of Business Journalism in the 1930s," *Business and Economic History* 28 (Winter 1999), 213–222.

8. Augspurger, *Economy of Abundant Beauty,* 21–118; see also Robert Vanderlan, *Intellectuals, Inc.: Politics, Art, and Ideas in Henry Luce's Media Empire* (Philadelphia, 2010), esp. 91–208, on the role that Luce's magazines played in the development of left and liberal intellectuals. On the Business Advisory Council and the Council for Economic Development, see Robert M. Collins, *The Business Response to Keynes, 1929–1964* (New York, 1981), 56–62, 81–87, 129–152.

9. Luce's prospectus is quoted in Augspurger, *Economy of Abundant Beauty,* 6; Young & Rubicam advertisement, *Fortune* 1 (February 1930), 105. On the new "hegemonic bloc," see Thomas Ferguson, "Industrial Conflict and the Coming of the New Deal: The Triumph of Multinational Liberalism in America," in Fraser and Gerstle, *Rise and Fall of the New Deal Order,* 3–31.

10. Henry Luce, "The American Century," *Life* 10 (February 17, 1941), 65.

11. Luce, "The American Century."

12. Luce, "The American Century," 65, 64.

13. Luce, "The American Century," 65, 63.

14. Rorty, *Our Master's Voice,* 30; the NBC publication is cited in David Jenemann, *Adorno in America* (Minneapolis, MN, 2007), 87, 86; see in general 47–104.

15. CBS broadcast cited in Jenemann, *Adorno in America,* 77–78; Adorno cited in Jenemann, *Adorno in America,* 102, 65, 78. Jenemann remarks that the CBS broadcast "makes a strong case not for the extremism of Adorno's critique but for its restraint" (78).

16. Steven Watts: *The Magic Kingdom: Walt Disney and the American Way of Life* (Columbia, MO, 2001 [1997]), 83–119, quotes on 107, 85.

17. Disney quoted in Watts, *Magic Kingdom,* 59, 108.

18. Gilbert Seldes, "Motion Pictures," *Scribner's* 103 (March 1, 1938), 65; Gilbert Seldes, *The Movies Come from America* (New York, 1937), 47.

19. Walter Benjamin, "Experience and Poverty" (1933), in *Walter Benjamin: Selected Writings,* vol. 2, *1927–1934,* ed. Michael Jennings et al., trans. Rodney Livingstone (Cambridge, MA, 1999), 735; "Mickey Mouse" (1931), unpublished ms., in Michael Jennings et al., *Walter Benjamin,* 545; Walter Benjamin, "The Work of Art in the Age of Its Reproducibility" (1936), in *Walter Benjamin: Selected Writings,* vol. 3, *1935–1938,* ed. Michael Jennings and Howard Eiland, trans. Edmund Jephcott et al. (Cambridge, MA, 2002), 118, 117.

20. Sergei Eisenstein, *Eisenstein on Disney,* ed. Jay Leyda (London, 1988), 3. On Eisenstein's stay in Hollywood and his friendship with Disney, see Leyda's introduction.

21. Eisenstein, *Eisenstein on Disney,* 2–3, 4, 49, 42.

22. My discussion of *Fantasia* in this and the next two paragraphs rests on the film itself and on Watts, *Magic Kingdom,* 83–89, 113–119, and John Culhane, *Walt Disney's Fantasia* (New York, 1983), the definitive account of the film's animation, sound, and narration.

23. Chris Hedges, *Empire of Illusion: The End of Literacy and the Triumph of Spectacle* (New York, 2009).

## 18. A New Order and Creed

1. Sanford M. Jacoby, *Employing Bureaucracy: Managers, Unions, and the Transformation of Work in the 20th Century* (Mahwah, NJ, 2004 [1985]), 124–204, covers the history of this period of managerial expansion, crisis, and consolidation.

2. James Burnham, *The Managerial Revolution: What Is Happening in the World* (New York, 1941); Elton Mayo, *The Human Problems of an Industrial Civilization* (New York, 1933).

3. Steve Fraser, "The 'Labor Question,'" in Fraser and Gerstle, *Rise and Fall of the New Deal Order,* 57–62, quotes on 59, 61; Steve Fraser, *Labor Will Rule: Sidney Hillman and the Rise of American Labor* (New York, 1991); Christopher L. Tomlins, *The State and the Unions: Labor Relations, Law, and the Organized Labor Movement in America, 1880–1960* (New York, 1985), 99–102.

4. Mary Parker Follett, "The Illusion of Final Authority," paper given to the Taylor Society, New York, December 10, 1926, in *Freedom and Co-Ordination: Lectures in Business Organization* (London, 1949), 8. On Follett's life and work, see Pauline Graham, "Mary Parker Follett: A Pioneering Life," in *Mary Parker Follett, Prophet of Management: A Celebration of Writings from the 1920s,* ed. Pauline Graham (Boston, 1995), 11–16. Despite her relative obscurity, there has been an enduring interest in her work for years: see, for instance, Henry S. Kariel, "The New Order of Mary Parker Follett," *Western Political Quarterly* 8 (September 1955), 425–440; Haber, *Efficiency and Uplift,*

126–128; Jean B. Quandt, *From the Small Town to the Great Community: The Social Thought of Progressive Intellectuals* (New Brunswick, NJ, 1970), 36–50; William Graebner, *The Engineering of Consent: Democracy and Authority in Twentieth-Century America* (Madison, WI, 1987), 71–73; and James Hoopes, *Community Denied: The Wrong Turn of Pragmatic Liberalism* (Ithaca, NY, 1998), 145–163.

5. Mary Parker Follett, *Creative Experience* (New York, 1924), 87, 132; Mary Parker Follett, "How Must Business Management Develop in Order to Become a Profession?," paper given to the New York Bureau of Personnel Administration, November 5, 1925, in Mary Parker Follett, *Dynamic Administration: The Collected Papers of Mary Parker Follett* (New York, 1941), 135, 137, 140–141.

6. Follett, *Creative Experience*, 54–55, 63, 91–116, 132, 203; Mary Parker Follett, "The Psychology of Control," paper given to Boston's Bureau of Personnel Administration, March 1927, in *Dynamic Administration*, 183–209. On Gestalt psychology, see Katherine Pandora, *Rebels within the Ranks: Psychologists' Critique of Scientific Authority and Democratic Realities in New Deal America* (Cambridge and New York, 1997), 36–40. Follett's ideas resembled the "social plant politics" theorized in Weimar Germany by Fritz Giese, whose *Philosophie der Arbeit* (1932) is described by Rabinbach as a "romantic philosophy of work": Rabinbach, *The Human Motor*, 282–284.

7. Mary Parker Follett, "Business as an Integrative Unity," in *Dynamic Administration*, 81, 88; Mary Parker Follett, "Leader and Expert," in *Dynamic Administration*, 247, 249.

8. Wallace Donham to Lawrence Lowell, cited in Robert M. Smith, *The American Business System and the Theory and Practice of Social Science* (New York, 1986 [1976]), 68; Alfred North Whitehead, *The Aims of Education and Other Essays* (New York, 1967 [1929]), 130, 132, 131.

9. Wallace Donham, "Business and Religion," *Harvard Business School Alumni Bulletin* 2 (May 1926), 122; Wallace Donham, "The Social Significance of Business," *Harvard Business Review* 5 (July 1927), 407, 417–418.

10. Elton Mayo, "The Great Stupidity," *Harper's* 151 (July 1925), 233; Elton Mayo, "Uncivilized Reason," *Harper's* 148 (March 1924), 527–535, and Elton Mayo, "Civilization: The Perilous Adventure," *Harper's* 149 (October 1924), 590–597; Mayo, *Human Problems of an Industrial Civilization*, 54, 100, 120, 185, 178; Fritz Roethlisberger, *Management and Morale* (Cambridge, MA, 1955 [1941]), 33, 52, 66; Elton Mayo, *The Political Problems of an Industrial Civilization* (Cambridge, MA, 1947), 23. The only biography of Mayo is the relatively uncritical R. C. S. Trahair, *The Humanist Temper: The Life and Work of Elton Mayo* (New Brunswick, NJ, 1984); see a much more damning portrayal in Duff McDonald, *The Golden Passport: Harvard Business School, the Moral Failure of the MBA Elite, and the Limits of Capitalism* (New York, 2017), 76–90. Critiques of Mayo include Daniel Bell, "Work and Its Discontents" (1956), in *The End of Ideology: On the Exhaustion of Political Ideas in the Fifties* (New York, 1962

[1960]), 245–249, and C. L. R. James, *American Civilization* (Cambridge, MA, 1993 [1950]), 181–184.

11. Drucker discusses his early life and career in *Adventures of a Bystander* (New Brunswick, NJ, 1994 [1978]), 9–82, 123–135, 158–186, 223–243. Secondary studies of Drucker include Berthold Freyberg, "The Genesis of Drucker's Thought," in *Peter Drucker: Contributions to Business Enterprise*, ed. Tony H. Bonaparte and John E. Flaherty (New York, 1970), 17–22; Steven Waring, *Taylorism Transformed: Scientific Management Theory since 1945* (Chapel Hill, NC, 1991), 78–103; Steven Waring, "Peter Drucker, MBO, and the Corporatist Critique of Scientific Management," in *A Mental Revolution: Scientific Management since Taylor,* ed. Daniel Nelson (Columbus, OH, 1992), 205–236; and Jack Beatty, *The World According to Peter Drucker* (New York, 1998).

12. Drucker, *Friedrich Julius Stahl: Konservative Staatslehre und Geschichtliche Entwicklung* (Tübingen, Germany, 1933); on Austrian corporatism, see Alfred Diamant, *Austrian Catholics and the First Republic: Democracy, Capitalism, and the Social Order, 1918–1934* (Princeton, NJ, 1960), esp. 99–207.

13. Adolf Berle and Gardiner Means, *The Modern Corporation and Private Property* (New York, 1932), esp. 345–357, quote on 356; John Maynard Keynes, *The General Theory of Employment, Interest, and Money* (New York, 1964 [1936]), 345; Burnham, *The Managerial Revolution;* James Burnham, *The Machiavellians: Defenders of Freedom* (New York, 1943), 88.

14. Robert Griffith, "The Selling of America: The Advertising Council and American Politics, 1942–1960," *Business History Review* 57 (Autumn 1983), 388–412; William Bird, *Better Living: Advertising, Media, and the New Vocabulary of Business Leadership, 1935–1955* (Evanston, IL, 1999), 10–143; Marchand, *Creating the Corporate Soul,* 202–248; Dawn Spring, *Advertising in the Age of Persuasion: Building Brand America, 1941–1961* (New York, 2011), 9–45; Jacoby, *Employing Bureaucracy,* 201.

15. Peter Drucker, *The End of Economic Man* (New York, 1939), 22, 44, 85–111; Peter Drucker, *The Future of Industrial Man* (New York, 1942), 99, 148–150. C. L. R. James, *American Civilization* (Cambridge, MA, 1993), 185–189, perceptively links Drucker to Robert Maynard Hutchins, Mortimer Adler, and other non-Catholic advocates of "Catholic humanism" as a ballast for bourgeois civilization. The religiosity of Drucker's early work belies his claim that he "never had much use for theology": Drucker, *Adventures of a Bystander,* ix.

16. Drucker, *Concept of the Corporation* (New York, 1946), 198, 6–7. Drucker recounts his relationship with GM in *Adventures of a Bystander,* 256–293, recalling that GM executives thought his book overly critical, even hostile (288). Alfred P. Sloan does not mention Drucker's report in *My Years with General Motors* (Garden City, NY, 1964). Marchand discusses the public relations image of the corporation as a "good neighbor" in *Creating the Corporate Soul,* 357–363.

## 19. Beauty as the New Business Tool

1. Rorty, *Our Master's Voice*, 210.

2. Lears, *Fables of Abundance*, 235–344, and Bogart, *Artists, Advertising, and the Borders of Art*, 125–302, nicely complement each other in chronicling the advertising profession between the wars. John B. Watson is quoted in Stephen Fox, *The Mirror Makers: A History of American Advertising and Its Creators* (New York, 1984), 86.

3. Rorty, *Our Master's Voice*, 333; James Wallen, "Emotion and Style in Copy," in *Masters of Advertising Copy*, ed. J. George Frederick (New York, 1925), 110–111; Merle Thorpe, quoted in Patricia A. Johnston, *Real Fantasies: Edward Steichen's Advertising Photography* (Berkeley, 2000), 34; William Allen White quoted in Fox, *The Mirror Makers*, 101; Franklin Roosevelt, "You Cannot Robotize Advertising," *Printer's Ink* 155 (July 18, 1931), 44; Edmund Wilson, "An Appeal to Progressives," *New Republic* 65 (January 14, 1931), 236.

4. Clement Greenberg, "Avant-Garde and Kitsch" (1939), in *Art and Culture: Critical Essays* (Boston, 1961), 10, 9, 8; Sherwood Anderson, *Poor White* (New York, 1920), 63–64; Rockwell Kent quoted in Bogart, *Artists, Advertising, and the Borders of Art*, 254; Rorty, *Our Master's Voice*, 19.

5. Art Directors' Club catalog quoted in Bogart, *Artists, Advertising, and the Borders of Art*, 128; on the significance of the 1925 Paris Exhibition for American advertisers and industrial designers, see Jeffrey Meikle, *Twentieth Century Limited: Industrial Design in America, 1925–1939* (Philadelphia, 2001 [1979]), 21–27.

6. Bogart, *Artists, Advertising, and the Borders of Art*, 257–273; Calkins, "Beauty the New Business Tool," 150.

7. Calkins, "The New Consumption Engineer," 127; on Paepcke and the Container Corporation, see James Sloan Allen, *The Romance of Commerce and Culture: Capitalism, Modernism, and the Chicago-Aspen Crusade for Cultural Reform* (Chicago, 1983); Paepcke quoted in Neil Harris, *Art, Design, and the Modern Corporation* (Washington, DC, 1985), 32; Frank Caspers, "Patrons at a Profit—Business Discovers Art as a Selling Force," *Art Digest* 17 (May 1943), 5.

8. *Printers' Ink* article quoted in Marchand, *Advertising the American Dream*, 143; Christine Frederick, *Selling Mrs. Consumer* (New York, 1929), 361; Lears, *Fables of Abundance*, 299–344.

9. Earnest Elmo Calkins, foreword to Frank H. Young, *Modern Advertising Art* (New York, 1930), 11, 9.

10. Bogart, *Artists, Advertising, and the Borders of Art*, 136; Matthew Josephson, "The Great American Billposter," *Broom* 2 (June 1922), 310; Richard Surrey, "Copy Writers with the Poet's Cast of Mind," *Printers' Ink* 131 (April 30, 1925), 133–139; Rorty, *Our Master's Voice*, 208, 203, 60, 201.

11. Marchand, *Advertising the American Dream*, 265; Lears, *Fables of Abundance*.

12. Wallen, "Emotion and Style," 93, 99; Glen Buck, *This American Ascendancy* (Chicago, 1927), 59; see also Glen Buck, "This American Ascendancy," *Nation's Business* 15 (March 1927), 15–17; Rene Clark quoted in Rorty, *Our Master's Voice,* 211.

13. Lejaren Hiller, "Illustrating Magazine Articles and Advertising by the Use of the Camera," *Commercial Photographer* 3 (October 1927), 18; "Hats—and Photographs That Sell Them," *Commercial Photographer* 1 (November 1925), 43. W. Livingston Larned, "Tricky Effects Obtained with Solid Black and White, *Printer's Ink* 130 (January 8, 1925), 125; W. Livingston Larned, "Magical Effects with Pen and Ink," *Printer's Ink* 130 (March 26, 1925), 34, 35; W. Livingston Larned, "When the Skirts of Romance Brush," *Printers' Ink* 139 (June 6, 1927), 152.

14. Marchand, *Advertising the American Dream,* 276–284; the Duco ad is on 278, figure 8.45.

15. Paul H. Nystrom, *Economics of Fashion* (New York, 1928), 68–69. On Nystrom, see Stuart Ewen, *Captains of Consciousness: Advertising and the Social Roots of the Consumer Culture* (New York, 2001 [1976]), 86; Lasch, *Culture of Narcissism,* 73–74; Lears, *Fables of Abundance,* 232.

16. Nystrom, *Economics of Fashion,* 68, 28.

17. Calkins, "The New Consumption Engineer," 127, 122; see also Ernest Elmo Calkins, "Advertising's Ingratiating Smile," *Scribner's* 73 (March 1923), 316–322; Ernest Elmo Calkins, "Advertising as an Art," *Saturday Review* 2 (October 10, 1925), 193; Ernest Elmo Calkins, "Business Has Wings," *Atlantic Monthly* (March 1927), 306–316.

18. Calkins, "Beauty the New Business Tool," 151; Calkins, "The New Consumption Engineer," 125; Ernest Elmo Calkins, *And Hearing Not: Annals of an Adman* (New York, 1946), 239.

19. Rorty, *Our Master's Voice,* 346; Stuart Chase, "The Tragedy of Waste: III. The Wastes of Advertising," *New Republic* 43 (August 19, 1923), 342; Stuart Chase and Frederick J. Schlick, *Your Money's Worth: A Study in the Waste of the Consumer's Dollar* (New York, 1927), 2–3; Theodore MacManus, "The Nadir of Nothingness," *Atlantic Monthly* (May 1928), 594–608; H. A. Batten, "Advertising Man Looks at Advertising," *Atlantic Monthly* 150 (July 1932), 53.

20. On the movement to regulate advertising in the 1930s, see Inger L. Stole, *Advertising on Trial: Consumer Activism and Corporate Public Relations in the 1930s* (Urbana, IL, 2006). Marchand analyzes the advertising of the decade in *Advertising the American Dream,* 285–334, quote on 300.

21. Meikle, *Twentieth Century Limited,* remains the best history of industrial design in America. Arthur J. Pulos, *American Design Ethic: A History of Industrial Design to 1940* (Cambridge, MA, 1986), is a less critical and more celebratory account of the movement. See also Orvell, *The Real Thing,* 180–197, who chronicles what he calls the "fetishism of the machine" among industrial designers (182). Calkins, "Beauty the New Business Tool," 156; Calkins, "The New Consumption Engineer," 126, 128–129.

22. Thomas L. Masson, "Of Such Stuff Are Dreams—and Business—Made," *Printers' Ink* 156 (July 16, 1931), 76; Norman Bel Geddes, *Horizons* (New York, 1972 [1932]), 277.

23. John Cotton Dana, *The Industrialist as Artist* (Woodstock, VT, 1927), 5–6; see also John Cotton Dana, "The Cash Value of Art in Industry," *Forbes* 22 (August 1, 1928), 16–18, 32; Richard F. Bach, "Machanalia," *American Magazine of Art* 22 (February 1931), 102.

24. Paul T. Frankl, *Form and Re-form: A Practical Handbook of Modern Interiors* (New York, 1930), 5; Christopher Long, *Paul T. Frankl and Modern American Design* (New Haven, CT, 2007), esp. 81–114, is a fine discussion not only of Frankl but also of the larger industrial design movement. Surrey, "Copy Writers with the Poet's Cast of Mind," 135; Robert Updegraff, *The New American Tempo* (New York, 1930), 15, 36–37.

25. Meikle, *Twentieth Century Limited,* quote on 22–23; on industrial design in the business press, see Meikle's summary on 235. "Home Furnishings=Modern Art," *Women's Wear Daily* (December 22, 1928), 17.

26. Meikle, *Twentieth Century Limited,* 48–187; Richard Guy Wilson, Dianne H. Pilgrim, and Dickran Tashjian, *Machine Age in America,* 65–90.

27. Sheldon Cheney, *The New World Architecture* (New York, 1930), 76, 172; Sheldon Cheney and Martha Cheney, *Art and the Machine: An Account of Industrial Design in 20th-Century America* (New York, 1936); Chase, *Men and Machines* (New York, 1929), 246; Margaret Bourke-White quoted in Angela Schonberger, *Raymond Loewy: Pioneer of Industrial Design* (New York, 1990), 64; Lewis Mumford, *Technics and Civilization* (Chicago, 2010 [1934]), 324; Alfred H. Barr, Jr., "Foreword," in *Machine Art* (New York, 1934), n.p.

28. Le Corbusier, *Towards a New Architecture,* trans. Frederick Etchells (New York, 1927 [1923]), 15, 271, 13, 14, 18, 6, 17, 25–31. I am indebted to Graham Ward's theological reading of Le Corbusier in *Cities of God* (London, 2000), 40–42. The modernist city described in Le Corbusier's work is "a secular dream," Ward writes, "that will reach its apotheosis in cyberspace and its electronic communities" (42).

29. Bel Geddes, *Horizons,* 5, 282, 285.

30. Walter Dorwin Teague, *Design This Day: The Technique of Order in the Machine Age* (New York, 1940), 37, 79, 5; Cheney and Cheney, *Art and the Machine,* viii, 92, 283.

31. Herbert Read, *Art and Industry: The Principles of Industrial Design* (London, 1935); Frankl, *Form and Re-Form,* 163.

32. Cheney and Cheney, *Art and the Machine,* xi, 299, 95, 217, 79, 224.

33. On Teague's life and career, see Meikle, *Twentieth Century Limited,* 43–48.

34. Teague, *Design This Day,* 32, 18, 27, 52–53, 7, 236, 242, 234.

35. Teague, *Design This Day,* 42, 244, 15, 63.

36. Nye, *American Technological Sublime,* 223. Accounts of the New York World's Fair include Nye, *American Technological Sublime,* 199–224; Meikle, *Twentieth Century Limited,* 189–210; Helen A. Harrison, ed., *Dawn of a New Day: The New York World's Fair, 1939/40* (New York, 1980); Marchand, *Creating the Corporate Soul,* 291–311.

37. Teague, "Industrial Art and Its Future" (1936), cited in Joseph P. Cusker, "The World of Tomorrow: Science, Culture, and Community at the New York World's Fair," in Harrison, *Dawn of a New Day,* 12; Grover Whalen quoted in Peter Conrad, *The Art*

*of the City: Views and Versions of New York* (New York, 1984), 262; Frank Monaghan and official guidebook quoted in *Official Guidebook of the New York World's Fair, 1939* (New York, 1939), 144, 39.

38. Quotes from Nye, *American Technological Sublime*, 214, 216

39. Quotes from Marchand, *Creating the Corporate Soul*, 301.

40. Quotes from Marchand, *Creating the Corporate Soul*, 303 (see entire discussion on 301–311), and Nye, *American Technological Sublime*, 218.

41. Nye, *American Technological Sublime*, 221.

42. Bogart, *Artists, Advertising, and the Borders of Art*, 290–302; Meikle, *Twentieth Century Limited*, 208–209.

## Part Six: Predicaments of Human Divinity

1. John Dewey, *The Public and Its Problems* (Athens, OH, 1954 [1927]), 141.

2. John Dewey, *Individualism Old and New* (New York, 1930), 21, 24, 5; Dewey, *A Common Faith,* 14; John Dewey, *Art as Experience* (New York, 2005 [1934]), 195.

3. Chesterton, *What I Saw in America,* 107–108, 11.

4. Chesterton, *What I Saw in America,* 34, 40, 44, 46.

5. G. K. Chesterton, *The Outline of Sanity* (1926), in *The Collected Works of G. K. Chesterton* (San Francisco, 1987), 5:169, 88, 188; G. K. Chesterton, *Utopia of Usurers* (1917), in *Collected Works of G. K. Chesterton,* 414.

6. Detlev Peukert, *The Weimar Republic: The Crisis of Classical Modernity* (New York, 1992 [1987]), 178–190, provides a nuanced survey of what in Germany was termed *Kulturkritik,* while Philippe Roger, *The American Enemy: The History of French Anti-Americanism,* trans. Sharon Bowman (Chicago, 2005 [2002]), esp. 373–410, covers similar sentiments in France. Frederick Lewis Allen reported that American intellectuals "lapped up the criticism of American culture offered by foreign lecturers imported in record-breaking numbers": *Only Yesterday: An Informal History of the 1920s* (New York, 1997 [1931]), 179.

7. D. H. Lawrence, *The Plumed Serpent* (Hertfordshire, England, 1995 [1926]), 37; D. H. Lawrence, *Studies in Classic American Literature* (New York, 1990 [1923]), 21; Aldous Huxley, *Brave New World* (New York, 2006 [1932]), 52, 34, 85.

8. James Rorty, *Where Life Is Better: An Unsentimental American Journey* (New York, 1936), 57.

## 20. The Mysticism of Numbers

1. William E. Akin, *Technocracy and the American Dream: The Technocrat Movement, 1900–1941* (Berkeley, 1977), is the most comprehensive study of the movement, but see also Segal, *Technological Utopianism,* 121–123, 141–145, and Andrew Ross, *Strange Weather: Culture, Science, and Technology in the Age of Limits* (New York, 1991), 117–122.

2. Veblen, *Absentee Ownership,* 281, 205–206, 180; Thorstein Veblen, *The Engineers and the Price System* (New York, 1921), 134–169.

3. Veblen, *Engineers and the Price System,* 98, 135, 151.

4. "Technocracy—Boom, Blight, or Bunk?," *Literary Digest* 114 (December 31, 1932), 5. Scott popularized the movement in Howard Scott, *Introduction to Technocracy* (New York, 1933), and in Howard Scott, "Technology Smashes the Price System: An Inquiry into the Nature of Our Present Crisis," *Harper's* 166 (January 1933), 129–142. The profile of Scott and his colleagues, "Technocrat," *Time* 20 (December 26, 1932), 22–24, is informative and slyly unflattering. Critiques include George Soule, "Technocracy: Good Medicine or Bedtime Story?," *New Republic* 73 (December 1932), 178–180; Bruce Bliven, "Technocracy and Communism," *New Republic* 73 (February 1933), 315–317; Henry Hazlitt, "Scrambled Eggs: An Examination of Technocracy," *Nation* 136 (February 1, 1933), 112–115; and Archibald MacLeish, "Technocracy," *Saturday Review* 9 (January 14, 1933), 373–374.

5. Howard Scott, *Introduction to Technocracy,* 15; "Technocrat," 22, 23; on Scott's and Loeb's backgrounds, see Akin, *Technocracy and the American Dream,* 28–29 and 118–119, respectively, and Howard Segal's introduction to Harold Loeb, *Life in a Technocracy: What It Might Be Like* (Syracuse, NY, 1996 [1933]), ix–xxxviii.

6. Akin, *Technocracy and the American Dream,* 97–130. One contemporary observer characterized Technocracy as "a product of petit-bourgeois discontent": Mauritz Hallgren, *Seeds of Revolt* (New York, 1933), 263.

7. Harold Loeb, *The Way It Was* (New York, 1959), 43–44.

8. Loeb, *Life in a Technocracy,* 178, 34, 105, 25, 27, 139–140.

9. Loeb, *Life in a Technocracy,* 108, 163, 166–167.

## 21. Secular Prayers and Impieties

1. Hugh Ferris, *The Metropolis of Tomorrow* (New York, 1929), 16, 38, 18. On these dissident designers, see Meikle, *Twentieth Century Limited,* 32–34.

2. Ferris, *Metropolis of Tomorrow,* 36, 61, 142–143.

3. On Vassos, see Meikle, *Twentieth Century Limited,* 40–41; P. K. Thomajan, foreword to John Vassos, *Contempo, Phobia, and Other Graphic Interpretations* (New York, 1976 [1929, 1931]), vii–xi; Danielle Schwartz, "Modernism for the Masses: The Industrial Design of John Vassos," *Archives of American Art Journal* 46 (2006), 4–23. Schwartz notes that John and Ruth collaborated on writing.

4. Vassos, *Contempo, Phobia, and Other Graphic Interpretations,* n.p.; John Vassos quoted in Meikle, *Twentieth Century Limited,* 83; Schwartz, "Modernism for the Masses," 7–8.

5. John Vassos, *Humanities* (New York, 1935), 6, 5, 92; Vassos, *Contempo,* plates 7, 6, frontispiece.

6. John Vassos and Ruth Vassos, *Ultimo: An Imaginative Narration of Life under the Earth* (New York, 1930), n.p.

7. Vassos and Vassos, *Ultimo,* n.p.

8. Susman, *Culture as History,* 80, 207; Denning, *Cultural Front,* 96–115. Susman himself was aware that the Popular Front could be interpreted as a substitute for religion, and he hedged on the point. Warning that it is "all too facile to describe the commitment to the Left as a religious surrogate," he nonetheless conceded that it was also "not far-fetched to see for some in the movement to the political Left quasi-religious motives" (Susman, *Culture as History,* 174, 179).

9. C. L. R. James, *American Civilization* (Oxford, 1993 [1950]), 144, 146, 149–165, 154–156.

10. Kenneth Burke, "Revolutionary Symbolism in America" (1935), in *The Strenuous Decade: A Social and Intellectual Record of the 1930s,* ed. Daniel Aaron and Robert Bendiner (Garden City, NY, 1970), 312, 315–316, 317.

11. Kenneth Burke, *Attitudes toward History* (New York, 1937), 321–327, 179, 93–94; Kenneth Burke, *Permanence and Change: An Anatomy of Purpose* (New York, 1935), 80–88.

12. John Dewey, "A Humanist Manifesto," *New Humanist* 6 (May–June 1933), 1–5; Dewey, *Individualism Old and New,* 120, 131; Dewey, *A Common Faith,* 31. See also John Dewey, *Liberalism and Social Action* (New York, 1935), where Dewey assigned liberalism the new role of creating "a spiritual authority that would nurture and direct the inner as well as the outer life of individuals" (30–31). On Dewey's religiosity, see Robert Westbrook, *John Dewey and American Democracy* (Ithaca, NY, 1991), 418–428, and Alan Ryan, *John Dewey and the High Tide of American Liberalism* (New York, 1995), 243–283.

13. Dewey, *Individualism Old and New,* 119, 134; John Dewey, *The Public and Its Problems* (Athens, OH, 1988 [1927]), 49–50. While Westbrook rightly maintains that religion was, to Dewey, "a more expansive aesthetic imagination" and that democracy was the "inclusive ideal" of *A Common Faith,* he sees no connection to "corporateness" and overlooks the persistence of professional-managerial hegemony; Westbrook, *John Dewey and American Democracy,* 424, 428.

Because Livingston equates the death of proprietary capitalism with the withering of the rage to accumulate, Dewey's oracular prophecy about "some kind of socialism" becomes, in his words, a choice between "a pecuniary measure of subjectivity and a 'social self.'" Yet Dewey's suggestion that "socialism" could be "capitalistic" contravenes Livingston's contention that the "social self" is necessarily non-pecuniary and that its presence heralds the extinction of corporate capitalism. Indeed, dispossession from the means of material and cultural production goes a long way toward explaining why, as Livingston himself observes, pragmatists and other prophets of post-pecuniary subjectivity "didn't notice what now seems obvious, that a 'social self' could be *more* susceptible than its predecessors to external manipulation." Livingston, *Pragmatism, Feminism, and Democracy,* 171–182.

14. Rorty's son Richard recalled the Trotskyite milieu in "Trotsky and the Wild Orchids" (1993), in *Philosophy and Social Hope* (New York, 1999), 3–22, quote on 6;

Daniel Pope, "His Master's Voice: James Rorty and the Critique of Advertising," *Maryland Historian* 19 (Spring 1988), 5–15, quote on 8. Little has been written about James Rorty. See Richard H. Pells, *Radical Visions and American Dreams: Culture and Social Thought in the Depression Years* (New York, 1973), 96–98 passim; Alan Wald, *The New York Intellectuals: The Rise and Decline of the Anti-Stalinist Left from the 1930s to the 1980s* (Chapel Hill, NJ, 1987), 54–56, 271–273; and Denning, *The Cultural Front*, 98, 431, who includes Rorty in the pantheon of "Western Marxism."

15. James Rorty, *Where Life Is Better: An Unsentimental Journey* (New York, 1936), 269; Rorty, *Our Master's Voice*, 177, 204, 208, 210.

16. Rorty, *Our Master's Voice*, 187, 282, 333, 256, 16; Rorty, *Where Life Is Better*, 108.

17. Rorty, *Where Life Is Better*, 30, 28, 50, 57.

18. Rorty, *Where Life Is Better*, 105–106, 177.

19. Rorty, *Where Life Is Better*, 21–22. Rorty was not, however, a supporter of Senator Joseph McCarthy; see James Rorty and Moshe Decter, *McCarthy and the Communists* (Boston, 1954), which excoriates its subject.

20. Max Horkheimer, *Eclipse of Reason* (New York, 1947), 37, 50; Theodor Adorno, *Minima Moralia: Reflections on Damaged Life* (New York, 2005 [1951]), 72.

21. Horkheimer, *Eclipse of Reason*, 125; on Horkheimer's and Adorno's time in Hollywood, see Jenemann, *Adorno in America*, 105–148.

22. Max Horkheimer and Theodor Adorno, *Dialectic of Enlightenment* (New York, 1997 [1944]), 11, xiii, 12; Horkheimer, *Eclipse of Reason*, 110.

23. Adorno, quoted in Jenemann, *Adorno in America*, 102, 64.

24. Horkheimer and Adorno, *Dialectic of Enlightenment*, 120–167.

25. Horkheimer and Adorno, *Dialectic of Enlightenment*, 170; Horkheimer, *Eclipse of Reason*, 45–48.

26. Theodor Adorno, "The Stars Down to Earth," in *The Stars Down to Earth and Other Essays on the Irrational in Culture* (New York, 2002 [1994]), 56, 51, 81, 57; Theodor Adorno, "Theses on Occultism," in *Stars Down to Earth*, 174.

27. Adorno, "The Stars Down to Earth," 157–158, 21, 57; "Theses on Occultism," in *Stars Down to Earth*, 179.

28. Horkheimer, *Eclipse of Reason*, 132; Adorno, *Minima Moralia*, 186–187.

29. Horkheimer, *Eclipse of Reason*, 24; Adorno, *Minima Moralia*, 15, 154, 247.

30. Randolph Bourne, "Twilight of Idols," in *The Radical Will: Selected Writings 1911–1918*, ed. Olaf Hansen (Berkeley, CA, 1977), 347; Horkheimer and Adorno, *Dialectic of Enlightenment*, 23.

31. Joe Woodward, *Alive Inside the Wreck: A Life of Nathanael West* (New York, 2010), is an invaluable introduction. Two indispensable literary studies of West are Rita Bernard, *The Great Depression and the Culture of Abundance: Kenneth Fearing, Nathanael West, and Mass Culture in the 1930s* (New York, 1995), 135–212, and Jonathan Veitch, *American Superrealism: Nathanael West and the Politics of Representation in the 1930s* (Madison, WI, 1997). Nathanael West, *A Cool Million* (New York, 1961 [1934]), 13.

32. West, *A Cool Million,* 10, 127–128, 58, 142.

33. West, *A Cool Million,* 114–116.

34. Nathanael West, *Miss Lonelyhearts and The Day of the Locust* (New York, 1969 [1933, 1939]), 4, 6, 32, 5, 23, 22, 8.

35. West, *Miss Lonelyhearts and The Day of the Locust,* 118, 61, 129.

36. West, *Miss Lonelyhearts and The Day of the Locust,* 142, 35, 6, 131–132.

37. West, *Miss Lonelyhearts and The Day of the Locust,* 142, 118, 177–178, 184. In Bernard's view, "for West, mass culture is certainly a sham, but so is religion: both gospels are equally mendacious": Bernard, *The Great Depression,* 205.

38. West, *Miss Lonelyhearts and The Day of the Locust,* 56–58, 184.

39. Zieger, *The CIO,* 227.

40. Steve Fraser, "The Labor Question," in *The Rise and Fall of the New Deal Order,* ed. Steve Fraser and Gary Gerstle (Princeton, NJ, 1989), 67; Jefferson Cowie and Nick Salvatore, "The Long Exception: Rethinking the Place of the New Deal in American History," *International Labor and Working-Class History* 74 (Fall 2008), 3–32, quotes on 3, 6; Cohen, *Making a New Deal,* 314–321; see also Alan Brinkley, *The End of Reform: New Deal Liberalism in Recession and War* (New York, 1996), 48–85, 201–272. The demurral of the CIO arguably commenced what Fraser has called "the age of acquiescence."

## 22. Small Is Beautiful

1. Cowley, *Exile's Return,* 190, 94, 210, 14. On the fear and loathing of cities in American history, see Steven Conn, *Americans against the City: Anti-Urbanism in the Twentieth Century* (New York, 2014), which traces the phenomenon back to the eighteenth century.

2. The literature on New Deal agricultural policy stresses its top-down, technocratic character: see, for instance, Theodore Saloutos, *The American Farmer and the New Deal* (Ames, IA, 1982); but see also Jess Gilbert, *Planning Democracy: Agrarian Intellectuals and the Intended New Deal* (New Haven, CT, 2015), which highlights a more participatory strain among New Dealers. Stuart Chase, *The Economy of Abundance* (New York, 1934), 235, 245, 247.

3. On the popular theology of the Depression in the Delta, see Alison Collis Greene's remarkable *No Depression in Heaven: The Great Depression, The New Deal, and the Transformation of Religion in the Delta* (New York, 2016), quotes on 53, 61; see 60–65 on Delta premillennialism.

4. Thomas Hart Benton, *The Arts of Life in America: A Series of Murals by Thomas Benton* (Whitney Museum of American Art, 1932), 5. See also Grant Wood's manifesto, *Revolt Against the City* (Iowa City, IA, 1935).

5. Waldo Frank, *The Rediscovery of America* (New York, 1947 [1929]), 148; Mumford, *Technics and Civilization,* 53–54; Willa Cather, *Death Comes for the Archbishop*

(New York, 1990 [1927]), 233; Stuart Chase, *Mexico: A Story of Two Americas* (New York, 1931).

6. Richard B. Ransom, "Corporate and Private Persons," in *Who Owns America? A New Declaration of Independence,* ed. Herbert Agar and Allen Tate (Boston, 1936), 72. On the Southern Agrarians, see Daniel Singal, *The War Within: From Victorian to Modernist Thought in the South, 1919–1945* (Chapel Hill, NC, 1982), 198–264, and Paul Murphy, *The Rebuke of History: The Southern Agrarians and American Conservative Thought* (Chapel Hill, NC, 2001), esp. 11–91.

7. John C. Rowe, "Agriculture and the Property State," in Agar and Tate, *Who Owns America?,* 41; Andrew Lytle, "The Small Farm Secures the State," in Agar and Tate, *Who Owns America?,* 244; Dorothy Day, editorial, *Catholic Worker* 14 (May 1947), 1.

8. John Crowe Ransom, "Reconstructed but Unregenerate," in Twelve Southerners, *I'll Take My Stand: The South and the Agrarian Tradition* (Baton Rouge, 1977 [1930]), 1; Lytle, "The Small Farm," 247; Donald Davidson, "A Mirror for Artists," in Twelve Southerners, *I'll Take My Stand,* 40; Dorothy Day, "Reflections on Work," *Catholic Worker* 13 (November 1946), 4.

9. Tate, "Remarks on the Southern Religion," in Twelve Southerners, *I'll Take My Stand,* 175; John Crowe Ransom, *God without Thunder: An Unorthodox Defense of Orthodoxy* (New York, 1965 [1930]), 20, 116–117.

10. Donald Davidson, "*I'll Take My Stand:* A History" (1935), in *The Southern Agrarians and the New Deal: Essays after I'll Take My Stand,* ed. Emily Bingham and Thomas A. Underwood (Charlottesville, VA, 2001), 95; Tate, "Remarks on the Southern Religion," 169; Frank Lawrence Owsley, "The Irrepressible Conflict," in Twelve Southerners, *I'll Take My Stand,,* 76; Robert Penn Warren, "The Briar Patch," in Twelve Southerners, *I'll Take My Stand,* 246–264; James Agee, untitled "period piece" in *The Collected Poems of James Agee,* ed. Robert Fitzgerald (Boston, 1968), 146.

11. On the religious character of the STFU, see Greene, *No Depression in Heaven,* 177–182; Anthony Dunbar, *Against the Grain: Southern Radicals and Prophets, 1929–1959* (Charlottesville, VA, 1981), 48–110; Mark Fannion, *Labor's Promised Land: Radical Visions of Race, Gender, and Religion in the South* (Knoxville, TN, 2003), 71–129; Robin D. G. Kelley, *Hammer and Hoe: Alabama Communists during the Great Depression* (Chapel Hill, NC, 1990), 107–108, 114–116, 148–149 (on the hymns at black locals); and Erik Gellman and Jarod Roll, *The Gospel of the Working Class: Labor's Southern Prophets in New Deal America* (Urbana, IL, 2011), who quote Williams on 47, 72; on the People's Institute of Applied Religion, see 50–115.

12. Howard Kester and Evelyn Smith, "Ceremony of the Land" (1937), in *America between the Wars, 1919–1941: A Documentary History,* ed. David Wilkey (Malden, MA, 2012), 142, 145; Williams, quoted in Gellman and Roll, *Gospel of the Working Class,* 70.

13. On Pentecostal and Baptist beliefs, see Jarod Roll, *Spirit of Rebellion: Labor and Religion in the New Cotton South* (Urbana, IL, 2010), 69; Whitfield's epiphany is retold in Gellman and Roll, *Gospel of the Working Class,* 73–74; Don West, "I've Seen God"

(1932), in Don West, *No Lonesome Road: Selected Poems and Prose,* ed. Jeff Biggers and George Brosi (Urbana, IL, 2004), 115. On West, see Chris Green, "The Tight Rope of Democracy: Don West's *Clods of Southern Earth,*" in *Radicalism in the South since Reconstruction,* ed. Chris Green, Rachel Rubin, and James Smelthurst (New York, 2006), 99–127.

14. Virgil Michel, "The Liturgy, The Basis of Social Regeneration," *Orate Fratres* 9 (November 2, 1935), 542–544. On the Catholic Worker and the liturgical movement in the 1930s, see McCarraher, *Christian Critics,* 82–88.

15. On Father Charles Coughlin, see Alan Brinkley, *Voices of Protest: Huey Long, Father Coughlin, and the Great Depression* (New York, 1982), 82–168; on Father John Ryan and Philip Murray, see McCarraher, *Christian Critics,* 72–74.

16. McCarraher, *Christian Critics,* 84; Peter Maurin, "Outdoor Universities," *Catholic Worker* 4 (January 1937), 1, 7.

17. Dorothy Day, "The Catholic Worker and Labor," *Catholic Worker* 6 (January 1939), 1.

18. Peter Maurin, "Maurin's Program," *Catholic Worker* 1 (June–July 1933), 4; Dorothy Day, *The Long Loneliness* (New York, 1952), 220.

19. Day, *Long Loneliness,* 222; John Crowe Ransom called agrarianism a "phantasy" in "Art and the Human Economy," *Kenyon Review* 7 (Autumn 1945), 686.

20. James T. Fisher, *The Catholic Counterculture in America, 1933–1962* (Chapel Hill, NC, 1989), 121; McCarraher, *Christian Critics,* 87.

21. David Cushman Coyle, "The Fallacy of Mass Production," in Agar and Tate, *Who Owns America?,* 7.

22. On Father Divine and the Peace Mission, I have relied on Robert Weisbrot, *Father Divine and the Struggle for Racial Equality* (Urbana, IL, 1983), esp. 122–144; Jill Watts, *God, Harlem U.S.A.: The Father Divine Story* (Berkeley, 1992), esp. 104–107, quotes on 106, 126; R. Marie Griffith, "Body Salvation: New Thought, Father Divine, and the Feast of Material Pleasures," *Religion and American Culture* 11 (Summer 2001), 119–153; and Judith Weisenfeld, *New World A-Coming: Black Religion and Racial Identity during the Great Migration* (New York, 2016), 73–87. The journalist was Edwin T. Buehrer, "Harlem's God," *Christian Century* 52 (December 11, 1933), 1592. For a representative white reaction, see John Hoshor, *God in a Rolls Royce: The Rise of Father Divine Madman, Menace, or Messiah* (New York, 1936).

23. Griffith, "Body Salvation," is a lucid examination of Father Divine's theology and communal banquets. For a contemporary description of one of the feasts, see Naomi Mitchison, "Epiphany in Heaven," *New Statesman and Nation* 9 (June 1935), 961–962.

24. On the impact of Catholic radicalism on the New Left, see Maurice Isserman, *If I Had a Hammer: The Death of the Old Left and the Birth of the New Left* (New York, 1989), 145–146, and McCarraher, *Christian Critics,* 116–119.

25. Leo Marx, "Lewis Mumford: Prophet of Organicism," in *Lewis Mumford: Public Intellectual,* ed. Thomas Hughes and Agatha Hughes (New York, 1990), 166; Lewis Mumford, *Faith for Living* (New York, 1940), 296. Mumford's life and work have

generated a considerable literature. I have benefited from Hughes and Hughes, *Lewis Mumford;* Blake, *Beloved Community;* Donald Miller, *Lewis Mumford: A Life* (New York, 1989); and Shuxue Li, *Lewis Mumford: Critic of Culture and Civilization* (Bern, Switzerland, 2009). The sharpest critique of Mumford is in Livingston, *Pragmatism and Political Economy,* 225–255, who indicts him as the point man in a "romantic acquiescence," an elegy for bourgeois individualism.

26. Lewis Mumford, *Sketches from Life: The Autobiography of Lewis Mumford, The Early Years* (New York, 1982), 144; letter to Patrick Geddes, October 10, 1922, in *Lewis Mumford and Patrick Geddes: The Correspondence,* ed. Frank G. Novak, Jr. (London, 1995), 136; see also Lewis Mumford, "Patrick Geddes, Insurgent," *New Republic* 60 (October 30, 1929), 295–296. For an introduction to Geddes's ideas, see Volker M. Welter, *Biopolis: Patrick Geddes and the City of Life* (Cambridge, MA, 2002).

27. Lewis Mumford, *Herman Melville: A Study of His Life and Vision* (New York, 1962 [1929]), 129; Mumford, *Technics and Civilization,* 76.

28. Lewis Mumford, *The Culture of Cities* (New York, 1938), 301; Mumford, *Technics and Civilization,* 368, 370; Mumford, *Faith for Living,* 203, 196.

29. Mumford, *Faith for Living,* 200; Lewis Mumford, *Sticks and Stones: A Study of American Architecture and Civilization* (New York, 1955 [1924]), 217–218, 222; Lewis Mumford, "Regions—To Live In," *Survey* 7 (May 1, 1925), 151; see also Lewis Mumford, "Devastated Regions," *American Mercury* 3 (October 1924), 217–220. On Mumford's work with the Regional Planning Association of America, see Miller, *Lewis Mumford,* 191–211.

30. Mumford, *Technics and Civilization,* 149.

31. Lewis Mumford, *The Golden Day: A Study in American Literature and Culture* (New York, 1926), 22, 26; Mumford, *Culture of Cities,* 28; Lewis Mumford, *The Story of Utopias* (New York, 1922), 209. Marc Greif, *The Age of the Crisis of Man: Thought and Fiction in America, 1933–1973* (Princeton, NJ, 2015), 56, locates Mumford among "medievalist" critics of modern industrial civilization.

32. Mumford, *Technics and Civilization,* 40, 13, 12, 3.

33. Mumford, *The Golden Day,* 22; Mumford, *Technics and Civilization,* 31, 94.

34. Mumford, *Technics and Civilization,* 369, 53, 45, 58.

35. Mumford, *Technics and Civilization,* 102, 176, 400, 173, 51, 178; Mumford, *Culture of Cities,* 278.

36. Mumford, *Faith for Living,* 25; Mumford, *The Golden Day,* 36, 69; Mumford, *Sticks and Stones,* 83, 174.

37. Mumford, *The Golden Day,* 193, 268.

38. Mumford, *Technics and Civilization,* 103, 105, 189 (on Marx, see 187–191 passim); Mumford, *The Golden Day,* 136.

39. Mumford, *Technics and Civilization,* 324, 363.

40. Mumford, *Technics and Civilization,* 312, 299, 292.

41. Mumford, *Technics and Civilization,* 205, 286–287, 227.

42. Lewis Mumford, "What I Believe," *Forum* 84 (November 1930), 263–268; Mumford, *Technics and Civilization,* 385, 354.

43. Mumford, *Technics and Civilization,* 213, 419; Lewis Mumford letter to Roderick Seidenberg, August 6, 1956, cited in Eugene Halton, *Bereft of Reason: On the Decline of Social Thought and Prospects for Its Renewal* (Chicago, 1995), 288 n. 13; Mumford, *Faith for Living,* 219.

44. Mumford, *Faith for Living,* 311, 317.

45. Mumford, *Faith for Living,* 3, 300, 331.

## 23. Human Divinity

1. F. Scott Fitzgerald, *This Side of Paradise* (New York, 1920), 282.

2. Joseph Wood Krutch, *The Modern Temper: A Study and a Confession* (New York, 1956 [1929]), 130, 13.

3. James Agee and Walker Evans, *Let Us Now Praise Famous Men* (New York, 1988 [1941]), xlvi.

4. F. Scott Fitzgerald, *The Great Gatsby* (New York, 1995 [1925]), 6, 189; Fitzgerald, letter to Ludlow Fowler, August 1924, in *F. Scott Fitzgerald: A Life in Letters,* ed. Matthew J. Bruccoli (New York, 1994), 78.

5. Fitzgerald, *This Side of Paradise,* 53–54; F. Scott Fitzgerald, *The Crack-Up* (New York, 2009 [1945]), 80; Fitzgerald, *The Great Gatsby,* 40; on the indelible Catholicism in Fitzgerald's work, see Paul Giles, *American Catholic Arts and Fictions: Culture, Ideology, Aesthetics* (New York, 1992), 169–188.

6. F. Scott Fitzgerald, "Absolution" (1924), in *The Short Stories of F. Scott Fitzgerald,* ed. Matthew J. Bruccoli (New York, 1989), 259–272.

7. Fitzgerald, *The Great Gatsby,* 104, 182, 105, 68.

8. Fitzgerald, *The Great Gatsby,* 98, 25, 44, 8, 73, 47, 61–62, 167, 69.

9. Fitzgerald, *The Great Gatsby,* 69, 169.

10. Fitzgerald, *The Great Gatsby,* 45, 189.

11. Agee, "Preliminaries," in Agee and Evans, *Let Us Now Praise Famous Men,* n.p.

12. Lionel Trilling, "Greatness with One Fault in It," *Kenyon Review* 4 (Winter 1942), 102.

13. Agee and Evans, *Let Us Now Praise Famous Men,* 99, 307; Evans, "James Agee in 1936," foreword, *Let Us Now Praise Famous Men,* xliv; Robert Fitzgerald quoted in John Hersey's introduction, *Let Us Now Praise Famous Men,* xxix.

14. Agee's remark about "leaden melodies" is from his autobiographical novel, James Agee, *The Morning Watch* (Boston, 1951), 40; "field between devil and God" is from a poem Agee recited in the pulpit, cited by Robert Saudek, "J. R. Agee, '32: A Snapshot Album, 1928–1932," in David Madden and Jeffrey J. Folks, eds., *Remembering James Agee* (Athens, GA, 1997), 18. Laurence Bergreen, *James Agee: A Life* (New York, 1985) is the best biography.

15. James Agee, "Dedication" (1934), from *Permit Me Voyage,* in *Collected Poems of James Agee,* ed. Robert Fitzgerald (Boston, 1968), 12; letter to Father James Flye, February 17, 1936, in James Agee, *Letters of James Agee to Father Flye,* ed. Robert Phelps (New York, 1962), 87.

16. Agee, "Dedication," from *Permit Me Voyage,* in *Collected Poems,* 11–12.

17. Augspurger, *Economy of Abundant Beauty,* 183; James Agee, "Folk Art," first published in *Partisan Review* (Spring 1944), in *Agee on Film: Criticism and Comment on the Movies* (New York, 2000 [1958]), 433–435; letter to Father Flye, March 8, 1940, in *Letters of James Agee to Father Flye,* 123.

18. James Agee, "Plans for Work: October 1937," in *The Collected Short Prose of James Agee,* ed. Robert Fitzgerald (Boston, 1968), 140; Agee and Evans, *Let Us Now Praise Famous Men,* 355, 356.

19. Agee and Evans, *Let Us Now Praise Famous Men,* 356, 249–250; Agee, "Preliminaries," n.p.

20. Agee and Evans, *Let Us Now Praise Famous Men,* 137, 134.

21. Agee and Evans, *Let Us Now Praise Famous Men,* 100–101, 107, 103. Agee's insistence on the human divinity of his subjects eludes Trilling's only criticism of the book: what he termed a "failure of moral realism," an "inability to see these people as anything but good" that stemmed from Agee's "guilt at his own relative freedom." "Poverty and suffering," Trilling admonished, "are not in themselves virtue." (Trilling, "Greatness," 102). Trilling thus exemplified the liberal moralism that Agee was seeking to overcome.

22. James Agee, "Christmas 1945," in *Collected Poems,* 161.

## Part Seven: One Vast and Ecumenical Holding Company

1. Nancy Mitford, *The Blessing* (New York, 2010 [1951]), 162–163.

2. Mitford, *The Blessing,* 163.

3. The February 1951 issue of *Fortune* was quickly published in book form as Russell Davenport and the editors of *Fortune, U.S.A.: The Permanent Revolution* (New York, 1951), 30, xi, xiii.

4. For the next few paragraphs I am quoting from Paddy Chayefsky's screenplay for *Network* (MGM, 1976); see also David Itzkoff, *Mad as Hell: The Making of Network and the Fateful Vision of the Angriest Man in Movies* (New York, 2014).

5. Guy Debord, *Society of the Spectacle* (New York, 1994 [1967]), 42, 20, 25.

6. Chayefsky, *Network.*

7. Thomas Frank, *One Market Under God: Extreme Capitalism, Market Populism, and the End of Economic Democracy* (New York, 2000).

8. Robert J. Griffith, "Dwight D. Eisenhower and the Corporate Commonwealth," *American Historical Review* 87 (February 1982), 87–122; John Kenneth Galbraith, *American Capitalism: The Concept of Countervailing Power* (Boston, 1952); Daniel Bell, *The End of Ideology: On the Exhaustion of Political Ideas in the Fifties* (Glencoe, IL,

1960), 393–408. On "managerial capitalism" after 1945, see Michael Useem, "Revolt of the Corporate Owners and the Demobilization of Business Political Action," *Critical Sociology* 16 (Summer–Fall 1989), 7–27, and Cesar J. Ayala, "Theories of Big Business in American Society," *Critical Sociology* 16 (Summer–Fall 1989), 91–120. Robert M. Collins, *More: The Politics of Economic Growth in Postwar America* (New York, 2000), 17–131, chronicles the rise and hegemony of "growth liberalism." Two contemporaneous studies of stockholder dispossession are Edward Ross Aranow and Herbert A. Einhorn, *Proxy Contests for Corporate Control* (New York, 1957), and Joseph A. Livingston, *The American Stockholder* (Philadelphia, 1958). For valuable discussions of the literature, see Doug Henwood, *Wall Street* (New York, 1997), 251–260, and Marjorie Kelly, *The Divine Right of Capital: Dethroning the Economic Aristocracy* (San Francisco, 2001), 51–56.

9. On investor capitalism, see Michael Useem, *Investor Capitalism: How Money Managers are Changing the Face of Corporate America* (New York, 1996); Paul Krugman, "For Richer," *New York Times Magazine* (October 20, 2002), 27.

10. Frank, *Conquest of Cool*, 25–33, discusses the shortcomings of the co-optation theory of the counterculture. Joel Dinerstein, *The Origins of Cool in Postwar America* (Chicago, 2017), provides a useful overview of "cool." On "virtuous consumerism," see Elaine Tyler May, *Homeward Bound: American Families in the Cold War Era* (New York, 1988), 165–167.

11. Sheldon Wolin, *Democracy Incorporated: Managed Democracy and the Specter of Inverted Totalitarianism* (Princeton, NJ, 2010), esp. 41–68.

## 24. God's in His Heaven, All's Right with the World

1. May, *Homeward Bound*, 13.

2. William Levitt, interview with Eric Larrabee, "The Six Thousand Houses that Levitt Built," *Harper's* (September 1948), 84; Lizabeth Cohen, *A Consumers' Republic: The Politics of Mass Consumption in Postwar America* (New York, 2003), 127; May, *Homeward Bound*, 166.

3. John Kenneth Galbraith, *The Affluent Society* (Boston, 1958), 101.

4. John Kenneth Galbraith, *The New Industrial State* (Boston, 1967), 187; Paul Baran and Paul Sweezy, *Monopoly Capital: An Essay on the American Economic and Social Order* (New York, 1966), 15–16.

5. Galbraith, *American Capitalism*, 17, 30; Will Herberg, *Protestant Catholic Jew: An Essay in American Religious Sociology* (Garden City, NY, 1960 [1955]), 74–90, quotes on 75, 78.

6. Davenport and the editors of *Fortune, U.S.A.: The Permanent Revolution*, x, viii, ix, 7, 67–68, 51.

7. Lionel Trilling, contribution to "Our Country and Our Culture," *Partisan Review* 19 (May–June 1952), 319, 321. For two representative rapprochements with business, see Bernard De Voto, "Why Professors Are Suspicious of Business," *Fortune* 43

(April 1951), 114–115, 139–142, who argued that intellectuals were just "dissatisfied customers," and Sidney Hook, "Bread, Freedom, and Businessmen," *Fortune* 44 (September 1951), 117, 176–188, who rhapsodized about the "irreducible quality in the experience of un-coerced choice." On the Aspen Institute, see Allen, *Romance of Commerce and Culture,* 119–290, esp. 237–267, quotes on 221, 233. For two contemporary accounts of the Aspen phenomenon, see "Business and Culture," *Newsweek* 37 (February 5, 1951), 76–77, and "Plato, Aristotle, and the Businessmen," *Newsweek* 44 (July 20, 1958), 79–80.

8. Eugene Staley, ed., *Creating an Industrial Civilization: A Report on the Corning Conference* (New York, 1952), 38, 176, 76, 159.

9. On Davenport's life and career, see John Knox Jessup, "Russell W. Davenport: A Sketch," introduction to Russell Davenport, *The Dignity of Man* (New York, 1955), 6–22. Russell Davenport, "The Greatest Opportunity on Earth," *Fortune* 40 (October 1949), 68.

10. Davenport, *Dignity of Man,* 88, 116, 120–121, 123, 100, 337.

11. Davenport, *Dignity of Man,* 263, 69, 275, 117, 323.

12. From among numerous discussions of corporate social responsibility, see Howard Bowen, *Social Responsibilities of the Businessman* (New York, 1953), 44; Howard Bowen, "How Public-Spirited Is American Business?," *Annals of the American Academy of Political and Social Science* 280 (March 1952), 82–89; Peter Drucker, "The Responsibilities of Management," *Harper's* (November 1954), 68; Peter Drucker, "Business and Society," *Saturday Review* 35 (January 19, 1952), 21–24; Clarence Randall, *A Creed for Free Enterprise* (New York, 1952); Clarence Randall, "Responsibility for What?," *Newsweek* 52 (September 22, 1958), 95; Eugene Jennings, "Make Way for the Business Moralist," *Nation's Business* 47 (September 1959), 90–92; Andrew Hacker, "Do Corporations Have a Social Duty?," *New York Times Magazine* (November 17, 1963), 21–24; Andrew Hacker, "Ideological Debate Dividing Businessmen," *Business Week* (September 12, 1964), 201–202. American Management Association, *Management Creeds and Philosophies: Top Management Guides in Our Changing Economy* (New York, 1958), includes some corporate "mission statements." Friedman expressed the laissez-faire view of corporate social responsibility when he wrote that the only responsibility borne by managers was to "make as much money for their stockholders as possible": Milton Friedman, *Capitalism and Freedom* (Chicago, 1962), 133.

13. Drucker, "Responsibilities of Management," 68; Crawford H. Greenewalt, "The Culture of the Businessman," *Saturday Review* 40 (January 19, 1957), 43; Crawford H. Greenewalt, "The Crown Princes of Business," *Fortune* 46 (October 1953), 266; Lili Foldes, "That Stuff Called Culture," *Nation's Business* 38 (March 1950), 31–34. See also Alfred Heidenreich, "Goethe and Enterprise," *Fortune* 40 (September 1949), 72. Augspurger, *Economy of Abundant Beauty,* 241–261, interprets *Fortune*'s postwar cultural politics as an effort to legitimize managerial professionalism.

14. Duncan Norton-Taylor, "Why Don't Businessmen Read Books?," *Fortune* 47 (May 1954), 117, 150. For two similarly ambivalent assessments of executive culture,

see Benjamin M. Selekman, "Wanted: Mature Managers," *Harvard Business Review* 24 (December 1946), 228–234, and Robert W. Wald, "The Top Executive: A First-Hand Profile," *Harvard Business Review* 32 (August 1954), 45–54.

15. Norton-Taylor, "Why Don't Businessmen Read Books?," 118, 154, 157; Galbraith, *Affluent Society*, 194; Kenneth Rexroth, "Poets, Old and New," in *Assays* (New York, 1961), 216–217.

16. "Fowler McCormick: Self-Made Man," *Fortune* 34 (August 1946), 111–114, 213–218.

17. Douglas McGregor, "Foreword," *Journal of Social Issues* 4 (Summer 1948), 4; Clarence Francis, "What's Ahead for Those in Industrial Relations Work?," *Industrial Relations* 11 (November 1946), 183; Frank W. Abrams, "Management's Responsibilities in a Complex World," *Harvard Business Review* 29 (May 1951), 29–30; Keith Davis, *Human Relations in Business* (New York, 1957), 1, 3, 444–466 passim, 468. For two representative accounts of human relations in the mainstream press, see "Human Relations: A New Art Brings a Revolution to Industry," *Time* (April 14, 1952), 26, and "Psychologists at Work," *Business Week* (September 19, 1953), 52. On postwar human relations theory and practice, see Stephen P. Waring, *Taylorism Transformed: Scientific Management Theory since 1945* (Chapel Hill, NC, 1991), 9–103, and Elizabeth Fones-Wolf, *Selling Free Enterprise: The Business Assault on Labor and Liberalism, 1945–1960* (Urbana, IL, 1994), 73–86.

18. Peter Drucker, The *New Society: The Anatomy of the Industrial Order* (New York, 1950), 38, 25–26, 348; Peter Drucker, *The Practice of Management* (New York, 1954), 344.

19. Drucker, *New Society*, 265, 105, 158–160, 49; Drucker, *Practice of Management*, 15, 121, 267.

20. On Auden's praise, see Chapter 23; Erich Fromm, *The Sane Society* (New York, 1955), 161–162; Clinton Rossiter, *Conservatism in America: The Thankless Persuasion* (New York, 1962 [1955]), 224.

21. David Riesman, *The Lonely Crowd: A Study of the Changing American Character* (New Haven, CT, 1961 [1950]), 81–83.

22. Bell, *End of Ideology*, 36.

23. "Sloan Wilson," obituary, *Economist* 367 (June 5, 2003), 79; Hodgins recounted his years at *Fortune* in his posthumously published autobiography, Eric Hodgins, *Trolley to the Moon* (New York, 1973); Sloan Wilson, *The Man in the Gray Flannel Suit* (New York, 1955), 164, 13, 76, 272. Wilson may have erred in his choice of wardrobe for Tom Rath. According to journalist Martin Mayer, "gray flannel was never really popular on Madison Avenue," though he adds the exculpatory observation that Tom "was in public relations rather than advertising, anyway": Martin Mayer, *Madison Avenue, U.S.A.* (New York, 1958), 13.

24. Eric Hodgins, *Blandings' Way* (New York, 1950), 64, 24–25, 47, 112, 314.

25. Whyte relates his wartime experiences in William H. Whyte, *A Time of War: Remembering Guadalcanal, A Battle without Maps* (New York, 2000) and describes his

early career as a salesman in William H. Whyte, *The Organization Man* (New York, 1956), 112–119; William H. Whyte, *Is Anybody Listening? How and Why U.S. Business Fumbles When It Talks with Human Beings* (New York, 1952), 32, 94; Frank, *Conquest of Cool*, 21. On Whyte as a social critic, see Richard H. Pells, *The Liberal Mind in a Conservative Age: Liberal Intellectuals in the 1940s and 1950s* (New York, 1985), 232–238, who expounds the conventional wisdom about Whyte as a critic of conformity; Paul A. Carter, *Another Part of the Fifties* (New York, 1983), 96–98, who considers Whyte's conclusion anticlimactic; John Patrick Diggins, *The Proud Decades: America in War and Peace, 1945–1960* (New York, 1988), 208–209, who reads in *The Organization Man* "a curious message, at once radical and conservative"; and Jackson Lears, "A Matter of Taste: Corporate Cultural Hegemony in a Mass-Consumption Society," in *Recasting America: Culture and Politics in the Age of Cold War,* ed. Lary May (Chicago, 1989), 44, who argues that, along with other postwar intellectuals, Whyte "tended to conflate aesthetics with more general 'spiritual' issues."

26. Whyte, *Organization Man,* 10–11.

27. Whyte, *Organization Man,* 3, 78, 74, 155, 361.

28. Whyte, *Organization Man,* 47, 6–7, 33.

29. Whyte, *Organization Man,* 35, 44, 29, 367.

30. Whyte, *Organization Man,* 365, 397, 166, 405.

31. Harold Rosenberg, "The Orgamerican Phantasy," in *The Tradition of The New* (New York, 1959), 283; Paul Goodman, *Growing Up Absurd: Problems of Youth in the Organized System* (New York, 1960), 59–60.

32. Alan Harrington, *The Immortalist: An Approach to the Engineering of Man's Divinity* (New York, 1969), 3.

33. Alan Harrington, *The Revelations of Dr. Modesto* (New York, 1955), 50.

34. Alan Harrington, *Life in the Crystal Palace* (New York, 1959), 20, 8, 12.

35. Harrington, *Life in the Crystal Palace,* 30, 25, 19–20, 24.

36. Harrington, *Life in the Crystal Palace,* 158–159, 248, 36, 38–39, 83, 209.

37. Harrington, *Life in the Crystal Palace,* 231–236.

## 25. Machines of Loving Grace

1. Whyte, *Organization Man,* 156, 403.

2. Luc Boltanski and Eve Chiapello, *The New Spirit of Capitalism,* trans. Gregory Elliott (New York, 2005 [1999]), esp. 55–342.

3. George Terborgh, *The Automation Hysteria* (New York, 1966), provides a judicious contemporary account of the phenomenon. Throughout this section, I have relied on David F. Noble, *Forces of Production: A Social History of Industrial Automation* (New York, 1984), and on Braverman's equally invaluable *Labor and Monopoly Capital,* 212–233. For examples of reportage and commentary in the business and opinion presses, see "On the Job, Automatic Tools Prove Virtuosos," *Business Week* (March 14, 1959), 73; "The Automatic Factory" and Eric W. Weaver and J. J. Brown, "Machines

without Men," *Fortune* 34 (November 1946), 160–164, 165, 192–204; "The Automatic Factory: A Roundtable," *Fortune* 48 (October 1953), 168–171, 178–180; "Technological Alarms," *Fortune* 51 (May 1955), 59–60; "More Jobs and a Sounder Dollar," *Fortune* 58 (November 1958); Peter Drucker, "The Promise of Automation," *Harper's* 210 (April 1955), 41–47; Charles Silberman, *The Myths of Automation* (New York, 1966), x; Gerard Piel, "Human Want Is Obsolete," *Saturday Review* (June 27, 1953), 9–11; Gerard Piel, "End of Toil: Science Offers a New World," *Nation* (June 17, 1961), 509–511; Gerard Piel, "Abundance and the Future of Man," *Atlantic* (April 1964), 84–90. Other enthusiastic endorsements of automation included "Special Report to Executives on Tomorrow's Management," *Business Week* (August 15, 1953), 158–160; "Push-Button Labor," *Fortune* 50 (August 1954), 50–52; "Push-Button Paradise," *Popular Science* 165 (November 1954), 147–149; "For Automation: A Broader View," *Business Week* (January 15, 1955), 164; "Automation: Blessing or Curse?," *Life* 38 (January 17, 1955), 35.

4. Thomas J. Watson, *A Business and Its Beliefs: The Ideas That Helped Build IBM* (New York, 1963), 24; Ralph Cordiner is cited in Robert P. Weeks, ed., *Machines and the Man: A Sourcebook on Automation* (New York, 1961), 176; David O. Woodbury, *Let ERMA Do It: The Full Story of Automation* (New York, 1956), 270–271, 279, 297.

5. Georges Friedmann, *Industrial Society* (Glencoe, IL, 1955), quote on 384; Georges Friedmann, *The Anatomy of Work: Labor, Leisure, and the Implications of Automation* (New York, 1961); Sigfried Giedion, *Mechanization Takes Command: A Contribution to Anonymous History* (New York, 1948), quote on 715; Jacques Ellul, *The Technological Society* (New York, 1964 [1954]).

6. James R. Bright, *Automation and Management* (Boston, 1958), 208; see also James R. Bright, "The Relationship of Automation and Skill Requirements," in National Commission on Technology, Automation, and Economic Progress, *The Employment Impact of Technological Change,* Appendix to vol. II, *Technology and the American Economy* (Washington, DC, 1966) 220; Daniel Bell, "The Bogey of Automation," *New York Review of Books* (August 26, 1965), 23; Ben Seligman, *Most Notorious Victory: Man in an Age of Automation* (New York, 1966), xiv, 317.

7. John von Neumann, "Can We Survive Technology?," *Fortune* 51 (June 1955), 106–108, 151–152; Donald N. Michael, *Cybernation, The Silent Conquest* (Santa Barbara, CA, 1962), 42, 39; Gerald Sykes, *The Cool Millennium* (Englewood Cliffs, NJ, 1967), 1.

8. Boulware quoted in Noble, *Forces of Production,* 156.

9. Neil W. Chamberlain, *The Union Challenge and Management Control* (New York, 1948), 87; all other quotes are from Noble, *Forces of Production,* 236, 235, 248.

10. Noble, *Forces of Production,* 57.

11. National Association of Manufacturers, cited in Weeks, *Machines and the Man,* 171; Russell Davenport and the editors of *Fortune, U.S.A.: The Permanent Revolution,* 26–27.

12. "The Automatic Factory," 163; and Weaver and Brown, "Machines without Men," 192, 194, 196, 199–200, 203–204.

13. On Wiener, see Noble, *Forces of Production*, 71–76, and Flo Conway and Jim Siegelman, *Dark Hero of the Information Age: In Search of Norbert Wiener, the Father of Cybernetics* (New York, 2005); on the early history of cybernetics, see Steve J. Heims, *Constructing a Social Science for Postwar America: The Cybernetics Group, 1946–1953* (Cambridge, MA, 1993). Norbert Wiener, "Moral Reflections of a Mathematician," *Bulletin of the Atomic Scientists* 12 (February 1956), 54, 56; Norbert Wiener, "A Scientist Rebels," *Atlantic Monthly* 179 (January 1947), 46.

14. Norbert Wiener, *The Human Use of Human Beings: Cybernetics and Society* (Boston, 1954 [1950]), 31–32, 159, 162; Norbert Wiener, "Science: The Megabuck Era," *New Republic* 138 (January 27, 1958), 10–11.

15. Norbert Wiener, *Cybernetics: Or, Control and Communication in the Animal and the Machine* (Cambridge, MA, 1965 [1948]), 176; *God and Golem, Inc.: A Comment on Certain Points Where Cybernetics Impinges on Religion* (Cambridge, MA, 1964), 53, 63, 95; Wiener, *Human Use of Human Beings*, 16.

16. Wiener, *God and Golem*, 47, 52.

17. Wiener's letter to Reuther is cited in Noble, *Forces of Production*, 76.

18. Wiener, *God and Golem*, 55. In his final years Wiener embarked on what Conway and Siegelman describe as a "personal reckoning with his own long-suppressed spiritual yearnings" and grew increasingly attracted to Hinduism: Conway and Siegelman, *Dark Hero*, 298–311, quote on 305.

19. Vonnegut quoted in Noble, *Forces of Production*, 359; see 359–360 on Vonnegut's experience at General Electric and the writing of *Player Piano*.

20. Kurt Vonnegut, *Player Piano* (New York, 1999 [1952]), 63, 332, 91, 30, 31, 128, 129.

21. Vonnegut, *Player Piano*, 117, 15, 123; on ENIAC and UNIVAC, see Noble, *Forces of Production*, 50–51.

22. Vonnegut, *Player Piano*, 8, 292, 289, 320, 341.

23. Vonnegut, *Player Piano*, 253; quote from foreword has no pagination.

24. McLuhan quoted in Paul Benedetti and Nancy DeHart, *Forward through the Rearview Mirror: Reflections on and by Marshall McLuhan* (Cambridge, MA, 1996), 70; Marshall McLuhan, "Catholic Humanism and Modern Letters" (1954), in *The Medium and the Light: Reflections on Religion and Media* (Eugene, OR, 2010 [1954]), 171; "Confronting the Secular: Letter to Clement McNapsy, S. J." (January 15, 1946), in McLuhann, *The Medium and the Light*, 202. The best biography of McLuhan is Philip Marchand, *Marshall McLuhan: The Medium and the Messenger* (Cambridge, MA, 1998 [1989]). Howard Brick, *The Age of Contradiction: American Thought and Culture in the 1960s* (Ithaca, NY, 2000 [1998]), 62–63, notes McLuhan's "thinly disguised antimodernism."

25. Marshall McLuhan, *The Mechanical Bride: Folklore of Industrial Man* (New York, 1951), 33, 11; Marshall McLuhan, "Catholic Humanism and Modern Letters," in McLuhan, *The Medium and the Light*, 164–165.

26. Marshall McLuhan, *Understanding Media: The Extensions of Man* (New York, 1966), 245; on McLuhan's career as an intellectual entrepreneur, see Marchand, *Marshall McLuhan,* 120–180.

27. Marshall McLuhan, *The Gutenberg Galaxy: The Making of Typographic Man* (Toronto, 2011 [1962]), 40, 37, 25, 312, 311, 160.

28. Galbraith, *New Industrial State,* 73–88; Frank, *Conquest of Cool,* 9.

29. Peter Drucker, *Landmarks of Tomorrow* (New York, 1959), 83, 45–59, 68; Peter Drucker, *America's Next Twenty Years* (New York, 1957), 17–34; Joseph Schumpeter, *Capitalism, Socialism, and Democracy* (New York, 2008 [1942]), 81–86. On Drucker as a forerunner of post-Fordism, see Nils Gilman, "Prophet of Post-Fordism: Peter Drucker and the Legitimation of the Corporation," in *American Capitalism: Social Thought and Political Economy in the Twentieth Century,* ed. Nelson Lichtenstein (Philadelphia, 2006), 109–134.

30. Alfred J. Marrow, *The Practical Theorist: The Life and Work of Kurt Lewin* (New York, 1970), covers its subject's life and work. Kurt Lewin, *Resolving Social Conflict: Selected Papers on Group Dynamics,* ed. Gertrude Lewin (New York, 1948), 82. On T-groups and sensitivity training, see Waring, *Taylorism Transformed,* 108–131; Robert Tannenbaum and W. R. Schmidt, "How to Choose a Leadership Pattern," *Harvard Business Review* 36 (March–April 1958), 95–102; see also Robert Tannenbaum, "Management of Differences," *Harvard Business Review* 38 (November–December 1960), 107–115, and Robert Tannenbaum, *Leadership and Organization: A Behavioral Approach* (New York, 1961). Abraham Maslow, *Motivation and Personality* (New York, 1954), 354; Carl Rogers, *On Becoming a Person: A Therapist's View of Psychotherapy* (Boston, 1961), 189.

31. Russell Jacoby, *Social Amnesia: A Critique of Conformist Psychology from Adler to Laing* (Boston, 1975), 53 (see 46–72); Abraham Maslow, "A Preface to Motivation Theory," *Psychosomatic Medicine* 5 (Winter 1943), 85–92; Abraham Maslow, *Toward a Psychology of Being* (New York, 1962), 70–95, quotes on 94. Maslow mused on the fecundity of his insights in Abraham Maslow, "Theory Z" (1969), in *The Farther Reaches of Human Nature* (New York, 1985 [1971]), 272. For an informative but relatively uncritical account of Maslow's life and work, see Edward Hoffmann, *The Right to Be Human: A Biography of Abraham Maslow* (New York, 1988).

32. Fromm, *The Sane Society,* xxxiv, 316 (see also 185–201); Erich Fromm, *The Art of Loving* (New York, 2008 [1956]), 119; Marcuse, *Eros and Civilization,* 266.

33. Douglas McGregor, *The Human Side of Enterprise,* (New York, 1960), vi, 4, 33–44, 195. On McGregor, see Warren G. Bennis's introduction to Bennis and Edgar Schein, eds., *Leadership and Motivation: Essays of Douglas McGregor* (Cambridge, MA, 1966), ix–xv, and Frank, *Conquest of Cool,* 22–23.

34. On Maslow's stay at NLS, see Hoffmann, *Right to Be Human,* 267–273; Maslow's account is in *Eupsychian Management: A Journal* (Homewood, IL, 1965), quotes on 146.

35. Maslow, *Eupsychian Management,* 20–21, 1, 62, 29, 105, 192–193.

36. McGregor, *Human Side of Enterprise*, 245; Maslow, *Eupsychian Management*, 41, xi, 10, 20, 70, 138.

37. Maslow, *Eupsychian Management*, xii; Kay quoted in "Where Being Nice to People Didn't Work," *Business Week* (January 20, 1973), 99.

38. Mayer, *Madison Avenue, U.S.A.*, 76; on the hegemony of "science" in advertising circles in the decade after World War II, see Frank, *Conquest of Cool*, 34–51.

39. David Ogilvy, *Confessions of an Advertising Man* (New York, 1971 [1963]), 19, 29; Frank, *Conquest of Cool*, 39; Frederic Wiseman, *The Hucksters* (New York, 1946), 88; Allen Ginsberg, *Howl and Other Poems* (San Francisco, 1956), 9, 16. On Ginsberg's years as a market researcher and adman, see Barry Miles, *Ginsberg: A Biography* (New York, 1989).

40. On the Creative Revolution, see Frank, *Conquest of Cool*, 52–103.

41. Ernest Dichter, *The Strategy of Desire* (Garden City, NY, 1960); Pierre Martineau, *Motivation in Advertising: Motives That Make People Buy* (New York, 1957), 4, 137; see also Pierre Martineau, "The Personality of the Retail Store," *Harvard Business Review* 36 (January–February 1958), 47–55. On motivational research, see Lears, *Fables of Abundance*, 251, 253–254, and Cohen, *A Consumers' Republic*, 296–297. Examples of motivational research writing include Ernest Dichter, "A Psychological View of Advertising Effectiveness," *Journal of Marketing* 14 (July 1949), 61–66; Warren J. Bilkey, "A Psychological Approach to Consumer Behavior Analysis," *Journal of Marketing* 18 (July 1953), 18–23; Norman Heller, "An Application of Psychological Learning Theory to Advertising," *Journal of Marketing* 20 (January 1955), 248–254.

42. "A New Language for Madison Avenue," *Business Week* (September 5, 1953), 40; see also "Behavior Research to Get Answers," *Business Week* (August 21, 1954), 140, 142–143; Thomas McCarthy, "Psyche and Sales," *Wall Street Journal* (September 14, 1954), 1; Robert Graham, "Adman's Nightmare: Is a Prune a Witch?," *Reporter* 8 (October 13, 1953), 27; Vance Packard, *The Hidden Persuaders* (New York, 1957); Ogilvy, *Confessions*, 20. Other critical accounts of motivational research included Mayer, *Madison Avenue, U.S.A.*, 233–256, and Joseph Seldin, "Selling to the Id," *Nation* 180 (May 21, 1955), 442–443.

43. Martineau, *Motivation in Advertising*, 2, 121, 66, 40–41, 147, 35. The urtext of market segmentation is Wendell R. Smith, "Product Differentiation and Market Segmentation as Alternative Marketing Strategies," *Journal of Marketing* 21 (July 1956), 1–11. Some of the earliest work in segmentation strategy is collected in James F. Engel, Henry F. Fiorillo, and Murray A. Cayley, *Market Segmentation: Concepts and Applications* (New York, 1972). For a historical perspective, see Cohen, *A Consumers' Republic*, 292–344.

44. Dichter, *Strategy of Desire*, 283; the letter is quoted in Dichter's memoir-cum-advice book: Ernest Dichter, *Getting Motivated* (New York, 1979), 33. On Dichter, see Daniel Horowitz, *The Anxieties of Affluence: Critiques of American Consumer Culture, 1939–1979* (Amherst, MA, 2005), 48–64. One early account of Dichter is "Psychologist

Dichter Tells Admen: You Either Offer Security or Fail," *Business Week* (June 23, 1951), 68, 70, 72, 74, 76. See also Mayer's highly ambivalent discussion of Dichter in *Madison Avenue, U.S.A.,* 233–242.

45. Dichter describes the Ivory Soap campaign in *Strategy of Desire,* 33–34, and *Getting Motivated,* 34–36.

46. The marketing director is quoted in Mayer, *Madison Avenue, U.S.A.,* 238. Packard mentions Dichter numerous times throughout *The Hidden Persuaders,* but his critique is so venomous that at one point he alludes to his subject's "broken English" (33). Dichter is quoted in Horowitz, *Vance Packard and American Social Criticism* (Chapel Hill, NC, 1994), 162; Dichter, *Strategy of Desire,* 85–86.

47. Dichter, *Strategy of Desire,* 91, 13, 16; see also Ernest Dichter, "How to Perpetuate Prosperity," *Motivations* 1 (April 1956), 3–11, and Ernest Dichter, "Persuasion: To What End?," *Motivations* 2 (June 1957), 14–20.

48. Ernest Dichter, *The Psychology of Everyday Living* (New York, 1947), 212; Dichter, *Strategy of Desire,* 167, 15, 21.

49. Dichter, *Psychology of Everyday Living,* 235–236; Dichter, *Strategy of Desire,* 86, 97–109. Compare the very similar psychological reading of commodities in Martineau, *Motivation in Advertising,* 54–64.

50. Dichter, *Strategy of Desire,* 86, 282, 263. On the "hostile kinship between religion and marketing" in Dichter's work, see Gabriele Sorgo, "Ernest Dichter, Religion, and the Spirit of Capitalism: An Exegete of Pure Cult Religion Serves Consumer Society," in *Ernest Dichter and Motivational Research: New Perspectives on the Making of Postwar Consumer Culture,* ed. Stefan Schwarzkopf and Rainer Gries (New York, 2010), 75–90, quote on 77.

51. On "expressive individualism," see Robert Bellah et al., *Habits of the Heart: Individualism and Commitment in American Life* (Berkeley, 2007 [1985]), 32–35, 48–50, 333–334. For one thoughtful historical study of the counterculture, see Grace Elizabeth Hale, *A Nation of Outsiders: How the White Middle Class Fell in Love with Rebellion in Postwar America* (New York, 2011), esp. 13–131. Though often and mistakenly read as a celebration of its subject, Theodore Roszak, *The Making of a Counter Culture: Reflections on the Technocratic Society and Its Youthful Opposition* (New York, 1969), remains an indispensable guide.

52. Charles Reich, *The Greening of America: How the Youth Revolution Is Trying to Make America Livable* (New York, 1970), 14. The vilification of Reich's book began almost immediately on its publication. Christopher Lasch was especially trenchant, dismissing Reich as "incorrigibly American" in his conviction that "great changes can take place without a great price having to be paid for them." Besides, he noted, Reich's "pinched and meager conception of the good life" owed much to "advertising and travel brochures": "The 'Counter-Culture'," in Lasch, *World of Nations,* 184, 186.

53. Roszak, *The Making of a Counter Culture,* 177; Reich, *The Greening of America,* 272, 171.

54. Richard Brautigan, "All Watched Over by Machines of Loving Grace" (1967), in *Richard Brautigan's Trout Fishing in America, The Pill Versus the Springhill Mine Disaster, and In Watermelon Sugar* (Boston, 1989 [1968]), 121.

55. Ross, *Strange Weather,* 75–100; Fred Turner, *From Counterculture to Cyberculture: Stewart Brand, the Whole Earth Network, and the Rise of Digital Utopianism* (Chicago, 2006); Robert Pirsig, *Zen and the Art of Motorcycle Maintenance* (New York, 1974), 16.

56. Turner, *From Counterculture to Cyberculture,* 41–68, quotes on 59; on the Trips Festival, see 65–67.

57. Turner, *From Counterculture to Cyberculture,* 69–111.

58. Turner, *From Counterculture to Cyberculture,* 99, 81–84 passim.

59. Turner, *From Counterculture to Cyberculture,* 99; Marshall McLuhan, "The Playboy Interview: Marshall McLuhan," *Playboy* (March 1969), 61.

60. Dichter quoted in *Advertising Age* (October 16, 1967), 34; Sam Blum, "Marijuana Clouds the Generation Gap," *New York Times Magazine* (August 23, 1970), 28; "The Touch-Touch Bang-Bang School of Creativity," *Marketing/Communications* 297 (February 1969), 32–34; see also "Agency Swingers Flourish Their Mini-Skirts," *Printers' Ink* 295 (August 11, 1967), 12–13.

61. Stephen Baker, "The Cultural Significance of Doyle Dane Bernbach," *Advertising Age* (November 1, 1965), 99. Frank, *Conquest of Cool,* 92–98, discusses the importance of creativity to the revitalization of professionalism in advertising.

62. Andy Warhol and Pat Hackett, *Popism: The Warhol Sixties* (New York, 1980), 3. On Pop, see Steven Madoff, *Pop Art: A Critical History* (Berkeley, 1997), and Hal Foster, *The First Pop Age* (Princeton, NJ, 2012).

63. Robert Hughes, "Andy Warhol," in *Nothing If Not Critical: Selected Essays on Art and Artists* (New York, 1990), 246.

64. Andy Warhol, *The Philosophy of Andy Warhol* (New York, 1975), 92, 134.

65. Warhol's brother John quoted in Jane Dillenberger, *The Religious Art of Andy Warhol* (New York, 1998), 17; see 17–24 on Warhol's early life and career. Although she attends primarily to Warhol's explicitly religious paintings, Dillenberger is sensitive to the iconographic character of his Pop productions, as is Giles, *American Catholic Arts and Fictions,* 278–294.

66. Warhol quoted in Dillenberger, *The Religious Art of Andy Warhol,* 27.

67. Charles A. Riley, *The Art of Peter Max* (New York, 2002), is a celebratory collection of Max's images that nonetheless acknowledges the distaste of most art critics. Although riddled with clichés, Max's memoir, *The Universe of Peter Max* (New York, 2013), is nonetheless informative.

68. Max, *Universe of Peter Max,* 69, 56, 72.

69. Max, *Universe of Peter Max,* 81, 85.

70. Max, *Universe of Peter Max,* 85, 101, 98.

71. Max, *Universe of Peter Max,* 125, 162; "The Mark of Max Is Everywhere," *Life* (September 5, 1969), 34–39.

72. Craig Karpel, "Das Hip Capital," *Esquire* (December 1970), 184; "Mark of Max Is Everywhere," 34, cover.

73. Alvin Toffler, *Future Shock* (New York, 1970), 188, 38, 431, 75, 95, 125.

74. Toffler, *Future Shock,* 109, 144; Robert Townsend, *Up the Organization: How to Stop the Corporation from Stifling People and Strangling Profits* (New York, 1970), 84.

75. Toffler, *Future Shock,* 319, 100–101, 122, 149.

76. Toffler, *Future Shock,* 221, 227, 233, 230, 321, 380, 382.

## 26. The New Testament of Capitalism

1. Maslow, "Theory Z," in *Eupsychian Management,* 273, 270, 278–279.

2. David Harvey, *A Brief History of Neoliberalism* (New York, 2006), 19.

3. Wendy Brown, *Undoing the Demos: Neoliberalism's Stealth Revolution* (Cambridge, MA, 2015), 67; Philip Mirowski, *Never Let a Serious Crisis Go to Waste: How Neoliberalism Survived the Financial Meltdown* (New York, 2014), 48, 55, 92, 108, 117.

4. Mirowski, *Never Let a Serious Crisis Go to Waste,* 104; President Ronald Reagan quoted in Daniel Rodgers, *Age of Fracture* (Cambridge, MA, 2011), 41 (which also contains the Rodgers quotation); Jasper Crane quoted in Kim Phillips-Fein, *Invisible Hands: The Businessmen's Crusade against the New Deal* (New York, 2009), 30.

5. Darren Dochuk, *From Bible Belt to Sunbelt: Plain-Folks Religion, Grassroots Politics, and the Rise of Evangelical Conservatism* (New York, 2011), 13.

6. Bethany Moreton, *To Serve God and Wal-Mart: The Making of Christian Free Enterprise* (Cambridge, MA, 2009), 6–48, maps the political economy of the South in the 1940s with admirable breadth and clarity; the preacher is quoted in Dochuk, *From Bible Belt to Sunbelt,* 117.

7. Lisa McGirr, *Suburban Warriors: The Origins of the New American Right* (Princeton, NJ, 2001), 94; Dochuk, *From Bible Belt to Sunbelt,* 17.

8. Fones-Wolf, *Selling Free Enterprise,* 237–245 (Pew quote on 237), covers the evangelical-business alliance in the first two decades after World War II. On the centrality of the Pew family to the postwar libertarian right, see Allan J. Lichtman, *White Protestant Nation: The Rise of the American Conservative Movement* (New York, 2009), 171–174, and Kevin Kruse, *One Nation under God: How Corporate America Invented Christian America* (New York, 2015), 20–22. Among contemporary reports on the prominence of religion in business circles, see especially Duncan Norton-Taylor, "Businessmen on Their Knees," *Fortune* 45 (October 1953), 254, and Clarence Woodbury, "Religion in Industry: 'Not Only to Make a Living . . . but a Life,'" *Nation's Business* 44 (June 1954), 30. On George Pepperdine and his university, see Dochuk, *From Bible Belt to Sunbelt,* 66–76, quotes on 70, 73, 71.

9. Phillips-Fein, *Invisible Hands,* 68–86, surveys this evangelical-capitalist complex. On Spiritual Mobilization in particular, see Eckard V. Toy, "Spiritual Mobilization: The Failure of an Ultraconservative Ideal," *Pacific Northwest Quarterly* 61

(April 1970), 77–86; Brian Doherty, *Radicals for Capitalism: A Freewheeling History of the Modern American Libertarian Movement* (New York, 2007), 271–276; and Kruse, *One Nation under God*, 11–27. Doherty, *Radicals for Capitalism*, 147–165, 198–205, covers Leonard Read, *The Freeman*, and the Foundation for Economic Education. On Rushdoony, see Michael McVicar, *Christian Reconstruction: R. J. Rushdoony and American Religious Conservatism* (Chapel Hill, NC, 2015); esp. 49–52. Although evangelical Protestants were champions of laissez-faire, they were not entirely comfortable with the moral and social consequences; see McGirr, *Suburban Warriors*, 163–168, on the convenient but uneasy alliance of economic libertarians and social conservatives. Darren E. Grem, *The Blessings of Business: How Corporations Shaped Conservative Christianity* (New York, 2016), provides an invaluable overview of the connections between evangelical religious culture and corporate business.

10. On Kershner and *Christian Economics,* see Ronald Lora and William Henry Longton, *The Conservative Press in Twentieth-Century America* (Greenwood, CT, 1999), 163–167, Kershner quote on 166. Kershner's work with the American Friends Service Committee was profiled in Dorothy Dunbar Bromley, "Europe's Children Are Hungry," *Life* (May 8, 1944), 56, 58. The proclamation about "free enterprise" was on the masthead of every issue of *Christian Economics.* Kershner's assertion about the "laws of economics" is in Ralph Lord Roy, "God, Free Enterprise, and Anarchy," *Christian Register* 132 (April 1953), 10.

11. Howard E. Kershner, *God, Gold, and Government: The Interrelationship of Christianity, Freedom, Self-Interest, and Economic Well-Being* (Englewood Cliffs, NJ, 1957), 24–25, 30, 71. On the place of gold in postwar free-enterprise ideology, see Francis X. Sutton Seymour Edwin Harris, Carl Kaysen, and James Tobin, *The American Business Creed* (Cambridge, MA, 1956), 239–245. Like their predecessors, Cold War goldbugs considered adherence to the gold standard as an application of "moral principles to monetary affairs" (243).

12. On Read's career, see Doherty, *Radicals for Capitalism*, 149–165; on "I, Pencil," see Doherty, *Radicals for Capitalism*, 284–285. Leonard Read, "I, Pencil," *Freeman* 8 (December 1958), 32–37. Read's earlier book *The Romance of Reality* (New York, 1937) has none of the former and little of the latter.

13. There is a sizeable literature on the resurgence of conservatism after 1945, including George Nash, *The Conservative Intellectual Movement in America since 1945* (Wilmington, DE, 2006 [1976]); Kevin Mattson, *Rebels All! A Short History of the Conservative Mind in Postwar America* (New Brunswick, NJ, 2008), and Patrick Allitt, *The Conservatives: Ideas and Personalities throughout American History* (New Haven, CT, 2009). The most incisive reflections on conservatism are in Corey Robin, *The Reactionary Mind: Conservatism from Edmund Burke to Sarah Palin* (New York, 2011), esp. 3–60, which clears away many of the cobwebs that obscure any consideration of conservative thought and politics, in particular the notion that conservatism entails a "respect for tradition." See also Mark Lilla, *The Shipwrecked Mind: On Political Reaction* (New York, 2016).

14. Lionel Trilling, *The Liberal Imagination: Essays on Literature and Society* (New York, 1950), 5; Hofstadter, *Age of Reform,* 13. For other examples of left-liberal response to conservatism in the 1950s, see Theodor Adorno, Else Frenkel-Brunswik, Daniel Levinson et al., *The Authoritarian Personality: Studies in Prejudice* (New York, 1950); Daniel Bell, ed., *The New American Right* (New York, 1955); and perhaps the best, Hofstadter, "The Paranoid Style in American Politics" (1964). Bell would later express a sincere (if desperate) interest in conservatism in *The Cultural Contradictions of Capitalism* (New York, 1976.) Russell Kirk, *The Conservative Mind: From Burke to Santayana* (Chicago, 1953), 7, 55, 8. James E. Person, ed., *The Unbought Grace of Life: Essays in Honor of Russell Kirk* (Peru, IL, 1994), is a colloquium on its subject's work. On Weaver and Kirk, see Nash, *The Conservative Intellectual Movement,* 52–62, 104–122, respectively, and Mattson, *Rebels All!,* 48–50.

15. Richard Weaver, *Ideas Have Consequences* (Chicago, 1948), 129, 134, 181, 132–133. Murphy, *Rebuke of History,* 151–178, provides a clear exposition and analysis of Weaver's thought. Joseph Scotchie, ed., *The Vision of Richard Weaver* (New Brunswick, NJ, 1995), is a collection of laudatory essays. See especially Ralph C. Ancil, "Richard M. Weaver and the Metaphysics of Property," in Scotchie, *Vision of Richard Weaver,* 61–75, for a lucid but also profoundly patriarchal elucidation of Weaver's thinking on this subject, endorsing the idea that "woman *is* property" (74).

16. Robin, *The Reactionary Mind,* 7, 15; Kirk, *The Conservative Mind,* 122, 412–413. See also the essays in Russell Kirk, *Beyond the Dreams of Avarice: Essays of a Social Critic* (Chicago, 1956), in which he rued that Americans "loll in Lotus-land, too fat and sleepy ever to give another twist to the rack of pleasure" (ix).

17. Kirk, *The Conservative Mind,* 434–435, 66. An impending "universal equalitarian domination," Kirk later feared, would obliterate "the freedom of the few who really deserve freedom" (Kirk, *Beyond the Dreams of Avarice,* 171–172). C. L. R. James's remarks on Weaver are worth noting here. After reading *Ideas Have Consequences,* James surmised that Weaver "would have no hesitation in linking himself up with any mass movement which promises to discipline the masses": James, *American Civilization,* 243. See also, in a similar spirit, C. Wright Mills's critique of Kirk, "The Conservative Mood" (1954), in *Power, Politics, and People: The Collected Essays of C. Wright Mills,* ed. Irving Louis Horowitz (New York, 1963), 208–220. Prevented by his own principles from appealing to reason, the conservative, Mills observed, is left with "gratefully accepting the leadership of some set of men whom he considers a received and sanctified elite" (210).

18. Edgar M. Queeny, *The Spirit of Enterprise* (New York, 1943); Ernest L. Klein, *How to Stay Rich: The Story of Democratic American Capitalism* (New York, 1950); Henry Grady Weaver, *The Mainspring of Human Progress* (New York, 1953); Friedrich Hayek, "Why I Am Not a Conservative," in *The Constitution of Liberty* (Chicago, 1960), 409, 401; Milton Friedman, *Capitalism and Freedom* (Chicago, 1962), 138, 6.

19. Quinn Slobodian, *Globalists: The End of Empire and the Birth of Neoliberalism* (Cambridge, MA, 2018), 2. On the early years of neoliberal thinking, see Slobodian,

_Globalists,_ esp. 27–145; Angus Burgin, _The Great Persuasion: Reinventing Free Markets since the Great Depression_ (Cambridge, MA, 2012), 12–185; see also Harvey, _Brief History,_ 5–119, Mirowski, _Never Let a Serious Crisis Go to Waste,_ 27–88, and Rodgers, _Age of Fracture,_ 41–48. For a comparative perspective, see Marion Fourcade-Gourinchas and Sarah L. Babb, "The Rebirth of the Liberal Creed: Paths to Neoliberalism in Four Countries," _American Journal of Sociology_ 108 (Summer 2002), 533–579. Erwin Dekker, _The Viennese Students of Civilization: The Meaning and Context of Austrian Economics Reconsidered_ (New York, 2016), esp. 46–108, sees Hayek, Mises, and other Austrian economists as engaged in a defense of liberal civilization against fascism and socialism. The importance of the Mount Pelerin Society is emphasized sympathetically by Ronald Hartwell, _A History of the Mount Pelerin Society_ (Indianapolis, IN, 1995), and far more critically by Philip Mirowski and Dieter Plehwe, eds., _The Road from Mount Pelerin: The Making of the Neoliberal Thought Collective_ (Cambridge, MA, 2009).

20. Doherty, _Radicals for Capitalism,_ 149–224, chronicles the formation of the neoliberal institutional network; Mirowski, _Never Let a Serious Crisis Go to Waste,_ 47; see also Slobodian, _Globalists,_ 125–127. Chicago School economics and its development are covered in Lanny Ebenstein, _Chicagonomics: The Evolution of Chicago Free Market Economics_ (New York, 2015), esp. 130–139, 154–187. The lives and thought of some of the leading figures are examined in the following books: Lanny Ebenstein, _Milton Friedman: A Biography_ (New York, 2007); Alan Ebenstein, _Friedrich Hayek: A Biography_ (New York, 2001); Israel M. Kirzner, _Ludwig von Mises: The Man and His Economics_ (Wilmington, DE, 2001); and Ross B. Emmett, _Frank Knight and the Chicago School in American Economics_ (New York, 2009). On the disastrous impact of Chicago economics on Chile, see Klein, _The Shock Doctrine,_ 59–159, and Juan Gabriel Valdes, _Pinochet's Economists: The Chicago School in Chile_ (New York, 1995).

21. Ludwig von Mises, _The Anti-Capitalistic Mentality_ (Princeton, NJ, 1956), 81; Murray Rothbard, "The Laissez-Faire Radical: A Quest for the Historical Mises," _Journal of Libertarian Studies_ 5 (Summer 1981), 253; Friedrich Hayek, _Law, Legislation, and Liberty,_ vol. 3, _The Political Order of a Free People_ (Chicago, 1979), 164–165; Milton Friedman, _Inflation: Causes and Consequences_ (New York, 1963), 1; Harberger quoted in Klein, _The Shock Doctrine,_ 61.

22. On Knight's early life, see A. M. C. Waterman, foreword to Emmett, _Frank Knight,_ xxvii–xxx; Knight quoted in William S. Kern, "Frank Knight on Preachers and Economic Policy," _American Journal of Economics and Sociology_ 47 (January 1988), 61; Frank Knight and Thornton Ward Merriam, _The Economic Order and Religion_ (New York, 1945), 45; Frank Knight, _Intelligence and Democratic Action_ (Cambridge, MA, 1960), 4; yet see also Burgin, _The Great Persuasion,_ 36, who notes that "Knight believed that a capitalist society could sustain itself only to the extent that it consisted of individuals whose behavior _departed_ from the norms it incentivized" (my italics). Mises agreed with Knight on the incompatibility of Christianity and capitalism. Since Jesus and his disciples exhibited a "resentment against the rich," so "a living Christianity

cannot, it seems, exist side by side with Capitalism": Ludwig von Mises, *Socialism: An Economic and Sociological Analysis* (New Haven, CT, 1951 [1922]), 419, 428–429.

23. Frank Knight, *On the History and Method of Economics* (Chicago, 1956), 280; Frank Knight, *Freedom and Reform: Essays in Economics and Social Philosophy* (New York, 1947), 196; Frank Knight, "The Newer Economics and the Control of Economic Activity," *Journal of Political Economy* 40 (August 1932), 455.

24. Friedrich Hayek, *Law, Legislation, and Liberty,* vol. 1, *Rules and Order* (Chicago, 1973), 51; Mirowski explains the "double-truth" nature of Hayek's cosmology in *Never Let a Serious Crisis Go to Waste,* 68–79. On Strauss, see Shadia B. Drury, *The Political Ideas of Leo Strauss* (New York, 1988) and Shadia B. Drury, *Leo Strauss and the American Right* (New York, 1999), which paint an unsettling portrait of its subject as the progenitor of a kind of right-wing nihilism. Perry Anderson aligns Hayek with Strauss, Carl Schmitt, and Michael Oakeshott as an intellectual quartet of reaction in *Spectrum: From Right to Left in the World of Ideas* (New York, 2005), 3–28.

25. Hayek, *Constitution of Liberty,* 112, 110; Friedrich Hayek, *Studies in Philosophy, Politics, and Economics* (New York, 1967), 88, 160–161; Friedrich Hayek, "The Use of Knowledge in Society," *American Economic Review* 35 (Winter 1945), 527; Friedrich Hayek, *The Road to Serfdom* (Chicago, 1944), 204–205. Because Hayek and others cast the market as "sublime and beyond capture" through representation, Slobodian goes so far as to characterize neoliberal economics as "a negative theology": *Globalists,* 87 (see 55–87 for a fuller discussion). On Hayek's career at Chicago in the 1950s, see Ebenstein, *Friedrich Hayek,* 171–183.

26. Hayek, *Road to Serfdom,* 205, 39, 42; Hayek, *Constitution of Liberty,* 378; Hayek, *Studies,* 161. Hayek went so far as to advocate a bicameral legislature whose upper chamber's electorate would be restricted to citizens older than forty-five: Hayek, *Law, Legislation, and Liberty,* 3:112–114.

27. Hayek, *Law, Legislation, and Liberty,* 1:45–46; Hayek, *Road to Serfdom,* 75; Hayek, *Studies,* 174–175.

28. Hayek, *Studies,* 164; Hayek, *Law, Legislation, and Liberty,* 1:18; Friedrich Hayek, *The Fatal Conceit: The Errors of Socialism* (London, 1998 [1988]), 137.

29. Hayek, *Road to Serfdom,* 57; Mises, *Anti-Capitalistic Mentality,* 81, 12.

30. Ludwig von Mises, "Economic Calculation in the Socialist Commonwealth" (1920), in *Collectivist Economic Planning,* ed. Friedrich Hayek (London, 1935), 105, 111; Ludwig von Mises, *Human Action* (New Haven, CT, 1949), 590–591. One socialist who wrong-headedly took up the challenge Mises posed in this essay was the British Marxist Maurice Dobb, who argued, not that socialism presumed an account of economic rationality different from that of capitalism, but that socialist planning was indeed compatible with it: see Maurice Dobb, *On Economic Theory and Socialism* (London, 1955), 55–92. For a brilliant critique of Mises, see Brown, *Life against Death,* 238–239.

31. Ludwig von Mises, "Economic Freedom in the Present-Day World" (1958), in *Economic Freedom and Interventionism: An Anthology of Articles and Essays by Ludwig von Mises,* ed. Bettina Bien Graves (Irvington-on-Hudson, NY, 1990), 238; Ludwig von

Mises, *Theory and History* (New Haven, CT, 1957), 168; Mises, *Anti-Capitalistic Mentality,* 75–76.

32. Rose Wilder Lane, "Credo," *Saturday Evening Post* 208 (March 7, 1936), 5–7, 30–35; see also Rose Wilder Lane, *Give Me Liberty* (New York, 1936), and Rose Wilder Lane, *The Discovery of Freedom: Man's Struggle against Authority* (New York, 1943). William V. Holtz, *The Ghost in the Little House: A Life of Rose Wilder Lane* (Columbia, MO, 1993), illuminates its subject's personality but treads lightly around her political convictions. Doherty, *Radicals for Capitalism,* 125–134, discusses Lane's work and her importance to the libertarian movement, while Jennifer Burns, *Goddess of the Market: Ayn Rand and the American Right* (New York, 2009), 119–122, discusses her friendship with Rand.

33. Paterson's reference to Social Security as a "swindle" is cited by Stephen Cox in his foreword to Isabel Paterson, *The God of the Machine* (New Brunswick, NJ, 2009 [1943]), xxix; subsequent quotes on 235, 55, 152, 62. Rand quoted in Doherty, *Radicals for Capitalism,* 122; see 117–125 on Paterson's significance to the postwar right.

34. Cameron Hawley, *Executive Suite* (Boston, 1952), 99, 118, 171, 328, 3; Cameron Hawley, *Cash McCall* (Boston, 1955). *Executive Suite* was made into a film in 1954; *Cash McCall,* in 1960. For an enthusiastic appreciation of Hawley's business fiction, see Marsha Enright, "Hawley's Heroes and the Romance of Business" (March 25, 2011), Atlas Society website.

35. Hawley, *Cash McCall,* 228, 153, 102.

36. Hawley, *Cash McCall,* 256, 154.

37. Rand, interview with Mike Wallace, quoted in Burns, *Goddess of the Market,* 3; Ayn Rand, *For the New Intellectual: The Philosophy of Ayn Rand* (New York, 1961), 2; Rick Perlstein, *Before the Storm: Barry Goldwater and the Unmaking of the American Consensus* (New York, 2001), 50–51. Perlstein later cites a student who told a reporter that the New Left had more in common with Randites than with "the great yawning masses of the middle" (109).

Rand and "Objectivism" have occasioned a sizable literature of exegesis and criticism. Many of the disputes can be as arcane and fierce as any in theology: the Ayn Rand Institute and the Institute for Objectivist Studies constitute, in effect, two spiteful sects who have excommunicated each other. On the sectarian warfare, see Jeff Walker, *The Ayn Rand Cult* (Chicago, 1999), 89–104. The first philosopher outside of Objectivist circles to take Rand seriously was Robert Nozick, *Anarchy, State, and Utopia* (New York, 1974), who cites her on 179, 344, 351. Chris Sciabarra, *Ayn Rand: The Russian Radical* (University Park, PA 1995), is a sympathetic but not uncritical account of its subject. Rand's detractors are as legion and resolute as her enthusiasts. Walker, for example, is unremittingly hostile; William O'Neill, *With Charity toward None: An Analysis of Ayn Rand's Philosophy* (Totowa, NJ, 1972), is an unsparing critique that focuses mainly on Rand's philosophical work but also provides insightful readings of her fiction.

Historians have only recently begun to seriously assess Rand's significance. Nash, *The Conservative Intellectual Movement,* 142–146, mentions her philosophical and fictional work only in passing, focusing instead on her abrasive personality. Burns, *Goddess of the Market,* is an incisive exploration both of her economic and political thinking and of her centrality to the American right; see also Doherty, *Radicals for Capitalism,* 135–147, 228–265, 537–546. In focusing on Rand's life, Anne C. Heller, *Ayn Rand and the World She Made* (New York, 2009), provides a fine complement to Burns.

38. Rand, journal entry, December 4, 1935, in Ayn Rand, *The Journals of Ayn Rand,* ed. David Harriman (New York, 1997), 80; letter to Channing Pollock, July 20, 1941, in Ayn Rand, *The Letters of Ayn Rand,* ed. Michael S. Berliner (New York, 1995), 5; Ayn Rand, *Atlas Shrugged* (New York, 1957), 1040.

Religious intellectuals on the right were well aware of and frightened by Rand's atheism. Kirk, for instance, condemned objectivism as an "inverted religion": Russell Kirk, *Confessions of a Bohemian Tory: Episodes and Reflections of a Vagrant Career* (New York, 1963), 181–182. William F. Buckley, Jr., founder and editor of the *National Review* and self-proclaimed guardian of conservative orthodoxy, was always wary of Rand and her circle, especially after she told him at their very first meeting that "you are too intelligent to believe in God": John B. Judis, *William F. Buckley, Jr.: Patron Saint of the Conservatives* (New York, 1988), 161. After Whittaker Chambers's searing polemic against *Atlas Shrugged* (discussed below), Rand never spoke to Buckley again and refused to remain in the same room with him. See Nash, *The Conservative Intellectual Movement,* 145–146, about the contretemps on the right over Rand's unbelief.

39. On Rand's life from her childhood in Russia to her exodus from left-wing Hollywood, see Heller, *Ayn Rand,* 1–122, and Burns, *Goddess of the Market,* 9–164. For a sample of Alan Greenspan's early work, see "The Assault on Integrity," *Objectivist Newsletter* 2 (August 1963), 31, where he dismisses consumer protection laws as "illusory": "it is precisely the 'greed' of the businessman . . . his profit-seeking, which is the unexcelled protection of the consumer." The films of Cecil B. De Mille provide some insight into Rand's work; see Steven J. Ross, *Working-Class Hollywood: Silent Film and the Shaping of Class in America* (Princeton, NJ, 1998), 173–211. Ross quotes de Mille's autobiography: "Your poor person wants to see wealth, colorful, interesting, exotic."

For two accounts of Rand's fawning testimony before the House Un-American Activities Committee, see Garry Wills's introduction to Lillian Hellman, *Scoundrel Time* (Boston, 1978), 3–4, and Victor Navasky, *Naming Names* (New York, 1980), 170.

40. Ayn Rand, "America's Persecuted Minority: Big Business," lecture at Columbia University, February 15, 1962, in *Capitalism: The Unknown Ideal* (New York, 1967), 44–62; letter to R. M. Lynch, December 14, 1957, *Letters,* 498; Ayn Rand, "Is Atlas Shrugging?," lecture at the Ford Hall Forum, Boston, April 19, 1964, in *Capitalism,* 158; Rand, *For the New Intellectual,* 5, 61, 63.

41. Rand, *The Fountainhead* (New York, 1943), 710–711, 715; Rand, *Atlas Shrugged,* 1027.

42. Rand, *Atlas Shrugged,* 390, 950; Ayn Rand, *The Virtue of Selfishness: A New Concept of Egoism* (New York, 1964), 31–32.

43. Rand, *Atlas Shrugged,* 538, 107, 242, 244; Rand, *The Fountainhead,* 231.

44. Ayn Rand, journal entry, December 4, 1935, *Journals,* 80; Ayn Rand, "Note on Charity," journal entry, April 23, 1946, *Journals,* 436, 434.

45. Rand, "Note on Charity," 435.

46. Rand, *Atlas Shrugged,* 424, 1019, 389; Rand, *The Fountainhead,* 4.

47. Robin, *The Reactionary Mind,* 90 (see 76–96 on Rand); Whittaker Chambers, "Big Sister Is Watching You," *National Review* 4 (December 28, 1957), 594.

48. Chambers, "Big Sister Is Watching You," 595.

49. Rand, *The Fountainhead,* 202, 337, 737, 660; Ayn Rand, *Anthem* (New York, 1995 [1937]); see Leonard Peikoff's introduction, v–xii, on the novel's publication history.

50. Rand, *Anthem,* 22–27, 29.

51. Rand, *Anthem,* 17, 95, 97, 94.

52. Rand, *Anthem,* 99. Chambers remarked on the "strenuously sterile" world of *Atlas Shrugged.* "Children probably irk the author," he added, "and may make her uneasy"; Chambers, "Big Sister Is Watching You," 595.

53. Chambers, "Big Sister Is Watching You," 596.

## 27. The Statues of Daedalus

1. For an account of the "kitchen debate," see May, *Homeward Bound,* 10–11.

2. Bell, *End of Ideology,* 275–407; on Niebuhr, see Richard Fox, *Reinhold Niebuhr: A Biography* (New York, 1985), esp. 224–234 on Niebuhr's impact on Cold War liberals. This account of the liberal mood in the decades after World War II relies on Pells, *Liberal Mind in a Conservative Age,* esp. 76–82, 117–173, 183–248; Andrew Ross, *No Respect: Intellectuals and Popular Culture* (New York, 1989), 42–64; Lears, "A Matter of Taste," in May, ed., *Recasting America,* 38–57; Denning, *Cultural Front,* 107–114. As Carl Schorske put it, postwar liberals both witnessed and launched "a revolution of falling political expectations": introduction to *Fin-de-Siécle Vienna: Politics and Culture* (New York: 1980), xxiii.

3. Howard Brick has outlined this account in "Optimism of the Mind: Imagining Post-Industrial Society in the 1960s and 1970s," *American Quarterly* 44 (September 1992), 348–380; Brick, *Age of Contradiction,* 1–22; Howard Brick, "The Post-capitalist Vision in Twentieth-Century American Social Thought," in Lichtenstein, *American Capitalism,* 21–46; and Howard Brick, *Transcending Capitalism: Visions of a New Society in Modern American Thought* (Ithaca, NY, 2006), esp. 152–218. See also Robert M. Collins, "Growth Liberalism in the Sixties: Great Societies at Home and Grand Designs Abroad," in *The Sixties: From Memory to History,* ed. David Farber (Chapel Hill, NC, 1994), 11–44, and Collins, *More,* esp. 40–97. The essays in Jonathan Bell and Timothy Stanley, eds., *Making Sense of American Liberalism* (Urbana, IL, 2012), contend that liberals and social democrats were more united than later polemicists suggested.

4. Riesman, *The Lonely Crowd,* 263; David Riesman, "Individualism Reconsidered" (1953), in *Individualism Reconsidered, and Other Essays* (Glencoe, IL, 1954), 35; Gal-

braith, *The Affluent Society,* 131; Michael Harrington, *The Accidental Century* (New York, 1965), 241–273, 78, 305; Tom Hayden, "The Port Huron Statement" (1962), appendix to James Miller, *Democracy Is in the Streets: From Port Huron to the Siege of Chicago* (New York, 1988), 365, 342, 332. See also Howard Brick and Christopher Phelps, *Radicals in America: The U.S. Left since the Second World War* (New York, 2015), 49–172.

5. Riesman, "Some Relationships between Technical Progress and Social Progress" (1953), in *Individualism Reconsidered,* 302–303; Galbraith, *New Industrial State,* 73–88, 347–364; David T. Bazelon, *The Paper Economy* (New York, 1965 [1963]), 418; Daniel Bell, *The Coming of Post-Industrial Society: A Venture in Social Forecasting* (New York, 1976 [1973]), 298.

6. Adolf Berle, foreword to Edward S. Mason, ed., *The Corporation in Modern Society* (Cambridge, MA, 1960), xii; Adolf Berle, *Power without Property: A New Development in American Political Economy* (New York, 1959), 138–139.

7. Bell, *End of Ideology,* 313–314; Trilling, *The Liberal Imagination,* 8. Although Lears contends that "the key fissure" in the "new class" was "between technicians and literati" (Lears, "A Matter of Taste," 53), Trilling's sense of cultural professionalism suggests, in my view, a large measure of affinity.

8. Ross, *Strange Weather,* 172–181, demonstrates that 1960s futurology represented both "the professionalization of the long gentleman-amateur tradition of intellectual prophecy" (Bacon, Wells, Verne, and Orwell) and "the consolidation, extension, and ultimately supersession of the scientific management principles that prevailed during the age of industrial Fordism" (175). The epitome of futurology can be sampled in the essays in Daniel Bell, ed., *Toward the Year 2000: Work in Progress* (Boston, 1968), first published in the summer 1967 issue of *Daedalus,* the journal of the American Academy of Arts and Sciences.

9. Bell, *Coming of Post-Industrial Society,* 349, 33.

10. Harrington, *The Accidental Century,* 25; Ross, *Strange Weather,* 176.

11. Daniel Bell, *The Reforming of General Education: The Columbia Experience in Its National Setting* (New Brunswick, NJ, 2011 [1966]), 310–311; Bell was referring to Brown, *Life against Death,* 216, 307–322, 116.

12. Paul Goodman, *New Reformation: Notes of a Neolithic Conservative* (New York, 1971 [1970]), 3; Roszak, *Making of a Counter Culture,* 50–51, 252; Theodore Roszak, *Where the Wasteland Ends: Politics and Transcendence in Post-Industrial Society* (New York, 1972).

13. Goodman, *New Reformation,* 6, 42, 59.

14. Robert Heilbroner, *An Inquiry into the Human Prospect* (New York, 1974), 138; Bell, *Cultural Contradictions of Capitalism,* 23, 26.

15. Heilbroner, *Inquiry into the Human Prospect,* 21, 17, 142, 82.

16. Bell, *Cultural Contradictions of Capitalism,* 83–84. Other examples of culturally conservative criticism include Philip Rieff, *The Triumph of the Therapeutic: Uses of Faith after Freud* (New York, 1966); Philip Rieff, *Fellow Teachers* (New York, 1973);

Christopher Lasch, *Haven in a Heartless World: The Family Besieged* (New York, 1977); and Lasch, *The Culture of Narcissism*. See also Trilling's discussion of the "adversary culture" in the preface to Lionel Trilling, *Beyond Culture: Essays on Literature and Learning* (New York, 1965 [1955]), xv–xvii.

17. Bell, *Cultural Contradictions of Capitalism*, 79, 28, 155–158, 167, 171.

18. The notion of enjoyment as a new form of capitalist command pervades the work of Slavoj Zizek; for an especially concise statement, see "You May!," *London Review of Books* 21 (March 18, 1999), 3–6.

19. Bell, *Cultural Contradictions of Capitalism*, 169.

## 28. To Live Instead of Making History

1. Bell, *End of Ideology*, 405; Riesman, *The Lonely Crowd*, 306.

2. C. Wright Mills, *The Causes of World War Three* (New York, 1958), 81–89; see also C. Wright Mills, *The Power Elite* (New York, 1956), 360, on the "men of decision" who impose their "crackpot definitions upon world reality"; C. Wright Mills, "The New Left" (1960), in *Power, Politics, and People: The Collected Essays of C. Wright Mills*, ed. Irving Horowitz (New York, 1963), 254; Brown, *Life against Death*, xvii, 305; Herbert Marcuse, *An Essay on Liberation* (Boston, 1969), 3–4. Joel Whitebrook asserts that the psychoanalytic criticism of Marcuse and Brown exemplifies "the not uncommon connection of utopian speculation and political despair": Joel Whitebrook, *Perversion and Utopia: A Study in Psychoanalysis and Critical Theory* (Cambridge, MA, 1996), 24–25. On Mills's significance for the New Left, see Daniel Geary, *Radical Ambition: C. Wright Mills, the Left, and American Social Thought* (Berkeley, 2009).

3. Brown, *Life against Death*, 34, 253, 236; Herbert Marcuse, "The End of Utopia" (1967), in *Five Lectures: Psychoanalysis, Politics, and Utopia* (Boston, 1970), 66; Marcuse, *Essay on Liberation*, 12.

4. Herbert Marcuse, *Eros and Civilization: A Philosophical Inquiry into Freud* (Boston, 1955), 160, 130; Brown, *Life against Death*, 216, 213, 316, 253.

5. Brown, *Life against Death*, 63; Marcuse, *Essay on Liberation*, 21; Herbert Marcuse, *Counterrevolution and Revolt* (Boston, 1972), 60; see also Marcuse, "End of Utopia," 62–63, where Marcuse contends that "decisive elements" of classical Marxism— especially the rigid and impassable boundary between the realms of necessity and freedom—are now "obsolete"; Mills, "The New Left," 256; C. Wright Mills, *White Collar: The American Middle Classes* (New York, 1951), 218, 222, 219; "Social Forces and the Frustrations of the Designer," address to the International Design Conference, Aspen, Colorado, June 28, 1958, published as C. Wright Mills, "The Man in the Middle: The Designer," in *Industrial Design* (November 1958), in Horowitz, *Collected Essays of C. Wright Mills*,386.

6. Marcuse, *Essay on Liberation*, 37; Marcuse, *Eros and Civilization*, 228, 130, 162; Brown, *Life against Death*, 307–322, quote on 318.

7. Herbert Marcuse, *One-Dimensional Man: Studies in the Ideology of Advanced Industrial Society* (Boston, 1964), 14; Marcuse, *Eros and Civilization*, 73; Marcuse, *Essay on Liberation,* 88–89. Greif, *Age of the Crisis of Man,* 260–261, takes Marcuse's work in the 1960s as emblematic of "the last stage of the discourse of man." On Marcuse's enduring commitment to a psychoanalytically inflected Marxism, see Paul Robinson, *The Freudian Left: Wilhelm Reich, Geza Roheim, Herbert Marcuse* (Ithaca, NY, 1990 [1969]), 202–258. Hill quoted Marcuse's *Essay on Liberation* at the end of *World Turned Upside Down* (414). Marcuse had written "in the great historical revolutions, the imagination was, for a short period, released and free to enter into the projects of a new social morality and of new institutions of freedom; then it was sacrificed to the requirements of effective reason": Marcuse, *Essay on Liberation,* 37. Looking, no doubt, at many of his rebellious Oxford undergraduates, Hill traced a line between them and earlier avatars of revolutionary imagination. "Now that the protestant ethic itself . . . is at last being questioned after a rule of three or four centuries, we can study with a new sympathy the Diggers, Ranters, and the many other daring thinkers who in the seventeenth century refused to bow down and worship it": Hill, *World Turned Upside Down,* 15.

8. Marcuse, *Counterrevolution and Revolt,* 59, 65, 60, 69. See also Marcuse, *Eros and Civilization,* 173, where Marcuse speculates that "nature would also be liberated from its own brutality and would become free to display the wealth of its purposeless forms which express the 'inner life' of its objects."

9. Marcuse, *Eros and Civilization,* 46; Marcuse, *One-Dimensional Man,* 4–6, 56–83; Marcuse, "End of Utopia," 77; Marcuse, *Essay on Liberation,* 4.

10. Marcuse, *Eros and Civilization,* 198; Marcuse, "End of Utopia," 68, 66. Students of industrial technology and management were already beginning to cast serious doubt on the linear conception of technological progress that not only beguiled Marcuse but also united liberals and much of the New Left. See, for instance, Braverman, *Labor and Monopoly Capital,* esp. 146–153; Stephen Marglin, "What Do Bosses Do?: The Origins and Functions of Hierarchy in Capitalist Production," *Review of Radical Political Economics* 6 (July 1974), 60–112; and Noble, *America By Design.* The most pointed criticism came from Lewis Mumford in *The Myth of the Machine,* vol. 2, *The Pentagon of Power* (New York, 1970), which I discuss in greater detail in Chapter 29.

11. Brown, *Life against Death,* 91, 259–260, xvii, 16, xviii, 111, 57. Surprisingly little has been written about Brown by historians. Brown wrote little about himself; his "Memoirs" in Jerome Neu, ed., *In Memoriam: Norman O. Brown* (Santa Cruz, CA, 2005), 3–38, provide a playfully illuminating start. Susan Mennel, "The Resurrection of the Body: Norman O. Brown and Modern Thought," Ph.D. dissertation, University of New Hampshire, 1990, treats Brown as a herald of postmodern rejections of objectivity and linearity. The essays in David Greenham, ed., *The Resurrection of the Body: The Work of Norman O. Brown* (Lanham, MD, 2006), cover his early work as a classical scholar as well as his later interests in psychoanalysis and mysticism.

12. Although Lasch perceptively identifies Brown's book as a "restatement of the romantic critique" of liberalism, Cartesian dualism, and the Enlightenment, he misses its religious quality: see Lasch's introduction to the second edition of Brown, *Life against Death*, vii–xiii. Rieff, *Fellow Teachers*, 197, alludes to Brown and other "contemporary false prophets" who enjoin us to become "ahistorical infants"; see also Daniel Bell, "Beyond Modernism, Beyond Self" (1977), in *The Winding Passage: Essays and Sociological Journeys, 1960–1980* (New York, 1980), 292–297. Brown, *Life against Death*, 30, 13, 16.

13. Brown, *Life against Death*, 3–10 (quotes on 13–14), 19.

14. Brown, *Life against Death*, 16, 284, 297.

15. Brown, *Life against Death*, 239–252, quotes on 240, 245, 252.

16. Brown, *Life against Death*, 202–233, quotes on 240, 215, 221, 216; see also 179–201 on Jonathan Swift. Brown's examination of Luther did not rely on Erik Erikson's *Young Man Luther: A Study in Psychoanalysis and History* (New York, 1958); I doubt that he would have found Erikson's rather tame version of psychoanalysis to his liking. In addition to perusing Luther's own work, Brown drew on Ernst Troeltsch, the German historian of Christian social teaching, and on Paul Tillich, "the theologian who has done most to disentangle Protestantism from its alliance with capitalism" (224). This is not the place to explore the affinities between Brown and Tillich, but let it suffice to say that both belong to the lineage of Romanticism. (Brown clearly took the title of his chapter on Luther—"The Protestant Era"—from Tillich's 1948 book of the same name.) Christopher Hill indicated an affinity with Brown: his chapter on seventeenth-century critics of the Protestant ethic in *World Turned Upside Down* (324–343) is entitled "Life against Death."

17. Brown, *Life against Death*, 305, 309, 236, 239; see 249–253 and 257–258 on Ruskin. Susan Sontag's comment is in "Psychoanalysis and Norman O. Brown's *Life against Death*," (1961), in *Against Interpretation: And Other Essays* (New York, 1966), 262.

18. Norman O. Brown, "Apocalypse: The Place of Mystery in the Life of the Mind," *Harper's* (May 1961), 49, 47; Norman O. Brown, *Love's Body* (New York, 1966), 254; Roszak, *Making of a Counter Culture*, 115. In characterizing Brown's position in *Love's Body* as one of "Zen-like transcendence," Brick, *Age of Contradiction*, 134, misses both its connection to *Life against Death* and its portrayal of an "eschatology of immanence."

19. Marcuse, "Love Mystified: A Critique of Norman O. Brown," *Commentary* 43 (February 1967), 71, 73, 74.

20. Norman O. Brown, "A Reply to Herbert Marcuse," *Commentary* 43 (March 1967), 83. Brown later made a similar point against the reactionary Rieff, who was, in his view, "trapped in the language of critical intellect" and therefore unprepared to greet a "fresh age of the gods": Norman O. Brown, "Rieff's '*Fellow Teachers*,'" *Salmagundi* 24 (Fall 1973), 45, 40.

## 29. Heaven Which Exists and Is Everywhere around Us

1. Thompson, *Making of the English Working Class,* 915; Williams, *Culture and Society.* On the post-Stalinist left in Britain, see Michael Kenny, *The First New Left: British Intellectuals after Stalin* (London, 1995).

2. Greil Marcus, *Lipstick Traces: A Secret History of the Twentieth Century* (Cambridge, MA, 1989), glamorizes the Situationist International, while Mackenzie Wark, *The Beach Beneath the Street: The Everyday Life and Glorious Times of the Situationist International* (London and New York, 2011), has been criticized by participants for numerous errors and misinterpretations. The best collections of Situationist writing are Tom McDonough, ed., *Guy Debord and the Situationist International: Texts and Documents* (Cambridge, MA, 2002), and Ken Knabb, ed., *The Situationist International Anthology* (Oakland, 2006). Raoul Vaneigem, *The Revolution of Everyday Life,* trans. Donald Nicholson-Smith (Oakland, 2012 [1967]), 178. Kristin Ross, *May '68 and Its Afterlives* (Chicago, 2002), traces the moment and its legacies.

3. Barrington Moore, Jr., "The Society Nobody Wants: A Look beyond Marxism and Liberalism," in *The Critical Spirit: Essays in Honor of Herbert Marcuse,* ed. Barrington Moore, Jr., and Kurt H. Wolff (Boston, 1967), 418; Roszak, *Making of a Counter Culture,* 3, xiii.

4. Roszak, *Where the Wasteland Ends,* 413–445; Roszak, *Making of a Counter Culture,* 252–268.

5. Dwight Macdonald, "The Root Is Man: Part One," *politics* 3 (April 1946), 97–115. On postwar personalism, see James J. Farrell, *The Spirit of the Sixties: The Making of Postwar Radicalism* (New York, 1997), esp. 21–170; Doug Rossinow, *The Politics of Authenticity: Christianity, Liberalism, and the New Left in America* (New York, 1998), 53–84, who prefers the term "Christian existentialism"; and McCarraher, *Christian Critics,* 112–146. Though he explicitly eschews the term "personalism," David Chappell describes a very similar worldview in *A Stone of Hope: Prophetic Religion and the Death of Jim Crow* (Chapel Hill, NC, 2004), 67–86. On *Liberation,* see Cristina Scatamacchia's remarkable unpublished manuscript, "Politics, *Liberation,* and Intellectual Radicalism," Ph.D. dissertation, University of Missouri, 1990.

6. Martin Luther King, Jr., "Sermon on Gandhi," February 2, 1959, in *The Papers of Martin Luther King, Jr.: Threshold of a New Decade, January 1959–December 1960,* ed. Clayborne Carson, Tenisha Armstrone, Susan Carson, Adrienne Clay, and Kieran Taylor (Berkeley, 1992), 159; Hayden, "Port Huron Statement," 332; Rev. James Lawson, "Statement of Purpose," *Student Voice* 1 (1960), 3, in *The Student Voice, 1960–1965: Periodical of the Student Nonviolent Coordinating Committee,* ed. Clayborne Carson (Westport, CT, and London, 1990). On the personalist roots of Women's Liberation, see Sara Evans, *Personal Politics: The Origins of Women's Liberation in the Civil Rights Movement and the New Left* (New York, 1979), esp. 156–232; see also Ruth Rosen, *The World Split Open: How the Modern Women's Movement Changed America* (New York, 2000), 143–262.

7. Simone Weil's reflections on "the Apparatus" were published posthumously in "Reflections on War," *politics* 2 (February 1945), 55, and "Factory Work," *politics* 3 (December 1946), 369–375; Editors, "A Tract for the Times," *Liberation* 1 (March 1956), 4; Buber, *Paths in Utopia*, 145, 135; David Dellinger, *From Yale to Jail: The Life Story of a Moral Dissenter* (New York, 1993), 62–63, 145–152; Staughton Lynd, *Living inside Our Hope* (Ithaca, NY, 1997), 48–50; on the Koinonia and experiments, see Charles Marsh, *The Beloved Community: How Faith Shapes Social Justice, From the Civil Rights Movement to Today* (New York, 2005), 51–86.

8. On the civil rights movement as a religious revival, see Chappell, *A Stone of Hope*, 87–104, esp. 90–101; the SNCC activist is quoted in Marsh, *Beloved Community*, 95–96; Martin Luther King, *Stride toward Freedom: The Montgomery Story* (Boston, 1986 [1958]), 125. My interpretation of King's political theology is influenced by Gregory, *Politics and the Order of Love*, 192–196, even though I remain unconvinced by his claim that King exemplified a "self-critical commitment to the (as yet unrealized) promise of American liberalism" (192).

9. Goodman, *Growing Up Absurd*, 138–142.

10. Macdonald, "The Root Is Man: Part Two," *politics* 3 (July 1946), 194–214. Many readers of the essay were put off not only by Macdonald's repudiation of Marxism but also by what they considered this newfound "religiosity": see Michael Wreszin, *A Rebel in Defense of Tradition: The Life and Politics of Dwight Macdonald* (New York, 1994), 164. Macdonald profiled Dorothy Day in "The Foolish Things of the World—I," *New Yorker* (October 4, 1952), 37–60, and "The Foolish Things of the World—II," *New Yorker* (October 11, 1952), 37–58; his later remarks are in Dwight Macdonald, "Revisiting Dorothy Day," *New York Review of Books* (January 28, 1971), 18.

11. On Cornell, see Deborah Solomon, *Utopia Parkway: The Life and Work of Joseph Cornell* (New York, 1997), who quotes Cornell's diary on 123, and Diane Waldman, *Joseph Cornell: Master of Dreams* (New York, 2006); see also Lears, *Fables of Abundance*, 403–414, who emphasizes Cornell's belief in Christian Science.

12. Rothko's remarks at the Pratt Institute are quoted in James E. B. Breslin, *Mark Rothko: A Biography* (Chicago, 1998), 389, 396–397; his 1959 interview is quoted in Anne Chave, *Mark Rothko: Subjects in Abstraction* (New Haven, CT, 1989), 78; Barnett Newman, "The Sublime Is Now" (1948), in *Barnett Newman: Selected Writings and Interviews,* ed. John O'Neill (Berkeley, 1992), 173.

13. Jed Perl, *New Art City* (New York, 2005); see esp. 426–432 on Rothko; Mark Rothko, *The Artist's Reality,* introduction by Christopher Rothko (New Haven, CT, 2004), 37.

14. Rothko, *The Artist's Reality,* 25, 37, 109. In an October 1943 radio interview with WNYC, Rothko and Adoph Gottlieb said that while the discovery of tribal art contributed to the rise of modernism, its "true significance" lay in "the spiritual meaning underlying all archaic works." While not "nostalgic for a past that seems enchanting because of its remoteness," the avant-garde was drawn to the "fancies and superstitions" of archaic peoples. Four months earlier, in a letter to the *New York Times* (June 7, 1943),

Rothko and Gottlieb had professed a "spiritual kinship with primitives and archaic art": Irving Sandler, *The Triumph of American Painting: A History of Abstract Expressionism* (New York, 1976), 63–64.

15. Henry Miller, *The Colossus of Maroussi* (New York, 1941), 45, 241; Henry Miller, *Tropic of Capricorn* (New York, 2007 [1937]), 42, 34. Miller's life is the subject of two notable biographies: Robert Ferguson, *Henry Miller: A Life* (New York, 1991), and Mary V. Dearborn, *The Happiest Man Alive: A Biography of Henry Miller* (New York, 1991). On Miller's years with Western Union, compare the rather different tales told by Ferguson, 62–66, and Dearborn, 64–74 passim. Ferguson portrays Miller as a humane and even "progressive" manager, while Dearborn asserts that he was an avidly corrupt figure who "ruled . . . like an Eastern potentate" (66). Citing some of Miller's own paperwork as well as reminiscences of his fellow employees, Ferguson seems, to me, more credible. Dearborn relies much too heavily and uncritically on the pyrotechnics of *Tropic of Capricorn.*

16. Miller, *Colossus of Maroussi,* 4, 241, 45, 57, 79, 24.

17. Henry Miller, *The Air-Conditioned Nightmare* (New York, 1945), 28, 27, 22–23, 36, 202, 56.

18. Henry Miller, *Remember to Remember* (New York, 1947), 41, 124–125; Miller, *Air-Conditioned Nightmare,* 57.

19. Ginsberg, *Howl,* 22; Allen Ginsberg, "Metaphysics" (1948), in *Allen Ginsberg: Collected Poems 1947–1980* (New York, 1988), 33; Gary Snyder, *Earth House Hold: Technical Notes and Queries to Fellow Dharma Revolutionaries* (New York, 1969), 113–116, 125–126, 133.

20. Roszak, *Where the Wasteland Ends,* 385, 118; Thomas Merton, *Raids on the Unspeakable* (New York, 1966), 106.

21. Kenneth Rexroth, "Revolt: True and False" (1958), in *World outside the Window: Selected Essays of Kenneth Rexroth,* ed. Bradford Morrow (New York, 1987), 75; Kenneth Rexroth, "Who Is Alienated from What?" (1967), in *The Alternative Society: Essays from the Other World* (New York, 1972), 126; Kenneth Rexroth, *An Autobiographical Novel* (New York, 1966), 335. Rexroth returned to the subject of Catholic theology and religious culture throughout his life: see, for instance, Kenneth Rexroth, "New Sex? New Church?" (1970) and "Faith in an Age of Faithlessness" (1969), in *With Eye and Ear* (New York, 1970), 78–92. Linda Hamalian, *A Life of Kenneth Rexroth* (New York, 1991), exhibits no interest in Rexroth's enduring religious and theological concerns. The best study of Rexroth's poetry in this regard is Donald Gutierrez, *"The Holiness of the Real": The Short Verse of Kenneth Rexroth* (Teaneck, NJ, 1996). Richard Candida-Smith, *Utopia and Dissent: Art, Poetry, and Politics in California* (Berkeley, 1996), 32–66, situates Rexroth in the region's postwar radical literary landscape.

22. Rexroth, *Autobiographical Novel,* 339, 252; Kenneth Rexroth, *The Signature of All Things: Poems, Songs, Elegies, Translations, and Epigrams* (New York, 1950), 15; Kenneth Rexroth, *The Dragon and the Unicorn* (New York, 1952), 70.

23. Roszak, *Making of a Counter Culture*, 205–238; Ginsberg, *Howl*, 21. Rexroth, *The Dragon and the Unicorn*, 92. Rexroth referred to "the Social Lie" in numerous venues, but for a pungent synopsis, see his interview in Lawrence Lipton, *The Holy Barbarians* (New York, 1959), 293–295.

24. Rexroth, *Dragon and the Unicorn*, 97.

25. Thomas Merton, *No Man Is an Island* (New York, 1983 [1955]), 28; Thomas Merton, "Letters to a White Liberal" (1964), in *Seeds of Destruction* (New York, 1964), 24. Merton has provided material for a thriving cottage industry of both spiritual and scholarly literature. Michael Mott, *The Seven Mountains of Thomas Merton* (New York, 1984), is the best biography, while George Woodcock, *Thomas Merton, Monk and Poet: A Critical Study* (New York, 1978), is a sympathetic anarchist exploration of Merton's religious and political thinking; see also Fisher, *Catholic Counterculture in America*, 205–247. Merton was not the only religious figure favored in bohemian circles: see also Brother Antoninus (nee William Everson), *The Crooked Lines of God: Poems 1949–1959* (Detroit, 1960), highly praised by Rexroth and Ginsberg.

26. Merton, "Letters to a White Liberal," 22–23.

27. Thomas Merton, "Rain and the Rhinoceros," in *Raids on the Unspeakable*, 9.

28. Thomas Merton, *Seeds of Contemplation* (New York, 1949), 105–106; Thomas Merton, *The New Man* (New York, 1961), 79; Thomas Merton, *The Silent Life* (New York, 1957), 27; Thomas Merton, *New Seeds of Contemplation* (New York, 1962), 19; see also Thomas Merton, *Life and Holiness* (New York, 1963), 124–129. Merton referred to himself and other Catholic leftists as "anarchists" in a letter to Martin E. Marty, September 6, 1967, in William H. Shannon, ed., *The Hidden Ground of Love: Letters of Thomas Merton on Religious Experience and Social Concern* (New York 1985), 458.

29. Snyder, *Earth House Hold*, 115, 112; Gary Snyder, "Buddhism and the Coming Revolution" (originally published in 1961 as "Buddhist Anarchism"), in *Earth House Hold*, 90–93, quote on 91; Gary Snyder, "Revolution in the Revolution in the Revolution," in *Regarding Wave* (New York, 1970), 39; Gary Snyder, "For the Children," in *Turtle Island* (New York, 1974), 90. On Snyder's significance in the West Coast radical counterculture, see Timothy Gray, *Gary Snyder and the Pacific Rim: Creating Countercultural Community* (Iowa City, IA, 2006). The verse is from Snyder, "For the Children."

30. Mumford, *Pentagon of Power*, 208, 269, 267.

31. Mumford, *Pentagon of Power*, 274, 175, 293, 297, 370 (see 175–185 for Mumford's critique of automation); Lewis Mumford, *Art and Technics* (New York, 2000 [1952]), 181, 162.

32. Mumford, *Pentagon of Power*, captions to photographs 26 and 27 following 340.

33. Lewis Mumford, *The Transformations of Man* (New York, 1956), 142; Mumford, *Art and Technics*, 12, 159; Lewis Mumford, *The Conduct of Life* (New York, 1951), 34.

34. Mumford, *Art and Technics*, 62, 49; Mumford, *Pentagon of Power*, 137.

35. Mumford, *Pentagon of Power*, 408, 433.

36. Mumford, *Pentagon of Power*, 413; Mumford, *Conduct of Life*, 113–114.

37. Roszak, *Where the Wasteland Ends*, 121, 106, xxiii–xxiv, xx, xxxi.

38. Roszak, *Making of a Counter Culture*, 155–177, 212; Roszak, *Where the Wasteland Ends*, 375–376.

39. Roszak, *Making of a Counter Culture*, 240; *Where the Wasteland Ends*, 125, 127, 134–135.

40. Roszak, *Where the Wasteland Ends*, 374, 281, 375, 373.

41. Roszak, *Where the Wasteland Ends*, 425, 426.

42. E. F. Schumacher, *Small Is Beautiful: Economics as If People Mattered* (New York, 1975 [1973]), 145, 52, 86, 93–94. Schumacher toured the United States shortly before his death in 1977. See also E. F. Schumacher, *Good Work* (New York, 1975), and E. F. Schumacher, *A Guide for the Perplexed* (New York, 1977). Theodore Roszak, introduction to Schumacher, *Small Is Beautiful*, 4–5, 8–9; Roszak, *Where the Wasteland Ends*, 436.

43. Roszak, *Where the Wasteland Ends*, 423, 44 (see also his introduction to *Small Is Beautiful*, 5, where he praises the *Whole Earth Catalog*); Lears, *Fables of Abundance*, 367. My criticism of Roszak here is similar to that of Christopher Shannon, *A World Made Safe for Differences: Cold War Intellectuals and the Politics of Identity* (Lanham, MD, 2005), 38–46.

44. Schumacher made this remark during his tour of the United States in 1977: see www.youtube.com/watch?v=9DtF9-owes4.

45. Thomas Merton, *The Wisdom of the Desert* (New York, 1970 [1960]), 3, 23–24.

46. Thomas Merton, *Mystics and Zen Masters* (New York, 1967), 157; Thomas Merton, *Zen and the Birds of Appetite* (New York, 1968), 140.

47. Thomas Merton, "Marxism and Monastic Perspectives," in *The Asian Journal of Thomas Merton*, ed. Naomi Burton (New York, 1975), 332–333, 329, 335, 338.

48. Kenneth Rexroth, preface to *Bird in the Bush: Obvious Essays* (New York, 1959), ix; Rexroth, "Who Is Alienated from What?," 129; Kenneth Rexroth, "The Second Post-War, the Second Interbellum, the Permanent War Generation" (1969), in *The Alternative Society*, 123.

49. Kenneth Rexroth, "Facing Extinction" (1969), in *The Alternative Society*, 186, 192, 196.

50. Kenneth Rexroth, "The Ecological Point of No Return," first published in the *San Francisco Bay Guardian*, May 1969, in *In the Sierra: Mountain Writings by Kenneth Rexroth*, ed. Kim Stanley Robinson (New York, 2012), 173; Kenneth Rexroth, *Communalism: From Its Origins to the Twentieth Century* (New York, 1974), 315; Kenneth Rexroth, "Poets Old and New," in *Assays* (New York, 1961), 208–209.

## Epilogue

1. Fraser, *Age of Acquiescence*, 416.

2. On investor capitalism, see Useem, *Investor Capitalism*; on the broader transformations of technology and labor processes since the 1970s, Harvey, *Condition of Postmodernity*, 141–200, remains an indispensable point of departure.

3. Fraser, *Age of Acquiescence,* 223–263. On the increasing intensity and precariousness of work life, see Steven Greenhouse, *The Big Squeeze: Tough Times for the American Worker* (New York, 2008), and Andrew Ross, *Nice Work If You Can Get It: Life and Labor in Precarious Times* (New York, 2009). For a concise account of economic developments in the United States since 1980, see Thomas Piketty's magisterial *Capital in the Twenty-First Century* (Cambridge, MA, 2014 [2013]), 368–381.

4. Bill Clinton is quoted in Andrew Bacevich, *American Empire: The Realities and Consequences of U.S. Diplomacy* (Cambridge, MA, 2002), 1, 38; John Mickelthwait and Adrian Woolridge, *A Future Perfect: The Promise and Challenge of Globalization* (New York, 2008 [2000]), 336, 341, 221–241, 337–339; Francis Fukuyama, *The End of History and the Last Man* (New York, 2006 [1992]), xii, 90, 108, 46.

5. Thomas Friedman, *The Lexus and the Olive Tree: Understanding Globalization* (New York, 2000 [1999]), 104; Thomas Friedman, "Senseless in Seattle," *New York Times,* December 1, 1999, A23; Thomas Friedman, "A Manifesto for the Fast World," *New York Times Magazine,* March 28, 1999, 40.

6. Tom Peters, *Liberation Management: Necessary Disorganization for the Nanosecond Nineties* (New York, 1992), 528; Frank, *One Market under God.*

7. Moreton, *To Serve God and Wal-Mart,* 89, 102–132; Lehmann, *The Money Cult,* 376.

8. Kathryn Lofton, *Oprah: The Gospel of an Icon* (Berkeley, 2011), 49, 209, 12, 65–66, 58.

9. Bill Gates, *The Road Ahead* (New York, 1995), 157–183; Bill Gates, *Business @ The Speed of Thought: Succeeding in the Digital Economy* (New York, 2000), 6, 15–38.

10. George Gilder, *Wealth and Poverty* (New York, 1981), 266; George Gilder, *Recapturing the Spirit of Enterprise* (New York, 1992 [1984]), 134; Kevin Kelly, *Out of Control: The New Biology of Machines, Social Systems, and the Economic World* (New York, 1994), 102, 469, 471; Kevin Kelly, "God Is the Machine," *Wired* 10 (December 2002), 183.

11. On the transformation of the Democratic Party into a vehicle of financial and technocratic capital, see Thomas Frank, *Listen Liberal: Or, Whatever Happened to the Party of the People?* (New York, 2016). Arlie Hochschild, *Strangers in Their Own Land: Anger and Mourning on the American Right* (New York, 2016), is invaluable for understanding the rancor that fueled Trump's ascent to power.

12. Chalmers Johnson, *The Sorrows of Empire: Militarism, Secrecy, and the End of the Republic* (New York, 2004), 23 ("Huxwellian" refers to a blend of Aldous Huxley's *Brave New World* and George Orwell's *1984*); Peter Frase, *Four Futures: Life after Capitalism* (New York, 2016), 47–90; Wolfgang Streeck, *How Will Capitalism End? Essays on a Failing System* (New York, 2016), 13, 35, 36.

13. Fraser, *Age of Acquiescence,* 337, 296, 301.

14. Naomi Klein, *This Changes Everything: Capitalism vs. The Climate* (New York, 2014), 178.

15. Jedidiah Purdy, "Bernie Sanders' New Deal Socialism," *New Yorker* (November 20, 2015), at http://www.newyorker.com/news/news-desk/bernie-sanderss -new-deal-socialism.

16. David Graeber, "Occupy Wall Street Rediscovers the Radical Imagination," *Guardian* (September 25, 2011), at https://www.theguardian.com/commentisfree /cifamerica/2011/sep/25/occupy-wall-street-protest; Rebecca Solnit, "Compassion Is Our New Currency," *TomDispatch* (December 22, 2011), at http://www.tomdispatch .com/post/175483/tomgram%3A_rebecca_solnit,_occupy_your_heart/.

17. Rebecca Solnit, *A Paradise Built in Hell: The Extraordinary Communities That Arise in Disaster* (New York, 2009), 17, 3.

18. Solnit, *A Paradise Built in Hell,* 65, Fraser, *Age of Acquiescence,* 421, 420, 305.

19. T. J. Clark, "For a Left with No Future," *New Left Review* 74 (March–April 2012), 56. Clark's essay should be indispensable reading for anyone who desires to move beyond capitalism to something more practicable and humane. "Many and bitter will be the things sacrificed," Clark informs his readers, "the big ideas, the revolutionary stylistics." Like Streeck, Clark muses that Marxism was "most productively a theory . . . of bourgeois society and how it would come to grief," but that "about bourgeois society's ending it was notoriously wrong." The secular left—for Clark, religion is not an option—must "learn to look failure in the face" and practice a politics "in the tragic key" (58, 62, 69, 72).

20. Pope Francis, *Laudato Si: On Care for Our Common Home* (Huntingdon, IN, 2015), 73.

21. Ruskin, "Unto This Last" (1862), in *Unto This Last and Other Writings,* ed. Clive Wilmer (New York, 1985), 189. On the new interest in craftsmanship, see Richard Sennett, *The Craftsman* (New Haven, CT, 2008), and Matthew Crawford, *Shop Class as Soulcraft: An Inquiry into the Value of Work* (New York, 2009), both of whom are indebted to Hannah Arendt's reflections on work in *The Human Condition* (Chicago, 1958), 79–135. The most vigorous and acerbic opposition to this revival is James Livingston, *No More Work: Why Full Employment Is a Bad Idea* (Chapel Hill, NC, 2016), 29–66. Jonathan Crary, *24/7: Late Capitalism and the Ends of Sleep* (New York, 2013), is a harrowing account of our contemporary addiction to work and social media.

22. Pope Francis, *Laudato Si,* 64. Peter Linebaugh has become the most passionate and prolific historian of "the commons": see *Magna Carta Manifesto; Stop, Thief! The Commons, Enclosures, and Resistance* (Oakland, 2014); Peter Linebaugh, *The Incomplete, True, Authentic, and Wonderful History of May Day* (Oakland, 2016).

23. Alasdair MacIntyre, *After Virtue: A Study in Moral Theory* (Notre Dame, IN, 2007 [1981]), 263; for an especially hysterical and preposterous example of Benedictine withdrawal, see Rod Dreher, *The Benedict Option: A Strategy for Christians in a Post-Christian Nation* (New York, 2017). Michael Hardt and Antonio Negri, *Empire* (Cambridge, MA, 2001), 413, 387; Taylor, *A Secular Age,* 732, 726.

# Acknowledgments

I worked for almost two decades on this book, and along the way I have had the encouragement and sympathetic criticism of a host of friends, colleagues, students, and other interlocutors.

To my parents, Eugene Thorne McCarraher (1929–2003) and Eleanor Marie McCarraher, I owe the gift of life and the virtue of resilience. Although my father did not live to see the publication of this book, his spirit informs every page. As always, my brother, Michael Patrick McCarraher, offered wisdom from his trove of classical learning. My in-laws, the D'Alonzos—Robert and Geraldine, as well as Robert, Mark, and Geri—have been unfailing sources of encouragement and humor.

No one is more keenly aware than I of the profound irony that a book like this has depended on the largesse of capital and the state. I have depended on the financial support of the National Endowment for the Humanities; the Lilly Endowment; the Pew Charitable Trusts; the Templeton Foundation; and the American Council of Learned Societies, whose Charles A. Ryskamp Fellowship enabled a much-needed sabbatical year of research and reflection. I must also thank Villanova University, which provided greatly appreciated time and research funding in the form of a Summer Research Grant and a VERITAS Faculty Research Award.

I've ventilated my thinking about enchantment, capitalism, and US history in various venues. Villanova's Robert M. Birmingham Program was an early forum for exchange and criticism. In the spring of 2002, Leigh Schmidt arranged for me to teach a course at Princeton University in which I broached some of my then-inchoate ideas; Eliot Ratzman and Vincent Lloyd (now a colleague at Villanova) deserve special thanks for their critiques and recommendations. David Solomon invited me to the Center for Ethics and Culture at the University of Notre Dame in the fall of 2002 to talk about enchantment and money. Michael Budde brought me out to DePaul University in the fall of 2005 to lecture about the perverse spirituality of capitalism. My thinking on the history of management theory received useful criticism at a conference of the Society for the Study of Christian Ethics at

Oxford University in the fall of 2007. In the fall of 2009, Andrew Bacevich included me in his lecture series at Boston University on "The Short American
Century," which provided an opportunity to showcase my thinking about the
contours of American history as a whole. In the spring of 2010, Eric Gregory invited me to Princeton University to test-drive my ideas with some graduate students in religion and history. The afternoon of vigorous questioning and discussion that ensued both convinced me that I was on the right path and that I needed
to be clearer about what that path was. I've also presented my ideas about enchantment, capitalism, and US history in talks at Baylor University, La Salle University, Rutgers University, Creighton University, and Columbia University.

Villanova University has been my institutional home for almost two decades,
and I remain indebted to John Doody for bringing me there. My friends and colleagues in the humanities department constitute a remarkable conventicle of
Christian humanism. Jesse Couenhoven, Margaret Grubiak, Mary Hirschfeld,
Kevin Hughes, Anna Moreland, Mark Shiffman, Thomas W. Smith, Helena
Tomko, Michael Tomko, and James M. Wilson all discussed and improved several chapters. James Wetzel undertook the herculean labor of reading an early
version of the manuscript; the book is much better on account of his effort. David
Bentley Hart also read the manuscript with his signature meticulousness and
stringency; when I passed his test, I knew that I had something worthwhile. I
might not have had a manuscript if Elisa Wiley hadn't saved me from technical
difficulties. Mary Di Lucia, Mary Agnes Edsall, Michael Hanby, David C.
Schindler, Jeanne Schindler, and Paul Wright are former colleagues at Villanova
who deserve my gratitude as early enthusiasts and critics of the work. Undergraduates provide a captive audience for scholars, and I shamelessly sketched
some of the intellectual background for this book in the honors-level seminar I
teach, "Interdisciplinary Studies III," as well as my humanities course on "The
Goods and the Good Life." Many thanks go to Nick Ader, Eric Aldieri, Kristin
Baskin, (Madeline Chera, Eduardo Crow, Katie Donahue, Charles Gillespie, P. J.
Gorre, (now Father) Bryan Kerns, Nick Morris, Tom Morris, Jeta Mulaj, Regina
Munch, Megan Murray, Joana Petrescu, Tara Powers, and Kim Reilly. Kristin,
Nick, Eduardo, P. J., and Madeline provided invaluable research assistance, while
Jeta and Regina have become good friends and critics.

Friends and colleagues elsewhere who read or listened to my ramblings include
William Cavanaugh, Eric Gregory, Stanley Hauerwas, Charles Marsh, Chuck
Mathewes, Wilfred McClay, Jay Tolson, and Lauren Winner. Charles and Jay read
the entire manuscript with generosity and rigorous discernment. I must also
thank Jay and Barbara McClay for allowing me to contribute to the *Hedgehog
Review,* John Wilson for indulging me at *Books and Culture,* and Paul Baumann
and Matt Boudway for granting me incredible latitude at *Commonweal.*

At what seemed like a gloomy moment for the book, my friend Greg Eskin took
me to lunch and offered much-needed wisdom and exhortation for which I'm

eternally grateful. At Villanova, Anthony Godzieba, Jane Morris, Angela Di Benedetto, Kathryn Getek-Soltis, and Mark Wilson deserve special commendation as stalwart friends and critics. Jane and Angela in particular have sustained me over the years through personal and professional highs and lows, and Mark has been nothing less than another brother. All of them have given me a glimpse of the beloved community that awaits us in the future.

John F. Thornton, my agent, has remained indefatigable and even exuberant in his support over the years, well past the time when any reasonable person would have given up hope. At Harvard University Press, Kathleen McDermott guided the manuscript through the acquisition and editorial process with remarkable skill, patience, and confidence. I must also thank the anonymous reviewers who offered keen criticism and vibrant encouragement. Melody Negron supervised the copyediting, indexing, and page-proofing with great precision and sensitivity.

Casey Blake and Jackson Lears are two friends to whom my debts are incalculable. A warm and insightful correspondent over the past two decades, Casey read the book with exquisite care and discernment. Jackson, too, read and critiqued several versions of the manuscript. As my mentor at Rutgers, he was and remains a model of generous, critical, and unaffected erudition. Jackson's faith in me and my work has been of inestimable value over the years, and I cherish the intellectual camaraderie and friendship that's developed. He and Karen Lears have provided a place of grace on earth.

My lovely daughters, Alexandra and Gabrielle, grew into young adults while this book gestated; by the time it's born, Alexandra will have married Kevin Edler. Whenever I see them, I know that the future is worth fighting for. One of my most ardent hopes is that this book can help, even if only slightly, to rescue them, their generation, and their descendents from the beguiling tyranny of Mammon.

Once again, my deepest gratitude goes to Alecia Rose D'Alonzo. In good times and bad, her abiding faith, patience, and endurance have afforded the dearest glimpse of a world beyond money. Whatever happens, her love has truly been a sacramental way of being. I remain, as always, enchanted.

*Ardmore, Pennsylvania*
*April 18, 2019*

# Index